NATION
OF NATIONS
Volume I: To 1877

Here is not merely a nation but a teeming nation of nations.
—WALT WHITMAN

NATION

OF NATIONS

A NARRATIVE
HISTORY
OF THE AMERICAN REPUBLIC

VOLUME I: TO 1877

JAMES WEST DAVIDSON

WILLIAM E. GIENAPP
The University of Wyoming

CHRISTINE LEIGH HEYRMAN
Brandeis University

MARK H. LYTLE
Bard College

MICHAEL B. STOFF
The University of Texas, Austin

McGRAW-HILL PUBLISHING COMANY
New York   St. Louis   San Francisco   Auckland   Bogotá   Caracas   Hamburg   Lisbon
London   Madrid   Mexico   Milan   Montreal   New Delhi   Oklahoma City   Paris
San Juan   São Paulo   Singapore   Sydney   Tokyo   Toronto

NATION OF NATIONS: A NARRATIVE HISTORY OF THE AMERICAN REPUBLIC
Volume I: To 1877

1 2 3 4 5 6 7 8 9 0   VNH   VNH   8 9 4 3 2 1 0 9

ISBN   0-07-557198-6

This book was set in Caledonia by York Graphic Services Inc.
The editors were Christopher J. Rogers and Judith Kromm;
the designer was John Lennard;
the production supervisor was Laura Lamorte.
Von Hoffmann Press, Inc., was printer and binder.

Cover Credit
John Lewis Krimmel, "Fourth of July Celebration in Center Square, Philadelphia, 1819"
Courtesy, The Historical Society of Pennsylvania.

Library of Congress Cataloging-in-Publication Data

Nation of nations: a narrative history of the American republic /
James West Davidson . . . [et al.].
    p.   cm.
    Includes bibliographical references.
    Contents: v. 1. To 1877.
    ISBN 0-07-557198-6 (v. 1)
    1. United States—History.   I. Davidson, James West.
E178.1.N346   1990
973—dc20
                                  89-14592

CONTENTS

PART 3

THE REPUBLIC TRANSFORMED AND TESTED   334

LIST OF MAPS AND CHARTS

PREFACE

History is both a discipline of rigor, bound by rules and scholarly methods, and something more: the unique, compelling, even strange way in which we humans define ourselves. We are all the sum of the tales of thousands of people, great and small, whose actions have etched their lines upon us. History supplies our very identity—a sense of the social groups to which we belong, whether family, ethnic group, race, class, or gender. It reveals to us the foundations of our deepest religious beliefs and traces the roots of our economic and political systems. It explores how we celebrate and grieve, sing the songs we sing, weather the illnesses to which time and chance subject us. It commands our attention for all these good reasons and for no good reason at all, other than a fascination with the way the myriad tales play out. Strange that we should come to care about a host of men and women so many centuries gone, some with names eminent and familiar, others unknown but for a chance scrap of information left behind in an obscure letter.

Yet we do care. We care about Sir Humphrey Gilbert, "devoured and swallowed up of the Sea" one black Atlantic night in 1583, about George Washington at Kips Bay, red with fury as he takes a riding crop to his retreating soldiers. We care about Octave Johnson, a slave fleeing through Louisiana swamps trying to decide whether to stand and fight the approaching hounds or take his chances with the bayou alligators, about Clara Barton, her nurse's skirts so heavy with blood from the wounded, she must wring them out before tending to the next soldier. We are drawn to the fate of Chinese laborers, chipping away at the Sierras' looming granite; a Georgian named Tom Watson seeking to forge a colorblind political alliance; and desperate immigrant mothers, kerosene in hand, storming Brooklyn butcher shops that had again raised prices. We follow, with a mix of awe and amusement, the fortunes of the quirky Henry Ford ("Everybody wants to be somewhere he ain't"), turning out identical automobiles, insisting his factory workers wear identical expressions ("Fordization of the Face"). We trace the career of young Thurgood Marshall, crisscrossing the South in his own "little old beat-up '29 Ford," typing legal briefs in the back seat, trying to get black teachers to sue for equal pay, hoping to get his people somewhere they weren't. The list could go on and on, spilling out as it did in Walt Whitman's *Leaves of Grass:* "A southerner soon as a northerner, a planter nonchalant and hospitable, / A Yankee bound my own way. . . . a Hoosier, a Badger, a Buckeye, a Louisianian or Georgian. . . ." Whitman embraced and celebrated them all, inseparable strands of what made him an American and what made him human:

> In all people I see myself, none more and not one a barleycorn less,
> And the good or bad I say of myself I say of them.

To encompass so expansive an America Whitman turned to poetry; historians have traditionally chosen *narrative* as their means of giving life to the past. That mode of explanation permits them to interweave the strands of economic, political, and social history in a coherent chronological framework. By choosing narrative, they affirm the multicausal nature of historical explanation—the insistence that events be portrayed in context. By choosing narrative, they are also acknowledging that, while long-term economic and social trends shape societies in deep and significant ways, events often take on a logic (or illogic) of their own, jostling one another, being deflected and redirected by unpredictable successions of personal decisions, sudden deaths, natural catastrophes, and chance. There are literary reasons, too, for preferring a narrative approach, since it supplies a dramatic force usually missing from more structural analyses of the past.

In some ways, surveys like this one are the natural antithesis of narrative history. They strive, by definition, to be comprehensive: to furnish a broad, orderly exposition of their chosen field. Yet to cover so much ground in so limited a space necessarily deprives readers of the pacing and context of more detailed accounts. Then, too, the resurgence of social history—with its concern for class and race, patterns of rural and urban life, the spread of market and industrial economies—lends itself to more analytic, less chronological treatments. The challenge facing historians is to incorporate these areas of research without losing the narrative drive that propels the story or sacrificing the chronological flow that orients readers to the more familiar events of our past.

Lately there has been increased attention to the worldwide breakdown of so many nonmarket economies, and by inference, to the greater success of the market societies of the United States and other capitalist nations. As our own narrative makes clear, American society and politics have indeed come together centrally in the marketplace. What Americans produce, how and where they produce it, and the desire to buy cheap and sell dear have been defining elements in every era. That market orientation has created unparalleled abundance and reinforced striking inequalities, not the least a society in which, for two centuries, human beings themselves were bought and sold. It has made Americans powerfully provincial in protecting local interests and internationally adventurous in seeking to expand wealth and opportunity.

It goes without saying that Americans have not always produced wisely or well. The insistent drive toward material plenty has levied a heavy tax on the global environment. Too often quantity has substituted for quality, whether we talk of cars, education, or culture. When markets flourish, the nation abounds with confidence that any problem, no matter how intractable, can be solved. When markets fail, however, the fault lines of our political and social systems become all too evident.

In the end, then, it is impossible to separate the marketplace of boom and bust and the world of ordinary Americans from the corridors of political maneuvering or the ceremonial pomp of an inauguration. To treat political and social history as distinct spheres or hostile camps is counterproductive. The primary question of this narrative—how the fledgling, often tumultuous confederation of "these United States" managed to transform itself into an enduring republic—is not only political, but necessarily social. In order to survive, a republic must resolve conflicts between citizens of different geographic regions and economic classes, of diverse racial and ethnic origins, of competing religions and ideologies. The resolution of these conflicts has produced tragic consequences, perhaps, as often as noble ones. But tragic or noble, the destiny of these states cannot be understood without comprehending the social dimension of the story.

A word about organization and strategies. The narrative is divided into six parts, each beginning with a brief essay setting American events of the period in a global context. We believe it important to make clear that the United States did not develop in a geographic or cultural vacuum and that the broad forces shaping it also influenced other nations. Thus we compare the extraordinary demographic growth of colonial America with the worldwide eighteenth-century rise in population; the effects of democratic and industrial revolutions here with those abroad; the massive voluntary migrations of the nineteenth century to many parts of the globe. We examine the rise of industrial societies of the twentieth century and the environmental constraints to growth as we approach the twenty-first. Each essay ends with a time line comparing political and social events in the United States with developments elsewhere.

Throughout the book we have sought to sustain a narrative approach, starting with introductory episodes for each chapter. Complementing the narrative for each chapter is a two-page essay, "Daily Lives," focusing on one of five topics that give insight into the lives of ordinary Americans: clothing and fashion; time and travel; food, drink, and drugs; political culture; public and private spaces. These topics recur regularly throughout the book, providing additional thematic continuity. Each chapter concludes with a summary of significant events; full and up-to-date bibliographies can be found at the back of the book.

For each of the book's six parts, we have included an essay, "Generations of the Republic," which takes one generation of Americans and charts its progress from birth, childhood, and adolescence through courtship, marriage, adulthood, and old age. In moving from the first Anglo-Americans (Part 1) to the baby-boomers born in the 1940s and 50s (Part 6), we have sought to integrate recent research on family structure and demographics with a sense of how national events affected the lives of ordinary citizens. In effect, we are applying a narrative approach to illuminating the intersection of biography and history.

Any account of a republic with a global reach must be geographically grounded. We have taken particular care in developing the maps for this book, working closely with the cartographers to create geographically detailed yet clear renderings. Full captions are provided whenever necessary; a number of maps are unique to this book, while many others include unusual information. In addition, six geographic essays explore such topics as the commercial and subsistence regions of the young republic, the economics of cotton in the post–Civil War South, and the geographic aspects of the war in Vietnam.

In addition to characterizing the American experience through a complement of paintings, photographs and drawings, we have tried to convey a sense of change over time by incorporating into the book's design contemporary printers' ornaments. The initial blocks opening each chapter have been taken from type specimen books of different eras; similarly, the decorative drawings have come from contemporary engravings.

Many people proved indispensable to the completion of this effort. In the editorial department, first at Alfred A. Knopf and then McGraw-Hill, Edna Shalev and Niels Aaboe somehow managed to keep control of the project's many facets, as did Project Manager Judith Kromm, Production Manager Laura Lamorte, and Photo Manager Safra Nimrod during production. John Lennard took our often inchoate suggestions of how this book might look and transformed them into a clean, elegant design. We are grateful, as well, to a host of readers whose comments and suggestions helped improve an earlier draft of this manuscript. They include Carol Berkin, Baruch College and the Graduate Center of the City University of New York; Roger W. Biles, Oklahoma State University; Carol Brown, Houston Community College; Victor Chen, Chabot College; Mario S. DePillis, University of Massachusetts, Amherst; Lynn Dumenil, Claremont McKenna College; Robert Elam, Modesto Junior College; Robert G. Fricke, West Valley College; James L. Gormly, Washington and Jefferson College; Peter Iverson, Arizona State University; George Juergens, Indiana University; Mark H. Leff, University of Illinois at Urbana-Champaign; John McCardell, Middlebury College; Gerald W. McFarland, University of Massachusetts, Amherst; Dennis C. Rousey, Arkansas State University; James C. Schneider, University of Texas, San Antonio; Lewright B. Sikes, Middle Tennessee State University; Gregory Holmes Singleton, Northeastern Illinois University; David Sloan, University of Arkansas, Fayetteville; Donna J. Spindel, Marshall University; Thomas E. Terrill, University of South Carolina; Stephen G. Weisner, Springfield Technical Community College; Frank J. Wetta, Galveston College; and William Bruce Wheeler, University of Tennessee, Knoxville. In addition, many friends and colleagues contributed their advice and constructive criticism in ways both small and large. These included Michael Bellesiles, Lawrence A. Cardoso, Dinah Chenven, James E. Crisp, R. David Edmunds, Drew McCoy, James McPherson, Stephen E. Maizlish, Harold Silesky, David J. Weber, and Virginia Joyner.

For a book to be successful, of course, the dialogue between readers and authors should continue. We welcome comments, criticisms, or suggestions, any of which will reach us addressed care of McGraw-Hill, College Department (History), 1221 Avenue of the Americas, New York, N.Y. 10020.

The division of labor for this book was determined by our respective fields of scholarship: Christine Heyrman, the colonial era, in which Europeans, Africans, and Indians participated in the making of both a new America and a new republic; William Gienapp, the ninety years in which the young nation first flourished, then foundered on the issues of section and slavery; Michael Stoff, the post–Civil War era, in which industrialization and urbanization brought the nation more centrally into an international system constantly disrupted by depression and war; and Mark Lytle, the modern era, in which Americans finally faced the reality that even the boldest dreams of national greatness are bounded by the finite nature of power and resources both natural and human. Finally, because the need to specialize inevitably imposes limits on any project as broad as this one, our fifth author, James Davidson, served as a general editor and writer, with the intent of fitting individual parts to the whole, as well as providing a measure of continuity, style, and overarching purpose. In producing this collaborative effort, all of us have shared the conviction that the best history speaks to a larger audience.

We began the writing of this book as friends; what is perhaps more unusual, given the strains of such undertakings, is that over the years our friendship deepened. The responsibility for such a happy outcome no doubt rests squarely on the shoulders of our editor, Christopher Rogers. He conceived the project, brought the authors together, consistently pushed us to make this the best book it could be, and marshalled the unstinting support of our publisher for its completion and production. Authors could ask for no more from an editor.

JAMES WEST DAVIDSON
WILLIAM E. GIENAPP
CHRISTINE LEIGH HEYRMAN
MARK H. LYTLE
MICHAEL B. STOFF

PART 1

THE CREATION OF A NEW AMERICA

It is now nearly half a millennium—a full 500 years—since the civilizations of Europe and Africa first made sustained contact with those of North America. The transformations arising out of that event have been astonishing. To gain a rough sense of the scale involved, both in time and space, we start not at the beginning of our story but somewhere nearer its midpoint: retracing the route taken by Meriwether Lewis, First Infantry, USA, as he embarked from Washington, D.C., July 4, 1803.

Lewis, on orders from President Thomas Jefferson, planned to cross the continent with his friend William Clark and a party of assistants; they would be the first Americans to do this. Leaving the cluster of buildings and muddy avenues then known as Washington, Lewis followed the rutted wagon road up the Potomac to Harpers Ferry and made his way across the Alleghenies, that range of mountains which had kept the English colonists hemmed in along the Atlantic coastal plain for 200 years. From Pittsburgh he proceeded by boat down the Ohio, where the wild squirrels were so numerous they could be seen crossing the river in herds. (Lewis' dog, Scannon, finding himself in canine heaven, jumped overboard and retrieved more than a few, which Lewis skinned, fried, and pronounced "a pleasant food.") Clark came aboard at Louisville and the two men continued down to the junction of the Mississippi, then beating upstream to the village of St. Louis.

The true journey began the following spring: up the broad Missouri, which,  together with the Mississippi, constituted one of the longest river systems in the world. The party passed first through lush, tall prairie grass ("from 5 to 8 feet high") and then into the short-grass plains. To Lewis, these resembled nothing so much as a "beautiful bowling-green in fine order," dotted by "immence herds of Buffaloe, deer Elk and Antelopes which we saw in every direction feeding on the hills and plains." The party pressed on through the Dakotas and Montana into the Rockies, seeking the ultimate headwaters of the Missouri. Finally, in August 1805, Lewis reached his watershed—a "handsome bold running Creek of cold Clear water," whose westward flow would eventually take him to the Pacific.

But stop for a moment with Lewis: midway between two oceans, straddling a continental divide and half a millennium of American history. From his vantage point, what can we see?

At first glance, we see pretty much what we expect to see at the beginning of American history: a magnificent and empty "virgin wilderness," rolling on and on across the continent. Even more to the point, because we live in the twentieth century, we tend to take for granted that this vast territory, stretching from ocean to ocean, will become united as a continental republic under a single national government; but only hindsight makes this proposition seem natural. In 1800 the sheer size of the land made the idea of unifying such a territory difficult to grasp. After all, Lewis had traveled a full 1200 miles merely to reach St. Louis, then another 2700 to the headwaters of the Missouri. In 1805 the nation amounted to over 1.5 million square miles. Vast as that was, nearly 2 million more square miles remained to be annexed before the United States would attain its present size.

But it was more than size that made the new "Louisiana Territory" which Lewis and Clark traversed hardly the stuff of continental republics. It was a diverse array of cultures, which for many years had been claimed by the Spanish but in fact was controlled primarily by scores of independent Indian nations. Some of these were hunter-gatherer societies, dispersed in bands across the land; others, especially to the south, had developed highly sophisticated urban cultures or the means of growing crops carefully cultivated through irrigation. Just how diverse the landscape was can be seen by the methods Lewis and Clark used to communicate. With no common language spanning the territory, speechmaking became a series of translations that reflected the route over which the party had traveled. In Idaho, for example, Clark addressed the Tushepaw tribe in English; his speech was translated into French by a trapper in the party; then a second  trapper translated into Minataree, a language which the trapper's Indian wife, Sacajawea, understood. Sacajawea, later renowned as the sole female member of the party, had grown up farther west with the Shoshone, so she in turn translated the Minataree into Shoshone, which a boy from the Tushepaw nation understood. He translated the Shoshone into his own people's tongue.

If the Louisiana Territory seemed a patchwork of governments and cultures, the rest of America was almost as heterogeneous. Spain, Britain, and Russia all continued to claim parts of it, with France too keeping an eye out for possible conquests. During the 1790s Clark had acted as an American intelligence agent, floating up and down the Ohio and Mississippi rivers keeping track of the foreign powers still active on what were then U.S. borders. The "U. States" themselves remained a group of colonies only recently unified. Jefferson, who possessed the vision to send Lewis and Clark on their continental mission, had nonetheless long been in the habit of referring to Virginia as "my country." Indeed, the various states contained a patchwork of languages and cultures nearly as diverse as those farther west. Dutch-speaking patroons could be found along New York's Hudson River, Welsh and German farmers along Pennsylvania's Lancaster Pike, Swedes in

Delaware, Gaelic-speaking Scots scattered up and down the Appalachian back-country, blacks using the African-English Gullah dialect along the Carolina coast. Many of these settlers knew more about their homelands in Europe or Africa than they did about other regions of North America.

In fact, many colonists gained a sense of what other regions were like only during the American Revolution. "Law! Is he a Yankee?" asked one Philadelphia lady of a soldier in the Continental Army. "I thought he was a Pennsylvanian. I don't see any difference between him and other people." Even in the nineteenth century, Americans might understandably be confused about the geography beyond their neighborhoods. Frederick Law Olmsted reported this conversation with a farmer riding on a train near Charleston, South Carolina, during the 1850s:

> "How do you go," the man asked, "w'en you get to Charleston?"
> "I am going on to New Orleans."
> "Is New York beyond New Orleans?"
> "Beyond New Orleans? Oh, no."
> "In New Orleans, is't?"
> "What?"
> "New York is somewhere in New Orleans, ain't it?"
> "No; it's the other way—beyond Wilmington."
> "Oh! Been pretty cold thar?"
> "Yes; there was a foot and a half of snow there, last week, I hear."
> "Lord o'massy! why! have to feed all the cattle!—whew!—ha!—whew! don't won-ner ye com' away."

Evidently this farmer had only vague ideas of the nation existing beyond his neighborhood. But even informed Americans of the 1850s doubted whether the United States could survive the bitter differences then growing between North and South. To resolve them took four years and the bloodiest war in the nation's history. It was by no means clear in the 1850s that a continental republic would survive.

Thus our first task in studying the American past becomes one of translation. We must view events not with the jaded eyes of the late twentieth century but with the innocent eyes of an earlier era. Then the foregone conclusions vanish. How does the American nation manage to unite millions of square miles of territory into one governable republic? How do New Orleans and New York come to be linked in a complex economy as well as in a single political system? Such questions take on even more significance when we recall that Europe—roughly the same size as the United States—is today still divided into 32 independent nations speaking some 33 languages, not to mention another 100 or so spoken within the Soviet Union. A united Europe has not emerged there, despite noble intentions and a Common Market economic system.

How, then, did this American republic—this "teeming nation of nations," to use Walt Whitman's phrase—come to be? In barest outline, that is the question which drives our narrative across half a millennium.

To Europeans in the mid-fifteenth century, of course, the idea of a republic across the sea was even more fantastic than the "Islands of the Blessed"—those mythical lands in the far mists of the Atlantic dreamed of by monks. Scandinavian seafarers had sailed as far west as Greenland by the end of the tenth century; in 1001 a party of men and women under Leif Ericsson established an encampment known as Vinland that endured several seasons, but news of his discoveries never reached the rest of Europe. In 1450, about the time Christopher Columbus was born, only the first stirrings of Western expansion had begun. Localism held sway even more than it did in Lewis and Clark's America.

Europe, in fact, was not a particularly formidable area of the globe. The fastest growing power in the region was the Turkish Ottoman Empire, which in 1453 had captured Constantinople as a beachhead for further expansion into Europe. True, the Italian city-states of Genoa and Venice controlled flourishing trading outposts in Asia Minor. But the Turks were also cutting into these. Within Europe, political organization remained fragmented. Italy was divided into five major states and an equal number of smaller territories. The Germanic peoples were united loosely in the Holy Roman Empire (which, as historians have long delighted in pointing out, was neither holy, Roman, nor an empire). French kings ruled over only about half of what is now France. Spain was divided into several kingdoms, with some areas held by Christians, others by Islamic Moors, whose forebears came from Africa. England, a contentious little nation, was beginning a series of bitter civil conflicts among the nobility, known eventually as the Wars of the Roses. The only country pushing beyond the boundaries of the known European world was Portugal, whose sailors were slowly advancing down the coast of Africa in search of gold and slaves.

Localism was evident in other ways. Europe in 1450 was far from being the urban commercial society it is today. London, which today has a population of 6 million or 7 million, held only about 50,000 people; Paris, something more than 100,000. Most people lived in rural or village settings. Moving goods from one region to another was extremely difficult. Land routes were by and large only rutted paths, except for the ancient Roman roads. Wheeled carts were sometimes used to haul loads, but more often it was simply pack animals or human porters bearing goods over the mountain passes of the Alps. Rivers and canals provided another option, but lords repeatedly taxed boats that crossed their territories. (On the Seine River, greedy tollkeepers lay in wait every six or seven miles.) Travel across the Mediterranean Sea and along Europe's northern coastlines was possible, but storms and pirates made the going dangerous and slow. Under good conditions, a ship might reach London from Venice in only 9 days; under bad, it might take 50. In addition, since 1347 western Europe had been repeatedly decimated by bubonic plague. A population once totaling more than 50 million had dropped to about 37 million by 1450.

European peoples at this time had some dealings—though not extensive—with Africa. What contact there was arose primarily from sharing the Mediterranean Sea. North African culture had been shaped since the seventh century by the religion of Islam, whose influence spread even up through Spain. Farther south in Africa, the kingdom of Songhai prospered along the Niger River. But Africans from these interior regions were linked with Europeans primarily through trading caravans, which made their way across the Sahara with African gold—essential to Europe's economy. The west African coast, which faced the Atlantic, was only beginning to receive the attention of the Portuguese. Their coming would drastically alter the patterns of African–European trade. Ultimately these changes would transform the Americas as well.

If Europe in 1450 was less unified and dynamic than we might have imagined, the civilizations of North and South America were more complex than they have sometimes been painted. We have already noted the popular image of America before 1492 as a "virgin wilderness." Yet this stereotype is profoundly misleading. Research over the past several decades indicates that North and South America were much more populous than historians once thought. Earlier estimates suggested that when Europeans arrived about 10 million people were living in Central and South America, with another million living north of Mexico. More recently these figures have been raised tenfold, to perhaps as many as 100 million people in Central and South America and 10 million north of Mexico.

Such numbers—which remain conjectural and imprecise—nevertheless lead to startling conclusions. In 1492, when Columbus landed on Hispaniola, that island alone may have held some 7 million to 8 million people—a number roughly equal to the entire population of Spain. (England at the time had only 4 million to 5 million people.) Tenochtitlán, capital of the Aztec empire, held an estimated 250,000 inhabitants, probably double the size of the largest European cities of the day. Such dense urban populations were supported by sophisticated agricultural techniques, including canals, irrigation, and drainage systems.

North America was far from being as heavily populated as the lands to the south, but neither was it sparsely settled. From one end of the continent to the other, native cultures actively shaped their environments, regularly burning the forests and plains to promote the growth of vegetation as well as animal populations, which they harvested. As we shall see, their agricultural achievements were so remarkable that they eventually revolutionized eating habits across the rest of the globe.

Here then are three worlds—Europe, Africa, the Americas—poised on the brink of contact. What social and economic forces led so many Europeans—desperate and opportunistic, high-minded and idealistic—to turn westward in pursuit of their dreams? How did the civilizations of North and South America react and adjust to the European invaders? And not least, how did the mix of cultures from Africa, Europe, and North America come together to create what was truly a new America, in which some of the most independent-minded individuals prospered in provinces that exhibited some of the harshest examples of human slavery? These are among the questions we seek to answer as our narrative unfolds.

CHRONOLOGY

AMERICAN EVENT	YEAR	GLOBAL EVENT
Leif Ericsson establishes Vinland in Newfoundland	1001	
	1215	Mongols begin 60-year conquest of China
	1271–1295	Marco Polo travels to China from Venice
Rise of the Aztec empire	ca. 1300	
	1347	Bubonic plague reaches Europe; population of 50 million drops 30–40 percent by 1400
Formation of the Iroquois League	late 1400s	
Columbus reaches America	1492	Reconquista drives Muslim Arabs from Spain
	1498	Vasco da Gama reaches India
	1517	Luther launches Protestant Reformation
European diseases waste central Mexico; population falls from ca. 25 million to 1 million in 1600, a 95% mortality	1520s	
Cortés conquers Aztec empire	1521	
Silver boom in Mexico, Bolivia	1550s	
	1602	Dutch East India Company founded
Jamestown established	1607	
Santa Fe founded	1610	
Pilgrims land at Plymouth	1620	
Sugar boom in Caribbean	1640s	
	1642	Outbreak of English Civil War
	1660	Restoration of English monarchy: Charles II ascends throne
Carolinas founded	1663	
Chesapeake labor system depends increasingly on black slavery	1680s	
La Salle follows the Mississippi	1682	
	1687	Isaac Newton's *Principia Mathematica*, on gravitation, published
	1688	Glorious Revolution in England; constitutional monarchy of William III and Mary
Glorious Revolution in America	1688–1691	
King William's War	1689–1697	War of the League of Augsburg
Rice boom in South Carolina	1700s	
Queen Anne's War	1702–1713	War of the Spanish Succession
French found New Orleans	1718	
The Great Awakening	1730s–1750s	
	1738	John and Charles Wesley begin preaching Methodism in England
King George's War	1740–1748	War of the Austrian Succession
Benjamin Franklin founds the American Philosophical Society	1743	

1

Old World, New Worlds

ll the world lay before them. Or so it seemed to mariners from England's seafaring coasts, pushing westward toward unknown lands in the far Atlantic.

The scent of the new land came first—not the sight of it, but the sounds and smells, wafted from beyond the horizon, delicious to mariners who had felt nothing but the rolling sea for weeks on end. In northerly latitudes around June, it would be the scent of fir trees or the sight of shore birds wheeling about the masts—signs of favor worthy of an Our Father or a Hail Mary from the grateful sailors. Straightaway the captain would call for a lead to be thrown overboard to sound the depths; at its end was a hollowed-out socket with a bit of tallow in it, so some of the sea bottom would stick when hauled up. Even out of sight of land, a good sailing master could tell where he was by what came up—"oosy sand," indicating a location north of the Scilly Isles, or perhaps "soft worms" or "popple-stones as big as beans." But if the ship was approaching unknown shores, the captain's hope would be to sight land early in the day, allowing time to work cautiously toward an untried harbor on uncharted tides.

Since the time of King Arthur, the English living along the rugged southwestern coasts of Devon and Cornwall had followed the sea. From the wharves of England's West Country seaports, like Bristol, Exeter, and Plymouth, ships headed west and north to Ireland, bringing back timber for houses, barrels and casks, and animal hides. Or they turned south, crossing the English Channel to trade with other Atlantic ports, bringing back wines from French Bordeaux and olive oil or luxurious figs and raisins from the Spanish and Portuguese coasts. In return, West Country ports offered woven woolen cloth and codfish, caught wherever the likeliest prospects beckoned.

In the early fifteenth century, prospects had taken West Country sailors north and west, toward Iceland. The amount of dried cod brought back had been not only essential for trade but also a crucial staple in the diet, especially over the barren winter months. By the 1480s, however, the West Country fisherfolk were taking a beating from the Icelanders, whose mariners preferred to keep the catch for themselves and trade with the Germans and the Danes. The brawling and killing that plagued the fishing grounds persuaded some of the more enterprising English to sail farther west. Old maps, after all, claimed that the bountiful *Hy-Brasil*—Gaelic for "Isle of the Blessed"—lay vaguely to the west of Ireland.

Over the next dozen years, a few ships ventured every other year or so

With sails bellying in a gale, the Dutch ship in this Verbeek painting has furled the rest of its canvas. When Humphrey Gilbert's ship went down in a similar storm, the last a nearby vessel saw was the stern lantern (visible on this ship too) wink out.

West Country fisherfolk from England weighed anchor and sailed from harbors like this one, painted during the 1480s. The ship at left is being towed by a longboat to a position where it can hoist sail and set off. In the foreground is a primitive lighthouse: an iron cresset on a pole, holding a smoky warning fire.

beyond the known routes, but with little luck. Into this eddy of interest stepped an Italian, a citizen of Venice named Giovanni Caboto, whom the English called John Cabot. Cabot had obtained the blessing of King Henry VII to hunt for unknown lands, and he wisely took to Bristol to outfit himself. In the spring of 1497 his lone ship set out to the west, and this time the return voyage brought news of a "new-found" island where the trees were tall enough to make fine masts and the codfish were plentiful. After returning to Bristol, Cabot marched off to London to inform His Majesty, received 10 pounds as his reward, and with the proceeds dressed himself in dashing silks. The multitudes of London flocked after him, wondering over "the Admiral"; then Cabot returned triumphantly to Bristol to undertake a more ambitious voyage—the search for a northwest passage to Asia. He set sail with five ships in 1498 and was never heard from again, presumably a victim of the North Atlantic.

Still, Bristol folk were not about to let a gale or two distract them from reports of cod. In the 1500s they began to fish regularly the relatively shallow Grand Banks off the island of Newfoundland, as it came to be called. The teeming waters attracted a swarm of Europeans, not only from England but also from Portuguese harbors like Aveiro and Viana, French ports scattered along Brittany and Normandy, and Spanish villages facing the Bay of Biscay. By 1550, perhaps 400 vessels and 1200 men arrived in Newfoundland for the annual fishing season.

The trip was not easy. Individual merchants or a few partners outfitted small ships with provisions, fishing boats, and a complement of guns to ward off both sea-roving pirates and "privateers"—pirates who looted with royal approval. As early in the season as they dared, crews of 10 or 20 would catch the spring easterlies, leaving astern the horizon of familiar roofs and the primitive lighthouse burning its smoky coal. Aboard ship, only the officers were given bunks; seamen slept in odd spaces below decks. Rats were such a constant plague that the law of the sea required carrying at least one cat aboard every ship. In Newfoundland waters, sailors had to look sharp for icebergs and even more dangerous "growlers"—chunks of ice the size of houses, which floated barely concealed just below the water, ready to do a ship in.

Weeks after setting sail the sailors sighted land—fog-shrouded beaches fringing thick pine forests, seals and walruses along the rocks offshore, and the encircling sea filled with cod and flounder, salmon and herring. Throughout the summer men launched little ketches from rickety, hastily constructed stages in each harbor and fished offshore all day and into the night. With lines and nets, and baskets weighted with stones, they scooped fish from the sea and then dried and salted the catch on the beach. Some of the Spanish went after whales, which they hauled ashore, cut up, and boiled into oil. And crews from every European country traded with the native Beothuks and Micmacs, who shared their summer fishing grounds and the skins of fox and deer.

For those who tired of the long weeks at sea, Newfoundland offered St. John's, which by the 1550s had become the hub of the North Atlantic fishery. Portuguese, English, and French fishing vessels all dropped anchor there, either to take on supplies in the spring or to prepare for the homeward voyage in autumn. Only the Spanish kept their distance. In St. John's, masters haggled over the price of fish and bartered for items they could not get at home. Here the port admiral, usually the master of the first vessel to arrive each season, struggled to settle disputes over stolen boats, contested beaches, and personal insults. And here, amid the swilling and scuffling and squabbling, there was always a great deal of talk, for these seafarers knew as much as anyone about the new world of wonders that was opening to Europeans. They were acquainted with names like Cristoforo Colombo, the Italian from Genoa whom Cabot might have known as a boy. They listened to Portuguese tales of sailing around the Horn of Africa in pursuit of spices and to stories of empires to the south, rich in gold and silver, which Spanish treasure ships were bringing home.

Indeed, Newfoundland was one of the few places in the world where so many ordinary folk of different nations could gather and talk, crammed aboard dank ships moored in St. John's harbor, huddled before blazing fires on its beaches, or crowded into smoky, makeshift taverns. And when the ships sailed home in autumn the tales went with them, repeated in the tiniest coastal villages by those pleased to have cheated death and the sea one more time. Eager to fish, talk, trade, and take profits, West Country mariners were almost giddy at the prospect of Europe's expanding horizons.

THE MEETING OF EUROPE AND AMERICA

Most of the captains, pilots, and seafarers who fished the waters of Newfoundland's Grand Banks remain anonymous today. Their lives are lost to the historical

The Geography of Exploration

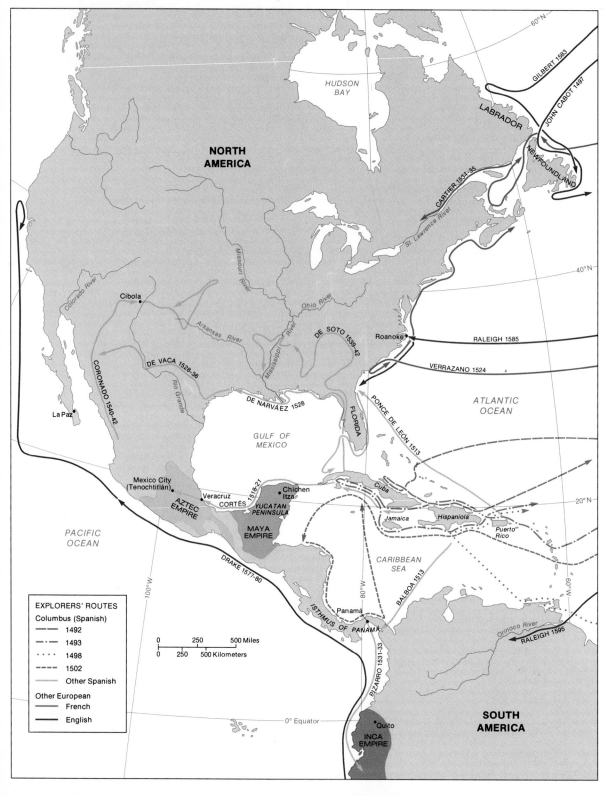

HUDSON BAY

GILBERT 1583

JOHN CABOT 1497

LABRADOR

NEWFOUNDLAND

CARTIER 1534-35

NORTH AMERICA

St. Lawrence River

Missouri River

Colorado River

Cibola

Ohio River

Arkansas River

Mississippi River

DE SOTO 1539-42

Roanoke

RALEIGH 1585

CORONADO 1540-42

DE VACA 1528-36

Rio Grande

VERRAZANO 1524

La Paz

DE NARVÁEZ 1528

FLORIDA

PONCE DE LEÓN 1513

ATLANTIC OCEAN

GULF OF MEXICO

40° N

60° N

20° N

Mexico City (Tenochtitlán)

Veracruz CORTÉS

1518-21

Chichen Itza

AZTEC EMPIRE

YUCATAN PENINSULA

MAYA EMPIRE

Cuba

Jamaica

Hispaniola

Puerto Rico

PACIFIC OCEAN

DRAKE 1577-80

100° W.

CARIBBEAN SEA

BALBOA 1513

80° W.

60° W.

ISTHMUS OF PANAMÁ

Panamá

PIZARRO 1531-33

Orinoco River

RALEIGH 1595

SOUTH AMERICA

0° Equator

Quito

INCA EMPIRE

EXPLORERS' ROUTES

Columbus (Spanish)

— — — 1492

—·—·— 1493

· · · · · 1498

– – – – 1502

〜〜〜 Other Spanish

Other European

——— French

——— English

0   250   500 Miles

0   250   500 Kilometers

Spain dominated the first hundred years of exploration and settlement in the Americas. Columbus and his successors first established a base of operations at Hispaniola and then subjugated Puerto Rico (1509), Jamaica (1510), and Cuba (1511). Ponce de León pressed north to Florida, Balboa traversed the Panamanian isthmus to discover the Pacific, and in 1519 Cortés began his conquest of the mainland.

But Spain was only one of several countries whose Atlantic coast encouraged them to press westward in search of profitable trade (top right). Spanish and French fisherfolk, whose ports lay on the Atlantic's Bay of Biscay, joined other French sailors from Brittany and Normandy as well as English "West Country boys" at the Grand Banks off Newfoundland, where the shallows of the continental shelf yielded abundant stores of cod and other fish.

Farther south, the Portuguese and Spanish had developed different strategies for sailing west (bottom right). During the fifteenth century, they used the prevailing breezes of the northeast trades to head south and west to the Madeira Islands, colonized by Portugal, and the Canaries, settled by Spain. But how to sail home, against the winds? The technique sailors hit upon was to travel farther *west*, but north as well, until they reached a latitude where the prevailing westerlies carried them back to Europe. The Portuguese called this maneuver the *volta do mar*—returning by sea.

Columbus and the Spanish who followed him applied the same technique on a grander scale: dropping south to the Canaries to catch the northeast trades to the Caribbean, then heading north on the return trip to pick up the westerlies. The technique was refined even further when the pilot of Ponce de León's expedition discovered the currents of the Gulf Stream that surged eastward between Florida and Cuba. Soon all Spanish fleets were returning home by sailing not south of Cuba but north, harnessing both ocean currents and the winds.

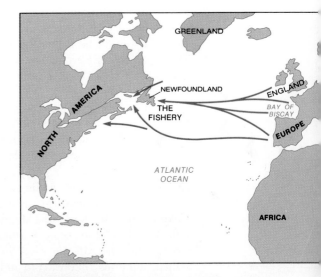

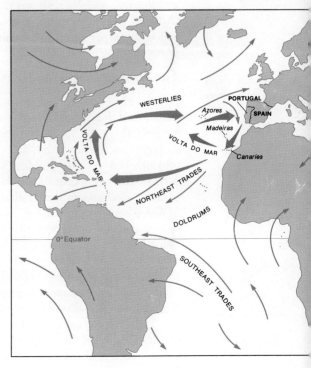

record except for a few recollections or a line or two in royal archives about voyagers who presented to the Crown exotic "hauwkes," wildcats, or "popinjays" (a bright bird of any unusual sort) "brought from the Newfounde Island." Yet it is well to begin with these anonymous fisherfolk, for the European discovery of the Americas cannot be looked upon simply as the voyages of a few bold explorers. The expansion of European peoples and culture that began in the 1450s could not have occurred without a series of gradual but telling changes in the fabric of European society.

Some of these changes were technological, arising out of advances in navigational skills, the art of shipbuilding, and the use of gunpowder. Some were social, involving the development of trade networks of the sort that linked Bristol with ports as far afield as those of Iceland and Spain. Some were demographic, bringing about a rise in Europe's population after a devastating century of plague. Some changes were religious, adding a dimension of devout belief to the political rivalries that fueled discoveries in the Americas. And some changes were political, making it possible for feudal kingdoms to centralize and extend their bureaucratic influence across the ocean. Portugal, Spain, France, and England—all possessing coasts along the Atlantic—led the way in exploration, spurred on by acclaimed Italian "admirals" like Caboto and Colombo, Spanish *conquistadores* like Cortés and Pizarro, and English sea dogs like Humphrey Gilbert and Walter Raleigh. Ordinary folk rode these currents too. The great and the small alike were propelled by forces that were remolding the face of Europe.

The Portuguese Wave

In 1450 all of the world known to western Europeans was Asia and Africa. Most mariners of the day confined their voyages to the coast of western Europe, inching gingerly along the shores between Norway and the southern tip of Spain, seldom daring to lose sight of land, and putting into port often. Since the beginning of the fifteenth century, the boldest seafarers had groped down the coast of western Africa—half-expecting to be boiled alive in the Atlantic as they approached the equator. Europeans had traded with Asia through the Muslims of the eastern Mediterranean and across an overland route called the "Silk Road," but they had only vague notions about the contours of "the Indies"—China and Japan, the Spice Islands, and the lands lying between Thailand and India. What little they knew, they had learned mainly from Marco Polo, whose account of his travels in the East was not published until 1477, more than 150 years after his death. Even then, many learned men in Europe doubted his reports of the Great Khan's Cathay (China) and dismissed his Cipango (Japan) as a mythical island.

But a revolution in the European knowledge of geography began in the middle decades of the fifteenth century. As the picture of the known world changed, so did the world itself. Ever-widening networks of travel and trade connected Europeans to new peoples, economies, and civilizations beyond western Europe. The Portuguese took the lead in pushing beyond the traditional bounds, encouraged by Prince Henry, known as the Navigator. The devout Henry, a member of Portugal's royal family in the middle of the fifteenth century, was not as much consumed by dynastic ambitions as he was curious about finding out "things which were hidden from other men, and secret." Like others of his day, he had heard tales of Prester John, a Catholic priest reputed to rule a Christian kingdom somewhere in Africa or Asia, on the eastern flank of the Muslim world. Henry dreamed of joining forces with Prester John and trapping the Muslims in a vise. To that end, he subsidized a series of expeditions down the coast of west Africa. And at Cape St. Vincent, the westernmost point of all Europe on the Portuguese coast, he founded an informal school of navigation, dispensing to shipmasters information about wind and currents, as well as navigational charts.

Portuguese merchants, who may or may not have credited the existence of Prester John, never doubted that there was money to be made in Africa. Unlike Spain, Portugal possessed no coast bordering the Mediterranean with easy access to its trade. As an alternative, its merchants invested in Prince Henry's voyages and in return gained trading monopolies of ivory and slaves, grain and gold. A few may have hoped that the voyages down the coast of west Africa would lead to a direct sea route to the Orient. By discovering such a route, Portugal would be able to lower the cost of importing Asia's silks, dyes, drugs, perfumes, and spices by cutting out the Muslim middlemen who controlled all of Europe's Asian trade through Mediterranean ports.

At the same time that Portugal's merchants were establishing trading posts or "factories" along the west coast of Africa, its mariners were discovering islands in the Atlantic. Before 1400, the Portuguese had found the Canary Islands, and in the 1420s they colonized both Madeira and the Azores; settlers planted sugar cane and grape vines and imported slaves from Africa to work their fields.

Portuguese mariners might have pressed farther west, but for the daring of Bartolomeu Dias. In 1488 Dias distracted the Portuguese from the Atlantic by rounding the Cape of Good Hope on the southern tip of Africa and sailing far enough up that continent's eastern coast to claim discovery of a sea route to India. Ten years later Vasco da Gama reached India itself, and Portuguese interests ultimately extended to Indochina and China. The Portuguese did not settle large numbers of their own people in Asia, but they scattered factories, garrisons, and missions throughout the Indies. And although Portugal's explorers never encountered the like of Prester John, its merchants replaced the Muslims as masters of trade to the Orient.

By the turn of the century, all of seafaring Europe eagerly sought the services of Portuguese pilots, prizing their superior maps and skills with the quadrant. That instrument made for a fairly accurate determination of latitude, allowing ships to plot their position after months out of the sight of land. The Portuguese had also pioneered the caravel, a light ship that afforded greater power against contrary winds and more maneuverability in rough seas than did heavier vessels. More seaworthy than the lumbering galleys of the Middle Ages, caravels combined longer, narrower hulls, a shape built for speed, with triangular lateen sails, which allowed for more flexible steering. Advances in firearms over the previous century led the Portuguese as well as other Europeans to mount cannons on their ships. The superior firepower made it possible to defeat Asian navies, even when the Europeans were outnumbered.

Following the discovery of a route to India, Portuguese attention turned largely to building an empire in the East Indies, although Portugal continued to

This stately ivory mask made by an African artist in the early sixteenth century for the Court of Benin (present-day Nigeria) is adorned with several small heads of white men, representing Portuguese explorers and traders who had first arrived in Benin in 1472.

dominate trade along Africa's west coast. When yellow fever, malaria, and other African diseases kept the Portuguese from colonizing the mainland, they set up way stations on islands off the African coast, such as the Cape Verdes and, farther south, São Tomé. There, Africans converted to Christianity by missionaries inter-married with European traders to form a culturally mixed society that became a linchpin of the Atlantic trade in African slaves. In the centuries to come, hundreds of thousands of slaves would be shipped to the Portuguese colony of Brazil, whose shores were discovered when a storm blew Pedro Álvares Cabral off course in 1500. But the Atlantic slave trade did not blossom in earnest until after Spain had made a much greater mark on the Americas.

The Spanish and Columbus

From among the international community of seafarers and pilots, it was a sailor from Genoa, Cristoforo Colombo, who led the Spanish to the Americas. Columbus (the Latinized version of his name survives) had knocked about in a number of harbors. In 1472 the red-haired, ruddy-faced young man of 25 traveled to Lisbon, picking up valuable navigation skills sailing Portugal's merchant ships to Madeira, west Africa, and the North Atlantic. His North Atlantic travels took him to Iceland and western Ireland, possibly even to England's West Country. In the Irish port of Galway, Columbus saw two boats drift into the harbor, bearing the dead bodies of "a man and a woman of extraordinary appearance." Most likely they were Lapps or Finns, the victims of a shipwreck. But everyone in Galway, including Columbus, assumed that they were Chinese, "blown across" the Atlantic.

That evidence only confirmed Columbus in his conviction that the quickest route to the Indies lay westward, across the Atlantic—and that his destiny was to prove it. Perhaps a mere 4500 miles, he reckoned, separated Europe from Japan. His wishful estimate raised eyebrows whenever Columbus asked European mon-archs for the money to meet his destiny. Most educated Europeans agreed that the world was round, but they also believed that the Atlantic barrier between themselves and Asia was far wider than Columbus allowed and that it was impossi-ble to navigate. The kings of England, France, and Portugal dismissed him as a crackpot.

Almost a decade of ridicule and rejection had grayed Columbus' red hair when Spain's monarchs, Ferdinand and Isabella, finally consented to subsidize his expedition in 1492. Even then, it was not so much confidence in Columbus as spite against Portugal that dictated Spanish support. For the past 20 years the two monarchs had worked to unite Spain and drive the Muslims out of their last stronghold on the peninsula, the Moorish kingdom of Granada. In 1492 they completed this *reconquista*, or battle of reconquest, expelling many Jews as well. Yet the Portuguese, by breaking the Muslim stranglehold on trade to Asia, had usurped the role of scourge of Islam that Spain coveted for itself. Ferdinand and Isabella were so desperate to even the score with their neighboring kingdom that jealousy overcame common sense: they agreed to take a risk on Columbus.

Columbus' first voyage across the Atlantic could only have confirmed his conviction that he was destiny's darling. His three ships, no bigger than fishing vessels that sailed to Newfoundland, plied their course over placid seas, south from Seville to the Canary Islands and then due west. On October 11, branches, leaves, and flowers floated by their hulls, signals that land lay near. And just after midnight, a sailor spied cliffs shining white in the moonlight. On the morning of

October 12, the *Niña*, the *Pinta*, and the *Santa Maria* made for a shallow, sapphire bay, and their crews disembarked and knelt on the white coral beach. Then Christopher Columbus, by the authority of Spain Admiral of the Ocean Sea and Governor and Viceroy of all he surveyed, christened the place San Salvador (Holy Savior).

Like so many men of destiny, Columbus did not recognize his true destination. Certain that God intended him to find the Indies, he resisted recognizing the novelty of his discovery. He was off by about 8000 miles. At first Columbus confused his actual location, the Bahamas, with an island off the coast of Japan. He coasted Cuba and Hispaniola (Haiti), expecting at any moment to catch sight of gold-roofed Japanese temples or to happen upon a fleet of Chinese junks. He encountered instead a gentle, generous people who knew nothing of the Great Khan, but who showed him around their islands. Columbus' journals note that they wore little clothing, but they did wear jewelry—tiny pendants of gold suspended from the nose. These trinkets they exchanged gladly for glass beads and hawks' bells, and they directed Columbus to the source of their finery, Hispaniola. He dubbed the Arawak people "Indians," as befitting inhabitants of the Indies.

Columbus crossed the Atlantic three more times between 1493 and 1504. On his second voyage he established a permanent colony at Hispaniola and explored other Caribbean islands; on his third voyage he reached "the Spanish Main" (or mainland)—Venezuela on the continent of South America; and on his last voyage he made landfalls throughout Central America—Honduras, Nicaragua, Costa Rica, and Panama. Everywhere he looked for proof that these lands formed part of Asia—probably, he came to believe, the Malay Peninsula.

Columbus died rich in titles, treasure, and tales—everything but recognition. During the last decade of his life, most Spaniards no longer believed that Columbus had discovered the Indies or anyplace else of significance. And shortly after his death in 1506, another Italian stamped his own name on the New World. Amerigo Vespucci, a Florentine banker with a flair for self-promotion, cruised the coast of Brazil in 1501 and again in 1503. His sensational report of his travels misled Martin Waldseemüller, a young German mapmaker, into giving Vespucci credit for discovering the barrier between Europe and Asia, and so naming it "America."

EARLY NORTH AMERICAN CULTURES

The Americas were a new world only to European latecomers. To the Asian peoples and their native American descendants who had settled the continents tens of thousands of years earlier, Columbus' new world was their own old world. But it is doubtful that the first nomadic hunters who crossed from Siberia over the Bering Strait to Alaska considered themselves discoverers or recognized what they had found—a truly new world, one wholly uninhabited by humans.

The First Inhabitants

The first passage of people from Asia to America probably took place during a prehistoric glacial period—either before 35,000 B.C. or about 10,000 years later—when huge amounts of the world's water froze into sheets of ice. Sea levels dropped so drastically that the Bering Strait became a broad, grassy plain. Across that land bridge between the two continents both humans and animals escaped icebound Siberia for ice-free Alaska. Whenever the first migration took place, the movement of Asians to America continued, even after 8000 B.C. when world temperatures rose again, and the water from melting glaciers flooded back into the ocean, submerging the Bering Strait. The 56-mile stretch of water froze in winter, paving an icy path to America; even in summer, small boats could hop from one continent to another across the Diomedes Islands. Over a span of 25,000 years settlement spread down the Alaskan coast, then up river valleys and along mountain passes deeper into the North American mainland, and finally throughout Central and South America.

Native Americans remained nomadic hunters and gatherers for thousands of years, as did many Europeans, Africans, and Asians of those millennia. Increasingly, however, American cultures diversified, especially after about 5500 B.C., when the peoples of central Mexico discovered how to cultivate food crops; this skill slowly spread north to other tribes. This "agricultural revolution" allowed native American societies to grow much larger, and each developed distinctive forms of economic, social, and political organization. By the end of the fifteenth century, the inhabitants of North America, perhaps 10 million people, spoke as many as 1000 languages, some as different from each other as English is from Chinese. Columbus erred doubly by calling the native Americans "Indians," not only mistaking continents but also attributing to peoples a cultural unity that had vanished long before 1492.

The simplest Indian societies were those that still relied on hunting and gathering—like the Shoshone of the Great Basin (parts of present-day Nevada, Oregon, and Idaho); the Eskimos of the Arctic; and the Serrano, Cahuilla, Luiseño, and Diegueño of southern California, Arizona, and the Baja peninsula of Mexico. Stark deserts and frozen tundra defied cultivation and yielded food supplies that could sustain nomadic bands numbering no more than about 50 people. Families occasionally joined together for a collective hunt or wintered in common quarters, but for most of the year they dispersed across the landscape, the women gathering plants and seeds, making baskets, and cooking meals while the men hunted for meat and hides. Political authority was invested in either the male family head or the "headman" of a small band; "shamans"—any tribesmen claiming spiritual powers—enlisted the supernatural to assist individuals.

Societies of Increasing Complexity

In the densely forested belt that stretched from Newfoundland to the Bering Strait, resources more generous than those of the tundra to the north made for larger populations and more closely knit societies. Northeastern bands like the Montagnais, the Micmac, and the Penobscot and northwestern tribes like the Yellowknife and the Beaver traveled forests of evergreen in moccasins and snowshoes, stalking deer, elk, moose, bear, and caribou; they speared fish in icy lakes and swift streams from birch-bark canoes. Their environment encouraged cooperative economic pursuits: leading men assigned several families to specific territories that they hunted together, dividing the returns among the whole band. Religious beliefs enhanced the solidarity of kin groups: each family had a "totem," a particular animal from which they claimed descent.

While men dominated Indian bands based on hunting by virtue of their skill

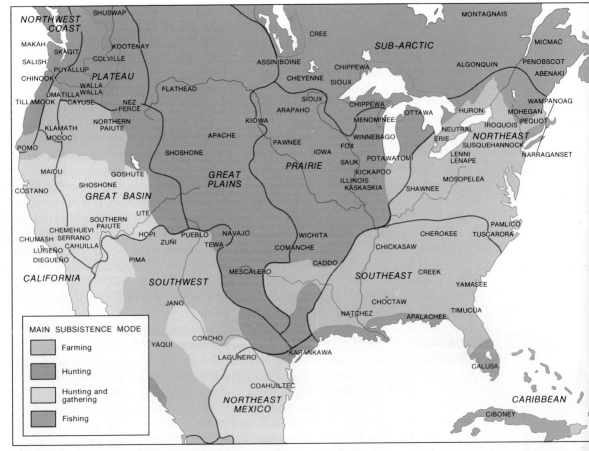

INDIANS OF NORTH AMERICA, CIRCA 1500

and knowledge of the terrain, women assumed more influence in societies that relied for part of their food on settled agriculture. Among the Pueblo peoples of Arizona and New Mexico, the Hopi and Zuñi tribes, men hunted bison and cultivated corn and beans, but women owned the fields, the crops, and even the tools. They also owned the sun-baked dwellings of adobe and stone, some of which rose to several stories, that housed the families of their daughters. By 1540 some 70 Pueblo villages flourished, harboring populations much larger than those of nomadic tribes. More reliable food supplies swelled the size and number of lineages or clans, families sharing a common ancestry, who together formed the Hopi and Zuñi tribes.

Despite the scale of Pueblo society, it remained egalitarian: a council of religious elders drawn from the different clans governed each village. But Pueblo religious ceremonies, in contrast to those of simpler Indian societies, involved the whole tribe, not just families or individuals. Elaborate rituals celebrated tribal unity and sought the gods' blessing for hunts and harvests that secured the common welfare. Thousands of miles to the northeast and in a natural setting far different from the semiarid Southwest, the Iroquois created a remarkably similar culture. There, too, property and inheritance passed through the mother's side of the family, and tribal councils united family kinship networks in a larger alliance.

More complex Indian civilizations arose in the bountiful environments of the Pacific Northwest and the coastal region reaching from Virginia to Texas. The seas and rivers from eastern Alaska to northern California teemed with salmon, cod, and halibut and hosted humpback whales, seals, and otters; the Southeast's fertile soil and temperate climate encouraged the cultivation of maize, rice, and a variety of fruits, and its forests were filled with deer, bear, and bison. Diligent harvesting of these resources and the development of techniques to preserve food supplies supported large, settled tribes.

Far less egalitarian than nomadic hunting bands or even the Pueblo and Iroquois, these tribes developed elaborate systems of status and distinct occupational groups, including a special caste of priests. Chiefs, if they won backing from powerful families, could exercise considerable authority: storing and redistributing food among the tribe's members, assigning certain families to fish, farm, or work at handicrafts, and conducting wars to expand tribal territories. In northwestern chiefdoms, each individual had a place in hierarchies based on lineage and wealth; the richest families kept slaves—captives taken in war—as emblems of their high rank. Among southeastern tribes like the Natchez, social divisions were even more firmly etched. Below the chief, or "Great Sun," stood his advisers, a hereditary nobility of lesser "Suns," who demanded elaborate deference from the lowly "Stinkards," the common people.

Even more advanced were the vast agricultural empires of Mesoamerica—south and central Mexico and Guatemala. As the Roman empire was declining in Europe, the civilization of the Mayas was flourishing in the lowland jungles of Central America. The Mayas established elaborate urban centers, filled with palaces, bridges, aqueducts, vapor baths, astronomical observatories, plazas, and temples topped by pyramids. Their priests developed a written language, their mathematicians discovered the zero, and their astronomers devised a calendar more accurate than any then existing and calculated the revolution of the moon and the recurrence of solar eclipses.

The Aztecs, who invaded central Mexico from the north in the fourteenth century, built on the achievements of the Mayas and later civilizations like the Toltecs. Within a century, conquest and diplomacy had created an empire of several million people that extended west from the Gulf coast to the Pacific and south to Guatemala. The Aztec capital, Tenochtitlán, transformed a once-marshy island on a lake into a glittering metropolis with a population in 1400 of perhaps a quarter of a million—several times the size of London. The Great Temple of the Sun dominated the center of the city, and through the causeways and canals leading to Tenochtitlán flowed gold, silver, exotic feathers, cotton cloaks, cocoa, and millions of pounds of maize, trade goods and tribute from other Mexican city-states conquered by the Aztecs.

Warfare enlarged and enriched the empire, but its primary purpose was to maintain a steady supply of human captives for sacrifice. Aztecs believed that they were the chosen people—chosen to nourish the earth by sustaining the life of the sun. Each year priests wielding razor-sharp obsidian knives sliced open the chests of thousands of captives and offered up to the sun hearts still beating, the essence of life.

Although early modern Europeans were shocked at the extent of the sacrifices and the accompanying cannibalism, crusading Christians should not have found unfamiliar the sense of mission and destiny underlying the Aztec ritual of human sacrifice. In other ways, too, the world of the Aztecs was not dissimilar to the societies of early modern Europe. Like Europe's peasants, Aztec farmers lived in permanent villages; their merchants and specialized craftworkers clustered in large cities, organized themselves into guilds, and clamored for protection from the government. And, as in Europe, noble and priestly classes commanding land and followers took the lead in politics and religion and exacted tribute from the common people. Although these Indian empires did not know the use of the wheel or iron, they had sophisticated methods of irrigation, architecture, and the manufacture of pottery, jewelry, and textiles.

Yet, for all their similarities, there was at least one crucial difference between Aztec civilization and that of Europe in 1500: Aztec territorial expansionism did not take the form of colonization or overseas settlement that spanned the oceans—indeed, the globe. That difference reflected a host of distinctive changes in European social, economic, and political development during the fourteenth and fifteenth centuries. It was these transformations that made it possible for bold sailors like Columbus and Cabot or anonymous fisherfolk and traders to dream of profit, glory, and empire.

THE EUROPEAN BACKGROUND OF AMERICAN COLONIZATION

Long before Europeans discovered America, they had invented it. Centuries before Columbus, stories abounded of an island across the Atlantic, a garden paradise of riches and plenty. Plato told of Atlantis, a kingdom lying beyond the Pillars of Hercules (Strait of Gibraltar), reputed for its wise men and valiant warriors. Medieval bards embellished the tale of St. Brendan, a fifth-century Irish abbot whose crew of monks, they claimed, sailed to islands in the Atlantic and encountered a whale that talked and birds that sang in Latin. Throughout the Middle Ages, wishful cartographers crowded the Atlantic with other enchanted islands like Hy-Brasil along with sea monsters and griffins.

Of course, the invention of America did not bring about its discovery. Not mere dreams but a complex constellation of historical circumstances impelled explorers of the fifteenth and sixteenth centuries to explode the boundaries of their old world. Europe in 1450 was slowly emerging from centuries of economic and political localism. It was recovering, too, from the onslaught of a continent-wide epidemic that had reduced its population by a third. As stronger, more centralized nation-states put advances in technology and trade at the service of their ruling monarchs, the temper of these vibrant, often chaotic times mixed a sense of crisis with a sense of possibility. It was this special blend of desperation and idealism that made the New World more than a dream of metaphysical philosophers and medieval monks.

Life and Death in Early Modern Europe

In the fourteenth and the fifteenth centuries, at the beginning of the Renaissance, Europe's interest in island paradises became especially keen. The Europe graced by the genius of Michelangelo and Leonardo da Vinci, Machiavelli and Petrarch, was also a world riddled with war, disease, and uncertainty. The conditions of life and death whetted the taste for fantasy and escapism. Ninety percent of Europe's people, widely dispersed in small villages, made their living from the land. But perhaps as few as one-fifth of all peasants owned enough land to feed themselves, and all faced the constant prospect of food shortages and outright famine. Warfare, bad weather, poor transportation, and low grain yields conspired to create a fragile food supply, and undernourishment produced a population prone to disease.

Under these circumstances, life was nasty, brutish, and usually short. One-quarter of all children died in the first year of life, and people who reached the ripe age of 40 counted themselves fortunate. Men and women usually married in their mid-twenties, and as a result, most children came to maturity having lost one or both parents. Parents deliberately tried to instill in their children the toughness needed to survive in a harsh world. Boys and girls of all classes commonly lived away from home between the ages of 7 and 10, receiving schooling or military training or serving apprenticeships as craftsworkers or domestic servants.

It was a world of sharp inequalities, where nobles and aristocrats enjoyed several hundred times the income of peasants or craftsworkers. It was a world with no strong, centralized political authority, where kings were weak and warrior lords held sway over small towns and tiny principalities. It was a world of hierarchy, dependence, and deference, where the upper classes provided land and protection for the lower orders. It was a world of violence and sudden death, where public executions commanded enormous crowds and where homicide, robbery, and rape occurred with brutal frequency. It was a world where security and order of any kind seemed so fragile that people clung to tradition and feared innovation and change.

Into that world in 1347 came the Black Death, which by 1351 had swept away one-third of Europe's population. The crisis of epidemic disease disrupted both agriculture and commerce, triggering a depression that lasted until the end of the fourteenth century. Recovery came slowly, over the course of a century. As Europe's population began to grow again after 1500, its cities sprang back to life; merchants revitalized old trading networks, and peasants reclaimed land for cultivation. Fewer people meant larger shares of wealth for all: the relative scarcity of workers and consumers made for better wages, lower prices, and more land.

But by the time of Columbus' arrival in America, nearly 150 years after the outbreak of the Black Death, Europe again confronted its old problem: too many people were competing for a limited supply of food and land. Throughout the sixteenth century most Europeans suffered a steady decline in the quality of their lives. Diets became poorer, land and work less available, wages lower, the peasantry more impoverished, and crime and begging more widespread. As Europe's population growth strained the limits of its resources, inflation compounded the recurrence of food and land shortages. Prices doubled at the end of the fifteenth century and then quadrupled between 1520 and 1590. To keep pace with the "Price Revolution," landlords raised rents, adding to the burden of Europe's peasantry.

The climate of scarcity, disorder, and uncertainty prevailing in Europe during the first century of exploration and colonization fostered among the hopeful and the desperate alike a belief that the New World offered an opportunity to renew the Old. That mixture of hope and desperation led Europeans to idealize America as a source of riches and plenty. Columbus wrote of Hispaniola: "This island and all others are very fertile to a limitless degree. . . . There are very large

St. Sebastian Interceding for the Plague-stricken City captures the desperation of Europeans during an outbreak of the Black Death. While a priest reads prayers over the bodies being buried in a common grave, a man suddenly taken by the plague writhes in agony. In the background, a cart moves through the street to collect more corpses. At the upper left St. Sebastian, a Christian martyr, intercedes with God to end the suffering.

tracts of cultivated land. . . . There are birds of many kinds, and fruits in great diversity. In the interior there are mines and metals, and the population is without number." Columbus and many of his contemporaries expected that the American cornucopia would provide land for the landless, work for the unemployed, and wealth beyond the wildest dreams of the daring.

The Conditions of Colonization

While the scale of scarcity and disruption in sixteenth-century Europe made colonizing the Americas attractive, other changes made settling the New World practical. The improvements in maritime technology that made travel at sea more precise—and made the Portuguese such respected pilots—led also to a general expansion of trade. By the late fifteenth century Europe had broken free from the limited, localized commercial exchange of the Middle Ages. Transcontinental trading networks now linked merchants in Lisbon, Seville, Amsterdam, and London to Africa and Asia. Europe's merchants and bankers created more efficient techniques of exchange and finance to support commerce across the longer distances. And if rising prices and rents pinched Europe's peasantry, inflation enriched those who had goods to sell, money to loan, and acreage to let. Wealth flowed into the coffers of sixteenth-century traders, financiers, and landlords, creating a pool of surplus capital that investors could plow into colonial development. Both the commercial networks and the private fortunes essential to sustaining overseas trade and settlement were in place by the time of Columbus' discovery.

The direction of Europe's political development during the fifteenth and sixteenth centuries also paved the path for American colonization. After 1450 strong monarchs enlarged the sphere of royal power in many European countries. Henry VII, the founder of England's Tudor dynasty, Francis I of France, and Ferdinand and Isabella of Spain initiated the trend, forging nation-states from the autonomous towns and tiny principalities of the Middle Ages and increasing royal authority at the expense of warrior lords who had earlier held sway over smaller areas. As European political organization became more coherent and as kings and queens tightened their control over territory, people, and resources, the prospects for overseas expansion flourished. The larger, more centrally organized states were able to marshal the resources necessary to support colonial outposts and to sustain the professional armies and navies capable of protecting empires abroad.

Successful colonization depended on more than dreams and daring. It was the growing power of monarchs as well as commercial and technological development in early modern Europe that allowed the Spaniards and the Portuguese, the Dutch, the French, and the English to establish permanent settlements—even empires—in another world lying an ocean away. That accomplishment had earlier eluded Scandinavians like Leif Ericsson because they lacked the political power that could be continuously and forcefully projected. They also lacked a network of trade dense enough to sustain colonies and the capital to back them in their formative years.

Similarly, the character of Aztec society limited its potential for expansion. For all of their sophistication in other technologies, the Aztecs lacked knowledge of ocean navigation, which not only limited the scope of their movement but also restricted commercial development and merchant wealth. Although their trading networks reached far into Central America and the North American Southwest, Aztec merchants relied entirely on overland routes and trafficked mainly in luxury goods for a limited market—precious stones and metals, jaguar skins, and rare feathers—a trade resembling medieval Europe's commerce with Asia. And while Europe's traders were enhancing their power and status, often in a partnership with aristocrats, Aztec merchants were losing out in a struggle with the nobility. By the end of the fifteenth century, Aztec nobles had succeeded in curbing the influence of commercial families, had even executed some merchants and seized their estates.

Equally important, Aztec political organization by 1500 had not become as centralized as that of western European states. Aztec rulers had not established their sovereign authority over powerful nobles and clans. These groups still raided neighboring city-states and evened scores with their enemies—with or without chiefly approval. The absence of centralized power made it impossible for the Aztecs to coordinate a more ambitious expansion and impeded the consolidation of their empire. While their armies put down disturbances in conquered territories, protected trade routes, and plundered subjugated peoples, the Aztecs never actively colonized, never exported their people or their way of life to other places. Nor did they integrate diverse subject tribes into their own culture. Instead, conquered city-states retained their distinctive languages and customs—and harbored a lingering hostility toward Aztec rule. The result was an empire vulnerable to division from within and to attack from abroad.

SPAIN'S EMPIRE IN THE NEW WORLD

By the reckoning of the Aztecs it was the year 12-House, a time, they believed, when the fate of the whole world hung by a thread. According to their calendar, a 52-year cycle had come to an end, a transition always pregnant with peril. Now the gods might extinguish the sun with a flood or a great wind, might even send the sky crashing down on the earth. The end of this particular cycle had been marked with chilling omens. Aztec scribes reported that a comet flared across the heavens, seeming "to bleed fire, drop by drop, like a wound in the sky"; mysteriously, a fire broke out in the Great Temple. And in one of the canals, fishermen caught a bird "the color of ashes" with a strange mirror in the crown of its head. They brought the creature to their ruler, Moctezuma II, who looked in the mirror and saw ranks of men mounted on animals resembling deer and moving across a plain. Everyone was terrified by the portents.

Two years later, the Aztecs' worst fears were fulfilled. Dust rose in whirlwinds on the roads from the hooves of horses and the boots of men in battle array, some glittering in iron from head to foot. Coats of mail and weapons crashed and rattled; flags flapped like bats above metal helmets; dogs raced ahead of the column, muzzles uplifted, ropes of saliva running from their jaws. "It was as if the earth trembled beneath them, or as if the world were spinning . . . as it spins during a fit of vertigo," one Aztec scribe recorded. This was no image in a magic mirror: Hernando Cortés and his army of Spaniards were marching on Tenochtitlán. By Cortés' calculations, it was A.D. 1519.

Spanish Conquest

To Cortés and the other Spanish explorers who had followed Columbus across the Atlantic over the previous quarter century, a new and remarkable world was opening. By 1513 the Spanish had explored and mastered the Caribbean basin. In that year too, Vasco Nuñez de Balboa crossed the Isthmus of Panama and glimpsed the Pacific Ocean. North and South America were revealed as continents of vast size, separated from Asia by another ocean. And Ferdinand Magellan finally did reach the Orient by sailing west across the vast Pacific; after his death in the Philippines in 1521, his shipmates completed the first circumnavigation of the globe.

From their bases in the islands of the Caribbean, the Spanish pressed outward, mounting expeditions in search of profits and treasure whenever an ambitious military commander could scrape together the necessary soldiers and supplies. To the north they met mostly with disappointment. Juan Ponce de León vainly scoured the shores of the Florida peninsula for the fabled "Fountain of Youth," while Pánfilo de Narváez trekked along the west side of Florida and over the Gulf Plains, a route that Hernando de Soto subsequently followed as far as the Mississippi River. Between 1540 and 1542 Francisco Vásquez de Coronado moved through Arizona, New Mexico, Texas, Oklahoma, and Kansas. But reports of fantastic cities of gold proved to be merely the stuff of dreams.

During these same decades, however, the Spanish found golden opportunities elsewhere. Those who had first rushed to Hispaniola immediately started scouring the island for gold—and enslaving Indians to work the mines. As for Cortés, when the envoys of Moctezuma met him on the road to Tenochtitlán in

1519 and attempted to appease him with gold ornaments and other gifts, an Indian witness recorded that "the Spaniards burst into smiles. . . . They picked up the gold and fingered it like monkeys. . . . Their bodies swelled with greed. . . . They hungered like pigs for that gold." For nearly half a year Cortés dominated the vacillating Moctezuma by imprisoning him in his own capital. The Aztecs drove the Spanish out after Moctezuma's death, but Cortés returned with reinforcements, set siege to Tenochtitlán, and in 1521 conquered it. The Aztec empire lay in ruins.

To the conquistadors—a motley lot of minor nobles, landless gentlemen, and professional soldiers—the Americas seemed not only a golden but also a most timely opportunity. Resentment of the Spanish monarchy's growing strength at home inspired in such men dreams of conquest abroad. Cortés and other conquistadors aimed to recreate in the New World a much older world. They dreamed of eluding the reach of expanding royal authority by establishing themselves as a powerful feudal nobility in America, one that would enjoy virtual independence from the Spanish Crown, buffered by the Atlantic.

For a time the conquistadors succeeded beyond their wildest expectations. By the 1540s Cortés and just 1500 men had taken all of Mexico and the southwestern portion of North America; by the 1550s the ruthless Pizarro brothers and an even smaller band of conquistadors had sailed along South America's Pacific coast and overthrown the Incas in Peru, an Andean civilization as impressive as that of the Aztecs. They also laid claim to Ecuador, Chile, Argentina, and Bolivia.

How did the conquistadors—a handful of Spanish gentlemen heading a rabble of soldiers, seamen, rustics, and criminals—bring down Indian empires in the span of a generation? To begin with, the Spanish enjoyed the edge of surprise and technological superiority. The sight of ships and the explosion of guns terrified the Indians. Just as strange and daunting were enormous mastiffs and mounted invaders, men on horseback whom the Indians took at first to be single creatures. The only domesticated animals known to the Aztecs were small dogs; the Spanish provided them with their first glimpse of horses and, later, cattle, sheep, oxen, pigs, goats, donkeys, mules, and chickens.

What delivered a more lasting shock to Indian civilizations was exposure to European infections. Smallpox, influenza, typhus, and measles, disease strains against which they had no defense, ravaged the people of entire villages and tribes. Tenochtitlán surrendered to Cortés after a siege of 85 days, during which many died from starvation but many more died of smallpox contracted from the Spanish. Everywhere that the conquistadors invaded, disease was their ally against Indian resistance.

An equally important factor in the rapidity of the conquest was the political disunity within Indian empires. The Aztecs and Incas had subjugated the native Indian populations of Mexico and Peru just 100 years before the Spanish invasion. They established themselves in cities as a noble and priestly aristocracy and collected tribute from Indian peasants, but they took no steps to conciliate the conquered. Disaffection with Aztec and Inca rule afforded the conquistadors eager

The dignity and grace of this Mexican woman drawn in the 1550s, possibly by a Spanish priest, may reflect the sympathetic influence of the missionary Bartolemé de Las Casas— sentiments most Spaniards did not share.

allies among the subject Indian tribes. But by aiding the Spanish overthrow of the Aztecs and the Incas, the native Indians only substituted one set of overlords for another.

Spanish Colonization

The conquistadors did not long enjoy their mastery over the New World. The Spanish monarchs who had just subdued a feudal aristocracy at home were not about to allow a new colonial nobility to arise across the Atlantic. The Crown bribed the conquistadors into retirement—or was saved the expense when bloodthirsty men like the Pizarro brothers were assassinated by their own followers. The task of governing Spain's new colonies passed from the conquistadors to a small army of officials, soldiers, lawyers, and Catholic bishops, all appointed by the Crown, reporting to the Crown, and loyal to the Crown. Headquartered in urban centers like Lima and Mexico City (the city that arose from the ashes of Tenochtitlán), an elaborate, centralized bureaucracy administered the Spanish empire, closely regulating every aspect of economic and social life.

Few Spaniards besides imperial officials settled in the New World. By the end of the sixteenth century only about 5 percent of the colonial population was of Spanish descent, the other 95 percent being either Indian or African. Even by 1800 only 300,000 Spanish immigrants had come to Central and South America. Indians remained on the lands that they had farmed under the Aztecs and the Incas, now paying Spanish overlords their taxes and producing valuable commodities for export, principally cochineal (a red dye) and livestock. The Indians were not enslaved outright by the Spanish, but they were compelled to work for their new masters for specified periods of time, a system of forced labor known as *encomienda*. The Spanish also established sugar plantations in the West Indies; these were worked by black slaves who were being imported from Africa in large numbers by 1520.

Spain's colonies returned even more spectacular profits to the mother country after 1540, when silver deposits were discovered in both Mexico and Peru. Silver mining developed into a large-scale capitalist enterprise requiring substantial investment and efficient production techniques. European investors and Spanish immigrants who had profited from cattle raising and sugar planting poured their capital into the necessary equipment—stamp mills, water-powered crushing equipment, and pumping machinery. To supply the mines' labor requirements, the Spanish government introduced another form of forced labor known as *repartimiento*. Whole villages of Indians were pressed into service in the mines, joining black slaves and free white workers employed there.

In the last decades of the sixteenth century the economies of Mexico and Peru revolved solely around the mines. By 1570 the town of Potosí, the site of a veritable mountain of silver, had become larger than any city either in Spain or its American empire, with a population of 120,000. Local farmers who supplied mining centers with food and Spanish merchants in Seville who exported European goods to Potosí profited handsomely. So, too, did the Spanish Crown, which claimed one-fifth of all the silver extracted from the mines. All told, between 1500 and 1600 some 16,000 tons of silver was exported from Spanish America to Europe.

The growth of Spain's New World empire strengthened the political and economic developments in Europe that had made colonization possible. The crea-

SPANISH AMERICA, CIRCA 1600

By 1600 Spain was extracting large amounts of gold and silver from Central and South America, as well as profits from sugar plantations in the Caribbean. Each year Spanish treasure ships ferried bullion from mines like Potosí to the Isthmus of Panamá, where it was transported by land to the Caribbean coast, and from there to Spain. An expedition from Acapulco sailed annually to the Philippines as well, returning with Asian spices and other trade goods.

tion of an imperial bureaucracy in Spanish America reinforced royal power by extending the Crown's dominion and enlarging the number of men in the monarch's service. Similarly, the growth of colonial economies returned large rewards to Europe's investors, concentrating more and more wealth in the hands of landlords, merchants, and bankers. In addition, the influx of American silver increased Europe's money supply, fueling inflation as well as increasing trade to eastern Europe and Asia, regions that demanded hard cash in return for their exports. Finally, the boom in Spanish America encouraged capitalist forms of economic organization, since the silver mines of Mexico and Peru were models of mass production. Brought into existence by the capital of private investors, they were more advanced than any enterprise existing in sixteenth-century Europe.

The Spanish colonization of America quickened the pace at which the Old

World developed more modern forms of economic and political organization. But that "progress" was purchased at a fearful human cost. The native population of the Americas in 1500 may have equaled that of Europe, but by 1600 it was not one-tenth of Europe's. Indian tribes were devastated not only by warfare and hard labor, but also by disease. The Indians of the Caribbean were virtually wiped out within a century; in Mesoamerica, a native population of 20 million was reduced to 2 million.

Well before European contact took its full toll among Indian tribes, the Spanish conquest came under attack. In the 1530s Bartolomé de Las Casas, a Spanish Dominican priest who became a bishop in southern Mexico, spoke out against the exploitation of the natives and called for the Spanish monarchy to return American lands to their rightful Indian owners. Las Casas' writings, reprinted in many translations and illustrated with gruesome drawings, circulated throughout Europe, becoming the basis of the "Black Legend" of Spanish tyranny and oppression in the New World.

Few of Las Casas' countrymen shared his scruples. They justified their conquest by claiming that they had "delivered" the Indians from Aztec and Inca tyranny. Enlightened emissaries of a superior culture, they were replacing native "barbarism" and "paganism" with European civilization and Christianity. The extent of the Spanish conquest itself fostered a heady sense of superiority. By the beginning of the seventeenth century Spain's dominions in the New World spanned 8000 miles, stretching from Baja California to the Straits of Magellan. It was the greatest empire known to Europe since ancient Rome. The prevailing mood was captured by the portrait of a Spanish soldier that adorns the frontispiece of his book about the West Indies. He stands with one hand on his sword and the other holding a pair of compasses on top of a globe. Beneath is inscribed the motto "By compasses and the sword/More and more and more and more."

THE PRELUDE TO ENGLAND'S AMERICAN COLONIZATION

While the Spanish reached for more in the Americas, England remained a small island nation. For the first several decades of the sixteenth century, the English Crown refused to entertain any schemes for poaching on Spain's colonial preserves. Caution was dictated by the strategic importance of Spain as an ally against a common rival, France, and the commercial value of England's cloth trade to the Netherlands, which was then controlled by Spain. To be sure, privateers like the senior Walter Raleigh looted Spanish silver ships, and buccaneers like John Hawkins tried to muscle in on the Caribbean slave trade. But these pirates—to use the less diplomatic term—only caused trouble for an England eager to conciliate imperial Spain. As the Spanish inched up the Atlantic coast in the 1560s, fortifying a base at St. Augustine, Florida, and claiming territory as far north as the Outer Banks of North Carolina, the English quietly abandoned a project to colonize the coast of present-day South Carolina.

Still, there were those English who remained restless. Sir Walter Raleigh senior was an expression of the same West Country culture that had sent enterprising fishermen across to Newfoundland. And his own swashbuckling career stamped a lasting impression on his impetuous brood of boys, especially his step-son, Humphrey Gilbert, and his namesake, the young Walter Raleigh. With Spain's empire looming before them, they envisioned more than plunder: they wanted to conquer the empire itself—or at least carve out for England an empire that would rival it. As they came of age during the 1560s and early 1570s they might have seriously disrupted English plans to remain on good terms with Spain, except that they were distracted by other alternatives to adventuring in America. One alternative lay in the upheavals arising out of the Protestant Reformation, which had turned all of sixteenth-century Europe into a battleground.

Backdrop to the Reformation

During the Middle Ages, the Roman Catholic church defined what it meant to be a Christian in western Europe. Like the other institutions of medieval society the Catholic church was a hierarchy. At the top was the pope in Rome, and under him were the descending ranks of other spiritual lords—cardinals, archbishops, bish-ops. At the bottom of the Catholic hierarchy were parish priests, each serving his own village, as well as monks and nuns living in monasteries and convents. But medieval popes were weak, their power felt little in the lives of most Europeans. Like political units of the era, religious institutions of the Middle Ages were local and decentralized.

Between about 1100 and 1500, the Roman Catholic church and the Papacy gradually increased their control over the lives of Europeans. Just as the kings of Europe were growing more powerful during those centuries, so too was the pope. Just as the nations of Europe were consolidating, so too was the Catholic church. As the church grew in wealth and power, a large bureaucracy of ecclesiastical officials emerged, and the Papacy exerted greater influence over Europe's politics. The Catholic church acquired land throughout Europe and added to its income with tithes (church taxes) and the sale of church offices. In the thirteenth century, church officials also began to sell "indulgences." For ordinary believers, who ex-pected to spend time after death purging their sins in purgatory, the purchase of an indulgence promised to shorten that punishment, by supposedly drawing on the "treasury of merit" amassed by the good works of Christ and the saints.

By the fifteenth century the Catholic church and the Papacy were enor-mously powerful, but both were weakened by their very success. Church officials had become caught up in bureaucratic concerns and secular politics. The more their affairs isolated them from the laity—the mass of ordinary believers—the less responsive they became to popular religious needs. Secular preoccupations all too often corrupted the church with a crass materialism. Popes and bishops flaunted their wealth. Poorly educated parish priests neglected their pastoral duties. Ca-tholicism in 1500 was no more corrupt than it had been a century earlier; but as the church gained power, its abuses became more visible.

Most lay people were not hostile to the church. They were indifferent. But although they found the institutional church irrelevant, a sharp anxiety over salva-tion and an intense need for religious assurance gripped Europeans in the fif-teenth and sixteenth centuries. Popular piety swelled in response to the sweeping and disorienting changes overtaking Europe—sporadic recurrences of the plague, the widening gulf between rich and poor, the new importance of commerce, the rise in prices, and the discovery of America. And with the invention of printing

St. Anthony Tormented by Demons evokes the sense of social and spiritual crisis pervading early modern Europe. The engraver, Martin Schongauer, was a contemporary of Luther.

with movable type in the mid-fifteenth century, more people had access to religious books and imagery.

The Teachings of Martin Luther

Into this climate of heightened spirituality stepped Martin Luther, a would-be lawyer who, thrown to the ground by a bolt of lightning from a passing thunderstorm in 1505, forsook his career and entered a monastery. Like many of his contemporaries, Luther was consumed by fears over his eternal fate. He was convinced that he was damned, and he could not find any consolation in the Catholic church. Catholic doctrine taught that men were saved by faith in God and by their own good works—by leading virtuous lives, partaking of the sacraments, making pilgrimages to holy places, and praying to Christ and the saints. Since he believed that human nature was innately evil, Luther despaired of being able to lead a life that "merited" salvation. If men and women are so bad, he reasoned, how could they ever win their way to heaven with good works?

Luther finally broke through his despair by reading the Bible, which convinced him that God did not require fallen mankind to earn salvation or to achieve grace. Salvation, he concluded, came by faith alone, the "free gift" of God to undeserving sinners. The ability to live a good life could not and must not be the *cause* of salvation, but its *consequence*: once men and women believed that they had saving faith, moral behavior was possible. That idea, known as "justification by faith alone," Luther elaborated between 1513 and 1517.

Luther's own experience put him in touch with the universal spiritual problem of his age, the need for assurance of salvation. At the same time, as Luther was ordained a priest and then assigned to teach at a university in Wittenberg, Germany, he was becoming more critical of the Catholic church as an institution. In 1517 he posted on the door of a local church 95 theses attacking the Catholic hierarchy for selling salvation in the form of indulgences.

What was new about Luther was not that he broke openly with Catholic teachings. Nor was it that he criticized the church as an institution. Challenges to Catholicism had cropped up throughout the Middle Ages, and some of the heretical groups of the fifteenth century—the Hussites of Bohemia, the Waldensians of Italy, and the Lollards of England—had anticipated some of Luther's theological ideas and his objections to the church. What was new about Luther was the passion and force that infused his attacks, his ability to write—in the blunt, earthy Germanic tongue—what many of this contemporaries thought and felt. The "gross, ignorant asses and knaves at Rome," he warned, should keep their distance from Germany, or else "jump into the Rhine or the nearest river, and take . . . a cold bath."

The pope and his representatives in Germany tried to silence Luther, as they had successfully suppressed earlier heretics. Their opposition only pushed the reformer toward more radical positions. He asserted that the church and its hierarchy were not infallible; only the Scriptures were without error. He argued that every person should read and interpret the Bible for himself or herself. The Catholic church, on the other hand, claimed that only certain theologians approved by the church had the necessary training to interpret Scripture—and that Martin Luther was not among them.

For defying the authority of the pope, Luther was excommunicated. He responded with an even more fundamental attack on the Catholic church in which he propounded an idea known as "the priesthood of all believers." Catholic doctrine held that salvation came only through the church and its clergy, a uniquely privileged group that was holier than the laity and possessed special access to God. Luther asserted that the whole hierarchy of popes, cardinals, and bishops was unnecessary and contrary to the Bible, that every person had the power claimed by priests. It followed for Luther that if the clergy had no special power to mediate between man and God, neither did the rituals and ceremonies that they performed. He believed that only two of the church's seven sacraments, baptism and communion, could be shown to exist in the Bible and that inner devotion and religious feeling were much more important than outward display and ceremony.

Although Luther had not intended to start a schism within Catholicism, independent Lutheran churches were forming in Germany by the 1520s. And during the 1530s, Luther's ideas spread throughout Europe, where they were eagerly taken up by other reformers.

The Contribution of John Calvin

The most influential of Luther's successors was John Calvin, a Frenchman who also had abandoned law for theology. Calvin agreed with Luther that men could not merit their salvation. But while Luther's God was a loving deity who extended his mercy to fallen, corrupt men, Calvin conceived of God as a majestic and terrible sovereign, all-knowing and all-powerful, the controlling force in human history who would ultimately triumph over Satan. To bring about that final vic-

Martin Luther.

tory, Calvin believed, God had designated certain people as his chosen agents for ushering in his heavenly kingdom. These people—"the saints," or "the elect"— had been chosen by a God who could foresee and shape the flight of the smallest sparrow. The elect alone were "predestined" for eternal bliss in heaven.

Calvin's emphasis on predestination led him to another distinctively Protestant notion—the doctrine of calling. How could a person learn whether he or she belonged to the elect who were saved? Calvin answered: strive to behave like a saint. God expected his elect to serve the good of society by unrelenting work in a "calling," or occupation, in the world. In place of the Catholic belief in the importance of good works, Calvin emphasized the goodness of work itself. Success in attaining discipline and self-control, in bringing order into one's own life and the entire society, revealed that a person was among the elect.

Calvin fashioned a religion to reshape the world. Out of his ideas flowed a militant, uncompromising, reformist impulse. Whereas Luther believed that Christians should accept the existing social order and established political authority, Calvin called on Christians to become activists, tailoring both society and government to conform with God's laws laid down in the Bible. He wanted all of Europe to become like Geneva, the Swiss city that he had converted into a holy commonwealth where the elect regimented the behavior and morals of everyone else.

Unlike Luther, Calvin was not a charismatic religious genius. But he had the French flair for systemizing doctrine in a way that could be applied to the work of reformation everywhere in Europe and, later, in America. And unlike Luther, who had aimed his writings primarily at a German audience, Calvin addressed his most important book, *The Institutes of the Christian Religion* (1536), to Christians throughout Europe who were dissatisfied with the Catholic church. Reformers from every country flocked to Geneva to learn more about Calvin's ideas.

The English Reformation

While the Reformation went forward, King Henry VIII of England was striving for a goal more modest than those of Martin Luther and John Calvin. He wanted only to sire a male heir to carry on the Tudor dynasty. When his wife, Catherine of Aragon, the daughter of the king of Spain, gave birth to a daughter, Mary, Henry decided to do something less modest: to prove that his marriage to Catherine had been unlawful and to get it annulled by the pope. Pope Clement VII, under pressure from Spain, refused, and so Henry divorced Catherine without papal consent in 1527 and married his mistress, Anne Boleyn.

Henry then widened this breach with Rome by dissolving England's monasteries, seizing all church lands, and making himself the head of the Church of England. In 1534 Parliament formalized the relationship with the Act of Supremacy. To ensure that the break with the pope would be permanent, Henry sold church lands at bargain prices to powerful members of the English gentry. But Henry, who fancied himself a theologian, had no fondness for Protestant doctrine. Under his leadership the Church of England remained essentially Catholic in teachings and rituals.

That changed in 1547 with the accession of Edward VI, the male heir that Henry had finally sired with his third wife, Jane Seymour. Anne Boleyn, who had produced another mere daughter, Elizabeth, had lost her head for that offense among others. During the brief reign of the boy king Edward, England's militant

Protestants began to press for a more radical reformation of the English church. They enjoyed considerable influence until Edward's early death in 1553 brought his elder half-sister, Mary, a Catholic and the wife of Philip II of Spain, to the English throne. Determined to reverse the English Reformation, "Bloody Mary" martyred many Protestants and drove others into exile on the Continent, some taking refuge in Geneva, Calvin's holy commonwealth. But Mary died before she could return England to the Catholic fold, and Anne Boleyn's "mere" daughter, Elizabeth I, took the crown in 1558, proclaiming herself "the Palladium of Protestantism."

With the accession of Elizabeth, the Protestants exiled by Mary rushed back to England, their enthusiasm to reform the church there burning hotter than before because of their stay in Geneva. But the new queen had other ideas. While she was willing to commit the Church of England to the Protestant cause, Elizabeth stopped short of embracing radical Calvinism. Her more zealous subjects remained a vocal minority, calling for the English church to purge itself of bishops, elaborate ceremonies, and other vestiges of Catholicism. Because of the austerity and zeal of such Calvinist reformers, their opponents proclaimed them "Puritans."

The Protestant Reformation shattered the unity of Christendom. Spain, Ireland, and Italy remained firmly Catholic, but England, France, Scotland, the Netherlands, and Switzerland developed either dominant or substantial Calvinist constituencies. Much of Germany and Scandinavia opted for Lutheranism. As competing religious loyalties coalesced, brutal wars and internal uprisings racked sixteenth-century Europe. Protestant and Catholic antagonists slaughtered each other in the name of Christianity.

In the long run, the Reformation's legacy of religious strife intensified European interest in colonization, as religious rivalries were played out in America. But in the 1560s France's bloody half-century of religious wars supplied some of England's young West Country gentlemen with a substitute for adventuring in America. In 1562 Humphrey Gilbert, followed by Walter Raleigh a few years later, crossed the English Channel to fight on the side of the Huguenots, French Calvinists locked in a struggle with French Catholics. And when the opportunities for winning Protestant supremacy and personal glory waned in France, Gilbert and the younger Raleigh looked elsewhere. By the late 1560s they had departed for Ireland.

The English Colonization of Ireland

The colonization of Ireland would serve as a rough model for later efforts in America. In 1565 the English began a concerted effort to bring Ireland under their control by military conquest and colonization. Fearing that Catholic Ireland would be used by the French or the Spanish as a base for invading England, Queen Elizabeth encouraged a number of her subjects, mainly gentlemen and aristocrats from the West Country, to sponsor private ventures for subduing the native Irish and settling English families on Irish land. The English enterprise in Ireland, like the Reformation in Europe, influenced the future course of American settlement.

Elizabethans saw Ireland as a place far outside the English periphery, a "famous island in the Virginia sea," peopled by a strange and savage race. Although all of Ireland professed Catholicism, the Irish church had never conformed completely to the worship prescribed by Rome, and many pre-Christian customs and traditions survived. The English invaders of Ireland, almost all ardent Protestants, regarded the native inhabitants as barbarians sunk in paganism and superstition. As one Englishman reported, "They blaspheme, they murder, commit whoredome, hold no wedlocke, ravish, steal and commit all abomination without scruple."

Thus did the English justify their conquest of Ireland by proclaiming their duty to teach the Irish the discipline of hard work, the rule of law, the refinement of manners, and the truth of Christianity. But before the Irish could be "delivered" from the darkness of superstition and their "thralldom" to Irish landlords, they had to be "civilized"—preferably as the servants and tenants of English landlords. And while they were learning civilized ways, the Irish would not be allowed to buy land or hold office or serve on juries or give testimony in courts or learn a trade or bear arms.

When the Irish rejected that program for their "liberation" and rebelled, the English savagely repressed native resistance, indiscriminately slaughtering men, women, and children, combatants and civilians. Most English in Ireland, like most Spaniards in America, believed that pagans and barbarians who resisted civilization and Christianity should be subdued at any human cost. No scruples stopped Humphrey Gilbert from planting the path to his camp in an insurgent county with the severed heads of Irish rebels.

The logic of England's conquistadors in Ireland was chilling: it sanctioned the savage repression of any "inferior race." More ominous still, not only Gilbert but also Raleigh and many other West Country gentry who colonized Ireland during the last half of the sixteenth century later turned their attention toward North America. After their apprenticeship in Ireland, where, Gilbert concluded, "neither reputation, or profytt is to be wonne," they wanted more.

ENGLAND'S ENTRY INTO THE NEW WORLD

After hard service in France and Ireland, Gilbert and Raleigh returned to England in the 1570s, assumed places at Elizabeth's glittering court, and flaunted their reputations as bold knights. Their more moderate and perhaps more modern contemporaries at court considered the two swaggering gentlemen insufferable if not downright dangerous, much as the Spanish officials distrusted their unbridled conquistadors. Cautious administrators who had been enlarging the royal bureaucracy ever since the reign of Henry VIII feared that the likes of Gilbert and Raleigh would never subordinate their pursuit of individual fame and family fortune to the larger aims of the Crown and the state. The court buzzed with gossip of Gilbert's vain boasting and Raleigh's epic pride, "which exceedeth [that] of all men alive."

Still, England in the 1570s was receptive to the schemes of such hotheaded warrior lords for challenging Spain overseas. English Protestantism, English nationalism, and English economic interests had fused to swell support for English exploration and colonization.

The turning point for the English came when the Calvinist Dutch rebelled during the 1570s against their rule by Catholic Spain. The Spanish retaliated savagely against the Netherlands' resistance, sacking the city of Antwerp and killing 8000 people. The destruction of Antwerp cost the English their major market for cloth on the continent of Europe, a loss that compounded the problems of Elizabethan merchants. Even before the troubles in the Netherlands, the market for English textiles was becoming saturated, the glut producing periodic depressions in the cloth industry and trade. Both difficulties prompted English merchants to look elsewhere for markets and investment opportunities. They combined in joint stock companies to develop a trade with Africa, Russia, the East Indies, and the Mediterranean. These private corporations, in which many shareholders pooled small amounts of capital, allowed investors to finance large ventures at minimal risk. These corporations also began to plow money into Atlantic privateering voyages and pressed Elizabeth to unleash England's sea rovers on Spain's silver ships.

Joining English merchants in the new interest in overseas exploration were gentry families, many of whom shared with traders a desire for new ventures in which to invest their capital. The gentry had a second concern as well. The high birth rate among England's upper classes throughout the sixteenth century had produced a surplus of younger sons, who stood to inherit no share of family estates. The shortage of land for their offspring at home stirred up support within gentry ranks for England to lay claim to land across the Atlantic.

With the support of England's landed and commercial elites, Elizabeth now needed little encouragement to adopt a more belligerent stance toward Spain. But she got more encouragement from Spain itself. The Spanish made no secret of wanting to restore England to the true faith of Catholicism, by armed invasion if necessary. In 1570 the pope excommunicated Elizabeth, and the Spanish ambassador plotted her assassination. By 1572 the queen was permitting her subjects to assist the Dutch rebels.

As Humphrey Gilbert stepped forward to aid the Dutch, he hoped that Elizabeth might be ready to challenge Spain in the New World as well. In 1577 he presented the queen with "A Discourse on How Her Majesty May Annoy the King of Spain," a proposal to conquer Spanish Cuba and Santo Domingo and then use the two islands as bases for destroying Spanish power on the mainland. Although Elizabeth probably agreed with Gilbert's view that Spanish Catholics were "at open and professed war with God himselfe," she was not prepared to annoy the king of Spain to the point of provoking open warfare. Even so, she winked at the freebooting of English pirates on the Spanish Main and closely watched with interest the exploits of a new generation of English explorers in North America.

The Failures of Frobisher and Gilbert

The adventurer who first caught the queen's eye was Martin Frobisher, a formidable professional sailor from Yorkshire, the veteran of slaving voyages to west Africa, privateering raids in the Atlantic, the fighting in Ireland, and other unsavory enterprises. A full-length contemporary portrait of Frobisher—face frozen in a glare, a horse-pistol fixed in his fist—conveys his character. In 1576 he set his sights on another search for the Northwest Passage to Asia.

After sailing as far as the bay north of Labrador that now bears his name, Frobisher returned to England with an Eskimo (plucked, kayak and all, from the Atlantic) and a shiny black stone. The unfortunate Eskimo died soon after, but experts attested that Frobisher's rock was gold ore. The sensational news prompted the queen and several of her courtiers to take the unusual step of forming a joint stock company to establish a military outpost and mining camp at this "new Peru." It was the closest that the English state had come to underwriting a colonial expedition.

Frobisher made two more voyages in 1577 and 1578, kidnaping three more Eskimos and hauling back nearly 2000 tons of black rock. These Eskimos also died shortly after arriving in England, and the rest of Frobisher's cargo, upon closer inspection, turned out to be "fool's gold." Frobisher's reputation fell under a cloud.

Because Gilbert had refused to invest in this fiasco, Frobisher's disgrace became Gilbert's opportunity. In 1578 Elizabeth granted Gilbert a vague patent—the first English colonial charter—to explore, occupy, and govern any territory in the New World "not actually possessed of any Christian prince or people." That charter, ignoring Indian claims to North America, made Gilbert the lord and proprietor of all the land lying between Florida and Labrador. His power was limited only by provisions that his colonists were to enjoy all the liberties and privileges of Englishmen and that his laws had to be "agreeable" to those of England.

In planning his American colony, Gilbert continued to dream of a mineral-rich empire that would rival Spain's holdings. But he hoped for more. For some years he had tried to interest Elizabeth in settling the New World with "such needie people of our Countrie which now trouble the common wealth, and through want here at home, are inforced to commit outragious offences, whereby they are dayly consumed with the Gallows." In the 1580s, his detailed plans for a settlement included encouraging the immigration of the English poor to his colony by providing them with free land and farm implements. Gilbert also provided his projected settlement with a civil government, consisting of a governor and 13 councilors "to be chosen by consent of the people," a legal code, and a system of Anglican parishes, schools, and clergymen.

It was the blueprint for building a better society, one that would guarantee land, employment, and liberty to England's poor. It was also a formula for recreating an older, nearly feudal world in America. Gilbert pictured himself and his heirs as manorial lords of an agricultural colony of grateful and loyal tenants, collecting rents, providing for defense, and, like Spain's conquistadors, enjoying considerable independence from the Crown.

In June 1583 Gilbert finally set sail. Ever the knight-errant, he took along a poet to set down in Latin verse "the gests and things worthy of remembrance happening in this discovery." By August, Gilbert had sailed into St. John's harbor to find the usual international crew of fishermen. Gilbert formally claimed the land for England (John Cabot's voyage of a century earlier having been forgotten by nearly everyone) and then set out to probe the coast of Nova Scotia when storms forced him to head for home. North of the Azores, the *Golden Hind* and the *Squirrel* met foul weather and high waves. Gilbert, commanding the smaller *Squirrel*, sat on deck with characteristic bravado, reading a book. "We are as neere to Heaven by sea as by land," he shouted across the heaving swells. The men aboard the *Golden Hind* recognized the words of Thomas More, whose *Utopia*—a description of an ideal society in the New World—Gilbert held in his hand. Gilbert was nearer to heaven than he knew: around midnight, the crew of

Martin Frobisher, 1588.

the *Golden Hind* saw the lights of the *Squirrel* extinguished and the ship "devoured and swallowed up by the sea."

Raleigh's Roanoke Venture

Raleigh had been eager to accompany his stepbrother's ill-fated expedition, but Elizabeth showered so many favors on him, it had been hard to leave. He was dining on food from palace kitchens, living in "a bravely furnished lodging," complete with a bed covered in green velvet and silver lace and adorned with spangled plumes of white feathers; he was supporting a retinue of 30 gallants, all sporting gold chains.

Still, Raleigh was restless. Even if Gilbert had perished at sea, others were succeeding spectacularly. Another West Country adventurer, Sir Francis Drake, had circumnavigated the globe by 1580. Drake had sailed around the southern tip of South America and surprised the Spanish treasure ships in the Pacific—which Spain looked on as its own sea in almost proprietary fashion. Drake then sailed north, claimed northern California for England, hunted for the Northwest Passage, crossed the Pacific and opened trade with the Portuguese Spice Islands in the East Indies, and then repeated the feat of Magellan's crew by sailing home. Elizabeth was impressed enough to knight him on the deck of his own ship.

And if Drake's daring voyage was not enough, two other men who never left England were calling attention to the possibilities of colonies abroad. Richard Hakluyt was a lawyer who neglected the law in favor of mastering the new geography of the world and corresponding with merchants in Spanish and Portuguese colonial possessions. He imparted to his nephew, a clergyman of the same name, a similar passion for spreading knowledge of overseas discoveries. From that time forward, the younger Hakluyt neglected his pastoral duties in favor of publicizing North America. The younger Hakluyt wrote for Elizabeth, at the behest of Raleigh, an eloquent plea for the English settlement of America, titled *A Discourse Concerning Westerne Planting*.

The temperate and fertile lands of North America, argued Hakluyt, would provide a perfect base from which to harry the Spanish, search for a Northwest Passage, and extend the influence of Protestantism. But he also stressed the commercial advantages of colonies—as sources of commodities that England could not produce, as markets for woolens that England could not sell nearer to home, and as havens for people whom England could not employ. Like Humphrey Gilbert, he believed that settling America would solve the problem of overpopulation.

Still wary of the king of Spain, Elizabeth stopped short of lending state support to any such venture. But in 1584 she granted Raleigh a patent to settle American lands nearly identical to the patent that she had given Gilbert. By the summer Raleigh had sent two able gentlemen of his retinue, Philip Amadas and Arthur Barlowe, across the Atlantic, their two small ships coasting the Outer Banks of present-day North Carolina. Amadas and Barlowe established cordial relations with the Roanoke tribe, exchanging gifts and hospitality with these "very handsome, goodly people" ruled by a "werowance," or chief, named Wingina. The expedition returned home, painting an idyllic picture of natives "most gentle, loving, and faithfull, void of all guile and treason," much as Columbus had to the

Sir Walter Raleigh, 1577.

Spanish almost a century before. The enthusiastic Hakluyt promptly envisioned a colony that would become the Mexico of England, full of tidewater plantations producing bananas, pineapples, and sugar cane, mulberry trees supporting a silk industry, and mountains yielding gold. Elizabeth immediately knighted Raleigh and allowed him to name the new land "Virginia," after his virgin queen. The following summer a full-scale expedition returned to Roanoke Island.

Raleigh apparently aimed to establish on Roanoke a mining camp and a military garrison modeled on Frobisher's venture of the 1570s. To lead the company of 108 men, he tapped a West Country relative, Sir Richard Grenville, and as governor of the new colony he named Ralph Lane: both were veterans of the Irish campaigns. He also recruited a scientist, Thomas Hariot, to study the country's natural resources and native cultures, and an artist, John White, to make drawings of the Virginia Indians. Their inclusion was a stroke of genius. *A Briefe and True Reporte of the New Found Land of Virginia* (1588), written by Hariot, illustrated by White, and translated into Latin, French, and German, served as one of the principal sources about North America and its Indian inhabitants for more than a century. But Raleigh's choice of Grenville and Lane to lead the expedition was a fatal error of judgment. Even his fellow conquistadors in Ireland considered Lane intolerably proud and greedy. As for Grenville, even Lane considered him intolerably proud, greedy, and violent: he was given to breaking wineglasses between his teeth and then swallowing the shards to show that he could stand the sight of blood, even his own.

Both men alienated the natives of Roanoke almost as soon as they set foot on American soil. After Grenville missed one of his silver cups, he accused the Indians of theft and burned one of their villages. Wingina overlooked the incident, invited the Englishmen to settle on Roanoke Island, supplied them with corn and built them weirs to trap fish. But after a year, with the English still apparently content to sponge indefinitely off the Indians—and indifferent when their cattle trampled Indian cornfields—Wingina's hospitality ran out. Rumors that the chief planned to weaken the English by starvation before finishing them off with bows and arrows prodded Lane to mount a preemptive strike. On the night of July 1, 1586, at the watchword "Christ our victory," Lane and his men attacked Wingina's main village, killing and beheading the chief. All that averted an overwhelming counterattack was the timely arrival of Drake and Frobisher, who had promised Raleigh that they would look in on his colony after freebooting up and down the Caribbean. They ended up evacuating the settlement's 102 survivors, who piled onto the pirate fleet and put an ocean between themselves and the avenging Roanokes.

Raleigh was not daunted, however. He decided to organize a second expedition to plant a settlement on a site farther north, in the Chesapeake Bay. And rather than colonizing with miners and military men, Raleigh projected an agricultural community modeled on Humphrey Gilbert's manorial dreams. He recruited 119 men, women, and children, members of the English middle class, granting each person an estate of 500 acres. He also appointed the artist John White as governor; the delighted White bought a suit of armor for ceremonial occasions.

From the moment of first landfall in July 1587, everything went wrong. Their expedition's pilot, Simon Ferdinando, insisted on putting off the colonists at Roanoke Island rather than the Chesapeake, so he could head off to raid Spain's annual convoy of silver ships. But even before Ferdinando weighed anchor, the settlers were skirmishing with the local Indians: one colonist killed, an Indian

Daily Lives

CLOTHING AND FASHION

"Barbaric" Dress—Indian and European

It was remarkable to sixteenth-century Europeans how many things seemed to be missing from Indian culture. Even more remarkable, the Indians themselves did not seem to notice. Michel de Montaigne, a French philosopher who had never been to America but liked to talk with explorers and read their accounts, managed to compile quite a list. According to Montaigne, Indians had "no kind of traffic [trade], no knowledge of letters, no intelligence of numbers, no name of magistrate, nor of politics, no use of service [servants], of riches, or of poverty, no contracts, no successions, no partitions, no occupation but idle, no apparel but natural. . . ." When other Europeans, with and without experience in America, made similar lists, they never failed to mention that last crucial item missing in Indian culture—clothing. Even European men and women who could not read and who never traveled beyond their villages associated America's inhabitants with nakedness, for woodcuts, engravings, and paintings showed native peoples either entirely nude or clad in the skimpiest of loincloths or grass skirts.

Europeans interpreted the simplicity of Indian dress in two different ways. Some saw the lack of clothing—like their supposed lack of commerce, law, government, and religion—as evidence of "barbarism." Andre Thevet, a shocked French visitor to Brazil in 1557, voiced this point of view when he attributed nakedness to native lasciviousness. If the Indians could weave hammocks, he sniffed, why not shirts? But other Europeans esteemed unashamed nakedness as the Indians'

badge of innocence. As remnants of a bygone "golden age," they believed, Indians needed clothing no more than government, laws, regular employment, or other corruptions of civilization. Jean de Lery, another French traveler to Brazil, remarked that the elaborate clothes and jewels worn by Parisian women were "without comparison a source of greater evils than the ordinary nudity of the savage women who in their natural state are not a whit less beautiful."

In fact, Indians were no more "naked" than they were without trade, politics, employment, or religion. While the simplest tribes of the Caribbean and Brazil wore little, the members of more advanced Indian cultures in Central and North America covered themselves with animal pelts sewn into mantles and robes, breechclouts, leggings, and moccasins. They wrought bird feathers into headdresses and ear decorations and fashioned reptile skins into belts and pouches. Even more formidably clad were the Eskimos of the far North, who dressed head to foot in sealskin suits with waterproofed seams, turning the furry side inward for warmth in the winter and outward in the summer.

By the late sixteenth century, Europeans, and especially the English, were paying more heed to what the Indians wore, hoping to assure prospective colonists that the natives would not affront European standards of modesty. Captain John Smith, for example, left detailed descriptions of the attire of Virginia's tribes, noting in a telling comparison that "the better sort use large mantels of deare skins not much differing in fashion from the Irish mantels." Even more reassuringly, Smith added, "The women are alwaies covered about their midles with a skin and very shamefast [modest] to be seen bare."

Daily Lives

Later accounts of Indian dress also advertised the riches of America. In a narrative of his voyage to Roanoke in 1584, Arthur Barlowe remarked that the wife of a local Indian leader sported a fur-lined cloak, a band of white coral about her forehead, and long pendant pearl earrings "of the bigness of good pease."

If natives struck whites as starkly underdressed, Europeans seemed, by the Indians' standards, grotesquely over-

Columbus meeting the natives on Hispaniola.

dressed. Indeed, European fashion was ill-suited to the environment between the Chesapeake and the Caribbean. Elizabethan gentlemen strutted in silk stockings attached with garters to padded, puffed knee breeches, topped by long-sleeved shirts and tight quilted jackets called "doublets." Men of lesser status wore coarse woolen hose, canvas breeches, shirts, and fitted vests known as "jerkins"; when at work, they donned aprons of dressed leather. Women wore gowns with long, full skirts, low-cut bodices, aprons, and hosiery held up by garters. Ladies went in silk and wore hoods and mantles to ward off the sun, while the rest dressed in flannels or canvas and covered their heads with linen caps or coifs. Both sexes favored long hair, and men sported mustaches and beards. Such fashions complicated life in the American environment, especially since heavy clothing and even shoes rotted rapidly from sweat and humidity. The pungent aroma of Europeans also compounded the discomfort of natives who came in contact with them. For despite sweltering heat, the whites who swaddled themselves in woolens and brocades also disdained regular bathing and regarded Indian devotion to daily washing as another uncivilized oddity.

It would have been natural for Indians to wonder why the barbaric newcomers did not adapt their dress to a new setting. The answer may be that for Europeans—entering an alien environment inhabited by peoples whom they identified as "naked savages"—the psychological risk of shedding familiar apparel was simply too great. However inappropriate or even unhealthy, heavy, elaborate dress afforded the comfort of familiarity and distinguished "civilized" newcomer from "savage" native in America.

village razed in retaliation, and an Indian executed. Sensing that the situation on Roanoke could rapidly become desperate, White sailed back with Ferdinando, hoping to bring reinforcements.

Unfortunately for White, he returned home just when King Philip of Spain had reached the end of his patience with England. It was 1588, and the massive Spanish navy, the Armada, was marshalling for an assault on England. Elizabeth was enlisting every seaworthy ship and able-bodied sailor in her realm to stave off invasion. Blocked by the war with Spain and distracted by another scheme to colonize a large plantation in Ireland, Raleigh left the Roanoke colonists to shift for themselves. White could not return to Roanoke Island until 1590, three years later. To herald his arrival, White's party sounded a trumpet, "and afterwards many familiar English tunes of songs, and called to them friendly." There was no answer. The empty fort, no more than a few cottages in a clearing, gave no clue of the colony's fate, save for a few letters carved on a post: CROATOAN. It was the name of a nearby island off Cape Hatteras.

Had the Roanoke colonists fled to Croatoan for safety? Had they moved to the mainland and joined Indian tribes in the interior? Had they been killed by Wingina's people? The historical record remains silent on the fate of the "lost colony." When a storm blew up, damaging his ship and spoiling his supplies, White was forced to sail back to England, leaving behind the little cluster of cottages that would soon be overgrown with vines and his suit of armor that was already "almost eaten through with rust."

All of the world lay before them. Or so it had seemed to the young men from England's West Country who dreamed of gold and glory, conquest and colonization. But the sixteenth-century world had defied the expectations and defeated the dreams of England's would-be conquistadors. In 1600, over a century after Columbus' first crossing, not a single English settlement existed anywhere in the Americas. The Atlantic had swallowed up Gilbert and his hopes for a manorial utopia; Raleigh's ventures foundered on the rock of royal ambition.

Raleigh had left behind his Virginia schemes to sail to South America in quest of El Dorado, a rich city somewhere near Guiana, rumored to be ruled by descendants of the Aztecs. But in 1603, Elizabeth's death brought to the English throne her cousin James I, the founder of the Stuart dynasty. The new king arrested the old queen's favorite for treason, and Raleigh languished for 15 years in the Tower of London. Set free in 1618 at the age of 64, he returned to Guiana, his lust for El Dorado undiminished. Along the way, he plundered some Spanish silver ships, defying James' orders. It was a fatal mistake, for England had made peace with Spain. By annoying the king of Spain, he had also annoyed the king of England: Raleigh lost his head.

James I did not want to annoy the king of Spain; he wanted to imitate him. The Stuarts were even more determined than the Tudors to enlarge the sphere of royal power. Royal ambition meant, among other things, that there would be no recreation of the old feudal world in America. It meant that there would be no role in America for a warrior nobility of conquistadors, no room for a kingdom ruled by the likes of Sir Walter Raleigh. Instead, there would be English colonies in America like the new outpost of Jamestown, planted on the Chesapeake Bay in Virginia in 1607. There would be English colonies in America named for English kings and queens and ruled by English royalty and their loyal, efficient bureaucrats. And there would be English colonies yielding commodities and revenues that enriched the English monarchy and the English state. Settling America would strengthen English monarchs, paving their path to greater power, just as the dominions of Mexico and Peru had augmented the authority of the Spanish crown. America would be the making of kings and queens.

Or would it? For some in the Old World, weary of the tyranny of conquistadors and sea rovers, the order and security that Crown rule and centralized states promoted in western Europe would be enough. But others, the desperate and idealistic men and women who sailed to the world that lay before them, would want more.

SIGNIFICANT EVENTS

ca. 50,000–25,000 B.P. (before the present)	First Asian penetration of the Americas
ca. 1300 A.D.	Rise of the Aztec empire
1271–1295	Marco Polo travels to China from Italy
1347	First outbreak of the Black Death
1420s	Portuguese settlements in the Atlantic islands
1488	Dias rounds the tip of Africa
1492	Columbus discovers America
1497	John Cabot discovers Newfoundland
1498	Da Gama reaches India
1517	Luther posts his 95 theses
1519–1522	Magellan circumnavigates the globe
1521	Tenochtitlán surrenders to Cortés
1540	Discovery of silver in Mexico and Peru
1558	Elizabeth I becomes queen of England
1565	England begins its conquest of Ireland
1576–1578	Frobisher searches for Northwest Passage
1583	Gilbert's quest for a North American colony
1584–1590	Roanoke voyages

2

The First Century of Settlement in the Colonial South

n the year 1617, as Europeans counted time, on a bay they called the Chesapeake, in a land they named Virginia, an old Indian chief surveyed his domain. It had all worked according to plan, and Powhatan, werowance of the Pamunkeys, had laid his plans carefully. While in his prime, the tall, robust man had drawn some 30 smaller tribes along the Virginia coast into a powerful confederacy. He had pressed southward, subjugating and exacting tribute from the other Algonkian-speaking tribes of the Tidewater. He had installed his relatives as their new leaders and as his new vassals. By 1607 Powhatan's confederacy numbered nearly 9000. In imposing political unity on the Virginia tribes, Powhatan conquered formidable obstacles. The natives of Virginia, like the tribes who inhabited the length of eastern North America, were a seminomadic people. They lived for most of the year in small villages and ranged seasonally with the game over tribal hunting and fishing grounds. Rivalries over trade, territorial boundaries, and leadership had often erupted into armed conflict. Some tribes in the Tidewater had fiercely resisted incorporation into the confederacy. To the west, another challenge had confronted Powhatan. From the gentle, rolling hill country lying between the falls of great rivers and the Appalachian Mountains the Monacans and Manahoacs had threatened the security of the infant confederacy. These interior tribes of the Piedmont had also controlled the trade in copper, a metal that the coastal tribes fashioned into decorative objects.

After 1607 Powhatan had been compelled to take into account yet another tribe as he consolidated his empire. They came by sea, crammed into three ships, 100 men and 4 boys, all clad in heavy, outlandish clothing, many dressed in gaudy colors. The English, as the tribe called themselves, followed a river deep into his territory and built a fort on a swampy, mosquito-infested site that they called Jamestown—a dubious way to honor their werowance, whom they called King James I.

Powhatan had not been surprised. His people had heard about, perhaps even encountered, other overdressed whites—the English settlers of the ill-fated Roanoke colony and the Spanish and French explorers, missionaries, and slavers who had scouted, preached, and plundered along the southeastern coast of North America during the late sixteenth century. The English had larger boats and louder, more lethal weapons than his own people possessed. But the Indians

The early southern gentry idealized their life as one of grace, plenty, and independence—qualities evoked by this painting, The Plantation. *Typically, this plantation fronts a river, ensuring good access to the markets for tobacco and rice across the Atlantic.*

quickly learned how to use guns, and they vastly outnumbered the English, who seemed, like those late of Roanoke, unlikely to live long and prosper in Powhatan's land.

Powhatan had not been frightened: he saw that the English were an inferior race of people. The feckless English could not manage to feed themselves, even in the rich Chesapeake region encompassing most of present-day Virginia and Maryland. Along the coast, where whites first settled, the forests abounded with deer, elk, and buffalo; the streams teemed with sturgeon and the shoals with shellfish. With bows and arrows, spears and nets, Indian men brought in an abundance of meat and fish. The fields tended by Indian women yielded generous crops of corns, beans, squash, and melon, and edible nuts and fruits—hickory and black walnuts, mulberries, grapes, and strawberries, plums and persimmons—grew wild. Still the English starved, and not just during the first few months of their settlement, but for several years thereafter.

Powhatan could understand why the English refused to grow food. Cultivating crops, like building houses, or making clothing, pottery, and baskets, or caring for children, was women's work, beneath manly dignity. And the English settlement included no women until two arrived in the fall of 1608. Yet even after more women came, the English still starved, and they expected—no, they demanded—that the Indians supply them with food.

Most incredible to Powhatan was that the inferior English considered themselves a superior people. They boasted incessantly about the power of their god—
they had only one—and spoke contemptuously of the Indians' "devil-worship" of
"false gods." The English also boasted incessantly about the power of their king,
who expected Powhatan to become his vassal. The English had even planned a
"coronation" at Jamestown to crown Powhatan as a "subject king." Powhatan had
not been impressed. "If your king has sent me presents," he responded, "I also am
a king, and this is my land. . . . Your father is to come to me, not I to him, nor yet
to your fort, neither will I bite at such a bait." In the end, the English did come to
Powhatan, only to find what "a fowle trouble there was to make him kneele to
receave his crowne . . . [he] indured so many perswasions, examples and instructions as tired them all. At last by leaning hard on his shoulders, he a little stooped,
and . . . put the Crowne on his head." In return for the English king's presents,
Powhatan sent James I his mantle and a pair of old shoes.

It was inconceivable to Powhatan—his kneeling before the English
werowance, the ruler of so savage a race. When his own subjects withheld food or
defended their land from these invaders, the English retaliated, not only by burning Indian villages, fields, and canoes, but also by murdering Indian women and
children. When the Indians made war, they killed the male warriors of rival
tribes, but adopted their women and children. And the English could not tell one
tribe from another. If an Indian tribe from outside the confederacy attacked a
white settlement, the English, in their confusion, were likely to retaliate by pillaging and murdering Indians allied to Powhatan. To make matters worse, the English could not even keep order within their own tribe. Too many of them wanted to
be chiefs, and they squabbled constantly among themselves.

Only one man among the English, a brash fellow called Captain John Smith,
had been able, briefly, in 1608, to impose discipline on the rest. Powhatan had
granted him a grudging respect, despite Smith's capacity for such extravagant
boasting that even other English seemed modest by comparison. Smith bragged
endlessly of his earlier exploits across the seas, where he had fought as a soldier of
fortune, and of his irresistible appeal to beautiful women, who had rescued him
from harrowing perils. A rough man, he had bullied the Indians for food and
would have enslaved them, had it been in his power. Even so, Smith had taken a
genuine interest in Indian ways and he, alone among the English, learned to tell
one tribe from another. Unfortunately, Smith returned to England in 1609 after
being injured when some of the whites' gunpowder blew up by mistake. Thereafter the English returned to squabbling and starving.

Small wonder that shortly after Smith's departure, the whole miserable tribe
of English had prepared to leave Jamestown for good. Only the arrival of another
ship carrying supplies and more settlers had turned them back. And small wonder
that some English had deserted their settlement to live among Powhatan's people.
Anyone could see the superiority of Indian culture to English ways.

The temptation to wipe out the helpless, troublesome, arrogant tribe of Eng-

No stranger to self-promotion, Captain John Smith included this portrait of himself and
verses celebrating his ennobling exploits at the beginning of his *Description of New England* (1616). After his brief stay in Jamestown, Smith explored the New England coast, but
he always hoped for an opportunity to return to Virginia.

lish—or simply to let them starve to death—had been almost overwhelming. But if Powhatan often wore a "sour look," as John Smith noticed, he had never launched a major offensive against the invaders. On the contrary, the food provided by his people was all that had kept Jamestown going for several years. Powhatan had allowed the source of his aggravation to survive because he had decided that even the English had their uses—as an addition to his empire. English manpower, English trading goods, and, most important, English guns would provide him with the support to quell resistance within his confederacy and to subdue his Indian rivals in the Piedmont. In 1614, Powhatan had cemented his claim on the English and their weapons with the marriage between his favorite child, Pocohontas, and a white settler, John Rolfe.

By 1617 events had vindicated Powhatan's strategy of suffering the English presence. His empire flourished, ready to be passed on to his brother, Opechancanough. Internal dissension within the confederacy had diminished, and the power of his Piedmont rivals had been broken. Powhatan's people still outnumbered the English, who seldom starved outright now but continued to quarrel and sicken and die. Only one thing had changed in the Chesapeake by 1617: the English were clearing woodland along the rivers and planting tobacco.

That was the doing of Powhatan's son-in-law, Rolfe, a man as strange as any of his tribe, all of them eager to accumulate wealth and worldly goods. Rolfe had been obsessed with finding a crop that could be grown in Virginia and then sold for gain across the sea. By the incomprehensible standards of the English, he had succeeded: his experiments with planting and selling a South American strain of tobacco were leading many other English to imitate the practice. Odder still, not women but men tended the tobacco fields. Here was more evidence of English inferiority. Men wasted long hours laboring when they might supply their needs with far less effort and enjoy the rest of the time allotted them by the gods.

In 1617 Powhatan, werowance of the Pamunkeys, surveyed his empire, and sometime in that year, he looked no longer. He had lived long enough to see the tobacco fields lining the riverbanks, straddling the charred stumps of felled trees. Knowing the English as he did, Powhatan had not been surprised by the sight of such plantations, and he had not been frightened. For he had overcome the greatest danger to his empire: he had prevailed over the other Indian tribes. He died believing that he had bent the English to his purposes—died, perhaps blessedly, before those stinking weeds spread over the length of his land and sent his hard-won empire up in smoke.

ENGLISH SOCIETY ON THE CHESAPEAKE

While the chief of the Chesapeake was expanding his dominions and consolidating his power, the king of England was doing the same. James I's ambition to enhance the wealth and power of his people and, not incidentally, himself, entangled the fate of England's infant empire with that of Powhatan.

The English and other European powers had an idea about how to attain national wealth and influence. That idea, which had been the guiding principle of Europe's commercial development and expansion for 200 years, was named "mercantilism" by the eighteenth-century economist Adam Smith. Mercantilists called for the state to supervise, regulate, and protect industry and commerce. Their primary objective was to enrich the nation by fostering a favorable balance of trade. Once the value of exports exceeded the cost of imports, they theorized, gold and silver would flow into home ports. If a nation could dispense entirely with imports from other countries, so much the better—and it was here that the idea of colonies entered the mercantilist scheme. Colonial planters and farmers, miners and loggers would supply raw materials that the mother country could not produce, while colonial consumers swelled demand for the finished goods and financial services that the mother country could provide. Convinced that colonies would enhance national self-sufficiency, mercantilists urged states to sponsor overseas settlements.

Mercantilist notions appealed to Europe's ambitious monarchs. A thriving trade meant that larger revenues from taxes and customs duties would fill royal coffers, increasing royal power. That logic led James I to lend his approval to the private venture that brought the first white settlers to the Chesapeake.

The Virginia Company

In 1606 the king granted a charter to Richard Hakluyt and a number of English merchants, gentlemen, and aristocrats, incorporating them as the Virginia Company of London. The members of the new joint stock company promptly sold stock in their venture to English investors, as well as awarding a share to those willing to settle in Virginia at their own expense. With the proceeds from the sale of stock, the company planned to send to Virginia hundreds of poor and unemployed people as well as scores of skilled craftsworkers. These laborers were to serve the company for seven years in return for their passage, pooling their efforts to produce any commodities that would return a profit to stockholders. Like Gilbert and Raleigh before them, the investors hoped to make money by discovering gold in the New World, as the Spanish had in the sixteenth century. If that failed, they hoped that North America might yield other valuable commodities—furs, pitch, tar, lumber, or sassafras, which Spanish merchants were hawking throughout Europe as a cure for a less popular American import, syphilis. In the spring of 1607, the Virginia Company's first expedition—104 men and boys aboard the *Godspeed*, the *Discovery*, and the *Susan Constant*—sailed into the Chesapeake Bay and up the Powhatan River, renaming it the James. Some 30 miles upstream, they founded Jamestown.

That was the first of many mistakes. Jamestown's first settlers had pitched their fort on an inland site ideally suited to prevent a surprise attack from the Spanish. Unfortunately, the marshy, thickly forested peninsula was also ideally conducive to malaria, especially during the steamy summer settling over the Chesapeake. Even for healthy men willing to work hard, cultivating such land would have been a daunting task. But Jamestown's settlers, weakened by bouts of malaria and then beset by dysentery, typhoid, and yellow fever, died by the scores, and those who survived were left listless and debilitated.

Many of Jamestown's first settlers—gentlemen who expected to lead rather than to work—had little taste for labor even before ill health claimed whatever inclination to work they might have had. Most other members of the early colonizing parties were gentlemen's servants and craftsmen—goldsmiths, jewelers, refiners, even a perfumer—men who were accustomed to labor but who did not regard growing crops as their line of work. The settlers resorted to bullying and begging

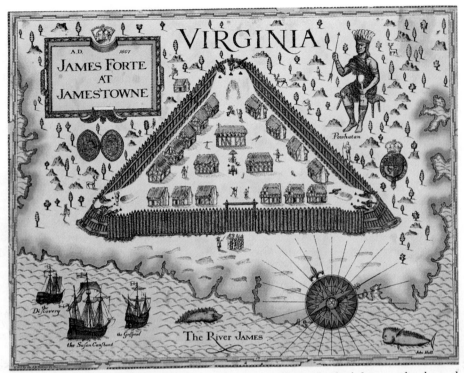

In Jamestown's early years its military orientation was clear. The fort's heavy palisades and its strategic location upriver and some distance inland underscore the colonists' concern for defense—as does the imposing figure of Powhatan seated at the right.

food from Powhatan's people, but the Indians' liberality was less than reliable, especially after the departure of John Smith. Food shortages produced chronic malnutrition, which heightened the colonists' susceptibility to disease, and even more drastic consequences. Only 60 of Jamestown's 500 inhabitants lived through the winter of 1609–1610, known as the "starving time." Some desperate colonists unearthed and ate corpses; one settler even butchered his wife.

Reports of starvation and staggering death rates stiffened the Virginia Company's resolve: in 1611 it imposed on the colonists what amounted to martial law. Company officials in Virginia organized the settlers into work gangs and inflicted draconian punishments on the lazy and the disorderly. Still the company failed to turn a profit. And after 1617, skirmishes with the Indians became more brutal and frequent, as rows of tobacco plants encroached on tribal lands farther and farther inland. The "noxious weeds" were equally an embarrassment to advocates of colonization at home in England. After a decade of settlement, Virginia's sole contribution to the empire was the smoke filling England's taverns and brothels. Even James I, whose standards of hygiene and morality often caused his own courtiers to wince, condemned the use of tobacco as a filthy and dissipated habit.

Reform and a Boom in Tobacco

Desperate to salvage their investment and their respectability, the company managers instituted in 1618 the sweeping reform program advocated by a principal stockholder, Sir Edwin Sandys. To attract more capital and colonists to Virginia, the company established a "headright" system for granting land to individuals. Those already settled in the colony received 100 acres apiece, new settlers each received 50 acres, and anyone who paid the passage of other immigrants to Virginia—either family members or servants—received 50 acres per "head." The company also dispensed with martial law, allowing the planters to elect a representative assembly, which, along with a governor and an advisory council appointed by the company, had the authority to make laws for the colony. The House of Burgesses met for the first time in 1619, commencing what would become a strong tradition of representative government in the English colonies. Finally, the company attempted to encourage a more diverse economy by ordering that no colonist could grow more than 100 pounds of tobacco annually and by dispatching to Virginia an assortment of skilled workers—vintners, ironworkers, brickmakers, and glassblowers.

The new measures to encourage migration met with immediate success. For several years both free immigrants and bound laborers surged into Virginia. Of the bound laborers, some were indentured servants who agreed to work a set number of years, usually four to seven, for the planters paying the cost of their passage. Others were sharecropping tenants who were to cultivate company land under the direction of its agents in the colony; for seven years they were to turn half of their earnings over to the Virginia Company, and at the end of their terms of service, they were to receive 50 acres.

Free immigrants poured into Virginia, too, for during the 1620s the tobacco economy took off. As demand soared and prices peaked in European markets, those with an eye for profits took their chances in Virginia, planted every inch of their farms in tobacco, and reaped windfalls. Because of the gains that free settlers stood to make by growing tobacco, the effort to diversify Virginia's economy failed. That was just one casualty of the tobacco boom; another was the lives of most English men and women who came to Virginia during the 1620s.

Those who crossed the Atlantic to Virginia during that decade were in the vanguard of an English migration to the Chesapeake that numbered between 130,000 and 150,000 over the seventeenth century. Drawn from the ranks of ordinary English working people, the immigrants were predominantly men, outnumbering women by six to one; typically young, ranging in age between 15 and 24; and generally, because of their youth, without skills or wealth. Three-quarters of all the newcomers arrived in the Chesapeake as indentured servants.

For most of the new servants, the crossing to Virginia was simply the last of many moves, each undertaken in the hope of finding work. While England's population had been expanding since the middle of the fifteenth century, changes in agriculture, chiefly the conversion of arable land for crops to pasturage for sheep, had steadily reduced the need for farm laborers. A severe recession in the English textile industry early in the seventeenth century augmented the problem of employing a growing number of people. The search for work pushed young men and women out of their villages, sending them through the countryside and then into the cities. Down and out in London, Bristol, or Liverpool, some decided to make their next move across the Atlantic and signed indentures. Pamphlets promoting immigration promised a bounteous natural environment, a balmy climate, and, once servants finished their terms, abundant land and quick riches. If the recruits to the Chesapeake did not credit completely these rosy promises, the lack of work, the low wages, and the high prices in old England made them desperate enough to try their luck in the New World anyway.

Even the most skeptical immigrants must have been shocked at what they found. The death rate in Virginia during the 1620s was higher than that of England during times of epidemic disease. The life expectancy for Chesapeake men who reached the age of 20 was a mere 48 years; for women it was lower still. Servants fared worst of all, since malnutrition, overwork, and abuse made them vulnerable to disease. And as masters scrambled to make quick profits, they extracted the maximum amount of work before death carried off their laborers. An estimated 40 percent of servants never regained their freedom because they did not survive to the end of their indentured terms.

The expanding cultivation of tobacco also claimed many lives by putting unbearable pressure on Indian land. Following Powhatan's death in 1617, leadership of the confederacy passed to Opechancanough, who watched, year after year, the tobacco mania grow. In March 1622 he coordinated a full-scale attack on white settlements that killed about one-fifth of the white population of Virginia. Swift English reprisals wiped out whole tribes and cut down an entire generation of young Indian men. As tragic as the casualties on both sides was the view of Indians that the events of 1622 fixed in the minds of the English—the belief that all Indians were treacherous and cunning, incapable of being civilized and incorporated into English colonial society. Back in England, John Smith predicted the consequence: the Virginians now saw "just cause to destroy them [the Indians] by all meanes possible."

The aftermath of the Indian war revealed to English investors the true state of their Virginia venture. It came to light that unscrupulous company officials in the

---

The Smokers, painted by Adriaen Brouwer, a seventeenth-century Dutch artist, suggests that the use of tobacco was both popular and disreputable. Native American peoples like the Costa Rican man shown at the right had been cultivating and smoking tobacco long before the arrival of Europeans.

colony had commandeered tenants to work their private plantations instead of company lands. The Virginia Company, despite the tobacco boom, was plunging toward bankruptcy. Nor was that the worst news. Stockholders discovered that their colony numbered just 1240 inhabitants after the upheaval in 1622. More than 3500 people had immigrated to Virginia after 1619, joining several hundred settlers who had arrived earlier. The Indian war had claimed 345 colonists. What accounted for the deaths of so many others? An investigation by the king brought out the whole truth: shiploads of servants and tenants, more dead than alive from scurvy, had been disgorged on Virginia shores without adequate supplies of food and clothing. Labor-hungry planters had snatched up the survivors, buying and selling their contracts like any other commodity, starving and driving human beings out of sheer greed. As one servant observed, Virginia masters used English men, women, and children "like damned slaves." James I dissolved the Virginia Company and took control of the colony himself in 1624.

Settling Down in the Chesapeake

The 1630s and 1640s brought beleaguered colonists some respite from the chaos of the first decades of Virginia's settlement. Although servants still streamed into the colony, the price of tobacco leveled off, which meant that planters were less likely to drive their servants to death in search of overnight fortunes. As the fever of the tobacco boom broke, a more settled social and political life emerged in Virginia. The same shrewd, ruthless tobacco planters who had become wealthy by monopolizing land now began to consolidate their gains through political power. They established local bases of influence in Virginia's counties, serving as justices of the peace and sheriffs, maintaining roads and bridges, collecting taxes, and supervising local elections. There they organized all able-bodied adult males into militias for local defense. There they established and served in vestries, the governing bodies of local Anglican parishes, hiring the handful of clergy who came to Virginia and providing for the neighborhood poor.

The biggest tobacco planters of each county also dominated colony politics. Even though King James had replaced the Virginia Company's government by charter with his own royal administration, the colony's elected assembly continued making laws for the colony. Along with the council (the upper house of the legislature), the assembly stoutly resisted interference in Virginia's affairs from the royal governor, the king's representative.

While the structure of colony and local government took shape, Virginia's population grew. As tobacco became less lucrative, planters raised more corn and cattle, and mortality rates declined as food supplies rose. The growing number of men who survived servitude found greater opportunity in the Chesapeake during the 1630s and 1640s than would have been theirs in England. The majority of freed servants, after a few years of working as hired hands or tenant farmers, managed to save enough money to buy their own land and become independent planters. That status was attained by few farmers in England, most of whom remained the tenants of gentlemen and aristocrats.

For the women who survived servitude in the Chesapeake, prospects were even better. With wives at a premium, single women stood a good chance of improving their status by marriage—far better than women back in England. Some impatient planters even bought women servants out of their indentures. If they outlived their husbands, widows inherited handsomely and often contracted even more advantageous second—and third—marriages.

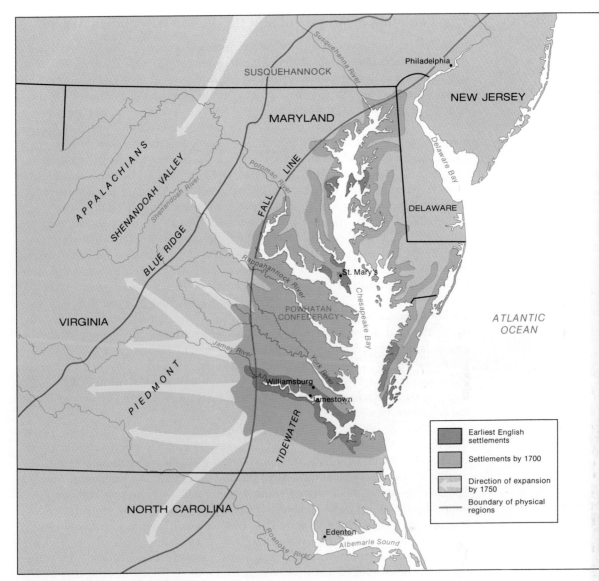

COLONIES OF THE CHESAPEAKE
Settlements in Virginia and Maryland spread out along the many bays of the Chesapeake, where tobacco could easily be loaded from plantation wharves. The "fall line" on rivers, dividing Tidewater and Piedmont regions, determined the extent of commercial agriculture, since ships could not pick up exports beyond that point.

By the middle of the seventeenth century, Virginia numbered about 15,000, with more servants and free immigrants coming to the colony every year. The increase of inhabitants and the rapid depletion of the soil by tobacco fed an eagerness for fresh land. But two impediments stood between the Virginians and the new territory that they coveted. The first problem was the creation of a second colony in the Chesapeake.

The Founding of Maryland and the Renewal of Indian Wars

In 1632 Cecilius Calvert, Lord Baltimore, received a charter from Charles I making him the absolute owner of 10 million acres on the Chesapeake Bay. Although Elizabeth I and her royal successors were suspicious of lordly gentlemen with designs on the New World, James I wanted to reward the loyalty of Cecilius' father, George. The king also wanted to please his queen, who, like the Calvert family, was Catholic. Lord Baltimore named the new colony Maryland in her majesty's honor and immediately set about fashioning in the New World a safe haven for what he valued in the Old World. To protect his cherished religion, Calvert established Maryland as a refuge for Catholics and extended complete religious freedom to all Christians. And to protect his cherished aristocratic order, Calvert attempted to recreate in Maryland a nearly feudal domain.

Unlike Virginia, which was first settled by a private corporation and later converted into a royal colony, Maryland was founded by a single aristocratic family. The first of several such "proprietary" colonies, Maryland was the private preserve of the Calverts, who held absolute authority to grant land, administer justice, and establish a civil government. All of these powers they exercised, granting estates, or "manors," to their friends, carving Calvert holdings into smaller farms for ordinary immigrants, and collecting annual "quitrents," fees for use of the land, from Calvert "tenants"—every settler in the colony. While the largest landowners dispensed local justice in manorial courts and made laws for the entire colony in a representative assembly, the Calverts appointed a governor and a council to oversee their own interests. Humphrey Gilbert and Walter Raleigh would have admired everything about the Calverts' lordly domain—except the toleration of Catholics.

Virginians, on the other hand, liked nothing at all about Maryland. Worse than the annoyance of Catholic neighbors was the problem of economic competition. By 1640 Maryland had 2000 inhabitants, virtually all of them pursuing the profitable business of planting tobacco on land desired by the Virginians. And the Marylanders were only one impediment to Virginia's expansion. The other was the remnant of the Powhatan confederacy, which had lost none of its determination to repel the white invaders. The solution was obvious: Virginians tried to incite the Indians to attack Calvert's colony.

But Opechancanough and his people had some old scores to settle, as well as some new resentments. They had not forgotten the reprisals of 1622, and by the 1640s Virginia's white settlers, blocked by Maryland from moving north and east along the Chesapeake Bay, were pressing west again onto Indian land. Opechancanough also had some new ideas about how to settle the score: he hoped that white Marylanders hated white Virginians enough to cast their lot with the Indians. Old and feeble but still formidable, Opechancanough rallied a new generation of Indians and in 1644 launched full-scale hostilities against the encroaching Virginia planters. The Indians again sustained the more severe losses, and the support they had hoped for from white Marylanders never materialized. Yet the Chesapeake tribes still mounted a determined resistance, one that in absolute numbers inflicted as many casualties on the Virginia planters as the attacks in 1622.

Virginians gradually resigned themselves to the existence of Maryland, and the two colonies came to resemble each other closely. Counties modeled on Virginia's system of local government replaced Calvert's manorial courts. The Maryland assembly became as obstreperous in resisting the power of the proprietor as

Virginia's legislature was in challenging the influence of the royal governor. But Maryland's imitation of Virginia was too faithful to be flattering. Maryland continued to develop an economy devoted to the cultivation of tobacco, and the competition continued to make Virginians miserable.

Changes in English Policy in the Chesapeake

In the 1630s and 1640s the king did not intervene, even belatedly, to ease tensions in the Chesapeake. Engulfed in a political crisis and then a civil war, England made no effort to protect the Indians by curbing white expansion or to reconcile Virginia and Maryland by diversifying the tobacco economy.

A storm gathered over England as the Stuarts, ever ambitious to enlarge the authority of the monarchy, found that they lacked the financial ability to pay for that authority. Throughout the first four decades of the seventeenth century James I and his son and successor, Charles I, sought to dispense with the nuisance of ruling with Parliament. James I made a great point of defending the right of kings to generally do whatever they pleased, and, in particular, to raise money through taxes and customs duties levied without the consent of Parliament. Even more eager than his father to dispense with Parliament, Charles dissolved that body in 1629 when its members condemned him for usurping the power of the purse. The landed gentlemen and merchants who sat in Parliament regarded representative government as indispensable, especially when it came to consenting to taxes, and they resisted royal bullying.

Unlike the successful absolutist monarchs of France and Spain, Charles had no way of getting money without Parliament's approval, no large royal bureaucracy, and no standing army. That left Charles no choice but to reconvene Parliament in 1640 when the Scots invaded England. By that time, many members of Parliament had decided that the Stuart kings themselves might be dispensable. In 1642 Parliament and its Puritan allies squared off against Charles I and his royalist supporters, defeated them in battle, and, in 1649, beheaded the king as a public criminal. For 11 years thereafter, from 1649 to 1660, England was a republic ruled by Oliver Cromwell, first as head of Parliament's New Model Army, and later as the Lord Protector.

Cromwell took advantage of the end of civil war to turn England's attention to its American colonies. Under his regime Parliament passed legislation that prohibited England's principal commercial rival, the Dutch, from trading with English possessions overseas. Taking a more aggressive tack, he sent English forces to attack the shipping and colonial settlements of Spain and France and in 1652, inaugurated a series of wars with the Dutch, conflicts that would flare up in 1664 and again in 1672.

Cromwell's death in 1658 ended the republican experiment in ruling without a king. Hatred of his repressive regime, which was more a military dictatorship than a true republic, restored to the throne of England a member of the Stuart family who promised never to dispense with Parliament. This was Charles II, the politically adroit son of the beheaded Charles I. Yet the determination of Cromwell and Parliament to make English colonies contribute to the parent country's prosperity outlived both the Lord Protector and the republic.

Indeed, almost immediately Charles II set out to implement a consistent colonial policy in a series of regulations known as the Navigation Acts. The first, passed in 1660, gave England and English colonial merchants a monopoly on the shipping and marketing of all colonial goods. It also specified certain "enumerated commodities" that the colonies could send only to England or other British ports, a list that included sugar, tobacco, cotton, ginger, and indigo (a blue dye). In 1663 Parliament added another regulation: the Staple Act gave Britain a virtual monopoly on the sale of European manufactured goods to Americans by stipulating that most imports going to the colonies had to pass through England. In 1673 a third Navigation Act levied duties on the coastal trade of the American colonies and provided for customs officials to collect imposts and enforce commercial regulations. Parliament later made minor modifications in the Navigation Acts, adding rice and naval stores (masts, pitch, tar, and turpentine) to the category of enumerated commodities in 1704 and 1705, prohibiting the colonies from exporting certain textiles by the Wool Act of 1699 and exporting hats by the Hat Act of 1732, and offering bounties and eliminating duties to encourage the colonial production of indigo and pig and bar iron. All of these regulations were designed to ensure that England—and no foreign nations or their merchants—would profit from all colonial production and trade.

CHESAPEAKE SOCIETY IN CRISIS

The turmoil of England's revolution had little lasting effect on Virginia and Maryland. The long decades of neglect only confirmed Chesapeake inhabitants in their inclination to act with considerable independence from their homeland. It was the measures instituted by Restoration kings Charles II and James II and their Parliaments that had a more dramatic impact on colonials. Accustomed to conducting their affairs as they pleased— and they were often pleased to trade with the Dutch—Chesapeake planters chafed under the new restrictions that limited their commerce to England. What was worse, the curtailing of colonial freedom after 1660 coincided with a downturn in colonial fortunes. In the effort to consolidate its empire, England inadvertently deepened the economic and social difficulties of Chesapeake society.

The Conditions of Unrest

Even before the passage of the Navigation Acts, the Chesapeake colonies had been headed for trouble. The problem began when inhabitants had started to live longer. More servants survived their terms of service, set up as independent tobacco planters, and competed with established growers for land and a share of the profits. More planters meant more production, and overproduction sent the price of tobacco plummeting, especially between 1660 and 1680. With the cost of land rising and the price of tobacco falling, opportunities for newly freed servants diminished sharply after the middle decades of the seventeenth century, especially in Virginia. To maintain their advantage, the biggest planters bought up all of the prime property along the coast. The scarcity of land forced freed servants to become tenants or to settle on unclaimed land in the interior. Either way, these poorer men lost. Depending on bigger planters for land and credit made the small farmers vulnerable to debt; moving to the frontier made them vulnerable to Indian attack.

Freed servants who managed to become small planters or tenants did not enjoy a comfortable livelihood or a secure existence. And after the passage of the Navigation Acts, demands on their slim resources included not only taxes levied by the county government and fees charged by local officials, but also export duties on tobacco collected by England. During the hard times after 1660, many small planters fell deeply into debt to those who had rented them land or advanced them credit, and some were forced back into servitude. By 1676 one-quarter of Virginia's free white men were landless.

An alarming number of former servants were unable to gain a foothold even as tenants. They became the vagabonds of Virginia, young bachelors who owned only the clothes on their backs—and their guns. They roamed from place to place, sometimes squatting on someone else's land, sometimes working as hired hands, sometimes living off whatever game they could shoot or livestock they could steal.

Diminishing opportunity in the 1660s and 1670s provided the tinder for social and political unrest. As the discontent of small planters mounted and the number of young, armed vagabonds multiplied, so did the apprehensions of Virginia's big planters. The assembly of the colony lengthened terms of servitude, hoping to limit the number of servants entering the free population, and curtailed the political rights of landless men, hoping to stifle opposition by depriving them of the vote.

Efforts to repress popular resentment only generated a spate of mutinies among servants and protests over rising taxes among small planters. By the early 1670s the situation had become so explosive that Virginia's royal governor, Sir William Berkeley, feared what might happen if the colony required defense from a European power or the Indians. If he mobilized the militia and marched them off to defend the coastline or the frontier, would Virginia's servants find in the absence of their masters a chance to rebel? Or would the militia—comprised mainly of small planters—turn their guns against the colony's government instead of the enemy? Berkeley's alarm deepened in 1673 when the Dutch, displeased at being excluded from the Chesapeake trade by the Navigation Acts, dispatched four armed vessels to Virginia and set fire to the tobacco fleet.

Bacon's Rebellion and Coode's Rebellion

Virginia survived the Dutch assault, but Berkeley's apprehensions were realized just three years later: civil war erupted in 1676. What set off the conflict among white Virginians was a renewal of hostilities with red Virginians. After Opechancanough's offensive of the 1640s, the Susquehannocks and several smaller Indian tribes living along the Potomac River had retreated to the northwest. By the 1670s white expansion again threatened these tribes, and they resisted with raids on frontier plantations. Berkeley favored a policy of building forts to contain the Indian threat, but frontier farmers opposed his plan as an expensive and ineffective way to defend their scattered plantations. As they clamored for a punitive expedition against the Indians, Nathaniel Bacon stepped forward to spearhead the bloody reprisals.

Wealthy and well connected, Bacon had arrived recently from England, expecting every consideration—including official permission to trade with the Indians from his frontier plantation. Berkeley, along with a few select friends, already held a monopoly on the Indian trade, and the governor declined to include Bacon. Stung by Berkeley's rebuff, Bacon switched his interests from Indian trading to

Indian fighting: he took up the cause of his poorer neighbors on the frontier against their common enemy, the governor. Bacon also received support from other monied, ambitious immigrants who resented being excluded from Berkeley's circle of power and patronage.

In the summer of 1676 Bacon appeared in Jamestown with a body of armed men and extracted from the assembly an authorization to kill Indians. While Bacon carried out that grisly business, indiscriminately slaughtering friendly as well as hostile tribes, Berkeley rallied his supporters and declared him a rebel. Bacon retaliated by turning his forces against those led by the governor. Both sides sought allies by offering freedom to servants and slaves willing to join their ranks. Many were willing: for months the partisans of Bacon and Berkeley plundered one another's plantations. In September 1676 Bacon reduced Jamestown itself to a mound of ashes. It was only his death from dysentery a month later that snuffed out the rebellion. Berkeley, with the belated assistance of 1000 soldiers from England, finally reimposed order.

On the heels of the civil war in Virginia, political upheaval engulfed Maryland. The extraordinary powers of that colony's proprietors, the Calvert family, had from the first created consternation among settlers. And after 1660, against a background of deepening economic depression, antagonisms intensified. A growing number of substantial Maryland planters, like some of Bacon's followers, resented their exclusion from political power and privilege. The Calvert family and their favorites, like Berkeley's circle in Virginia, monopolized political offices. Maryland's small farmers, like Virginia's, suffered from taxes and customs duties that siphoned off their profits and from new laws that whittled away their political privileges. They too wanted a less expensive and more representative government. Compounding the tensions in Maryland were religious enmities: the Calverts and their friends were Catholic, but many of the colony's inhabitants, including its most successful planters, were Protestants.

The unrest among Maryland planters, both humble and powerful, came to a head in July 1689. John Coode, a former member of the assembly, gathered an army, captured the proprietary governor, seized the Calvert family's plantation, and took the grievances of his Protestant Association to authorities in England. There Coode received a sympathetic hearing; the Calverts' charter was revoked and not restored until 1715, by which time the family had embraced Protestantism.

After 1690 the warring factions within the Chesapeake colonies' elite gradually worked out an accommodation that eased competition among them. The leading planters, newer as well as earlier settlers in Virginia, Protestants as well as Catholics in Maryland, parceled out among themselves the spoils of political office. That more inclusive distribution of power and privilege ensured that no future Nathaniel Bacon or John Coode could mobilize disgruntled elites against the government. The great planter families dominated the assembly and the council of both colonies, and by acting in concert, they managed to curb the power of royal and proprietary governors for decades thereafter.

The greater unity among the Chesapeake's leading families did not redress that region's most fundamental problem. The sharp inequality of white society, a gulf between rich and poor planters etched ever more deeply by the troubled tobacco economy, persisted long after Bacon's Rebellion in Virginia and Coode's Rebellion in Maryland. All that saved white society in the Chesapeake from a renewal of internal crisis was the growth of black slavery.

From Servitude to Slavery

Like the tobacco plants that came to command the length of Powhatan's land, a labor system based on slavery had not figured in the first plans for the Chesapeake. Both early promoters and planters had preferred importing English servants to importing alien African slaves. Black slaves, because they served for life, were more expensive than white workers, who served for several years. Since neither whites nor blacks lived long, cheaper servant labor was the logical choice. The number of blacks in the Chesapeake remained small for most of the seventeenth century, comprising just 5 percent of all inhabitants in 1675.

The first blacks landed in Virginia in 1619, brought by the Dutch, who dominated the slave trade until the middle of the eighteenth century. The lives of those blacks, and the lives of those who followed during the next few decades, resembled those of white servants, with whom they shared harsh work routines and living conditions. White and black bound laborers socialized with each other and formed sexual liaisons; they conspired to steal from their masters and ran away together—and if caught, they endured similar punishments. There was more common ground: many of the first blacks did not arrive directly from Africa, but

---

THE AFRICAN TRANSATLANTIC TRADE: 1450–1760

Of all the American colonies, Brazil received the largest proportion of slaves (about 32 percent), although the total numbers shipped to the Caribbean sugar islands during this period were greater. Only 4 percent of the trade went to North America. As the map indicates, the Islamic slave trade also continued to flourish, carrying roughly as many slaves along its routes across the Sahara, the Red Sea, and the Indian Ocean.

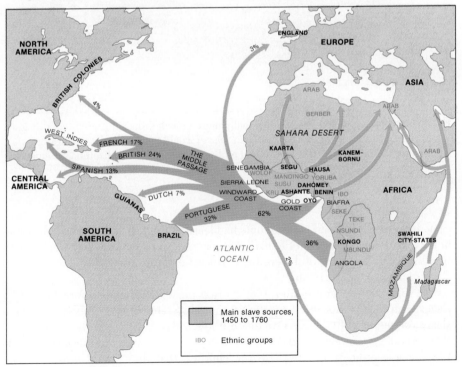

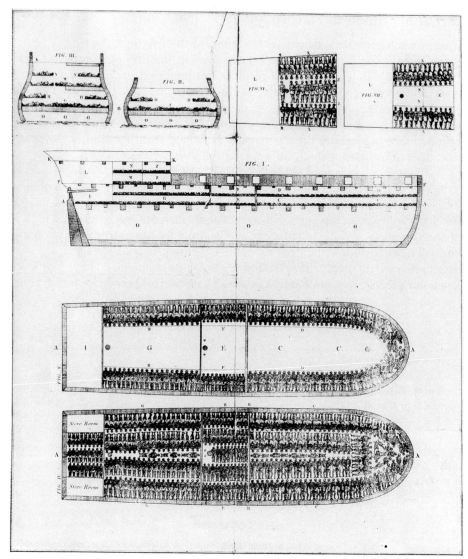

Eighteenth-century slave ships were actually more crowded than this architect's diagram suggests, because traders expected that many slaves would die during the Atlantic crossing. Congestion only contributed to the spread of disease and high rate of shipboard mortality.

came from the Caribbean, where some had learned English and adopted Christian beliefs. And not all blacks in the early Chesapeake were slaves: a few were indentured servants and a handful were free. At least one free black Virginian owned a slave himself.

A number of changes after 1680 caused planters to invest more heavily in slaves than in servants. First, declining mortality rates in the Chesapeake made slaves the more profitable investment. Although slaves were still more expensive than servants, planters could now expect to get many years of work from their bondspeople—and title as well to the children that they would now live long enough to have. At the same time, the flow of white servant migrants was falling off, in response to rumors of brutal conditions in the colonies and a new interest in keeping English workers at home to labor in new English factories and textile mills. Finally, while the supply of white servants was dwindling, the pool of available black labor was widening. When the Royal African Company lost its monopoly on the English slave trade in 1698, other merchants entered the market and swelled the number of Africans sold by British dealers to 20,000 annually.

More than 80 percent of the blacks caught up in the forced migration to America during the decades after 1680 came directly from Africa. They came mainly from agrarian tribes in Angola on the southwest coast of Africa and from the hinterlands of Senegambia, the Windward Coast, and the Gold Coast, an area lying between the Senegal and Niger rivers and the Gulf of Benin. Seized by other Africans, the captive blacks were yoked together at the neck and marched hundreds of miles through the interior to the coast. Some attempted suicide by eating clay; others died of hunger, exhaustion, and exposure. When slaves arrived at coastal trading posts, they were held in pens until their numbers constituted a full cargo for sale and shipment by European dealers.

For those who survived the trauma of capture and the long trek to the ocean, there remained the deadly hurdle of the Middle Passage, a journey of 5000 miles across the Atlantic to America. Perhaps 100 to 200 black men, women, and children were crowded onto each slave ship, but an estimated one out of every six did not live through the crossing. Shipmasters crammed their human cargo onto platforms built between the decks of their vessels, tiers spaced so low that even sitting upright was impossible. Among white sailors and slaves alike, the death toll from disease, especially dysentery, was staggering. Some of the captives tried to starve themselves to death; others fomented mutinies. Both forms of resistance were met with brutal repression.

Those captives who survived the Middle Passage reached their destinations in American ports numb and exhausted; now they faced more challenges to staying alive. The first year in the colonies was the most lethal for new, unseasoned slaves. The sickle cell genetic trait gave blacks a greater immunity than whites had to malaria, but slaves were highly susceptible to respiratory infections. One-quarter of all blacks died during their first year in the Chesapeake, and among Carolina and Caribbean slaves, mortality rates were even higher. In addition to the new disease environment, Africans were forced to adapt to lives without freedom in a wholly unfamiliar country and culture.

The Chesapeake's conversion from a labor system based on servitude to one based on slavery transformed the size, composition, and character of its black population. By 1740 forty percent of all Virginians were black, and most were African-born. Unlike blacks who had arrived earlier, they had no familiarity with English language and culture. Not only larger and more distinctively African, the black community was also locked into a more debased status by the late decades of the seventeenth century. Laws limiting manumission, the freeing of slaves by masters, inhibited the growth of a free black population. Other legislation systematically separated the races: free blacks were forbidden to own white servants; interracial marriages and sexual relationships were punished by stiff penalties. The legal code also fostered white contempt for blacks: while masters were prohibited from whipping their white servants on the bare back, slaves had no such protection. And "any Negro that shall presume to strike any white" was to receive 30 lashes for the rash act.

By consigning blacks to a servile status and defining them as property, the new laws both reflected and encouraged racism among whites of all classes. The spread of racism greatly reduced the likelihood that antagonism between rich and poor would erupt into armed conflict. White servants and small planters came to perceive slaves as inferiors; racial hatred alienated and exploited whites from exploited blacks. Instead of identifying with the plight of the slaves, the Chesapeake's poor whites prided themselves on being free, the formal equals of the great planters.

The leaders of the Chesapeake colonies cultivated white supremacy and white solidarity by improving economic prospects for freed servants and lesser planters. The Virginia assembly made provisions for servants to get a better start once they became free, ensuring that fewer would falter as small farmers and slip back into servitude. Legislators also lowered taxes, allowing lesser planters to keep more of their earnings, and widened the franchise, affording most white male Virginians a channel to express their grievances through voting. Economic trends also contributed to the greater security and prosperity of poorer whites after the last decades of the seventeenth century. In response to a moderate but steady swell of demand in Europe, tobacco prices rose slightly and then stabilized. As a result of Bacon's genocidal campaign against the Virginia Indians in 1676, new land became available. Even the domestic lives of lesser men improved as the numbers of men and women in the white population evened out around the turn of the century.

After 1700 the Chesapeake evolved into a more stable society. Gone were the bands of wild, landless, young bachelors one step ahead of the law, the small body of struggling lesser planters one step ahead of their creditors, and the great mass of exploited servants one step away from rebellion. Virginia and Maryland became colonies of farming families, most of them small planters who owned between 50 and 200 acres, who held no slaves—or at most two or three—and who accepted, usually without question, the social and political leadership of their acknowledged "superiors." The ruthless tobacco barons and swaggering conquistadors of the seventeenth century were supplanted at the top of society by great planters who styled themselves the "gentry."

The Chesapeake Gentry

The new Chesapeake gentry were the sons of well-to-do London merchant families, powerful commercial clans whose capital and connections had allied them, by interest and intermarriage, with England's landed gentlemen. Entrepreneurial fathers, some of them investors in the old Virginia Company, sent their sons to the Chesapeake between 1640 and 1670 to create prosperous plantations and to establish family interests in the New World. Their coolly calculating sons and their descendants achieved those objectives, not by the feckless gambling and heedless exploitation practiced by the Chesapeake's former profiteers, but by shrewd use of family land, capital, and influence, careful planning, and skillful estate management.

Their fortunes rested in part on the cultivation of tobacco on thousands of acres by hundreds of slaves. But the gentry made their real money from even more lucrative commercial sidelines: they collected and marketed the tobacco crops of their lesser neighbors; they sold these smaller families English manufactured goods from stores maintained on their home plantations; they provided legal

George Booth, the son of a wealthy planter family in Gloucester County, Virginia, was being raised for mastery. The young man's self-assured stance, the bow and arrows, the dog at his feet clutching the kill, the classical busts of women flanking his figure, and his family estate in the distance all suggest the gentry's concern for controlling the natural and social worlds.

advice, lent money, speculated in land, dispensed medical services, and hired out slaves to the whole county. Unlike the rough-hewn barons of the tobacco boom, the gentry's profit did not depend on wringing work from poor whites. It hinged instead on wringing work from black slaves while converting their white "inferiors" into modestly prosperous small planters and paying clients.

But the gentry wanted more than money: they wanted respect. The earliest leaders of the Chesapeake, men of no breeding or learning, had been satisfied with making their fortunes and then heading home for England. The merchants' sons who succeeded them at the top of society, men with better educations and higher social ambitions, planned to stay in the Chesapeake and to acquire not only wealth, but also the dignity and status of gentlemen.

The gentry sought—and received—the deference of the colony's lesser inhabitants in a host of ways. In the realm of politics, they looked forward to election days, when most men in the county came to cast their ballots, each in turn approaching the gentleman candidate of his choice. Some yeomen offered a brief, flattering speech before awarding their vote, and the winning candidate afterward treated his supporters to "bumbo," a potent rum punch. On militia days, when every able-bodied man in the county over the age of 16 mobilized to perform military drills, gentlemen officers led the exercises and then invited everyone to their plantations for refreshments. On court days, defendants and plaintiffs testified respectfully before gentlemen justices of the peace, bedecked in wigs and robes and seated on raised benches, and during recesses all participants repaired to the neighboring tavern. And each Sabbath morning, when many in the county came to worship at the Anglican chapel, families filed soberly into the church in order of their social rank, with the gentlemen vestry heading the procession. The little enclaves for public assembly that sprang up at the central crossroads of each county—courthouse and church, tavern and training field—served as theaters in which the new Chesapeake gentry dramatized their superiority and lesser men displayed their deference.

The plantation societies of Virginia and Maryland remained as unequal after 1700 as they had been a century earlier—indeed, even more so, for the conversion to slavery steadily deepened economic and social distinctions within the white population. Those who owned slaves enjoyed a decided edge over those who did not. And leading men still had little but disdain for poorer whites: the gentry regarded small planters and white servants alike as a lazy, stupid, and dissipated lot. But while extreme economic inequality persisted, social tension among whites eased. The naked domination of white servants and poorer planters by unscrupulous scoundrels was replaced with the exploitation of slaves by great planters who fancied themselves the equals of English gentlemen and the patriarchs of Chesapeake society.

As "fathers" to county and colony, the gentry cultivated reputations for responsibility. They served in political office not only to pursue private interest but also to advance the public good. And as "fathers" of their plantations and neighborhoods, the gentry kept a close watch over the public and private affairs of everyone, both black and white, bound and free. They decided whether to advance more credit or sue a lesser planter struggling with debt; whether to beat or administer medicine to a slave complaining of sickness; whether to indulge or discipline a white overseer or servant drinking to excess.

While maintaining strong ties to local society, the Chesapeake gentry also enjoyed a more cosmopolitan culture. Unlike their lesser neighbors, the great planter families were connected to a world wider than the county. As major marketers of tobacco, they hosted the visiting captains of English commercial vessels that sailed upriver from Chesapeake Bay to dock at their plantations. As representatives to the assembly or members of the governor's council, they convened to hear the latest news from England and to conduct public business in the tiny capitals of Williamsburg, Virginia, and Annapolis, Maryland. And as proud fathers, they sent their sons to England for a university education, rather than entrusting them to the Chesapeake's only institution of higher learning, the College of William and Mary, which was chartered in 1693.

The gentry prized such contacts with the greater Anglo-American world. They prized them so much that they were slow to recognize that their dependence on England might someday expose them to a dangerous contradiction. Their dilemma was that in addition to wealth and respect, the new Chesapeake gentry also wanted independence. "I am dependent upon no one but Providence," boasted William Byrd, one of Virginia's biggest planters.

He was wrong. True, Byrd and other members of the gentry dominated Chesapeake society and politics with little interference from England for decades after 1700. But planter power remained subject to check by authorities in the parent country—the monarchy and Parliament. Equally crucial, control over the tobacco trade, the basis of gentry prosperity and prestige, rested elsewhere. English and Scottish merchants supplied credit, banking, and marketing services, while Parliament determined imperial economic policy.

Gentlemen planters like Byrd were dependent in other ways as well. While the great gentry families created in their counties nearly self-sufficient home plantations, it was slave skill and slave labor that supported their operation. Black men and women grew the food, planted the tobacco, erected the buildings, tended the livestock, sewed the clothing, cobbled the shoes, and performed the host of other tasks that sustained gentry "self-sufficiency." And it was the clientage and acknowledgment of small planters that contributed to gentry profit and prestige.

The Chesapeake gentry, who so prized independence, also wanted wealth and respect, for which they had to depend on England, on lesser planters, and on their own slaves. That contradiction—of being independent-minded and dependent at the same time—would eventually undermine the stable social world over which the Chesapeake gentry held sway.

FROM THE CARIBBEAN TO THE CAROLINAS

During the same decade that the English invaded Powhatan's land, they began to colonize the Caribbean. A century earlier, Columbus had charted the route: ships picked up the trade winds off Madeira and the Canary Islands and headed west across the Atlantic. Dolphins and flying fish trailed in their wake, and paradise awaited at journey's end. There the surf broke over shores rimmed with white sand and jagged rocks; beaches rose sharply to coral terraces, then to broad plateaus or mountain peaks shrouded in rain forests and lush jungles. Wild hogs and cattle, turtles, fish of every sort, and figs and oranges, pomegranates, pineapples, papayas, guavas, melons, and yams promised a life of ease and plenty to all comers.

Paradise was lost to the Indians of the Caribbean, or at least to those few remaining alive. European diseases, combined with Spanish exploitation, had eliminated virtually all the natives of Hispaniola by the 1520s; over the next century those living in Cuba, Puerto Rico, and Jamaica would follow. Disease, spread by Spanish slaving expeditions, guaranteed the same fate for the Bahamas and the Lesser Antilles Islands. And the "paradise" that remained was filled with plants and animals that would have been strange to natives only a century earlier. The hogs and cattle, now wild, had been imported by Europeans, as had the figs, oranges, pomegranates and African yams. This ecological migration of flora and fauna would continue to transform the Caribbean, as well as the Americas, in the century to come.

Paradise was lost to the English as well. At first they came to the Caribbean intending not to colonize but to steal from the Spanish. Even after 1604 when some English settled on the islands, few intended to stay. Yet the English ended up not only establishing permanent plantation colonies in the West Indies, but also extending themselves from the Caribbean to a new colony on the North American mainland. Because of the strong West Indian influence, South Carolina developed a social order in some ways distinct from that of the Chesapeake or, indeed, any place in America north of paradise. But white society in early South Carolina moved toward stability and consolidation in a manner similar to that of Virginia and Maryland.

Paradise Lost Beyond the Line

The English had traded and battled with the Spanish in the Caribbean since the 1560s. During the decades of war with Spain after 1588 the islands served as bases for English privateers, staging grounds from which they conducted an illicit trade with Spanish settlements, sacked the coastal towns, and plundered silver ships bound for Seville. Until the 1630s English investors plowed more money into commerce and piracy in the Caribbean than any other overseas venture.

Even after the war with Spain ended in 1604, fighting in the Caribbean continued, for the West Indies lay "beyond the line," outside of the territorial claims ratified by European treaties. That left any nation with the courage to face the Spanish free to settle and trade in the Caribbean. And that left the Spanish free to wipe out any interlopers, if they had the strength. But they did not. Weakened by decades of warfare, Spain could not hold the West Indies; the Dutch drove a wedge into Caribbean trade routes, and the French and the English began to colonize the islands.

In the 40 years after 1604, some 30,000 immigrants from the British Isles planted crude frontier outposts on St. Kitts, Barbados, Nevis, Montserrat, and Antigua. The settlers—some free, many others indentured servants, and almost all young men—devoted themselves to working as little as possible, drinking as much as possible, and returning to England as soon as possible. They cultivated for export a poor quality of tobacco, which returned just enough to maintain straggling settlements of small farms.

Then, nearly overnight, sugar cultivation transformed the Caribbean. In the 1640s Barbados planters learned from the Dutch how to process sugar cane. The Dutch also supplied African slaves to work the cane fields and marketed the sugar for high prices in the Netherlands. Sugar plantations and slave labor rapidly spread to other English and French islands as Europeans developed an insatiable sweet tooth for the once scarce commodity. In meeting the demand, West Indian planters outstripped all of their competitors in the Mediterranean and Portuguese Brazil. Caribbean sugar made more money for England than the total volume of commodities exported by all of the mainland American colonies. Barbados, the largest and most prosperous island, became the jewel of the Caribbean, and the Caribbean, the diadem of England's overseas empire.

The biggest planters of Barbados and the other islands battened on the sugar boom. In the 50 years after 1640 a few hundred families claimed the best growing land and imported thousands of slaves; they amassed fabulous fortunes and dominated island politics. They housed and fed themselves with unbridled extravagance; they dressed with opulent vulgarity; they entertained with frantic gaiety. By 1680 Caribbean nabobs were the richest people in English America.

But even its great planters could not have confused the West Indies with paradise. Throughout the seventeenth century, yellow fever and other tropical diseases took a fearful toll, and island populations grew only because of immigration. A precarious food supply compounded the problem of disease: with every acre of land planted in sugar, West Indians had to import all that they consumed from Britain and North America. The scramble for land shunted small farmers, still the majority of the white population, onto tiny plots that supported bare subsistence.

The desperation of bound laborers posed another threat. After the conversion to sugar, black slaves gradually replaced white indentured servants in the cane fields. By the end of the seventeenth century a quarter of a million Africans had been transported to the English West Indies; a few decades later, blacks outnumbered whites by a ratio of four to one. Fear of servant mutinies and slave rebellions frayed the nerves of island masters. They tried to contain the danger by imposing harsh slave codes and inflicting brutal punishments on white and black laborers alike. But planters paid a high price for their security: they lived under a constant state of siege. One visitor to Barbados observed that whites fortified their homes with parapets from which they could pour scalding water on attacking servants and slaves. During the first century of settlement, seven major slave uprisings shook the English islands.

As more people, both white and black, squeezed onto the islands, some settlers looked for a way out. With all of the land in use, the Caribbean no longer offered opportunity to freed servants or even planters' sons. It was then that the West Indies started to shape the history of the American South.

The Founding of the Carolinas

At the end of England's civil war, Sir John Colleton, a royalist friend of Charles I, had gone into exile beyond the line in the Caribbean. After the restoration of the Stuarts in 1660 Colleton returned to England, hoping to obtain a charter for a mainland colony to be settled by the overflow from the Caribbean. In England Colleton met Sir William Berkeley, the newly appointed royal governor of Virginia, who knew that the inhabitants of his colony needed room to expand as well. Together the two men set their sights on the area south of Virginia and enlisted in their venture a number of other aristocratic, influential favorites of Charles II. By 1663 they had become joint proprietors of a place they called, in honor of the king, the Carolinas.

The northernmost part of that proprietary grant already harbored a few hardy souls from Virginia who had squatted around Albemarle Sound. The proprietors duly dispatched a governor and granted a representative assembly to that desolate region, and about 40 years later, in 1701, they set it off as a separate colony, North Carolina. The place quickly proved a disappointment. Lacking good harbors and navigable rivers to the interior, the colony had no convenient way of marketing its produce. Settlement aroused little enthusiasm among either the proprietors or any prospective inhabitants. North Carolina remained a small, poor colony, its sparse population engaged in general farming and the production of naval stores.

The southern portion of the Carolina grant held far more promise, especially in the eyes of one of its proprietors, Sir Anthony Ashley Cooper, earl of Shaftesbury. In 1669 he sponsored an expedition of a few hundred English and Barbadian immigrants, who planted the first permanent settlement in South Carolina. By 1680 the colonists, now numbering about 1000, established the center of economic, social, and political life at the confluence of two rivers called the Ashley and the Cooper after Sir Anthony and named the site itself Charleston after the king.

Cooper had big plans for his Carolina colony. Charleston's location at the hub of a network of river routes leading into the interior would permit full exploitation of the region's commercial potential. The favorable prospects for trade, coupled with the proprietors' provisions for liberal land grants and promises of complete religious toleration and representative government, would lure settlers in droves. These droves of settlers would enrich the proprietors by paying quitrents, a halfpenny per acre annually.

Such plans were big enough to satisfy most of the Carolina proprietors, who regarded their venture simply as land speculation. But Cooper, like Gilbert and Raleigh before him, and like the Calverts of Maryland, hoped to create an ideal

Daily Lives

FOOD/DRINK/DRUGS

A Taste for Sugar

It is said that shortly before his death in A.D. 735, the Venerable Bede, an English abbot, bequeathed a precious treasure to his brother monks. His legacy consisted of a cache of spices, including a little stock of sugar. What separated Bede's world, where sugar was counted a costly luxury, from twentieth-century Americans' world of ever-present sweetness was the discovery of America and the establishment of plantation economies in the Caribbean and Brazil.

Europeans acquired their first knowledge of sugar from the cultural exchange produced by an earlier surge of expansion—the Arab conquests in the Mediterranean, North Africa, and Spain during the seventh and eighth centuries. From then until the fourteenth century, Europe's merchants imported small quantities of sugar at great expense from Arab plantations, as well as from distant Persia and India, countries that had produced sugar since A.D. 500.

Throughout the Middle Ages and the early modern era, only the royal and the rich of Europe could indulge their desire for sugar, and even those privileged classes partook sparingly. Europeans classified sugar as a spice, like the equally scarce and exotic pepper, nutmeg, ginger, and saffron. Apothecaries doled out small doses as medicine for sore throats, stomach disorders, and infertility; it was also used as a remedy for the Black Death and tooth decay. The cooks of castle kitchens seasoned food and sauces with a pinch of sugar or sprinkled it on meat, fish, fowl, and fruit to preserve freshness—or to conceal rot. Only on great occasions did the confectioners of noble families dare to splurge, fashioning for courtly feasts and rituals great baked sugar sculptures of knights and kings, horses and apes, called "subtleties." Until the eighteenth century, those who consumed sugar as a medicine, spice, preservative, or decorative dessert were distinguished from the ranks of commoners as persons of consequence.

For the rest of Europe, life was not as sweet. While the rich and royal savored sugary treats, the diets of ordinary people

---

Once harvested, sugar cane in the West Indies was crushed, as in this sugar mill. The juice was collected and channeled to the sugar works, where it was concentrated through boiling and evaporation. This neat diagrammatic picture belies the harsh conditions of labor and high mortality slaves experienced: sweetness came at a steep price.

The Sugar Mill.

Daily Lives

ran to monotonous, meager starches. The staff of everyday life consisted of bread, peas, beans, and, in good years, a little milk, butter, and cheese. The occasional pig slaughtered, rabbit trapped, or fish caught supplied stray protein for the poor. Sugar, like the other trappings of power and status, only lordly families possessed.

That pattern of consumption started to change as Europeans turned to African slave labor to grow sugar for them. The sugar plantations established by Spain and Portugal in the fourteenth century on Madeira and the Canary Islands became steppingstones across the Atlantic to the creation of veritable sugar factories in the Caribbean colonies of England and France.

The impact of American sugar production on European diets manifested itself slowly but dramatically over a long span of time. By the sixteenth and seventeenth centuries, Europe's merchant classes could imitate elite patterns of eating by pouring sugar into pastries and puddings. And by the middle of the eighteenth century, an increasingly large and inexpensive supply from the Caribbean was making sugar essential to the poorest Europeans. Among England's laboring classes, another colonial import—Indian tea, laced heavily with sugar—emerged as the preferred complement to an otherwise cold supper of bread. Sweet tea and bread comprised the entire diet of those at the bottom of English society. Cheaper, warmer, and more stimulating than milk or beer (its principal competitors), sugared tea won the loyalty of England's mass market and ranked as the nonalcoholic beverage of national choice. By the nineteenth century, English working families were also combining sugar and starch by pouring treacle (molasses) over porridge and spreading jams or marmalades on their bread.

Europe and America affected each other in many ways, but diet figures among the more fundamental conditions of life altered by colonization. More than coffee, chocolate, rum, or tobacco—indeed, more than any of the other "drug foods" produced by the colonies except tea—sugar provided a major addition to the diet of the English and other Europeans. In Britain alone, consumption per capita rose about 400 percent over the eighteenth century as more and more people used more and more sugar.

Even though sugar changed gradually from a coveted luxury belonging only to the lordly to a basic foodstuff commanding a mass market, its association with power persisted. But by the eighteenth century, it was no longer the *consumption* of sugar that bestowed status. On the contrary, as sweeteners found their way into the barest cupboards, the rich and royal probably used less sugar than the poor and powerless. Instead, after 1700 it was the *production* of sugar that conferred power. Planters who grew it, merchants who shipped and sold it, industrialists who refined it, and statesmen who taxed it discovered in sugar sources of profit and distinction less perishable than the "subtleties" of noble banquets or the legacy of the Venerable Bede.

society in America. Cooper's utopia was one in which a few landed aristocrats and gentlemen would rule with the consent of many smaller propertyholders. With his personal secretary and physician, John Locke, Cooper drew up an intricate scheme of government, the Fundamental Constitutions. The design provided Carolina with a proprietary governor and a three-tiered order of hereditary nobility—proprietors, landgraves, and caciques. These nobles would constitute a Council of Lords and recommend all laws to a Parliament elected by lesser landowners.

The Fundamental Constitutions met the same fate as other grand manorial dreams for America. Frontier conditions defied all efforts to establish elaborate feudal domains. Instead, both of the Carolinas plunged into the political contention typical of other proprietary regimes like Maryland: assemblies resisted the great powers granted to the proprietary governors; ordinary settlers protested against paying quitrents claimed by the proprietors. Political unrest in North Carolina triggered three separate rebellions against proprietary rule between 1677 and 1711, with near-anarchy prevailing in intervening years. In South Carolina opposition to the proprietors gathered strength more slowly, but in the end it exploded with equal force.

Early Instability

Immigrants from Barbados, the most numerous among the early settlers, quickly assumed a dominant role in South Carolina politics, and, just as quickly, they voiced objections to proprietary power. To offset the influence of the Barbadians, most of whom were Anglican, the proprietors encouraged the migration of other groups—principally French Huguenots and English Presbyterians and Baptists—and awarded them political office. Their arrival in the colony only compounded tensions, cleaving South Carolinians into two camps with competing political and religious loyalties.

While both factions battled over proprietary rule, settlers dispersed along the coastal plain north and south of Charleston, establishing scattered plantations and searching for a profitable export. The first colonists raised grains and grazed cattle, foodstuffs that they regularly exported to the West Indies. South Carolinians also developed a large trade in deerskins and other animal pelts with coastal tribes like the Yamasee and the Creeks of the interior. More numerous than the Indians of the Chesapeake and even more deeply divided by old antagonisms, the Carolina tribes competed to become the favored clients of white traders. Southeastern Indian economies quickly became dependent on English guns, rum, and clothing.

Out of all these circumstances there developed another profitable sector of the early Carolina economy—Indian slavery. To satisfy their debts to white traders, Indians enslaved and sold to white buyers large numbers of men, women, and

---

THE CAROLINAS AND THE CARIBBEAN
The map underscores the geographic link between West Indian and Carolina settlements. Emigrants from Barbados dominated politics in early South Carolina, while Carolinians provided foodstuffs, grain, and cattle to the West Indies. As South Carolinians began growing rice, Caribbean slave ships found it an easy sail north and west to unload their cargoes in Charleston.

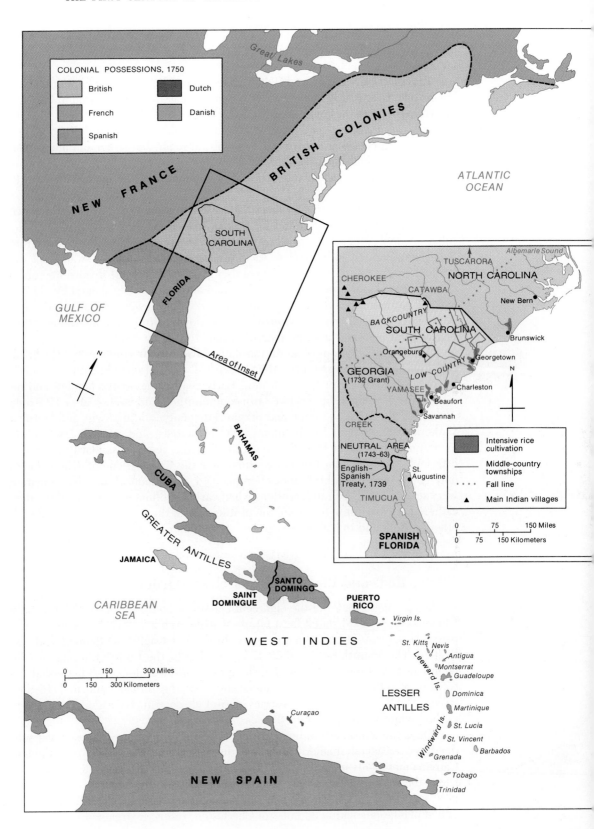

children from rival tribes taken in war. Although Carolinians exported many of the captives to New England and the West Indies, Indian slavery existed in the colony for a century.

Provisions, deerskins, and Indian slaves proved less lucrative for South Carolinians than rice. Paddy fields sprouted from the marshy lowlands around Charleston as rice became the colony's cash crop by the opening decades of the eighteenth century. Commanding good prices and being in constant demand in Europe, rice yielded less spectacular rewards than Caribbean sugar, but larger and more reliable returns than Chesapeake tobacco. It made South Carolina the richest colony and South Carolina rice planters the richest people on the mainland of North America.

Unfortunately, South Carolina's natural environment, so well suited for rice production, was less well suited for human habitation. For a century after the colony's initial settlement, appalling mortality rates prevented many planters from living long enough to appreciate their prosperity. The miasmic swamps of the lowland coast, perfect breeding grounds for mosquitoes and deadly microbes, defied survival and reproduction among men and women. Weakened by chronic malaria, settlers succumbed in epic numbers to yellow fever, smallpox, and respiratory infections. The white population grew slowly, through immigration rather than natural increase, and numbered a mere 10,000 by 1730.

The first generations of South Carolinians had little in common but the harsh conditions of frontier existence. Most colonists lived on isolated plantations, making only occasional trips to Charleston. Early deaths fragmented families and inhibited the development of native-born communities. Immigration after 1700 only intensified the colony's ethnic and religious diversity, adding Swiss and German Lutherans, Scots-Irish Presbyterians, Welsh Baptists, and Spanish Jews. Local institutions that might have enhanced order and a sense of solidarity remained extremely weak for more than a century after the first settlement. The colony's only courts were in Charleston; churches and clergymen of any denomination were scarce. On those rare occasions when early Carolinians came together, they gathered at Charleston to escape the pestilent air of their plantations, to sue each other for debt and to haggle over prices, or to fight over religious differences and proprietary politics.

White, Red, and Black: The Search for Order

By the opening decades of the eighteenth century, South Carolina, like the early Chesapeake, seemed slated for a future of strife. While internal weaknesses impaired social stability, external dangers threatened English settlement with extinction. The Spanish rattling their sabers in Florida, the French filtering into the Gulf region, and the pirates lurking along the North Carolina coast imperiled the security of settlement. But most menacing were the Indians, and in 1715 they struck. The Yamasee launched a series of carefully coordinated assaults that nearly pushed white Carolinians into the sea.

Once the allies and trading partners of white settlers, the Yamasee had subdued and enslaved smaller tribes like the Tuscarora. Then their own debt to Carolina merchants mounted, and the Yamasee realized that they might share the fate of the shattered Tuscarora. Allied with the Creeks, the Yamasee executed the most successful pan-Indian offensive in the eighteenth-century South. As Indians raided plantations within 30 miles of Charleston, refugees streamed into the city, and rumors flew throughout North America that Yamasee success would inspire assaults all along the coast. All that saved South Carolinians was their timely alliance with the Cherokee, another strong interior tribe. The Cherokee had also become dependent on English trading goods, and to meet their own needs, they were willing to make common cause with white Carolinians and to mount a counterattack against the Yamasee and the Creeks.

Although white settlement in South Carolina survived the Yamasee uprising, proprietary rule did not. As colonists reeled from the devastation of the Indian war, opposition mounted against the proprietors, who had done nothing to protect their vulnerable colony from the Spanish, the French, and the Indians. The proprietors were equally indifferent to the economic difficulties arising from the cost of defense. Military expenditures had saddled Carolinians with a depreciating currency, rising taxes, and growing indebtedness, but the proprietors had been unable to brake the colony's descent into economic crisis. Even Presbyterians, Baptists, and Huguenots, once the mainstay of proprietary support, had shifted their sympathies because they disapproved the proprietors' attempts to establish the Church of England as South Carolina's officially sanctioned religion.

Unified in their hatred of the proprietors yet divided over the route to economic recovery, planters and merchants waged a bitter struggle that nearly tore the colony apart during the 1720s. Mass meetings and mob actions so disrupted government that it all but ground to a halt during the latter years of that decade. Finally, in 1729, the Crown formally established royal government; the following year economic recovery did much to ease local tensions. Even more important in bringing greater political stability to South Carolina, whites in the colony recognized that unity within their ranks was essential, if they were to counter the Spanish in Florida and the French and their Indian allies to the southwest. Still more crucial for white Carolinians was maintaining a unified front against black Carolinians.

Black slaves brought by their Barbadian masters had been among the earliest inhabitants of South Carolina. During the first decades of settlement, frontier conditions and the scarcity of labor had forced masters to temper their treatment of slaves and to allow them greater freedom within bondage. Whites and blacks shared chores on small farms, and on isolated stockraising plantations, called "cowpens," black cowboys ranged freely over the countryside, chasing the cattle being fattened for market. The pioneer economy accorded blacks considerable autonomy and a variety of employments, and their familiarity with subtropical environments gave them an advantage over all whites except the Barbadian emigrants. White settlers could not have confused lowland South Carolina with the English countryside, but blacks found southern topography and climate remarkably similar to those of West Africa. Masters had much to learn from slaves who could identify useful plants and animals and suggest methods of cultivation and stockraising best suited to the environment. Black contributions to the defense of the colony also reinforced racial interdependence and muted white domination. From the first years of settlement to the Yamasee War, whenever the Spanish, the French, or the Indians threatened, blacks were enlisted in the militia.

After white Carolinians turned to rice as their cash crop, they depended on blacks no less—in fact, planters began to import slaves in larger numbers because of West African skill in rice cultivation. But whites now feared their dependence on blacks a great deal more. As early as 1708 blacks had become a majority in the colony, and by 1730 they outnumbered whites by two to one. Like Caribbean planters, white Carolinians instituted repressive slave codes that converted their colony into an armed camp and snuffed out the freedoms that blacks had enjoyed earlier.

The ever-present threat of revolt on the part of the black majority gave all white South Carolinians, whatever their religion, politics, or ethnic background, an incentive to cooperate among themselves. Despite the persistence of high death rates and cultural differences, despite the continuing isolation of planter families and the lack of strong local civil and religious institutions—against all odds, white South Carolinians prospered and political peace prevailed after 1730. Any course except harmony would have extracted too high a price.

In South Carolina there emerged a society both more opulent and more embattled than that of the Chesapeake. In its extremes of planter prosperity and black degradation, the surface splendor of Charleston and the actual vulnerability of the entire colony, South Carolina resembled the English Caribbean more closely than it did Virginia or Maryland. On the other hand, white Carolinians, like Chesapeake planters, tied their fortunes to a single staple crop, found themselves in debt to British merchants and financiers, prided themselves on being white and free, and held in contempt the enslaved black and Indian population. Even more than the Chesapeake's biggest planters, low country Carolina's leading men depended for their wealth on the very people whom they deeply feared—the black slaves who tended their rice fields and the Indians who supplied them with pelts and slaves.

The Founding of Georgia

After 1730 South Carolinians could take comfort not only from their new prosperity and new political harmony, but also from the founding of a new colony on their southern border. South Carolinians liked Georgia a great deal more than the Virginians had liked Maryland, for the colony formed a defensive buffer between British North America and Spanish Florida.

Enhancing the military security of South Carolina was only one reason for the founding of Georgia. More important to General James Oglethorpe and other idealistic English gentry was the aim of aiding the "worthy poor" by providing them with land, employment, and a new start in a better society. They projected a colony of hardworking small farmers who would produce silk and wine, sparing England the need to import both commodities from other countries. That dream seemed within reach when George II made Oglethorpe and his friends the trustees of the new colony in 1732, granting them a charter for 21 years, after which time Georgia would revert to royal control.

Unlike the Virginia Company's inadequate and haphazard provisions for Jamestown, Georgia's trustees exercised strict oversight in their colony. They selected with meticulous care those poor families who were to be transported "on charity," a group including not only English but Germans, Swiss, Austrians, Scots, and even a few Italians. The trustees did not, as legend has it, empty England's debtors' prisons to populate Georgia: they freed few debtors but recruited from every country in Europe paupers who seemed willing to work hard— and who professed Protestantism. They sponsored their resettlement and provided each with 50 acres of land, tools, and a year's worth of supplies. They also encouraged settlers who could pay their own way to immigrate, by allotting them larger tracts of land. Much to the trustees' consternation, that generous offer was

The Yuchi were neighbors of one of Georgia's early settlements, and one of the newly emigrated German colonists painted this watercolor of a Yuchi celebration. Judging from the guns hanging at the back of the shelter, these Indians were already trading with whites.

taken up not only by many hoped-for Protestants, but also by several hundred Ashkenazim (German Jews) and Sephardim (Spanish and Portuguese Jews), who established a thriving community in early Savannah.

The trustees enforced several regulations to ensure that Georgia became a small farmers' utopia. Rather than selling land the trustees simply gave it away, but none of the colony's settlers could receive more than 500 acres. The trustees also prohibited Georgians themselves from selling land or from willing their farms to female heirs, thus preventing daughters from combining their inheritances with their husbands' land to form large estates. As a further precaution against great plantations, the trustees outlawed slavery, not out of any concern for blacks but to cultivate habits of industry and to sustain equality among whites. The same considerations led the trustees to ban the importation and consumption of all hard liquor.

This design for a virtuous and egalitarian utopia for poor families was greeted with little enthusiasm by Georgians. They lobbied for the opening of a free market in land, claiming that many of the individual grants made by the trustees consisted only of sandy soil and pine trees, acreage not suited to farming. They also argued that the colony could never prosper until the trustees revoked their ban on slavery and followed the example of booming South Carolina. Since the trustees had provided for no elective assembly, settlers could express their discontent only by moving across the border—which many did during the early decades.

Careful planning and good intentions had not been enough to realize the trustees' utopian dreams. As mounting opposition to their policies threatened to depopulate the whole colony, the trustees caved in. They revoked their restrictions on land, slavery, and liquor a few years before the king assumed control of the colony in 1752. The death of the trustees' vision made Georgia a magnet for immigrants from Europe, the West Indies, and the other mainland North American colonies. Under royal control, Georgia continued to develop an ethnically and religiously diverse society, similar to that of South Carolina, and a comparable economy based on rice cultivation and the Indian trade.

THE SPANISH BORDERLANDS

When the English founded Jamestown, Spanish claims in North America extended from a feeble fort at St. Augustine, Florida, in the east to a western flank of garrison towns (*presidios*) and Catholic missions in New Mexico. During the seventeenth century, as Chesapeake planters developed a tobacco economy and Carolinians cleared their frontier, the Spanish sustained their initial colonizing efforts in the Southwest. Juan de Oñate founded Santa Fe in 1610; the Jesuit Eusebio Francisco Kino established missions in Arizona and Baja California later in the seventeenth century. As English colonial societies matured in the Southeast over the first half of the eighteenth century, the Spanish were establishing more missions and *presidios* at San Antonio and elsewhere in Texas. The spread of Spanish influence to California took place later, possibly because of a persistent misconception among Europeans that California was an island. It was not until the last half of the eighteenth century that Spanish soldiers and missionaries led by the Franciscan friar Junípero Serra established 20 communities along California's coastal plain.

Since the borderlands of the Southwest lacked the mineral wealth and the large native populations of Mexico and Peru, Spain took relatively little interest in that part of its empire and the region developed slowly. Cattle-raising became the basis of the borderlands' economy: mounted cowboys, *vaqueros*, rounded up the herds that roamed over the vast open ranges of scattered ranches, or *haciendas*. After the roundup, or *rodeo*, the cattle were slaughtered for sale to the south and to supply the soldiers of the *presidios*. The garrisons, in turn, protected Spanish settlements in the Southwest from the French, who infiltrated the region in the eighteenth century, and they protected Spanish claims in northern California from English and Russian traders.

The Spanish also attempted to strengthen their hold on the borderlands by incorporating native tribes into colonial society. The principal instrument for attaining that objective was the mission community. Each mission consisted of a quadrangle, dominated at the center by a large church. Homes, workshops, granaries, and stables clustered around the church. Spanish missionaries, chiefly members of the Franciscan and Dominican orders, gathered the Indians into the missions and taught them European agricultural techniques and crafts, as well as the Spanish language and Catholic doctrine. Native Indian men sometimes served mission villages as civil officials and judges, but always under the close scrutiny of the Catholic clergy.

Unlike the English, the Spanish projected a place in their colonies for the Indians, and they made sustained efforts to "civilize" and Christianize them. The role that the Spanish envisioned for the Indians in their settlements was a subservient one—docile servants for Spanish officers, pious agricultural laborers and artisans for Spanish missionaries and *hacendados* (ranchers), willing laborers for Spanish mine owners. The Indians might not have accepted such a fate without a determined struggle, but the deadly contagion of European diseases had devastated the small southwestern and Pacific coastal tribes.

The Indians still managed to mete out defiance. The Apache adopted the horses introduced by the Spanish and became expert cattle rustlers. Indians forced into the missions regularly ran away and occasionally organized major insurrections. The Yaqui uprising of 1740 in northwest Mexico left over 1000 Spanish dead. The Tepehuanes and the Tarahumaras of northern Mexico and the Hopi of the American Southwest also held out against Spanish rule for long periods.

The most sustained and successful Indian resistance was the Great Pueblo Revolt in 1680, which drove the Spanish out of New Mexico for more than a decade. Popé, an Indian spiritual leader in Taos, coordinated an uprising of several Pueblo tribes that vented the full force of their hatred of Spanish rule. They murdered priests, piled their bodies on altars, and set the churches on fire. They killed families in outlying *haciendas* and burned their Spanish-style houses to the ground. They even exterminated the livestock introduced by the Spanish. The attack wiped out one-fifth of the Spanish population of 2500 and sent survivors scurrying for refuge down Dead Man's Road to El Paso, Texas. After the Pueblo victory, one candid colonial official observed that "they are very happy without religious [Catholic missionaries] or Spaniards." Only after four attempts at reconquest and the outbreak of a plague among the Pueblos did the Spanish reassert their control over New Mexico.

The Spanish in the Southwest attempted to regulate every aspect of native life by drawing local tribes into missions. Here, Catholic priests have marshalled the Indian inhabitants of a mission in Carmel, California, to welcome a visiting European dignitary.

Empire . . . utopia . . . independence. . . . For more than a century after the founding of Jamestown, those dreams inspired the inhabitants of the Chesapeake, the Carolinas, and Georgia, the Caribbean, and the American Southwest. The regions served as staging grounds where kings and commoners, free and unfree, men and women, red, white, and black played out their hopes. Most met only disappointment and many, disaster.

The dream of an expanding empire faltered for the Spanish, who found no new El Dorado to the north. It failed the expectations of England's early Stuart monarchs, who found themselves embroiled in revolution at home. And the dream foundered fatally for Powhatan's successors, who were unable to resist both white diseases and land-hungry tobacco planters. So, too, the dream of a feudal utopia carried by the Calvert family into Maryland and by Cooper into the Carolinas sank like Gilbert's ship, buffeted by the frontier and finally engulfed by swells of opposition to lordly rule. The Georgian trustees could not transplant across the Atlantic their dream of a utopia for the poor, and the dream of a Spanish Catholic utopia brought by missionaries to the American Southwest dimmed with Indian resistance.

The dream of independence proved the most deceptive of all, especially for the inhabitants of England's colonies. Just a bare majority of the white servant immigrants to the Chesapeake survived to enjoy freedom, and not all of those earned freedom from hardship and insecurity. Not only in the Chesapeake but also in the Caribbean and the Carolinas, real independence eluded the English planters. Poorer people relied on richer people for land and leadership; the richest looked to England as the ultimate source of economic and political power. And everywhere in the American South and Southwest, white people's lingering dreams could be realized only through the labor of the least free members of colonial societies—Indians and blacks, whose own dreams of empire or independence had met an even more cruel defeat.

SIGNIFICANT EVENTS

late 1500s	Formation of Powhatan's confederacy
1603	James I becomes king of England; beginning of Stuart dynasty
1604	First English settlements in the Caribbean
1607	English settle Jamestown
1610	Founding of Santa Fe
1619	First blacks arrive in Virginia
1620s	Tobacco boom in Virginia
1622	White–Indian warfare in Virginia
1624	Virginia becomes a royal colony
1625	Charles I becomes king of England
1632	Calvert founds Maryland
1640s	The sugar boom begins in the Caribbean
1660	Parliament passes the first of the Navigation Acts
1669	First permanent settlement in South Carolina
1676	Bacon's Rebellion in Virginia
1680	Pueblo Revolt in New Mexico
1689	Coode's Rebellion in Maryland
ca. 1700	Rice boom begins in South Carolina
1715	Yamasee uprising in South Carolina
1732	Chartering of Georgia

3

The First Century of Settlement in the Colonial North

hey came to her one night while she slept. Into her dreams drifted a small island, and on the island were tall trees and living creatures, one of them wearing the fur of a white rabbit. When she told of her vision, no one took her seriously, not even the wise men among her people, shamans and conjurers whose business it was to interpret dreams. No one, that is, until two days later, when the island appeared to all, floating toward shore. On the island, as she had seen, were tall trees, and on their branches—bears. Or creatures that looked so much like bears that the men grabbed their weapons and raced to the beach, eager for a good hunt and hungry for a great feast sent by the gods. They were disappointed. The island was not an island at all, but a strange wooden ship planted with trees. And the bears were not bears at all but a strange sort of men whose bodies were covered with hair. Strangest among them, as she had somehow known, was a man dressed all in white. He commanded great respect among the bearlike men as their shaman, or "priest."

In that way, foretold in the dreams of a young woman, the Micmac Indians living along the north Atlantic coast in 1869 recounted their tribe's first meeting with whites more than two centuries earlier. Uncannily, the traditions of other northern tribes record similar dream portents of the European arrival: "large canoes with great white wings like those of a giant bird," filled with pale, bearded men bearing "long, sharp knives" and "long black tubes." Perhaps the dreamers gave shape in their sleep to stories heard from other tribes who had actually seen white strangers and ships. Or perhaps the Indians of the north Atlantic coast and Canada, long before they ever encountered Europeans, imagined them, just as medieval monks fantasized the Isles of the Blessed. The first whites seen by those tribes might have been English or Dutch, but probably, like the party met by the Micmacs, they were French, the most avid early adventurers in the northern reaches of the New World.

While Indians dreamed of ships and strangers, the dreams of some French explorers were more fabulous and far-fetched. At first, in the sixteenth century, the French dreamed of finding a northwest passage to Asia, a discovery that would bring their nation riches rivaling those of the Spanish and the Portuguese. That quest captivated Giovanni de Verrazzano, a Florentine navigator in the service of Francis I, who coasted the continent from North Carolina to Nova Scotia in 1524.

Mrs. Elizabeth Freake and Baby Mary, *by an anonymous New England artist (1670–1674). Unlike the South, where family life developed slowly, northern colonial society was based from the beginning on the family.*

The same prospect shimmered before the hopeful eyes of Jacques Cartier, whose quarry also included "Saguenay," a kingdom of fabulous riches reputed to exist in northern reaches just as surely as Prester John's principality thrived somewhere in the Muslim world. Instead of Saguenay, Cartier discovered the St. Lawrence River in 1535. The French attempted to settle at the present site of Quebec several years later, but, failing to find precious minerals, they confined their efforts to fishing and fur trading for the next 50 years. The French did not plant a permanent colony in North America until 1605, when a company of merchants established Port Royal in Acadia (Nova Scotia).

The French quickly realized the limits of Port Royal's location: the Appalachian highlands cut off Acadia from the rest of Canada. Eager for access to the vast North American hinterland, the French shifted the center of their settlement back to the St. Lawrence valley, where Samuel de Champlain founded Quebec in 1608. He planned to follow from Quebec the elaborate network of rivers and lakes leading into the interior, exploring the continent for the furs that it would yield and for the passage to the Pacific that it might hold. With the returns of the fur trade, he hoped to finance the immigration of settlers, who would build a strong colony for France in America.

A quarter of a century after the founding of Quebec, Canada had neither attracted a large contingent of colonists nor revealed a northwest passage. But the handful of settlers in New France—about 100 soldiers, traders, and missionaries—had established amicable relations with the local Indian tribes. There were the Algonquin and Montagnais of the St. Lawrence valley, skilled nomadic hunters and eager traders who rubbed the arms and torsos of the French in gleeful greeting. In the broad, fertile meadows and rich forests around Georgian Bay there was Huronia, a nation of expert fishermen, woodsmen, and hunters, 25,000 strong. More settled than the St. Lawrence tribes, the Huron lived in a score of semipermanent villages, longhouses enclosed by a palisade and surrounded by the corn fields that women tended.

The French formed profitable partnerships with these native peoples. Tribesmen hunted beaver, otter, and raccoon and then wore the pelts until they turned soft and supple enough to be converted into felt for fashionable European hats. Indians also supplied the skins of mink and marten, finery favored by European government officials and churchmen to display their rank. The French had a name for what New France had become by 1630—a *comptoir*, a storehouse for the skins of dead animals, not a proper colony.

That began to change when other Frenchmen with their own dreams took responsibility for Canada. Louis XIII and his chief minister, Cardinal Richelieu, hoped that American wealth might be the making of France and its monarchs. In the 1630s, they granted large tracts of land and a trading monopoly to a group of private investors, the Company of the Hundred Associates. The Associates brought a few thousand French farmers across the Atlantic, dispersed them over 200 miles of company lands along the St. Lawrence, and established upstream from Quebec the towns of Montreal and Trois-Rivières.

Religious zeal, as much as the hope of profit, spurred France to renew its commitment to colonization. The Catholic Church throughout Europe was basking in a revival of religious piety and confidence as a result of the Counterreformation, an effort to correct those abuses that had prompted the Protestant Reformation. Catholic reformers called for ending the sale of indulgences and church offices, improving the education of parish priests, enforcing celibacy among the clergy, and making the church more responsive to popular spiritual needs. To reclaim members lost to Protestantism and to arrest the spread of Lutheran and Calvinist "heresies," the Counterreformation launched an aggressive campaign of repression in Europe and missionary work abroad. In France, the Catholic majority persecuted Protestant Huguenots and targeted Canada as a field ripe for religious imperialism. The shock troops of the Counterreformation, not only in the Americas but also in India and Japan, were the Jesuits. One of several new religious orders founded during the Counterreformation, the Jesuits, whose order is the Society of Jesus, specialized in educating the sons of upper-class families and in spreading Catholic teachings to foreign lands. With Richelieu's encouragement, Jesuit missionaries streamed into Canada to assist other French settlers in bringing the Indians the "right" kind of Christianity.

In the Jesuits' dreams began France's formidable "responsibility" in America. The Indians of the north Atlantic coast shared with the southern tribes a supreme confidence in the superiority of their own cultures. The Jesuits, at least at first, seemed unlikely to shake that conviction. In Indian eyes, the Jesuits were a joke—men encumbered by their effeminate robes, deformed by their "very ugly" beards, and disqualified from physical pleasure by their vow of celibacy. The Jesuits were also a nuisance. Not content with establishing missions in French settlements and Indian villages, they undertook "flying" missions to the nomadic tribes, tagging along with Indian trappers. Once in the wilderness, the Jesuits were a disaster—tangling their legs as they tried to master snowshoes, trying for a first and last time to stand in a bark canoe, refusing to carry any weapons, and sponging off the Indians for food and shelter.

Some Indians gradually formed a better opinion of the French and their priests. The French were brave. Their traders, known as *coureurs du bois*, and their soldiers often adopted the Indian way of life and married Indian women. Even better, the French were still relatively few. Interested primarily in trade, they had no designs on Indian land. The Jesuits, too, won acceptance among some tribes. Their sincere lack of interest in Indian land, Indian furs, and Indian women made them a novelty among white men, while their relative immunity to the diseases that killed many Indians confirmed their claims to superior power. And once the Jesuits got the hang of native tongues, they exhibited a talent for smooth talk that the Indians, who prized able oratory, greatly admired. The Jesuits returned the admiration: unlike many of their countrymen, they saw the Indians not as savage brutes, but as innately civil and good.

Jesuit persistence slowly paid off. Missionaries reached every tribe within a radius of several hundred miles from Quebec. Christian factions formed in many tribes, especially those in which shamans or important families embraced the new religion. Part of the Jesuits' appeal was that they accepted and even appreciated much of Indian culture. The Jesuits never wavered in their determination to supplant Indian religions with Catholicism, but they did not try to convert the Indians into French men and women. If the natives chose to become Catholics in their religion, while retaining the rest of their culture, it was all to the good—a good deal better than their becoming English and Protestant.

THE FOUNDING OF NEW ENGLAND

The English regarded the northern part of North America as a place that only the mad French could endow with possibility. English fishermen who strayed from

Newfoundland to the coast of Acadia and New England carried home descriptions of the long, lonely stretch of coast, rockbound and rugged, washed by the waves of the slate gray Atlantic. Long winters of numbing cold and heavy snowfalls alternated with short summers of steamy heat. There were no minerals worthy of mining, no crops worthy of export, no large population of natives suitable for enslaving. To prospective investors and settlers the Chesapeake, with its temperate climate and long growing season, appeared a more likely spot.

In truth, of course, Indian tribes had successfully inhabited the territory that came to be called New England for at least 10,000 years. Each spring they set fires while the forests were still wet, to burn away the underbrush and make traveling and hunting easier. Such burnings encouraged the growth of deer and other game populations and gave early New England forests an almost parklike appearance. Elsewhere, Algonkian women tended fields of corn, beans, and pumpkins—not one crop per field as Europeans did, but mixed together in single patches, to help keep down weeds. By the beginning of the seventeenth century, perhaps 100,000 Algonkian-speaking men and women hunted, fished, and farmed in the area reaching from the Kennebec River in Maine to Cape Cod.

Until 1620, the English remained unimpressed with the region's potential. Increasingly, however, deteriorating conditions in the Old World began to produce the peculiarly intense blend of desperation and idealism that was required to settle an uninviting, unknown world. Just as the crusading militancy of the Catholic Counterreformation shaped the French colonization of Canada, the uncompromising zeal of John Calvin's followers inspired the first English settlements on the north Atlantic coast. Because of the Protestant Reformation, religious faith became more and more a matter of controversy during the seventeenth century. Compounding the religious crisis were mounting political tensions and continuing problems of unemployment and recession. Times were bad—so bad that the anticipation of worse times to come swept men and women to the shores of New England. The drama that unfolded there differed in almost every way from the ordeal taking place at the same time in the Chesapeake colonies and the Carolinas.

The Puritan Movement

The settlement of New England started with a king who chose his enemies unwisely. James I, shortly after succeeding Elizabeth I in 1603, vowed to "harry out" of his realm radical Protestant reformers. That angered the Puritans, the radicals whom James had in mind, and it angered some members of Parliament with Puritan sympathies. Next the king attempted to levy taxes without the consent of Parliament. That angered every member of Parliament and many other English besides. The anger of these two groups did not bode well for James' reign. In Parliament, he faced politically ambitious landowners and merchants, who were convinced that law was on their side. And in the Puritans he faced a determined band of zealots who were convinced that God was on their side.

The Puritans were less remarkable for what they believed than for the intensity with which they believed it. Like all Christians, Protestant and Catholic, the Puritans believed that God was all-knowing and all-powerful. And like all Calvinists, the Puritans emphasized that idea of divine sovereignty known as predestination. At the center of their thinking was the belief that God had determined the outcome of history, including the eternal fate of every human being, before the beginning of time. Logically, believing in predestination should have made men and women despairing or passive, resigned to their preordained fates. But psychologically, the effect on the Puritans was just the opposite: predestination was the engine driving their social and political activism.

Far from sinking into pessimism, the Puritans called predestination "a comfortable doctrine," because it provided their lives with meaning, order, and a clear sense of purpose. They had the assurance that a sovereign God was firmly directing the fate of individuals, nations, and all of creation. Far from lapsing into passivity, the Puritans strove to play their parts in the divine drama of history and to discover in their performances some evidence of personal salvation.

The divine plan, as the Puritans understood it, called for them to reform evils in both church and society along the lines laid down by John Calvin. What stood between them and the reformation of England was the state. Instead of promoting purity in the churches and order in society, the English government, it seemed to the Puritans, impeded the progress of reform. It tolerated drunkenness, theatergoing, gambling, extravagance, public swearing, and Sabbath-breaking. It condoned popular pastimes rooted in pagan custom and superstition—sports like bear-baiting and maypole-dancing and festivals like the celebration of Christmas and saints' days. What was worse, the state had not gone far enough in purifying the English church. The Puritans deplored the "corruptions" of Roman Catholicism that still infected the Church of England: the hierarchical offices of bishops and archbishops, ecclesiastical courts, elaborate ceremonies in which priests wore ornate vestments, making communion a kind of literal sacrifice, in which wine was turned into blood before an altar. Too many Anglican clergy were "dumb dogges" in Puritan eyes, too poorly educated to instruct the laity in the truths of Scripture or to deliver a decent sermon. Finally, the Church of England included everyone in the nation, saint and sinner alike. To the Puritans, belonging to a church was no birthright. They wished to limit church membership and the privileges of baptism and communion to the visibly godly.

The refusal of English monarchs to take stronger measures to reform church and society turned the Puritans into their outspoken critics. Elizabeth I had tolerated this opposition, but James I would not endure it and intended to rid England of these malcontents. With some of the Puritans, known as the Separatists, he seemed to succeed.

The Pilgrim Settlement at Plymouth Colony

The Separatists were Puritans who concluded that the Church of England was too corrupt to be reformed from within. They abandoned Anglican worship and met secretly in small congregations of like-minded men and women. From their first appearance in England during the 1570s, the Separatists suffered persecution from the government—fines, imprisonment, and in a few cases, execution. Always a tiny minority within the Puritan movement, the Separatists were pious people from humble backgrounds, craftworkers and farmers without the resources or the numbers or the inclination to challenge the state. By 1608 one Separatist congregation, a group at Scrooby, had become so dismayed by the depravity of Stuart England that they migrated to Holland.

The move to Holland proved to be just the first of their trials. Although the Dutch government permitted complete freedom of religion, the Separatists were disappointed by low-paying jobs, alarmed when their children adopted Dutch customs, and distressed by desertions from their own ranks to other religions.

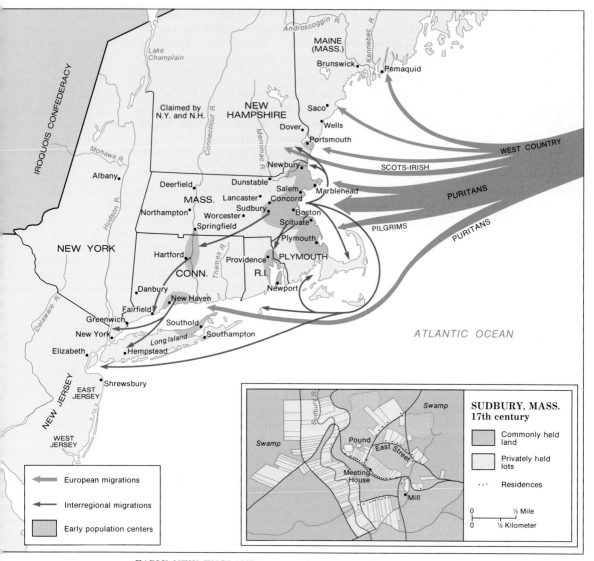

EARLY NEW ENGLAND
Despite some variety among emigrants to New England, the region remained relatively homogenous and stable, with everyday life centered in small towns like Sudbury (located to the west of Boston). Most families lived close to one another in houses clustered around the meetinghouse, in contrast to the decentralized plantations of the South. The privately held farm lots were mixed together as well, so that neighbors worked and lived in close contact with each other.

They wanted a place where their pure churches and communities could flourish, free of hardship, corruption, distraction, and competition. Some decided to move to Virginia.

What fate would have greeted the gentle, unworldly Separatists of Holland if they had actually settled in the Chesapeake during the decade of the tobacco boom can only be imagined. But a series of mistakes—including an error in charting the course of their ship, the *Mayflower*—landed the little band in New England instead. In November 1620, some 88 Separatist "Pilgrims," sick with scurvy, weakened by malnutrition, and shaken by a shipboard mutiny, disembarked at a place that they called Plymouth on the coast of present-day southeastern Massachusetts. Neither the site nor the season seemed auspicious, as one of their leaders, William Bradford, later remembered:

> For summer being done, all things stand upon them with a weatherbeaten face, and the whole country, full of woods and thickets represented a savage hue. If they looked behind them, there was the mighty ocean which they had passed and was now as a main bar and gulf to separate them from all the civil parts of the world.

For some, the shock was too great. Dorothy Bradford, William's wife, is said to have fallen overboard from the *Mayflower* as it lay anchored off Plymouth. It is more likely that she jumped to her death.

Few Pilgrims could have foreseen founding the first permanent white settlement in New England, and many did not live long enough to enjoy the distinction. The season was far too late to plant crops, and the colonists had failed to bring an adequate supply of food with them. By the spring of 1621, half of the immigrants had died. Plans for attaining self-sufficiency through hunting and fishing proved impractical too, for the Separatists knew little of firearms and even less about fish. Their efforts to establish a summer fishery on Cape Ann ended in an inglorious retreat after a company of English fishermen laid claim to the same spot with muskets leveled. English merchants who had financed the *Mayflower* voyage failed to send supplies to the struggling colony.

Plymouth might have become another doomed colony if the Pilgrims had not received better treatment from native inhabitants than they did from their English backers. Samoset and Squanto, two Indians who had learned to speak English from visiting fishermen, introduced the settlers to native strains of corn and arranged a treaty between the Pilgrims and the region's main tribe, the Wampanoags, who sought the English as allies against their enemies, the Narragansetts. Peace with them prevailed for 50 years, enabling the white settlers of Plymouth to survive.

The Pilgrims also set up a government for their colony, the basis of which was the Mayflower Compact. That agreement provided for a governor and several assistants to advise him, all to be elected annually by Plymouth's adult males. The Plymouth settlers had no clear legal sanction for their claim to land or their government, for they had neither a royal charter nor approval from the Crown. But English authorities, distracted by more pressing problems, left the tiny colony of farmers alone.

The Puritan Settlement at Massachusetts Bay

Among the Crown's distractions were other Puritans—the Presbyterians and the Congregationalists—who were still striving to reform church and society in England. But the 1620s brought them only fresh discouragements. In 1625 Charles I inherited his father's throne and all of his enemies in Parliament and among the Puritans. Charles dealt with political dissent by dissolving Parliament in 1629. He dealt with religious dissent by supporting a group of archconservative Anglicans led by Archbishop William Laud, proponents of stringent measures for suppressing Puritanism. Laud purged England's parishes of ministers with Puritan leanings and reintroduced Roman Catholic rituals and practices into the Church of England.

Increased persecution appeared to the Puritans a fearful portent that England was slipping toward the edge of apocalypse. Many believed that great catastrophes were at hand which would usher in the second coming of Jesus Christ. As their disillusionment deepened into desperation, some concluded that it might be more prudent to cross the Atlantic—then press for reform and await Christ's return.

The Puritans who became interested in American colonization came from the ranks of the Congregationalists. They shared with the Separatists in Old and New England a commitment to Calvinism and a common view of church government. Both groups believed that each congregation should be self-governing and independent of any higher authority. But the Congregationalists differed from the Separatists in their desire to remain within the Church of England, as well as in their social background and temperament.

It was a group of energetic, experienced, and established Congregationalist merchants, landed gentlemen, and lawyers who organized the Massachusetts Bay Company in 1629. Alienated from their own society, these able Puritan leaders aimed to build a better society in America, an example to the rest of the world. Unlike the Separatists, they were imbued with a strong sense of mission and destiny; they claimed that they were not abandoning the English church but regrouping for another assault on corruption from across the Atlantic. They began by organizing a mass exodus to Massachusetts Bay that had the precision and efficiency of a military maneuver and the aggressive, martial spirit of a crusade. One of the immigrants, Edward Johnson, described his fellows as "Soldiers of Jesus Christ," who "for England's sake . . . are going from England to pray without ceasing for England."

The Massachusetts Bay Company first dispatched advance parties of several hundred settlers, who established the town of Salem as a Puritan foothold on the coast well north of Plymouth. Then the company procured a royal charter confirming its title to most of present-day Massachusetts and New Hampshire and securing its rights to govern the region. That accomplished, the stockholders promptly voted to transfer the company to Massachusetts Bay and elected as their first governor John Winthrop, a pious, tough-minded Puritan lawyer and landed gentleman. Winthrop sailed from England in 1630, taking with him a dozen other company stockholders and a fleet of men and women committed to the Puritan cause. "We shall be as a city on a hill," Winthrop declared during the crossing to his fellow passengers on the ship *Arbella*. The Winthrop fleet steered a straight course for Salem, landing on the spot as spring planting season began.

To guarantee that the settlers would govern themselves without interference from London, Winthrop carried across the Atlantic the royal charter of the Massachusetts Bay Company. Leaders of the migration believed that the charter supplied them with an unimpeachable title to settle and to rule, and they made the most of their opportunity. Once established in the Bay Colony, Winthrop and the other stockholders transformed the charter for a mere trading company into the framework of government for a colony. The company's governor became the

John Winthrop, the first governor of the Massachusetts Bay Colony.

colony's chief executive and the company's other officers, the governor's assist-ants. The charter provided for annual elections of the governor and his assistants by company stockholders, the freemen. But to create a broad base of support for the new government, Winthrop and his assistants expanded the freemanship in 1631 to include every adult male church member. Being committed to Puritanism rather than owning company stock became the requirement for political participa-tion. "The way of God hath always beene to gather his churches out of the world," Winthrop remarked; "Now the world, or civill state, must be raised out of the churches."

The governor, his assistants, and the freemen together comprised the Gen-eral Court of the colony, which passed all laws, levied taxes, established courts, and made war and peace. In 1634 the whole body of the freemen stopped meeting and instead each town elected representatives or deputies to the General Court. Ten years later, the deputies constituted themselves as the lower house of the Bay Colony legislature, and the assistants formed the upper house. By refashioning a company charter into a civil constitution, Massachusetts Bay Puritans gained full control of the government under which they would live. In the New World they fulfilled their dream of shaping society, church, and state to their liking.

NEW ENGLAND COMMUNITIES

Contrary to all expectations, New England proved more hospitable to the English than did the Chesapeake. The character of the initial migration itself gave New England settlers an advantage, for most arrived not as young, single, indentured servants, but in family groups. The heads of New England's first households were typically free men—farmers, artisans, and merchants, most of whom were skilled and literate. Since husbands usually migrated with their wives and children, the ratio of three men to two women within the population was fairly evenly balanced at the outset. There was never in New England a large number of young, single men like those who contributed to the volatility of Virginia society.

Most immigrants, some 21,000, came in a cluster between 1630 and 1642. Thereafter the flow of new arrivals tapered off because of the outbreak of the English Civil War. The concentrated settlement of New England within the short span of 12 years meant that these colonies, unlike the Chesapeake, escaped the strain of absorbing a steady stream of newcomers throughout the seventeenth century. Rapid settlement also made for social solidarity, because immigrants shared a common set of experiences and ideals. The "Great Migration" of 1630 to 1642 was a movement of Puritans unified by persecution and a strong sense of religious mission—the desire to create a purer church and to establish an ordered society modeled on Scripture.

New England Families

Like-minded Puritan emigrants and their progeny lived long and prospered in New England, and their very longevity fostered a sense of continuity. New Eng-landers lived nearly twice as long as Virginians and about 10 years longer than English men and women. The first generation of colonists lived to an average age

Daily Lives

PUBLIC SPACE/PRIVATE SPACE

The Rituals of Mourning

Two hours past midnight on a Boston Sabbath, Samuel Sewall awoke to the cries of his eldest daughter, Hannah, and rushed downstairs to her bedside. The 44-year-old woman was in a "restless" state and, from the looks of the sober-faced attending relatives, near death. Sewall roused his wife, Hannah's stepmother, and sent for his son, the Reverend Joseph Sewall, and other neighborhood clergy, who joined the family, watching and reading psalms at the deathbed. Later that morning he pinned a note to the door of the Old South meetinghouse: "Prayers are desired for Hannah Sewall as drawing Near her end." Then he attended Sabbath services, where the minister led the prayers for the dying woman. When he returned from public worship, Sewall found his daughter dead.

Like most New Englanders, Hannah Sewall died at home, and there her body remained for a period of private mourning. In her case, this period of necessity would be short, for both the sweltering mid-August heat and the nature of her illness dictated that burial take place quickly, within two days. By Monday Hannah lay in a coffin in the "best room" of her father's house; near the windows "opened for coolness," Sewall's slave, a man named "Boston," kept vigil over the corpse through the night. "Her pleasant Countenance was very Refreshing to me," Sewall noted in his diary. "I hope God had delivered her from her fears."

Samuel Sewall was practiced at pious resignation to divine will, for death had stopped often at his household, more frequently than at most New Englanders'. By the time of Hannah's death, he had buried

On the elaborate headstone of John Foster (d. 1681) Father Time attempts to stay the hand of a skeletal Death from extinguishing the candle of earthly life; the sun of redemption rises above both figures, promising eternal life to the godly. The Foster headstone contains more biographical allusions than most other early markers. The Latin inscription below, composed by Increase Mather, a Boston minister, celebrates Foster's career as an astronomer and publisher of almanacs. It reads: "Living thou studiest the stars; dying, mayest thou, Foster, I pray, mount the skies and learn to measure the highest heaven."

two wives; of his 16 children, 7 had died in infancy and another was stillborn. Hannah's death might also have come as a relief: she had "languished" for a long time and possibly suffered from ill health all her life, for she died, at age 44, unmarried. But however familiar death was to his family or however welcome Hannah's release from suffering, Sewall deeply felt his loss. Grief and distraction intruded as he listed in his diary his last efforts to comfort his

Daily Lives

daughter and to ready her corpse for burial: "I do not remember the exact order of these things," he admitted.

To master his sorrow, Sewall threw himself into preparations for Hannah's funeral, the ritual of public mourning. By 1724, the year of her death, New England funerals had become elaborate and costly affairs, especially those for members of leading families like the Sewalls. They began the public ritual of death by sending a pair of gloves, a symbol of fellowship, to each person invited to the funeral. They also presented relatives, friends, and local clergy with mourning rings, bands wrought of gold and engraved or enameled with death's heads (winged skulls), coffins, and skeletons. On Tuesday, August 18, the Sewall family, outfitted in elegant black mourning clothes, were joined by other relatives and friends in a solemn procession behind Hannah's coffin, to which were pinned elegies composed by Boston clergy. Although New England funerals were civil ceremonies, one of the ministers would offer a prayer before the burial, once the pallbearers and the horse-drawn hearse had led the assembly to a nearby graveyard.

To those attending Hannah Sewall's burial, cemeteries, although public property, were steeped in spiritual significance. Puritans regarded the graveyard not as a final resting place but rather as a way station between this world and the next. Like other Christians, they viewed death as both destructive and regenerative: the dissolution of the body but, for the elect, the final stage of the spiritual resurrection that had begun in the conversion experience. The shape of the gravestones suggested a doorway, a passage from earthly life to eternal afterlife; the most popular motifs of gravestone art— the winged skull of death's head and the winged head of a cherub—represented the ascent of the soul to heaven. Less common images of peacocks, flowering vines, and hearts also bespoke immortality, as did more elaborate allegorical designs: skeletons grasping scythes and seated on winged hourglasses, representing death's reign over time. Above them might stand a giant sun, signifying Christ's ultimate victory over the natural process of decay.

Such gravestones, carved by local stonecutters and often erected weeks and sometimes years after burial had taken place, served many purposes. Epitaphs recorded the age, date of death, and, occasionally, more detailed biographical information, philosophical reflection, or moral exhortation. Although most epitaphs expressed solemn sentiments ("READER/ REMEMBER DEATH"), a few adopted a lighter tone. Consider, for example, the punning inscription for one Captain Hezekiah Stone:

Beneath this Stone Death's Prisoner Lies
The Stone Shall move the Prisoner Rise.

Like the other rituals surrounding the Puritan way of death, both private and public, gravestones helped console friends and relatives to the loss of loved ones and remind the living of their own mortality. At the same time, these memorials served as reminders for future generations, inscribing on New England's landscape the lives and deaths of individuals and, indeed, whole families, who had sustained the Puritan mission in the New World.

of 70, and nearly one-fifth survived into their eighties. Rates of mortality among infants and children in New England were also significantly lower than those in the Chesapeake and England. Ninety percent of all children reached adulthood, and most young people grew up knowing both of their parents and even their grandparents. While the premature deaths of parents splintered Chesapeake families, two adult generations were often on hand to encourage order within New England households.

The probable cause of New Englanders' longer lives was their less temperate but more healthful northern climate. They also managed to escape infection from the epidemics that devastated both the Chesapeake and seventeenth-century Europe. Whatever the cause of longevity, the consequence for New England was a dynamic rate of population growth. While the populations of Europe and the Chesapeake barely reproduced themselves, the number of New Englanders doubled about every 27 years. Families were large, the typical household consisting of seven or eight children who survived to maturity. Along with low mortality rates, a more balanced sex ratio contributed to the brisk rate of reproduction. Because there were roughly equal numbers of men and women in the population, most New Englanders could and did marry. By 1700, New England and the Chesapeake each had populations of approximately 100,000. But whereas the southern population grew because of continuing immigration, New England's expanded through natural increase.

Local Life in Early New England

As immigrants arrived in the Bay Colony after 1630, they spread out rapidly from the first centers of settlement at Salem, Charlestown, and Boston, establishing an arc of small villages around the Massachusetts Bay. Within a decade settlers pressed into Connecticut, Rhode Island, and New Hampshire. Connecticut and Rhode Island received separate charters from Charles II in the 1660s, securing to their inhabitants title to land and power to govern. But as early as the 1640s, Massachusetts successfully staked its claim to New Hampshire, which did not become a separate colony until 1679; by 1658 the handful of families settled along the coast of present-day Maine had also accepted the Massachusetts Bay Colony's authority.

The families who spread throughout the New England landscape proceeded in an orderly way that laid the groundwork for a coherent organization of local life. Unlike the Virginians, who scattered across the Chesapeake to isolated plantations, most New Englanders distributed themselves into tightly knit communities that resembled the places that they had left behind in England. Often families who had left the same village or congregation back in England formed a community together in the New World. They petitioned the colony government for a tract of land in order to establish a town. All prospective adult townsmen initially owned in common this free grant of land, along with the right to set up a local government.

Townsmen gradually parceled out among themselves the land granted by the colony, with each family receiving a lot for a house, lying at the center of the village, along with farmland in adjacent fields. The distribution of land was remarkably even, the typical family holding about 150 acres. But farmers left much of their acreage uncultivated, a legacy for future generations, for most had only the labor of their own families to develop their farms. While the early Chesapeake abounded with discontented servants, tenant farmers, and landless men, almost every adult male in rural New England owned property.

The economy that supported most of New England's families and towns offered few chances for anyone to get rich. By diligent cultivation, farmers could coax enough yield from the land to feed their families, but the climate and soil would not support the production of a cash crop like tobacco, rice, or sugar. Lacking the resources to sustain a profitable commercial agriculture, New England farmers also lacked the Chesapeake planters' incentive to import shiploads of servants and slaves or to create large plantations.

The farmers who labored for subsistence in the New England countryside established strong institutions that contributed to the coherence of social life. First and foremost was the family, described by the Puritans as a "little commonwealth," a government in miniature that was the basis of social and civil order. The strong patriarchal fathers who governed the "little commonwealth" of the Puritan family exacted strict obedience from all of their children, even after they had reached maturity.

To foster local order New Englanders created, quite deliberately, another important institution—the village leadership. Few members of the English upper class migrated to New England, but the Puritan colonists, like most other seventeenth-century English, believed firmly in the importance of hierarchy. They thought that a measure of social inequality was natural, inevitable, and essential to a stable society. Because early New Englanders desired to be less equal than they were, each town favored certain families in its land distribution, awarding them a little more than the average allotment. The heads of these favored families were often ministers or other men who had received university degrees. Or they were millers or other artisans who possessed some skill of unusual service to the community. Or they were men who had enjoyed some wealth and standing back in England. They became the "town fathers" and took the lead in directing local affairs. The rest of the community generally accepted their authority, for all agreed that some men were more suited to rule than others. The trust that most New Englanders accorded their leaders had no counterpart in the Chesapeake experience, where the credibility of the early elite was constantly challenged.

Equally important in preserving local order was the church. Unlike Chesapeake immigrants, New Englanders arrived in the colonies with a full supply of ministers. Settlers formed churches as quickly as they founded towns. In the churches, the Puritans realized their ideal form of ecclesiastical organization—the independent, self-governing congregation. Each village church conducted its own affairs, hiring and dismissing ministers, admitting and disciplining members. The autonomy of each congregation guaranteed that local churches never clashed with higher religious authorities, for none existed. Bishops and synods had been left behind in the Old World. And membership in the churches was voluntary: men and women joined Congregational churches by consent, not compulsion.

But membership in New England churches was not available to anyone for the asking. Candidates for membership had to submit to a rigorous scrutiny to satisfy the church that they had experienced "conversion." The Puritans understood conversion to mean a turning of the heart and soul toward God, an inward transformation that was reflected by an outwardly godly and disciplined life. Believers who had some hope that they had experienced this inner spiritual rebirth and gained admission to church membership on that basis were called "visible saints."

Most early New Englanders sought and received church membership, a status that entitled them to receive communion and to have their children baptized. Widespread membership enabled the churches to oversee public morality and to discipline backsliders for a variety of offenses ranging from drunkenness to adultery. Although the churches of New England could not inflict corporal punishment on their members or fine them, as church courts did in England, Puritan churches could and did censure and excommunicate wayward members for misbehavior. And everywhere in New England except Rhode Island, civil laws obliged every settler to attend worship services on the Sabbath and every taxpayer to contribute to the support of the Puritan clergy.

Another feature of New England's religious life spared its clergy from becoming the targets of criticism and controversy. Although the Congregational churches exerted enormous informal influence over public and private life alike, they held no formal, legal power. Puritan ministers did not serve as officers in the civil government, and the Congregational churches owned no property. Even the meetinghouse was the property of the town, not the congregation. The separation between church and state in New England was not complete, but it had progressed further there than in most nations of the Old World. Catholic and Anglican church officials wielded real temporal power in European states, and the churches held extensive tracts of land.

Finally, there was the town meeting, the basis of local self-government. In every New England village, all white adult male inhabitants gathered regularly at the meetinghouse to decide matters of local importance, and virtually all of them could vote for town officials. The town fathers generally took the lead at these meetings, presenting an agenda of public business and making recommendations. But decisions were reached by the unanimous agreement of the entire body of townsmen. Consensus was a practical necessity, because the town fathers had no way to enforce unpopular decisions, no means to bring into line a reluctant majority or even a recalcitrant minority.

Colony governments in early New England also evolved into representative and responsive political institutions. Typically the central government of each colony, like the General Court of Massachusetts Bay, consisted of a governor and a bicameral legislature, including an upper house, or council, and a lower house, or assembly. These officials were elected annually by the freemen—white adult males entitled to vote in colony elections. Voting qualifications for colony elections varied in New England but the number of men entitled to vote comprised a much broader segment of society than in seventeenth-century England. Many qualified voters, however, did not bother to exercise their right to elect colony officials. For most ordinary farmers, town elections and local affairs loomed much larger than colony politics. And New England's small, inexpensive colony governments intruded little into the daily lives of most settlers. The Bay Colony's General Court, like its counterparts in other New England colonies, concerned itself mainly with parceling out land to new towns, making war and peace with native peoples, and mediating relations with England.

Deviance and Dissent

Although most aspects of life in early New England fostered order, its inhabitants had not fashioned wholly harmonious communities. The Puritans sometimes disagreed among themselves, and there were some people in New England who found the Puritans themselves most disagreeable.

Along the edges of New England settlement, several communities departed dramatically from typical patterns of Puritan life—and their inhabitants had no desire to conform. One such outpost was Marblehead, a fishing port north of Boston on the Massachusetts coast. Marbleheaders were a volatile mixture of immigrant fisherfolk from England's West Country, Wales, Ireland, and the French-speaking Isle of Jersey in the English Channel. Most eked out a spare subsistence as suppliers and employees of Boston merchants, who managed Marblehead's fishery and pocketed most of its profits. Fishermen and mariners competed fiercely for credit and customers in Boston—and for the company of the few women in Marblehead. They sought solace for the shortage of both at the town's many taverns, which inspired frequent street brawls and drunken cavorting. Since most Marbleheaders had come to New England mainly to catch fish, they had little commitment to creating a community life of any kind, let alone the Puritan variety. Local government remained weak for most of the seventeenth century, and inhabitants managed to avoid founding a local church for 50 years.

Similar problems blighted Springfield in western Massachusetts, a frontier settlement in the fertile Connecticut River valley. A single powerful family, the Pynchons, founded Springfield as a center of the fur trade and later developed a thriving commercial agriculture. The Pynchon family recruited most of Springfield's inhabitants—a motley assortment of Scottish convicts and English indentured servants—for their labor rather than their lives of piety and restraint.

Raucous, chaotic "company towns" like Marblehead and Springfield had more in common with the settlements of the early Chesapeake than with the rest of New England. Financed by profit-minded merchants, these places suffered from severe social disarray because of the great gulf between rich and poor and the exploitation of labor. Puritan Massachusetts tolerated these towns because their inhabitants produced what few commodities New England could trade to the rest of the world. Outside of the Connecticut River valley, New England's stony soil yielded just enough to feed farming families. But Marblehead's abundant supplies of fish found a ready market in Catholic Spain and Portugal and among the slaves of English sugar planters in the West Indies. Similarly, the surplus of Springfield's grain and livestock commanded a good price among Caribbean planters, and English consumers coveted furs. In exchange, New Englanders acquired wine, sugar, molasses, textiles, and iron goods—commodities that they needed but could not produce.

Still, less-than-Puritan places like Marblehead and Springfield were few and far between. A more common cause of conflict in early New England than ethnic diversity and economic inequality was the tension that resulted when immigrants of different English backgrounds tried to live together. Variations in English local customs produced disagreement among townsmen about the proper way of distributing land or farming it, regulating livestock, or allocating rights to marshes and woodlands.

As the first generation passed from the scene, disagreements of this sort died and other quarrels arose to take their place. The typical town conflict of the late seventeenth century was triggered by the movement of households. As local population expanded and the centers of towns became overcrowded, many young families relocated in outlying districts, village "suburbs." Since moving made churches and schools at the center of towns too distant, the "outlivers" petitioned the town meeting to create convenient institutions of their own or to split off as a separate town. Reluctant to lose taxpayers, the town meeting often resisted, and a running battle between the two factions resulted.

These conflicts within New England towns were little more than tempests in a teapot. Most discord amounted to little more than petty quarrels among members of a community who agreed on fundamentals. A far more serious source of conflict in early New England was religion.

Heresy

While most of the men and women who settled in New England called themselves Puritans, that name did not imply a single, uniform code of belief and practice. Instead, Puritanism encompassed a spectrum of religious persuasions, all aimed at carrying out the impulse of the Protestant Reformation and the ideas of John Calvin. The Puritan Separatists in Plymouth Colony, for example, believed that religious purity required renouncing the Church of England, while the Bay Colony's Puritans clung to the hope of reforming the Anglican Church from within. The Puritans of the Bay Colony even differed among themselves about how to organize church life. Because individual Congregational churches were free to go their own way, each had its own distinctive way of admitting members, conducting divine worship, or hiring a minister. Over time, the diversity among Congregational churches inevitably increased. Many adopted more liberal standards for determining who might be admitted, be baptized, or take communion.

During the earliest years of settlement, religious diversity led to the founding of new colonies in New England. In 1636 Thomas Hooker, the minister of Cambridge, Massachusetts, led part of his congregation to Connecticut, where they established the first English settlement. Somewhat more liberal than other Bay Puritans, Hooker favored less stringent standards for church membership. He also opposed the Bay's policy of restricting its civil franchise to church members. By contrast, New Haven, a separate colony until its incorporation by Connecticut in 1662, started in 1638 as the preserve of strict Puritans who found Massachusetts a little too liberal. Massachusetts recognized its southern neighbors, including Separatist Plymouth, as colonies within the Puritan fold, respectable suburbs of Winthrop's city on a hill.

The same could not be said about Rhode Island, for that little colony on Narragansett Bay began as a ghetto for heretics. While voluntary migration formed Connecticut and New Haven, enforced exile filled Rhode Island with Puritans whose radical ideas unsettled the rest of Massachusetts.

Roger Williams, Rhode Island's founder, had come to New England in 1631, serving as a popular and respected minister of Salem. But soon Williams announced that he was a Separatist, like the Pilgrims of Plymouth. He encouraged his congregation and the entire Bay Colony to break all connections to the corrupt Church of England. He also urged a more complete separation of church and state than most Puritans were prepared to accept, and later in his career he endorsed full religious toleration. Finally, Williams denounced the Bay's charter—the legal document that justified Massachusetts' existence—on the grounds that the king had no right to grant land that he had not purchased from the Indians. Even more provocatively, he urged Massachusetts to inform the king of his mistake immediately. With Charles so hostile to Puritans, Massachusetts leaders hardly wished to call attention to themselves and so ordered that Williams be deported to England. Instead he chose to flee the colony in the dead of winter to live with the Indians. In 1636, Williams became the founder and first citizen of Providence, later to be part of Rhode Island.

The artist who sketched this Quaker meeting called attention to one of that sect's most controversial practices by placing a woman at the center of his composition. Women were allowed to speak in Quaker worship services and to preach and proselytize at public gatherings of non-Quakers. The Puritans roundly condemned this liberty as contrary to the teachings of St. Paul.

Another brilliant and charismatic heretic from Massachusetts arrived soon after. Anne Hutchinson, a skilled midwife and the spouse of a wealthy merchant, emigrated to Boston in 1634 for the pleasure of hearing John Cotton, formerly her minister in England. Enthusiasm for Cotton's eloquence started her on a course of explaining his sermons to gatherings of her neighbors—and then to elaborating ideas of her own in which many of the Bay's leaders detected the dangerous heresy of "Antinomianism," meaning "against the law."

The Bay Puritans, like all Calvinists, denied that men and women could "earn" salvation by conforming their lives to God's laws. That stark denial of human ability—the insistence that divine grace alone could save fallen mankind—offered individuals little incentive for good behavior. But most Puritans tempered that conviction with another belief that did more to encourage orderly and disciplined conduct: they held that individuals might be able to discern in their capacity to lead a godly life the *sign* that they had been saved by divine grace. A minority in the Puritan movement, including Anne Hutchinson, rejected the notion that upright living could constitute evidence of salvation; she contended that outward obedience to God's commandments indicated nothing whatsoever about the inward state of the soul. She was certain that those predestined for salvation knew it intuitively and could recognize the same grace in others.

When most of the Bay Colony's ministers denounced her, Anne Hutchinson denounced them. Her attack on the clergy, along with the popularity of her preaching among many important merchant families, prompted the Bay Colony government to expel Hutchinson and her followers for sedition in 1638. Despite a spirited and intelligent defense of her position during her trial, she made a fatal slip by claiming that she had received divine revelation directly from the Holy Spirit. That assertion sealed her fate, for the Puritans held that revelation had ended in biblical times and that those who believed otherwise belonged in Rhode Island. Anne Hutchinson stopped there briefly before moving on to Long Island, where she died in an Indian attack—to the satisfaction of many in Massachusetts Bay.

The devil of religious controversy assumed the shape of a woman in later cases of dissent as well. The Quakers, one of the most radical religious groups spawned by the Protestant Reformation in England, sent Ann Austin and Mary Fisher as their first missionaries to the Bay, and women were among the most active and determined early converts. Mary Dyer was hanged for her persistence along with three Quaker men in 1656. Like the Antinomians, the Quakers attached great significance to an inward state of grace, called the "Light Within." Through that inner light, the Quakers claimed, God revealed his will directly to believers, enabling men and women to attain spiritual perfection. Because they held that everyone had immediate access to God, the Quakers also dispensed with a clergy and the sacraments.

Goodwives

If Anne Hutchinson and Mary Dyer had been men, their ideas would still have been deemed heretical. On the other hand, if these women had been men, they might not have become heretics. As men, they might have found other ways to assert their extraordinary intelligence and magnetism, other avenues to power and approval. But life in colonial New England offered women, especially married women, little scope to exercise their ability and authority.

Most adult women were hardworking farm wives who cared for large households of children, to which a new baby was added every two years. Between marriage and middle age, most New England wives were pregnant except when breast-feeding. When they were not nursing or minding children, mothers were producing and preparing much of what was consumed and worn by their families. They planted vegetable gardens and pruned fruit trees, salted beef and pork and pressed cider, milked cows and churned butter, kept bees and tended poultry, cooked and baked, washed and ironed, spun, wove, and sewed. Most women had only their daughters to assist in this exhausting round of chores. Their contributions to feeding, clothing, and raising their families left farm wives little time for tidy housekeeping—as more leisured and affluent female visitors from larger towns like Boston churlishly observed.

What farm women themselves minded more than the drudgery and dirt—conditions that they shared with men—was the tedium of their repetitive household duties. While husbands and sons engaged in jobs on the farm that changed with the seasons, conducted business in town, took trips to the village mills, and went off to hunt or fish, housebound wives and daughters were locked into a humdrum daily routine with little time for themselves. "A continual sameness reigns throughout the year," complained one New England matron.

Most women suffered legal disadvantages as well, because English common law and colonial legal codes accorded married women no control over property.

Wives could not sue or be sued; they could not make contracts; and they surrendered to their husbands any property that they possessed before marriage. Divorce was almost impossible to obtain until the late eighteenth century. Only widows and a few single women had the same legal rights as men, and even these women could not vote in colony elections.

The one arena in which women could attain something approaching equal standing with men was the churches. Although Puritan women could not become ministers, after the 1660s they comprised the majority of church members. In some congregations, membership enabled them to vote for ministerial candidates and to voice opinions in cases of admission and discipline. For many New England women, religion was a source of social identity.

Whites and Indians in Early New England

New England Puritans were far more concerned to define and perfect the principles of the Protestant Reformation among themselves than to impart their faith to other peoples. While French missionaries carried Catholicism to tribes in every place reached by traders, the Puritans made only a few halfhearted efforts to bring Protestantism to the natives of New England.

Although most white settlers in New England, like those in the Chesapeake, insisted on the "savagery" of the Indians, the Puritans had much in common with native peoples. Both groups relied on the same resources and the same combination of seasonal activities—fishing in spring and summer, hunting in winter, cultivating and harvesting food crops in spring and fall. And, to an even greater degree than among the Puritans, Indian political authority was local. No central government like Powhatan's confederacy or the English colonial governments consolidated New England's tribes. Within each village, a single leader known as the "sachem" or "sagamore" directed economic life, administered justice, and negotiated with other tribes and English settlers. And like the officials of New England towns, a sachem's power depended on keeping the trust and consent of his people. Like the town fathers, the sachems cultivated reputations for spirituality to enhance their claims to leadership.

The Indians of New England shared one other characteristic with the English: no love was lost among neighboring nations. The antagonism among the English, Spanish, Dutch, and French was equaled in intensity by the animosities among the Abenaki, Pawtucket, Massachusett, Narragansett, and Wampanoag tribes of the north Atlantic coast. The rivalries kept different tribes from forging an effective defense against white colonials. New England settlers, like those in the Chesapeake, exploited Indian disunity, playing one tribe off against another. What made the white strategy of "divide and conquer" easier still was that the competition for trade magnified rivalries among the tribes, just as it heightened conflict among European nations.

If the New England tribes had been able to unify, they might have resisted the English longer. Still, they would have confronted a deadly enemy against which they had no defense—disease. Even before the Pilgrims landed, an epidemic introduced in 1618 by visiting fishermen ravaged the Massachusett and Pawtucket tribes, leaving the coast of New England "a widowed land." As contact with Europeans increased, epidemics recurred with deadly frequency, drastically reducing tribal populations.

With only the shattered remnants of the coastal tribes inhabiting the areas where New England colonials first settled, conflicts between the two groups occurred infrequently at first. But when white settlers began to push into Connecticut, they encountered the Pequots, a tribe still numerous and strong enough to marshal a staunch resistance. Had the Pequots allied with their neighbors, the Narragansetts, they could have retarded English expansion southward. But the Narragansetts, bitter enemies of the Pequots, cast their lot with the English instead. Together they prosecuted a brutal campaign that virtually destroyed the Pequots in 1637. A few years later, in 1643, the English, eyeing Narragansett lands, turned against their former allies, joined forces with the Narragansetts' rivals, the Mohegans, and mobilized for an assault. To avoid following the Pequots into oblivion, the Narragansetts ceded a large tract of their territory to white settlers. As the Puritans established themselves as "the dread and sovereign lords" of the Connecticut River valley, only a few objected to their aims and methods, among them Roger Williams. "God Land," he warned one of Connecticut's leaders, "will be (as it now is) as great a God with us English as God Gold was with the Spanish."

The destruction of the Pequots and the submission of the Narragansetts left the Wampanoags of Plymouth as the only coastal tribe capable of resisting Puritan encroachment. For nearly 50 years they had been allied with Plymouth settlers, but in the 1660s their sachem Metacomet, whom the English called King Philip, decided that Indian clients of the English inevitably lost their lands, their lives, and their dignity. In 1675 he organized a pan-Indian uprising: the Narragansetts, Mohegans, and Nipmucs joined the Wampanoags in an offensive that devastated white settlements throughout the New England frontier. By the spring of 1676, Metacomet's forces were pressing toward the coast, raiding towns that lay within 20 miles of Boston.

What finally halted the Indian advance was not a successful colonial counterattack, but shortages of food and ammunition and the outbreak of disease. Metacomet called for assistance from the Abenaki, a powerful Maine tribe, and from the Iroquois of New York. His efforts were in vain; these tribes withheld their support, not wishing to jeopardize their trade with the English. By the summer of 1676 the Indian offensive had collapsed. Some of the tribes surrendered, while others fled for refuge farther west. Metacomet met his death in battle, and his wife and son along with many other Indians were sold as slaves to Caribbean planters. The remnants of the surviving tribes submitted to resettlement in villages supervised by the white victors.

In seventeenth-century New England, as in the Chesapeake, the clash between the tribes and white settlers culminated in violence that threatened the very survival of both groups. Ultimately, the Puritans broke the back of Indian resistance, but at a fearful cost to both sides. Perhaps 20,000 English and Indians lost their lives in Metacomet's War; scores of colonial towns and tribal villages lay in ruins.

THE MIDDLE COLONIES

The settlements planted between Connecticut and Maryland are aptly called the Middle Colonies, for while the inhabitants of New York and New Jersey, Pennsylvania and Delaware enjoyed more secure lives than most southerners, they lacked the basis for consensus that lent New England its remarkable stability. Instead, in each of the Middle Colonies an assortment of ethnic and religious groups vied for wealth from farming and the fur trade and chafed under the rule of political institutions less responsive and representative than those to the north and south.

The Founding of New Netherlands

By the beginning of the seventeenth century the Calvinist Dutch had finally freed their homeland from Spanish domination. Having won independence, they were equally determined to compete with Spanish merchants and to contain the spread of Spanish Catholicism. Along the Amazon River and the African coast, forts and trading posts of the Dutch West India Company protected and promoted Dutch commerce while harrying Spanish competitors. Least important to the company was its sole outpost in North America, New Netherlands, founded in 1624. The company had some interest in tapping the furs of the interior, scattering a few trading posts along the Hudson, Connecticut, and Delaware rivers. But the Dutch did not intend to plant permanent communities in America; enjoying both prosperity and religious freedom at home, they were far less inclined than the English to emigrate.

Thus New Netherlands' population was as small and scattered as New England's was large and concentrated. Most of the few settlers were clustered in the village of New Amsterdam on the tip of Manhattan Island at the mouth of the Hudson. One-hundred and fifty miles upriver lay Fort Orange (Albany). By the

New Amsterdam (later New York City) in about 1626. Despite having this outpost in New Netherlands, the Dutch had far more interest in vying with the Portuguese for control of commerce with the Far East than in competing with the English for the fur trade in North America.

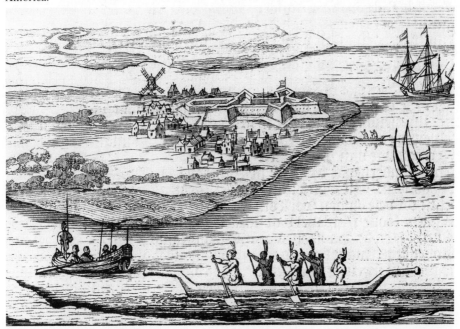

1660s a few other farming villages dotted the west end of Long Island, upper Manhattan Island, Staten Island, and the lower Hudson valley. In all, there were fewer than 9000 New Netherlanders—a diverse array of Dutch, Belgians, French, English, Portuguese, Swedes, Finns, and Africans. The first blacks had arrived in 1626, imported as slaves; some later became free, intermarried with whites, and even owned white indentured servants.

This ethnic diversity ensured a variety of religions. Although the Dutch Reformed Church predominated, other early New Netherlanders professed Lutheranism, Congregationalism, Quakerism, and Catholicism. There were Jews as well, refugees from Portuguese Brazil, who were required by law to live in a ghetto in New Amsterdam. To New Englanders, accustomed as they were to more homogeneous communities, New Netherlands must have seemed a veritable Babel, a bustling confusion of languages, customs, and beliefs. Nevertheless, as early as the 1640s, a substantial number of New Englanders, drawn by promises of cheap land and local self-government, planted farming communities on eastern Long Island.

New Netherlanders recognized that their differences complicated the creation of a stable civic order, and the Dutch West India Company did little to ease the strain. Most of the colony's governors were inefficient, corrupt, and dictatorial, and no elective assembly was established. New Netherlanders felt little loyalty to either the company or its representatives. To make matters worse, the company provided scant protection for its outlying settlers; when it did attack neighboring Indian nations it did so savagely, leading to an increased level of violence. By the time the company went bankrupt, in 1654, it had virtually abandoned its American colony.

New Englanders on Long Island, who had insisted on a free hand in regulating their own villages, began to demand a voice in running the colony as well. Their example prompted Dutch towns to advance claims to self-government. By the 1660s, the New Englanders had gone further still, openly challenging Dutch rule and calling for English conquest of the colony.

English Rule in New York

The English were, of course, already in the midst of an ongoing rivalry with Holland for maritime and commercial supremacy. In 1652 antagonism flared into a conflict that lasted for two years, the first Anglo-Dutch War. Four years later the English were spoiling for a renewal of hostilities. More than 100 English ship captains complained to Oliver Cromwell in 1658 that "the Dutch eat us out of our trade at home and abroad . . . and call us 'English Dogs,' which doth much grieve our English spirits. They will not sail with us, but shoot at us and by indirect courses bring their goods into our ports, which wrongs not only us but you in your customs."

Charles II took up the challenge, tempted by the disarray of New Netherlands. Brushing aside Dutch claims, he granted his brother James, the duke of York, a proprietary charter that included all of New Netherlands to Delaware Bay, as well as Maine, Martha's Vineyard, and Nantucket Island. In 1664 James sent an invading fleet, whose mere presence caused the Dutch to surrender without even a show of resistance. Governing the new colony, however, proved more of a problem.

The establishment of English rule in New York, as it was renamed, improved the efficiency of colonial administration but did little to ease ethnic tensions, encourage settlement, or promote political stability. James made a determined effort to appease the Dutch. He allowed them to remain in the colony, confirmed their land titles, permitted their merchants direct trade to Holland, and tolerated the Dutch Reformed Church. But the Dutch remained restive under English rule. When Holland briefly reconquered the colony during the third Anglo-Dutch War in 1673, they rejoiced. When New York was returned to England by treaty a year later, they reluctantly submitted again to foreign rule. Only a generation of intermarriage and acculturation would finally ease these frictions.

James also failed to win the goodwill of Long Island's Puritans. He instituted a legal code based on English practice, the Duke's Laws; but he refused to establish an elective assembly. The settlers, in turn, refused to pay taxes to what they termed his "arbitrary" government. James, whose aversion to assemblies dated from the beheading of his royal father at the direction of Parliament, grudgingly gave in to the demand for such a body in 1683. But he repudiated the first act of the new assembly, the Charter of Liberties, which would have guaranteed New Yorkers basic civil and political rights. On top of everything else, James' Catholicism aroused suspicion and antagonism among both Long Island Puritans and Dutch Calvinists.

Political upheaval and discontent discouraged settlers from coming to New York. By 1698 the whole colony numbered only 18,000 inhabitants. New York City, the former New Amsterdam, was an overgrown village of a few thousand, still dependent on Boston for shipping and trade. James enjoyed little in the way of revenues from his proprietary colony.

The League of the Iroquois

The Indian tribes around New York City and the lower Hudson valley fell prey to the same forces that shattered the natives of New England and the Chesapeake. They resisted English land hunger for decades, but recognized too late the importance of united action. Farther into the interior, however, contact with European fur traders strengthened the Iroquois nation, which had already united in a remarkable league.

The dynamics of the situation resembled those at work in early South Carolina. Like the tribes of South Carolina, the Indians of northern New York became important suppliers of fur pelts to white traders. As in the Carolinas, powerful tribes dominated the upper Hudson, far outnumbering whites. The handful of Dutch and, later, English traders had every reason to cultivate goodwill among the Indians. But while mutual economic interests promoted peace between white New Yorkers and Indians, the fur trade heightened tensions among the northern interior tribes. At first the Mahicans had supplied furs to the Dutch, but by 1625 the game in their territory had been exhausted and the Dutch had taken their business to the Iroquois. When the Iroquois faced the same depletion of fur-bearing animals in the 1640s, they found a solution. With Dutch encouragement and Dutch guns, the Iroquois hunted the neighboring Huron nation virtually to extinction and seized the rich Canadian forests where the Huron had trapped for the French. In every respect except the conduct of a slave trade in Indian captives, the brutal warfare in the north resembled the conflicts that competition for English trade had also brought upon Carolina's tribes.

The extermination of the Huron left the Iroquois undisputed Indian lords of the northern frontier. More successfully than Powhatan's confederacy in the Ches-

Converts of the French Jesuits, these women of the Caughnawaga tribe are kneeling before a statue of the Virgin Mary taking vows of celibacy. One cuts her hair, in imitation of the practice of Catholic nuns. Both French Catholic and English Protestant missionaries condemned the long hair favored by Indian women and men alike as a symbol of native pride.

apeake or Canada's Huronia, the Iroquois managed to consolidate disparate tribes into a coherent political unit, 12,000 strong. This union of the Five Nations (to become six after the Tuscaroras joined them in 1712) included the Mohawk, Oneida, Cayuga, and Seneca tribes, stretching from the lands around the upper Hudson in the east to the Genesee River in the west.

Iroquois legend attributes the consolidation to the work of Hiawatha, a Mohawk sachem, who was inspired by a vision to unify the northern tribes. By the late sixteenth century a council of 49 chiefs presided over the League of the Iroquois, making decisions for all villages and prohibiting feuding and blood revenge among them. Political strength enabled the Iroquois to deal effectively with their Algonkian rivals in New England as well as European newcomers. As the favored clients of the Dutch and, later, the English, they became opponents of the French, who had allied with the Hurons.

The League's remarkable achievement rested on an even more remarkable form of political and social organization, one in which both sexes shared authority. The most powerful women anywhere in colonial North America were the matriarchs of the Iroquois. Matrilineal kinship formed the basis of Iroquois society, as it did among the Pueblos of the Southwest: when men married, they joined their wives' families, households over which the eldest female member presided. But unlike Pueblo women, Iroquois matriarchs wielded political influence as well. The most senior Iroquois women selected the confederation's council of chiefs, advised them, and "dehorned"—removed from office—those deemed unfit. Throughout the eighteenth century, the League of the Iroquois would continue to figure as a major force in North America.

The Founding of New Jersey

The colony of New Jersey took shape in the shadow of its more notable neighbors to the north. Its inhabitants were less united and powerful than the Iroquois, less wealthy and influential than New Yorkers, and less like-minded and self-governing than New Englanders.

New Jersey's beginnings had promised greater distinction. In 1664 James, duke of York, bestowed on two of his favorites, Lord Berkeley and Sir George Carteret, 5 million fertile acres lying west of the Hudson and east of the Delaware River. To attract settlers, New Jersey's new proprietors adopted the same strategy that they were using in their other colonies, the Carolinas. They guaranteed religious freedom, generous land grants, and self-government in a representative assembly to all inhabitants in exchange for a small quitrent, an annual fee for the use of the land. The proprietors' terms and the lure of rich land appealed to a group of Puritans, who moved there from New Haven. There they encountered another group of Puritans from eastern Long Island.

The Long Islanders, however, had settled in New Jersey not at the invitation of Berkeley and Carteret, but under a conflicting grant from Governor Richard Nicolls of New York, whose colony claimed title to New Jersey. Unaware that James had already given New Jersey to his friends, Nicolls granted the Long Islanders land there, as well as the right to government by their own assembly. The Long Islanders announced that they had not come to New Jersey to pay quitrents or to submit to autocratic rule.

To complicate matters even more, Berkeley and Carteret decided to divide New Jersey into east and west and sell both halves to Quaker investors. New Jersey's Puritan inhabitants, unhappy with any proprietorship, became apoplectic at the prospect of heretical Quakers running their colony. But New Jersey was not destined to develop as the center of Quaker settlement in the New World. Although some English Friends migrated to West Jersey, the Quakers quickly decided that neither of the Jerseys compared favorably with Pennsylvania and sold both to speculators. In the end, the Jerseys were dominated neither by Puritans nor by Quakers, but became patchwork colonies of English, Scots, Irish, Dutch, French Huguenots, Germans, and West Indians. These settlers established small family farms and clustered in neighborhoods where inhabitants shared a common religion or national origin. When the Crown reunited east and west and converted New Jersey into a royal colony in 1702, it was still overshadowed by more notable settlements to the north and, now, to the south.

Quaker Odysseys

A spirit of religious and political idealism similar to that of New England infused the settlement of Pennsylvania, making it an oddity among northern proprietary colonies. The oddity began with an improbable founder, William Penn. Young Penn devoted his early years to disappointing his distinguished father, Sir William Penn, an admiral in the royal navy. After being expelled from college, he traveled in Europe, dabbled in law, and seemed generally at loose ends, until at last he settled upon a career that may have made his eminent father yearn for mere disappointment. For the son had been captivated by the doctrines of the Quakers; this youthful interest in the Society of Friends quickly deepened into a lifelong commitment to put into practice its teachings. By the 1670s William Penn had emerged as one of the movement's acknowledged leaders.

English Quakerism had by the 1660s shed some of its more extreme practices, taken up during the previous heady decade of revolt and religious enthusiasm. But the Friends still adhered to ideas that most people regarded as odd. They affected a deliberately plain and severe manner of dress. They withheld from their social superiors the customary marks of respect, such as bowing, kneeling, and removing their hats. They refused to swear oaths or to make war. They allowed women to speak in their meetings and to travel about preaching as "Public Friends." That pattern of behavior bespoke their disdain of pride and worldliness and their embrace of egalitarian ideals. It was the logical conclusion of the Quaker belief that all men and women shared equally in the "Light Within." Some 40,000 English merchants, artisans, and farmers embraced Quakerism by 1660, and many suffered for their convictions, paying fines and enduring imprisonment and corporal punishment.

Since the English upper class has always welcomed eccentricity among its members, it is perhaps less surprising that young William Penn's Quakerism did nothing to diminish his standing at the Stuart court or his friendship with Charles II. More surprising is that royal favor took the extravagant form of presenting Penn with all the land between New Jersey and Maryland. A royal charter of 1681 made the 37-year-old Penn the absolute proprietor of the only ungranted land left along the North American coast, a territory nearly as large as England. Perhaps the king was repaying Penn for the large sum that his father had lent the Stuarts. Or perhaps the king was hoping to export England's troublesome Quakers to a preserve presided over by his trusted personal friend.

Whatever the reason for Charles' generosity, the energetic Penn lost no time in making the most of his New World windfall. He envisioned planting a prosperous settlement that would provide a refuge for persecuted Quakers and produce revenue for its proprietor in the form of quitrents. Recruiting settlers required planning, because the pace of English migration to America had slowed by the 1680s, and Quaker meetings, the most likely source of colonists, were scattered throughout the British Isles and the continent of Europe. To publicize his colony, Penn printed pamphlets in several languages extolling its attractions.

The response was overwhelming. In 1682, just a year after being chartered, Pennsylvania received 4000 settlers. Within five years its population had tripled, and by 1700 it stood at 21,000. The only early migration of equal magnitude was the Puritan colonization of New England.

Perhaps half of Pennsylvania's settlers arrived as indentured servants: the families of free farmers and artisans made up the rest of the immigrants. The majority were English, Irish, and Welsh Quakers, but newcomers also included

William Penn, the founder of Pennsylvania.

Catholics, Lutherans, Baptists, Anglicans, and Calvinists. Not all new Pennsylvanians came from the British Isles; Quakers from Germany and Holland joined the exodus. And in 1682 when Penn purchased and annexed the Three Lower Counties (later the colony of Delaware), his settlement included the Dutch, Swedes, and Finns living there, about 1000 people. Finally, Quakers from other American colonies—West Jersey, Maryland, and New England—flocked to the new homeland.

These experienced American farmers and established merchants brought with them agricultural skills and trading connections that contributed to Pennsylvania's spectacular economic growth. Industrious Quaker landowners speedily sowed their rich lands into a sea of wheat, which was exported along with pork, beef, and lumber to the Caribbean by enterprising Quaker merchants. The center of the colony's trade was the seaport of Philadelphia, a superb natural harbor situated at the confluence of the Delaware and Schuylkill rivers. Boasting a population of 5000 by 1700, Philadelphia equaled New York City in size and soon outstripped its northern competitor.

Rural settlement radiated rapidly from Philadelphia, first stretching along the Delaware River. After 1700 settlers moved west along the Schuylkill and later across the Susquehanna River. In contrast to New England's landscape of villages, the Pennsylvania countryside was dotted with dispersed farmsteads. Commercial agriculture required larger farms, which kept settlers at some distance from one another. As a result, the county rather than the town became the basic unit of local government in Pennsylvania.

Another reason that farmers did not need to cluster their homes within a central village was that the local Indian tribe, the Lenni Lenapes (also called Delawares by the English), posed no threat. Thanks to two of the odder Quaker beliefs—their commitment to pacifism and their conviction that the Indians rightfully owned their land—peace prevailed between native Pennsylvanians and newcomers. Before he sold any land to white settlers, Penn purchased it from the Indians. He also prohibited the sale of alcohol to the tribe, strictly regulated the fur trade, and learned the language of the Lenni Lenapes. "Not a language spoken in Europe," he remarked, "hath words of more sweetness in Accent and Emphasis than theirs."

"Our Wildernesse flourishes as a Garden," Penn declared late in 1683, and in fact, his colony lived up to all of its advance promises. New arrivals readily acquired good land on liberal terms; Penn's Frame of Government instituted a representative assembly and guaranteed all inhabitants the basic English liberties of habeas corpus (the right to bail) and trial by jury. In addition, all faiths enjoyed complete freedom of worship.

Like the Puritans, Penn yearned to reform the political and religious errors of Europe by creating a model society across the seas. And like the Puritans, he believed that government should be based on contract and consent. Penn even shared with the Puritans the view that the state should by law promote morality, virtue, and Christian values. But he parted company with most New England Puritans on the point of religious toleration. While the Puritans believed that the government should support "true religion" and persecute dissenters, Penn vehemently opposed religious establishments. Undeviating in his devotion to liberty of conscience, he endorsed a nearly complete separation of church and state.

Despite Pennsylvania's prosperity and religious peace, political harmony did not follow. Because Penn believed that the colony would survive and prosper only with the backing of the wealthy, he sold rich investors large tracts of land to persuade them to settle. As an added inducement, he conferred on them trade monopolies and political power. Penn's Frame of Government gave the sole right to initiate legislation to the council, a body comprised of those large landowners. The colony's representative assembly could only accept or reject bills sent down by the council. The citizens of Pennsylvania, having been given much, wanted more. Members of the assembly battled relentlessly for the right to initiate legislation. Farmers opposed Penn's efforts to make orderly allotments of land and to collect quitrents. The Dutch, Swedish, and Finnish inhabitants of the Three Lower Counties, non-Quakers who felt no loyalty to Penn, chafed at being annexed to the colony and agitated for separation.

Adding insult to injury, even the Quaker merchants and landowners who owed their privileges to Penn tried to increase their influence by challenging proprietary rule. Their attacks found a receptive audience among settlers, fully half of whom could vote. Penn's carefully laid plans ran afoul of his prickly fellow Quakers who, accustomed to defying civil and religious authority in the Old World, bristled against proprietors in America.

Penn finally bought peace in the place that he now called "this licentious wilderness"—but at the price of approving a complete revision of his original Frame of Government. In 1701 the Charter of Privileges, Pennsylvania's new constitution, stripped the council of its legislative power, leaving it only the role of advising the governor. The charter also limited Penn's privileges to the ownership of ungranted land and the power to veto legislation. A unicameral assembly, the only single-house legislature in the colonies, dominated Pennsylvania's government.

Pennsylvania continued to prosper, and Philadelphia became the commercial and cultural center of England's North American empire. The colony's Quaker inhabitants continued to squabble over politics, both among themselves and with their Anglican and Presbyterian neighbors. And as the interior of the colony became peopled with groups with no "odd" ideas about Indian rights—mainly Germans and Scots-Irish—the Lenni Lenapes and other tribes were intimidated into moving farther west. As for William Penn, he returned to England and spent some time in a debtors' prison after being defrauded by his unscrupulous colonial agents. He died in 1718, an ocean away from his American utopia.

ADJUSTMENT TO EMPIRE

In the year 1685, from the city of London, a new English king surveyed his American domains. The former duke of York, now James II, had hoped that America might contribute to the making of England and, incidentally, to the making of kings and queens. Like earlier Stuart monarchs, James hoped to ride to power on a wave of imperial wealth, just as Spain's monarchs had during the sixteenth century. The Stuarts had chartered the private trading companies of Virginia, Plymouth, and Massachusetts Bay, and they had handed out to their aristocratic favorites huge tracts of land—Maryland, the Carolinas, New York, New Jersey, and Pennsylvania—all in the name of encouraging colonial settlement. But Stuart expectations had exceeded Stuart commitments. Their governments had resisted supplying military or financial assistance to the new outposts, leaving those details to private investors. Until Parliament passed the first Navigation Acts in 1660, England had lacked even a coherent policy for regulating colonial trade.

As a result, when James II came to the throne in 1685, there were a great many places in North America named for English monarchs, but only three colonies, New Hampshire, New York, and Virginia, over which England exercised direct rule through royally appointed governors and councils. What was worse, ungrateful colonists were resisting their obligations to enrich the English state and its rulers. While Chesapeake planters grumbled over the customs duties levied on tobacco, New Englanders flouted the Navigation Acts altogether and traded openly with the Dutch. The Puritans could have paid the tariffs and prospered still, but they delighted in defying the dictates of Stuart monarchs and Restoration Parliaments. The New Yorkers were shaping up as an equally intractable lot, as James, the former duke of York, remembered all too well. Elsewhere—in New Jersey, the Carolinas, and Pennsylvania—settlement was still too raw and recent to seem anything but anarchic. Yet even in the new colonies, the stirrings of resistance to proprietary authority did not bode well.

What was needed, in James' view, was first to bring Massachusetts to heel. Because of their charter, the inhabitants of the Bay Colony were, as one English statesman observed, "a people almost upon the brink of renouncing any dependance of the Crowne." James' brother, Charles II, had laid the groundwork for dealing with truculent Massachusetts. In 1664 he had authorized the same commission charged with seizing New Netherlands to look in on Massachusetts Bay. Their reports of flagrant violations of the Navigation Acts prompted Parliament in 1673 to authorize the placement of customs agents in colonial ports to suppress illicit trade.

The commission also inspired Charles II to form the Lords of Trade and Plantations, a committee charged with overseeing colonial affairs. In 1679 the Lords of Trade further tightened the reins of command by rejecting the Bay's longstanding claim to New Hampshire, making it a separate royal colony instead. When reports of Puritan defiance continued to surface, Charles II delivered the decisive blow: an English court annulled the charter of Massachusetts in 1684, leaving the Bay Colony without a legal basis for its claim to the privilege of self-government. The presiding judge declared that Massachusetts was "a Company of Rebells the King should send a fleet to subdue."

The Dominion of New England

Charles died the following year, leaving James II to complete the reorganization of Massachusetts' affairs. In 1686, at the king's urging, the Lords of Trade consolidated the colonies of Connecticut, Plymouth, Massachusetts Bay, Rhode Island, and New Hampshire into a single entity to be ruled by a royal governor and a royally appointed council. By 1688 he had added New York and New Jersey to his royal domain, now called the Dominion of New England. Indulging the Stuart distaste for representative government, James also abolished all northern colonial assemblies. The king's aim to centralize authority over such a large territory made the Dominion not only a royal dream but a radical experiment in English colonial administration.

The transition to royal rule proceeded without opposition; even Massachusetts submitted without armed intervention from England. Yet the Dominion government assumed from the outset a military cast. Sir Edmund Andros, a tough professional soldier sent to Boston as the Dominion's royal governor, quickly came to vie with his king for the title of most unpopular man north of Pennsylvania. Andros imposed autocratic rule and implemented policies guaranteed to alienate every segment of New England society, even those few colonial leaders who had at first urged accommodation to royal government. He strictly enforced the Navigation Acts, thus stagnating trade and infuriating not only merchants, but sailors, fishermen, dockworkers, and artisans in the maritime trades. He appropriated a Congregationalist meetinghouse for Anglican worship and immediately angered devout Puritans. He invalidated all title to land granted under the old charter, incensing farmers and speculators. He imposed arbitrary taxes, censored the press, and prohibited town meetings, thereby outraging virtually everyone.

The Aftershocks of a Glorious Revolution

While northern colonials endured Andros with a great deal of ill humor, the English were deciding that they had taken enough from his royal master. James II had revealed himself as the wrong sort of Stuart—one who tried to dispense with Parliament and who embraced Catholicism. As they had before with Charles I, Parliament dispensed with the king. In a quick, bloodless coup d'état known as the Glorious Revolution, Parliament forced James into exile in 1688 and placed on the throne of England his daughter, Mary, and her Dutch husband, William of Orange. Mary was the right sort of Stuart, a staunch Protestant who would abide by her agreement to rule with Parliament as a monarch limited by the unwritten English constitution of customs and law. The accession of William and Mary halted the drift toward royal power in England and America and established the supremacy of Parliament.

The deposing of James II was so popular among New Englanders that they rose in revolt against his Dominion governor even before Parliament officially proclaimed the succession of William and Mary. On April 18, 1689, as soon as news reached Boston that William had landed in England, the town's militia seized Andros and sent him home to England. Bay leaders restored the old charter government, while Increase Mather, an eminent minister from Boston, negotiated in London with the new monarchs.

William and Mary officially dismembered the Dominion and reinstated representative assemblies everywhere in the northern colonies. Connecticut and Rhode Island retained their old corporate charters, but Massachusetts received a new charter in 1691. The terms of that charter incorporated Massachusetts, Plymouth, and present-day Maine into a single royal colony headed by a governor appointed by the Crown rather than elected by the people. It also made property ownership rather than church membership the basis of the franchise and imposed religious toleration. Henceforth the Bay Colony's civil goverment had no power to persecute religious dissidents like Anglicans and Quakers, and these groups were also exempted from paying taxes to support the Congregationalist clergy.

The new charter did not satisfy all New Englanders, accustomed as they were to virtual independence from the Crown and from official suppression of religious dissent. And many were badly shaken by the years of uncertainty and upheaval after the old charter had been revoked in 1684. Those anxieties and the search for scapegoats may have found an outlet in the mass accusations of witchcraft that began at Salem Village, Massachusetts (now Danvers), in 1692. Like most early modern Europeans, New Englanders believed in wizards and witches, men and women who acquired supernatural powers by signing a compact with Satan. Before 1692 courts in both Massachusetts and Connecticut had tried scores of people accused of practicing witchcraft, usually women of middle age or older, and some of those convicted had been executed. What was unique about the Salem Village outbreak was its scale and intensity: hundreds of people were accused of witchcraft, more than 100 were imprisoned, and 20 were executed.

No single cause seems to have triggered the Salem episode. Bitter rivalries among families lay behind some of the accusations; others grew out of disputes between near neighbors over boundaries and livestock. These antagonisms may have festered into charges of witchcraft because the revocation of the old charter in 1684 dismantled the judicial system, which usually had settled such petty grievances, and new courts were not established until 1692. The first court created under the new charter was empowered to investigate only the witchcraft charges that had started to crop up in Salem Village, a restriction that probably encouraged many people with old grudges to accuse their adversaries of witchcraft. Religious hatreds could have fueled the hysteria, too, for many of the accused witches were kin, spouses, or close friends of Baptists, Quakers, or Anglicans—heretical groups feared and despised by a Puritan majority now bound by law to tolerate dissent.

If the tragedy at Salem Village vented tensions that had built up over a period of drastic change, it was the last aftershock of the political earthquake that had shaken New England. Its inhabitants adjusted to the political realities of royal rule and quickly came to regard their new charter as a decided improvement on the Dominion. That rapid adaptation both reflected and reinforced the basic stability of New England society. By contrast, the violence and vicious political infighting that plagued New York after 1691 at once reflected and reinforced that colony's essential instability.

Leisler's Rebellion

Word of revolution in England and rebellion in Massachusetts galvanized New Yorkers into armed opposition in May 1689. Declaring their loyalty to William and Mary, the New York City militia forced from office Francis Nicholson, the young, arrogant military officer who served as the Dominion's lieutenant governor. In his place they appointed one of their own leaders, Jacob Leisler, a German immigrant who had attained modest prosperity as a merchant.

Since James II had won few friends in New York, there was no opposition to the rebellion. But Leisler could not consolidate the support for his authority, strongest among Protestant Dutch farmers, artisans, and small shopkeepers. At the same time, the leaders of the colony—an intermarried elite of English and Dutch merchants—considered Leisler a dangerous upstart and a threat to their own influence. After royal rule was restored to New York in 1691, Colonel Henry Sloughter, the new governor, adopted the merchants' suspicions of Leisler. In May 1691 a jury comprised entirely of Englishmen convicted Leisler and his son-in-law, Jacob Milburne, of treason. Their executions lent a long life to the bitter political rivalries that the rebellion had intensified in New York. When Leisler and Milburne were reburied in a Dutch cemetery in 1698, some 1200 people, a quarter of New York City's population, marched in the funeral procession. For decades thereafter, political factions fought each other for advantage.

Royal Authority in America in 1700

In the wake of political upheaval at home and abroad, England confined its colonial efforts to reaping maximum profit from the American trade. A series of measures passed in 1696 put more muscle into monitoring colonial commerce. Parliament enlarged the number of customs officials stationed in each colony to oversee the Navigation Acts. Colonial governors took oaths to uphold the regulations, and customs officers received broader legal powers to search warehouses for contraband goods. To help prosecute smugglers, Parliament established colonial vice-admiralty courts, tribunals without juries presided over by royally appointed justices. And to keep current on all colonial matters, the king appointed a new Board of Trade to replace the old Lords of Trade. The new enforcement procedures generally succeeded in curtailing the contraband traffic, channeling colonial trade through England, and quelling American resistance to the Navigation Acts.

That was enough for England and its monarchs for half a century thereafter. With the Glorious Revolution, the steam went out of the Stuart drive to consolidate their empire. English kings and queens forswore any aspirations to impose on North America the strict, centralized administration of colonial life that the Dominion had attempted. Political readjustment at home and the distractions of wars with Spain and France dictated a policy toward the colonies that Edmund Burke, an English political philosopher, later termed "salutary neglect."

True, there were at the end of the seventeenth century more American colonies directly ruled by the Crown. By 1700 royal governments had been established in Virginia, New York, Massachusetts, and New Hampshire; New Jersey, the Carolinas, and Georgia would shortly be added to the list. Proprietary rule persisted only in Pennsylvania and Maryland; Connecticut and Rhode Island alone retained their old corporate charters granting full powers of self-government. Royal rule meant that the monarch appointed governors and (everywhere except Massachusetts) also appointed their councils. Royally appointed councils could veto any law passed by the representative assembly, royally appointed governors could veto any law passed by both houses; and the Crown could disallow any law passed by both houses and approved by the governor.

Still, the sway of royal power remained more apparent than real after 1700. The Glorious Revolution had established once and for all that Parliament's authority would be supreme in the governing of England, putting distinct limits on royal power. In the colonies, members of representative assemblies grew more adept at dealing with royal governors and more entrenched in power. They protected most jealously their strongest lever of power—the right of the lower houses to levy taxes.

The political reality of the assemblies' power reflected a social reality as well. The colonies of 1700 were no longer mere beachheads along the Atlantic, run from 2000 miles away by English joint stock companies. They were no longer the blueprints of absentee proprietors with dreams of establishing lucrative feudal domains or benevolent utopian kingdoms. The close-knit Puritan towns of New England, the heterogeneous farmlands of the Middle Colonies—even the plantation economies of the Chesapeake and the Carolinas—were becoming more firmly rooted societies with social dynamics of their own. Their laws and traditions were based not only on what they had brought from England, but on the conditions of life in America. The Stuarts had hoped that America might be the making of English kings and queens, and the Glorious Revolution swept away that hope. But social realities had already ensured that Stuart hopes of controlling American development would prove no more practical than proprietary dreams or joint stock ventures.

Still, the dream of empire would revive among England's rulers in the middle of the eighteenth century—in part because the same dream had never died among the rulers of France. By 1663, Louis XIV had decided that kings could succeed where the enterprise of private French traders had failed: he placed New France under royal rule. Thereafter France's fortunes in America steadily improved. Soldiers strengthened Canada's defenses; colonists and traders expanded the scope of French influence; the Jesuits made more converts among the tribes of the interior—and even among the Iroquois, who had previously been raiding French farms and trading posts. Under the Sun King, as Louis was known to admiring courtiers, royal rule became absolute and the hopes for empire grew absolutely. Louis and his heirs would continue their plans for the making of France by contending for empire with the English, both in the Old World and in the New.

SIGNIFICANT EVENTS

late 1500s	Formation of the League of the Iroquois
1535	Cartier discovers the St. Lawrence
1608	Champlain founds Quebec on the St. Lawrence; Separatists flee to Holland
1620	Pilgrims land at Plymouth
1624	Dutch found New Netherlands
1630	Winthrop fleet arrives at Massachusetts Bay
1637	Pequot War
1642–1648	English Civil War
1649	Charles I executed
1660	English monarchy restored: Charles II becomes king
1664	New Netherlands becomes English New York; founding of New Jersey
1675–1676	Metacomet's War
1681	Founding of Pennsylvania
1685	James II becomes king of England
1686	Dominion of New England established
1688	Glorious Revolution; William and Mary become monarchs of England
1689	Massachusetts Bay overthrows Andros; Leisler's Rebellion in New York
1692	Witchcraft trials in Salem
1696	Creation of the Board of Trade and Plantations

Generations of the Republic

The First Anglo-Americans
(1640–1700)

Thirteen-year-old Rachel lay awake in the dark loft, listening to the regular breathing of her two stepbrothers and the servant girl who lay beside her. In the darkness of the small, half-story room squeezed under the steep roof of her stepfather's Maryland house, she drifted toward sleep. Waking with a sudden start, she whispered the word that now described her: *orphan*. Not only was she an orphan, but her mother, dead three days, had named no guardian for her. At the sound of footsteps in the hall room beneath her, Rachel sat upright and crept quietly from her straw mattress to the ladder leading below and listened intently to the exchange that might determine her fate.

She could identify each person in the hall. She recognized the commanding voice of a local gentleman, a wealthy planter and member of the county court, the body charged with appointing guardians for orphans. She heard the respectful responses of her few remaining kinfolk and friends. There was her 21-year-old brother, Thomas, who worked the small farm he had inherited from their parents. There were her godparents, who had attended her baptism into the Anglican church at the crossroads 10 miles distant.

And there was her stepfather, the man who had become her mother's second husband.

Rachel's natural father had died five years earlier. Like most men in the Chesapeake, he had come out of England as a young indentured servant. Unlike many, he had survived the rigors of servitude, then worked for a few years as a hired hand, and finally, in his late twenties, scraped together enough money to buy his own land. A year later he married Rachel's mother, a former servant herself, in her mid-twenties. Like many immigrant brides, she was pregnant with her husband's son at the time of their marriage. Rachel's father considered himself luckier than most men along the Chesapeake, where males outnumbered females by six to one and a quarter remained bachelors all their lives. And he had lived to the ripe old age of 48, the average life expectancy for men, before succumbing to typhoid fever.

Rachel's mother had fared well after her husband's death. His will granted her full responsibility for the farm and the children. Like most people in the early Chesapeake, he had no other kin who could have assumed those obligations. But the estate had not amounted to much: it included no servants or slaves. The new widow might have been forced to bind out

her children as servants, simply to provide for their support, if a neighboring planter had not promptly proposed marriage.

Rachel and Thomas had not resented their mother remarrying. Most widows in the Chesapeake took a second and even a third husband, and most marriages were broken within 10 years by the death of one partner. And when Rachel and Thomas moved into their new stepfather's household, which included two young sons from his previous marriage, they took it in stride. Many other children up and down the Bay lived in complicated households that included stepparents, stepsiblings, and half-siblings.

But then her mother had become pregnant. Rachel had watched the matrons from neighboring plantations gather in the hall of her stepfather's home to help her mother from the bed to the birthing stool. Her mother, by then in her early forties, delivered what might have been her last baby even if she had been healthy. But only hours later the infant died, and a few days later Rachel's mother succumbed to complications of childbirth compounded by malaria—the chronic condition that dogged so many settlers, month in and out, and which pregnancy made worse. Many other women in the Chesapeake met the same fate. And many of their children found themselves orphaned, as had Rachel: one-fifth of all youngsters lost both parents before their thirteenth birthday and one-third by their eighteenth birthday.

Even so, Rachel knew that she was lucky just to be alive, since so many of the other children she had seen at church over the years had died of one malady or another. Indeed, one out of every four children born in the Chesapeake did not survive into their teens. And in a society dominated by immigrants with few ties to one another, she was lucky to still have a small circle of adults who might look after her. The county court usually bound out orphans without kin or friends as servants to any planter looking for another laborer. She was lucky, too, because her mother, before her remarriage, had deeded the major part of her first husband's land to Thomas, securing his future as a small planter, and reserved two cows as her daughter's inheritance and modest dowry.

What would the future hold? If Rachel became the ward of her stepfather, or her godparents, or even her brother, they might mismanage her inheritance or mistreat her. Even if they did not, she would be obliged to work for part of her keep, since her inheritance would not yield enough income for her support. If she remained with her stepfather, he would surely favor his own boys over Rachel—or he might marry yet again, perhaps to a woman who would resent the young girl. On the other hand, Rachel could expect to marry out of any unpleasant situation in a few years. Most native-born girls who were not indentured to a master married between 16 and 19, much earlier than their servant-mothers had. And since men

still outnumbered women—by a ratio of three to one in Rachel's generation—even the orphaned daughter of a small planter could choose among suitors. Choose she would, too, and freely, for Rachel no longer had parents alive to influence her selection of a husband.

Still, the world of the Chesapeake did not present a particularly wide array of choices. Rachel and her brother Thomas expected to replicate their parents' lives, he as a small planter, she as a small planter's wife, both of them marrying into nearby farm families. They did not look for futures of greater wealth, higher social rank, education exceeding bare literacy, or travel to distant places. The possibility of real change, of not repeating their parents' lives, never occurred to them.

Far to the north of the tiny, weather-beaten frame house where Rachel listened from the loft, hundreds of miles up the coast, a slightly larger home of similar design nestled amid some 60 others in a small New England village. This house offered even less privacy than that of Rachel's stepfather, for its occupants included a family of eight, and their neighbors lived moments rather than miles away. But Edward, a boy of about Rachel's age, found nothing exceptional in his crowded life.

While Edward's family—his father, mother, and several brothers and sisters—constituted an average New England household, only folk far wealthier than ordinary farmers enjoyed more commodi-

ous living quarters. But what most families lacked in space within their homes, they more than made up for in the acres that they owned outdoors: long strips of land for crops, radiating out from the village center, and fat plots of meadow, marsh, and woodland for grazing, hay, and fuel—scattered where nature saw fit. Although the typical New England farm was half the size of a Chesapeake plantation, Edward's father was still rich in land beyond the wildest dreams of any English yeoman.

That land, coupled with a healthy northern climate, allowed early New Englanders to become rich in children—and rich in relatives of every kind. Rachel counted herself fortunate that her parents had lived into their forties and left her among a few familiar faces; Edward's family formed a phalanx of interminable and seemingly indestructible kin. Both sets of his grandparents, who had emigrated from England as young married couples with small children and settled in this very village, were still alive in their sixties. And they might live 10 or even 20 years longer. Most of their now-grown children—Edward's mother and father and his legion of aunts and uncles—had reached maturity and married in the same village. There they bore their own children, wives becoming pregnant every two years, as soon as they weaned their most recent baby. While Edward's parents, grandparents, aunts, and uncles each maintained separate households, the intimate scale of village society ensured that he encoun-

tered his near and distant kin every day of his life.

The land, too, gave New England's long-lived fathers great authority over their children. Land commanded power, respect, and submission to parental standards, for sons and daughters relied on legacies of farms in order to marry and establish their own families. The subordination to patriarch rule extended for some sons even into middle age, for most fathers waited until the end of their long lives before deeding land to their heirs.

Long before he realized that his future livelihood depended on his father's pleasure, Edward had learned to submit to authority. After his second birthday, his parents started to discipline him whenever he stubbornly misbehaved, making plain by a severe look, a scolding, or a switching their expectation that Edward conform his will to their wishes. At the age of 10 he was sent by his parents to serve his uncle's household, where he lived for two years. It was a common practice among New England parents, an antidote to their fears of coddling and indulging beloved children. During his several winters of study at the village school, Edward learned that his willful ways were the legacy of Adam and Eve to the whole human race. "In Adam's Fall, We Sinned All," read his primer. Twice each week in the meeting house the minister taught the same lesson, urging upon his congregation that conversion alone could make "a new creature," a Christian who preferred

God's will to his or her own. Throughout the long sermons, which seemed even longer on winter Sabbaths so cold that the bread froze and rattled on the communion plate, Edward and the other village boys wriggled and dozed in the drafty back pews under the watchful eye of the sexton, who rang the steeple bell, buried the dead, and kept order among the young.

The lessons took. Edward and most members of his generation accepted the authority of their elders and came to understand parental discipline as a sign of affection and concern. They adopted and celebrated their values, admired and even lionized their parents and grandparents. As adults they sought to imitate and replicate patriarchal culture. And since New England parents lived long enough to be more than memories to their offspring, they exerted considerable influence over the choices of mates and careers made by the next generation. Matters in the Chesapeake were very different. Even if parents there attempted to discipline their children, early death made that authority impossible to sustain. By their teens, many southern youngsters were already independent, making their own way without assistance from kin or friends. The broken, discontinuous families that afforded a full measure of freedom but little certainty stood in sharp contrast to the secure but insulated existences of young people in New England.

4

The Mosaic of Eighteenth-Century America

y the time the hundred and fifty or so Iroquois sat facing the colonial commissioners the morning of June 29, 1754, the rain had passed and the sky had cleared—a good thing, considering the downpours of the past few days. The Hudson River had risen nearly 14 feet, overflowing its banks, tearing sloops from their moorings, drowning the corn in nearby fields, and even pushing up against the palisade fence surrounding the frontier settlement of Albany, New York. The rains, though, had not stopped the meeting. In front of the governor's house, servants had set up about 10 long wooden planks, upon which the delegates from the Six Nations of the Iroquois now sat. The commissioners themselves, 25 in all, were not about to make do with planks; each had his own chair. They represented seven colonies, from Massachusetts Bay on the north to Maryland on the south.

Governor James DeLancey of New York stood and read a proclamation of welcome, pledging to "brighten the Chain of Friendship" between the Iroquois and the English and to keep that "antient Covenant Chain . . . Inviolable and Free from Rust." As each paragraph of the governor's speech was translated, the Iroquois were presented with a decorative belt, to which they responded with a ceremonial *"Yo-heigh-eigh,"* shouted in unison. The noise sounded little more than "a kind of universal Huzzah" to one of the New Hampshire commissioners, who was new to such meetings. But sharper ears were more attuned to Iroquois diplomacy. Normally, each nation voiced its agreement individually: six *Yo-heigh-eighs* coming one after another. By mixing them together, noted one observer, the delegates "had a mind to disguise that all the Nations did not universally give their hearty assent to the Covenant." The Iroquois League was not as united in its friendship as first appearances indicated.

Unity—and not merely the unity of the Iroquois—was very much on the mind of one commissioner from Philadelphia. Several chairs to the left of Governor DeLancey sat the most influential member of the Pennsylvania delegation, Benjamin Franklin. Forty-eight years old and in the prime of life, Franklin recognized that the question of whether the Iroquois would unite in an alliance was only half the issue for this congress at Albany. Equally important was whether the British colonies could unite, to deal in an effective way with France's threat throughout North America. Franklin had a plan for bringing the colonies together, but whether they would pay any heed remained an open question.

By the mid-eighteenth century, Philadelphia was the largest city in the colonies and the second largest in all the British empire. Its busy harbor served not only as a commercial hub but also as the disembarkation point for thousands of immigrants.

In a sense, the plan grew out of a lifetime of experience, for the imperial rivalry between England and France had begun well before Franklin's birth and had flared, on and off, throughout his adult years. In 1689, in the wake of the Glorious Revolution, England had joined the Netherlands and the League of Augsburg (several German-speaking states) in a war against Louis XIV, France's ambitious Sun King. While the main struggle raged on the continent of Europe, French and English colonials, joined by their Indian allies, skirmished across the Atlantic in what was known as King William's War. The Treaty of Ryswick in 1697 signaled a brief interlude in the fighting, but the Anglo-French struggle resumed in 1702, four years before Franklin was born, and continued throughout his early childhood, until the treaty of Utrecht brought peace in 1713.

At stake between the two imperial powers was not so much control over people or even territory but control over trade. In North America France and England vied for access to the rich sugar islands of the Caribbean, a monopoly on the supply of manufactured goods to New Spain, and title to the fur trade. For a quarter of a century following the peace of Utrecht, France and England waged a kind of cold war, vying for position and influence. The British had the advantage of numbers: nearly 400,000 subjects in the colonies in 1720, compared to only about 25,000 French spread along a thin line of fishing stations and fur trading posts. The French, however, had strengthened their chain of forts, stretching from the mouth of the Mississippi north through the Illinois country and into Canada. The forts helped channel the flow of furs from the Great Lakes and the Mississippi River valley into Canada, thus keeping them out of the clutches of English traders.

And strategically, the forts neatly encircled England's colonies, confining their settlement to the eastern seaboard. By midcentury, about 50,000 farmers, traders, and missionaries lived in French America, and wheat had joined furs as a profitable export.

When fighting again engulfed Europe and the colonies in 1744, the results were inconclusive. King George's War, as the colonials dubbed it, was ended by the peace of Aix-la-Chappelle (1748), which essentially restored the status quo. The French, seeing English traders and settlers filter steadily into the Ohio River valley, moved in 1752 to protect their interests in the region, building a new line of forts south of Lake Erie to the Ohio River. Two years later they erected Fort Duquesne at the strategic forks of the Ohio, flush against the border of Franklin's Pennsylvania. The news of Fort Duquesne startled Pennsylvania and other colonies into sending commissioners to Albany in 1754 to coordinate efforts to deal with the worsening crisis. Franklin put the message plainly in his newspaper, the *Pennsylvania Gazette*, in a cartoon of a snake cut into segments. It was inscribed "Join, or Die."

Throughout this imperial maneuvering, the Iroquois League maintained a cool neutrality toward its white rivals. Where once the League had been willing to attack New France in order to maintain control of the fur trade, by the eighteenth century it had become equally suspicious that the English were perhaps using the Iroquois merely as "a Pack of Hounds" to hunt the French. On July 2, three days after Governor DeLancey's welcoming speech, the Albany commissioners heard the frank reply of Hendrik, a Mohawk chief. The English and the French "are both Quarrelling about lands which belong to us," Hendrik complained. "And such a Quarrel as this may end in our destruction." Furthermore, while English farmers from Pennsylvania and Virginia continued to settle on Indian lands, English soldiers seemed incapable of resisting the French. "Look about your Country and see," Hendrik concluded contemptuously,

> you have no Fortifications about you no not even to this City, tis but one step from Canada hither and the French may easily come and turn you out of your Doors. . . . Look at the French, they are Men, they are fortifying every where—but we are ashamed to say it, you are all like Women, bare and Open without any Fortifications.

For the time being, the commissioners could do little to satisfy Iroquois doubts, except lavish as much hospitality as their straitened budgets would allow. In the end, Hendrik and the other delegates made evasive promises of loyalty, and then hauled away 30 wagons full of presents.

But would the colonies themselves unite? That was Franklin's worry. On the way to the Albany Congress he had sketched out a tentative political framework for colonial cooperation. Working with several others at the meeting, he proposed establishing a federal council composed of representatives from each colony, presided over by a president-general appointed by the Crown. The council would assume all responsibility for colonial defense and Indian policy, defraying the cost of building forts and patrolling harbors by taxes levied on all Americans. The commissioners were bold enough to accept the plan, having experienced face to face the reluctance of the Iroquois and the reality of the French threat. Franklin sailed back down the Hudson with his plan endorsed and a call from the commissioners to establish "one general government" for British North America.

But the union born at Albany was smothered by the jealous colonies, who were unwilling to sing *yo-heigh-eigh* either in unison or separately. Not a single assembly approved the Albany Plan of Union. New Englanders and Pennsylvanians did not want to help secure the claims of Virginians to the upper Ohio valley. Virginians, along with New Jerseyans, had refused even to attend the congress. And no American legislature was ready to surrender its cherished and exclusive right to tax inhabitants of its own colony—not to a federal council or any other body. "Everyone cries, a union is necessary," Franklin wrote Governor Shirley of Massachusetts in disgust; "but when they come to the manner and form of the union, their weak noodles are perfectly distracted." If the Albany Congress proved one thing, it was that American colonials were emphatically and hopelessly divided.

FORCES OF DIVISION

Franklin, of course, should have known better. He was a practical man, not given to idle dreams, and he certainly recognized the many forces of disunion at work in America. He knew that the colonies were divided by ethnic, racial, and religious differences and prejudices. Year after year small wooden ships sailed into American seaports to disgorge a bewildering variety of immigrants—especially in Philadelphia, where Franklin had lived since 1723. From his efforts to reorganize the post office Franklin knew, too, that Americans were separated by vast distances, poor transportation, and slow communications. And he knew how much frontier districts distrusted seaboard communities and how the eastern seaboard disdained the backcountry. Taken all in all, the British settlements in America were, in the eighteenth century, a diverse and divided lot.

Immigration and Natural Increase

One of the largest immigrant groups—250,000 black men, women, and children—had come to the colonies from Africa not by choice but in chains. White arrivals included a substantial number of English immigrants, but also a quarter of a million Scots-Irish, the descendants of seventeenth-century Scots who had regret-

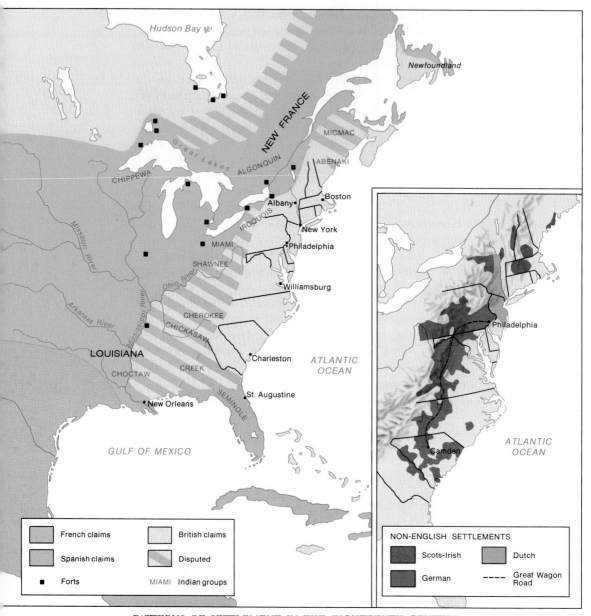

PATTERNS OF SETTLEMENT IN THE EIGHTEENTH CENTURY

The French, English, and Indian nations all jockeyed for power and position across North America during the eighteenth century. The French expanded their fur trade through the interior, while English settlement at midcentury began to press the barrier of the Appalachians. Many non-English settlers spilled into the backcountry: the Scots-Irish and Germans followed the Great Wagon Road through the western parts of the Middle and southern colonies while the Dutch and Germans moved up the Hudson River valley. Albany, where Franklin journeyed in 1754 for the Albany Congress, was one natural pivot point in the rivalry—a place where Iroquois, French, and Indian interests converged.

ted settling in northern Ireland; perhaps 135,000 Germans; and a sprinkling of Swiss, Swedes, Highland Scots, and Spanish Jews. Most non-English white immigrants were fleeing lives rent by famine, warfare, and religious persecution. All of the voyagers, English and non-English, risked the hazardous Atlantic crossing. And many mortgaged their freedom to redeem the price of passage by signing indentures to work as servants in the New World.

The immigrants and slaves who arrived in the colonies between 1700 and 1775 swelled an American population that was already growing dramatically from natural increase. The birth rate in eighteenth-century America was triple what it is today. Most women bore between five and eight children, and most children survived to maturity. Even larger families of 10 or more children were not uncommon—Franklin was the youngest son in a family of 17 children. After about 1700, low rates of infant mortality and long life expectancy, the rule in the northern colonies since the seventeenth century, also became more typical in the South.

Franklin knew, better than most colonials, the dimensions of American growth, both from immigration and through reproduction. In a 1751 essay on the subject, he recognized the social and political consequences of the population explosion. People of different races speaking different languages, believing in different religions, and cherishing different customs created distinctive environments that ranged over a wide expanse of territory. This diversity, coupled with the hectic pace and sheer scale of expansion after 1700, made it hard for Americans to share any common identity. Far from fostering political union, almost every aspect of social development set Americans at odds with one another.

Older Rural Communities

Once they disembarked at American ports, the free immigrants needed places to live and ways of earning a livelihood. So, too, did the burgeoning ranks of native-born Americans coming of age every year: about half of the colonial population in 1775 was under 16. The places that probably appealed to many immigrants and younger Americans were the scores of older rural communities lining the coast or lying a few miles inland.

Even after a century of colonization, most northern settlements remained isolated villages of several hundred inhabitants living in simple family farmsteads built of logs, stone, or brick. In the older parts of New England, family farms of about 100 acres radiated along dirt roads from country towns, the centers of social life. Here farmers bartered small stocks of produce at village stores for what their families could not make at home—sugar, molasses, rum, spices, salt, chocolate, tea, iron ploughs and scythes, and English textiles. Here men and women gathered at village taverns to tipple, smoke, and gossip. Here families flocked on the Sabbath to worship at white steepled meetinghouses and to listen to long sermons delivered by the best educated man in the community, the village minister. Here, several times during the year, men convened at the same meetinghouse to discuss village business.

The stony soil of New England's coast, now worn with a century of use, afforded most families just enough to feed themselves. Outside of the rich Connecticut River valley, it was almost impossible to turn a profit by farming. But most farmers owned the land they worked, and there were no marked extremes of wealth or poverty.

Daily Lives

TIME AND TRAVEL

Transatlantic Trials

A mountain of water swelled from the slate gray Atlantic, towering over the *Jamaica Packet*, then toppled onto the small wooden passenger ship. The impact hurled Janet Schaw and her maid about their cabin like rag dolls. As seawater surged in, the two women struggled to grasp something, anything, to keep from drowning. Outside, it was panic and pandemonium as the ship pitched wildly, "one moment mounted to the clouds and whirled on the pointed wave," the next plunging prow first into the heaving ocean. Four men lashed to the helm fought for control, while the rest of the crew worked with hands "torn to pieces by the wet ropes." The ship's provisions—hogsheads of water, coops of chickens, and barrels of salted meat—snapped from their fastenings and careened across the deck before bouncing overboard.

For more than two days the *Jamaica Packet* hurtled in the grip of the gale. Then its foremast splintered, and the ship flipped onto its side. Passengers, crew, and furniture crashed "heels over head to the side the vessel had laid down on." Schaw found herself "swimming amongst joint-stools, chests, [and] tables" in her cabin and listening to the sound of "our sails fluttering into rags." It would have been the end of the *Jamaica Packet* if, at that moment, its masts had not washed overboard. With the weight of the masts gone, the ship righted itself, reeling all aboard "with equal violence to the other side," as "a second deluge of sea water" swept the vessel.

Schaw, "a lady of quality," as she described herself, was traveling by the finest accommodations from Great Britain to America in the age of sail. For those passengers who could not pay full fare for a private cabin on the *Jamaica Packet*, the storm was worse. Twenty-two or more indentured servants from Scotland in that year of 1774 were bound aboard ship for the West Indies. Unlike ladies and gentlemen "of quality," these desperate, impoverished families of farmers and fishermen had agreed with British merchants to work for labor-hungry American masters in return for the costs of passage. And, like the thousands of others who came to America in the eighteenth century, they were consigned to steerage, the between-decks area or "upper hold."

Perhaps four to five feet high, that space was a congested, foul-smelling dormitory, crowded with narrow wooden bunks arranged in tiers about two feet apart. It was impossible for most people to stand in steerage or to sit up in a bunk, where as many as four people huddled together at night. Sanitary facilities consisted of a few wooden buckets filled with seawater; candles and fish-oil lanterns

Daily Lives

supplied the only light; the sole source of air was the hatch opening onto the deck.

When the storm struck, the hatch had been closed and fastened tightly to keep the holds from filling with water. But as waves dashed over the decks, water seeped and then streamed into steerage, forcing its occupants to stand, clutching their children to keep them from being crushed or suffocated as the storm tumbled everyone from one side of their dark, watery prison to the other. For nine days they stood in water, soaked to the skin, without a fire or any food except raw potatoes and moldy biscuit. And they were without light or fresh air, except for one young man and his pregnant wife. During the storm the woman miscarried, and her "absolutely distracted" husband, Schaw reported, somehow forced open the hatch and carried her up to the deck, reviving the unconscious woman and saving her life. When at last the servants were allowed to come up on deck, they discovered that all of their belongings had been swept overboard.

What followed the servants up to the deck, to the horror of all, was a stench "sufficient to raise a plague aboard." But the luck of the *Jamaica Packet* held, for it escaped not only shipwreck but epidemic disease. Passengers on other transatlantic voyages were not so fortunate. Throughout the eighteenth century notices of ships "lost at sea" or of passengers who slipped overboard in storms filled colonial newspapers. Even on voyages graced with good weather, all aboard suffered from a week of seasickness. Outbreaks of epidemic disease—smallpox, influenza, typhus, and diphtheria—were common. Contributing to the problem of pestilence were the cramped, airless quarters of most travelers bound for America: indentured servants and some convict laborers. Although even cabin passengers complained of wet and cold, they could stroll the deck at will. But servants and convicts were confined to the hold for most of the voyage—anywhere from two to three months.

Along with poor ventilation and primitive sanitation, meager diets left steerage occupants prey to infection. Full-paying passengers received the same rations as ships' officers and often brought a private stock of provisions, but those in steerage subsisted on a stingy allotment of oatmeal, molasses, bread, and meat, much of it wet, moldy, or spoiled. Often their water was brackish. Aside from a few peas, they had no vegetables or fruit. Debilitated by malnutrition, dysentery, and fever, they became vulnerable to deadlier microbes. Although there are no reliable statistics for shipboard mortality during the eighteenth century, estimates range from 3 percent of all passengers to as high as 10 to 15 percent, a rate comparable to that for slave ships during the Middle Passage across the Atlantic.

For all who ventured abroad, transatlantic travel was tedious and dirty at best, fraught with hazard and horror at worst. Those who risked the crossing routinely made out wills and sought the prayers of friends and relatives. But disease and danger at sea discriminated against the poor, indentured servants, and convict laborers who comprised the majority of eighteenth-century emigrants.

In the Middle Colonies, farms of slightly larger size lay at a greater distance from smaller central places, often only a crossroads where all of the county occasionally gathered at a tavern, a country store, a courthouse, or a church. The fertile soil south of Connecticut afforded farm families there not only subsistence but often a surplus of livestock and grain, which they sent to Philadelphia or New York City for export. Because of such commercial opportunities, wider disparities in wealth existed in some settled communities of the Middle Colonies. But since most farmers owned land, inequality was not pronounced.

In established northern rural communities, there had emerged a local "squirearchy" comprised of the wealthier farmers. These families, at the pinnacle of the village pecking order, owned more land than their neighbors and supplemented their farm income by keeping stores, milling wheat or logs, or practicing law. Year after year, they provided leadership for their localities, directing civic life and church affairs.

In the oldest counties of the Virginia and Maryland Tidewater and in the Carolina low country, stability and prosperity also prevailed. Like the rural areas of the Middle Colonies, coastal southern counties specialized in commercial agriculture. Chesapeake planters cultivated tobacco for export; low-country farmers grew rice and indigo. But southern farms were even larger than those in the Middle Colonies, and even greater distances isolated planters from each other. Not only longer physical distances, but also greater social distances separated inhabitants of settled plantation districts. Through a combination of farming, shopkeeping, land speculation, and professional practice, the gentry amassed estates that far exceeded those of ordinary planters. And after 1700, gentry property included a growing number of black slaves. Wealth won the deference of lesser planters: social authority and political office passed from one generation of southern gentlemen to the next. Like their northern counterparts, these local leaders administered justice, supervised civic life, and oversaw public order and morality.

To white immigrants from Europe, weary of war or worn by want, America's settled towns and counties must have seemed safe havens. But by the beginning of the eighteenth century, many coastal communities could no longer accommodate even the children of long-time settlers, let alone newcomers from Europe. In older New England towns, three and four generations were putting pressure on a limited supply of land, while wasteful farming practices had depleted the soil of its fertility. Farther south, earlier settlers had already snatched up the choice farmland of Philadelphia's outlying counties, the prime tidewater tobacco property, and the best low-country rice swamps.

With older rural communities offering few opportunities to either native-born or newly arrived white families, both groups were forced to create new communities in new places. Blacks alone among eighteenth-century immigrants were settled in established rural districts, the plantations of the tidewater and the low country. The uprooting and resettlement of Europeans, Africans, and native sons and daughters created three distinctive kinds of societies in eighteenth-century America: the raw frontier county, the urban seaport, and the plantation slave community.

The Settlement of the Backcountry

The obvious outlet for hard-pressed settlers was the frontier. A few hardy Scots-Irish established enclaves in Maine and in the territory that was to become Vermont. But for the most part, the peopling of New England's interior was left to the descendants of old Yankee families. Throughout the eighteenth century, young men, often brothers or cousins who had grown up in the same coastal village, brought their brides to Maine, New Hampshire, or Vermont. There they felled trees, planted farmsteads, and named tiny hamlets after their hometowns back in southern New England.

Better opportunities to acquire plentiful land at cheaper prices lay south of New York, especially in the backcountry of Pennsylvania, Virginia, and the Carolinas. There, Germans, Scots-Irish, and other settlers formed farming communities that were distinct from both the plantation districts of the southern coast and the rural villages of the North. Backcountry families dispersed across the landscape, enduring greater isolation than any other Americans. In one new Virginia Piedmont county, about 3000 settlers were scattered over 5000 square miles. Farm families spread over this distance seldom had contact with anyone outside of the members of their own households. The nearest courthouse could lie as far as a day's ride from many farmsteads; taverns and churches were often just as distant.

If the isolation of the frontier inhibited the development of strong social bonds, so did the rapid rate at which people came to and left western communities. Many Americans migrated west only to roam restlessly within the backcountry: some families pulled up stakes three and four times before settling down permanently. It was not uncommon for as many as one-third of the members of a frontier county to move on after a few years—to be replaced by an even larger number of newcomers. Houses reflected the transiency of frontier settlements. Framed structures were the exception; most families crowded into filthy, fragile, one-room shacks, earth-fast structures built on posts sunk in the ground and walled with mud, turf, or crude logs.

Backcountry economies afforded most families a bare existence. Large portions of the interior were cut off from access to water transport, lying on unnavigable rivers above the fall line. Unable to float their crops downriver to seaport markets or to drive cattle or cart crops overland on primitive dirt paths, farmers grew only enough to feed their households, selling to new settlers whatever small surplus remained. Not only poor transportation but also the lack of labor kept frontier farmers from tapping the commercial potential of their lands. Most backcountry inhabitants could not afford to invest in a slave or even a servant. They had at their disposal only the labor of family members.

The lack of opportunity to engage in trade or to buy bound labor made the frontier, more than anywhere else in America, a society of equals. Most backcountry families lived on their own farms of about 200 to 400 acres. They had sons enough to cultivate a small fraction of that total acreage, and daughters enough to help with the never-ending household chores of cooking, weaving, spinning, sewing, making candles and soap. Together, their efforts yielded just enough to sustain their families. All of the worldly goods of a typical family consisted of livestock, farm implements, a few pots, knives, and blankets.

What the frontier gained in equality it may have lost in stability. In the backcountry there were no southern gentlemen or northern squires to supply continuous, experienced local leadership. There was only a handful of farmers in each county set above their neighbors by a few extra acres or a single slave. To these relatively inexperienced and uneducated men fell the thankless tasks of overseeing public order as justices of the peace or officers in the local militia or representatives to colonial assemblies. It was hard for men who had so little authority over

This log cabin, built in the North Carolina backcountry in 1782, would have been dark inside, given the lack of windows. The spaces between the logs in such cabins were usually chinked with thin stones or wedges of wood, then daubed with mortar.

their fellows to police sprawling backcountry communities; not surprisingly, coarse and aggressive behavior dominated frontier life. Backcountry men and women mated out of wedlock, swore in public, drank to excess, and brawled at any provocation.

Nor were the churches much help in promoting law and order. Most westerners could not at first afford to build churches, and their widely dispersed homesteads deterred them from attending public worship. The few clergy willing to endure the rigors of preaching from one backcountry neighborhood to another were either exceptional zealots or, as frontier folk described them, "notorious evil-livers"—drunkards, womanizers, and other scoundrels. While churches loomed large in the lives of Americans on the coast, most western families, although often deeply pious, had only haphazard or occasional contact with organized religion.

Among the least enviable lives in eighteenth-century America were those of frontier women. Besides doing the usual chores of farm women, western wives and daughters joined male family members in the fields. One traveler from the East expressed his astonishment at seeing German women in western Pennsylvania "at work abroad on the Farm mowing, Hoeing, Loading Dung into a Cart." Perhaps even more difficult to endure than the greater demands on their labor was the loneliness of their lives. Most women had little enthusiasm for moving far away from family and old friends, and they often had trouble adjusting to the primitive conditions of the backcountry. Equally distressing was the distance separating their homesteads from those of female neighbors. The reactions of women to being uprooted and resettled in a wilderness cabin can be guessed at from the assurance that one Scottish husband offered his wife: "We would get all these trees cut down . . . [so] that we would see from house to house."

Social Conflict on the Frontier

Benjamin Franklin knew about the lure of the frontier. He had observed the hordes of Scots-Irish and German immigrants disembarking at Philadelphia and lingering there just long enough to scrape together the purchase price of western land. He had seen workers in his own printshop grow restless with city life and light out for the frontier. From his point of view, the backcountry performed a valuable service by siphoning off surplus people from congested eastern settlements and endowing them with enough land to make a living. But he knew, too, that the frontier was an American Pandora's box: once opened, the West unleashed discord and conflict. Backcountry communities were themselves volatile and violent places. And the settlement of the frontier fostered deep political divisions between the eastern seaboard and the backcountry.

These fissures fueled struggles in almost every colony, and in some, they widened into violent conflict. In Pennsylvania, Franklin himself mediated one contest between East and West. In 1763 a band of Scots-Irish farmers known as "the Paxton Boys" protested the government's inadequate protection of frontier settlers by killing a number of Indians. Then they took their protests and their guns to Philadelphia, marching as far as Lancaster before Franklin intervened and promised redress of their grievances.

North and South Carolina did not get off as easily. In both colonies, legislatures dominated by coastal planters refused to grant equitable political representation and extend basic legal institutions to inland settlers. In response to eastern intransigence, two protest movements emerged in the Carolina interior, each known as the Regulation.

Beginning in the 1760s, backcountry South Carolinians sought to "regulate" into extinction gangs of horse thieves and cattle rustlers who preyed on farm families. The outlaws stormed into lonely plantations, burned farm buildings, stole livestock, kidnaped and raped women, tortured and murdered men. Disgusted by the inaction of South Carolina's assembly, which refused to set up courts in the backcountry, westerners formed vigilante groups and administered grisly frontier justice to the marauders, as well as to any hapless drifters and trappers caught in their dragnets. Threats to march on Charleston itself finally panicked eastern political leaders into extending the court system, but bitter memories of eastern indifference lingered among the Regulators.

If local government in western South Carolina was nonexistent, in North Carolina it was corrupt. Here frontier disaffection ran even deeper. Wealthy lawyers and merchants, backed by big eastern planters, moved into the western parts of the colony, shouldered aside local farmers, and seized control of politics. The new leaders used the machinery of government to exploit frontier settlers, charging exorbitant fees for legal services, imposing high taxes, and manipulating debt laws. Led by the largest local planters, frontier settlers petitioned the governor and the assembly for redress in 1766 and tried to vote the corrupt out of office. When that failed, a virtual civil war erupted in the backcountry. Dubbing themselves the "Regulation," western farmers seized county courts, liberated their jailed leaders, and at last squared off 2000 strong against an eastern militia led by the governor. The militia won at the Battle of Alamance in 1771, but the brutal repression of frontier discontent left westerners in North Carolina with an enduring hostility to the seaboard.

Ethnic differences exacerbated the political tensions between East and West. While people of English extraction predominated along the Atlantic coast, Germans, Scots-Irish, and other white minorities were concentrated in the interior. Many English colonials eyed the new immigrants with disdain and mistrust, regarding them as culturally inferior and even politically subversive. In 1729 Bostonians greeted the arrival of a boatload of Irish immigrants with a riot; a few years later, a mob in Worcester, Massachusetts, set fire to a Scots-Irish Presbyterian church. Farther south, the Scots-Irish also stirred strong animosities. Charles Woodmason, an Anglican missionary in the South Carolina backcountry, deplored the influx of "5 or 6000 Ignorant, mean, worthless, beggarly Irish Presbyterians, the Scum of the Earth, the Refuse of Mankind," who "delighted in a low, lazy, sluttish, heathenish, hellish life."

German immigrants were generally credited with greater industry as well as higher standards of sexual morality and personal hygiene. But like the clannish Scots-Irish, the Germans preferred to live, trade, and worship among themselves. They exhibited little admiration for English political institutions, even less interest in citizenship, and a decided aversion to military service. By 1751 Franklin was warning that the Germans would always retain their separate language and customs: instead of Anglicizing the Germans, the Pennsylvania English would be overrun by "the Palatine Boors." Even in South Carolina, a colony desperate for white settlers because of its black majority, the assembly considered restricting German immigration.

Boundary Disputes and Tenant Wars

The settlement of the frontier also triggered disputes between colonies over their boundaries. At the root of the confusion were the old colonial charters, whose vague definitions of western borders allowed groups of settlers and land speculators from different colonies to lay claim to the same tract of land. Thus was New York drawn into frays with Connecticut and Massachusetts, and Pennsylvania with Connecticut and Virginia.

The most serious of these border wars pitted New York against some farmers from New England who had settled in present-day Vermont: Ethan Allen and the Green Mountain Boys. In the 1760s, New York, backed by the Crown, claimed land that Allen and his friends had already purchased from New Hampshire. When New York tried to invalidate New England land titles and to extend its political jurisdiction over Vermont, it reaped a whirlwind of opposition. For more than a decade Allen spearheaded a successful guerrilla resistance, harassing Yorker settlers and officials, occupying Yorker courthouses, and setting up a competing judicial system in the Green Mountains.

The spread of settlement also set the stage for mass revolts by farm tenants in areas where proprietors controlled vast amounts of land. While outright ownership of land was the exception among rural folk in Europe, it was the rule in America. Throughout the eighteenth century, colonial governments regularly granted or sold land to any interested buyers; for those willing to settle in remote western districts, allotments were liberal and prices affordable. Even those who started out renting farms managed to end up as independent landowners. Still, in a few areas of the Middle Colonies, tenancy struck a deeper root. In eastern New Jersey, prominent proprietors pressed squatters for quitrents on land that had become increasingly populated and therefore more valuable. When the squatters, many of them strong-willed migrants from New England, refused to pay rents, buy the land, or move, the proprietors began evictions, touching off riots in the 1740s.

In New York's Hudson River valley several prominent merchant families had received large manorial estates in the 1680s from the royal governor. They established themselves on these tracts as resident landlords and recruited poor Dutch and German immigrants as tenants. By the middle of the eighteenth century, there were about 30 manors around New York City and Albany, totaling some 2 million acres and worked by several thousand tenants. Their labor produced a large surplus of wheat and livestock and a handsome profit for the great Yorker landlords.

The terms of tenancy in the Hudson valley were fairly generous, because Yorker landlords had to compete with other colonies to attract laborers. But tenancy under any terms was unacceptable to the New Englanders who had moved there. They squatted on Yorker manors, fended off all attempts at eviction, and preached their ideas about owning land to Dutch and German tenants. Armed insurrection exploded in 1757 and again, more violently, in 1766. Tenants refused to pay rents, formed mobs, stormed the homes of landlords, and prepared to march on New York City. The rebels dispersed only when a regiment of British soldiers arrived armed with a cannon.

Eighteenth-Century Seaports

Most Americans on the move found homes, if not havens, in frontier communities. Others, drawn by opportunity or desperation, made places for themselves in a different environment—colonial seaports. Cities like Boston, New York, Philadelphia, and Charleston, founded as coastal villages in the seventeenth century, became magnets for migrants and mushroomed into major commercial centers by the opening decades of the eighteenth century.

Benjamin Franklin's Philadelphia offered a waterfront fringed with wharves and dotted with warehouses, streets crowded with a jumble of shops, taverns, and homes, and a skyline punctuated by the spires of churches and the towers of public buildings. It was the second largest city of all the British empire, but by modern standards Philadelphia was small, with just 35,000 inhabitants in 1770. New York, Boston, Charleston, and Newport were its closest competitors in the colonies. The scale of city life was small in another way too. All of New York City was clustered at the southern tip of Manhattan Island; all of Boston could be traversed in a walk of less than an hour. Only Philadelphia's population had sprawled into suburbs. And it was a rare building that rose more than two stories high.

Because of their tiny total area, colonial seaports were teeming, congested places. Human occupants competed for places on crude sidewalks and narrow streets of gravel or rough cobblestone with cattle and sheep being driven to the butcher and with carts, carriages, and horses conveying produce and passengers, often at breakneck pace. Pedestrians, vehicles, and livestock alike vied for right of way with roaming herds of swine and packs of dogs. Despite the density of settle-

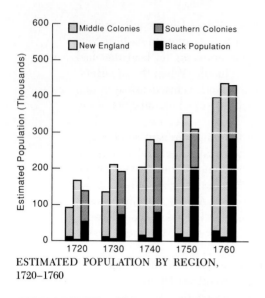

ESTIMATED POPULATION BY REGION,
1720–1760

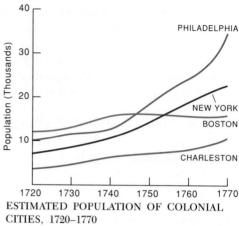

ESTIMATED POPULATION OF COLONIAL
CITIES, 1720–1770

While Boston's population remained stable
after 1740, it was surpassed by the sharp
growth of New York and, especially, Philadelphia.

ment and traffic, colonial cities were relatively clean compared to European towns
of equal size. While public sanitation still left much to be desired, most city
governments improved the state of sewers, drains, and streets during the eighteenth century. Only New York remained so filthy that it defied human habitation.

The size of cities fostered intimacy among inhabitants. Most faces seen on the
streets were familiar, and nearly everyone could recognize one group—the merchants. They managed commerce, the lifeblood of urban economies. Traders in
New York and Philadelphia dealt in the produce of their towns' rich hinterland,
dispatching corn, wheat, cattle, and horses to feed West Indian planters and to
power island sugar mills. New England merchants trafficked in fish, a staple in the
diet of Caribbean slaves and Iberian Catholics; masts and timber, items in demand
by the British navy; and rum, a popular export to almost any place. Charleston's
dealers sent indigo and rice to Britain, the indigo for English dyemakers, the rice
for shipment to Europe. With the returns of the export trade, merchants in every
colonial city imported the coveted luxuries produced in England—fine cloth, pottery, and tea—along with large lots of cheaper textiles and farming implements.

Their wealth made merchants a dominant force in political as well as economic life. They monopolized city governments and shared power in colonial
assemblies with lawyers and the largest farmers and planters. By the middle of the
eighteenth century, an increasing amount of wealth and political influence was
concentrated in the hands of urban trading families. But the merchant class was
not a closed oligarchy: new entrepreneurs with ready skills or fortunate marital
connections were always entering the ranks of the city elite.

Most of those mobile citizens rose from the ranks of skilled craftworkers, the
artisans who comprised the middling classes of colonial cities. No large-scale domestic industry produced goods for a mass market. Instead, the households of
master craftworkers, usually including a few younger and less skilled journeymen
artisans and very young, unskilled apprentices, filled orders for specific items
placed by individual purchasers. Some artisans specialized in the maritime trades,

the greater rewards going to master mariners, shipbuilders, and blacksmiths who forged anchors and iron fittings, the lesser returns to ropemakers and sailmakers who fashioned rigging. Master craftworkers who processed and packed raw materials for export—butchers, millers, and rum distillers—might also realize a substantial profit, as could those artisans in the luxury trades—gold- and silversmiths, jewelers, cabinet and carriage makers. Ranking below the master craftworkers in the most lucrative trades were those who served the basic needs of city dwellers— the men and, occasionally, women who baked bread, mended shoes, combed and powdered wigs, sewed simple clothing, cut hair and beards, and tended shops and taverns.

On the lowest rung of the city's social hierarchy were free and bound workers. The free labor force included journeymen artisans who were still perfecting their skill in a particular craft and young, able-bodied men who shipped out as sailors and fishermen or who loaded cargo onto ships docked in harbors. At the very bottom of the social order were unfree laborers—young boys serving apprenticeships to local master craftworkers and indentured servants doing menial labor for merchants or artisans.

Black men and women also made up a substantial part of the bound labor force of colonial seaports, not only in southern Charleston but in northern cities as well. While the vast majority of slaves imported from Africa were destined for a lifetime in tobacco fields and rice swamps, a smaller number were sold to urban merchants and craftsmen. Working as porters at the docks, assistants in craft shops, or as servants in wealthy households, blacks made up almost 20 percent of New York City's population and accounted for 10 percent of the inhabitants of Boston and Philadelphia.

The character of northern slavery changed decisively during the middle of the eighteenth century, when wars raging in Europe strangled the supply of white indentured servants to the colonies. Northern whites turned to slaves as substitutes for servants and started importing large numbers of blacks directly from Africa. In the two decades after 1730, one-third of all immigrants arriving in New York harbor were black; by 1760, blacks comprised over three-quarters of all bound laborers in Philadelphia. The preference of white merchants for importing African men upset what had been an equal balance of black men and women in colonial seaports, making it difficult for the newcomers to enjoy a normal family life. The recently arrived Africans also lacked immunity to American diseases, and many did not survive their first northern winter: the death rate among urban blacks was double that for whites.

But those who did survive infused into urban black culture a new awareness of a common West African past. The resurgence of African traditions appeared most vividly in an annual event known as "Negro election day." The festival, similar to one conducted throughout West Africa, was celebrated by blacks in seaports throughout New England and the Middle Colonies. The day's revels began with black men and women—some dressed in their masters' clothes or mounted on their horses—parading to the music of fiddles, banjos, drums, and tambourines. They proceeded to select black "kings," "governors," and "judges," who duly "held court" and settled minor disputes among white and black members of the community. "Negro election day" did not challenge the established racial order with its temporary and ritualized reversal of roles. But it did allow the black community to honor their own leaders.

The availability of black maids and cooks as well as the pool of free domestic

The Old Plantation affords a rare glimpse of life in the slave quarters. At this festive gathering, both men and women dance to the music of a molo (a stringed instrument similar to a banjo) and drums. The insets show a gudugudu drum and a stringed kora, instruments common throughout Africa and similar to those depicted in the painting.

servants made for leisured lives among women from well-to-do white families in colonial seaports. Even those women who could not afford the luxury of household help spent less time and energy doing domestic work than farming wives and daughters. Although some housewives grew vegetables in backyard gardens or kept a few chickens, large markets stocked by outlying farmers supplied most of the food for urban families. Most women were also relieved of the laborious chore of spinning and weaving: they bought their cloth at dry goods stores instead. Because they purchased what farm women had to produce, urban wives could devote more time to keeping up houses and appearances. The daughters of the well-to-do, in particular, had greater leisure for visiting friends and reading. Unlike girls in rural areas, whose labor was vital to family welfare, these young urban women learned "the mysteries of housewifery" only to prepare themselves for their future domestic roles.

All colonial women were expected to devote themselves to caring for households, husbands, and children and to find fulfillment in the domestic sphere. But cities offered to women who had to support themselves a number of employments.

Young single women from poorer families commonly spent a few years before marriage working in more affluent households as maids, cooks, laundresses, seamstresses, or nurses for infants and the infirm. Prostitution was another possible line of work, but less secure because of public opposition. More respected and lucrative occupations for women, all requiring long apprenticeships and expert skill, included midwifery, millinery, and "mantua making"—the "Genteel way of Making up" fashionable dresses and cloaks. Although wives of artisans and retailers sometimes assisted in their husbands' businesses, and, as widows, often continued to manage groceries, taverns, and printshops, most women worked in jobs that more closely resembled traditional female roles. And even in cities, less than one out of every ten women worked outside their own homes.

The people who lived in cities, perhaps one out of every twenty Americans, enjoyed a more stimulating and diverse environment than most colonials. The wealthiest could attend an occasional ball or concert; those living in liberal New York or Charleston might even see a play performed by touring English actors. The middling classes could choose among weekly newspapers and a varied stock at local bookshops and could converse with other tradespeople at private social clubs and fraternal societies. The lower classes, along with their betters, found diversion in drink, horse racing, cockfighting, and bull and bear baiting. Occasionally members of all social classes converged at taverns to see traveling exhibitions of trained dogs and horses, exotic displays of "Great White Bears" and "Arabian camels," or the spectacular waxworks of one John Dyer, featuring "a lively Representation of Margaret, Countess of Herrinburg, who had 365 Children at one Birth."

But city dwellers, then as now, paid a price for the variety of their lives. Commerce was fraught with risk: ships sank, small markets abroad glutted, and wars disrupted trading patterns. Natural and human disasters could send shock waves through the delicate economies of colonial seaports, bankrupting merchants and leaving craftworkers and laborers out of work. When trade slowed down, the lowest classes were the first to feel the pinch. The ups and downs of seaport economies, combined with the steady influx of immigrants, swelled the ranks of the poor in all cities by the mid-eighteenth century. While the major seaports established workhouses to employ the able-bodied poor, these institutions were a place of last resort for their intended occupants. Cities continued to aid most of the dependent by doling out small subsidies of money, food, and firewood.

Not only economic life but often life itself was more precarious for city dwellers, who endured epidemic disease more frequently than country folk. The deadly microbes of smallpox and yellow fever, introduced to American ports by sailors and immigrants, spread rapidly among closely packed populations. And because of urban congestion, fire was an ever-present danger as well. Although buildings of brick were slowly supplanting the wooden frame structures of an earlier era, a spark from a single clogged chimney flue could quickly set afire surrounding dwellings, engulfing overcrowded neighborhoods in a catastrophic blaze.

Social Conflict in Seaports

Cities were social tinderboxes too. Just as rapid westward movement churned up trouble on the frontier, the swelling of urban populations sparked discord in seaports. The jumbled assortment of English, Scots-Irish, Germans, Swiss, Dutch, French, and Spanish jostled uneasily against one another in the compact quarters of Philadelphia and New York. To make matters worse, religious differences contributed to ethnic animosities. Jewish funerals in New York, for example, drew crowds of the hostile and the curious to cemeteries, where they heckled the mourners. Even when hostility did not turn to violence, ethnic and religious differences often split city residents in urban political contests.

Antagonism between rich and poor also stirred up unrest. Some merchant families flaunted their wealth, building imposing mansions in town and maintaining country estates. Merchants clad in scarlet coats clambered out of elegant carriages and strutted to their counting houses in gaudily striped shoes. Their wives shivered in fashionably low-cut gowns of French design, encumbered by hoop petticoats and weighed down with lavish jewelry. During hard times, symbols of merchant opulence like expensive coaches and full warehouses became favorite targets of mob vandalism. Crowds also congregated to intimidate and punish other groups who provoked popular hostility—unresponsive politicians, prostitutes, and "press gangs." Impressment, attempts on the part of the British navy to dragoon colonial service, triggered some of the most violent urban riots.

SLAVE SOCIETIES IN THE EIGHTEENTH-CENTURY SOUTH

The divisions and social diversity of seaports paled, however, when set beside those of another society in eighteenth-century America. There was no colonial environment so deeply unequal, varied, and violent as the plantation district of the southern coast.

When Thomas Jefferson wrote the Declaration of Independence in 1776, nearly half of the people in his own colony of Virginia were slaves. Even by the first decade of the eighteenth century, a majority of South Carolinians were black, and by 1720 slaves made up two-thirds of that colony's population. By 1775 one out of every five Americans was of African ancestry, and over 90 percent of all American blacks lived in the South, most along the seaboard. Here, on tobacco and rice plantations, slaves fashioned an African-American society and culture as distinctive as the other provincial settings of the eighteenth century. But blacks began to build stable families and communities only late in the eighteenth century, and against formidable odds.

Whether a slave was auctioned off to the Chesapeake or to the Lower South shaped his or her future in important ways. Slaves in the low country of South Carolina and Georgia lived on plantations with as many as 50 other blacks, about half of whom were African-born. Slaves residing in large lowland quarters, virtually black villages, had infrequent contact with either their masters or the rest of the sparse white population. In some districts of South Carolina there were seven or eight blacks for every white. Planters who could afford the luxury of absentee ownership escaped the lowland malarial climate for the healthier air of Charleston. Other masters owned several plantations and traveled from one to another. In their absence, white overseers and black "drivers," the most experienced slaves, supervised work routines.

That work was arduous, for rice required constant cultivation. Blacks tended young plants and hoed fields in the sweltering summer heat of the mosquito-infested lowlands. After midcentury when some planters adopted "tidal cultivation," irrigating their fields by regulating the flow of rivers, slaves spent the winter

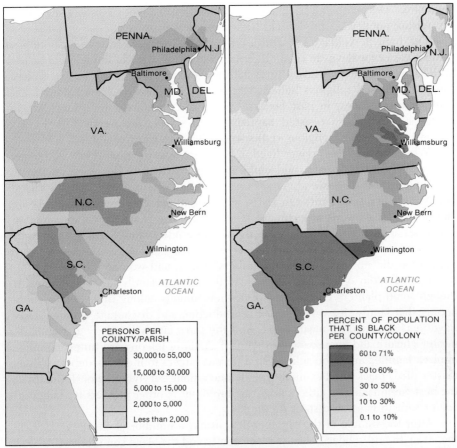

THE DISTRIBUTION OF THE AMERICAN POPULATION, 1775
The African-American population expanded dramatically during the eighteenth century, especially in the southern colonies. While the high volume of slave imports accounts for most of the growth in the first half of the century, natural increase was responsible for the rising black population during later decades.

and early spring building dams and canals and the summer overseeing sluices and floodgates.

Many Chesapeake slaves, like those in Carolina, were African-born, but most lived on smaller plantations with fewer fellow blacks. Throughout the eighteenth century, more than half lived on plantations of less than 20 slaves. Less densely concentrated than in Carolina, Chesapeake slaves also had more contact with whites. Unlike Carolina's absentee owners, gentlemen in the Upper South actively managed their estates and subjected their slaves' performance to closer scrutiny.

The Slave Family and Community

By contrast, in the Carolina low country, the density of black settlement afforded slaves the opportunity to cultivate a separate sphere in the quarters. The widespread use of the "task system" rather than gang labor on Carolina plantations also widened the window of freedom within slavery. When a slave had completed his assigned task for the day, one planter explained, "his master feels no right to call upon him." During such free time blacks tended garden plots, growing vegetables and raising poultry to supplement their own diets or to sell.

The high percentage of African-born blacks everywhere in the South also made it easier for slaves to retain their tribal cultures. African influence appeared in the slaves' distinctive agricultural skills and practices, folktales, music, dances, superstitions, and religious beliefs. Christianity won few converts among eighteenth-century slaves, in part because most blacks preferred traditional African religions. Whites also resisted baptizing their slaves, fearing that blacks who shared their masters' religious status would become less tractable.

Whenever possible, slaves lived in family groups, the typical household consisting of a husband, wife, and children. Some gradually developed elaborate kinship networks that extended over several plantations in a single neighborhood, maintaining family ties through visits, with or without their masters' permission. But not all slaves were so fortunate. The smaller size of Chesapeake plantations narrowed opportunities for slaves in the Upper South to find partners, and in the Lower South, two out of every three slaves were male. The South Carolina slave population did not contain equal numbers of men and women until 1790.

Even for slaves fortunate enough to find mates, family life was fragile. Although some planters encouraged permanent unions among their bondspeople, hoping that family ties would foster reproduction and discourage running away, slave marriages had no legal status. And the slave family was only as stable as a master's health and finances were sound. If a planter fell on hard times, members of black families might be sold off to different buyers to meet his debts. When a master died, black families might be divided among surviving heirs. Even under the best circumstances, fathers might be hired out to other planters for long periods or sent to work in distant quarters.

After the middle of the eighteenth century, a number of changes enhanced the strength and solidarity of the black family and the slave community. As slave importation began to taper off, the rate of natural increase among blacks started to climb. In the Tidewater and the Virginia Piedmont, the black population grew more rapidly than the white, and even in the Lower South, slave communities began to increase because of reproduction rather than importation. As the proportion of new Africans dropped and the number of native-born blacks grew, the ratio of men to women in the slave community became more equal. Those changes and the appearance of more large plantations, even in the Chesapeake, created more opportunities for blacks to form families.

As the number of native-born blacks increased, so did a distinctive African-American culture in the slave quarters. Glimpses of it begin to appear in planters' diaries and travelers' accounts toward the end of the eighteenth century. In 1774, one young English visitor to the Maryland Tidewater described "a Negro Ball" held on one spring Sabbath day, "the only days that these poor creatures have to themselves." To the music of a banjo, a gourd fitted out with four strings, the assembled slaves danced. They also sang together, "very droll music indeed," which related "the usage they have received from their Masters or Mistresses in a very satirical stile and manner."

Slave Resistance in the Eighteenth Century

What the young Englishman had witnessed at the "Negro Ball" was not only an African-American entertainment, but also a subtle expression of resistance and a strategy for survival. While the influx of white immigrants to the backcountry contributed to upheaval on the frontier, the concentration of slaves on the southern coast generated conflict in plantation districts.

Slave resistance took several forms. Among newly arrived Africans, collective attempts at escape were most common. Groups of "saltwater" slaves, often made up of newcomers from the same tribe, fled inland and formed "Maroon" communities of runaways. These efforts were usually unsuccessful because the Maroon settlements were large enough to be easily detected; Carolinians even enlisted the Cherokee to return runaways for a reward.

More acculturated blacks adopted subtler ways of subverting slavery. William Byrd, a Virginia planter, unwittingly recorded in his diary a catalogue of the range of resistance tactics deployed by slaves on his plantation. He complained about house servants challenging his orders, damaging his furniture, stealing his liquor, and engaging him and his wife in elaborate contests of will; he fretted over field hands who broke his tools and dragged out their tasks. Domestics and field hands alike faked illness, feigned stupidity and laziness, pilfered from the storehouse, hid in the woods for weeks at a time, or simply took off to visit other plantations. It never dawned on Byrd that there was a pattern to slave behavior and that every recalcitrant act was another grain of sand scattered in the gears of his plantation.

The more that slaves became accustomed to English ways, the more likely they were to resist their condition and to escape—successfully. The largest group of blacks who made good on a flight to freedom were slave artisans. Because of their work, these craftworkers were accustomed to moving about the countryside from one job to another on different plantations. Because they spoke fluent English and possessed valuable skills, they could survive once they slipped away from their masters. And because they ran away individually, the slave artisans were more difficult to track down. Most disappeared into colonial seaports, where they practiced their craft or became sailors.

Rebellion against bondage also involved violence. Whites in communities with substantial numbers of blacks lived in gnawing dread of arson, poisoning, and insurrection. Four slave conspiracies were reported in Virginia during the first half of the eighteenth century. In South Carolina, more than two decades of abortive uprisings and insurrection scares culminated in the Stono Rebellion of 1739, the largest slave revolt of the colonial period. Nearly 100 blacks, led by a slave named Jemmy, seized arms from a store in the low-country district of Stono and killed several whites before they were caught and killed by the white militia.

The Stono Rebellion triggered other unsuccessful slave uprisings and reports of slave conspiracies throughout the colonies in 1740 and 1741. But throughout the eighteenth century, slave rebellions occurred far less frequently on the mainland of North America than in the Caribbean or Brazil. Whites outnumbered blacks in all of the colonies except South Carolina, and only there did rebels have a haven for a quick escape—Spanish Florida. Faced with these odds, most slaves reasoned that the risks of rebellion outweighed the prospects for success—and most sought opportunities for greater personal freedom within the slave system instead.

Despite the growing rebelliousness of blacks, southern planters continued to import African slaves in large numbers during the eighteenth century. The practice mystified Franklin, revealing at least one gap in his knowledge—the crucial importance of slavery in the southern economy. But unlike some of his Quaker neighbors in Pennsylvania, who were beginning to object to slavery on moral and humanitarian grounds, Franklin's reservations—like his opposition to German immigration—were overtly racist. "Why increase the sons of Africa by planting them in America," he asked, "where we have so fair an opportunity, by excluding all blacks and tawnys, of increasing the lovely white and red?"

ENLIGHTENMENT AND AWAKENING IN AMERICA

All of the differences among eighteenth-century Americans resulted in more than clashes of economic interests and conflicts between regions, races, and ethnic groups. Diversity also made for fundamental differences in the ways that Americans thought and believed. City dwellers were more attuned to European culture than were people living in small inland farming villages, and both were more cosmopolitan than settlers scattered across the frontier. White males from well-to-do families of English ancestry were far more likely to receive college educations than those from poorer or immigrant households, white women of every class and background were excluded from higher education, and slaves received no education at all. Where they lived, how well they lived, whether they were male or female, native-born or immigrant, slave or free—all these variables fostered among Americans distinctive world views, differing attitudes and assumptions about the individual's relationship to nature, society, and God.

The Enlightenment in America

The diversity of Americans' inner lives became even more pronounced during the eighteenth century because of the Enlightenment, an intellectual movement that started in Europe during the seventeenth century. The leading figures of the Enlightenment, the "philosophes," stressed the power of human reason to promote progress by revealing the laws governing both nature and society. By acquiring a clear understanding of these laws, they believed, people could control their lives and improve the quality of society and government. The philosophy of the Enlightenment struck a shallow root in the American colonies. Its influence was confined mainly to the most skilled seaport artisans and some elite colonial families of city merchants, northern country squires, and southern planters. Only well-to-do families had the resources, the leisure, and the education to read the latest books from Europe. The new outlook that they adopted contrasted sharply with that of less privileged and well-educated colonials.

Franklin's career epitomized the Enlightenment's impact on the colonies. Like other Americans who imbibed the "new learning," he was most impressed by its emphasis on useful knowledge and experimentation. He pondered air currents and then invented a stove that heated houses more efficiently. He toyed with electricity and then invented lightning rods to protect buildings in thunderstorms. Other amateur American scientists also hoped to understand and master the natural world: they constructed simple telescopes to observe the transits of Venus and Mercury; they filled botanical gardens with plants and identified and classified animal species native to North America; they sought to explain epidemics in terms of natural causes and supported inoculation, a new medical procedure for immunizing people against smallpox. They experimented with new farming techniques and wrote treatises on increasing the productivity of agriculture.

Clubs were organized to discuss the latest European ideas about science, philosophy, literature, and social betterment. Typical of these groups was the American Philosophical Society, founded by Franklin in 1743 and dedicated to "Experiments that let Light into the Nature of Things, tend to increase the Power of Man over Matter, and multiply the Conveniencies or Pleasures of Life."

Enlightenment ideas were also disseminated among young men of affluent families through American colleges. While many scions of colonial families were still educated in England, six colleges had been established in America by 1763: Harvard (1636); William and Mary (1693); Yale (1701); the College of New Jersey (later Princeton, 1746); King's College (later Columbia, 1754); and the Academy and College of Philadelphia (later the University of Pennsylvania, 1755). The founders of some of these institutions had intended them primarily to train ministers, but by the eighteenth century their graduates included lawyers and merchants, doctors and scientists. Most colleges offered courses in mathematics and the natural sciences that taught students algebra and such advanced theories as Copernican astronomy and Newtonian physics.

Even some clergy educated at American colleges were touched by the Enlightenment, the new spirit being reflected in the more liberal theology that they developed and preached to their congregations. By 1740, this "rational Christianity" commanded a small following among Americans, usually Anglicans or liberal Congregationalists. In place of the Calvinist religion of mystery and miracle, rationalists asserted the essential reasonableness of Christianity. Their God was not the Calvinists' inscrutable Jehovah, but a benevolent, nearly genial deity who opened salvation to all, not just a small, predestined elite. According to the rationalists, religious life consisted in doing good works: they muted the Calvinist emphasis on human sinfulness and dispensed altogether with the Calvinist insistence on a heart-wrenching conversion. Some reduced religion to a moral science— Franklin drew up lists of virtues in a ledger and then kept an account of his progress toward perfection.

Enlightenment philosophy and rational Christianity did not affect the outlook of most Americans. Even among members of the elite the appeal of these newer currents was far from universal. The great majority of colonials still looked for ultimate truth in God's revelation in the Bible rather than human reason, and explained the workings of the world in terms of divine providence rather than natural law. By the mid-eighteenth century, over half of all white men (and a smaller percentage of white women) were literate, and most children of every class except slaves received some training in reading, writing, and basic arithmetic at home, in village "dame schools" run by widows or unmarried women, or in schools set up for apprentices by their masters. Even so, such rudimentary educations could not have carried most American readers through such learned treatises of the philosophes as John Locke's essay on human psychology, Newton's explanation of the law of gravity, or Voltaire's attacks on traditional Christianity.

The inroads of rationalism in America, although slight, still convinced some clergy that they needed to promote among colonials not only religion but "true religion"—Calvinism. Out of their concerns came the revival that swept the colonies during the middle decades of the eighteenth century.

The First Great Awakening

The westward flow of immigrants, the concentration of more people in seaports, and the forced settlement of many slaves in the coastal South—all three movements of people over the eighteenth century—set the stage for mounting social

To Nathan Cole, a Connecticut farmer who witnessed one of George Whitefield's sermons, the preacher appeared "almost angelical; a young, slim, slender youth before thousands of people with a bold, undaunted countenance. . . . He looked as if he was clothed with authority from the Great God . . . and my hearing him preach gave me a heart wound."

tensions. And in the 1740s, a single dramatic episode supplied Americans with yet another source of division. Ironically, that event was a religious revival. Even more ironically, participation in the revival, known as the first Great Awakening, was the only experience that a large number of people everywhere in the colonies had in common. And the man who sparked the Great Awakening, George Whitefield, an English evangelist and one of the founders of the Methodist Church, was the only public figure whose name was known to all eighteenth-century Americans.

Of course, Americans had been fighting over religion well before the Great Awakening. In most New England colonies, minorities of Anglicans, Baptists, and Quakers had battled the established Congregational Church for more than a century, first seeking relief from outright persecution and political discrimination and later exemptions from paying taxes to support the Puritan clergy. In the southern colonies, even smaller congregations of Presbyterians, Baptists, and Quakers had waged a similar struggle against the established Anglican Church. And in the Middle Colonies, where religious toleration prevailed, a patchwork of denominations and smaller sects—Quakers, Presbyterians, Lutherans, Mennonites, Dunkards, and others—competed ferociously for members.

The spread of population westward heightened the competition and fostered a sense of crisis in American church life. The clergy recognized that many inhabitants of the backcountry were deprived of religious consolation and the ordered social life offered by churches. And many ministers, especially the strict Calvinists among the Congregationalists, Presbyterians, and Reformed, feared that large numbers of lay people might abandon the faith of their ancestors and embrace rational Christianity—or lose all faith.

The first stirrings of religious excitement began among the congregations of a handful of evangelical Calvinists who urged the necessity of conversion. There was William Tennent, a Scots-Irish immigrant who settled with his four sons, all ministers, in Bucks County, Pennsylvania. The Tennents aroused religious enthusiasm among their fellow Presbyterians throughout the Middle Colonies and in the 1730s founded the "Log College"—the institution that came to be called Princeton—to train other preachers. Among New England Congregationalists, clergy awakened "backsliders" to a proper anxiety over salvation by preaching about local epidemics or earthquakes or the premature deaths of young people. Among them was Jonathan Edwards, a tall, thin, intensely intellectual Yale graduate who served as the pastor at Northampton, Massachusetts. By the mid-1730s, Edwards' preaching, which combined lyrical descriptions of God's saving grace with sheer psychological terrorism, had promoted "frontier revivals" throughout the Connecticut River valley. "The God that holds you over the pit of hell, much as one holds a spider or some loathsome insect over the fire, abhors you and is dreadfully provoked," Edwards declaimed to one congregation, ". . . there is no other reason to be given, why you have not dropped into hell since you arise in the morning, but that God's hand has held you up."

These local revivals were mere tremors compared to the earthquake of enthusiasm that shook the colonies with the arrival in the fall of 1739 of George Whitefield, the handsome, cross-eyed "boy preacher." What Whitefield preached in the churches and open fields of America was nothing more than what other Calvinists had been saying for centuries: sinful men and women were totally dependent for salvation on the mercy of a pure, all-powerful God. But Whitefield presented the message in novel ways. He and his many eager imitators among colonial ministers turned the church into a theater. With dramatic gestures and sometimes copious tears, in low, ominous monotones or in ringing cadences, divines preached sermons laden with vivid, terrifying images of the torments of hellfire. The pathos, simplicity, and stark violence of such performances appealed to people of all classes, ethnic groups, and races. Whitefield toured America from New England to Georgia; by the time he sailed back to England in January 1741, thousands of awakened souls were joining churches, many of them newly formed.

The Aftermath of the Great Awakening

Whitefield also left in his wake a gathering storm of controversy. Throughout the colonies, conservative and moderate clergy questioned the unrestrained emotionalism of the evangelicals and the disorder and discord that attended the revivals. "Our presses are forever teeming with books, and our women with bastards," one antirevivalist sighed. Many members of the awakened laity now openly criticized their old ministers as cold, unconverted, and uninspiring. To supply the missing fire, some laymen—"and even Women and Common Negroes"—took to "exhorting" any audience willing to listen. The most popular prorevival ministers turned "itinerants," traveling like Whitefield from one town to another. Battles raged within congregations and whole denominations over the challenge to clerical authority by lay exhorters and itinerants, as well as the evangelical approach to conversion from "the heart" rather than "the head."

The Awakening left Americans sharply polarized along religious lines. Quakers (who by now had become much soberer than their seventeenth-century forebears) gained new members among conservatives who disapproved of the revivals' excesses. So did the Anglicans. On the other hand, Baptists and "Separate" Congregationalists gained a host of evangelical radicals, who demanded pure churches of converted believers. The largest single group of churchgoing Americans remained within the Congregational and Presbyterian denominations, but they divided internally between advocates and opponents of revivals.

While congregations splintered and denominations bickered, the fires of revivalism spread to the frontier. As the enthusiasm on the seaboard burned down to embers, the Presbyterians of the Middle Colonies and the Baptists of New England spread the gospel in the backcountry of Pennsylvania, Virginia, the Carolinas, and Georgia. From the mid-1740s until the 1770s, scores of new churches were formed. As in the East, the "awakenings" caused contention. Ardent Presbyterian converts in the Carolina backcountry harassed Anglican priests and disrupted their services by loosing packs of dogs in local chapels. In parts of Virginia, Anglicans took the offensive against the somber Baptists. Their severe, ascetic, and egalitarian morality sounded a silent reproach to the hard-drinking, high-stepping, horse-racing, slaveholding Chesapeake gentry. County officials, prodded into action by resentful Anglican parsons, fined Baptist ministers, intimidated and imprisoned them, and occasionally even whipped them.

While the West was turning toward evangelical Calvinism, the most powerful people on the southeastern coast remained Anglican, and, in the Middle Colonies, Quaker. As a result, the seaboard and the backcountry residents found themselves quarreling over religious as well as political and ethnic issues. Inevitably, civil governments were drawn into the fray. In colonies where one denomination received state support, other churches lobbied legislatures for disestablishment, an end to the favored status of Congregationalism in Connecticut and Massachusetts and of Anglicanism in the southern colonies.

And so a divided and diverse lot of Americans found themselves at odds with one another—whether over religion, ethnic origins, or backcountry versus seaboard disputes. And Benjamin Franklin, who made it his business to know, knew well the extent of the divisions as he made his way toward Albany in the spring of 1754, dreaming improbably of American political union. He had himself counted his fellow citizens, despairing over the influx of Germans, Scots-Irish, Africans, and other non-English newcomers. He had lived in two booming seaports, and he had felt the explosive force of the frontier. He personified the Enlightenment—and he knew all about the Great Awakening. The day that George Whitefield preached on the steps of the Philadelphia courthouse, there stood Franklin, an unrepentant rationalist, ignoring the sermon and working his way through the crowd to compute the distance traveled by the evangelist's voice.

Why, then, could Franklin, who knew how little held the colonials together, sustain his hopes for political unity? The answer may be that even in 1754, the majority of colonial men and women were of English descent. And these free, white Americans liked being English. That much they had in common.

THE ANGLO-AMERICAN WORLDS OF THE EIGHTEENTH CENTURY

Most Americans prided themselves in being English. When colonials named their towns and counties, they named them after places in their parent country. When colonials established governments, they turned to England for their political models. They frequently claimed "the liberties of freeborn Englishmen" as their birthright. Even in diet, dress, furniture, architecture, and literature colonists adopted English standards of taste.

Yet the physical separation of the colonies across the wide Atlantic meant that American society had developed in ways significantly different from Great Britain.* Americans who visited their parent country quickly discovered the differences, which set them to thinking what it really meant to be English. Some differences made Americans feel inferior, ashamed of their rustic manners when compared with London's sophistication. But Americans also came to appreciate the comparative simplicity of their culture and the greater equality of their society. In particular, they judged colonial political arrangements to be more representative and responsive than those in England. Most Americans still liked being English, but they especially liked being English in America.

Urban Life in England and America

England was a more urban society than America. Although three-quarters of England's people lived in the countryside, a considerable number passed some part of their lives in cities. While most Americans on the move struck out for the frontier, the English gravitated toward urban settings. Perhaps one out of every six English men and women lived for a time in London, a teeming colossus by eighteenth-century standards with a population of 675,000 in 1750.

Nothing in their experience at home could have prepared colonials for their first exposure to London. Ninety percent of all Americans lived in towns of less than 2000, and the complexity of life even in major colonial seaports was dwarfed by that of London. Those who could afford to gloried in London's luxury and elegant diversions. They roamed the British Museum. They gawked at cathedrals and lounged in coffeehouses. They strolled through fashionable shops, fingering fine textiles, trying on spectacles, and inspecting handsome carriages. They had their portraits painted by celebrated artists like Joshua Reynolds. They savored concerts and operas, and they could even be found in Drury Lane, enjoying, perhaps with a twinge of Puritan guilt, English stage plays.

But the underside to this splendor left colonials with grave misgivings. London seethed with filth, crime, and desperate poverty. The poor and the unemployed, beggars and thieves, pickpockets and prostitutes crowded into its gin-soaked slums, taverns, and brothels. The city's death rate was double the birth rate, in large part because of heavy consumption of alcohol by the poor. The contrast between the polite refinements enjoyed by a wealthy few Londoners and the abject misery of the many disquieted colonial observers. Ebenezer Hazard, an American Quaker, knew for certain that he was not in Philadelphia, but instead in "a Sink of Sin."

Economic Development and Inequality

What sustained the growth of London and the urbanization of all England was a higher level of commercial and industrial development than existed in any of the

---

*When England and Scotland were unified in 1707, the nation as a whole became known officially as Great Britain, its citizens as British.

colonies. Most English men and women worked at agriculture, but it had become a big business, aimed at producing surplus food for city dwellers or for export abroad. By the mid-eighteenth century, the average English farm was a large-scale capitalist enterprise. Members of the gentry rented their estates to tenants, members of the rural middle class, or entrusted the management of their lands to stewards. Tenants and stewards then hired men and women from the swollen ranks of England's landless to perform the actual farm labor. At most, a mere quarter of the English actually owned the land that they farmed.

Bigness was the byword in other sectors of the economy as well. Mines and textile factories had become familiar sights, backed by large financial institutions and corporations like the Bank of England, Lloyd's of London, and the East India Company. By contrast, the average American family farm was small—a few hundred acres of land owned by the people who worked it. Production on most farms outside of the coastal South and the Delaware and Hudson valleys was geared to subsistence rather than trade. Manufacturing remained limited both by British mercantilist restrictions and the inclinations of colonials to farm instead.

The opportunities for great wealth provided by England's more developed economy created deep class distinctions, as did the inherited privileges of the aristocracy. The gulf between the rich and the poor yawned widest in London, but inequality of every kind was woven into the fabric of society. The members of the English upper class, the landed aristocracy and gentry, made up less than 2 percent of England's population but owned 70 percent of its land. By right of birth, English aristocrats claimed membership in the House of Lords; by custom, certain powerful gentry families dominated the other branch of Parliament, the House of Commons. England's titled gentlemen shared power and wealth and often family ties with the rich men of the city—major import and export merchants, successful lawyers, and lucky financiers. They too exerted political influence through the House of Commons.

The colonies had their own elites, but no true aristocracy or formally titled ruling class, no group gaining political privilege by hereditary right. On the contrary, the biggest American merchants and planters could trace their ancestries no higher than to England's merchants and minor gentlemen, and most derived from humbler backgrounds. Even the wealthiest colonial families lived in markedly less magnificence than their English counterparts. Probably the finest mansion in eighteenth-century America, William Byrd's Westover plantation, was scarcely a tenth the size of the marquis of Rockingham's country house, which was longer than two football fields.

If the English upper classes were more splendid, its lower classes were larger and worse off than their American counterparts. Less than a third of England's inhabitants belonged to the "middling sort" of traders, professionals, artisans, and tenant farmers. More than two-thirds eked out marginal existences at the bottom of society. By contrast, the colonial middle class took in nearly three-quarters of the white population, who prospered thanks to the availability of relatively cheap land. With labor scarce and wages for both urban and rural workers 100 percent higher in America than in England, it was much easier for Americans to accumulate savings and then buy a farm of their own. Most whites who began life on the bottom of society did not remain there throughout their lives.

Americans were divided in their opinion of England's social and economic development. On the one hand, gentlemen planters from the colonies envied the techniques English estate managers had introduced to make their fields more

Coffeehouses like this establishment in London were favorite gathering places for eight-eenth-century Americans visiting Britain. Here merchants and mariners, ministers and students, lobbyists and tourists warmed themselves, read newspapers, and exchanged gossip about commerce, politics, and social life.

productive. Colonial entrepreneurs admired the ingenuity of English mills, mines, and canals. And they saw nothing amiss in women and children working long hours in factories. On the other hand, Americans disdained some members of the English upper class, whose incomes from land sustained extravagant, slothful, and dissolute habits. Just as alarming was the eagerness among London's big bankers and brokers to speculate in stocks or engage in shady financial maneuvering.

Americans were equally fascinated and uneasy about the habits of royalty and aristocracy. Benjamin Rush, a Philadelphia physician, felt in the House of Lords as if he "walked on sacred ground," begged his guide for permission to sit on the throne therein, and, once ensconced, sat "for a considerable time." Other colonials gushed over the grandeur of aristocratic estates and imported suits of livery for their servants, tea services for their wives, and wallpaper for their drawing rooms. They exported their sons to Britain for college educations at Oxford and Cambridge, medical school at Edinburgh, and legal training at London's Inns of Court.

But the aping of English ways was accompanied by a tinge of apprehension. One Philadelphia Quaker ordered an elegant English coach complete with coat-of-arms—but then reconsidered and removed the crest. When sons educated in England came home wearing dandified silks and affecting foppish manners, planter and merchant fathers complained that higher education had left their boys not only incompetent but impertinent. Fashionable English slang such as "Split me, Madam!" "By Gad!" and "Dam me!" fell hard on parental ears.

Americans harbored even greater doubts about English inequality. They recognized that England's ruling classes purchased their luxury and leisure at the cost of the rest of the nation. In his *Autobiography*, Benjamin Franklin painted a devastating portrait of the idle, dissipated, and degraded lives of his fellow workers in a London printshop. With no hope of bettering themselves, the printers drowned their disappointments by drinking throughout the workday, even more excessively on the Sabbath, and then faithfully observing the holiday of "St. Monday's" to nurse their hangovers. Franklin wondered about a society that suffered the many to live "below the Savage State so that a few may be raised above it." While accepting hierarchy as natural and desirable, many Americans felt that gross inequality of wealth would endanger liberty. They regarded the idle parasites among England's rich and poor alike as ominous signs of a degenerate nation.

Politics in England and America

American sentiments about English government were simpler. They venerated the British constitution of government but abhorred the actual workings of English politics. That judgment was ungenerous at best, for British political life had become remarkably stable over the eighteenth century. In large part it had done so because those who governed England ignored theories of what was supposed to be in favor of what worked.

In theory, England's "balanced constitution" was designed to give every order of English society some place in the workings of government. While the Crown represented the monarchy and the House of Lords the aristocracy, the House of Commons represented the democracy, the people of England. An ideal equilibrium was supposed to exist among the three elements of monarchy, aristocracy, and democracy, and that balance produced political harmony. In fact, the monarch's executive ministers had become dominant by adroit "managing" of the legislative branch, Parliament. The executive created support for their policies through a system of "influence" or patronage—or, put more bluntly, bribery.

Over the course of the eighteenth century, a large executive bureaucracy had evolved, in order to enforce laws, collect taxes, and prosecute the nearly constant wars in Europe and America. The power to appoint all military and treasury officials, customs and excise collectors, judges and justices of the peace lay with the monarch and his or her ministers. They used the spoils of office to win support among members of Parliament. By the middle of the eighteenth century, almost half of all members of Parliament also held Crown offices or government contracts.

Royal patronage was also deployed to manipulate parliamentary elections. In some of England's smaller districts, the majority of the electorate were royal officeholders. In other cases, the executive branch used money or liquor to bribe local voters into selecting their candidates. The small size of England's electorate fostered executive influence. Perhaps just one-fifth of all adult males were enfranchised. And many electoral districts were not adjusted to keep pace with population growth and resettlement. The notorious "rotten boroughs" each elected a member of Parliament to represent fewer than 500 easily bribable voters, while some large cities like Manchester and Leeds, newly populous because of industrial growth, had no representation in Parliament at all.

Americans liked to think that their colonial governments replicated the ideal structure of the English constitution. In terms of formal organization, there were similarities. Every colony except Connecticut and Rhode Island had a royal governor who represented the monarch in America. Every colony also had a bicameral (two-house) legislature: the democratically elected lower house or assembly, like the House of Commons, stood for popular interests, while the upper house or council, some elected and others appointed, more roughly approximated the House of Lords. Like members of Parliament, most colonial legislators came from among the elite.

But these formal similarities masked real differences between English and colonial governments. On the face of it, royal governors had much more power than the English Crown. Unlike kings and queens, royal governors could veto laws passed by assemblies; they could dissolve those bodies at will; they could create courts and dismiss judges. However, governors who asserted their full powers quickly ran afoul of their assemblies, who objected that such overwhelming authority endangered popular liberty. And in any showdown with their assemblies, most royal governors had to give way, for they lacked the lubricant of English politics—the lucrative government offices and contracts that bought loyalty. The colonial legislatures possessed additional leverage, since all of them retained the sole authority to levy taxes.

But even if the governors had enjoyed greater patronage powers, their efforts to "manage" colonial legislatures would have been stymied by the sheer size of the American electorate. There were too many voters in America to bribe. Over half and possibly as many as 70 percent of all white adult colonial men were enfranchised. Property requirements were the same in America as in England, but widespread ownership of land in the colonies allowed most men to meet the qualifications easily.

The American electorate was not only too big to bribe, but it was also more watchful. Representatives were required to reside in the districts that they served, and a few even received binding instructions from their constituents about how to vote. Representation was also apportioned according to population far more equitably than in England. Eighteenth-century Americans endorsed the notion of "actual representation": they believed that officials should serve the local interests and needs of those who directly elected them. Since they were so closely tied to their constituents' wishes, American legislators were far less susceptible than members of Parliament to executive pressure and influence.

All these peculiarities of American political life fostered a phenomenon historians have called "the rise of the assemblies." The royal governors' lack of patronage steadily diminished executive influence over colonial legislatures, allowing assemblies a decided edge in any political contest. Increasingly confident of their power and importance, the assemblies styled themselves miniature Parliaments, entitled to all of the privileges of the original body in England.

The English Opposition and American Political Thought

The desire of colonial legislatures to emulate Parliament was part of the wider reverence in which Americans held the English constitution. But while Americans agreed that the English constitution was nothing short of "the most happy and excellent form of government" ever devised, many were appalled by the reality of English politics. John Dickinson, a young Pennsylvanian training as a lawyer in London, recoiled in horror from the conduct of a parliamentary election in 1754. The king and his ministers had spent over 100,000 pounds to sway support for their candidates, he wrote to his father, and "If a man cannot be brought to vote as he is desired, he is made dead drunk and kept in that state, never heard of by his family and friends, till all is over and he can do no harm."

The English artist William Hogarth's satirical rendition of an English election mirrored the reservations of many Americans about the political culture of the mother country.

Americans like John Dickinson found their own dark conclusions reinforced by the writings of a group of English known as the "Country Party," also called "the Opposition." The Opposition drew their inspiration from the English Civil War a century earlier, when thinkers like John Milton, Algernon Sydney, and James Harrington had consistently upheld the rights of the individual against the power of the state. Even now, the Opposition argued, the danger to liberty still loomed. The Glorious Revolution of 1688 had not gone far enough in reforming English politics. The ever-expanding executive branch of government was steadily corrupting Parliament and depriving the electorate of its liberty.

Underlying the Opposition's conception of politics was a nearly Calvinist view of sinful human nature. In their eyes humankind was not ruled by principle but driven by passion and insatiable ambition. Politicians, the most selfish and depraved of all people, would always conspire against liberty to enhance their own power. They had to be watched at all times: the price of liberty was eternal vigilance. In pressing their case for reform, the Opposition advocated adult manhood suffrage and proportional representation. They also favored binding representatives to their constituencies by residential requirements and instructions. Only the reform of politics and the restoration of virtue to public and private life, the Opposition believed, could save England from certain disaster.

Such sentiments were strongly put, but in fact, Opposition thinkers occupied only the fringes of English political life. They drew from radicals and religious dissenters on the extreme left and conservative landed gentlemen on the extreme right of the political spectrum. An odd lot, they included the gifted historian Catherine Macaulay; Henry St. John Bolingbroke and Robert Viscount Molesworth, two aristocratic politicians out of power; Benjamin Hoadley, an Anglican priest; and Joseph Priestley, a clergyman and chemist. Best known to Americans were John Trenchard, a lawyer, and Thomas Gordon, a schoolteacher, who collaborated on *Cato's Letters*, a series of scathing essays against the political establishment. But whether intellectuals, teachers, or clergy, they had drifted far from England's political mainstream.

American colonists, however, revered the English Opposition. Their assessment of English society confirmed American anxieties about England, while their program for political reform bore a flattering resemblance to how colonial politics operated. The Opposition also shared with Americans a lurking suspicion of people at the center of power—for both groups were far enough on the fringes of imperial politics to imagine the worst.

The Imperial System Before 1760

In England most citizens remained complacent and unconcerned about the condition of government. In their view, the Glorious Revolution of 1688 had worked: peace prevailed in public life, except for the mutterings of the Opposition. As for the Americans, the English thought about them little, understood them less, and wished neither to think more about them nor to understand them better.

It would be hard to overstate just how insignificant North America was in the English scheme of things. Those few Britons who thought about America at all saw colonials as seedy rustics who resembled the "savage" Indians more than the "civilized" English. As a London acquaintance remarked to Thomas Hancock, it was a pity Mrs. Hancock had to remain in Boston when he could "take her to England and make her happy with Christians." Americans on the receiving end of British scorn bristled, like the Marblehead fish merchant Robert Hooper, who complained to his London agent about being cheated by an English trader. "Do tell him," Hooper fumed, "that we are not quite Indians, although living in an Indian country."

The same indifference contributed to England's haphazard administration of its colonies. The Board of Trade and Plantations, created from the Lords of Trade in 1696, remained for the rest of the colonial period the major agency monitoring American affairs. The Board gathered information about Atlantic trading and fishing, reviewed laws and petitions drawn up by colonial assemblies, and exchanged letters and instructions with royal governors. But the Board of Trade was only an advisory body, reporting to the king's ministers and passing on information to other government agencies but unable to act. The English bureaucrats who knew the most about America were not the same bureaucrats who decided on colonial policies.

Real authority over the colonies was scattered among an array of other agencies—the secretary of state for the Southern Department, the Treasury, the Admiralty Board, and the War Office. Each agency staked out its own tiny administrative area: the Treasury oversaw customs and gathered other royal revenues; the Admiralty Board enforced regulations of trade; the War Office orchestrated colonial defense. But these departments were distracted by domestic and international responsibilities; colonial affairs stood at the bottom of their agendas. Furthermore, most British officials in America seemed equally indifferent to America. While some governors, customs collectors, and other officials were honest and competent, the king and his ministers commonly passed out the plums of colonial jobs in payment for political support, not in recognition of administrative ability. That standard saddled the colonies with some choice royal officials, eager to profit

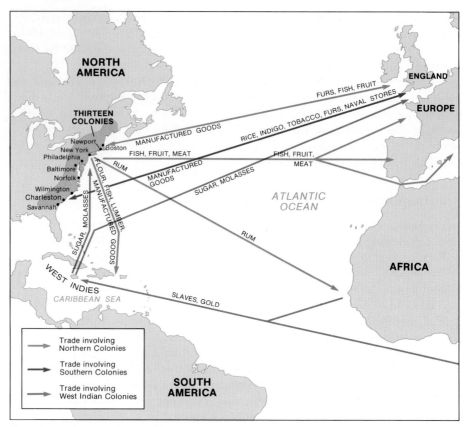

OVERSEAS TRADE NETWORKS
Commercial ties to Spain and Portugal, Africa, and the Caribbean sustained the growth of both seaports and commercial farming regions on the British North American mainland and enabled colonials to purchase an increasing volume of finished goods from England. The proceeds from exports in foodstuffs and lumber to the West Indies and trade in fish to Spain and Portugal enabled northern merchants and farmers to buy hardware and clothing from the mother country. Southern planters financed their consumption of English imports and their investment in African slaves with the profits from the sale of tobacco, rice, and indigo abroad.

from their office and then retire. Some royal appointees never even set foot in America, selling their offices to the highest bidder.

But no group in England's government was more indifferent to America than Parliament. Members were content to consign colonial affairs to the king's ministers and the executive bureaucracy. Aside from passing an occasional law to regulate trade, restrict manufacturing, or direct monetary policy, Parliament made no effort to assert its authority in America. The Lords and Commoners assumed that their sovereignty extended over the entire empire, and nothing had occurred to make them think otherwise.

In sum, England's decentralized colonial administration was chaotic, inefficient, and corrupt. And for the colonies, it worked quite well. The very weakness of imperial oversight minimized the chances for conflict and left Americans with a great deal of freedom.

Even England's regulation of trade rested lightly on the shoulders of Americans, for most colonial commerce flowed naturally into the channels prescribed by mercantilist restrictions. Southern planters were obliged to send their rice, indigo, and tobacco to Britain only, but they enjoyed favorable credit terms and experienced wholesaling from English merchants. Colonials were prohibited from finishing iron products and exporting hats and textiles, but they had no strong interest in developing domestic industries. Americans were required to import all manufactured goods through England, but by doing so, they acquired high-quality goods at low prices. At little sacrifice, Americans abided by imperial regulations: illicit trade was minimal in volume, sugar, molasses, and tea being the only commodities routinely smuggled.

Basking in benign neglect, the colonies prospered. During the eighteenth century America steadily produced more, earned more, and consumed more imported goods. American exports commanded high prices and met with steady demand. And by doing almost nothing about the colonies, England benefited as well, reaping a harvest of raw materials and a burgeoning market of ready colonial consumers. By 1770 one-third of England's total trade went to the colonies.

In this manner, the British empire muddled on to the mutual satisfaction of most people on both sides of the Atlantic. Prosperity and political autonomy allowed most Americans to like being English, despite their misgivings about the mother country. The beauty of it was that Americans could be English in America, enjoying higher birth rates, less squalid cities, more economic opportunity, greater political equality, and superior virtue. If imperial arrangements had remained as they were in 1754, the empire might have muddled on indefinitely. But because of the French and the Indians on the American frontier, the British empire began to change. And those changes made it increasingly hard for Americans to be English in America.

TOWARD THE SEVEN YEARS' WAR

In the late spring of 1754, while Benjamin Franklin dreamed of unifying Americans, a young man from Virginia dreamed of military glory. As Franklin rode toward Albany, the young man, an inexperienced, impulsive officer, led his company of Virginia militia toward Fort Duquesne, the French stronghold on the Forks of the Ohio.

Less than a year earlier, the king's ministers had advised royal governors in America to retard—by force if necessary—the French advance into the Ohio country. Virginians welcomed the order, for many leading politicians there held stock in the Ohio Company, a group of speculators who claimed hundreds of thousands of acres in the disputed territory. The Virginia government organized an expedition against Fort Duquesne, placing at its head the tall, strapping, red-haired young planter. He combined an imposing presence with the aloof self-possession of an English gentleman, and he wanted, more than anything, to become an officer in the regular British army.

But events in the Ohio country during that spring and summer did not go George Washington's way. French soldiers easily captured Fort Necessity, the crude outpost near Fort Duquesne that Washington's troops had hastily constructed. In early July, as the Albany Congress was debating, Washington was surrendering to a French force in the Pennsylvania backcountry and beating a retreat back to Virginia. By the end of 1754, Washington had resigned his militia command and retired to his plantation at Mount Vernon. His humiliation at Fort Necessity had dashed his dreams of martial glory and a regular army commission: he had no future as a soldier.

With the rout of Washington and his troops, the French grew bolder and the Indians, more restless. The renewal of war between England and France was imminent by the beginning of 1755. This time the contest between the two powers would be conclusive, the question of sovereignty over North America decided once and for all. That, at least, was the dream of William Pitt, who was about to become the most powerful man in England.

Even by the standards of English politicians, William Pitt was an odd character. Egotistical and devious, he inspired the loathing of his king, George II, and many of his colleagues. He also suffered devastating bouts of gout and depression that disabled him for months, even years, at a stretch. Yet despite his opportunism, his cold, disdainful manner, and his fragile health, Pitt always managed to recoup his political losses and return to power.

What kept Pitt alive was a strong sense of destiny—his own and that of England. His dream for England, imparted by his grandfather, "Diamond Pitt," a bloody-minded India merchant, was commercial supremacy. England must seize the world's trade, for trade meant wealth and wealth meant power. As early as the 1730s, Pitt knew that the only power in Europe that stood between England and its destiny was France—and that the balance of power in Europe would be decided in America. Deprived of Canadian timber, French planters in the West Indies would lack fuel, driving up the price of their sugar, and the French navy would lack masts, driving down their strength at sea. The entire market for manufactured goods in the New World would be lost to France. And, incidentally from Pitt's point of view, the British colonies would enjoy complete security.

During King George's War, Pitt had repeatedly mesmerized the House of Commons and the nation with his spellbinding oratory about England's imperial destiny. But troubled by the mounting cost of fighting, the government opted to accept peace with France in 1748, dismissing Pitt's proposal to mount an attack on Quebec, the key to all of Canada. In dejection and frustration Pitt retired from public life.

But while Pitt sulked in his library and nursed his gout, the rivalry for the American frontier moved toward a showdown. The French pressed their front lines eastward; the English pushed for land westward; chiefs like Hendrik maneuvered for position. Sustained by every dispatch from America, Pitt clung to his dream of English commercial dominion and French defeat. And by the late spring of 1754, as Benjamin Franklin and George Washington rode toward their defeats, William Pitt knew that he would have his war and his way.

Other dreams would wait longer for fulfillment. The Albany Congress had demonstrated that a few enlightened Americans like Franklin had seen beyond the diversity of a divided colonial world—beyond backcountry Presbyterians who quarreled with Philadelphia's Quaker pacifists, parochial Yankee Congregationalists who confined their charity to New England, and prickly Anglican gentry who projected the borders of the southern colonies to the Pacific Ocean. But it would take another war, one that restructured an empire, before some Americans saw in themselves a likeness that was not English.

SIGNIFICANT EVENTS

1636	Harvard College founded
1689–1697	King William's War (War of the League of Augsburg)
1701	Yale College founded
1702	Anne becomes queen of England
1702–1713	Queen Anne's War (War of the Spanish Succession)
1714	George I becomes king of England, beginning Hanover dynasty
1727	George II becomes king of England
1730s	Tennents' "Log College" founded (becomes College of New Jersey at Princeton in 1746)
1730s–1740s	Rise in importation of black slaves in northern colonies
1739	George Whitefield's first preaching tour in America; Stono Rebellion in South Carolina
1743	Franklin founds the American Philosophical Society
1744–1748	King George's War (War of the Austrian Succession)
1751	Franklin's essay on population
1754	The Albany Congress; Washington surrenders at Fort Necessity
1760–1769	South Carolina Regulation
1763	Paxton Boys march in Pennsylvania
1766	Tenant rebellion in New York
1766–1771	North Carolina Regulation (Battle of Alamance, 1771)

PART 2

THE CREATION OF A NEW REPUBLIC

As the shrewd Benjamin Franklin had observed in the course of his wide involvement in colonial affairs, the population of British North America was doubling approximately every 25 years. This astonishing rate was quite possibly the fastest in the world at the time. Even so, the North American surge in population was merely the most striking example of a more general global trend at work in the second half of the eighteenth century. In terms of sheer numbers, China led the way. Its population of 150 million in 1700 had doubled to over 313 million by the end of the century. African and Indian populations seem to have risen too, although historians have analyzed trends there less closely. Europe's total rose from about 118 million in 1700 to about 187 million a century later, the greatest growth coming on its eastern and western flanks, in Great Britain and Russia.

This worldwide rise, unprecedented in previous history, occurred for a variety of reasons. Climate may have been one: in Europe, at least, warmer and drier seasons produced generally better harvests.* Furthermore, health and nutrition improved globally with the spread of native American crops. Irish farmers discovered that a single acre planted with the lowly American potato could support an entire family. The tomato added crucial vitamins to the Mediterranean diet, while maize provided more calories per acre than any European or African grain. In China, the American sweet potato made great headway, being planted in hilly regions where rice would not grow.

Not only plants but diseases also were carried back and forth by European ships, and these too affected world population. As we have seen, contact between previously isolated peoples produced extreme mortality from epidemics, enabling European invaders like Hernando Cortés to conquer populous civilizations. Similarly, the Pilgrims unwittingly blessed Divine Providence for allowing them to take over deserted fields that had been cleared and farmed by Indians only recently struck down by disease. By 1800 the more globally isolated peoples—those living in Australia or on the North American plains, for instance—still remained at risk, but increased biological resistance to European and African diseases allowed the Indian and mestizo populations in Peru and Mexico to grow rapidly. The frequent circulation of diseases worldwide led to a more stable environment, in which populations began to swell.

During the same years that Europeans were explor-

*The already dry Middle East seems to have been one area whose population was not expanding, and it may have been hurt by the climate changes.

ing the Atlantic frontiers of North and South America, Slavic and Romanian pioneers were pushing eastward into the Eurasian steppes, turning sparsely settled pastoral lands into feudal manors and farms. Farther north in forested lands unsuitable for farming, Russian fur traders had crossed the Urals by 1580 and were advancing steadily eastward across the river systems of Siberia, until they reached Okhotsk on the Pacific in the 1630s. By the 1780s the advance guard of Russian pioneers (*zemleprokhodtsy*, the "crossers of land") had reached Alaska and the Pacific American coast, encountering western Europeans who had been trapping their way across the forests and streams of Canada.

Both flanks of this European thrust often depended on forced labor, especially in agricultural settings. As we have seen, the institution of slavery in North America became increasingly restrictive over the course of the seventeenth century. And the number of slaves imported to North America paled when compared with the thousands shipped by the Portuguese to the slave markets of Rio de Janeiro. Similarly, along the frontiers of eastern Europe, the plight of serfs worsened from 1500 to 1650, as empty lands were being taken up and the demand for labor increased. In 1574 Polish nobles received the right to do entirely as they pleased with their serfs—including execution, if they chose. By 1603, Russian peasants were forbidden to move from one estate to another, being routinely sold along with the land they worked; in 1649 the czar issued even more restrictive laws.

As the currents of European Enlightenment swirled along the frontier peripheries of North America during the eighteenth century, so too they penetrated eastern Europe. Russia's Peter the Great absorbed many ideas when he traveled, sometimes incognito, to England and western Europe, and he attempted to Westernize Russia during his reign (1689–1725). Even more artistically enlightened was Catherine the Great (1762–1796), who imported Western architects, sculptors, and musicians to her court at St. Petersburg. But her limits to toleration were made brutally clear in 1773. The same year that a group of rowdy Americans were dumping tea into Boston harbor, a Cossack soldier named Emelian Pugachev launched a peasant rebellion, grandly proclaiming himself emperor and issuing decrees abolishing serfdom and taxes. Serfs in the Ural and Volga river valleys flocked to his ragtag army. Catherine ruthlessly executed Pugachev and scattered his followers; in 1775 she granted Russian nobles even more absolute control over their serfs.

To make the obvious comparison—between a failed Russian revolution for liberty and the triumph of American colonials—would be somewhat smug. Liberty-loving American merchants like John Hancock and genteel tobacco planters like George Washington were hardly in the position of serfs. A more appropriate link might be made between Russian serfs and American slaves, since both groups supplied the forced labor along the frontiers of European expansion. But the slaves, whose African homelands lay thousands of miles away, found the long odds of rebellion equally as formidable as did Russian serfs. Ironically, white Americans may have been able to fight so vigorously for their liberties precisely because they had made revolt by a class of forced laborers so difficult.

Americans rebelled in 1775 not out of a serf's desperation; quite the opposite. The Seven Years' War ended in 1763 with the French being driven out of North America, the British colonists thriving thanks to a wartime boom, and American hopes high. Thomas Mayhew, a respected Boston minister, voiced the opinion of many colonials when he envisioned a glorious empire spreading across the continent in the century to come. "I do not mean an independent one," he added carefully, but in 1763 the qualification was hardly necessary. Most white Americans were quite pleased with the prospect of being English. With the significant exception of the slave class, the distance between the poorest and richest Americans was smaller than anywhere in Europe. And the British tradition of representative government ensured a broader involvement of citizens in colonial government. Thus the American Revolution was hardly inevitable in 1776—and most certainly it did not appear so in 1763. The timing of the break with Great Britain was the result of specific decisions made on both sides of the Atlantic.

America's isolated position on the periphery of European expansion certainly created conditions that made separation likely at some point. Most colonials, used to relative social equality among white Americans, blanched at what they saw as English luxury and corruption—as we have seen. English governing elites, when they bothered to notice Americans, usually found them provincial and naive. Under different circumstances, the move for independence might have come in 1800, or even 1867, as it did for Canada. But the break came earlier, and surprisingly—given the experience of the Albany Congress of 1754—ended in the creation of a new American Republic.

CHRONOLOGY

AMERICAN EVENT	YEAR		GLOBAL EVENT
	1630s		Russian fur traders reach the Pacific Coast
English found Hudson's Bay Company, rival for French fur trade	1670		
English and French increase penetration of Ohio valley	1740s–1750s		
	ca. 1750		Global population rise
Franklin publishes essay on population	1751		
	1751–1772		Denis Diderot's *Encyclopedia* published, popularizing the ideas of the Enlightenment
Albany Congress meets	1754		
French and Indian War	1754–1763		Seven Years' War
	1762		Catherine the Great becomes empress of Russia
	1763		Proclamation of 1763 issued, to contain British colonials east of the Alleghenies
	1764		Sugar Act passed, beginning British attempt to increase colonial revenues
Stamp Act protests and riots	1765		
Boston Tea Party	1773		Pugachev leads revolt of Russian peasants
American Revolution	1775–1783		
Paine's *Common Sense* published	1776		
Noah Webster publishes American spelling book	1783		
Constitutional Convention meets	1787		Wolfgang Amadeus Mozart composes *Don Giovanni*
First presidential inauguration	1789	WASHINGTON	French Revolution begins
	1797	ADAMS	
	1799		Napoleon comes to power in France
First peaceful transfer of power between rival parties	1801	JEFFERSON	
	1803		Britain and France resume war
Tecumseh organizes Pan-Indian confederacy	1809	MADISON	
Treaty of Ghent ends War of 1812	1814		Congress of Vienna meets to bring political stability to Europe
Jackson defeats British at New Orleans	1815		Napoleon defeated at Waterloo
	1817	MONROE	
	1820		King George III dies
Monroe Doctrine proclaimed	1823		
	1825	ADAMS	

5

Toward the War for American Independence

mericans liked being English. They had liked being English from the beginning of colonial settlement, and they liked it even more as time went on. But Americans most liked being English for a few golden years after 1759. One wonderful day during those golden years— September 16, 1762—Bostonians turned out to hear a sermon preached by a local minister, the Reverend Jonathan Sewall. Later that day they began to imbibe inspiration from another source, just as Puritan and almost as potent: they drank "many loyal healths" and consumed "a vast quantity of liquor." Doubly inspirited, the inhabitants of Boston savored the pageantry of a public celebration. Soldiers mustered on the Common in stirring martial display; bells pealed from the steeples of local churches; the charge of guns fired from the battery resounded through towns; strains of orchestra music from a concert floated over the city's crowded streets and narrow alleys. As daylight drifted into darkness, bonfires illuminated the city's neighborhoods. Many loyal healths later that evening, General John Winslow of Marshfield leapt onto a table and danced to the tinkle of glassware shattering on the tavern floor. But no matter. It was a day to make merry. And Winslow was a local hero, an officer who had served in the Seven Years' War.

The occasion of Boston's celebration was the Spanish surrender to British forces at Havana, Cuba. Spain's capitulation in August 1762 marked the end of the Seven Years' War, sometimes called the French and Indian War. When the great news reached the North American mainland in early fall, celebrations like the one in Boston broke out all over the colonies. But the party in America had begun long before, with a string of stellar British triumphs in French Canada in the glorious year of 1759, and it continued through 1760 when all of Canada fell to Anglo-American forces and the youthful King George III acceded to the throne of England. The revels resumed in 1762, when the British conquered all comers, and climaxed in February of 1763 with the Treaty of Paris, which formally ended the war. Britain had become the new Rome, the largest and most powerful empire in the Western world. Americans were among His Majesty's proudest subjects.

Thirteen years after the celebration of 1762, Boston was a different place. In less than a generation, deep affection for Britain had been supplanted by deadly enmity. Pride in belonging to the empire had shriveled to a shrill conviction that England conspired to enslave its colonies. Boston led the way, drawing the other colonies deep into the logic of resistance and, by 1775, into outright rebellion. Bostonians had initiated many of the colonial petitions and resolves against British authority. They had ignited the rioting, when words did not work. They had

"To have a standing army!" wrote one Bostonian in 1768. "Good God! What can be worse to a people who have tasted the sweets of liberty! Things are come to an unhappy crisis!" Paul Revere engraved this print of British redcoats arriving in Boston.

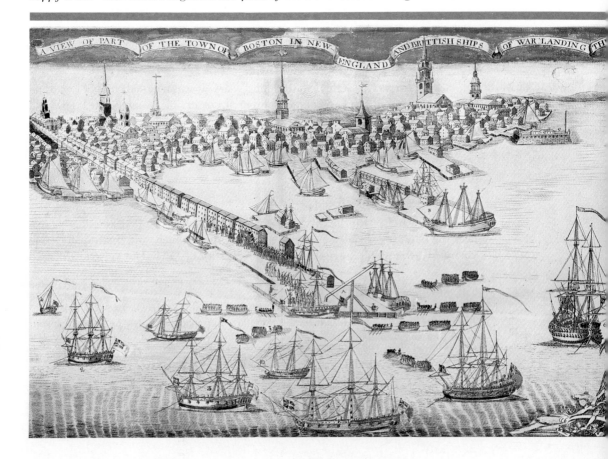

harassed British officials, baited British troops, and destroyed British property. In 1775, they were laying plans for war against the British empire.

Oddly enough, Americans, even Bostonians, still liked being English, even as they readied for war in 1775. It was only the inhabitants of England that they couldn't stand. History plays tricks of all sorts on the dead. But few twists in history are more ironic than the fate dealt that generation of Americans who loved being English. In the light of historical hindsight, they were members of a revolutionary generation, the men and women who made the war for independence. But by their own lights, they were members of a postwar generation, jealous of their rights as Britons and elated at belonging to the all-conquering empire. It was that intense pride in being British that drove Americans into rebellion. After 1763, both a long process of evolution and the individual men who ran the empire would not allow Americans to be English.

Even before the Seven Years' War, some Americans recognized that divergent courses of social and political development made them different from the English. After the Seven Years' War, events demonstrated to more Americans that they were not considered the political equals of the English who lived in England. Colonials did not accept easily the defeat of their dreams of being English. But as their disillusionment with the British empire deepened, they began to discover a new identity as Americans. As that discovery unfolded, they declared their independence from being English.

THE SEVEN YEARS' WAR

The Seven Years' War actually lasted nine years. It was a global conflict fought on four continents by the two reigning imperial powers of the eighteenth century. The struggle pitted Britain and its ally, Prussia, against France, in league with Austria and Spain. The battle raged from 1754 until 1763, and it ranged over the continent of Europe, the coast of west Africa, India, the Philippines, the Caribbean, and North America.

The Years of Defeat

The war started in the Pennsylvania backcountry after the longstanding contest over the Ohio River valley among the English, the French, and the Indians led to George Washington's surrender at Fort Necessity in 1754. The episode stiffened

THE SEVEN YEARS' WAR IN AMERICA
After Washington's surrender and Braddock's defeat in the Pennsylvania backcountry, the British and French waged their final contest for supremacy in North America in upstate New York and Canada.

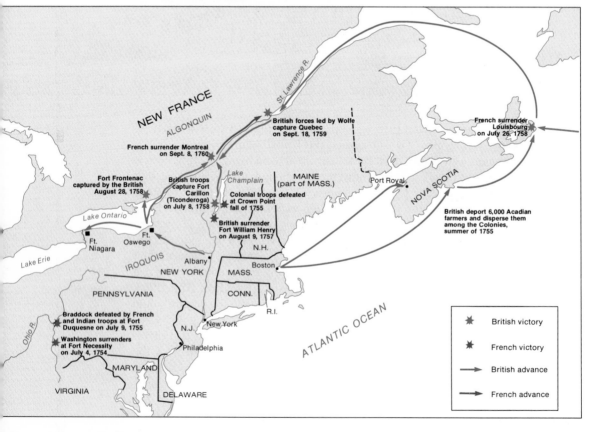

Britain's resolve to remove French encroachments along the American frontier and to assert its claims to the Ohio country. In the summer of 1755, two under-strength British regiments led by an underskilled commander, Major General Edward Braddock, slowly advanced through the densely forested backcountry toward the French outpost at Fort Duquesne on the Forks of the Ohio. On July 9, as the British approached Duquesne, they were ambushed and cut to pieces by a party of French and Indians. Washington led the mortally wounded Braddock and the remnants of his army in a retreat.

During the summer of Braddock's defeat, New Englanders fared somewhat better against the French. New England forces expelled French defenders from two small garrisons along the Nova Scotia frontier and then deported 6000 Acadian farmers. Most Acadians professed to be neutral, but their ancestors had been French; the English suspected they might be susceptible to intrigue from nearby Quebec. Their lands were confiscated, and they were dispersed throughout the colonies. Farther to the west in the fall of 1755, troops from New York and New England tried and failed to capture the French stronghold at Crown Point on Lake Champlain. The Americans got only as far as the head of Lake George when they were beset by a party of French and Indians. Colonials billed the costly but indecisive encounter as a victory and on the site of the battle built Fort William Henry.

But no amount of doubletalk could put a better face on the failures that followed for two disastrous years. When England and France formally declared war in May 1756, John Campbell, the fourth earl of Loudoun, took command of the North American theater. Loudoun insisted on personal command over provincial troops in all of the colonies, as well as sufficient money and men on demand from colonial assemblies. Provincial soldiers and civilian leaders alike hated Lord Loudoun. They balked at his efforts to centralize control over the military and dragged their heels at his demands for troops and supplies.

Meanwhile, the French moved to strengthen their position in Canada, appointing a new commanding general, Louis Joseph, the marquis de Montcalm. Montcalm immediately smashed British defenses at Fort Oswego on the southern shore of Lake Ontario, plunging New Yorkers into a panic. Then he snuffed out American hopes to advance up Lake Champlain, by fortifying French strength on its southern end with Fort Carillon. From Carillon Montcalm pressed south toward Lake George and laid siege to Fort William Henry. Its British defenders surrendered in August 1757, after just six days, alarming New Englanders. While Montcalm prospered in North America, the British and their Prussian allies were taking a beating from the French in Europe and in India as well. The lethal combination of Loudoun's ineptitude and Montcalm's daring brought the American war effort almost to a standstill by the end of 1757.

During the years when the French juggernaut seemed unstoppable, Americans looked for help from the strongest tribes of the interior—the Iroquois in the North, the Creek, Choctaw, and Cherokee in the South. Instead, Benjamin Franklin's worst fears were realized: most tribes adopted neutrality or joined the French. After Braddock's defeat in 1755, Indian raiders set ablaze English frontier settlements from New England to Georgia. Over the next three years, as France seemed certain to carry the continent, the attacks mounted in intensity.

The Years of Victory

As the news of the war worsened throughout 1756 and 1757, in England the political fortunes of William Pitt improved. By 1758 Pitt had ended his retirement, maneuvered himself into the head of the ministry, and assumed personal control over the war, "I know that I can save this country and that no one else can," he declared. Whatever his weaknesses may have been, Pitt was a great war minister. He knew exactly how to handle the French. Leaving the fighting in Europe to the Prussians, Pitt lobbed the mortar of British muscle at North America, mobilizing the British army and navy as well as American troops for an amphibious assault against the French fortress at Louisbourg. He dispatched other naval squadrons to blockade France itself, cutting off the lifeline to Canada.

Pitt also knew just how to handle the Americans. He recalled Lord Loudoun, replaced him with James Abercromby, a new commander who had far more limited authority over colonial troops, and sent new requests for men and money directly to each colonial assembly—accompanied by promises of reimbursement in gold and silver. Americans, who found the combination of political and military autonomy and real money irresistible, renewed their enthusiasm for the war effort.

France enjoyed its last victory on North American soil in July 1758, when Montcalm beat back a British assault on Fort Carillon. Less than three weeks later, the British seized control of the St. Lawrence when Louisbourg fell before the combined force of the Royal Navy, the British regular army, and provincial troops led by Lord Jeffrey Amherst. In August of 1758, Lieutenant Colonel John Bradstreet and a force of New England volunteers strangled France's frontier defenses by capturing Fort Frontenac on the northeast shore of Lake Ontario at the western end of the St. Lawrence. The fall of Frontenac left isolated and indefensible Forts Niagara and Detroit on the Great Lakes and the chain of posts lining the Ohio valley. By the end of 1758, the French had been routed in the interior and abandoned by their Iroquois allies. The Indians, seeing the turning tide of the battle, switched their allegiance back to the English. Anglo-American troops, George Washington among them, even claimed Fort Duquesne, the site of Braddock's defeat, renaming it Pittsburgh.

The British succeeded even more brilliantly in 1759. During July of that year, forces under Amherst pushed the French first from Fort Carillon, renamed Ticonderoga, and then from Crown Point. Meanwhile, more than 200 miles to the north, Brigadier General James Wolfe was proceeding more impulsively. As soon as the spring ice had melted, Wolfe sailed up the St. Lawrence with 9000 men and waited outside the walls of Quebec. Within lay Montcalm and his army. Months passed, and Quebec towered still secure atop a well-fortified palisade. On September 13, Wolfe gambled and won, decoying and splitting French defenses with a daring and dangerous stratagem. Naval squadrons landed Wolfe's men beneath a steep path leading up the bluff to Quebec. They scaled the heights to a plateau known as the Plains of Abraham. Montcalm might have won by holding out behind the walls of his fortress and awaiting reinforcements, but he matched Wolfe's recklessness and offered battle instead. Five days later both Wolfe and Montcalm lay dead, along with 1400 French soldiers and 600 British and American troops. Quebec had fallen.

The tide of war turned toward Britain in other theaters as well during 1759. John Clive routed the French in India; English offensives captured French sugar islands in the Caribbean and French trading posts in Africa; the British navy destroyed its rival's fleet when the French attempted to break the blockade; the Prussians, subsidized by Pitt, held their own in Europe.

The campaigns of 1760 ended the fighting in North America. Three branches

Executing General Wolfe's daring strategy, British soldiers climb the cliffs to the Plains of Abraham, laying siege to the city. The fall of Quebec in 1759 presaged the end of France's empire in North America.

of the Anglo-American army closed in on Montreal. The city and its surrounding territory were defenseless, with enemy forces in control of Louisbourg, the major strategic points on the St. Lawrence, Frontenac and Quebec, and Crown Point and Lake Champlain. On September 8, the governor general of New France surrendered, and New France was no more.

Elsewhere in the world, the war was also winding down—much to the dismay of William Pitt. He wanted to press the British advantage by attacking Spain's colonial possessions. But the new king of England, George III, liked Pitt even less than had his grandfather, George II. The king also worried over the expense of the war—the mounting national debt and high taxes. When George III refused to carry the struggle to Spain, Pitt resigned in protest. Spain vindicated Pitt by entering the war on the side of France in 1762, and intermittent conflict continued until the British subdued Manila in the Philippines and Havana a few months later, bringing the Spanish to the bargaining table.

The Treaty of Paris, signed in February 1763, ended the French presence on the continent of North America. The terms confirmed British title to all French territory east of the Mississippi as well as to Spanish Florida. France ceded to its ally Spain all of its land lying west of the Mississippi and the port of New Orleans. Despite Britain's overwhelming victory, France retained and regained some valuable colonial possessions and commercial rights—its sugar islands in the West Indies, its trading posts and slave stations in west Africa, and its factories and warehouses in India. Britain's generosity to its defeated rival was the doing of Pitt's replacement as first minister, Lord Bute, who believed that England's future security lay in balancing power among European nations.

The peace made at Paris was welcomed by most war-weary Britons, but it did not please everyone. "Like the peace of God," jeered the English radical John

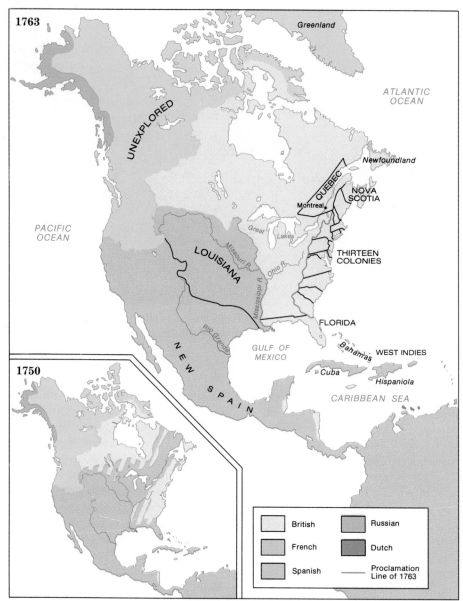

EUROPEAN CLAIMS IN NORTH AMERICA, 1750 AND 1763
The British victory in the Seven Years' War secured their title to a large portion of the present-day United States and Canada. While colonials hoped to settle the newly won territory, statesmen in London intended to restrict westward movment with the Proclamation of 1763.

Wilkes, "it passeth all understanding." And the concessions to French commerce disgusted Pitt, dashing his dreams of undisputed dominion for British trade. Crippled by gout, exhausted, and almost incapable of speech, he roused himself to denounce the treaty before the House of Commons: "We retain nothing although we have conquered everything."

Postwar Expectations

While Pitt fumed, the colonies overflowed with great expectations. The end of the war, they were sure, meant the end of high taxes. The terms of the peace, they were confident, meant the opening of the Ohio valley's limitless tracts of fertile land. It was certainly the start of an era of security and prosperity—and to some Americans, nothing less than the dawning of the millennium. In a sermon much like the one Jonathan Sewall gave during the bonfires and celebrations of 1762, the Reverend Thomas Barnard told his congregation in Salem, Massachusetts,

> Now commences the Aera of our quiet Enjoyment of those Liberties. . . . Safe from the Enemy of the wilderness. . . . Here shall be the late founded Seat of Peace and Freedom. Here shall our indulgent Mother, who has most generously rescued and protected us, be served and honoured with Growing Numbers, with all Duty, Love, and Gratitude till Time shall be no more.

The prosperity of the war years alone made for a mood of optimism. British military spending and Pitt's subsidies had created a boomlet for farmers, merchants, artisans, and anyone else who had anything to do with supplying the army or navy. Provincials also took pride in their contributions to the winning of the war. Only a few colonies had withheld appropriations altogether. The rest, led by Virginia and Massachusetts, raised an average of 20,000 troops every year until 1762 and despite Pitt's subsidies, paid about half of the cost themselves. And although the British regular army had shouldered much of the actual fighting, the provincial irregular troops had participated in most major engagements.

Even more impressive to Americans than their own contributions to the struggle were the blood and treasure expended by England in defense of the colonies. In global terms, William Pitt cared relatively little about securing the American frontier, but that did not stop colonials from flattering themselves on their importance to the empire. William Smith, Jr., a New York lawyer, was confident that Britain's wealth and power had been "vastly enhanced since the Discovery of the New World." A fellow colonial waxed even more self-congratulatory, contending that without America's trade, "the people in Britain would make but a poor figure, if they could even subsist as an independent nation." Postwar Americans fully expected to be accorded more consideration within the British empire, a larger and more equal status. Now, as one anonymous pamphleteer put it, Americans would "not be thought presumptuous, if they consider[ed] themselves upon an equal footing" with English in the parent country.

If Americans took pride in being British, most English officials in America thought that they had done a poor job, during the war, of showing it. Many complained that local assemblies had been downright niggardly in supporting the fighting. Although the American contribution was actually substantial, the version of their role put forward, predictably, by Lord Loudoun was the one that stuck in the minds of Britons back home. Colonial legislators, he charged, "assumed to themselves what they call Rights and Privileges . . . to screen them, from giving any Aid." British commanders also heaped abuse on provincial troops. Wolfe, considered by Americans a demigod of martial valor, had not returned the compliment. Before meeting his end at Quebec he had remarked that "the Americans are in general the dirtiest, most contemptible, most cowardly dogs that you can conceive."

What enraged British officials more than Americans' lack of generosity or bravery was their determination to turn a profit from the war. Customs officials and royal governors reported a sharp rise in violations of the Navigation Acts, alleging that there was "scarce a man in all that country who was not concerned in the smuggling trade." The worst of it was the insouciance of American merchants and mariners. Caught redhanded with contraband tea from the neutral Dutch and even illegal molasses from the enemy French, the smugglers coolly explained that their illicit trade helped to pay for the fighting!

The British on the scene concluded that the Americans were selfish and self-interested, unconcerned with the welfare of the empire as a whole. In the defense of the colonies, Britain had accumulated a huge national debt that would saddle the nation with high taxes for years to come. And they were repaid with American ingratitude—or perhaps even worse. With the French finally removed from North America, some Britons suspected that colonials would make a bid for independence. As early as 1755, Josiah Tucker, a respected English political economist, had warned that "to drive the French out of all North America would be the most fatal step we could take." Ironically, independence entered the calculations of some people in England long before it was ever considered by Americans.

What might prevent or at least forestall independence, the British recognized, was the depth of intercolonial division. In fact, the few leaders who gave any thought at all to America counted on continuing disunity to diffuse any sentiment for independence. Yet the rivalries over western land and local quarrels also promoted an instability that threatened the British presence in North America. The more observant English worried about what Americans, especially those on the frontier, might do to each other and to the Indians.

Americans in 1763 were not revolutionaries-in-the-making. They were patriotic British subjects of the postwar generation. Americans in 1763, deeply divided among themselves, were not even "Americans." But most postwar English colonials expected to enjoy a greater and more equal status in the empire. And most Britons had no inclination to accord them that influence. The differing expectations of the colonies' place in the empire poised the postwar generation for crisis. A conflict was not inevitable, but it came in the course of human events.

THE IMPERIAL CRISIS

It was common sense. Great Britain had waged a long and costly war to secure its empire in America; it needed now to consolidate its gains. Whatever the deficiencies of Americans in English eyes, the value of their land, labor, and trade contributed greatly to the wealth of England. The empire's North American territory required adequate protection, its administration needed centralization and tightening, and its colonies had to be made as profitable as possible to the parent nation. The decision to centralize the empire dictated the British decision to leave several thousand troops in America after the Seven Years' War. The British army would prevent France from trying to regain its lost territory. Maintaining a military presence would also ensure the submission of the non-English inhabitants in the newly conquered provinces—the French in Canada, the Spanish in Florida.

New Troubles on the Frontier

Keeping troops in North America made sense because of the Indians, too. The fall of New France made native Americans restless. They knew that with the removal of the French from the West, English traders, speculators, and settlers would swarm into the region. The Indians also knew that without the French as trading partners, the tribes were in a weaker position to resist white incursions. No longer could they play the French off against the British to gain favorable trading terms. No longer could they count on a steady supply of arms and ammunition from European rivals competing for their furs. Many tribes had hoped to preserve the balance of power among Europeans by throwing their support to the French during the Seven Years' War—until English victory became imminent. Now, with the French gone, the Indians were edgy, expecting the worst, and the British were worried.

Even as Anglo-American forces, joined by the Iroquois, fought to victory in Canada, the Cherokees had started terrorizing backcountry settlements in South Carolina. The Cherokee War raged until 1761, when troops under Amherst crushed the Indian insurgents. Deprived of French guns, shot, and powder, the Cherokee cause was doomed to defeat. Only an alliance with the other Indian power of the southern interior, the Creeks, could have turned the tide of battle toward the Cherokees. But the Creeks had long memories: the Cherokees had refused to come to their assistance earlier, during the Yamasee War of 1715. Now it was the Creeks who stayed on the sidelines, forcing the Cherokees to submit to a peace treaty in 1761. Despite the Cherokee surrender, the British believed that it was only a matter of time before colonials blundered into another Indian war.

Events bore out British fears. In the early 1760s, a Lenni Lenape prophet, Neolin, began advising the tribes to return to their ancient ways and resist the spread of white settlement. Pontiac, an Ottawa chief, embraced Neolin's message of renaissance and rebellion. In May 1763 he organized an attack on Fort Detroit, a British outpost on the Great Lakes. Other tribes joined Pontiac's offensive—the Shawnee, Chippewa, Huron, Lenni Lenape, Miami, Potawatomi, and Seneca. Throughout the summer of 1763, as the defenders of Detroit held out, the Indians captured all of the other British outposts west of Pittsburgh. British troops and American militia finally smothered Pontiac's Rebellion, as shortages of supplies again forced the tribes to terms. But deadly skirmishing bled backcountry settlements in Pennsylvania, Maryland, and Virginia until the end of 1764.

After the outbreak of Pontiac's Rebellion, British policymakers found another use for troops in America—to enforce the newly issued Proclamation of 1763. This order, issued by the administration's Board of Trade, prohibited white settlement past the crest of the Appalachian Mountains. Restricting westward movement might mollify Indian fears, the British hoped, and so preclude future conflicts. It might also keep the combustible colonials confined to the seaboard, where they were more easily subject to the control of colonial administrators. It might even encourage Americans to settle in the new territories of Nova Scotia and Florida, diluting the strength of potentially disloyal French and Spanish inhabitants.

George Grenville's New Measures

A final reason for keeping troops in the colonies occurred to the British by 1764: an armed presence could encourage American compliance with other new and equally sensible measures for tightening the empire. Those new measures were the solutions of George Grenville, the First Lord of the Treasury, to the fiscal problems confronting England after the Seven Years' War.

Britain's national debt had doubled in the decade after 1754, and adding to that burden was the drain of supporting troops in the colonies. Grenville recognized that English taxpayers alone could not shoulder the costs of winning and maintaining an empire: heavy taxes and a postwar trade recession were already triggering sporadic protests among hard-pressed Britons. Americans, by contrast, paid comparatively low taxes to their colonial governments and little in trade duties. Indeed, Grenville discovered that the colonial customs service paid out four times more in salaries to its collectors than it gathered in duties, operating at a net loss of 6000 pounds sterling every year. The returns from customs were negligible, because Americans systematically evaded the Molasses Act of 1733.

The Molasses Act imposed a hefty duty of six pence on every gallon of molasses imported from the French and Dutch sugar islands. Parliament had designed that tariff to encourage colonists to consume more British molasses, which carried a higher price but came duty-free. But New England merchants, who distilled molasses into rum and then traded it to the southern colonies and to west Africa, claimed that the British sugar islands could not keep pace with the demands of their distilleries. Regrettably, the merchants were compelled to import more molasses from the French and Dutch. More regrettably, to keep their costs low and the price of their rum competitive, they were compelled to bribe customs officials. With the going rate for bribes ranging from a halfpenny to a penny and a half per gallon, the entire arrangement offered a substantial break to merchants and a tidy sum for customs inspectors. Highly regrettable; highly profitable.

George Grenville reasoned that if Americans could pay out a little under the table to protect an illicit trade, they would willingly pay a little more to go legitimate. Parliament agreed and in April 1764 passed the Revenue Act, commonly called the Sugar Act. On the face of it, Americans benefited because the act lowered the duty on foreign molasses to three pence a gallon. But this time Grenville intended to enforce the duty and to crack down on American smugglers. The Sugar Act required shipmasters to submit elaborate papers enumerating every item in their cargoes when entering or clearing colonial ports. Even common sailors had to declare the contents of their sea chests. Those caught on the wrong side of the law were to be tried in admiralty courts, where verdicts were handed down by royally appointed judges—not juries of Americans more likely to sympathize with their fellow citizens than to convict.

By tightening customs enforcement, Grenville hoped to realize a more substantial revenue from the American trade. His were modest aims: he did not expect Americans to help reduce England's national debt or even to defray the entire cost of their defense. To meet his objectives, Grenville made other modest proposals, all approved by Parliament. In the same month as the Sugar Act was passed, Parliament also approved the Currency Act, which prohibited the colonies from making their paper money legal tender. That prevented Americans from paying their debts to British traders in currency that had fallen to less than its face value. Then there was the Quartering Act, passed in May 1765, which obliged any colony in which troops were stationed to provide them with suitable accommodations. That contributed to the cost of keeping British forces in America. And a few months earlier, in March 1765, Parliament had passed the Stamp Act.

The Stamp Act placed taxes on legal documents, customs papers, newspa-

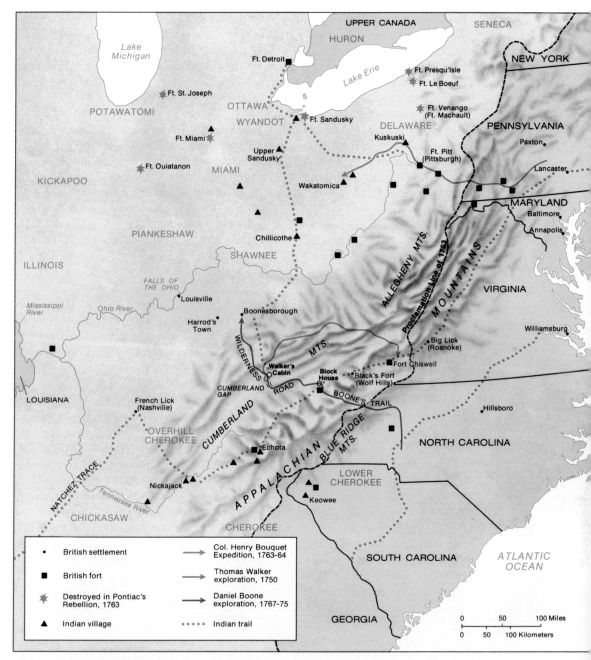

THE APPALACHIAN FRONTIER, 1750–1775

Made bold by the presence of British forts and soldiers, land-hungry colonials spilled into the west through the Cumberland Gap, a notch in the chain of mountains stretching the length of the North American interior. Only Indians and some white hunters knew of the Cumberland Gap before it was scouted in 1750 by Dr. Thomas Walker and a party of Virginians on behalf of a company of land speculators. In 1763, Indians led by Pontiac seized eight British forts before troops under Colonel Henry Bouquet stopped the offensive at Bushy Run, Pennsylvania. In 1775 Daniel Boone took the first large party of pioneers through the Cumberland Gap and established a fort at Boonesborough in present-day Kentucky.

pers, almanacs, college diplomas, playing cards, and dice. After November 1, 1765, all these items had to bear a stamp signifying that their possessor had paid the tax. Violators of the Stamp Act, like those infringing the Sugar Act, were to be tried without juries in admiralty courts. The English had been paying a similar tax for nearly a century, so it seemed to Grenville and Parliament that Americans could have no objections, especially since the revenues raised would help to pay for American defense.

Every packet boat from London that brought Americans news of another one of Grenville's measures dampened postwar optimism. For all of the real differences between the colonies and England, Americans still held much in common with the English, including definite ideas about why the British constitution, British customs, and British history all served to protect liberty and the rights of the empire's free-born citizens. And for that reason, the new measures, which seemed like common sense to Grenville and Parliament, did not make sense to Americans.

The Beginning of American Resistance

Like the English, Americans feared and mistrusted standing armies. They were familiar with a classic pamphlet, *An Argument, Shewing, that a Standing Army Is Inconsistent with a Free Government* (1697), by John Trenchard, one of the English Opposition politicians to whom Americans paid such close heed. Trenchard, and others like him, had pointed out that an army unchecked by firm civilian control could all too easily use its power to reduce citizens to slavery, as the Turkish empire and other "despotic kingdoms" demonstrated. And while English redcoats were hardly Turkish mercenaries, Americans did not take kindly to any sort of army standing between them and the coveted lands to the west.

Like the English, Americans believed that they should be taxed only by assemblies of their representatives. Like the English, Americans adhered to the axiom laid down by the liberal philosopher John Locke: property guaranteed liberty. Property, in this view, was not merely real estate, or wealth, or material possessions; it was the source of strength for every individual, providing the freedom to act, to live according to one's own lights, as one pleased. Protecting the individual's right or property was the principal responsibility of government, for if personal property was not sacred, then neither was personal liberty. The obvious corollary in this equation of power and liberty was that no people should be taxed without their consent or that of their elected representatives. The power to tax was the power to deprive a person of property; therefore, it was the power to destroy. Yet both the Sugar Act and the Stamp Act were taxes passed by members of Parliament, none of whom had been elected by colonials.

Finally, Americans, like the English, prized the right of trial by jury as one of their basic constitutional liberties. Yet both the Sugar Act and the Stamp Act would prosecute offenders in the admiralty courts, not through the duly constituted local courts. The acts thus deprived colonials of the freedom claimed by all other English men and women.

In sum, Grenville's new measures implied that Americans were not the political equals of the English living in England. They were not entitled to protection from standing armies, to taxation by consent, or to trial by jury. The psychological impact on Americans was devastating. The sting of British social snobbery, always a sore point among provincial visitors to London, now assumed a more ominous political cast. To be treated like second-class citizens wounded Americans' pride and mocked their postwar expectations. George Grenville had reduced colonials to political nonentities. The great dreams of the role that the colonies would play in the British empire evaporated, leaving behind the bitter dregs of disappointment. And after the passage of the Stamp Act, dismay mushroomed into militant protest.

Britain's determination to centralize its empire after 1763 was a disaster of timing, not just psychologically but also economically. By then, Americans were in the throes of a recession. The boom produced in the colonies by government spending during the war had collapsed once subsidies were withdrawn. American merchants were left with full stocks of imported goods gathering dust on their shelves; farmers lost the brisk and lucrative market of the army.

American response to the Sugar Act reflected a preoccupation with painful postwar readjustments. New England merchants led the opposition, objecting to the Sugar Act principally on economic grounds. They contended that enforcing a lower duty on foreign molasses would ruin the rum trade, a cornerstone of the suddenly shaky colonial economy. But with the passage of the Stamp Act, the terms of the imperial debate widened, and resistance within all of the colonies intensified.

The Stamp Act hit all Americans, not just New England merchants. It laid a levy on anyone who made a will, filed a deed, traded out of a colonial port, bought a newspaper, consulted an almanac, graduated from college, took a chance at dice, or played cards. More important, the Stamp Act represented the first outright attempt by Parliament to tax the colonies directly. In the past, Parliament had passed legislation affecting the colonies and had regulated their trade. These regulations often amounted to a kind of indirect tax: the Sugar Act raised revenues at the same time that its tariff regulated trade, and the Quartering Act also required an outlay of public funds. But the Stamp Act served notice that Parliament possessed the rightful authority to raise a revenue by directly taxing the colonials.

That assertion provoked an unprecedented development: the first display of American unity. A nearly unanimous chorus of outrage greeted Parliament's claim that it could tax the colonies. During the spring and summer of 1765, American assemblies passed resolves denying Parliament that authority. The right to tax Americans belonged to colonial assemblies alone, they argued, by the law of nature and the liberties guaranteed in charters and in the British constitution.

Virginia's assembly, the House of Burgesses, took the lead in protesting the Stamp Act, prodded by Patrick Henry. Just 29 years old in 1765, Henry had tried his hand at planting in western Virginia before recognizing his real talent—demagoguery. Blessed with the eloquence of an evangelical preacher, the dashing charm of a southern cavalier, and a mind uncluttered by much learning, Henry parlayed his popularity as a fast-talking lawyer into a place among the Burgesses. He took his seat just 10 days before introducing the Virginia Resolves against the Stamp Act. Although Henry's heated attack on Parliament's authority alienated some of the older Burgesses, his defiant rhetoric stirred the blood of younger members. It also aroused the admiration of another westerner, a gangly young law student with political ambitions who watched the debate over the Stamp Act from the back of the chamber. His name was Thomas Jefferson.

The Burgesses passed Henry's resolutions upholding their exclusive right to tax Virginians. But they stopped short of adopting those that called for outright resistance to the Stamp Act. When news of Virginia's stand spread to the rest of

Visual imagery brought home the urgency of resistance to Americans who could not read political pamphlets or radical newspapers. This detail from an engraving by Paul Revere includes a liberty tree, from which is hung an effigy of the Boston stamp distributor, and a beast busily destroying the Magna Carta while trampling American colonials. The date on the tree, August 14, 1765, marked the first Stamp Act riot in Boston.

the colonies, other assemblies followed suit, affirming that the sole right to tax Americans resided in their elected representatives. In October 1765, delegates from nine colonies convened in New York, where they prepared a joint statement of the American position and petitioned the king and Parliament to repeal both the Sugar Act and the Stamp Act.

Meanwhile, American political leaders turned to the press to arouse popular opposition to the Stamp Act. Disposed by the writings of the English Opposition to think of politics in conspiratorial terms, they warned that Grenville and the king's other ministers schemed to deprive the colonies of their liberties by unlawfully taxing their property. The Stamp Act was only the first step in a sinister design to impoverish and then to enslave Americans. Whether or not dark fears of a ministerial conspiracy haunted most Americans in 1765, many resisted the Stamp Act. The merchants of Boston, New York, and Philadelphia agreed to stop the importation of English goods to pressure British traders to lobby for repeal. In every colony, organizations emerged to ensure that the Stamp Act, if not repealed, would never be enforced.

The new extralegal resistance groups, which styled themselves the "Sons of Liberty," consisted of traders, lawyers, and prosperous artisans. With great success, they mobilized the middling and lower ranks of seaport society in opposition to the Stamp Act. In every colonial city, crowds of sailors, dockworkers, poor artisans, apprentices, and servants burnt the stamp distributors in effigy, insulted them on the streets, demolished their offices, and attacked their homes. One hot night in August 1765, a mob went further than the Sons of Liberty had planned. They set on the stately mansion of Thomas Hutchinson, the unpopular lieutenant governor of Massachusetts and the brother-in-law of the colony's stamp distributor, looting and all but leveling the place by morning. Committed to a resistance in the name of protecting private property, the Sons of Liberty afterward took care to keep crowds under tighter control. In most cases, the mere show of popular force sufficed: by the first of November, the day that the Stamp Act took effect, all of the stamp distributors had resigned.

As American port dwellers rioted and colonial assemblies resolved, a reprieve from the Stamp Act was already in the works back in England. The man who came—inadvertently—to America's relief was none other than George III. The young king was a good man, industrious and devoted to the empire, but he was also immature and not overendowed with intellect. Unfortunately, George knew his limitations, and the anxiety that he was unequal to his great responsibilities compounded his emotional instability. These insecurities made the young king an irksome master, and he ran through ministers as rapidly as his father Frederick had run through mistresses. By the end of 1765, George had dismissed Grenville for reasons unrelated to the uproar in America and appointed a new first minister, the marquis of Rockingham. Rockingham had opposed the Stamp Act from the outset, and he had no desire to enforce it. He received support from London merchants, who were beginning to feel the pinch of the colonists' nonimportation campaign and so pushed for repeal. Although Parliament was prepared to stand by the Stamp Act, especially after hearing reports of rioting and insolent colonial resolves from across the Atlantic, Rockingham and his merchant allies secured repeal in March 1766.

When news of the Stamp Act's demise reached America in May, jubilant celebrations erupted throughout the colonies. As fireworks and rockets soared over seaports, repeal restored to some Americans their earlier optimism. In truth, celebrations were not in order: the Stamp Act crisis did not augur well for the future of imperial relations. It had decided nothing about the extent of Parliament's authority in America, and it had demonstrated dramatically to Americans just how similar in political outlook they were to one another and just how different they were from the British.

Americans had found that they shared the same assumptions about the meaning of representation. To counter colonial objections to the Stamp Act, Grenville and his supporters had claimed that Americans *were* represented in Parliament, even though they had elected none of its members. Americans were virtually represented, Grenville insisted, for each member of Parliament stood for the interests of the whole empire, not just those of the particular constituency that had elected him.

Americans could see no virtue in virtual representation, and they rejected the British view that divorced representation from direct election. The newly recognized American consensus was that colonials could be truly represented only by those whom they had actually elected. Their view, known as actual representation, emphasized that elected officials were directly responsible for their constituents.

Americans also had discovered that they agreed about the extent of Parliament's authority over the colonies: it stopped at the right to tax. Colonials did not contend that Parliament had no authority over them; they readily conceded its right to legislate and to regulate trade for the good of the whole empire. But taxation, in the American view, was no part of the power to pass laws or to regulate trade: taxation was the free gift of the people through their representatives.

Members of Parliament were not amused by the American assessment of their rightful power. They brushed aside colonial petitions and resolves, all but ignoring their constitutional argument. To make its authority perfectly clear, Parliament accompanied the repeal of the Stamp Act with a Declaratory Act, asserting that it had the power to make laws for the colonies "in all cases whatsoever." But the Declaratory Act clarified nothing: did Parliament understand the power of legislation to include the power of taxation?

Daily Lives

POLITICAL CULTURE

The Rituals of Revolutionary Protest

On the first night of November 1765, the city of New York glowed with unaccustomed light. The Stamp Act was to have taken effect on that date, but the colony's stampmaster had long since resigned his office. What had frightened him into resignation could be seen in the ominous moving shadows of men, women, and children, hundreds of them. The flaring torches and flickering candles that they carried aloft through the city's crooked streets cast on storefronts and doorways dark images of a crowd protesting the "death of Liberty."

Bringing up the rear of the procession was a seaman, bearing atop his head an old chair in which was seated a paper effigy. It represented Cadwallader Colden, "the most hated man in the province" and—as New York's temporary governor—the local representative of British authority. The crowd marched to the center of town, shouting insults at Colden's figure and peppering it with pistol shots. When some of the marchers decided that their effigy should evoke the Roman Catholic pope, the chief symbol of arbitrary power to colonial Americans, they broke into Colden's stable and appropriated his fine coach for a proper papal throne. A second group joined the crowd, bearing their own carefully designed piece of portable political theater—a gallows illuminated with two lanterns. Hanging from the gallows were effigies of Colden and the devil, the "grand Deceiver of Mankind." The entire assembly climaxed the evening by burning the effigies in a bonfire and then vandalizing homes of several Stamp Act supporters.

Similar protests had been staged throughout the colonies, in major seaports and small hamlets, following Boston's rioting against the Stamp Act. Some crowds held mock trials of local stampmasters or unpopular British officials and then tarred and feathered, beat, hung, or burned their effigies. Other crowds enacted mock funerals, parading effigies in carts or coffins to the accompaniment of tolling church bells. Despite local variations, certain symbols appeared repeatedly: devils and gallows, lanterns and the paraphernalia of papal authority. And virtually every town that protested the Stamp Act acquired in the process another political symbol, the "liberty tree." Whether a living tree or a rough-hewn pole, the liberty tree became the center of protests and celebrations, bedecked with lanterns or adorned with flagstaffs used to signal meetings of the local Sons of Liberty. Townsfolk gathered under liberty trees to protest measures like the Townshend duties and the Tea Act, to intimidate loyalists and customs informers with mock trials, and to mark the anniversaries of events like the Boston Massacre.

The frequency and the political focus of this rioting were new to the decade preceding the Revolution. Still, the actions taken resembled those of earlier colonial crowds in their direction and restraint. Previous protests against merchants who hoarded goods, houses of prostitution, or supporters of smallpox inoculation had not been spontaneous, uncontrolled outbursts of popular passion. Crowds chose their targets and their tactics carefully and then carried out the communal will with a minimum of violence and destruction.

Equally striking, the resistance after 1765 drew on rituals and symbols surrounding traditional forms of protest, pun-

Daily Lives

A Pope's Day parade in mid-eighteenth-century Boston. Boys dressed as the devil's imps accompany a cart bearing an effigy of the pope.

ishment, and celebration. For centuries before the Revolution, for example, crowds on both sides of the Atlantic had meted out to prostitutes, adulterers, or henpecked husbands punishments known in England as "rough music." That ritualized round of humiliation and abuse included tarring and feathering or placing around the neck of the malefactor a halter with a placard naming his or her crime. The targets of rough music were also ridden "skimmington": placed on the back of a donkey, pelted with mud and dung, and driven out of town to the accompaniment of hooting laughter and beating drums.

An even more important inspiration for resistance rituals came from Pope's Day, an elaborate annual celebration of anti-Catholic sentiment which started in Boston early in the eighteenth century. Craftworkers and apprentices from both the North End and South End of town fashioned a cart bearing a lantern, effigies of the pope and the devil, and signs reading "The devil take the pope" and "North [or South] End Forever." Local boys with blackened faces and jester's caps played the part of the "devil's imps," taunting the

pope's effigy as laboring people from both ends of town paraded their carts through the streets. Each group tried to destroy the other's creation before the final bonfire at the end of the evening.

As Americans appropriated the symbols of the past for their rituals of political resistance, their borrowing took an odd twist. Pope's Day, the ritual prototype for later protests, was in fact a colonial adaptation of an English celebration of monarchy, Guy Fawkes Day. In 1605 Fawkes, a Catholic, had been foiled in his attempt to assassinate James I, a failure that the English annually commemorated with a parade ending with burning the conspirator in effigy. In colonial America an effigy of the pope took the place of the Catholic Fawkes; in resistance rituals after 1765 hated British officials took the place of the pope. Beginning in 1776 Americans celebrated public readings of the Declaration of Independence by parading, burning, and burying effigies of George III. Strangely enough, Americans had converted symbols and ceremonies designed to honor monarchy to represent the ritualized killing of a king.

The Townshend Acts

In the summer of 1766, George III—again inadvertently—gave Americans what should have been an advantage by changing ministers again. The king replaced Rockingham with William Pitt. Suddenly popular with his king, Pitt was doubly the darling of the Americans for his prosecution of the Seven Years' War and his opposition to the Stamp Act. Almost alone among British politicians, Pitt had grasped and agreed with the colonists' constitutional objections to taxation.

During the debate over repeal of the Stamp Act, Pitt rose in the House of Commons to affirm that Parliament's sovereignty over the colonies notwithstanding, Americans possessed all the rights of English citizens. Those rights included being taxed only by their representatives. Grenville's application of virtual representation to the colonies Pitt dismissed as "the most contemptible idea that ever entered into the head of man." America's spirited opposition to the Stamp Act drew Pitt's admiration, and he warned Parliament of the perils of threatening colonial liberties: "America, if she fell, would fall like a strong man. She would embrace the pillars of the state and pull down the constitution along with her." Grenville rose to defend his modest proposals: "Tell me when the colonies were emancipated?" he asked. "I desire to know when they were made slaves!" Pitt shot back.

If the man who believed that Americans were "the sons not the bastards of England" had been well enough to govern, matters between Great Britain and the colonies might have turned out differently. But almost immediately after Pitt took office, his health collapsed, and he went into seclusion. Power passed into the hands of Charles Townshend, the brilliant but erratic Chancellor of the Exchequer.

Unlike Pitt, Townshend had little understanding of the colonies and even less comprehension of their constitutional objections to taxation. His twin concerns were to strengthen the authority of Parliament and the power of royal officials in the colonies at the expense of American assemblies and to raise more revenue at the expense of American taxpayers. In 1767, he persuaded Parliament to tax the lead, paint, paper, glass, and tea that Americans imported from Britain.

To clip the wings of colonial assemblies, Townshend advanced several strategies. First, he instructed the royal governors to take a firmer hand with their recalcitrant legislatures. To set the example, he singled out for punishment the New York legislature, which was refusing to comply with provisions of the Quartering Act of 1765. The troops that were left on the western frontier after the Seven Years' War had been pulled back into colonial seaports in 1766, in part to economize on costs, but also to quiet agitation over the Stamp Act. The largest contingent came to New York. That colony's assembly protested, claiming that the cost of quartering the troops constituted a form of indirect taxation. But Townshend was determined to enforce the Quartering Act, and Parliament backed him, suspending the New York assembly in 1767 until it agreed to toe the mark.

In an even more ominous encroachment on colonial autonomy, Townshend dipped into the revenue from his new tariffs to free royal officials from their financial dependence on the assemblies. Governors and other officers like customs

This 1766 porcelain of *Lord Chatham and America* attests to the popularity of William Pitt, Earl of Chatham, among Americans who resisted the Stamp Act. The artist's representation of "America" as a black kneeling in gratitude echoes the colonists' association of taxation with slavery.

collectors and judges had heretofore received their salaries from colonial legislatures. The assemblies lost that crucial leverage when Townshend found a different way to pay colonial bureaucrats.

Townshend's policies not only liberated royal officials from colonial control but also enlarged their numbers. To ensure more effective enforcement of all the duties on imports, he created an American Board of Customs Commissioners, who appointed in turn a small army of new customs collectors. Townshend also established three new vice-admiralty courts in Boston, New York, and Charleston to bring smugglers to justice. At the same time, he instituted a new cabinet office for handling American affairs, the secretary of state for the colonies.

In Townshend's efforts to centralize the British empire, Americans saw new evidence that they were not being treated like the English. In newspapers and pamphlets colonial leaders reiterated their earlier protests against taxation. The most widely read publication, "A Letter from a Farmer in Pennsylvania," was the work of John Dickinson. If not quite a Pennsylvania farmer, Dickinson had developed from a young law student disgusted by the corruption of British politics into a Philadelphia lawyer disgusted by the policies of Parliament. He urged Americans to protest the Townshend duties with a show of superior virtue. Through hard work, thrift, simplicity, and home manufacturing, Americans could reduce their consumption of imported English luxuries. American self-reliance, Dickinson argued, would advance the cause of repeal.

As John Dickinson's star rose over Philadelphia, the Townshend Acts also dealt the destiny of another man farther north. He was 46 years old in 1768, and had failed at almost everything. His aspirations of becoming a minister he had surrendered while still a student at Harvard; his ventures as a merchant ended in bankruptcy; his improbable stint as a tax collector left all of Boston in the red. These credentials disqualified Samuel Adams for any career except politics. By the 1760s, he was a leader in the Massachusetts assembly. The Townshend Acts made him the consummate political organizer and agitator in America. First his enemies and later his friends claimed that Adams had decided on independence for America as early as 1768.

Adams started small. In February 1768, he persuaded the Massachusetts assembly to send other colonial legislatures a circular letter condemning the Townshend Acts and calling for a united American resistance. He got more than he had expected. From Virginia, the House of Burgesses responded in May with hopes for "a hearty union" against any British measures that "have an immediate tendency to enslave them [the colonies]."

While John Dickinson and Samuel Adams whipped up public indignation against the Townshend Acts, the Sons of Liberty surfaced again in every colonial seaport, orchestrating the opposition in the streets. Customs officials, like the stamp distributors before them, became targets of popular hatred. But the customs collectors gave as good as they got, using the flimsiest pretexts to justify seizing American vessels for violating royal regulations and shaking down American merchants for what amounted to protection money. The racketeering in the customs service brought tensions in Boston to a flashpoint in June 1768 after officials seized and condemned the *Liberty*, a sloop belonging to one of the city's biggest merchants, John Hancock. Bostonians vented their anger in a night of

John Dickinson, a moderate who defended American rights but hoped for reconciliation.

rioting. A crowd of several thousand swept through the streets, searching out and roughing up customs officials.

The new secretary of state for the colonies, Lord Hillsborough, raised the ante. He dispatched two regiments of troops to Boston to protect the customs collectors and to wrest control of the city from the Sons of Liberty. The presence of British soldiers in Boston affronted its inhabitants in every way. The redcoats disembarked in the fall of 1768 and paraded into town under the cover of warships lying off the harbor. In the days and months that followed, citizens accustomed to coming and going as they pleased bristled when challenged on the streets by armed sentries. Even more disturbing to Bostonians was the execution of British military justice on the Common: British soldiers were whipped savagely for breaking military discipline, and desertion was punished by execution.

Despite the risk, desertion was fairly common because of the disadvantages of being a British soldier in Boston. They were regularly reviled by the citizenry and occasionally pelted with stones, snowballs, dirt, and human excrement. The British regulars were particularly unpopular among Boston's laboring classes because they competed with them for jobs. Off-duty soldiers were permitted to moonlight as maritime laborers, and they sold their services at much cheaper rates than the wages paid to locals. By 1769, brawls between British regulars and waterfront workers broke out with disturbing frequency.

With some 4000 redcoats coming into contact daily with some 15,000 Bostonians under the sway of Samuel Adams, what happened on the night of March 5, 1770 was almost inevitable. A crowd gathered around the customshouse for the sport of heckling its guard of 10 soldiers. When the confrontation turned ugly, the redcoats panicked: they fended off the volley of insults, snowballs, and chunks of ice hurled by the mob with live fire, hitting 11 rioters and killing 5. Adams and other propagandists seized upon the incident: labeling the bloodshed "the Boston Massacre," they publicized the "atrocity" throughout the colonies. The radical *Boston Gazette* framed its account in an eye-catching black-bordered edition complete with a drawing of five coffins.

Even before the Boston Massacre, intercolonial resistance had been gathering momentum. The *Liberty* riot of 1768 and the arrival of British troops in Boston a few months later galvanized colonial assemblies into action. Most legislatures joined Virginia's Burgesses in endorsing the Massachusetts circular letter and in protesting the Townshend Acts. The colonies also adopted agreements not to import or to consume British goods. The reluctance among some merchants to revive nonimportation in 1767 gave way to greater enthusiasm by 1768, and by early 1769, such agreements were in effect throughout the colonies.

The Stamp Act crisis had also called forth intercolonial cooperation and tactics like nonimportation. But the protests against the Townshend Acts raised the stakes by creating new institutions to carry forward the resistance. Subscribers to the nonimportation agreements established "committees of inspection" to enforce the ban on trade with Britain. Merchants who refused to stop importing opened themselves to retribution meted out by the committees, who claimed authority from "the people." The committees denounced recalcitrant traders in the newspapers, vandalized their warehouses, forced them to stand under the gallows, and sometimes resorted to tar and feathers. In effect, the committees of inspection, although they had no formal, legal sanction, operated like shadow governments.

After 1768, the resistance also brought a broader range of Americans into the politics of protest. Artisans, who recognized that nonimportation would spur domestic manufacturing, began to organize as independent political groups. In many towns, women took an active part in opposing the Townshend duties. The "Daughters of Liberty" took to heart John Dickinson's recommendations: they forswore English finery in favor of homespun clothing, served coffee instead of tea, and boycotted shops that persisted in selling British goods.

While Townshend's policies intensified the insurgency in America, at least part of his program was meeting with opposition in England as well. Finally the obvious had dawned on members of Parliament: by taxing British exports of paint, lead, paper, and glass, they were losing more in trade than they gained in colonial revenues. Duties only discouraged sales to Americans and encouraged them to manufacture at home. The argument for repeal was overwhelming, and the way had been cleared by the unexpected death of Townshend shortly after Parliament adopted his proposals.

But American defiance of the Townshend Acts stiffened the spine of Parliament. The stalemate was broken only by the king's appointment of Lord North as his new first minister at the beginning of 1770. North convinced Parliament to repeal all of the Townshend duties except the one on tea, allowing that tax to stand as a source of revenue and as a symbol of Parliament's authority.

Resistance Revived

For more than two years, colonial protest subsided. Repeal of the Townshend duties took the wind from the sails of American resistance, restoring to imperial relations some of their former harmony. And internal problems preoccupied Americans after 1770—the Regulator movements in the Carolinas and the contest over western land waged by Connecticut, Pennsylvania, and Virginia. But the quiet was deceptive, for the controversy between England and the colonies had not been resolved. Americans still paid the Sugar Act's duty on molasses and Townshend's tariff on tea, taxes to which they had not consented. Americans were still subject to trial in admiralty courts, tribunals that operated without juries. Americans still lived with a standing army in their midst, a threat to basic freedoms. Beneath the banked fires of protest burned the live embers of Americans' political inequality. Any shift in the wind could fan those embers into flames.

The wind shifted on Narragansett Bay in 1772, running aground the *Gaspee*, a British naval schooner. Since the ship had been in hot pursuit of Rhode Island smugglers, eight boatloads of Providence residents, led by a prominent merchant, celebrated its misfortune in the middle of the night with a bonfire built on the deck of the *Gaspee* after the ship had been boarded and its crew beaten up and put ashore. British officials sent a special commission to look into the burning of the ship, intending once again to bypass the established colonial court system. That violation of common law procedure reignited the imperial crisis, and American resistance flared again.

It did so through an ingenious mechanism, the committees of correspondence. Established all across the colonies by the legislative assemblies, the committees took it upon themselves to draw up statements of American rights and grievances, to distribute these documents within and among the colonies, and to solicit responses from towns and counties. The brainchild of Samuel Adams, the committee structure constituted a new communications network, one designed to

Samuel Adams, a radical who masterminded colonial resistance tactics.

foster an intercolonial consensus on resistance to British measures. Adams had worked too long as a politician not to recognize the need to develop allies, to coordinate plans of action, to embolden wavering supporters to act through the example of others. The arguing and cajoling, the evening meetings at taverns— such techniques might work in lining up local support for a Boston town meeting, but the committees of correspondence provided the badly needed means to rally support on an intercolonial basis. The strategy succeeded admirably, and not only between colonies. The committees spread the scope of the resistance from colonial seaports into rural areas, engaging farmers and other country folk in the opposition to Britain.

The committees had much to talk about when Parliament passed the Tea Act in 1773. The law was an effort to bail out the bankrupt East India Company by granting that corporation a monopoly on the tea trade to Americans. Since the company could use agents to sell its product directly, cutting out the middlemen, the new low price undercut that charged by colonial merchants—even when the duty of three pence per pound was added, and even when smugglers tried to compete using illegal Dutch tea. Thus although the Tea Act would hurt American merchants, it promised to make tea cheaper for ordinary Americans. Still, many colonials saw the act as Parliament's ploy to lull them into accepting its authority to tax the colonies. They set out to deny that power, once and for all.

By the fall of 1773, the Sons of Liberty had resumed their agitation in American seaports. Colonial newspapers denounced the merchants to whom the East India Company had consigned shipments of tea; mobs collected around their warehouses; mass meetings gathered to decry the latest step in the plot to enslave the colonies. In early winter of 1773, the tempest over the Tea Act peaked in Boston, with popular leaders calling for the cargoes to be returned forthwith to England. Thomas Hutchinson, now the governor of Massachusetts, was determined that the tea would be landed and stored.

On the evening of December 16, thousands of Bostonians, as well as farmers from the surrounding countryside, packed into the Old South Meetinghouse to hear Samuel Adams announce that Hutchinson had denied clearance to vessels attempting to carry the detested tea back to England. Some members of the audience knew that Adams had more on the evening's agenda than denouncing the governor, and they awaited their cue. It came when Adams told the meeting that they could do nothing more to save their country. War whoops rang through the meetinghouse, the crowd spilled onto the streets and out to the waterfront, and the Boston Tea Party commenced. From the throng emerged 50 "Indians" clad in blankets, their faces smeared with paint to disguise their identities. The party boarded three vessels docked off Griffin's Wharf, broke open casks containing 90,000 pounds of tea, and brewed a beverage worth 10,000 pounds sterling in Boston harbor.

The Empire Strikes Back

George III, his ministers, and Parliament responded to the destruction of the tea first with shock, then with disgust, and finally with grim determination. The Tea Party proved to British satisfaction that Americans aimed at independence. Lord North concluded that "we are now to dispute whether we have, or have not, any authority in that country."

To show that they did, Parliament speedily assented to the Coercive Acts,

While the new political activism of some American women often amused male leaders of the resistance, it inspired the scorn of some partisans of British authority. When the women of Edenton, North Carolina, renounced imported tea, this British cartoon mocked them.

dubbed in the colonies the "Intolerable Acts." In March 1774, two months after hearing of the Tea Party, Parliament passed the Boston Port Bill, closing that harbor to all oceangoing traffic until such time as the king saw fit to reopen it. He would not see fit until America recompensed the East India Company for their tea. During the next three months, Parliament approved three other "intolerable" laws designed to isolate and punish Massachusetts. The Massachusetts Government Act handed over the colony government to royal officials: henceforth, the Crown would nominate that colony's council and the royal governor would appoint and remove most officials. Sheriffs would become royal appointees rather than freemen, and it was given to them to select juries. Town meetings henceforth would require royal permission. The Impartial Administration of Justice Act permitted any royal official accused of a crime in Massachusetts to be tried in England or in another colony. The Quartering Act allowed the billeting of British troops in private households—not only in recalcitrant Massachusetts, but in all the colonies.

Many Americans saw the Coercive Acts as proof of a deliberate plot to enslave the colonies. The taxes and duties, laws and regulations of the last decade— measures that the king's ministers and Parliament regarded as commonsensical steps to centralize British authority in America—many colonials perceived as a sinister conspiracy against their liberties.

The source of this conspiratorial interpretation of the recent past lay in the writings of the English Opposition, which held that human history recorded the same story, time and time again. It was a tale of power overwhelming liberty. Those who had power would always seek more; those who had more power would inevitably become corrupt, unless checked by a virtuous and vigilant people. An especially popular treatment of this theme appeared in a series of essays by Trenchard and Gordon, *Cato's Letters* (1720–1723), which was reprinted repeatedly in America. Trenchard, Gordon, and others of the Opposition asserted that ambitious politicians always pursued the same strategies to supplant representative government and popular freedom with tyranny and despotism. They pointed to the sad lessons of the ancient republics of Greece and Rome, whose citizens had fallen prey to the powers of tyrants and dictators. They held up more recent examples of Venice, Sweden, and Denmark, whose republican traditions had all degenerated within the past century. Power overwhelming liberty: colonials discerned that same dark scenario unfolding in America.

First, English theorists warned, the people of a republic were impoverished by costly wars—something the colonists could well appreciate after the Seven Years' War. Then the government loaded the people with taxes to pay for those wars—as in the case of the Sugar Act or the Stamp Act or the Townshend duties. Next the government stationed a standing army in the country, ostensibly to protect the people, but actually to consolidate the strength of those in power. And of course, troops had been unloaded in Boston harbor, were quartered in New York, and were making trouble wherever they appeared. Then, the Opposition warned, worthless and wicked men were favored with public offices and patronage to secure their loyalty and support for the foes of liberty. And how else could one describe the royal governors, customs collectors, and judges whose salaries derived from the revenues of the Townshend duties? Then those in power would deliberately promote luxury, idleness, and extravagance to weaken the moral fiber of the people—like the consumption encouraged by the low prices ensured by the Tea Act. Finally, those in power would try to provoke the people to violence in order to justify new oppression. And week after week in the spring of 1774, reports of the Coercive Acts and other legislative outrages came across the waters.

With the passage of the Coercive Acts, many more Americans came to believe not only that distant powers plotted to enslave the colonies but also that the conspirators included a large number of British political leaders. At the time of the Stamp Act and again during the agitation against the Townshend Acts, most Americans had confined their suspicions to the king's ministers. By 1774, those implicated in that conspiracy included more than a handful of ministers—Parliament itself had fallen under suspicion. Americans everywhere were thoroughly alarmed. The Coercive Acts prompted an outpouring of support for "suffering Boston," and the committees of correspondence worked unceasingly to rally support. From one colony after another came calls for an intercolonial congress—like the one that had met during the Stamp Act crisis—to determine the best way to defend their freedom.

In 1754 the Albany Congress had found the colonies too divided to agree on any course of action in the common defense. In 1765 the Stamp Act Congress had shown greater resolve, but the occasion for action passed. In 1774 Americans were united in opposition, convinced that the threat to their liberties was real. But many remained unsettled about where the logic of their actions might be taking them: toward a denial that they were any longer English.

TOWARD THE REVOLUTION

By the beginning of September 1774, when the First Continental Congress met, the news from Massachusetts was bad. The colony verged on anarchy, it was reported, as its inhabitants resisted the enforcement of the Massachusetts Government Act. When British soldiers had raided an arsenal at Charlestown where radical leaders were stockpiling arms and ammunition, thousands of militia throughout the colony had mobilized and marched to defend Boston. On that occasion, known as "the Powder Alarm," the volunteers had finally dispersed, and the episode ended without bloodshed. But the 55 delegates meeting at Carpenter's Hall in Philadelphia feared that there would be more confrontations and more violence.

In the midst of this atmosphere of crisis, they also had to take one another's measure. Many of the delegates had not traveled outside their native provinces; even those who had were hardly familiar with all the customs and circumstances of the other colonies. (All but Georgia sent representatives.) Lawyers compared notes on how their respective colonial governments justified their rights as British subjects, how their laws were encoded. Delegates learned more about their distant neighbors' economies, customs, and temperaments. Although the representatives encountered a great deal of diversity, they quickly discovered that they held in common an esteem of certain "republican" virtues: simplicity and self-reliance, industry and thrift, and, above all, disinterested commitment to the public good. Individual delegates were delighted to discern among men from other colonies those virtues that they had once attributed only to themselves. Most members of the Congress also shared a common mistrust of England, associating the mother country with vice, extravagance, and corruption.

Still, as delegates took one another's measure, they found that their perceptions were not entirely in accord. Massachusetts in particular brought with it a reputation—well deserved, considering Samuel Adams was along—for radical action and a willingness to use force to accomplish its ends. John Adams, another delegate (and a cousin of Samuel Adams), reported that other colonies were suspicious of the Massachusetts representatives. "We have been obliged to keep ourselves out of sight, and to feel pulses, and to sound the depths; to insinuate our sentiments, designs, and desires by means of other persons, sometimes of one province, and sometimes of another."

The First Continental Congress

In an atmosphere charged with apprehension and excitement, the delegates settled down to business. Their agenda was to reach a consensus on the basis of American rights, the limits of Parliament's power, and the proper tactics for resisting the Coercive Acts. Congress quickly agreed on the first point. They affirmed what most Americans had argued since 1765: the law of nature, the colonial charters, and the British constitution were the foundations of American liberties. On the two other issues, Congress plied a middle course between the demands of the more radical delegates and the reservations of conservatives.

In a Declaration of Rights and Grievances, adopted on October 14, 1774, the delegates asserted the right of the colonies to tax and legislate for themselves. Since the time of the Stamp Act, most Americans had insisted that Parliament had no authority to tax the colonies. Subsequent events—including the suspension of the New York legislature, the Gaspee Commission, and, most recently, the Coercive Acts—had demonstrated that Parliament could undermine colonial liberties by legislation as well as by taxation. The Declaration of Rights reflected that recognition, defining the limits of Parliament's power over Americans more narrowly than colonials had a decade earlier.

The repudiation of Parliament's power to legislate for the colonies doomed to defeat a strategy for accommodation with England favored by the most conservative members of the Congress. Their leading advocate, Joseph Galloway of Pennsylvania, proposed a plan of union with Britain similar to the one set forth by the Albany Congress in 1754: a grand council of the colonies would handle all common concerns, its enactments subject to review and veto by Parliament, and all acts of Parliament affecting America would require the approval of the grand council. A majority of delegates judged that Galloway's proposal left Parliament too much leeway in legislating for Americans, and they rejected his plan. Galloway, who knew a good politician when he saw one, blamed Samuel Adams' maneuverings for his defeat. Adams, he commented, "eats little, sleeps little, thinks much, and is most decisive and indefatigable in the pursuit of his objects."

Although the Congress denied Parliament the right to impose taxes or to make laws, delegates stopped short of declaring that it had no authority at all in the colonies. They grudgingly approved Parliament's regulation of trade, but "only from the necessity of the case," that is, because of the interdependent economy of the empire. And although some American pamphleteers were attacking the king for plotting against American liberties, Congress acknowledged the continuing allegiance of the colonies to George III. In other words, the delegates called for a return to the situation that had existed in the empire before 1763, with Parliament regulating trade and the colonies exercising all powers of taxation and legislation.

On the question of resistance, Congress acceded to the desires of its most radical delegates by drawing up the Continental Association, an agreement to cease all trade with Britain until the Coercive Acts were repealed. They agreed that their fellow citizens would immediately stop drinking East India Company tea, and that by December 1, 1774, merchants would no longer import goods of any sort from Britain. A ban on the export of American produce to Britain and the West Indies would go into effect a year later, during September 1775—the lag being a concession to southern rice and tobacco planters, who wanted to market their crops.

Although the Association provided for the total cessation of trade favored by radical delegates, Congress did not approve another part of their agenda—making preparations for war. From the outset of the convention, Samuel Adams and some of the other Massachusetts delegates had quietly worked to commit the Congress to mobilizing colonial defenses. Adams' designs were not farfetched. A story had been spreading among the delegates that George Washington, when he heard of the Boston Port Bill, had "offered to raise and arm and lead one thousand men at his own expense, for the defense of his country."

On September 16, a Boston silversmith named Paul Revere rode breathlessly into Philadelphia with news. Revere had worked with Adams before, providing the press with more than a few inflammatory engravings to strengthen the radicals' causes, including one of the Boston Massacre. Now he had a copy of the Suffolk Resolves, drawn up by Bostonians and other inhabitants of Suffolk County a month earlier. The resolutions set forth the sufferings of Massachusetts in inflammatory language and called for civil disobedience to protest the Coercive Acts. Congress endorsed the Suffolk Resolves to underscore American solidarity.

But when Revere rode into town again on October 16, this time to announce that the British were fortifying Boston, he received a cooler response from Congress. A few of the southern delegates joined in the spirit of the Boston radicals: Patrick Henry thundered that "Arms are a Resource to which We shall be forced";

Christopher Gadsden of South Carolina proposed an immediate attack on British troops in Boston; Richard Henry Lee of Virginia wanted Congress to call for the evacuation of the city. Among the majority of delegates, however, restraint prevailed. They refused to be stampeded by the manipulation of Adams, the saber-rattling of southern hotspurs, or the histrionics of Revere. Congress approved a defensive strategy of civil disobedience but drew the line at authorizing proposals to strengthen and arm colonial militias.

The First Continental Congress, although determined to bring about repeal of the Coercive Acts, held firm in its resistance to a revolutionary course of action. If British officials had responded to its recommendations and restored the status quo of 1763, the war for independence might have been postponed—perhaps indefinitely. On the other hand, even though the Congress did not go to the extremes urged by the radicals, its decisions drew Americans further down the road to independence.

The successful conduct of a continental congress itself fostered the cause of American unity. Despite the differing backgrounds of delegates and the separate interests of individual colonies, the Congress forged compromises and attained remarkable unanimity on the key issues of colonial rights and the tactics of resistance. More important, the delegates discovered that they shared a common set of values—a commitment to the republican virtues of simplicity and industry—embodied in the Association. To their mutual satisfaction, members of Congress came away concluding, with Caesar Rodney of Delaware, that "more sensible, fine fellows you would never wish to see."

The Last Days of the
British Empire in America

Most Americans shared the delegates' enthusiasm for the achievements of the First Continental Congress. They expected that the Association would bring about a speedy repeal of the Coercive Acts. But most of the delegates, although proud of their unity, were less sanguine about the future. They anticipated war with England, even if they were unwilling to commit Congress itself to preparing for it.

The same apprehension that America was slipping toward a showdown with Britain led other men to denounce the doings of Congress. Joseph Galloway warned his countrymen that he had detected within Congress "the ill-shapen diminutive brat, Independency." Conservatives dreaded that outcome. If the authority of Parliament was denied, they predicted, the colonies would be in "a perfect state of nature," destitute of any supreme director to settle differences among themselves. Americans would quarrel over land claims and other contended issues, and the result would be civil war. Conservatives also warned that a break with Britain would mean the triumph of democracy in America. They believed that the colonies had more to fear from the certain anarchy and mob rule that would follow independence than from the British Parliament.

The man in America with the least enthusiasm for the actions of the Continental Congress was the one who sat in the hottest seat in the colonies, that of the governor of Massachusetts. He was General Thomas Gage, who had replaced Thomas Hutchinson in 1774 and now watched as royal authority crumbled in Massachusetts and the disintegration spread to other colonies.

In October 1774, a desperate Gage dissolved the Massachusetts legislature, which then reconstituted itself as a Provincial Congress and assumed the government of the colony. The new Provincial Congress promptly took over tax collection, appropriating 20,000 pounds for arms and ammunition and creating a committee to supply and direct the militia. Gage then started to fortify the Boston Neck with cannon and pleaded with the ministry for more troops—only to find his fortifications damaged by saboteurs and his requests for reinforcements ignored by Britain. Gage at last dispatched scouts to map the roads leading out of Boston, but his scouts were detected and sent packing by farmers. And when he made a show of drilling his troops, the Provincial Congress announced it would muster the militia if more than 500 British regulators moved out of Boston.

Outside Boston, the friends of royal authority fared no better. Farmers in western Massachusetts forcibly closed the county courts, turning out royally appointed justices and establishing their own tribunals. Popularly elected committees of inspection charged with enforcing the Association took over towns everywhere in Massachusetts, not only restricting trade, but also regulating every aspect of local life. The committees converted their communities into "Christian Spartas," societies of virtuous republicans who condemned "effeminate" English luxuries like tea and fine clothing and "corrupt" leisure activities like dancing, gambling, and racing. The committees also dispatched spies to report on any citizen unfriendly to the resistance. "Enemies of American liberty," who engaged in illegal trade, illicit consumption, or "disloyal" behavior, faced public censure, and in some places, intimidation and punishment at the hands of angry mobs.

Throughout the colonies a similar process was under way. During the winter and early spring of 1775, provincial congresses, county conventions, and local committees of inspection were emerging as de facto governments, supplanting royal authority at every level. As the spectacle unfolded before General Gage, he concluded that only force could subdue the colonies. But it would take more than he had at his command.

With Massachusetts on the verge of armed revolt, most Britons received reports from the colonies with utter indifference. The chaos in America merited hardly a mention during the parliamentary elections held in November 1774. In most English circles, Edmund Burke observed, "any remarkable highway robbery on Hounslow Heath would make more conversation than all of the disturbances in America."

By the end of 1774, Gage had persuaded the king and Parliament that the colonies were in rebellion, but most politicians still regarded the American resistance as the work of "a rude rabble" in Boston fired by a few radical agitators like Samuel Adams. Few British policymakers understood the seriousness of the situation, but one who did was William Pitt. No longer a minister but now a member of Parliament, Pitt put before that body a radical program for reconciliation in January 1775. He urged the withdrawal of all troops from Boston, the repeal of the Coercive Acts and all other measures objectionable to Americans, and the passage of legislation promising that the colonies could not be taxed without their consent. In return for these concessions, the colonies would grant the Crown a perpetual revenue.

Would the adoption of Pitt's proposals have undermined the momentum of the resistance and restored the colonies to the empire? There is no way to know: Parliament spurned Pitt's program and instead, in February, approved an address to the king declaring that the colonies were in rebellion. A few weeks later, it approved a carrot-and-stick policy proposed by Lord North as a final means to settle the dispute. For the stick, Parliament closed the Atlantic fishery to New

England ships and restricted their trade to Britain and the West Indies. Balancing this punishment with a conciliatory offer, Parliament agreed to suspend its taxation of any colony that made adequate provision on its own for the support of civil and military government. But no mention was made of how much revenue would be required or what each colony's proportion might be. It hardly mattered, for no one in America took Lord North's offer seriously.

The Fighting Begins

As spring came to Boston, the city waited. A band of artisans in the North End, organized as spies and express riders by Paul Revere, watched General Thomas Gage, waiting for him to act. Gage waited for word from Lord North and watched the hostile town. On April 14, word from North finally arrived: the general was to seize the leaders of the Provincial Congress. That would behead the rebellion, North said. If the arrest of resistance leaders triggered violence, Gage was to suppress the insurrection with force. That would nip revolution in the bud. General Gage knew better—the situation required more than a quick police action—but he also knew that he had to do something.

On the night of April 18, the sexton of Christ Church in Boston's North End hung two lamps in the steeple. It was a signal that British troops were moving out of Boston by water. They had crossed the Back Bay in boats around midnight, beginning a march toward the arms and ammunition stored by the Provincial Congress in Concord. As the lamps flashed the signal to Charlestown, Revere and a comrade, William Dawes, set out on a hard ride to arouse the rest of the countryside.

When the news of a British march reached Lexington, the local militia of about 70 farmers, chilled and sleepy, mustered on the Green at the center of the little rural town. Lexington Green lay directly on the road to Concord. At about four in the morning, 700 British troops appeared on the Green, and their commander, Major John Pitcairn, ordered the Lexington militia to disperse. The Americans, badly outnumbered and probably overawed, began to comply. A shot rang out—whether the British or the Americans fired first is unknown—then two volleys burst from the ranks of the redcoats. With a cheer, the British set off for Concord, five miles distant, leaving eight Americans dead on Lexington Green.

By dawn, hundreds of volunteers from nearby towns were surging into Concord. From as far west as Worcester other companies were on the march, heading for the same site. The British entered Concord at about seven in the morning and encountered no opposition as they moved on their target, a house lying across the North Bridge that spanned the Concord River. While three companies of British soldiers conducted a futile search for American arms, three others, posted on the bridge itself, had the misfortune to find American arms—borne by the rebels and fired at the badly deployed redcoats with deadly effect. By noon, the British were retreating to Boston.

The narrow road from Concord to Boston's outskirts became a corridor of carnage, Americans in pursuit firing on the column of fleeing redcoats from the cover of fences and forests. By the end of April 19, the British had sustained 273 casualties; the Americans, 95. It was only the beginning. By evening of the next day, perhaps 20,000 militia had converged on Boston and were digging in for a long siege.

Common Sense

The bloodshed at Lexington Green and Concord's North Bridge irrevocably committed Americans to a course of rebellion—and that course of rebellion, to independence. That was the conclusion drawn by Thomas Paine, who urged other Americans to do the same.

In point of fact, Paine was hardly an American at all. He was born in England, apprenticed first as a corsetmaker, appointed later a tax collector, and fated finally to become midwife to the age of republican revolutions. Paine came to Philadelphia late in 1774, set up as a journalist, and made the American cause his own. "Where liberty is, there is my country," he declared. In January 1776, he wrote a pamphlet to inform Americans of their identity as a distinct people and their destiny as a nation. *Common Sense* enjoyed tremendous popularity and wide circulation, selling 120,000 copies within three months of its publication.

After Lexington and Concord, Paine wrote, as the imperial crisis passed "from argument to arms, a new era for politics is struck—a new method of thinking has arisen." That new era of politics for Paine was the age of republicanism. He derided monarchy as a foolish and dangerous form of government, one that ran counter to the dictates of reason as well as the word of the Bible. King George himself Paine rechristened as "the Royal Brute of Britain," a "sullen Pharaoh" who had enslaved the chosen people of the new age—the Americans.

By ridicule and remorseless argument, Paine severed the ties of America's allegiance to the king. George III was no well-meaning but misinformed monarch in the thrall of evil ministers and a corrupt Parliament. In Paine's view, George III was the principal villain of the piece, nothing more than "a crowned ruffian," like all other kings before him. Nor did Paine stop there. He rejected the idea that Americans were or should want to be English. Britain, he told his readers, had nurtured the colonies out of self-interest rather than attachment. Far from being a tender parent, the so-called mother country was a parasite on colonial wealth and a predator on colonial liberties. That the colonies occupied a huge continent an ocean away from the tiny British Isles proved that nature itself had fashioned America for independence. There was more: "By the common order of nature, it is evident that they belong to different systems. England to Europe, America to itself." England lay locked in Europe, doomed to the corruption of an Old World. The New World liberated America to become an "asylum of liberty."

Americans liked being English, but being English hadn't worked. Perhaps that is another way of saying that over the course of nearly two centuries colonial society and politics had evolved in such a way that the identity between Americans and English no longer fit. By the end of the Seven Years' War, the colonies had established political institutions—institutions that made the rights of "freeborn Britons" more evident and available to ordinary citizens in America than in the nation that had created those liberties. Perhaps, then, most Americans had succeeded *too* well at becoming English, regarding themselves as political equals entitled to basic constitutional freedoms. No matter. In the space of less than a generation, the logic of events made clear that for all the English and Americans

Thomas Paine, author of *Common Sense*.

shared, in the distribution of political power they were fundamentally at odds. And the call to arms at Lexington and Concord made retreat impossible.

On that point Paine was clear. It was the destiny of Americans to be republicans, not monarchists. It was the destiny of Americans to be independent, not subject to British dominion. It was the destiny of Americans to be American, not to be English. That, according to Thomas Paine, was common sense.

SIGNIFICANT EVENTS

1755 — Braddock defeated by French and Indians
1756 — England and France declare war
1759 — Decisive English victory at Quebec
1760 — George III becomes king of England
1763 — Treaty of Paris ends the Seven Years' War; Pontiac's Rebellion; royal proclamation prohibits settlement west of the Appalachians
1764 — Sugar Act; Currency Act
1765 — Stamp Act; Quartering Act
1766 — Repeal of the Stamp Act; Declaratory Act
1767 — Townshend duties; Parliament suspends New York assembly
1770 — Boston Massacre; repeal of most Townshend duties
1772 — Gaspee Commission
1773 — Boston Tea Party
1774 — Coercive Acts; First Continental Congress meets at Philadelphia
1775 — Battles of Lexington and Concord

6

The American People and the American Revolution

t was a perfect morning in the middle of June. From a high place in the city—Beacon Hill, perhaps, or Copse Hill—General Thomas Gage looked down on the peninsula of Boston. His gaze traveled over the church belfries and steeples, the roofs of brick and white frame houses basking serenely in the warm air of early summer. Then he shifted his spyglass, focusing on a figure far in the distance across the Charles River. The man was perched on the parapet of a crude fortification on Breed's Hill, an elevation lying a little below Bunker Hill on the Charlestown peninsula. Gage took the measure of his enemy: an older man, past middle age, clad all in homespun, a sword swinging beneath his coat, a broad-brimmed hat shading his eyes. As he passed the spyglass to his ally, a king's man, an American loyalist, Gage asked Abijah Willard if he knew the man on the parapet. Willard peered across the Charles and identified his own brother-in-law, Colonel William Prescott. The member of an eminent Massachusetts family and a veteran of Amherst's assault on Louisbourg during the Seven Years' War, Prescott was now a leader in the rebel army laying siege to Boston. Atop the parapet, Prescott deliberately exposed himself to British fire from Boston harbor, a gesture to hearten his men.

"Will he fight?" Gage wondered aloud. The loyalist studied his kinsman. "I cannot answer for his men," Willard replied, "but Prescott will fight you to the gates of hell."

Fight they did on June 17, 1775, both William Prescott and his men. The evening before, three regiments drawn from the thousands of New England militia who had converged on British-occupied Boston after the bloodshed at Lexington and Concord followed Prescott from Cambridge to the Charlestown peninsula. There, all through the hot, dusty night, they built on Breed's Hill a redoubt of deep trenches and high earthen walls. At the first light of day, General Gage awakened to the boom of a cannonade from Boston harbor: his warship, the *Lively*, had spotted the new rebel outpost on Breed's Hill and opened fire. By noon barges were ferrying British troops under Major General William Howe across the half-mile of river that separated Boston from Charlestown. The 1600 raw rebel troops tensed at the sight of scarlet-coated soldiers streaming ashore, glittering bayonets grasped at the ready. Their eyes stung from the acrid smoke of bombardments fired from British warships and the battery on Copse Hill. Their ears re-

Eleven years after the event, the American artist John Trumbull painted Battle of Bunker's Hill *(1786), a canvas executed in the currently fashionable mode of grand historical painting, designed to commemorate (and elevate) an occasion of note.*

sounded with the din of guns roaring and an enemy massing. The rebels were farmers and craftworkers, not professional soldiers, and they were frightened out of their wits.

But Prescott and his men held their ground. The British charged Breed's Hill twice, and both times the defenders allowed them to close before raining lead into their lines. Howe watched in horror the stream of fire felling his troops. Finally, during the third British frontal assault, the rebels ran out of ammunition and were forced to withdraw; redcoats swarmed over the redoubt, savagely bayoneting its handful of remaining defenders. By nightfall the British had taken Breed's Hill and the rest of the Charlestown peninsula. They had bought a dark triumph at the cost of 228 dead and 800 wounded. The British could not afford to win another such victory, one officer remarked, and Howe agreed.

The cost came high in loyalties as well. The fighting on Breed's Hill fed hatred of Britain, the sense of betrayal that had been building since April. Throughout America, preparations for war intensified: militia in every colony mustered; communities stockpiled arms and ammunition. From as far south as Virginia came reports that "a phrenzy of revenge" had "seized all ranks of people." Back in New England, civilians fled Charlestown, which had been ravaged in a fire lit by the British shelling of Breed's Hill. Fearful of another British strike, the inhabitants of neighboring communities also sought refuge farther inland with friends and kinfolk. "The roads filled with frightened women and children, some in carts with their tattered furniture, others on foot fleeing into the woods," recalled Hannah Winthrop, one of their number. Militia companies from every town and hamlet in the colony started to converge on the hills around Boston, cordoning off the capital. From nearby Watertown the rebel leader James Warren reported that "it is Impossible to describe the Confusion in this place, Women and Children flying into the Country, armed Men Going to the field, and wounded Men returning from there fill the Streets."

The bloody and indecisive fight on the Charlestown peninsula known as the Battle of Bunker Hill actually took place on Breed's Hill. And the exchange between Thomas Gage and Abijah Willard that is said to have preceded the battle may not have taken place at all. But the story has persisted in the folklore of that war for colonial liberation called the American Revolution. Whether it really happened or not, the conversation between Gage and Willard raised the question that both sides wanted answered: were Americans willing to fight for independence from British rule? It was one thing, after all, to oppose the British ministry's policy of taxation; it was another to support a rebellion for which the ultimate price of failure was hanging for treason. It was fine enough to be stirred by the rhetoric of Thomas Paine's *Common Sense;* it was another matter for farmers and their wives to find soldiers marching through newly sown fields, stealing their chickens. And it was another matter entirely for men to wait nervously atop a hill as the seasoned troops of one's own "mother country" marched toward them with the firm intent to kill.

Indeed, the question "will they fight?" was revolutionary shorthand for a host of other, deeper queries concerning how ordinary men and women would react to the tug of loyalties between long-established colonial governments and a long-revered parent nation and monarch. For recent immigrants, the question of loyalties concerned their feelings about their neighbors and their new-found land. For slaves, the question revolved around their allegiance to masters who spoke of liberty, or to their masters' enemies, who promised liberation. For those who led the rebels, it was a question of strengthening the resolve of the undecided, coordinating resistance, instilling discipline—translating the *will* to fight into the ability to do so. And for those who believed the rebellion was a madness whipped up by artful politicians, it was a question of whether to remain silent or risk speaking out; whether to take up arms for the king or flee. All these questions were raised, of necessity, by the act of revolution. But the barrel of a rifle shortened them to a single, pointed question: will you fight?

THE DECISION FOR INDEPENDENCE

The delegates to the Second Continental Congress gathered on May 10, 1775, just one month after the battles at Lexington and Concord. As the armies of Britain and America faced each other across the siege lines surrounding Boston, the delegates meeting together again at Philadelphia considered whether independence or reconciliation offered the best way to protect the liberties of their colonies.

For a brash, ambitious lawyer from Braintree, Massachusetts, British depravity dictated only one course. "The Cancer [of official corruption] is too deeply rooted," wrote John Adams, "and too far spread to be cured by anything short of cutting it out entire." Yet during the spring and summer of 1775, even ardent advocates of independence like Adams and his kindred spirit, Virginia's Richard Henry Lee, did not openly seek a separation from Britain. Even the impulsive Adams recognized that reconciliation still appealed to many both in Congress and in the colonies. If the radicals' objective of independence was ever to be achieved, greater agreement among Americans had to be attained. Moderates and conservatives clung to the hope of reconciliation and harbored deep misgivings about independence: they had to be brought along slowly.

The Second Continental Congress

To bring them along, Congress adopted the "Olive Branch Petition" in July 1775. Drawn up by Pennsylvania's John Dickinson, the document affirmed American loyalty to George III and asked the king to disavow the policies of his principal ministers. At the same time, Congress issued a declaration denying that the colonies aimed at independence. Yet, less than a month earlier, Congress had authorized the creation of a rebel military force, the Continental Army, and had issued paper money to pay for the troops. Americans had taken up arms only to protect their rights, the delegates insisted, and would lay them down once Britain had redressed their grievances.

Congress not only mobilized for war but also cast about for allies among Britain's other colonies. The planters of the British West Indies, too remote and too dependent on England, were dismissed as potential supporters, but the "oppressed Inhabitants of Canada" were invited to send delegates to the Second Continental Congress. Some Americans had regarded Canadians as "fellow sufferers" for a "common liberty" ever since Parliament passed the Quebec Act in 1774. That legislation provided for the rule of Canada by a royal governor and a council, but no representative assembly; it also officially recognized the Roman Catholic church and extended the bounds of the province to include all land between the Mississippi and Ohio rivers. While the Quebec Act outraged the partisans of American liberty, Protestantism, and land speculation, the 80,000 inhabitants of Canada, most of whom were Catholic, applauded Parliament's toleration of their religion and the expansion of their territory. Since most Canadians were also French, they had little sympathy for a struggle for "British liberties." When Canadians declared either loyalty to the king or indifference to the American cause, Congress sponsored several unsuccessful invasions of Canada, approving the first almost immediately after it created the Continental Army.

A Congress that sued for peace while preparing for war was a contradiction that British politicians did not even try to fathom, least of all Lord George Germain, the new, tough-minded American secretary. Germain would hear nothing of negotiating: he was determined to bring Americans to heel by force. George III proved just as stubborn. He refused to receive the Olive Branch Petition, and in the fall of 1775 he informed Parliament of "a desperate conspiracy" for independence in America. By the end of that year Parliament had shut down all trade with the rebellious colonies and had ordered the Royal Navy to seize colonial merchant ships on the high seas. The remaining royal governors also lent their influence to snuffing out any chance of reconciliation. In November 1775, Virginia's Lord Dunmore offered freedom to any slaves who would rebel against their masters and join

In John Trumbull's painting the Committee of Five, including Adams (left), Jefferson (second from right), and Franklin (right) submit the Declaration of Independence to the Continental Congress. John Hancock, the president of the Congress, is reported to have remarked, "We must be unanimous; there must be no pulling different ways; we must all hang together." Franklin is said to have rejoined, "Yes, we must indeed all hang together, or most assuredly, we shall all hang separately."

the British. During January of the next year, Dunmore ordered the shelling of Norfolk, Virginia, reducing that town to a smoldering rubble.

The blast of British belligerence withered the cause of reconciliation within Congress and the colonies. Support for independence gained momentum from the overwhelming public reception of Thomas Paine's *Common Sense* in January 1776. The radicals in Congress realized that the future was theirs and were ready to act. In April 1776 the delegates opened American trade to every nation in the world except Great Britain; a month later Congress advised the colonies to establish new state governments. And on June 7, Richard Henry Lee offered the motion "That these United Colonies are, and of right ought to be, free and independent States, that they are absolved from all allegiance to the British Crown, and that all political connection between them and the State of Great Britain is, and ought to be, totally dissolved."

Congress debated Lee's motion but then postponed a final vote until July. There was still some lingering opposition among delegates from the Middle Colonies, and a committee appointed to write a declaration of independence needed time to complete its work. That committee included some of the premier political leaders in Congress: John Adams, Benjamin Franklin, Connecticut's Roger Sherman, and New York's Robert Livingston. But the man who did most of the drafting was a young planter and lawyer from western Virginia, a learned and imaginative devotee of the Enlightenment.

Thomas Jefferson was just 33 years old in the summer of 1776 when he sequestered himself in his second-floor lodgings on the outskirts of Philadelphia, pulled a portable writing desk onto his lap, and wrote the statement that would explain American independence to a "candid world." In the document's brief opening section, Jefferson set forth a general justification of revolution that invoked the "self-evident truths" of human equality and "unalienable rights" to "life, liberty, and the pursuit of happiness." To underscore the finality of America's break with Britain, the Declaration's case for revolution rested squarely on the doctrine of natural rights. These rights had been "endowed" to all persons "by their Creator," the Declaration pointed out; thus there was no need to appeal to the narrower claim of the "rights of Englishmen."

While the first part of the Declaration served notice that Americans no longer considered themselves English, its second and longer section implicitly denied Parliament any authority in the colonies. In its detailed history of American grievances against the British empire, the Declaration alluded only once to Parliament. Instead, for every infringement of American liberty, the Declaration blamed the last acknowledged link between Britain and the colonies—George III. This second section specifically justified an American revolution by showing the "long train of abuses and usurpations," the design for "absolute despotism" authored by the king. Unlike Paine's *Common Sense*, the Declaration indicted only the reigning king of England; it did not attack the institution of monarchy itself. But like *Common Sense*, the Declaration affirmed that government originated in the consent of the governed and upheld the right of the people to overthrow oppressive rule. And it referred hopefully to Americans as "one people."

Later generations have debated what Jefferson meant by "the pursuit of happiness" and whether he had either women or black Americans in mind when he wrote the famous phrase "all men are created equal." His own contemporaries in Congress did not pause to consider these questions: they adopted the Declaration of Independence on July 4, 1776.

American Loyalists

Colonial political leaders edged toward independence, drawn by their own interests, their commitment to preserving constitutional liberty, and events that extinguished any prospect of reconciliation. In the end, they embraced independence because they believed that a majority of Americans would support a revolution to bring it about.

But the sentiment for independence was not universal. Those who would not back the rebellion, partisans of the king and Parliament, who numbered perhaps one-fifth of the population in 1775, proclaimed themselves "loyalists." Their rebel opponents dubbed them "tories"—"a thing whose head is in England, whose body is in America, and whose neck ought to be stretched." That division made the Revolution a conflict that pitted Americans against one another as well as the British. In truth, the war for independence was the first American civil war.

Many who took up the king's cause had not lacked sympathy for the resistance. Loyalist leaders like Joseph Galloway, Daniel Dulany, and Daniel Leonard actually opposed the Stamp Act in 1765 and disapproved of imperial policy thereafter. It was not until the crisis reached a fever pitch in 1774, after the Boston Tea Party, that a large number of colonials cast their lot with the king. Even then many

Daily Lives

CLOTHING AND FASHION

Radical Chic and the Revolutionary Generation

Women and men of revolutionary America sought to invest themselves with virtue as they escaped British "corruption." The most zealous partisans of colonial rights took that "investiture" to a literal extreme: they made and wore particular clothing as an emblem of political commitment and aspiration. What workshirts, faded denim jeans, and "love beads" were to student radicals of the 1960s, gowns, shirts, and breeches made of "homespun" were to members of the revolutionary generation. In the 1760s homespun, any coarse cloth made in America, became a badge of imperiled innocence and cultural alienation.

Donning homespun bespoke the wearer's virtue: he or she had forsworn fine fabrics along with all the other "effeminate" and "enslaving" English luxuries. Clothes sewn from domestic textiles identified the men and women who wore them as friends of liberty, freed from the vanity and foppishness of British fashion and the humiliating dependence on British imports. As early as 1766 the radical press called for increased domestic industry to offset American reliance on English cloth and beamed its pleas particularly at the women who managed colonial households. A Rhode Islander writing in the *Providence Gazette* remarked in 1767, "We must after all our efforts depend greatly upon the female sex for the introduction of œconomy among us."

By 1769 radical propaganda had produced a new ritual of American resistance, the patriotic spinning competition. Wives and daughters from some of the wealthiest and most prominent families, women who had heretofore vied to outdo each other in acquiring the latest English finery, were the featured players in this novel form of political theater. Its setting was usually the home of a local minister where, early in the morning, "respectable" young ladies, all dressed in homespun, assembled with their spinning wheels. They spent the day spinning furiously, stopping only to sustain themselves with "American produce . . . which was more agreeable to them than any foreign Dainties and Delicacies" and to drink herbal tea. At the end of the day the minister accepted their homespun cloth and delivered an edifying sermon to all present. That was a large group, often including from 20 to 100 "respectable" female spinners as well as hundreds of other townsfolk who had come to watch the competition or to provide food and entertainment. The Reverend Ezra Stiles of Newport, Rhode Island, hosted a spinning bee that drew, by his estimate, 600 spectators.

Women reveled in the new attention and value that the male resistance movement and the radical press now attached to a common and humdrum domestic task. By the beginning of 1769 New England newspapers were giving extensive coverage to spinning bees and their female participants, sometimes termed the "Daughters of Liberty." Front pages overflowed with praise of female patriotism: "The industry and frugality of American ladies must exalt their character in the Eyes of the World and serve to show how greatly they are contributing to bring about the political salvation of a whole Continent."

Spinning competitions and the vogue of wearing homespun served two political purposes. First, the bees actively enlisted American women in the struggle against Britain. The wives and daughters from families of every rank were made to feel

Daily Lives

Hunting shirts like the one worn by this rifleman (second figure from the right) captured the imagination of the French army officer in America who made these watercolor sketches of uniforms of revolutionary soldiers. The enlistment of blacks (infantryman at the far left) drew the artist's attention as well.

that they could play an important role in the resistance by imitating the elite women showcased in public spinning spectacles. Every woman could display her devotion to liberty by encouraging industry and frugality in her own household. Many women took pride in the new political importance that radical propaganda attributed to domestic pursuits. Writing to her English cousin, Charity Clarke of New York City cast herself as one of America's "fighting army of amazones . . . armed with spinning wheels." Although "heroines may not distinguish themselves at the head of an Army," the young woman assured her cousin, American women could still defend their "new arcadia" from "arbitrary power" by clothing its inhabitants "with the work of our hands."

Spinning bees and "dressing down" in homespun also contributed to the solidarity of the resistance by narrowing the visible distance between rich and poor Americans. In accounts of spinning competitions, the radical press emphasized that the spinners came from "as good families as any in town," demonstrating that even daughters of the elite sacrificed for the cause of resistance by embracing domestic economy and simplicity. And what genteel women wove, leading men wore. On public occasions throughout the revolutionary crisis, radical leaders appeared in homespun, an ostentatious display of both their patriotic virtue and their identification with poorer Americans who could not afford British finery. When they returned to their home counties to muster local militia companies, many southern gentlemen—indeed, most members of the Virginia House of Burgesses—adopted homespun "hunting shirts," long, loose, full-sleeved frocks that reached past the thigh. This staple of the attire of ordinary frontiersmen since the beginning of the eighteenth century at once united the gentry with ordinary men of the backcountry while declaring their superiority to the corrupt mother country.

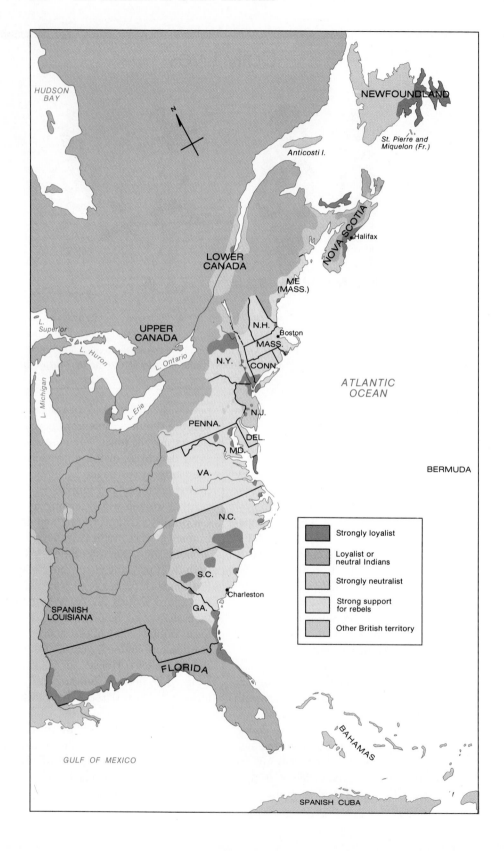

who did so voiced objections to the Tea Act. But worse than British taxation, in their view, was the radicalism of American resistance—the dumping of tea into Boston harbor, the forming of the Association, and the flouting of royal authority.

If any single characteristic distinguished the loyalists' thinking, it was their deep conviction of the divisiveness and instability of colonial society. If Americans won independence, they feared, the chaos of civil war would envelop the continent. Without the British around to maintain order, controversies among Americans would mushroom into armed conflicts. On the eve of the Revolution, Jonathan Boucher, a New York loyalist of uncanny prescience, warned:

> See ye not that after some few years of civil broils all the fair settlements in the middle and southern colonies will be seized on by our more enterprising and restless fellow-colonists of the North. . . ? O 'tis a monstrous and unnatural coalition; and we should as soon expect to see . . . the wolf and the lamb feed together, as Virginians to form a cordial union with the saints of New England.

Predictably, the king and Parliament commanded the strongest support in New York, New Jersey, Pennsylvania, and the Carolinas, colonies that had been wracked by severe internal strife earlier in the eighteenth century. In these colonies a history of struggle not only sharpened worries of future upheaval, but old adversaries also took different sides in the Revolution. The Carolina backcountry emerged early as a stronghold of loyalist sentiment, principally because some former frontier Regulators refused to make common cause with their old enemies, the coastal planters, most of whom advocated independence. The same reasoning held among the former land rioters of New York and New Jersey. If their old landlord opponents opted for the rebel cause, the tenants took up loyalism. Everywhere that controversies over land tenure and political representation had raged before the Revolution, the losers in those contests gravitated toward loyalism during the Revolution.

Other influences also fostered allegiance to the king. About 10 percent of the loyalists were government officials who owed their jobs to the empire or major city merchants who depended on British trade. Those Anglicans living outside the South retained strong ties to the parent country because of their membership in the Church of England. Loyalists were also disproportionately represented among recent emigrants from the British Isles. The inhabitants of Georgia, the newest colony, inclined toward the king, as did the Highland Scots, many of whom had arrived in the colonies as soldiers during the Seven Years' War or had worked for a short time in the southern backcountry as tobacco merchants and Indian traders.

Although a substantial minority, loyalists were the least of the problems facing republican leaders. While there were supporters of the king in all the colonies, they never became numerous enough anywhere to pose a serious threat to the Revolution. A more serious problem was posed by the British army, the most formidable in Europe. An even more serious problem was posed by those very Americans who claimed that they wanted independence. For the question remained: would they fight?

PATTERNS OF ALLEGIANCE
While most New Englanders rallied behind the rebel cause, support for the Revolution was not as widespread in the Middle and southern colonies.

THE FIGHTING IN THE NORTH

Perhaps more numerous than either diehard loyalists or dedicated rebels, at least in the summer of 1775, were Americans who wished to remain neutral. Strictly from a military standpoint, staying neutral made a lot more sense than fighting for independence. Even the most ardent advocates of American rights had reason to harbor second thoughts, given the odds against the rebel colonists defeating the armed forces of the British empire. And no friend of the American cause sized up the dismal chances of a rebel victory more accurately than George Washington.

June of 1775 found Washington, 43 years old, in Philadelphia, a delegate to the Second Continental Congress. He attended its deliberations dressed—a bit conspicuously—in his officer's uniform. The other delegates listened closely to his opinions on military matters, for Washington was the most celebrated American veteran of the Seven Years' War still young enough to lead a campaign. Better still, he was a southerner, who, if chosen to command Congress' forces, could bring his region into what thus far had remained mostly New England's fight. John Adams proposed that Congress accept the volunteer forces surrounding British-held Boston as a Continental Army and appoint a commander-in-chief. He made no secret of his preference for Washington, and the Congress followed his lead.

The Two Armies at Bay

So Washington found himself, only a month later, outside Boston in the once-quiet college town of Cambridge, the commander-in-chief of the Continental Army. Maturity had muted some of the impulsiveness and ambition that marred his performance at Fort Necessity in 1754. But the grave, dignified Virginia planter who took charge of the rebels massing around Boston had lost none of his admiration for the British army.

There was much to admire. Highly trained, ably commanded, and efficiently equipped, the king's troops were seasoned professionals. Rigorous drills and often savage discipline administered by an aristocratic officer corps welded rank-and-file soldiers, men drawn mainly from the bottom of British society, into a formidable fighting machine. They marched in precise formations, loaded and discharged their muskets on orders, held ranks under fire, and fought with the courage instilled by stringent military regimen. At the height of the campaign in America, reinforcements brought the number of British troops to 50,000, their strength augmented by some 30,000 Hessian mercenaries from Germany and the support of half the ships in the British navy, the largest in the world.

Washington was more modest about the army under his command, and he had a great deal to be modest about. At first Congress recruited his fighting force of 16,600 rebel "regulars," the Continental Army, from the ranks of local militia bands, armed civilians from everywhere in New England who converged on Boston in 1775. Although a flurry of patriotic enthusiasm swelled enlistments briefly during 1775, for the rest of the war Washington's Continentals suffered chronic shortages of men and supplies. Even strong supporters of the Revolution did not want to join the regular army. They disdained the low pay and strict discipline and feared the disease and danger that were the lot of a professional soldier. Most men preferred to fight instead as members of local militia units, the "irregular" troops who turned out as adjuncts to the regular army whenever British forces came close to their neighborhoods.

The general reluctance to join the Continental Army created a host of difficulties for its commander and for Congress. Washington wanted and needed an army whose size and military capability could be counted on in long campaigns. He could not create an effective fighting force out of civilians who mustered out occasionally with the militia or enlisted for short stints in the Continental Army. Washington's insistence on a professional military establishment clashed with the inclinations of most republican leaders. They feared standing armies and idealized "citizen-soldiers," volunteers who took up arms whenever needed, as the backbone of the common defense. "Oh, that I was a soldier," John Adams rhapsodized in 1775, "I will be.—I am reading military books. Everyone must and will and shall be a soldier."

But not everyone became a soldier. The dwindling number of volunteers gradually overcame republican scruples about standing armies. In September 1776 Congress set terms in the Continental Army at a minimum of three years or for the duration of the war and assigned each state to raise a certain number of troops. They offered every man who enlisted in the army a cash bounty and a yearly clothing issue; enlistees for the duration were offered 100 acres of land as well. Still the problem of recruitment persisted. Less than a year later, Congress recommended that the states adopt a draft. Some passed conscription laws, but Congress had no authority to compel the states to meet their troop quotas.

Even in the summer of 1775, before enlistments fell off, Washington was worried. As his Continentals laid siege to British-occupied Boston, he measured them against the adversary and found them wanting. Not only were his Continentals complete strangers to military drill and discipline, they regularly shirked the most basic responsibilities of soldiers. The rank and file slipped away from camp at night; they left sentry duty before being relieved; they took potshots at the British; they tolerated filthy conditions in their camps. Inexperienced officers provided no real leadership. And the several thousand militia lending occasional support around Boston were even more stubbornly independent, undisciplined, and dirty.

Then there were "the Women of the Army." When American men went off to fight, their wives usually stayed at home. To women then fell the sole responsibility for running farms and businesses, raising children, and keeping households together. They helped to supply the troops by sewing clothing, making blankets, and saving rags and lead weights for bandages and bullets. Other women on the home front organized relief for the widows and orphans of soldiers and protests against merchants who hoarded scarce commodities. But the wives of poor men who joined the army were often left with no means to support their families. Thousands of such women—one for every 15 soldiers—drifted after the troops. In return for half-rations, they cooked and washed for the soldiers, and, after battles, nursed the wounded, buried the dead, and scavenged the field for clothing and equipment. An even larger number of women accompanied the redcoats: their presence was the only thing that Washington did not admire about the British army and could barely tolerate in his own. From the beginning to the end of the Revolution, Washington fumed that women were "a clog upon every movement" of the Continentals.

It was fortunate that Washington no longer lusted for fame and military glory, because his army seemed likely to bring him humiliation and defeat. He could only set aside his doubts about the prospects for military victory and set about imposing discipline on officers and men alike. As soon as Washington assumed command, he issued orders that covered everything from the proper procedure for standing guard to restrictions on "profane cursing, swearing, and drunkenness." He tried repeatedly to get rid of the "Women of the Army" as well—without success. The services that they performed were indispensable, and women followed the troops throughout the war.

Laying Strategies

At the same time that he tried to bring order to the ranks, Washington designed a defensive strategy to compensate for the weakness of his army. To avoid exposing raw rebel troops on "open ground against their Superiors in number and Discipline," he planned to fight the British from strong fortifications. In March 1776, Washington barricaded his Continentals on Dorchester Heights, an elevation commanding Boston harbor from the south.

Even before the besieging rebels encroached on Dorchester Heights, General William Howe, who had replaced Gage as the head of the British land forces in North America, had decided to back out of Boston. Now the certain peril that rebel artillery on the Heights would pose to British warships in Boston harbor prodded Howe into an immediate evacuation. By March 27, 1776, the occupying army of 5000 British regulars had departed for Halifax, Nova Scotia.

The evacuation of Boston marked Britain's abandonment of their first strategy for reclaiming colonies—strangling the insurgency in Massachusetts—in favor of another approach. By now the British had discerned that they were up against more than a Yankee rabble aroused by a few agitators. More than a quick, directed strike against New England would be required to arrest the cancer of resistance. Instead, the situation called for Britain to wage a conventional war in America, capturing major cities and crushing the Continental forces in a decisive battle. Military victory, the British believed, would enable them to restore political control and reestablish imperial authority.

The first target was New York City. General Howe and Lord George Germain, the new American secretary charged with overseeing the war, chose that seaport for its central location, its excellent harbor, and—they hoped—its large loyalist population. They planned for Howe's army to move from New York City up the Hudson River, meeting ultimately with a smaller complement of British troops under General Sir Guy Carleton coming south from Canada. Either the British drive would lure Washington into a major engagement, drubbing the Continentals, or, if unopposed, the British offensive would cut America in two, smothering resistance to the south by isolating New England.

The strategy seemed sound enough, but the two men charged with its execution hobbled British efforts from the outset. General Howe took to extremes the conventional wisdom of eighteenth-century European warfare, which aimed as much at avoiding heavy casualties as winning victories against the enemy. The difficulty and expense of recruiting, training, and maintaining professional soldiers dictated conservative strategies of battle. Concern for preserving manpower dominated Howe's approach throughout his American campaigns, addicting him to caution when greater daring would have carried the day. Howe's brother, Admiral Lord Richard Howe, the head of naval operations in America, also refrained from pressing the British advantage. A true eccentric among the English of his day, Richard Howe actually liked Americans. Torn between the ministry's orders to subdue the colonies by military force and his personal desire for reconciliation, Admiral Howe prosecuted the war halfheartedly. The reluctance of both of the

Howe brothers to fight became the formula for British frustration in the two years that followed.

The Campaigns in New York and New Jersey

However cautiously, General William Howe and his army sailed from Halifax and landed on Staten Island in New York harbor during July 1776. Admiral Richard Howe followed with reinforcements by sea. The Continentals marched from Boston and fortified Brooklyn Heights on Long Island, the key to the defenses of New York City on Manhattan Island. By mid-August, 32,000 British troops, including 8000 Hessians, the largest expeditionary force of the eighteenth century, faced Washington's army of 23,000.

At dawn on August 22, the Howe brothers moved on Long Island. Although the British easily pushed the rebel army from Brooklyn Heights back across the East River to Manhattan, the Howe brothers lingered on Long Island for almost a month. While the rebel militia deserted in droves and his supplies dwindled, Washington waited in Manhattan, wondering whether to defend New York City or withdraw. Just as he prepared to pull out, marching his army north through Harlem, the Howe brothers at last lurched into action, ferrying their forces to Kip's Bay, just a few miles south of Harlem. When the British landed, the handful of rebel defenders at Kip's Bay fled—straight into the towering wrath of Washington, who happened on the scene of their humiliation. Enraged by the rout, the general lost his habitual self-restraint, flogged both officers and men with his riding crop, and came close to being captured himself.

On the next day, September 16, the rebels managed to hold back the wave of British advance at Harlem Heights. The Howe brothers, still reluctant to hit hard with everything they had, let Washington's army escape from Manhattan to Westchester County on the mainland. Throughout the fall of 1776, General Howe's forces followed as Washington's fell back, first northward into New York and then southward into New Jersey. By mid-November the British advance picked up speed, and the rebels stepped up their retreat across New Jersey into a desperate race for the Delaware River. With the pursuing British army at his heels, Washington reached Trenton and ferried his forces across the river to Pennsylvania on December 7. There Howe suspended his pursuit, pulling back most of his army to winter in New York City and leaving the Hessians to hold the British line of advance along the New Jersey side of the Delaware River.

In spite of everything, Washington decided that the campaign of 1776 was not over. Although the British had harried the Continentals from their positions throughout New York and New Jersey, although the retreat had shriveled rebel strength to only 3000 men, half of whose enlistments would end with the year, and although the winter cold had settled over the Northeast, Washington wanted to play one last card.

His gamble paid off. On a frosty Christmas night, as it rained, sleeted, and snowed, Washington floated his forces back across the Delaware, their boats dodging chunks of ice. As dawn broke, the Continentals picked their way across roads sheeted with ice and blanketed with snow and finally slid into Hessian-held Trenton at eight in the morning. One thousand German soldiers, disabled by their spirited Christmas celebration and caught completely by surprise, quickly surrendered.

When word of Washington's daring exploit reached Howe in New York City, he ordered to Trenton forces under his subordinate officer, Charles, Lord Cornwallis. But Washington's luck held. On January 3, 1777, the Continentals slipped past Cornwallis' main force and struck at a smaller British detachment on the outskirts of Princeton, New Jersey. The rebel victories at Trenton and Princeton whittled away the British hold on New Jersey. Cornwallis withdrew to New Brunswick, while Washington's army watched the enemy from their winter camp at Morristown, just 25 miles from New York City.

The rebels enjoyed the view from Morristown. During that winter of 1776–1777, the British alienated the very civilians whose loyalties they had hoped to cultivate. In New York City the presence of the main body of the British army brought shortages of food and housing and fostered constant friction between soldiers and city dwellers. In the New Jersey countryside still held by the Hessians, the situation was even worse. Forced to live off the land, the Germans aroused resentment among local farmers by seizing "hay, oats, Indian corn, cattle, and horses, which were never or but very seldom paid for," as one loyalist admitted; ". . . in many instances their families were insulted, stripped of their beds with other furniture—nay, even of their very wearing apparel." The Hessians ransacked and destroyed homes and churches; they kidnaped and raped young women.

Instead of protecting civilians and nurturing loyalist sentiment, the British army menaced local peace and prosperity. Americans who had had enough of the king's men could take their allegiance elsewhere, for Washington had demonstrated at Trenton and Princeton the credibility of the Continental Army as a fighting force. The result was a surge of popular support for the revolutionary cause throughout the region: bands of militia irregulars on Long Island, along the Hudson River, and all over New Jersey rallied and raided British patrols and foraging parties.

Capturing Philadelphia

Spring came and passed into summer in 1777 before word filtered down to the anxious Continentals in Morristown that the British were on the move again—boarding ships in New York harbor. General Howe had not changed his strategy: he still hoped to entice the Continentals into a decisive engagement or to seize a major American seaport, control the surrounding countryside, and solicit loyalist support. But Howe had now decided to goad the Americans into battle by capturing Philadelphia. Rather than risk his army on a march through hostile New Jersey, he intended to approach the rebel capital by sea. In July Howe's army of 15,000 set sail, leaving behind a force of 7300 to hold New York.

In early August rebel spies sighted on the Chesapeake Bay the British convoy carrying Howe's army. As the redcoats disembarked on the Maryland shore and headed for Philadelphia, 50 miles away, Washington's army, swelled to 11,000, hurried south from New Jersey. Washington had hoped to stay on the strategic defensive, holding his smaller army together, harassing the enemy, but avoiding full-scale engagements. Howe's march on Philadelphia made that impossible: he could not allow the British to seize the fledgling nation's capital.

On September 11 the two armies joined battle at Brandywine Creek, where the British scored a major victory and the Continentals beat a disorganized retreat. The rebels managed to stay between the advancing British and the city until September 26, when Howe decoyed the Continentals up the Schuylkill River and

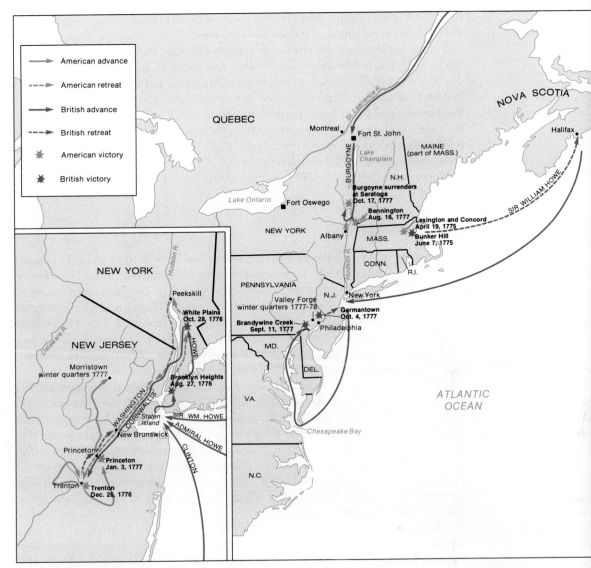

THE FIGHTING IN THE NORTH, 1775–1777

claimed Philadelphia. He quartered his main force of some 9000 men in German-town, a village five miles northwest of the city. Washington struck back quickly, surprising the British at Germantown in the dawn of October 4, but Howe's troops recovered and forced another rebel retreat.

Germantown was a miss for Washington—but it was a near miss, too close for Howe's comfort. The Americans could take satisfaction not only from a new pride that sustained the army even in defeat, but also from the difficulties that blighted the British even in victory. Although the British held Philadelphia, rebel-held forts along the Delaware blocked the flow of supplies and reinforcements into the capital until mid-November. The natives of the conquered city were restless, too. In Philadelphia, as in New York, British occupation jacked up demand and prices for food, fuel, and housing. While inflation hit hardest at the poor, the wealthy resented British officers who became their uninvited house guests. Everyone in Philadelphia complained of redcoats looting their shops, trampling their gardens, and harassing them on the streets. Elizabeth Drinker, the wife of a Quaker merchant, confided in her diary that "I often feel afraid to go to bed."

Even worse, the British march through Maryland and Pennsylvania had terrified and outraged civilians, who fled before the army and then returned to find their homes and barns bare, their crops and livestock gone. Everywhere Howe's men went in the middle states, they left in their wake Americans with compelling reasons to support the rebels. But worst of all, just days after Howe marched his occupying army into Philadelphia in the fall of 1777, another British commander in North America was surrendering his entire army to rebel forces at Saratoga, New York.

Disaster at Saratoga

The calamity that befell the British at Saratoga had been in the making ever since the previous winter. While Washington was reclaiming parts of the New Jersey countryside and Howe was simmering in New York City, another general, back in London, was jockeying for an independent command. Glamorous, glory-mongering John "Gentleman Johnny" Burgoyne had served under Sir Guy Carleton in Canada. After Carleton bungled a drive into New York during the summer of 1776, Burgoyne went back to Britain to urge Germain and George III to attack from Canada again, this time under more aggressive leadership—his own.

Burgoyne proposed to cut off New England by pressing down Lake Champlain and then south along the Hudson River to Albany. He left vague exactly what he would do once he got as far as Albany and exactly how his maneuvering would isolate New England, but Germain and the king asked no questions. Nor did they try to coordinate Burgoyne's drive with the movements of Howe's army, who might have assisted by heading north up the Hudson. Howe, bent on taking Philadelphia and unwilling to share military glory with Burgoyne, offered no support; and Burgoyne, bent on taking Albany and unwilling to share military glory with anyone, requested none.

Burgoyne began his campaign by calling for support from those "friendly civilians" whom the British consistently expected to find in great numbers. Few stepped forward, especially after Burgoyne's bullying threat to unleash the Iroquois against frontier settlements. Nevertheless, at the end of June 1777 Burgoyne set out from Quebec with a force of 9500 redcoats, 2000 women and children, and an elaborate baggage train that included the commander's silver dining service, his dress uniforms, and numerous cases of his favorite champagne. As the British marched into New York, a handful of Continentals and a horde of New England militia assembled at Bemis Heights, an elevation 200 feet above the Hudson River and several miles below Saratoga, under the command of General Horatio Gates. An elderly, rough-hewn man, "Granny" Gates enjoyed great popularity with his troops, but he exercised little discipline and shared with the Howe brothers a lack of daring.

If the rebels in New York lacked an effective commander, the British under Burgoyne faced an even more formidable disadvantage—the treacherous terrain from Quebec to Albany. The route before them led over a winding road, broken by boulders and felled trees and knit together with long, ramshackle bridges that swayed over yawning ravines. Burgoyne's huge entourage lumbered southward like a stately royal caravan gone astray, the rigors of the journey exhausting men, horses, and supplies. To replenish his stocks, Burgoyne dispatched a foraging party of 600 Hessians to the Connecticut River, only to have them stopped at Bennington, Vermont, and mauled by a much larger rebel force under Brigadier General John Stark.

As the dispirited Burgoyne continued his halting advance toward Albany, Gates and several thousand rebels were fortifying Bemis Heights. On September 19, scouts nested high in the trees spied the glitter of bayonets and alerted Gates to the British approach. Benedict Arnold, a dashing young officer who had organized several heroic but futile rebel forays into Canada, persuaded a reluctant Gates that British fire would pry open the rebel fortifications. Arnold led the forces that descended from Bemis Heights and swarmed into the surrounding woods, meeting Burgoyne's men in a clearing at Freeman's Farm. Arnold spearheaded repeated charges across the clearing, and the British rallied and returned the assaults. At the end of the day, British reinforcements finally pushed the rebels back from a battlefield piled high with the bodies of soldiers from both sides. Burgoyne's army, bleeding after its mangling at Freeman's Farm, hemorrhaged as it started back toward Canada with the rebels in deadly pursuit. On October 17, Burgoyne stopped his flight at Saratoga and surrendered his entire army to Gates.

Saratoga changed everything. With Burgoyne's surrender, the British did not lose their military superiority in America, but they lost something just as important: the conviction that the war was theirs to win. And with Burgoyne's surrender, the rebels did not gain irresistible momentum on the battlefield, but they did succeed in convincing France that, with a little help, the Americans might well reap the fruits of victory. The new British uncertainty and the new French alliance soon transformed the American Revolution into a global war.

THE TURNING POINT

France had been waiting since 1763 for revenge against Britain. Humiliated by defeat in the Seven Years' War, the French yearned for an opportunity to reclaim their fisheries in the North Atlantic, to secure their colonies in the Caribbean, and to reassert their supremacy in Europe. Since the mid-1760s, as France's agents in America sent home reports of a rebellion brewing, a scheme for evening the score with Britain had been taking shape in the mind of the French foreign minister, Charles Gravier de Vergennes. In the disaffected Americans he reckoned that France might find willing allies against Britain.

An Alliance Formed

Vergennes approached his prospective allies cautiously. He wanted to make certain that the rift between Britain and its colonies would not be reconciled. He also wanted to make certain that the rebels in America stood a fighting chance. Although France had been secretly supplying the Continental Army with guns and ammunition since the spring of 1776, Vergennes would go no further than covert assistance—until Saratoga.

Congress approached their former French enemies with equal caution. In November 1775 they deputized a secret committee to solicit foreign aid, and after declaring independence they aimed at open recognition and assistance from France. But would France, the leading Catholic monarchy in Europe, make common cause with the republican rebels? A few years earlier American colonials had fought against the French in Canada; only recently they had renounced a king; and for centuries they had overwhelmingly adhered to Protestantism. And if Congress contracted an alliance with France, what would the French want in return?

The string of defeats dealt the Continental Army during 1776 convinced Congress that they needed the French enough to accept both the contradictions and the costs of such an alliance. In November Congress appointed a commission to negotiate not only aid from France but also a formal alliance. That commission included Silas Deane of Connecticut, Arthur Lee of Virginia, and a past master at achieving the improbable, Benjamin Franklin, whose arrival in Paris created a sensation.

Because of their sophistication, the French prized innocence, which they associated with America. In spite of their sophistication, they mistook Benjamin Franklin for an American innocent. From the moment Franklin stepped onto French soil, sporting a simple fur cap and a pair of spectacles (something no fashionable Frenchman wore in public), he was hailed as a homespun sage, sprung from the unspoiled wilderness of Philadelphia. While Franklin basked in his popularity among the Parisians, who stamped his face on everything from the top of snuffboxes to the bottom of porcelain chamber pots, he knew that public adulation would not produce the alliance sought by Congress. Franklin could do nothing more to advance the rebel cause—until Saratoga.

British officials played nicely into his hands, for at the beginning of 1778, just weeks after news of Burgoyne's surrender crossed the Atlantic, they authorized a commission headed by Lord Carlisle to negotiate a peace settlement. The Carlisle Commission made an offer that Congress could not have refused two years earlier. They invited Americans to return to the empire as it had existed before 1763—no parliamentary taxes, no oppressive legislation, but also, of course, no independence. Franklin knew that Congress would dismiss the peace overtures, but the anxious Vergennes did not. So the simple, straightforward American turned the screws, playing on French fears that the Carlisle Commission might reconcile Britain with its former colonies.

Determined to weaken England and convinced by Saratoga that the Continental Army could win, Vergennes willingly succumbed to Franklin's pressure. In February 1778, France signed a treaty of commerce and friendship and a treaty of alliance, which Congress approved in May. Under the terms of the treaties, both parties agreed to accept nothing short of independence for America, and France pledged to renounce all future claims in continental North America and to relinquish any territory captured in the war. The alliance left the British no option other than to declare war on France. Less than a year later Spain joined France, hoping to recover territory lost to England in earlier wars.

As the Revolution widened into a European war after 1778, the British could take some comfort from being able, once again, to think about Americans as little as possible. Hostilities with France and Spain posed a grave peril, but at least the British understood how to wage and win a war against European powers. The same could not be said about the struggle in America. There the British had fought bravely, captured major cities, and gained important victories—but their con-

The French public's infatuation with Franklin knew no bounds, as this painting, entitled *The Genius of Franklin*, illustrates.

quests failed to restore political control. They knew how to win battles, but they could not figure out how to extinguish the rebellion. After 1778, few British officials even tried to figure it out. The struggle with France and Spain absorbed their attention; the war in America became a sideshow.

Winding Down the War in the North

Preparing to fight France dictated a reorganization of British strategy and command in America. No longer could the British concentrate on crushing the Continental Army; instead they would disperse their forces to fend off challenges all over the world. George III and his ministers also decided to deploy some of the troops in America to attack France's possessions in the West Indies, the rich sugar islands. In May, Sir Henry Clinton replaced William Howe as commander-in-chief and received orders to cut his commitments in Philadelphia and withdraw to New York City. There, and in Newport, Rhode Island, Clinton was to maintain defensive bases for harrying northern coastal towns. But the strategic future lay southward. Clinton planned to dispatch some 5000 men to the Caribbean and another 3000 to Florida. In addition, the British laid plans for a new offensive drive in the American South.

Before dawn on June 18, 1778, the British army of 10,000 men started out of Philadelphia and overland toward New York. That same morning, word of the British march reached rebel headquarters. Clinton's cumbersome column of men and supply trains snaking slowly northward was a target too tempting to be resisted by Washington and his Continentals at Valley Forge.

Some 11,000 rebel soldiers had passed a harrowing winter in that isolated spot, starving for want of food, freezing for lack of clothing, huddling in miserable huts, and hating the British who lay 18 miles away in Philadelphia. The army also cursed their own countrymen, for the misery of the soldiers resulted from congressional weakness and disorganization and civilian corruption and indifference. Congress lacked both money to pay and maintain the army and an efficient system for dispensing provisions to the troops. And most farmers and merchants preferred contracting to supply the British, who could pay handsomely, to doing business with financially strapped Congress and the Continentals. What little did reach the army often was food too rancid to eat or clothing too rotten to wear. Perhaps 2500 perished at Valley Forge, the victims of cold, hunger, and disease.

Why did civilians who considered themselves patriotic allow the army to suffer? Probably because by the winter of 1777, the Continentals came mainly from social classes that received little consideration at any time. The middle-class farmers and artisans who had laid siege to Boston in 1775 had stopped enlisting. Respectable, propertied rebels wanted nothing to do with the Continental Army. As for the virtuous "citizen-soldier" rising to the defense of the Republic, "I knew it to be impossible," John Adams snapped, in an abrupt change of mind. Serving in their stead were single men in their teens and early twenties, some who joined the army out of desperation, others who were drafted, still others who were hired as substitutes for the more affluent. The landless sons of farmers, unemployed laborers, drifters, petty criminals, vagrants, indentured servants, slaves, even captured British and Hessian soldiers—all men with no other means and no other choice—were swept into the Continental Army. "The most undisciplined, profligate Crew that were ever collected," was how James Warren of Massachusetts described the army. The social composition of the rebel rank and file had come to resemble that of the British army.

It is the great irony of the Revolution: a war to protect liberty and property

The soldiers depicted in this 1777 illustration condemn civilian neglect and the profiteering of private contractors who supplied the Continental Army. Such grievances would provoke mutinies within the army before the end of the fighting.

First Soldier: "Keep up courage, my boys, we will soon bring those villains to terms."

Second Soldier: "These d__d Extortioners are the worst enemies to the country."

Third Soldier: "I serve my country for sixteen pence a day, pinched with cold."

was waged by those Americans who were poorest and least free. The army did not forget the misery that they endured not only at Valley Forge, but also for the two winters that followed.

The beginning of spring in 1778 brought a reprieve. Supplies arrived at Valley Forge, and so did a fellow calling himself the Baron von Steuben. A penniless Prussian soldier of fortune, the Baron came to the Continental Army recommended by Franklin. Although Washington's men had shown spirit and resilience ever since Trenton, they still lacked discipline and training. Those defects and more von Steuben began to remedy. Barking orders and spewing curses in German and French, the Baron (and his translators) drilled the rebel regiments to march in formation and to handle their bayonets like proper Prussian soldiers. By the summer of 1778, morale had rebounded as professional skill and pride fused solidarity among Continental ranks in the crucible of Valley Forge.

Spoiling for action after their long winter, Washington's army, now numbering nearly 13,500, set out to harass Clinton's army as it headed for New York. The Continentals caught up with the British force on June 28 at Monmouth Courthouse and got more than they bargained for. The long, confused battle ended in a draw; after both armies retired for the night, exhausted by combat and summer heat, Clinton's forces slipped away. A week later the British reached safety in New York City.

With the Battle of Monmouth Courthouse, the Continental Army had come of age, holding its own against the best army in Europe. Washington longed to launch an all-out assault on New York City, but he lacked the necessary numbers. And with the defenses of New York secured, Clinton had fulfilled his objectives: he would not offer battle. The main force of the Continental Army camped at White Plains outside of occupied New York City and waited. The war in the north had stalemated.

Now the fighting between the Continental Army and civilian rebel leaders began. While Washington waited outside New York City, his army started to come apart. During two hard winters, resentments mounted among the rank and file over spoiled food, inadequate clothing, and arrears in pay. Petitions to Congress and the state legislatures produced pensions for the officers but no improvements for their men. The army responded with mutinies. Between 1779 and 1780 officers managed to quell uprisings in three New England regiments. But in January 1781 both the Pennsylvania and New Jersey lines mutinied outright and marched on Philadelphia, where Congress had reconvened. Order returned only after Congress promised back pay and provisions and Washington put two ringleaders in front of a firing squad.

Trouble also loomed on the western frontier. From a fortress at Detroit, a British official named Henry Hamilton, known, for good reason, as the "Hair Buyer," stirred up the Great Lakes tribes to attack settlers in Kentucky and West Virginia. In October 1778 Hamilton himself led some Indians south into the Illinois–Indiana country and took Vincennes from a handful of rebel Virginians. A few months later, the rebels, led by a burly young Virginian named George Rogers Clark, known—since scalping was hardly restricted to the Indians—as "Long Knife," drove the "Hair Buyer" from Vincennes.

After the disastrous winter at Valley Forge, Baron Friedrich Wilhelm von Steuben helped to restore the morale and to improve the military skills of Continental soldiers.

While Clark and his few hundred troops helped to contain Indian raids in the Old Northwest, General John Sullivan led an expedition against the Iroquois in upstate New York. From Fort Niagara loyalists under Major John Butler and Iroquois fighters under a Mohawk chief, Thayendanegea (called Joseph Brant by the English), had conducted a series of bloody raids along the New York and Pennsylvania frontiers. Sullivan and his expedition routed the marauders and retaliated, burning over 40 Indian villages.

Both the British and the rebels sought support from the Indians, because the most powerful tribes determined the balance of power on the frontier. Most of the tribes maintained their neutrality, but those who took sides usually joined the British, who had tried to stem the tide of Americans taking Indian lands.

The Home Front in the North

While fighting continued on the frontier and English and Hessian troops made occasional attacks on Connecticut coastal towns in 1779, the stalemate in the North afforded most civilians a welcome respite from the war. Since the outbreak of the fighting at Lexington and Concord, every movement of troops—or rumor of movement—had pitched the inhabitants of threatened neighborhoods into a panic. Refugees on foot and in carts hastily packed with their belongings filled the roads, fleeing the advancing armies. "By this time the Cannon began to roar," wrote Mary Silliman, a Connecticut mother who escaped a British coastal raid with her two-year-old son Selleck, "which pleased Selleck, and he would mimic them by saying *bang, bang.* But they were doleful sounds in our ears." Those who remained to protect their homes and property ran multiple risks. They might be caught in the crossfire of contending forces, endangered by the fighting itself, or cut off from supplies of food and firewood. Loyalists who remained in areas occupied by rebel troops faced harassment, imprisonment, or the confiscation of their property; rebel sympathizers endured similar fates in regions held by the British. Disease, however, was no respecter of political allegiances: military camps and occupied towns spawned epidemics of dysentery and smallpox that devastated civilians as well as soldiers, rebels and loyalists alike.

When the war moved on, the families who had remained and the refugees who returned confronted their losses—crops and livestock stolen, fences and barns demolished, churches and meetinghouses converted into barracks and stables. While plundering armies destroyed and damaged civilian property wherever they marched, military demands disrupted family economies throughout the northern countryside. The seasons of intense fighting drew men off into military service just when their labor was most needed on family farms. Wives and daughters were left to assume the "outside duties" of husbands and sons while coping with loneliness, anxiety, and grief. Often enough, the disruptions, flight, and loss of family members left lasting scars. Two years after she fled before Burgoyne's advance into upstate New York, Ann Eliza Bleecker confessed to a friend, "Alas! the wilderness is within: I muse so long on the dead until I am unfit for the company of the living."

Although such wounds could be searing, many women vigorously supported the revolutionary cause in a variety of ways. The Daughters of Liberty continued to join their brethren in harassing loyalists who refused to commit themselves to the rebel cause; one outspoken dissident found himself surrounded by Daughters who stripped off his shirt, covered him with molasses, and plastered him with flower petals. In Massachusetts a crowd of some 400 women marched on a local merchant who was hoarding coffee, newly popular in the wake of the tea boycotts. In more genteel fashion, a group of well-to-do women founded the Ladies Association of Philadelphia, an organization that divided the city into districts and went door-to-door, collecting contributions. The idea spread to four other states, with women collecting not only money but medicines, food, and pewter to melt for bullets.

THE STRUGGLE IN THE SOUTH

Between the fall of 1778 and the summer of 1781, while Washington waited outside New York City and tried to control his mutinous army, the British stormed the American South. The few English politicians and generals who were still thinking about America after 1778 believed that the war could be won in that region. Loyalists, they believed, lay thick on southern ground, especially in the backcountry. Festering resentment of the seaboard, a rebel stronghold, bred among frontier folk a readiness to take up arms for the king at the first show of British force. On the other hand, southern rebels—especially the vulnerable planters along the coast—could never afford to turn their guns away from their slaves. So, at least, the British theorized. All that was needed, they concluded, was for the British army to establish a beachhead in the South and then, in league with loyalists, drive northward, pacifying the population while pressing up the coast. The idea had been already tried in the summer of 1776, when Clinton and Admiral Peter Parker had attempted an invasion of Charleston. Although some in the backcountry stood ready to support the British, the rebels held the coast, and their fire from Sullivan's Island in Charleston harbor drove the British back to sea. By 1778 the British were ready to try again.

The Siege of Charleston

The southern strategy worked well for a short time in a small place. In November 1778, Clinton detached 3500 troops to Savannah, Georgia. The resistance in the tiny colony quickly collapsed, and a gratifyingly large number of loyalists turned out to help the British invaders subdue the remnants of rebel forces and to reimpose royal control over Georgia. Everything was proceeding according to plan until the British reached South Carolina.

During the last days of 1779, an expedition under Clinton himself set sail out of New York City; for nearly a month, rain, snow, and high waves buffeted the British fleet. After drying out on Tybee Island off the Georgia coast, the troops mucked through the malarial swamps of Johns and James islands to the mainland of South Carolina. By then, April had arrived in the low country. Unseasonably warm weather made the area a heaven for sandflies and mosquitoes and a hell for human beings. Sweltering and swatting, redcoats weighted down in their woolen uniforms inched their siegeworks down the peninsula lying between the Ashley and Cooper rivers. At the tip of that neck of land stood the city of Charleston, and every night of burrowing in the soggy sand brought the British closer.

But they advanced at great cost. From "the Citadel," a fortification constructed across the northern end of the neck, more than 5000 Continental soldiers and South Carolina militia commanded by Major General Benjamin Lincoln threw everything that they had at the British. All day long the rebels fired rifles and muskets: by night they bombarded the enemy with a deadly assortment of projectiles—shards of glass, broken shovels, pickaxes, hatchets, and flatirons. The redcoats battered back with mortar shells and canisters filled with bullets. As the British pushed onward, each side could see by day the carnage in the other's camp; by night more men were maimed and killed in the murky, humid darkness. By the beginning of May, Clinton's siege lines lay within yards of the rebel Citadel, and his shelling was setting fire to houses within the city. On May 12 Charleston surrendered.

Much to Clinton's relief, he had not been obliged to destroy Charleston in order to save it for the British. His aim was not to devastate the city, but to pacify its defenders. To woo support, he paroled and pardoned many of his prisoners of war. Then he erred fatally by insisting that both military and civilian leaders take an oath of loyalty to the British cause. That demand rankled the rebels, forcing many back into active opposition. Even worse, Clinton's tender of pardons and paroles provoked the resentment of South Carolina's loyalists.

But Clinton did not stay in his conquered city long enough to experience the opposition aroused by his policies. By the end of June 1780 he was sailing back to New York, leaving behind 8300 men to reclaim the rest of South Carolina for the king and to carry the British offensive northward to Virginia. The man that Clinton left in command was his jealous and ambitious, but able subordinate, Charles, Lord Cornwallis.

The Partisan Struggle in the South

Even before Congress declared independence, civil war had erupted between local bands of rebels and loyalists in the South. Although loyalists were scarce in Charleston and along the coast, the king's supporters were more numerous in the Carolina backcountry. The rebel slogan "no taxation without representation" rang hollow to western farmers denied an equitable voice in eastern-dominated Carolina legislatures. The legacy of the Regulator movements had convinced many on the frontier that the Crown would be their best defense in any future contest with the coast. In fact, some frontier loyalists regarded the seaboard's strong support for independence as nothing more than a strategy for gaining a free hand in dealing with the backcountry.

In the summer and fall of 1775 the supporters of Congress and the new South Carolina revolutionary government denounced, mobbed, tortured, and imprisoned men who refused to sign the newly adopted Association. But these attacks only hardened loyalist resolve, as roving bands seized ammunition, mobilized to break their leaders out of jail, and besieged rebel outposts. Still, South Carolina's revolutionary government kept the upper hand. Reinforcements from the coast joined rebel militia on the frontier in defeating and disbanding loyalist forces in the backcountry.

But the fall of Charleston in 1780 aroused the dormant loyalists on the frontier, while the loss of the entire Continental line at Charleston made southern revolutionaries more willing to adopt new and unconventional modes of warfare. Out of loyalist vengefulness and rebel desperation issued the brutal partisan strug-

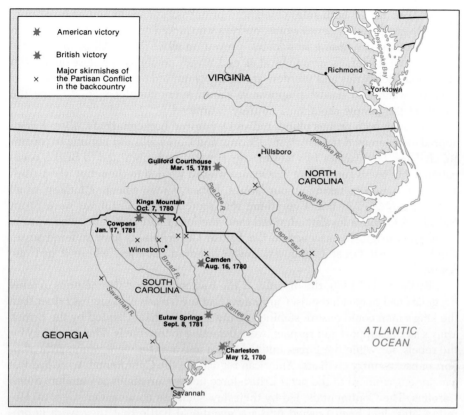

American victory

British victory

x Major skirmishes of the Partisan Conflict in the backcountry

VIRGINIA

Richmond

Chesapeake Bay

Yorktown

Roanoke R.

Hillsboro

Guilford Courthouse
Mar. 15, 1781

NORTH
CAROLINA

Neuse R.

Pee Dee R.

Kings Mountain
Oct. 7, 1780

Cowpens
Jan. 17, 1781

Cape Fear R.

Winnsboro

Broad R.

Camden
Aug. 16, 1780

SOUTH
CAROLINA

Savannah R.

Santee R.

Eutaw Springs
Sept. 8, 1781

GEORGIA

ATLANTIC
OCEAN

Charleston
May 12, 1780

Savannah

THE FIGHTING IN THE SOUTH, 1780–1781

gle that seared the southern backcountry after 1780. A bloody guerrilla war of ambush, arson, and atrocity, reprisal and counterreprisal raged in the Carolinas for the duration of the Revolution. Neighbors and even families fought and killed each other as members of roaming rebel and tory militias.

By the fall of 1780, the resistance had gathered real momentum, as rebel irregulars picked up victories and popular support. Francis Marion, the "Swamp Fox," and his band of white and black raiders cut British lines of communication between Charleston and the interior. Another rebel leader, the "Gamecock," Thomas Sumter, bloodied loyalist forces throughout the central part of South Carolina. Farther west, rebel over-the-mountain men capped the successes of Marion and Sumter at the Battle of King's Mountain in October 1780. The revolutionaries surrounded loyalist forces on a ridge running across the border between North and South Carolina and then, from the cover of pine trees, picked off enemy soldiers with long rifles.

Most families on the Carolina frontier wished only for a restoration of order. Like civilians in the middle states, those in the South lost property to pillaging soldiers: crops and livestock were snatched, slaves were stolen, and fences, fruit trees, and farm buildings were pulled down for firewood. But the intensity of partisan warfare in the backcountry produced unprecedented desolation and destruction. British troops and their loyalist allies plundered plantations and assaulted local women; rebel militias whipped suspected British supporters and burned their farms; both sides committed brutal assassinations and tortured prisoners. To make matters even worse, outlaws who lurked around the fringes of both armies, sometimes posing as soldiers, preyed on all civilians. All of society, observed one minister, "seems to be at an end. Every person keeps close on his own plantation. Robberies and murders are often committed on the public roads. . . . Poverty, want, and hardship appear in almost every countenance . . . and the morals of the people are almost entirely extirpated."

Although both armies plundered and terrorized backcountry families, British depradations created the greatest suffering, and Cornwallis did nothing to conciliate civilians. One farmer in a western district that had submitted to British occupation wrote to his cousin that "no sooner we had yielded to them but [the British army] set to Rob us taking all our livings, horses, Cows, Sheep, Clothing, of all sorts, money . . . in fine Everything that sooted them. Untill we were Stript Naked." A Carolina loyalist admitted that "the lower sort of People, who were in many parts originally attached to the British Government, have suffered so severely . . . that Great Britain has now a hundred enemies, where it had one before."

By the end of 1780, the disorder in the backcountry and the victories of rebel irregulars had persuaded most Carolinians that the friends of Congress rather than the king's men could ensure stability. Many loyalists, disenchanted by the British army's lack of support and respect, were defecting to the rebels. That was lucky for the rebels, for while the forces under Marion and Sumter were winning the support of backcountry civilians, American regulars in the Continental Army had lost a major engagement to the main British force under Cornwallis at Camden, South Carolina. The Continentals, led by their new southern commander, General Horatio Gates, had been pushed into a conventional battle that they were unprepared to fight. On a brutally hot August day, redcoats scattered the rebels in all directions, with their general himself leading a headlong scramble back to safety in Hillsboro, North Carolina. Gates' rapid retreat, in the irreverent view of Washington's young aide, Alexander Hamilton, "did admirable credit to the activity of a man at his time of life." In the fall of 1780, Congress replaced Gates with Washington's candidate for the southern command, Nathanael Greene, an able, energetic, 38-year-old Rhode Islander and a veteran of the northern campaigns.

Greene Takes Command

Greene vindicated Washington's confidence by intuitively grasping the military situation in the South. He understood the needs of his men—1400 hungry, ragged, and demoralized troops—and instructed von Steuben to lobby Virginia for food and clothing. He understood the importance of the rebel irregulars, and sent Lieutenant Colonel Henry "Lighthorse Harry" Lee to assist Marion's raids. He understood the weariness of southern civilians, and insisted that his men refrain from plundering the countryside for provisions. He understood the problems of the backcountry terrain, and directed Thaddeus Kosciuszko, a Polish officer and engineer who had lent his services to the rebels, to scout the fords of rivers and to build flatboats for quick crossings.

Above all, Greene understood that his forces could never hold the field

General Nathanael Greene.

against the whole British army. That led him to break the first rule of conventional warfare: he divided his army. In December 1780, he dispatched to western South Carolina a detachment of 600 men under the command of his comrade from the northern campaigns, Brigadier General Daniel Morgan of Virginia.

Back at the British camp, Cornwallis and Lieutenant Colonel Banastre Tarleton could hardly believe their intelligence reports. Tarleton urged a quick assault on Greene, but Cornwallis worried that Morgan and his rebels, if left unchecked, might mobilize the entire Carolina backcountry. On the other hand, Cornwallis reckoned that he could not commit his entire army to the pursuit of Morgan's men, for then Greene and his troops might try to retake Charleston. The only solution, unconventional to be sure, was for Cornwallis to divide *his* army. That he did, sending Tarleton and 1100 men west after Morgan. Cornwallis had played right into Greene's hands: the rebel troops might be able to defeat a British army split into two pieces. And if some of the redcoats could be tired out even before the battle by weeks of running after Morgan, so much the better.

For two weeks Morgan's men led Tarleton's troops on a breakneck chase across the Carolina countryside, until mid-January 1781, when the British finally cornered the rebels at an open meadow called Cowpens. With the Broad River at their backs, Morgan's troops had nowhere to run, so they stood and fought. For once it was the British who panicked and lost the fight, prodded into a premature and disorganized attack by the impetuous Tarleton.

When Cornwallis took up the chase, Morgan and Greene reconnoitered and agreed to keep going until the British army wore out. After another month of running, Cornwallis called a temporary respite at Hillsboro, North Carolina, and issued invitations to all local loyalists to join his forces. Few recruits appeared. By now Cornwallis was beginning to suspect that there were not many loyalists left in the Lower South. To ensure that loyalist ranks remained thin, Greene decided to make a show of rebel force. He chose as his battleground Guilford Courthouse, a tiny village set on a hill overlooking a forested valley. On a brisk day in March, the two sides joined battle, each sustaining severe casualties. Cornwallis finally forced Greene to retreat rather than risk the loss of his army. But the high cost of victory at Guilford Courthouse convinced Cornwallis to end his pursuit. "I am quite tired of marching about the country in quest of adventures," he informed Clinton.

Cornwallis now conceded that he could not put down the rebellion in the Carolinas. He realized that the British had wildly exaggerated the strength of southern loyalism. But unlike Washington, Cornwallis had not put behind him the hunger for military glory. Outfoxed in the Carolinas, he still believed he could win the war with a decisive victory against the Continental Army. The theater that he chose for the showdown was the Chesapeake Bay.

While Cornwallis turned north, the rebel militia routed loyalist defenders from most of their forts in the South Carolina interior. By the end of May, as the entire backcountry arrayed against them, the British were planning to evacuate Camden. Even the redcoats' ability to beat back Greene's army in a final encounter at Eutaw Springs in September gained them no advantage. The remaining British garrisons at Charleston and Savannah simply waited out the end of the war.

The southern campaign could have gone differently. If the British had swept into the Carolinas with a stronger force in 1776, if they had seized Charleston then, and if they had nursed loyalist support in the backcountry, they could have crushed the Revolution. But when the British were repulsed at Charleston in 1776, they neglected the South for nearly four years and abandoned the king's

Rebel Americans were able to hold the southern backcountry because of the courage and determination of militias like the one depicted in this nineteenth-century painting. Francis Marion's company was unusual among southern militias because it included blacks.

supporters to the Carolina rebels. During those four years, the rebels smothered loyalism and proved that the revolutionary governments could maintain order. Even after Charleston finally fell to the British in 1780 and loyalists renewed their opposition, the rebels, working through their militia, still commanded the support of most civilians. In 1780, as in 1775, the rebels held the edge in the struggle for the hearts and minds of southern civilians. The resilience of their militia sowed the seeds of British frustration and, finally, British defeat.

Most American officers had few kind words for the militia. They complained constantly about the militia's lack of discipline, its habit of melting away when homesickness set in or harvest approached, and its record of cowardice under fire in conventional engagements. But if the militia faltered and fled from set-piece battles, they shone in guerrilla fights. When set the task of ambushing supply trains and dispatch riders, harrying bands of local loyalists, or making forays against isolated British outposts, the militia came through. The majority of southerners refused to join the British or to provide the redcoats with food and information, because they knew that once the British army left their neighborhoods, the rebels would always be back. The Continental Army in the South lost many conventional engagements, but the irregulars kept the British from restoring political control over the backcountry.

African Americans in the Age of Revolution

The British lost the South not only because they overestimated loyalist sentiment and underestimated the rebel militia, but also because they did not enlist widespread support among those Americans who would have fought for liberty *with* the British—the slaves.

Black Americans, virtually all in bondage, made up one-third of the population between Delaware and Georgia. White revolutionaries fully expected the British to turn slave rebelliousness to their strategic advantage. As early as 1775, rumors spread throughout the colonies that the British were planning to instigate slave revolts and that the slaves were waiting to assist the British in return for freedom. Janet Schaw, an English woman visiting her brother's North Carolina plantation in July of 1775, reported that his neighbors had heard that the loyalists were "promising every Negro that would murder his master and family he should have his Master's plantation. . . . The Negroes have got it amongst them and believe it to be true."

Wracked by the fear of slave conspiracies, southern revolutionaries began to take precautions. Marylanders disarmed blacks and issued extra guns to the white militia. Charlestonians hanged and then burned the body of Thomas Jeremiah, a free black and a highly skilled harbor pilot, who was convicted of urging others that the British "were come to help the poor Negroes." Throughout the South, white loyalists accused of stirring up the slaves were mobbed, tarred and feathered, and, in one instance, packed off to Britain. When he invaded the South in 1779, Clinton repeated Lord Dunmore's offer to free all slaves who joined the British.

But in London there was considerable opposition to the policy of encouraging slave runaways and recruiting blacks into the army. British leaders dismissed Dunmore's ambitious scheme to raise a black army of 10,000 and another plan to create a southeastern sanctuary for black loyalists. Turning slaves against masters, they recognized, was not the way to conciliate southern whites.

Southern fears of insurrection made the rebels even more reluctant to enlist blacks as soldiers. Since the beginning of the resistance to Britain, white southerners had worried that the watchwords of liberty and equality would spread to the slave quarters. As Charlestonians protested the Stamp Act in 1765, Henry Laurens, a local merchant and political leader, reported that local blacks "in thoughtless imitation" took up the cry of "Liberty." The spectacle of slaves shouting "Liberty!" in the streets so unsettled white Charlestonians that the city "was thrown under arms for a week" and the countryside was alerted. By 1775 southerners were even more concerned that blacks would seize on the disruption to make a revolution of their own.

That fear prompted Congress to bar blacks from the Continental Army. But as the rebels became more desperate for manpower, policy changed. Northern states actively encouraged black enlistments, and in the Upper South, some states allowed free blacks to join the army or permitted slaves to substitute for their masters. Even in South Carolina, where resistance to arming blacks remained intense, a few fought in racially mixed militias like Marion's raiders.

Blacks themselves sought freedom from whichever side seemed most likely to grant it. Even before Dunmore invited Virginia slaves to desert their masters in 1775, a group of blacks offered him their services, and at least 800 reached his floating headquarters off Norfolk harbor. Thousands more flocked to Clinton's forces after the fall of Charleston. For many the hope of liberation proved an illusion: they died of disease in army camps or were sold back into slavery in the West Indies. But some served the British army as laborers, spies, and soldiers. An estimated 5000 blacks served in the revolutionary army in the hope of gaining freedom. In addition, the number of runaways soared during the Revolution, especially in the Upper South, where there was a more acculturated black population, familiar with the countryside and fluent in English. All told, some 55,000 slaves fled to freedom, some escaping behind British lines, others into the North.

While several thousand solitary fugitives fought on either side and thousands of other individuals and families ran for freedom, the slave revolts so dreaded by southern whites never materialized. Possibly the boldest slaves were drawn off into the armies; possibly greater white precautions discouraged would-be insurrectionists. In South Carolina, where the potential for revolt was greatest, slaves preferred staying on plantations to risking a collective resistance and escape in the midst of the fierce partisan warfare.

THE WORLD TURNED UPSIDE DOWN

It was a perfect summer on the Chesapeake. A glove of warm, moist air gathered over the fingers of deep green peninsulas and smaller spits and necks of land

The world turned upside down: The British lay down their arms at Yorktown.

reaching into the bay. The scent of salt wafted from the creeks and coves, rivers and swamps cleaving the mainland. That soothing June of 1781 was all the sweeter to Charles, Lord Cornwallis, because waiting for him on the Chesapeake was an ally—a king's man—the newly turned loyalist, Benedict Arnold.

Arnold was a disillusioned man. Distressed by his personal finances and disgusted by Congress' shabby treatment of the Continental Army, he had started exchanging rebel secrets for British money in 1779 before defecting outright in the fall of 1780. But disappointment and disgrace had not lessened his ambition. A few months later, Arnold and 1500 redcoats were marauding along the Virginia coast, striking as far inland as Richmond. And in that perfect summer of 1781 he joined forces on the Chesapeake with another disillusioned man whose ambition had also survived disappointment and disgrace. Together Cornwallis and Arnold set about fortifying a site on the tip of the peninsula formed by the York and James rivers, a place called Yorktown.

Meanwhile, Washington and his French ally, the Comte de Rochambeau, met in Connecticut to plan a major attack. An able strategist, Rochambeau urged a coordinated land–sea assault on the Virginia coast: he had learned that a large French fleet from the West Indies might be in the Chesapeake Bay to blockade

Cornwallis. Washington insisted instead on a full-scale offensive against New York City. Just when the rebel commander was about to have his way, Clinton received a daunting number of Hessian reinforcements, and word arrived that a French fleet under the Comte de Grasse was headed for the Chesapeake.

By the end of September, 7800 Frenchmen, 5700 Continentals, and 3200 militia had sandwiched Yorktown between the devil of an allied army and the deep blue sea of French warships. "If you cannot relieve me very soon," Cornwallis wrote to Clinton, "you must expect to hear the worst." At last the British navy did arrive—seven days after Cornwallis surrendered to the rebels on October 19, 1781. When Germain carried the news from Yorktown to the king's first minister, Lord North replied, "Oh, God, it is over." Then North resigned, Germain resigned, and even George III murmured something about abdicating.

It need not have ended at Yorktown. But Cornwallis' defeat drained away what little was left of British resolve to smash the American rebellion. The timing of Yorktown made all the difference. At the end of 1781 and early in 1782, the British army received setbacks in the other theaters of the war: India, the West Indies, and Florida. The French and the Spanish were everywhere in Europe as well, gathering in the English Channel, planning a major offensive against Gibraltar. The cost of the fighting was already enormous. British leaders recognized that the rest of the empire was at stake and set about cutting their losses in America.

The Treaty of Paris, signed on September 3, 1783, was a diplomatic triumph for the American negotiators, Benjamin Franklin, John Adams, and John Jay. They dangled before Britain the possibility that a magnanimous settlement might weaken American ties to France. The British jumped at the bait. They recognized the independence of the United States and agreed to generous boundaries for the new nation: the Mississippi River on the west, the 31st parallel on the south, and the present boundary of Canada on the north. American negotiators then persuaded a skeptical France to approve the treaty by arguing that, as allies, they had to present a united front to the British. When the French finally persuaded Spain, the third member of the alliance, to reduce its demands on Britain for territorial concessions, the treaty was an accomplished fact. The Spanish settled for Florida and Minorca, an island in the Mediterranean.

Those present at Yorktown on that clear autumn afternoon in 1781 watched as the second-in-command to an "indisposed" Lord Cornwallis surrendered his superior's sword—first, in a face-saving gesture, to the French commander Rochambeau, who politely demurred and pointed to the American general, Washington, who proudly demurred and pointed to *his* second-in-command, Benjamin Lincoln. Some witnesses recalled that British musicians arrayed on the green played "The World Turned Upside Down." Their recollections may have been faulty, but the story has persisted as part of the folklore of the American Revolution—and with some justification. The world *had*, it seemed, turned upside down with the coming of American independence. The colonial rebels shocked the British with their answer to the question: would they fight?

The answer had been yes—but on their own terms. By 1777 most propertied Americans avoided fighting in the Continental Army. Yet whenever the war reached their homes, farms, and businesses, sufficient numbers of Americans gave their allegiance to the new confederation by turning out with rifles or supplying homespun clothing, food, or ammunition. The men fought in the militia, rallying around Washington in New Jersey, Gates in upstate New York, Clark on the frontier, Greene and Lincoln, Marion and Sumter in the Carolinas. Middle-class

Americans fought, some from idealism, others out of self-interest, but always on their own terms, as members of the militia. At Saratoga and in the Carolina back-country, these "citizen-soldiers" turned the world upside down by defeating professional armies.

Of course, the militia did not bear the brunt of the fighting. That responsibility fell to the Continental Army, which by 1777 drew its strength from the poorest ranks of American society. Yet even the Continentals, despite their desperation, managed to fight on their own terms. Some asserted their rights by raising mutinies, until Congress redressed their grievances. All of them, as the Baron von Steuben observed, behaved differently from European soldiers. Americans followed orders only if the logic of commands was explained to them. The Continentals, held in contempt by most Americans, turned the world upside down by sensing their power and asserting their measure of personal independence.

Thus did a revolutionary generation turn the world upside down. Descended from desperate, idealistic, and self-interested men and women who settled colonies named for kings and queens, ruled by kings and queens whose absolutist and mercantilist ideals sought to enrich the power of their bureaucratic states—these Americans rebelled against a king. They wanted more than a monarch. But what more did they want? What awaited in a world turned upside down by republican revolutionaries?

SIGNIFICANT EVENTS

1775 — Second Continental Congress convenes at Philadelphia; Congress creates the Continental Army; Battle of Bunker Hill

1776 — Publication of *Common Sense;* British troops evacuate Boston; Declaration of Independence; British occupy New York City, forcing Washington to retreat through New Jersey into Pennsylvania; Washington counterattacks at Battle of Trenton

1777 — British summer drive to occupy Philadelphia: battles of Brandywine Creek, Germantown; Burgoyne surrenders at Saratoga; Continental Army encamps for winter at Valley Forge

1778 — Carlisle Commission sues for peace; France allies with rebel Americans; France and Britain declare war; British shift focus to the South: Savannah falls

1780 — British occupy Charleston; partisan warfare of Marion, Sumter; rebel victory at King's Mountain, South Carolina; Nathanael Greene takes southern command

1781 — Engagements at Cowpens, Guilford Courthouse; Cornwallis surrenders at Yorktown

1783 — Treaty of Paris

7

Crisis and Constitution

 am not a Virginian, but an American," Patrick Henry declaimed to the Virginia House of Burgesses. Most likely he was lying. Certainly no one listening took him seriously, for the newly independent patriots did not identify themselves as members of a nation. They would have said, as Thomas Jefferson did, "Virginia, Sir, is my country." Or as John Adams wrote to another native son, "Massachusetts is our country." Jefferson and Adams were men of wide political vision and experience: both were leaders in the Continental Congress and more inclined than most to think nationally. But like other members of the revolutionary generation, they harbored strong local loyalties. "Americans" identified deeply with their home states and even more deeply with their home counties and towns.

When did the inhabitants of 13 separate states begin to think of themselves as Americans? The war for independence itself fostered a new sense of national identity among some participants. Marching together from one state to another in ragged uniforms, enduring enemy fire from British cannon—not to mention soggy "firecake," a flatbread from their own army commissary—Washington's Continentals were the first group whose experience awakened a camaraderie and an allegiance to a truly national institution, the army. These men may have been the first "Americans."

But if military men came to think in terms of loyalty to a national cause, most political leaders did not. Allegiance to the states, not the Union, determined the shape of the first republican political experiments. For a decade after independence, the revolutionaries were less committed to creating an American nation than to organizing 13 separate state republics. The Declaration of Independence referred explicitly not to *the* United States, but *these* United States. It envisioned not one republic so much as a federation of 13, like the independent but linked city-state republics of Switzerland.

Only when peace was restored during the decade of the 1780s were Americans forced to think through the consequences of their revolution. The Declaration proclaimed that these "free and independent states" had "full power to levy war, conclude peace, contract alliances, establish commerce." Did that mean that New Jersey, as a free and independent state, could sign a trade agreement with France, excluding the other states? If the United States was to be more than a loose federation, how could it assert power on a national scale? Similarly, American borderlands to the west presented problems. If these territories were settled

During the summer of 1787 the Constitutional Convention met at the old State House in Philadelphia (pictured here in 1799). Because passersby strolled by the windows, the delegates kept them closed to maintain privacy—and sweltered in the summer heat.

The portraits of Captain and Mrs. Samuel Chandler, a New England couple, project the virtuous rectitude of the new republican era. Husband and wife share the same direct, disarming gaze, a mixture of wariness and resolution. To the portrait of Captain Chandler, a proud veteran of the Revolution, the artist added a battlefield scene in the background.

by Americans, would they eventually join the United States? Go their own ways as independent nations? Become new colonies of Spain or England? None of these political questions had been fully answered.

Such problems were more than political; they were rooted in social realities. For a political union to succeed, Americans needed some sense of national identity. There had to be social bonds linking one citizen with another. When it came right down to it, what united a Vermont farmer working his stubborn, rocky fields and a South Carolina nabob, presiding over a vast rice plantation? What bonds existed between a leather-shirted Kentuckian rafting the Ohio River and a Salem merchant sailing all the way to China for porcelain? Could a republic be strong enough to unite these "Americans" politically yet still reflect their widely different identities? Could it be strong enough to raise money and regulate trade without unfairly promoting one economic class or geographic region at the expense of another?

And in a society where all citizens were said to be "created equal," the inevitable social inequalities had to be confronted. How could women participate in the Revolution's bid for freedom if they were not free to vote or to hold property? How could blacks feel a bond with white Americans when so often the only existing bonds had been forged with chains? To these questions there were no answers in 1781, none, at least, with the ring of finality. And as the decade progressed, the sense of crisis deepened. Americans worried that the center could not hold, that factions and selfish interest groups would pull "these" United States irrevocably apart. The republican union that had been formed, spread out as it was over so many miles, constituted a truly unprecedented venture. A good deal of experimenting would be needed if it was to succeed.

REPUBLICAN EXPERIMENTS

The enduring hold of local loyalties accounts in part for the enormous enthusiasm among revolutionary leaders for creating new state governments, but it also accounts for the lack of concern about designing national institutions. After independence was declared in July 1776, many of America's best political minds were engaged in drawing up constitutions for their individual states. Thomas Jefferson deserted the Continental Congress, leaving the conduct of the war and national affairs to other men. He wanted to address the more important business of creating Virginia's new government.

In truth, the state constitutions were crucial political experiments, the first efforts at applying republican principles to American actualities. The states faced the task of designing institutions that would carry out the republican commitment to a government of and by the people. All of the revolutionaries agreed that the people—not a king or a few privileged aristocrats—should rule. Giving effective form to that ideal might require some trial and error, but of one thing Americans were absolutely certain: republican governments were not suited to large territories. That axiom appeared in the writings of every major republican thinker read by Americans, the most influential being Montesquieu.

Americans took the axiom to heart. Inevitably, they believed, national legislatures grew indifferent to popular concerns, being distant from their far-flung constituents. Without being under the watchful eye of the people, they escaped popular control and soon degenerated into despotism. Thus revolutionary leaders thought of republican government in terms of the states. Efforts to form a single national republic would be doomed to failure, they reasoned. A federation of small state republics would stand a far better chance of enduring.

The State Constitutions

Colonial experience as well as republican theory shaped the framing of the first state constitutions. The states retained the basic form of their old colonial governments, most providing for a governor and a bicameral legislature. Only Georgia and Pennsylvania dispensed with both the governor and the upper house of the legislature. But while the structure of most new constitutions resembled those of the old colonial regimes, the balance of power among the branches of government shifted dramatically.

From the republican perspective in 1776, the greatest problem of any government lay in curbing executive power. What had driven Americans into rebellion was the abuse of authority by the king, his ministers, and their agents in the colonies, the royal governors. To ensure that the executive could never again threaten popular liberty, the new states either accorded almost no power to their governors or abolished that office entirely. The governors had no authority to convene or dissolve the legislature. They could not veto the legislatures' laws. They could not grant land or erect courts. Most important from the republican point of view, governors had few powers to appoint other state officials. All these limits were designed with one aim in mind: to deprive the executive of any patronage or other form of influence over the legislature. By reducing the governor to a cipher, Americans hoped to preserve their states from the corruption that they deplored in British political life.

What the state governors lost, the legislatures gained. In the decade after

1776 most American republicans believed that liberty would be best served by making legislatures the dominant force in the government. The colonial assemblies, after all, had led the staunch opposition to Britain, defended American freedom, and embodied the will of the people. The course for state constitution makers was clear: grant legislatures a lion's share of power and take steps to make assemblies truly representative.

To realize the ideal of actual representation, the new constitutions called for annual elections and stipulated that candidates for the legislature had to live in the district they represented. Some states also reapportioned representation on the basis of population, and many asserted the right of constituents to instruct the men elected to office. Although no state granted universal manhood suffrage, most reduced the amount of property required of qualified voters. American republicans believed that the major purpose of government was to protect property and that only men who owned property possessed the independence necessary to participate in political life. But the new property qualifications were low enough to allow most white men the vote, and Georgia and Pennsylvania went as far as opening the franchise to all taxpayers.

While the legislatures reigned supreme over state executives, the judiciary was also rendered dependent on popular favor. State supreme courts were either elected by the legislatures or appointed by an elected governor. In one sense, the sum of these constitutional changes was fairly democratic. A majority of voters within a state could do whatever they wanted, unchecked by governors or courts. On the other hand, the arrangement opened the door for legislatures to turn as tyrannical as governors. The revolutionaries brushed that prospect aside: republican theory assured them that the people would never oppress themselves.

By investing all power in popular assemblies, Americans abandoned the British system of mixed government. In an equally momentous departure from British

Americans responded to independence with rituals of "killing the king," like this New York crowd in 1776, which is pulling down a statue of George III. Americans also expressed their mistrust of monarchs and their ministers by establishing new state governments with weak executive branches.

practice, the revolutionaries insisted on written state constitutions. They were determined to set down the fundamental law in an actual document that defined the extent of government's power and the full scope of popular liberty. Whenever government appeared to exceed the limits of its authority, Americans wanted to have at hand the contract between rules and ruled. Americans had discovered the necessity for written constitutions in their experience with the British constitution. That much-admired system of government was an unwritten constitution— not an actual document but a collection of parliamentary laws, customs, and precedents. When eighteenth-century Englishmen used the word "constitution," they meant the existing arrangement of government. But Americans believed that a constitution should be a written code that stood apart from and above government, a law superior to government, a yardstick against which the people measured the performance of their rulers. If Britain's constitution had been written down, available for all to consult, would American rights have been violated? No, the republican rebels reasoned, and so they came to write their own state constitutions. These documents circulated widely on both sides of the Atlantic, were translated and published in France and other European countries, and were touted as models of enlightened political organization.

From Congress to Confederation

While Americans were lavishing attention on their state constitutions, the national government nearly languished, a neglected stepchild during the decade after 1776. With the coming of independence, the Second Continental Congress assumed responsibility for conducting the common business of the federated colonies. It created and maintained the Continental Army, issued currency, and negotiated with foreign powers. But while Congress functioned as a central government by common consent, it lacked any legal basis for its authority. To redress that need, in July 1776 Congress appointed a committee to draft a constitution for a national government. The more urgent business of waging and paying for the war made for delay, as did the consuming interest in framing state constitutions. Congress finally approved the first national constitution in November 1777, but it took four more years for all of the states to ratify these Articles of Confederation.

The Articles of Confederation provided for a government by a national legislature—essentially a continuation of the Second Continental Congress. This body had the authority to declare war and make peace, conduct diplomacy, regulate Indian affairs, appoint military and naval officers, and requisition men from the states. In affairs of finance it could coin money and issue paper currency. Extensive as these responsibilities were, Congress lacked important powers. It could not levy taxes or even regulate trade. The crucial power of the purse rested entirely with the states, which were to contribute funds to the common expense at congressional request. Nor could Congress do more than recommend particular policies to the states; it had no authority to enforce its resolutions. All final power to make and execute laws lay with the states. In addition, the states retained control over a potential source of large revenues, the undistributed tracts of western land granted to them under their old colonial charters.

Beyond these limitations, the very organization of the new government fostered a weak, discontinuous leadership. Delegates to Congress were appointed annually by state legislatures, and no delegate could serve more than three out of every six years. Often the states dispatched men of little ability to sit as their representatives in Congress, and even after the fighting had ended, its meetings shifted from Philadelphia to Princeton to Annapolis to New York City. Even worse, the national government had no distinct executive branch. Congressional committees, constantly changing in their membership, not only had to make laws but had to administer and enforce them as well. With no executive to carry out the policies of finance, war, and foreign policy, the federal government's influence was extremely limited.

These weaknesses appear more evident in hindsight than Congress perceived in 1777. It was no easy task to frame a new government in the midst of a war. Day in, day out, delegates were harried enough keeping up with news of battles, demands from the army for more arms and men, squabbles over which general should command which troops, complaints from individual states—even the threat of their own capture by the British, which caused them to pack their bags hastily on several occasions.

Beyond such distractions, most American statesmen of the 1770s had given little thought to federalism, the organization of a United States. Political leaders simply had not yet perceived the need for a defined distribution of power between the states and the central government. With the new nation in the midst of a military crisis, Congress assumed—correctly in most cases—that the states did not have to be forced to contribute men and money to the common defense. To have given significant powers to the national government would only have aroused opposition among the states, each jealous of its independence. Sam Adams, the Boston rebel leader, expressed the consensus of political opinion when he declared that "every legislature of every colony ought to be the sovereign and uncontrollable Power within its own limits of territory." Creating a strong national government would also have antagonized many Americans, who after all had just rebelled against the distant, centralized authority of Britain's king and Parliament. As Edward Rutledge of South Carolina observed, "The inhabitants of every Colony consider themselves at liberty to do as they please on almost every occasion."

Primed by republican political theory and guided by their experience as colonials, the revolutionaries set about creating a loose confederation of 13 independent state republics under a nearly powerless national government. They succeeded so well that the United States almost failed to outlast the first decade of its independence. The problem was that republican theory and lessons from the colonial past were not always apt guides to postwar realities. Only when events forced Americans to think nationally did they begin to consider the possibility of reinventing "these United States"—this time under the yoke of a truly federal republic.

THE TEMPTATIONS OF PEACE

The surrender of Lord Cornwallis to George Washington's forces at Yorktown in 1781 marked the end of military crisis in America. But as the threat from Britain receded, so did the source of American unity. No longer endangered by a common enemy, the 13 independent states fell to bickering among themselves. The many differences among Americans, most of which lay submerged during the struggle for independence, surfaced in full force. And neither the states nor the national government proved equal to the conflicts arising from the intrigues of foreign powers or the domestic dislocations of the postwar period.

The Temptations of the West

The greatest opportunities and the greatest problems for postwar Americans awaited in the West. The frontier, of course, had long provided land for an expanding population. Even before the Revolution, settlers had pushed into the backcountry, especially of Pennsylvania, Virginia, and the Carolinas. Some hardy frontiersmen had even defied British authority by crossing the Proclamation Line of 1763 and had risked Indian retaliation by venturing into tribal lands over the Appalachians. After the Revolution, the movement to the western portions of the new states assumed such massive scale that the population of the backcountry outstripped that of the seaboard in some places. And with the boundary of the United States now set at the Mississippi River, more migrating families spilled across the Appalachians, planting farmsteads and raw frontier towns throughout Ohio, Kentucky, and Tennessee.

Frontier growth was explosive. By 1790 places that had been almost uninhabited by whites in 1760 held over 2.25 million people, one-third of the nation's population. By 1800 that proportion approached one-half. The scope of movement attained momentous dimensions; except for the first colonization of the early seventeenth century, never before or since has such a large percentage of white Americans lived in newly settled communities.

The frontier was explosive in another sense too. After the Revolution, as before, the West was a source of sharp conflict. American claims to sovereignty all the way to the Mississippi were by no means taken for granted by covetous European powers. And even if Americans could ignore the intrigues of Europeans or the claims of Indians, they faced a question of their own national identity. How would the nation incorporate the newly settled territories? Would they come in as states on an equal footing with the original 13 states? Would they be ruled as dependent colonies? Could the federal government reconcile conflicting interests, cultures, and traditions over so great an area? The fate of the West, in other words, constituted a crucial test of whether "these" United States could grow and still remain united.

With independence won, the Confederation still faced the problem of enforcing American claims to its northwestern and southwestern frontiers. Both the British from their base in Canada and the Spanish in Florida and Louisiana hoped to chisel away at American boundaries. Their considerable success in the 1780s exposed the weakness of Confederation diplomacy. Before the ink was dry on the Treaty of Paris, Britain's ministers were secretly instructing Canadians to maintain their forts and trading posts inside the United States' northwestern frontier. They reckoned—correctly—that with the Continental Army disbanded, the Confederation had no troops to force the British to withdraw. When Congress protested this treaty violation, the British pointed out that Americans were in violation too. The treaty required that neither side hinder the collection of private debts contracted before the war and that Congress recommend that the states restore confiscated loyalist property. But several states had passed laws prohibiting British subjects from suing to recover debts and property in America. Congress could do nothing to compel the states to abide by the terms of the treaty and repeal the offending legislation. With Congress unable to bring the states into line or to raise troops for defense, the British stayed on in their northwestern garrisons and savored the humiliation of the Confederation.

The British also attempted mischief along the Confederation's northern borders, principally with Vermont. For decades, Ethan Allen and his Green Mountain Boys had waged a war of nerves with neighboring New York, which claimed Vermont as part of its territory. The Vermonters kept the controversy going after the Revolution, petitioning Congress for statehood and demanding independence of both New York and New Hampshire. When Congress dragged its feet, the British tried to woo Vermont into their empire as a province of Canada. That flirtation with the British pressured Congress into granting Vermont statehood in 1791.

The loyalty of the southwestern frontier was far less certain. By 1790 more than 100,000 settlers had poured through the Cumberland Gap to reach Kentucky and Tennessee. Along with the farmers came speculators, who bought up large tracts of land from the Indians. But the commercial possibilities of the region depended entirely on access to the Mississippi and the port of New Orleans, since it was far too costly to ship southwestern produce over the rough trails east across the Appalachians. And the Mississippi route was still dominated by the Spanish, who controlled Louisiana as well as forts along western Mississippi shores as far north as St. Louis. The Spanish, seeing their opportunity, closed the Mississippi to American navigation in 1784, hoping to sway the Southwest into their empire. Without free access to an ocean port, the inhabitants of western Virginia, Kentucky, and Tennessee seriously considered secession from the United States. Already dissatisfied by the neglect of the states and Congress, they were clamoring as well for protection from local Indians, who had occasionally reacted to white settlements on their land with retaliatory raids. While the Confederation temporized, unable to do anything to guarantee frontier military or economic objectives, western loyalties hung in the balance.

The West posed not only international difficulties but also internal problems. Throughout the colonial era, frontier settlers had protested their lack of influence in legislative affairs. Although most northern states moved quickly to extend representation to frontier districts, the southern states proceeded more slowly. North Carolina, whose western Regulators had nearly launched a civil war before the Revolution, once again saw protests and riots erupt when its constitution did not extend full representation to the western counties. A new state of Franklin was actually formed and its legislature met for several years in the mid-1780s. Virginia experienced similar problems.

Even more demoralizing were the continuing arguments among states over conflicting land claims. The old royal charters for some colonies—Georgia, the Carolinas, Virginia, Connecticut, Massachusetts, and New York—had extended their boundaries all the way to the Mississippi and beyond. But the charters were as vague as they were generous, granting both Massachusetts and Virginia, for example, undisputed possession of present-day Wisconsin. An even knottier problem arose because the charters of other states—Maryland, Delaware, Pennsylvania, Rhode Island, and New Jersey—limited their territories to within a few hundred miles of the Atlantic coast. "Landed" states like Virginia wanted to secure control over their chartered territory. "Landless" states like Maryland called on Congress to restrict the boundaries of landed states and to convert western lands into a domain administered by the Confederation.

The landless states had good reasons for favoring control over the West by

WESTERN LAND CLAIMS, 1782–1802
The Confederation's settlement of conflicting western land claims was an achievement essential to the consolidation of political union. Some states asserted that their original charters extended their western borders to the Mississippi River. A few states, like Virginia, claimed western borders on the Pacific Ocean.

Congress. The landed states, they argued, enjoyed an unfair advantage from the large revenue that could be gained from selling their western claims. That revenue would allow landed states to reduce taxes, and lower taxes would lure settlers from the landless states. Meanwhile, landless states would have to raise taxes to make up for the departed citizens, forcing a continuing downward cycle.

The landless states had a few less high-minded reasons for opposing the landed states. Before the Revolution, speculators, who numbered among the most prominent citizens of landless Pennsylvania, Maryland, and New Jersey, had purchased tracts in the West from Indians, and some had nearly received royal approval of their purchases before independence inconveniently intervened. These speculators now joined forces with the political leaders of the landless states to lobby for congressional ownership of all western lands except those tracts that they had already purchased from the Indians.

The landless states, however, had lost the opening round of the contest over ownership of the West. The Articles of Confederation acknowledged the old charter claims of the landed states. But Maryland, one of the smallest landless states, refused to ratify the Articles. Since every state had to approve the Articles before they were formally accepted, the fate of the United States hung in the balance. One by one the landed states relented. The last holdout, Virginia, in January 1781 ceded its charter rights to land north of the Ohio River. In a moment of uncharacteristic modesty, the Virginians conceded that they might have trouble extending republican government over the entire territory allotted them in their charter—a substantial portion of the North American continent. Once Virginia ceded, Maryland stepped into line, ratifying the Articles in February 1781, four long years after Congress had first approved them.

The West triggered controversy in yet another way: by the sort of people being elected to political office. The state legislatures of the 1780s were both larger and less aristocratic than the old colonial assemblies. A newer, more democratic spirit leavened legislative proceedings. The new representatives were often less wealthy, less socially prominent, and less educated. Before the Revolution no more than a fifth of the men serving in the assemblies were middle-class farmers or artisans; government was almost exclusively the domain of the wealthiest merchants and planters. After the Revolution twice as many state legislators were men of moderate wealth. The shift was more marked in the North, where middle-class men predominated among representatives; but in every state, some men of the middling sort attained political power.

This spread of democracy resulted chiefly from the surge of westward settlement. As backcountry districts grew, the number of their representatives increased, swelling both the size of state legislatures and western influence within them. One telling sign of the change was that many states moved their capitals from the coast farther inland to sites more accessible for frontier delegates. The new western influence also guaranteed that more men who were not rich or cultivated would sit in legislatures, since backcountry districts tended to be less developed economically and culturally. Voters did not repudiate the wealthy leaders who had led the movement for independence, but because of greater western representation, older elites became a much smaller and less powerful group within the legislatures.

Some republican gentlemen accepted the new situation. One eminent Virginian observed that the House of Burgesses in 1776 was "composed of men not quite so well dressed, nor so politely educated, nor so highly born as some I have formerly seen, but they are the people's men (and the People in general are right)." Not all patriots were as pleased, however. Some gentlemen—no doubt a minority—condemned all notions of "the equality of mankind," preferring the more cynical doctrine that "the many were made for the few." Others, while endorsing government by popular consent, still doubted whether the people themselves were fit to rule.

The problem, conservative republicans argued, was that the new legislators lacked a "larger view" of politics. Rougher, blunter, more single-minded, the new western delegates concerned themselves only with the narrow interests of their particular constituents, not with the good of the whole. They were too wedded to their localities and too easily swayed by the demands of a short-sighted and often selfish electorate. They seemed, to conservatives at least, to lack the cardinal republican virtue of "disinterestedness." And if state legislatures could not rise above petty bickering and narrow self-interest, how long would it be before civic virtue and a concern for the general welfare simply withered away?

By the early 1780s movements were already afoot in many states to amend the new constitutions by reducing the powers of democratic legislatures. Furthermore, fears of democratic excess influenced policy at the national level when Congress finally came to decide what to do with the Northwest Territory.

Carved out of the land ceded by the states to the national government, the Northwest Territory comprised the present-day states of Ohio, Indiana, Illinois, Michigan, and Wisconsin. With so many white settlers moving into these lands, Congress was faced with a crucial test of its federal system. As the national government, how could it expand the confederation of states beyond the original 13 colonies? If a peaceful and orderly way could not be devised, the new territories might well break off and become independent countries or even colonies of Spain or Britain. Congress dealt with the issue of expansion by adopting three ordinances.

The first, drafted by Thomas Jefferson in 1784, proposed a division of the Northwest Territory into 10 states, each to be admitted to the Union on equal terms as soon as its population equaled that in any of the existing states. In the interim, Jefferson provided for democratic self-government of the territory by all free adult males according to any state constitution. A second ordinance of 1785 set up an efficient mechanism for dividing and selling public lands. The Northwest Territory was surveyed into townships of six square miles along lines running east–west and north–south. Each township was then divided into 36 lots of one square mile, or 640 acres. Congress also established land offices in all of the states to organize public auctions, stipulating that a lot was the smallest unit that could be purchased and setting the price per acre at not less than one dollar in specie.

Eager for anticipated revenue, Congress waited—in vain—for buyers to flock to the land offices. The cost of even a single lot—$640—was too steep for most farmers, especially since Congress required payment in specie, not paper money. Disappointed by the dearth of buyers and desperate for funds, Congress finally succumbed to a proposition submitted by a private company of land speculators who offered to buy some 6 million acres in present-day southeastern Ohio, using badly depreciated paper money. That several members of Congress numbered among the company's stockholders no doubt added to enthusiasm for the deal.

The transaction concluded, Congress sweetened the bargain by calming the speculators' worries that incoming settlers might enjoy too much self-government. For decades, eastern entrepreneurs had been warning that backcountry folk were "uncivilized, and little better than barbarians.—They are lazy, licentious, and lawless—and, instead of being useful members of society, are become seditious and dangerous to the community." In short, these were not the sort of people the speculators wanted to trust with self-government. Congress accordingly scrapped Jefferson's democratic design and substituted the Northwest Ordinance of 1787.

That ordinance swept aside self-government and provided for a period in which Congress held sway in the territory through its appointees—a governor, a secretary, and three judges. When the population reached 5000 free adult males, a legislature was to be established, although its laws required the governor's approval. A representative could sit in Congress but had no vote. When the population reached 60,000, the inhabitants might apply for statehood, and the whole Northwest Territory was to be divided into not less than three or more than five states. The ordinance also guaranteed basic rights—freedom of religion and trial by jury—and provided for the support of public education.

Congress' settlement ignored just one important consideration: the Indian nations who were settled on the land had never relinquished their claim to it. That

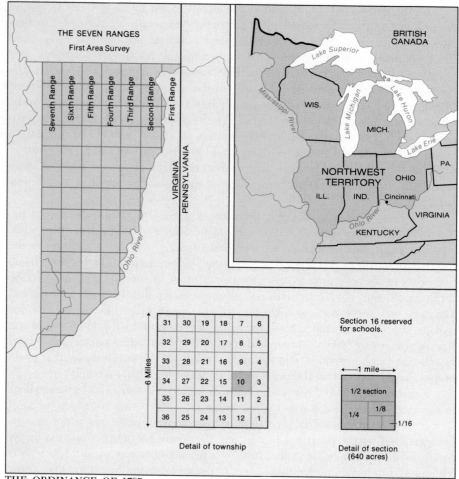

THE SEVEN RANGES

First Area Survey

Seventh Range | Sixth Range | Fifth Range | Fourth Range | Third Range | Second Range | First Range

VIRGINIA
PENNSYLVANIA

Ohio River

BRITISH CANADA

Lake Superior

Mississippi River

WIS.

Lake Michigan

Lake Huron

MICH.

Lake Erie

NORTHWEST TERRITORY   OHIO   PA.

ILL.   IND.   Cincinnati

Ohio River

VIRGINIA

KENTUCKY

31	30	19	18	7	6
32	29	20	17	8	5
33	28	21	16	9	4
34	27	22	15	10	3
35	26	23	14	11	2
36	25	24	13	12	1

6 Miles

Detail of township

Section 16 reserved for schools.

←—1 mile—→

1/2 section

1/4   1/8

1/16

Detail of section
(640 acres)

THE ORDINANCE OF 1785

Surveyors entered the Northwest Territory in September of 1785, imposing on the land regular grids of six square miles to define new townships, as shown on this range map of a portion of Ohio. Farmers purchased blocks of land within townships, each one mile square, from the federal government or from land speculators. This pattern was followed in mapping and settling public lands all the way to the Pacific Coast.

the British had ceded the territory to the states and the states to the Confederation made no difference to the Shawnee, the Chippewa, the Ottawa, and the Potawatomi, who had never ceased to regard the land as theirs. After the Revolution, these nations formed a league to enforce their right of ownership and to stop white settlement at the Ohio River. Confrontation could not be avoided indefinitely, but in 1790, only about 4300 whites had settled in the Northwest, the largest number around Cincinnati.

In the final analysis, the Northwest Ordinance slighted tribal land rights, discriminated economically against small farmers, and retreated politically from Jefferson's ideal of self-governing democracy for the frontier. On the other hand, Congress had succeeded in extending republican government to the West and incorporating the frontier into the federal system. It did not make the mistake of keeping its new territories as dependent colonies of the older, more powerful states. In that sense, the Northwest Ordinance became the most enduring legacy of government under the Articles of Confederation.

Congress left the Northwest another legacy: it outlawed slavery throughout the territory. And this had an unlooked-for, almost ironic consequence. The Northwest Ordinance went a long way toward establishing a federal system that minimized tensions between the East and the West, which had been a major source of postwar conflict. The Republic now had a peaceful, orderly way to expand its federation of states. Yet by limiting the spread of slavery in the northern states, Congress deepened the critical social and economic differences between North and South, evident already in the 1780s. For the time being, conflict between the two sections remained muted. But the tensions that erupted into civil war in 1860 were mounting in the wake of the Revolution.

Slavery and Sectionalism

When white Americans declared their independence, they owned nearly half a million black Americans. African-Americans of the revolutionary generation, most of them enslaved, comprised 20 percent of the total population of the colonies in 1775, and nearly 90 percent of them lived in the South. But few political leaders, either in Congress or in the state legislatures, directly confronted the issue of whether slavery should be permitted to exist in a truly republican society.

On the rare occasions when political discussion strayed toward the subject of slavery, southerners bristled defensively. Theirs was a difficult position, fraught with contradictions, especially for ardent republicans. On the one hand, they had condemned parliamentary taxation as tantamount to political "slavery" and had rebelled, declaring that all men were "created equal." On the other hand, enslaved blacks formed the basis of the South's plantation economy. To surrender slavery, southerners believed, would be to usher in economic ruin. And in much of the South, slavery was an entrenched part of the social system.

Some planters in the Upper South resolved the dilemma they felt by freeing their slaves. In any case, the economies of Maryland and Virginia were shifting away from tobacco toward wheat, a crop demanding a good deal less labor. With less need to maintain a large slave work force, Virginia and Maryland liberalized their manumission statutes, laws providing for freeing slaves. Between 1776 and 1789, most southern states also joined the North in prohibiting the importation of slaves, and a few antislavery societies appeared in the Upper South. But no southern state legally abolished slavery. Most planters continued to hold human property and defended their right to do so in the name of republicanism.

To modern eyes, the irony in that position is obvious. Yet it is important to remember that equality was not the only ideal held by eighteenth-century republicans. For them the concept of property was equally crucial. Property provided a man and his family with security, status, and wealth. More important, it provided a measure of independence: to be able to act firmly and rationally, without fear or favor of other men. People without property were dangerous, republicans believed, because the poor could never be politically independent. When English republicans discussed people without property, they were concerned chiefly with their country's large number of white poor and unemployed. Some political theorists there even recommended that the state enslave propertyless people or incarcerate them in workhouses.

Negro Methodists Holding a Meeting in a Philadelphia Alley evokes the vibrancy of African-American religious life in the city that became a haven for free blacks. The artist, Pavel Petrovich Svinin, was a Russian diplomat who traveled throughout America, praised its religious freedom, and predicted the end of slavery.

Republicans in the American South followed a similar line of reasoning. Slavery was necessary, they argued, because free, propertyless black people would constitute a political threat to the liberty of propertied whites. Ending slavery would undermine the stability of the new nation. And, of course, to the white masters who held them, slaves were property, assets that provided wealth, status, independence. Subordinating human rights to property rights, southern republicans reached the paradoxical conclusion that freedom—for whites—depended on keeping one-fifth of the population in bondage.

The North followed a different course. Because its economy was far less dependent on slave labor, emancipation did not run counter to entrenched economic interests. Antislavery societies, the first founded by the Quakers in 1775, spread throughout the northern states during the next quarter century. Over the same period, the legislatures of most northern states provided for the immediate or gradual abolition of slavery. Freedom for most northern blacks came slowly, but by 1830 there were fewer than 3000 slaves out of a total northern black population of 125,000.

The Revolution, which had been fought for liberty and equality, did little to change the status of most black Americans. All the same, a larger number of blacks than ever before became free during the war and in the decades following. Some had escaped slavery by serving in the military. Both the British and the Americans emancipated slaves who joined their ranks. The British evacuation at the end of the war also liberated tens of thousands of slaves, who were resettled in England, Canada, the West Indies, and Sierra Leone. Furthermore, an unprecedented number of blacks took advantage of the chaos created by the war in the South, fleeing from the plantations in an escape to freedom. And after the war, while the northern states took steps to abolish slavery, manumissions rose sharply in the Upper South.

All these developments fostered the growth of free black communities, especially in the Upper South and in northern cities. By 1810 free blacks comprised 10 percent of the total population of Maryland and Virginia. The composition of the postwar free community changed as well. Before independence, most free blacks had been either mulattoes—the offspring of interracial unions—or former slaves too sick or aged to have value as laborers. By contrast, the free population of the 1780s became darker skinned, younger, and healthier. This group injected new vitality into black communal life, organizing independent schools and churches for the growing number of "free people of color."

Yet for all those changes, there were more blacks enslaved in 1800 than in 1776. Slavery had continued to grow in the Lower South as the rice culture of the Carolinas and Georgia expanded and as the new cotton culture spread to the backcountry districts and beyond, into the Alabama and Mississippi frontiers. Because of the high demand for slaves in the Lower South, most Virginia and Maryland planters who had turned to growing wheat did not release their slaves, but sold them to ready buyers among rice and cotton growers. And in the Lower South, the commitment to slave labor meant that virtually no free black communities or white-sponsored antislavery societies could prosper.

After the Revolution, slavery ceased to be a national institution. It became the "peculiar institution" of a single region, the American South. Because the overwhelming majority of black Americans lived in the South, the end of slavery as a national institution affected few blacks. But it determined the political future for white Americans. The isolation of slavery in one section set North and South on radically different courses of social development, sharpening economic and political divisions. As early as 1778, South Carolina's William Henry Drayton predicted that northern and southern interests would naturally diverge "from the nature of the climate, soil, and produce of the several states." That phrase was Drayton's delicate device to avoid even mentioning the word slavery.

Wartime Economic Disruption

With the outbreak of the Revolution, Americans had suffered an immediate and costly loss of the manufactured goods, markets, and credit that Britain had formerly supplied. Hardest hit were southern planters, who had to seek new customers for their tobacco, cotton, and rice as well as finding new sources of capital to finance production. British bounties had for years encouraged the indigo plantations of South Carolina. Without that subsidy, the industry was dealt a crippling blow from which it never recovered. And the liberation of tens of thousands of slaves deprived many masters of their investment in a labor force.

Northerners faced hard times as well. Most northern cities were occupied for a time by British troops, whose presence disrupted commercial activity. Even after the army had departed, British naval vessels and privateers patrolled northern harbors, crippling the fishing industry and menacing the carrying trade. Thrown out of work, maritime craftsmen, dockside laborers, and sailors migrated to rural areas or joined the army.

Matters did not improve with the coming of peace. Desperate for markets,

Americans now found that both the British and the French colonies in the Caribbean were closed to their trade. But both France and Britain flooded the new states with their manufactures, and postwar Americans, eager for luxuries, indulged in a most unrepublican spending spree. The flurry of buying left some American merchants and consumers as deeply in debt as their governments. When loans from private citizens and foreign creditors like France and Holland had proved insufficient to finance the fighting, both Congress and the states printed paper money—a whopping total of $400 million. The paper currency was backed only by the government's promise to redeem the bills with money from future tax receipts, since politicians balked at the unpopular alternative of levying taxes during the war. For the bills to be redeemed, the government had to survive. Consequently, each rebel military reversal was followed by a decline in the value of American currency.

By the end of 1776, when Continental forces sustained a series of defeats, paper money started to depreciate dramatically. By 1781 it was virtually without value, and Americans coined the expression "not worth a Continental." The printing of paper money combined with a wartime shortage of goods set off an inflationary spiral of scarcer and scarcer goods costing more and more worthless dollars. In this spiral, creditors were gouged by debtors, who paid them back with depreciated currency. At the same time, soaring prices for food and manufactured goods eroded the buying power of wage earners and small farmers. And the end of the war brought on demands for prompt repayment from the new nation's foreign creditors as well as from soldiers seeking back pay and pensions.

Under the Articles of Confederation, Congress was hamstrung by the crisis. With no power to regulate trade, it could neither dam the stream of imported goods rushing into the states nor stanch the flow of gold and silver to Europe to pay for these items. With no power to prohibit the states from issuing paper money, it could not halt depreciation. With no power to regulate wages or prices, it could not curb inflation. And with no power to tax, it could not make any headway in reducing the public debt. Efforts to grant Congress greater powers met with determined resistance from the states. In 1781 and again in 1783, a group that included Alexander Hamilton, John Jay, and Robert Morris proposed that Congress be allowed to levy a 5 percent duty on all imports. The income generated by the impost would have given the Confederation a source of independent revenue to help repay the national debt. But the states still jealously guarded their power to tax. They refused Congress any revenue of its own, fearing the first steps toward "arbitrary" and "aristocratic" government.

Within states, too, economic problems fomented disaffection and discord. War always offers the chance for large profits, especially for those with an eye to the main chance. Some major merchants, creditors, and large commercial farmers had profited handsomely by selling supplies to the army at high prices or by preying on enemy vessels as privateers. Eager to protect their windfall, they lobbied state legislatures for an end to inflationary monetary policy. That meant passing high taxes to pay wartime debts, a paper currency that was backed up with gold and silver, and an active policy to encourage foreign trade.

Small farmers and urban artisans retaliated, pressing legislatures for programs that met their needs. Rural subsistence farmers, often in debt, pitted themselves against merchant and creditor interests, urging low taxes, a moratorium on debt payments, and a policy of cheap money and easy credit. Artisans opposed merchants by calling for protection from low-priced foreign imports that competed with the goods they produced. They set themselves against farmers as well by demanding price regulation of the farm products they consumed. In the continuing struggle, the state legislatures became the battleground of competing economic factions, each bent on gaining its own particular advantage.

As the 1780s wore on, conflict mounted toward crisis. The original political structures created by American revolutionaries proved poorly equipped to cope with postwar social and economic divisions. So long as the individual states remained sovereign, jealously guarding their prerogatives and the power of the purse, the Confederation was crippled—unable to conduct foreign affairs effectively, unable to set coherent economic policy, unable to deal with discontent in the West—in short, "frittered down to the impotent condition in which it now stands," as one observer noted in 1787. And political leaders who had counted on the civic virtue of their countrymen found that private interest proved more powerful than republican disinterestedness. With the body politic slowly rending itself to pieces, leaders like George Washington and James Madison of Virginia, James Wilson and Robert Morris of Pennsylvania, and Alexander Hamilton and John Jay of New York became convinced that the only way to quell the clashes among Americans was to strengthen the central government. Whether the states could be convinced to surrender power remained to be seen.

REPUBLICAN SOCIETY

While leaders with power and influence tried to decide how America should define itself politically, ordinary men and women were finding their own ways to reshape American society and culture. Inspired by the Declaration's ideal of equality, some Americans chafed at the subordinate position assigned to them under the old colonial order. Westerners, newly wealthy entrepreneurs, urban artisans, and women all claimed greater liberty, power, and recognition. These groups differed in their aspirations and goals, but all of them were, in some sense, challenging "patriarchy." The authority of the traditional "fathers" of government, society, and the family came under a new scrutiny; the impulse to defer to social superiors became less automatic. The new assertiveness demonstrated how deeply egalitarian assumptions were taking root in American culture.

The New Men of the Revolution

The Revolution gave rise to a new sense of social identity and a new set of ambitions among several groups of men who had once accepted obscurity. Westerners, especially, had rising expectations that sprang from the rapidly changing conditions of frontier communities. As one Kentuckian explained to James Madison, the western migrants "must make a very different mass from one which is composed of men born and raised on the same spot. . . . They see none about them to whom or to whose families they have been accustomed to think themselves inferior." Contemporaries saw clearly that frontier mobility weakened deference to eastern elites.

The war also offered opportunities to clever entrepreneurs, and these men too had their aspirations. Often these entrepreneurs were not the same men who

Daily Lives

FOOD/DRINK/DRUGS

The Spirits of Independence

If God had intended man to drink water, Ben Franklin remarked, He would not have made him with an elbow capable of raising a wine glass. Colonials from all across America, regardless of their theology, agreed with Franklin on the virtues of drink. The ruddy glow of colonial cheeks (still visible in the portraits hung in museums) reflected not only good health and ardent republican virtues, but also substantial daily doses of alcohol. Colonials consumed about twice as much alcohol as Americans today, though in different forms. Beer was not popular, the only sort consumed being a weak, homemade "small beer" containing about one percent alcohol. Only the wealthy, like Franklin, could afford imported Madeira and port wines. On the other hand, the produce of apple orchards allowed Americans northward from Virginia to drink their fill of hard cider. Far and away the most popular distilled liquor was rum, a potent 90 proof beverage (45 percent alcohol) that they sipped straight or mixed with water and sugar to make "toddies."

    Special occasions were especially convivial. The liquor flowed freely at ministerial ordinations in New England towns, at court days in the tidewater South, at house-raisings, corn-huskings, and quilting bees on the frontier, and at weddings, elections, and militia musters everywhere in the colonies. But Americans did not confine their drinking to occasional celebrations. Some, like John Adams, started the day with a tankard of hard cider. Others, merchants and craftworkers, broke the tedium of late mornings and early afternoons by sending the youngest apprentice in the shop out for

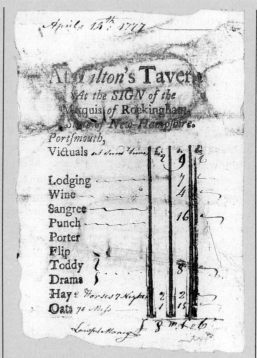

This tavern bill from New Hampshire indicates that in 1777 whiskey was still too rare to be listed.

spirits. Laborers in seaport docks and shipyards, fishermen and sailors at sea, and farm workers in the countryside commonly received a daily allotment of liquor as part of their wages. And at night, men of every class enjoyed a solitary glass at home or a sociable one at a local tavern.

    Socialization into the drinking culture started in childhood. Parents permitted youngsters to sip the sweet dregs of a glass of rum, and when young men entered their teens, they joined their fathers at the tavern. Women drank too, although more often at home, and they sometimes explained their use of distilled liquor as serving some "medicinal" purpose. Even slaves got their share, despite laws restricting their consumption of alcohol.

Daily Lives

Thomas Jefferson, whose presidential administration invented the Washington cocktail party, complained that for every glass of wine drunk by his guests, his resourceful slaves stole three.

Early Americans did not drink because they regarded alcohol as healthful, but their faith that it provided an added comfort. Until the middle of the eighteenth century, most colonials (and Europeans) considered spirits a source of physical strength and an essential supplement to their diet, as well as a remedy for colds, fevers, snakebite, and, ironically, depression. They did not condone public drunkenness, but they saw nothing amiss in the regular use of alcohol or even in occasional intoxication.

The easy acceptance of drinking prevailed for most of the colonial period for two reasons. First, until about 1760s, frequent access to the strongest spirits, rum, lay beyond the means of most Americans. Second, the leaders of local communities were able to oversee most public drinking and to keep disorder to a minimum. But by the middle of the eighteenth century some Americans developed misgivings about the drinking culture. Increased production and importation led the price of rum to drop anywhere from 30 to nearly 50 percent. With a gallon of rum selling so cheaply, an ordinary laborer could earn enough in a day to stay "drunk as a lord" for the rest of the week. And as distilled liquor became cheaper, taverns proliferated, making it impossible for community leaders to monitor the popular consumption of alcohol.

The new concern that the drinking of rum fostered crime and social disruption prompted the first steps toward temperance reform. By the 1770s, Quakers like Anthony Benezet were urging that alcohol, like slavery, was an "unrepublican vice," for both forms of bondage deprived their victims of liberty and the capacity for rationality and self-control. Some members of the medical profession also joined early temperance ranks, most notably Benjamin Rush, who publicized new theories about the detrimental effects of drink upon health which he had learned in Edinburgh.

While the advocates of more moderate consumption won support among some educated elites, most Americans altered their drinking habits by consuming *more* hard liquor. Rum, the liquor of choice, received a setback during the Revolution when the British blockade cut drastically the import of both rum and the molasses from which it was made. It became so scarce that Patrick Henry, while governor of Virginia, was embarrassed into serving his guests home-brewed beer. After the war distillers tried to recover their trade, but consumption dropped from 8 million gallons in 1770 to only 7 million in 1789, even though the American population had nearly doubled during that time. Rum lost much of its ground to a new rival, whiskey. Before the 1780s few Americans drank whiskey or were even familiar with it. But significant numbers of immigrants, arriving from Scotland and Ireland in the last quarter of the eighteenth century, brought with them the techniques of efficient, small-still grain distilling.

Whiskey was democratic and cheap, for it could be made in the lowliest backcountry farmhouse. It was patriotic, since it did not depend on imports from the Caribbean. Gradually these "spirits of independence" supplanted rum, not only in the frontier West but also in the urban East. Consumption of alcohol was on a steady rise that would finally result, half a century after the Revolution, in calls for temperance reform.

had prospered before the war, for the fair fortunes and high social position of some families did not survive the Revolution. The biggest losers were loyalists, whose ranks included a disproportionate number of government officials, large landowners, and major merchants. At a stroke independence swept away their political prominence while revolutionary governments confiscated their properties. Whig politicians, some men of humble social backgrounds, assumed loyalist power and government offices. Land speculators, gambling on an American victory, bought up loyalist property, selling off tracts to smaller buyers at a handsome profit.

The loyalists were not alone in suffering reversals. Wartime disruptions ruined some major merchants and planters who had supported independence. But others with a quick eye for profit stepped in. Some northern merchants turned to privateering; others profited from military contracts; many large commercial farmers in the Middle Colonies made a killing from the high prices for food caused by wartime scarcity and army demand.

The Revolution effected no dramatic redistribution of wealth; in fact, the gap between rich and poor increased during the 1780s. Many elite families weathered the war years well, retaining their property and prestige into the nineteenth century. But those families newly enriched by the Revolution came to demand and receive status and power during the postwar period. Their wealth allowed them to compete with established elites, the former "fathers" of colonial society, for social recognition and political influence. The republican ideal of "an aristocracy of merit" justified their claims to social leadership.

Urban Artisans

The dominance of society's traditional "fathers" met with resistance from city craftsmen as well. Before the imperial crisis, manufactured items had been produced in houses and small shops. Presiding was the master craftsman, who imparted the "mystery" of his art to younger, less experienced journeymen and even younger, unskilled apprentices. Journeymen and apprentices not only worked under their master's roof but usually lived under it also. The master supervised their private lives as well as their initiation into his trade. After the Revolution the "patriarchal" organization of the crafts began to give way to a more impersonal, contractual system of production. As domestic manufacturing expanded, the distinction between home and shop grew. Journeymen and even apprentices moved out of their masters' households and away from paternalistic supervision. They took their pay in cash rather than in room and board. Recognizing that their interests were often distinct from those of masters, journeymen formed new organizations to secure higher wages. Between 1786 and 1816, skilled urban laborers organized the first major strikes in American history. A new sense of solidarity among urban laborers translated into political activism, and workers expressed their objectives in republican rhetoric.

The New Women of the Revolution

Not long after the fighting with Britain had broken out, Margaret Livingston of New York wrote to her sister Catherine, "You know that our Sex are doomed to be obedient in every stage of life so that we shant be great gainers by this contest." By war's end, however, Eliza Wilkinson from rural South Carolina was complaining boldly to a woman friend: "The men say we have no business with political matters

. . . it's not our sphere. . . . [But] I won't have it thought that because we are the weaker Sex (as to bodily strength my dear) we are Capable of nothing more, than minding the Dairy . . . surely we may have enough sense to give our Opinions."

What separated Margaret Livingston's resignation from Eliza Wilkinson's assertion of personal worth and independence was the Revolution. For many American women, the war was a politicizing experience. Eliza Wilkinson, for one, had managed her parents' plantation during the war and defended it from British marauders. Other women discovered similar reserves of skill and resourcefulness. When soldiers returned home, some were surprised to find their wives and daughters, who had been running family farms and businesses, less submissive and more self-confident.

Beyond savoring their newfound independence, some women took republican promises of equality to heart, claiming greater political and domestic liberty. Like westerners, self-made capitalists, and city artisans, these women challenged traditional authority. They objected to men monopolizing political life and husbands ruling the family like patriarchs of old. Their protests were seldom heeded.

American men had not fought a revolution for the equality of American women. In fact, male revolutionaries gave no thought whatsoever to the role of women in the new nation, assuming that those of the "weaker sex" were incapable of making informed and independent political decisions. The English Opposition tradition, the main influence on American republican thought, contributed to the widespread conviction that women were politically irrelevant. These radical thinkers—among them, ironically, the gifted historian Catherine Macaulay— wrote virtually nothing about the relationship of women to the state. Most women of the revolutionary generation agreed that the proper female domain was the home, not the public arena of politics. Those with political interests and opinions usually apologized for expressing their views on public matters. When the widow of the head of Georgia's revolutionary government, Ann Gwinnet, wrote to warn the Continental Congress that the officer corps in her state was rife with loyalists, she added, "These things (tho from a Woman, and it is not our sphere, yet I cannot help it) are all true."

But occasionally women of the revolutionary generation openly displayed their keen political interests and advanced their claims to political consideration. When a loosely worded provision regarding voting requirements in the New Jersey state constitution enfranchised "all free inhabitants" owning a specified amount of property, white widows and single women went to the polls. Until 1807, when the state legislature amended the law, unmarried women qualified as legal voters and exercised that right.

Even though women's primary sphere remained the home, the Revolution brought about changes. Reformers like Benjamin Rush and Judith Sargent Murray argued that only educated and independent-minded women could raise the informed and self-reliant citizens that a republican government required. The notion of "republican motherhood" contributed to the most dramatic change in the lives of women after the war—the spread of female literacy.

Mercy Otis Warren, the sister of James Otis and the wife of James Warren, another Massachusetts political leader, lent her talent as a writer to the causes of American independence and education for women.

Between 1780 and 1830, the number of American colleges and secondary academies rose dramatically, and some of these new institutions were devoted to educating women. Not only did the number of schools for women increase, but these schools also instituted a solid academic curriculum. At the Young Ladies Academy of Philadelphia, which Rush helped to establish in 1787, students learned reading, arithmetic, English grammar and composition, rhetoric, and geography. Missing from the female curriculum were natural philosophy (science), advanced mathematics, and classics, subjects still restricted to male scholars. On the other hand, needlework no longer dominated the course of instruction for women.

The reform of women's education that began after the war resulted in a closing of the literacy gap between the two sexes. By 1850—for the first time in American history—there were as many literate women as there were men. That change came slowly, hampered by the view shared by members of both sexes that academic study for women was self-indulgent, useless, or even dangerous—a luxury that made women "masculine," ridiculous, and, above all, unfit for domestic life. To counter popular prejudices, the defenders of female education contended, schooling for women would produce the ideal republican mother. An educated woman, as one graduate of a female academy claimed, would "inspire her brothers, her husband, or her sons with such a love of virtue, such just ideas of the true value of civil liberty . . . that future heroes and statesmen shall exaltingly declare, it is to my mother that I owe this elevation."

The Revolution also prompted a number of states to reform their marriage laws, making divorce somewhat easier. In New England divorce rates rose, reflecting less willingness on the part of wives to tolerate domestic tyranny and more sensitivity on the part of judges to the rights of women within marriage. Divorce was still extremely unusual in the North and almost impossible in the South, yet the Revolution at least raised the possibility that equality should affect private as well as public lives.

While women won better schooling and greater freedom to divorce, they actually lost ground in the realm of property rights. After the Revolution courts became more lax about preserving dower rights, the widow's legal claim to one-third of her spouse's real estate. Married women still could not sue or be sued, make wills or contracts, or buy and sell property; any wages that they earned went to their husbands. All personal property that wives brought into a marriage became the possession of their spouses, as did the rents and profits of any real estate.

Even the new notion of "republican motherhood," while enhancing the significance of what women did within the home, relegated them to the domestic sphere. In the end, women as independent actors in the political world remained as invisible to the framers of the federal constitution in 1787 as they had been to John Adams when Abigail petitioned him in 1776 to act on behalf of "the ladies." The only reference to women in *The Federalist Papers* warns that the intrigues of mistresses and courtesans often threatened the stability of governments.

The Attack on Aristocracy

Why wasn't the American Revolution more revolutionary? Independence secured the full political equality of white men who owned property, but most had enjoyed such equality before the war. The Revolution fostered greater personal freedom for women and prompted some states and individuals to emancipate slaves, but by and large it left the major legal barriers to equality unchanged. Women were still deprived of political rights, blacks of human rights. Why did the revolutionaries stop short of extending equality to the most unequal groups in American society— and with so little sense that they were being inconsistent?

In part, the lack of concern was rooted in republican ideas themselves: lacking property, women and blacks were easily read out of the political nation, consigned to the custody of husbands and masters. In part, the oversight was the product of prejudice: the perception of women and blacks as naturally inferior beings. But it was also the product of a deep conservatism among the revolutionaries. Political innovators though they were, American republicans in their social vision looked backward. Their obsession with traditional inequities kept them from conceiving of social justice in more progressive terms.

The revolutionaries thought of themselves as engaged in a great struggle for equality, and so they were. Yet most defined that battle in traditional and limited terms. During the Middle Ages, the feudal system had created a class of princes, dukes, knights, and other aristocrats, who had become bloated with the power of inherited privileges. Bishops, archbishops, and other "spiritual lords" had also come to rule over the thoughts and beliefs of free citizens. In the eyes of republicans, the real threat to liberty lay in the privileges of those "lords spiritual and temporal"—privileges that had to be eliminated from the political system, root and branch. Republicans were interested in leveling off the top of society, not in raising up the bottom. When they looked for legal abuses, they saw the unfair legal practices inherited from medieval Europe, but they remained blind to the legal inequalities that kept blacks enslaved and women dependent.

No matter that America was devoid of aristocrats and bishops and that no individuals or groups enjoyed formal privileges. Republicans sought out and exposed any traces of aristocracy they could find. If elaborate powdered wigs smacked of lordly privilege, then city crowds might find themselves treated to a Fourth of July parade like the one in Philadelphia witnessed by a local resident: a dirty woman wearing a "very high Head dress" was "exhibited thro the Streets" with an eager mob swirling around her, symbolically beating "Drums etc. by way of ridiculing that very foolish fashion." In similar spirit, reformers attacked the Society of Cincinnati, a group organized by former officers of the Continental Army in 1783. The society, which was nothing more sinister than a social club for veterans, was harried for its policy of passing on its membership rights to eldest sons. In this way, critics charged, the Cincinnati was creating artificial distinctions and perpetuating a hereditary warrior nobility. Bowing to public pressure, the society eventually disbanded.

More significant was the dismantling of state-supported churches. Every state except Delaware, New Jersey, Pennsylvania, and Rhode Island had a religious establishment—the Anglican church in New York and the South, the Congregational church in New England. Since the 1740s, dissenters who did not worship at state churches had protested laws that taxed all citizens to support the clergy of established denominations. They also objected to the licenses that colonial governments required their own ministers to have. After the Revolution, dissenters argued that if all citizens were to be treated as equals, the privileges of religion had to be ended. Pointing to their contributions to winning the war for independence, dissenters urged that they were entitled to a full share of liberty in the new republic. As more and more dissenters became voters, state legislators paid heed and finally abolished the special legal privileges of the Anglican and Congregational churches. But the trend toward disestablishment had been under way well before the Revolution, and the new laws were mainly the capstone of the process.

Many of the republican efforts at reform seem in retrospect misdirected and occasionally ridiculous. While only a handful of revolutionaries worked for the education of women and the emancipation of slaves, enormous zeal went into fighting threats from a feudal past that had never existed in America. Yet if most revolutionaries struck at shadows, the darkness of aristocrats and bishops seemed real to them—and indeed remained real in many parts of Europe. Their determination to sweep away every residue of formal privilege ensured that these forms of inequality never took root in America. And if eighteenth-century Americans did not extend equality to women and racial minorities, it was a failure that they shared with later revolutionary movements that promised more. The political institutions that American republicans created did not by any stretch of the imagination bring total equality. But over the years the strength of those institutions has allowed the extent of equality to grow.

FROM CONFEDERATION TO CONSTITUTION

While Americans sought to realize the republican commitment to equality in many walks of life, leaders in Congress wrestled with the problem of preserving the nation itself. By the mid-1780s the survival of the United States was in doubt. Two events—one foreign, one domestic—brought American republicans to the disturbing conclusion that neither the Confederation nor the state legislatures were able to remedy the fundamental difficulties facing the nation.

The Jay–Gardoqui Treaty

The international episode that pushed the United States to the brink of dissolution was a debate over a proposed treaty with Spain. In 1785 settlers along the southwestern frontier remained restive over their trade route to New Orleans. Accordingly, Congress instructed its secretary of foreign affairs, John Jay, to negotiate an agreement with Spain preserving American navigational rights on the Mississippi River. The Spanish emissary, Don Diego de Gardoqui, proved the more formidable diplomat. He inveigled Jay into an arrangement by which the United States would actually relinquish all rights to the Mississippi for 25 years. In return, Spain would acknowledge American territorial claims in the Southwest and grant trading privileges to American merchants.

Jay, a New Yorker, leapt to the bait. He knew northern merchants took a keen interest in finding new markets, and he chose to overlook the expense to the South at which this northern opportunity was gained. Southwestern settlers in the Ohio valley, most of them migrants from Virginia and the Carolinas, regarded the proposed treaty as nothing short of betrayal, and they told Congress so. The treaty was never ratified, but the hostility stirred up during the debate revealed how strong sectional feelings were. Gardoqui's clever bid to deepen southwestern mistrust of the Confederation worked. Southwestern leaders like James Wilkinson, a former Revolutionary War general, and Daniel Boone began accepting bribes from the governor of New Orleans with the understanding that they would encourage pro-Spanish sympathies among their neighbors.

Shays' Rebellion

On the heels of the Confederation's foreign humiliation came an internal ruckus that challenged the notion that individual states could maintain order in their own territories. The problem surfaced in western Massachusetts, where many small farmers were close to ruin. By 1786 farm wages and prices had fallen sharply and farmers were selling little produce. Yet they still had to pay mortgages on their farms, still had other debts, and were perpetually short of money. The time-honored tactics that legislatures used to help debtors were to lower taxes and fees and simply to print more money. Stay laws could be passed, too, temporarily forbidding creditors from foreclosing on farmers' property. (Foreclosures could include more than land: sometimes creditors took away farmers' personal tools, household goods, and even clothing.) In 1786 the lower house of the Massachusetts legislature obliged the farmers with a package of relief measures.

But creditors in eastern Massachusetts, determined to safeguard their own investments, persuaded the upper house to defeat the measures. The farmers then took matters into their own hands. In the summer of 1786 they met in extralegal conventions, demanding that the upper house of the legislature be abolished and that the relief measures go into effect. By autumn the farmers had turned from words to deeds, rising 2000 strong in armed rebellion. Led by Captain Daniel Shays, a veteran of the Revolution, mobs closed the county courts to halt creditors from foreclosing on their farms and marched on the federal arsenal at Springfield. The state militia quelled the uprising by February 1787, but the insurrection left many in Massachusetts and the rest of the country thoroughly shaken.

Alarmed conservatives saw Shays' Rebellion as the consequence of democracy carried to radical extremes. "The natural effects of pure democracy are already produced among us," lamented one republican gentleman; "it is a war against virtue, talents, and property carried on by the dregs and scum of mankind." But the farmers who took up arms under Daniel Shays were no impoverished rabble. They were reputable members of western communities who wanted their property protected and believed that government existed to provide that protection. The Massachusetts state legislature had been unable to safeguard the property of farmers from the inroads of recession or to protect the property of creditors from the armed debtors who closed the courts. It had failed, in other words, to fulfill the most fundamental aim of republican government.

What if such violent tactics spread? Other states with discontented debtors feared what the example of western Massachusetts might mean for their own future—not to mention the future of the Confederation itself. But by 1786 Shays' Rebellion supplied only the sharpest jolt to the movement toward creating a stronger national government already under way. Even before Shays rose in arms, a group of Virginians had urged Congress to authorize a meeting of the states that would consider setting up a uniform system of commercial regulations. Once assembled at Annapolis in September 1786 the delegates from five states agreed to a more ambitious undertaking. They called for a second, broader meeting in Philadelphia, which Congress approved, for the "express purpose of revising the Articles of Confederation." The die was now cast; but the outcome was by no means certain.

The Framing of the Federal Constitution

It was the wettest spring anyone could remember. The 55 men who traveled to Philadelphia in May 1787 came over muddy roads and through unceasing rainstorms, arriving drenched and bespattered. They wondered if the honor of being chosen a delegate to the convention made up for the discomfort. Fortunately, most of the travelers were men in their thirties and forties, young enough to survive a good soaking. And since most were gentlemen of some means—planters, merchants, and lawyers with powdered wigs and prosperous paunches—they could recover from the rigors of their journey in the best accommodations offered by America's largest city.

The delegates came from all of the states except one. Rhode Island, ever the maverick, refused to send a representative. The rest of New England supplied shrewd backroom politicians—Roger Sherman and Oliver Ellsworth from Connecticut, and Rufus King and Elbridge Gerry, Massachusetts men who had learned a trick or two from Sam Adams. The middle states marshaled much of the intellectual might: two Philadelphia lawyers, John Dickinson and James Wilson, and one Philadelphia financier, Robert Morris. There was Alexander Hamilton, the mercurial and ambitious young protégé of Washington, and his fellow New Yorker, the aristocratic Gouverneur Morris. South Carolina provided fiery orators, Charles Pinckney and John Rutledge.

It was "an assembly of the demi-gods," gushed Thomas Jefferson, who was not there. Along with John Adams, Jefferson was serving as a diplomat in Europe when the convention met. In fact, the only delegate who looked even remotely divine was the convention's presiding deity. Towering a full half foot taller than most of his colleagues, George Washington exuded his ineffable self-possession from a chair elevated on the speaker's platform where the delegates met, in the Pennsylvania State House.

It would have been hard to find a less likely candidate for patriotic icon than Washington's fellow Virginia delegate, James Madison. Short and slightly built, bookish and retiring, the 36-year-old Madison had no profession except hypochondria; he read a great deal and dressed in black. He was not a commanding presence like Washington or as celebrated as other Virginia delegates like George Mason, the author of that state's bill of rights, or Edmund Randolph, its eccentric governor. Nonetheless, Madison was an astute politician. He possessed limitless patience and was brilliant without being dogmatic. The convention belonged to him: more than anyone else, James Madison shaped the framing of the federal Constitution.

The delegates from 12 different states had two things in common. First, they were men of considerable political talent and experience. Most had served in Congress; others had drafted state constitutions or served as state governors. One-third were veterans of the Continental Army and 34 were lawyers. Second, the delegates all recognized the need for a stronger national government. So when the Virginia delegation introduced Madison's outline for a new central government, the convention was ready to listen.

James Madison, the scholar and statesman whose ideas and political skill shaped the Constitution.

What Madison had in mind was a truly national republic, not a confederation of independent states. His "Virginia Plan" proposed a central government with three branches—legislative, executive, and judicial—with Congress having the power to veto all state legislation. In place of the Confederation's single assembly, Madison substituted a bicameral legislature, with a lower house elected directly by the people and an upper house chosen by the lower from nominations made by state legislatures. Representatives to both houses would be apportioned according to population—a change from practice under the Articles, in which each state had a single vote in Congress. Madison also revised the structure of government that had existed under the articles by adding an executive, who would be elected by Congress, and an independent federal judiciary.

After two weeks of debate over the Virginia Plan, William Paterson, a lawyer from New Jersey, presented a less radical counterproposal. While his "New Jersey Plan" increased Congress' power to tax and to regulate trade, it kept the national government as a unicameral assembly, with each state receiving one vote in Congress under the policy of equal representation. Smaller states like New Jersey opposed proportional representation because it would give larger, more populous states greater influence in Congress. The delegates summarily dispatched Paterson's plan, rejecting it within four days. Most recognized the need for stronger measures and supported Madison's design for changing the structure of the central government. But the delegates were seriously divided over the apportionment of representation. While smaller states pressed for each state having an equal vote in Congress, larger states backed Madison's provision for basing representation on population.

Underlying the dispute over representation was an even deeper rivalry between southern and northern states. While northern and southern populations were nearly equal in the 1780s, and the South's population was growing at the more rapid rate, the northern states were more numerous. Giving the states equal votes would put the South at a disadvantage. Southerners feared being outflanked in Congress by the northern states and felt that only proportional representation would protect the interests of their section.

As the wettest spring that anyone could remember burned off into the hottest summer, the division over representation deepened into a deadlock. Temperatures soared, tempers shortened, and the delegates suffered the daily torture of staring at a large sun emblazoned across the speaker's chair occupied by Washington. The stifling heat was made even worse because the windows remained shut all day, to keep any news of the proceedings from drifting out onto the Philadelphia streets and upsetting the delicate negotiations.

Finally, as the heat wave broke, so did the political impasse. On July 2 a committee headed by Benjamin Franklin, who at 81 had been trying to form a national union before some of the delegates were born, weighed in with a compromise. States would be equally represented in the upper house of Congress, each state legislature appointing two senators to six-year terms. That appeased the smaller states. But in the lower house of Congress, which alone could initiate money bills, representation was to be apportioned according to population: every 30,000 inhabitants would elect one representative for a two-year term. A slave was to count as three-fifths of a free person in the calculation of population, and the slave trade was to continue until 1808. That appeased the larger states and the South.

The Constitution was drawn up and debated, and by the end of August the

As the Constitution is signed, Benjamin Franklin, second from left, looks on; Washington presides. "The business being closed," Washington wrote, "the members adjourned to the City Tavern, dined together and took cordial leave of each other."

convention was prepared to approve the final draft. The delegates agreed that the executive, now called the president, would be chosen every four years. Direct election, however, seemed out of the question—after all, how could citizens in South Carolina know anything about a presidential candidate who happened to live in distant Massachusetts, or vice versa? But if voters instead chose presidential electors, those eminent men likely would have been involved in national politics, would have known the candidates personally, and would be prepared to vote wisely. Thus the Electoral College was established, with each state's total number of senators and representatives determining its share of electoral votes. It was a cumbersome device, but one that guaranteed that the president would not owe his office to Congress.

An array of other powers assured that the executive would remain independent and strong: he would have command over the armed forces, authority to conduct diplomatic relations, responsibility to nominate judges and officials in the executive branch, and the power to veto congressional legislation. Just as the executive branch was made independent, so too the federal judiciary was separated from the other two branches of government. Madison believed that this clear separation of powers was essential to a balanced republican government.

Madison's only real defeat came when the convention refused to give Congress veto power over state legislation. Still, the new bicameral national legislature enjoyed much broader authority than Congress had under the Confederation, including the power to tax and to regulate commerce. The Constitution also clipped the wings of state legislatures, prohibiting them from levying import and export duties, coining money or issuing paper currency, relieving debtors of their contractual obligations, and conducting foreign relations. The Constitution and the acts passed by Congress were declared the supreme law of the land, taking precedence over any legislation passed by the states. And changing the Constitution would not be easy—amendments could be proposed only by a two-thirds vote of both houses of Congress or in a convention requested by two-thirds of the state legislatures. Ratification of amendments required approval by three-quarters of the states.

On September 17, 1787, thirty-nine of the forty-two delegates remaining in Philadelphia signed the Constitution. It was fortunate that the signatories included so many lawyers, for the summer's proceedings had been of such dubious legality that a battery of skilled attorneys would be needed to make them seem otherwise. Charged only to revise the Articles, the delegates had instead written a new frame of government. Not only had they written a new constitution, but one with no bill of rights—the majority of delegates had deemed that unnecessary. In addition, to speed up ratification, the convention decided that the Constitution would go into effect after only nine states had approved it, overlooking the fact that even a revision of the Articles would have required the assent of all state legislatures. As for the state legislatures, the delegates determined to bypass them altogether, declaring that the people themselves would pass judgment on the Constitution in special ratifying conventions. To serve final notice that the new central government was a republic of the people and not merely another confederation of states, Gouverneur Morris of New York hit on a happy turn of phrase to introduce the Constitution. "We the People," the document begins, "in order to form a more perfect union. . . ."

Ratification

With grave misgivings on the part of many, the states called for conventions to decide whether to ratify the new Constitution. Those with the gravest misgivings—the anti-Federalists as they came to be called—voiced familiar republican fears. Expanding the power of the central government at the expense of the states, they warned, would lead to corrupt and arbitrary rule by new aristocrats. Extending a republic over a large territory, they cautioned, would separate national legislators from the interests and close oversight of their constituents. With so many different regions and interests and classes of people, factions would soon tear the government apart.

Madison responded to these objections in *The Federalist Papers,* a series of 85 essays written with Alexander Hamilton and John Jay and published in a New York City newspaper during the winter of 1787–1788. He countered anti-Federalist concerns over the centralization of power by pointing to the ingenious system of checks and balances built into the Constitution. Each separate branch of the national government would, Madison explained, keep the others within the limits of their legal authority. The mechanism would prevent the executive from oppressing the people while preventing the people from oppressing themselves.

To answer anti-Federalist objections to a national republic, Madison drew on the iconoclastic ideas of an English philosopher, David Hume. According to Hume, the conventional wisdom of Montesquieu and other liberal thinkers was all wrong: large size was not a liability but an asset for a republic. The larger a territory, the more likely were multiple political interests and parties—so many that no single faction could dominate. Instead, each would cancel out the others.

Ratification of the Constitution

STATE	DATE	VOTE FOR	VOTE AGAINST
Delaware	December 8, 1787	30	0
Pennsylvania	December 12, 1787	46	23
New Jersey	December 18, 1787	38	0
Georgia	January 2, 1788	26	0
Connecticut	January 9, 1788	128	40
Massachusetts	February 16, 1788	187	168
Maryland	April 26, 1788	63	11
South Carolina	May 23, 1788	149	73
New Hampshire	June 21, 1788	57	47
Virginia	June 25, 1788	89	79
New York	July 26, 1788	30	27
North Carolina	November 21, 1789	194	77
Rhode Island	May 29, 1790	34	32

Madison reformulated Hume's argument in his famous tenth essay in *The Federalist Papers,* arguing that in a great republic, "the Society becomes broken into a greater variety of interests, of pursuits, of passions, which check each other, whilst those who may feel a common sentiment have less opportunity of communication and contact."

The one criticism Madison could not get around—and the issue that became the core of anti-Federalist opposition to the Constitution—was the absence of a bill of rights. The convention delegates had not drawn up a specific national bill of rights because they believed that provisions in the Constitution as well as the state constitutions themselves provided sufficient protection for personal freedoms. But the anti-Federalists were not assured, and they called for an explicit statement of rights to secure the freedoms of individuals and minorities from being violated by the federal government. Madison finally promised to place a bill of rights before Congress immediately after the Constitution was ratified.

Throughout the early months of 1788, anti-Federalists continued their opposition. Although their followers were widespread, they lacked the articulate and influential leadership that rallied behind the Constitution and commanded greater access to the public press. In the end, too, anti-Federalist fears of a tyrannical centralized power proved less compelling than federalist prophecies of the chaos that would follow if the Constitution was not adopted. Many agreed with Hamilton that the alternative to ratification was "anarchy and Convulsion."

By June 1788 all of the states except three had voted in favor of ratification— New York, North Carolina. The last holdout—to no one's surprise Rhode Island— finally accepted the Constitution in May 1790. Madison's pledge to provide a bill

The American artist Thomas Sully's idealized likeness of Patrick Henry conveys his subject's intensity. Henry's eloquence and passion as on orator made a vivid impression on his contemporaries.

of rights took the form of the first 10 amendments to the Constitution, adopted by three-quarters of the states by the end of 1791. The amendments protected the freedoms of speech, religion, press, and assembly, as well as the right to bear arms and to trial by jury. In a real sense, they were the anti-Federalists' most impressive legacy.

Within the life span of a single generation, Americans had declared their independence twice. In many ways the liberation claimed from Britain in 1776 was less remarkable than the intellectual freedom that Americans achieved by assenting to the Constitution. The Constitution represented a triumph of political imagination and pragmatism and a repudiation of some ancient and cherished republican axioms. It was a recognition that experience could be the only reliable guide to politics.

Americans were afraid to change their minds, but many did. Committed at first to limiting executive power and asserting legislative supremacy, Americans at last ratified a constitution that provided for an independent executive and a balanced government. Committed at first to preserving the sovereignty of the states, Americans at last established a national government with authority independent of the states. Committed at first to the proposition that a national republic was impossible, Americans at last created an impossibility that still endures. Such thinking was hardly consistent, but "a foolish consistency," wrote philosopher Ralph Waldo Emerson half a century after 1787, "is the hobgoblin of small minds." It would have been a fitting epitaph for the revolutionary generation.

Not all of the old revolutionaries agreed. The narrow majorities by which the Constitution was ratified reflect the continuing influence of localistic sentiments. Among the loyal supporters of undiluted state sovereignty was Patrick Henry. He refused to attend the Constitutional Convention in 1787 because he "smelt a rat." He became an ardent anti-Federalist, lending his impassioned oratory to the cause of defeating ratification. "I am not a Virginian, but an American," Henry had once declared. Most likely he was lying. Or perhaps Patrick Henry, a southerner and a slaveholder, could see his way clear to being an "American" only so long as sovereignty remained firmly in the hands of the individual states. That was a position which, 70 years later, would rise again to haunt the Union.

SIGNIFICANT EVENTS

1777	Continental Congress approves the Articles of Confederation
1781	Articles of Confederation ratified
1784	Spain closes the Mississippi River to American navigation
1785	Jay–Gardoqui Treaty negotiated but not ratified
	Shays' Rebellion; Annapolis convention calls for revising the Articles
1787	Congress adopts the Northwest Ordinance; Constitutional Convention
1787–1788	Publication of *The Federalist Papers*
1788	New Hampshire becomes ninth state to ratify Constitution
1791	Bill of Rights adopted

Generations of the Republic

The First African-Americans
(1740–1800)

What were their memories of the world as first they found it? Perhaps some remembered the snug darkness or the dank, dirt floor of home, a spare one-room hut. Perhaps some remembered its familiar objects—straw bedding, coarse woolen blankets, wooden barrels that served as seats, a grindstone for making corn into meal. Perhaps they remembered their mother or father, sitting before the fireplace, smiling, calling the familiar name they had been given by someone else: Molly or Betty, Jack or Jemmy.

Or did the world outdoors leave more of an impression? Some may have remembered the yard fronted by identical huts, an enclosed space filled during the day with chickens and small children—their brothers and sisters, cousins and playmates—and presided over by an ancient woman, wrinkled by the sun, worn by work—their grandmother, or even great-grandmother. Perhaps they remembered glimpsing in the distance the dark figures of mothers and fathers, aunts and uncles, older brothers and sisters, as they weeded, hoed, or harvested from daybreak to sundown in tobacco fields and rice swamps. Perhaps they remembered watching their mothers breaking from work long enough to suckle the infants left lying in the shade.

Evenings in the quarters no doubt etched themselves vividly. The whole village of kin, in-laws, and friends came together, often cooking a communal meal of cornbread and bits of pork. Perhaps they remembered the men after supper sharing liquor and stories of how they had contrived to get the contraband spirits. Perhaps they remembered the runaways who sometimes came after dark to take shelter in the quarters.

Many must have remembered fondly Sundays and holidays, when family members not seen every day came to visit—fathers, grown brothers and sisters, and more distant kin and friends from neighboring plantations. Exuberant singing and dancing to the beating of drums and the strumming of banjos marked these reunions. Cross-plantation networks of families and friends also convened more solemn gatherings—meetings for religious worship and commemorations of the dead. Funerals, usually held a month after bur-

ial, often included a ritual of drinking the dead to a new home, as some said, in west Africa.

The African-American children born into slavery on southern plantations could not count west Africa among their memories. It was only through their immigrant parents that these native-born children came to know of the world their elders had lost. The older generation told of the initiation ceremonies and puberty rites, the marriage customs and religious beliefs, the hunting and farming practices, the legends and tales of conjuring and sorcery of tribes to which they had once belonged: the Ibos and Ibidios, the Efkins and Mokos. They told of African relatives they would never see again and African names they no longer heard.

Equally foreign to the black children growing up after 1750 was the earlier America of their parents, the Africans brought to the Chesapeake and the Carolinas in the four decades after 1700, the time of heaviest importation. This older generation had survived the trauma of captivity, the Middle Passage, and sale at slave auctions. They had been thrust into a bewildering new world: a sea of unfamiliar faces, a clamor of different languages, a host of demands from men and women who called themselves masters. Theirs was a world of ceaseless, monotonous labor, performing the plantation's most menial tasks. Theirs was a world of count-

less efforts to escape. Theirs was a world in which death stalked life, especially during the first grim year of "seasoning," when one-quarter of all black immigrants succumbed to disease or despair.

The earliest generations of enslaved Africans confronted a world of constant struggle and conflict, not only with deadly diseases against which they had no immunity and with masters against whom they had few defenses, but also with their fellow slaves. Coming from a number of diverse west African tribes, each with a separate language or dialect and distinctive cultures and kinship systems, the "new Negroes" often had little in common with one another, and even less in common with the American-born black minority. Native-born blacks enjoyed better health, command of English, and experience in dealing with whites. They were also more likely to enjoy a family life, for their advantages probably made them the preferred partners of black women, who were outnumbered two to one by black men. And since immigrant women waited two or three years before marrying, some immigrant men died before they could find a wife, and many never married. Africans resented native-born men as rivals in the competition for wives, and some immigrants held in particular contempt native converts to Christianity.

But by the 1730s in the Chesapeake, and a few decades later in the Carolinas,

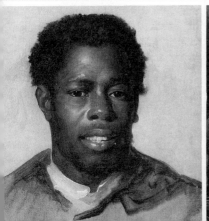

births began to outnumber deaths in the slave quarters. As the black population began to grow by natural increase, slave importations tapered off. As native-born blacks predominated, the balance between men and women started to even out, reinforcing the growth of population by reproduction. As the black population expanded, the size of plantations also grew apace. In the Chesapeake as well as in the Carolinas, slave quarters on larger plantations came to resemble black villages of interrelated kin. And as the immigrant generations were replaced by native-born blacks, earlier sources of tension and division within the slave community disappeared.

Forming a family had also become somewhat easier by the 1750s. Because men still outnumbered women, most black males married later than whites, around age 30; black women married in their late teens, at about the age of southern white brides. Although some newly married black couples set up their own households after the birth of their first child, most black wives, even on larger plantations, did not share that home with their husbands. For unlike southern whites, blacks refused to marry their cousins, a taboo that forced many young men to choose mates from neighboring plantations. These husbands and fathers resided in barracks with other men on separate plantations, visiting their wives and children as often as they could.

Because of these changes, black children of the mid-eighteenth century came of age in a plantation society more stable than that known by earlier generations. These members of a new African-American majority generally lived in households with their mothers and some of their brothers and sisters, and more than half of all youngsters on larger plantations lived with both parents. In addition, many members of a child's extended family—grandparents, uncles, aunts, and cousins—often lived on the same plantation or close enough to allow frequent visits.

African-Americans coming of age later in the eighteenth century not only had fuller domestic and social lives, but some also engaged in work more varied than heavy labor in the fields. White masters, especially the owners of large plantations, trained some native blacks in skilled trades that did not require literacy, apprenticing them as blacksmiths, coopers, masons, potters, carpenters, miners, shoemakers, millers, and boatmen. Slave women acquired skills as cooks, laundresses, dairymaids, and nurses. In the 1770s, a large number who learned the crafts of weaving and spinning supplied much of the cloth previously imported from England. The determination of white masters to make their plantations as self-

sufficient as possible fostered a class of skilled black workers, both male and female.

To be sure, the harsh realities of slavery still intruded into the lives of African-American children. Masters, not slave parents, named the infants born on their plantations, and their preferences ran to diminutives and nicknames. Between the ages of 7 and 10, youngsters were sent to work alongside adult slaves in the fields, and between the ages of 10 and 14, many either left their parental home to live with relatives or were sold to neighboring planters.

The most basic conditions of life remained fraught with uncertainty. Virtually every southern slave experienced a forced separation from the family at some time in his or her life. Although some planters encouraged permanent unions among their bondspeople, hoping that family ties would increase reproduction and discourage runaways, slave marriages had no legal status. And the slave family was only as stable as a master's health and finances were sound. If a master fell on hard times, members of black families might be sold off to different buyers to meet his debts. When a master died, slave families were divided among the heirs. Even in the best circumstances, fathers might be separated from their families for long periods, hired out to other planters or sent to work on distant quarters.

Two other developments disrupted black efforts to fashion domestic and communal bonds. Most important was the migration of many white slaveholding families from the coast to the interior. Between 1755 and 1782, masters on the move resettled fully one-third of all adult blacks living in Tidewater Virginia, mostly men and women in their teens and early twenties, in the valleys of the Piedmont, hundreds of miles from their families and friends. There these young people had to begin again the long process of establishing families and elaborating kinship networks. Another unsettling event was the American Revolution, when southern blacks were confronted with a choice between remaining on their plantations or risking a trek across the embattled countryside to escape behind British lines. Perhaps 2 to 3 percent of the Chesapeake's slave population—3000 to 5000 people— cast their lot with the British, nearly half of them women with children.

8

The Republic Launched

he news spread outward from the centers of ratification like ripples from pebbles dropped in a pond. Normally news traveled slowly in the eighteenth century, but express riders spurred their horses through the night. New Hampshire, the ninth state to ratify, sent messengers south on June 21 and in three days New York City had received the news. The next day Philadelphia learned and the ripple kept spreading: through Delaware, on to Maryland, and then farther south. Meanwhile in Richmond, the Virginia convention ratified on June 25, and its news began traveling north, the two ripples crossing at about two hours before dawn on June 28, in the village of Alexandria. New Hampshire to Virginia—500 miles in one week.

West of the Alleghenies in Pittsburgh, rumors were spreading so fast that eager Federalists persuaded themselves that Virginia had ratified five days before it actually did. Some 1500 citizens assembled on Grant's Hill to hear an orator proudly announce that the Anti-Federalist "frogs of the marsh" would no longer threaten the Republic because their pond was "about to be dried up." In Albany, New York, opponents of the Constitution accepted the news less calmly. Filling their pockets with stones, they bombarded the local Federalist parade. Out in the Southwestern Territory, word of the new union didn't reach the Creek nation until April 1789, when American officials announced, somewhat pompously, that the United States was "now governed by a President who is like the old King over the great water. He commands all the warriors of the thirteen great fires . . . and when peace shall be established he will be your father, and you will be his children." The Creeks were neither impressed nor notably inclined to become anyone's children.

As always, the celebrations were symbolic. The crowd at Pittsburgh lit nine bonfires—each representing a state that had ratified—and then let the flames spread to four other brush piles, those states yet to join. When Pennsylvania ratified, a few seamen managed to load a boat onto a wagon and haul it through Philadelphia's streets. One of the sailors stood in the bow, throwing out a sounding line and calling, "Three and twenty fathoms, foul bottom," or sometimes, "Six-and-forty fathoms, sound bottom, safe anchorage." Onlookers were puzzled about the meaning until someone realized that the number of fathoms referred to the vote: the Federalists had won by a margin of 46 to 23. Up in Boston, citizens

The corner of Wall and Water Streets in New York City was the location of the Stock Exchange and the Tontine Coffee House, both meeting places for the merchants and brokers of commercial America.

sang an epic poem about ratification to the tune of "Yankee Doodle." Its final stanza concluded:

> So here I end my Fed'ral song,
> Composed of thirteen verses;
> May agriculture flourish long
> And commerce fill our purses!

The symbols were important, illustrating as they did Americans' hopes for the Republic and what it might become. Yet the bonfires, parades, and solemn pronouncements could not mask large uncertainties. Joining together under the "new federal roof" involved more than wrangling over political philosophy. Could the new government succeed in uniting so many diverse factions and regions? The visions Americans had for the nation were formed largely by the social backgrounds from which they came. A Yankee merchant from Salem whose "purse," as the song put it, was being filled by commerce from the new China trade had economic interests and cultural traditions quite different from a farmer in the Virginia backcountry whose agriculture was "flourishing long" by the raising of hogs and tending of a few acres of corn. What were the social contours of the American Republic as its new federal government was launched?

1789: A SOCIAL PORTRAIT

When the Constitution went into effect, the United States stretched from the Atlantic Ocean to the Mississippi River. The first federal census, compiled in 1790, put the population at approximately 4 million people, divided about evenly between the northern and southern states. Virginia, the largest and most populous state, contained over half again as many residents as Pennsylvania, its nearest rival. New York, whose settlers lived primarily in the Hudson River valley, ranked only fifth, behind not only Virginia and Pennsylvania, but also Massachusetts and North Carolina. Formal boundaries could be deceptive, however, since the Republic's population was overwhelmingly concentrated along the eastern seaboard within 50 miles of the Tidewater. Only about 100,000 settlers lived beyond the Appalachians in the Tennessee and Kentucky territories, which were soon to become states. The area north of the Ohio River was virtually unsettled by whites. The great westward surge of population, which would be a major phenomenon of the nineteenth century, was just beginning.

Within the Republic's boundaries were two major social groups that lacked effective political influence: African-Americans and Indians. In 1790 blacks numbered 750,000, almost one-fifth of the total population. Over 90 percent lived in the southern states from Maryland to Georgia, most of them slaves who worked on tobacco and rice plantations. But there were free blacks as well, their numbers increased by the ideals of liberty that the Revolution had fostered. In 1790 the free black population was larger, relative to the total African-American population, than at any time before the Civil War. The census did not count the numbers of Indians living east of the Mississippi. North of the Ohio, the powerful Miami Confederacy discouraged settlement, although during the 1780s a smallpox epidemic had decimated their numbers. To the south, five strong, well-organized tribes with a total population somewhere between 50,000 and 100,000—the Creeks, Cherokees, Chickasaws, Choctaws, and Seminoles—dominated the region below the Ohio from the Appalachians to the Mississippi River. In 1790 in other words, Indian nations wielded effective control of more territory within the United States than the United States itself did.

That situation would soon change, however, as the white population continued to double approximately once every 22 years. Immigration contributed only a small part to this astonishing increase, for on average, fewer than 10,000 incoming Europeans arrived annually between 1790 and 1820. The primary cause was natural increase, making the United States preeminently a nation of youth. In 1790 almost half of all white Americans were under 16 years old and the average American woman gave birth to nearly eight children. Because of the extremely high birth rate (no nation in the world today can match it), women did not live as long, and thus males made up slightly more than half the population, at least among whites.* The age at first marriage was about 25 for men, 24 for women; because of the preponderance of males on the frontier, it was significantly lower in newly settled areas (on average perhaps 21 for males and less for females), which contributed to the high birth rate.

---

*Because the 1790 census did not include significant data on the black population, many of the statistical figures quoted for this era apply only to whites.

This youthful, burgeoning population remained overwhelmingly rural. Only 24 towns or cities boasted a population of 2500 or more, and 19 out of 20 Americans lived outside them. In fact, in 1800 over 80 percent of American families engaged in agriculture, a figure more than double that for England, the most industrialized country of the day. Throughout rural America, the movement of people, goods, and information was slow. The news of the Constitution's ratification traveled much faster than most newspapers, letters, or cargoes. Most roads were still little more than dirt paths hacked through the forest, with stumps cut off at 16 inches (so axles would just clear them) and large trees sometimes left in the roadway. They choked with dust in dry periods and became a sea of mud after rains. When the new government took office, there was not a soundly paved road anywhere in the country. South of Richmond and westward over the Appalachians, travel conditions were even worse.

The primary means of written communication were the mails and newspapers. The United States had a regular postal system, but it was so expensive that it was used principally by businesses rather than individuals. In 1790 the country had 92 newspapers, published weekly or semiweekly, mostly in towns and cities along major avenues of transportation. There were few post offices—only 75 in 1790 to serve a population of almost 4 million. Americans off the beaten path led isolated lives, with only an occasional traveler offering a window to the larger world.

Life in such isolated regions contrasted markedly with the bustling environment of urban centers like New York and Philadelphia. But perhaps the most basic division in American society lay not so much between the cities and the countryside, important as that was. What would divide Americans most broadly over the coming decades was whether they were primarily subsistence farmers, living on the produce of their own land and labor, or whether they were tied more closely to the larger commercial markets of a far-flung world. As the United States began its life under the new federal union, the distinction between a subsistence economy and a commercial economy was a crucial one.

The Subsistence Economy of Crèvecoeur's America

Most rural Americans lived off the produce of their own land in a barter economy. It was this world of small American farms and farm families that a French naturalist and author, Hector St. John de Crèvecoeur, described so well.

Crèvecoeur arrived in the British colonies in 1759 and almost immediately began wandering: riding over the rutted roads that led to the farms of New England and New York, fording the streams between the scattered settlements of Ohio and Kentucky, knocking the dust of Virginia off his clothes, stopping to talk at taverns along the roads to Philadelphia, and finally settling for a number of years as a farmer in the Hudson River valley. A surveyor and a salesman, he visited not only the older settled areas along the Atlantic coast but also the interior, crossing the Appalachians and traveling down the Ohio River and through the region of the Great Lakes. Crèvecoeur was not only curious but literate as well, and his *Letters from an American Farmer*, published in 1783, asked the question that had so often recurred to him: "What then is the American, this new man?"

For Crèvecoeur, what distinguished American society was the widespread equality of its people, especially the rural farmers. Americans were hostile to social pretensions and anything that smacked of aristocratic privilege. Further-

Subsistence and Commercial America

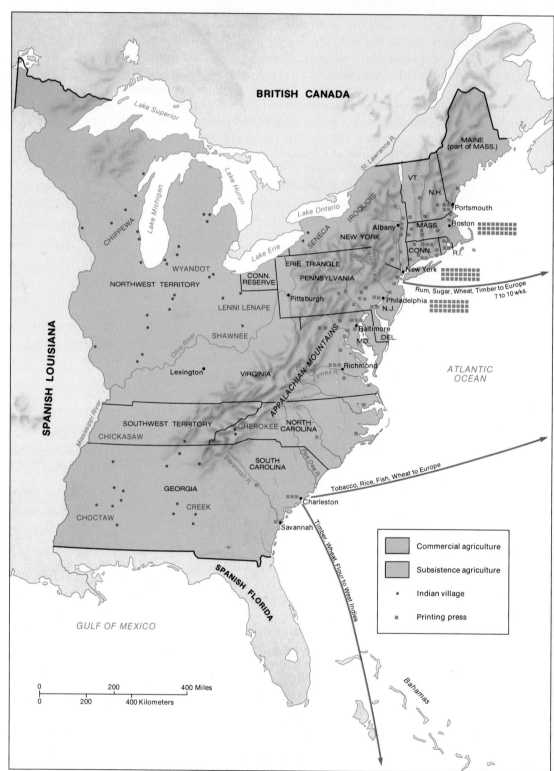

BRITISH CANADA

Lake Superior

Lake Michigan

Lake Huron

St. Lawrence R.

MAINE
(part of MASS.)

VT.

N.H.

Portsmouth

Lake Ontario

IROQUOIS

Albany

MASS.

Boston

SENECA

NEW YORK

CONN.

R.I.

CHIPPEWA

Lake Erie

ERIE TRIANGLE

CONN.
RESERVE

PENNSYLVANIA

New York

WYANDOT

NORTHWEST TERRITORY

Pittsburgh

Philadelphia

N.J.

Rum, Sugar, Wheat, Timber to Europe
7 to 10 wks.

LENNI LENAPE

Delaware R.

SHAWNEE

Baltimore

MD.

DEL.

Ohio River

Richmond

ATLANTIC
OCEAN

Lexington

VIRGINIA

APPALACHIAN MOUNTAINS

James R.

SPANISH LOUISIANA

Mississippi River

SOUTHWEST TERRITORY

CHEROKEE

NORTH
CAROLINA

CHICKASAW

SOUTH
CAROLINA

Savannah R.

Pee Dee R.

GEORGIA

Tobacco, Rice, Fish, Wheat to Europe

CREEK

Charleston

CHOCTAW

Savannah

Timber, Wheat, Flour to West Indies

SPANISH FLORIDA

GULF OF MEXICO

Bahamas

0   200   400 Miles
0   200   400 Kilometers

Commercial agriculture

Subsistence agriculture

•   Indian village

■   Printing press

The geography of the young Republic played a large part in determining which areas would become commercial and which would remain semisubsistent. To prosper, commerce demanded relatively cheap transportation to move goods; hence the commercial economy was largely confined to settled areas along the coast and to navigable rivers below the fall line. Since commerce depended on an efficient flow of information and goods, newspapers flourished in these areas. As we have already seen in Chapter 4 (see map on page 137), the highest proportion of blacks were concentrated along the commercial southern coasts and rivers. In limited areas of Kentucky and Tennessee, commercial agriculture based on slavery had begun to take root, but full-scale operations could not develop in the trans-Appalachian West so long as Spain controlled the mouth of the Mississippi River.

Population density was greater in commercial areas (left), not only because of the presence of cities, but also because domestic markets flourished as labor became more specialized. (Workers who did not raise their own food needed to buy it, along with other necessities.) Population density decreased in some older settled regions, as in New England, where the shortage of good land drove young men westward in search of opportunity. In southeastern Pennsylvania, an area of intensive commercial agriculture, the high birth rate and declining farm size were beginning to exert similar pressure on the younger generation.

The linkage of western migration and economic opportunity produced distinctive sex ratios in different areas of the country (bottom right). In New England, the migration of young men westward created a surplus of females in older areas, a sign of declining economic prospects stemming from poor soil, excess population, and exhausted fields. By the same token, males predominated in frontier regions. Many pioneers were unmarried men, and only after they established farms and achieved a measure of economic security did they marry and begin to raise a family.

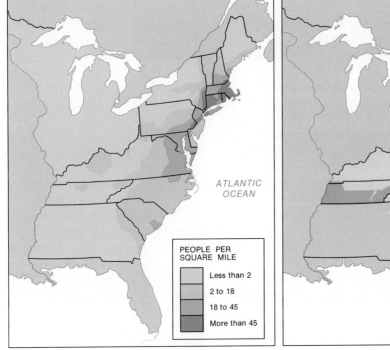

PEOPLE PER SQUARE MILE

Less than 2

2 to 18

18 to 45

More than 45

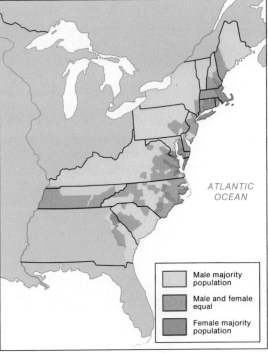

Male majority population

Male and female equal

Female majority population

ATLANTIC OCEAN

more, the conditions of the country promoted equality. The abundance of land provided citizens with the freedom and opportunity to live decently, rather than go hungry or idle, as in Europe. In effect, Crèvecoeur was describing a freehold utopia—a society of small farms, where property was widely distributed, where people supported themselves by growing what they needed, and where the population was not divided into the wealthy few and the desperate many. (Like most of his contemporaries, Crèvecoeur glided rather quickly over the plight of black slaves.) "We are the most perfect society now existing in the world," he boasted.

Although Crèvecoeur waxed romantic about the conditions of American life, he painted a reasonably accurate portrait of most of the interior of the northern states and the backcountry of the South. Wealth in those areas was hardly distributed equally, but it was spread fairly broadly. And subsistence remained the goal of most families. "The great effort was for every farmer to produce anything he required within his own family," one European visitor noted. In such an economy, women played a key role. In addition to helping care for the children and maintaining the home, a wife had to be skilled in making articles such as clothes, hats, candles, and soap, since the cost of buying such items was prohibitive. In his report on manufacturing in the 1790s, Alexander Hamilton estimated that household manufacturing produced two-thirds to three-fourths of the clothing in this country. The prevalence of homemade articles, with their awkward shapes and ill-fitting cut, was responsible for the rustic appearance that set off the rural inhabitant from the city dweller.

With labor scarce and expensive, farmers also depended on the cooperation of their neighbors, who helped one another in clearing fields, building homes, and harvesting crops. What small surplus farmers produced was used in local exchange rather than sold for cash in a distant market. In this barter economy, money was seldom seen and was used primarily to pay taxes, settle accounts, and purchase imported goods. "Instead of money going incessantly backwards and forwards into the same hands," a French traveler wrote, residents in the countryside "supply their needs . . . by direct reciprocal exchanges. The tailor and the bootmaker go and do the work of their calling at the home of the farmer who requires it and who, most frequently, provides the raw material for it and pays for the work in goods. . . . They write down what they give and receive on both sides and at the end of the year they settle a large variety of exchanges with a very small quantity of coin." Even ministers were often paid in kind. In 1798 John Shackleford's Baptist parishioners in South Elkhorn, Kentucky, paid him by donating wheat, pork, flour, beef, sugar, tallow, and whiskey; only a handful gave cash.

Indian economies throughout the backcountry were also based primarily on subsistence. In the division of labor, women were responsible for raising crops, while men fished or hunted—not only for meat, but also for skins to make clothing. Indians did not domesticate cattle, sheep, or pigs, but they managed and "harvested" deer more than was evident at first glance. Once or twice a year, villagers would burn the surrounding forests, resulting in an almost parklike environment free of underbrush, full of large, well-spaced trees and open meadows. The Indians fired the forests, noted one perceptive Yankee traveler, "to produce fresh and sweet pasture for the purpose of alluring the deer to the spots on which they had been kindled." Because Indians followed game more seasonally than white settlers, their villages were moved to several different locations over the course of a year. But both whites and Indians in a subsistence economy moved periodically to new fields after the old ones were exhausted. Indians consumed

He that by the plough would thrive, Himself must either hold or drive.

Work in semisubsistence rural families was done by both sexes and often involved cooperation among neighbors. While a woman milks the cow, a group of men assist in the difficult
labor of burning felled trees and plowing a new field with an eight-oxen team.

firewood more prodigiously than whites and were forced to relocate villages closer
to new supplies of timber, but they exhausted agricultural lands less quickly than
most whites, because they planted beans, corn, and squash in the same field, a
technique that better conserved soil nutrients.

Despite the popular image of both the independent "noble savage" and the
self-reliant yeoman farmer, virtually no one in the rural backcountry operated
within a truly subsistence economy. While farmers tried to grow most of the food
their families ate, they normally bought salt, sugar, coffee, and molasses. Often
they depended on trade with their neighbors for extra food and agricultural produce. In addition, necessities such as iron, glass, lead, and powder had to be
purchased, usually at a country store, and many farmers hired artisans to make
items such as shoes and to weave cloth. Similarly, even before white contact,
Indians had wide trade networks of their own (obsidian, mined in the Rockies and
used for arrowheads, made its way by trade as far east as the Mississippi valley).
And Indians quickly became enmeshed in the wider realm of European commerce, exchanging furs for iron implements or items of ornamentation and dress.

The Commercial Economy of Franklin's America

Outside the backcountry, other regions of the United States were tied much more
closely to a commercial economy, where specialized merchants, artisans, and even
farmers did not subsist on what they produced, but instead sold goods or services
in a wider market and lived on their earnings and profits. Cities and towns, of
course, played a key part in the commercial economy, but so did the agricultural
regions near the seaboard and along navigable rivers. Farmers in these areas, such
as Virginia planters who exported tobacco to London and Pennsylvania farmers
who shipped grain to Barbados, were part of a much wider commercial network.

For commerce to flourish, goods had to move from producers to market cheaply enough to reap profits. Cost-effective transportation was available to the planters of the Tidewater South, and city merchants used their access to the sea to establish trading ties to the West Indies and Europe. But urban artisans and workers were also linked to this market economy, as were many farm families in the Hudson valley, southeastern Pennsylvania, and southern New England. Where transportation was limited or prohibitively expensive, an economy of barter and semisubsistence persisted, since it cost as much to ship goods a mere 30 miles over primitive roads as to ship by boat 3000 miles across the Atlantic to London. And because backcountry farmers could sell produce only locally, they had no reason to increase production. "It was of no importance to the farmer, that his fields, with careful cultivation, would yield from 50 to 100 bushels of corn per acre," an Ohio pioneer recalled, "when a fourth part of the quantity would answer his purpose, there being no market for a surplus."

Good transportation and the opportunity to profit from wider markets set commercial society apart from Crèvecoeur's world in another way: its wealth was less equally distributed. In the Tidewater South, a small number of planter families monopolized wealth and status. Most backcountry southerners, although not poor, were clearly inferior socially to the planter class. Similarly, American cities were becoming more stratified as the number of propertyless citizens increased and the wealthiest families controlled a greater percentage of a city's total wealth. By 1790, the richest 10 percent of those living in cities and plantation districts owned about 50 percent of the wealth. In the backcountry, the top 10 percent was likely to own 25 to 35 percent.

Crèvecoeur argued that the American tradition of equality had sustained a society of small farm families, bound together in a community of relative equals. But he failed to see how much that equality rested on isolation. Without access to market, one could aspire only so high. Where the market economy operated more fully, however, Americans were more acquisitive and materialistic. Europeans were struck by this desire for wealth and emphasis on money. Material well-being was increasingly the means to status in American society, and the Revolution and its aftermath stimulated the competitive spirit. "Man here weighs everything, calculates everything, and sacrifices everything to his interest," one foreign visitor reported. Although semisubsistence farm families were eager to rise in life and acquire material goods, only those in the commercial economy could realistically pursue these dreams.

The man who gained international renown as a self-made citizen of commercial America was Benjamin Franklin. In his writings and in the example of his own life, Franklin offered a vision of the new nation that contrasted with Crèvecoeur's ideal of a subsistence America. Franklin symbolized the urban and commercial order that was emerging from colonial society, a process that extended from the Revolution into the early nineteenth century. He had arrived in Philadelphia as a runaway apprentice, but by hard work and natural talent rose to be one of the leading citizens of his adopted city.

The preface to Franklin's popular *Poor Richard's Almanack*, as well as his countless essays, spelled out simple maxims for Americans seeking the upward path. "The way to wealth is as plain as the way to market," he advised. "It depends chiefly on two words, industry and frugality." The aphorisms flowed effortlessly from his pen. "Remember that time is money." "Keep thy shop, and thy shop will keep thee." "God gives all things to industry." To Franklin, success and wealth were moral obligations, and success was a reflection of one's virtue. Though he did not say so explicitly, the kind of success he preached depended on taking advantage of commerce and a wider market. As a printer, Franklin's hard work paid off because he could distribute his almanacs and newspapers to ever-greater audiences. As an inventor, he trafficked in a marketplace of ideas that could flourish only in an urban culture, where libraries and social interchange spread ideas freely. As a land speculator hoping to make money in the Ohio backcountry, he anticipated the market price of land being driven up by the spread of settlement and markets westward. Franklin lived what he preached: the commercial life of acquisition and wealth, of social mobility and the potential of the free individual.

By the time he died in 1790, the commercial economy had reached a plateau. The markets for American agriculture were so limited that most farmers had no incentive to increase their yields by adopting the newer techniques of crop rotation and fertilizing with manure. Without profits made from shipping surplus produce to market, American agriculture suffered from a scarcity of capital. Thus farmers lacked the means to boost farm efficiency by increasing the size of their farms, by specializing in the production of a single grain, or by buying better tools. The high birth rate created population pressures that compounded this problem, as farms were further divided from one generation to the next. Even in prosperous commercial regions such as southeastern Pennsylvania, the declining size of farms reduced their profitability; a growing number of farmers were tenants rather than independent operators. Although the West acted as a magnet to draw off surplus population, since Indians still held much of the prime agricultural land and the Spanish controlled the mouth of the Mississippi River, opportunity was severely constricted. Even when western farmers were allowed to ship their surplus to market through New Orleans, their livelihood remained subject to foreign control.

The ethics of Franklin's marketplace, which looked forward to the opening up of opportunity in American society, threatened to destroy Crèvecoeur's egalitarian America. In 1790, the ideal that Crèvecoeur had so eloquently described still held sway across much of America. But the political debate of the 1790s showed clearly that Franklin's world of commerce and markets was slowly transforming the nation.

The Constitution and Commerce

In many ways, the fight over ratification of the Constitution represented a struggle between the commercial and the subsistence-oriented elements of American society. Urban merchants and workers as well as commercial farmers generally rallied behind the Constitution. They participated in a larger market and took a broader, more cosmopolitan view of the nation's future. As a result, they were much more willing to see the government play a role in the economy and especially in promoting foreign trade. Franklin, predictably, supported the Constitution. So did Madison and Washington, both planters whose wealth depended on trade and commerce. Robert Morris, another framer at the convention, was a leading merchant whose expertise in finance helped the young Republic during the Revolution.

Americans who remained a part of the subsistence barter economy tended to oppose the Constitution. More provincial in outlook, they feared concentrated power and harbored deep suspicions of cities and commercial institutions, were outspoken foes of aristocracy and special privilege, and in general just wanted to be left alone. They were a majority of the population, but they were not easily mobilized, lacked prestigious leaders, and did not have the access to communication that their opponents enjoyed. In defeat they remained suspicious that a powerful government would tax them to benefit the commercial sectors of the economy. They clung, like Crèvecoeur, to a vision of a rural, freehold utopia.

And so in 1789 the United States embarked on its new national course, with two rival visions—both somewhat hazy and not clearly expressed—of the direction that the fledgling Republic should take. Whose vision of America would prevail? This question—as much social as it was political—increasingly divided the generation of revolutionary leaders during the 1790s.

THE NEW GOVERNMENT

Whatever the Republic was to become, Americans were agreed on one thing: George Washington personified it. The certainty that Washington would be the nation's first president induced the delegates at the Constitutional Convention to invest more power in the executive than they might otherwise have done. His prestige aided the Federalists immensely in rallying support for ratification. When the first Electoral College cast its votes, Washington was unanimously elected, the only president in history so honored. John Adams became vice president.

Washington knew full well the challenges that faced him. "My movements to the chair of government will be accompanied by feelings not unlike those of a culprit who is going to the place of his execution," he confessed, for he was loath to leave his plantation at Mount Vernon. But his strong sense of duty obliged him to bow to the inevitable, and in April 1789 he journeyed to New York, the temporary federal capital. Along the route crowds gathered for a glimpse of him and to cheer. Almost every town organized an official welcome and celebration, culminating in a gigantic reception in New York City, complete with arches over the streets, booming guns in the harbor, and girls strewing flowers ahead of him as he made his way to his living quarters.

The Federalists—supporters of the Constitution—called the new government "the great experiment," for they were intensely aware that throughout history democratic republics had ultimately degenerated into quarreling factions, as with the city-states of ancient Greece, or ended in dictatorships, as had happened in Cromwell's England and Caesar's Rome. No republic—not England, or Rome, or the Swiss city-states—had stretched over a territory as large as the United States' 890,000 square miles. Loyalty to the new Republic, with its new and untried form of government and diversity of peoples and interests, rested to a great degree on the trust and respect Americans accorded Washington.

Washington's Character

Time has transformed Washington from a man into a monument: remote and unknowable, stiff, unbowing, impenetrable. Even during his own lifetime, Washington had no close friends in public life and discouraged familiarity, even among his closest acquaintances. "I could never be on familiar terms with the General—a man so cold, so cautious," one foreigner testified after visiting Mount Vernon. In a famous story, perhaps apocryphal but widely circulated because it captured the essence of Washington's character, Gouverneur Morris on a dare put his arm on the general's shoulder and greeted him casually; Washington stepped back, icily removed Morris' hand, and glared at him until the poor man fled in mortification. Washington cultivated his aloofness deliberately, believing it would enhance his power and sense of command.

As much as he craved honor and military fame, Washington did not hunger for power. Although he had a temper described as "volcanic" when it exploded, he learned with age to control it. He tried to endure criticism patiently, yet he bitterly resented it, a feeling that deepened during his presidency because he had accepted the office reluctantly. In an age of brilliant political theorists, Washington was not an original thinker, although he was far from dull. At a loss to give an instant opinion, he fell into the habit of asking for advice and then making his decision only after he had weighed the options carefully. But once he adopted a policy, he always assumed responsibility for it.

The president also provoked criticism by the pomp with which he conducted the government. Washington, who was one of the richest men in America, enjoyed the luxuries that wealth brought. Critics complained about his formal public receptions, the large number of servants, and the coach emblazoned with his coat of arms—all aristocratic habits. James Madison remarked that "the satellites and sycophants which surround him [Washington] had wound up the ceremonials of the government to such a pitch of stateliness which nothing but his personal character could have supported, and which no character but his could ever maintain."

Organizing the Government

Washington realized that as the first occupant of the executive office, everything he did was fraught with significance. "I walk on untrodden ground," he commented. "There is scarcely any part of my conduct which may not hereafter be drawn into precedent."

The Constitution made no mention of a cabinet. Yet the drafters of the Constitution, aware of the experience of the Continental Congress under the Articles of Confederation, clearly assumed that the president would have some system of advisers. Congress authorized the creation of four departments—War, Treasury, State, and Attorney General—whose heads were to be appointed with the consent of the Senate. Under Madison's guidance, Congress rejected the proposal that these department heads could be removed only with the Senate's approval, thereby reaffirming the independence of the executive.

Washington chose Alexander Hamilton to be secretary of the treasury and Thomas Jefferson to head the State Department. For the other two positions, Washington selected men of lesser note: Henry Knox, an old colleague from the Revolution, for secretary of war, and Edmund Randolph of Virginia as attorney general. Initially the president did not meet regularly with his advisers as a group, but gradually the idea of a cabinet that met to discuss policy matters evolved. Any meaningful role for the vice president, whose duties were largely undefined by the Constitution, soon disappeared. Washington gradually excluded Adams from cabinet discussions, and before the end of the first term, the vice presidency had sunk into the political backwaters from which it has never emerged.

Congress faced several crucial decisions, including the establishment of a system of federal courts. The Constitution created a federal Supreme Court, but beyond that was silent about the court system. The Judiciary Act of 1789 set the size of the Supreme Court at six members; it also established 13 federal district courts and three circuit courts of appeal. Supreme Court justices spent much of their time serving on these circuit courts, a distasteful duty whose long hours "riding the circuit" caused one justice to grumble that Congress had made him a "traveling postboy." The Judiciary Act made it clear that federal courts had the right to review decisions of the state courts and specified cases over which the Supreme Court would have original jurisdiction. Washington appointed John Jay of New York, a staunch Federalist, as the first chief justice.

The Bill of Rights

Congress also confronted the demand for a bill of rights, which had become an issue during the debate over ratification. Among the 200 some amendments suggested during the ratification debates, there were about 80 proposed changes to the Constitution. They included a prohibition of standing armies (the bane of Republicans) and, most ominous to proponents of the Constitution, a restriction of the federal power to tax. Already critics in some states had called for a new convention to revise the Constitution. Madison sought to forestall any large-scale tinkering by submitting a bill of rights more to his liking in the House of Representatives, where he led the Federalist forces. By focusing on civil liberties, he hoped to win over well-meaning opponents of the Constitution without weakening federal power.

Ultimately Congress sent 12 amendments to the states. The 10 that were ratified—known as the Bill of Rights—became part of the Constitution in December 1791. Their passage by Congress helped persuade North Carolina (1789) and Rhode Island (1790), the two holdouts, to join the Union. So Madison's shrewd tactic succeeded. The advocates of strong federal power, like Hamilton, were relieved that "the structure of the government, and the mass and distribution of its powers" remained unchanged. At the same time, the Bill of Rights fixed firmly the 10 amendments that were destined to be of such importance in defining personal liberty in the United States.

Among the rights guaranteed were freedom of religion, the press, and speech, as well as the right to assemble and petition and the right to bear arms. The amendments also established clear procedural safeguards, including the right to a trial by jury and protection against illegal searches and seizures. They prohibited excessive bail, cruel and unusual punishment, and the quartering of troops in private homes. The last two amendments were intended to calm fears about the federal government having unlimited power and to silence the objection that by enumerating certain basic rights, other, unlisted rights would be denied the people. Madison was careful, however, to phrase these amendments in the most general terms. The Tenth Amendment, for example, declared that "the powers not delegated to the United States by the Constitution, nor prohibited by it to the States, are reserved to the States respectively, or to the people." At the same time, an attempt in Congress to apply these same guarantees to state governments failed, and almost a century would pass before Congress moved, during Reconstruction, to prevent states from interfering with certain basic rights.

Hamilton's Financial Program

Before adjourning, Congress called on Alexander Hamilton, as secretary of the treasury, to prepare a report on the nation's finances. Hamilton undertook the assignment eagerly, for he did not intend to be a minor figure in the new administration.

Hamilton never forgot that he was a self-made man. His father was a Scottish merchant of noble birth, his mother the talented, headstrong daughter of a West Indies physician. But Hamilton's parents never married, and his father eventually deserted the family. Raised largely by his mother, who became a storekeeper, Hamilton grew up on the islands of the West Indies, scarred by the stigmas of poverty and illegitimacy. To compensate, he became a driven personality, who craved respectability and money and remained extremely sensitive about his reputation. "My blood is as good as that of those who plume themselves upon their ancestry," he once asserted. Marriage to the daughter of a wealthy New York politician gave him influential connections he could draw on in his political career. As a military aide to Washington during the Revolution, his devotion was so great as to suggest that the general had become the father figure he lacked as a child.

Ever restless, searching always for the bold or masterful stroke, Hamilton was unable to curb his penchant for intrigue, his feelings, and his tongue, characteristics that made him many enemies. Moreover, he was haughty and overbearing, and, for all his ability, he was jealous and could not tolerate any rival. He was a brilliant thinker and, at times, a shrewd leader, yet he was a turbulent and explosive personality who felt out of place in the new, increasingly democratic society that was emerging around him. Hamilton's political principles were unique among the leaders of the Revolution. He deeply admired British culture and the British

HAMILTON'S FINANCIAL SYSTEM
Under Hamilton's financial system, over 80 percent of federal revenues went to pay the interest on the national debt.

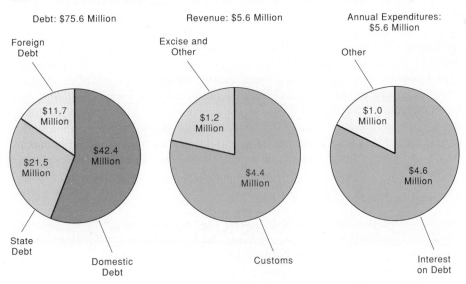

Debt: $75.6 Million

Foreign Debt
$11.7 Million
$21.5 Million
$42.4 Million
State Debt
Domestic Debt

Revenue: $5.6 Million

Excise and Other
$1.2 Million
$4.4 Million
Customs

Annual Expenditures: $5.6 Million

Other
$1.0 Million
$4.6 Million
Interest on Debt

constitution, and he abhorred democracy. "All communities divide themselves into the few and the many," he declared. "The first are rich and wellborn, the other the mass of the people. . . . The people are turbulent and changing; they seldom judge or determine right."

Still, despite the accusations of his enemies, he was not a monarchist. At the Constitutional Convention he had proposed that the president serve for life, but had not wanted the office to be hereditary. His experience in the army impressed on him the necessity of a vigorous government, so that he was more inclined to use force than most of his colleagues. Convinced that human nature was fundamentally selfish, Hamilton believed that the government needed to appeal to the self-interest of the rich and wellborn in order to succeed. "Men," he observed succinctly, "will naturally go to those who pay them best." He took as his model Great Britain, whose greatness he attributed to its system of public finance and its preeminence in commerce and manufacturing. Thus Hamilton set out to achieve two goals: to use federal power to encourage manufacturing and commerce, to make the United States economically strong and independent of Europe; and to link the interests of the wealthy with those of the new government.

Neither of these goals could be achieved until the federal government solved its two most pressing financial problems: revenue and credit. Without revenue, it could not be effective. Without the faith of merchants and other governments that it would repay its debts, it would lack the ability to borrow money. Hamilton proposed not only that all $52 million of the federal debt be paid in full (or funded), but that the government also assume responsibility for the remaining $25 million in debts that individual states owed. He hoped that these twin policies of funding and assumption would put the new federal government on a sound financial footing and enhance its power. Convinced that the critical power of government was the power to tax, Hamilton also proposed a series of excise taxes to help pay off the debt, including a controversial 25 percent levy on whiskey.

After heated debate, Congress deadlocked over funding and assumption. Several southern states, especially Virginia, were unhappy about assumption, because they had already paid off part of their debts and did not relish the prospect of being taxed to assist heavily indebted states like Massachusetts. Finally, over dinner with Hamilton, Jefferson and Madison of Virginia agreed to support his proposal if, after 10 years in Philadelphia, the permanent seat of government was located in the South, on the Potomac River between Virginia and Maryland. Aided by this understanding, funding and assumption finally passed Congress. In 1791 Congress also approved a 20-year charter for the first Bank of the United States. The bank would hold government deposits and issue bank notes that would be received in payment of all debts owed the federal government, thus providing the country with a sound paper currency. Congress proved less receptive to the remainder of Hamilton's program, although a limited tariff to encourage manufacturing and several excise taxes, including the one on whiskey, won approval.

Opposition to Hamilton's Program

The passage of Hamilton's program caused a permanent rupture among supporters of the Constitution. Madison, who had collaborated closely with Hamilton in the 1780s, broke with his former ally over funding and assumption. Jefferson, who disliked personal confrontation, finally went over to the opposition when Hamilton announced plans for a national bank. Eventually the two warring factions

A study in contrasts, Jefferson and Hamilton increasingly came into conflict in Washington's administration. Despite his aristocratic upbringing, Jefferson (left) was awkward, loose-jointed, reserved, and ill-at-ease in public. Testifying before a congressional committee, he casually lounged in a chair and spoke in a rambling, nonstop manner. "Yet he scattered information wherever he went," conceded Senator Maclay of Pennsylvania, "and some even brilliant sentiments sparkled from him." Hamilton, though short of stature, cut a dashing figure with his erect bearing, strutting manner, meticulous dress, and carefully powdered hair. Declared the wife of the British ambassador: "I have scarcely ever been more charmed with the vivacity and conversation of any man."

organized themselves into political parties: the Republicans, led by Jefferson and Madison, and the Federalists, led by Hamilton and Adams.* But the divisions emerged slowly over several years.

Hamilton's program rekindled many of the concerns that had surfaced during the struggle over ratification of the Constitution, for it promoted the commercial sector at the expense of subsistence-agrarian groups. The ideology of the Revolution had long stressed that republics were extremely fragile, and that they always contained groups who sought power in order to destroy popular liberties and overthrow the republic. Having escaped an alleged British conspiracy to enslave them, some Americans saw in Hamilton's program an internal threat to establish a privileged and powerful financial aristocracy—perhaps even a monarchy, given the high-handed and intriguing methods of the secretary of the treasury. Even worse, there was considerable doubt that Hamilton ever intended to retire the national debt, which he planned to convert into a source of credit in society.

Who, after all, would benefit from the funding proposal? As the value of notes issued by the Continental Congress diminished during and after the Revolution, speculators had bought them up for a fraction of their face value from small farm-

*The Republican party of the 1790s, sometimes referred to as the Jeffersonian Republicans, is not to be confused with the modern-day Republican party, which originated in the 1850s.

ers and workers. If the government ultimately redeemed the debt, speculators would profit accordingly. By 1790 an estimated four-fifths of this paper was in the hands of speculators. Equally disturbing, some members of Congress had been buying up the notes prior to the adoption of Hamilton's program. Nearly half of the members of the House owned U.S. securities. Madison urged that only the original holders of the debt be reimbursed in full, and that subsequent purchasers be paid the market value before funding (about 50 percent of the face value), but Hamilton rejected this idea. Merchants and commercial speculators were precisely that class of people he hoped to bind to the new government.

Similarly, when stock in the Bank of the United States went on sale, speculators snapped up all the shares in an hour. The price of a share skyrocketed from $25 to $300 in two months. Jefferson was appalled by the mania Hamilton's program encouraged. "The spirit of gambling, once it has seized a subject, is incurable," he asserted. "The taylor who has made thousands in one day, tho he has lost them the next, can never again be content with the slow and moderate earnings of his needle."

The national bank struck its critics as a dangerous mimicking of English corruption. After all, the Bank of England played a powerful role not only in fueling the English economy but in controlling Parliament by making loans to members, electing directors and stockholders, and attaching the new moneyed men to the government. Hamilton's program, Benjamin Rush warned, would inexorably "introduce among us all the corruptions of the British funding system." Jefferson railed that bank directors and members of Congress with loans from the bank would take their marching orders from the Treasury Department rather than represent their constituents. English-style corruption seemed to be taking root as "paper men" became rich not by producing anything substantial with their own hard work, but by shuffling paper, trading notes, and benefiting from the financial legislation they themselves passed. These fears were heightened by the fact that Americans had little experience with banks—only three existed in the country when the Bank of the United States was chartered. One congressman expressed a common attitude when he said that he would no more be caught entering a bank than a house of prostitution.

Then, too, banks and commerce were a part of the urban environment that rural Americans so distrusted. To them, cities seemed sores of corruption, teeming with propertyless and dependent citizens under the control of the rich. Although most granted that a certain amount of commerce was necessary, they believed that it should remain subordinate. Hamilton's program, in contrast, would encourage manufacturing and urbanization, developments that history showed to be incompatible with liberty and equality. Moreover, the tariff favored one group in society—the manufacturers—at the expense of other groups. Such favoritism would enrich the few, concentrate wealth, and destroy the values and social fabric necessary to preserve republicanism.

As wealth became concentrated, so would power in the hands of the federal government. Republicans had long been suspicious of concentrated power, and after Congress approved the bank bill, Washington hesitated to sign it, uncertain of its legality. When he consulted his cabinet, Jefferson and Randolph argued that the Constitution did not specifically authorize Congress to charter a bank. (Madison, who supported them, recalled that the Constitutional Convention had rejected a proposal that Congress be authorized to charter corporations.) All three men upheld the idea of strict construction—that the Constitution should be interpreted narrowly and the federal government restricted to powers expressly delegated to it. To allow Congress to decide that a bank charter was constitutional would make the federal government the judge of its own powers. There would be no safeguard against the abuse of power.

Hamilton countered that the Constitution contained implied as well as enumerated powers. He particularly emphasized the clause that permitted Congress to make all laws "necessary and proper" to carry out its duties. A bank would be useful in carrying out the enumerated powers of regulating commerce and maintaining the public credit; therefore Congress had a right to decide whether the specific means proposed should be employed. The Constitution, after all, could not possibly anticipate all emergencies and future developments. To be effective, the government needed flexibility to meet its responsibilities. In the end, Washington was persuaded by Hamilton's forceful arguments and signed the bill.

The Specter of Aristocracy

The alarm over what a "standing army" might do, the threat posed by a powerful bank, the secretary of the treasury's outspoken efforts to woo the rich—all these concerns made Hamilton's opponents fear the rise of an aristocracy in the United States. While Americans did not insist on an equal division of property and wealth, they did cherish the Revolutionary ideal that all individuals were of equal moral worth. They were hostile to arrogance and haughtiness among the upper classes, and to anything that harked back to the aristocratic traditions of Europe. Because Hamilton's program deliberately aided the rich and created a class of citizens whose wealth derived from the federal government, it strengthened these traditional fears. "Money will be put under the direction of government," charged Philip Freneau, a leading Republican editor, "and the government will be put under the direction of money."

Many who opposed Hamilton's financial program had also been against the Constitution, but leadership of the opposition fell to Jefferson and Madison, who had staunchly worked for ratification. The political divisions of 1788 did not survive intact into the 1790s, but Anti-Federalism generally carried over into the emerging Republican party. Although Jefferson and Madison were planters, and well accustomed to the workings of the marketplace, they still distrusted cities and commerce and Hamilton's aristocratic ways.

Economically Hamilton's program was a success. With the government's credit restored, it was able to borrow at home and abroad. The national bank checked the inflation of the previous two decades and created a sound currency. And the government's policies stimulated investment and capitalistic enterprise. At the same time, the administration demonstrated that the federal government would not be paralyzed as it had been under the Articles. Hamilton's theory of implied powers and broad construction gave the nation the flexibility necessary to respond to unanticipated crises.

EXPANSION AND TURMOIL IN THE WEST

Under terms of the peace treaty of 1783, Britain ceded to the United States the territory between the Appalachian Mountains and the Mississippi River. Nevertheless, when the new government began functioning, British troops continued to hold the forts in the Northwest and Indian tribes controlled most of this region. To demonstrate the government's effectiveness, the Washington administration moved to extend control over the West.

The Resistance of the Miamis

In the Treaties of Fort Harmar, made in 1789 with the Iroquois and the Miami Confederacy (composed of eight western tribes headed by the Miami), the United States recognized the rights of Indians to their lands and their right to negotiate as sovereign powers. The government promised that land would be transferred through treaties rather than by separate negotiations of land companies and individual settlers to negotiate with tribes. Nevertheless, the government was determined to clear Indian titles in order to promote white settlement and to prevent costly wars on the frontier. Recognition of Indian sovereignty was only a tactic to hasten Indian removal.

Although Indian titles to most of Kentucky and about one-quarter of Tennessee had been cleared by 1790, north of the Ohio the Miami Confederacy still blocked white settlement. Standing together, the Miami, Shawnee, and Lenni Lenape refused to make any cessions. The Washington administration decided to resort to force, but the Indians defeated American military expeditions under General Josiah Harmar in 1790 and General Arthur St. Clair in 1791. St. Clair's defeat, in which over 600 soldiers were killed, was particularly devastating. Encouraged by their victory, the Miami Confederacy insisted that peace would be possible only if the United States accepted the Ohio River as the boundary dividing white from Indian lands.

Washington responded by mounting yet another military expedition, this one led by General Anthony Wayne, a hero of the Revolution. Although British officials in the area encouraged Indians to resist American settlement, they refused to come to their allies' aid. Wayne marched an army of 2000 into the Ohio wilderness and at the Battle of Fallen Timbers in August 1794 won a decisive victory, breaking the Indians' hold on the Northwest. In the Treaty of Greenville, negotiated in 1795, Wayne forced the tribes to cede the southern two-thirds of the area between Lake Erie and the Ohio River. No previous Indian cession had been larger, and it opened up the Northwest to white settlement.

The Whiskey Rebellion

Westerners approved of the administration's military policy against the Indians, but they were far less pleased with the enactment in 1791 of a new excise tax on distilled liquors. No other action brought the question of federal power more directly to the attention of the ordinary citizen. Indeed, since Hamilton pushed the whiskey tax precisely to demonstrate the power of the new government, he was almost eager for an outbreak of popular resistance. Farmers in the western districts of several states, especially Pennsylvania, defied federal officials and refused to pay. In the barter economy west of the Appalachians, where barrels of whiskey were sometimes used as currency, about the only way farmers could profitably export surplus grain was to distill it and bring the liquor to market. But Hamilton saw the matter as a question of authority. "Shall there be government, or no government?" he asked.

The West during the 1790s was a society in turmoil. Most property owners

Frontier farmers in Pennsylvania tar and feather a federal tax collector during the Whiskey Rebellion. In response to such acts of violence and defiance, Washington called out the army in 1794. Marching to western Pennsylvania, the troops restored order but found few rebels.

along the frontier found it hard to make ends meet, and a number were forced to sell their land and become tenants on what had been their own property. Thus wealth became more concentrated in the hands of fewer individuals. The whiskey tax was unpopular in many rural areas, but opposition was strongest on the frontier, where residents fiercely resisted any outside control and where the sale of whiskey made the greatest difference in providing poor families with a bit of extra income. Resistance was most pronounced in areas with the greatest number of tenants, who resented the more commercially minded larger landowners of their region. Many of these miserably poor farmers turned out at mass meetings to condemn the tax and protest against having to support government officials and the burdensome national debt. Beset by economic dislocation, they directed their resentment not just at the authorities, but also at wealthy landowners, merchants, and other symbols of an alien urban cosmopolitan culture.

When the protests flared into the Whiskey Rebellion, an alarmed Washington led an army of 13,000 men—larger than he had commanded at Yorktown—into the Pennsylvania countryside to awe the populace and subdue the rebels. He soon returned to Philadelphia, but the zealous Hamilton accompanied the army the entire way to Pittsburgh. To his disappointment the army met no organized resistance; it had to be satisfied with taking 20 prisoners, all obscure men who posed no threat to the government. Two were convicted of treason, but Washington pardoned both since they were mentally incompetent. As Jefferson scoffed, "An insurrection was announced and proclaimed and armed against, but could never be found." Even some of Hamilton's allies conceded that he had overreacted. "Elective rulers can scarcely ever employ the physical force of a democracy," one remarked, "without turning the moral force, or the power of public opinion, against the government."

Pinckney's Treaty

Less controversial was Washington's effort to strengthen the hold on the West by negotiating a treaty with Spain. That nation still controlled Florida and the mouth of the Mississippi and had never agreed to a northern boundary between its possessions and the United States. Increasingly afraid that the United States might form an open alliance with Great Britain, the Spanish government readily agreed to all concessions sought by Washington's emissary, Thomas Pinckney of South Carolina. Pinckney's Treaty set the 31st parallel as the southern boundary of the United States and granted Americans free navigation of the Mississippi, with the right to deposit goods at New Orleans for reshipment to ports in the East and abroad. Not surprisingly, the Senate approved the treaty unanimously in 1796. No longer could Spain try to detach the western settlements from American control by promising to open the Mississippi to their trade.

THE EMERGENCE OF POLITICAL PARTIES

It is ironic that political parties developed in the 1790s, because members of the revolutionary generation fervently hoped that they would not take root in the United States. "If I could not go to heaven but with a party, I would not go at all," remarked Jefferson. Yet the United States was the first nation to establish truly popular parties.

The fear of parties was a heritage of the Revolution and English political thought. Radical English theorists like John Trenchard and Thomas Gordon condemned parties because they divided society, were dominated by narrow special interests, and placed selfishness and party loyalty above a concern for the public welfare. This was a rather accurate portrait of parties in Britain, where personal and factional advantage often outweighed other considerations and many members of Parliament routinely exchanged their votes for offices, pensions, and lucrative contracts. American thinkers differed over whether it was possible to keep parties down permanently, but no influential leader embraced the idea that they were necessary or good.

In an aristocratic society like that of Great Britain, where most common people could not vote, political factions were much freer to pursue their own private interests. But in the United States, if party members hoped to hold office, they had to offer a broad program attractive to a wider constituency. Thus the material contours of American society actually aided the rise of parties. Because property ownership was widely diffused, the nation had a broad suffrage, and the Revolution, by lowering property requirements in many states, had increased the number of voters still further. As representatives of economic and social interest groups, parties were one way a large electorate could make its feelings known. In addition, the United States had the highest literacy rate in the world and the

largest number of newspapers, further encouraging political interest and participation. Finally, the fact that well-known patriots of the Revolution ended up in
both the Federalist and the Republican camps helped defuse the charge that
either party represented continued hostility to the Revolution or the Constitution.

The French Revolution

While domestic issues initially split the supporters of the Constitution, divisions
over foreign affairs crystallized the new parties. Since the creation of the Republic,
Americans had argued that their mission was to serve as an example to other
nations. The American Revolution would be a beacon for the oppressed in other
societies. Thus when the French Revolution began in 1789, Americans hailed it as
the first stirring of liberty on the European continent. Each new ship from overseas brought exciting news: the Bastille prison had been stormed in July; the new
National Assembly had abolished feudal privileges and adopted the Declaration of
the Rights of Man. France seemed on the way to establishing its own just society.

By 1793, however, enthusiasm for the French Revolution began to cool, as
word came that the king and queen had been executed and that the radical Jacobin
party had inaugurated a reign of terror. Some 20,000 French men and women,
including many of the nobility and other "enemies" of the Revolution, met their
end on the guillotine. The French republic even outlawed Christianity and substituted the worship of Reason. Finally in 1793 republican France and monarchical
England went to war. Whether America should continue its old alliance with
France or support Great Britain fundamentally divided American politics.

Hamilton and his allies viewed the French Revolution as sheer anarchy. Its
mad leaders seemed to be destroying the very institutions that held civilization
together: the church, social classes, property, law and order. The United States,
Hamilton argued, should renounce the treaty of alliance with France signed in
1778 and side with Britain. Fisher Ames, a congressman from Massachusetts,
spoke for the Federalists when he declared: "Behold France, an open hell, still
ringing with agonies and blasphemies, still smoking with suffering and crimes, in
which we see perhaps our future state." For Jefferson and his followers, the issue
was republicanism versus monarchy. France was a sister republic, and despite
deplorable excesses, its revolution was spreading the doctrine of liberty. Britain
remained repressive and corrupt, presided over by the same tyrannical king who
had made war on the colonies. As secretary of state, Jefferson argued that the
United States should maintain its treaty of alliance with France and insist that as
neutrals, Americans had every right to trade with France as much as with England.

As tempers flared between the two factions, each side suspected the worst of
the other. To the Jeffersonians, Hamilton and his friends seemed part of a monarchist conspiracy—"monocrats," they dubbed them. "The ultimate object of all
this," Jefferson said of Hamilton's policies, "is to prepare the way for a change,
from the present republican forms of Government, to that of a monarchy." As for
the Hamiltonians, they viewed Jefferson and his faction as "mobocrats"—
domestic agents of an international conspiracy designed to import the subversive
doctrines of the French Jacobins. Foreign affairs became a distorting lens through
which each party perceived an alternate destiny that threatened the Republic.
Years later, when calm reflection was possible, John Adams conceded that both
parties had "excited artificial terrors."

Washington's Neutral Course

Although Washington did not actively involve himself in the economic affairs of the government, from the beginning he took a keen interest in foreign affairs. Furthermore, he entered office convinced that the United States must remain independent of Europe and its incessant quarrels and wars. Thus Washington repeatedly tempered Jefferson's efforts to support France.

Under international law, neutrals could trade with belligerents as long as the trade had existed prior to the outbreak of hostilities and did not involve war supplies. Neither France nor Great Britain, however, was willing to respect neutral rights in the midst of their desperate struggle. They began intercepting American ships and confiscating cargoes. In addition, Britain, which badly needed manpower to maintain its powerful navy, impressed into service American sailors it suspected of being British subjects. Despite these abuses, Hamilton still supported a friendly policy toward Britain. Beyond his horror of the French Revolution, he realistically recognized, as did Washington, that the United States was not strong enough to challenge Britain militarily. It therefore needed to maintain commercial ties between the two nations, avoid an open alliance, and gain time for the nation to grow and develop.

In addition, the secretary of the treasury's domestic program depended critically on trade with Britain, which purchased 75 percent of America's exports (mostly foodstuffs and naval supplies), as well as providing 90 percent of imports. The war in Europe stimulated the demand for American grains, drove the price up on the world market, and created unprecedented prosperity in America. During

Typifying the rising party spirit of the 1790s, this anti-Republican cartoon portrays Washington with American troops repulsing an invasion of bloodthirsty French radicals. Jefferson and Citizen Genêt attempt to hold his chariot back, while a dog (presumably an ardent Federalist) sprays a Republican newspaper.

the decade, the total value of American exports increased nearly fourfold. At the same time, American ships almost completely took over the carrying trade between the United States and Europe. All parts of the commercial economy shared in this new prosperity, not only merchants, but also workers and businessmen in the cities, sailors, the shipbuilding industry, and farmers who sold their surplus at high prices in the domestic or European market.

While Hamilton and Jefferson struggled within the cabinet for Washington's support, the arrival in April 1793 of "Citizen" Edmond Genêt, the French minister to America, further muddied the diplomatic waters. As the minister traveled from Charleston to Philadelphia, he was greeted by enthusiastic crowds sympathetic to the French cause. Genêt, a hot-blooded zealot without much of a head on his shoulders, became giddy from the reception. "I live in a round of parties," he boasted to the French government. "Old man Washington can't forgive my success." He embarrassed even Jefferson when he began commissioning American privateers to attack British shipping in the Caribbean and set up courts in American ports, run by French consuls, who officially condemned the seized cargo. Washington, who had already issued a proclamation of American neutrality, angrily demanded the French minister's recall. Genêt's American popularity collapsed, and when a new French government at home called for his arrest, he decided rather hastily to settle in New York rather than return to France and lose his head permanently.

For its part, Great Britain continued to run roughshod over American rights on the high seas and to maintain the garrisons in U.S. western territories that it had promised to evacuate in 1783. In addition, it closed the West Indies, a traditional source of trade, to American ships. In March 1794 Washington appointed John Jay as a special minister to negotiate the differences between the two countries. Unfortunately, Jay had little leverage with which to bargain, and Hamilton undercut his position further by secretly informing the British minister that the United States would take no action regardless of the outcome of Jay's mission. In the end, Jay persuaded the British only to withdraw their troops from the western territories, but the West Indies remained closed to American shipping except under the most restrictive conditions (which the Senate subsequently refused to accept). Britain continued to impress sailors and violate neutral rights. Jay's Treaty, in essence, reinforced the United States' position as an economic satellite of Britain; only reluctantly did Washington submit it to the Senate.

The treaty debate was bitter. Republicans denounced Jay and hung him in effigy, a mob stoned Hamilton in the streets, and Washington testified that the public was agitated "in a higher degree than it has been at any period since the Revolution." At the center were the old Revolutionary fears of an external threat to American independence (whether France or Great Britain) and of an internal threat (either from secret monarchists or subversive democrats). In June 1795, the Senate approved Jay's Treaty by exactly the two-thirds vote required, 20–10.

The Federalists and Republicans Organize

The war in Europe, Jefferson commented, "kindled and brought forward the two parties with an ardour which our own interests merely, could never excite." Likeminded members of Congress had worked together planning strategies and votes almost from the beginning, but by the mid-1790s they were organizing on a national basis. At first, Hamilton had given no thought to forming a party; he intended merely to rally support for the government and his policies. Yet the Federalist party grew naturally out of the voting bloc in Congress that enacted Hamilton's legislative program and, once formally organized, represented an important break with the past. Increasingly, Washington drew closer to Federalist advisers and policies. In effect, he became the symbol of the party, although he clung to the vision of a nonpartisan administration and never recognized the extent to which he had become a party leader.

The guiding genius of the opposition movement was Hamilton's one-time colleague James Madison. Jefferson, who resigned as secretary of state at the end of 1793, became the symbolic head of the party, much as Washington headed the Federalists. But, unconvinced of the wisdom and necessity of such a party, he was reluctant to lead it. Madison acted much more vigorously, conferring over strategy and lining up the Republican voting bloc in the House. The disputes of 1794 and 1795—Jay's Treaty, the whiskey tax—gave the Republicans issues with which to take the offensive, and they began organizing on the state and local levels. Unlike the Federalists, who cloaked themselves in Washington's mantle and claimed to be the upholders of the government and the Constitution, the opposition had to overcome the ingrained idea that an opposition party was seditious and therefore illegitimate. Because of broad support for the Constitution, Republican leaders had to be careful to distinguish between opposing the administration and opposing the Constitution. For in an atmosphere where French revolutionary tribunals routinely overthrew one another and British factions constantly intrigued, it was by no means clear that an opposition party could arise without threatening the very government itself.

As the two parties took shape, voting in Congress became increasingly partisan, with more and more members allying with one faction or the other. In the first two Congresses, party votes occurred mostly on Hamilton's economic program and the organization of the government. In the third and fourth Congresses, party questions included foreign affairs and domestic issues such as western problems and the Whiskey Rebellion. By 1796 even minor matters were debated in party caucuses and decided by partisan votes.

Gradually, party organization filtered downward to local communities. John Beckley, the clerk of the House of Representatives, was a key Republican partisan who took the lead in setting up effective party machinery. In 1796 Beckley managed the Republican campaign in Pennsylvania. In an age when deference remained a central feature of American politics, Beckley recruited prominent residents to endorse the Republican cause, relying on them to distribute political pamphlets and handbills. A shrewd tactician, he secretly sent copies of one Anti-Federalist broadside over primitive mountain trails to circulate in the western part of the state, and only later work its way east, so that the Federalists in Philadelphia would have no time to issue a counterattack. Once party leaders had agreed on a list of presidential electors, Beckley hired express riders to distribute tickets throughout the state. Since voters at the polls had to write out the name of the electors and could not use printed lists, Beckley also instructed local leaders to use friends and family members to write out as many tickets as possible beforehand, to be given to unprepared voters. In a state where only 12,000 votes were cast in the election, he distributed 30,000 electoral tickets and thousands of handbills and addresses. It was an unprecedented effort.

The 1796 Election

As long as Washington remained head of the Federalists, they enjoyed an insurmountable advantage over their opponents. But in 1796 the weary president, stung by the vituperation heaped on him by the opposition press, announced that he would not accept a third term in office. Just as he had refused during the Revolution to assume dictatorial powers, so in 1796 he voluntarily relinquished power, setting a two-term precedent that other presidents would follow until Franklin Roosevelt. In his Farewell Address to his fellow citizens, he warned against the dangers of parties and urged a return to the earlier nonpartisan system. Since the "nonpartisan" system envisioned the Federalists guiding the government, the manifesto amounted to an electioneering tract; still, it voiced Washington's genuine fear of party strife. But that vision had become obsolete: parties were an effective way of expressing the interests of different social and economic groups within the nation. When the Republicans chose Thomas Jefferson to oppose John Adams, the possibility of a nonparty constitutional system disappeared.

The framers of the Constitution did not anticipate that political parties would run competing candidates for both the presidency and the vice presidency. They assumed that, of those running for president, the candidate with the most electoral votes would win and the second highest would become vice president. Hamilton, ever the intriguer, disliked both Adams and Jefferson and tried to manipulate the electoral vote so that the Federalist vice presidential candidate, Thomas Pinckney of South Carolina, would be elected president. Hamilton attempted to persuade several Federalist electors to vote for Pinckney but not Adams; the scheme backfired when some of Adams' supporters learned of the plan and refused to vote for Pinckney. In the ensuing confusion, Adams won with 71 electoral votes, and his rival, Jefferson, gained the vice presidency with 68 votes.

In their constituencies, the two parties reflected basic divisions in American life. Geographically, the Federalists were strongest in New England, with its extensive commercial ties to Great Britain and its powerful tradition of hierarchy and order. Moving farther south, the party became progressively weaker. Of the southernmost states, the Federalists enjoyed significant strength only in aristocratic South Carolina. The Republicans won solid support in subsistence areas like the West, where Crèvecoeur's farmers were only weakly linked to the market. The middle states, with more complicated economic and social divisions, were closely contested, although the most cosmopolitan and commercially oriented elements remained the core of Federalist strength.

The Republicans won over most of the old Anti-Federalist opponents of the Constitution, and their coalition contained some who had firmly backed the new union. These supporters included some commercial farmers in the North and planters in the South and, increasingly, urban workers and small shopkeepers who were repelled by the aristocratic tone of the Federalists. In many communities, especially towns that were rising economically, the Republicans were led by ambitious men of new wealth who felt excluded by the entrenched Federalist elite. For similar reasons, Jefferson attracted the support of immigrants from France and Ireland, who felt culturally excluded, as well as members of religious sects such as the Baptists and Methodists, who resented the power and privileges of New England's established Congregational Church.

Federalist and Republican Ideologies

In different ways, each party was drawn toward certain traditions of the past as well as toward newer social currents that would shape America in the nineteenth century.

Most Federalists viewed themselves as a kind of natural aristocracy making a last desperate stand against the excesses of democracy. They clung to the notion that a nation's political and social leaders should be identical, that the upper class should rule over their social and economic inferiors. In supporting the established social order, most Federalists opposed unbridled individualism. They believed that society's needs took precedence over the individual's and that each class fulfilled a particular role in society. Government should regulate individual behavior for the good of society and protect property from the violent and unruly. Pessimistic in their view of human nature, Federalists were almost obsessed by fear of the "mob." Unthinking and easily manipulated, the masses were dangerous when led by a demagogue who sought power by setting the poor against the rich. In a republic, they argued, popular power had to be restrained, and the role of the people was to choose leaders from society's best men.

Although the Federalists resolutely opposed the rising tide of democracy and individualism, they were remarkably forward-looking in their economic ideas. (Hamilton and his allies here took the lead.) They sensed that the United States would become the major economic and military power of their vision only by prospering through commerce and economic development. To that end, the government ought to use its power not only to protect property, but to actively encourage growth of commerce and manufacturing.

The Republicans, in contrast, viewed Federalist attitudes and policies as evidence of corruption that was eating away at American morals, just as had occurred in England prior to 1776, when Americans finally declared their independence. Thus Republican ideology harked back to the traditional Revolutionary fear that government power threatened liberty, that agriculture had to be dominant over commerce, that wealth and luxury threatened to corrupt the ideals of American society. Over and over Republicans emphasized the threat of corruption: the Treasury was too powerful and was corrupting Congress; the anti–Whiskey Rebellion army would be used to enslave the people; broad construction of the Constitution would make the federal government all-powerful.

Despite their emphasis on agriculture, Republican leaders like Jefferson and Madison recognized that commerce was essential. Yet they were not forward-looking in their economic ideals. The only real need they saw for commerce was to sell America's agricultural surplus abroad; hence they insisted that commercial interests remain secondary to agriculture. When Jefferson considered the merits of developing industry, he instinctively felt republican values would be preserved by limiting it to household manufacturing. And Republicans failed to appreciate the role financiers played in accumulating capital and promoting economic development. Instead, Republicans focused on the abuses of "paper wealth"— speculators, bank directors, stockjobbers, and holders of the public debt.

Whereas the Jeffersonians looked backward in their economic values, rejecting the ideals of urbanization and industrialization that would dominate American society in the nineteenth century, they were more farsighted in matters of equality and personal liberty. Their faith in the people put them much more in tune with the emerging egalitarian temper of society. Eagerly they embraced the virtues of individualism, hoping to reduce government to the bare essentials in order to free individuals to develop to their full potential without interference. And they looked to the West as the means to preserve opportunity and American values.

THE PRESIDENCY OF JOHN ADAMS

As president, John Adams became the nominal head of the Federalists, but in many ways he was out of step with his party. Unlike Hamilton, he felt no pressing need for the government to aid the wealthy, nor was he fully committed to the commercial–industrial vision that Hamilton held. As a crusty revolutionary leader who in the 1780s had served in England as American minister, Adams also opposed any alliance with Britain. Increasingly he and Hamilton clashed, not only over policies but also over party leadership. Part of the problem stemmed from personalities. Adams was so abrasive and thin-skinned, it was difficult for anyone to get along with him, and Hamilton's secret intrigues in the 1796 election had not improved relations between the two men. Although Hamilton had resigned from the Treasury Department in 1795 to practice law in New York City, key members of Adams' cabinet remained loyal to him and turned to him on a regular basis for advice. Indeed, they opposed Adams so often that the frustrated president sometimes dealt with them, according to Jefferson, "by dashing and trampling his wig on the floor." The feud between the two rivals did not bode well for the Federalist party.

John Adams, who believed that pageantry and pomp were essential to government, proposed in 1789 that the president's title be "His Highness the President of the United States and Protector of the Rights of the Same." He wore this sword at his own inauguration in the vain hope that it would lend dignity. Sarcastic Republicans, noting his paunchy figure, gleefully bestowed a title of their own: "His Rotundity."

The Quasi-War with France

Adams began his term trying to balance relations with both Great Britain and France. Since the terms of Jay's Treaty had been so favorable to the British, the French in retaliation set their navy and privateers to raiding U.S. shipping. To resolve the conflict, in 1797 Adams sent three envoys, John Marshall, Charles Cotesworth Pinckney, and Elbridge Gerry, to France. In what became known as the XYZ Affair (because in the official documents the administration substituted the letters X, Y, and Z for the names of the French officials involved), the French minister Talleyrand demanded a personal bribe of $250,000 and a "loan" of $12 million to the French treasury before negotiations could even begin. The American representatives refused and Marshall and Pinckney returned home. When the affair became known, a tremendous public outcry against France ensued.

Confronted with such deeply felt anger, Federalist leaders saw a chance to retain power by exploiting the national emergency and going to war with France. With war fever running high, Congress in 1798 repudiated the French treaty of 1778, authorized 40 ships for a newly created Department of the Navy, and created a new army of 12,500 men. Republicans suspected that the purpose of the army was not to fight the French army—none existed in North America—but to crush the opposition party and establish a military despotism. All that remained was for Adams to whip up popular feeling and lead the nation into war.

But Adams hesitated, afraid he would become a scapegoat if his policies failed. He preferred to have France declare war in order to unite the country solidly behind his leadership. Furthermore, he distrusted standing armies and preferred the navy as the nation's primary defense. So an unofficial naval war broke out—the so-called Quasi-War—as ships in each navy openly and freely raided the fleets of the other, while Britain continued to impress American sailors and seize ships suspected of trading with France.

Believing that war with France offered a solution to all his party's problems, Hamilton took the lead in getting Congress to enlarge the army without Adams' support. Then, when Adams summoned Washington out of retirement to head the American forces, the aged general insisted that Hamilton be his second in command. Since Washington was only a figurehead, Hamilton wielded effective control of the army. He dreamed of seizing Louisiana and Florida, which were held by France's ally Spain, as a way to make the army acceptable to the American people, and even toyed with the idea of marching the army through Virginia in order to provoke resistance and justify suppression of the Republican party. Urging that Virginia be put "to the test of resistance," he disclosed that he was ready to use the army "to subdue a *refractory and powerful State.*"

But Hamilton's hot-headed behavior helped cool Adams' martial ardor. The president delayed accepting enlistments and commissioning officers, and the new army never reached more than a third its authorized size. Moreover, the British defeat of the French fleet in 1798 ended any threat of French invasion. Adams recognized that only in times of crisis could a standing army gain widespread support, and as he caustically observed in 1799, "At present there is no more chance of seeing a French army here than there is in Heaven."

Suppression at Home

Before the threat of war had diminished, however, Federalist leaders attempted to suppress disloyalty at home. In the summer of 1798 Congress passed several measures known together as the Alien and Sedition Acts. The Alien Act authorized the president to arrest and deport aliens suspected of having "treasonable or secret" leanings. Although never used, the act directly threatened nonnaturalized immigrants, many of whom were prominent Jeffersonians. Immigrant voters—again, most of them Republican—were also penalized by the Naturalization Act, which increased from 5 to 14 years the length of residency before a newcomer could become a naturalized citizen. Most controversially, the Sedition Act established heavy fines and even imprisonment for writing, speaking, or publishing anything of "a false, scandalous and malicious" nature against the government or any officer of the government. To cries that such censorship violated the First Amendment's guarantees of freedom of speech and the press, Federalists replied that sedition and libel were not protected by the Constitution.

Because of the heavy-handed way it was enforced, the Sedition Act quickly became a symbol of tyranny. Federalists directed it with single-minded zeal against a number of prominent Republican editors, convicting and imprisoning them. Several Republican papers ceased publication, and the act even brought to justice one unfortunate tippler who had proclaimed his fervent hope that a cannonball might hit the president in his rear. In all, 25 were arrested under the law and 10 convicted and imprisoned, including Matthew Lyon, a Republican member of Congress from Vermont. What would have been an unpopular law in any event became doubly obnoxious because of the partisan fashion in which Federalists used it.

The crisis over the Sedition Act forced Republicans to develop a broader concept of freedom of the press. The prevailing view had been that newspapers ought not to be restrained before publication, but that they could be punished afterward for libel. Jefferson and others now argued that the American government was uniquely based on the free expression of public opinion—not just in elections every two years, but in continuous discussion and debate. Thus criticism of the government was not a sign of criminal intent. Only overtly seditious acts, not opinions, should be subject to prosecution. The courts eventually adopted this view, although once in power the Republicans did not hesitate to prosecute Federalist editors for libel, especially in the state courts. Finally, the Supreme Court settled the issue in *United States v. Hudson and Goodwin* (1812), ruling that there was no such crime as seditious libel under the Constitution. The decision heralded a new and more absolute view of freedom of speech guaranteed by the First Amendment.

Meanwhile, however, the Republican-controlled legislatures of Virginia and Kentucky responded to the crisis of 1798 by each passing a set of resolutions. Written secretly by Madison for Virginia and Jefferson for Kentucky, they formulated the doctrine of state interposition. The Constitution, they claimed, was a compact between sovereign states, which delegated strictly limited powers to the federal government. When the government exceeded those limits and threatened the liberties of citizens, states had the right to interpose their authority. The logical conclusion of this reasoning was that the states, and not the federal courts, had the authority to decide whether the federal government had exceeded its power.

But Jefferson and Madison were not ready to rend a union that had so recently been forged. They hoped the Virginia and Kentucky resolutions would rally public opinion to the Republican cause, but they did not encourage Virginia or Kentucky to resist federal authority by force. And other states openly rejected the doctrine. As the Adams administration came to a close, the Alien Act quietly expired in June 1800 and the Sedition Act in March 1801. Once in power, the Republicans repealed the Naturalization Act.

The Election of 1800

With a naval war raging on the high seas and the Alien and Sedition Acts precipitating a storm at home, Adams suddenly shocked his party by appointing three new commissioners to reopen negotiations with France. It was a courageous act, for Adams not only split his party in two, but also ruined his own chances for reelection by forcing Hamilton's pro-British wing of the party into open opposition. Yet the nation as a whole benefited, for France signed a peace treaty ending its undeclared war. Adams, who bristled with pride and independence, termed this act "the most disinterested, the most determined and the most successful of my whole life."

With the Federalist party split, Republican prospects for 1800 brightened. Again the party chose Jefferson to run against Adams, along with Aaron Burr for vice president. Their efficient party organization coordinated the campaign, subsidizing Republican newspapers, circulating the Virginia and Kentucky resolutions as propaganda, and mobilizing supporters. In contrast, the Federalists' high-handed policies, disdain for the masses, and insensitivity to public opinion doomed them in a republic where the suffrage was so broad. The political journalist Noah Webster put his finger on his fellow Federalists' problem when he said: "They have attempted to resist the force of public opinion, instead of falling into the current with a view to direct it."

Sweeping to victory, the Republicans won control of both houses of Congress for the first time, gaining 40 seats from the Federalists in the House alone. Jefferson outdistanced Adams, 73 electoral votes to 65, although Adams ran ahead of his party and proved more popular with the rank-and-file Federalists and the southern wing of the party. But once again, the election demonstrated the fragility of the fledgling political system. Jefferson and Burr received an equal number of votes, but the Constitution, with no provision for political parties, did not distinguish between the votes for president and vice president. With the election tied, the decision lay with the House of Representatives, where each state was allotted one vote. Since Burr refused to step aside for Jefferson, the election remained deadlocked for almost a week, until the Federalists, who eventually decided that Jefferson represented the lesser of two evils, allowed his election on the thirty-sixth ballot. In 1804 the Twelfth Amendment corrected the problem, specifying that electors were to vote separately for president and vice president.

Political Violence in the Early Republic

It had been a tense moment: the leadership of the Republic hanging on bitter party votes in the House, Federalists willing to chance the unscrupulous Burr to escape "the fangs of Jefferson." Some even swore they would "go without a constitution and take the risk of civil war." Indeed, the hindsight of a later day makes it easy to forget how violent and unpredictable the politics of the 1790s had been.

Some of the violence was physical. Irate crowds roughed up federal marshals who tried to enforce the whiskey tax; Benjamin Bache, the leading Republican newspaper editor in Philadelphia, plunged into a street brawl with his Federalist

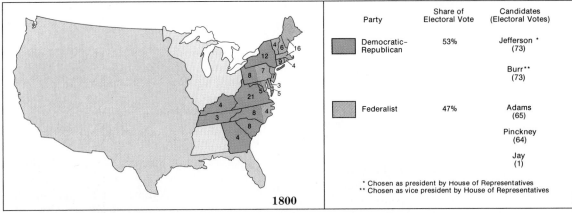

Party	Share of Electoral Vote	Candidates (Electoral Votes)
Democratic-Republican	53%	Jefferson * (73)
		Burr** (73)
Federalist	47%	Adams (65)
		Pinckney (64)
		Jay (1)

* Chosen as president by House of Representatives
** Chosen as vice president by House of Representatives

1800

THE ELECTION OF 1800

rival, John Fenno; Representative Matthew Lyon of Vermont spit in the eye of Representative Roger Griswold of Connecticut, the two of them wrestling on the floor of Congress, going at each other with cane and fire tongs. Mobs threatened the leaders of both parties, and at the height of the crisis of 1798–1799, President John Adams actually smuggled guns into his home for protection. But most of the violence was emotional and rhetorical, as reflected in the era's abusive political language. Republicans accused patriots like Washington and Hamilton of being British agents, tyrants, and monarchists; Federalists portrayed Jefferson as an irreligious Jacobin, and the Republicans as "blood-drinking cannibals." Washington complained that he was abused "in such exaggerated and indecent terms as could scarcely be applied . . . to a common pickpocket." In 1797 Jefferson noted that normally political differences did not extend to social relations, but "it is not so now. Men who have been intimate all their lives, cross the streets to avoid meeting, and turn their heads another way, lest they should be obliged to touch their hats."

What accounts for this remarkable estrangement of the leaders of the Revolution and the amount of violence—both real and rhetorical—in the first decade of the Republic? For one, Federalists and Republicans alike knew how fragile a form of government republicanism had proved over the long course of history. Its repeated failure created grave uncertainty about the American experiment. Then too, the ideology of the American Revolution stressed the need to be on constant guard against conspiracies to subvert liberty. Domestic suspicions were all too quickly magnified by turbulent foreign events, as Federalists perceived threats to the country from the subversive and violent French Revolution, and Republicans detected the age-old corruptions of power and aristocracy in an alliance with the British.

In such overheated circumstances, both Republicans and Federalists readily assumed the worst of one another. In 1798, for example, Washington contended that the Republican party aimed at nothing less than to "change the nature" of the government and "subvert the Constitution." American leaders lacked a satisfactory intellectual framework with which to interpret events of the 1790s. Neither side grasped that in a democracy, political parties were essential institutions, needed to express the differences between social and competing interests and to

Daily Lives

POLITICAL CULTURE

The Rise of "Vile Electioneering"

When George Washington launched the new federal government in 1789, American politics remained a relatively hierarchical affair. Most ordinary citizens deferred to their social "betters," accepting the notion that political leadership belonged to the rich, the educated, and the articulate. Politics was not a full-time profession, and politicians devoted only part of their energies to public life. Nominations, which were the result of deliberations among a handful of leaders, were simply announced in the local press, and elections were decided on a personal rather than a party basis. As a result, most voters did not bother to participate in the political process. In Newburyport, Massachusetts, for example, only 12 percent of the town's eligible voters cast ballots in the 1792 congressional election.

The rise of political parties in the 1790s transformed America's political culture, involving ordinary citizens more than ever before. Previously, competition for voters' support had been limited to the South, where candidates were expected to treat voters to drinks on election day and, in some communities, to stand at the polls soliciting support. But extensive campaigning for weeks before the election was unusual and often condemned.

By 1800, however, "the vile practice of electioneering," as one contemporary termed it, had spread throughout the nation. Since the Jeffersonian Republicans were at first excluded from most avenues of power, they took the lead in electioneering, holding mass meetings at which they dispensed free food and drinks while party leaders addressed the crowd. They arranged so many political barbecues that

Federalist leader Fisher Ames, looking down his aristocratic nose, dismissed Republicans as "ox-eating fools." They also organized campaign committees, furnished written or published ballots in states where these were required, and distributed party propaganda far and wide. On election day, volunteers manning a fleet of vehicles transported supporters to the polls, where party leaders addressed those waiting to vote and had an ample supply of tickets and often liquor on hand.

Believing themselves the natural leaders of society and equating electioneering with corruption, Federalists at first spurned the new techniques as "too degrading." Instead, they tried to stymie Republican electioneering through intimi-

In this detail of an early nineteenth-century painting by Rudolf Krimmel, party workers bring electors to the Philadelphia polls in carriages, while voters argue about candidates and celebrate.

dation. In the 1799 election in New York City, for example, wealthy Federalist merchants warned cartmen that they would be fired if they voted the Republican ticket; and then they stood watch in laboring wards on election day to observe how individuals voted. (Voting by secret ballot did not appear in American politics until after the Civil War.) By 1800, however, a number of Federalists began to electioneer in a frantic effort to keep the despised Jefferson out of the presidency.

The new partisan attitudes spilled over into virtually all areas of daily life. Federalists in Salem, Massachusetts, expelled Republicans from the local dancing club, even though the Republicans came from respected and wealthy families. In commercial centers, Federalists and Republicans established rival banks, rival insurance companies, and even rival wharfs. Party members began attending different churches, hoping in part to hear partisan sermons blasting the opposition. As a result of these agitations, election-day proceedings became much more tumultuous. Even in normally staid Boston, "confusion, wrangling, and even uproar" prevailed as rival organizations distributed their ballots outside the polls.

Both parties developed ingenious methods to swell their vote: they paid the taxes of poorer voters, transferred workers to doubtful districts, and delayed ships' scheduled departures to herd the crews to the polls. In the sharply contested 1800 election, resourceful New Jersey Federalists took advantage of the state's ambiguous election law and beat back the Republican challenge with the votes of wives, daughters, and other women. In Charleston, Federalists handed out specially colored tickets, so that merchants, bankers, and other influential men could be sure of how their employees voted.

The hardest-fought contest in 1800 occurred in New York City. Both parties mounted all-out efforts in the April legislative election, since the legislature would select the presidential electors. For the Republicans, the wily Aaron Burr kept a record on virtually every voter in the city, assigned party members to collect contributions from well-heeled sympathizers, presided over countless strategy sessions, and had party workers plaster the city with handbills. One merchant wrote in his diary: "Col. Burr kept open house for nearly two months, and Committees were in session day and night. . . . Refreshments were always on the table and mattresses for temporary repose in the rooms." The Federalists, led by Alexander Hamilton, overcame their scruples at mixing with the masses and pitched in. "I have not eaten dinner for three days and have been constantly upon my legs from 7 in the morning till 7 in the afternoon," reported one Federalist at the climax of the campaign. Burr's hard work paid off when the Republicans carried New York City by only 250 votes, assuring them of the state's electoral vote. The election of Jefferson in 1800 was truly a party triumph, in which efficient organization paved the way to success.

The American party system had not yet become entirely modern. Politics continued to be a sideline rather than a career for party leaders, and party coalitions depended on networks of friends, relatives, and business associates. A good deal of political activity remained secret, while parties were still looked on with suspicion. Nevertheless, in the decade since the adoption of the Constitution, political culture had been fundamentally transformed.

help resolve them peacefully. Instead, each party considered the other a faction, and therefore illegitimate; and each hoped fervently to reestablish a one-party system. Not until after 1815 did there develop an American political ideology that recognized the necessity of parties and the government's role in promoting economic development.

As John Adams prepared to leave office, he looked back on the 12 years that his Federalist party had held power with mixed feelings. Under Washington's firm leadership and his own, the Federalists had made the Constitution a workable instrument of government. They had proved that republicanism was compatible with stability and order, and they had established economic policies and principles of foreign affairs that even their opponents would continue. The Union had been strengthened, the Constitution accepted, and prosperity had returned. Perhaps those achievements, along with the Revolution's glorious heritage, would be a monument that history would long remember.

But most Federalists took no solace in such reflections. For the forces of history seemed to be running against them. With the world they knew and sought to preserve rapidly disintegrating, they had waged one last desperate battle to save it—and had lost. The champions of order and hierarchy, of government by the well-born, of a society in which social betters guided their respectful inferiors, had been vanquished by the ignorant and unwashed rabble, led by that archdemagogue Thomas Jefferson. Federalists shared fully the view of the British minister, who concluded in 1800 that the entire American political system was "tottering to its foundations."

The great American experiment in republicanism had failed. Of this most Federalists were certain. And surely, if history was any judge, the destruction of liberty and order would soon follow.

SIGNIFICANT EVENTS

1789	First session of Congress; Washington inaugurated president; French Revolution begins; Judiciary Act passed
1790	Funding and assumption approved; Harmar's defeat
1791	Bank of the United States chartered; St. Clair's defeat; first ten amendments (Bill of Rights) ratified
1792	Washington reelected
1793	Execution of Louis XVI; war breaks out between France and England; Washington's Neutrality Proclamation; Genêt Affair
1794	Battle of Fallen Timbers; Whiskey Rebellion
1795	Jay's Treaty ratified; Treaty of Greenville signed
1796	Pinckney's Treaty ratified; first contested presidential election—Adams defeats Jefferson
1798	XYZ Affair; Alien and Sedition Acts passed; Virginia and Kentucky resolutions
1798–1799	Quasi-War with France
1800	Adams sends new mission to France; Jefferson defeats Adams
1801	The House elects Jefferson president

9

The Jeffersonian Republic

 n September 29, 1800, after a long and rocky courtship, Margaret Bayard quietly married Samuel H. Smith. In many ways, there was nothing unusual in their union. Despite religious differences (she was a Presbyterian, he belonged to no church), they had much in common: they were from prominent families, well educated, accustomed to life's comforts, and at ease in society. Still, even though they were second cousins, Margaret's father consented to the marriage only reluctantly, for the Bayards were staunch Federalists, and Smith was an ardent Republican. Indeed, Thomas Jefferson had asked Smith, a Republican editor in Philadelphia, to follow the government to Washington, D.C., and establish a party newspaper in the new capital. After the wedding ceremony, the couple traveled to the new seat of government on the banks of the Potomac River.

The Smiths arrived in the capital in early October. Renting two adjacent buildings, Samuel established a printing office in one, while Margaret set up housekeeping in the other. On the last day of the month, he began publishing the *National Intelligencer*, the first national newspaper in the United States. Servants were scarce and unreliable, so Margaret had to prepare meals for her husband's employees as well as her family. Moreover, Washington was little more than a raw village of 3200 souls, offering few social outlets. Yet thanks to her husband's connections, Margaret soon became acquainted with the nation's political leaders. Her social charm and keen intelligence made her home a center of Washington society.

Predisposed by her upbringing to view Federalists as models of refinement and intelligence, Margaret Smith expected the head of the Republican party to be coarse and vulgar. Instead, when she met Jefferson about a month after her arrival, she found herself captivated by his gracious manners, sparkling conversation, and gentlemanly bearing. Whatever remained of her Federalist sympathies vanished, and she became (perhaps as her father feared) a devoted supporter of the new president.

On March 4, 1801, in eager anticipation, she went to the Senate chamber to witness Jefferson's inauguration. The chamber was packed, but the members of Congress nonetheless reserved one side for the ladies present. To emphasize the change in attitude that the new administration represented, Jefferson walked to the capitol, accompanied by a few government officials and well-wishers, along with a small body of Maryland militia carrying flags and beating drums. Absent

"We have met the enemy and they are ours," reported Captain Oliver Perry after defeating the British on Lake Erie in 1813. His triumph, revealed in this contemporary painting (detail), was celebrated by an increasingly nationalistic citizenry.

were the elaborate ceremonies and flourishes of the Federalists; absent too were the silver-buckled shoes, knee breeches, and wigs that had been the hallmarks of a Revolutionary gentleman. As cannon roared in the background, Jefferson ascended the capitol steps at noon. Since the new president delivered his inaugural address in almost a whisper, few of the assembled crowd heard much of what he said. Then Chief Justice John Marshall, a Virginian but a Federalist whom Jefferson deeply distrusted, administered the oath of office. When the ceremony was over, the new president returned to his lodgings at Conrad and McMunn's boardinghouse, where he declined a place of honor and instead took his accustomed seat at the foot of the table. Only several weeks later did he finally move to his official residence.

As Margaret Smith proudly watched the proceedings, she could not help thinking of the most striking feature of this transfer of power: it was peaceful. "The changes of administration, which in every government and in every age have most generally been epochs of confusion, villainy and bloodshed, in our happy country take place without any species of distraction, or disorder." After the violence of the Revolution, the fierce controversies of the previous decade, and the harsh rhetoric of the election of 1800, the peaceful assumption of power by the opposing party—the first such occurrence in the nation's history—was indeed remarkable.

After the inauguration, Mrs. Smith returned home. A steady stream of visitors called during the day to offer congratulations and celebrate the party's triumph. With a mixture of surprise and pride, she reported that even three Federalists (one her cousin) called and stayed for two hours, drinking tea with members of the other party. With memories still fresh of the heated campaign and the struggle in the House before Jefferson was finally elected, this display of civility was noteworthy. The Republic had weathered a serious trial.

Like Margaret Bayard Smith, the country had shifted its allegiance to the Republican party. The new president's inauguration represented a break with the Federalist past, and once in power, Jefferson ambitiously set out to reshape the government and society in accord with Republican principles. Jefferson later referred to his election as "the Revolution of 1800," asserting that it "was as real a revolution in the principles of our government as that of 1776 was in its form." That statement is an exaggeration, perhaps. But the rule of the Republican party during the following two decades set the nation on a distinctly more democratic tack. And in working out its relationship with Britain and France, as well as with the Indian nations of the West, America achieved a sense of its own nationhood that came only with time and the passing of the Revolutionary generation.

JEFFERSON IN POWER

Thomas Jefferson was the first president to be inaugurated in the new capital of Washington, D.C. In 1791 George Washington had commissioned Pierre Charles L'Enfant, a French architect and engineer who had served in the American Revolution, to draw up plans for the new seat of government. L'Enfant designed a city with broad avenues, statues and fountains, parks and plazas, and a central mall. The capitol building and the president's home dominated L'Enfant's design, with streets radiating out from these and other major buildings and crossing the rectangular pattern of streets at various angles. In keeping with their belief that government was the paramount power in a nation, the Federalists intended that the city would be a new Rome—a cultural, intellectual, and commercial center of the Republic.

The New Capital City

The reality of the new city, however, fell far short of this grandiose dream. The site selected by Washington was located in a swampy river bottom near the head of navigation on the Potomac. The surrounding low-lying hills rendered the spot oppressively hot and muggy during the summer. Removed as it was from the thriving commercial centers of the country, the capital had no business or society independent of the government. Nondescript boardinghouses, where members of Congress and government officials lived when in town, represented the main commercial activity. Cattle roamed the Mall, as they would throughout much of the century. The streets were filled with tree stumps and became impenetrable seas of mud after a rain. Much of the District was covered with woods and virtually all of it remained unoccupied. Residents and visitors boasted of the excellent hunting along the streets and even around the capitol's walls. So undeveloped was the town that in 1801 a group of congressmen returning from a party wandered lost in the woods all night.

When the government moved to its new residence in 1800, the capitol, built on a small hill to emphasize the dominance of the legislative branch in a republic, was not yet finished. The Senate chamber, where Jefferson took the oath of office,

Washington in 1800 barely resembled L'Enfant's grand design. When Jefferson was inaugurated, only one wing of the capitol was completed, and a primitive Pennsylvania Avenue ran more than a mile through the woods to connect it with the unfinished executive mansion.

was the only part of the capitol that had been completed. The executive mansion was unfinished as well, although it had been occupied since November when the Adamses had moved in for the last few months of John Adams' presidency. Except for its classical architecture, the city gave no indication of emulating the great centers of antiquity. A British diplomat grumbled over leaving Philadelphia, the previous capital, with its large population, bustling commerce, regular communication with the outside world, and lively society, to conduct business in "what was . . . scarce any better than a mere swamp."

Yet the isolated and unimpressive capital reflected the new president's attitude toward government. Distrustful of centralized power of any kind, Jefferson deliberately set out to remake the national government into one of limited scope. He took as his ideal precisely what the Federalists had striven to avoid—a government, in Hamilton's words, "at a distance and out of sight," which commanded little popular attention and touched few people's daily lives.

Jefferson's Character

Jefferson himself reflected that vision of modesty. Even standing nearly 6 feet, 3 inches, with red hair now mostly gray, the 57-year-old president lacked an impressive presence. He dressed so carelessly in frequently ill-fitting clothes that William Plumer, a New Hampshire Federalist, mistook him for a servant when he called at the executive mansion. Despite his wealth and genteel birth into Virginia society, Jefferson disliked pomp and maintained an image of republican simplicity. His habit of conducting business in a frayed coat and slippers dismayed dignitaries who called on him decked out in ribbons and lace.

Contemporaries noted his genial disposition. Although he wrestled with occasional bouts of despair, he was on the whole an unshakable optimist. "I steer my bark with Hope in the head," he once declared, "leaving fear astern." Although he was a writer of literary elegance, his "soft and gentle" voice made him a poor public speaker, prompting him to send written messages to Congress rather than deliver them in person, as Washington and Adams had done. And he preferred to accomplish his political business in private conversations or at his renowned dinner parties, where he charmed his guests with his easy conversation and informal manners. The normally critical John Quincy Adams, who eventually abandoned the Federalist party for the Republicans, declared, "You never can be an hour in this man's company without something of the marvelous."

Jefferson's Political Philosophy

Jefferson spelled out his political principles in the Declaration of Independence and his first inaugural address. For him, every person possessed certain inherent natural rights, which he defined as "life, liberty, and the pursuit of happiness." As John Locke had argued, government existed to secure these rights and derived its authority from the consent of the governed. Defending the wisdom of the people, Jefferson considered "the will of the majority" to be "the Natural law of every society" and "the only sure guardian of the rights of man." Although he conceded that the masses might err, he was confident they would soon return to correct principles. His faith in human virtue exceeded that of most of the founding generation, yet in good republican fashion, he feared those in power. Government seemed to Jefferson a necessary evil. Unlike the Federalists, he wanted to free individuals from its economic regulations and incentives and let the market control the distribution of goods and rewards in society.

In Jefferson's vision of the ideal society, agriculture was a morally superior way of life. "Those who labour in the earth are the chosen people of God, if ever he had a chosen people," he wrote in *Notes on the State of Virginia* (1787). Like Crèvecoeur, Jefferson praised rural life for nourishing the values of honesty, independence, and virtue that were essential in a republic. Government would "remain virtuous . . . as long as [the American people] are chiefly agricultural," he assured his associate James Madison. "When they get piled upon one another in large cities, as in Europe, they will become corrupt as in Europe." Rather than encouraging the development of large-scale factories, Jefferson wanted to preserve small household manufacturing, which was an integral part of the rural economy. Commerce should exist primarily to sell America's agricultural surplus. He was never able to overcome his earlier conviction, rooted in the classical republican ideology of the Revolution, that cities and commerce promoted speculation, greed, and useless luxury and self-indulgence.

Jefferson was a product of the Enlightenment, with its faith in the power of human reason to perfect society and decipher the universe. A self-taught architect of considerable merit, he designed the first buildings at the University of Virginia, in which he took a special interest because of his belief in the importance of education. He also submitted a plan for the president's home in the new capital. As an amateur scientist, he kept meticulous records of his observations and farming activities and invented many practical gadgets, including a more efficient plow and a machine that made a copy of his letters to help him carry on his voluminous correspondence. His estate at Monticello reflected his multifaceted interests. The house, which he designed, was built from bricks manufactured on the premises. Its rooms were filled with his inventions, scientific equipment, including a telescope and a set of meteorological instruments (he recorded data for years in hopes of being able to predict the weather), and specimens and artifacts collected from all over the world. His library of 6500 volumes, reputedly the finest in the country, was ultimately purchased by the government and became the nucleus of the Library of Congress.

Although Jefferson asserted that "the tree of liberty must be refreshed from time to time by the blood of patriots and tyrants," his reputation as a radical was undeserved. He did not support universal suffrage, he did not speak out for women's rights, and he did not advocate allowing women to vote. He clung to the traditional republican idea that voters should own property and thus have a stake in society. He proposed to broaden the suffrage, not by abolishing property requirements, which he believed would allow men dependent on others to control elections, but by giving propertyless men 50 acres from the public domain. Such a policy would maintain his cherished agrarian community. After 1790 his once-bold condemnation of slavery grew increasingly mute, and in the last years of his life he rebuked critics of the institution who sought to prevent its expansion westward. One of the largest slaveholders in the country, he treated his slaves indulgently yet took steps to protect his investment by tracking down runaways and, on occasion, selling slaves. Nor did his belief in free speech mean that he rejected the traditional idea that seditious libel was an offense government could prosecute. Although he did not seek to renew the Sedition Act, which had expired with Adams' presidency, Jefferson had no qualms about state governments punishing seditious behavior.

Slaveholding aristocrat and apostle of democracy, lofty theorist and pragmatic politician, Jefferson was an exceedingly complex, and at times contradictory, personality. But like most politicians, he was flexible in his approach to problems and tried to balance ends and means. And like most leaders, he quickly discovered that he confronted very different problems in power than he had in opposition.

Republican Principles

Once Jefferson settled into the executive mansion, he took steps to return the government to the republican ideals of simplicity and frugality. In place of the elaborate presidential receptions held by Washington and Adams, he opened his office to all callers and received them in order of arrival. At social affairs he paid no attention to rank or seniority, much to the discomfort of foreign dignitaries and upper-crust guests left to scramble for places at the table.

When the inaugural address was printed and circulated, it proved to be a carefully crafted work laying out what Jefferson termed "the essential principles of republican government." The states rather than the federal government, he asserted, were "the most competent administrators for our domestic concerns and the surest bulwarks against antirepublican tendencies." He stressed too that the civil authorities must always retain control of the military, long a firm republican conviction. He also affirmed his belief in individualism and a government that would leave people "free to regulate their own pursuits of industry and improvement." Jefferson particularly went out of his way to conciliate the vanquished Federalists. "Though the will of the majority is in all cases to prevail," he concluded, " . . . the minority possess their equal rights, which equal law must protect, and to violate would be oppression." In acknowledgment of Hamilton's fiscal policies, he promised to uphold the government's credit and protect commerce as the "handmaiden" of agriculture. Agreeing with Washington, he proposed friendship with all nations and "entangling alliances" with none. Urging Americans to unite for the common good, he declared, "We have called by different names brethren of the same principles. We are all republicans—we are all federalists."

The election of 1800 established the legitimacy of an opposition party in American politics, and Jefferson, in his inaugural address, seemed to endorse the validity of a party system. In reality, he hoped to restore one-party rule to the country by winning over moderate and honest Federalists and isolating the party's extremists, whom he still attacked as monarchists. "Nothing shall be spared on my part to obliterate the traces of party and consolidate the nation," he pledged, "if it can be done without the abandonment of principle."

Jefferson's Economic Policies

But what would Jefferson do about Hamilton's economic program? As he promised in his inaugural address, Jefferson proceeded to cut spending, reduce the size of the government, and begin paying off the national debt. Unless the debt was paid, he warned Albert Gallatin, his talented secretary of the treasury, "we shall be committed to the English career of debt, corruption and rottenness, closing with revolution." Even though the government was absurdly small by modern standards, with almost no employees other than those in the post office and army and navy, Jefferson considered it much larger than necessary. He abolished the internal taxes enacted by the Federalists, including the notorious tax on whiskey, and thus was able to get rid of all tax collectors and inspectors. "What farmer, what mechanic, what laborer, ever sees a tax gatherer in the United States?" boasted Jefferson in 1805. Land sales and the tariff duties would supply the funds needed to run the government.

The most serious spending cuts were made in the military branches, upon which the Federalists had placed such emphasis. Jefferson slashed the army budget in half, reducing the army to 3000 men stationed in the West. In a national emergency, Jefferson reasoned, the militia would be adequate to defend the country. He reduced the navy to an even greater extent. During the Quasi-War with France, the Federalists had launched a program to strengthen and expand the navy; Jefferson brought this work to a halt and replaced the navy's frigates with a fleet of small gunboats designed to guard the coast. The gunboats captured Jefferson's fancy because they were cheap, but in the long term they proved totally inadequate to defend the nation in war.

By such steps, Jefferson made significant progress toward paying off Hamilton's hated national debt. He lowered it from $83 million to only $57 million by the end of his two terms in office, despite the added financial burden of the Louisiana Purchase. Still, Jefferson did not dismantle entirely the Federalists' economic program. Funding and assumption could not be reversed—the nation's honor was pledged to paying these debts, and Jefferson fully understood the importance of maintaining the nation's credit. The tariff had to be retained as a source of revenue to meet the government's expenses. But more surprising, Jefferson argued that the national bank should be left to run its course until 1811, when its charter would expire. In fact, he actually expanded the bank's operations and began to contend, in words reminiscent of Hamilton, that he favored "making all the banks Republican, by sharing deposits among them in proportion to the [political] dispositions they show." His goal, he confessed to Gallatin, was "to detach the mercantile interest from its enemies and incorporate them into the body of its friends."

In effect, practical politics had triumphed over agrarian economics. "We can never get rid of his [Hamilton's] financial system," Jefferson confessed. "It mortifies me to be strengthening principles which I deem radically vicious, but this vice is entailed on us by the first error." Throughout his presidency, Jefferson frequently put pragmatic considerations above unyielding principles. As he himself expressed it, "What is practicable must often control what is pure theory." Other Republicans were less happy with such compromises. A small, intransigent wing of the party, led by John Randolph and John Taylor, both of Virginia, accused Jefferson of abandoning the principles of strict construction and agrarian virtue that had called the party into being.

John Marshall and Judicial Review

Having lost both the presidency and control of Congress in 1800, the Federalists moved before Jefferson took office to shore up their control of the remaining branch of government by expanding the size of the federal court system. The Judiciary Act of 1801 created 6 circuit courts and 16 new judgeships, along with a number of marshals, attorneys, and clerks. Federalists justified these "midnight appointments" executed by Adams in the last hours of his term on the grounds that the expanding nation required a larger judiciary. Jefferson, however, understandably saw matters differently. "The Federalists, defeated at the polls, have retired into the Judiciary," he fumed, "and from that barricade . . . hope to batter down all the bulwarks of Republicanism." In 1802, by a strict party vote, Congress repealed the 1801 law. Elimination of the new courts left their judges without jobs, prompting Federalists to protest that the action was illegal because the Constitution provided that judges were appointed for life and could be removed from office only for misconduct. The Republicans, determined to bring the judiciary under party control, forged ahead.

Under newly appointed Chief Justice John Marshall, the Supreme Court declined to challenge Congress' action on the courts. But before leaving office Adams had made a number of last-minute appointments, among them William Marbury as justice of the peace for the District of Columbia. When James Madison assumed the office of secretary of state under the new administration, he found a batch of undelivered commissions, including Marbury's. Wishing to appoint a loyal Republican, Jefferson instructed Madison not to hand over these commissions, whereupon Marbury sued under the Judiciary Act of 1789. Since that act gave the Supreme Court original jurisdiction in cases against federal officials, the case of *Marbury v. Madison* went directly to the Court in 1803.

Chief Justice Marshall, himself a Federalist, faced a dilemma. If he persuaded his colleagues to rule in favor of Marbury, Jefferson and Madison would almost certainly defy the Court and badly damage its prestige. On the other hand, a ruling in favor of Madison would amount to conceding that the Court had no legitimate check on the executive branch—a responsibility that Marshall believed the Constitution had clearly given the Court. In writing the majority opinion, the chief justice showed himself to be politically adroit and judicially farsighted. He avoided both pitfalls by ruling against Marbury on technical grounds, while at the same time affirming the Court's greatest power, the right to review statutes and interpret the meaning of the Constitution.

"It is emphatically the province of and duty of the judicial department to say what the law is," he wrote in upholding the doctrine of judicial review. This idea meant that the Court "must of necessity expound and interpret" the Constitution and the laws when one statute conflicted with another or when a law deviated from the Constitution. Marshall found that the section of the Judiciary Act of 1789 that granted the Supreme Court original jurisdiction in the case was unconstitutional. Since the Constitution specified those cases the Court had such jurisdiction over, they could not be enlarged by statute. Thus Marshall was able both to deny Marbury's petition and to assert that the executive branch was not above the law. Jefferson could hardly defy the ruling, since it required no action on his part. *Marbury v. Madison* was so critical to the development of the American constitutional system that it has been called the keystone of the constitutional arch.

Marshall and his colleagues subsequently asserted the power of the Court to review the constitutionality of state laws in *Fletcher v. Peck* (1810) when it struck down a Georgia law. It also brought state courts under the scrutiny of the Supreme Court in *Martin v. Hunter's Lessee* (1816), denying the claim of the Virginia Supreme Court that it was not subject to the authority of the federal judiciary, and in *Cohens v. Virginia* (1821), in which it asserted its right to review decisions of state courts on issues arising under the Constitution. During his tenure on the bench, Marshall extended judicial review to all acts of government. It

John Marshall.

took time for the doctrine to be accepted, but since Marshall's time the Supreme Court has successfully defended its position as the final arbiter of the meaning of the Constitution.

The Jeffersonian Attack on the Judiciary

Having disposed of Adams' last-minute appointments, the Republicans proceeded to attack Federalist judges who had been particularly obnoxious during the party battles of the 1790s. Jefferson argued that impeachment was not limited to criminal acts but was an appropriate political device to remove any judge who was unacceptable to two-thirds of the Senate. That, he claimed, would make the judiciary responsive to the public will. The administration began by seeking to remove John Pickering of New Hampshire, a federal district judge. Pickering, who was both insane and an alcoholic, had delivered rambling tirades against the Republican party from the bench. In 1803, after the House had impeached him, he was convicted and removed by the Senate.

Encouraged by this success, the administration turned its attention to Associate Justice Samuel Chase of the Supreme Court. An ultra-Federalist, Chase had interpreted the Sedition Act in a blatantly partisan fashion to ensure convictions against Republicans. In continuing their attack, Jefferson and his advisers ignored the uneasiness of some Republicans over using the impeachment process to remove judges who had committed no crime but merely held opinions opposed to those of the party in power. The House impeached Chase on political charges, but in the Senate trial his lawyers argued that impeachment was limited to indictable offenses. While acknowledging that Chase had perhaps been indiscreet, they claimed he had committed no crime. A majority of senators voted to convict, but since a two-thirds vote was necessary for removal, Chase was acquitted. A number of Republican senators refused to expand the meaning of impeachment to include political transgressions.

In the end, even Jefferson, who believed the trial had been mismanaged, accepted Chase's acquittal without protest. Republicans decided to wait for death and retirement to give them eventual control of the remaining branch of the government through presidential appointments.

JEFFERSON AND WESTERN EXPANSION

The Federalists feared the West as a threat to social order and stability. Thus when they passed an act in 1796 authorizing the sale of federal land, they regarded it as a revenue measure rather than the means to develop the country and kept the price of land high. It sold for a minimum of $2 an acre, with a required purchase of at least 640 acres, over four times the size of the typical American farm. Jefferson and the Republicans, on the other hand, viewed the West as the means to preserve the values of an agrarian republic. In 1801, the Republican Congress reduced the minimum purchase to 320 acres and established a four-year credit system to pay. The intention was to encourage rapid settlement of the interior, and in fact land sales boomed under the new law. Most of the sales, however, were to speculators and land companies rather than individual settlers.

Jefferson realized that as settled regions of the country became crowded, the excess population would seek opportunity elsewhere. Without fresh, cheap land to the west, many rural residents would migrate to the cities in search of work. Such a development, he believed, would be a calamity for the security of an agrarian republic, since western society evidenced a greater degree of equality in day-to-day affairs. Wealth and property were more widely distributed than in the East, where urbanization and commercial development led to a growing concentration of wealth. America's vast spaces provided land that would last for a thousand generations, Jefferson predicted in his inaugural, enough to transform the United States into "an empire of liberty." Moreover, the West was overwhelmingly Republican, and thus the admission of each new state would also strengthen his party and hasten the demise of the Federalists. From the Jeffersonian perspective, western expansion was a blessing economically, socially, and politically.

The Louisiana Purchase

Jefferson recognized the importance of the Mississippi River to western interests. Because Spain's New World empire was disintegrating, Americans were confident that before long they would gain control of Florida and of the rest of the Mississippi, either through purchase or military occupation.

This comforting prospect was shattered, however, when Spain secretly ceded Louisiana, which encompassed the territory between the Mississippi River and the Rocky Mountains, to France. That nation had emerged from the convulsions of revolution led by a bold young military commander, Napoleon Bonaparte. Under his rule, France had become the most powerful nation on the European continent, with the military might to protect its new colony and block American expansion. American anxiety intensified when Spain, while still in control of Louisiana, suddenly revoked Americans' right to navigate the lower Mississippi guaranteed by Pinckney's Treaty (page 282). Americans believed (incorrectly, it turned out) that Spain had acted at the behest of France. Western farmers, who were thus denied access to the sea, angrily protested Spain's high-handed action. If this were not enough, word came that Spanish officials, dangling the bait of access to the Mississippi, were intriguing again with American settlers in the West to detach the region from the United States.

Jefferson saw that if he could buy New Orleans and West Florida from the French, the United States would gain control of the entire Mississippi. He dispatched James Monroe to Paris to join Robert Livingston, the American minister, in negotiations. "There is on the globe one single spot, the possession [i.e., possessor] of which is our natural and habitual enemy," Jefferson reminded them. "It is New Orleans." Should they fail to acquire the city, he instructed them to seek an alliance with Great Britain, whose navy offered the only possible protection. "The day that France takes New Orleans, we must marry ourselves to the British fleet and nation," he observed with a notable lack of enthusiasm.

In the meantime, however, Napoleon lost interest in Louisiana. He had intended to use the region to feed the slaves on the sugar-rich island of Santo Domingo (Haiti), but a military expedition to reestablish French control ended in disaster. Furthermore, with war looming again in Europe, he desperately needed money, so in April 1803 he offered to sell not just New Orleans, but all of Louisiana to the United States. This proposal flabbergasted Livingston and Monroe. Their instructions said nothing about acquiring all of Louisiana; and they certainly had not been authorized to spend what the French demanded. On the other hand, here was an unprecedented opportunity to dramatically expand the boundaries of the United States. Pressed for an immediate answer, Livingston and Monroe wanted to consult Jefferson but worried that the French might withdraw the offer as suddenly as they had made it. So the American ministers haggled over a few details, took a deep breath, and agreed to purchase Louisiana for approximately $15 million. Striking one of the most extraordinary bargains in the history of the United States, they had doubled its size by adding some 830,000 square miles.

Such was Talleyrand's haste to conclude the agreement that the boundaries of Louisiana were not even specified. When Livingston pointed out this omission, the opportunistic French foreign minister characteristically replied, "You have made a noble bargain for yourselves, and I suppose you will make the most of it." The millions of acres of fertile farmland, untold natural resources, and control of the vital Mississippi River and its tributaries were indeed a noble bargain, and Livingston recognized it. "From this day," he asserted, "the United States take their place among the powers of the first rank."

Jefferson, naturally, was immensely pleased at the prospect of acquiring so much territory, which seemed to guarantee the survival of his agrarian republic. At the same time, he found the legality of the act deeply troubling. He himself had set forth the doctrine of strict construction in the Kentucky resolutions of 1798, and clearly, the Constitution did not specifically authorize the acquisition of territory by treaty. Jefferson went so far as to draw up a constitutional amendment authorizing the acquisition of Louisiana, but ratification would take time, and Livingston and Monroe urged haste. In the end, Jefferson sent the treaty to the Senate for ratification, noting privately, "The less we say about constitutional difficulties the better." Once again pragmatism had triumphed over theory in Jefferson's presidency. His desire for an agrarian empire of liberty took precedence over his states' rights principles.

The Louisiana Purchase was generally popular, even in Federalist New England. The Senate ratified the treaty 24–7 and Congress appropriated the necessary funds. West Florida, which bordered part of the lower Mississippi, remained in Spanish hands, and Jefferson's efforts to acquire this region, either by threats or by purchase, were unsuccessful. Nevertheless, western commerce could flow down the Mississippi unimpeded to the sea. The Louisiana Purchase would rank as the greatest achievement of Jefferson's presidency.

Lewis and Clark

As early as the 1780s Jefferson's interest in the West had led him to propose an expedition to California. The project had never gotten off the ground, but early in 1803, even before the Louisiana Purchase was completed, Congress secretly appropriated $2500 to send an exploring party up the Missouri River to the Pacific. To head this expedition, Jefferson selected his private secretary, Meriwether Lewis, a Virginian who had served in the army in the West and who was an acute and knowledgeable observer. Lewis selected William Clark, a younger brother of Revolutionary War hero George Rogers Clark, as co-commander.

Jefferson instructed Lewis and Clark to map the region and make detailed observations concerning the soil, climate, rivers, minerals, and plant and animal life. They were also to investigate the feasibility of an overland route to the Pacific, particularly whether the Missouri River "may offer the most direct and practicable water communication across this continent for the purposes of commerce." When the Spanish minister inquired about the purposes of the expedition (once across the Rockies, it would be in Spanish territory), Jefferson blandly informed him they were solely geographic. But in truth, he hoped also to engage in diplomacy with the Indians in the West and assure them of the United States' friendship (and weaken their ties to Spain). Equally important, by pushing onward to the Pacific, Lewis and Clark would strengthen the American title to Oregon, which several nations claimed but none effectively occupied.

In the spring of 1804, Lewis and Clark, accompanied by 48 men, embarked from near St. Louis. They laboriously pushed their boats up the Missouri River to present-day North Dakota, where they spent the winter with the Mandans. The next spring, they headed west again. In their difficult trek over the Rockies, they were aided by a French-Canadian trader and his wife Sacajawea, a member of the Shoshone tribe who served as guide and interpreter in dealing with various Indian peoples. Only with great difficulty did the expedition get through the rugged mountains ahead of the winter snows. Having crossed the Continental Divide, the party floated down first the Snake and then the Columbia River to the Pacific.

EXPLORATION AND EXPANSION: THE LOUISIANA PURCHASE
The vast, largely uncharted Louisiana Purchase lay well beyond the most densely populated areas of the United States. The Lewis and Clark expedition along with Lieutenant Zebulon Pike's exploration of the upper Mississippi River and the Southwest opened the way for westward expansion.

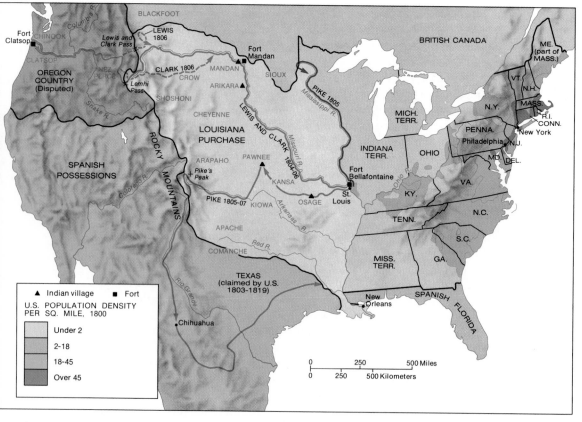

After spending a bleak winter in Oregon, vainly waiting for a ship that would take them back, the company returned in 1806 over the Rockies. Having traveled across half the continent in both directions, navigated countless rapids, and conducted negotiations with numerous tribes, Lewis and Clark arrived in St. Louis in September, two and a half years after they had departed. The expedition fired the imagination of Americans about the exotic lands of the newly acquired Louisiana Purchase, as well as the Pacific Northwest. Lewis and Clark had collected thousands of useful plant and animal specimens (for a time, two grizzly bear cubs they had captured were kept on the grounds of the White House). They discovered several passes through the Rockies and produced a remarkably accurate map, their most valuable contribution to western exploration.

WHITES AND INDIANS ON THE FRONTIER

In their trek across the continent, Lewis and Clark fought only one skirmish with Indians. The expedition's dealings remained peaceful partly through vigilance and caution, but also because a small party of whites hardly threatened the Indians living west of the Mississippi. The situation was different farther east, where for some years settlers had been streaming through the passes and into the fertile lands of the Ohio River valley. Whereas in 1790 only about 100,000 whites lived in the West, by 1800 that number had jumped to almost 400,000, and a decade later, to over a million. By 1820 more than 2 million whites lived in a region they had first entered only 50 years earlier.

In this backcountry, where white and Indian cultures mixed and often clashed, both peoples experienced the breakdown of their own traditional cultural systems. White immigrants pushing into Indian territory often lacked the structures of community such as churches, schools, and legal institutions. Indians, for their part, were attracted to some elements of white culture, such as the benefits of trade goods. But whites, with their unceasing hunger for Indian land, their more settled agricultural ways, domesticated animals, and fenced-in fields, placed severe stress on Indian cultures.

The Course of White Penetration

Following the Treaty of Greenville (page 280), white settlers poured into the Ohio Territory. Travelers were amazed at the number of people heading west by wagon and flatboat. "From what I have seen and heard," one girl wrote while crossing Pennsylvania bound for the West, "I think the State of Ohio will be well fill'd before winter,—Waggons without number, every day go on." The pattern of settlement remained the same: in the first wave came backwoods families who laboriously cleared a few acres of forest by girding the trees, removing the brush, and planting corn between the dead trunks. Their isolated one-room log cabins were crude, dark, and windowless, with mud stuffed between the chinks, the furniture and utensils sparse and homemade. Such settlers were mostly squatters, without legal title to their land, depending largely on their own resources. As a region began to fill up these incurably restless pioneers usually sold their improvements and headed west again.

The waves of settlement that followed were more permanent. These men and women completed the work of clearing the land and improving a farm. Many were young unmarried men who left crowded regions in the East seeking new opportunities. Their migration, which relieved population pressures back home, contributed to the imbalance of males and females on the frontier. Once established, they quickly married and started families. Like the pioneers before them, most engaged in semisubsistence agriculture; as their numbers increased and a local market developed, they switched to surplus agriculture, growing and making much of what the family needed while selling or exchanging the surplus to obtain essential items. "The woman told me that they spun and wove all the cotton and woollen garments of the family, and knit all the stockings," a visitor to an Ohio farm wrote. "Her husband, though not a shoemaker by trade, made all the shoes. She manufactured all the soap and candles they used." The wife sold butter and chickens to get money to buy coffee, tea, and whiskey.

The Second Great Awakening

It was the most sparsely settled regions that became famous for a second wave of revivals that swept across the nation beginning in the 1790s. Like the first national outpouring of religious concern 50 years earlier, the Second Great Awakening was not limited to the frontier. Revivals flourished among Congregationalists in New England and Presbyterians in central New York and Pennsylvania. They roused young students at college campuses like Hampden-Sydney and Washington College in Virginia (1787) and at Yale in Connecticut (1802). But even in the East, there was widespread concern that the newer, less developed areas of the country needed religion most. Beginning in 1798 the Congregationalists set up a missionary society to send ministers westward, and the Baptists and Presbyterians quickly followed suit.

The Methodists, however, had the most effective organization for spreading the gospel in remote areas. As soon as a district could be organized, a devout "circuit rider"—not necessarily a minister—would be appointed to travel the countryside, stopping at isolated cabins, handing out tracts, and preaching to small groups anywhere he could. One competing Presbyterian missionary ruefully noted that "into every hovel I entered I learned that the Methodist missionary had been there before me." It became common wisdom among country folk that when blizzards or thunderstorms were especially severe, "nobody was out but crows and Methodist preachers."

In June 1800 three Presbyterian ministers and a Methodist held an especially successful four-day meeting along the Red River in Kentucky. The audience, moved to tears by their sins and the prospect of eternal life, began to fall to the ground and shriek for mercy as John McGee, the Methodist preacher, begged them to "let the Lord Omnipotent reign in their hearts." News of the meeting spread quickly; several more meetings were held in the area during the summer, and people came from 50 and 100 miles around, camping in makeshift tents and holding services out of doors. This new form of worship, the camp meeting, reached its climax at Cane Ridge, Kentucky, in August 1801. At a time when the largest city in the state had only 2000 people, over 10,000 gathered for a week to hear dozens of ministers.

Men and women earnestly examined their hearts; scoffers came, half-mocking, half-fearful of what they might see. For rural folk accustomed to going to bed

Although the clergy at camp meetings were male, women played prominent roles, often pressing husbands to convert. The audience here is predominantly female, including those sitting on the "anxious bench" below the preacher.

soon after dark, the sight of hundreds of campfires flickering throughout the woods far into the night, reinforced by the endless singing, praying, and crying, was a powerful tonic indeed. "The vast sea of human beings seemed to be agitated as if by storm," recalled one skeptic, who himself was converted at Cane Ridge. "I counted seven ministers all preaching at once. . . . Some of the people were singing, others praying, some crying for mercy in the most piteous accents. . . . At one time I saw at least 500 swept down in a moment as if a battery of a thousand guns had been opened upon them, and then immediately followed shrieks and shouts that rent the very heavens." In the overwhelming emotion of the moment, converts might dance, bark, laugh hysterically, or jerk uncontrollably, hair flying, the whole body shaking, as they sought to gain assurance of their salvation.

In the South, blacks, including slaves, attended camp meetings and enthusiastically participated in the tumultuous services. Indeed, revivals were a major force in spreading Christianity to African-Americans and producing slave conversions. Revivalists' clear and vivid speech, their acceptance of the moral worth of every individual regardless of race, and their emphasis on the conversion experience rather than the forms of religion and abstract theology had the same appeal to blacks, who had little formal schooling, as it did to poorly educated whites. Blacks worshiped separately from and sometimes together with whites. The revivals also produced black preachers, who exhorted whites as well as blacks. Some slaveholders, especially in eastern plantation districts, worried that camp meetings might foster racial egalitarianism, but revivalists concentrated on bringing slaves to Christ rather than questioning society's institutions. As with whites, the Baptist and Methodist churches received the bulk of African-American converts.

The revivals quickly found critics, who decried the emotionalism and hysteria they produced. For a time Presbyterians and Baptists withdrew from camp meetings, leaving the field to the more enthusiastic Methodists. But as the country became more settled, even the Methodists took pains to set well-defined limits on camp meeting revivals. They restricted admittance, patrolled the grounds, and attempted to maintain a sober atmosphere.

Daily Lives

PUBLIC SPACE/PRIVATE SPACE

The Frontier Camp Meeting

The Cane Ridge revival, one of the earliest along the frontier, was a chaotic and disorganized affair. But as western clergy became more experienced with outdoor camp meetings, they standardized the format. About a week in advance, organizers chose a forest clearing, removed nearby underbrush, erected pulpits, and constructed benches for the worshipers. Usually the camp went up near an established church, which provided lodging for the ministers. Since an adequate water supply was essential, camps were located near springs, creeks, or rivers. Being near a navigable river also improved access to the meeting. A good site needed dry ground, shade so worshipers could escape the blazing sun, pasturage for the horses, and wood for tent poles and fuel.

The meeting site might be laid out in a horseshoe, a rectangle, or, most popularly, a broad circle. But in each case the tents of the worshipers formed a ring around the outdoor auditorium where services were held. As participants began to arrive, a supervisor directed drivers where to park carriages or wagons, tether animals, and pitch tents. At a large meeting, where as many as 200 tents covered the site, they were set up in several rows with streets in between to allow easy access. To help people find their lodgings, the streets were sometimes even named. This outer perimeter constituted the meeting's private spaces. Here, beneath tents of sailcloth or even shelters patched together from old blankets and sheets, individuals could withdraw from the larger group to find relative solitude, cook meals in front of campfires, and sleep on rude

beds of straw or simply on the ground. Often several families shared a tent.

Worshipers were naturally drawn toward the central public space, where they filled bench after bench at the periodic call of a bugle. Few would have been inclined to fall asleep at such meetings, but the benches made it difficult to do so, for unlike most church pews they had no backs. Rising above the listeners, at one or both ends of the clearing, stood the preachers' pulpit. Sometimes it was merely a 10-foot-square platform on stilts, other times it was more elaborate, with several levels and a roof. Services were held in the open, where neither rain nor thunderstorms would interrupt them. At night time, the dancing light and shadows produced by the candles, torches, campfires, and fire altars (earthen covered platforms) at each corner created a spectacular effect and heightened the feeling of awe.

The democracy of the frontier did not automatically break down customary social constraints. For reasons of authority as well as practicality, the ministers' pulpit rose above the congregation. And the audience itself was segregated: women were seated on one side of the clearing, men on the other. In the South, blacks who attended camp meetings were relegated to an area behind the pulpit, where they set up their own camp and conducted their own services.

Since the avowed purpose of camp meetings was to "revive" religion and produce an alteration in listeners' hearts, the meeting site provided what was known as an "anxious bench" for those whose souls struggled in the agony of conversion. Several rows of planks were set aside for such "mourners," directly in front of the pulpit. Thus the design of the space focused the attention of both the congregation and the

Daily Lives

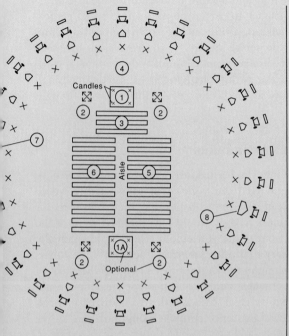

CODE

X Cooking fires—illumination also from candles in trees
△ Tents
🛏 Wagons
▭ Horses
1. Speakers' stand—candles for illumination
2. Earthen covered fire platforms
3. Mourners' bench
4. Blacks' worship area
5. Seats—women's side
6. Seats—men's side
7. Preachers' tent
8. Boarding tent

Source: Adapted from Charles A. Johnson, *The Frontier Camp Meeting: Religion's Harvest Time* (Dallas: SMU Press, 1955), pp. 43 and 47.

ministers on the mourners, who were exhorted and prayed over in hopes that they would receive a new birth in Christ. Sometimes the anxious bench became so crowded with the stricken that they could hardly move. As camp meetings became increasingly organized, separate mourning tents were set up on the edge of the arena near the anxious benches. (Again, curtains separated the male and female sections, and blacks had their own mourning tents.)

But the demarcations between public and private, male and female, and even black and white could be broken down. As excitement grew, several services might be held simultaneously, some people praying, others singing, shouting, or listening to ministers who stood on wagons or makeshift platforms of felled trees. And when formal services ended, men and women often continued singing and exhorting in small groups, going into the woods to pray, and searching one another's souls by campfires late into the night. Indeed, the social mixing and spontaneous excitement were great enough that meeting sponsors quickly learned that supervision was necessary to prevent unseemly activities. The nearby forest, the many tents, and nightfall all offered temptations for drinking, carousing, or lovemaking. Official patrols regularly investigated suspicious activities and monitored sleeping arrangements.

On the final day whites and blacks would join together in a singing and marching festival before disbanding to their more humdrum daily routines. Successful camp meetings depended on more than the talents of the clergy and the enthusiasm of participants. In their layout they were carefully planned and regulated communities in the forest, designed to reduce the distance between public and private space and thereby instill a sense of religion in all of the activities that took place in the meeting, as well as those that would be resumed in the regular world.

Revivals like Cane Ridge provided an emotional release from the hard and isolated life on the frontier. For a moment, pioneers could forget the drabness and squalor of their lives, the pains and sorrows they endured as they struggled to carve an existence out of the forest. For families that enjoyed little social interaction with others, revivals offered a chance to participate in a wider social gathering, to renew old friendships and make new ones, while relieving pent-up emotions. For those at the bottom of the social hierarchy, the revivalists' message emphasized an individual's ability to gain personal triumph and salvation, regardless of his or her station in life. In the swiftly changing borderlands north and south of the Ohio River, where society seemed constantly in flux, revivals brought a sense of uplift and comfort.

Black Hoof and the Choice of Assimilation

As white settlers continued to pour into the backcountry, the pressure to acquire Indian lands increased. Jefferson endorsed the policy that Indian tribes would either have to assimilate into American culture by abandoning their seminomadic hunting practices and becoming farmers or they would have to move west of the Mississippi River. There, isolated from white settlement, they could gradually develop the skills and values necessary to fit into American society. While Jefferson defended these alternatives as being in the best interests of the Indians, since otherwise they faced extermination, he also understood that such a policy would conveniently enable the government to clear Indian titles to lands east of the Mississippi. By adopting an agricultural existence, Indians would be able "to live on smaller portions of land," he noted, adding, "While they are learning to do better on less land, our increasing numbers will be calling for more land." And call they did. Between 1800 and 1810 whites pressed Indians into ceding more than 100 million acres in the Ohio River valley.

The hard truth about white policies toward the Indians was that however enlightened individuals might be, the demographic pressure of high birth rates and aggressive expansion ensured conflict between the two cultures. Anglo-Americans—whether Crèvecoeur's yeoman farmers or Franklin's commercial traders or devout Methodist circuit riders—never doubted the superiority of their ways. As William Henry Harrison, governor of the new Indiana Territory, confessed in 1801, "A great many of the Inhabitants of the Fronteers consider the murdering of the Indians in the highest degree meritorious." And even a student of the Enlightenment like Jefferson could become cynical. Corresponding with Harrison, he encouraged the policy of selling goods on credit, in order to lure Indians into debt. "When these debts get beyond what the individuals can pay," the president observed, "they become willing to lop them off by a cession of

---

THE INDIAN RESPONSE TO WHITE ENCROACHMENT
With land cessions and white western migration placing increased pressure on Indian cultures after 1790, news of the Prophet's revival fell on eager ears. It spread especially quickly northward along the shores of Lake Michigan and westward along Lake Superior and the interior of Wisconsin. Following the Battle of Tippecanoe, Tecumseh eclipsed the Prophet as the major leader of Indian resistance, but his trips South to forge political alliances met with less success.

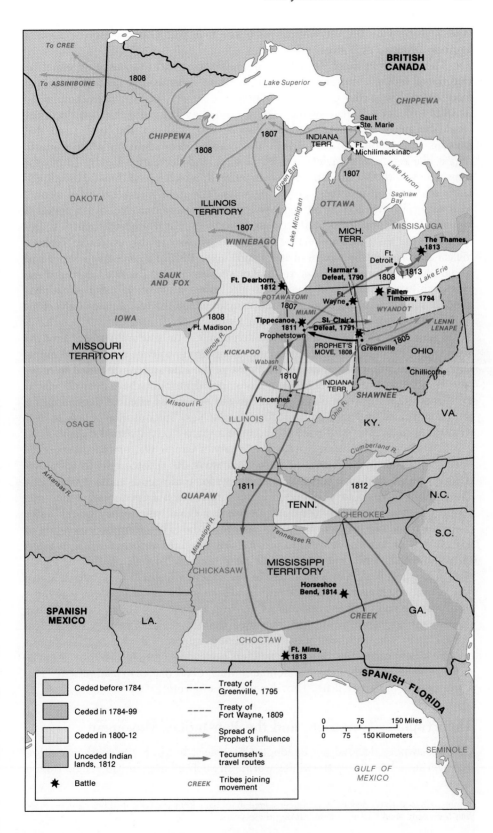

lands." Such were the rationalizations of the man who hoped to spread a white agrarian "empire of liberty" westward.

The loss of so much land to white settlement had a devastating effect on traditional Indian cultures by reducing hunting grounds and making game and food scarce. "Stop your people from killing our game," the Shawnees complained in 1802 to federal Indian agents. "At present they kill more than we do. They would be angry if we were to kill a cow or hog of theirs, the little game that remains is very dear to us." Tribes also became dependent on white trade to obtain blankets, guns, metal utensils, alcohol, and decorative beads. To pay for these goods with furs, Indians often overtrapped, which forced them to invade the lands of neighboring tribes, provoking wars. The debilitating effects of alcohol were especially marked during these years. Indians turned to alcohol as a means of coping with cultural stress, and increased production in white backcountry settlements during the 1790s and early 1800s made whiskey readily available. Technological advances in the design of small stills made distilling corn much easier and by far the most profitable way to market surplus grain.* Indeed, during these years, white consumption of alcohol was also rising, a symptom of the adjustment of white society to urban and industrial stresses which the temperance movement of the 1820s and 1830s attempted to deal with.

Among the Shawnees in the Ohio River valley, the cultural stresses brought about by white expansion led to alcoholism, growing violence among tribe members, family disintegration, and the collapse of the clan system designed to regulate relations among different villages. These problems might have been alleviated by separating from white culture, but the Shawnees had become dependent on trade for articles they could not produce themselves. The question of how to deal with the encroaching white culture became a matter of anguished debate.

Chief Black Hoof, one signer of the Treaty of Greenville, embraced assimilation, hoping to help his people adapt to white ways. He accepted the treaty provisions ceding some Shawnee lands in exchange for trade goods and a government annuity and traveled to Washington in 1801 to request a deed guaranteeing his people the remaining Shawnee lands in western Ohio, where they would "raise good Grain and cut Hay for our Cattle" as whites did. The astonished secretary of war, Henry Dearborn, refused to provide any deed (Jefferson, after all, wanted *Indians* to cede land, not whites); but he promised "ploughs and other useful tools." So a group of Shawnees settled in permanent villages in the Auglaize River valley, built log houses, wore garments like those of whites, and, aided by government officials and Quaker missionaries, took up agriculture. For several years the experiment appeared promising, but after the government refused to pay the federal agent who had been providing technical support, Black Hoof's followers became discouraged. As their independence steadily eroded and they became more dependent on their government annuities, even Black Hoof admitted, "The white people has spoiled us. They have been our ruin."

The Prophet, Tecumseh, and the Pan-Indian Movement

Other Shawnees decided not to adopt white ways, but to revitalize their culture by severing all ties with the white world. In such efforts, Indian religion often

---

*From 1802 to 1815 the federal government issued more than 100 patents for distilling devices, more than 5 percent of all patents granted during these years.

played a central role. During the 1790s a revival of religious fervor led by Handsome Lake took hold among the Iroquois, following the loss of most of the Iroquois lands and the collapse of their military power in western New York. Among the Shawnees, Lalawethika, also known as the Prophet, sparked a religious revival. The Prophet's early life was undistinguished: he was a poor hunter and as a child accidentally blinded himself in the right eye with an arrow. His portly build and homely looks reinforced his unsightly appearance, and the ridicule of his fellow tribe members drove him to alcoholism. Then suddenly in April 1805 he lapsed into a trance so deep that he was given up for dead. When he revived, he spoke of having died and been reborn. In this vision and others he later received, he outlined a new creed for the Shawnee. Renouncing alcohol, he took a new name, Tenskwatawa (The Open Door), to express his mission to "reclaim the Indians from bad habits and to cause them to live in peace with all mankind."

He urged the Shawnee to renounce whiskey and white goods and return to their old ways of hunting with bows and arrows and eating traditional foods like corn and beans. "You must not dress like the White Man or wear hats like them," he exhorted, ". . . and when the weather is not severe, you must go naked Excepting the Breach cloth, and when you are clothed, it must be in skins or leather of your own Dressing." Seeking to revitalize Shawnee culture, the Prophet condemned intertribal violence, promoted monogamous marriage, and denounced the idea of private instead of communal property. Except for guns, which could be used in self-defense, his followers were to discard all items made by whites.

Not only trade but also fraternizing with Americans was forbidden. Indian wives of white men were to leave their husbands and return to the tribe, and children of mixed parentage were to be barred from the village. Setting up his headquarters first in Greenville, Ohio, and then at his own village of Prophetstown in Indiana in 1808, Tenskwatawa led a religious revival among the tribes of the Northwest, who were increasingly concerned about the loss of their lands. Just as thousands of white settlers traveled to Methodist or Baptist camp

Tenskwatawa, "the Open Door," shown in traditional dress, led a religious movement to revitalize Shawnee culture. After the Battle of Tippecanoe, he was supplanted as leader of the movement by his brother Tecumseh, who advocated political unity to preserve Indian lands and cultures.

meetings deep in the woods, where preachers denounced the evils of liquor and called for a return to a purer way of life, so thousands from northern tribes as far away as Wisconsin and Minnesota traveled to the Prophet's village for inspiration.

While Tenskwatawa's strategy of revitalization was primarily religious, his older brother Tecumseh turned to political and military solutions. William Henry Harrison described Tecumseh as "one of those uncommon geniuses which spring up occasionally to produce revolutions and overturn the established order of things." Tall and athletic, an accomplished hunter and a renowned warrior, Tecumseh at first played only a secondary role in his brother's religious movement. But in 1809 when the Lenni Lenape and Miami tribes ceded yet another 3 million acres in Indiana and Illinois under the Treaty of Fort Wayne, Tecumseh concluded that spiritual revival was inadequate to safeguard Indian lands. Repudiating this treaty, he urged tribes to forget their ancient animosities and unite under his leadership to protect their lands from white incursions. As he traveled throughout the Northwest, preaching his message of unity and resistance, hundreds of young braves rallied to his movement. Tecumseh's confederacy brought together the Wyandot, Chippewa, Sauk and Fox, Winnebago, Potawatomi, and other tribes. As Tecumseh began to overshadow the Prophet, Harrison aptly termed him "really the efficient man—the Moses of the family."

Tecumseh's message of pan-Indian unity and centralized authority ran counter to many facets of traditional Indian cultures. He asked villages to pay less attention to their local leaders and join his larger movement; he also called on tribes to unite with their traditional enemies in a common cause. While the amount of support he received was impressive, his following never matched that of the Prophet's earlier revivals. After proselytizing among the northwestern tribes, Tecumseh in 1811 toured through the South, where he encountered greater resistance. In general, the southern tribes were more prosperous, more acculturated, and felt less immediate pressure on their land base than did northern tribes. In addition, the Choctaws and Chickasaws refused to forget longstanding feuds with northern tribes.

So Tecumseh's southern mission ended largely in failure. To compound his problems, while he was away, a force of Americans under Governor Harrison fought off an attack launched by the Prophet at the Battle of Tippecanoe in November and then destroyed Prophetstown. As a result, Tecumseh had to continue his uphill battle for unity under discouraging circumstances. He became convinced that the best way to contain white expansion was to play off the Americans against the British, who maintained their interest in the Great Lakes region. Indeed, by 1811 the two nations were on the brink of war.

THE SECOND WAR FOR AMERICAN INDEPENDENCE

As Tecumseh pushed his campaign for a pan-Indian alliance, Jefferson, paying much more attention to partisan politics, looked to restore American political unity by wooing all but the most extreme Federalists into the Republican camp. Jefferson easily won reelection in 1804 over Charles Cotesworth Pinckney, the Federalist candidate, carrying 15 of 17 states. With the Federalists discredited by their vocal reactionary wing, and with the Republicans controlling three-quarters of the seats in Congress, Jefferson's goal of one-party rule seemed near at hand.

That unity was threatened, however, by growing Republican factionalism and, more important, by renewed fighting in Europe. Only two weeks after Napoleon agreed to sell Louisiana to the United States, war broke out between France and Great Britain. As in the 1790s, the United States found itself caught between the world's two greatest powers. In his struggle to maintain American neutrality, Jefferson's controversial policies momentarily revived the two-party system.

Neutral Rights

Initially, the war's disruption of European agriculture stimulated the American economy, since raw materials, especially foodstuffs, were in great demand overseas. As the fighting drove most nonneutral ships from the seas, American shipping dominated the carrying trade. The nation's foreign trade doubled between 1803 and 1805. Moreover, because the British navy prevented any direct trade with the French colonies, the reexport trade flourished. American ships transported sugar, coffee, and other goods from colonies in the West Indies and Latin America to an American port, unloaded the cargo and paid a duty, then reloaded the cargo and carried it to Europe. Britain initially ignored these broken voyages, but in 1805 its Admiralty courts ruled that such voyages violated the British blockade, and therefore the ships and cargo could be seized.

Adding to American anger, the British navy again resorted to impressment of sailors and even passengers from American ships. British authorities refused to recognize the right of its citizens to emigrate and become Americans, insisting that even if naturalized by the United States, they remained subjects of the Crown. Anywhere from 4000 to 10,000 sailors were impressed by British naval officers, who were not always terribly concerned about distinguishing between naturalized and native-born Americans. Isaac Clark, for example, was a native of Randolph, Massachusetts, yet he was taken from the American ship *Jane* in June 1809 after it was stopped by the British. When he presented papers attesting to his American citizenship, the English captain tore them up and threw them overboard. Refusing to work, he was put in irons, given a daily allowance of a biscuit and a pint of water, and once a week received two dozen lashes. Finally, half-starved and physically broken, Clark gave in. He served in the British navy for over two and a half years until wounded in action against a French frigate. While in a hospital he was freed through the intervention of the American consul. Voicing American indignation over such cases, John Quincy Adams characterized impressment as an "authorized system of kidnapping upon the ocean."

By 1805, the war had demonstrated the British navy's clear superiority on the sea, while Napoleon's army enjoyed a similar decisive edge on land. Adopting a strategy of attrition, each country began to raid America's ocean commerce with the other side. Between 1803 and 1807, Britain seized over 500 American ships, France over 300. Insurance rates soared, yet trading with the belligerents was so profitable that American merchants willingly ran the risks. Knowledgeable observers claimed that even if only one ship in three reached its destination, the owner reaped a handsome profit.

But in 1806 the British government tightened the screws further by proclaiming a blockade of France and northern Europe. Napoleon in turn issued the Berlin Decree of 1806, which established his own "Continental System" prohibiting British merchants and shipping from European markets. The following year the British adopted a set of regulations over neutral shipping known as the Orders in Council, which stipulated that any ship trading with France or its satellites had to

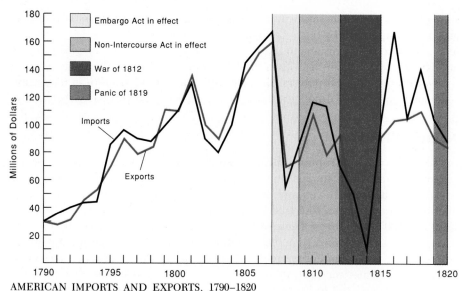

AMERICAN IMPORTS AND EXPORTS, 1790–1820
The prosperity of the 1790s is reflected in steadily rising foreign trade. Note the sharp drop after the Embargo Act and during the war.

stop first at a British port, pay a duty, and get a license. Napoleon retaliated with the Milan Decree of 1807, which announced that any ship that stopped in Britain in conformity with the Orders in Council would be treated as a British ship, subject to seizure. American merchants, caught in the middle, saw the number of seized ships again increase. An irate Jefferson said of France and England, "The one is a den of robbers, the other of pirates."

The war of nerves came to a head in June 1807, when the British frigate *Leopard* stopped the U.S. warship *Chesapeake* while still in American territorial waters just outside Norfolk, Virginia. When the British demanded the right to search the ship and seize British deserters, the American commander indignantly refused, since no nation claimed the right to impress sailors from a warship. The *Leopard* then fired three salvoes point blank into the *Chesapeake*, killing 3 and wounding 18. When the American ship struck its colors, a British boarding party seized four sailors who had deserted from the Royal Navy, three of them Americans (including two blacks). News of the high-handed British behavior inflamed public opinion, as politicians and editors called for the country to redress the humiliations it had suffered. Jefferson testified that "never, since the battle of Lexington, have I seen the country in such a state of exasperation as at present."

The Embargo

Yet Jefferson shrank from declaring war. He announced instead a program of "peaceable coercion," designed to protect neutral rights without war. The plan not only prohibited American ships from trading with foreign ports, it stopped the export of all American goods. Staying at home would keep American ships out of trouble on the high seas. In addition, Jefferson was confident that American exports were so essential to the two belligerents, they would quickly agree to respect American neutral rights. In December 1807 Congress passed the Embargo Act.

The president had seriously miscalculated. France did not depend on American trade and so managed well enough, while British ships quickly took over the carrying trade as American vessels lay idle. Under the embargo, American exports plunged from $108 million in 1807 to a mere $22 million a year later; simultaneously, imports fell from $138 million to less than $57 million. As the center of American shipping, New England port cities were hurt the most and protested the loudest.

More disturbing, American merchants and shippers resorted to smuggling and open defiance of the law, outdoing one another in devising ways to circumvent the regulations. Congress passed a series of supplementary laws to close loopholes, and the administration resorted to increasingly harsh enforcement procedures that could be justified only by a loose reading of the Constitution. Jefferson stubbornly refused to admit his mistake, but during his last months in office he simply gave up trying to enforce the act.

Madison and the Young Republicans

Following the example set by Washington, Jefferson did not seek a third term. A caucus of Republican members of Congress selected James Madison, Jefferson's secretary of state and close political collaborator, to run against Federalist Charles Cotesworth Pinckney. Influenced by younger members, who recognized the necessity of party organization and appeals for popular support, the Federalists mounted an energetic campaign, yet in the end Madison triumphed easily. Still, Pinckney swept all of New England, where feeling against the embargo was highest, and his party gained 24 seats in Congress. To younger Federalists, who advocated accommodation to the prevailing political attitudes and techniques, the party seemed on the verge of a revival.

Few men have assumed the presidency with more experience than James Madison. A leading nationalist in the 1780s, the father of the Constitution, a key floor leader in Congress, the founder of the Republican party, Jefferson's secretary of state and closest adviser, Madison had spent over a quarter of a century in public life. Yet his tenure as president proved disappointing, in large degree because of his character. Few had maneuvered more adeptly in the House or performed more loyally in the cabinet. But Madison lacked the force of leadership and the inner strength to impose his will on less capable men. Slight and frail-looking, he suffered from periodic seizures and was terrified that he was an epileptic. (It is not clear from what disease, if any, the seizures stemmed.) His weak voice, lack of personal charm, and failure to appeal to women scarred him further. He married his vivacious wife, Dolley, late in life, only to have his inadequacy heightened when the union produced no children. Madison compensated by pursuing intellectual achievement with a furious intensity, but his brilliant accomplishments never overcame his sense of inferiority.

With a president reluctant to fight for what he wanted, leadership passed from the executive branch to Congress. In the process, the Republican party, which had begun to fragment under Jefferson, became more factionalized. In 1810, of the 142 members of the House of Representatives 63 were swept out of office. They were replaced by a new generation of Republicans, led by the adroit and magnetic 34-year-old Henry Clay of Kentucky, who gained the rare distinction of being elected Speaker in his first term. These younger Republicans were much more nationalistic than the generation led by Jefferson and Madison. They sought an ambitious program of economic development and were aggressive expansionists, especially those from frontier districts. Their feisty willingness to go to war earned them the name of War Hawks. Though they numbered fewer than 30 in Congress, they quickly became the driving force in the Republican party.

The Decision for War

During Jefferson's final week in office in early 1809, Congress had repealed the Embargo Act, replacing it with the more moderate Non-Intercourse Act. Hoping to induce the two great powers to respect neutral rights, the new act reopened trade with all nations except Britain and France; it authorized the president to resume trade with either nation that lifted its trade restrictions. In 1810, Congress passed an even more poorly thought-out piece of legislation, Macon's Bill Number 2, introduced by Nathaniel Macon of North Carolina. It authorized trade with France and England, but decreed that if one of the two belligerents agreed to stop interfering with American shipping, trade with the other would be prohibited.

In this situation, Napoleon cleverly outmaneuvered the British by announcing that he would not enforce his Continental System. Madison eagerly took the French emperor at his word and reimposed a ban on trade with England. It soon became clear that Napoleon had no intention of lifting restrictions, and French raiders continued to seize American ships. But Madison, who had boxed himself into a corner, refused to rescind his order unless the British revoked the Orders in Council. In the disputes that followed, American anger focused on the British, who seized many more ships than the French and continued to impress American sailors. Westerners also accused the British of stirring up hostility among the Indian tribes.

Jefferson's and Madison's policies had a cumulative effect. With the Continent closed to British goods and with exports to the United States cut by some 80 percent, hard times fell on British merchants. As the depression in England deepened, pressure mounted for the government to modify its policy. Finally, on June 16, 1812, the British ministry suspended the Orders in Council. But it was too late. Two days earlier, unaware of the impending British decision, the United States had declared war on Britain.

Angered by the continued British violations of American neutrality and pressed by the War Hawks to defend American honor, Madison on June 1 asked for a declaration of war. The vote for war was 79 to 49 in the House and 19 to 13 in the Senate; to a large extent, the division followed party lines, with every Federalist voting against war. As the representatives of commercial interests, particularly in New England, Federalists were convinced that war would ruin American commerce; they also still identified with Britain as the champion of order and conservatism. The handful of Republicans who joined the Federalists represented coastal districts, which were most vulnerable to the Royal Navy.

Clearly, the vote for war could not be explained as a matter of outraged Americans protecting neutral rights. The coastal areas, which were most affected,

Jefferson in rags because of the Embargo Act.

preferred trade over high principle, while members of Congress from the South and the West, regions that had a less direct interest in the issue, clamored most strongly for war. The War Hawks were led by Henry Clay of Kentucky, John C. Calhoun of South Carolina, Felix Grundy of Tennessee, and Peter Porter of western New York. Their constituents were consumed with a desire to seize additional territory in Canada or in Florida (which was owned by Britain's ally Spain) and were outraged by British intrigues with the Indians along the frontier.

Overriding all these considerations was the conviction that Britain had never accepted the verdict of the American Revolution. American independence, the War Hawks were convinced, hung in the balance. A war against Great Britain would destroy both the internal and external enemies of republicanism by forcing the British to respect American rights and by strengthening the Republican party at home against its domestic foes. For insecure Americans, hungering for acceptance in the community of nations, nothing rankled more than being treated by the British as colonials. John Quincy Adams expressed this point of view when he declared: "In this question something besides dollars and cents is concerned and no alternative [is] left but war or the abandonment of our rights as an independent nation."

National Unpreparedness

With Britain preoccupied by Napoleon, the War Hawks expected that the United States would win an easy victory. The British fleet certainly posed no threat to the interior of the country. The conquest of Canada, Jefferson asserted, was simply a matter of marching.

In truth, the United States was totally unprepared for war. While a handful of frigates like the U.S.S. *Constitution* (known affectionately as *Old Ironsides*) fought commendably in individual actions, collectively they were woefully outnumbered. Against the world's most powerful navy, Jefferson's vaunted gunboats could do nothing to lift the British blockade of the American coast, which bottled up the country's merchant marine and most of its navy. But the Great Lakes, which were inaccessible to the Royal Navy, held the key to the naval war, and when hostilities began neither side had an advantage on these waters. The American army included only a few thousand men, led largely by inexperienced junior officers or Revolutionary War veterans well past their prime. The militia numbered an additional 690,000, but the best units were in disaffected New England. When Congress moved to increase the size of the army to 75,000, even the most hawkish states failed to meet their quotas. Congress was also reluctant to levy taxes to finance the war.

Full of hope, the American army launched a three-pronged invasion of Canada from Detroit in the West, Niagara in western New York, and Lake Champlain along the New York–Canada border. In the West, the timid General William Hull marched only a few miles into Canada before suddenly returning to Detroit, where he surrendered to the British without firing a shot. The invasions from New York also proved a fiasco when militia units refused to leave the state and cross into Canada. American forces were defeated at Niagara, and the march on Montreal from Plattsburgh also had to be abandoned.

American forces fared better in 1813, as both sides raced to build a navy on the strategically located Lake Erie. Led by Commander Oliver Hazard Perry, the Americans prevailed in the decisive battle at Put-in-Bay. Fighting between the

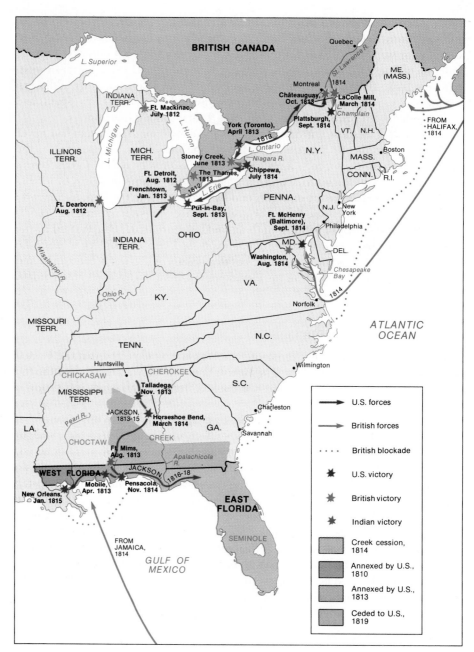

THE WAR OF 1812

After the American victory on Lake Erie and the defeat of the western Indians at the Battle of the Thames, the British adopted a three-pronged strategy to invade the United States, culminating with an attempt on New Orleans. But they met their match in Andrew Jackson, whose troops marched to New Orleans after fighting a series of battles against the Creeks and forcing them to cede a massive tract of land.

two squadrons was fierce, and at one point Perry transferred to another ship to continue the battle after his flagship was knocked out of commission. This victory gave the United States control of Lake Erie and greatly strengthened the American position in the Northwest.

"A Chance Such as Will Never Occur Again"

While the United States struggled to rally its forces, Tecumseh saw the need for the Indians to drive Americans out of the western territories. When a number of chiefs spoke in favor of siding with the Americans against the British, Tecumseh retorted, "Here is a chance . . . such as will never occur again—for us Indians of North America to form ourselves into one great combination." Joining up with the British, Tecumseh traveled south in the fall to talk again with his Creek allies. To coordinate a concerted Indian offensive for the following summer, he left a bundle of red sticks with eager Creek soldiers. They were to remove one stick each day from the bundle and attack when the sticks had run out.

A number of the older Creeks were more acculturated and preferred an American alliance. But about 2000 younger "Red Stick" Creeks launched a series of attacks, culminating with the destruction of Fort Mims along the Alabama River in August 1813. Andrew Jackson, the major general of the Tennessee militia, summoned 2000 volunteers and set out after the Creeks. Once again, the Indians' lack of unity was a serious handicap. Warriors from the Cherokee, Choctaw, and Chickasaw tribes, who were the Creeks' traditional enemies, joined Jackson's army. At the Battle of Horseshoe Bend in March 1814, these allied forces soundly defeated the Red Sticks. Jackson promptly dictated a peace treaty under which the Creeks ceded 22 million acres of land in the Mississippi Territory. They and the other southern tribes still retained significant landholdings, but Indian military power had been broken in the Southwest.

Farther north, Perry's victory on Lake Erie meant trouble for Tecumseh. With his supply lines cut, British General Henry Proctor abandoned the area around Detroit and retreated north. American forces under General William Henry Harrison pursued, and in October they defeated the British and their Indian allies at the Battle of the Thames. In the midst of heavy fighting Tecumseh was slain—and with him died any hope of a pan-Indian movement. In the short time of his power, he could not overcome the divisions and suspicions among tribes, especially in the South, where the forces of acculturation had taken stronger hold.

The British Invasion

As long as the war against Napoleon continued, the British were unwilling to divert army units to North America. But in 1814 Napoleon was at last defeated. Free to concentrate on the war in America, the British devised a coordinated strategy to invade the United States in the northern, central, and southern parts of the country. The main army headed south from Montreal but was checked when Captain Thomas Macdonough destroyed the British fleet on Lake Champlain.

In the meantime, a smaller British force landed in Maryland, marched on Washington, burned a number of public buildings, including the capitol and the president's home, and withdrew. To cover the scars of this destruction, the executive mansion was painted with whitewash and became known as the White House. The burning of the capital was a humiliating event (President Madison and his wife

During the Battle of New Orleans, American troops under Jackson entrenched behind breastworks, while their artillery raked the advancing British forces with deadly fire. The ladders needed to scale the American works quickly became entangled in the disorganized British assault. The portrait of Jackson (right) was done shortly after the battle.

Dolley were abruptly forced to flee, leaving their dinner to be eaten by the British), but the defeat had little military significance. The main objective of the British forces was Baltimore, where for 25 hours their fleet bombarded Fort McHenry in the city's harbor. Francis Scott Key, an American detained aboard a British ship, saw "the rockets' red glare, the bombs bursting in air"—and, at dawn, the American flag still flying above Fort McHenry. He hurriedly penned the verses of "The Star Spangled Banner," which was eventually adopted as the national anthem. The British abandoned their attempt to capture Baltimore.

The third British target was New Orleans, where a formidable force of 7500 British troops, mostly veterans fresh from the European theater, faced a motley collection of American regulars, western frontiersmen from Kentucky and Tennessee, citizens of the city, including several companies of free African-Americans, Choctaws, and—for an added dash of color—a group of pirates. The Americans were commanded by Major General Andrew Jackson, who had crushed the Red Stick Creeks. Not satisfied with defeating the Creeks, Jackson had invaded Spanish Florida contrary to his orders and occupied Pensacola and Mobile, solidifying American control of all of West Florida, over which the United States now assumed jurisdiction.

Taking charge of the defense of New Orleans, Jackson deployed his forces on a carefully chosen site five miles below the city. Protecting his flanks were the Mississippi and a swamp; in front lay an open field over which the enemy would have to advance. The Americans constructed a set of breastworks behind a dry canal bed and dug in. When the British attacked on January 8, 1815, the ladders needed to scale the American earthworks were at the rear rather than in front of the attacking column. When this mix-up was discovered, the attacking troops halted within range of the American guns while those to the back attempted to bring the ladders forward. In the prevailing confusion, Jackson's artillery raked the enemy with deadly fire, and the British finally broke and ran. In the two-hour battle, British losses exceeded 2000 men, of whom 291 were killed and over 1200 wounded (another 500 were missing); Jackson lost only 21: 8 killed and 13 wounded. It was a stunning victory, which made the general an overnight hero. As the victor over hardened British veterans who themselves had vanquished Napoleon, Jackson enabled Americans to forget the war's many failures and to boast that once again the United States had humbled the world's greatest military power.

The Hartford Convention

In December 1814, while Jackson was organizing the defense of New Orleans, New England Federalists met in Hartford to map strategy against the war. Yankee merchants, contemptuous of "Mr. Madison's War," had continued to trade with the enemy during the war, while New England governors declined to make available the state militias. Finally the Massachusetts legislature called for a convention to discuss New England's grievances. Connecticut and Rhode Island sent delegates, but only three counties in New Hampshire and one in Vermont were represented.

The delegates endorsed a series of proposed amendments to the Constitution which showed their displeasure with the government's economic policies. Embargoes could be enforced for no more than 60 days; Congress would not be permitted to restrict foreign trade or declare war without a two-thirds vote. The delegates indicated their resentment of southern power by proposing the abolition of the three-fifths clause of the Constitution, which provided that five slaves would count as three free persons in determining congressional representation, a measure that boosted southern representation in Congress. To limit the power of the West, they proposed that Congress require a two-thirds vote to admit new states. Although a few extremists thought secession from the Union might be necessary, the moderates in control at Hartford merely sent a committee to Washington to present the convention's demands. To their dismay, it arrived in the capital just as news of Andrew Jackson's victory was being trumpeted on the streets. The burst of national pride badly undercut the Hartford Convention's position, as did a second piece of news from across the Atlantic: American negotiators in Ghent, Belgium, had signed a treaty ending the war. Hostilities had ceased, technically, on Christmas Eve 1814, two weeks before the Battle of New Orleans.

Like the war itself, the Treaty of Ghent accomplished little of significance. Impressment, neutral rights, the boundary between the United States and Canada, American trade and fishing rights—all these issues were either ignored or referred to future commissions for settlement. As John Quincy Adams succinctly commented, "Nothing was adjusted, nothing was settled—nothing in substance but an indefinite suspension of hostilities was agreed to." Both sides were simply relieved to end the conflict.

AMERICA TURNS INWARD

In the wake of the war's end came an outburst of American nationalism—one that could not have flowered in 1776, when "these United States" had first fought Britain for independence. Those states had united before their citizens could develop a strong sense of national identity. But the War of 1812, capped by Jackson's victory, strengthened Americans' confidence in their country's destiny.

The upsurge in nationalism sounded the death knell of the Federalist party. The resistance of New England Federalists to the embargo and their disloyalty during the war had already weakened the party elsewhere, and the Hartford Convention tainted it with disunion and treason. Although it had made its best showing in years at the outbreak of the war (Madison had been reelected in 1812 by a margin of only 128 electoral votes to 89), the party's support collapsed in the 1816 election. Madison's secretary of state, James Monroe, handily defeated Federalist Rufus King of New York. In 1820 Monroe ran for reelection unopposed. The Federalists' strength in the House likewise collapsed; by 1818 they could count only 27 members of the House, compared to 156 Republicans.

Monroe's Presidency

The spirit of postwar harmony produced the so-called Era of Good Feelings, presided over by James Monroe, the last president of the Virginia dynasty and of the revolutionary generation. Monroe, like Jefferson before him, hoped to eliminate political parties, which he considered unnecessary in a free government. Like Washington, he thought of himself as the head of the nation rather than of a party.

Monroe's greatest achievements were diplomatic, accomplished largely by his astute secretary of state, John Quincy Adams. Adams, the son of President John Adams, already had compiled a distinguished diplomatic record, for while often harsh and overbearing, he was nevertheless a skillful negotiator. Adams thought of the Republic in continental terms; he was intent on promoting expansion to the Pacific, which he considered the avenue of trade with the Orient. Such a vision required dealing with Spain, which had never recognized the legality of the Louisiana Purchase. In addition, between 1810 and 1813 the United States had occupied and unilaterally annexed Spanish West Florida.

Spain, however, was preoccupied with events farther south in the Americas. In the first quarter of the nineteenth century, its colonies one after another had revolted and established themselves as independent nations. These revolutions increased the pressure on the Spanish minister to America, Luis de Onís, to come to terms with the United States. Furthermore, in 1818 Jackson marched into East Florida and captured several Spanish forts. Jackson had exceeded his instructions, but Adams understood well enough the additional pressure this aggression put on Onís and refused to disavow it.

Fearful that the United States might next invade Texas or other Spanish territory, Spain agreed to the Transcontinental, or Adams–Onís Treaty in February 1819. Its terms set the boundary between American and Spanish territory all the way to the Pacific. Spain not only relinquished its claims to the Pacific Northwest, but also ceded Florida in exchange for the U.S. government assuming $5 million in claims against Spain by American citizens. In exchange for the line to the Pacific, the United States abandoned its contention that Texas was part of the Louisiana Purchase. Adams had wanted Texas, but he wanted the line to the Pacific even more, understanding the strategic commitment to expanding across the continent. "The acknowledgement of a definite line of boundary to the South Sea [Pacific] forms a great epoch in our history," he confided to his diary.

The Monroe Doctrine

The United States came to terms not only with Spain, but, even more important, with Great Britain as well. Following the War of 1812, the British abandoned their

Thomas Sully's portrait of John Quincy Adams (1825) includes an open map symbolizing his significant contribution to national expansion during his eight years as secretary of state.

connections with the western Indian tribes and no longer attempted to block American expansion to the Rocky Mountains. In a growing spirit of cooperation, the two countries signed a commercial treaty that ended British discrimination against American trade, a sore point ever since the Revolution. The Rush–Bagot Agreement in 1817 limited naval forces on the Great Lakes and on Lake Champlain. In 1818 the countries agreed to the 49th parallel as the northern boundary of the Louisiana Purchase and also to joint control of the Oregon Territory for 10 years, subject to renewal.

In this atmosphere of goodwill, George Canning, the British foreign secretary, proposed in August 1823 that the United States and Britain issue a joint statement that would keep European powers from meddling in Latin America. Spain was clearly too weak to reestablish control of its former colonies, but Britain feared that Russia, Austria, and Prussia, which had joined together in the Holy Alliance, or France might intervene on Spain's behalf. Canning proposed that the United States and Britain declare that neither sought to expand in Latin America and that they opposed the transfer of Spain's colonies to any foreign power.

Monroe was inclined to accept the British offer, and both Jefferson and Madison urged him to do so. But John Quincy Adams forcefully argued that the United States should not make any pledge against acquiring territory in the future, particularly in Texas, Mexico, and the Caribbean, where Americans thought Cuba might come under its sway. Adams also worried that in any joint statement the United States would appear to be merely a junior partner, coming along "as a cock-boat in the wake of a British man-of-war." In addition, Adams was concerned over Russia's steady advance down the west coast of North America. Monroe finally agreed to make an independent statement.

He included it in his annual message to Congress, on December 2, 1823. Monroe reaffirmed that the United States would not intervene in European affairs, a principle of American foreign policy since Washington's Farewell Address. And he also announced that the United States would not interfere with already established European colonies in the Western Hemisphere. But any intervention, he warned, in the new republics of Latin America would be considered a hostile act: "The American continents . . . are henceforth not to be considered as subjects for future colonization by any European powers." The essence of this policy, which was Adams' handiwork, was the concept of two worlds, one old and one new, each refraining from interfering in the other's affairs.

Canning, upon hearing of Monroe's message, was irked: it was the British fleet, not any presidential declaration, that blocked European intervention in Latin America. American public opinion hailed Monroe's statement and then promptly forgot it. Only years later would it be referred to as the Monroe Doctrine. Still, it represented the culmination of the American quest since 1776 for independence and sovereignty. The very fact that Britain had proposed a joint declaration demonstrated that, at last, the parent nation recognized its offspring as a legitimate and sovereign nation. Monroe's declaration underlined that the United States would not act in world affairs as a satellite of Britain. Ever since the adoption of the Constitution, the issue of independence had been at the center of American politics: in Hamilton's quarrel with Jefferson over whether to favor Britain or France, in the response to the French Revolution, in the debate over the embargo, and finally in 1812 with the second war for American independence.

The End of an Era

The growing reconciliation with Great Britain ended the external threat to the Republic. Isolated from Europe and protected by the British fleet, the United States was free to turn its attention inward, to concentrate on expanding across the vast continent and on developing its resources. Yet how would the nation be developed? Jefferson had dreamed of an "empire of liberty," delighting in western expansion because it would preserve a nation of small farmers, like those Crève-coeur had written about during the 1780s. Indeed, Jefferson seemed to have achieved his political goal of a one-party system, for by 1820 the Federalist party had dwindled to insignificance. "Our government is now so firmly on it's republican tack, that it will not be easily monarchized by forms," he assured Lafayette.

Yet the younger, more nationalistic Republicans were speaking of internal improvements, protective tariffs to help foster American industries, better roads and canals to link farmers with towns, cities, and wider markets. The tone of these new Republicans was not aristocratic, like the Federalists of old, but their dream of a national, commercial republic resembled Franklin's and Hamilton's more than Jefferson's. The new young westerners were aggressive: they looked to profit from speculation in land, from the increasing market for cotton, from the new methods of industrial manufacturing. If these people represented the rising wave across America, what would be the fate of Crèvecoeur's semisubsistence farm communities? The answer was not yet clear.

In one of those remarkable coincidences that Americans hailed as a sign of Providence's favor, Thomas Jefferson and John Adams died within hours of each other on July 4, 1826, the fiftieth anniversary of the adoption of the Declaration of Independence. The lives of these two giants of the Revolution—Jefferson, the ever-hopeful, self-styled revolutionary Virginia gentleman, and Adams, the prickly, independent Federalist of Braintree—intertwined with one another in the fabric of the nation's development. Partners in the struggle to secure American independence, they had become bitterly estranged in the heated party battles of the 1790s and resumed a warm friendship only after their public careers had drawn to a close. Their reconciliation was in tune with the rise of American nationalism, but their time was past. Leadership belonged now to a new generation of Americans who confronted different problems and challenges. Revolutionary America had passed from the scene. The dawn of a new nation was at hand.

SIGNIFICANT EVENTS

1790s	Second Great Awakening begins
1801	Adams' "midnight" appointments; Marshall becomes chief justice; Jefferson inaugurated in Washington; Cane Ridge revival
1802	Judiciary Act of 1801 repealed
1803	*Marbury v. Madison*; Louisiana Purchase; war resumes between Great Britain and France
1804–1806	Lewis and Clark expedition
1805	Prophet's revivals begin
1806	Non-Importation Act
1807	*Chesapeake* affair; Embargo Act passed
1808	Madison elected president
1809	Non-Intercourse Act passed; Tecumseh's confederacy organized
1810	Macon's Bill Number 2; *Fletcher v. Peck*
1810–1813	West Florida annexed
1811	Battle of Tippecanoe
1812	War declared against Great Britain
1813	Battle of Lake Erie; Tecumseh killed
1813–1814	Creek War
1814	Washington burned; Hartford Convention; Treaty of Ghent
1815	Battle of New Orleans
1816	*Martin v. Hunter's Lessee*; Monroe elected president
1817	Rush–Bagot Agreement
1818	United States–Canada boundary fixed to the Rockies; Joint occupation of Oregon
1819	Transcontinental Treaty; United States acquires Florida
1819–1823	Panic and depression
1820	Monroe reelected
1823	Monroe Doctrine

PART 3

THE REPUBLIC
TRANSFORMED AND
TESTED

Two remarkable transformations began sweeping the world in the late eighteenth century; so wrenching and far-reaching were these changes that both have been called revolutions. The first was a cascade of political revolts that led to increased democratic participation in the governing of many nation-states. The other was the application of machine labor and technological innovation to agricultural and commercial economies known as the industrial revolution.

Proclaiming the values of liberty and equality, Americans in 1776 led the way in what would become a succession of democratic revolutions. As we have seen, the bold act of revolution did not in itself solve the question of how regional and economic antagonisms could be adjusted peacefully in the new nation-state. Not until the Republicans succeeded the Federalists was a tradition of peaceful political change established within the framework of the Constitution. And not until a new generation of leaders arrived on the scene during the second war for independence did a national consciousness fully bloom.

These were notable milestones, but internationally, the center of revolutionary attention had shifted in 1789 to France. There, as in America, the ideals of the Enlightenment played a part in justifying democratic revolution; and French liberals like the Marquis de Lafayette were also inspired by the example of the United States. Still, the crowds marching through the streets of Paris adopted a more radical and violent stance, reflecting the onerous burdens that the feudal system exacted from peasants and workers as well as other pressures affecting

France. The worldwide rise in population of the previous half-century had left the French capital overcrowded, underfed, and thoroughly unruly—and the French citizenry that much more willing to arm themselves and march on the Bastille, on the palace at Versailles, against any perceived enemies of the Revolution. The countryside, too, suffering from a series of bad harvests, rose up in protest, sometimes brutally. Paradoxically, the population pressure that had pushed matters to a crisis was relieved as the Revolution gave way to the emperor Napoleon, whose wars of conquest killed almost as many French soldiers as the nation's natural in-

334

crease was producing. When Napoleon was at last defeated at the Battle of Waterloo (1815), Louis XVIII reestablished the French monarchy.

In Latin America, however, movements of democracy and nationalism spread. Just as England had attempted to pay for its colonial defenses with additional revenue from its colonies, so the Spanish Crown raised taxes in the Americas, with predictable results. The Creole class—Spanish who had been born in America—resented the preferential treatment given the *peninsulares*—colonial residents born in Spain—who often held a monopoly on administrative positions. Although the Spanish colonies lacked the tradition of representative assemblies found in North America, the writings of Jefferson and Thomas Paine circulated, as did translations of the French *Declaration of the Rights of Man.* From 1808 to 1821 Spain's American provinces declared their independence one by one. Democracy did not always root itself in the aftermath of these revolutions, but democratic ideology remained a powerful social catalyst.

The industrial revolution was less violent but no less dramatic in its effects. It began in Great Britain, where an increasing proportion of that nation's burgeoning population had begun to develop a more diversified commercial economy. A string of canal-building projects improved its transportation network toward the end of the eighteenth century, just as a similar movement would develop in the 1820s and 1830s in the United States. In Britain, too, James Watt in 1769 invented an engine that harnessed the power of steam, and innovations in textile production led to the use of water and later steam power to drive mechanical looms. As steam power was applied to transportation, both in ships and rail locomotives, the reach of commercial markets widened. Regular shipping made it possible to bring Egyptian cotton from Alexandria to factories in British Manchester and American cotton from the Arkansas Red River country to New England. Just as  skilled workers like Samuel Slater smuggled the new technology out of England to the United States, others like William Cockerill set up factories in Europe, as the capabilities of steam and industrial manufacturing spread to the continent.

In many ways the narrative of the young American republic is the story of how one nation worked out the implications of these twin revolutions, industrial and democratic. It was only after the War of 1812 that a market economy began rapidly to transform the agricultural practices of Crèvecoeur's subsistence America. Urban areas of the North became more diversified and industrial, as young women took jobs in textile mills and young men labored at flour mills processing grain to be shipped east. The impact of industry on the North is probably clear enough in the popular imagination; what is sometimes less appreciated is how the industrial revolution transformed the rural South. Cotton would never have become king there without the demand for it created by textile factories or without the ability to "gin" the seeds out of cotton by Eli Whitney's invention. (The "gin" in *cotton gin*, after all, is a clipped southern pronunciation of the word "engine.") Nor could cotton production have flourished without industrial advances in transportation, which allowed raw materials and factory goods to be shipped worldwide.

As the industrial and democratic revolutions developed side by side, the United States had to resolve the conflicts that the two presented each other. On the one hand, the advances in industry and commerce made it possible for resourceful entrepreneurs to reap profits on a scale that Americans of Crèvecoeur's day could never have imagined. They also created a labor force more impoverished than most Americans had been. The industrial revolution, in other words, made possible a society in which Americans could become both richer and poorer than they had ever been before—a society more stratified and more unequal. At the same time, the democratic revolution spreading across America was calling for greater equality among all citizens. This potential contradiction was one Americans wrestled with throughout the era.

Furthermore, although the industrial revolution transformed both the North and the South, it transformed them in conflicting ways. Although the economies of the two regions depended on each other, slavery came increasingly to be the focus of disputes between them. The industrial revolution's demand for cotton increased both southern profits and a demand for slave labor. Yet the spread of democratic ideology worldwide was creating increased pressure to abolish slavery everywhere. In France, the revolutionary government struck it down in 1794; the British empire outlawed it in 1833, about the time that American abolitionists, influenced by their British friends, became more active in opposing it. In eastern Europe, the near-slavery of feudal serfdom was being eliminated as well: in 1848 within the Hapsburg empire; in 1861 in Russia; in 1864 in Romania.

If the purpose of a democratic republic is to resolve conflicts among its members in a nonviolent manner, then in 1860 the American republic failed. It took four years of bitter fighting to reconcile the twin paths of democracy and industrial development. Given the massive size of the territory involved in the dispute and the different ways in which industry affected the North and South, it is perhaps not surprising that a union so diverse did not hold without the force of arms. That the separation was not final—that in the end, reunion emerged out of conflict—is perhaps one reason why the tale is so gripping.

CHRONOLOGY

AMERICAN EVENT	YEAR		GLOBAL EVENT
Stamp Act Congress	1765		Spinning jenny invented
	1769		Steam engine invented
American Revolution begins	1775		
	1789	WASHINGTON	French Revolution begins
First American textile mill	1790		
Whitney invents cotton gin	1793		
Slave revolt in Haiti	1794		France abolishes slavery
	1797	ADAMS	
	1801	JEFFERSON	
Wars for independence in Latin America	1804–1824		
	1809	MADISON	
Cotton trade is the major expansive force in the American economy	1815–1839		
	1817	MONROE	
Erie Canal completed	1825	ADAMS	First rail line in England
Mexico abolishes slavery	1829	JACKSON	
Total U.S. rail mileage, 13 miles	1830		Revolutionary movements in Europe
Indians removed from Southwest	1830–1838		
American Anti-Slavery Society founded	1833		Slavery abolished within British empire
McCormick patents mechanical reaper	1834		
	1837	VAN BUREN	
Total U.S. rail and canal mileage, 3300 miles each	1840		
	1841	HARRISON TYLER	
	1845	POLK	Irish potato famine begins
Outbreak of Mexican War	1846		Repeal of British Corn Laws
Immigration from Europe rises			
Seneca Falls convention for women's rights	1848		Serfdom abolished within Hapsburg empire Revolutions in Europe
	1849	TAYLOR	
Total U.S. rail mileage, 8900 miles	1850	FILLMORE	Total rail mileage: Britain, 15,900; Germany, 9500; France, 4700
	1853	PIERCE	
Kansas–Nebraska Act; Thoreau's *Walden* published	1854		Crimean War begins
	1857	BUCHANAN	
	1860		Italy unified
Civil War begins	1861	LINCOLN	Serfdom abolished in Russia
Emancipation Proclamation	1863		
Reconstruction begins	1865	JOHNSON	
	1868		Meiji Restoration in Japan
	1869	GRANT	
	1871		Germany unified
End of Reconstruction	1877	HAYES	

10

The Opening of America

I n the years before the Civil War, the name of Chauncey Jerome could be found traced in neat, sharp letters in a thousand different places across the globe: everywhere from the fireplace mantels of plantation nabobs to the log huts of Illinois prairie farmers, the residences of English greengrocers, and even in Chinese hongs, the trading houses along the banks of the Pearl River at Canton. For Chauncey Jerome was a New England clockmaker, whose clever, inexpensive, and addictive machines had conquered the markets of the world.

Truly a self-made man, Jerome was born in 1793 in Canaan, Connecticut. His father was a blacksmith and wrought-iron maker. After just three winters of schooling he went to work at the age of nine, first in his father's smithy and then as an apprentice to a house carpenter. When the carpentry business turned slack during the winter months, he worked making dials and cases for clocks. Duty called during the War of 1812, but when peace came, Jerome tried several jobs before buying some clock movements and wood veneers and setting up a clock-making business. For several years he eked out a living peddling his products from farmhouse to farmhouse.

Then in 1824 Jerome's career took off. The epitome of the Yankee mechanic, he designed a "very showy" bronze looking-glass clock, whose models sold as fast as he could manufacture them. Between 1827 and 1837 his factory produced more clocks than any other in the country. But when the Panic of 1837 struck, Jerome's business dropped off so sharply that he had to scramble to avoid ruin.

Looking for a new opportunity, he set out to produce an inexpensive brass "one-day" clock—so called because its winding mechanism kept it running that long. Traditionally, only the movements of expensive eight-day clocks had been fashioned from brass. The wood in one-day clocks was cheaper, but it had to be seasoned for an entire year and the clock's wheels and teeth had to be painstakingly cut by hand. Furthermore, wooden clocks could not be exported overseas because the humidity on board ship swelled the wood and ruined them. Jerome's new brass version proved more accurate than earlier types and cheaper to boot. Costs came down further when he began to use interchangeable parts and combined his operations for making cases and movements within a single factory in New Haven, Connecticut. By systematically organizing the production process, Jerome brought the price of a good clock within the reach of ordinary people. So popular were the new models that his hapless competitors began attaching Jerome labels to their own inferior imitations.

"There are very many young ladies at work in the factories that have given up milinary dressmaking and school-keeping for to work in the mill," wrote Malenda Edwards in 1839. This young woman was one of them.

Disaster struck again in 1855, when Jerome went into partnership with several unreliable associates. Within a few years, his business faltered, then failed. At the age of 62, the once-prominent Chauncey Jerome found himself working again in a clock factory as an ordinary mechanic. He lived his last years in poverty.

Jerome rose higher than most Americans of his generation, and he fell further. Yet his fellow citizens shared his dreams of wealth and success and at the same time were haunted by the fear—so vividly illustrated in his own life—of losing everything. Not only material comforts vanished; so did respect. "One of the most trying things to me now," he confessed in his autobiography, "is to see how I am looked upon by the community since I lost my property. I never was any better when I owned it than I am now, and never behaved any better. But how different is the feeling towards you, when your neighbors can make nothing more out of you. . . . You are passed by without notice."

Chauncey Jerome's life spanned the transition from the old master–apprentice system of production to the beginnings of mechanization and the rise of the factory system. By 1850 the notion of independent American farmers subsisting primarily on what they themselves produced (Crèvecoeur's vision of the 1780s) had become a dream of the past. In its place stood a commercial republic, in which a full-blown national market encompassed most settled areas of the country.

The notion of the market is crucial here. Americans tied themselves to one another eagerly, even aggressively, through the mechanism of the free market. They sold cotton or wheat and bought manufactured cloth or brass one-day clocks. They sold pork, beef, or tobacco and purchased shoes or the new ladies' magazines. They mortgaged land and houses not merely to establish a family estate, but to speculate and profit. They relied, even in many rural villages, on cash and paper money instead of bartering for goods and services. In short, a market economy bound Americans to one another in increasingly complex ways. American life moved from less to more specialized forms of labor; from subsistence-oriented to more commercially oriented outlooks; from face-to-face local dealings to impersonal, distant transactions; from the mechanically simple to the technologically complex; and from less dense patterns of settlement to more complex arrangements in cities and towns. Such were the changes Chauncey Jerome witnessed—indeed, changes he helped to bring about himself, with his clocks that divided the working days of Americans into more disciplined, orderly segments.

As these changes swirled around him, Jerome sensed that somehow society had taken on a different tone—that the marketplace and its ethos had become dominant. "It is all money and business, business and money which make the man now-a-days," he complained. "Success is every thing, and it makes very little difference how, or what means he uses to obtain it." The United States, according to the foreign visitor Francis J. Grund, had become "one gigantic workshop, over the entrance of which there is the blazing inscription '*No admission here except on business.*'"

THE MARKET REVOLUTION

A truly national system of markets began to grow following the War of 1812 and was in full swing by the 1820s, when the United States entered a period of unprecedented economic expansion. As it grew, the economy became varied enough to sustain and even accelerate its growth. Before the war, it had been tied largely to international trade. The United States exported staples like cotton, wheat, tobacco, and timber; if the nations that bought these commodities suddenly stopped doing so, as happened during the European wars of the 1790s and again after 1803, the domestic economy suffered. Since so many Americans remained rural and primarily self-sufficient—as in the America idealized by Crèvecoeur—they could not absorb any increase in producer goods.

But the War of 1812 marked the turning point in the creation and expansion of a domestic market. First the embargo and then the war itself stimulated the growth of manufacturing, particularly in textiles. In 1808 the United States had 8000 spindles spinning cotton thread; by 1811 the number had risen to 80,000 and at the end of the war there were around 130,000—a greater than 15-fold increase in less than a decade. War had also bottled up capital in Europe, and when peace was restored this capital flowed into the United States, further stimulating growth. Finally, the war experience led the federal government to adopt policies designed to spur economic growth, particularly a protective tariff, the national bank, and aid for internal improvements.

The New Nationalism

In the aftermath of the war with Britain, leadership passed to a new generation of the Republic—younger men such as Henry Clay, John C. Calhoun, and John Quincy Adams, who were ardent nationalists eager to use the power of the federal government to promote the rapid development of the nation. Increasingly dominant within the Republican party, they were impatient with the old-fashioned ideas of Jefferson and Madison and advocated the "New Nationalism," a set of economic policies designed to foster the prosperity of all regions of the country and bind the nation more tightly together.

Even Madison saw the need for increased federal activity, especially given the problems the government experienced during the war. The national bank closed its doors in 1811, when its charter expired, and in its absence state bank notes had multiplied, and their variety and uncertain value had produced financial chaos. In his message to Congress in December 1815, Madison, who had led the fight against Hamilton's national bank in 1791, noted that the country had changed a great deal since the adoption of the Constitution, and that a national bank had become essential for the American economy. Congress responded by chartering the Second Bank of the United States for a period of 20 years. It had a capital of $35 million (compared to $10 million for Hamilton's first bank), which made it easily the largest and most powerful bank in the country.

The war had also highlighted the need for greater economic independence. Madison thus endorsed a mildly protective tariff to aid the fledgling American industries that had sprung up during the embargo and the war. The tariff of 1816 set an average duty of 20 percent on imports of woolen and cotton cloth, iron, sugar, and other items. Because duties raised the prices of imported goods, competing American products gained an advantage in the domestic market. The Middle Atlantic states and the West voted for the tariff by a large margin, while even Federalist New England, whose prosperity was closely tied to imports, lent the Republican measure moderate support. But in a portent of sectional tensions, many southern representatives opposed the tariff.

Madison also recommended that the government provide aid for internal improvements such as roads, canals, and bridges. The war had demonstrated how cumbersome it was to move troops or supplies overland. Madison, however, believed that a constitutional amendment was needed to permit federal funds to be used for local projects. To nationalists such as Clay and Calhoun, this proposal was one more example of Madison's outmoded ideas. Calhoun brushed aside Madison's constitutional scruples and championed the so-called Bonus Bill, under which the $1.5 million bonus the national bank paid the government for its charter was to be distributed to the states for internal improvements. The president vetoed the bill, but this represented only a temporary setback for the nationalists. Even Madison was willing to support projects broader in scope, and his successor, James Monroe, approved additional ones.

The Cotton Trade

The most important cause of American economic development after 1815 was the growth of the cotton trade. By the end of the eighteenth century, southern planters had discovered that cotton would grow in the lower part of the South. At first, however, the only profitable type of cotton was the long-fibered, silky variety that flourished in a narrow band along the South Carolina and Georgia coast and on the islands offshore. A short-fibered variety grew upland, but it contained sticky green seeds that could not be easily separated from the lint by hand. The necessary technological breakthrough occurred in 1793, when Eli Whitney, a Connecticut Yankee working as a tutor on a Georgia plantation, invented a simple but ingenious device that removed seeds from the cotton.

The impact of the cotton gin was dramatic. Whereas before, a slave could clean only a pound of cotton a day by hand, with a gin one person could clean 50 pounds. The heavy demand for cotton by British textile mills sent prices on the world market soaring. By 1840 the South produced over 60 percent of the world supply, which accounted for almost two-thirds of all American exports.

The cotton trade was the major expansive force in the economy until 1839—and not only in the South. Northern factories increasingly made money by turning raw cotton into cloth, while northern merchants reaped profits from shipping the cotton and then reshipping the textiles. Planters used the income they earned to purchase foodstuffs from the West and goods and services from the Northeast. After 1839 the cotton trade became less of an economic stimulus, but its explosive expansion in the critical earlier period enabled the country to sustain internal economic growth.

The Transportation Revolution

For a market economy to become truly national, a transportation network linking various parts of the nation was essential. The network was crucial not so much for moving people as it was for moving goods. (A market economy, after all, did not require a farmer to travel regularly to St. Louis or New York, but his grain had to get there efficiently and cheaply.) The economy had not become self-sustaining earlier partly because the only means of transporting goods cheaply was by water. Thus trade was limited largely to coastal and international markets, for even on rivers, bulky goods moved easily in only one direction—downstream.

Whitney's cotton gin.

All that changed, however, with the revolution in transportation. New areas were drawn quickly into the market, while the speed and cost required to move goods across land dropped dramatically. From 1825 to 1855—the span of a single generation—the cost of transportation on land fell 95 percent, while its speed increased fivefold.

The Canal Age

Canals attracted considerable investment capital, especially after the success of the wondrous Erie Canal. Built between 1818 and 1825, the Erie Canal stretched 364 miles from Albany on the Hudson River to Buffalo on Lake Erie. Its construction, the dream of Governor De Witt Clinton of New York, was an act of faith, for in 1816 the United States had only 100 miles of canals, none longer than 28 miles. Jefferson, hardly a man of limited vision, called the idea of such a canal "little short of madness."

For much of its distance the Erie Canal ran through forest, disease-ridden swamps, and unsettled wilderness. The canal's engineers, headed by Benjamin Wright, were largely self-taught, but they made up in ingenuity what they lacked in training. Improving on European tools, they devised a special scraper for excavating, a cable and screw that allowed one man to pull down even the largest trees, and a stump-puller that could remove up to 40 stumps a day. Along the route they discovered limestone, which made a superior cement that hardened under water. Still, no ingenuity could get around the grueling work of clearing trees when the route led straight through a swamp.

The Erie Canal promoted urban growth, economic development, and bustle along its route. Here boatmen guiding their craft past busy laborers on shore provide an indication of the commerce that quickly flourished on the waterway.

When finished in 1825, the canal was 40 feet wide and 4 feet deep; it had 83 locks with a combined ascent and descent of 675 feet and 18 aqueducts across various rivers. The one at Little Falls was 1184 feet long with a massive central arch 70 feet across. The project, which cost New York $7.5 million, paid for itself within a few years. Indeed, traffic was so heavy that it soon strained the Erie's capacity. Before its completion, shipping a ton of goods from Buffalo to New York City had cost over 19 cents a mile; with the canal in operation the cost dropped to less than 3 cents, and by 1860 it had fallen to less than a penny. Where its busy traffic passed, settlers flocked, and with them came commerce and new markets. Haphazardly constructed towns like Syracuse, Rochester, and Lockport sprang up and thrived by moving goods, serving markets, and creating new demand. Between 1820 and 1840 the number of people employed in manufacturing in the region rose 262 percent, while those engaged in commerce and navigation swelled by 1000 percent. "Everything in this bustling place appears to be in motion," wrote one English traveler about Rochester in 1827. "Here and there we saw great warehouses, without window sashes, but half-filled with goods, and furnished with hoisting cranes, ready to fish up the huge pyramids of flour barrels, bales, and boxes lying in the streets." And the steady flow of goods eastward gave New York City a dominant position in the scramble for control of western trade.

Indeed, New York's rivals such as Philadelphia and Baltimore were soon frantically trying to build their own canals to the West. Western states like Ohio and Indiana constructed canals to link interior regions with the Great Lakes. Wasted money and a number of foolish schemes brought several overextended state governments to the verge of bankruptcy, but the general attitude among citizens was that without cheap transportation and access to markets, farmers in the state could never prosper. The public's enthusiasm for canals increased support for government involvement in the economy. By 1840 the nation had completed over 3300 miles of canals—a length greater than the distance from New York City to Seattle—at a cost of about $125 million. Almost half of that amount came from state governments.

By 1850 the canal era was over. The depression of 1839 caused several states to halt or slow their construction, especially since many poorly planned canals lost money. Still, whether profitable or not, canals sharply reduced transportation costs and stimulated economic development in a broad belt along their routes.

Steamboats

Because of its vast expanse, the United States was particularly dependent on river transportation. But shipping goods downstream from Pittsburgh to New Orleans took 6 weeks, while the return trip required 17 weeks or more in keelboats pushed laboriously by hand against the current. Consequently, only the lightest and most valuable goods could be profitably shipped upstream. Steamboats, however, substantially reduced both the cost and time of river travel. A trip from New Orleans to Louisville dropped from 90 to 8 days, while upstream costs were cut by 90 percent.

John Fitch, an ingenious mechanic, had exhibited a working prototype of a steamship to the members of the Constitutional Convention in Philadelphia in 1787, but his work was ignored. Twenty years later Robert Fulton demonstrated the commercial possibilities of propelling a boat with steam when his ship, the *Clermont,* traveled from New York City to Albany on the Hudson River. But the

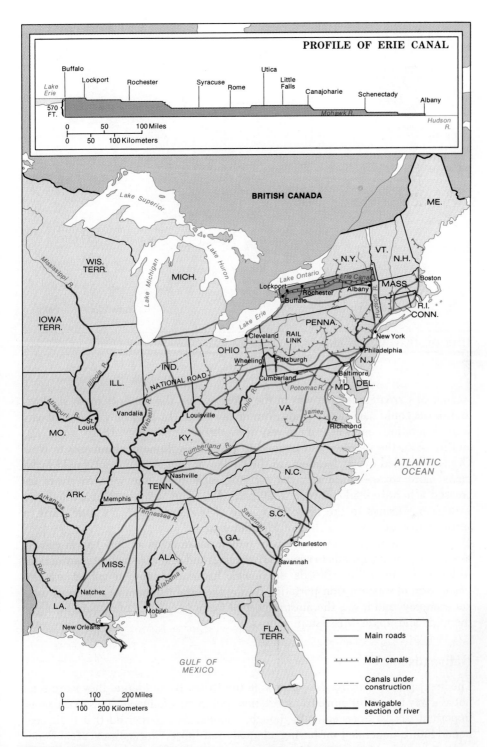

PROFILE OF ERIE CANAL

Buffalo
Lockport
Rochester
Syracuse
Rome
Utica
Little Falls
Canajoharie
Schenectady
Albany
Lake Erie
570 FT.
Mohawk R.
Hudson R.

0   50   100 Miles
0   50   100 Kilometers

BRITISH CANADA

ME.

Lake Superior

Lake Michigan

Lake Huron

WIS. TERR.

MICH.

N.Y.

VT.   N.H.

Lake Ontario
Lockport   Erie Canal
Rochester   Albany
Buffalo

MASS.   Boston

R.I.
CONN.

IOWA TERR.

Lake Erie

PENNA.

Cleveland   RAIL LINK

Hudson R.

New York

OHIO

Wheeling   Pittsburgh

Philadelphia

IND.

N.J.

ILL.

NATIONAL ROAD

Cumberland

Baltimore

MD.   DEL.

Potomac R.

Mississippi R.

Illinois R.

Ohio R.

VA.

James R.

Vandalia   Louisville

Richmond

Missouri R.
St. Louis

MO.

KY.

Cumberland R.

ATLANTIC OCEAN

Nashville

N.C.

ARK.

TENN.

Memphis

Tennessee R.

Savannah R.

S.C.

GA.

Charleston

MISS.

ALA.

Savannah

Red R.

Natchez

Alabama R.

LA.

Mobile

New Orleans

FLA. TERR.

Arkansas R.

GULF OF MEXICO

0   100   200 Miles
0   100   200 Kilometers

— Main roads

+++++ Main canals

----- Canals under construction

— Navigable section of river

THE TRANSPORTATION NETWORK OF A MARKET ECONOMY, 1840
Canals played their most important role in the Northeast, where they linked eastern cities to western rivers and the Great Lakes. On the Erie Canal, a set of locks raised and lowered boats in a series of steps along the route. Steamboats were most crucial in the extensive river systems of the South and the West.

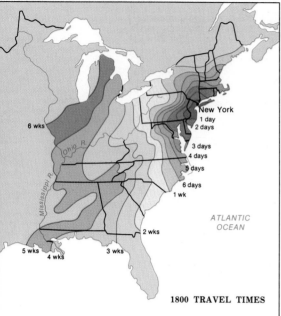

TIME OF TRAVEL, 1800 AND 1830

steamboat's greatest impact was in the West, where the flat-bottomed, shallow-draft boats could haul heavy loads even in low water. In 1817 only 17 steamboats were operating on western rivers; just three years later there were 69, and by 1855, the number had jumped to 727. The volume of shipments to New Orleans doubled every decade until the Civil War. Since steamboats could make many more voyages annually, the carrying capacity on the western rivers increased a hundredfold between 1820 and 1860. The steamboat, marveled one westerner, "brings to the remotest village of our streams . . . a little Paris, a section of Broadway, or a slice of Philadelphia."

Governments did not invest as heavily in steamboats as they had in canals, except for providing funds to remove river snags and other obstacles to navigation. Although by 1860 the railroads' dominance had ended, the steamboat was the major form of western transportation during the establishment of a national market economy, and it was the most important factor in the rise of manufacturing in the Ohio and upper Mississippi valleys.

Railroads

The first significant railroads appeared in the 1830s. By and large, they were seen not as a way to revolutionize transportation, but merely as feeder lines to the more important canals. Soon enough, though, communities perceived that their economic future depended on having adequate rail links. Chicago's eventual dominance among western cities grew out of its early commitment to railroads, and Boston, Baltimore, and Charleston, which all lacked important inland waterways, led the way in the construction of regional rail networks.

The country had only 13 miles of track in 1830, but 10 years later railroad and canal mileage were almost exactly equal (3325 miles). During the next decade, the railroad network rapidly expanded, reaching a total of 8879 miles by 1850. Railroads did not always cut the cost of transporting goods over land; canals and steamboats were usually cheaper. But railroads were approximately twice as fast as steamboats, offered more direct routes, and could operate year-round. After 1850, railroads would increasingly become the dominant form of transportation in the country, but initially canals and steamboats were the key to creating a national market.

Agriculture in the Market Economy

The new forms of transportation had a remarkable impact on Crèvecoeur's yeoman farmer. Before the canal era, a farmer could not ship corn profitably outside his immediate neighborhood—unless, of course, he transformed it into a more transportable commodity such as whiskey. Wheat, for example, could be shipped at a profit no farther than 50 miles. But once cheap transportation became available, farmers eagerly sought to increase their yields and ship the surplus to distant markets for sale. Output per worker surged upward as farmers began cultivating more acres and working longer hours. They also began adopting scientific farming methods, including crop rotation and the use of manures as fertilizer. State governments encouraged the circulation of agricultural information through fairs and state agricultural departments, while farm journals advised interested subscribers on the latest advances in fertilizers, plows, and plant varieties.

The transportation revolution also encouraged regional agricultural specialization. Marginal lands in New England and the Northeast could no longer compete with wheat yields of western farms. Eastern farmers, if they did not pull up and move west, shifted to other crops and particularly engaged in dairying and truck farming, for they could now sell milk, vegetables, and fruit to the rapidly growing urban areas. Other farmers began raising sheep. The center of wheat production moved steadily westward, so that by 1850, Wisconsin and Illinois were developing into major wheat-producing states.

All these changes linked farmers more tightly to a national market system. They were now more likely to deal in cash and credit, forsaking the barter system previously used between neighbors. Instead of marketing crops themselves, as they had in the past, farmers dealt with regional merchants, middlemen in a far-flung distribution system. Like southern planters, western wheat farmers increasingly sold in a world market. Poor harvests in Europe, as well as the repeal of Britain's protectionist Corn Laws in the 1840s, created a great demand for American wheat. Banks and distributors advanced farmers credit, and those who anticipated the ups and downs of prices in markets hundreds of miles away were most likely to profit from this system. More and more, farmers competed in a market controlled by impersonal forces centered in distant locations.

As transportation and market networks spread, they fed on themselves, growing larger, connecting more areas of the nation, and allowing further specialization. The South increasingly concentrated on staple crops for export and the West grew foodstuffs, particularly grain, while the Northeast became the center of manufacturing. Although foreign commerce expanded too, it was overshadowed by the dramatic growth in domestic markets, which absorbed more and more of the goods and services being produced. Even though Americans were producing

Daily Lives

TIME AND TRAVEL

Floating Palaces of the West

Plying the Mississippi River and its many tributaries, the western steamboat carried both freight and passengers, but it won its greatest fame as a mode of travel. The most luxurious boats, dubbed "floating palaces," offered accommodations far beyond the experience of the average American. Steamboats also provided the cheapest form of inland transportation before the Civil War: by midcentury, cabin passage for the 1400-mile trip from Louisville to New Orleans was only $12 to $15.

On the earliest steamboats, passengers were housed on the main deck along with the cargo. As the boats became larger, designers added a second or boiler deck (which, despite its name, was not where the boilers were located). Eventually a third level was added, the hurricane or texas, which contained additional accommodations for the officers and passengers. The boiler deck's saloon was the center of steamboat society, with the ladies' parlor at one end and the barroom at the other. Besides serving as a dining room and lounge, it provided the sleeping quarters. Berths were arranged in two tiers on both sides of the saloon and, at least on the better boats, each contained bedding and a mattress. Gentlemen were not allowed in the ladies' cabin except by invitation or if they were traveling with their wives. Women entered the saloon only for meals.

Steamboats also offered passage on the main deck for about one-fifth the price of a regular ticket. Primarily the poor, immigrants, and blacks, these passengers had no living quarters or toilet facilities and had to provide their own food. Then too, boiler explosions, collisions, and sinkings from snags caused a much higher loss of life among lower deck passengers, who were closer to the water and had less warning. Between 1811 and 1851, some 44 steamboats collided, 166 burned, 209 exploded, and 576 hit obstructions and sank. And in the four years before 1852, when Congress passed a law governing steamboat safety, more than 1500 people lost their lives in steamboat accidents.

The steamboat was, as many travelers remarked, a "world in miniature," carrying slaves and planters, farmers and manufacturers, merchants and frontier families, soldiers and Indians, ministers and professional gamblers. Regular passengers generally had little contact with those on the lower deck, but as fares steadily dropped, people of widely different wealth and position were thrown together in the main cabin and mingled with a democratic familiarity. Women spent their time talking, sewing, caring for children, and strolling the deck. Men passed the time in conversation, drinking, and gambling. The bar was the center of the male social world, where as one minister remarked, "whiskey is used just as freely as water." Gambling was rife on steamboats, as many men, temporarily freed from the moral restraints of home, eagerly dealt themselves into card games.

The most famous vessels on the rivers boasted intricately carved gingerbread facings, painted a glistening white and trimmed in gold leaf—an architectural style known as Steamboat Gothic. Sophisticated Europeans found the effect garish and vulgar: "an indefinable sham splendor all around, half disgusting and wholly comical." To rustic westerners and southerners, however, the decor represented elegance beyond anything they had seen. Some, unaccustomed to the finery, gave the furnishings rather hard usage. Owners

The luxurious saloon furnishings on the Mississippi steamboat, the *Princess*.

had to post rules against whittling the furniture and sleeping with boots on.

For all their luxurious veneer, steamboats lacked amenities that later travelers would take for granted. Most six-by-six staterooms had two narrow shelves to sleep on and no lighting or heat. The washrooms in the main cabin contained tin basins and pitchers of cold water, a comb and brush, and a communal toothbrush. One traveler complained that there were only two towels for 70 men on one boat. Water, both for drinking and washing, came directly from the river and was laden with silt. Furthermore, the average riverboat hardly lived up to the standards of the most famous packets. In 1843 John James Audubon journeyed from Louisville to St. Louis on what he described as "the very filthiest of all filthy old rat-traps I ever traveled in." He grumbled particularly about a leaky roof, threadbare sheets, and pillows filled with corn husks.

Steamboat food was ample but often poorly prepared and saturated with grease. In the main cabin 30 or more dishes were placed on the table and diners grabbed whatever they wanted. Unused to such variety, some passengers simply gorged themselves on the dishes near at hand rather than selecting what they wanted. It was a common saying that "steamboat living was entirely too rich for any one to stand it long without ruining the stomach."

In maintaining law and order, the captain was aided by the passengers, who, in the tradition of the frontier, sometimes formed their own courts to deal with those charged with minor offenses. Travelers accused of theft, illicit sexual relations, or gambling disputes might find themselves flogged or put ashore at some desolate spot. In one case, when a young man and woman traveling together as "cousins" aroused suspicion, the passengers insisted on an investigation by the boat's officers, who discovered the pair sharing a berth. At the next stop, while the boat waited, indignant passengers marched the couple ashore, rounded up a minister, and compelled them to get married.

Despite the discomforts of swarming mosquitoes, heat from the boilers, and noisy engines at all hours of the night, observers agreed that journeying by steamboat was far more pleasant than taking a stagecoach, the principal alternative in the West before 1850. With their churning paddlewheels, gingerbread decks, and belching smokestacks, these gaudy vessels were the grandest showpieces of life on the Mississippi.

more goods than ever before, only in 1835 did American exports exceed those of 1807, the last year before the embargo.

Thus the cities of the East no longer looked primarily to the sea; they looked to southern and western markets. That, indeed, was a revolution in markets.

John Marshall and the Promotion of Enterprise

For a national market system to flourish, a climate favorable to investment had to exist. As it happened, the Supreme Court became the branch of the federal government most aggressive in protecting the new forms of business central to the growing market economy.

As chief justice, John Marshall presided over the Court from 1801 to 1835. Despite his informal, almost sloppy personal manners, he was a commanding figure: tall and slender, with twinkling eyes and a hearty laugh that was as contagious as it was disarming. His forceful intellect was reinforced by his genial ability to persuade. A strong nationalist, he convinced his colleagues time after time to uphold the supremacy of the federal government over the states, its power to promote economic growth, and the sanctity of private property.

In the case of *McCulloch v. Maryland* (1819), the Court had to decide whether the Second Bank of the United States, chartered by Congress in 1816, was constitutional. Maryland had levied a tax on the Baltimore branch of the national bank, which John McCulloch, the cashier, refused to pay, and the case went to the Supreme Court. Asserting that "the power to tax involves the power to destroy," Marshall, speaking for the Court, upheld the constitutionality of the national bank and struck down the tax. Just as Alexander Hamilton had argued during the 1790s in the debate over the first national bank, Marshall pointed out that the Constitution gave Congress the power to make all "necessary and proper" laws to carry out its delegated powers. If Congress believed that a bank would help it meet its responsibilities, such as maintaining the public credit and regulating the currency, then it was constitutional. The bank only had to be useful, not essential. "Let the end be legitimate," Marshall wrote, "let it be within the scope of the Constitution, and all means which are appropriate, which are plainly adapted to that end, which are not prohibited . . . are constitutional." By upholding Hamilton's doctrine of implied powers, Marshall enlarged federal power to an extraordinary degree.

He also encouraged a more freewheeling commerce in *Gibbons v. Ogden* (1824). Under a New York law, Aaron Ogden held a monopoly on steamboat traffic on the Hudson River between New Jersey and New York City. Gibbons, who had a federal license to operate a steamboat, set up a competing line and Ogden sued. The case gave Marshall a chance to define the greatest power of the federal government in peacetime, the right to regulate interstate commerce. In striking down the New York monopoly, the chief justice gave the term *commerce* the broadest possible definition, declaring that it covered all commercial intercourse, and that Congress' power over interstate commerce could be "exercised to its utmost extent." The result was increased business competition, not just on the Hudson but throughout society.

At the heart of most commercial agreements were private contracts, made between individuals or companies. Marshall took an active role in defining the meaning of contract law, which was then in its infancy. The case of *Fletcher v. Peck* (1810) showed how far he was willing to go to protect private property. The case grew out of a grant of land the Georgia legislature made in 1795 to a group of speculators. When it was discovered that the speculators had bribed some of the representatives, the next legislature rescinded the grant. Because some individuals had already purchased property from the original grantees, thinking their title was valid, the case eventually made its way to the Supreme Court. The justices unanimously struck down the law rescinding the land grant. A grant was a contract, Marshall declared, and since the Constitution forbade states from impairing "the obligation of contracts," the legislature could not interfere with the grant once it had been made. Although the framers of the Constitution probably meant contracts to refer only to agreements between private parties, Marshall made no distinction between public and private agreements, thereby greatly expanding the meaning of the contract clause.

In another decision (*Sturges v. Crowninshield*, 1819), the Court also defined a debt as a binding contract and limited the power of state legislatures, through bankruptcy laws, to interfere with the collection of debts. But the most celebrated decision Marshall wrote on the contract clause was in *Dartmouth College v. Woodward*, also decided in 1819. This case arose out of the attempt of the state of New Hampshire to alter the charter that George III had granted in 1769 to the college's trustees. The Court overturned the state law on the grounds that state charters were also contracts and could not be altered by later legislatures. By this ruling, Marshall intended to protect corporations, which conducted business under charters granted by individual states. Yet his arguments could be used to preserve monopolies from competition and to defend corporations from regulation in the public interest. So extreme was Marshall's position that courts eventually had to modify some of his decisions.

Thus the Marshall Court sought to encourage economic risk taking by protecting property and contracts, by limiting state interference, and by creating a climate of business confidence. Like other Federalists, Marshall distrusted the masses and believed that state laws were the major obstacle to economic development. During his years on the bench, he upheld the view that commerce and economic enterprise were the agents of progress.

General Incorporation Laws

Corporations were not new in American business, but as the economy expanded they grew in numbers. From the beginning, banks had been established by acts of incorporation, and their success encouraged other businesses to adopt this mode of organization. Corporations continued beyond the lives of the individuals who created them, and by pooling investors' resources, they provided a means to raise capital for large-scale undertakings. Corporations also offered the advantage of limited liability: an investor was liable for the corporation's debts only to the extent of the amount he or she had invested. A recent innovation, this legal concept put limits on a person's financial risk. Small and medium-sized businesses continued to be run as partnerships and individual ventures, but banks, insurance companies, railroads, and manufacturing firms, which required greater capital, increasingly were incorporated.

Originally, state legislatures were required to approve a special charter for each new corporation. But with the number of applications steadily increasing, this procedure became too cumbersome. Beginning in the 1830s, states adopted general incorporation laws. Any applicant who met certain minimum qualifications would automatically be granted a corporation charter. This reform made it much easier and faster to secure a charter and stimulated organization and manipulation of the national market.

A RESTLESS TEMPER

"An American . . . wants to perform within a year what others do within a much longer period," observed Francis Lieber, a German who emigrated and became a noted American political scientist. Between 1815 and 1850, as new markets were opened up, fresh fields plowed, canals dug, and faster steamboats built, the nation reverberated with almost explosive energy. The famous French commentator Alexis de Tocqueville was astonished, like most Europeans, at the restless mobility of the average American. "Born often under another sky, placed in the middle of an always moving scene, himself driven by the irresistible torrent which draws all about him, the American has no time to tie himself to anything, he grows accustomed only to change, and ends by regarding it as the natural state of man."

This emphasis on speed—seen in the mobility of Americans, the expansiveness of the new market, the sense of boundless possibilities—affected nearly every aspect of American life. Steamboat captains vied with one another for the honor of having the fastest boat on the river, their sweaty stokers in the boiler rooms piling log after log into the fires until—all too often—the pressurized engines exploded, ripping the vessel apart. To the visiting English novelist Charles Dickens, traveling under these conditions seemed like taking up "lodgings on the first floor of a powder mill." In railroad cars, Americans could not sit still long enough to abide the European system of providing individual passenger compartments; instead, American cars had a center aisle, allowing their ever-restless passengers to wander the length of the train. American transportation technology emphasized speed over longevity: unlike European railroads, which were sturdy and heavy, American railroads were lightweight, hastily constructed, with little heed paid to the safety or comfort of passengers. Americans even ate quickly, looking neither right nor left, only at their plates, bolting the food down in complete silence. In America, insisted one disgruntled European, food was "pitchforked down."

The new American way of building manifested a similar emphasis on speed. Before the 1830s, American houses were held together with mortises and joints. This method of construction was sturdy, but it required master craftsmen to hew the joints by hand. The pressure to build many houses quickly in areas with few skilled carpenters led to the use of new light frames, made of two-by-fours nailed together, to which the walls, roof, and floor were also attached with nails. Derisively called "balloon frame" houses, they cost less than half the price of a traditional house, and they could be built in a week by workers with only minimal training. Ironically, balloon frame houses proved stronger and lasted longer than traditional houses. Moreover, they were perfectly adapted to the American penchant for moving: the owner simply removed the nails, hauled the lumber to a new site, and reassembled the building.

Horatio Greenough, an American sculptor who returned to the United States in 1836 after an extended stay abroad, was amazed and a bit frightened by the pace

Europeans were shocked that Americans bolted their food or gorged themselves on any-thing within reach, as this English drawing indicates. Such habits reflected both the indif-ferent preparation of food and the frenetic tempo of American life.

that confronted him. "Go ahead! is the order of the day," he observed. "The whole continent presents a scene of scrambling and roars with greedy hurry." If the economic hallmark of this new order was the growth of a national market, there were social factors that also contributed to the new, restless America.

Population Growth

The American population continued to double about every 22 years—more than twice the birth rate of Great Britain. The census, which stood at fewer than 4 million in 1790, surpassed 9 million in 1820. By 1850, there were 23 million people living in the United States. Although the birth rate peaked in 1800, it evidenced only a slow decline before 1840. In the 1840s, which was a period of rapid urbanization, it dropped about 10 percent, the first significant decrease in American history. In cities, couples tended to be older at marriage and families were smaller, in part because the labor of children was not as critical to the family's welfare. At the same time, many basic population characteristics changed little throughout the first half of the nineteenth century: life expectancy did not improve significantly, the population was very young, and early marriage and family formation remained the norm, especially in rural areas.

From 1790 to 1820, natural increase accounted for virtually all of the country's population growth. But immigration, which had been disrupted by the Napoleonic Wars in Europe, revived after 1815. In the 1830s, some 600,000 immi-grants arrived, more than double the number in the quarter century after 1790, and this increase was just a foretaste of the flood of newcomers that reached America beginning in the late 1840s.

The vast areas of land available for settlement absorbed much of the burgeon-ing population. "Old America seems to be breaking up, and moving westward," Morris Birkbeck, an Englishman, declared in 1817. By 1850 almost half of the

American population lived outside the original 13 states, and well over 2 million lived beyond the Mississippi River. The population west of the Appalachian Mountains doubled in the decade 1810–1820, and it doubled again the following decade. By 1840, more than one American in three lived in the trans-Appalachian West.

The Federal Land Rush

As the tide of settlers pushed west, the federal government avidly encouraged them. In the great prosperity after 1815, speculation in western lands reached frenzied proportions as the government sold land on credit. Whereas in 1800 only 68,000 acres of the public domain had been sold, 1.3 million acres were sold in 1815, mostly to speculators, and in 1818 sales peaked at a staggering 3.5 million acres, an area larger than the state of Connecticut. In the ensuing depression that began in 1819, numerous speculators were ruined, and many farmers lost their farms. Congress reacted by abolishing credit sales and demanding full payment in cash, but it tempered this policy by lowering the price of the cheapest lands from $2.00 an acre to $1.25 (the best lands, sold at auction, fetched considerably higher prices, however). It also reduced the minimum tract to 80 acres, which meant that an ordinary farm could be purchased for a hundred dollars.

Squatters on public land, however, clamored for the right of preemption: the right to buy at the minimum price the land they had cleared and put into production before it was offered for sale at auction. Under federal law, squatters who had moved onto land before it had been surveyed and legally opened could be evicted without compensation by the rightful owner, although the owner, to avoid trouble, often paid something for the improvements. The issue of preemption divided those who favored rapid settlement of the West from those who wanted to increase federal revenue. In the 1830s, Congress moved toward the right of preemption by passing a series of special acts, which allowed the preemption of certain lands in the public domain. Finally, in 1841, it approved a general preemption law.

Even with these new laws, speculators purchased most of the public lands sold, since there was no limit on the amount of acreage an individual or land company could buy. These land speculators, who intended to hold property until it rose in value and then sell it, played a leading role in settlement of the West. Naturally, they could not afford to allow land to remain unsettled indefinitely, so to hasten sales, they usually sold land partially on credit—a vital aid to poorer farmers. They also provided loans to purchase needed tools and supplies. To repay these loans, farmers had to grow a commercial crop, and hence they needed access to markets. Many farmers became speculators themselves, buying up property in the neighborhood, keeping it until the population increased, and then selling their surplus to latecomers at a tidy profit. "Speculation in real estate has been the ruling idea and occupation of the western mind," one Englishman reported in the 1830s. "Clerks, laborers, farmers, storekeepers merely followed their callings for a living while they were speculating for their fortunes."

With the westward surge of the population came the admission of new states. In the 20 years before 1810, only four states entered the Union, whereas during the next decade no fewer than five were added. Four more came in by 1840, including Missouri and Arkansas, both west of the Mississippi. By 1860 seven additional states had joined the Union, including California and Oregon on the Pacific Coast.

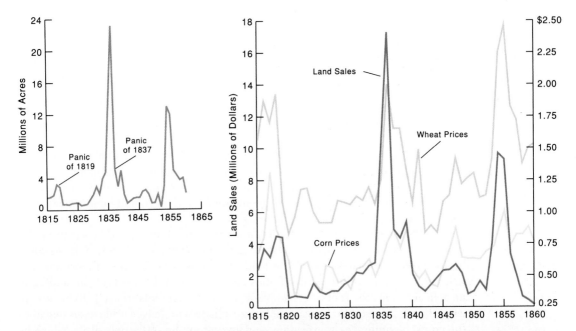

WESTERN LAND SALES AND THE PRICE OF CORN AND WHEAT

Western farmers' expectations of future income were tied to the price of corn and wheat. As commodity prices rose, farmers eagerly bought land on credit, anticipating that future profits would enable them to pay off their mortgages. As the chart illustrates, when wheat and corn prices fell sharply in the Panic of 1819, land sales plummeted and many farmers who had purchased on credit found themselves unable to pay their debts; a similar pattern is apparent in the 1830s. In the South there was a comparable relationship between land sales and the price of cotton.

Purchases of Public Land

YEAR	PRICE PER ACRE	MINIMUM ACREAGE	TERMS OF SALE
1785	$1.00	640	Cash
1796	2.00	640	One-half cash; 1 year to pay balance
1800	2.00	320	Payment over 4 years
1804	2.00	160	Payment over 4 years
1820	1.25	80	Cash
1832	1.25	40	Cash
1841	Preemption (squatter could buy up to 160 acres at minimum price of $1.25 per acre)		
1854	Graduation (price of unsold lands reduced over time to a minimum of 12.5 cents per acre)		

Geographic Mobility

Given such rapid settlement, geographic mobility became one of the most striking characteristics of the American people. The 1850 census revealed that nearly half of all native-born free Americans lived outside the state where they had been born. In Boston from 1830 to 1860 perhaps one-third of the inhabitants changed their place of residence each year. Unlike European peasants, who had a strong attachment to the village where their families had lived for generations, the typical American "has no root in the soil," visiting Frenchman Michel Chevalier observed, but "is always in the mood to move on, always ready to start in the first steamer that comes along from the place where he had just now landed." Americans had become much more mobile than they were during the colonial or Revolutionary era, and Chevalier thought the national emblem should be a steamboat or locomotive.

It was the search for opportunity, more than anything else, that accounted for such restlessness. An American moved, noted one British observer, "if by so doing he can make $10 where before he made $8." Alexis de Tocqueville commented that "in the United States a man builds a house to spend his latter years in it, and he sells it before the roof is on; he plants a garden, and lets it just as the trees are coming into bearing; he brings a field into tillage, and leaves other men to gather the crops; he embraces a profession, and gives it up; he settles in a place, which he soon afterwards leaves to carry his changeable longing elsewhere."

Urbanization

Even with the growth of national markets, the United States remained a rural nation. Nevertheless, a significant rise in urbanization occurred during the period. In 1820 there were only 12 cities with a population of more than 5000; by 1850, there were nearly 150. In 1820 the census classified only about 9 percent of the American people as urban (living in towns with a population of 2500 or more). Forty years later, the number had risen to 20 percent. Indeed, the four decades after 1820 witnessed the fastest rate of urbanization in American history. As a result, the ratio of farmers to urban dwellers steadily dropped from 15 to 1 in 1800 to 10.5 to 1 in 1830, and 5.5 to 1 in 1850. The most heavily urbanized area of the country was the Northeast, where in 1860 more than a third of the population was urban.* The South, with only 10 percent of its population living in cities, was the least urbanized. Improved transportation, the declining productivity of many eastern farms, the beginnings of industrialization, and the influx of immigrants all stimulated the growth of cities.

In 1850 six cities had populations exceeding 100,000. The largest, New York (which then did not include the city of Brooklyn), contained over half a million people, and older cities like Philadelphia, Boston, Baltimore, and New Orleans continued to be major urban centers. Equally significant was the rise of cities in the West. By 1850 Cincinnati and St. Louis each had over 100,000 people, and Chicago, which in 1830 had only about 8000 inhabitants, topped 50,000. Indeed, at the century's midpoint, 40 percent of the nation's total urban population lived in interior cities.

---

*The Northeast includes New England and the Middle Atlantic states (New York, Pennsylvania, and New Jersey). The South comprised the slave states plus the District of Columbia (page 455n).

St. Louis, a major urban center that developed in the West, depended on the steamboat to sustain its commerce, as this 1859 illustration makes clear.

All of these changes—the amazing growth of the population, the quickening movement westward, and the rising migration to the cities—pointed to a fundamental reorientation of American development. Expansion was the keynote of the new America, and the prospects it offered thrilled Americans. "Our population is destined to roll its resistless waves to the icy barriers of the north, and to encounter Oriental civilization on the shores of the Pacific," proclaimed former New York governor William H. Seward in 1846.

THE RISE OF FACTORIES

Another crucial element in the country's accelerating economic growth was the beginning of industrial manufacturing. This development required not only technological innovation but also a reorganization of the labor used to manufacture goods.

Before 1815 manufacturing had been done in homes or shops by skilled artisans, who turned out a small number of finished goods, often made to order for local customers. As master craftworkers, they imparted the secrets of their trades to apprentices and journeymen. In addition, women often worked in their homes part-time under the putting-out system, in which merchant capitalists supplied raw material from which these women made finished or partially finished articles. Weaving was traditionally done at home by both men and women, and many farm families manufactured items such as brooms and fans during the winter months.

After 1815, however, this older form of manufacturing began to give way to large-scale factories with machinery tended by unskilled or semiskilled laborers. The creation of a domestic market, the development of cheap transportation, the rise of cities, and the availability of capital and credit all stimulated the shift to factory production.

Technological Advances

Many of the earliest technological innovations were developed in England, including James Watt's steam engine (1769), spinning machinery, and the power loom. But Americans often improved on these inventions or adapted them to more extensive uses. In contrast to the more traditional societies of Europe, "everything new is quickly introduced here," one visitor commented in 1820. "There is no clinging to old ways; the moment an American hears the word 'invention' he pricks up his ears." To encourage experimentation, the United States established the Patent Office in 1790 and provided that inventors would enjoy exclusive use of a registered patent for 17 years. The number of patents averaged 77 a year during the first decade of the nineteenth century; by 1850 it had risen to nearly 1000 a year. Indeed, from 1790 to 1860 the United States granted more patents than England and France combined.

To protect their economic advantage, the British forbade the export of any textile machinery or drawings of such machines as well as the emigration of any craftworker trained in their design and construction. American legislatures countered by offering rewards to those who could provide plans, and in 1790, a 21-year-old English mill worker named Samuel Slater emigrated, pretending to be a farmer and carrying the necessary plans in his head. Backed by Moses Brown, a Providence merchant, Slater designed and built the first textile mill in America. Two decades later, the Boston merchant Francis Cabot Lowell imitated British designs for a power loom and then improved on them. In fact, American tinkering and innovation soon made the home-built models more efficient than the English originals.

The first machines were often complex and required highly skilled workers to build and repair the individual gears, cogs, and other parts. Eli Whitney had a better idea. Having won a contract to produce 10,000 rifles for the government, he developed machinery that would mass produce parts that were interchangeable from rifle to rifle. Such parts had to be manufactured to very rigid specifications, and it took Whitney a number of years to achieve the precision needed. But once the process was perfected, these parts allowed a worker to assemble a rifle quickly with only a few tools. As an experiment, a British commission studying Whitney's techniques disassembled a set of guns Whitney had produced over a 10-year period and mixed the parts together. Then one of Whitney's workers astonished the commission by selecting parts at random and assembling a gun without difficulty. Simeon North applied the same principle to the production of clocks and made the famous Connecticut clock affordable for the first time to most families; Chauncey Jerome followed North's example and soon surpassed him.

What rail and steam engines did for transportation, Samuel F. B. Morse's telegraph did for communications. Morse patented his device in 1837, but it was not until 1844 that he used a government subsidy to construct an experimental line from Washington to Baltimore. Soon telegraph lines fanned out in all directions, linking various parts of the country in instantaneous communication. By 1852 there were 23,000 miles of lines laid, and by 1860, over 50,000 miles. The telegraph to California was completed the following year. The new form of communication sped business information, helped link the transportation network, and allowed newspapers to provide their readers with up-to-date news.

Indeed, the invention of the telegraph and the perfection of a power press (1847) by Robert Hoe and his son Richard revolutionized journalism. The mechanical press sharply increased the speed with which sheets could be printed over the old hand method. Mass-produced newspapers, crammed with the latest news, became readily available. The penny press—newspapers costing only a penny, which was within reach of ordinary families—gained huge circulations through a skillful combination of news, gossip, and sensationalism. "These papers are to be found in every street, lane, and alley; in every hotel, tavern, counting-house, [and] shop," one editor noted. "Almost every porter and dray-man, while not engaged in his occupation, may be seen with a paper in his hands." Hoe's press had a similar impact on book publishing, as thousands of copies could now be printed at a price that mass audiences could afford.

Lacking a large pool of highly skilled workers, the United States took the lead in inventing machine tools that did not require great skill to operate. Whenever possible, American manufacturing relied on mechanization over human labor. The use of light machine tools and interchangeable parts constituted the American system of manufacturing.

Textile Factories

The factory system originated in the Northeast, where through lucrative foreign trade investors had accumulated the capital needed for expensive equipment, water power was abundant, good transportation facilities were available, and banks and other commercial institutions already existed. As in England, the production of cloth was the first manufacturing process to make use of the new technology on a large scale. Initially, factories like Samuel Slater's merely spun thread, which was then put out to be handwoven. But ultimately all of the processes of manufacturing cloth were brought together in a single location, from opening the cotton bales to weaving the cloth, and machines did virtually all the work.

In 1813 a group of wealthy Boston merchants, the most important of whom were Francis Cabot Lowell and Nathan Appleton, chartered the Boston Manufacturing Company and established the first fully integrated textile factory at Waltham, Massachusetts. Expanding their highly profitable operations, these investors, known as the Boston Associates, then organized the Merrimack Manufacturing Company and set up operations at Chelmsford—which was renamed Lowell, Massachusetts. Intended as a model community, Lowell soon became the most famous center of textile manufacturing in the country.

Its founders sought to avoid the misery and wretchedness that characterized the factory system in England. Instead of relying primarily on child labor or a permanent working class, Lowell employed daughters of New England farm families, and thus women were the first factory workers in the United States. Male supervisors lived in company houses; female workers stayed in company boardinghouses under the watchful eye of a matron. To its many visitors, Lowell presented an impressive scene, the town "new and fresh," with "a pile of huge factories, each five, six or seven stories high," wrote one visitor. "By the side of these larger structures rise numerous little wooden houses, painted white, with green blinds, very neat, very snug, very nicely carpeted, and with a few small trees around them. . . . [There are also] fancy-goods shops . . . vast hotels in the American style . . . canals, water wheels, water falls, bridges, banks, schools, and libraries." Female workers were encouraged to attend lectures and use the library; they even published their own magazine, the *Lowell Offering*. In this seemingly utopian setting, the Boston Associates intended to combine paternalism with high profits.

In reality, factory life involved a regimen of punctuality, strict work rules, and long hours of tedious, repetitive work. At Lowell, for example, workers could be fined for lateness or misconduct, such as talking on the job. The company forbade alcohol as well as cards and gambling in the shop or mill yard. Employees who did not go to church on the Sabbath were to remain inside, improving themselves by reading, writing, or other uplifting activities. The women's morals in the boardinghouses were strictly guarded; male visitors were allowed only in the presence of a chaperone, and there was a 10 p.m. curfew. Work typically began at 7 a.m. (earlier in the summer) and continued until 7 at night, six days a week. With only 30 minutes for the noon meal, many workers had to run to the boardinghouse and back to avoid being late. Winter was the "lighting up" season, when work began before daylight and ended after dark. The only light after sunset came from whale oil lamps that filled the long rooms with smoke. Even in summer the factories were poorly lit and badly ventilated. Although the labor was hard, the female operators received wages that were considered good by the standards of the time. They earned from $2.40 to $3.20 a week, depending on their skill and position, compared to less than a dollar a week for domestic servants and seamstresses, two of the most common jobs women held.

The average "mill girl," as they were called, was between 16 and 30 years of age. Contrary to a widely held assumption, most were not working to support their families back home on the farm. Their departure reduced the financial burden on the family, but most of the women kept their earnings in order to accumulate some money for perhaps the first time in their lives, to sample some of life's pleasures, and to save for a marriage dowry. "I must . . . have something of my own before many more years have passed," Sally Rice wrote when her parents asked her to return home to Somerset, Vermont. "And where is that something coming from if I go home and earn nothing? . . . I have but one life to live and I want to enjoy myself as well as I can." Like Rice, few women in the mills intended to work permanently, and most stayed no more than five years before marrying, taking up housekeeping, and raising a family. Mill workers often quit periodically to return home, then came back and, if they had left in good standing, resume work. These interruptions from the tedious routine, the sense of sisterhood that united women in the boardinghouses, and their view of the situation as temporary rather than permanent, all made it easier for farm daughters to adjust to the stress and regimen the factory imposed on them.

Mary Paul went to work in the Lowell mills in November 1845 at the age of 15. The daughter of a rural New England family, she was working as a domestic servant when she asked her father for permission to go to Lowell. "I am in need of clothes which I cannot get about here," she explained, "and for that reason I want to go to Lowell or some other place." Two friends from her hometown of Barnard, Vermont, helped her find her first job, from which she earned $128 in 11 months; apparently she did not send any of it back to her father. After four years she returned home, but now found the "countryfied" style too confining and eventually left again. During the next seven years, she moved about and supported herself in several occupations, until at age 27 she married the son of a former Lowell boardinghouse keeper. Mary Paul's urban experiences had altered her outlook, and like the majority of mill workers traced in one study, she did not return to farm life, settling down instead in nearby Lynn, where her husband got a job in the marble works.

As competition in the textile industry intensified, factory managers undertook

Long hours and punctuality: that is the message of this Lowell time-table. Often accustomed to a less regimented life on a farm, laborers complained of the pace of the machines and the tyranny of the factory bell that summoned and dismissed them each day.

TIME TABLE OF THE LOWELL MILLS,
To take effect on and after Oct. 21st, 1851.

The Standard time being that of the meridian of Lowell, as shown by the regulator clock of JOSEPH RAYNES, 43 Central Street

	From 1st to 10th inclusive.				From 11th to 20th inclusive.				From 21st to last day of month.			
	1st Bell	2d Bell	3d Bell	Eve. Bell	1st Bell	2d Bell	3d Bell	Eve. Bell	1st Bell	2d Bell	3d Bell	Eve. Bell
January,	5.00	6.00	6.50	*7.30	5.00	6 00	6.50	*7.30	5.00	6.00	6.50	*7.30
February,	4.30	5.30	6.40	*7.30	4.30	5.30	6.25	*7.30	4.30	5.30	6.15	*7.30
March,	5.40	6.00		*7.30	5.20	5.40		*7.30	5.05	5.25		6.35
April,	4.45	5.05		6.45	4.30	4.50		6.55	4.30	4.50		7.00
May,	4.30	4.50		7·00	4.30	4.50		7.00	4.30	4.50		7 00
June,	"	"		"	"	"		"	"	"		"
July,	"	"		"	"	"		"	"	"		"
August,	"	"		"	"	"		"	"	"		"
September,	4.40	5.00		6.45	4.50	5.10		6.30	5.00	5.20		*7.30
October,	5.10	5.30		*7.30	5.20	5.40		*7.30	5.35	5.55		*7.30
November,	4.30	5.30	6.10	*7.30	4.30	5.30	6.20	*7.30	5.00	6.00	6.35	*7.30
December,	5.00	6.00	6.45	*7.30	5.00	6.00	6.50	*7.30	5.00	6·00	6.50	*7.30

* Excepting on Saturdays from Sept. 21st to March 20th inclusive, when it is rung at 20 minutes after sunset.

YARD GATES,
Will be opened at ringing of last morning bell, of meal bells, and of evening bells; and kept open Ten minutes.

MILL GATES.
Commence hoisting Mill Gates, Two minutes before commencing work.

WORK COMMENCES,
At Ten minutes after last morning bell, and at Ten minutes after bell which " rings in " from Meals.

BREAKFAST BELLS.
During March "Ring out".........at....7.30 a. m......... "Ring in" at 8:05 a. m.
April 1st to Sept. 20th inclusive.....at....7 00 " " .... " " at 7.35 " "
Sept. 21st to Oct. 31st inclusive.....at....7.30 " " .... " " at 8.05 " "
Remainder of year work commences after Breakfast.

DINNER BELLS.
" Ring out"..... ....12.30 p. m......... "Ring in".... 1.05 p. m.

In all cases, the *first* stroke of the bell is considered as marking the time.

to raise productivity. In the mid-1830s the mills began to increase the workloads. The most commonly used methods were the speed-up (increasing the speed of the machines), the stretch-out (increasing the number of machines each operator tended), and the premium system (paying bonuses for high productivity). Skilled women could make more money under the new system, but they had to work much harder to do so. The average worker's productivity rose by 71 percent, but her wages went up only 16 percent. Even these changes in work rules failed to maintain previous profits, and on several occasions factories cut wages.

The decline of paternalism and the ever-quickening pace of work finally provoked resistance among the women in the mills. Several times in the 1830s wage cuts precipitated strikes in which a minority of workers walked out. Management retaliated by firing strike leaders, hiring new workers, and blacklisting women who refused to return. In the 1840s, workers' protests focused on the demand for a 10-hour day. Perhaps a third of the female workers signed petitions calling for the shorter workday, but the legislature, siding with the owners, concluded that working conditions were not the state's responsibility.

As the mills expanded, a smaller proportion of the workers lived in company boardinghouses and moral regulations were relaxed. But the greatest change was a shift in the work force from native-born females to Irish immigrants. The Irish, who had comprised only 8 percent of the Lowell work force in 1845, made up almost half by 1860. In addition, 30 percent of the workers were men, and the number of children in the mills (many of whom also were Irish) doubled. The arrival of the Irish, who were desperately poor and did not view their situation as temporary, signaled the creation of a permanent working class. It also eventually led to a lowering of wages and a narrowing of the gap between the highest and lowest paying jobs in the factory.

Industrial Work

The transition to an industrial labor force with values and behavior patterns that were attuned to factory work was not a smooth one. Before the rise of the factory, artisans had worked within the home. Apprentices were considered part of the family and subject to the discipline and control of the master. Masters were responsible not only for teaching their apprentices a trade, but also for providing them some education and for supervising their moral behavior. Journeymen took pride in their work, knowing that if they developed their skills and were frugal, they could eventually set themselves up in a shop and become respected master artisans. Nor did skilled craftsmen work by the clock, at a steady pace, but rather in bursts of intense labor alternating with slow seasons, their work frequently interrupted for a pint of ale, a bit of gossip, or even a prank or two.

The factory, however, changed that. Pride in craftsmanship gave way to rates of productivity. Goods produced by factories were not as finished or elegant as those done by hand. Instead, the emphasis was on mass producing articles of lower quality that could be sold cheaply. At the same time that workers lost pride in their work, they were required to discard old habits. Industrialism demanded a worker who was sober, dependable, and self-disciplined. The machines, whirring and clacking away, set a strict schedule that had to be followed. Absenteeism, lateness, and drunkenness hurt productivity and, since work was specialized, disrupted the regular factory routine. Thus industrialization not only produced a fundamental change in the way work was organized, but also transformed the very nature of work.

The first generation to experience these changes did not adopt the new attitudes easily, and many workers persisted in the old ways. The factory clock became the symbol of the new work rules. One mill worker who finally quit complained revealingly about "obedience to the ding-dong of the bell—just as though we are so many living machines." With the loss of personal freedom also came the loss of pride in one's work and a sense of place in the community. Unlike the master–apprentice relationship, factories sharply separated workers from management, and few workers rose through the ranks to supervisory positions. In areas of the economy where factory production became dominant, even fewer could achieve the artisan's dream of setting up one's own business, since handcrafted goods were too expensive to be sold to any but the wealthy. Even well-paid workers sensed their decline in status.

The Shoe Industry

Shoemaking illustrates one way the artisan tradition came to be undermined. If Lowell was the symbol of the textile industry, nearby Lynn was the center of shoe manufacturing. Traditionally, a skilled cobbler possessed a good knowledge of leather, had the ability to cut out the various parts of a shoe, and could stitch and glue those parts together. He then sold the shoes in the same shop where he and his apprentices made them. Unlike the textile industry, shoemaking was not rapidly transformed by a shift to heavy machinery. That came only later, in the 1860s. But expanding transportation networks and national markets nevertheless fundamentally altered this business.

Micajah Pratt began selling shoes in 1812, a business in which his father John had prospered by selling to customers in New England. However, the younger Pratt found that if he could meet the demand for cheaply made shoes, there were ready markets in the South and West that he could ship to, beyond his father's traditional customers. Responding to these new opportunities, he hired workers to produce shoes in larger and larger central shops. He cut costs further by using new production techniques, such as standardized patterns and sole-cutting machines. Pratt eventually employed as many as 500 men and women and produced about a quarter-million pairs of shoes annually. Other shoe manufacturers adopted similar strategies.

With the shoe industry serving as a magnet, Lynn's population doubled every 20 years, yet so great was the national market that manufacturers could not keep pace with demand. More and more they hired farmers, fishermen, and their families, many of whom lived in other towns, putting out part-time work at home. Women and girls sewed the upper parts of a shoe, and men and boys attached the bottoms. While slow, this mode of production allowed wages to be reduced still further. A few highly paid workers performed critical tasks like cutting the leather, but most of the work was done either in large central shops or in homes. No longer able to make an entire shoe, workers lost their sense of craftsmanship and with it their status. In little more than a generation, shoemaking ceased to be a craft. Though not organized in a factory setting, it had become essentially an assembly-line process.

The Labor Movement

In this newly emerging economic order, workers sometimes organized to protect their rights and traditional ways of life. In the 1820s, workers formed political parties in several eastern cities. Such craftsmen as carpenters, printers, and tailors organized, and in 1834 individual unions came together in the National Trades' Union.

The leaders of these groups argued that labor was degraded in American society: workers endured long hours, low pay, and low status. Instead of a society where individuals were rewarded according to the value of their labor, the idle rich enslaved the industrious poor. Thus labor leaders, unlike most American social thinkers of the day, accepted the idea of conflict between different classes. They did not believe that the interests of workers and employers could be reconciled, and they blamed the plight of labor on monopolies, especially banking and paper money, and on machines and the factory system.

If the unions' rhetoric sounded radical, the solutions they proposed were moderate. Reformers agitated for public education, abolition of imprisonment for debt, political action by workers, and effective unions as the means to guarantee social equality and restore labor to its former honored position. In that sense, labor reformers looked to the ideology of the Revolution rather than to the notion of a working-class movement. Proclaiming the republican virtues of freedom and equality, they attacked special privilege, denounced the lack of equal opportunity, and decried workers' loss of independence. "As our fathers resisted unto blood the lordly avarice of the British ministry," affirmed the Lowell strikers in 1836, "so we, their daughters, never will wear the yoke which has been prepared for us."

The labor movement gathered some momentum in the decade before the Panic of 1837, but in the depression that followed, labor's strength collapsed. During hard times, few workers were willing to strike or engage in collective action. Nor did skilled craftsmen, who instituted the union movement, feel a particularly strong community of interest with semiskilled factory workers and unskilled laborers. More than a decade of agitation did finally bring the 10-hour day to most industries by the 1850s; and unions also campaigned hard for the right to strike, something that the authorities had long looked upon as an illegal conspiracy to restrain trade. Unions also confronted hostile public opinion, which held them guilty of price fixing contrary to the public good. In 1842, however, Chief Justice Lemuel Shaw of the Massachusetts Supreme Court upheld the basic right to strike in the case of *Commonwealth v. Hunt*. Gaining this right was a milestone in the history of the labor movement, but in the years before the Civil War the ruling had little impact.

Workers were united in their resentment of the industrial system and their loss of status, but they were divided by ethnic and racial antagonisms, gender, conflicting religious perspectives, occupational differences, party loyalties, and disagreements over tactics. And despite their longing for Revolutionary equality, most workers were unable to do much to ease the changes brought by the technologies of the factory system. For them, the factory and industrialism were not agents of opportunity but reminders of their loss of independence and a measure of control over their lives.

SOCIAL STRUCTURES OF THE MARKET SOCIETY

Laborers, farmers, and merchants were among the social groups affected by the rapidly developing economy. The revolution in markets, however, also restructured American society as a whole.

Historian William McNeill observes that "civilized societies were created and are sustained by dint of occupational differentiation and specialization." Clearly, the opening up of America to the market allowed society to become much more specialized. Transportation networks made it possible for farmers to concentrate on producing certain crops, while factories could focus on making a single item such as cloth or shoes. The growth of cities with their dense patterns of settlement made possible the development of more complex social relationships among buyers, sellers, and distributors. The rise of the factory system made the process of manufacturing more specialized through a division of labor. No longer did cobblers produce a pair of shoes from start to finish; the operation was broken down into more specialized (and less skilled) tasks. There was, as McNeill puts it, more "occupational differentiation."

This process evolved at different rates. Textiles and milling were completely mechanized, whereas other sectors of the economy, such as shoes and men's clothing, depended little on machinery. Slow to use steam engines, American manufacturing relied largely on water power. Moreover, large factories were the exception rather than the rule; except in fully mechanized industries, much of the manufacturing was done in smaller shops with few employees. Nevertheless, the tendency was toward more technology, greater efficiency, and increasing specialization. Textile factories illustrated this latter development. Initially textile companies built their own machinery and marketed their products, but eventually they began to purchase machines from firms that specialized in machinery construction and they sold their cloth to wholesalers who in turn marketed it.

These more complex structures had consequences for the home as well as the workplace. For the average eighteenth-century American woman, the home was a workplace where she produced items like thread, cloth, clothing, and candles. With the growth of factories, household manufacturing all but disappeared. As a result, women lost many of the economic functions they had previously performed in the family unit. Again, textiles are a striking example. Between 1815 and 1860, the price of a yard of cotton cloth fell from 18 to 2 cents. Because it was cheaper, smoother, and more brightly colored than homespun, most women purchased cloth rather than make it themselves. Similarly, the development of ready-made men's clothing reduced the amount of sewing women did. In urban centers, more men purchased clothing from retail stores. As Chapter 12 will make clearer, the growth of industry led to an economic reorganization of the family and a new definition of women's role in society.

The Distribution of Wealth

As American society became increasingly specialized and differentiated, greater extremes of wealth began to appear. Chauncey Jerome and Micajah Pratt demonstrated that if one's market were the nation—or even the world—greater riches could be amassed than by selling door to door, or even town to town. And as the new markets created fortunes for the few, the factory system lowered the wages of many ordinary workers by dividing labor into smaller and less skilled tasks.

Indeed, recent studies of local tax records have documented a growing concentration of wealth at the top of the social pyramid after 1815. Wealth was most highly concentrated in large eastern cities and in the cotton kingdom of the South, but everywhere the tendency was for the rich to get richer and own a larger share of the community's total wealth. In New York, Brooklyn, Boston, and Philadelphia, the top 1 percent of the wealthholders owned a quarter of the total wealth in 1825; by 1850, they owned half. Similar trends appeared in western cities, such as Cincinnati and St. Louis.

In contrast, those at the base of the social pyramid held a smaller percentage of a community's wealth. In Connecticut towns during the years 1831 to 1851 the number of inhabitants listed as having no property increased by 33 percent. In Cincinnati the bottom half of the city's taxpayers held 10 percent of the wealth in 1817; in 1860 their share had dropped to less than 3 percent. By 1860, in fact, 5 percent of American families owned more than 50 percent of the nation's wealth. Significantly, in villages where the market revolution had not penetrated, wealth tended to be less concentrated. Among rural towns in Massachusetts, wealth was most evenly distributed in precisely those towns that were the most economically stagnant.

In a market society, the rich were able to build up their assets because those with capital were in a position to increase it dramatically by taking advantage of new investment opportunities. As a result, family fortunes generally persisted from one generation to the next. Although a few men, such as Cornelius Vanderbilt and John Jacob Astor, vaulted from the bottom ranks of society to the top, most of the nation's richest individuals came from wealthy families. In one study of four major eastern cities, over 90 percent of the rich had wealthy parents, whereas only 2 percent had been born poor.

Social Mobility

The existence of great fortunes is not necessarily inconsistent with the idea of social mobility or property accumulation. Although the gap between the rich and the poor widened after 1820, even the incomes of most poor Americans rose, because the total amount of wealth produced in America had become much larger. From about 1825 to 1860, the average per capita income almost doubled to $300, a figure that exceeded that of western Europe. Europeans were impressed by how hard Americans worked, and also by their high standard of living. A Scottish immigrant testified that "the generality of working people in the United States live more sumptuously than most middle class people in England." Voicing the popular belief, a New York judge proclaimed, "In this favored land of liberty, the road to advancement is open to all."

Recent research indicates that such social mobility existed, but not to the degree claimed by contemporaries. In Philadelphia, during each decade between 1820 and 1860, perhaps 15 percent of the population who remained in the city improved their income or place of residence. At the same time, the proportion of those who lost wealth or status increased sharply until it roughly equaled the rate of upward mobility. Movement up and down was highest among those who worked in the lowest paying jobs. In the end, most laborers—or more often their sons—did manage to move up the social ladder, but only a rung or two. Few unskilled workers rose higher than to a semiskilled occupation. Even the children of skilled workers normally did not escape the laboring classes and enter the middle-class ranks of clerks, managers, or lawyers. For most workers, improved status came in the form of a savings account or home ownership, which gave them some security during economic downswings and in old age.

Materialism

Europeans who visited the United States during these years were struck by the degree to which Americans were preoccupied with material goods and achievements. The new generation did not invent materialism, but the spread of the market after 1815 made it much more evident. "I know of no country, indeed," Tocqueville commented, "where the love of money has taken stronger hold on the affections of men." And in 1836 the American writer Washington Irving coined the classic phrase that captured the spirit of the age when he spoke, in one of his stories, of "the almighty dollar, that great object of universal devotion throughout the land."

In a nation that had no legally established aristocracy, no established church, and class lines that were only informally drawn, wealth became the most obvious symbol of status. As one magazine explained, "Wealth is something substantial. Everybody knows that and feels it. Birth is a mere idea, which grows everyday more and more intangible." Materialism reflected more than a desire for physical comfort and luxury. It also represented a quest for respect and recognition. "Americans boast of their skill in money making," one contemporary observed, "and as it is the only standard of dignity and nobility and worth, they endeavor to obtain it by every possible means."

The emphasis on money and material goods left its mark on the American character. Often enough, it encouraged sharp business practices and promoted a greater tolerance of wealth acquired by questionable means. Families were rated by the size, not the source, of their fortunes. Americans also emphasized practicality over theory. "In no country in the civilized world," remarked Tocqueville, "is less attention paid to philosophy than in the United States." The esteem of the founding generation for intellectual achievement was often lost in the scramble for wealth that seemed to consume those who were developing new markets.

The Redefinition of Time

It was no accident that Chauncey Jerome's clocks spread across the land along with the market economy. The new methods of doing business required that society be structured more precisely. Actually, rural Americans who paced themselves according to the natural rhythms of a day were, in their own way, quite sophisticated about time. An Illinois farmer, for example, divided the last hours before sunrise into no less than eight different stages: long before day, just before day, just coming day, just about daylight, good light, before sunup, about sunup, and finally sunup. Factory life, however, required a more regimented time, where work commenced at the sound of a bell, workers kept machines going at a constant pace, and the day was divided into hours and even minutes.

Clocks began to invade private as well as public space. Before Chauncey Jerome and his competitors began using standardized parts, only the wealthy could afford clocks. But beginning in the 1830s, even farmers became more sensitive to time as they became integrated into the marketplace. As one frontier traveler reported in 1844, "In Kentucky, in Indiana, in Illinois, in Missouri, and here in every dale in Arkansas, and in cabins where there was not a chair to sit on, there was sure to be a Connecticut clock."

The Market at Work: Three Examples

To sense how much America was leaving behind Crèvecoeur's vision of a land of subsistence farmers, consider three examples of the new market economy, from a small city on the East Coast to the distant frontier of the Rocky Mountains.

In 1820, Kingston, New York, was a small, rural-oriented community of 1000 people, located along the Hudson River halfway between New York City and Albany. But in 1828 the Delaware and Hudson Canal linked Kingston with the Pennsylvania coal fields, jolting the town out of its economic lethargy. The rise of the coal trade stimulated local commerce, marked the shift to a cash economy, and greatly increased the number of banks and the variety of businesses. While still seasonal, the rhythm of life in Kingston changed. With the spring thaw still came a quickening of activity, but it now focused on the docks, stores, and canal boats rather than on planting and harvest. By 1850 Kingston had a population of 10,000, ten times that of 1820.

Its landscape changed too. Whereas in 1820 most storekeepers and craftsmen conducted business from their homes, by 1850 a commercial district had developed. As had already happened in the largest cities, Kingston's stores became specialized, some handling china and glassware, others dry goods, clothing, or jewelry and watches. Some blocks of the downtown area were devoted almost entirely to one type of trade or business. In addition, most of the manufacturing facilities were confined to two sections on the city's outskirts. Residential areas were separate from the commercial center and had become segregated along class lines, with the elite of the community, skilled workers, and unskilled laborers each living in their own neighborhoods. By midcentury, street signs and gas lamps were going up, and numbers were being assigned to buildings. Kingston had passed the urban threshold.

A thousand miles west, the small settlement of Sugar Creek, Illinois, presented an even more rural setting. The first white settlers had moved to Sugar Creek in 1817, just as the market revolution was getting under way. At that point, the village's pioneers were less worried about the market than about simply surviving. The land they plowed was not on the prairie (the available plows could not cut prairie grass roots), but in forests, where girdled trees often remained standing among the crops until they could be cleared. The roads to larger towns like Springfield were mere cart paths, winding hither and yon among the trees.

By the 1840s and 1850s, the market economy had made inroads at Sugar Creek. True, a farmer like Eddin Lewis might still keep an account book noting that James Wilson came by for "six days work planting corn [$]3.00." That was the traditional barter system in action, for no cash actually changed hands—Lewis was simply keeping tabs, noting also when he helped Wilson, so that eventually the account could be balanced. But Lewis had also begun to drive pigs down the road to St. Louis, where he received cash in return. By 1848 he was shipping south 6000 pounds of barreled pork, as well as lard and 350 bushels of corn. Wealth had become more concentrated in Sugar Creek, too: the richest farmers owned more land, which they rented to poorer tenants. Well-to-do farmers grew a few lucrative crops, which freed their wives from having to produce large amounts of butter for the market to make ends meet. Sugar Creek, in other words, was becoming more specialized, more stratified in terms of wealth, and more tied into regional and national markets.

Another thousand miles west a different sort of American roamed, who might at first seem the least connected to the bustle of urban markets. These were the legendary mountain men. Traveling across the Great Plains, along upland streams, and over the passes of the Rockies, hard-bitten outdoorsmen like Jim Bridger, Jedediah Smith, and James Walker wore buckskin hunting shirts, let their unkempt hair grow to their shoulders, and stuck pistols and tomahawks in their belts. In good times they feasted on buffalo blood, raw liver, and roasted hump; when game was scarce, some were not above holding their hands "in an ant-hill until they were covered with ants, then greedily [licking] them off," as one veteran trapper recalled. Wild and exotic, the mountain men quickly became romantic symbols of the American quest for individual freedom.

Yet these wanderers too were inextricably tied to the market. During their heyday, from the mid-1820s to the early 1840s, they hunted beaver, whose pelts were shipped east and turned into fancy hats for gentlemen. The fur trade was not a sporting event but a business, dominated by organizations like John Jacob Astor's American Fur Company, and the trapper was the agent of a vast economic structure that stretched from the mountains to the eastern cities and even to Europe. The majority of these men went into the wilderness not to flee civiliza-

Alfred Jacob Miller's *Caravan en Route* shows the annual procession of trade goods being shipped west during the fur trappers' heyday. Despite their colorful lifestyle, trappers were employees in a large-scale business enterprise organized along corporate lines and dominated by large fur companies.

tion, but to make money, and their ultimate goal was to accumulate capital in order to set themselves up in society. Of those who survived the fur trade, almost none remained permanently outside the bounds of civilization. In one sample of 446 trappers whose careers could be traced, only 5 stayed in the wilderness; 36 became ranchers or farmers, 22 transformed themselves into shopkeepers and traders, 10 became skilled workers, and 2 became bankers. Seven, capitalizing on their fame, entered politics. Far from repudiating society's values, the mountain men sought respectability and success as defined by the society they had temporarily left. They, like farmers, were expectant capitalists for whom the West was a land of opportunity.

PROSPERITY AND ANXIETY

The mountain men, the farmers of Sugar Creek, and the workers of Kingston were all alert to the possibilities of the market. Indeed, many citizens, buoyed by the expansion of their nation's frontiers and its economy, began to view history in terms of an inevitable and continuous improvement. "The irresistible tendency of the human race is therefore to advancement," historian George Bancroft argued in 1835. "The movement of the species is upward, irresistibly upward."

In fact, however, the path of commerce was not steadily upward. Rather it advanced in a series of wrenching boom–bust cycles: accelerating growth, followed by a crash and then a depression. The country remained extraordinarily prosperous from 1815 until 1819, only to sink into a depression that lasted from 1819 to 1823. The next cycle extended from 1823 to 1843, the economy expanding slowly during the 1820s, followed by almost frenzied speculation and investment in the 1830s. Then came the inevitable contraction in 1837, and the country suffered an even more severe depression from 1839 to 1843. The third cycle stretched from 1843 to 1861, again following the familiar pattern: gradual economic growth during the 1840s, followed by frantic expansion in the 1850s, and a third depression that began in 1857 and lasted until the Civil War began in 1861. In each of these depressions, thousands of workers were thrown out of work, overextended farmers lost their farms, and many businesses closed their doors.

In such an environment, prosperity, like personal success, seemed all too fleeting. Because Americans believed the good times would not, could not last—that the bubble would burst and another "panic" set in—their buoyant optimism was often tinged with a sense of insecurity and anxiety. They knew too many individuals like Chauncey Jerome, who had been rich and then lost all their wealth in a downturn. With the economy subject to such extreme fluctuations and seemingly impersonal forces, a person could be dragged down through no fault of his or her own.

The Panic of 1819

The initial shock of this boom-and-bust psychology came with the Panic of 1819, the first major depression in the nation's history. And like most American economic disasters, it was tied to events in Europe. From 1815 to 1818 cotton had commanded truly fabulous prices on the Liverpool market, reaching 32.5 cents a pound in 1818. The high prices meant high profits, and as eager investors looked for new opportunities, the federal government extended liberal credit to those who bought land. Similarly, the new national bank encouraged merchants and farmers to expand and buy more land and catch the rising tide. In the heady prosperity of the new economic order, few Americans preached the old republican values of simplicity and frugality.

But in 1819 world demand for American staples suddenly dropped. The price of cotton collapsed and took the rest of the economy with it. As the inflationary bubble burst, land values, which had been driven to unprecedented heights by the speculative fever, plummeted 50 to 75 percent almost overnight. As the economy went slack, so did the demand for western foodstuffs and eastern manufactured goods and services, sending the nation into a severe depression.

Because the market economy had spread to new areas, this economic downturn affected many Americans. The impact of the panic was not confined to cities and commercial centers, but it was felt in the countryside as well. Many farmers, especially in newly settled regions, had bought their land on credit, and farmers in established areas had expanded their operations in anticipation of future returns. When prices fell, both groups were hard-pressed to pay their debts. Moreover, because so many new cotton plantations had sprung up in the Southwest, many more southerners were now deeply enmeshed in the market. And because they sold most of their staples abroad, their income was especially vulnerable to fluctuations in the world market.

The Missouri Crisis

The Panic of 1819 brought an end to the optimism that had followed the War of 1812. The New Nationalism's spirit of cooperation gave way to jealousy and conflict between competing interests and social groups. Scrambling to weather the economic storm, southern planters, Yankee merchants, and western farmers looked first to their own welfare. So it was probably not surprising that smoldering sectional animosities flared again in 1819, when the Missouri Territory applied for admission as a slave state.

Before the crisis over Missouri, slavery had not been a major issue in American politics. Congress had debated the institution when Jefferson called for the prohibition of the African slave trade in 1808, the earliest year this could be done under the Constitution. Antislavery forces prevailed then, and Congress had outlawed the trade. Louisiana entered the Union in 1812 as a slave state—the first from the Louisiana Purchase—and in 1818 Missouri asked permission to come in too. It did not have a climate suitable for growing cotton and was thus unlikely to be a substantial slaveholding state. In the absence of any specific federal legislation, however, slavery had crossed the Mississippi River into the Louisiana Purchase. By 1820 there were 10,000 slaves in the Missouri Territory out of a total population of 66,000.

Since the adoption of the Constitution, four free states (Vermont, Ohio, Indiana, and Illinois), and five slave states (Kentucky, Tennessee, Alabama, Mississippi, and Louisiana) had been admitted to the Union. That made the tally in Congress 11 free and 11 slave states. As the federal government became stronger and more active, both the North and the South became increasingly anxious about maintaining their political power. The North's greater population gave it a majority in the House of Representatives, 105 to 81. The Senate, of course, was evenly balanced, since each state had two senators regardless of population. But Maine, which up to now had been part of Massachusetts, requested admission as the

THE MISSOURI COMPROMISE AND THE UNION'S BOUNDARIES IN 1820

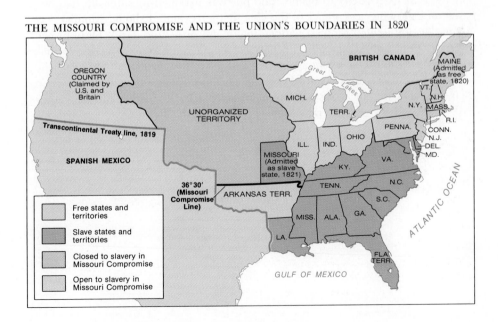

twelfth free state, which would upset the balance unless Missouri came in as a slave state. This was the delicate state of affairs in 1819 when Representative James Tallmadge of New York suddenly introduced an amendment designed to establish a program of gradual emancipation in Missouri.

The debate that followed was bitter. One New York paper argued that the issue "involves not only the future character of our nation, but the future weight and influence of the free states. If now lost—it is lost forever." The Richmond *Enquirer* made the same point from the southern perspective when it declared that if the North prevailed, "Virginia influence will be heard of no more." In addition, for the first time Congress directly debated the morality of slavery. The House approved the Tallmadge amendment, but the Senate refused to accept it, and the two houses deadlocked.

When Congress reconvened in 1820, Henry Clay of Kentucky, the Speaker of the House and a leading spokesman for the New Nationalism, proposed what came to be known as the Missouri Compromise. Under its terms, Missouri was admitted as a slave state and Maine as a free state. In addition, slavery was forever prohibited in the remainder of the Louisiana Purchase north of 36°30′ (the southern boundary of Missouri). This division gave the North most of the Louisiana Purchase. The only remaining portion where slavery could exist was Arkansas, which was organized as a slave territory and eventually admitted as a slave state (1836). Clay's proposal, the first of several sectional compromises he would engineer in his long career, won congressional approval, ending the crisis. But southern fears for the security of slavery and northern fears about its spread remained. As Thomas Jefferson had gloomily predicted, "A geographical line, coinciding with a marked principle, moral and political, once conceived and held up to angry passions of men, will never be obliterated; and every new irritation will mark it deeper and deeper."

Yet sectional tensions, while ominous, tended to ebb and flow with events. The Panic of 1819 affected the political life of the nation in even more direct ways, for as the depression deepened and hardship spread, Americans saw government policies as at least partly to blame. The postwar nationalism, after all, had been based on a growing acceptance of the idea that government should stimulate economic development through a national bank and protective tariff, by improving transportation, and by opening up new lands. As Americans struggled to make sense out of their new economic order and their own personal situation, they began to take more direct control of the government that was so actively shaping their lives. During the 1820s, the popular response to the market and the Panic of 1819 produced a strikingly new kind of politics in the Republic.

SIGNIFICANT EVENTS

1790	Slater's textile mill opens
1793	Eli Whitney invents the cotton gin
1798	Whitney develops system of interchangeable parts
1807	Fulton's *Clermont* initiates regular steamboat service on the Hudson River
1810	*Fletcher v. Peck*
1810–1820	Cotton boom begins in the South
1811	First steamboat trip from Pittsburgh to New Orleans
1813	Waltham system initiated
1816	Second Bank of the United States chartered; protective tariff enacted
1818–1825	Erie Canal constructed
1819	*Dartmouth College v. Woodward*; *McCulloch v. Maryland*; *Sturges v. Crowninshield*
1819–1823	Panic and depression
1820	Missouri Compromise; Lowell mills established
1824	*Gibbons v. Ogden*
1825–1850	Canal era
1830	Baltimore and Ohio Railroad begins passenger service
1834	National Trades' Union founded
1837	Panic
1839–1843	Depression
1841	Preemption Act
1842	*Commonwealth v. Hunt*
1844	Samuel F. B. Morse sends first telegraphic message
1847	Rotary printing press invented

11

The Rise of Democracy

The notice, printed in the small but estimable newspaper of Monticello, Mississippi, made the rounds along the Pearl River. The readers peered at the advertisement by candlelight, in rough log cabins tucked along the piney woods trails; or perhaps together, among a knot of idlers lounging comfortably outside the county courthouse; or perhaps even over in Natchez, shooting billiards barefoot in the late afternoon light while trying to keep the mosquitoes at bay. Someone who knew how to read might happen on the notice and then, grinning, share it with the rest of the crowd. A traveler, the advertisement proclaimed, had lost a suitcase while fording the Tallahala River; the contents included "6 ruffled shirts, 6 cambric handkerchiefs, 1 hair-brush, 1 tooth-brush, 1 nail-brush. . . ."

And as the list went on, the reaction of the listeners would inevitably shift from amusement to disdain and beyond. ". . . 1 pair curling tongs, 2 sticks pomatum . . . 1 box pearl-powder, 1 bottle Cologne, 1 [bottle] rose-water, 4 pairs silk stockings, and 2 pairs kid gloves." The howls of derision that filled the air could only have increased upon learning that anyone finding said trunk was requested to contact the owner—Mr. Powhatan Ellis of Natchez.

Powhatan Ellis was no ordinary backcountry traveler. Born into a genteel Virginia family that claimed descent from Pocahontas, Ellis had moved in 1816 to the raw Southwest to seek his fortune. With his cultivated tastes, careful dress, and stately dignity, he upheld the tradition of the gentleman politician. In Virginia he would have commanded respect—indeed, in Mississippi he had been appointed district judge and United States senator. But for the voters along the Pearl River, the advertisement for his trunk of ruffled shirts, hair oils, and fancy "skunkwater" proved to be the political kiss of death. His opponents branded him an aristocrat and a dandy, and his support among the piney woods farmers evaporated faster than a morning mist along Old Muddy on a sweltering summer's day.

No one was more satisfied with this outcome than the resourceful Franklin E. Plummer, one of Ellis' political enemies. In truth, while the unfortunate Powhatan Ellis had lost a trunk fording a stream, he had never placed the advertisement trying to locate it. That was the handiwork of Plummer, who well understood the new playing field of American politics in the 1820s. If Powhatan Ellis typified the passing political world of the revolutionary era, Plummer was a product of the raucous democratic system emerging in its place. Leaving his home in New England during the hard times following the Panic of 1819, he had worked

A Whig parade in Philadelphia, 1840, painted by Francis Schell. "It seems as though every man, woman, and child preferred politics to anything else," wrote one politician at the end of the campaign.

his way downriver to New Orleans, then headed inland to Mississippi. Settling in a new community, he set himself up as an attorney, complete with a law library of three books. Plummer's ambition, shrewdness, and oratorical talent compensated for his lack of legal training, and he became the first member of the legislature elected from his county.

Plummer's ambition soon flowed beyond the state capital. In 1830 he announced his candidacy for Congress against Colonel James C. Wilkins, a wealthy Natchez merchant, military hero, and member of the state's ruling political clique. The uncouth Plummer seemed overmatched against such a distinguished opponent, and at first few observers took his candidacy seriously. In his campaign, however, he boldly portrayed himself as the champion of the people battling against the aristocrats of Natchez. Contrasting his humble background with that of his opponent, Plummer proclaimed: "We are taught that the highway to office, distinction and honor, is as free to the *meritorious poor* man, as to the *rich;* to the man who has risen from obscurity by his own individual exertions, as to him who has inherited a high and elevated standing in society, founded on the patrimony of his ancestors." Taking as his slogan "Plummer for the People, and the People for Plummer," he was easily elected.

Plummer was a campaigner who knew how to affect the common touch. Once, while canvassing the district with his opponent, the pair stopped at a farmhouse. When his opponent, seeking the farmer's vote, kissed the daughter, Plummer picked up a toddling boy and began picking red bugs off him, telling the enchanted mother, "They are powerful bad, and mighty hard on babies." On another occasion, while his opponent slept, Plummer rose at dawn to help milk the family's cow—and won another vote. He was a master at secretly planting false stories attacking himself in the press, and then bringing forth personal testimonials of well-known men defending his character and denouncing the charges against him.

As long as Plummer maintained his image as one of the people, fighting their battles against aristocrats, he remained invincible. But in 1835 when he became a candidate for the U.S. Senate, his touch deserted him. Borrowing money from a Natchez bank, he purchased a stylish coach, put his servant in a uniform, and campaigned across the state. Having become beholden to the wealthy, he abruptly dropped his attacks on banks and aristocrats. His followers abandoned him and he was soundly defeated. He died in 1852 in obscurity and poverty. Ah, Plummer! Even the staunchest of nature's noblemen may stumble, prey to the temptations of power and commerce!

Indeed, Franklin Plummer was being pulled two ways by the forces transforming American society. As the previous chapter explained, the growth of commerce and new markets opened up opportunities for more and more Americans during these years. "Opportunity" was one of the bywords of the age. Through his connections with bankers and the well-to-do, Plummer saw the opportunity to accumulate wealth, to hire a servant and a coach, to gain status and respect. It was the growth of a market economy that made these opportunities possible, not only for Plummer, but also for farmers speculating in western lands and shoe merchants in Lynn seeking profits by selling throughout the country.

Yet at the same time that new markets were producing a more stratified, unequal society, the nation's politics were becoming more democratic. The new political system that developed after 1820 was strikingly different from the system of the early Republic. Just as national markets linked the regions of America

As this nattily dressed oyster seller suggests, clothes were not much help in sorting out social status in America. Although the clothing of the upper class was often made of finer material and was more skillfully tailored, by the 1820s the less wealthy were wearing similar styles. One visitor expressed amazement at seeing common workers in sleek coats, glossy hats, and doeskin gloves.

economically, the new system of national politics involved more voters than ever before, adopted more democratic electioneering techniques, and created a new class of politicians. Plummer's world reflected that new political culture. And its central feature—another byword on everyone's lips—was "equality." What was the relation between the new equalities of politics and the new opportunities of the market?

EQUALITY AND OPPORTUNITY

Middle- and upper-class Europeans who visited the United States during these decades were especially sensitive to how much of an egalitarian society America had become. Coming from the more traditional and stratified society of Europe, they were immediately struck—often unfavorably—by the "democratic spirit" that had become "infused into all the national habits and all the customs of society." Europeans spent only a few days traveling American roads before the blunt contours of Franklin Plummer's world were brought home to them.

To begin with, they discovered that only one class of seats was available on stagecoaches and rail cars. And these were filled according to the rough-and-ready rule of first come, first served. In steamboat dining rooms or at country taverns, everyone ate at a common table—sitting alongside their fellow "democrats," sharing food from the same serving plates, and ordering from a common menu. As one upper-class gentleman complained, "The rich and the poor, the educated and the ignorant, the polite and the vulgar, all herd on the cabin floor, feed at the same table, sit in each others laps, as it were." Being ushered to bed at an inn, visitors found themselves lodged 10 to 12 people a room, often with several bodies occupying a single bed. Fastidious Europeans were horrified at the thought of sleeping with unwashed representatives of American democracy.

Indeed, the democratic "manners" of Americans seemed positively shocking. Europeans were used to social inferiors speaking only if spoken to. But Americans felt free to strike up a conversation "on terms of perfect equality," with no sense that they were intruding. Frances Trollope, the mother of the English novelist Anthony Trollope, was offended by the "coarse familiarity of address" between classes, while another visitor complained that in a nation where every citizen felt free to shake the hand of another, it was impossible to know anyone's social station. This informality—a forward, even *rude* attitude—was not limited to shaking hands. At theaters, it was hard to get patrons to remove their hats so those behind them could see. And American men seemed always to be slouching when they sat, their feet propped up on a nearby stool, legs dangling this way or that, bodies lying full length on a bench; "perfectly indescribable," sniffed Mrs. Trollope. Not only that, they chewed tobacco and spit constantly—in the national Capitol, in courts and hospitals, even on the floor in homes (although one visitor at least claimed that no gentleman would spit in the living room). Fanny Kemble, an English actress who toured the United States and eventually married an upper-class southerner, reported that on an American steamboat "it was a perfect shower of saliva all the time."

When Plummer took on airs, he made the mistake of dressing his servant in a formal uniform. Few servants in America stood for such unrepublican treatment. An American "will not wear a livery," one visitor explained, "any more than he will wear a halter around his neck." Those who did hire themselves out refused to be called "servants," insisting on the term "help" and on being treated as part of the family. They took their meals at the same table and refused to be summoned by bells. Indeed, except in the South, where black slaves served their owners through the legally enforced system of slavery, no permanent class of domestic servants existed in America. Before the first large wave of immigration began in the mid-1840s, wealthy families often could not hire "help" at any price.

Americans were self-consciously proud of such democratic behavior, which they viewed as a valued heritage of the Revolution. One European reported that a tailor refused to come to his room to fit him for a suit, since to do so would be "unrepublican." And the keelboaters who carried the duke of Orléans—the future King Louis-Philippe of France—on a trip down the Mississippi made their republican feelings plain when the keelboat ran aground. "You kings down there!" called the captain. "Show yourselves and do a man's work, and help us three-spots pull off this bar!" The ideology of the Revolution made it clear that, in the American deck of cards at least, "three-spots" counted as much as jacks, kings, and queens. Kings were not allowed to forget that—and neither was Franklin Plummer.

The Tension Between Equality and Opportunity

While Americans extolled opportunity and equality, a fundamental tension existed between these values, because widespread opportunity would inevitably produce inequality of wealth. In Crèvecoeur's America, a rough equality of wealth and status had prevailed because of the lack of opportunity. In 1800, shoemakers in Lynn, with no way to ship large quantities of shoes across the country, could not become wealthy. Without steamboats or canals, farmers in Jefferson's day could not market surplus grain for profit. But by the 1820s and 1830s, as the opportunities of the market expanded, wealth became much more unevenly distributed. Thus the new generation had to confront contradictions in the American creed that their parents had been able to conveniently ignore.

By equality, Americans did not mean equality of wealth or property. Calls for the redistribution of property were doomed to failure. "I know of no country where profounder contempt is expressed for the theory of permanent equality of property," Alexis de Tocqueville wrote. Thomas Skidmore, a New York City labor leader, did argue that inherited property should be confiscated and redistributed. But even the workers' movement spurned him as too radical. Nor did equality mean that all citizens had equal talent or capacity. Americans realized that individuals possessed widely differing abilities, which inevitably produced differences in wealth. "Distinctions in society will always exist under every just government," Andrew Jackson declared. "Equality of talents, or education, or of wealth cannot be produced by human institutions."

What Americans upheld, in the final analysis, was the equality of opportunity, not equality of condition. Self-made men such as John Jacob Astor, whose fortune came from the western fur trade, were celebrated as the fulfillment of the American dream—examples to be emulated. "True republicanism requires that every man shall have an equal chance—that every man shall be free to become as unequal as he can," one American commented. In a world of expanding markets, increasing national wealth, and an economy that could go bust as well as boom, Americans agreed that one of the primary objectives of government was to safeguard opportunity. Thus the new politics of democracy walked hand in hand with the new opportunities of the market.

THE NEW POLITICAL CULTURE OF DEMOCRACY

The stately James Monroe, with buckled shoes and breeches, his hair powdered and tied in a queue, was not part of the new politics. The last president of the Revolutionary generation, he was suspicious of political parties and rejoiced in the Era of Good Feelings, when party competition seemed to be dying. But as he neared the end of his second term in 1824, a host of new leaders in the Republican party looked to succeed him. Traditionally, a congressional caucus selected the party's presidential nominee; in 1824, the Republican caucus settled on William H. Crawford of Georgia. But Crawford's rivals condemned "King Caucus" as undemocratic. Rejecting the party's official nominee, three other Republicans continued to seek the presidency, all of them ardent nationalists. John Quincy Adams, son of the second president, had once been a Federalist, but as Monroe's secretary of state he strongly pushed for American expansion. John C. Calhoun, Monroe's secretary of war, and Henry Clay, the Speaker of the House, both supported the national bank, a protective tariff, and federal aid for internal improvements.

None of these men bargained on the sudden emergence of another Republican candidate, Andrew Jackson, the hero of the Battle of New Orleans. Jackson was an unexpected choice, for among all previous presidents, only Washington had been a military leader; the others had each spent a long apprenticeship in public office. Jackson had served in the House and the Senate for only three years, and he had briefly been governor of the Florida Territory. At first no one took his candidacy seriously, including Jackson himself. But soon the general's supporters and rivals began receiving reports of his popularity. One of Calhoun's lieutenants in Pennsylvania sent word that Jackson sentiment was strong among "the grog shop politicians of the villages and rabble of Philadelphia and Pittsburgh." From Cincinnati an observer wrote, "Strange! Wild! Infatuated! All for Jackson!" Savvy politicians soon flocked to his standard, but it was the people who first made Jackson a serious candidate.

The Election of 1824

Calhoun eventually dropped out of the race, but that still left four candidates, none of whom received a majority of the popular vote. Jackson led the field, however, and finished first in the Electoral College with 99 votes. Adams had 84, Crawford 41, and Clay 37. Under the Twelfth Amendment, the House was to select a president from the top three candidates. Clay, though himself eliminated, held enough influence as Speaker of the House to name the winner. After a private meeting between the two, he threw his support to Adams, who was elected.

Two days later, Adams announced that Clay would be his new secretary of state; in each of the previous three administrations, the secretary of state had succeeded to the presidency. Jackson and his supporters promptly took up the charge of a "corrupt bargain" between Adams and Clay. Before Adams had even assumed office, the 1828 race was under way.

Even more significant, the election of 1824 had shattered the old party system. The Federalists were long gone, the Republicans hopelessly divided. Political competition would not wither away in a permanent era of good feelings, for the simple reason that differing economic, social, and regional elements in society would continue to advance conflicting interests. But as the old system was breaking up, what would replace it? Henry Clay and John Quincy Adams began to organize a new party, known as the National Republicans to distinguish it from Jefferson's old party, while Jackson's disgruntled supporters were beginning to call themselves Democrats. To muddy the waters even further, a third party arose out of a controversy that erupted in 1826.

Anti-Masonry and the Defense of Equality

The controversy centered on a secret organization known as the Freemasons (or simply Masons), a fraternal group whose chapters had spread through Europe and America during the eighteenth century. Members like George Washington and Benjamin Franklin shared the Enlightenment's belief in the power of reason and the idea of progress, while embracing the Masons' moral commitment to temperance, charity, and hard work. Members were taught this code through secret initiation rituals as they gradually rose through various "degrees" of membership. By 1826, the 150,000 American Masons were predominantly business leaders, manufacturers, and professionals, and the order especially attracted ambitious young men eager to take advantage of the contacts it provided. While Masons were often above average in wealth, their power and prestige stemmed more from the number of public offices they held. In Genesee County, New York, for example, where the Erie Canal was spawning new markets and new fortunes, half of the county's officeholders and an even larger proportion of town officers were Masons.

It was along the canal that William Morgan, a disgruntled Mason, announced

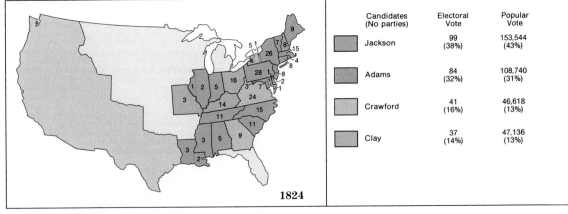

Candidates (No parties)	Electoral Vote	Popular Vote
Jackson	99 (38%)	153,544 (43%)
Adams	84 (32%)	108,740 (31%)
Crawford	41 (16%)	46,618 (13%)
Clay	37 (14%)	47,136 (13%)

1824

ELECTION OF 1824

in 1826 that he intended to publish a book exposing the secrets of the order. Not long after, he was seized by a group of Masons and, crying "Murder," forced into a closed carriage and spirited off into the night. Morgan was never seen again, but little doubt exists that he was murdered, allegedly near Niagara Falls. Indignant citizens in western New York demanded an investigation, and when prominent Masons used their power to thwart it, the Anti-Masonic movement, which demanded eradication of the order, mushroomed. By 1830 the Anti-Masons had organized in 10 states as a political party. William Wirt, Monroe's former attorney general, ran for president on its ticket in 1832.

In national terms, Morgan's disappearance was a relatively minor incident, but it touched raw nerves in an egalitarian society. The Masons, with their secret rituals and shadowy influence, seemed a sinister threat to equality and opportunity. One of the secret oaths its members swore was to advance a "brother's" best interest "by always supporting his military fame and political preferment in opposition to another." Confronted with the power of such an "aristocratic" order, how could ordinary citizens compete? "The direct object of freemasonry," one Anti-Masonry writer charged, "is to benefit the few at the expense of the many, by creating a privileged class, in the midst of a community entitled to enjoy equal rights and privileges." The Anti-Masons argued that in a society of equals, the rule of law should settle disputes—not aristocratic power or secret connections. They looked for new ways to organize politically, to involve more citizens in politics, and to reform society through public opinion and voting.

As a rule, Anti-Masonry was strongest in the most populous, rapidly developing, market-oriented towns. Poor farmers who lacked access to markets but wanted it, as well as farmers in newly opened areas who had become dependent on city banks and merchants for credit or who wanted new roads or canal lines to come their way, were often suspicious of Masonic officeholders. Anti-Masonry also represented a fervent desire to Christianize society and root out organizations like the Masons that exalted reason over traditional religion. The movement was especially powerful in communities with many churches, and it attracted strong support from evangelical Protestants, particularly Baptists, Methodists, Presbyterians, and Congregationalists. In attacking Masonry as an infidel society, the Anti-Mason movement represented a protest against the increasingly secular aspects of American life, which the spread of the market had strengthened.

The new parties were one indication of how much the political system was in flux. By the mid-1830s, what historians now call the second American party system would be in place. The National Republicans gave way to the Whigs, a new party whose organization absorbed many members of the fading Anti-Masons. The Democrats, as the other major party, came together under the leadership of Andrew Jackson. Once established, the second American party system dominated the nation's politics until the 1850s.

Social Sources of the New Politics

Why was it that a new style and new system of politics emerged in the 1820s? We have already seen that a revolution in markets was under way: stimulated by new transportation networks, a more diversified economy, and a more stratified and urbanized society, was emerging. We have seen, too, the immense westward migration, the scramble to bring new land into the market, and the speculative land boom that collapsed in the Panic of 1819. The rise of the new political culture was rooted in these social conditions. During the sharp depression that followed, many Americans became convinced that government policy had aggravated, if not actually produced, hard times. Consequently, they decided that the government had a responsibility to relieve distress and promote prosperity.

The connection made between government policy and economic well-being was the fundamental cause of a rising popular interest in politics during the 1820s. For the first time, large numbers of Americans saw politics as relevant to their daily lives. As agitation mounted for government, especially at the state level, to provide assistance, voters demanded leaders who would respond to the popular will. In several states, notably Kentucky, a movement arose for the legislature to provide debtor relief by enacting a moratorium on the collection of debts. Elections soon became the means through which the majority expressed its policy preferences, by voting for candidates pledged to specific programs. The older style of politics, where a representative took the lead in shaping opinion rather than following it, gave way to the notion that representatives were to carry out the will of the people, as expressed in the results of elections.

As more citizens championed the "will of the people," pressures mounted to open up the political process. Most states had traditionally required voters to own a certain amount of property, to guarantee that they had a "stake in society" if they were to vote on matters concerning the common good. By 1824, only four states (Virginia, North Carolina, Rhode Island, and Louisiana) maintained significant property qualifications for voting. In the others, something approximating white manhood suffrage, under which all free white males were allowed to vote, prevailed. Similarly, property requirements for officeholders were reduced or dropped.

Presidential elections became more democratic as well. In 1800, when Jefferson was elected, only two states allowed the voters rather than the legislature to choose presidential electors. By 1832 South Carolina was the only state that had not reformed its system. States also began casting their electoral votes for president in a single bloc, rather than by districts. This winner-take-all principle increased the power of the most populous states and made it all but impossible for minor parties to wield power or control the election of president. And because a candidate had to carry a number of states in different sections of the country, the backing of a national party, with effective state and local organizations, became essential.

As Jefferson's old Republican party splintered, reformers objected to the legislative caucus as a way of choosing party candidates. Other techniques were tried, such as Jackson's nomination by the Tennessee legislature and Calhoun's endorsement in a public letter signed by a small number of congressmen. But it was the Anti-Masons who pioneered what they argued was a more democratic approach: a party convention to nominate candidates and approve a platform on the crucial issues of the election. By 1832 the other parties were also bringing delegates together at conventions to select state and local tickets, write party platforms, and celebrate partisan fellowship.

As the new reforms went into effect, voter turnout soared. In the 1824 presidential election, only 27 percent of eligible voters bothered to go to the polls. Four years later, the proportion had more than doubled to 56 percent, and in 1840, the apex of the second party system, 78 percent of eligible voters cast ballots, probably the highest turnout in American history. In some states over 90 percent voted in national elections. As the Democrats and the Whigs became truly national parties fielding competitive slates, voter interest intensified.

The Acceptance of Parties

All these developments worked to favor the rise of a new type of politician: one whose life was devoted to party service and who often depended for his living on public office. As the number of state-sponsored internal improvement projects increased during the 1820s, so did the number of government jobs that could support party workers. No longer was politics primarily the province of the wealthy, who often served out of a sense of duty and spent only part of their time on public affairs. Instead, the profession became an important avenue of social mobility. Political leaders were much more likely to come from the middle ranks of society, especially outside the South. Many became economically established after entering politics, but as Franklin Plummer demonstrated, large sums of money were not required to conduct a campaign. Indeed, given the new state of affairs, a successful politician had to mingle with the masses, voice their feelings, and identify with them—requirements that put the wealthy elite at a disadvantage.

In many ways, Martin Van Buren epitomized the new political leader. The son of a New York tavernkeeper, Van Buren was a self-made man who used his success as a lawyer to launch his political career. A master organizer and tactician, he built alliances and gained power even though he lacked a charismatic style. Like Van Buren, whose career took him to the U.S. Senate and eventually the White House, the new breed of politician was beholden to the party system and highly adept at manipulation and party management.

Indeed, it was Van Buren who played a decisive role in promoting a dramatic new attitude toward political parties. The older Revolutionary generation, like Washington, Jefferson, and Monroe, regarded political parties as dangerous and destructive—necessary evils at best. Van Buren took a more positive attitude. Parties were not only "inseparable from free governments," he argued, but "in many and material respects . . . highly useful to the country." He conceded that they were subject to abuse, like any organization, but insisted that they were essential for dealing with the inevitable conflicts that arose in any free political system. Competing parties would scrutinize each other and check abuses, at the same time that they kept the masses informed and politically involved.

"The Will of the People the Supreme Law" reads the banner at this county election. One of the few occasions when most of the men would assemble at the village, election day remained an all-male event, as well as a time of excitement, heated debate, and boisterous celebration. As citizens give their oath to an election judge, diligent party workers dispense free drinks, solicit support, offer party tickets, and keep a careful tally of who has voted. Liquor and drinking are prominently featured: one voter enjoys another round, a prospective voter who is too drunk to stand is held up by a faithful party member, and on the right one groggy partisan is obviously the worse for wear.

Parties also subjected private individuals to discipline and control. If leaders were to be politically successful, they had to consider more than their own personal ambitions. In addition, patronage became a crucial means of holding parties together by rewarding members for faithful service. Finally, parties, by uniting the different sections in a single political organization, helped dampen sectional rivalries. For Van Buren, who had been badly shaken by the Missouri crisis of 1820, parties and the discipline they wielded provided the means to keep the slavery issue out of national politics—which virtually all politicians agreed was essential if the Union was to be preserved.

The Politics of the Common Man

The Jacksonian era has been called the Age of the Common Man. Certainly in politics the ordinary citizen was celebrated as never before. Andrew Jackson, one of the first political leaders to grasp this change, invoked the often-expressed refrain of American politics when he insisted, "Never for a moment believe that the great body of the citizens . . . can deliberately intend to do wrong." To be born in a log cabin became a great advantage, and party leaders everywhere avoided aristocratic airs when on the stump. "I have always dressed chiefly in *Home spun* when among the people," one North Carolina congressman explained. "If a Candidate be dressed Farmerlike he is well received and kindly remembered by the inmates of the Log Cabin, and there is no sensation among the children or the *chickens.*"

Politics became mass entertainment, with campaign hoopla frequently overshadowing issues. Parades complete with floats and marching bands, massive rallies sometimes involving thousands of people, glee clubs, torchlight processions, barbecues, picnics, and free whiskey were used to rouse voters. Treating to drinks became an almost universal campaign tactic. One Kentucky politician admitted that electoral success depended on understanding that "the way to men's hearts is down their throats." Although politicians talked often about principles, political parties were pragmatic organizations, intent on gaining and holding power, and no party could long survive if it did not have a realistic chance of electing a president.

The new politics created an enthusiastic electorate with strong loyalties. By the time the second party system reached maturity, most voters identified with one of the two major parties and supported its candidates through thick and thin. Given such strong loyalties, elections became deeply felt battles between two competing armies, led by men who claimed that the very survival of the Republic hinged on the outcome.

Certainly the politics of the "common man" had distinct limits. Women and slaves were not allowed to vote, nor could free African-Americans (except in a few states) and Indians. Nor did the parties always deal effectively with (or even address) basic problems in society. Still, the importance of Van Buren's insight was fundamental. If the United States was to expand and prosper, the political system had to resolve peacefully differences among competing interest groups, regions, and social classes.

JACKSON'S RISE TO POWER

The new democratic style of politics first appeared on the state and local levels: Van Buren deftly working behind the scenes in New York; Amos Kendall of Kentucky campaigning in favor of debtor relief; Davy Crockett of Tennessee carefully dressed in frontier garb and offering voters a drink from a jug of whiskey and a chew from a large plug of tobacco. But the national implications of these changes were not clear until Andrew Jackson came to power in 1829 as the head of a new, well-organized party. John Quincy Adams might have created a mass-based party when he assumed the presidency in 1825, but while Adams could think nationally—even continentally—about America's future, he was temperamentally unsuited to the task.

John Quincy Adams' Presidency

Adams had been a talented diplomat and a great secretary of state. Intelligent and far-seeing, he was eminently fit to be president—except that he had hardly a political bone in his body. The cold and tactless Adams could build no popular following, and his first message to Congress even urged members not to be "palsied by the will of our constituents." As a committed nationalist, he proposed a series of far-reaching programs to promote internal improvements, manufacturing and agriculture, and exploration of the interior, as well as to support the arts, literature, and the sciences. But such sweeping recommendations left his opponents aghast, and since Adams would not deign to seek support for them, his proposals languished.

Nor would Adams take any steps to gain reelection, though he earnestly desired it. Despite urgent pleas from Henry Clay and other advisers, he declined to remove from federal office men who actively opposed him. Since Adams refused to be a party leader, Clay undertook to organize the National Republicans. But with a reluctant candidate at the top of the ticket, Clay labored under serious handicaps.

Meanwhile, Jackson and his advisers were putting together a new party, the Democrats, to promote his candidacy. Because the party was made up of conflicting interests, its leaders decided against adopting any specific platform, and Jackson remained vague about his own position on many issues. Under these conditions, the 1828 campaign quickly degenerated into a series of scurrilous attacks on the candidates' personal characters, splattering mud on all involved. Meanwhile, party lieutenants (like Van Buren and Calhoun for Jackson and Clay for the National Republicans) organized meetings and barbecues, mobilized the party apparatus, and got out the vote.

Aided by enormous majorities in the South, Jackson won the election handily. Adams carried New England and ran well in the mid-Atlantic states, but he showed little strength in the South and West. In one sense, the significance of the election was clear. It marked the beginning of politics as Americans have practiced it ever since, with two disciplined national parties actively competing for votes, an emphasis on pageantry over issues, and the resort to mass electioneering techniques. Yet in terms of public policy, the meaning of the election was anything but clear. The people had voted for Jackson as a national hero without any real sense of what he would do with his newly won power.

President of the People

Certainly the people looked for change. "I never saw such a crowd here before," Daniel Webster wrote as inauguration day approached. "Persons have come 500 miles to see General Jackson, and they really seem to think that the country is rescued from some dreadful danger!" Some 15,000 supporters cheered wildly after Jackson was sworn in, and only with difficulty did he make his way through the crowd that rushed up the capitol steps to congratulate him.

At the White House, pandemonium reigned. Elbowing aside the invited dignitaries, thousands of ordinary citizens pushed inside to catch a glimpse of their idol. The new president had to flee after being nearly crushed to death by well-wishers. The crowd trampled on the furniture, broke glass, smashed mirrors, and ruined carpets and draperies. Finally the refreshments were moved to the lawn to disperse the mob and keep the executive mansion intact. "It was a proud day for the people," boasted Amos Kendall, one of the new president's advisers. "General Jackson is their own president." Supreme Court Justice Joseph Story was less enraptured: "I never saw such a mixture. The reign of King Mob seemed triumphant."

Whether loved as a man of the people or hated as a demagogue leading the

mob, Jackson was the representative of the new democracy. The first president from west of the Appalachians, he was a product of the frontier, where so many Scotch-Irish families like his own had settled. As a young lawyer, he moved to the Tennessee frontier and became the new state's attorney general. He had a quick mind but limited schooling and little use for learning; after his death a family intimate acknowledged that the general had never believed that the Earth was round. A man of action rather than thought, his decisiveness served him well as a soldier and also in the booming economy around Nashville, where he established himself as a large landowner and slaveholder.

Tall and wiry, with flowing white hair, Jackson carried himself with a soldier's bearing. He had mellowed with age, yet he was never a man to provoke. His troops had nicknamed him Old Hickory out of respect for his toughness, but that strength sometimes became arrogance, and he could be a bully and a tyrant. Toward his enemies he was vindictive, taking opposition as a personal slight. So sensitive was he about his and his wife's reputations that he engaged in several duels and carried a bullet from one near his heart for the rest of his life. Upon leaving the presidency he remarked that his only regret was that he had never had the opportunity to shoot Henry Clay or hang John C. Calhoun.

For all these flaws, Jackson was a shrewd politician. He knew how to manipulate men and could be affable or abusive as the occasion demanded. He would sometimes burst into a rage to get his way with a hostile delegation, only to chuckle afterward, "They thought I was mad." He also displayed a keen sense of public opinion, reading the shifting national mood better than any of his contemporaries.

As the nation's chief executive, he defended the spoils system, under which public offices were awarded to political supporters, as a democratic reform. Rotation in office, he declared, would guard against insensitive bureaucrats who believed that they held their positions by right. During eight years he replaced about 20 percent of the 10,000 federal employees—more than his predecessors, but hardly a wholesale housecleaning. The cabinet, he believed, existed more to carry out his will than to offer counsel, and he had no qualms about removing members who disagreed with him. For advice, Jackson turned more regularly to an informal group of friends, who soon came to be known as the "Kitchen Cabinet." Throughout his term he remained a strong executive who insisted on his way—and usually got it.

The Political Agenda in the Market Economy

Jackson took office at a time when the market economy was spreading through America and the nation's borders were expanding geographically. The three major problems his administration faced were directly caused by the growing pains of this expansion. First, the demand for new lands put continuing pressure on Indians, whose valuable cornfields and hunting grounds could produce marketable commodities like cotton and wheat. Second, as the economies of the North, South, and West became more specialized, their rival interests forced a confrontation over the tariff. Jackson was faced with the difficult question of how the national government might resolve the disputes among different regions. And finally, the booming economy focused attention on the role of credit and banking in society, and on the new commercial attitudes that had become a central part of the developing market economy. The president attacked all three issues in his characteristically combative style.

DEMOCRACY AND RACE

As a planter, Jackson well understood the international demand for cotton that was drawing new lands into the market. He had gone off to the Tennessee frontier in 1788, a rowdy, ambitious young man who could afford to purchase only one slave. Swept up in 1795 in the speculative mania, he bought 50,000 acres on the future site of Memphis. By 1820 44 slaves worked his plantation, the Hermitage; that number grew to nearly 100 by the time he became president. In other words, Jackson pursued the opportunities of the market like so many other Americans on the frontier, and his popularity derived not only from defeating the British, but also from subduing Indians and opening their lands to white settlement. Through military fighting and treaty negotiating, he was personally responsible for obtaining about a third of Tennessee for the United States, three-quarters of Florida and Alabama, a fifth of Georgia and Mississippi, and a tenth of Kentucky and North Carolina.

Even so, in 1820 an estimated 125,000 Indians remained east of the Mississippi River. In the Southwest, the Choctaws, Creeks, Cherokees, Chickasaws, and Seminoles—known as the five "civilized" tribes because their activities and institutions most closely approximated those of whites—retained millions of acres of prime land in the heart of the cotton kingdom. Led by Georgia, southern states demanded that the federal government clear these titles. In response to this mounting pressure, Monroe in 1824 proposed to Congress that the remaining eastern tribes be relocated west of the Mississippi River.

As white pressure for removal intensified during the Jacksonian era, a shift in the attitude toward Indians and race became increasingly apparent. Earlier leaders like Jefferson had argued that although Indian and white cultures could not long coexist side by side, Indians might gradually adopt white ways. By the 1820s, however, more and more Americans began to argue that the Indian could never be "civilized" but was a permanently inferior savage who would always block progress. Before 1815, whites had generally attributed cultural differences among whites, blacks, and Indians to the environment; after 1815 the dominant white culture stressed "innate" racial differences that could never be eradicated.

Accommodate or Resist?

The clamor among southern whites for removal placed the southwestern tribes in a difficult situation. Understandably, they all strongly rejected the idea of removal from their lands. They diverged, however, over how to respond. Among the Seminoles, mixed-bloods (those with white as well as Indian ancestry) took the lead in urging military resistance to any attempt to expel them. Among the Cherokees, on the other hand, mixed-bloods led by John Ross argued that resistance was hopeless and advocated a program of accommodation. They would adopt white ways and live in a manner that would make removal legally impossible. After a bitter struggle, the mixed-blood accommodationists carried the day and in 1827 the Cherokees adopted a written constitution modeled after that of the United States. They also declared themselves an independent nation, enacting the death penalty for any member who sold tribal lands to whites without consent of the governing general council. Developing their own alphabet, they published a bilingual newspaper, *The Cherokee Phoenix*. Similarly, the neighboring Creeks moved to centralize authority by strengthening the power of the governing council at the ex-

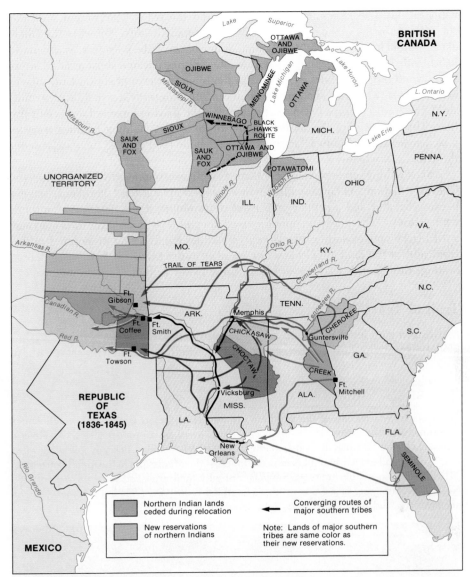

INDIAN REMOVAL

During Jackson's presidency, the federal government concluded nearly 70 treaties with Indian tribes, in the Old Northwest as well as in the South. Under their terms, the United States acquired approximately 100 million acres of Indian land.

pense of local towns. They too made it illegal for individual chiefs to sell any more land to whites.

The division between traditionalists and those favoring accommodation reflected the fact that Indians had been drawn into a web of market relationships too. Indeed, their production of commercial crops such as cotton reinforced the perception among whites that these tribes were more "civilized." While the Cherokee tribe as a whole had prospered, more and more families began clearing their own land and selling the surplus rather than sharing property communally, as they had in the past. Cherokee society became more stratified and unequal, just as white society had. Economic elites dominated the tribal government, and not surprisingly, many of the new laws dealt with property rights. Nor were the Cherokees untouched by the cotton boom. Some of the tribe's leaders, particularly half-bloods who could deal easily with white culture, became substantial planters who owned large numbers of slaves and thousands of acres of cotton land. Slaveholders were wealthier, had investments in other enterprises such as gristmills and ferries, raised crops for market, and were the driving force behind acculturation. Three-fourths of the members of Cherokee slaveholding families were of mixed ancestry, and a much larger proportion could read English than was true for the tribe as a whole.

Slaveholding created value conflicts as well as economic divisions within the Cherokee nation. As cotton cultivation expanded among the Cherokees, slavery became harsher and a primary means of determining status, just as in southern white society. The general council passed several laws forbidding intermarriage with blacks and excluding blacks and mulattoes from voting or holding office. Ironically, at the same time that white racial attitudes toward Indians were deteriorating, the Cherokees' view of blacks drew closer to that of white society.

Trail of Tears

As western land fever increased and racial attitudes hardened, a policy of accommodation was the last thing that whites welcomed. Jackson, who shared these

---

The Choctaws were one of the southern tribes forcibly removed by the United States government in the 1830s. Here, a Choctaw family, led by a proud male, walks along a Louisiana bayou. Tocqueville watched one group, which included sick and wounded, newborn babies, and elderly members near death, cross the Mississippi in the middle of winter. "They possessed neither tents nor wagons, but only their arms and some provisions. . . . No cry, no sob, was heard among the assembled crowd. . . . Their calamities were of ancient date, and they knew them to be irremediable."

feelings, was determined as president to bring the matter of Indian removal to a head. During his first year in office, he watched sympathetically as the Georgia legislature overturned the Cherokee constitution and declared Cherokee laws null and void. It also decreed that Indians would be tried in state courts, although it excluded them from sitting on juries or testifying against whites. Pointing to these developments, the president prodded Congress to allocate funds for Indian removal. In 1830 Congress finally passed a removal bill.

But the Cherokees brought suit in federal court against Georgia's actions, as did sympathetic white missionaries. In 1832 in the case of *Worcester v. Georgia,* the Supreme Court, in an opinion written by Chief Justice John Marshall, sided with the Cherokees. Indian tribes had full authority over their lands, Marshall ruled, and thus Georgia had no right to extend its laws over Cherokee territory. Pronouncing Marshall's decision "stillborn," Jackson ignored the Court's edict and went ahead with plans for removal.

Although Jackson assured Indians that they could be removed only voluntarily, he paid no heed when state governments harassed tribes into surrendering lands. Under the threat of coercion, the Choctaws, Chickasaws, and Creeks reluctantly agreed to move to tracts in present-day Oklahoma. In the process, Indians unaccustomed to white law and notions of property fell victim to shameful frauds. Land-hungry schemers forged sales contracts, enticed intoxicated Indians to sign papers they did not understand, and conspired with the state courts to cheat tribal members. As much as 90 percent of the western land allotments may have fallen into the hands of speculators. Then too, the lure of easy money influenced some tribal leaders to push for emigration. Chief Greenwood LeFlore, a prosperous and powerful Choctaw slaveowner, urged his tribe to relocate, even though he remained behind on his plantation in Mississippi.

The Cherokees held out longest, but to no avail. In order to deal with more pliant leaders of the tribe, Georgia authorities kidnapped Chief John Ross, who had led the tribe in resisting relocation, and threw him into jail. Ross was finally released but not allowed to negotiate the settlement, which stipulated that the Cherokees leave their lands no later than 1838. When that time came, most refused to go. In response, President Martin Van Buren had the U.S. Army round up resistant members and put them in detention camps. Many, leaving the lands they knew so intimately, touched the trunks of trees one last time before they were forced, at bayonet point, to join the westward march. Of the 15,000 who traveled this Trail of Tears, approximately one-quarter died along the way of exposure, disease, and exhaustion. John Ross' wife was one, succumbing to pneumonia after she had given her blanket to a sick child during a snowstorm. As for the western tracts awaiting the survivors, they were smaller and generally inferior to the rich lands that had been taken from the Cherokees.

Some Indians chose resistance. In the Old Northwest, a group of the Sauk and Fox led by Black Hawk recrossed the Mississippi into Illinois in 1832 and were crushed by federal troops and the militia. More successful was the resistance of a minority of Seminoles under the leadership of Osceola. Despite his death, they held out until 1842 in the Everglades of Florida before being subdued at a cost of some $50 million and more than 1500 soldiers' lives. Seminole casualties were

The leader of the antiremoval faction, Cherokee chief John Ross was the son of a mixed-blood mother and a Scottish trader.

equally high by the time most had been removed to Oklahoma. In the end, only a small number of southern tribe members were able to escape removal. Most were relegated to worthless lands that whites did not want.

Except for a few missionaries and eastern reformers, Americans expressed little regret over the treatment of the eastern tribes. In his Farewell Address in 1837, Jackson defended his policy by piously asserting that the eastern tribes had been finally "placed beyond the reach of injury or oppression, and that [the] paternal care of the General Government will hereafter watch over them and protect them." Indians knew the bitter truth of the matter. Without effective political power, they found themselves at the mercy of the pressures of the marketplace and the hardening racial attitudes of white Americans.

Free Blacks in the North

Unlike Indian removal, discrimination against free blacks and the lessening of black opportunity in this period did not depend directly on presidential action. Still, it was Jackson's Democratic party, which so vigorously trumpeted its belief in democracy, that was also the most strongly proslavery and the most hostile to black rights. The intensifying racism that paradoxically accompanied the emergence of democracy in American life bore down with particular force on free African-Americans. "The policy and power of the national and state governments are against them," commented one northerner. "The popular feeling is against them—the interests of our citizens are against them. Their prospects . . . are dreary, and comfortless."

In the years before the Civil War, the free states never had a significant free black population.* In 1860, about 226,000 free blacks, one-quarter of whom were mulattoes, lived in the North. Although they constituted less than 2 percent of the North's population, most states enacted a series of laws to keep African-Americans in an inferior position.

Most northern blacks lacked any meaningful political rights. Black males could vote on equal terms with whites in only five New England states. In New York, the only other state where any African-Americans could vote, they were required to have property worth at least $250, which effectively disfranchised all but a handful of black males. (White males, in contrast, did not have to meet any property requirement.) In 1840, some 93 percent of the northern black population lived in states that completely or practically excluded them from the franchise. Moreover, in New Jersey, Pennsylvania, and Connecticut, blacks lost the right to vote after having previously enjoyed that privilege.

Blacks were also denied basic civil rights that whites enjoyed. Five states prohibited blacks from testifying against whites, and either law or custom excluded African-Americans from juries everywhere except Massachusetts. In addition, Ohio, Indiana, and Illinois passed black exclusion laws prohibiting free blacks from immigrating into the state. These laws were seldom enforced, but they were available to harass the African-American population, as were laws requiring free blacks to post bonds of $500 to $1000 (a sum beyond the means of most whites as well as blacks) for "good behavior." When officials in Cincinnati, following an anti-black riot, enforced such a law in 1829, fully half the city's African-American residents departed.

*For a discussion of free blacks in the South, see Chapter 13, pages 430–431.

THE SPREAD OF WHITE MANHOOD SUFFRAGE
Although white manhood suffrage became the norm during the Jacksonian era, in a number of states free black males who had been voting by law or by custom (until 1834 in Tennessee) actually lost the right to vote. After 1821 a $250 property requirement disfranchised about 90 percent of adult black males in New York.

Segregation, or the physical separation of the races, was widely practiced in the free states. African-Americans were excluded from or assigned to special, separate sections on railroads, steamboats, stagecoaches, and omnibuses. Throughout the North, they could not go into most hotels and restaurants, except as servants of wealthy whites, and if permitted to enter at all, they sat in the corners and balconies of theaters and lecture halls. If they worshiped in white churches, they were relegated to separate pews and took communion after white members. In virtually every community, black children were excluded from the public schools or forced to attend overcrowded and poorly funded separate schools. Commented one English visitor: "We see, in effect, two nations—one white and another black—growing up together . . . but never mingling on a principle of equality."

During these years, whites took to the streets to vent their hostility against blacks in a number of cities with a significant African-American population. No fewer than five major anti-black riots occurred in Philadelphia between 1832 and 1849. After the 1849 riot, Frederick Douglass, the most prominent African-American leader in the North, observed: "No man is safe—his life—his property—and all that he holds dear, are in the hands of a mob, which may come upon him at any moment—at midnight or mid-day, and deprive him of his all."

Discrimination relegated African-American males to the lowest paying and most unskilled jobs in society: servants, sailors, waiters, and common laborers. In Philadelphia in 1838, 80 percent of employed black males were unskilled laborers, and three of five black families had less than $60 total wealth. African-American women normally continued working after marriage, mostly as servants, cooks, laundresses, and seamstresses, since their wages were critical to the family's well-being. Fearing economic competition and loss of status, white workers were overtly hostile to black workers, and skilled black artisans found it increasingly difficult to practice their craft. Excluded from trade unions, African-Americans willingly became strikebreakers. "Whenever the interests of the white man and the black come into collision," one foreign observer noted, "the black man goes to the wall. It is certain that, wherever labor is scarce, there he is readily employed; when it becomes plentiful, he is the first to be discharged." Forced into abject poverty, free blacks suffered from inadequate diet, were more susceptible to disease, and in 1850 had a life expectancy 8 to 10 years less than that of whites.

"At times I feel it almost impossible not to despond entirely of there ever being a better day for us," despaired Charlotte Forten, a free black in Philadelphia. "None but those who experience it can know what it is—this constant, galling sense of cruel injustice and wrong."

The African-American Community

African-Americans responded to this oppression by founding self-help societies, and the black community centered on institutions such as black churches, schools, and mutual aid societies. African-American leaders often emphasized the importance of thrift, industry, and morality as the means to rise in society, but these qualities could not negate white prejudice. A black convention movement began in the early 1830s, bringing together representatives of these various state and local societies. These conventions agitated against slavery in the South and for equal rights in the North. After 1840 black frustration generated a nationalist movement that emphasized racial unity, self-help, and for some, renewal of ties with Africa.

Because of limited economic opportunity, the African-American community was not as diversified as white society in terms of occupation and wealth. But there were distinctions, made not only in terms of wealth but of skin color. In general, lighter skinned blacks, called mulattoes, had greater opportunity to become more literate and skilled than their darker neighbors, had a better chance of finding employment and thus were better off economically, and were more likely to be community leaders. Mulattoes' feelings of superiority were reflected in marriage choices. In Philadelphia, for example, only 8 percent of black marriages in 1850 were between mulattoes and darker-skinned blacks. "They have as much caste among themselves as we have," lamented the abolitionist Sarah Grimké, "and despise the poor as much I fear as their pale brethren."

Minstrel sheet music (left) illustrates the racist attitudes that pervaded Jacksonian democracy. Blacks, played by whites, were made to appear ridiculous through grotesque physical features, exaggerated poses, and pretentious airs. In contrast, the black sawyer (right) working in New York City evidences the dignity free blacks maintained in the face of hostility and discrimination.

The Minstrel Show

During the first half of the nineteenth century, a popular culture directed toward the masses developed in response to rising urbanization. Originating in the 1830s and 1840s and playing to packed houses in cities and towns throughout the nation and even in the gold fields of California, the minstrel show became the most popular form of entertainment in Jacksonian America. Featuring white actors performing in blackface, these shows revealed the deep racism embedded in American society. They dealt in the broadest of racial stereotypes; their advertisements ridiculed blacks, with bulging eyeballs, flat noses, large lips, and gaping mouths, as physically different. The skits themselves portrayed blacks as buffoons, speaking in heavy dialect, performing outlandish dances, and singing almost compulsively.

Although popular throughout the country, minstrelsy's primary audience was in northern cities, and its basic message was that African-Americans could not cope with freedom and therefore did not belong in the North. Blacks in slavery were portrayed as happy and contented, whereas free blacks were invariably caricatured either as strutting dandies who aped white ways or as helpless ignoramuses. Longing to return to the South, one character declared, "Dis being free is worser den being a slave." Drawing its patrons from workers, Irish immigrants, and the poorer elements in society, minstrelsy assured these white champions of democracy that no matter what their situation, they were superior to blacks.

The unsettling economic, social, and political changes of the Jacksonian era heightened white anxiety. Under intense pressure to succeed, whites were haunted by the fear of failure, and this fear was magnified because of the popular yet unrealistic expectation that anyone could become rich. In truth, 20 to 40 percent of white adult males during this period never accumulated any property. Their lack of success stimulated racism, which served as an effective outlet to relieve personal tensions. Subjecting blacks to legal disabilities ensured that even the poorest whites would enjoy an advantage in the race for wealth and status. "The prejudice of race appears to be stronger in the states that have abolished slavery than in those where it still exists," Tocqueville noted, "and nowhere is it so intolerant as in those states where servitude has never been known."

Racism, whether directed against African-Americans or Indians, offered whites a refuge from the frustrations of uncertain status in a supposedly egalitarian society. The power of racism in Jacksonian America stemmed in part at least from the fact that equality remained part of the nation's creed, while it steadily receded as a social reality.

THE NULLIFICATION CRISIS

Indian removal and black discrimination provided one answer to the question of who would be given equality of opportunity in the new democracy of the 1820s and 1830s. Indians and African-Americans would not. The issue of nullification raised a different, but equally pressing question. In a republic as large as the United States, how would various regions or interest groups accommodate their differences? The market revolution, we have seen, led the North, South, and West to specialize economically. Each region had its own particular interests, and when economic conditions became especially severe, the conflicts became more evident.

The Growing Crisis in South Carolina

South Carolina had been particularly hard hit by the depression of 1819. When prosperity returned to the rest of the nation, many of the state's cotton planters remained economically depressed. With lands exhausted from years of cultivation, they could not compete with the fabulous yields of frontier planters in Tennessee, Alabama, and Mississippi. To make matters worse, the policy of Indian removal opened up millions of acres of rich new land that competed with their own.

Under these difficult conditions, South Carolinians increasingly viewed federal tariffs as the cause of their miseries. Congress raised the duty rates in 1816 and again in 1824. The tariff of 1824 included high duties on imported agricultural goods such as wool, hemp, wheat, and liquor, which protected western farmers. Duties on imported textiles encouraged manufacturing in New England, and iron duties were particularly important to Pennsylvania's mining and forging industries. Southerners bitterly assailed the tariff as an unfair tax that raised the prices of goods they imported by as much as 50 percent, while benefiting other regions of the nation.

South Carolina, the one southern state in which blacks outnumbered whites, had been growing progressively more sensitive about the institution of slavery. Moreover, in 1822 a slave conspiracy led by Denmark Vesey, a free black carpenter in Charleston, had been thwarted only at the last moment. A brilliant leader, highly intelligent, literate, and well traveled, Vesey argued that slavery was a violation of republicanism and Christianity. He devised a careful plan to seize control of the city in a series of coordinated attacks and raise the standard of black liberty, but several slaves betrayed the conspiracy shortly before it was scheduled to go into operation. Alerted to the impending danger, Charleston authorities arrested Vesey and his lieutenants, who were speedily tried, convicted, and either executed or banished. Nevertheless, whites remained panic-stricken, since they were convinced that many conspirators had escaped detection and were still in their midst.

With popular fears aroused, South Carolinians felt strongly that additional constitutional protection was needed for slavery. They feared that the constitutional doctrine of broad construction and implied powers, which was used to justify enactment of protective tariffs, might also be used to end slavery. "In contending against the tariff, I have always felt that we were combatting against the symptom instead of the disease," argued Chancellor William Harper of South Carolina. "Tomorrow may witness [an attempt] to relieve . . . your slaves."

Other southern states opposed the 1824 tariff as well, though none so vehemently as South Carolina. When Congress, over the protests of the state's representatives, raised the duty rates still higher in 1828 with the so-called Tariff of Abominations, South Carolina's legislature defiantly published a response, the *South Carolina Exposition and Protest*. This document outlined for the first time the theory of nullification. Only later was it revealed that the author was the second highest official of the federal government itself: Vice President John C. Calhoun.

Calhoun's Theory of Nullification

Educated at Yale and at the most distinguished law school in the country, Calhoun was the most impressive intellect of his political generation. A humorless, driven man, he displayed a fondness for theoretical abstractions that set him apart from his more practical-minded colleagues. During the 1820s, as the crisis in South Carolina deepened, Calhoun made his slow but steady journey away from nationalism toward an extreme states' rights position. When he was elected Jackson's vice president, South Carolinians assumed that tariff reform would be quickly forthcoming. But not long after Jackson took office, he and Calhoun quarreled over a number of matters, and Calhoun lost all influence in the administration.

In his theory of nullification, Calhoun grappled with the problem of how to protect the rights of a minority in a political system based on the rule of the majority. Madison and Jefferson had addressed this question in the Virginia and Kentucky resolutions (page 291), but Calhoun was the first to work out a fully coherent theory. The Union, he argued, was a compact between sovereign states. Thus the people of each state, acting in special conventions, had the right to nullify any federal law that exceeded the powers which the Constitution had granted Congress. If a popular convention declared a law unconstitutional, it would become null and void in that state. Congress then could either yield and repeal the law or propose a constitutional amendment expressly giving it the power in question. If the amendment was ratified and added to the Constitution, the nullifying state could then either accept the decision or exercise its ultimate right as a sovereign state and secede from the Union.

When Senator Robert Hayne of South Carolina explained Calhoun's theory

As Daniel Webster outlines his nationalist theory of the Constitution and the Union, Senator Robert Hayne of South Carolina sits (front, center) with his hands together. Leaning forward on his desk at the extreme left, Vice President Calhoun listens intently. The Senate gallery is filled, with most of the seats occupied by women, evidence of widespread interest in politics.

on the floor of the Senate, Senator Daniel Webster of Massachusetts replied sharply that the Union was not a compact of sovereign states. The Constitution began with the words "We the people," and it was the people, and not the states, who had created it. "It is the people's constitution, the people's government, made for the people, made by the people, and answerable to the people." Webster also argued that the federal government did not merely act as the agent of the states, but that it had sovereign powers in those areas where it had been delegated responsibility. Finally, Webster pointed out that the doctrine of judicial review gave the Supreme Court, and not the states, the final authority to determine the meaning of the Constitution. Expressing the hope that he would never see the Union rent by "fraternal blood," Webster closed with the affirmation, "Liberty and Union, now and forever, one and inseparable."

The Nullifiers Nullified

When Congress passed another tariff in 1832 that failed to give the state any relief, South Carolina's legislature called for the election of delegates to a popular convention, which overwhelmingly adopted an ordinance in November that declared the tariffs of 1828 and 1832 "null, void, and no law, nor binding upon this state, its officers or citizens" after February 1, 1833. The convention established legal penalties for any state or federal officer who attempted to collect the tariff duties and prohibited any appeals to the federal courts.

Jackson, who had spent much of his life defending the nation and expanding its borders, was not about to tolerate any defiance of his authority or the federal government's. In his Proclamation on Nullification, issued in December 1832, he reiterated Webster's nationalist arguments and added a last one of his own—the idea that the Union was perpetual. Under the Constitution, he insisted, there was no right of secession. The United States was a nation, not a league, and secession would destroy the nation. Surprisingly, it had taken 40 years since the adoption of the Constitution to develop this point. Warning the citizens of South Carolina that nullification was treason, Jackson vowed that he would unflinchingly enforce the tariff laws. To reinforce his threat, in March Congress passed the Force Bill, a largely symbolic law that reaffirmed the president's powers to use the army and navy to quell any insurrection.

Yet Jackson was also a skillful politician. At the same time he threatened South Carolina, he urged Congress to reduce the tariff rates. By holding out the hope of tariff reform, he managed to isolate South Carolina from the rest of the southern states. With no other state willing to follow South Carolina's lead, Calhoun reluctantly joined forces with Henry Clay to work out a compromise tariff, which Jackson signed on March 1, the same day he signed the Force Bill. The nullifiers eagerly accepted the compromise, reassembled their popular convention, and repealed the nullifying ordinance. Then, in a move of symbolic defiance, the delegates nullified the Force Bill! Jackson, however, chose to ignore this meaningless gesture, and the crisis came to an end.

The nullification crisis was a triumph of nationalism, and Jackson quickly became a nationalist hero and a symbol of the Union. Whatever its virtues as a theory, Calhoun's doctrine had proven too radical in practice for the rest of the South. No doubt the fact that Jackson was a southerner had also helped. And the resulting compromise had managed to balance the economic interests of the North, South, and West.

But the controversy did strengthen the sense among many southerners that they were becoming a permanent minority. "It is useless and impracticable to disguise the fact," concluded nullifier William Harper, "that we are divided into slave-holding and non-slaveholding states, and this is the broad and marked distinction that must separate us at last." As that feeling grew, it was not nullification, but the threat of secession that ultimately became the South's primary weapon. Although few Americans recognized it then, by 1832 the time had passed when a state might secede peacefully.

THE BANK WAR

Jackson comprehended the political ties that bound the nation, but he understood less well the economic and financial connections that linked different regions of the country through banks and national markets. In particular, the president was suspicious of the national bank and the power it possessed. His clash with the Second Bank of the United States brought on the greatest crisis of his presidency.

The National Bank and the Panic of 1819

Chartered by Congress in 1816 for a 20-year period, the Second Bank of the United States suffered in its early years from woeful mismanagement. During the frenzied speculation between 1816 and 1818, it recklessly overexpanded its operations. When the depression hit in 1819, the Bank, under new management, rigorously contracted credit by calling in loans. The West and the cities were especially hard hit. Senator Thomas Hart Benton of Missouri charged that the national bank foreclosed on so much property that it owned entire towns. Cautious policies put the Bank on a sound financial footing again, but William Gouge, a Philadelphia journalist and economist, charged, "The Bank was saved and the people were ruined." Critics viewed the Bank's policies not as a consequence, but as the cause of the financial downswing. To many Americans, the Bank had already become a monster.

The psychological effects of the Panic were almost as momentous as the economic. The American people had been rapidly pulled from the old agrarian order into a national market economy. From the midst of dizzying prosperity and unbounded optimism, they were suddenly plunged into privation and despair. The shock made the 1820s a time of soul searching, during which many uneasy farmers and workers came to view the hard times as punishment for having lost sight of the revolutionary virtues of simplicity, frugality, and hard work. The call to restore the old Republic and its values found a ready audience. For such Americans, unsettled by the changes that were sweeping the land, banks became a symbol of the commercialization of American society and the rapid passing of a simpler way of life.

Biddle's Bank

In 1823 Nicholas Biddle, a rich, 37-year-old Philadelphia businessman, became president of the national bank. Biddle was intelligent, well educated, and thoroughly familiar with the banking system, but he was also impossibly arrogant. Setting out boldly to restore the Bank's damaged reputation and provide the nation with a sound credit system, he made the Bank of the United States something like a central bank that regulated the amount of credit available in the economy. Government revenues, which came primarily from tariff duties and land sales, were paid largely in state bank notes—paper money issued by state-chartered banks. Because the Treasury Department deposited United States funds in the national bank, the notes of state banks from all across the Union came into its possession. If Biddle believed that a state bank was overextended and had issued more notes than was safe, he presented them to that bank and demanded they be redeemed in specie (gold or silver). Because banks rarely had enough specie reserves to back all the paper money they issued, the only way a state bank could continue to redeem its notes was to call in its loans and reduce the amount of its notes in circulation. This action had the effect of lessening the amount of credit in the economy.

On the other hand, if Biddle felt that a bank's credit policies were reasonable, he simply returned the state bank notes to circulation without presenting them for redemption. Being the government's official depository gave Biddle's Bank enormous power over state banks and over the economy. As Biddle tactlessly commented under questioning by a congressional committee, "There are very few [state banks] which might not have been destroyed by an exertion of the powers of the bank."

Yet Biddle did not use this power irresponsibly. By skillfully regulating the credit supply, he gave the United States a sound paper currency, which the expanding economy needed. Many appreciative bankers supported the national bank, although in the West, where the need for credit was particularly acute, some resented its restraints. Critics also noted that whatever public services it performed, the Bank was a private institution that put stockholders' profits first. Under Biddle's direction, it had opened 29 branches by 1830 and was a financial colossus. The Bank made 20 percent of the country's loans, issued one-fifth of the total bank notes, and held fully a third of all deposits and specie.

Although the Bank had strong support in the business community, workers were often critical of the paper money system. They were frequently paid in depreciated state bank notes that could be redeemed for only a portion of their face value, a practice that deprived them of part of their wages. To avoid being cheated, they called for a "hard money" system—using only gold and silver for currency. Hard money advocates viewed bankers and financiers as profiteers who manipulated the paper money system to enrich themselves at the expense of honest, hardworking farmers and laborers.

The Clash Between Jackson and Biddle

Jackson's own experiences left him with a deep distrust of banks and paper money. In 1804 his Tennessee land speculations had brought him to the brink of bankruptcy, from which it took years of painful struggle to free himself. Reflecting on his personal situation, he became convinced that banks and paper money threatened to corrupt the Republic. He also concluded that the Constitution prohibited banks and that gold and silver were the only constitutional currency. Lacking an understanding of how a credit system and paper money contributed to economic expansion, Jackson had no appreciation of the vital services performed by the national bank.

As president, Jackson periodically called for reform of the banking system, but Biddle refused even to consider curbing the Bank's powers. Already distracted by the nullification controversy, Jackson warned Biddle not to inject the bank issue into the 1832 campaign. Wishing to generate an issue for the upcoming election, Clay and Webster prodded Biddle into applying for a renewal of the Bank's charter in 1832, four years before it was to expire. When Biddle did so, Jackson was furious. "The Bank is trying to kill me," he stormed to Van Buren, "*but I will kill it.*"

Despite the president's opposition, Congress passed a recharter bill in the summer of 1832. Immediately Jackson vetoed it as unconstitutional (rejecting Marshall's earlier ruling in *McCulloch v. Maryland*). He went on to condemn the Bank as an agent of special privilege and as inconsistent with the republican principle of equality, because it made "the rich richer and the potent more powerful." Holding up the Bank as a symbol of aristocracy, the president pledged to protect "the humble members of society—the farmer, mechanics, and laborers" against "the advancement of the few at the expense of the many."

As Jackson's veto message revealed, to a large extent the struggle over the national bank pitted traditional farmers and workers against the world of commerce and national markets. Jackson's strongest supporters were workers and farmers outside the commercial economy and those who were ill at ease over or hurt by the changes that the market produced in their lives. Speculators who desired an inflationary credit system also hailed Jackson's opposition to the Bank— not because they distrusted banks and wanted a "hard money" policy, but because they wanted all restraints lifted from state banks. Individuals who were more comfortable with the new commercial ethos rallied to the Bank's defense. Ultimately, most of them would end up as members of the opposing Whig party.

The Bank Destroyed

When Congress failed to override Jackson's veto, the recharter of the Bank became a central issue of the 1832 campaign. Jackson's opponent was Henry Clay, a National Republican who eagerly accepted the support of Biddle and his national bank. Indeed, Biddle may have spent as much as $100,000 of the Bank's funds in the futile campaign to defeat Jackson. Once reelected, the president was determined to destroy the Bank. He believed that as a private corporation the Bank wielded a dangerous influence over government policy and the economy, and he was justly incensed over its intervention in the election.

His strategy was simple. Since the government had nearly $10 million in Biddle's vaults, the president would cripple the Bank by ordering the deposits withdrawn. When his secretary of the treasury pointed out that such a policy was against the law, Jackson transferred him to another office. When the new secretary also refused, Jackson fired him. Finally, he found in Roger Taney a secretary of the treasury willing to carry out his edict. Taney (pronounced "Taw-ney") did not withdraw the deposits en masse; he merely began drawing against them to pay the government's debts, while depositing new revenues in state banks. The Senate censured Jackson for his action, but Old Hickory remained defiant.

Biddle fought back by deliberately precipitating a brief financial panic in 1833. As the Bank contracted credit, businessmen flocked to Washington seeking relief. Jackson was unmoved. "Go to Biddle," he snapped. "I never will restore the deposits. I never will recharter the United States Bank, or sign a charter for any other bank." Again, Biddle had blundered in this naked display of the Bank's power, for he alienated many supporters in the business community and eventually had to relent. Jackson's victory was complete. When the Bank's charter expired in 1836, no national banking system replaced it. Instead, Jackson continued depositing federal revenues in selected state banks, soon nicknamed "Pet Banks" by his opponents. While some were responsibly managed, political considerations carried more weight in their selection, as a large majority were controlled by Democrats.

Jackson's Impact on the Presidency

Jackson approached the end of his administration in triumph. Indian removal was well on its way to completion, the nullifiers had been confounded, and the "Monster Bank" had been destroyed. A strong-willed general who had never been shy about acting forcefully, Jackson immeasurably enlarged the power of the presidency. "The President is the direct representative of the American people," he lectured the Senate when it opposed him. "He was elected by the people, and is responsible to them." With this declaration, Jackson redefined the character of the presidential office and its relationship to the people.

Jackson also converted the veto into an effective presidential power. During his two terms in office, he vetoed 12 bills, compared with only 9 for all previous presidents combined. Moreover, where previous presidents had vetoed bills only on strict constitutional grounds, Jackson felt free to block laws simply because he thought them bad policy. The threat of such action became an effective way to shape pending legislation to his liking, which fundamentally strengthened the power of the president over Congress. The development of the modern presidency began with Andrew Jackson.

VAN BUREN AND DEPRESSION

With the controls of the national bank removed, state banks rapidly expanded their loans and the amount of paper money in circulation. The total value of bank notes jumped from $82 million in January 1835 to $120 million in December 1836. As the currency expanded, so did the number of banks: from 329 in 1829 to 788 in 1837. A spiraling inflation set in, as prices rose 50 percent after 1830 and interest rates by half as much. Anti-bank Democrats were aghast. Fumed Senator Thomas Hart Benton: "I did not join in putting down the Bank of the United States to put up a wilderness of local banks."

As prices rose sharply, so did speculative fever. By 1836 land sales, which had been only $2.6 million four years earlier, approached $25 million. Almost all of these lands were bought entirely on credit with bank notes, many of which had little value. The opening of extensive Indian tracts for sale fueled the fever. Men seeking land poured into the Old Southwest, and as one observer wryly commented, "under this stimulating process prices rose like smoke." In July 1836, Jackson, seeking to apply the brakes to the economy, issued the Specie Circular, which decreed that the government would accept only specie for the purchase of public land. Land sales drastically declined, but the speculative pressures in the economy were by now too great to be reversed. The Specie Circular remained in effect until May 1838, when Congress repealed it.

"Van Ruin's" Depression

During Jackson's second term, his opponents had gradually coalesced into a new party, the Whigs. Taking their name from the English party that had resisted monarchical tyranny, they charged that "King Andrew I" was a tyrant who abused his veto power, trampled on the Constitution, and dangerously concentrated power in the presidency. Henry Clay led the new party, and his American System, designed to spur national economic development through a protective tariff, a national bank, and federal aid for internal improvements, formed the core of its program. In 1836 the Democrats' presidential nominee was Martin Van Buren, who had replaced Calhoun as Jackson's vice president during his second term. The Whigs ran not one candidate but three: Daniel Webster in New England, Hugh Lawson White in the South, and William Henry Harrison in the West. In so doing, the party hoped to prevent Van Buren from getting a majority of the electoral votes and thus send the election to the House. But while Van Buren was a lackluster candidate, he carried the election and assumed office in March 1837.

Van Buren had less than two months in office to savor his triumph before the speculative mania of the previous few years collapsed. An oversupply drove down the price of cotton on the international markets, and nervous investors began a rush on banks to redeem paper notes for hard cash. In May, as the New York banks ran out of gold and silver reserves, they suspended specie payments. The

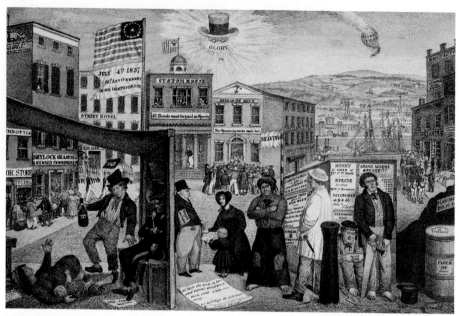

This Whig cartoon blames the Democratic party for the depression that began during Van Buren's administration. Barefoot workers go unemployed and women and children beg and sleep in the streets. Depositors clamor for their money from a bank that has suspended specie payments, while the pawnbroker and liquor store do a thriving business and the sheriff rounds up debtors.

news spread as fast as stagecoaches and steamboats could travel, and everywhere banks faced the same crisis. The economy recovered partially, but in 1839, following a record crop and declining British demand, the bottom fell out of the cotton market and the country entered a serious depression. Arising from causes that were worldwide, the depression demonstrated how deeply the market economy had penetrated American society. It was not until 1843 that the economy revived.

But public opinion identified hard times with the policies of the Democratic party. As federal revenues declined, Van Buren cut government spending, further constricting the economy. He also steadfastly opposed a new national bank and instead sought to divorce government from banking. In 1840 Congress approved his proposal for an Independent Treasury to keep the government's funds. Its offices were forbidden to accept paper currency, issue any bank notes, or make any loans. The government's money would be safe, as Van Buren intended, but it would also remain unavailable to banks to make loans and stimulate the economy. In addition, the system produced a perpetual shortage of specie as it accumulated in Independent Treasury vaults, thus further curtailing economic investment.

Whigs countered by demanding a protective tariff, continuation of state internal improvement projects, protection of corporations, and expansion of the banking and credit system. In states where the Whigs gained power, they increased the number of banks, expanded the supply of paper money, and called for positive government programs to promote economic recovery.

As the depression deepened, thousands of workers were unemployed and countless businesses failed. Cotton prices, which had stood at 17 cents a pound before the depression, fell to a low of 6 cents. Suffering was particularly acute among urban workers and their families. An estimated 50,000 were unemployed in New York City, 2000 shoemakers representing 40 percent of the work force were thrown out of work in Lynn, and the mills in Lowell were idle; nationally wages fell 30 to 50 percent. "Business of all kinds is completely at a stand," wrote New York businessman and civic leader Philip Hone in 1840, "and the whole body politic sick and infirm, and calling aloud for a remedy."

The Whigs' Triumph

For the 1840 presidential campaign the Whigs turned to William Henry Harrison, a military hero who had defeated the Shawnee at Tippecanoe and the British at the Battle of the Thames during the War of 1812. By 1840 the Whigs had done much to perfect their party's national organization, and they entered the campaign in high spirits, especially since the Democrats had rather glumly renominated Van Buren. The Whigs' strategy was simple. In the midst of the worst depression of the century, they employed the democratic electioneering techniques that Jackson's supporters had perfected to portray Harrison as a man of the people. Van Buren, of course, was painted in the opposite colors. Whig broadsides claimed that he wore a corset, ate off gold plates with silver spoons—even that "Sweet Sandy Whiskers" indulged in the effeminate custom of using cologne. Shades of Franklin Plummer!

In contrast, when one Democratic newspaper editor (allegedly quoting a disgruntled Whig) sneered that Harrison would be content to spend his days drinking hard cider in a log cabin, Whig rallies began featuring hard cider and log cabins to reinforce Harrison's image as a man of the people. Ironically, Harrison had been born into one of Virginia's most aristocratic families and was living in a 16-room mansion in Ohio. But the Whig campaign, by portraying the election as a contest between aristocracy and democracy, was perfectly attuned to the prevailing national spirit.

Both parties used the new campaign techniques—parades, barbecues, liberty pole raisings, and mass meetings—to stir up enthusiasm among the voters. And just as the Panic of 1819 had roused the voters to action, the depression and the two parties' response to it kindled voters' interest. The result was a record turnout, as nearly four-fifths of the eligible voters went to the polls. Some 900,000 new voters were mobilized between 1836 and 1840, and the Whigs won over three-fifths of them. Voters who were hurt most severely by falling prices blamed the Democrats for hard times and strongly backed the Whigs. Democrats, on the other hand, recruited thousands of new voters who feared the probanking legislation passed by Whigs in various states in 1838 and 1839. Although the popular vote was fairly close (Harrison led by about 150,000 votes out of 2.4 million cast), in the Electoral College he won an easy victory, 234 to 60.

The "log cabin" campaign marked the final transition from the deferential politics of the Federalist era to the stridently egalitarian politics that had emerged in the wake of the Panic of 1819. The Whig and Democratic parties, now closely competitive and national in their organization, attracted great popular support. As the *Democratic Review* conceded after the Whigs' victory in 1840, "We have taught them how to conquer us."

Daily Lives

POLITICAL CULTURE

The Log Cabin Campaign

"Political life to an American citizen, has all the fanaticism of religion and all the fascination of gambling." So concluded one knowledgeable American during the Jacksonian era, and he spoke accurately enough. The Whigs' legendary "log cabin" campaign of 1840 was in many respects the first modern presidential campaign, with both parties involving ordinary Americans in a multitude of ways.

The sheer number of participants in 1840 was unprecedented. Whigs, who led the way in innovation, organized a rally on the battlefield at Fort Meigs, in Ohio, which reputedly attracted more than 25,000 men, women, and children. Thousands marched in parades in New Jersey and Ohio, but the largest political demonstration the country had ever seen occurred in Baltimore at the Young Men's Whig Convention. Spectators jammed rooftops, balconies, and sidewalks to witness the three-mile-long parade of delegates accompanied by artillery, bands, carriages with dignitaries, at least eight log cabin floats, and over a thousand banners and transparencies. The festivities, which continued for two full days, included hour after hour of speeches, a balloon ascension, and a fancy-dress ball.

Although women lacked the right to vote, by 1840 they were cheering party processions, riding on floats, and attending political meetings. This was a sharp break with tradition, and at first women caught up in the excitement felt uneasy. In 1840 Mary Todd, the future wife of Abraham Lincoln, confessed that her support of Harrison had led her into the rather "unladylike profession" of politics. "Yet at such a crisis," she countered, "whose heart could remain untouched?" Once again the Whigs were innovators, specifically inviting women to attend party rallies. As Thomas Corwin, the Whig candidate for governor in Ohio, declared, "Ladies should become interested in subjects affecting the welfare and very existence of our common country."

Most women remained in the background of the campaign, but some became more active, delivering political speeches and conducting meetings. On Harrison's behalf, Lucy Kenney published *The Strongest of All Governments Is That Which is Most Free*, one of the first political pamphlets written by an American woman. "This way of making politicians of their women is something new under the sun," acknowledged one Georgia Democrat. Democrats initially resisted the trend, but of necessity soon plunged in.

In an era when social diversions were relatively limited, the new political techniques aimed to entertain as they forged bonds of party commitment. The variety of activities was limited only by the imagination of party organizers: political clubs, pole raisings, bonfires, fireworks, barbecues and picnics, debates and stump speaking. Before a mammoth 1840 Whig meeting in Ohio, party volunteers baked 20,000 pounds of bread and prepared 200 bushels of potatoes, 600 pounds of butter, 70 sheep, 80 slabs of bacon, 21 steers, and "numerous other provisions" for the expected throng. (Small wonder that Whigs saluted the contribution of women in their songs and speeches.) One member of Congress acknowledged that it was a hardship for many voters to attend rallies, but added that "the fun, the joy, the excitement . . . repaid them for the loss of time and the necessary expenditures of money and energy it required."

Daily Lives

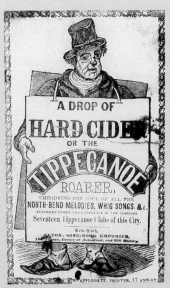

Whig song book, 1840.

The Whigs' 1840 campaign for the first time popularized party songs. Male and female glee clubs sang partisan tunes, publishers brought out campaign song books, and newspapers printed the most popular lyrics. "Nobody cared how sorry the doggerel might be," one western politician recalled, "if it contained a hit at the opposite party . . . or a rattling chorus." In the best democratic tradition of Franklin Plummer, Whigs crooned:

Old Tip he wears a homespun coat
He has no ruffled shirt-wirt-wirt.
But Mat he has the golden plate
And he's a little squirt-wirt-wirt.

Democrats countered with a serenade mocking General Harrison's tactful silence during the campaign:

Another gourd for General *Mum*,
Whose fame is like his fav'rite drum;
Which when most empty makes
    most noise,
Huzza for General Mum, my boys!

Even if the lyrics were mostly nonsense, commented Whig editor Horace Greeley, "people like the swing of the music," and "after a song or two they are more ready to listen to the orators."

Drinking went hand in hand with the new democratic politics: rural taverns and urban saloons were frequently centers of party activity, and liquid refreshment was mandatory at rallies. Whig gatherings featured barrels of hard cider (and sweet cider for the temperate). Capitalizing on the fervor of 1840, Edmund C. Booz, an enterprising distiller, hit on the brilliant strategy of marketing his liquor in bottles shaped like log cabins. Soon known as booze bottles, they added a new word for liquor to American speech.

Party souvenirs, too, were widely marketed for the first time. Arising in the morning, a loyal Whig could shave with Tippecanoe Shaving Soap, don a Harrison suit complete with log cabin buttons, knot his Harrison necktie, fold his Harrison handkerchief, and pin on a Tippecanoe badge. He could check the weather forecast in the *Harrison Almanac*, write his friends on Harrison stationery, and smoke Tippecanoe Tobacco. In the evening, with his wife outfitted in a dress made from calico printed with Harrison's picture and log cabins and carrying a Harrison fan, he might saunter down to Whig headquarters to sing selections from *The Tippecanoe Roarer*.

Witnessing the popular fervor of the 1840 campaign, former president John Quincy Adams wrote in his diary, "Here is a revolution in the habits and manners of the people. Where will it end?" Adams' terminology was apt: nothing less than a revolution in the structure and behavior of American politics had occurred. Enthusiastic popular involvement would remain the hallmark of the party system for the remainder of the nineteenth century.

THE JACKSONIAN PARTY SYSTEM

It is easy, given the hoopla of hard-cider campaigning, to be distracted from the central fact that the new political system was directly shaped by the social and economic strains of an expanding nation. Despite the efforts of both parties to avoid campaigning on the issues, Whigs and Democrats held different attitudes toward the changes brought about by the market, banks, and commerce.

Democrats, Whigs, and the Market

The Democrats had supported Jackson in his war against a national bank and stuck with Van Buren through the depression, as he tried to check the harm of speculating banks. Through it all, they tended to view society as a continuing conflict between "the people"—farmers, planters, and workers—and a set of greedy aristocrats—bankers, stock jobbers, and investors—who manipulated the banking system for their own profit. Idle social parasites, this paper money aristocracy was the enemy of the nation's traditional Revolutionary virtues, for it encouraged speculation and the desire for sudden, unearned wealth. For Democrats, the Bank War became a battle to restore the old Jeffersonian Republic, to preserve the values of simplicity, frugality, hard work, and independence. The Bank was a monster, a symbol of the corporate power that menaced the Republic. This is what Jackson meant when he said that removal of the deposits from Biddle's Bank would "preserve the morals of the people."

Jackson shrewdly understood the power private banks could wield and the dangers they posed to a democratic society. Yet Democrats, in effect, wanted the rewards of the market without sacrificing the virtues of a simple agrarian republic. They wanted the wealth that the market offered, without the competitive, changing society, the complex dealings, the dominance of urban centers, and the loss of independence that came with it. Whigs, on the other hand, were more comfortable with the market. For them, commerce and economic development were agents of civilization. "Our course is onward, straight onward, and forward," Daniel Webster proclaimed. ". . . we shall elevate [our country] to a pitch of prosperity and happiness, of honor and power, never yet reached by any nation beneath the sun."

Nor did the Whigs envision any conflict in society between farmers and mechanics on the one hand and businessmen and bankers on the other. Economic growth would benefit everyone by creating jobs, stimulating demand for agricultural products, raising national income, and expanding opportunity. The government's responsibility was to provide a well-regulated economy that guaranteed opportunity for citizens of ability. In such an economy, banks and corporations were not only useful but necessary, as was a sound currency that was at least partly paper. A North Carolina Whig well expressed the party's vision of society: "We are all one family. . . . All should be mutual friends and helpers to each other, and who ever aids and assists his fellow men from good motives, by lending money, by affording employment by precept or example, is a benefactor to his fellow men."

Whigs and Democrats differed not only in their attitudes toward the market, but also about how active government should be. Despite Andrew Jackson's inclination to be a strong president, Democrats as a rule believed in limited government, particularly at the federal level. They feared power as a threat to individual-

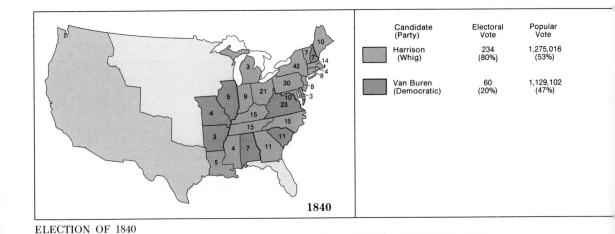

Candidate (Party)	Electoral Vote	Popular Vote
Harrison (Whig)	234 (80%)	1,275,016 (53%)
Van Buren (Democratic)	60 (20%)	1,129,102 (47%)

1840

ELECTION OF 1840

ism and freedom. To restrain excessive power, they believed that government had a responsibility to destroy monopolies and special privileges and open the market to equal access and free competition. As one New Jersey Democratic newspaper declared, "All Bank charters, all laws conferring special privileges, with all acts of incorporation, for purposes of private gain, are monopolies, in as much as they are calculated to enhance the power of wealth, produce inequalities among the people and to subvert liberty."

In *Charles River Bridge v. Warren Bridge* (1837), the Supreme Court strengthened the vision of an expanding capitalistic society undergirded by free competition. The opinion was written by Chief Justice Roger B. Taney, whom Jackson had appointed in 1835 to succeed John Marshall. At issue was whether the state of Massachusetts, which had given a charter to the Charles River Bridge Company to build a toll bridge, could give another company a charter to construct an adjacent free bridge. The toll bridge company sued, claiming that construction of the competing bridge would make its property worthless. In his opinion, Taney held that the public interest was an overriding concern, and that any ambiguity in the charter should be resolved in favor of the people. By striking down the idea of implied monopolies, the Court sought to promote equality of opportunity and economic progress.

In keeping with this philosophy of limited government, Democrats also rejected the idea that moral beliefs were the proper sphere of government action. Religion and politics, they believed, should be kept clearly separate. More fearful of concentrated power, Democrats believed that limited government would best preserve individual liberty, and they viewed humanitarian legislation as an interference with personal freedom. On the other hand, they supported debtor relief, which in their view curbed the wealthy aristocrats who tyrannized the common worker.

The Whigs, in contrast, viewed government power positively. They believed that it should be used to protect individual rights and public liberty, and that it had a special role where individual effort was futile. By regulating the economy and competition, the government could assure equal opportunity. In the absence of government control, the rich would monopolize power and wealth.

But for Whigs the concept of government promoting the general welfare went beyond the economy. Northern Whigs in particular also believed that government power should be used to foster the moral welfare of the country. They were much more likely to favor temperance or antislavery legislation, aid to education, and the reform of prisons or asylums. Whigs portrayed themselves not only as the party of prosperity, but also as the party of respectability and proper behavior.

The Social Bases of the Two Parties

In some ways, the social makeup of the two parties was similar. To be competitive, Whigs and Democrats both had to have significant support among farmers, the largest group in society, and workers. Since most Americans were in the middle ranks of society, neither party could carry an election by appealing exclusively to the rich or the poor.

The Whigs, however, enjoyed disproportionate strength among the business and commercial classes, especially after the Bank War drove a number of businessmen out of the Democratic party. They appealed to planters who needed credit to finance their cotton and rice trade in the world market, to farmers who were eager to ship their surpluses at a profit, and to workers who were eager to improve themselves. Democrats attracted farmers isolated from the market or uncomfortable with it, workers alienated from the emerging industrial system, and rising entrepreneurs who felt excluded and were eager to break monopolies and open the economy to newcomers like themselves. The Whigs were strongest in the towns, cities, and rural areas that were fully integrated into the market economy, whereas Democrats dominated areas of semisubsistence farming that were more isolated and were economically languishing or declining. Attitude toward the market, rather than economic position, was more important in determining party affiliation.

The Triumph of the Market

Clearly, then, Jacksonian politics evolved out of the social and economic dislocation produced by rapidly expanding economic opportunity. Yet efforts to reverse some of the effects of the market while preserving its benefits were doomed to failure. Some Democrats followed up the destruction of the national bank by mounting a drive to eliminate all state banks as well. But in the states where they succeeded, so much hardship and financial chaos ensued that some system of banking was soon restored. The expansion of the economy after 1815 had caught farmers as well as urban residents in an international network of trade and finance, tying them with a tightening grip to the price of cotton in Liverpool or the interest rates of the Bank of England. There was no rolling back the market in a return to the ideals of Crèvecoeur.

Still, Americans had evolved a system of democratic politics to deal with the conflicts that the new order produced. The new national politics—like the new markets spreading across the nation—had become essential structures uniting the American nation. They provided an ideology of equality and opportunity, which stood as a goal for the nation even if crucial elements of society, like women, blacks, and Indians, were excluded. The new politics developed a system of truly national parties, competing with one another, involving large numbers of ordinary Americans, resolving differences through compromise and negotiation. Along with the market, democracy had become an integral part of American life.

SIGNIFICANT EVENTS

1819–1823	Panic and depression
1822	Denmark Vesey conspiracy
1823	Biddle becomes president of the Bank of the United States
1824	Tariff duties raised; Jackson finishes first in presidential race
1825	House elects John Quincy Adams president
1826	William Morgan kidnapped
1827	Cherokees adopt written constitution
1828	Tariff of Abominations; *South Carolina Exposition and Protest*; Jackson elected president
1829	Cherokee blood law
1830	Webster–Hayne debate; Indian Removal Act
1830–1838	Indians removed from Southwest
1831	Anti-Masonic party holds first nominating convention
1832	*Worcester v. Georgia*; Jackson vetoes recharter of the national bank; Black Hawk War; Jackson reelected; South Carolina nullifies tariff; Jackson's Proclamation on Nullification
1833	Force Bill; Tariff duties reduced; Jackson removes deposits from the Bank of the United States
1833–1834	Biddle's panic
1834	Whig party organized
1835–1842	Second Seminole war
1836	Specie Circular; Van Buren elected president
1837	*Charles River Bridge* case; Panic
1838	Trail of Tears
1839–1843	Depression
1840	Independent Treasury Act; Harrison elected president
1842	First professional minstrel troupe.

12

The Quest for Perfection

nyone unfamiliar with Boston would have mistaken the short, plain, rustic fellow for a stranger. His speech, with talk of God's "creeturs" or "nat'ral" occurrences, was that of a rural Yankee, a pious farmer, perhaps, come to gaze reverently upon the imposing Hanover Street Church. Spanking new in 1826, the church boasted a facade of rough-hewn granite and a main floor that sloped toward the pulpit, allowing every member of its thriving congregation to see as well as hear anyone who spoke from it. All the more curious, then, was the purposeful, almost proprietary way that this unkempt man bustled about the church. Come Sunday morning, however, visitors understood the unusual behavior of this rough-hewn man. For then he would mount the stairs to the pulpit, fasten his wide-set, burning eyes on his audience, and blaze forth denunciations of dancing, drinking, dueling, or "infidelity," all the while punctuating his sermon with pump-handle strokes of the right hand. In 1826 the Reverend Lyman Beecher was probably the most celebrated minister of the Republic, and the pulpit of Hanover Street was his to command.

Nor were Beecher's ambitions small. His goal was nothing less than to bring the kingdom of Christ not only to Boston but to the nation and the entire world as well. Like most respectable clergy of the day, Beecher had studied the intriguing final book of the New Testament, the Revelation to John. The Revelation set forth visions of what would come to pass in the latter days of the Earth. It foretold a thousand years of peace and triumph, when the saints would rule and evil would be banished from the world. These obscure prophecies of a glorious millennium had been analyzed for years, not only by noted ministers like Jonathan Edwards but also by scientists like Isaac Newton and Joseph Priestley, the discoverer of oxygen. Beecher was convinced that the long-awaited millennium might well begin in the United States.

Personal experience had long reinforced this unfailing optimism. Born to a shrewd, sturdy lineage of New England blacksmiths in the year before the colonies declared their independence, Beecher entered Yale College during the high tide of postwar nationalism—and, some said, the lowest ebb of religion among young people. Many of his fellow Yale students boasted of reading deist books like Thomas Paine's *Age of Reason,* which ridiculed the "superstitions" of the Bible. Yale's devout president, Timothy Dwight, did not silence Yale's young infidels; instead, he challenged them to open and frank debate. His energetic arguments, vigorous eloquence, and sheer endurance swept students up in the revivals of the

The Way of Good and Evil extolls the importance of family, religion, education, and hard work, all virtues in the millennial quest for perfection.

Second Great Awakening that came to many colleges in 1802. Among those converted was Beecher.

As a minister, Beecher first did the Lord's work in a small Long Island fishing town, then moved in 1810 to Litchfield, Connecticut, a prosperous community noted for its fine law school and excellent female academy. But his boundless energy also went into raising a family of 11 children, every one of whom he prayed would take leading roles in bringing the kingdom of God to America. Beecher was no stodgy Puritan. He loved to wrestle on the floor with his sons or climb the highest trees, scrambling energetically for nuts. With his daughters he went "berrying," and young Harriet Beecher delighted in such expeditions, coming back "with a six quart pail full of berries and her dress wet up to her knees." But the religious dimension of their lives was constant: two services on Sunday, a weekly prayer meeting, and a monthly "concert of prayer," where the devout met to pray for the conversion of the world. Beecher's son Thomas remembered the daily prayers and the commanding, deep voice of his father: "Overturn and overturn till He whose right it is shall come and reign, King of nations and King of saints."

If the kingdom were to come, there would clearly have to be a sweeping transformation of the world, not only of individual souls but also of families, communities, and entire nations. Beecher joined other Protestant ministers in supporting a host of religious reforms and missionary efforts. In 1810 the American Board of Commissioners for Foreign Missions was established, followed by the American Bible Society (1816) and the American Tract Society (1825), whose Bibles and religious pamphlets blanketed every sleepy hamlet in the country. Societies sprang up to promote Sunday schools and minister to sailors and the poor. By 1830 the most important of these organizations made up the loosely united "Benevolent Empire." To Beecher these were signs of the coming kingdom.

In 1826, as the new pastor at Hanover Street, Beecher was determined to combat Unitarianism, which seemed to him Boston's most threatening perversion of Christianity. Upper-class and cultured, Unitarian churches counted among their members many of Boston's merchant and banking elite, as well as lawyers, judges, and Harvard professors. They were the sort of people who borrowed many books from the Boston Atheneum, who attended concerts of the Haydn and Handel Choral Society, who employed exotic Asian servants and stocked their private gardens with peacocks. To Beecher their liberal, rational theology was little more than a "halfway house on the road to infidelity," for Unitarians rejected the divinity of Jesus, referring to him only as Teacher and Redeemer, not as the Son of God. They disdained revivals as entirely too emotional and distrusted the notion that a conversion experience was essential to leading a Christian life. Beecher's aim as "the great gun of Calvinism" was to destroy these pernicious beliefs, "roots and all."

But he had artillery enough left over for other targets. Constantly Beecher denounced the sins of playing cards and gambling with dice. He agitated to outlaw

Lyman Beecher (center) with his family in 1855. Five of his six sons, all of whom were ministers, stand in back. In front, daughters Catharine (holding his arm to steady it for the long exposure) and Isabella are on the left; Harriet, the author of *Uncle Tom's Cabin*, is at the far right.

lotteries that were so popular among the lower classes. He outspokenly condemned those who drank to excess, and he sought to close the booths that sold grog on the Boston Common. And he denounced Roman Catholic priests and nuns as superstitious, devious agents of "Antichrist"—that seven-headed, ten-horned beast described so vividly in the book of Revelation. By the late 1820s a new wave of immigrants had begun to arrive in the United States, many of them Catholics from Ireland and Germany. Such newcomers, as well as other working people who enjoyed rum, whiskey, or lotteries, did not appreciate Beecher's efforts at "moral reform." When a blaze broke out in the basement of his church in 1830, local firefighters rushed to Hanover Street—for the pleasure of watching while that splendid structure burned to the ground. The fires of spiritual reform had been checked, temporarily, by a blaze of a literal sort.

Any fire, real or spiritual, is a bit unpredictable as it spreads from one scrap of tinder to the next. So it proved with reform movements of the 1820s and 1830s: they moved in diverging, sometimes contradictory ways. What did it mean, after all, to bring in Christ's kingdom? The goals of the early reform societies were moral rather than social. Leaders like Beecher sought to convert individuals and to church the unchurched, with the help of religious revivals and benevolent associations. Their conservative aim, as he expressed it, was to restore America to "the moral government of God." Other Christians, however, began to focus on social abuses and to demand more radical solutions. The degradation of slavery, the inequality of women in society, the abuses of prisons and asylums—these social evils needed to be attacked directly, they argued. Ironically, while Lyman Beecher remained in the conservative mainstream, many of his children went well beyond his own strategies for hastening the millennium. They spoke out for abolition, women's rights, and education in ways that left their father distinctly uncomfortable. In their activities, Beecher family members reflected the diversity of the reform impulse itself.

REVIVALISM AND THE SOCIAL ORDER

Society during the Jacksonian era was undergoing deep and rapid changes. It was expanding economically through the revolution in markets, as its citizens competed for status and wealth through the gospel of democratic individualism. In a nation where fortunes could be won and lost almost overnight, some reformers sought stability and moral order in religious community. The bonds of unity created by a revival brought a sense of peace in the midst of a society in change. Revivals could provide a sense of strength and discipline, too, in an emerging industrial culture that demanded sobriety and regular working habits. Other reformers, however, sought to check the excesses of Jacksonian America by radically remaking institutions or devising utopian, experimental ways of living and working together. The drive for renewal, in other words, led reformers sometimes to preserve social institutions, other times to overturn them. It led them sometimes to liberate, other times to control. And the conflicting ways in which these dynamics operated could be seen as the revivals of the Second Great Awakening were transformed by the electric career of Charles Grandison Finney.

Finney's New Measures

In 1821, before Lyman Beecher had even moved his family to Boston, a young lawyer in western New York experienced a soul-shattering religious conversion. Immediately he abandoned his legal career and announced that he was now on retainer to God. He began preaching throughout New York as an itinerant free-lance revivalist, joining with settled ministers who invited him to address their congregations. Eventually he was ordained in the Presbyterian church, although he lacked any formal theological training. Then he conducted a series of spectacu-lar revivals in the booming port cities along the new Erie Canal between the mid-1820s and the early 1830s—the final, climactic phase of the Second Great Awakening. As a result of these revivals in upstate New York, Charles Finney, lawyer-turned-evangelist, gained national attention.

There were many reasons for his extraordinary appeal. Tall and spare, a hand-some man with a penetrating gaze, Finney, like George Whitefield before him, had a marvelous voice that he could project a great distance and modulate at will. His power over an audience was such that when he described the descent of a sinner into hell, those in the back of the hall rose to witness the final plunge. The secret of his success lay less in his presence than in his use of special revivalistic techniques—"the new measures"—and his casual attitude toward religious doc-trine.

The new measures that Finney popularized in upstate New York had been developed on the frontier in places like Cane Ridge. They included using blunt, direct speech; holding "protracted meetings" night after night to build up excite-ment and emotion; praying for sinners by name; encouraging women to testify in public gatherings; and placing sinners on the "anxious bench" at the front of the church, where the entire congregation could witness their struggle for conversion. "A revival is not a miracle," Finney coolly declared, "it is a purely scientific result of the right use of constituted means." He even wrote a manual for ministers explaining how to "work up" a revival with the new measures.

The Philosophy of the New Revivals

Finney walked in the footsteps of a long tradition of Protestant evangelicals.* But by his day, many optimistic, individualistic Americans found the traditional doc-trines of John Calvin and Jonathan Edwards difficult to endorse. A mysterious, inscrutable God who predetermined the fate of every human being seemed unrea-sonable and undemocratic to citizens of a republic founded on common sense and natural rights. And Calvin's insistence that men and women had inherited Adam's original sin and could do nothing to attain salvation hardly appealed to a genera-tion that condemned hereditary distinctions, celebrated human dignity, and praised ability and activity.

These strict Calvinist doctrines had already been modified by a fast friend of Lyman Beecher, Professor Nathaniel Taylor of the Yale Divinity School. His "New

---

*The word *evangelical* derives from a Greek word meaning the bringing of good news—in this case, the Gospel. Protestant evangelicals consistently stressed the need for individuals to undergo an emo-tionally wrenching conversion experience and subsequent rebirth stemming from an awareness of sinful guilt, and Christ's act of atoning, through his death, for their sins.

Charles Finney, about 1834.

Haven theology" rejected the doctrine of original sin, in which Adam and Eve's sin had been passed on in human nature as a hereditary taint. Although men and women would inevitably sin, Taylor acknowledged, as rational beings they had sufficient free will to resist their natural inclination toward evil. Taylor thus denied that salvation was exclusively the doing of God; instead it was the duty of ministers to induce sinners to accept of their own free will God's gift of salvation.

Finney popularized these notions, couching liberal Calvinism in a language that his audience could easily understand. But that process pushed him further than Taylor dared go toward minimizing human sinfulness and emphasizing human free will. Leaving the Lord little role in the drama of human deliverance, Finney insisted that men and women were free moral agents and that all who wanted to could be saved. To those anxious about their salvation, he thundered, "Do it!" Finney's approach also made emotion paramount. While his revivals were not as tumultuous as those on the southern frontier, shrieks and groans, the cries of agonized prayers, and uncontrolled crying resounded throughout the hall. Like the camp meetings, Finney's methods were designed to precipitate outbursts of emotion and to prepare sinners to accept conversion. He justified their use on the grounds of success, pointing to the large numbers who had been saved.

With such changes within reach of every individual, what might be in store for the society at large? "If the church would do her duty," Finney confidently predicted, "the millennium may come in this country in three years." He advised his young converts that they should take as their goal "the complete reformation of the whole world." And by the 1830s Finney had taken to preaching not merely faith in human progress, but something more—human perfectibility. This new theology of "perfectionism" maintained that a benevolent God was progressively revealing his will to a reasonable mankind—so plainly that in time even the common people would understand these ultimate truths and successfully live up to them. Finney boldly asserted that all Christians should "aim at being holy and not rest satisfied until they are as perfect as God."

By bringing more aggressive techniques to the practice of revivalism, by preaching an optimistic message of free will and salvation to all, Finney and his many eager imitators among western ministers transformed Protestantism. But not all clergy applauded his achievement. For Beecher, as well as many supporters of the Second Great Awakening, Finney's new measures went too far, the emotionalism of his revivals ran to excess, and his theology of perfectionism verged on heresy. When the two men met at New Lebanon, Connecticut, in 1827 to discuss their differences, Beecher warned that if Finney tried to bring his brand of revivalism to Massachusetts, "I'll meet you at the State Line, and call out all the artillery-men, and fight you every inch of the way to Boston." Undeterred, Finney promoted his new measures in New York, western Pennsylvania, and even New England. As for Beecher, by 1832 he had decided to outflank all of his adversaries—Finney in upstate New York, the Unitarians in Boston, even the pope in Rome—by moving west to take over the presidency of Lane Seminary in Cincinnati. There he planned to train the right sort of revivalists to save the frontier for true religion and to bring about the kingdom of God in America.

Religion and the Market Economy

The controversies over revivalism and perfectionism were not remote theological disputes. Revival audiences responded to the call for reform partly because they were disquieted by the rapid social changes Americans were experiencing. In the

North, evangelical religion proved strongest not in isolated backwaters, but in areas emerging from the frontier stage and entering the market economy. Rochester, New York, a burgeoning flour-milling center on the Erie Canal, epitomized the social environment that spawned revivals. When Charles Finney came to town in the winter of 1830–1831, Rochester was a community in crisis. It had grown in a decade and a half from a village of 300 souls to a commercial city of more than 20,000. That wrenching expansion produced sharp divisions among the town's leaders, a large working class that increasingly lived apart from employers and beyond their moral control, and a rowdy saloon culture catering to canal boatmen and other transients. Many members of the business community were indifferent to religion and the spiritual state of their employees.

Finney preached almost daily in Rochester for six months. One resident remembered that "you could not go upon the streets and hear any conversation, except upon religion." In cooperation with the local ministers, Finney brought thousands to accept his message of voluntary salvation. Church membership doubled during the revival, and by the time he left, members were actively at work in the community, spreading the gospel. Religion helped bring order to what had been a chaotic and fragmented city.

Although revivals like Finney's Rochester triumph drew converts from all segments of American society, they appealed especially to the middle class: lawyers, merchants, retailers, and manufacturers—men who played central roles in the larger market economy and invested in factories and railroads. The market put intense pressure on these upwardly mobile citizens, who regarded success as a moral obligation and a reflection of individual character. At the same time, the oscillations of the economy—boom, then bust—intensified their fear that success would be fleeting. Religion provided a way in which to cope with the tensions and uncertainties of their own lives.

In addition to businessmen and professionals, workingmen were among the converted. Joining a church symbolized their desire to get ahead in the new economy by accepting moral self-discipline. To a striking degree, social mobility walked hand in hand with church membership. In Rochester two-thirds of the workers who were church members improved their occupational status in a decade: they were far more likely than unchurched workers to own their own shop or business or to become skilled employees. By contrast, workingmen who did not join a church rarely stayed in town more than a few years, and those who stayed were likely to decline in status.

Although revivalists like Finney cared more about saving souls than about savings accounts, evangelical Protestantism reinforced values that were necessary to succeed in the new competitive economy. The market and the factory required a disciplined, reliable, responsible work force. Churchgoers accepted the values of hard work, sobriety, and punctuality; they internalized the demand for restraint and self-control. Religion was also a means of social control in a disordered society. Again, that aim was far from the purpose of the revivalists, who had their gaze fixed firmly on the millennium. But the revivals promoted social order through the mechanism of self-restraint. And many employers put pressure on workers to give up their drinking habits, on and off the job, and to embrace religion.

The Significance of the Second Great Awakening

Tocqueville claimed that he knew of "no country in the world where the Christian religion retains a greater influence over the souls of men than in America." He did not exaggerate. And as a result of the Second Great Awakening, the dominant form of Christianity in America became evangelical Protestantism. Membership in the major Protestant churches of pre–Civil War America—Congregational, Presbyterian, Baptist, and Methodist—soared during the first half of the nineteenth century. By 1840 an estimated half of the adult population was nominally connected to some church, with the Methodists emerging as the largest Protestant denomination in both the North and the South. Numbering just 58,000 members in 1790, Methodists claimed over a million members in 1844. Unlike the more Calvinistic Congregationalists, Presbyterians, and Baptists, the Methodists from the beginning embraced the doctrine of free will and honed their revival skills.

Evangelicalism was in harmony with the basic values of early nineteenth-century Americans. Its emphasis on the ability of the individual to bring about his or her salvation endorsed the American belief in individualism. The revivals appealed to ordinary people and catered to a mass audience without social distinctions, which reinforced the American belief in democracy and equality. Anti-intellectual in their thrust, revivalists emphasized the individual's feelings and conscience as the source of truth and scorned carefully reasoned theological discourses. Success oriented, the revivals varied tactics to gain the most converts and were invincibly optimistic. Finney's doctrine of perfectionism was perfectly attuned to the spirit of the age.

WOMEN'S SPHERE

But not all—or even a majority—of Americans who flocked to revivals or joined reform societies were men. On the contrary, female converts outnumbered males by about three to two. Usually the initial convert in a family was a woman, and many men who converted were related to women who had come forward earlier. In Utica, New York, for example, the majority of men who joined the churches were relatives of women who had preceded them in membership.

Women and Revivalism

Women played such a prominent role in the Second Great Awakening in part because of changes in their own social universe. During the early nineteenth century, Americans placed increasing emphasis on romantic love as a factor in marriage. In the new conjugal marriage, couples married less often to enhance property and status, and more often because they shared a mutual affection. With sons and daughters demanding the right to choose their own partners, parents played a smaller part in arranging marriages. Marriage was still deemed important for a woman's happiness, and it remained essential for her economic security. But a woman's prospects for marriage became less certain with the decline of the parental role in matchmaking. And in older areas such as New England, this uncertainty was compounded by the migration of so many young men to the West, creating a shortage of eligible bachelors.

The new unpredictability of their lives drew young women toward religion. Although everywhere in America women made up the backbone of the churches, those between the ages of 12 and 25 were especially susceptible to conversion. Joining a church heightened a young woman's sense of initiative and gave her a sense of purpose. Church membership also provided friendships and support and, by establishing respectability and widening her social circle, enhanced her chances of marriage.

Furthermore, the changing economic order of the Jacksonian era brought unfamiliar pressures to bear on wives and mothers. Most men now worked outside the home, while the rise of factories led to a decline in part-time work such as spinning, which women had once performed to supplement family income. Moreover, except on the frontier, home manufacturing was no longer essential, for the family purchased articles that women previously had made, such as clothing, shoes, soap, and candles. A number of occupations that had been open to women earlier, including medicine and shopkeeping, were now closed to them.

The Ideal of Domesticity

This increasing separation of the household from the workplace converted the home into a female domain. As such, it took on a new social identity. Idealized as a repository of virtue and a barrier against the disorder of the outside world, the home became a sanctuary and the mother its patron saint. This new view of women's role—almost a "cult of domesticity"—was elaborated largely by clergy and female authors in countless sermons, advice manuals, and pieces of sentimental fiction for an urban middle-class audience. But the ideal's significance and acceptance had far-reaching consequences.

The cult of domesticity was based on the notion of separate sexual spheres. Each sex, it was said, had a part of life in which it reigned supreme. Whereas men were breadwinners responsible for the family's financial security, women were care-givers, concerned with and finding fulfillment in others. If men's sphere was the outside world, women's sphere was the home, where they were to dispense love and comfort and teach moral values to husbands and children. "Love is our life our reality, business yours," Mollie Clark told one suitor. Women were also held to a higher standard of sexual purity. Although regarded as physically weaker and therefore reliant on male protection, women were believed to be stronger morally. A man's sexual infidelity, while hardly condoned, brought no lasting shame. But for a woman to "fall" before marriage or to stray afterward was to court everlasting disgrace and social isolation. Under this double standard, men were expected to be aggressive, while women were to be passive, to submerge their identities in those of their husbands. Tocqueville commented that "in no country has such constant care been taken, as in America, to trace two clearly distinct lines of action for the two sexes, and to make them keep pace with the other, but in two pathways which are always different."

Most Jacksonian women did not see this ideology as a rationale for male dominance. On the contrary, women played an important role in creating the cult of domesticity, none more than Lyman Beecher's daughter Catharine. Like the earlier advocates of "republican motherhood," she argued that making the home a female domain gave women real power as moral custodians of the nation's future. To raise children in Christian virtue and to provide solace for family members were crucial responsibilities. So too was the proper care of a middle-class household, and she wrote several books on the "science" of domestic management, detailing the most efficient, economical, and sanitary methods of preparing food and keeping house. Catharine Beecher was also a leading advocate of training women to become schoolteachers. Conceiving of the school as an extension of the

As business affairs grew increasingly separate from the family in the nineteenth century, the middle-class home became a female domain. As a wife and mother, a woman was to dispense love and moral guidance to her husband and her children.

home, she maintained that teachers, like mothers, should instill sound moral values in children. Because of their naturally pious character and their affection for children, women were ideally suited to be teachers and should receive greater educational opportunities.

Most women hardly had the time to make the ideal of domesticity the center of their lives. Farm women had to work hard and constantly, while lower-class families could not get by without the wages of female members. Still, most middle-class women accepted and tried to live up to the ideal, and many found the effort confining. "The great trial is that I have nothing to do," one complained. "Here I am with abundant leisure and capable, I believe, of accomplishing some good, and yet with no object on which to expend my energies." For such women, religion and reform offered two socially accepted outlets for their talents.

Their socially defined role as the guardians of religion and morality helps explain the prominence of women among revival converts, but religious activities offered other rewards as well. It was the one way that women could exert influence over society and the one area where wives were freed from subordination to their husbands. Finney allowed men and women to pray together, and he permitted women to lead the congregation in prayer. For some male critics, this was the most dangerous of his new measures, for it implied a certain equality between the sexes. One unhappy man in Rochester complained about the effect of Finney's visit to his home: "He *stuffed* my wife with tracts, and alarmed her fears, and nothing short of meetings, night and day, could atone for the many fold sins my poor, simple spouse had committed." Then, getting to the heart of the matter, he added, "She made the miraculous discovery, that she had been 'unevenly yoked.' From this unhappy period, peace, quiet, and happiness have fled from my dwelling, never, I fear, to return."

Daily Lives

CLOTHING AND FASHION
Early Bloomers

As Elizabeth Smith Miller cultivated her garden in the spring of 1851, her thoughts wandered from the flowers and vegetables to her muddy, bedraggled skirt. Those long, trailing flounces seemed to catch on every stalk and branch; layers of stiff petticoats made stooping to weed and plant almost impossible; her snug corset kept her short of breath. Irritated and uncomfortable, Miller resolved then and there to free herself from bondage to those "fettering folds" by designing a simpler outfit. The result was a loose-fitting dress that reached a few inches below her knees and a pair of trousers that tapered at the ankle, resembling "harem pants." "It would be suitable dress for a journey to California," one dubious but diplomatic family member remarked. Miller remained undaunted. "What is Life," she rejoined, "but a journey to California—to that Eldorado of higher development in pursuit of which one should cast off every impediment."

In her eagerness to "cast off every impediment," Elizabeth Miller epitomized the perfectionist spirit of early Victorian America, and her chosen object of reform became women's dress. The daughter of Gerrit Smith, a wealthy landowner and merchant from upstate New York who endorsed abolition, temperance, and women's rights, Miller enlisted in the cause of dress reform feminists like her cousin, Elizabeth Cady Stanton, and Amelia Bloomer, the editor of a temperance newspaper, *The Lily*. After Bloomer's newspaper publicized Miller's design, other journalists dubbed the outfit "bloomers," and Cady Stanton, along with many other women prominent in the suffrage movement, adopted the costume.

Dress reform attracted adherents with a variety of social agendas. Some feminists, like Elizabeth Miller, simply sought greater freedom of movement. Cady Stanton, for example, commended bloomers to all busy wives and mothers "who wash and iron, bake and brew, carry water and fat babies upstairs and down, bring potatoes, apples, and pans of milk from the cellar, run our own errands, through mud or snow, shovel paths, and work in the garden." "'The drapery,'" she concluded, "is quite too much—one might as well work with a ball and chain." Other feminists went further, seeing dress reform as essential to establishing the equality of the sexes. Sarah Grimké contended that "so long as we submit to being dressed like dolls, we can never rise to the stations of duty and usefulness from which they [men] desire to exclude us." Many women members of utopian socialist communities like Oneida, Brook Farm, and New Harmony adopted the bloomer costume for similar reasons, applauding dress reform as a leveling, democratic influence.

A consensus concerning the need to simplify women's dress reached well beyond the ranks of feminists and utopian thinkers. Health reformers like the followers of Sylvester Graham joined with more orthodox members of the medical community in condemning the vogue of "tight-lacing" corsets. Some physicians warned that tight lacing impaired the ability of women to bear healthy children by narrowing the pelvis, while others charged that the practice could result in broken ribs, collapsed lungs, weakened abdominal walls, and uterine disorders. Catharine Beecher, who instituted a regimen of health-promoting calisthenics at her female seminaries, agreed with feminists that confining corsets and "seas" of crino-

Daily Lives

line petticoats restricted ease of movement. The members of female moral reform societies also took up the cause, contending that addiction to fashion and finery encouraged prostitution. A similar suspicion of high style pervaded sentimental novels of the period, literature written largely by and for women.

But not all Victorians agreed on the need for dress reform. *Harper's Bazaar,* a popular women's magazine, stood with tradition by declaring that "we believe in the petticoat as an institution older and more sacred than the Magna Carta." Critics associated bloomers with the radicalism of upstate New York's "Burned-Over District," where it had been created, and with the free love theories of the Oneida Community, where it reigned as the prevailing fashion. Others charged that bloomers resembled the garments worn by prostitutes in big city brothels, while pious skeptics pointed to the biblical prohibition against women wearing trousers. Most middle-class Americans, steeped in both Scripture and the doctrine of "separate spheres," strongly identified wearing pants with masculinity and believed that bloomers would make women men's "rivals" rather than their "counterparts." Even Cady Stanton's father lamented that she had made "a guy" of herself by appearing in the new costume.

By the 1860s, bloomers had fallen from favor even among feminists. The outfit proved difficult to make, and even Elizabeth Miller admitted that her creation did not "sit" gracefully. More to the point, the flurry over fashion distracted attention from the cause of women's rights. Susan B. Anthony abandoned bloomers when she noticed that men stared at her ankles instead of listening to her talk. Perhaps most important, many suffragists became convinced that women's degradation was rooted in laws and institutions, not in dress. "We have no reason to hope that pantaloons would do more for us than they have done for man himself," Cady Stanton wrote. "The negro slave enjoys the most unlimited freedom in his attire . . . yet in spite of his dress and his manhood, too, he is a slave still."

Despite the new importance of affection in marriage, women gave emotionally much more to other family members than they received in exchange, and they turned to other women for comfort and support. Thus benevolent organizations supplemented religious revivals, weekly services, and prayer in consoling women and providing an outlet for expression. These societies fostered close friendships among women eager for companionship. This "sisterhood"—the common sense of identity and shared experiences—helped sustain not only home missionary societies and maternal associations, but also other reform movements launched by women to aid females of the lower classes, including movements to reclaim prostitutes.

The Middle-Class Family in Transition

As the middle-class family adapted to the increased pressures of a competitive market society by becoming a domestic haven of moral virtue, it developed a new structure and new set of attitudes closer in spirit to the modern family. One basic change was the rise of privacy. The family was increasingly seen as a sheltered retreat from the outside world. It became the center of emotional comfort, reassurance, and support. In addition, the pressures to achieve success led middle-class young adults to delay marriage. A man was expected to be sufficiently established to support a wife before he married. Owning a house and having a wife who did not work became important symbols of success.

Smaller family size was a result of the delay in marriage as well, since wives began bearing children later. But especially among the urban middle class, women began to use birth control to space children further apart and minimize the risks of pregnancy. The methods were primitive by modern standards: abstinence from intercourse, extended breastfeeding, condoms, and crude vaginal diaphragms and sponges. In addition, it has been estimated that before 1860 one abortion was performed for every five or six live births. These practices contributed to a decline in the birth rate, from slightly more than 7 children per family in 1800 to 5.4 in 1850—a 25 percent drop. Although the birth rate had been falling gradually since the turn of the century, it dropped more abruptly beginning in the 1830s. Family size was directly related to the success ethic. A smaller family indicated an effort at self-restraint, but, more important, it showed that the family recognized the necessity of living within its means. In the cities, large families were increasingly identified with low-status immigrants and were viewed as evidence of economic irresponsibility. An economic asset on the farm, children were a financial burden in the new society, where extended education and special training were needed to succeed.

Indeed, more parents showed greater concern about providing their children with advantages in the race for success. Middle-class families were increasingly willing to bear the additional expense of educating their sons to prepare them for a career in business. Sons remained in the family longer and entered the work force later; often they were in their early twenties by the time they left home. In general the parents' sacrifice accomplished its purpose: sons who went to school longer and left home later tended to be more successful and achieve a higher status. Middle-class families also frequently equalized inheritances rather than giving priority to the eldest son or favoring sons over daughters.

AMERICAN ROMANTICISM

American Protestantism, with its drive for millennial perfection, played a central role in the reform movements of the Jacksonian era—whether it was Charles Finney "praying up" a revival or Catharine Beecher reordering the habits of American women. Yet the temper of those movements would have been strikingly different without another influential current of thought, that of Romanticism.

As an intellectual movement, Romanticism began in Europe as a reaction to the Enlightenment. The Enlightenment had placed reason at the center of human endeavor; Romanticism emphasized instead the importance of intuition and emotion as sources of truth. It gloried in the unlimited potential of the individual, who might soar if freed from the artificial restraints of oppressive institutions. Romanticism extolled humanitarianism; it sought to experience and identify with the suffering of the oppressed, in the way that Lord Byron, the tempestuous English poet who died in 1824 working for Greek independence, did.

All of these attitudes, values, and thought helped separate the world of Jacksonian America from the Enlightenment temperament of the Revolutionary generation. In exalting inner feelings and heartfelt convictions, Romanticism reinforced the emotionalism of religious revivals. Philosophically, its influence was strongest among intellectuals who took part in the Transcendental movement and in the dramatic flowering of American literature. And like millennial revivalism, Romanticism offered its own paths toward perfection.

Emerson and Transcendentalism

Above all, Romanticism produced individualists. Thus Transcendentalism is difficult to define, for its members resisted being lumped together. It blossomed in the mid-1830s, when a number of Unitarian clergy like George Ripley and Ralph Waldo Emerson resigned their pulpits, loudly protesting the church's smug, lifeless teachings. To Lyman Beecher, Unitarians were threatening because their rationalism took them too far toward infidelity. To Ripley and Emerson, Unitarian rationalism did not go far enough. "In how many churches, by how many prophets, tell me," demanded Emerson, "is man made sensible that he is an Infinite Soul; that the heavens and the earth are passing into his mind; that he is drinking forever the soul of God?" The new "Transcendentalist Club" attracted a small following among other young Boston intellectuals who were likewise unhappy, including Margaret Fuller, Bronson Alcott, and Orestes Brownson.

Like European Romantics, American Transcendentalists emphasized feeling over reason, seeking a spiritual communion with nature. By *transcend* they meant to go beyond or to rise above—specifically above reason and beyond the material world. Every human being contained a spark of divinity, Emerson avowed, by participating in what he called the "Over-Soul," the divine force flowing through all of creation. Transcendentalists also shared in the Romantic's glorification of the individual. "Trust thyself. Every heart vibrates to that iron string," Emerson ad-

Ralph Waldo Emerson.

vised. "The root and seed of democracy is the doctrine, judge for yourself." If freed from the artificial constraints of traditional authority, the individual had infinite potential. So optimistic was Transcendentalism in its view of human nature, it essentially denied the existence of evil.

Transcendentalism had much in common with Jacksonian America— optimism, individualism, and an egalitarian spirit. "I am *Defeated* all the time," Emerson declared, "yet to Victory I am born." The psychology of boom-and-bust left no place for the finality of defeat. Although the details of Emerson's philosophy lay beyond the grasp of all but a handful of intellectuals, thousands flocked to hear him lecture. Like the devout at Finney's revivals, who sought to perfect themselves and bring about the millennium, those who heard Emerson were infused with the spirit of optimistic reform.

As the currents of Romanticism percolated through American society, the country's literary tradition came of age. In 1820 educated Americans still tended to ape the fashions of England and Europe: American readers bought seven English books for every three written in the United States. But as the population grew and education expanded, American writers developed their own distinctive styles and examined the customs, opinions, and character of American society. Improved printing presses allowed for cheaper, mass-produced American books, and better transportation made possible a wider distribution of printed material across the nation. By 1850 for every British book, two American books were sold in the United States.

Emerson's address "The American Scholar" (1837) constituted a declaration of literary independence. "Our long dependence, our long apprenticeship to the learning of other lands draws to a close," he proclaimed. "Events, actions arise, that must be sung, that will sing themselves." His call inspired a generation of writers.

The Clash Between Nature and Civilization

At the time Emerson spoke, James Fenimore Cooper was already making his mark as the first distinctive American novelist. In the Leatherstocking Tales, a series of five novels written between 1823 and 1841, Cooper chronicled the life of the frontiersman Natty Bumppo. Leatherstocking, as Bumppo was also known, was hardly drawn with realism; decades later, Mark Twain would hoot at Cooper's crude dialogue, and the poet James Russell Lowell gleefully said of Cooper that "the women he draws from one model don't vary/ All sappy as maples and flat as a prairie."

But the tales did examine two basic yet contradictory impulses within American culture. On the one hand, Natty Bumppo represented the nobility and innocence of the wilderness. At the same time, the novels portrayed the culture of the frontier as a threat to the civilization Cooper prized so highly. In one scene in *The Pioneers* (1823), as villagers along the New York frontier slaughter thousands of pigeons, Leatherstocking laments the wanton destruction, only to hear a townsman express surprise that anyone would "grumble at the loss of a few pigeons. . . . If you had to sow your wheat twice, and three times, as I have done," he continues, "you wouldn't be so massyfully feeling'd toward the devils. Hurrah, boys! scatter the feathers." As the market expanded and the hinterlands began to develop and exploit their resources, American thought betrayed an inward dread that the advance of civilization would destroy the natural simplicity of the land.

Natty Bumppo, the self-reliant solitary individual, stood halfway between the savage and civilized worlds, not comfortable embracing either.

Henry David Thoreau, too, used nature as a backdrop for his literary explorations; he also was concerned with the conflict between the unfettered individual and the constraints of society. A disciple of Emerson, Thoreau grew up in Concord, Massachusetts, where he became part of Emerson's circle. Eventually he undertook to live by himself to demonstrate the advantages of self-reliance. Building a cabin on the edge of Walden Pond on land owned by Emerson, Thoreau lived in relative solitude for 16 months, recording his observations in his journal, which became the basis for one of the classics in American literature, *Walden* (1854).

Thoreau argued that only in nature could one find true independence, liberty, equality, and happiness. By living simply, it was possible to master oneself and the world. Thoreau's own isolation from society, however, was less than total. When lonely or hungry, he walked to Emerson's home nearby for conversation and a slice of Lidian Emerson's apple pie, and most of the materials he used to build his "wilderness" cabin were store-bought. Still, *Walden* eloquently denounced the frantic competition in an industrial society for material goods and wealth. "Money is not required to buy one necessity of the soul," Thoreau maintained. "I see my townsmen, whose misfortune it is to have inherited farms, houses, barns, cattle, and farming tools. . . . Who made them serfs of the soil?" It seemed only too clear that "the mass of men lead lives of quiet desperation."

Thoreau's individualism was so extreme that he rejected any institution of society that contradicted his personal sense of right. "The only obligation which I have a right to assume, is to do at any time what I think right," he wrote in his essay "On Civil Disobedience." He extolled the individual over the democratic will of the majority. "Any man more right than his neighbors constitutes a majority of one already," he claimed. Thoreau's anarchism finally led him to refuse to pay his poll tax as a protest against the Mexican War. After spending a night in jail, he was released when his aunt paid the tax. Voicing the anti-institutional impulse of Romanticism, he took individualism to its antisocial extreme.

Songs of the Self-Reliant and Darker Loomings

In contrast to Thoreau's exclusiveness, Walt Whitman was all-inclusive, embracing American society in its infinite variety. A journalist and laborer in the New York City area, Whitman proclaimed that "the genius of the United States is . . . always most in the common people. Their manners, speech, dress, friendships . . . are unrhymed poetry." In taking their measure in *Leaves of Grass* (1855), he pioneered a new, modern form of poetry, unconcerned with meter and rhyme and using the line as the basic unit. Baffled by his innovative free verse, put off by his informal use of slang, most critics were offended by his frank imagery and sexual references.

"Simmering, simmering," as he later said, when Emerson "brought me to a boil," Whitman accepted fervently the idea that America was the hope of the future. Conceiving himself the representative of all Americans, he exuberantly

Walt Whitman, poet of democracy.

titled his first major poem "Song of Myself."

> I am your voice—It was tied in you—In me it began to talk.
> I celebrate myself to celebrate every man and woman alive.

Like the Transcendentalists, Whitman exalted the emotions, nature, and the individual, while endowing these ideas with a more joyous, democratic spirit.

More brooding in spirit was Nathaniel Hawthorne, who lived for a time in Concord and also participated in the Transcendental commune at Brook Farm. After his father's death, Hawthorne's mother withdrew into herself, leaving Nathaniel to make his way emotionally on his own. He became gloomy and introspective, unable to partake of Emerson's sunny optimism and repelled by the self-centered outlook of Thoreau. Convinced of the power of the past to shape future generations, Hawthorne wrote of the reality of evil and its place in the human heart. In *The Scarlet Letter* (1850), set in New England's Puritan era, Hawthorne spun the tale of Hester Prynne, condemned to wear the scarlet A (adulteress) for bearing an illegitimate child. His sympathies obviously lay with Prynne, even though she was guilty of the sin of pride, while his greatest condemnation fell on her neighbors, who judged her without compassion. Like the Puritans, who both attracted and repelled him, Hawthorne had no illusions about creating a world without evil, and he rejected the American belief that a person or society could free itself from the past.

Hawthorne found a soul mate in Herman Melville, who became a close friend. But unlike Hawthorne, who was recognized by his contemporaries and supported himself by his writing, Melville died in poverty and obscurity. Not until the twentieth century did literary scholars elevate him to the first rank of American authors. His masterpiece, *Moby-Dick* (1851), drew on his youthful experiences aboard a whaling ship. The novel's Captain Ahab relentlessly drives his ship and crew in pursuit of the great white whale Moby-Dick, to whom he had lost a leg. In his unbridled quest for success the fierce captain becomes, in Melville's telling, a powerful symbol of American character and values: the prototype of the ruthless businessman despoiling nature's resources. "Swerve me?" he asks at one point. "The path to my fixed purpose is laid with iron rails, whereon my soul is grooved to run. Over unsound gorges, through the rifled hearts of mountains, under torrents' beds, unerringly I rush!" In *Moby-Dick* Melville repudiated the materialistic emphasis of American individualism.

Even more adamantly than Hawthorne, Melville rejected the spark of divinity that Emerson saw within each individual. Ahab is Emerson's self-reliant man, but in him, self-reliance is transformed into a dangerous monomania. A law unto himself, Ahab chases the whale with such relentless ferocity that he destroys his ship, its crew, and himself. *Moby-Dick*'s universe is morally ambiguous, rejecting the view that goodness must always triumph. Instead, individuals find themselves isolated and in spiritual anguish, doomed to a lifelong pilgrimage in search of the meaning of life and one's proper place in the infinite cosmos.

More clearly than any other writer, Melville recognized the dilemma created by Romanticism's emphasis on emotion and the individual. On the one hand,

Herman Melville.

Americans celebrated the unlimited power of the free individual. Liberated from institutional restraints, human possibilities seemed unlimited to Romantic philosophers. Yet as older traditions and institutions dropped away, the new individualism also led to a competitive materialism devoid of the older sense of community. How, Melville seemed to be asking, could American society be made perfect, if it was based on self-interested materialism and individualism?

But awash in the unbounded opportunities opening before them, most Americans preferred to celebrate, with Emerson, the glories of democracy and the individual's quest for perfection.

THE AGE OF REFORM

Both Romanticism and perfectionism held the potential for inspiring radical democratic change. While the earlier benevolent societies had aimed at a more conservative reformation of individual sinners, the more radical offshoots of Romanticism and perfectionism sought to remake society at large. The new ideas invited ordinary people to determine what good needed doing independent of the clergy and to equate their decision with the Lord's will.

Some schemers and dreamers for a better world harbored decidedly eccentric notions. The reformer Sylvester Graham, who argued that diet determined character, won lasting fame by having a cracker named after him. Graham also advocated frequent bathing, exercise, wearing loose-fitting clothing, and avoiding sex except for purposes of procreation. While he gained a small following, most Americans ignored him—except for commercial bakers, who, knowing a threat when they saw one, mobbed this champion of homemade bread.

Even stranger than Graham's theory of diet was the vogue of phrenology. Based on an alleged science of the mind, phrenology purported to chart aspects of human character by studying the form and shape of the head. Eager urban audiences paid for lectures explaining the system, rural families subscribed to mail order courses, and thousands visited salons to have bumps on their heads examined and their character analyzed, including young men uncertain about a career, for phrenology promised to discover the occupation that would best match a person's talents. In all, the fad suited the needs of a people anxious to succeed.

Utopian Communities

Other reformers proposed more radical changes in society by establishing utopian communities. These experiments aimed at reforming the world through example, and all sought to restore a spirit of unity and cooperation in place of competitive individualism. Some were directly linked to religion, but even the secular communities shared the optimism of perfectionism and millennialism.

One of the most long-lived utopian experiments had its sources in an eighteenth-century millennial movement: the Shakers, led by Ann Lee. The illiterate daughter of an English blacksmith, Lee believed that God had a dual nature, part male and part female. In a series of ecstatic visions, she became convinced that, just as Christ had come to earth exemplifying the male side of God, through her own person a spiritual Second Coming would be achieved. Persecuted in England, she left for America in 1774 with eight followers.

Mother Ann, as she was known, died in 1784, after making a number of converts in New England and New York. But the Shakers' greatest growth came during the years of the Second Great Awakening, when Lee's successors traveled to revivals (including the great camp meeting at Cane Ridge, Kentucky) to make their own converts. The new disciples founded about 20 communal settlements to put into effect Mother Ann's teachings. Influenced by the Quakers, Lee had preached a life of spiritual simplicity. Like the early Quakers, she and her followers sometimes shook in the fervent public demonstration of their faith—hence the name Shakers. Convinced that the end of the world was at hand and that there was no need to perpetuate the human race, Shaker communities practiced celibacy, separating the sexes as far as practical. Men and women normally worked apart, ate at separate tables in silence, entered separate doorways, and had separate living quarters. The Shakers' religious services provided an emotional release in their otherwise carefully regimented lives. Central to these services was dancing, which was sometimes carefully regulated, other times wild and spontaneous. At its peak after 1820, the sect had an estimated 6000 members.

Shaker communities accorded women unusual authority and equality. Community tasks were generally assigned along sexual lines, with women performing household chores and men laboring in the fields. But leadership of the church was split equally between men and women. Since marriage and families had been abolished, women were freed from many traditional burdens. By the mid-nineteenth century, a majority of members were female.

Property in Shaker settlements was owned communally and controlled by the church hierarchy. The sect's members worked hard, lived simply, and impressed outsiders with their cleanliness and order. They prospered through a combination of agriculture and crafts, and they became famous for the clean, simple lines of their architecture and furniture. Lacking any natural increase, membership began to decline after 1850, and by the end of the century the Shakers had been reduced to a small remnant.

The Oneida Community, founded by John Humphrey Noyes, also set out to alter the relationship between the sexes, though in a rather different way. Noyes, a convert of Charles Finney, was expelled from his ministry in the Congregational church for his heretical ideas on perfectionism. While Finney argued that men and women should strive to achieve perfection, Noyes announced that he had reached this blessed state. Unlike Finney, he contended that once a person was saved, he or she became incapable of sinning. Settling in Putney, Vermont, with a band of like-minded followers, Noyes relieved women of what he termed "kitchen slavery." Under his system, they cooked only at breakfast and thereafter were free from household duties until the next morning.

Noyes' ideas of liberation, however, went beyond the kitchen. After he had been spurned by the woman he wished to marry, he evolved the doctrine of "complex marriage." Exclusive love for one person was antisocial and dangerous to a community, he argued, since all members should be bound to one another. Rejecting traditional marriage, Noyes concluded that it was not sinful for the members of his commune to have sexual relations with one another. Confronted with the hostility of his Vermont neighbors, who emphatically did not share these views, Noyes in 1848 moved his unorthodox community to Oneida, New York.

The practice of complex marriage did not lead to unrestrained self-indulgence. Oneida couples were allowed to have intercourse only with the approval of the community and after a searching examination of their motives. Eventually Noyes even undertook experiments in planned reproduction. Acting on his conviction that good character was inherited, a committee of Oneidans selected "scientific" combinations of parents to produce morally superior children. Despite his radical ideas about marriage and women's work, Noyes was hardly a feminist. He unambiguously believed that men were superior to women and that this superiority was part of the order of the universe. In his eyes, the ultimate ideal for a woman was to become "what she ought to be, a female man."

Noyes' real concern was not to liberate women but to overcome social and intellectual disorder and in so doing, achieve a new synthesis between religion and society. Under his charismatic leadership, the Oneida Community grew to over 200 members in 1851. But in 1879 an internal dispute drove him from power, and without his guiding hand the community soon fell apart. In 1881 its members reorganized as a joint stock company and prospered by manufacturing silver, an enterprise still in existence.

Robert Owen and New Harmony

The hardship and poverty that accompanied the growth of industrial factories sparked another attempt at utopian reform by Robert Owen, himself a Scottish industrialist. Determined to create a society that balanced both agriculture and manufacturing, Owen believed that the character of individuals was shaped by their surroundings, and that by changing those surroundings, one could change human character. In this sense he was an environmentalist. His utopianism was based on science and reason, not religion, yet he shared the belief in the perfectibility of human nature and society.

Owen came to the United States in 1824 and purchased property in Indiana to found his community of New Harmony. Confident that he could reform anyone, he accepted all who wanted to join. Unfortunately, most of the 900 or so volunteers who flocked to New Harmony lacked the skills, commitment, and discipline needed to make the community a success. Bitter factions that split the settlement were made worse when Owen tried to ease frictions through open discussion and debate. Owen also rashly surrendered control of the textile mill, the economic basis of the community, to its members; this socialist scheme soon failed. Having lost most of his own fortune, Owen dissolved the community in 1827. Over 20 other American communities were founded on Owen's theories, none particularly successful.

By 1840 Owen had been eclipsed in socialist circles by a French theorist and reformer, Charles Fourier. Fourier also envisioned communities of cooperative labor, but his system was not true communism, for investors shared profits produced by the community, as in a business corporation. Instead of adopting environmentalism, Fourier based his theories on his own science of human nature. An individual's personality was determined by the mixture of 12 passions, Fourier argued; laborers who took jobs suited to their personalities would find work a pleasure, not drudgery. Because Fourierism attracted support from some intellectuals and received lavish publicity in Horace Greeley's New York *Tribune*, it gained much attention in the United States. At least 28 cooperative communities were established, but none lasted long.

The experience of New Harmony and other communities demonstrated that the United States was poor soil for socialistic experiments. Wages were too high and land too cheap to interest most Americans in collectivist ventures. And individualism was too strong to create a commitment to cooperative action.

The Temperance Movement

The most significant reform movements of the period sought not to withdraw from society, but to change it directly. One of the most determined of these was the temperance movement.

The origins of the campaign lay in the heavy drinking of the early nineteenth century. Liquor had been part of American life since the founding of the colonies, but after the Revolution, alcohol consumption reached unprecedented levels. From 1800 to 1830 the annual per capita consumption of distilled spirits rose from three gallons to more than five, the highest level in American history and nearly triple present-day levels. The per capita figure, of course, included women and children, who did much less imbibing than men; on average in the late 1820s, an adult male drank nearly half a pint daily of whiskey, gin, brandy, or rum. Whiskey was cheap and plentiful, and anxiety-ridden Americans sought relief in the bottle, as well as drinking routinely at house raisings, quilting parties, weddings, and funerals. Anne Royale, whose travels often took her cross country by stage, reported, "When I was in Virginia, it was too much whiskey—in Ohio, too much whiskey—in Tennessee, it is too, too much whiskey!" The social costs for such habits were high: broken families, abused and neglected wives and children, sickness and disability, poverty and crime. The temperance movement undertook to eliminate these problems by curbing drinking.

Led largely by clergy, the movement initially focused on drunkenness and did not oppose moderate drinking. But in 1826 the American Temperance Society was founded, taking voluntary abstinence as its goal; during the next decade approximately 5000 local temperance societies were founded. Three important changes occurred in the antidrinking movement between 1820 and 1850, reflecting this shift toward total abstinence. First, ardent spirits were redefined to include beer and wine, whose consumption was no longer acceptable. Second, temperance advocates increasingly concentrated their attack on the liquor traffic rather than the consumer. And finally, the movement entered the political arena and lobbied for state laws to prohibit the manufacture and sale of liquor. Despite legal setbacks and the unwillingness of many politicians to lend support, the temperance movement produced a sharp decline in the annual per capita consumption of alcohol after 1830. By the middle of the next decade it had fallen below two gallons.

The temperance movement lasted longer and attracted many more supporters than other reforms: it appealed to young and old, to men and women, to urban and rural residents, to workers and businessmen. And it was the only reform movement with significant support in the South. One reason for its wide appeal was the campaign's use of revival techniques. The Washington Temperance Society, founded by reformed alcoholics, aimed to save drunkards through personal testimony, using the language of the common people and deliberately emphasizing emotion. At the climax of these meetings, members of the audience were invited to step forward, like converts in a revival, and take the pledge.

Other factors strengthened the movement's appeal. The rise of democracy

ANNUAL CONSUMPTION OF DISTILLED SPIRITS, PER CAPITA, 1710–1920

necessitated sober voters; the rise of industry required sober workers. Temperance also appealed to the upwardly mobile—professionals, small businessmen, and skilled artisans anxious to improve their social standing by acquiring reputations for self-discipline. Finally, the temperance movement strongly appealed to women. To a striking degree, its literature stressed the suffering that men inflicted on women and children. As defenders of the home, women saw drinking as a threat to family security; participation in the temperance campaign provided an important avenue of self-assertion and a way for women to uphold their domestic mission.

Educational Reform

In 1800 Massachusetts was the only state requiring free public schools supported by community funds. The well-to-do generally were educated in private academies or by tutors, and some of the poor attended church or charity schools. Even where public schools existed, the one-room buildings crowded in as many as 80 students of various ages and ability levels, to be taught by a single harassed, overworked, and underpaid teacher.

The call for tax-supported education arose first among workers, as a means to restore their deteriorating position in society. But middle-class reformers quickly took control of the movement, with an intent to uplift common citizens, educate boys to vote wisely when they came of age, and make equal opportunity a reality. Horace Mann, the leading proponent of common schools, hailed education as "the great equalizer of the conditions of men" and contended that it would eliminate poverty. Reformers appealed to business leaders by arguing that the new economic order needed educated workers.

Mann convinced Massachusetts to create a state board of education, which he oversaw from 1837 to 1848. Under his leadership, the state adopted a minimum-length school year, provided for training of teachers, increased their pay, and improved the curriculum by including subjects such as history, geography, and various applied skills. Massachusetts also took the lead in requiring every town with a population of 500 or more to establish a high school. This innovation was slow to catch on elsewhere; by 1860 the nation could count only about 300 high schools, fully a third of which were in Massachusetts. Moreover, compulsory attendance was rarely required, and out of necessity many poor parents sent their children to work instead of school, particularly at the secondary level. Still, by the 1850s the number of schools, attendance figures, and school budgets had all increased sharply. Educational reformers enjoyed their greatest success in the Northeast and the least in the South, where planters opposed paying taxes to educate poorer white children.

Educational opportunities for women also expanded. Teachers like Catharine Beecher and Emma Hunt Willard established a number of private girls' schools, putting to rest the objection of many male educators that fragile female minds would not be able to absorb large doses of mathematics, physics, or geography. In 1833 Oberlin became the nation's first coeducational college; four years later Mary Lyon founded Mount Holyoke, the first American college for women. Students at Holyoke led a rigorous life, not only studying hard but helping out with the housekeeping. On Thanksgiving Day one relieved student recorded that "we all had the privilege of sleeping as long as we wished in the morning, provided we were ready for breakfast by 8 o'clock. I rose at five, an hour later than usual and worked two hours and a half before breakfast."

The Asylum Movement

After 1820 there was also a dramatic increase in the number of asylums of every sort—orphanages, jails, and hospitals. The proponents of asylums called for isolating and separating the criminal, the insane, the ill, and the dependent from outside society, and the goal of care shifted from confinement to reform.

The prison reform movement tried to separate youthful offenders from older, hardened criminals, to end imprisonment for debt, and to abolish public executions. But it was American efforts to rehabilitate prisoners that attracted international attention. Tocqueville originally came to the United States to examine and report on prisons. Pennsylvania and New York developed systems to isolate prisoners, introducing the measures of solitary confinement and absolute silence to give inmates time to reflect on their past errors. The reformers assumed that environment produced criminal behavior and that the new prison regimen would rehabilitate criminals. The new measures were not very effective, however: under the strain of isolation, some inmates went insane or committed suicide.

Other reformers lobbied to improve care for the mentally ill. Dorothea Dix, a Boston schoolteacher, took the lead in advocating state-supported asylums for the insane. She attracted much attention to the movement by her report detailing the horrors to which the mentally ill were subjected, including being chained, kept in cages and closets, and beaten with rods. In response to her efforts, 28 states maintained mental institutions by 1860.

Like other reform movements, the push for new asylums and better educational facilities reflected overtones of both liberation and control. Asylums freed prisoners and the mentally ill from the harsh punishments and abuses of the past, but the new techniques of rehabilitation forced prisoners to march in lockstep. Education brought with it freedom, but some enthusiastic reformers seemed to hope that schools would become as orderly as prisons.

ABOLITIONISM

Late in the fall of 1834, Lyman Beecher was in the midst of his own continuing efforts to "overturn and overturn" on behalf of the kingdom of God. As planned, he had left Boston in 1832 to assume leadership of Lane Seminary, which boasted a distinguished faculty, handsome new buildings, an ample library, and a hilltop setting commanding a panoramic view of Cincinnati and the Ohio River. The school made an admirable beachhead for converting and evangelizing the West, for it had everything that an institution for training ministers needed—everything, that is, except students. In October 1834, all but 8 of Lane's 100 students had deserted after months of bitter fighting with Beecher and the trustees over the issue of abolition.

Beecher knew the source of his troubles: a disheveled, charismatic student named Theodore Dwight Weld, who had been firing up his classmates at Lane, filling their heads with the necessity for immediately freeing the slaves of America. Beecher was not surprised, for Weld had been converted by that firebrand Finney. He knew, too, that Theodore Weld had been influenced by the arguments of William Lloyd Garrison, whose abolitionist newspaper had, in 1831, sent shock waves across the entire nation. Indeed, Beecher's troubles at Lane Seminary provided only one example of how reform, when loosed, could move in paths unexpected by those who began it.

The Beginnings of the Abolitionist Movement

William Lloyd Garrison symbolized the transition from a moderate antislavery movement to the more militant abolitionism of the 1830s. A sober, religious youngster deeply influenced by his Baptist mother, Garrison apprenticed as a printer and in the 1820s edited a newspaper sympathetic to many of the new reforms. In 1829 he was enlisted in the antislavery cause by the Quaker Benjamin Lundy. The Quakers had long opposed slavery, and Lundy had founded antislavery societies in several southern states and edited a Baltimore newspaper, *The Genius of Universal Emancipation*. Calling for a gradual end to slavery, he supported colonization, a strategy for overcoming southern fears of emancipation by transporting free blacks to Africa. Under the auspices of the colonizationists, the first group of former slaves was sent to Liberia in West Africa in 1822.

Once engaged in the antislavery cause, Garrison developed views far more radical than Lundy's. Within a year of moving to Baltimore to help edit Lundy's paper, he was convicted of libel and imprisoned. Upon his release, he hurried back to Boston, determined to publish a new kind of antislavery journal. On January 1, 1831, the first issue of *The Liberator* appeared, and abolitionism was born. In appearance, the bespectacled Garrison seemed frail, almost mousy, but in print he was abrasive, vituperative, and uncompromising. "On this subject, I do not wish to think, or speak, or write with moderation," he proclaimed. "I am in earnest—I will not equivocate—I will not excuse—I will not retreat a single inch—AND I WILL BE HEARD." Repudiating gradual emancipation and embracing "immediatism," he declared that freedom had to come at once. He denounced colonization as a racist movement and upheld the principle of racial

William Lloyd Garrison (shown left at age 30) and Theodore Dwight Weld represented different wings of the abolitionist movement. Garrison's growing radicalism led him to repudiate organized religion in the struggle against slavery. Weld, on the other hand, preferred to work through the evangelical churches and cooperated with the clergy.

equality. He insisted on no compensation to slaveowners and urged the use of "moral suasion" to convince southerners voluntarily to renounce slavery as a sin.

Garrison attracted the most attention, but other abolitionists spoke with equal conviction. Wendell Phillips, from a socially prominent Boston family, could hold listeners spellbound with his speeches; Lewis Tappan and his brother Arthur, two New York City silk merchants, boldly placed their wealth behind the causes they believed in; James G. Birney, a southern slaveholder, converted to abolitionism after wrestling with his conscience; and Angelina and Sarah Grimké, the daughters of a South Carolina planter, left their native state to speak against the institution. And there was Angelina's future husband, Theodore Weld, the restless student at Lane Seminary who had fallen so dramatically under Garrison's influence.

To abolitionists, slavery seemed a contradiction of the principle that all human beings had been created with natural rights. Then too, it went against the Romantic spirit of the age, which celebrated the individual's freedom and self-reliance. Already involved with other humanitarian campaigns, reformers condemned slavery as the most inhumane of institutions, because of the breakup of marriages and families by sale, the harsh punishment of the lash, the lack of access to education, and the sexual abuse of black women. But most of all, abolitionists condemned slavery as outrageously contrary to Christian teaching. So persistent and firmly made were their religious objections that the churches were forced to face the question of slavery head-on. In the 1840s the Methodist and Baptist churches split into northern and southern organizations over the issue. In making their indictment of slavery, abolitionists did not debate how abolition might affect the economy of the South or southern whites. To them, slavery was a moral, not an economic question. As one Ohio antislavery paper declared, "We believe slavery to be a sin, always, everywhere, and only, sin—sin, in itself."

The Spread of Abolitionism

Garrison and others organized the New England Anti-Slavery Society in 1832 with about 75 members. In 1833 he joined with merchant Lewis Tappan and with Theodore Weld to establish a national organization, the American Anti-Slavery Society, which served as an umbrella for a loosely affiliated network of state and local societies. During the years before the Civil War, perhaps 200,000 northerners belonged to an abolitionist society.

Abolitionists were concentrated in the East, especially New England, and areas that had been settled by New Englanders, such as western New York and northern Ohio. The movement was not strong in cities or among businessmen and workers. Most abolitionists were young, generally in their twenties and thirties when the movement began, and had grown up in rural areas and small towns in middle-class families. Intensely religious, many had been profoundly affected by the revivals of the Second Great Awakening. Whatever their background, they shared a deep alienation from American society—its materialism, its crass politics. More and more they came to feel that slavery was the fundamental cause of the Republic's degraded condition.

Certainly Theodore Weld felt that way when in 1833 he enrolled in Lane Seminary. Immediately he began to implement a plan endorsed by Tappan and Garrison for making Lane Seminary a strategic western center of abolitionist activity. He culled a nucleus of abolitionist sympathizers from the ranks of his fellow students and assigned each an uncommitted classmate, a man who needed to be convinced that slavery was not simply *a* problem, but *the* problem facing the nation. "Thus we carried one after another," Weld recalled. By the time Beecher arrived to assume the Lane presidency a year later, he confronted a student body dominated by committed abolitionists, impatient of any position that stopped short of Garrison's immediatism.

The radicalism of Lane students was also made clear in their commitment to racial equality. Unlike some abolitionists, who opposed slavery but disdained blacks as inferior, Lane students mingled freely with Cincinnati's large free black community. Rumors that the town's residents, alarmed by the "amalgamation" of free blacks and students, intended to demolish the school panicked Beecher and Lane's trustees into taking drastic measures in the summer of 1834. They prohibited any discussion of slavery on campus, dissolved Lane's antislavery society, restricted contact with the black community, and ordered students to return to their academic work. The response of the Lane rebels was decisive. "Who that has an opinion and a soul will enter L. Sem now?" one asked, "Who can do it without degrading himself?" All except a few left the school and enrolled at Oberlin College. That desperate, debt-ridden institution agreed to their demands for guaranteeing freedom of speech, admitting black students, and hiring Charles Finney as professor of theology.

But Finney fared no better than Beecher with the Lane rebels. In the end, he too concluded that reform generated discord, distracting Christians from the greater good of promoting revivals. Both men conceived of sin in terms of individual immorality, not unjust social institutions and prejudices. To the abolitionists, most of them younger men and women, America could never become a godly nation until slavery was abolished. "Revivals, moral Reform, etc. will remain stationary until the temple is cleansed," concluded Weld bluntly.

As such sentiments spread, free blacks, who always constituted the majority of subscribers to Garrison's *Liberator*, became a mainstay of the movement. Their unwavering support provided them with an opportunity to strike a blow against the discrimination and hostility that pervaded northern society. Many abolitionists challenged discrimination as a denial of the American principle of equality, and free African-Americans provided important support and leadership for the movement.

Frederick Douglass assumed the greatest prominence. Having escaped from slavery in Maryland, he became an eloquent critic of its evils. Initially a follower of Garrison, Douglass eventually broke with him and started his own newspaper in Rochester. Other important black abolitionists included Martin Delany, William Wells Brown, William Still, and Sojourner Truth. Most blacks endorsed peaceful means to end slavery, but David Walker in his *Appeal to the Colored Citizens of the World* (1829) urged slaves to use violence to end bondage. Aided by many others of their race, these men and women battled against racial discrimination in the North as well as slavery in the South.

A network of antislavery sympathizers developed in the North to convey runaway slaves to Canada and freedom. While not as extensive or as tightly organized as contemporaries claimed, the Underground Railroad hid fugitives and transported them northward from one station to the next. Free blacks, who were more readily trusted by wary slaves, played a leading role in the Underground Railroad. One of its most famous conductors was Harriet Tubman, an escaped slave of great daring and resourcefulness. Returning to the South at least 19 times, she escorted more than 200 slaves, including several members of her own family, to freedom.

An escaped slave, Harriet Tubman (far left) made several forays into the South as a "conductor" on the Underground Railroad. Shown here with one group that she led to freedom, she was noted for her stealth and firm determination, qualities that helped her repeatedly to outwit her pursuers.

Opponents and Discontents

The drive for immediate abolition faced massive obstacles, no matter how fervent its advocates. With slavery increasingly pivotal to the economic life of the South (Chapter 13), the abolitionist cause was received there with extreme hostility. And in the North racism was equally entrenched, as the case of Prudence Crandall demonstrated. A Quaker schoolteacher, Crandall opened a boarding school for black girls in 1833 in Canterbury, Connecticut, with the backing of several well-known abolitionists. Town residents harassed her by breaking her windows, poisoning her well with manure, and attempting to destroy the school building. When all else failed, town officials induced the legislature to pass a law closing the school, and Crandall was arrested and imprisoned. Racism was so deeply ingrained that even abolitionists like Garrison, whose attitudes were far in advance of the general public's, treated blacks paternalistically, contending that they should occupy a subordinate place in the antislavery movement.

As support for abolition spread, opponents reacted harshly. Southerners, immune to "moral suasion," forced opponents of slavery to flee the region. In the North anti-abolitionist mobs attacked antislavery speakers. A Boston mob seized Garrison in 1835 and paraded him with a noose around his neck; another mob burned to the ground the headquarters of the American Anti-Slavery Society in Philadelphia. And in 1837 in Alton, Illinois—across the river from the slave state of Missouri—Elijah Lovejoy was murdered when he tried to protect his printing press from an angry crowd. The leaders of these anti-abolitionist mobs were not the rabble of the streets but, as one of their victims noted, "gentlemen of property and standing." Prominent leaders in the community, they reacted vigorously to the threat that abolitionists posed to their power and prosperity, and to the established order.

The progress of the abolitionists was further limited by divisions among the reformers themselves. Given the Romantic individualism of the era, it became all too easy for groups of reformers to splinter and diverge. Finney, maintaining that revivals provided the road to perfection, watched in dismay as his convert Theodore Weld became a rabid abolitionist. Lyman Beecher, more conservative than Finney, saw his son Edward put aside his preaching to stand guard over Elijah Lovejoy's printing press the evening before the editor's murder. Within another decade, Beecher would see his daughter Harriet Beecher Stowe write the most successful piece of antislavery literature in the nation's history, *Uncle Tom's Cabin*. And finally the abolitionists themselves splintered, shaken by the harsh opposition they encountered and unable to agree on the most effective response. The more conservative reformers argued that abolitionism needed to broaden its appeal to northerners. Confident that American society, although in need of reform, was basically sound, they counted on political action to end slavery. But for Garrison and his followers, the mob violence demonstrated that slavery was only part of a deeper national disease. All American institutions must be overthrown, all values changed.

By the end of the decade, Garrison had formulated a program for the total reform of society—root-and-branch abolitionism. He embraced perfectionism and pacifism, denounced the clergy, urged members to leave the churches, and called for an end to all government. Adopting the slogan "No Union with Slaveholders," he condemned the Constitution as proslavery—"a covenant with death and an agreement with hell"—and publicly burned a copy one July 4th. Finally, he argued that politics was inherently corrupting and that no person of conscience could vote or otherwise participate in the political system. This platform was radical enough on all counts; but the final straw for Garrison's opponents was his endorsement of women's rights as an inseparable part of abolitionism.

The Women's Rights Movement

Women faced many disadvantages in American society. They were kept out of most jobs, denied political rights, and given only limited access to education beyond the elementary grades. And they had no legal control over their property. When a woman married, her husband became the legal will of the marriage and gained complete control of her assets. If a marriage ended in divorce, the husband was awarded custody of the children. Any unmarried woman was made the ward of a male relative.

When abolitionists divided over the issue of female participation, women found it easy to identify with the situation of slaves, since both were victims of male tyranny. The attacks on female abolitionists and attempts to keep them from exerting influence in the movement produced the first major documents of American feminism. Sarah and Angelina Grimké took up the cause of women's rights after they were criticized for speaking to audiences that included men as well as women. Sarah responded with *Letters on the Condition of Women and the Equality of the Sexes* (1838), arguing that women deserved the same rights as men. Abby Kelly, another abolitionist, remarked that women "have good cause to be grateful to the slave," for in "striving to strike his irons off, we found most surely, that we were manacled *ourselves.*"

Two abolitionists, Elizabeth Cady Stanton and Lucretia Mott, launched the women's rights movement after they were forced to sit behind a curtain, screened from other delegates, at a world antislavery convention held at London in 1840. In 1848 Stanton and Mott organized a conference in Seneca Falls, New York, that attracted an attendance of about a hundred. The meeting issued a Declaration of Sentiments (modeled after the Declaration of Independence) that began, "All men and women are created equal." There followed a catalog of the wrongs that men had inflicted on women, a device paralleling the first Declaration's indictment of George III.

The Seneca Falls convention approved resolutions calling for educational and professional opportunities for women, passage of laws giving them control over their property, recognition of legal equality, and repeal of laws awarding the father custody of the children in divorce. The most controversial proposal, and the only resolution that did not pass unanimously, was one demanding the right to vote. Thus the Seneca Falls convention established the arguments and the program for the women's rights movement for the remainder of the century.

The women's rights movement won few victories before 1860. Several states gave women greater control over their property, and a few made divorce easier or granted women the right to sue in courts. But disappointments and defeats far outweighed these early victories. Still, many of the important leaders in the crusade for women's rights that emerged after the Civil War had already taken their places at the forefront of the movement. They included Stanton, Susan B. Anthony, Lucy Stone, and—as Lyman Beecher by now must have expected—one of his daughters, Isabella Beecher Hooker.

Elizabeth Cady Stanton, one of the instigators and guiding spirits at the Seneca Falls convention, photographed with two of her children about that time.

The Schism of 1840 and the Decline of Abolitionism

It was Garrison's position on women's rights that finally split antislavery ranks already divided over other aspects of his growing radicalism. The showdown came in 1840 at the national meeting of the American Anti-Slavery Society, where the key battle was waged over allowing women to hold office in the organization. Some of Garrison's opponents favored women's rights but opposed linking this question to the slavery issue, insisting that it would drive off potential supporters. By packing the convention, Garrison carried the day, and his opponents, led by Lewis Tappan, resigned to found the rival American and Foreign Anti-Slavery Society.

The schism of 1840 marked the end of abolitionism as an important movement in American society. Crippled by the division of resources and supporters, neither national organization was of much significance thereafter. Although abolitionism heightened moral concern about slavery, it failed to convert the North to its program, and throughout its existence its supporters remained an infinitesimal minority. For all the courage they showed—and that was considerable, given the scorn of so many of their neighbors—their movement suffered from an excess of individualism and a repeated tendency toward extremism. Furthermore, the abolitionists had no realistic, long-range plan for eliminating so deeply entrenched an institution. When attempts at moral persuasion failed, they fell back on harsh rhetoric. Garrison even boasted that "the genius of the abolitionist movement is to have *no* plan." Abolitionism demonstrated the severe limits of Emersonian self-reliance as a solution to deeply rooted social problems.

REFORM SHAKES THE PARTY SYSTEM

The crusading idealism of revivalists and reformers inevitably collided with the hard reality that society could not be perfected by converting individuals. Despite the arguments of the temperance movement, some Americans continued to drink. For all the zeal of the abolitionists, slavery showed no signs of disappearing. Even the revivalist tide had lost its force by the end of the 1830s. Several campaigns, including those to establish public schools and erect asylums, had operated within the political system from the beginning. But a growing number of other frustrated reformers abandoned the principle of voluntary persuasion and looked to governmental coercion to achieve their goals. In America's democratic society, politics promised a more effective means to impose a new moral vision on the nation. Declared a writer in the *American Temperance Magazine*, "The speculative has yielded to the practical. . . . In this sense, moral suasion is moral balderdash."

Old-line politicians did not particularly welcome the new interest. Moral questions such as temperance and antislavery, which cut across party lines, threatened to detach regular party members and disrupt each party's unity and voting base. Because the Whig and Democratic parties had formed around economic questions rather than moral ones, both drew on evangelical and nonevangelical voters. Yet it was precisely for this reason that moral reform, by mobilizing evangelical voters, threatened the Jacksonian party system.

Both religion and reform helped shape that system, through ethnic and religious loyalties. Whigs attracted immigrant groups that most easily merged into the dominant culture, such as the English, Welsh, and Scots. Democrats, on the other hand, recruited more Germans and Irish, whose drinking habits, more lenient observance of the Sabbath, and (among Catholics) use of parochial schools made native-born citizens suspicious. As the self-proclaimed party of respectability, Whigs especially attracted the support of high-status native-born church groups, including the Congregationalists and Unitarians in New England and Presbyterians elsewhere. Democrats appealed to the lower-status Baptists and Methodists. For all their evangelical ways, these groups usually lacked the prestige and social acceptance of the Presbyterians and Congregationalists, with whom they often clashed. Both parties also attracted freethinkers and the unchurched, but the Democrats had the advantage because they resisted demands for temperance and sabbatarian laws, such as the prohibition of Sunday travel.

Women and the Right to Vote

As the focus of change and reform shifted toward the political arena, women in particular lost influence. As major participants in the benevolent organizations of the 1820s and 1830s, they had circulated petitions, sought new members, and used their efforts on behalf of "moral suasion." But since women could not vote, they felt excluded when reformers turned to electoral action to accomplish their goals. By the 1840s, female reformers increasingly demanded the right to vote as the means to reform society. Nor were men blind to what was at stake: one reason they so strongly resisted female suffrage was because it would give women real power.

The temperance and abolitionist movements, both of which turned to political action in the 1840s, helped convince women of the importance of gaining the ballot. Previously, many female reformers had accepted the right of petition as their most appropriate political activity. But *The Lily*, a women's rights paper, soon changed its tack. "Why shall [women] be left only the poor resource of petition?" it asked. "For even petitions, when they are from women, without the elective franchise to give them backbone, are of but little consequence." The right to vote would remain the key demand of the women's rights movement until 1920, when the Nineteenth Amendment was ratified.

The Maine Law

The political parties could resist the women's suffrage movement, since most of its advocates lacked the right to vote. Less easily put off were temperance advocates. As early as 1825 Lyman Beecher had called for banning the sale of distilled spirits, and the antiliquor crusade turned to political action in the 1840s. Although drinking had significantly declined in American society, it had not been eradicated, and the arrival after 1845 of large numbers of German and Irish immigrants, who were accustomed to drinking, made voluntary prohibition even more remote. In response, temperance advocates decided to attack the supply of liquor by enacting state laws outlawing the manufacture and sale of alcoholic beverages; they demanded stiff penalties, including jail sentences, for individuals guilty of selling liquor. Antiliquor reformers reasoned that if liquor was unavailable, the attitude of drinkers was unimportant—they would be forced to reform whether they wanted to or not.

In taking up the cause of prohibition, the antidrinking movement gained the support of the evangelical churches, which condemned drinking even in moderation. Consequently, the issue of prohibition cut across party lines, with large numbers of Whigs and Democrats on both sides of the question. When party leaders tried to dodge the issue, the temperance movement adopted the strategy of endorsing for the legislature only candidates who pledged to support a prohibitory law. As a result, a growing number of legislators committed themselves to the antiliquor cause. To win additional recruits, temperance leaders emulated techniques used in political campaigns, including house-to-house canvasses, parades and processions, bands and singing, banners, picnics, and mass rallies.

The major triumph came in 1851 in Maine's legislature. The Maine Law, as it was known, provided stiff penalties for selling liquor in the state; it also provided for search and seizure of private property, thereby strengthening the powers of enforcement. In the next few years a number of states enacted similar laws, although most were struck down by the courts or subsequently repealed. Nevertheless, prohibition remained a divisive political issue throughout the century.

While prohibition was temporarily defeated, the issue badly disrupted the unity of the two parties. It detached a number of voters from both coalitions, greatly increased the extent of party switching, and brought to the polls a large number of new voters, including many "wets" who wanted to preserve their right to drink. By dissolving the ties between many voters and their party, the temperance issue played a major role in the eventual collapse of the Jacksonian party system in the 1850s.

Abolitionism and the Party System

Abolition remained the most divisive issue to come out of the benevolent movement. Even during the 1830s, when abolitionists were not focusing on the political
arena, a dispute arose over the use of the federal mails. In 1835 abolitionists
distributed over a million pamphlets through the post office. Since these were
sent to southerners as well as northerners, a wave of excitement swept over the
South when the first batches arrived. Former senator Robert Hayne led a Charleston mob that burned sacks of United States mail containing abolitionist literature,
and postmasters in other southern cities refused to deliver the material. The Jackson administration allowed southern states to censor the mail and close the post
office to abolitionists, who protested that their civil rights had been violated. In
reaction, the number of antislavery societies in the North nearly tripled.

With access to the mails impaired, abolitionists began flooding Congress with
petitions against slavery. Most called for its abolition within the District of Columbia, which was under the jurisdiction of Congress. Asserting that Congress had no
power over slavery, angry southern representatives demanded action, and the
House adopted the so-called gag law in 1836. The provision automatically tabled
without consideration petitions dealing with slavery. Claiming that the right of
petition was also under attack by slavery's champions, abolitionists gained new
supporters. In 1844 the House finally repealed the controversial rule.

The censorship of the mails and the attack on the right of petition were
serious tactical mistakes by southern leaders. These acts allowed abolitionists to
speak out as defenders of white civil liberties and to broaden significantly the
appeal of the antislavery movement. Abolitionists outside William Lloyd Garrison's circle were convinced that by forming a third party they could force the
slavery issue into the political arena. In 1840 these political abolitionists founded
the Liberty party and nominated for president James Birney, a former slaveholder
who had converted to abolitionism. Birney received only 7000 votes, but the
Liberty party was the seed from which a stronger antislavery political movement
would grow.

Since they were not tied to either major party, political abolitionists were
freed from the restraints that national parties imposed on their members in order
to maintain unity. Always seeking to enlarge their popular support, abolitionists
did not hesitate to push controversial questions. In doing so, they functioned like a
pressure group on the major parties, goading them to commit themselves, to take
more radical positions. In closely divided northern states their votes continued to
be critical.

After two decades of fiery revivals, benevolent crusades, utopian experiments, and Transcendental philosophizing, the ferment of reform had spread
through urban streets, canal town churches, frontier clearings, and congressional
halls. Part and parcel of the era, it shared the nation's individualistic, optimistic
temperament. But the sheer diversity of reform—its conservative impulse to control as well as its more radical, liberating tendencies—meant that its effects varied. The quest for perfection could impel Henry Thoreau to secede temporarily
from society altogether or convince Sarah Grimké to engage in activities formerly
restricted to men. It could reinforce the new order of industrial labor by preaching
the virtues of sobriety or scandalize the God-fearing with tales of communal marriage. Fires, once burning, spread in unpredictable ways.

Abolition, potentially the most divisive issue, seemed still under control in 1840. Birney's small vote, along with the disputes between the two national anti-slavery societies, encouraged party leaders in the belief that the slavery issue had run its course—that the party system had successfully turned back this latest threat of sectionalism. But the growing northern concern about slavery highlighted differences between the two sections. Despite the strength of evangelicalism in the South, the reform impulse spawned by the revivals was largely confined to the North. Discredited by their association with abolitionism, reform movements generally found little support below the Mason–Dixon line, a situation that heightened southern distinctiveness. The party system confronted the difficult challenge of holding together sections that, although sharing much, were also diverging in important ways. To the residents of both sections, the South increasingly seemed to be a unique society with its own distinctive way of life.

SIGNIFICANT EVENTS

1787	First Shaker commune established
1821	New York constructs first penitentiary
1824	New Harmony established
1824–1837	Peak of revivals
1826	James Fenimore Cooper's *The Last of the Mohicans* published; American Temperance Society founded
1829	David Walker's *Appeal to the Colored Citizens of the World*
1830–1831	Charles Finney's revival at Rochester
1831	*The Liberator* established
1833	American Anti-Slavery Society founded; Oberlin College admits women
1834	Lane Seminary rebellion
1835	Abolitionists' postal campaign
1836	Transcendental Club established
1836	Gag law passed
1837	Massachusetts establishes state board of education; Ralph Waldo Emerson delivers "The American Scholar" address; Mount Holyoke Seminary commences classes; Elijah Lovejoy killed
1838	Sarah Grimké's *Letters on the Condition of Women and the Equality of the Sexes* published
1840	Schism of American Anti-Slavery Society; Liberty party founded
1841	Fourierist phalanx established
1843	Dorothea Dix's report on treatment of the insane
1844	Gag law repealed
1848	Oneida Community established; Seneca Falls convention
1850	Nathaniel Hawthorne's *The Scarlet Letter* published
1851	Maine adopts prohibition law; Herman Melville's *Moby-Dick* published
1854	Henry David Thoreau's *Walden* published
1855	Walt Whitman's *Leaves of Grass* published

Generations of the Republic

Families of the New Democracy (1815–1875)

An Englishman, Frederick Marryat, was visiting the United States in the 1830s when he witnessed a scene—all too common, for his taste—of youthful disobedience. The youngster in question was only three years old, scampering about in the rain. "Johnny my dear, come here," his mother called.

"I won't," cried Johnny.

"You must, my love, you are all wet, and you'll catch cold."

"I won't," repeated the lad.

"Come, my sweet, and I've something for you."

"I won't."

At this point the exasperated mother begged her husband, "Do, pray, make Johnny come in."

"Come in, Johnny," called the father.

"I won't."

"I tell you, come in directly, sir—do you hear?"

"I won't," replied the child, as he ran off. The father smiled at Marryat and remarked, "A sturdy republican, sir." To Marryat the conclusion was obvious: "Anyone who has been in the United States must have perceived that there is little or no parental control."

Whether or not the American family was consistently different from its European counterpart, its character was evolving steadily away from that of earlier generations of Americans. As the young Republic expanded, families adapted to the changes that were transforming society: unprecedented mobility, heightened commercialization, accelerating industrialization and urbanization. In conjunction, a new concept of the family emerged, more democratic in structure and modern in orientation.

To begin with, American families were getting smaller. After a century of extraordinary population growth, the birth rate began to decline. Between Jefferson's election in 1800 and the Civil War, the fertility rate dropped almost 25 percent. By twentieth-century standards American families remained large, averaging 5.5 children in 1850, but the average before 1800 had been 8 children. Family size was diminished by infant mortality, which remained at about 20 percent among whites and was even higher on the frontier and among African-Americans.

The smaller size of families reflected economic choices, a new conception of

marriage and the family, and a desire among women for greater personal freedom. Such considerations surfaced first among the urban middle class created by the market economy. Separating themselves from the working class, these families consciously reduced the number of children in order to increase their own standard of living and improve their children's prospects for success. The birth rate was higher among immigrants and working-class families, who spent less money on education and sent children to work at an earlier age, but it also gradually declined. The birth rate of African-Americans, on the other hand, showed no significant falling off, and would not until after emancipation. Blacks had a strong sense of family, but the economic incentives that motivated whites to reduce family size affected them less, since slaves were denied control over their own lives. Because free blacks were allowed to work only in the lowest paying jobs, they depended, as did poor immigrant families, on the income of children to make ends meet.

The ideal of the democratic family that developed after 1800 was based on greater personal affection, not only between husband and wife, but also between parents and children. The new family was child-centered: relations with children were emotionally less distant and—as Marryat observed—discipline was less severe. Children were seen as individuals

with special needs, and companies began producing books, toys, and furniture designed specifically for children. By mid-century the concept of the family vacation had developed, along with new family-oriented celebrations such as Christmas, Thanksgiving, and birthday parties.

With fewer children, mothers could lavish more attention on each child. Anxious about raising their sons and daughters properly, women read a host of books on child nurture directed specifically at them. Whereas the Puritan tradition had stressed the "breaking and beating down" of a child's "natural pride," nineteenth-century parents emphasized the importance of affection rather than strict control.

The new generation of children also tended to remain at home longer. Eighteenth-century parents had put out older children as apprentices and servants in order to reduce their financial burden, but families now delayed their children's departure in order to extend their education and increase their chances of success. A growing number of children, especially among the urban middle class, lived at home until their late teens and even early twenties. Adolescence (a term that now came into common use) was recognized as a separate stage of life, distinct from childhood, with its own needs and problems.

In the new world of the market, aspiring parents hoped to raise children who were independent, responsible, orderly,

and self-disciplined. Too strict control of children would stifle self-reliance, an essential quality in an intensely competitive society. Yet these attitudes were a source of tension, too. Because sons remained at home longer, they were more dependent economically and emotionally on their parents; at the same time, they spent a larger part of their days at school away from home and were expected to be independent, "sturdy" republicans. Daughters felt new pressures as well. Since they had no crucial economic role at home, more of them received a better education and supported themselves by working in factories and teaching. Yet upon marriage they were expected to sacrifice their interests to being a wife and mother.

The independence of youth extended to choosing a marriage partner. The colonial custom of parents arranging suitable marriages was no longer observed. Financial considerations, although still important, took second place to physical attraction and emotional compatibility. Earlier generations had identified romantic love with immaturity, but the new generation, taking its cue from novels and popular literature, elevated love to the central force in marriage. Still, falling in love could be risky—how could one know if such feelings were deceptive? "Of all the foolish things under the sun, the most foolish and saddest is for very young and ignorant people to rush into marriage under the impression that they are 'in love,'" reflected Lydia Sigourney. "'In love' they are crazy, and they make themselves miserable for life, for want of a little sense."

Most parents did not interfere with courtship and couples were allowed considerable time alone. But young women especially were responsible for seeing that passionate exchanges did not lead to premarital intercourse. Emma Hadley, a clever young Quaker, said of youthful courting:

The boys they go courting they dress very
    fine
To keep the girls up 'tis all their design
They will hug them and kiss them
    and flatter and lie
And keep the girls up till they are ready to
    die.

As etiquette books formulated a new set of rituals designed to solemnize marriage, weddings among the urban upper and middle class became more elaborate. Church services supplanted civil ceremonies, and instead of only a few close family members in attendance, weddings became gala social events. Earlier, American brides had often worn gray or brown, but now social convention dictated a white dress, veil, and a wreath of flowers in the hair. Most couples had one or two bridesmaids and groomsmen, but elaborate weddings involved as many as a dozen.

Because of the cost, wedding ceremonies for most working-class and rural families remained simple and were held at home. And slaves were often denied any formal ceremony, allowed only to observe the tradition of "jumping the broomstick" before the slave community.

After the wedding, new responsibilities greeted husband and wife. "An entirely new life opened," Priscilla Page recalled; "duties, interests, associations hitherto unknown forcibly presented themselves; new cares and anxieties replaced the old ones, and life together assumed a more serious aspect." The transition to married life was often more difficult for women, since marriage now represented a sharp break in women's lives, with new work and responsibilities.

On a much greater scale than with any previous American generation, war disrupted families and lives. In 1861 in both the North and the South, lovers, sons, brothers, and fathers marched off to war. Many never came back; many others returned maimed and disabled, unable to resume their former roles in society. For slaves, emancipation brought control over their families, and in freedom African-Americans quickly sought to model their family life after that of whites. Among whites, the war left countless women widows and children without fathers. Few white families on either side were not touched by personal loss. With so many shattered lives, the Civil War was a wrenching experience for this generation.

In old age and retirement, parents depended on their own resources, and if necessary their children, for care and support. With no pension plans (except for Union veterans), and with most couples able to save only limited amounts for later years, perhaps 70 percent of men over 65 continued to work. Some fathers sought to provide for the couple's final years by giving a son the family farm or business in exchange for being taken care of in old age. Care for elderly parents put pressures on both generations. Having worked hard all their lives, parents worried about falling into poverty in their final years, while their children's independence was limited by continuing obligations and parental supervision. Couples might be able to spend a few years in retirement together after their children were grown, but these years tended to be few. Indeed, at mid-century in half of the families one of the parents died before the youngest child was married.

Thus the family too was touched by the nineteenth-century revolution in markets, urban development, and industry. The new democratic family developed gradually, flourishing at different rates and in different places. But the changes were revolutionary nonetheless. Frederick Marryat had good reason to be surprised at these "sturdy republicans."

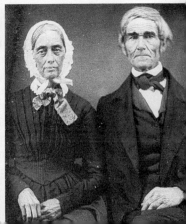

13

The Old South

The myth of the Old South has long engaged the popular imagination. It was, in legend, a land of chivalrous gentlemen and ladies fair, of moonlight and magnolias, of elegant aristocrats and dutiful slaves. But the reality of the Old South was far more complex. Where, then, is the real Old South to be found?

The impeccably dressed Colonel Daniel Jordan, master of 261 slaves at Laurel Hill, strolls down his oak-lined lawn to the dock along the Waccamaw River, a day's journey north of Charleston in All Saints Parish. Here he boards the steamship *Nina*, which on its regular run passes other rice plantations with names like True Blue, Weehawka, Forlorn Hope, and Oryzantia, whose vast irrigated fields front the river on either side. On Fridays, it is Colonel Jordan's custom to visit the exclusive Hot and Hot Fish Club, founded by his fellow low-country planters, to play a game of lawn bowling or billiards, and be waited on by black servants in livery as he sips a mint julep—or even more remarkable, a shivering-cold glass of ice water—in the refined and genteel atmosphere that for him is the South.

Several hundred miles to the west another steamboat, the *Fashion*, makes its way along the Alabama River, tying up to take on cotton at landings so crude that trees offer the only available moorings. Near the village of Claiborne, one of the passengers is upset by the steamboat's slow pace. Tall and thin, he is wearing a ready-made suit, which unfortunately seems to have been tailored with a short, fat figure in mind. The hilt of a large knife protrudes from his waistcoat. He has been away from his plantation in the Red River country of Texas and is eager to get back. "Time's money, time's money!" he mutters to anyone who will listen. "Time's worth more'n money to me now; a hundred percent more, 'cause I left my niggers all alone; not a damn white man within four mile on 'em." When asked what they are doing, since the cotton crop has already been picked, he says, "I set 'em to clairin', but they ain't doin' a damn thing—not a damn thing, they ain't. . . . I know that as well as you do. That's the reason time's an object. I told the capting so, when I came aboard: says I, 'Capting,' says I, 'time is in the objective case with me.' No sir, they ain't doin' a damn solitary thing; that's what they are up to. . . . But I'll make it up, I'll make it up when I get thar, now you'd better believe." For this Red River planter, time is money and cotton is his world—indeed, cotton is what the South is all about. "I am a cotton man, I am, and I don't car who knows it," he proclaims. "I know cotton, I do. I'm dam' if I know anythin' but cotton."

Plantation Burial, *painted about 1860 by John Antrobus, portrays a black slave community from a Louisiana plantation burying a loved one. Religion played a central role in the life of slaves.*

In the bayous of the Deep South, only a few miles from where the Mississippi Delta meets the Gulf, the South is a far different place. There, Octave Johnson hears the dogs coming: as many as 20, he judges, from the strength of their baying. Johnson is a runaway slave and has been for over a year. He fled from a Louisiana plantation in St. James Parish when the work bell rang so early it was too dark to see, and his overseer threatened to whip him for staying in bed. To survive, he hides in the swamps four miles behind the plantation—stealing turkeys, chickens, and pigs when he gets the chance. Some days he meets slaves at work in the field and swaps his meat for their cornmeal or some matches. The example his freedom sets, uncertain a life as it is, seems alluring to his fellow slaves. Over the year, nearly 30 others have joined him. The band sleeps on logs and burns cypress leaves to keep away the mosquitoes.

The sound of the dogs warns Johnson and his companions that the hound master Eugene Jardeau is out again. This time when the pack bursts upon them, the slaves do not flee, but set about killing as many dogs as possible. Then they throw themselves into the bayou, the hounds following, and alligators make short work of another six. Johnson isn't pleased by the notion of mixing with alligators, but he isn't terrified either. "The alligators [prefer] dog flesh to personal flesh," he explains later. For Octave Johnson, the real Old South is a matter of weighing one's prospects between the uncertainties of alligators and the overseer's whip— and deciding when to say no.

Ferdinand Steel and his family were not forced, by the flick of the lash, to rise

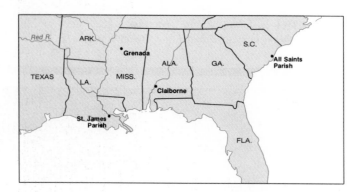

at five in the morning. They rose because the land demanded it; and it was their duty to do the work of the Lord. Steel, in his twenties, owned 170 acres of land in Carroll County, Mississippi, not many miles from the Yalobusha River. Not yet married, he had moved there from Tennessee with his widowed mother, sister, and brother in 1836, only a few years after the Choctaws had been compelled to give up the region and march west. His life was one of continuous hard work. After family prayers each morning, he would milk the cows, feed the horses, and then come to breakfast. Except for a midday respite, he was out in the fields until sundown, tending corn, a little wheat, and some watermelons. His mother Eliza and sister Julia had plenty to keep them busy: making lye soap by the long, messy process of boiling ashes with animal fat, or fashioning dippers out of gourds, or sewing dresses, shirts, and "pantiloons" for the men. Always there was work to do, droughts to worry about, or accidents and misfortune. Steel had castrated a calf and it had died—probably, he felt, because he had performed the operation when the moon was in the wrong phase.

The Steel family grew cotton, too, but not with the single-minded devotion of the planter aboard the *Fashion*. Self-sufficiency and family security always came first, and Steel's total crop amounted to only five or six bales. His profit was never sufficient to consider buying even one slave. In fact, he would have preferred not to raise any cotton. "We are to[o] weak handed," he wrote in his diary. "We had better raise small grain and corn and let cotton alone, raise corn and keep out of debt and we will have no necessity of raising cotton." But the five bales meant cash, and cash meant that when he went to market at nearby Grenada on Saturday afternoons, he could buy sugar and coffee for the family, gunpowder and lead, a bit of calico for the women, and quinine to treat the malaria that was so common in those parts. Sunday was the Lord's day, and often Steel's family found their hearts melted to tenderness by the sermon of an itinerant Methodist preacher. Though fiercely independent, Steel and his scattered neighbors came together often enough, to help each other raise houses, clear fields, shuck corn, or quilt. Worshiping or playing, working or eating, they depended on one another and were bound together by blood, religion, obligation, and honor. For rural farmers like Ferdinand Steel, these ties were the real South.

The portraits could go on: different people, different Souths, all of them real. Such contrasts underscore the futility of trying to isolate one "true" South, or even of trying to define a regional identity. The label itself—the *South*—suggests a definition based on geography; yet the South was a land of great geographic diversity. Encompassing in 1860 the fifteen slave states plus the District of Columbia, it extended from the Tidewater coastal plain along the Atlantic seaboard to the prairies of Texas; from the Shenandoah and Tennessee valleys to the Gulf coast, from the hill regions and mountains of western Virginia and North Carolina to the swampy Mississippi Delta with its semitropical climate. Nor did geographic boundaries set the South apart from the rest of the country. Only the Ohio River separated the North and South, and it was an avenue of trade rather than a source of division.

Yet despite its many differences of people and geography, the South was bonded by ties so strong, they eventually outpulled those of the nation itself. Sectional loyalty led in the end to civil war. To understand what made the South a region, we cannot merely take one particular portrait and elevate it: we cannot decide, for example, that Octave Johnson rather than Colonel Jordan was the "real" South. Instead, we must see how so many different people and races and classes formed a single southern society.

At the heart of this unity was an agricultural system that took advantage of the region's warm climate and long growing season. Cotton required 200 frost-free days, and rice and sugar even more, which meant that in the United States these crops could be grown only in the South. These staples tied the South to the international economy. Furthermore, the emphasis on staple crops and the prestige accorded agriculture discouraged the growth of cities and made it more difficult for a diversified economy to develop. And most important, this rural agricultural economy was based on the institution of slavery, which had far-reaching effects on all aspects of southern society. It shaped not only the culture of the slaves themselves, but the lives of their masters, and even of farmers and herdsmen in the hills and backwoods, who saw few slaves during their day-to-day existence. To understand the Old South, then, we must understand how the southern agricultural economy and the institution of slavery affected the social class structure of both whites and blacks.

THE SOCIAL STRUCTURE OF THE COTTON KINGDOM

We have already seen (Chapter 10) that the spread of cotton stimulated the nation's remarkable economic growth after the War of 1812, both in the North, with its textile factories, and the South, with the expansion of the plantation system. Demand sent the price of cotton soaring on the international market and southerners scrambled westward to reap the profits to be made in the cotton sweepstakes. Just as tobacco had turned the Chesapeake Bay region into a boom country during the seventeenth century, cotton produced new fortunes in the 1820s, 1830s, and 1840s from the fresh lands of the Southwest.

The Boom Country Economy

Letters, newspapers, and word of mouth all brought tales of the "black belt" region of Alabama, where the dark, loamy soil was particularly suited to growing cotton. Tremendous yields also came from the alluvial soils deposited along the Mississippi River's broad reaches. As southern agricultural practices rapidly exhausted the soil in older fields, the policies of Indian removal soon opened up new tracts in Alabama, Mississippi, Louisiana, and then Arkansas. "The *Alabama Fever* rages here with great violence and has *carried off* vast numbers of our Citizens," a North Carolinian wrote in 1817. "I am apprehensive if it continues to spread as it has done, it will almost depopulate the country." A generation later, in the 1830s, immigrants were still "pouring in with a ceaseless tide," an Alabama observer reported, including "'Land Sharks' ready to swallow up the home of the redmen, or the white, as opportunity might offer."

By the 1840s, planters even began to leave Mississippi and Alabama—virgin territory at the turn of the century—to head for the new cotton frontier along the Red River and up into Texas. A traveler in 1845 saw many abandoned and desolate farms in Mississippi, which a decade later the northern visitor Frederick Law Olmsted called "Gone to Texas" farms. Texas cotton production jumped from 58,000 bales in 1850 to 432,000 in 1860. Indeed, by the eve of the Civil War the Gulf states produced three-fourths of all the cotton grown in the United States. Equally amazing, nearly a third of the total crop came from *west* of the Mississippi River.

As Senator James Henry Hammond of South Carolina boasted in 1858, cotton was king in the Old South. True, the region devoted more acreage to corn, which was the major crop of nonslaveholders, but cotton was the primary export and the major source of southern wealth. It accounted for over half of America's exports from 1815 to 1860, and by 1860 the United States produced three-fourths of the world's supply of cotton.

In this romanticized Currier and Ives print of a cotton plantation, field hands are waist-deep in the fields while other slaves haul the picked cotton to be ginned and then pressed into bales. Looking on are the owner and his wife. Picking began as early as August and continued in some areas until late January. Because the bolls ripened at different times, a field had to be picked several times.

This boom fueled the southern economy so strongly that, following the depression of 1839–1843, it grew faster than the northern economy. Southern per capita income (with slaves included) was 20 percent lower than the national average in 1860, but it was higher than that of the Northwest, which had been settled at the same time as the cotton belt. Moreover, among whites, per capita income in the South actually exceeded that of the free states, though wealth was not as evenly distributed in the plantation South as in northern agricultural areas. Yet the gap between the richest and the poorest southern whites was not significantly different from the gap in northern cities.

The surface of prosperity, however, masked basic problems in the economy—problems that would become more apparent after the Civil War. Much of the South's new wealth resulted from migration of its population to more productive western lands. The amount of unsettled prime land was not unlimited, and once it was settled, the South could not sustain forever its rate of expansion. Nor did the shift in population alter the structure of the southern economy, stimulate technological change, or improve the way goods were produced and marketed. Fundamentally dependent on its exports, the South failed to develop internal markets, which would have generated economic growth and increased specialization among its citizens.

The Upper South's New Orientation

As cotton transformed the boom country of the Deep South, agriculture in the Upper South also adjusted.* Improved varieties and more scientific agricultural

*The Upper South included the border states (Delaware, Maryland, Kentucky, and Missouri) and Virginia, North Carolina, Tennessee, and Arkansas. The states of the Deep South were South Carolina, Georgia, Florida, Alabama, Mississippi, Louisiana, and Texas.

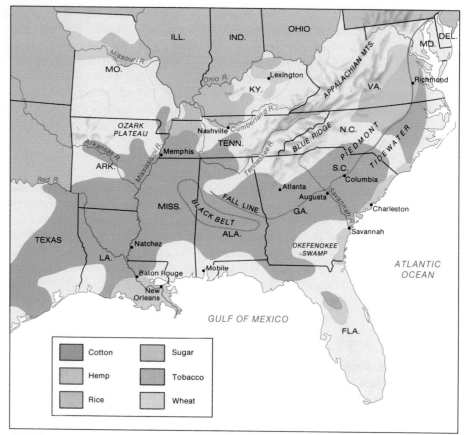

COTTON AND OTHER CROPS OF THE SOUTH
By 1860, the cotton kingdom extended across the Lower South into the Texas prairie and up the Mississippi River valley. Tobacco and hemp were the staple crops of the Upper South, where they competed with corn and wheat. Rice production was concentrated in the swampy coastal region of South Carolina and Georgia as well as the lower tip of Louisiana. The sugar district was in southern Louisiana.

practices reversed the decline in tobacco, which had begun in the 1790s. More important, however, farmers in the Upper South made wheat and corn their major crops. As early as 1840 the value of wheat grown in Virginia was twice that of tobacco.

Because the new crops required less labor, planters in the Upper South found themselves with a surplus of slaves, whom they regularly sold to cotton and sugar planters in the Deep South. This flow of slaves strongly shaped the southern economy—indeed, some planters in the Upper South maintained a profit margin only by selling surplus slaves. The demand in the Deep South for field hands drove their price steadily up from 1820 to 1860. By the late 1850s a prime field hand, who would have sold for $600 in the early 1840s, commanded as much as $1500. Even with increased labor costs, southern agriculture flourished. In 1800 a slave's labor produced less than $15 worth of crops on average, but by 1860, the figure had risen to about $125.

The Rural South

The Old South, then, was expanding, dynamic, and booming economically. But the primary focus on agriculture meant that its social structure would remain overwhelmingly rural. In 1860 in the South, 84 percent of the labor force was engaged in agriculture, compared to 40 percent in the North. Although the South on the eve of the Civil War had slightly less than 40 percent of the population, it raised 50 percent of the nation's cattle, 60 percent of the hogs, 90 percent of the mules, and 50 percent of the corn. And of course it had no competition in the production of tobacco, cotton, sugar, rice, and hemp.

Conversely, the South lagged badly in manufacturing. A few towns like Columbus, Alabama, had small textile factories where "cracker girls" from the countryside earned from $8 to $12 a month running the spindles, but less than 15 percent of the capital invested in manufacturing went to southern factories. Because these were built on a smaller scale than those in the North, they produced only 9 percent of the nation's manufactured goods. The South even trailed the new states of the Northwest like Indiana and Illinois, where the manufacturing capital invested was greater than that of the seven states of the Deep South combined. During the 1850s, some southern propagandists urged greater investment in industry to diversify the South's economy, but so long as the high profits from cotton continued, the movement made little headway. Most slaveholders did not encourage the development of an industrial, urban economy, which would have undermined their power.

With so little industry, few cities developed in the South. New Orleans, with a population of 169,000 in 1860, was the only city of significant size. (Baltimore and St. Louis, both located in slave states, were not really southern in their value systems or economic orientation.) Whereas in 1860 Indiana and Illinois had 40 cities with a population over 2500, the entire Deep South combined had only 33. North Carolina, Alabama, Mississippi, Arkansas, and Texas did not contain a single city with a population of 10,000. Only 1 in 10 southerners lived in cities and towns in 1860, compared to 1 out of 3 persons in the North.

Innovation and education often accompany an urban culture, and the South evidenced far less interest in education. The nation's best colleges were in the North, and many wealthy southerners sent their sons to these schools, much to the dismay of some southern leaders. At the secondary level, southern facilities were virtually nonexistent, except for private academies serving the children of the rich. Southern politicians, who spoke for the planter class, argued that education was the responsibility of the family, not the state. Thus free public schools were rare, especially in the rural districts that comprised most of the South. Georgia in 1860 had only one county with a free school system, and Mississippi had no public schools outside its few cities.

The net effect of fewer schools, lower attendance, and shorter school terms was that white children on average spent only one-fifth as much time in school as did their northern counterparts. Since laws forbade the education of black slaves, and whites were seldom in school, illiteracy rates were much higher in the South. Among native-born whites, the 1850 census showed that 20 percent were unable to read and write. The comparable figure was 3 percent in the Middle states and 0.4 percent in New England. In some areas of the South, over a third of all whites were illiterate.

Distribution of Slavery

Even more than agrarian ways, slavery set the South apart. In 1776, slavery had been a national institution. Legally enslaved African-Americans could be found rolling barrels on the wharves of Boston, serving meals in the mansions of Rhode Island merchants, tending stock on New Jersey farms, and stoking iron forges in Pennsylvania. One by one, however, the northern states freed their slaves, so that by the 1820s, slavery was virtually confined to the states south of Pennsylvania and the Ohio River. It became the South's "peculiar institution." Thus slavery must be

---

THE SPREAD OF SLAVERY, 1820–1860

Between 1820 and 1860, the slave population of the South shifted south and westward, concentrating especially heavily in coastal South Carolina and Georgia, in the black belt of central Alabama and Mississippi (so named because of its rich soil), and in the Mississippi valley. Small farms with few slaves predominated in cotton-growing areas that lacked good transportation, such as northern Georgia, and in regions with poor soil, such as the piney woods of southern Mississippi.

understood not only in the searing personal terms of human bondage, but also as a social and economic system that bound southern whites and blacks together in a multitude of ways.

Slaves were not evenly distributed throughout the region. More than half lived in the Deep South, where blacks outnumbered whites in both South Carolina and Mississippi by the 1850s. Elsewhere in the Deep South, the black population exceeded 40 percent in all states except Texas. In the Upper South, on the other hand, whites greatly outnumbered blacks. Only in Virginia and North Carolina did the slave population exceed 30 percent. In Delaware, it was a minuscule 1.5 percent.

The distribution of slaves showed striking geographic variations within individual states as well. Virginia's Tidewater and Piedmont regions, for example, had significant slave populations, whereas the hilly and mountainous western part of the state had relatively few slaves. A similar pattern prevailed in most other states. In areas of fertile soil, flat or rolling countryside, and good transportation, slavery and the plantation system dominated; in the pine barrens, areas isolated by lack of transportation, and hilly and mountainous regions, small family farms and few slaves were the rule.

Almost all slaves, male and female, were used in agriculture, with only about 10 percent living in cities and towns. On large plantations, a few slaves were domestic servants, and others were skilled artisans—blacksmiths, carpenters, or bricklayers—but most toiled in the fields. Some slaves found work in extractive industries such as turpentine production and lumbering, others along the docks, or in industry. But by and large, the demand for slaves as agricultural workers drove their purchase price so high that they were seldom used elsewhere in the southern economy. Only about 5 percent of the South's manufacturing employees in the 1850s were slaves.

Slavery as a Labor System

Slavery was, first and foremost, a system to manage and control labor. Other than the work performed by farm families, slaves supplied virtually all southern agricultural labor. Southern whites, like northern farmers, refused to hire out as farm laborers, except to save enough money to buy a farm of their own. The plantation system, with its extensive estates and large labor forces, could never have developed without slavery, nor could it have met the world demand for cotton and other staples. Slavery, in other words, made the mass production of agricultural staples possible.

And it remained a highly profitable investment. The average slaveowner spent perhaps $30 to $35 a year to support an adult slave; some expended as little as half that. Allowing for the cost of land, equipment, and other expenses, a planter could expect one of his slaves to produce more than $78 worth of cotton—which meant that even at the higher cost of support, the planter expropriated about 60 percent of the wealth produced by a slave's labor. For those who pinched pennies and drove slaves harder, the profits were even greater. In terms of investment, planters generally received about as high a return on human property as they would have by putting their money into land, factories, or railroads. As a result, slaves represented an enormous capital investment, worth more than all the land in the Old South.

By concentrating wealth and power in the hands of the planter class, slavery shaped and influenced the tone of southern society. Planters were not aristocrats in the European sense of having special legal privileges or formal titles of rank. Still, the system encouraged southern planters to think of themselves as a landed gentry upholding the aristocratic values of pride, honor, family, and hospitality. The planters gained wealth and prestige from their ownership of other human beings, and the law gave masters wide discretion in controlling plantation slaves— just as medieval lords had exercised nearly absolute power over their serfs.

Whereas slavery had existed throughout most of the New World at the beginning of the century, by the 1850s the United States, Cuba, and Brazil were the only slaveholding nations left in the Americas. Public opinion in Europe and in the North had grown more and more hostile to the institution, causing southern whites to feel increasingly like an isolated minority defending an embattled position. Yet white southerners tenaciously clung to slavery, for it was the base on which the South's economic growth and way of life rested. As one Georgian observed on the eve of the Civil War, slavery was "so intimately mingled with our social conditions that it would be impossible to eradicate it."

CLASS STRUCTURE OF THE WHITE SOUTH

Tradition divided southern society into three classes: planters, slaves, and poor whites. In reality, the class structure of the Old South was considerably more complex. Because of the institution of slavery, the social structure of the antebellum South differed in important ways from that of the North. Even so, southern society was remarkably fluid and as a result class lines were not rigid.

The Slaveowners

In 1860 the region's 15 states had a population of 12 million, of which roughly two-thirds were white, one-third were black slaves, and about 2 percent were free

SOUTHERN POPULATION, 1860

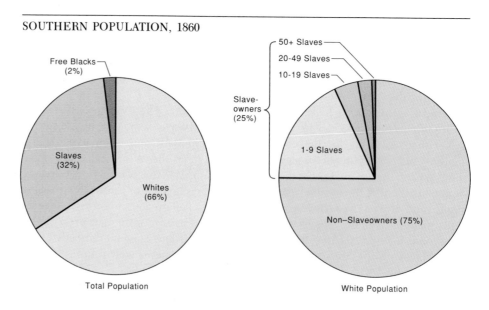

Total Population

White Population

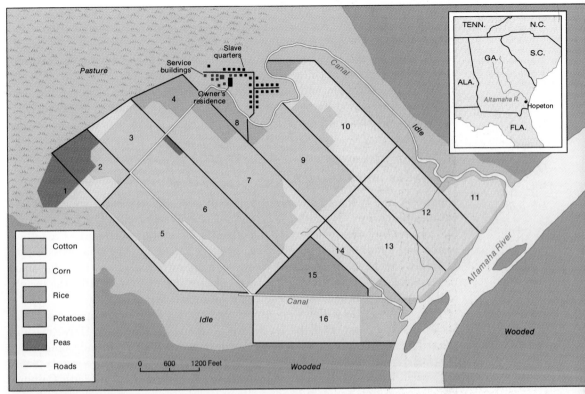

A PLANTATION LAYOUT

Often covering a thousand acres or more, a plantation contained several fields and usually extensive uncleared woods. Service buildings might include a smoke house, stables, a gin house (for cotton) or a rice mill, and an overseer's dwelling. Like most large plantations, Hopeton produced a considerable amount of foodstuffs, but it grew both rice and cotton as staples. Most plantations concentrated on a single cash crop.

blacks. Of the 8 million whites, only about 2 million, or one-quarter, either owned slaves or were members of slaveowning families. Thus the typical white southerner was not a slaveowner at all, but belonged to a yeoman farmer family whose members worked the land themselves. Moreover, most slaveowners owned only a few slaves, usually at most one slave family. If one uses the census definition of a planter as a person who owned 20 or more slaves, only about 1 out of every 30 southern whites belonged to families of the planter class.

A planter of consequence, however, needed to own at least 50 slaves, and there were only about 10,000 such families—less than 1 percent of the white population. This privileged group made up the aristocracy at the top of the southern class structure. Owners of large numbers of slaves were very rare. Out of 8 million southern whites, only about 2000 like Colonel Daniel Jordan owned 100 or more slaves. Although limited in size, the planter class nevertheless owned over half of all slaves and controlled over 90 percent of the region's total wealth. The average slaveholder was 14 times as rich as the average nonslaveholder.

The typical plantation had 20 to 50 slaves and 800 to 1000 acres of land. On a larger estate, slaves would have to walk more than an hour to reach the farthest fields, losing valuable work time. Thus larger slaveowners usually owned several plantations. An overseer managed the slaves on each, while the owner attended to administrative and business matters. The slaves were divided into field hands, skilled workers, and house servants, with one or more slaves serving as "drivers" to assist the overseer. Planters pioneered the application of capitalistic methods, including specialization and division of labor, to agriculture, and the best-run plantations resembled "factories in the fields." Yet they remained labor-intensive operations. Of the southern staples, only the production of sugar was heavily mechanized.

Tidewater and Frontier

Southern planters shared a commitment to preserve slavery as the source of their wealth and stature. Yet in other ways they were a diverse group. On the one hand, the tobacco and rice planters of the Atlantic Tidewater were part of a settled region and a culture that reached back 150 to 200 years. Alabama, Mississippi, Arkansas, and Texas, by contrast, were just emerging from the frontier stage, since the vast majority of their settlers had arrived after 1815. Consequently, the society of the Southwest was newer, rawer, and more volatile.

It was along the Tidewater, especially the bays of the Chesapeake and the South Carolina coast, that the legendary "Old South" was born. Here, masters erected substantial homes, some—especially between Charleston and Columbia— the classic white-pillared mansions in the Greek revival style. For Virginia planters, social life centered on their plantations, in contrast to the South Carolina nabobs, who often gravitated to the city of Charleston, especially during the gay winter social season. While these planters were practical men rather than philosophers, more than a few were urbane and polished. Upriver from the Tidewater, most country gentry were more rustic. They enjoyed a leisurely life, fought duels to defend their reputations, and were bound to one another by strong ties of kinship.

The ideal of the Tidewater South was the country gentleman of the old English tradition. An Irish visitor observed that in Maryland and Virginia the great plantation residences were "exactly similar to the old manor houses of England" and that their occupants lived in "a style which approaches nearer to that of the English country gentleman than what is to be met with anywhere else on the continent." As in England, the Episcopal Church remained the socially accepted road to heaven; also as in England, the local gentry often served as justices of the peace, administering the local courts and dispensing justice. Here, too, family connections continued to be important in politics: there were fewer upstart Franklin Plummers to challenge aristocrats like Powhatan Ellis.

While the newer regions of the South boasted planters with cultivated manners (Jefferson Davis of Mississippi was one), as a group the cotton lords were a different breed. They were basically entrepreneurs who had moved west for the same reason so many other Americans had: to make their fortunes. Some were planters fleeing the exhausted soils of the Tidewater; others were the sons of planters seeking to improve their lot. Not a few were northerners with an eye for opportunity, such as Henry Watson, who went south as a young tutor, settled in Greensboro, Alabama, and became a leading planter. Overseers sometimes rose into the ranks of slaveowners, as Ephraim Beanland of Mississippi did. Merchants and businessmen like Maunsel White of New Orleans invested their profits in a plantation; land speculators rode the land grabs of the 1830s into the ranks of the elite. But by and large, the wealthy planters of the cotton gentry were self-made men, who through hard work, aggressive business tactics, and good luck had risen from ordinary backgrounds. For them, the cotton boom offered the opportunity to move up in a new society that lacked an entrenched elite.

"Time's money, time's money." For men like the impatient Texan, time was indeed money, slaves were capital, and cotton by the bale signified cash in hand. This business orientation was especially apparent in the cotton kingdom, where planters sought to maximize profits and constantly reinvested their returns in land and slaves. As one visitor remarked of Mississippi slaveholders: "To sell cotton in order to buy negroes—to make more cotton to buy more negroes, 'ad infinitum,' is the aim and direct tendency of all the operations of the thorough-going cotton planter: his whole soul is wrapped in the pursuit." One shocked Virginian who visited Vicksburg claimed that its citizens ran "mad with speculation" and did business "in a kind of phrenzy." And indeed there was money to be made. The combined annual income of the richest thousand families of the cotton kingdom approached $50 million, while the wealth of the remaining 666,000 families amounted to only about $60 million.

Stately mansions could be found in a few areas, especially along the Mississippi between Natchez and Vicksburg and below Baton Rouge. In general, though, elegant homes were uncommon in the cotton South, coming into their own only during the 1850s and later. Most planters lived more humbly. Although they ranked among the richest citizens in America, their homes were often simple one- or two-story, unpainted wooden frame houses. A visitor to one Georgia plantation reported that the house did not have a pane of glass in the windows, a door between the rooms, or a ceiling other than the roof. A traveler in central Mississippi in 1839 spent the night in "the *Mansion House* of the plantation, a cabin with two rooms and a passage between, the one room was occupied by barrels of pork, flour, and plough and its appendages, a few old saddles, some peas spread on the floor, etc. The other served as a parlour, dining room, chamber, etc." "If you wish to see people worth millions living as [if] they were not worth hundreds," advised one southwestern planter in 1839, ". . . come to the land of cotton and negroes."

Few of the new cotton lords had a strong commitment to education; fewer still absorbed the culture and learning of the traditional country gentleman. During his extensive journeys in the South, the noted New Yorker Frederick Law Olmsted declared that he "did not see, except perhaps in one or two towns, a thermometer, nor a book of Shakespeare, nor a piano or sheet of music, nor a good reading lamp, nor an engraving or copy of any kind, or a work of art of the slightest merit. A large majority of all these houses were residences of slaveholders, a considerable proportion cotton planters."

The Master at Home

Whether tending a Tidewater plantation or carving out a cotton estate on the Texas frontier, the master had to coordinate a complex agricultural operation. He gave daily instructions concerning the work to be done, settled disputes between slaves and the overseer who supervised the slaves, and generally handed out the rewards and penalties. In addition, the owner made the critical decisions concerning which fields to use, what crops to plant, and when to send crops to market. Planters had to watch expenses and income carefully, and they often sought to expand their production by clearing additional fields, buying more land or slaves, or investing in machinery such as cotton gins. As in any business, these decisions required a sound understanding of the domestic and international market as well as anticipation of future swings.

In performing his duties, the plantation owner was supposed to be the "master" of his crops, his family, and his slaves. Defenders of slavery often held up this paternalistic ideal—the care and guidance of dependent children—as the keystone of southern society. With slaves, as with children, the relationship included instilling proper behavior by any discipline necessary. White southerners expected that the duties and responsibilities each had for the other would promote a genuine bond of affection between the caring master and his loyal slaves.

In real life, the forces of the market and a desire for success made this paternalistic ideal less evident among masters. Some conservatives, located in the more traditional, long-settled areas of the South, did condemn the increasingly material scramble for wealth on the cotton frontier, a pursuit that led to an excessive exploitation of slaves and land. Still, Tidewater planters were concerned with money and profits as much as the self-made cotton lords were. Indeed, some of the most brutal forms of slavery existed on the rice plantations, where the absenteeism of many Tidewater planters, combined with the sheer numbers of slaves, made close personal ties impossible. Except for a few domestic servants, owners of large plantations generally had little contact with their slaves. Nor could paternalism mask the reality that slavery everywhere rested on violence, racism, and exploitation.

The Plantation Mistress

Upper-class southern white women, like those in the North, grew up with the ideal of domesticity, reinforced by the notion of a paternalistic master who was lord of the plantation. The proper southern woman was religious, pure, and submissive, and she focused attention on family and home. As the guardian of moral standards, she dispensed love and comfort along with moral guidance in her role as wife and mother. But the plantation mistress soon discovered that, given the demands placed on her, the ideal was hard to fulfill.

A genteel lady, after all, enjoyed a certain amount of leisure. Once a young southern woman married and became a plantation mistress, she was often shocked by the magnitude of her responsibilities. Nursing the sick, making clothing, tending the garden, caring for the poultry, and overseeing every aspect of food preparation were all her domain. She also had to supervise and plan the work of the domestic servants and distribute clothing. "This morning I got up late having been disturbed in the night," wrote one harried Carolina mistress, "hurried down to have something arranged for breakfast, . . . had prayers, got the boys off to town. Had the [sewing] work cut out, gave orders about dinner, had the horse feed fixed in hot water, had the box filled with cork: went to see the carpenters working on the negro houses . . . now I have to cut out the flannel jackets." Small wonder that Sarah Williams, the New York bride of a North Carolina planter, admitted that her mother-in-law "works harder than any Northern farmer's wife I know."

Unlike female reformers in the North, upper-class southern women did not openly challenge their role, but there is evidence that they found their sphere confining. The greatest unhappiness stemmed from the never-ending task of managing the slaves. "These women have less chance to live their own lives than if

Sarah Pierce Vick, the mistress of a plantation near Vicksburg, Mississippi, pauses to speak to one of her slaves, who may be holding feed for her horse. A plantation mistress had many duties and, while enjoying the comforts brought by wealth and status, often found her life more difficult than she had anticipated before marriage.

they were African missionaries," Mary Chesnut, the wife of a prominent South Carolina planter, observed. "They have a swarm of blacks about them like children under their care." Another southern woman, voicing her dislike for her position, confessed, "I do not see how I can live my life amid these people! To be always among people whom I do not understand and whom I must guide, and teach and lead on like children. It frightens me." Yet without the labor of slaves, the lifestyle of these women was an impossibility.

Some women drew a parallel between their situation and that of the slaves. Both in some sense were victims of male dominance, and independent-minded women found the subordination of marriage difficult. Commented Mary Chesnut, "There is no slave, after all, like a wife." And Susan Dabney Smedes, in her recollection of growing up on an Alabama plantation, recalled that "it was a saying that the mistress of a plantation was the most complete slave on it." Some women particularly bristled at their lack of independence and at the necessity of obeying men. "How men can go blustering around, making everybody uncomfortable, simply to show that they are masters and we are only women and children at their mercy!" exclaimed Mary Chesnut. Her father-in-law, she observed, was amiable so long as those beneath him did as he expected, "but he is as absolute a tyrant as the Czar of Russia . . . or the Sultan of Turkey."

Many women were deeply discontented, too, with the widespread double standard for sexual behavior and with the daily reminders of miscegenation some had to face. A man who fathered illegitimate children by slave women suffered no social or legal penalties, even in the case of rape (southern law did not recognize such a crime against slave women), whereas a white woman guilty of adultery lost all social respectability. Miscegenation placed a particular strain on the ideals of plantation mistresses. Like all wives, their duties required them to preserve the sanctity of marriage and the wholesomeness of family life. But they were also required to oversee the welfare of their slaves as additional "family"—at the same time that they knew their husbands might be siring children out of wedlock and violating the lines of racial caste so crucial to maintaining the peculiar institution."

Mary Chesnut, who knew the reality of miscegenation firsthand from her father-in-law's liaisons with slave women and discussed it more frankly than most, sneered in her diary at the assumptions of male superiority. "All the time they seem to think themselves patterns—models of husbands and fathers," she fumed, bitter at the enforced silence among wives. "Like the patriarchs of old, our men live all in one house with their wives and concubines; and the mulattoes one sees in every family partly resemble the white children. Any lady is ready to tell you who is the father of all the mulattoes one sees in everybody's household but her own. Those, she seems to think, drop from the clouds. My disgust sometimes is boiling over." She discovered that her views were shared by other planters' wives. One spoke of "violations of the moral law that made mulattoes as common as blackberries," and another recalled, "I saw slavery in its bearing on my sex. I saw that it teemed with injustice and shame to all womankind and I hated it."

Even women whose husbands or sons had not engaged in such behavior often felt constrained and chafed at the legal restraints marriage imposed. Some preferred to work for themselves, often running their own businesses, and thus maintain control of their own property. Married women found such lack of control a particular grievance. The ups and downs of cotton prices and the boom–bust cycles of the economy finally led some southern states to protect the property women brought with them when they married by establishing a separate estate over which women had greater control.

Still, only a small minority of women questioned either their place in southern society or the corrosive influence of slavery. Even fewer were willing to forgo the physical and material comforts that slavery made possible, despite the burdens it imposed on them. Racism was so pervasive within American society that the few white southern women who privately criticized the institution displayed little empathy for the plight of slaves themselves, including black women. Whatever the burdens of the plantation mistress, the experiences that made her a "slave" to her duties as an upper-class woman were hardly akin to the bondage of slavery itself.

Yeoman Farmers

In terms of numbers, yeoman farmers and their families were the backbone of southern society, accounting for well over half the southern white population. They owned no slaves and farmed the traditional 80 to 160 acres, like northern farmers. About 80 percent of the males owned their own land and the rest rented or hired themselves out to other farmers, hoping one day to acquire their own homestead. They settled almost everywhere in the South, except in the rice and sugar districts and valuable river bottomlands of the Deep South, which were monopolized by large slaveowners. Like Ferdinand Steel, most were semisubsistence farmers who raised primarily corn and hogs, along with perhaps a few bales of cotton or some tobacco, which they sold to obtain the cash needed to buy items like sugar, coffee, and salt. The more enterprising sought to produce a surplus of food to sell locally or in a more distant market, and in areas like Virginia's Shenandoah Valley, wheat production thoroughly tied yeoman farmers and small slaveowners to the commercial economy. Some were not so much farmers as herdsmen, who set large herds of scrawny cattle or pigs to forage in the woods until it was time for the annual drive to market. Yeoman farmers lacked the wealth of planters, but they had a pride and dignity that earned them the respect of their richer neighbors.

Southern farmers led more isolated lives than their northern counterparts. The population density was thinner, towns were less numerous, and there were

A majority of white southerners were members of nonslaveholding yeoman farm families. Respected and relatively prosperous, these families nevertheless often lacked many comforts. A number, such as this German farm family in Texas, lived in log cabins.

fewer roads, canals, or railroads to ease travel. Yet the social activities of these people were not much different from those of northern farmers. Religion played an important role, and the church was the center of the community. Camp meetings, held in late summer after the crops were laid by but before harvest time, were both a soul-wrenching experience and a valued time for socializing. As in the North, neighbors also met to exchange labor and tools, always managing to combine work with play. Men raised a house for a new family or for a bride and groom, the women prepared a feast, then everyone had a square dance in the evening. The men rolled logs to clear fields of dead trees, turning the activity into a contest of strength. Women met for quilting bees, where they pieced such traditional patterns as log cabin, flying geese, and oak leaf cluster. Adults and children alike would gather at a barn to shuck corn; in the evening glow of lanterns, the jug would be passed around, rival teams would compete, or a couple of the stoutest voices would lead a chorus of "Round up the corn, boys, round up the corn . . . pull off the shucks, boys, pull off the shucks" and "Give me a dram, sir, give me a dram." County fairs, court sessions, militia musters, political rallies—these too were occasions that brought rural folk together.

Hard work helped improve the lot of these farm families, but the southern economic system put limits on how far ordinary farmers could progress. Planters monopolized the best farmlands, particularly those tracts along riverways with ready access to market. Since yeoman farmers lacked cheap slave labor, adequate transportation, and access to credit, they could not compete with planters in the production of staples. And when it came to selling their corn and wheat, small farmers conducted only limited business with planters, who usually grew as much of their own foodstuffs as possible. In the North, cities became a market for small farmers, but in the South, where the staple economy did not stimulate the growth of towns and cities, this internal market was much smaller.

Thus while southern yeoman farmers were not poor, they suffered from a chronic lack of money and the absence of conveniences that northern farm families enjoyed, such as cast iron stoves, sewing machines, ready-made clothing, and good furniture. And the lack of public schooling hurt ordinary farmers more than wealthy planters, who could afford private tutors. A few chafed at the absence of greater opportunities. Josiah Hinds, who hacked a farm out of the isolated woods of northern Mississippi, worried that his children were growing up "wild" and complained, "Education is but little prized by my neighbours, although honest and industrious . . . and if the corn and cotton grows to perfection . . . it is enough, provided it brings a fare price, and hog meat is at hand to boil with the greens."

In some ways, then, the worlds of the yeoman farmers and the upper-class planters were not only different, but also in conflict. Still, a hostility between the two classes did not emerge. Yeoman farmers admired planters and looked up to them. Realistically or not, they aspired to join the gentry themselves. And even whites who owned no slaves accepted slavery as a means of controlling blacks. If slaves were freed, they would compete directly with white farmers; as slaves, they remained members of an inferior social caste based on race. "Now suppose they was free," one poor farmer told Frederick Law Olmsted. "You see they'd all think themselves as good as we." Racism and fear of blacks were sufficient to keep nonslaveholders loyal to southern institutions. In 1849 in Kentucky, where nearly 90 percent of the voters were nonslaveholders, support for a program of gradual emancipation won only 10,000 votes—showing how firmly whites of all classes supported slavery.

Urban Society

In many ways urban society paralleled rural society in the South. At the top were the merchants, businessmen, and professionals, who generally allied themselves with the planters. Down a notch were the mechanics and tradesmen, part of the southern middle class. They ranked higher than farm laborers or factory workers, and a few even owned slaves. At the bottom were the unskilled white laborers, who did work such as building the canals and railroads of the South. To avoid losing valuable slaves, planters often hired Irish workers to perform such dangerous jobs as draining malarial swamps. The most notable feature of all these groups was their small size—less than 8 percent of the population in 1860 lived in towns with a population over 4000—which reflected the minor role urban life played in the South.

Poor Whites

The poorest white southerners lived on land that no one else wanted: the wiregrass region of southeastern Georgia, the sand hills of central South Carolina, the pine barrens of the coastal plains from Virginia to southeastern Mississippi. In their backgrounds, they were similar to other southerners, but they were the least efficient, the least enterprising, and the least lucky of the rural white population. Shiftless and lazy, extremely superstitious, and largely illiterate, they lived in squalor in rude, unchinked, windowless log cabins. They resided in the remotest areas, inaccessible to market, and were often squatters without title to the land they were on. Many of the men were not really farmers, but spent their time hunting and fishing while women did the domestic work, including what farming they could manage. Other southern whites scorned them as crackers, white trash, sandhillers, and clay eaters.

Circumstances made their poverty difficult to escape. Consuming a monotonous diet of corn, pork, and whiskey, they suffered from malnutrition. And the poor lands they inhabited were prime country for malaria and the hookworm parasite, afflictions which sapped their energy, made them listless, and gave them yellow, sallow complexions. Olmsted described one woman whom he found sitting before the fire in her piney woods cabin: "apparently young," but her face "dry and impassive as a dead man's. . . . Once in about a minute, [she] would suddenly throw up her chin, and spit with perfect precision into the hottest embers of the fire."

The number of poor whites in the Old South has been difficult to estimate. They were found more often in the eastern coastal plain than in the new regions of the Southwest. Their numbers were probably magnified by visitors to the South, who tended to classify most natives they encountered either as wealthy planters or poverty-stricken squatters, ignoring the vast majority of "plain folk." There may have been as few as 100,000 poor whites or as many as a million; probably they numbered about 500,000, or a little more than 5 percent of the white population.

Because poor whites often traded with slaves, exchanging whiskey for stolen goods, planters considered them a nuisance as well as contemptible, and often bought them out, simply to rid the neighborhood of them. For their part, poor whites resented planters much more than did most yeoman farmers. Still, their hostility toward blacks grew stronger. Poor whites refused to work alongside slaves, to perform any work commonly done by them, and vehemently opposed ending slavery. Emancipation would remove one of the few symbols of their status—that they were, at least, free.

THE PECULIAR INSTITUTION

Slaves were not free. That overwhelming fact must be understood before anything is said about the kindness or the cruelty individual slaves experienced; before any consideration of healthy or unhealthy living conditions; before any discussion of how slave families coped with hardship, rejoiced in shared pleasures, or worshiped in prayer. The lives of slaves were affected day in and day out, in big ways and small, by the basic reality that slaves were not their own masters. If a slave's workload was reasonable, it remained so only at the master's discretion, not because the slave determined it to be. If slaves married or visited family or friends on a nearby plantation, they could do so only with the master's permission. If they raised a family, they could remain together only so long as the master did not separate them by sale. Whatever slaves wanted to do, they had always to consider the response of their masters.

When power is distributed as unequally as it was between masters and slaves, every action on the part of the enslaved involved a certain calculation, conscious or unconscious. The consequences of every act, of every expression or gesture, had to be considered. In that sense, the line between freedom and slavery penetrated every corner of a slave's life, and it was an absolute and overwhelming distinction. Not even the most miserable, poverty-stricken white, wearing rags or going hungry or living in the draftiest log hovel, ever asked to be a slave.

One other stark fact reinforced the sharp line between freedom and slavery: slaves were distinguished on the basis of color. While the peculiar institution was an economic system of labor, it was also a caste system based on race. The color line of slavery made it much easier to brand blacks as somehow different. It made it easier to rationalize the institution of slavery and to win the support of yeoman farmers and poor whites, even though in many ways the system held them back. And when emancipation finally arrived, the practice of racism remained, in both the North and the South. All this is to say that slavery must be understood on many levels: not only as an economic system, but as a racial and cultural one; not only in terms of its outward conditions of life and labor, but also through the inner demands it made on the soul.

Work and Discipline

The vast majority of African-Americans in the South were slaves, but the conditions they encountered varied widely, depending on the size of the farm or plantation, the crop being grown, the personality of the master, and whether he was an absentee owner. On small farms, slaves worked in the fields with the owners and had much closer contact with whites. The Upper South, where such holdings were common, had a reputation for treating slaves less harshly. On large plantations, on the other hand, most slaves rarely saw the master. Instead, they dealt with the overseer, who had not invested in them personally, was being paid for the size of the harvest he brought in, and was therefore often harsh in his approach. The largest plantations, which raised rice and sugar, also required the longest hours and the most grueling labor.

On large plantations, the house servants and the drivers were accorded the highest status. Skilled artisans such as carpenters and blacksmiths were also given special recognition and, like house servants, worked in the fields only in emergencies. The hardest work was done by the field hands, both men and women. Sometimes field hands were separated into specialties. In the summer of 1854, Olmsted watched a group of Mississippi slaves return to work in the fields after a thunderstorm. "First came, led by an old driver carrying a whip, forty of the largest and strongest women I ever saw together; . . . they carried themselves loftily, each having a hoe over the shoulder, and walking with a free, powerful swing like [soldiers] on the march." Behind them were the plowhands on the mules, "the cavalry, thirty strong, mostly men, but a few of them women." Bringing up the rear was "a lean and vigilant white overseer, on a brisk pony."

Toil began just before sunrise and continued until dusk. Tasks varied according to the crop, but plantations required a year-round routine, and masters were always able to find work for slaves. One Alabama planter informed his father in Connecticut, "There is no leisure, no long sleeping season such as you have in New England." In addition, most planters tried to grow a substantial portion of their food supply, which meant that slaves also had charge of corn and livestock (mostly hogs). Corn and cotton required attention in alternating sequences, and therefore many planters preferred to plant both crops to keep the slaves constantly busy.

Some planters used a gang system for working their slaves, in which an overseer or a driver supervised gangs of 20 to 25 adults. Although this approach ex-

Black slave driver.

tracted long hours of reasonably hard labor, the gangs had to be constantly supervised and shirkers were difficult to detect. Other planters preferred the task system, under which each slave was given a specific daily assignment. An able-bodied man, for example, would be required to break up 1200 square feet of rice field with a spade, or a woman to sow half an acre with rice seed. Slaves could work at their own pace, and when the assigned tasks were completed, they were finished for the day. This system gave slaves an incentive to do rapid but careful work and freed overseers from having to closely supervise the work. On the other hand, slaves resisted vigorously if masters tried to increase the workload. The task system was most common in the rice fields, whereas the gang system predominated in the cotton districts. Many planters used a combination of the two.

During cultivation and harvest, slaves were in the field 15 to 16 hours a day, eating a noonday meal there and resting before resuming labor. Work was uncommon on Sundays, and frequently only a half day was required on Saturdays. Even so, the routine was taxing by the standards of the day. "We get up before day every morning and eat breakfast before day and have everybody at work before day dawns," an Arkansas cotton planter reported. "I am never caught in bed after day light nor is any body else on the place, and we continue in the cotton fields when we can have fair weather till it is so dark we can't see to work."

Often masters gave rewards to slaves who worked diligently. A field hand whose tools passed inspection at the end of the year might receive a week's extra ration of rice, peas, molasses, meat, and tobacco. But the threat of punishment was always present. Slaves could be denied passes to visit other plantations on Sunday; their food allowance could be reduced or their workload increased; and if all else failed, they could be sold. The most common instrument of punishment was the whip, emblem of the master's authority. The frequency of its use varied from plantation to plantation, but few slaves escaped the lash entirely. "We have to rely more and more on the power of fear," planter James Henry Hammond acknowledged. "We are determined to continue masters, and to do so we have to draw the reign tighter and tighter day by day to be assured that we hold them in complete check."

Slave Maintenance

Planters generally bought cheap cloth for slave clothing and each year gave adults at most only a couple of outfits and a pair of shoes. By the end of the year, field hands were usually in tatters. Few had enough clothing or blankets to keep warm when the weather dipped below freezing. Some planters provided well-built housing, but more commonly slaves lived in cramped, poorly built cabins that were leaky in wet weather, drafty in cold, and furnished with a few crude chairs, benches and a table, perhaps a mattress filled with corn husks or straw, and a few pots and dishes. The floor was dirt, and cooking was done in the fireplace, which also supplied the heat for the cabin.

Sickness among the hands was a persistent problem for slaveowners. In order to keep medical expenses down, they treated sick slaves themselves and called in a doctor only for desperate cases. One overseer included among the skills necessary for the job "a tolerable knowledge" of medicines and sufficient skill in surgery "that he may be able with *safety* to open a vein, extract a tooth, or bandage a broken limb." Even conscientious masters often employed harmful treatments and dispensed quack patent medicines that promised to cure a wide variety of ailments. Conditions varied widely, but on average, a slaveowner spent less than a dollar a year on medical care for each slave.

Some plantations had hospitals to care for the sick; other slaveowners expected slaves who were sick to be cared for by family members. When she took up residence on her husband's plantation in Georgia, Fanny Kemble was shocked that the hospital had only a dirt floor, the rooms were filthy, and the patients did not have a bed or mattress but simply lay on the floor.

Defenders of slavery exaggerated when they claimed that the standard of living for American slaves exceeded that of free workers in the North. On the other hand, slaves fared much worse in Latin America, where the heavy imbalance of males over females prevented anything like a normal family life, and harsher treatment, harder labor, and greater incidence of disease resulted in a much higher mortality rate. Only by continually importing new slaves from Africa could Latin American societies maintain their labor force. The United States, by contrast, was the only slave society in the Americas where the slave population increased naturally—indeed, at about the same rate as the white population.

Still, a deficient diet, inadequate clothing and shelter, long hours of hard toil, and poor medical care resulted in a lower life expectancy among slaves compared to whites in the United States. Infant mortality among slaves was more than double that of the white population; for every 1000 live births among southern slaves, more than 200 died before the age of five. For those who survived infancy, slaves had a life expectancy about 8 years less than whites. As late as 1860, fewer than two-thirds of slave children survived to the age of 10.

Resistance

Given the wide gulf between freedom and slavery, it was only natural that slaves resisted the bondage imposed on them. The most radical form of resistance was rebellion. In Latin America, slave revolts were relatively frequent, involving hundreds and even thousands of slaves and pitched battles in which large numbers were killed. Such struggles were rare in the United States. Unlike slave societies such as Brazil and Jamaica, in the Old South whites outnumbered blacks almost everywhere, and the influence and power of the civil government was much stronger. Then too, the South offered less suitable terrain to establish the fugitive slave colonies that developed in Latin American jungles and mountains. Furthermore, African-born slaves, most of whom had grown up free, were most likely to revolt in Latin America, whereas the African slave trade had been closed off much earlier in the United States. By 1820, a majority of U.S. slaves were native-born. Finally, in the United States slave family life was stronger and more important, which mitigated against desperate rebellion. Slaves recognized the odds against them, and many potential leaders became fugitives instead. What is remarkable is that American slaves revolted at all.

Early in the nineteenth century several well-organized uprisings were barely thwarted. In 1800 Gabriel Prosser, a slave blacksmith, carefully recruited perhaps a couple hundred slaves in hopes of marching on Richmond, setting fire to the city, and capturing the governor. But a heavy thunderstorm postponed the attack and a few slaves then betrayed the plot. Prosser and other leaders were eventually captured and executed. Denmark Vesey's conspiracy in Charleston in 1822 met a similar fate (page 396). Both of these rebellions were elaborately planned, and both were hurt by their sheer size. The larger any group of conspirators, the greater chance that the plot would be betrayed.

The most famous slave revolt, led by a Virginia slave preacher named Nat Turner, was smaller and more spontaneous. Turner, who lived on a farm in the southeastern part of the state, enjoyed unusual privileges. His master, whom he described as a kind and trusting man, allowed him to read and write, encouraged him to study the Bible and preach to other slaves on Sundays, and gave him great personal freedom. Spurred on by an almost fanatic mysticism, Turner became convinced from visions of white and black angels fighting that God intended to punish whites, and that he had been selected "to carry terror and devastation" throughout the countryside. One night in 1831 following an eclipse of the sun, he and six confederates stole out and murdered Turner's master and family. Gaining some 70 recruits as they went, Turner's band eventually killed 57 white men, women, and children. Along the way, the members voiced their grievances against slavery and announced that they intended to confiscate their masters' wealth.

The revolt lasted only 48 hours before being crushed. In the aftermath as many as 200 slaves, most of whom were innocent, were killed by unnerved whites. Turner himself eluded pursuers for over two months but finally was captured, tried, and executed. This uprising was quickly put down, but it left whites throughout the South with a haunting uneasiness. Turner's master had been kind; Turner himself seemed a model slave. Yet in a world where masters held such power over human property, who could read the true emotions behind the mask of obedience?

Few slaves followed Turner's violent example. But there were other, more subtle ways of resisting a master's authority. Whatever the theory, in practice slavery was an institution in which the master was not all-powerful and the slave helpless; slaves found countless ways to disrupt the daily routine. Most dramatically, they could do as Octave Johnson did: say no, put down their tools, and run away. With the odds stacked heavily against them, few runaways escaped safely to freedom except from the border states. More frequently, slaves fled to nearby woods or swamps to avoid punishment or protest their treatment. Often they remained away for weeks while other slaves served as intermediaries in negotiations with the owner or overseer. Some runaways stayed out only a few days; others, like Johnson, held out for months.

Many slaves resisted by abusing their masters' property. They mishandled animals, broke tools and machinery, misplaced items, and worked carelessly in the fields. Many of these misdeeds arose simply from the lack of incentive to perform well; others, however, were conscious obstruction. Olmsted observed one field gang that stopped hoeing every time the overseer turned his back. Slaves also sought to trick the master by feigning illness or injury and by hiding rocks in the cotton they picked. Slaves complained directly to the owner about an overseer's mistreatment, thereby attempting to drive a wedge between the two. The most common form of resistance, and a persistent annoyance to slaveowners, was theft. Slaves became adept at stealing produce from the master's garden, watermelon, chickens (telltale feathers had to be buried, not burned, for masters recognized the smell), hogs (clubbed quickly, to keep them from squealing), and even cattle. Slaves often distinguished between "stealing" from each other and merely "taking" from white masters. "Dey allus done tell us it am wrong to lie and steal," recalled Josephine Howard, a former slave in Texas, "but why did de white folks steal my mammy and her mammy? Dey lives clost to some water, somewhere over in Africy. . . . Dat de sinfulles' stealin' dey is."

In the end, the typical slave was neither a rebel a childlike adult, but an individual who lived his or her life with as much dignity as possible. To do so often required the slave to wear an "impenetrable mask," as one bondsman recalled. "How much of joy, of sorrow, of misery and anguish have they hidden from their tormentors." Slaves learned to outwit their masters. Frederick Douglass, the most famous fugitive slave, explained that "as the master studies to keep the slave ignorant, the slave is cunning enough to make the master think he succeeds." When emancipation came, former slaves dropped their masks, and white masters were amazed at the transformation. "We planters could never get at the truth," one slaveowner wrote after the Civil War. "So deceitful is the Negro that as far as my own experience extends I could never in a single instance decipher his character."

SLAVE CULTURE

Trapped in bondage, facing the futility of revolt, slaves could at least forge a culture of their own. By the nineteenth century, American slaves had been separated from much of their traditional African heritage, but that did not mean they had fully accepted the dominant white culture. Instead, slaves combined strands from their African past with customs that evolved from their life in America. This slave culture was most distinct on big plantations, where the slave population was large and slaves had more opportunity to live apart from white scrutiny.

The Black Family

Maintaining a sense of family was one of the most remarkable achievements of African-Americans in bondage, especially given the odds against it. Southern law did not recognize slave marriages as legally binding, slave parents did not have complete authority over themselves or their children, black women faced the possibility of rape by the master or overseer without legal recourse, and husbands, wives, and children had to live with the fear of being sold and separated. From 1820 to 1860 more than 2 million slaves were sold in the interstate slave trade, one of the greatest forced migrations in world history, and perhaps 600,000 husbands and wives were separated by such sales. The chance that a slave family would be broken up—children taken from parents, brothers separated from sisters—was even greater.

Still, family ties remained strong, as slave culture demonstrated. The marriage ceremony among slaves varied from plantation to plantation: sometimes it consisted of the tradition of jumping over a broomstick in the presence of the slave community; sometimes it was no more than the master giving verbal approval; sometimes there was a formal religious ceremony in the planter's Big House. Whatever the ceremony, slaves viewed the ritual as a public affirmation of commitment to the couple's new duties and responsibilities. Although young men and women often engaged in premarital sex, they were expected to settle down, choose a partner, and become part of a stable family. It has been estimated that at least one in five slave women had one or more children before marriage, but most of these mothers eventually married. "The negroes had their own ideas of morality, and they held them very strictly," the daughter of a Georgia planter recalled.

None of the slaves for sale at this Richmond auction betrays outwardly the pain and anguish of being sold, bid upon, and physically inspected by prospective owners. Mary Chesnut, an upper-class South Carolinian, was once walking with a European visitor past a sidewalk slave sale. "If you can stand that," she remarked, "no other Southern thing need choke you."

"They did not consider it wrong for a girl to have a child before she married, but afterwards were very strict upon anything like infidelity on her part."

The traditional nuclear family of father, mother, and children was the rule, not the exception, among slaves. Families headed by the mother and with an absent father (unless sold by the master) were not typical. Within the marriage, the father was viewed as the traditional head of the family; wives were to be submissive and obey their husbands. Labor in the quarters was divided according to sex: women did the indoor work such as cooking, washing, and sewing, and men did outdoor chores, such as gathering firewood, hauling water, and tending the animals and garden plots. The men also hunted and fished to supplement the spare weekly rations. "My old daddy . . . caught rabbits, coons an' possums" recalled Louisa Adams of North Carolina. "He would work all day and hunt at night."

Beyond the nuclear family, slaves developed strong kinship networks. Normally the master allowed a slave couple to name their children, and most were named after a relative. The ties of kin also promoted a sense of community. Aunts and uncles were expected to look after children who lost their parents through death or sale. When children were sold to a new plantation, a family in the slave quarters took them in. Thus all members of the slave society drew together in an extended network of mutual obligation.

Slave Songs and Stories

In the songs they sang, slaves expressed some of their deepest feelings about love and work and the joys and sorrows of life. "The songs of the slave represent the sorrows of his heart," commented Frederick Douglass. Surely there was bitterness as well as sorrow when slaves sang.

Daily Lives

FOOD/DRINK/DRUGS

A Slave's Daily Bread

Once a week on most plantations, slaves lined up to receive their rations from the master. Though the allotments varied from one plantation to the next, they were predictable enough: for each adult slave about a peck of cornmeal, three or four pounds of bacon or salt pork, and some molasses for sweetener. Some masters added vegetables, fruits, or sweet potatoes in season, but only on rare occasions did slaves receive wheat flour, beef, lean meat, poultry, eggs, or milk (which was reserved for children when it was available at all, and was usually in soured form).

In terms of simple calories, this ration was ample enough to sustain life. Frederick Law Olmsted, who traveled extensively in the South in the 1850s, reported that slaves had enough to eat but that their fare was generally "coarse, crude, and wanting in variety." A careful modern study of slave diet concludes that on the eve of the Civil War, the standard daily ration was over 3000 calories, and that adult slaves received almost 5400 calories, which exceeds today's recommended levels of consumption. But over 80 percent of the daily calories came from corn and pork, and this monotonous fare of hog-and-hominy, while sufficient in bulk, lacked several essential nutrients as well as enough protein. Diet-related diseases such as pellagra and beriberi were often noted among the slave population. This malnutrition was due more to ignorance than miserliness or willful neglect on the part of masters. Although slaveowners and their families enjoyed more variety in their food and better cuts of meat, they too lacked a balanced diet.

On some plantations, masters left all cooking to the slaves, who would make breakfast and their noon meal before going to work in the morning, taking dinner with them to eat in the fields. After the day's labor was done, they came home to fix a light supper. Other masters established a plantation kitchen where regular cooks prepared breakfast and dinner, though supper remained the responsibility of the individual slave or family. On these plantations, a noon meal was brought to the fields. In general, the quality of food preparation was better under this system because slaves were often too exhausted after work to put much time or care into cooking. Naturally enough, however, slaves preferred to fix meals according to their own taste and eat as a family in some privacy, even if their quarters were hardly luxurious. Fanny Kemble reported that on her husband's Georgia plantation the slaves sat "on the earth or doorsteps, and ate out of their little cedar tubs or an iron pot, some few with broken iron spoons, more with pieces of wood, and all the children with their fingers." The cooking itself was done in front of a large fireplace, perhaps four feet wide, using long-handled frying pans, dutch ovens that nestled in the coals, or pots that were hung from poles swung over the fire.

Slaves resorted to various means to enliven their drab diet. Wherever their masters permitted it, they tended their own vegetable gardens after work or raised chickens and other animals. Not only did this practice provide eggs and other items not included in the weekly rations, but it also enabled slaves to sell their surplus to the master or in town and use their earnings to buy small quantities of luxuries such as coffee, sugar, and tobacco. Slaves also raided the master's smokehouse, secretly slaughtered his

Daily Lives

When slaves working in the fields became dizzy from the heat, they sometimes called out, "I see a monkey." "Monkey pots" like this one brought water and relief.

De way ter cook de 'possum nice,
Carve 'im to de heart,
First parbile 'im, stir 'im twice,
Carve 'im to de heart.

Den lay sweet taters in de pan,
Carve 'im to de heart;
Nuthin' beats dat in de lan'.
Carve 'im to de heart.

Squirrel meat, though tougher, could be boiled long enough to soften it up for squirrel pie served with dumplings. Rabbits, especially young ones, were tender enough to fry.

Along with such meat might come "hoecakes," a popular dish made by slapping a bit of cornmeal dough on the blade of a hoe and holding it over the coals. Vegetables were boiled in a pot with a bit of hog jowl, each new vegetable thrown in at the appropriate cooking time: beans first, then cabbage when the beans were half done, then squash, and finally okra. Whenever they could get them, slave cooks used spices to flavor their dishes. Some spices, such as sesame seeds, had come from Africa with the slaves. Red pepper, native to the Americas, added zing to innumerable dishes.

Holidays on the plantation, when the master would provide a banquet for the hands, provided a welcome break from the usual daily fare. On these occasions, slaves could fill up on beef, mutton, roast pig, coffee, wheat bread, pies, and other dishes only rarely tasted. Although masters generally tried to keep whiskey away from their slaves, some slaveowners made an exception at Christmas. Feasting was one of the slaves' "principle sources of comfort," one ex-slave testified. "Only the slave who has lived all the year on his scanty allowance of meal and bacon, can appreciate such suppers."

stock and killed his poultry, and stole from neighboring plantations. Richard Carruthers, a former slave, recalled, "If they didn't provision you 'nough, you just had to slip round and get a chicken." Even slaves who received relatively large rations resorted to midnight forays to obtain higher-quality food and to trade stolen goods for tobacco and whiskey.

Hunting and fishing provided fresh meat as well as variety. Slaves who worked all day still had plenty of incentive to stir out at night to hunt raccoon or opossum. "The flesh of the coon is palatable," admitted Solomon Northup, a black who had tasted both southern and northern cooking, "but verily there is nothing in all butcherdom so delicious as a roasted 'possum." Possum was parboiled to soften it up and then roasted with lard over the fire, along with sweet potatoes. As one slave song put it:

> We raise the wheat
> They give us the corn
> We bake the bread
> They give us the crust
> We sift the meal
> They give us the husk
> We peel the meat
> They give us the skin
> And that's the way
> They take us in

Yet songs were also central to the celebrations held in the slave quarters: for marriages, Christmas revels, and after harvest time. And a slave on the way to the fields might sing,

> Saturday night and Sunday too
> Young gals on my mind.
> Monday morning 'way 'fore day,
> Old master's got me gwine.
> Peggy does you love me now?

Slaves expressed themselves through stories as well as song. Most often these folk tales used animals as symbolic models for the predicaments slaves found themselves in. The best known of these, the cunning Brer Rabbit, was a weak fellow who defeated larger animals like Brer Fox and Brer Bear by using his wits. Such stories passed from generation to generation in the slave quarters. Some undoubtedly had their origins in traditional African "trickster" folk tales; others grew out of the slaves' own experiences. Sometimes the identity of the trickster was no longer symbolic, but the slave. Because these latter stories contained more overt hostility to whites, slaves usually told them only among themselves. But the message, whether direct or symbolic, was much the same: to laugh at the master's foibles and teach the young how to survive in a hostile world.

The Lord Calls Us Home

At the center of slave culture was religion. Slaveowners encouraged a carefully controlled form of religion among slaves, based on their own version of the gospel, as an effective means of social control. Masters provided slaves with a minister (often white), set the time and place of services, and usually insisted that a white person be present. "Church was what they called it," one former slave protested, "but all that preacher talked about was for us slaves to obey our masters and not to lie and steal. Nothing about Jesus was ever said and the overseer stood there to see that the preacher talked as he wanted him to talk." Disenchanted, some slaves repudiated all religion. Henry Bibb, a fugitive slave, maintained that "this kind of preaching has driven thousands into infidelity." Others continued to believe in conjuring, voodoo, and various practices derived from African religion.

Most slaves, however, sought a Christianity firmly their own, beyond the control of the master. On many plantations, they met secretly at night, in the quarters or at "hush harbors" in the safety of the woods, where a rhythmic singing and dancing, modeled on the ring shout of African religion, would begin: some "clapping their hands and beating time with their feet," one witness reported;

others "walking around in a ring . . . [striking] into the shout step, observing most accurate time with the music." As one slave preacher recalled, "The way in which we worshiped is almost indescribable. The singing was accompanied by a certain ecstasy of motion, clapping of hands, tossing of heads, which would continue without cessation about half an hour. The old house partook of the ecstasy; it rang with their jubilant shouts, and shook in all its joints." In an environment where slaves, for most of the day, were prevented from expressing their deepest feelings, such meetings served as a satisfying emotional release.

Religion also provided slaves with values to guide them through their daily experiences and give them a sense of self-worth. From their gospel's Christian roots, slaves learned that God, through the love of Jesus, would redeem the poor and downtrodden and raise them one day to honor and glory. Rejecting the teaching of some whites that slavery was punishment, slave preachers told their congregations that they were the chosen people of God, and that on the final Day of Judgment, masters would be punished for their sins. "This is one reason why I believe in hell," a former slave declared. "I don't believe a just God is going to take no such man as my former master into His Kingdom."

Again, song played a central role. Slaves sang religious "spirituals" at work and at play as well as in religious services. Seemingly meek and otherworldly, the songs often contained a hidden element of protest. Frederick Douglass disclosed that when slaves sang longingly of "Canaan, sweet Canaan" they were thinking not only of the Bible's Promised Land, but of the North and freedom. When slaves heard "Steal Away to Jesus" sung in the fields, they knew that a secret devotional meeting was scheduled that evening. Songs became one of the few ways slaves could openly express their yearning for freedom, in the approved language of Christianity. While a song's lyrics might speak of an otherworldly freedom from sin in heaven, their hearts were considering a this-worldly escape from physical bondage. Even so, slaves sometimes ran afoul of white authority. At the beginning of the Civil War one group of slaves was jailed in South Carolina for singing "We'll soon be free/When the Lord calls us home."

Religion, then, served not only to comfort slaves after days of toil and sorrow. It also strengthened the sense of togetherness and common purpose and held out the promise of eventual freedom in this world and the next. The faith that "some ob dese days my time will come" was one of the most important ways that slaves coped with bondage and resisted its pressure to rob them of their self-esteem.

The Slave Community

While slaves managed with remarkable success to preserve a sense of self-worth in a culture of their own, the hard reality of slavery made it impossible to escape fully from white control. Whites constantly intruded in slaves' daily lives and in a wide variety of ways tried to make them dependent. Even the social hierarchy within the slave quarters could never remain entirely free from the white world. Slave preachers, conjurers, and herb doctors held status that no white conferred, but the prestige of a slave driver rested on the authority of the white master. Similarly, skilled slaves and house servants often felt superior to other slaves, an attitude masters consciously promoted. "I considered my station a very high one," one master's body servant confessed. Light-skinned slaves sometimes deemed their color a badge of superiority. Fanny Kemble recorded that one woman begged to be relieved of field labor, which she considered degrading, "on 'account of her color.'"

But the realities of slavery and white racism inevitably drove blacks closer together in a common bond and forced them to depend on each other to survive. Slaves who helped masters capture runaways or curried favor by reporting other slaves' misbehavior were unusual. And new slaves on a plantation were immediately instructed in the mysteries of the quarters, including such vital matters as the best strategies for avoiding punishment. The slave community was their only sanctuary in an otherwise hostile environment. Walled in from the individualistic white society beyond, slaves out of necessity created their own community.

Free Blacks in the South

Of the 4 million blacks living in the South in 1860, only 260,000—about 7 percent—were free. Over 85 percent of them lived in the Upper South, with almost 200,000 in Maryland, Virginia, and North Carolina alone. Mississippi, by contrast, had only 773 free blacks in the entire state, and of all African-Americans living in the Deep South, only 1.5 percent were free. Free blacks were also much more urban than either the southern white or slave populations. In 1860 almost a third of the free African-Americans in the Upper South, and over half in the Lower South, lived in towns and cities. As a rule free African-Americans were more literate than slaves, and they were disproportionately female. They were also much more likely to have mixed ancestry, especially in the Lower South. Only 10 percent of all slaves were classified as mulattoes, compared to four times as many free blacks. Compared to free African-Americans in the North, a greater proportion in the South were skilled artisans and were materially better off.

Still, most free blacks lived in rural areas, although usually not near plantations. Planters adamantly refused to hire them or sell them land, fearing their presence would corrupt slaves. Most eked out a living in low-paying unskilled jobs, but some did well enough to own slaves themselves. In 1830 about 3600 did, although commonly their "property" was their own wives or children, purchased because they could not be emancipated under state laws. A few, like William Tiler Johnson of Natchez, were full-blown slaveowners, however. Johnson invested his earnings from barbering in a farm and eventually hired a white overseer to supervise his 15 slaves. As one of the free African-American elite, he went to the theater, attended horse races, gave his daughters music lessons, and subscribed to six newspapers. In 1852, however, he came to a tragic end when he sued a white neighbor in a boundary dispute. Johnson won in court, but his white adversary murdered him in revenge, and since the witnesses were black, and state law forbade blacks from testifying against whites, the murderer was acquitted.

While highly unusual, Johnson's life illustrated the limits placed on even extraordinarily talented free blacks. And after Nat Turner's rebellion of 1831, southern legislatures moved to restrict free blacks even further. Most states in the Deep South prohibited whites from freeing slaves in their wills, and some required any emancipated slaves to leave the state. All states forbade the entry of free African-Americans, and those already living there were subject to ever greater restrictions. They had to carry their free papers, could not assemble when they wished, were subject to a curfew, often had to register or be licensed to work, and could not vote, hold office, or testify in court against whites. In the final analysis, free African-Americans were hedged in so tightly because they were a glaring contradiction of the idea that bondage was the natural condition of blacks.

As Johnson's life also illustrated, lighter-skinned free blacks in the South, as in the North, tended to set themselves apart from darker-skinned blacks, free or slave. In such cities as Charleston and New Orleans, they established separate social and cultural organizations and maintained their own exclusive social network. Economically dependent on white customers, they developed close connections with whites, yet were never accepted in the white world. Free African-Americans occupied an anomalous position in southern society, well above black slaves but distinctly beneath even poorer whites. They were victims of a society that had no place for them.

SOUTHERN SOCIETY AND THE DEFENSE OF SLAVERY

From wealthy planters to yeoman farmers, from free black slaveholders to poor white mountain families, from cotton field hands to urban craftworkers, the South was a remarkably diverse region. But as we have seen, it was united by its dependence on staple crops and above all by the "peculiar institution" of slavery, the labor system that supported those crops. As the South's economy became more and more dependent on slave-produced staples, and even poor farmers shared the dream of becoming "cotton gentry," slavery became more central to the life of the South, to its culture and its identity.

The Virginia Debate of 1832

At the time of the Revolution, the leading critics of slavery had been southerners—Jefferson, Washington, Madison, and Patrick Henry among them. But beginning in the 1820s, in the wake of the controversy over admitting Missouri as a slave state, southern leaders became less apologetic about slavery and more aggressive in defending it. The turning point occurred in the early 1830s, when the South found itself increasingly under attack. It was in 1831 that William Lloyd Garrison began publishing his abolitionist newspaper, *The Liberator*, and in that year too, Nat Turner launched his revolt, which frightened so many white southerners.

In response to the Turner insurrection, a number of Virginia's western counties, where there were few slaves, petitioned the legislature to adopt a program for gradual emancipation. Between January 16 and 25, 1832, the House of Delegates engaged in a remarkable debate over the merits of slavery. Some antislavery advocates advanced the traditional religious and moral arguments; others pointed to the American belief in natural rights. But most often they focused on how much slavery hurt whites, by retarding southern economic development and draining Virginia of its white population by driving nonslaveholders to free states in the West. These arguments did not sway the more powerful slaveowning classes, even in the Upper South. In the end, the legislature refused, 73–58, to consider legislation to end slavery. The majority was unwilling even to label slavery an evil.

The Virginia debate represented the last significant attempt of southerners to take action against slavery. Most felt that the subject was no longer open to debate. Only in Tennessee, when a constitutional convention in 1834 rejected by a lopsided vote any consideration of gradual emancipation, and in Kentucky, when candidates pledged to gradual emancipation failed to win a single seat in the 1849 state constitutional convention, was the issue raised again. Instead, during the

1830s and 1840s, southern spokesmen defended slavery as a positive good, not just for whites but for blacks. As John C. Calhoun proclaimed in 1837, "I hold that in the present state of civilization, where two races of different origin, and distinguished by color and other physical differences, as well as intellectual, are brought together, the relation now existing in the slaveholding states between the two is, instead of an evil, a good—a positive good."

The Proslavery Argument

Politicians like Calhoun were not alone. Southern leaders, whether slaveholders or not, justified slavery in a variety of ways. Those favoring religious sanction argued that under the law of Moses, Jews were authorized to enslave heathens; and throughout the Bible, no Old Testament prophet, no Apostle, not even Christ himself had ever condemned slavery. Some proslavery writers suggested that God had brought blacks and whites into existence through two separate (and unequal) creations, but for orthodox southern Christians this was heresy. Instead, most white southerners accepted the idea of a single creation and traced slavery's origins instead to the curse of Canaan, in which Canaan (the allegedly black grandson of Noah) was made a servant in punishment for his father's sin. Jefferson Davis summarized the biblical defense of slavery when he declared that slavery "was established by the decree of Almighty God."

Defenders of the institution also pointed out that classical Greece and Rome depended on slavery. The Greek philosopher Aristotle had argued that individuals of superior talent properly became masters over those of inferior ability. They even cited John Locke, that giant of the Enlightenment, who had recognized slavery in the constitution he drafted for the colony of Carolina. Slavery, however, benefited not only "civilization" and its masters, but also slaves themselves. Blacks belonged to an intellectually and emotionally inferior race, apologists argued, and therefore lacked the ability to care for themselves and were sexually licentious. "Providence has placed [the black man] in our hands for his good, and has paid us from his labor for our guardianship," contended James Henry Hammond, an eminent planter and senator from South Carolina, whose "guardianship" of several hundred slaves had netted him a tidy fortune.

Apologists sometimes argued that slaves in the South lived better than factory workers in the North. Masters cared for slaves for life, whereas northern workers had no claim on their employer when they were unemployed, old, or no longer able to work. In making this argument, southerners exaggerated the material comforts of slavery and minimized the average worker's standard of living—to say nothing, of course, about the value of freedom. Still, to many southerners, slavery seemed a more humane system of labor relations, one that kept southern society free from the social turmoil and disorder that plagued the North. George Fitzhugh, the most original of the proslavery writers, placed heavy emphasis on these ideas in his book *Cannibals All!* and other writings. Fitzhugh advanced a class-based theory of society in which superior individuals by right dominated those who were inferior.

Defenders of slavery did not really expect to influence opinion in the North. Their target was more often slaveowners themselves. As Duff Green, a southern editor and one of Calhoun's advisers, explained, "We must satisfy the consciences, we must allay the fears of our own people. We must satisfy them that slavery is of itself right—that it is not a sin against God—that it is not an evil, moral or politi-

This 1841 proslavery cartoon contrasts the treatment of American slaves, who are allegedly well fed, clothed, and cared for, with the plight of unemployed, sick, and starving English factory workers. Defenders of slavery made the same comparisons with northern laborers.

cal. In this way only," he went on, "can we prepare our own people to defend their institutions."

Closing Ranks

Of course, not all southerners could quell their doubts. To take only one example, Robert Scott, an antislavery advocate in the Virginia debate of 1832, was publicly calling slavery "an institution reprobated by the world" as late as 1849. Still, a remarkable change in southern opinion seems to have occurred in the three decades before the Civil War. Outside the border states, few southern whites after 1840 would admit even in private that slavery was wrong. And those who opposed slavery found themselves harassed and sometimes assaulted. Southern newspapers refused to print articles criticizing slavery, and southern mobs destroyed the presses of antislavery papers and threatened the editors into either keeping silent or leaving the state for their personal safety. Southern mails were closed to abolitionist propaganda, and by the 1850s there were even attempts to prevent the circulation of northern magazines or newspapers. Academic freedom also came under attack, as defenders of the South's institutions scrutinized textbooks, administrators, and faculty members. By suppressing even minor dissent on slavery, southern leaders helped to effect greater unity by intimidating critics or driving them into exile. Southerners like James Birney and Sarah and Angelina Grimké left their native region to carry on the fight against slavery from the free states.

Increasingly, too, the debate over slavery spread to the national political arena. Before 1836, Andrew Jackson's enormous popularity in the South blocked the formation of a competitive two-party system. His strong stand against South Carolina and nullification and his destruction of the national bank alienated some groups in the South, who became the nucleus of the Whig party, but Jackson remained overwhelmingly popular with the masses. The emergence of the abolitionist movement in the 1830s left many southerners uneasy, and when the Democrats nominated the northerner Martin Van Buren in 1836, southern Whigs seized the opportunity to build up their party. Emphasizing the need to safeguard southern institutions, they charged that Van Buren could not be counted on to meet the abolitionist threat. The Whigs made impressive gains in the South in 1836, carrying several states and narrowing the margin between the two parties significantly. The election marked the beginning of party rivalry in the South.

In later presidential elections, both parties in the South exploited the politics of slavery by attacking the opposing party through its northern supporters. This tactic was less successful in state elections, however, since both parties were led by slaveholders and were committed to protecting slavery. In addition, the depression that began in 1837 focused the attention of southern voters on economic matters. Southern Whigs appealed to the commercially oriented members of society: planters, business leaders and merchants, bankers, professionals, residents of cities and the plantation black belts. Democrats won their share of slaveowners, but the party's strongholds were the more isolated regions of small independent farmers. As in the North, class and occupation were less important than one's economic and moral outlook. Southern voters most comfortable with the market and the changes it brought gravitated toward the Whig party. And since Whigs supported tariffs to stimulate local industries, hemp growers in Kentucky and sugar planters in Louisiana supported the Whigs, for their crops needed protection from cheaper imports. On the other hand, those farmers who feared the loss of personal independence that banks and commercial development brought with them tended to support the Democratic party.

During the Jacksonian era, most southern political battles did not revolve around the slavery issue. Still, Whigs and Democrats had to be careful to avoid the stigma of antislavery. And politicians who hoped to suppress or ignore the slavery issue came under mounting pressure from John C. Calhoun and his followers. Frustrated in his presidential hopes by the nullification crisis in 1832–1833, Calhoun's sincere wish to preserve the South's way of life merged imperceptibly with his national ambitions. Insistently, even recklessly, he agitated the slavery issue, introducing inflammatory resolutions in Congress upholding slavery, seizing on the abolitionist mailing campaign to demand censorship of the mails, leaping to his feet to insist on a gag law to block antislavery petitions. During the 1830s and early 1840s, few southern politicians followed his lead, but they did become extremely careful about being the least critical of slavery or southern institutions. They knew quite well that, even if their constituents were not as fanatical as Calhoun, southern voters overwhelmingly supported slavery. And such agitation, along with the continued debate between proslavery and abolitionist forces, contributed to the eventual emergence of slavery as a national issue.

Sections and the Nation

Viewing the events of the 1830s and 1840s with the benefit of hindsight, one cannot help but concentrate on the Civil War looming on the horizon, a sharp reminder of the major differences dividing the North and the South. Yet both northerners and southerners had much in common as Americans.

The largest group in both sections was composed of independent farmers who cultivated their own land with their own labor and were devoted to the principles of personal independence and social egalitarianism. Although southern society was more aristocratic in tone, both sections were driven forcefully by the quest for material wealth and prosperity. The Texas Red River planter for whom "time was in the objective case" did not take a back seat to the Yankee clockmaker Chauncey Jerome in the scramble for success and status. White Americans in both sections aspired to rise in society, and they looked to the expanding opportunities of the market to help them do so. Moreover, both northerners and southerners linked geographic mobility to opportunity, and both pushed westward with astonishing frequency in search of better land and a new start.

Many Americans, North and South, also adhered to the teachings of evangelical Protestantism, viewing emotion as central to the religious experience and accepting the need for atonement and rebirth. Southern churches were less open to social reform, primarily because of its association with abolitionism; and southern churches, unlike most in the North, defended slavery as a Christian institution. Eventually both the Methodist and the Baptist churches split into separate northern and southern organizations over this issue, but their attitudes on other matters often coincided.

Finally, northerners and southerners shared a belief in democracy and white equality. Southern as well as northern states embraced the democratic reforms of the 1820s and 1830s, and the electorate in both sections favored giving all white males the vote and making public officeholders responsible to the people. The existence of the planter class created greater tensions in southern society between democracy and the aristocratic side of southern life. But in both sections running for public office required celebrating the "voice of the people." Southerners insisted that the equality proclaimed in the Declaration of Independence applied only to whites (and really only to white males), but the vast majority of northerners in practice took no exception to this attitude. Both sections agreed on the necessity of safeguarding equality of opportunity rather than equality of wealth.

With so much in common, it was not inevitable that the two sections should come to blows. Indeed, economically they complemented one another, since to a large extent they did not compete in the crops they grew or the articles they manufactured. Certainly, before 1840 few politicians believed that the differences between the two sections were decisive. It was only in the mid-1840s, when the United States embarked on a new program of westward expansion, that the slavery issue began to loom ominously in American life, and Americans began to question whether the Union could permanently endure, half slave and half free.

SIGNIFICANT EVENTS

1800	Gabriel's revolt
1815–1860	Spread of the cotton kingdom
1822	Denmark Vesey conspiracy
1830–1840	Proslavery argument developed
1830–1860	Agricultural reform movement in Upper South
1831	Nat Turner Rebellion
1832	Virginia debate on slavery
1844	Methodist church divides into northern and southern organizations
1845	Baptist church divides

14

Western Expansion and the Rise of the Slavery Issue

At first the Crows, Arapahos, and other Indians of the Great Plains paid little attention to the new people moving out from the forests far to the east. After all, nations like the Crow had hunted buffalo for as long as they could remember and had called the plains their own. But the new arrivals were not to be taken lightly. Relentlessly they pushed westward: up the Missouri River, along the Platte, toward the Rocky Mountains. Armed with superior weapons and bringing a great many women and children, their appetite for land seemed unlimited. They attacked the villages of the Plains Indians, ruthlessly massacred women and children, and forced defeated tribes to live on reservations and serve their economic interests. In conflict after conflict, they drove the Mandans off their homelands, made the Arikara scatter up the Missouri, and looked to take over the hunting grounds of the Cheyenne and the Crow. In little more than a century and a half—from the first days when only a handful of their hunters and trappers had come into the land—they had become the masters of the plains.

The invaders who established this political and military dominance were *not* the strange "white men," who also came from the forest. During the 1830s and early 1840s, whites were still few in number. The more dangerous people—the ones who truly worried the Plains tribes—were the Sioux.

Although westward expansion is a firmly entrenched part of the American myth, it is usually told as a one-dimensional tale, centering on the wagon trains pressing on toward the Pacific. But frontiers, after all, are the boundary lines between contrasting cultures or environments; and during the nineteenth century, those in the West were shifting, skirmishing with one another, and adapting. Frontier lines moved not only east to west, as with the white and Sioux migrations, but also from south to north, as Spanish culture diffused; and west to east, as Asian immigrants came to California. Furthermore, frontiers marked not only human but animal boundaries as well. Horses, cattle, and pigs, all of which had been imported from Europe, moved across the continent, usually in advance of European settlers, and often transformed the way Indian peoples lived. Frontiers

486

The Spirit of Progress dominates John Gast's painting of Manifest Destiny. *In reality, the movement of the frontier was hardly one-dimensional, as Hispanic, Indian, Asian, and white cultures clashed.*

could also be technological, as in the case of trade goods and firearms. Moreover, as we have already seen, disease moved across the continent, with disastrous consequences for natives who had not acquired immunity to European microorganisms.

Three frontiers altered the lives of the Sioux: those of the horse, the gun, and disease. The horse frontier spread originally from the southwest, where the Spanish first taught Indians to ride. As horses began to run wild or were stolen by neighboring tribes, their habitat spread north and east, well ahead of white settlement. On the other hand, the Spanish, unlike English and French traders, refused to sell firearms to Indians, so the gun frontier moved in the opposite direction, from northeast to southwest. The two waves met and crossed along the upper Missouri during the first half of the eighteenth century—at a time when Ben Franklin rode to Albany, New York, along his western frontier, the Spanish remained a thousand miles to the south, and only a few French traders had penetrated the Mississippi valley. For the tribes that possessed them, horses provided greater mobility, both for hunting bison and for fighting. Guns, too, conferred obvious advantages, and the arrival of these new elements inaugurated an extremely unsettled era for Plains Indian cultures.

The Sioux were first lured from the forest onto the Minnesota prairie during the early 1700s to hunt beaver, whose pelts could be exchanged with white traders for manufactured goods, and buffalo, whose meat offered a reliable food supply. Having obtained guns in exchange for furs, the Sioux could drive the Omahas, Otos, Cheyennes, and Missouris (who had not yet acquired guns) south and west. Much like the Iroquois in New York a century earlier, the Sioux used their strategic position to dominate the western fur trade. But by the 1770s their previous advantage in guns had disappeared, and any further advance up the Missouri was blocked by powerful tribes such as the Mandans and Arikaras. These peoples were primarily horticultural, raising corn, beans, and squash and living in well-fortified towns. They also owned more horses than the Sioux, which made it easier for them to resist attacks.

But the third frontier, disease, threw the balance of power toward the Sioux after 1779. European traders inadvertently brought smallpox with them onto the prairie. The horticultural tribes were hit especially hard because they lived in densely populated villages, where the epidemic spread more easily. Observing this decimation, the Sioux abandoned their tentative experiments with agriculture and instead developed a nomadic culture centered on the buffalo hunt. They began a second wave of westward expansion in the late eighteenth century, so that by the time Lewis and Clark came through in 1804, they firmly controlled the upper Missouri as far as the Yellowstone River.

The Sioux's nomadic life enabled them to avoid the worst ravages of disease, especially the smallpox epidemic of 1837, which reduced the plains population by as much as half. They also benefited from government vaccination programs in the 1830s and 1840s, after several U.S. forts were established on the Missouri. Indeed, the Sioux became the largest tribe on the plains and was the only one whose high birth rate approximated that of whites, their population doubling perhaps every 20 years. From an estimated 5000 in 1804, they grew to 25,000 by the 1850s. Their numbers increased Sioux military power as well as the need for new hunting grounds. During the first half of the nineteenth century, they pushed farther up the Missouri, conquered the plains west of the Black Hills, and won control of the hunting grounds on the Platte River. By the 1840s, when whites began to traverse the region in large numbers, the Sioux had become the most powerful tribe on the plains.

So the "Sioux frontier" was multidimensional, involving shifting boundaries of trade, animals, guns, and disease. Each of these factors disrupted the political and cultural life of the Great Plains. And as white Americans moved westward, their own frontier lines produced similar disruptions, not only between white settlers and Indians, but also between Anglo-American and Hispanic cultures. To Americans in the East, hearing tales of covered wagons along the Platte, the frontier saga seemed a stirring tale of "progress" moving west. To ranchers in New Mexico or California, this migration threatened their status as the predominant upper class. For the Chinese who had come to the gold fields of California, it meant creating a civilized enclave among the *fon kwei* (foreign devils), who mocked long pigtails and wore incredibly coarse clothes.

Ironically, perhaps the greatest instability created by the moving frontiers occurred in established American society. As the political system of the United States struggled to incorporate territories, the North and South engaged in a fierce debate over whether the new lands should become slave or free. What, after all, was the destiny of "these" United States? (Americans, remember, still used the plural.) Just as the Sioux's cultural identity was brought into question by the moving frontier, so too was the identity of the American Republic.

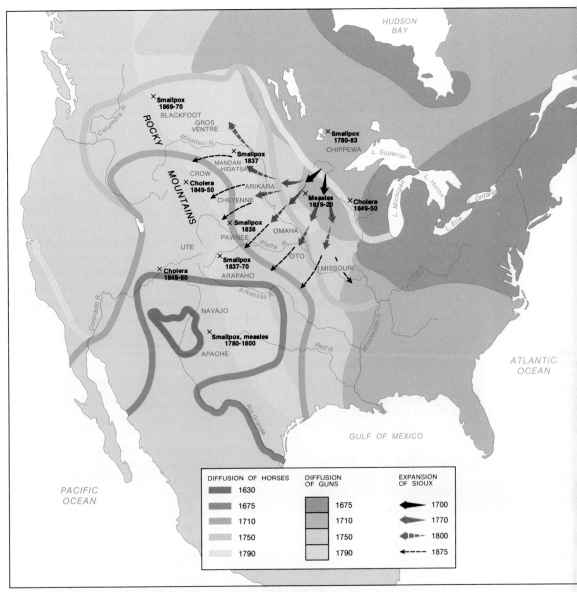

SIOUX EXPANSION AND THE HORSE AND GUN FRONTIER
In 1710 the horse and gun frontiers had not yet crossed, but by 1750 the two waves began to overlap. The Sioux pushed west during the early eighteenth century thanks to firearms; they were checked from further expansion until the 1770s, when smallpox epidemics again turned the balance in their favor.

DESTINIES: MANIFEST AND OTHERWISE

"Make way . . . for the young American Buffalo—he has not yet got land enough," bellowed one American politician in 1844. "We will give him Oregon for his summer shade," Texas "as his winter pasture," and "the use of two oceans—the mighty Pacific and the turbulent Atlantic" to quench his thirst.

In the space of a few years, the United States acquired Texas, California, the lower part of the Oregon Territory, and the lands between the Rockies and California: nearly 1.5 million square miles in all. To many a "young Buffalo," such acquisitions seemed only proper. John L. O'Sullivan, a prominent Democratic editor in New York, struck a responsive chord when he declared that it had become the United States' "manifest destiny to overspread the continent allotted by Providence for the free development of our yearly multiplying millions." The cry of "Manifest Destiny" soon echoed in other editorial pages and in the halls of Congress.

The Roots of the Doctrine

Many Americans had long believed that their country had a special, even divine mission. The Protestant version of this conviction could be traced back to John Winthrop, who assured his fellow Puritans that God intended them to build a model "city upon a hill" for the rest of the world to emulate. During the Revolution, many Americans, including the Reverend Ebenezer Baldwin of Danbury, Connecticut, expected that the colonies would one day become "a great and mighty Empire; the largest the World ever saw." Revivalists of the Second Great Awakening like Charles Finney (pages 416–417) spoke similarly of a coming Christian "millennium": a thousand years of peace and prosperity toward which America, by its example, would lead the way.

Manifest Destiny also contained a political component, inherited from the ideology of the Revolution. Baldwin, for example, had argued that the holy American empire would be founded on the "principles of Liberty and Freedom, both civil and religious." In the mid-nineteenth century, future president James Buchanan echoed this dream of a nation "extending the blessings of Christianity and of civil and religious liberty over the whole North American continent." By "civil liberty," he meant a democracy with widespread suffrage, no king or aristocracy, and no established church. In that sense, Manifest Destiny reflected the democratic reforms of the Jacksonian era. But it was a social and economic system, too, that Americans believed should spread around the globe. That system, they argued, encouraged a broad ownership of land, individualism, and the free play of economic opportunity. This doctrine had its self-interested side, of course, for American business interests recognized the value of the fine harbors along the Pacific Coast and hoped to make them American. As Senator Thomas Hart Benton proclaimed, the West was the road to India. By traveling it, a lucrative trade with the Orient would grow and flourish.

Finally, underlying other assumptions about Manifest Destiny was a persistent and widespread racism. The same belief in racial superiority that was used to justify Indian removal under Jackson, to uphold slavery in the South, and to excuse segregation in the North also proved handy to defend expansion westward. The United States had a duty to regenerate the backward peoples of America, declared politicians and propagandists. Their reference was not so much to Indians—who stubbornly refused to assimilate into American society—but to Mexicans, whose Christian nation had its roots in European culture. The Mexican race "must amalgamate and be lost, in the superior vigor of the Anglo-Saxon race," proclaimed O'Sullivan's *Democratic Review*, "or they must utterly perish."

Before 1845 most Americans assumed that expansion would be achieved peacefully. American settlement would spread westward and, when the time was ripe, neighboring provinces, like ripe fruit, would fall into American hands natu-rally. Neither mountains nor deserts nor (in their eyes) backward cultures could stand in the way. Nor did Americans doubt in which direction their country's destiny pointed. Texas, New Mexico, Oregon, and California—areas that were sparsely populated and weakly defended—dominated the American imagination. As this destiny became more manifest (to them, at least), Americans became less willing to wait patiently for the fruit to fall.

The Mexican Borderlands

The heart of Spain's American empire was Mexico City, where spacious boule-vards spread out through the center of the city and the University of Mexico, the oldest university in North America, had been accepting students since 1553, a full 85 years longer than Harvard. From the Mexican point of view, the frontier was 1000 miles to the north, reached over rutted trails by burro caravan, a four-week journey to Texas, another two weeks to New Mexico, and three months by land and sea to the missions of California. Spain had established these provinces as buffers to protect its flanks from the Russians, whose traders had been wandering down the California coast, and from French settlements in Louisiana. But being so isolated, the provinces of California, New Mexico, and Texas developed largely free from supervision.

California's settlements were anchored by four coastal *presidios*, or forts, built by the Spanish at San Diego, Santa Barbara, Monterey, and San Francisco. Between them lay 21 Catholic missions, each 14 leagues, or one day's journey, from the next. Run by a handful of Franciscans (there were only 36 at the time of Mexican independence), the missions controlled enormous tracts of land and were the center of California's economic activity. Gigantic herds of cattle and irrigated fields were tended by about 20,000 Indians, nominally converted to the Christian faith, who worked for all practical purposes as slaves. In 1834 the missions' hold-ings included 400,000 cattle, 300,000 sheep and swine, and 60,000 horses.

Following Mexican indepen-dence, the demand for cattle hides and government redistribution of church lands created a flamboyant new society in Mexican California centered on the *rancho*. Forming a rural aristocracy, the *rancheros* controlled gigantic estates and vast herds of cattle, supervised by workers who were virtual slaves.

When Mexico won its independence from Spain in 1821, California at first was little affected. But as the Mexican Congress began carrying out reforms, it freed the Indians of California in 1833 and stripped the Catholic Church of its lands. These were turned over to Mexican cattle ranchers, usually in massive grants of 50,000 acres or more. The new *rancheros* ruled their estates much like great planters of the antebellum South. Labor was provided by Indians, who once again were forced to work for little more than room and board. Indeed, the mortality rate of Indian workers was twice that of southern slaves and four times that of the Mexican Californians. The *rancheros* lived in as much ease and comfort as their isolated existence allowed. They became famous for their lavish hospitality, horsemanship, broad-brimmed hats, and brightly decorated clothes. At this time the Mexican population of California was approximately 4000.

By the 1820s and 1830s, Yankee traders were sailing around South America and up the Pacific to California, bringing everything from cloth and axes to brass buttons adorned with eagles. Ships moved up and down the coast trading for dried hides and tallow; when their holds were full they set sail for home. As ranchers began to play off rival merchants, the Yankees established their own agents in California to buy hides year-round and store them in warehouses until a company ship arrived. These agents were the first Americans to settle permanently in California, and their glowing letters home lured others west. Still, in 1845 the American population amounted to only 700.

Spanish settlement of New Mexico was more dense: the province had about 44,000 inhabitants in 1827. But like California, its society was dominated by *ranchero* families who grazed large herds of sheep along the upper Rio Grande valley between El Paso and Taos. A few individuals controlled most of the wealth, while their workers eked out a meager living. Mining of copper and gold was also important, and here too, the profits enriched a small upper class. Spain had long outlawed any commerce with Americans, but in 1821 several traders from Missouri ventured forth, returning with the news (as one ingenious speller phrased it) that "the mackeson [Mexican] province Has de Clared Independence of the mother Cuntry and is desirous of a traid With the people of the united States." Soon yearly caravans were making the long journey along the Santa Fe Trail, banding together for safety in a single wagon train. Approaching their destination, the traders would wash, don bright handkerchiefs, and parade into town shooting pistols, cracking whips, and wending their wagons through the plaza to the cheers of Santa Fe's 3000 inhabitants. While this trade flourished over the next two decades, developments in the third Mexican borderland, neighboring Texas, eroded relations between Mexico and the United States.

The Texas Revolution

Just as the new government in Mexico had opened New Mexico to trade, it hoped to encourage emigrants to Texas, where only about 3000 Mexicans, mostly ranchers, lived. In 1821 Moses Austin, an American, received a grant from the Spanish government to establish a colony of 300 families. When Austin died, his son Stephen took over the project, laying out the little town of San Felipe de Austin along the Brazos River. By 1824 over 300 families had received large grants of land at almost no cost and the colony's population exceeded 2000. Stephen Austin was only the first of a new wave of American land agents, or *empresarios*, who obtained permission from Mexican authorities to settle families in Texas. Ninety

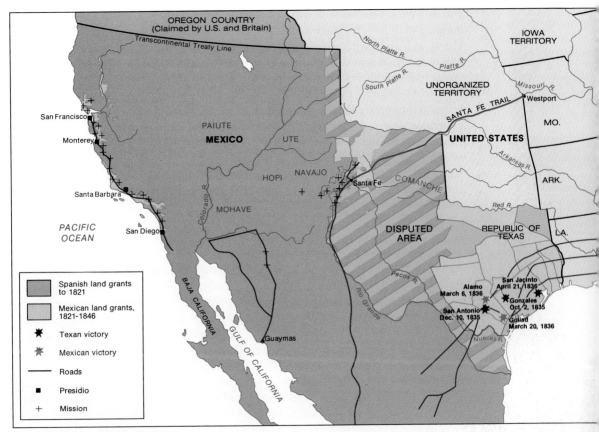

THE MEXICAN BORDERLANDS

percent of the new arrivals came from the South, and some, intending to grow cotton, brought slaves with them.

Tensions between Mexicans and Americans grew with the Texas economy. Most settlers from the States were Protestant, and although the government did not enforce its law that all citizens become Catholic, it barred Protestant churches. In 1829 Mexico abolished slavery, then looked the other way when Texas slaveholders evaded the law by forcing workers to sign lifetime indenture contracts. In the 1830s the Mexican government began to have second thoughts about American settlement and passed laws prohibiting any new immigration and levying stiff duties on goods imported from the United States. But Texans were most disturbed because they had little say in their government. Their province was allotted only 2 of 12 representatives in the more densely populated state of Coahuila, whose capital lay 700 miles away.

For a time, the Mexicans enforced these policies only erratically and in 1833 allowed American immigration to resume. But the flood of new settlers only made the situation worse, for by 1835 the American white population of 30,000 was nearly 10 times the number of Mexicans in the territory. The government also seemed determined to enforce the abolition of slavery. Hoping to work out a compromise, Stephen Austin journeyed to Mexico City in 1833, only to be thrown in jail because he advocated a Texan government independent of Coahuila. Events the following year seemed even more threatening when Antonio Lopez de Santa Anna, a general with large ambitions, dissolved the Mexican Congress, abolished the state legislatures (including the one in Texas–Coahuila), and proclaimed himself dictator. Worried Texans intercepted an official dispatch reporting that Santa Anna was sending troops north to reinforce the corrupt customs officials.

To Americans reared on tales of their own Revolution, the sequence of events seemed ominously familiar. Hadn't the English refused to grant the colonists full representation in Parliament? And hadn't a tyrannical king sent troops to America to support corrupt customs officials? As in the American Revolution, "committees of safety and correspondence" spread among the settlements, and when Santa Anna led a disciplinary military expedition north, a ragtag Texas army drove back the advance party and then captured Mexican troops in nearby San Antonio. A full-scale revolution was under way.

The Texas Republic

As Santa Anna massed his troops for a decisive attack, a provisional government on March 2, 1836, proclaimed Texas' independence. The constitution of the new republic of Texas borrowed heavily from the U.S. Constitution, except that it explicitly prohibited the new Texas Congress from interfering with slavery. Meanwhile, Santa Anna's troops overran a Texan garrison at an old mission in San Antonio known as the Alamo and killed all of its 187 defenders, including the legendary western figures Davy Crockett, Jim Bowie, and William Travis. The Mexicans, however, paid dearly for the victory, losing over 1500 men. The massacre of another force at Goliad after it had surrendered further inflamed American resistance.

But anger was one thing; organized resistance was another. It fell to the commander of the Texas forces, Sam Houston, to discipline his troops. Of striking physique and something of an eccentric, Houston had a flair for wearing gaudy clothing to attract attention (he once set tongues wagging by appearing at a ball in a suit of black velvet lined with white satin and sporting a large hat trailing plumes of feathers). His successful political career in his home state of Tennessee might have continued, except that the failure of his marriage led him to resign abruptly as governor and go live with the Indians. Eventually he made his way to Texas, where his intellectual ability, courtly manner, and unexcelled talent as a stump speaker propelled him to the forefront of the independence movement. His sturdy six-foot frame enabled him to endure great physical hardship, a quality that served him well as commander of the small Texas army. Steadily retreating eastward, Houston adeptly forged his ragged army into a disciplined fighting force.

By late April Houston was ready to fight. Reinforced by eager volunteers from the United States, Houston's army advanced along the San Jacinto River, taking advantage of the Mexican army's habit of enjoying an afternoon siesta. "Hold your fire! God damn you, hold your fire!" Houston commanded as his troops fell upon Santa Anna's startled men. With the first Mexican volley rattling overhead, the Texans fired and charged, shouting "Remember the Alamo!" Fif-

Sam Houston, the first president of the Texas Republic, often sported gaudy clothing. A staunch nationalist, he worked for the annexation of Texas to the United States. This detail from a portrait painted between 1846 and 1859 shows the aging lion's firm determination.

teen minutes of spirited combat ended in total victory and the capture of Santa Anna.

Threatened with execution, the Mexican commander signed treaties recognizing Texas' independence and establishing the Rio Grande as the southern boundary of the Texas Republic. The Mexican Congress (which had been reestablished in 1835) later repudiated the agreements as having been signed under duress and launched several invasions into Texas, none of which was successful. In the meantime, Houston assumed office in October 1836 as the first president of the new republic, determined to bring Texas into the Union as quickly as possible. (In a referendum, only 61 of the 6000 who cast ballots opposed annexation.)

As an old Tennessee crony of Andrew Jackson, Houston assumed that the United States would find the acquisition of such a rich and inviting territory irresistible. But Jackson worried that such a step would revive the debates over slavery and sectionalism. Since that might hurt Martin Van Buren's chances in the 1836 presidential election, Jackson temporized. Only on his last day in office did he extend formal diplomatic recognition to the Texas Republic. Van Buren, distracted by the economic panic that erupted shortly after he took office and fearful of stirring up sectional tensions, took no action during his term.

Rebuffed, Texans decided to go their own way and strengthen their economy. In the 10 years following independence, the Lone Star Republic attracted over 100,000 immigrants by offering free land grants of 1280 acres to families and 640 acres to single men. As Texas sought diplomatic recognition and economic aid from Europe, some of its citizens talked grandly of expanding their republic to the Pacific. But Mexico refused to recognize Texas' independence, and the vast majority of its citizens still wished to join the United States, where most of them, after all, had been born. There matters stood when the Whigs and William Henry Harrison won the presidency in 1840.

THE TREK WEST

As thousands of Americans were moving into Texas, a much smaller trickle headed toward the Oregon country. Since 1818 the United States and Great Britain had occupied that territory jointly, as far north as latitude 54°40′, but the only white settlement of any size was the trading headquarters of the Hudson's Bay Company, along the Columbia River. Then in 1833, in response to a fanciful report that Indians in Oregon wanted to be instructed in the white man's "Book of Heaven," several denominations eagerly sent missionaries west. The first, Methodist Jason Lee, erected a settlement in the Willamette valley in 1834, only to discover that the Indians there had been largely wiped out by an epidemic. But what Lee lacked in converts he made up for by publicizing Oregon's virtues back East. By 1836 American settlers outnumbered the British in the Willamette valley.

Pushed by the Panic of 1837 and six years of depression and pulled by tales of Oregon's lush, fertile valleys and the frost-free climate along California's Sacramento River, many American farmers struck out for the West Coast. Missouri was "cleaned" out of money, worried farmer Daniel Waldo, and his wife was even more adamant about heading west: "Well, Dan Waldo, if you want to stay here another summer and shake your liver out with the fever and ague, you can do it;

Daily Lives

TIME AND TRAVEL

Seeing the Elephant on the Overland Trail

In an era when traveling circuses proved a welcome though rare attraction, Americans used the expression "I have seen the elephant" to indicate they had gotten all—or considerably more—than they had bargained for. To the quarter of a million men and women who migrated overland to the Pacific coast, "seeing the elephant" meant ceasing to be a greenhorn by overcoming hardship and succeeding. The greeting, "Have you seen the elephant?" became the unofficial password of the Overland Trail.

Some walked, rode horseback, or accompanied mule pack trains, but the overwhelming majority of emigrants traveled in wagons. There were faults aplenty with these: they were cumbersome, liable to break, and difficult to maneuver. But they could haul more pounds per animal, did not have to be packed each day, could carry the sick and injured, and could be arranged in a defensive circle at night. Most often, emigrants modified a common farm wagon, about 10 feet long, for their purposes. The wooden bed, which had to be of seasoned hardwood to withstand the extremes in temperature and moisture, was arched over by cloth or waterproofed canvas that could be closed at each end. Many owners adorned their wagon covers with personal information and slogans or decorated them with paintings and pictures of animals (the elephant was a popular choice), so they would stand out in the crowd. Because of the many streams and rivers to be crossed, the bottom was caulked or covered with canvas so it would float.

Pulled usually by four to six oxen, one wagon provided sufficient space to carry provisions and gear for a family of four. Most farm families were larger, however, and took at least one additional wagon. Packed within was a supply of bacon, breadstuffs (mostly flour), and coffee. Because fuel was scarce on the treeless prairie and water boiled at lower temperatures at high altitudes, rice and beans were not taken in large quantities. For sleeping, families brought blankets and frequently a tent; a well-equipped wagon might have a feather bed laid over the packed possessions in the wagon. Parents normally slept there for privacy while children used the tent.

Before starting, the adult male members of a company elected their leaders. In the first years, when trains often ran to 30 wagons or more, a complex set of rules and procedures was adopted. With experience, these were simplified. Often decisions were openly discussed and then made by majority vote. Disputes inevitably arose, and leaders were sometimes deposed midjourney. Samuel Tetherow recalled that his father, the captain of an 1845 train, "was capable as well as popular. . . . But if you think it's any snap to run a wagon train of 66 wagons with every man in the train having a different idea of what is the best thing to do, all I can say is that some day you ought to try it."

At first, overlanders were gripped by a spirit of adventure; this feeling soon passed, as the monotonous daily routine set in. Women rose before daybreak to cook breakfast and food for lunch; the men followed at around 5 to care for the animals; the train was off at 7 with the call of a bugle. Men and older sons walked alongside the team or herded stock in the rear. Women and children could ride in the wagon as it jolted along, but before long

Daily Lives

Leaving home   Arrival in California

Joseph Goldsborough Bruff's sketches of "Seeing the Elephant" on the way west included a confident overlander leaving home—and arriving in California.

they walked as much as possible to conserve the animals' strength. After a noonday stop for a cold lunch, the journey resumed; by midafternoon the men seemed almost asleep as they plodded under the baking sun beside their teams. At evening camp the men attended to the animals, which, in addition to the oxen, usually included at least one horse used for hunting, rounding up stray livestock, and scouting. Many emigrants drove cattle too, and families with small children often took a milk cow. Meanwhile, the women and children collected buffalo dung for fuel and hauled water. Women cooked the evening meal and afterward washed the dishes, took care of the bedding, cleaned the wagons, aired provisions, and mended clothes. After a guard was posted, the exhausted emigrants turned in for the night.

For most of the trip, travelers relied on the family as the basic unit of labor. Yet mutual assistance was critical, especially once the Great Plains were crossed and the Rockies loomed ahead. The final third of the route lay across deserts, along twisting rivers with numerous and difficult crossings, on narrow paths barely wide enough for a wagon, and over the Sierra Nevada. Wagons had to be double- and triple-teamed up steep grades, and hoisted over canyon walls with ropes, chains, and winches. Since most wagons lacked brakes, drivers locked the wheels when going down steep slopes, dragged a weight behind, or lowered the wagon by a rope attached to a tree. Company members also worked cooperatively by selling or trading food, taking in individuals abandoned along the trail, and helping when members were too sick to work. At some desert crossings, a tradition developed: travelers used supplies left by earlier groups, then hauled water and grass back after they had safely crossed, to replenish the supplies for the next party.

Improvements in the 1850s shortened the trip and reduced the hardships. Still, it required considerable courage to embark on the journey and resilience and fortitude to complete it. "To enjoy such a trip," an anonymous overlander testified, "a man must be able to endure heat like a Salamander, . . . dust like a toad, and labor like a jackass. He must learn to eat with his unwashed fingers, drink out of the same vessel with his mules, sleep on the ground when it rains, and share his blanket with vermin. . . . It is a hardship without glory." When they reached their new homes, those who traveled the Overland Trail could boast that they had, indeed, seen the elephant.

but in the spring I am going to take the children and go to Oregon, Indians or no Indians. They can't be any worse than the chills and fever!" The wagon trains began rolling west.

The Overland Trail

Only a few hundred emigrants reached the West in 1840 and 1841, but in 1843 over 800 crossed the mountains to Oregon, and from then on, they came by the thousands. Every spring brought a new rush of families to Independence or later St. Joseph, Missouri, or to Council Bluffs, Iowa, where they waited for the spring rains to end and the trails to become passable. Meantime, they traded horses or mules, bought blankets and frying pans at street auctions, compared trail guide-books, and practiced snapping the whip over oxen to get the wagons moving. "Whoo ha! Go it boys! We're in a perfect *Oregon fever.*" The migration was primarily a family enterprise, and many couples had only recently married. Most adults were between 20 and 50, since the hard journey discouraged the elderly. Furthermore, the price of emigration was high enough to exclude most poor. A family of four needed about $600 to outfit their journey, although they could recoup two-thirds of the cost at the end of the trip by selling the wagon and oxen.

The Oregon Trail followed the Platte River to South Pass, where it made a relatively easy crossing of the Rockies, and then turned north and followed the Snake and the Columbia rivers to the Willamette valley. Several forks angled southwest to northern and central California. Caravans of 20 to 30 wagons were not uncommon the first few years, but after 1845, parties traveled in smaller trains of 8 to 10 wagons. Large companies used up the grass quickly, discipline was more difficult to maintain, and breakdowns (and hence halts) were more frequent. The trip itself lasted about 6 months, since the wagons normally covered only 15 miles a day, and the weather, repairs, deaths, and other eventualities necessitated occasional halts.

Women on the Overland Trail

The journey west placed a special strain on many wives and mothers, for the rugged life along the trail disrupted the sense of the home as a moral center and nursery for the family. What lay ahead, in an unsettled country far from older family ties? Not all wives were as eager as Dan Waldo's to find the answer. "Poor Ma said only this morning, 'Oh I wish we never had started,'" one daughter reported, "and she looks so sorrowful and dejected." Another disgruntled woman wondered "what had possessed my husband, anyway, that he should have thought of bringing us away out through this God forsaken country."

Sheer necessity put new demands on women and eventually altered their roles. At first, parties divided work by sex, as had always been done back home. Women cooked, washed, sewed, and took care of the children, while men drove the wagons, cared for the stock, stood guard, and did other heavy labor. Within a few weeks, however, women found themselves engaged in the distinctly unlady-like task of gathering buffalo dung for fuel on the treeless plains, or pitching in to help repair wagons or construct a river bridge. When men became exhausted, sick, or injured, women stood guard and drove the oxen. The change in work assignments proceeded only in one direction: few men undertook "women's work." And no matter how late the previous night's chores had continued, women had to be up before daybreak, ahead of the men, fixing a fire and the next morning's meal.

The extra labor did not bring women new authority or power within the family, nor, by and large, did they seek it. Women resisted efforts to blur the division between male and female labor and struggled to preserve their traditional role and image. Quarrels over work assignments often brought into the open long-simmering family tensions. One woman reported that there was "not a little fighting" in their company, "invariably the outcome of disputes over divisions of labor." The conflicting pressures a woman might feel were well illustrated by Mary Ellen Todd, a teenaged daughter who spent hours practicing how to crack the bullwhip. "How my heart bounded," she recalled, "when I chanced to hear father say to mother, 'Do you know that Mary Ellen is beginning to crack the whip.' Then how it fell again when mother replied, 'I am afraid it isn't a very lady-like thing for a girl to do.' After this, while I felt a secret joy in being able to have a power that set things going, there was also a sense of shame over this new accomplishment."

As women strove to maintain a semblance of home on the trail, they often experienced a profound sense of loss. The Sabbath, which had been ladies' day back home and an emblem of women's moral authority, was often spent working or traveling, especially once the going got rough. "Oh dear me I did not think we would have abused the sabbath in such a manner," wrote one guilt-stricken female emigrant. Women also felt the lack of close companions, to whom they could turn for comfort. One woman, whose husband separated their wagon from the train after a dispute, sadly watched the other wagons pull away: "I felt that indeed I had left all my friends to journey over the dreaded plains without one female acquaintance even for a companion—of course I wept and grieved about it but to no purpose."

Often fatigued, their sense of moral authority eroded, their ultimate home uncertain, women complained, as one put it, that "we had left all civilization behind us." Civilization to women meant more than law, government, and schools; it also meant their homes and domestic mission. Once settled in the West, they strove to reestablish that order.

Indians and the Trail Experience

The nations whose lands were crossed by white wagon trains reacted in a number of ways to the westward tide. The Sioux, who had long been trading with whites, were among the tribes who regularly visited overlanders to trade for blankets, clothes, cows, rifles, and knives. The Sioux were sharp negotiators, who "in every case get the best of the bargain," remarked one overlander, while another, Catherine Haun, asserted that the Indian was "a financier of no mean ability and invariably comes out A1 in a bargain." As white migrants flooded the overland routes, they took a heavy toll on the Plains Indians' way of life: the emigrant parties scared off game and reduced buffalo herds, overgrazed the grass, and depleted the supply of wood. Having petitioned unsuccessfully in 1846 for government compensation, the Sioux decided to demand payment from the wagon trains crossing their lands. Whether parties paid or not depended on the relative strength of the two groups, but whites complained bitterly of what seemed to them naked robbery.

Their fears aroused by sensational stories, overland parties were wary of Indi-

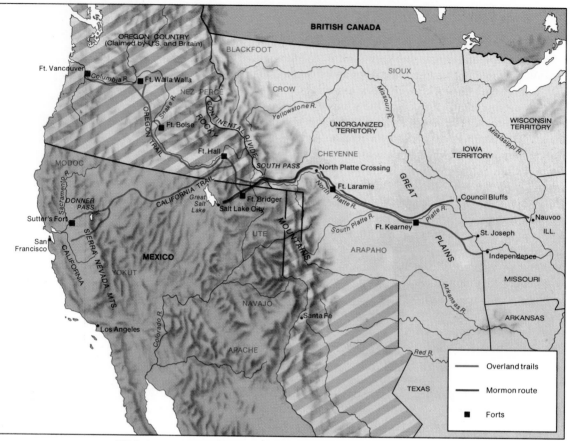

THE OVERLAND TRAIL
Beginning at several different points, the Overland Trail followed the Platte and Sweet-
water rivers across the plains to South Pass, where it crossed the Continental Divide. The
trail split again near Fort Hall. Between 1840 and 1860 over a quarter of a million emigrants
made the trek. With news of the gold strikes in 1849, the flow of westward emigrants
increased and shifted toward California.

ans, but this menace was greatly exaggerated, especially on the plains. Few wagon
trains were attacked by Indians, and less than 4 percent of deaths on the trail were
caused by Indians; in actuality, emigrants killed more Indians than were killed by
Indians. Most attacks occurred during the last third of the trip, which was the
most dangerous segment. Violence flared occasionally between whites and Indians, mostly after the number of travelers rose sharply during the 1850s, but for
overlanders the most aggravating problem posed by Indians always was theft of
stock. Many companies completed the journey without encountering a single hostile Indian, and others received valuable assistance from Indians, who acted as
guides, directed them to grass and water, transported stock and wagons across
rivers, and traded various goods.

    As trail congestion and conflict increased, the government constructed a
string of forts to protect emigrants and in 1851 summoned the Plains Indians to a
conference at Fort Laramie. Although some tribes refused to attend, about 10,000

Indians assembled. The United States government agreed to make an annual payment as compensation for the damages caused by the wagon trains but also required tribes to confine themselves to areas north or south of a corridor through which the Overland Trail ran. This first treaty with the Plains Indians foreshadowed the reservation approach already in use east of the Mississippi. Some tribes were unwilling to surrender their freedom of movement and refused to agree; the Sioux, the most powerful tribe on the plains, signed and then ignored the terms.

THE POLITICAL ORIGINS OF EXPANSION

President William Henry Harrison made the gravest mistake of his brief presidential career when he ventured out one raw spring day, bareheaded and without an overcoat, to buy groceries at the Washington fish and meat markets. Shortly after, the 68-year-old president caught pneumonia and died, only a month into his administration.

For the first time in the nation's history, a vice president succeeded to the nation's highest office upon the death of the president. The prospect pleased virtually no one. John Tyler of Virginia had been a Democrat who supported states' rights so strongly that, during the nullification crisis, he was the only senator to vote against the Force Bill. After that, Jackson and the Democrats would have nothing to do with him, so Tyler joined the Whigs. The Whigs were hardly overjoyed, since Tyler was a strict constructionist and often suspicious of Whig plans to use federal power to develop the economy. But in 1840 they put him on the ticket with Old Tip anyway, in order to balance the ticket sectionally. In the rollicking 1840 campaign, the Whigs sang all too accurately: "And we'll vote for Tyler, therefore,/Without a why or wherefore."

Tyler's Texas Ploy

A proud Virginia planter, Tyler was extremely vain, a quality his marriage to a glamorous heiress 30 years his junior had only puffed up further. His courteous manner and personal warmth masked a rigid, doctrinaire mind. Repeatedly, when Henry Clay and the Whigs in Congress passed a major bill, Tyler opposed it. After Tyler twice vetoed bills to charter a new national bank, disgusted congressional Whigs held a caucus and expelled their president from the party, sarcastically referring to him as "His Accidency." Most Democrats, too, avoided the man they viewed as an untrustworthy "renegade."

Tyler, in short, was a man without a party. Surrounded by a small group of flatterers whom critics sneered at as "the corporal's guard," the president had almost no support in the country except among federal officeholders, who could be fired if they did not endorse him. Still, Tyler's intense ambition led him to covet a term of his own. His advisers, nursing their own personal and political dreams, convinced him that the right popular issue could win him another four years in the White House, either as a Democrat or as an independent candidate. These political operators began to whisper in Tyler's ear that the issue he needed to carry the 1844 election was the annexation of Texas.

That advice came mostly from Democrats disgruntled with Martin Van Buren and his followers. Van Buren was, in their eyes, an ineffective leader who had stumbled through a depression and in 1840 gone ignominiously down to defeat. They "mean to throw Van overboard," reported one delighted Whig, who caught wind of the plans. "There is music ahead." Van Buren's principal opponent was Robert Walker, a Pennsylvania Democrat who had moved to Mississippi. Walker and his allies set out in 1842–1843 to propagandize on behalf of annexing Texas. The campaign included rumors (inaccurate, as it proved) that Britain was ready to offer economic aid if Texas would abolish slavery. An independent Texas would block American expansion westward, and a free Texas would, in southern eyes, threaten slavery in the United States. Under his advisers' prompting, Tyler secretly opened negotiations to bring Texas into the Union. Convinced the nation would rally behind him, he sent the resulting treaty to the Senate for ratification in April 1844.

Van Overboard

As the politicians watched this drama unfold, they looked to see what position Clay and Van Buren, the two presidential front runners, would take on Texas. Although rivals, Clay and Van Buren were both moderates who wanted to avoid dividing their parties over slavery. The previous fall, Van Buren had paid a two-day social call on Clay in Kentucky, and they apparently agreed to keep Texas out of the campaign. In late April, both men issued letters opposing annexation on the grounds that it threatened the Union and would provoke war with Mexico.

As expected, the Whigs unanimously nominated Clay on a platform that ignored the expansion issue entirely. The Democrats, however, had a more difficult time. Under Walker's lead, the Democratic convention adopted a rule (used in 1836 and then dropped in 1840) requiring a two-thirds vote to nominate a candidate. When Van Buren won a majority but not two-thirds, the convention deadlocked. Finally, on the ninth ballot, the delegates turned to James K. Polk of Tennessee. Polk had been a supporter of both Jackson and Van Buren, but he was also pro-Texas. Having served in Congress for 14 years, four of them as Speaker, he was hardly unknown, but no one had expected him to be selected. The 1844 Democratic platform called for the "reannexation" of Texas (under the claim it had been part of the Louisiana Purchase) and the "reoccupation" of Oregon, all the way to its northernmost boundary at 54°40'.

Angered by their defeat, Van Buren's supporters in the Senate joined the Whigs in decisively defeating Tyler's treaty of annexation, 35–16. But during the presidential campaign, the issue would not go away. Tyler, who had been nominated as an independent candidate by an assembly of federal officeholders, was finally flattered into bowing out, leaving the pro-Texas voters to Polk. Henry Clay, on the other hand, found many southerners slipping out of his camp because he opposed annexation; backtracking, he announced that he would be glad to see Texas annexed if it could be done without war or dishonor and without threatening the Union. And in the North, a few antislavery Whigs turned to James G. Birney, running on the Liberty party ticket.

In the end, Polk squeaked through by 38,000 votes out of nearly 3 million cast. A 5000-vote margin in New York decided the election in his favor. If just half of Birney's 15,000 ballots there had gone to Clay, Clay would have carried the state and been narrowly elected president. Whigs poured out their wrath on the political abolitionists, charging that by refusing to support Clay, they had made the annexation of Texas, and hence the addition of slave territory to the Union, inevitable. And indeed, with only a few months remaining in his term, Tyler again asked Congress to annex Texas—this time by a joint resolution, which required only a majority in both houses rather than a two-thirds vote for a treaty in the Senate. In the new atmosphere following Polk's victory, the resolution passed (just barely in the Senate) and on March 3, 1845, his last day in office, Tyler invited Texas to enter the Union.

To the Pacific

Hardworking and intense, the humorless Polk pursued his objectives as president with a dogged determination. He lacked personal charm, was calculating and often deceitful, and was not particularly brilliant in his maneuvering. But the life of politics consumed him, he knew his mind, and he could take the pounding when the political brawling got rough. Embracing a continental vision of the United States, Polk not only endorsed Tyler's offer of annexation but looked beyond, hoping to gain the three best harbors on the Pacific: San Diego, San Francisco, and Puget Sound. That meant wresting Oregon from Britain and California from Mexico.

The new president brushed aside any notion of continuing joint occupation of Oregon with Britain. The American title was "clear and unquestionable," he claimed. To pressure the British, he convinced Congress to give the required one-year notice terminating the joint occupation of the territory. "Great Britain was never known to do justice to any country . . . on her knees before her," Polk insisted. His blustering was reinforced by the knowledge that American settlers in Oregon outnumbered the British 5000 to 750. On the other hand, Polk hardly wanted war with a nation as powerful as Great Britain. So when the British offered, in June 1846, to divide the Oregon Territory along the 49th parallel, he readily agreed.* The arrangement gave the United States Puget Sound, which had been the president's objective all along. Even more important, the settlement left Polk free to deal with Mexico, for by June the two nations were already at war.

The Mexican War

Texas, of course, had been the issue. In 1845 Congress admitted it to the Union as a slave state, but Mexico had never formally recognized Texas' independence and insisted, moreover, that its southern boundary was the Nueces River. Texans countered that Santa Anna had accepted the Rio Grande, 130 miles to the south, as the boundary. In fact, Texas had never controlled the disputed region, and if its claim had been taken literally, the Rio Grande border would have encompassed New Mexican territory all the way to Santa Fe—lands still controlled by Mexico. Polk, already looking toward the Pacific, supported the Rio Grande boundary.

When Mexico broke off diplomatic relations after Texas came into the Union, Polk countered by sending American troops under General Zachary Taylor across

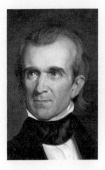

*Britain retained Vancouver Island, however, where the Hudson's Bay Company headquarters was located.

James K. Polk, continentalist (detail from an 1846 portrait by George Healy).

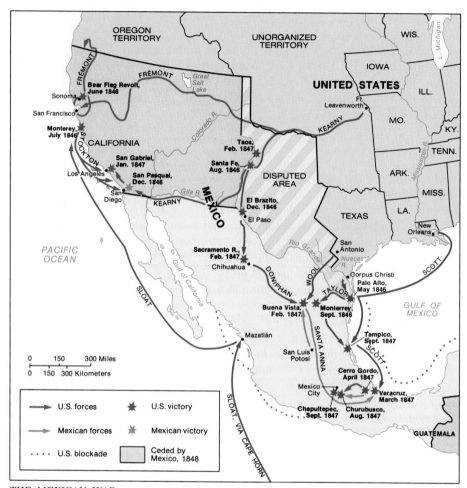

THE MEXICAN WAR

the Nueces. At the same time, knowing that the unstable Mexican government desperately needed money, he attempted to buy territory to the Pacific. Sending John Slidell of Louisiana to Mexico as his special minister, Polk was prepared to offer $2 million in return for clear title to the Rio Grande boundary, $5 million for the remaining part of New Mexico, and up to $25 million for California. But Mexican public opinion was so hostile to the idea of ceding more territory that the Mexican government collapsed for even permitting Slidell to set foot in the country. "Depend upon it," reported Slidell, as he departed in March 1846, "we can never get along well with them, until we have given them a good drubbing."

On orders from Washington, General Taylor had cautiously crossed the Nueces with 4000 troops in July 1845. For almost six months he camped on the south bank, hoping to prevent any clash between his forces and the Mexican army. Once the Slidell mission had failed, Polk ordered Taylor to proceed south to the Rio Grande. From the Mexican standpoint, the Americans had invaded their country and occupied their territory. For his part, Polk wanted to be in position to defend the disputed region if the two countries went to war. He also hoped that the Mexican army might attack Taylor's force and make war inevitable.

On May 9, the president resolved to send Congress a war message that cited Mexico's refusal to negotiate with Slidell as the reason to begin hostilities. As he began work on it, word arrived that on April 25 Mexican forces had crossed the Rio Grande and attacked some of Taylor's troops, killing 11 Americans. Polk quickly revised his war message, placing the entire blame for the war on Mexico. "Now," he told Congress on May 11, "after reiterated menaces, Mexico has passed the boundary of the United States, has invaded our territory, and shed American blood upon American soil. War exists, and notwithstanding all our efforts to avoid it, exists by the act of Mexico herself." The administration sent a bill to Congress calling for volunteers and requesting money to supply American troops.

Opposition to the War

The war with Mexico posed a dilemma for Whigs. They were convinced (correctly) that Polk had provoked it in order to acquire more territory from Mexico, and many northern Whigs accused the president of seeking to extend slavery. But they remembered, too, that the Federalist party had doomed itself to extinction by opposing the War of 1812. If Mexico had attacked American soldiers, it seemed political suicide to vote against Polk's request for supplies. Throughout the conflict, they voted for supply bills, but at the same time they strenuously attacked the conduct of "Mr. Polk's War." One young member of the House, Abraham Lincoln of Illinois, submitted a set of resolutions asking Polk to inform Congress whether the Mexicans living in the area where Taylor was attacked "have ever submitted themselves to the government or laws of Texas or of the United States, by consent or by compulsion, either by accepting office, or voting at elections, or paying tax, or serving on juries, or having process served on them, or in any other way." Lincoln, of course, knew the answer was no. Crossing the Nueces was invasion, pure and simple.

Sentiment for the war was strongest in the Old Southwest and most of the Old Northwest. It was much weaker in the East, where antislavery "Conscience Whigs" were prominent. "If I were a Mexican," Senator Thomas Corwin of Ohio affirmed in the Senate, "I would tell you, . . . 'we will greet you with bloody hands and welcome you to hospitable graves.'" In 1847 the Massachusetts legislature resolved that the war was unconstitutionally begun by the president, and that it was being fought to extend slavery and strengthen the South. With their party deeply divided over the issue of the expansion of slavery, Whigs opposed the acquisition of any territory from Mexico.

The Price of Victory

When the war began, a military exploring party under the command of Colonel John C. Frémont was already in California, and the Pacific squadron was off the coast of Monterey, waiting for official word that war had started. (In 1842, the previous American commander, under the mistaken notion that war had broken out with Mexico, had stormed into Monterey Bay and captured the town, only to return it with great embarrassment to Mexican authorities when he discovered his error.) In addition, Polk immediately ordered Colonel Stephen W. Kearny to march from Fort Leavenworth, capture Santa Fe, and then proceed to California.

Before word of hostilities arrived in California, a group of impetuous American settlers around Sacramento launched the "Bear Flag Revolt" in June and

The fortified heights of Chapultepec fell in 1847 to Winfield Scott's invading forces, but not without fierce resistance by young Mexican cadets. Like the partisans of the Alamo, who gained fame in Texas lore, the defenders of Chapultepec won an honored place in Mexican history.

proclaimed California an independent republic. Aiding the rebels, Frémont attacked the Mexican forces at Monterey and assumed command of the rebellion. The American navy squadron quickly captured Monterey and San Francisco and then transported Frémont's troops to the southern part of the state, where resistance continued. Kearny and his force soon arrived to aid in mopping up. By January 1847 California was safely in American hands.

Meanwhile, Taylor moved south from the Rio Grande, and in a hard-fought battle took possession of the major Mexican city of Monterrey. His popularity soared when a Mexican army under Santa Anna, who was back in power, attacked him at the Battle of Buena Vista. Although outnumbered four to one, Taylor's forces had the advantage of highly mobile artillery, which throughout the campaign helped him beat back Mexican assaults. Once Santa Anna retreated, the war in the northern provinces was essentially over.

Military victory gave Polk the territory he sought from the beginning; now he wanted only peace. But the Mexican people, inspired by nationalist fervor, refused to support any government that sued for peace, and so Polk decided to invade the heart of the country. An American army commanded by General Winfield Scott sailed to Veracruz in March 1847 and captured that key port. Scott then moved inland, brilliantly fighting a series of engagements, beginning with a decisive victory in the Battle of Cerro Gordo and culminating with the storming of the stone palace of Chapultepec, overlooking Mexico City. On September 14, Scott entered the capital and Mexico surrendered.

The war had cost $97 million and 13,000 American lives, mostly as a result of disease. Yet the real cost was even higher. By bringing vast new territories into the Union, the war forced the explosive slavery issue to the center of national politics and threatened to upset the balance of power between North and South. When the Mexican War began, Ralph Waldo Emerson had been prophetic: "The United States will conquer Mexico," he wrote, "but it will be as the man who swallows the arsenic which brings him down in turn. Mexico will poison us."

The Rise of the Slavery Issue

When the second party system emerged during the 1820s, Martin Van Buren had championed political parties as one way to forge links between North and South that would strengthen the Union. But the widening gulf between northern and southern interests so stretched the bonds of union that politicians from the two sections found it increasingly hard to work with one another. On the Democratic side, President Polk did nothing to ease this problem.

Polk was a politician to his bones: constantly maneuvering, promising one thing, doing another, making a pledge, taking it back—using any means to accomplish his ends. As his term wore on, the pro-southern bent of this Tennessee slaveholder embittered Democrats from the North and West. Western Democrats, for example, had struck a deal for southern votes to pass a bill to improve harbors and river navigation, voting in return with southern Democrats to lower the tariff. But then Polk vetoed the river and harbors bill. Northerners also complained that Polk had compromised with the British on Oregon at the same time that he had used military force to defend Texas' absurd boundary claims.

This festering discontent finally erupted in August 1846 when Polk requested $2 million from Congress, as he vaguely explained, to "facilitate negotiations" with Mexico. Everyone in Washington knew that the purpose of the money was to bribe the Mexican government to cede territory to the United States.

A group of northern Democrats had come to the end of the line. On August 8, David Wilmot, an obscure Pennsylvania congressman, startled Democratic leaders by introducing an amendment to the $2 million bill. The Wilmot Proviso, as the amendment became known, barred slavery from any territory acquired from Mexico. The measure passed the House of Representatives several times, only to be rejected in the Senate. Still, it revealed mounting sectional tensions. When first introduced, every northern congressman except two (both Democrats) voted in favor of the proviso, while every southern representative except two (both Whigs) voted against it.

Wilmot himself was hardly an abolitionist. Indeed, he hoped to keep not only slaves but all blacks out of the territories. Denying any "morbid sympathy for the slave," he rose to "plead the cause of the rights of white freemen. I would preserve for white free labor a fair country . . . where the sons of toil, of my own race and color, can live without the disgrace which association with negro slavery brings upon free labor." The Wilmot Proviso aimed not to destroy slavery in the South, but to confine the institution to those states where it already existed. Northerners who opposed slavery on moral grounds rallied behind the proviso, but the issue also attracted a much larger group of people—who felt that both slavery and blacks were a curse.

Abolitionists had long contended that slaveholders were an oligarchy—a "Slave Power"—that dominated the South and were consciously plotting to extend their sway over the rest of the country. The political maneuverings of slave-holders like Tyler, and especially Polk, convinced growing numbers of northerners that the Slave Power existed. To them, slavery seemed an aristocratic institution, which threatened the republican society established by the Revolution. Northern fears of a Slave Power, like southern fears of abolitionist conspiracies, disclosed the growing sensitivity to regional differences.

The issue of slavery in the territories became more than an abstract debate once Polk's representative in Mexico, Nicholas Trist, negotiated the Treaty of Guadalupe Hidalgo. Under the treaty, ratified in 1848, the United States acquired New Mexico and Upper California in return for approximately $18 million. That translated into a half million square miles of territory along with about 75,000 Spanish-speaking inhabitants. After the Louisiana Purchase, it was the largest territorial acquisition in American history. And with the United States in control of the Pacific Coast from San Diego to Puget Sound, Polk's continental vision had become a reality.

NEW SOCIETIES IN THE WEST

As Hispanic, Indian, Asian, and Anglo-American cultures mixed, the patterns of settlement along the frontier varied widely. Some recreated the farm economies and small towns of the Anglo-American East; others continued the cattle-ranching life of the Hispanic West. In California the new settlements were overwhelmingly shaped by the rush for gold after 1848. And in the Great Basin around Salt Lake, the Mormons established a society whose sense of religious mission was as strong as that of the Puritans.

Farming in the West

The overlanders expected to replicate the societies they had left behind. Once a wagon train arrived at its destination, members scattered in search of employment, a good farm site, or a town in which to practice a profession. Most families who completed the marathon trip were so low on supplies, they could hardly afford to waste time. "Friday, October 27.—Arrived at Oregon City at the falls of the Willamette," read one pioneer diary. "Saturday, October 28.—Went to work." For farmers, that meant clearing land and building a home. The high cost of transport made supplies and equipment expensive; furthermore, credit was not readily available, and markets were small and inaccessible. The Overland Trail took its toll on family possessions too, so that many of the cabins lacked the amenities that farm families had become accustomed to back East. "I baked 18 loaves of bread," recorded Mary Walker in Oregon. "A hard job for our old baker. What a handy thing an oven would be."

In the Willamette valley, the first large group of emigrants adopted a constitution setting up the machinery of government. Elsewhere, the process was repeated over and over again. Although violence was frequent on the frontier, farming communities, which contained many families, tended to resolve problems by traditional means. Churches took longer to establish, for ministers were hard to recruit, congregations were often not large enough to support a church, and many frontier settlers had grown indifferent if not hostile to religion. As the population grew, however, a more conventional society evolved: towns and a middle class developed, the proportion of women increased, and the population became more stable. The presence of women, both as teachers and as strong advocates of education, made possible the establishment of schools.

As towns expanded to serve the neighboring countryside, they provided stores, newspapers, cultural institutions, and better transportation. While opportunity was greater on the frontier than in the East and early arrivals had a special advantage, the development of the market and a transportation network meant that success and wealth would not be equally distributed throughout the community. More and more, the agricultural frontier of the West resembled the older society of the East. Wealth became concentrated, some families fell to the lower rungs of society, and those who were less successful left, seeking yet another fresh start.

The Gold Rush

In January 1848, while constructing a sawmill along the American River, a carpenter and engineer named James Marshall noticed gold flecks in the millrace. More discoveries followed, and by May eager prospectors were stampeding to the Sierra foothills. Word took a season to trickle east, then spread like wildfire, and the following spring the Overland Trail was jammed with eager "forty-niners." Some 80,000 emigrants journeyed to California that year, about 55,000 of whom took the overland route. The popular song that had once serenaded travelers to the boom country of Louisiana was quickly updated: "Oh, Susannah, don't you cry for me, / I'm gone to California with my wash-bowl on my knee." In only two years, from 1848 to the end of 1849, California's population jumped from 14,000 to 100,000. By 1852 it stood at twice that figure, and in 1860 it was 380,000. California's glittering promise would always have a special allure for restless Americans.

For those intent on making a fortune and returning home, there was no question of putting down roots. Camps literally appeared and died overnight, as word of a new strike sent miners racing off to yet another canyon, valley, or streambed. Most settlements were hardly more than a single street, littered with debris and lined with stores, buildings, and miners' shacks—dirty, uncomfortable, and often no more than blankets or cloth tacked to a wooden frame in order to hold down costs. Almost always a saloon and gambling hall, which might double as a hotel and sometimes a brothel, was the most prominent building in town. Over 80 percent of the prospectors who poured into these settlements were Americans; most hailed from the Mississippi valley, but Yankees and free African-Americans were there as well. Mexicans, Australians, Hawaiians, Chinese, French, English, and Irish also came. Whatever their nationality, the new arrivals were overwhelmingly unmarried men in their twenties and thirties.

The constant movement, the hard labor of mining, the ready cash, and the rootlessness all contributed to the instability of camp society. "There is an excitement connected with the pursuit of gold which renders one restless and uneasy—ever hoping to do something better," explained one forty-niner. Removed from the traditional forms of social control, miners felt and behaved as if they had left civilization behind. Gambling, swearing, drinking, and fighting were commonplace. As a Denver paper complained during that territory's gold rush a few years later, as soon as "men of decent appearance" reached a mining camp, they "sang low songs, walked openly with the painted courtesans with whom the town teems, and generally gave themselves up to what they term 'a time!'" Secure in the knowledge that "their women folks were safe and snug in their distant homes . . . these [former] gentlemen announced that they were going 'the whole hog or none.'"

Only about 5 percent of gold rush emigrants were women or children; given this relative scarcity, men were willing to pay top dollar for women's domestic skills. Women supported themselves by cooking, sewing, and washing, as well as running hotels and boarding houses. "A smart woman can do very well in this country," one woman informed a friend in the East. "It is the only country I ever was in where a woman received anything like a just compensation for work." Yet women's earnings depended on those of the miners, and as the mines played out, their wages declined accordingly. Regardless, they suffered no shortage of suitors. "Even I had men come forty miles over the mountains, just to look at me," Eliza Wilson recalled, "and I never was called a handsome woman, in my best days, even by my most ardent admirers."

Women went to the mining frontier to be with their husbands, to make money, or to find adventure. By far the class most frequently seen in the diggings were prostitutes, who numbered perhaps 20 percent of female Californians in 1850. Many had practiced their trade elsewhere before coming to the mining districts. Those handsome enough to set themselves up in "high-class" houses made tidy fortunes. But for those who had aged or were less attractive, "cribs" were rented: tiny, foul, windowless rooms with a cot, a chair, and a blur of faces at 50 cents apiece. In such circumstances, life was grim, violent, and uncertain.

Predictably, mining the miners offered one of the more reliable roads to prosperity. Perhaps half the inhabitants of a mining town were shopkeepers, businessmen, and professionals who serviced prospectors; also conspicuous were gamblers, card sharks, and other shady characters, all bent on separating the miner from his riches. In such an atmosphere, violence was prevalent, so when a new camp opened, miners adopted a set of rules and regulations to govern it, including a mining code and local government. Justice was dispensed promptly, either by a vote of all the miners or by an elected jury. After witnessing one such trial, a European visitor commented, "I never saw a court of justice with so little humbug about it." While effective when administered fairly, the system at times degenerated into lynch law.

Observers spoke of the democratic spirit in the diggings. "The only capital required is muscle and an honest purpose," boasted one. Yet such assertions overlooked strongly held nativist prejudices: when frustrated by a lack of success, American miners directed their hostility toward foreigners, whom they scorned with such derogatory names as "greasers" (Mexicans) and "chinks" (Chinese). The miners ruthlessly exterminated the Indians in the area, mob violence drove Mexicans out of nearly every camp, and the Chinese were confined to claims abandoned by Americans as unprofitable. Efforts to exclude all foreigners from mining failed, but the state eventually enacted a foreign miners' tax, which fell largely on the Chinese. Free African-Americans felt the sting of discrimination as well, both in the camps and in state law. White American miners proclaimed that "colored men were not privileged to work in a country intended only for American citizens."

Before long, the most easily worked claims had been played out. Moreover, with 100,000 miners in the state by 1852, competition steadily drove down the average daily earnings from $20 in 1848 to $6 in 1852. That was still higher than eastern wages, but goods and services cost significantly more too. As gold became increasingly difficult to extract, highly capitalized companies using heavy equipment dominated the industry. Shafts were dug deep into the ground, high-pressure water jets tore away ore-bearing gravel, and veins of quartz rock were blasted out and crushed in large stamping mills. Virtually all of this was done by miners working for wages rather than prospecting for themselves. Thus control of the mining industry passed into the hands of capitalists and corporate executives. Men who had come to California filled with visions of wealth usually found only shovels of mud. And as the era of the individual miner passed, so too did most mining camps and the unique society they spawned.

Instant City: San Francisco

When the United States assumed control of California, San Francisco had a population of perhaps 200. But thousands of emigrants took the water route west, passing through San Francisco's harbor on their way to the diggings. Some stayed, others returned from the mines to settle down, and by 1856 the city's population had jumped to an astonishing 50,000. In a mere eight years the city had attained the size New York had taken 190 years to reach.

The product of economic self-interest, San Francisco developed in a helter-skelter fashion. Land prices soared, speculation was rampant, and commercial forces became paramount. The business streets presented a bedlam of noise and commotion, one visitor reporting that "the throng of men of all classes, characters, and nations, with carts and animals, equaled Wall Street before three o'clock." The city plan was a neat gridiron, but it paid no heed to the hilly terrain, and streets along the waterfront were projected precariously into the bay on piles driven into the water, until dirt from the hills being leveled could be carted down to fill in the cove. To complicate matters, south of Market Street the streets were laid out at a 45° angle to the original survey, which clogged the flow of traffic.

Commercial sentiment was so strong that almost no land was reserved for public use, and the city government took virtually no role in directing development. The town appeared insubstantial, with people living in tents or poorly constructed, half-finished buildings. Junk and rubbish littered the streets and goods were piled everywhere because of the lack of warehouse space. Property owners defeated a proposal to widen the streets, prompting the city's leading newspaper to complain, "To sell a few more feet of lots, the streets were compressed like a cheese, into half their width." The city's population was strikingly heterogeneous, and visitors reported that an amazing assortment of languages could be heard. Ethnic neighborhoods included Little Chile for South Americans, a French quarter, Sydneytown, where Australians dominated, Chinatown, and a Jewish section. In 1860, the city was 50 percent foreign-born.

The most distinctive of the ethnic groups was the Chinese. They had come to *Gum San*, the land of the golden mountain, because China in the 1840s had experienced considerable economic distress. Between 1849 and 1854, some 45,000 Chinese went to California. Like the other gold seekers, they were overwhelmingly young and male, and they wanted only to accumulate savings and return home to their families. (Indeed, only 16 Chinese women were recorded as arriving before 1854.)

When the Chinese were harassed in the mines, many found work in San Francisco as launderers. The going rate at the time for washing, ironing, and starching shirts was an exorbitant $8 per dozen; many early San Franciscans actually found it cheaper to send their dirty laundry to Canton or Honolulu, to be returned several months later. The Chinese quickly stepped in, for it took little capital to start a laundry—soap, scrub board, iron, and ironing board. Soon the price for washing shirts dropped to $2 a dozen. Other Chinese around San Francisco set up restaurants or worked in the fishing industry. In these early years, they found Americans less hostile, so long as they stayed away from the gold fields. In 1850 a San Francisco newspaper, the *Alta California,* predicted optimistically that "the China Boys will yet vote at the same polls, study at the same schools and bow at the same altar as our countrymen." As immigration and the competition for jobs increased, however, anti-Chinese sentiment intensified.

Gradually, San Francisco took on the trappings of a more orderly community. The city government established a public school system, erected street lights, created a municipal water system, and halted further filling in of the bay. Fashionable neighborhoods sprouted on several hills, as high rents drove many residents from the developing commercial center of the city. Industry was relegated to the area south of the city; several new working-class neighborhoods grew up near the downtown section. Churches and families became more common. By 1856, when the city and county were consolidated, the city of the gold rush had been replaced by a new city whose stone and brick buildings gave it a sense of permanence.

The Mormon Experience

The society spawned by the gold rush—in the makeshift mining towns and the chaotic progress of San Francisco—was a product of largely uncontrolled economic pressures. The society that evolved in the Great Basin of Utah exhibited an entirely different but equally remarkable growth. Salt Lake City became the center of a religious kingdom established by the Church of Jesus Christ of Latter-day Saints. Church members, known generally as Mormons, streamed west by the thousands during the 1840s. But unlike most families on the Overland Trail, they were united by a common faith and closely bound by persecution. Salt Lake City reflected the discipline and unity of their movement, whose roots reached back to the "Burned-Over District" of western New York, an area where the religious fires of revivalism flared up regularly.

The church had been founded in Palmyra, New York, by a young man named Joseph Smith. In 1827, at the age of only 22, Smith announced that he had discovered a set of golden tablets on which was written the *Book of Mormon.* The tablets, translated by Smith, told the story of some lost tribes of Israel, who came to America and established a Christian civilization, only to be exterminated by the Indians. Proclaiming that he had a commission from God to reestablish the true church, Smith gathered a group of devoted followers. Although he was a robust, cheerful, and magnetic person, Smith's unorthodox teachings provoked bitter persecution wherever he went: first in Ohio and then Missouri, where mob violence hounded his settlement out of the state. Finally he obtained a charter from the Illinois legislature to establish a Mormon community at Nauvoo. Thousands of followers settled there, but hostility again mounted after rumors circulated around the state that Smith had announced to his inner circle a new revelation sanctioning plural marriage, or polygamy. In 1844, following a dispute with dissident Mormons, the state threw him in jail in Carthage, Illinois, where an anti-Mormon mob murdered him.

Leadership of the church fell to Brigham Young, who lacked Smith's religious mysticism but was a brilliant organizer. Studying the reports of various explorers, Young decided to move his followers to the Great Basin. In 1844, the region was still part of Mexico, which had not authorized any settlement, but it could be farmed with irrigation and was a thousand miles from settled areas of the United States, promising the freedom to live and worship without interference. In 1847 the first thousand settlers began building at Salt Lake, the vanguard of thousands more who extended Mormon settlement throughout the valley of the Great Salt Lake. Thanks to energetic mission work in Great Britain and Scandinavia as well as the East, over 30,000 emigrants had moved to Utah by 1860, and the Mormons had established over 96 separate communities. In 1849 they erected the state of Deseret with Brigham Young as governor and applied for admission to the Union.

The Mormon success rested on a community-oriented effort firmly controlled by the church elders and Brigham Young. Families were given only as much farmland as they could use. Water for irrigation was owned by the community and the bishops assigned each user an appropriate share. And since church officials also held the government positions, church and state were not separated. Young had supreme power in legislative, executive, and judicial matters as well as religious affairs.

The most controversial church teaching was the doctrine of polygamy, which Young finally sanctioned publicly in 1852. Although the arrangement might have been expected to place special pressures on Mormon wives, visitors reported with surprise that few seemed to rebel against the practice. Some plural wives developed close friendships; indeed, in one sample almost a third of plural marriages included at least two sisters. If the wives lived together, the system allowed them to share domestic work. When the husband established separate households, some wives enjoyed greater freedom, since the husband was not constantly present. Many women testified that plural marriage was difficult to accept, yet because polygamy distinguished Mormonism from other religions, plural wives saw it as a badge of pride and as an expression of their religious faith. "I want to be assured of *my position in God's estimation,*" one plural wife explained. "If polygamy is the Lord's order, we must carry it out."

Temple City: Salt Lake City

Brigham Young and his advance party had laid out the "temple city" of Salt Lake in 1847, determined to avoid the commercial worldliness, speculation in property, and competitive individualism that had plagued the earlier Mormon settlement at Nauvoo. City lots were not sold but distributed by lottery; they could not be subdivided for sale, and real estate speculation was forbidden. Water and timberlands were held in common and their use was governed by church leaders. As one church apostle recalled, these rules "created a community of interest which could not have been felt under other circumstances."

The city itself was conceived on a grand scale, in a checkerboard grid well suited to the level terrain. Streets were all 132 feet wide (compared with 60 feet in early San Francisco), and each square block contained eight home lots of 1.25 acres each. Unlike early San Francisco, the family was the basic social unit in Salt Lake City, and almost from the beginning the city had an equal balance of men and women. Families were to use part of their lot to grow food in order to increase the community's self-sufficiency. Regulations specified that sidewalks were to be a standard width, and homes were to be set 20 feet back from the sidewalks and constructed of adobe. The planners also provided for four public squares in various parts of the city. As with the kingdom of Deseret itself, Salt Lake City lacked any traditional secular authority. The city was divided into 18 wards, each under the supervision of a bishop. Holding civil as well as religious power, the bishops were responsible for fencing, constructing irrigation ditches, and building and maintaining the bridges across the ditches in their wards.

By 1853 the city already covered four square miles. As the city expanded, the original plan had to be modified to accommodate the developing commercial district by dividing lots into sizes more suitable for stores. Experience and growth also eventually dictated smaller blocks and narrower streets, but the city still retained its spacious appearance and regular design. Through religious and economic discipline church leaders succeeded in preserving a sense of unity and common purpose in an urban setting, while making a "desert bloom."

Shadows on the Moving Frontier

Transformations like Salt Lake City and San Francisco were truly remarkable. But it is important to remember that Americans were not coming into a trackless, unsettled wilderness. As frontier lines crossed, 75,000 Mexicans had to adapt to the new American rule.

In theory, the Treaty of Guadalupe Hidalgo guaranteed that Mexicans would be "maintained and protected in the free enjoyment of their liberty and property." So long as Mexicans continued to be a sizable majority in a given area, their influence was strong. But as Anglo emigrants became more numerous, they scorned Mexicans and demanded conformity to American customs. When Mexicans remained faithful to their heritage, language, and religion, these cultural differences worked to reinforce Hispanic powerlessness, social isolation, and economic exploitation.

New Mexico had the largest Hispanic population as well as the fewest Anglos in the former Mexican territory. As a result, the upper-class Mexicans who owned the land and employed large numbers of mixed-blood workers on their ranches managed to maintain their position. This class had established American allies during the Santa Fe trade, and their connections grew stronger as American businessmen slowly entered the territory in the 1850s. Neither group had much interest in the lower-class Hispanics, whom both exploited.

In contrast, the rush of American emigrants quickly overwhelmed Hispanic settlers in California and Texas. Even in 1848, before the discovery of gold, Americans in California outnumbered Mexicans two to one, and by 1860 Hispanics amounted to only 2 percent of the population. Ironically, the descendants of the Spanish, who had opened their own American frontier three centuries earlier by exploiting Indians in the silver mines, now found themselves subject to the California "foreign" miners' tax and driven out of the gold fields by Anglo mobs who had equally firm notions about their own superiority.

During the gold rush, the 200 or so *ranchero* families (who together owned about 14 million acres) prospered because of the demand for beef to feed the miners. But changes in California land law required verification of the *rancheros'* original land grants by a federal commission. Since the average claim took 17 years to complete and imposed complex procedures and hefty legal fees, many *ranche-*

ros lost large areas of land to Americans. Lower-class Mexicans scratched out a bare existence on ranches and farms, or in the growing cities and towns. Despised by the dominant Anglo majority and without skills and resources, they were often reduced to extreme poverty.

Mexicans in Texas were also greatly outnumbered: they totaled only 10 percent of the population in 1840 and 6 percent in 1860. Stigmatized as inferior, they were the poorest group in free society. One response to this dislocation, an option commonly taken by persecuted minorities, was social banditry. Just as the Shawnee prophet Tenskwatawa a half century earlier sought to drive out American intruders and restore the purity of Indian cultures, a number of Mexican bandits gained fame by attacking and robbing Anglos. The most famous was Joaquín Murieta of California, a semifictional character whose legend actually drew on the exploits of several men. Another folk hero, less shrouded in legend, was Juan Cortina. A member of a displaced landed family in southern Texas, Cortina was driven into resistance in the 1850s by American harassment. He began stealing from wealthy Anglos to aid poor Mexicans, proclaiming, "To me is entrusted the breaking of the chains of your slavery." His sizable band of followers staged a daring attack on Brownsville in 1859, then eluded the U.S. Army by retreating into Mexico. Cortina continued to raid Texas border settlements until the Mexican army, under intense American pressure, finally imprisoned him. While failing to produce any lasting change, Murieta and Cortina demonstrated the depth of frustration and resentment among Hispanics over their abuse at the hands of the new Anglo majority.

ESCAPE FROM CRISIS

With the return of peace, Congress continued to debate what to do with its newly won territories, especially whether to allow slavery within them. David Wilmot had already thrown down the gauntlet of the northern opposition with his proviso to outlaw slavery in any new territory. John C. Calhoun, representing the extreme southern position, countered that slavery ought to be legal in all territories. The federal government had acted as the agent of all the states in acquiring the land, he argued, and southerners had a right to move there and take their property with them, including slaves. Only when the residents of a territory drafted a state constitution could they decide the question of slavery.

Between these extremes were two moderate positions. One proposed extending the Missouri Compromise line of 36°30′ to the Pacific. That approach would have continued the policy, dating back to the 1780s, of dividing the national domain between the North and the South. The other proposal, championed by Senators Lewis Cass of Michigan and Stephen A. Douglas of Illinois, was to allow the people of the territory rather than Congress to decide the status of slavery. This solution, which became known as popular sovereignty, was left deliberately ambiguous. Could settlers of a new territory prohibit slavery any time they wished or only at the time it was admitted as a state, as Calhoun argued? Hoping to avoid further polarization, Cass, Douglas, and other supporters of popular sovereignty left northerners and southerners to draw their own conclusions.

In 1848 the two moderate approaches would probably have appealed to most

Americans. Over the next decade, however, they became increasingly unacceptable to both the North and the South. When Congress organized the Oregon Territory in 1848, under pressure from the northern-controlled House, it prohibited slavery there, since even southerners admitted that the region could not support slave-labor crops like cotton, rice, and tobacco. But this seemingly straightforward decision made it impossible to apply the Missouri Compromise to the other territories. Without Oregon as a part of the package, the greater share of the remaining land would be open to slavery, something the North balked at. Almost inadvertently, one of the two moderate solutions by the summer of 1848 had been discarded.

A Two-Faced Campaign

In the election of 1848, both major parties tried to avoid disrupting national politics with the slavery issue. The Democrats nominated Lewis Cass, a supporter of popular sovereignty. The Whigs bypassed all their prominent leaders and nominated General Zachary Taylor, still basking in the fame of his victories in the Mexican War. Taylor was a southerner and a slaveholder, but he had not previously identified with the Whig party and had taken no position on any public issue. In fact, he had never even voted. The Whigs adopted no platform and planned instead to emphasize the general's war record.

But the slavery issue would not quietly go away. A number of dissatisfied factions came together to form the new antislavery Free Soil party. Alienated by Polk's policies and still angry over the 1844 convention, northern Democrats loyal to Van Buren spearheaded its creation, and they were joined by "Conscience Whigs," who repudiated Taylor's nomination because he was a slaveholder. Furthermore, political abolitionists like Salmon P. Chase left the Liberty party in favor of this broader coalition. To widen its appeal, the Free Soil platform focused on the dangers of extending slavery rather than on the evil of slavery itself. Allow it to exist in the present slave states, party members agreed, but any new states entering the Union must be free. "Free soil" as much as antislavery was the key. Ironically, the party's convention named as its candidate Martin Van Buren—the man who for years had struggled to keep the slavery issue out of politics. William Lloyd Garrison and other strong abolitionists saw the choice of Van Buren as an example of the compromises reformers would be forced to make in the political arena.

With the Free Soilers strongly supporting the Wilmot Proviso, the Whigs and Democrats could not ignore the slavery question. Since Taylor had taken no position on the subject, the Whigs ran a deliberately sectional campaign. Northern party leaders promised audiences that Taylor would not veto the Wilmot Proviso if it passed Congress, while southern Whigs insisted he would protect the interests of his native South. Similarly, northern Democrats claimed that popular sovereignty would allow the new territories to vote themselves free, while southern Democrats assured slaveholders that they would have equal access to territories won with the nation's common blood and treasure.

In this two-faced, sectional campaign, the Whigs won their second national victory. Taylor kept the core of Whig voters in both sections (Van Buren as well as Cass, after all, had long been Democrats). But especially in the South, where the contest pitted a southern slaveholder against two northerners, Taylor won many more votes than Clay had in 1844. As one southern Democrat complained, "We have lost hundreds of votes, solely on the ground that General Cass was a North-

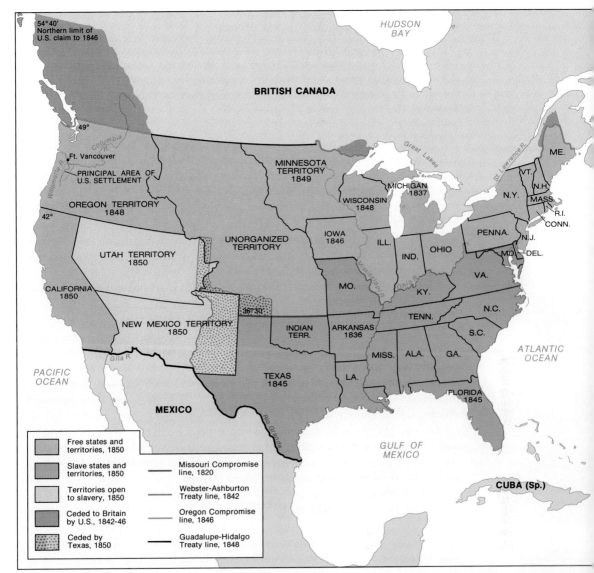

TERRITORIAL GROWTH AND THE COMPROMISE OF 1850

erner and General Taylor a Southern man." Furthermore, Van Buren polled five times as many votes as the Liberty party had four years earlier, further splitting the nation along sectional lines. It seemed that the national system of political parties was being gradually pulled apart.

The Compromise of 1850

Once he became president, Taylor could no longer remain silent. The territories gained from Mexico had to be organized; California, crowded with would-be miners, even in 1849 had gained enough population to be admitted as a state. In the

Senate the balance of power between North and South stood at 15 states each. Whichever way California went, it would break the sectional balance.

Taylor was a forthright man of action ("Old Rough and Ready," his troops called him), but he was an utter political novice. As an ardent nationalist, he decided that the way to end the territorial crisis was simple. Even Calhoun conceded that entering states had the right to ban slavery. The solution, Taylor therefore reasoned, was to skip the controversial territorial stage. So the president sent agents to California and New Mexico with instructions to set the machinery in motion for both territories to draft constitutions and apply for statehood directly. Even more shocking to southern Whigs, he indicated his support for admitting both as free states because he was convinced that slavery would never flourish in them. When Congress convened in December 1849, California had drafted a constitution and applied for admission as a free state. Taylor indicated that New Mexico (which then included most of Arizona, Utah, and Colorado) would soon do the same. All that remained was for Congress to admit these two free states and the crisis would be over. Instead, Taylor touched off the most serious sectional crisis the Union had yet confronted.

Into this turmoil stepped Henry Clay, now 73 years old and nearing the end of his career. Clay had been a savvy cardplayer all his life; he loved the bargaining, the wheeling and dealing, the late-night trade-offs eased along by a pint of bourbon. Thirty years earlier he had engineered the Missouri Compromise, and in 1833 he had helped defuse the nullification crisis. Clay decided that a grand compromise was now needed to end all disputes between the North and South and save the Union. Already, Mississippi had summoned other southern states to meet in a convention at Nashville to discuss the crisis, and extremists were pushing for secession. The issues rankling both sides went beyond the question of the western territories. Many northerners considered it disgraceful that slaves were bought and sold in the nation's capital, where slavery was still permitted. Southerners complained bitterly that northern states ignored the 1793 fugitive slave law and prevented them from reclaiming runaway slaves.

Clay's compromise, submitted in January 1850, addressed all of these issues. California, he proposed, should be admitted as a free state, which represented the clear wishes of most settlers there. The rest of the Mexican cession would be organized as two territories, New Mexico and Utah, under the doctrine of popular sovereignty. Thus slavery would not be prohibited from these regions. Clay also proposed that Congress abolish the slave trade but not slavery itself in the District of Columbia, and that a new, more rigorous fugitive slave law be passed. To reinforce the idea that both North and South were yielding ground, Clay combined most of these provisions (and several others adjusting the Texas–New Mexico border) in a larger package known as the Omnibus Bill.

With the stakes so high, the Senate debated Clay's proposal for six months. Daniel Webster of Massachusetts, always solemn and deep-voiced, seemed more somber than usual when he delivered a pro-compromise speech on the seventh of March. "I wish to speak today not as a Massachusetts man, not as a Northern man, but as an American. . . . I speak today for the preservation of the Union. Hear me for my cause." Calhoun, whose aged, crevassed face mirrored the lines that had been drawn so deeply between the two sections, was near death and too ill to deliver his final speech to the Senate. But he listened, a silent specter, as a colleague read it for him. The "cords of Union," he warned—those ties of interest and affection that held the nation together—were snapping one by one. Only

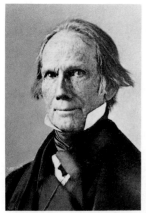  

The Great Triumvirate, Clay, Webster, and Calhoun, served the public together for almost four decades. Clay (left) and Webster (center) supported the Compromise of 1850, whereas the dying Calhoun's last speech opposed it. By midcentury, power was passing to a new generation of politicians more accustomed to sectional conflict and less amenable to compromise. (All pictures are details from portraits.)

equal treatment of the South and an end to the agitation against slavery could preserve the Union. William Henry Seward of New York, a younger voice speaking for the antislavery forces, proclaimed that "all legislative compromises . . . [are] radically wrong and essentially vicious." In the matter of human bondage, "a higher law" than the Constitution had to be obeyed.

Clay, wracked by a hacking cough, spent long hours trying to line up the needed votes. But for once, the great whist enthusiast had misplayed his hand. The Omnibus Bill required that the components of the compromise be approved as a package. But extremists in Congress from both regions combined against the moderates and rejected the bill. With Clay exhausted and his strategy in shambles, Democrat Stephen A. Douglas assumed leadership of the pro-compromise forces. One by one, he submitted the individual measures for a vote. By September 17, all the separate bills had passed and become law. Northern representatives provided the necessary votes to admit California and abolish the slave trade in the District of Columbia, while southern representatives supplied the edge needed to organize the Utah and New Mexico territories and pass the new fugitive slave law. On the face of it, everyone had compromised. But in truth, only 61 members of Congress, or 21 percent of the membership, had supported all of the Compromise or had abstained on one vote and supported the remaining measures. Nearly 80 percent had voted against some part of it.

Away from the Brink

President Taylor had threatened a veto, but he died suddenly on July 9, and the new president, Millard Fillmore, threw his support behind Clay and Douglas. The Compromise of 1850 became law and the Union, it seemed, was safe.

The general public, both North and South, rallied to the Compromise. At the convention of southern states in Nashville, the fire-eaters—the radical proponents of states' rights and secession—found themselves voted down by more moderate voices. Even in the Deep South, coalitions of pro-Compromise Whigs and Democrats soundly defeated secessionists in subsequent state elections. Nevertheless, most southerners felt that a firm line had been drawn. With California's admission, they were now outnumbered in the Senate, so it was even more crucial that slaveholders be granted equal legal access to the territories. They announced that any breach of the Compromise of 1850 would justify secession. During the 1830s and 1840s, few southerners had asserted the right of secession; but by 1850 a majority accepted it in the abstract as the South's ultimate recourse, although they refrained from exercising it.

The North, for its part, found the new fugitive slave law the hardest measure of the Compromise of 1850 to swallow. Denying an accused runaway a trial by jury, it provided that the case was to be decided by a special commissioner. The commissioner would receive a $5 fee if he freed the accused fugitive but $10 if he returned him or her to slavery. In addition, the law required that all citizens assist federal marshals in its enforcement. Harriet Beecher Stowe's popular novel *Uncle Tom's Cabin* (1852) presented a powerful moral indictment of the law—and of slavery as an institution. Despite sentimental characters, a contrived plot, and clumsy dialect, Stowe's story profoundly moved its readers. It described the plight of the slave without resorting to the harsh rhetoric of the abolitionists. Emphasizing the duty of Christians toward the downtrodden in this crisis, the book reached a greater audience than any previous abolitionist work, heightening moral opposition to the institution.

In reality, however, fewer than 1000 slaves a year ran away to the North, and many of those never reached freedom. Despite some cases of well-publicized resistance, the 1850 fugitive slave law was generally enforced in the free states. From 1850 to 1856, an estimated 200 blacks were arrested under its provisions, and only 12 of them were forcibly rescued. Many northerners did not like the law, but they were unwilling to tamper with the Compromise. Stephen Douglas spoke accurately when he boasted in 1851, "The whole country is acquiescing in the compromise measures—everywhere, North and South. Nobody proposes to repeal or disturb them."

And so calm returned. In the lackluster 1852 presidential campaign, both the Whigs and the Democrats endorsed the Compromise, and Franklin Pierce, a little-known New Hampshire Democratic politician, soundly defeated the Whig candidate Winfield Scott. Even more significant, the antislavery Free Soil candidate received only about half as many votes as Van Buren had four years before. The slavery issue was losing political force. To maintain party unity, both parties had abandoned sectional issues, and public opinion seemed willing to stand by the Compromise of 1850. It appeared that the Republic had weathered the storm unleashed by the Wilmot Proviso and could direct its attention once more to the economic development of the continent.

But the moving frontier still had changes to work. It had leaped from the Mississippi valley all the way to the Pacific, but in between remained territory still unorganized. And as the North became increasingly industrialized and the South more firmly committed to an economy based on cotton and the peculiar institution, the conflict between the two sections would shatter the Jacksonian party system, reinvigorate the slavery issue, and shake the Union to its foundation.

SIGNIFICANT EVENTS

1725–1850	Sioux expansion on the Great Plains
1821	Mexico wins independence; Santa Fe trade opens
1823	First American settlers in Texas
1829	Mexico tries to abolish slavery in Texas
1830	Mexico attempts to halt American migration to Texas; Joseph Smith founds Mormon church
1835	Texas Revolution
1836	Texas Republic established; Battle of the Alamo; Santa Anna defeated at San Jacinto
1841	Tyler becomes president
1842	Webster–Ashburton Treaty
1843	Large-scale migration to Oregon begins
1843–1844	Tyler's secret negotiations with Texas
1844	Tyler's Texas treaty rejected by the Senate; Joseph Smith murdered; Polk elected president
1845	United States annexes Texas; phrase "Manifest Destiny" coined
1845–1846	Slidell's unsuccessful mission
1846	War declared against Mexico; Bear Flag Revolt in California; Oregon Treaty ratified; Wilmot Proviso introduced
1847	Mormon migration to Utah; U.S. troops occupy Mexico City
1848	Gold discovered in California; Treaty of Guadalupe Hidalgo; Free Soil party founded; Taylor elected president
1849	Gold rush; California drafts free state constitution
1850	Nashville convention; Taylor dies and Fillmore becomes president; Compromise of 1850 enacted
1850–1851	South rejects secession
1851	Fort Laramie Treaty
1852	Harriet Beecher Stowe's *Uncle Tom's Cabin* published; Pierce elected president

15

The Union Broken

I nto town they rode, several hundred strong, their faces flushed with excitement. They were unshaven, big, rough-talking men, "wearing the most savage looks" and "armed . . . to the teeth with rifles and revolvers, cutlasses and bowie-knives." Out in front of the procession, an American flag flapped softly in the warm May breeze. Alongside it was another flag, a crouching tiger emblazoned on black and white stripes, followed by banners proclaiming "Southern Rights," "South Carolina," and "The Superiority of the White Race." At the rear rolled five artillery pieces, which were quickly dragged into range of the town's main street. Josiah Miller, the editor of the Lawrence *Kansas Free State*, watched intently from a window in his office. "Well, boys," he predicted, "we're in for it."

For the residents of Lawrence, Kansas, a community of less than 1000 people along the banks of the Kansas River, the worst seemed at hand. Founded by the New England Emigrant Aid Company, a Yankee association that recruited settlers in an effort to preserve Kansas for freedom, Lawrence was the headquarters of the free state movement in the territory. Accepting Stephen Douglas' idea that the people should decide the status of slavery, the town's residents intended to see to it that under popular sovereignty Kansas entered the Union as a free state. Emigrants from the neighboring slave state of Missouri were equally determined that no "abolition tyrants," "negro thieves," or "philanthropic knaves" control the future of the territory. There had been conflict in Kansas almost immediately: land disputes, horse thievery, shootings on both sides—even two tar-and-featherings. (Actually, lacking feathers, the proslavery vigilantes had settled for tar and cotton.)

In the ensuing turmoil, the federal government seemed to back the proslavery forces, much to the anger of the free-staters. Finally, in the spring of 1856, a U.S. District Court indicted several of Lawrence's leading citizens for treason and federal marshal Israel Donaldson called for a posse to help make the arrests and to put down any resistance. That was all the encouragement proslavery forces needed. "War to the knife, and knife to the hilt," raged one proslavery newspaper, the *Squatter Sovereign*. Donaldson's posse, swelled to an army by eager volunteers from across the Missouri border, arrived outside Lawrence on the night of May 20.

Meanwhile, Lawrence's "committee of safety" had agreed on a policy of nonresistance. The next morning it instructed residents to give no provocation, not even to congregate in groups on the streets. Most of those indicted had prudently fled, but Donaldson arrested two men without incident; then, hoping to cement the uneasy peace, the proprietors of the newly completed Free State Hotel in-

A torchlight parade staged by the Republican Wide-Awakes, New York City, 1860. In remarkably few years, the new sectional party sensed victory within its reach in the presidential election.

vited several of the group to dinner, including Donaldson and former U.S. senator David Rice Atchison of Missouri. After the meal, Donaldson returned and dismissed his posse, announcing that his purpose had been accomplished. But Sheriff Samuel Jones, one of its members, had a score to settle. During his previous visit to Lawrence, someone had taken a potshot that wounded him in the back; now the irate sheriff, falsely claiming that he had a court order, took over the band and led its cheering members into the hated free state town at three o'clock in the afternoon.

The thoroughly liquored "army" quickly degenerated into a mob and, ignoring the pleas of some leaders, went on a drunken spree. The mob burst into the offices of two newspapers, the *Herald of Freedom* and the *Kansas Free State*, smashed the presses, broke up type, and threw assorted printing material into the Kansas River. Then the crowd unleashed its wrath on the now-deserted Free State Hotel, which, with its 18-inch-thick walls, concealed portholes, and parapet, resembled a fort. Sheriff Jones and his followers unsuccessfully attempted to batter it down with cannon fire; they then set off two kegs of gunpowder in the basement to no avail. Finally, after carefully confiscating the hotel's liquor supply, they put a torch to the building. After destroying additional private property, the mob, with a few final whoops and hurrahs, rode off, leaving the residents of Lawrence unharmed but thoroughly terrified. As they departed, a worried Atchison exclaimed, "And the eyes of the nation are on Kansas!"

Retaliation by free state partisans was not long in coming. Hurrying north along a different road to Lawrence, an older man with a grim visage and steely eyes that would not be shaded by his dirty straw hat heard the news the next morning that the town had been sacked. Old Man Brown, as everyone called him, was on his way with several of his sons to provide reinforcements. A severe, God-fearing Calvinist (some of his neighbors would have called him a fanatic), John Brown was also a staunch abolitionist who had once remarked to a friend that he believed "God had raised him up on purpose to break the jaws of the wicked." News that the free-staters had not resisted the "slave hounds" from Missouri made him livid. Brooding over these events, Brown decided not to push on to Lawrence; instead, he ordered his followers to sharpen their heavy cutlasses. When one of the other volunteers warned Brown to behave with caution, he exploded. "Caution, caution, sir. I am eternally tired of hearing the word caution. It is nothing but the word of Cowardice."

On the night of May 24, 1856, three days after the Lawrence raid, Brown headed toward Pottawatomie Creek with a half dozen others, including four of his sons. As a damp wind beat against their coats, the party silently approached a dark cabin, cutlasses drawn. When James Doyle, a proslavery man from Tennessee, opened the door, Brown and his men charged in, declaring that they were "the Northern Army" come to serve justice. Terrified, Doyle's wife Mahala stood in the shadows with her young daughter, crying. As Brown marched Doyle and his three sons off, she begged him to spare her youngest, and the old man relented. The others were led no more than 100 yards down the road before Owen and Salmon Brown set upon them, broadswords slashing and hacking, until the three men lay in a bloodied heap along the trail. Old Man Brown then walked up to James Doyle's body and put a bullet through his forehead. Before the night was done, two more cabins had been visited and two more proslavery settlers brutally executed. Not one of the five murdered men owned a single slave or had any connection with the attack on Lawrence.

In the days that followed, as guerrilla bands prowled the plains, prudent

The Free State Hotel was destroyed and burned by the proslavery band that attacked Lawrence, Kansas, on May 21, 1856. News of the so-called "Sack of Lawrence" greatly agitated northern public opinion and strengthened the struggling Republican party.

Kansans armed themselves when traveling. Families refused to open their doors at night; and the news of the tumult, as Senator Atchison had predicted, soon reached outraged audiences in both the North and the South. "Everybody here feels as if we are upon a volcano," remarked one congressman in Washington.

The country was indeed atop a smoldering volcano that would finally erupt in the spring of 1861, showering death and destruction across the land. Popular sovereignty, the last remaining moderate solution to the controversy over the expansion of slavery, had failed dismally in Kansas. The violence and disorder in the territory provided a stark reply to Stephen Douglas' proposition: What could be more peaceable, more fair than the notion of popular sovereignty?

SECTIONAL CHANGES IN AMERICAN SOCIETY

The road to war was not a straight or short one. Six years elapsed between the Compromise of 1850 and the crisis in "Bleeding Kansas"; another four would pass before the first blows between North and South were struck. And the process of separation involved more than hot tempers, bumbling politicians, and an unwillingness to negotiate. As we have seen, Americans were bound together by a growing transportation network, by national markets, and by a national political system. These social and political ties—the "cords of Union," Calhoun called them—could not be severed all at once. Increasingly, however, the changes occurring in American society heightened sectional tensions. As the North continued to industrialize, its society came increasingly into conflict with that of the South, while the Old Northwest, which had long been an ally of the South, became more closely linked to the East. The coming of Civil War, in other words, involved changes in the social and economic systems as well as the political.

The Growth of a Railroad Economy

By the time the Compromise of 1850 produced a lull in the tensions between North and South, the American economy had left behind the depression of the early 1840s and was roaring again with speculative optimism. The basic structure of the economy, however, was changing. Cotton remained the nation's major export, but it was no longer the driving force for American economic growth. After 1839, this role was taken over by the construction of a vast railroad network covering the eastern half of the continent.

By the 1840s most states recognized that railroads were essential to a thriving commerce, and construction of a national rail network was under way. By 1850, the United States possessed more than 9000 miles of track; 10 years later, it had over 30,000 miles, more than the rest of the world combined. During the 1850s, much of the new construction occurred west of the Appalachian Mountains—over 2000 miles in Ohio and Illinois alone. The South lagged behind the North, yet in 1860 almost a third of the nation's total mileage was located in the southern states. As rail networks expanded, they were also combined into integrated systems, or trunk lines, that brought long sections of track under a single management. The New York Erie, for example, ran all the way from the Hudson River north of New York City to Lake Erie. Soon after, Erastus Corning, an Albany banker and financier, created a rival line, the New York Central, by merging a number of small lines running from Albany to Buffalo.

To help secure adequate transportation, businessmen and farmers subscribed to railroad company stock. In heavily populated areas, where the freight and passenger traffic was heavy, investors usually profited quickly. Western railroads, however, ran through less settled areas and were especially dependent on public aid. State and local governments made loans to rail companies, invested in their stocks and bonds, backed them with government credit, and sometimes exempted them temporarily from taxes. About a quarter of the cost of railroad construction came from state and local governments, but federal land grants were crucial too. In 1850 the Illinois Central, which was charted to run south from Chicago to Mobile on the Gulf of Mexico, received almost 2.6 million acres of land from the public domain along its tracks. By mortgaging or selling the land to farmers, the railroad raised most of the needed construction capital and also stimulated settlement, which increased its business and profits. By 1860 Congress had allotted about 28 million acres of federal land to 40 different companies.

The effect of the new lines rippled outward through the economy. Farmers along the tracks began to specialize in cash crops and market them in distant locations. With their profits they purchased manufactured goods that earlier they might have made at home. A newspaper in Athens, Tennessee, noted that before the railroad reached its region, the surrounding counties produced about 25,000 bushels of wheat, which sold for less than 50 cents a bushel. Once the railroad came, farmers in these same counties grew 400,000 bushels and sold their crop at a dollar a bushel. Railroads also stimulated other areas of the economy, notably the mining and iron industries. By 1860 half of the domestic output of bar and sheet iron was used by railroads, and pig iron production stood at 920,000 tons, almost triple what it had been only 20 years earlier.

On a national map, the rail network in place by 1860 looked impressive, but appearances were deceiving. Roadbeds had not yet been standardized, so that no fewer than 12 different gauges, or track widths, were in use. Furthermore, cities at the end of rail lines jealously strove to maintain their commercial advantages, not wanting to connect with competing port cities, for fear freight would pass through to the next city down the line. Philadelphia, for example, was linked to the west through the Pennsylvania Railroad, to the north with two lines running toward New York, and to the south with a line toward Baltimore. But the two lines from New York stopped well short of Philadelphia, and the lines from the south and west did not connect with each other, even though they used the same gauge.

Still, the new rail networks shifted the direction of western trade. Traditionally, the mighty Mississippi, the Ohio, and the Missouri rivers linked the Old Northwest with the South. In 1840 most grain produced upstream was shipped by water to the bustling port of New Orleans. But there were disadvantages to water travel, even by steamboat. Low water made travel risky in summer; and by the time farmers in Missouri, Illinois, and the country of the upper Mississippi were finished harvesting crops, ice began shutting down river travel. Products such as lard, tallow, and cheese quickly spoiled if stored in New Orleans' sweltering warehouses. And transferring freight at the crowded harbor of St. Louis or New Orleans was woefully inefficient.

With the new rail lines, traffic from the Midwest increasingly flowed west to east. Chicago, which had no rail connections at the beginning of 1848, was served by over 2000 miles of track by 1855. It became the region's hub, connecting the farms of the upper Midwest to New York and other eastern cities. Loading and unloading freight was a lot easier beside rail warehouses and grain elevators than at river ports, where water levels rose and fell unpredictably. Whereas eastern merchants had enough capital to extend credit to western shippers, in New Orleans, as elsewhere in the South, capital was largely tied up in slaves. Thus while the value of goods shipped by river to New Orleans continued to increase, the South's overall share of western trade dropped dramatically. The old political alliance between the South and West, based on shared economic interests, was weakened by the new patterns of commerce.

The New Commercial Agriculture

The growing rail network was not the only factor that led farmers in the Northeast and Midwest to become more commercially oriented. Another was the sharp rise in international demand for grain. After 1846, the repeal of the protective English corn laws opened up English markets. European crop failures and the Crimean War (1853–1856) also increased demand. Wheat, which in 1845 commanded $1.08 a bushel in New York City, fetched $2.46 in 1855; the price of corn nearly doubled during the same period. Farmers responded by specializing in cash crops, borrowing to purchase more land, and investing in equipment to increase productivity.

Improved technology made it possible to meet the increased demand. John Deere's steel plow allowed midwestern farmers to cut through the thick roots of prairie grass without the soil sticking to the blade. Cyrus McCormick refined a

The Geography of Railroads

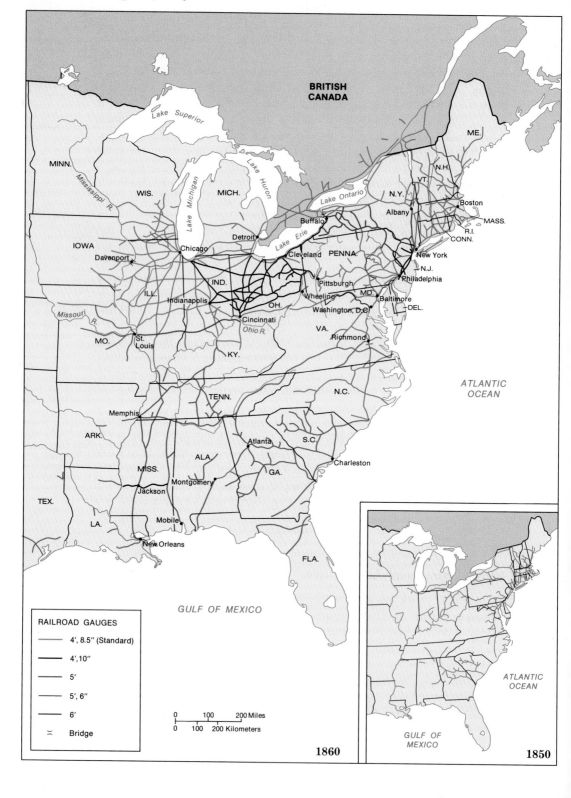

RAILROAD GAUGES

— 4', 8.5" (Standard)

— 4',10"

— 5'

— 5', 6"

— 6'

⋈ Bridge

0   100   200 Miles
0   100   200 Kilometers

1860

1850

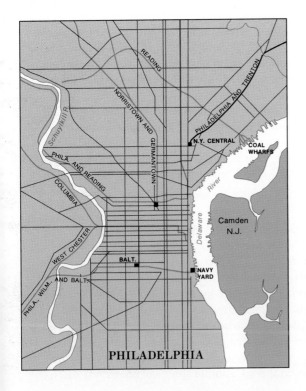

PHILADELPHIA

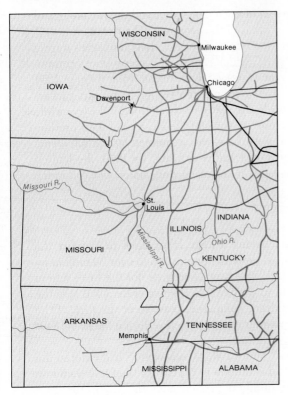

During the 1850s, a significant amount of railroad track was laid in the United States. Total track mileage is misleading, however. Despite the cobweb of lines crisscrossing the nation, the United States still lacked a fully integrated rail network in 1860. A few trunk-line roads had combined a number of smaller lines into a single system to facilitate shipment; the Baltimore and Ohio, for example, extended to Wheeling on the Ohio River, and the Pennsylvania connected Philadelphia and Pittsburgh. But the existence of five major track gauges, as well as additional minor ones, meant that passengers and freight often had to be transferred from one line to the next. North-south traffic was disrupted not only by gauge differentials, but also by the lack of bridges over the Ohio.

Even in a city like Philadelphia, where most of the railroads were the same gauge, traffic was hindered by the failure to connect the different lines. Passengers and freight had to be transported in wagons, carts, and coaches through the city's crowded streets to another line. Teamsters, cartmen, stagecoach drivers, and others whose livelihood depended on the need for local transportation bitterly fought efforts to link rail lines.

In the decade before the Civil War, railroad construction produced a dramatic shift in the economic orientation of the West. Before 1850, western trade had flowed primarily down the Ohio and Mississippi rivers on steamboats to St. Louis and New Orleans. In the 1850s, however, railroads transported an increasing proportion of western grains and foodstuffs eastward to New York, Philadelphia, and other major cities. Recognizing this threat to the steamboat industry, the St. Louis Chamber of Commerce tried to prevent construction of a crucial railroad bridge over the Mississippi near Davenport, Iowa; indeed the Chamber's attorney was even jailed on suspicion of attempted arson. But by the end of the decade, Illinois rail lines reached into Iowa and Missouri, and Chicago had emerged as the major rail hub of the Midwest.

mechanical reaper. Problems in harvesting had long limited the amount of grain farmers could grow, for they had only a short time to cut it before it spoiled. The reaper allowed as much as 14 times more wheat to be harvested with the same amount of labor. John Deere established a factory in Moline, Illinois, in 1847, the same year that McCormick set up headquarters in Chicago. McCormick was soon selling 1000 reapers a year and could not keep up with demand, while Deere turned out 10,000 plows annually.

By 1860 midwestern states produced for market more wheat, corn, beef, and pork than any other region. Again the shift in commercial agriculture had an effect on the political balance. "The power of cotton over the financial affairs of the Union has in the last few years rapidly diminished," the *Democratic Review* remarked in 1849, "and bread stuffs will now become the governing power."

Rising Industrialization

On the eve of the Civil War, 60 percent of the American labor force was still employed in agriculture. But in 1860 for the first time, less than half the workers in the North were engaged in agriculture. The expansion of commercial agriculture spurred the growth of industrial labor, for out of the 10 leading American industries, 8 processed raw materials produced by agriculture; these included flour milling and the manufacture of textiles, shoes, and woolens. The only exceptions were iron and machinery. Industrial growth also spurted during the 1850s as water power was increasingly replaced by steam. Only a fixed number of rivers and falls were available for water-power sites, and in the Northeast, these had largely been occupied. For industry to spread, another source of power was essential.

Most important, the factory system of organizing labor and the technology of interchangeable parts spread to other areas of the economy. The textile industry, we have seen, first brought workers together in factories. Many industries during the 1850s adopted interchangeable parts, which required that a product's components be machined to very fine tolerances. Isaac Singer began using them in 1851 to mass produce sewing machines, an invention patented only five years earlier. In turn, sewing machines made possible the ready-made clothing industry, while shoe manufacturers adapted the machines to concentrate all steps of their production under a single roof. Similarly, the workers who assembled farm implements performed a single step in the process over and over again. By 1860, the United States had nearly a billion dollars invested in manufacturing, almost twice as much as in 1849.

Immigration

The surge of industry depended on having a large labor force to support the factory system. Natural increase helped swell the population to over 30 million by 1860, but this accounted for only part of the new labor force, for the birth rate in the United States had actually begun to decline. On the eve of the Civil War the average white mother bore five children, compared to seven at the turn of the century. But the beginning of mass immigration to America during the mid-1840s kept population growth soaring.

In the 20 years from 1820 to 1840, about 700,000 newcomers had entered the United States. That figure jumped to 1.7 million in the 1840s, then to 2.6 million in the 1850s. Though even greater numbers arrived after the Civil War, as a percentage of the nation's total population, the wave from 1845 to 1854 was the largest influx of immigrants in American history. From the British Isles alone, a fleet of 1000 ships transported immigrants back and forth; in 1854, one of the heaviest years, 51 ships left Liverpool in June, carrying nearly 22,000 passengers. Whether traveling as individuals or as families, most of the newcomers were young people in the prime of life: in 1856 out of 224,000 arrivals, only 31,000 were under 10 and 20,000 were over 40.

Although fares were low, the journey, which lasted from six weeks to three months depending on the weather, was anything but comfortable. The cheapest passage was the cramped, crowded quarters of steerage, where the food was bad, the air noxious, and sanitation inadequate. Sickness weakened the passengers, and sometimes epidemics decimated them. "Dyin' like rotten sheep thrown into a pit," one Irish immigrant recalled, "and the minit the breath is out of our bodies, flung into the sea to be eaten up by them horrid sharks." Once disembarked in the United States, newcomers were set upon by runners for various boardinghouses and railroad companies, as well as swindlers who tried to take advantage of them. Tickets, printed with enticing pictures of a train, steamboat, or canal packet, were hawked at exorbitant rates, after which hopeful immigrants might find themselves herded, for example, onto a "night boat" from New York to Albany, with no shelter from the rain or cold, and only a hard deck to sleep on. Deaths from exposure on the lines to Albany alone were estimated in the thousands.

Certainly the booming economy and the lure of freedom drew immigrants to America, but they were also pushed by deteriorating conditions in Europe. In Ireland, a potato blight which struck in 1846 produced widespread famine. Already desperately poor and oppressed by English landlords, the Irish faced hunger, starvation, and the ravages of epidemics that swept across the Emerald Isle. Out of an Irish population of 9 million, as many as a million perished, while a million and a half more emigrated, two-thirds to the United States. The tide continued, though at a lesser rate, even after the potato crop recovered in 1849.

The Irish tended to be poorer than other immigrant groups of the day, generally younger sons and daughters of farm families, who had become a burden to their families because Irish landholdings and farms were so small. Mostly unmarried, they often arrived as individuals rather than as part of a family, and they sent money home to support their relatives. Although the Protestant Scotch-Irish con-

New York was the major port of entry for immigrants in the 1840s and 1850s. Here a group of Irish immigrants debark at New York in 1847.

tinued to emigrate, as they had in large numbers during the eighteenth century, the decided majority of the Irish who came after 1845 were Catholic. Because they were poor and unskilled, the Irish congregated in the cities, where the women performed domestic service and took factory jobs and men did manual labor.

Germans and Scandinavians also had economic reasons for leaving Europe. They might be small farmers whose lands had become marginal or who had been displaced by landlords, or skilled workers thrown out of work by industrialization. Others fled religious persecution. Some, particularly among the Germans, left after the liberal revolutions of 1848 failed. Many celebrated the free institutions of the United States and advertised them in letters home. "I am living in God's noble and free soil, neither am I a slave under others," wrote a Swede who settled in Iowa in 1850. Since coming to America, he added, "I have not been compelled to pay a penny for the privilege of living. Neither is my cap worn out from lifting it in the presence of gentlemen." An approving Dutch woman reported that schools were free, taxes low, and while "the finery is great, one cannot discern any difference between the cobbler's wife and the wife of a prominent gentleman."

Immigration reached its highest levels during periods of prosperity, then declined significantly after 1857, when the country entered another depression. Newcomers testified that the pace of work was faster and more regular in the United States, but wages were high and the food abundant and cheap. "Nearly all people eat meat three times a day," marveled a woman from Holland.

Although many Germans and Scandinavians arrived in modest straits, few were truly impoverished, and many could afford to buy a farm or start a business. Scandinavians and the Dutch were most often farmers; Germans included workers and shopkeepers, who settled throughout the countryside and in cities and towns. Unlike the Irish, Germans tended to emigrate as families, and wherever they settled they formed social, religious, and cultural organizations to maintain their language and customs. Whereas the Scandinavians, Dutch, and English immigrants were Protestant, half or more of the Germans were Catholics.

As a result of the immigrant tide, many American cities by 1860 contained a sizable foreign-born population. The Irish were especially numerous in eastern cities, particularly Boston, New York, and Philadelphia. Germans had established enclaves there too, but they were more dominant in western cities like Cincinnati, Chicago, Milwaukee, and St. Louis. By 1860 a majority of the population in Chicago, St. Louis, and San Francisco was foreign-born.

Factories came more and more to depend on immigrant labor, since newcomers would work for lower wages and were less willing to protest harsh working conditions. The meager pay seldom supported a family, so both parents and all but the youngest children often had to work. The shift to an immigrant work force could be seen most clearly in the textile industry, where over half the workers in New England mills were foreign-born by 1860. Mostly Irish, they found that American employers gave them only the lower paying jobs and excluded them from company housing. Rising ethnic tensions between native- and foreign-born workers, as well as among immigrants of various nationalities, made it difficult for workers to unite.

The massive influx of immigrants also strained city resources. Immigrants who could barely make ends meet were forced to live in overcrowded, unheated tenement houses, damp cellars, and even shacks. A building might appear as "a high, respectable-looking brick house on the outside," one New York journalist reported, but "within, the hall was dark and reeking with the worst filth. . . . The upper part of the house was filled with little narrow rooms, each one having five or six occupants; all very filthy. The people seemed very poor, honest Irish, not long here, and without work, usually." Such urban slums became notorious for crime and drinking, which took a heavy toll on families and the poor. In the eyes of many native-born Americans, immigrants were to blame for driving down factory wages and pushing American workers out of jobs. Overarching these complaints was a fear that America might not be able to assimilate the new groups, with their unfamiliar social customs, strange languages, national pride, and foreign traditions. Such fears precipitated an outburst of political nativism in the mid-1850s.

Southern Complaints

Industrialization affected the South, too, though in different ways. With British and northern factories buying cotton in unprecedented quantities, southern planters prospered in the 1850s. Like those of northern commercial farmers, their operations became more highly capitalized to keep up with the demand. But northern capital went into machinery like McCormick's harvester; white south-

---

SLAVE PRICES VERSUS COTTON PRICES
From 1815 to 1850, cotton and slave prices generally moved together, as southerners plowed their profits from growing cotton into buying more land and slaves. During the 1850s, however, the booming southern economy and bumper cotton crops drove the price of slaves steeply upward compared to cotton prices, squeezing slaveowners' profit margins and heightening southern anxieties about the future.

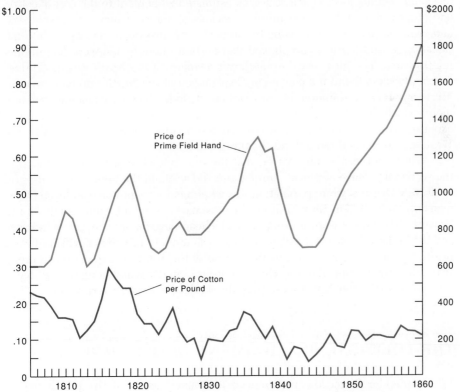

erners invested in slaves. During the 1850s, the price of prime field hands reached record levels at New Orleans and other southern markets.

Still, a number of southern nationalists, who advocated that the South should be a separate nation, pressed for greater industrialization to make the region more independent. "At present, the North fattens and grows rich upon the South," one Alabama newspaper complained in 1851.

> We purchase all our luxuries and necessities from the North. . . . Our slaves are clothed with Northern manufactured goods, have Northern hats and shoes, work with Northern hoes, ploughs, and other implements. . . . The slaveholder dresses in Northern goods, rides in a Northern saddle . . . sports his Northern carriage . . . reads Northern books. . . . In Northern vessels his products are carried to market, his cotton is ginned with Northern gins, his sugar is crushed and preserved by Northern machinery; his rivers are navigated by Northern steamboats.

So long as investments in cotton and slaves absorbed most of the South's capital, efforts to promote southern industry were doomed. Even with northern rail networks siphoning away the trade of western farmers, southern planters found railroads a less attractive investment, since these roads' profits were limited by the region's dispersed population, lack of cities, and restricted domestic market.

Despite southern prosperity, the section's leaders repeatedly complained that the North had used its power over banking and commerce to convert the South into a colony. In the absence of any significant southern shipping, northern middlemen controlled the South's commodities through a complex series of transfers from planter to manufacturer. Storage and shipping charges, insurance, port fees, and commissions, which added an estimated 20 percent to the cost of cotton and other commodities, went into the pockets of northern merchants, shippers, and bankers. Rather than viewing this as part of the process necessary for international trade, southerners complained that northern middlemen were nonproducing parasites. The idea that the South was a colony of the North was inaccurate, but southerners found it a convincing explanation of the North's growing wealth. More important, it reinforced their resistance to federal aid for economic development, which they were convinced would inevitably enrich the North at southern expense. This attitude further weakened the South's political alliance with the West, which needed federal aid for transportation.

White southerners also feared that the new tide of immigration would shift the sectional balance of power. Immigrants did settle in the South's few cities (in 1860 New Orleans' white population was 44 percent foreign-born) and some German farmers settled in Texas. But for the most part immigrants shunned the South because they did not want to compete with cheap slave labor. The lack of industry and the limited demand for skilled labor also shunted immigrants northward. As a result, the North surged even further ahead of the South in population, thereby strengthening its control of the House of Representatives and heightening southern concern that the North would rapidly settle the western territories.

THE POLITICAL REALIGNMENT OF THE 1850s

When Franklin Pierce (he pronounced it "Purse") assumed the presidency in 1853, he was only 48 years old, the youngest man yet to be elected president. He

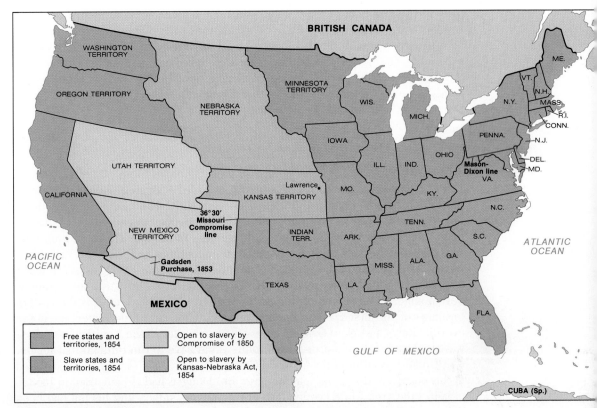

THE KANSAS-NEBRASKA ACT

When the Kansas-Nebraska Act of 1854 opened the remaining portion of the Louisiana Purchase to slavery under the doctrine of popular sovereignty, conflict between the two sections focused on control of Kansas, directly west of the slave state of Missouri.

was also a supporter of the "Young America" movement of the Democratic party, which enthusiastically anticipated extending democracy across the globe, securing new markets to promote American prosperity, and annexing additional territory to the United States. Its boastful spirit was epitomized in 1853 by a Philadelphia newspaper that spoke of the United States as bound on the "East by sunrise, West by sunset, North by the Arctic Expedition, and South as far as we darn please."

The believers in Young America considered themselves a dynamic, can-do lot, who felt it idle to argue about slavery and sectionalism when the nation could be developing. But they failed to comprehend how deeply American society was divided, and how each new plan for annexation would stir up renewed opposition. In 1853 Pierce did manage to conclude the Gadsden Purchase, thereby gaining control of about 45,000 square miles of Mexican desert and the most feasible southern route for a transcontinental railroad.

Pierce's major goal, Cuba, generated even fiercer debate. For years many Americans had assumed the United States would eventually acquire Cuba, and in 1848 Polk had authorized offering Spain up to $100 million for the island. Pierce was ready to raise the price, but Spain showed no interest. Then in 1854, three American ministers meeting at Ostend in Belgium sent the president a confidential recommendation. If Cuba could not be purchased, they argued, it should be seized. The contents of this "Ostend Manifesto" soon leaked, with predictable results. The acquisition of Cuba, a rich sugar-producing region where slavery had once been strong and still existed, was inexorably linked to the question of slavery expansion. The notion of acquiring it through naked aggression was so unpopular that Pierce was forced to repudiate the suggestion. In any case, he soon had his hands full with the proposals of another Democrat of the Young America stamp, Senator Stephen A. Douglas of Illinois.

The Kansas–Nebraska Act

Douglas too was eager to revive the fortunes of the sagging Democratic party. Stocky and short of stature (5 feet, 4 inches), the Little Giant was ambitious, bursting with energy, brimming with self-confidence, impatient to get things done, pugnacious in debate—always, it seemed, in motion. He could improvise strategies on the spot, but his impetuosity sometimes led him into rash judgments. As chairman of the Senate's Committee on Territories, Douglas was eager to organize federal lands west of Missouri as part of his program for economic development. As a citizen of Illinois, he wanted Chicago selected as the eastern terminus of the first transcontinental railroad. Chicago would never be chosen over St. Louis and New Orleans unless the remainder of the Louisiana Purchase was organized, for any northern rail route would have to run through that region.

Under the terms of the Missouri Compromise of 1820, slavery was prohibited in this portion of the Louisiana Purchase. But Douglas had already tried in 1853 to organize the area while keeping the ban on slavery intact, and his bill had been defeated by southern votes in the Senate. Douglas reintroduced his bill organizing this territory in January 1854. Bowing to a good deal of southern pressure, the Illinois leader agreed to remove the prohibition on slavery that had been in effect for 34 years, although he acknowledged that this action would "raise a hell of a storm."

As finally written, the bill created two territories: Kansas, directly west of Missouri, and a much larger Nebraska Territory, located west of Iowa and the Minnesota Territory. The Missouri Compromise was explicitly repealed. Instead, popular sovereignty was to determine the status of slavery in both territories, though it was left unclear whether residents of Kansas and Nebraska could prohibit slavery at any time, or only at the time of statehood, as southerners insisted. Still, most members of Congress assumed that Douglas had split the region into two territories so that each section could claim another state: Kansas would be slave and Nebraska free.

The Kansas–Nebraska Act outraged northern Democrats, Whigs, and Free Soilers alike. The Missouri Compromise was not just another statute, they argued, but an inviolable compact between the two sections. Critics rejected Douglas' contention that popular sovereignty would keep the territories free; the bill, they charged, was meant to give the Slave Power new territory. As always, most northerners spoke little of the moral evils of slavery; it was the expansion of slavery and the Slave Power that concerned them. So great was the northern outcry that Douglas joked he could "travel from Boston to Chicago by the light of my own [burning] effigy."

Once President Pierce endorsed the bill, Senate passage was assured. The real fight came in the House, where the North held a large majority. The president put intense pressure on his fellow northern Democrats, and finally the bill passed by a narrow margin, 113–100. Pierce signed it on May 30, 1854, and the Missouri Compromise was repealed.

The Collapse of the Second American Party System

In a sense, the furor over the Kansas–Nebraska Act was like the fault line of an earthquake zone. The jagged scar across the political landscape was visible evidence of the underlying social and economic tensions that had developed between the North and South. Since the 1820s and 1830s, the Jacksonian party system had bound the Union together. Both the Whig and the Democratic parties were national in scope, bringing together like-minded leaders from the North and the South. But as the moving frontier brought in new territories, the balance of political power tipped and the second American party system collapsed. Voters who had been loyal to one party for years, even decades, began switching allegiances, while new voters were mobilized. By the time the process of realignment was completed, a new party system had emerged, divided this time along clearly sectional lines.

In part, the old party system decayed because new problems had replaced the traditional issues of both Whigs and Democrats. Jacksonian Democrats had achieved many of their political reforms, and the latest round of prosperity undermined their campaign against banks as the agents of economic "privilege." The Whigs, whose strength lay within the Protestant mainstream, tried to expand their base by appealing to Catholics and recent immigrants, a tactic that backfired by alienating many of the party's traditional supporters. Then too, after 1850 Protestant reformers began agitating for the prohibition of alcohol, a question that deeply divided Whigs. In several key states the party was in complete disarray by the end of 1853. Finally, both the Whigs and Democrats were targets of a popular feeling that the existing parties were little more than corrupt engines of plunder designed "to keep a lot of 'Old Fogies' in office." Some citizens called for reform; others simply stopped voting. "There is prevailing generally a sort of 'don't care a damn' spirit," admitted one Ohio Whig in 1853.

Thus the party system was already weakened when the Kansas–Nebraska Act divided the two major parties along sectional lines. The northern Whigs, who unanimously opposed the bill, found themselves deserted by all of their southern colleagues, except for a few border-state Whigs. Indeed, many southern Whigs soon left the party for the Democrats. Although Franklin Pierce had convinced half the northern Democratic representatives to vote for Douglas' bill, the party paid the price in the elections that fall, losing 66 of the 91 northern Democratic seats and control of the House of Representatives.

In such an unstable atmosphere, with party loyalties badly weakened, independent parties flourished. The antislavery forces, which had earlier sparked the Liberty and Free Soil parties, united with Whigs and anti-Nebraska Democrats in the new antislavery Republican party. Their hopes were jolted, however, when another new party capitalized upon widespread fears aroused by the recent flood of immigrants and surged to the political forefront.

The Know-Nothings

New York City was the primary gateway for immigrants, and it was here in 1850 that a secret society, the Order of the Star-Spangled Banner, was formed. The society, which entered the political arena as the American party, proclaimed its unbridled hostility to the growing political power of Catholics and immigrants. Its members were sworn to secrecy and instructed to answer inquiries by replying "I know nothing." In 1853, the Know-Nothings (as they were quickly dubbed) began organizing in several other states; after only a year they had become the fastest growing party in the nation. Not coincidentally, 1854 also marked the peak of the new wave of immigration.

Taking as its slogan "Americans should rule America," the American party advocated that immigrants be forced to wait not 5 but 21 years before becoming naturalized citizens, and it called on voters to oust from office corrupt politicians who openly bid for foreign and Catholic votes. Know-Nothings denounced illegal voting by immigrants, the rising crime and disorder in urban areas, and immigrants' more easygoing observance of the Sabbath. (Germans, for example, enjoyed congregating on Sunday in beer gardens rather than engaging in solemn contemplation at home.) Indeed, because the Irish as well as the Germans often drank more heavily than native-born Americans, the prohibition movement had strong nativist overtones and gained the support of many Know-Nothings. Behind a great many of their specific complaints lay a virulent anti-Catholicism. Know-Nothings were convinced that the "undemocratic" hierarchy of priests, bishops, and archbishops, controlled by the pope in Rome, was conspiring to undermine American democracy.

The party especially attracted the support of young native-born American workers, who bore the brunt of the economic dislocations caused by industrialization and had to compete with immigrants for jobs. To workers, their jobs threatened and their status declining, immigrants and Catholics seemed obvious symbols of the unwanted transformation. And in the election of 1854, joined by sympathetic farmers and some members of the middle class, they voted in remarkable numbers for nativist candidates in key northern states like New York, Pennsylvania, Ohio, and Massachusetts.

The Know-Nothing triumph spelled doom for the Whigs, as the rank and file deserted in droves to the Know-Nothings. Fueled by its success, the American party turned its attention south, and in a few months it had organized in every state of the Union. By 1855, perhaps a million voters had enrolled in its lodges, as Know-Nothing candidates triumphed for the first time in Maryland, Kentucky, and Texas. Know-Nothing leaders confidently predicted that they would elect the next president.

Yet only a year later—by the end of 1856—the party had collapsed as quickly as it had risen. Lack of experience was one reason. Many Know-Nothing officeholders proved woefully incompetent, while in some states ambitious politicians quickly took over the movement and used it for their own purposes. Worse, party members often fell to bickering among themselves and failed to enact their program: voting reforms, a longer period of naturalization, and laws meant to check the power of the Catholic church. When firm deeds failed to follow strong words, supporters became disillusioned. The party's secrecy, too, seemed out of tune with a free republican spirit and in some cities, Know-Nothing gangs stole ballot boxes or attacked immigrants to prevent them from voting. Such actions made a mockery of the American party's claim to be a patriotic reform organization.

But the death knell of the party was rising sectional tensions. In 1855 a majority of northern delegates walked out of the American party's national convention when it adopted a proslavery platform. The 1856 convention brought a repeat of the same scene. This time, however, the bulk of the northern Know-Nothings left for good and joined the other new party, the Republicans. This party, unlike the Know-Nothings, had no base in the South. It intended to elect a president by sweeping the free states, which controlled a majority of the electoral votes. With Democratic strength concentrated more and more in the South, and the Republicans gaining in the North, the party system was realigning along sectional rather than national lines.

The Republicans and Bleeding Kansas

Initially, the Republicans looked no more like a viable party than any of the other short-lived antislavery parties of the period. In the summer of 1854, following passage of the Kansas–Nebraska Act, party organizers tried to capitalize on antislavery sentiment to attract Whigs, anti-Nebraska Democrats, and Free Soilers, but voters seemed more concerned about other issues: immigration in some states, temperance in others, and longstanding partisan antipathies in still others. To many moderate Whigs and Democrats, the Republican party seemed too radical. In 1855 Republican candidates met defeat almost everywhere they ran. A Democratic newspaper expressed the prevailing view when it declared, "Nobody believes that this Republican movement can prove the basis of a permanent party."

Such predictions, however, did not take into account the Kansas issue, and the emotions that it stirred. Most early settlers migrated to Kansas for the same reasons other Americans headed west—the chance to prosper in a new land. But Douglas' idea of popular sovereignty transformed the settlement of Kansas into a referendum on slavery in the territories: people voted with their feet. Thus a group of Massachusetts free-staters organized the New England Emigrant Aid Company, a joint stock venture designed to make a profit by investing in Kansas land and improvements while peopling the territory with antislavery advocates. This was one Yankee venture that failed on both counts; it sent few settlers to Kansas, and it was soon bankrupt.* But to the proslavery residents of Missouri's western counties, free state communities like Lawrence appeared as ominous threats. "We are playing for a mighty stake," former senator David Rice Atchison insisted. "If we win, we carry slavery to the Pacific Ocean; if we fail we lose Missouri, Arkansas and Texas and all the territories; the game must be played boldly."

In 1854 and 1855, during the first Kansas elections to select a delegate to Congress and a territorial legislature, Missourians took Atchison's advice to heart. In these elections they poured over the Kansas border, seized the polls, overawed the election judges, and voted en masse. Later congressional investigations concluded that over 60 percent of the votes were cast illegally. This massive fraud tarnished popular sovereignty at the outset and greatly aroused public opinion in the North. It also provided proslavery forces with a commanding majority in the Kansas legislature, where they promptly expelled the legally elected free state members and enacted a stringent legal code designed to intimidate antislavery

---

*It sent no more than 750 settlers in 1854 and fewer than 900 the following year; of these, perhaps a third left.

settlers. This Kansas Code, which attacked such time-honored rights as freedom of speech, impartial juries, and fair elections, became for northerners a symbol of tyranny. Mobilized into action, the free-staters in the fall of 1855 organized a separate government in Topeka, drafted a state constitution prohibiting slavery, and asked Congress to admit Kansas as the seventeenth free state in the Union.

Such a polarized situation triggered increased violence between the two factions in 1855 and again in the spring of 1856. Some of the bloodshed was typical of the anarchy common to most frontiers and had little to do with the slavery question. But since Kansas was distant from the more settled areas of the country, each report became fodder for propagandists on either side. For southerners, the free state Kansans were abolitionists preaching moral righteousness as an excuse to cheat southerners out of their property and rights. For their part, northern Republicans made little distinction between whiskey-soaked "border ruffians" and more peaceable southern settlers.

The Caning of Charles Sumner

In the ensuing congressional debate over the situation in Kansas, few were more heated in condemning the proslavery electoral frauds and violence than Senator Charles Sumner, a Republican from Massachusetts. A strong antislavery man, Sumner made no secret of his contempt for those who defended what he saw as an evil institution. In May, only a few days before the proslavery attack on Lawrence, he delivered a scathing speech entitled "The Crime Against Kansas," which included several deliberately insulting remarks about the state of South Carolina and one of its senators, 60-year-old Andrew P. Butler, a courtly, well-liked gentleman.

Butler was not in Washington at the time, but his cousin Preston Brooks was. A congressman from South Carolina, Brooks was especially outraged because Sumner had insulted an elderly blood relation, mocking his state and section. Several days later, on May 22, Brooks strode into the Senate after it had adjourned and approached Sumner, who was seated at his desk addressing mail. Announcing that he considered the speech "a libel on South Carolina and Mr. Butler," Brooks took his gutta-percha cane and struck the senator sharply on the head. Sumner, surprised and stunned by the blow, struggled to rise but his desk, bolted to the floor, restrained him. The emotion of the moment swept Brooks up and, furiously, he delivered blow after blow to Sumner's bleeding head, his cane shattering into three pieces from the vehemence of the attack. Sumner finally wrenched the desk from the floor with his legs and staggered forward, blinded by blood and vainly trying to ward off the blows. Brooks continued hitting him until another member of Congress finally restrained him. Sumner collapsed unconscious.

Northerners were electrified to learn that a senator of the United States had been beaten senseless in the Senate chamber. The next day, news of the "sack of Lawrence," which had occurred one day earlier, arrived. But what caused even greater consternation in the North was southern reaction to Sumner's caning, for in his own region, Preston Brooks was promptly lionized as a hero. Resolutions endorsed his action, souvenir canes descended on him, and supporters feted him with dinners and receptions. Influential papers like the Richmond *Enquirer* urged that other notable Republican members of Congress "be lashed into submission." Instantly, the Sumner caning breathed life into the fledgling Republican party. Its claims about "Bleeding Kansas" and the Slave Power now seemed credible. Sumner, whose injuries proved severe enough to keep him away from the Senate until

The caning of Senator Charles Sumner by Representative Preston Brooks of South Carolina inflamed public opinion. In this northern cartoon, the fallen Sumner, a martyr to free speech, raises his pen against Brooks' club. In the background several prominent Democrats look on in amusement. Rushing to capitalize on the furor, printmakers did not know what the obscure Brooks looked like and thus had to devise ingenious ways of portraying the incident. In this print, Brooks' face is hidden by his raised arm.

SOUTHERN CHIVALRY — ARGUMENT versus CLUB'S.

1860, was reelected anyway in 1857 by the Massachusetts legislature, his chair left vacant as a symbol of southern brutality.

The Election of 1856

Given the storm that had arisen over Kansas, Democrats concluded that no candidate associated with the repeal of the Missouri Compromise had a chance to win. That eliminated President Pierce and the ever-ambitious Senator Douglas. Instead, the Democrats turned to James Buchanan of Pennsylvania, an old party warhorse whose supreme qualification was that he had been out of the country when the Kansas–Nebraska Act was passed.

The American party, which had been badly split by the Kansas issue, nominated former president Millard Fillmore. The Republicans chose John C. Frémont, the western explorer and adventurer who had helped liberate California during the Mexican War. Considerably younger than Fillmore and Buchanan, the dashing Frémont seemed to many a fresh face. His only known opinions were on the subject of slavery, which he opposed in the territories. That suited the Republicans, whose platform denounced slavery as a "relic of barbarism" and who demanded that Kansas be admitted as a free state. Throughout the summer the party hammered away on Bleeding Sumner and Bleeding Kansas. "A constantly increasing excitement is kept up by the intelligence coming every day from Kansas," wrote one knowledgeable observer. "I have never known political excitement—I ought rather to say exasperation—approach that which now rages."

A number of basic principles guided the Republican party, especially the ideal of free labor. Slavery degraded labor, Republicans argued, and would inevitably drive free labor out of the territories. Condemning the South as a stagnant, hierarchical, and economically backward region, Republicans extolled the North as a fluid society of widespread opportunity, where enterprising individuals could improve their lot through hard work and self-discipline. Stopping the expansion of slavery, in Republican eyes, would preserve this heritage of opportunity and economic independence for white Americans. This notion of free labor, which drew a great deal from the traditional Protestant ethic, was of course an idealized vision. Republicans by and large remained blind to the growing concentration of wealth in the North and the extent to which industrialization closed off avenues of social mobility for poor laborers.

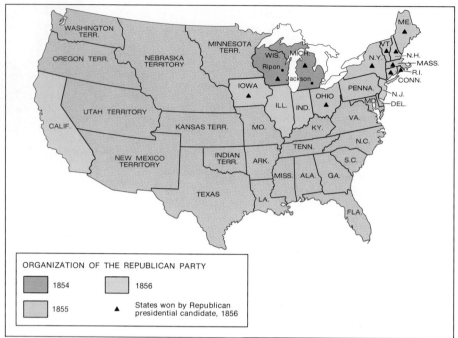

THE EMERGENCE OF THE REPUBLICAN PARTY
In the first two years after its founding in 1854, the Republican party enjoyed only limited success in the North. The turning point came in 1856, when Frémont won a plurality of the popular vote in the North, carried all but five of the free states, and finished second in the presidential contest.

Also important was the moral opposition to slavery, which works like Harriet Beecher Stowe's *Uncle Tom's Cabin* had strengthened. Republican speakers and editors stressed that slavery was a moral wrong, that it was incompatible with the ideals of the Republic and Christianity. Emerging as a prominent Republican leader, Abraham Lincoln spoke out eloquently in the decade against the evil of slavery. "Never forget," he declared on one occasion, "that we have before us this whole matter of the right and wrong of slavery in this Union, though the immediate question is as to its spreading out into new Territories and States."

More negatively, Republicans gained support by shifting their attacks from slavery itself to the Slave Power, or the political influence of the planter class. Since the party's founding, the New York *Times* explained, its "specific aim was to dislodge the slaveholding interest from the ascendency it had acquired over the Federal government, and to render it forever impossible for it to regain that supremacy." Pointing to the Sumner assault and the incidents in Kansas, Republicans contended that the Slave Power had set out to destroy the liberties of northern whites. Since concern for the welfare of blacks was weak in the North, the focus on the rights of whites gave Republicans a more potent appeal. "The issues now before the people," one Republican insisted in the 1856 campaign, "are those of Despotism or Freedom. The question has passed on from that of slavery for negro servants, to that of tyranny over free white men."

All these fears played on a strong northern attachment to the heritage of the

American Revolution. Republicans argued that just as the nation's founders had battled against slavery, tyranny, aristocracy, and minority rule, so the North faced the unrepublican Slave Power. "If our government, for the sake of Slavery, is to be perpetually the representative of a minority, it may continue republican in form, but the substance of its republicanism has departed," argued the Cincinnati *Commercial*. And a New Hampshire Republican paper warned in 1856 that "the liberties of our country are in tenfold the danger that they were at the commencement of the American Revolution. We then had a distant foe to contend with. Now the enemy is within our borders."

News of the violence in Kansas and Sumner's caning nearly won Frémont the presidency, despite his inexperience. He ran ahead of both Buchanan and Fillmore in the North, and won 11 free states out of 16. Had he carried Pennsylvania plus one more, he would have been elected. Still, Buchanan all but swept the South (losing only Maryland to Fillmore) and won enough free states to push him over the top, with 174 electoral votes to Frémont's 114 and Fillmore's 8. Clearly, the Republican party had supplanted the Whigs in the two-party system. For the first time in American history, an antislavery party based entirely in the North threatened to elect a president and snap the bonds of union.

THE WORSENING CRISIS

President James Buchanan had spent much of his life in public service: over 20 years in the House and the Senate, secretary of state under Polk, as well as minister to Russia and to Great Britain. A tall and heavy-set man with flowing white hair, Buchanan struck White House visitors as exceptionally courteous; an eye defect caused him to tilt his head slightly forward and to one side, which reinforced the impression of deference and attentiveness. Yet underneath this facade, he was cold, humorless, and calculating. At bottom a timid man, he had a strong stubborn streak, deeply resented opposition, and overrated his ability to enforce party discipline on those who disagreed with his policies. Throughout his career, Buchanan had taken the southern position on sectional matters. His closest associates remained southerners, and he proved remarkably insensitive to the concerns of northern Democrats.

Moderates in both the North and the South hoped that the new president's diplomatic skills would steer the country clear of Republican radicals and secessionists of the Deep South, popularly known as "fire-eaters." But on March 6, 1857, only two days after Buchanan's inauguration, the Supreme Court gave the new administration a jolt with one of the most controversial decisions in its history.

The *Dred Scott* Decision

The owner of a Missouri slave named Dred Scott had taken him to live for several years in Illinois, a free state, and in the Wisconsin Territory, where slavery had been banned by the Missouri Compromise. Scott had returned to Missouri as a slave, but aided by some antislavery people eventually sued for his freedom. Residence in a free state and a free territory had made him free, he argued. His case ultimately went to the Supreme Court, which had to decide two questions. First, was Scott, a black person, a citizen of Missouri who had the legal right to sue in federal court? And second, if he could sue, was he free by virtue of his having resided in free territory? The Court's decision was so complex that every justice wrote his own opinion, but all five southern members of the Court, plus two northerners, ruled 7–2 that Scott remained a slave. In the majority opinion Chief Justice Roger Taney argued that Scott had voluntarily returned to Missouri and that under Missouri law, which took precedence, he was a slave.

Had the Court stopped there, the public outcry would have been minimal. But the Court majority believed that they had a judicial responsibility to deal with the larger controversy between the two sections, and Chief Justice Taney, in particular, wanted to strengthen the judicial protection of slavery. Taney, a former Maryland slaveowner who had emancipated his slaves, ruled that blacks could not be and never had been citizens of the United States. Instead, he insisted that at the time the Constitution was adopted, blacks were "regarded as beings of an inferior order, so far inferior that they had no rights which the white man was bound to respect." In addition, since Scott had based part of his appeal on the fact that the Missouri Compromise outlawed slavery in the western part of the Wisconsin Territory, the Court ruled that the Compromise was unconstitutional. Congress, it declared, had no power to ban slavery from *any* territory of the United States.

While southerners rejoiced at this unexpected outcome, Republicans were flabbergasted. Their platform declared, after all, that Congress ought to prohibit slavery in all territories. In effect, the Court had ruled their central goal unconstitutional and upheld the extreme southern position. Horace Greeley, the Republican editor of the New York *Tribune*, fumed that the decision was "entitled to just so much moral weight as would be the judgment of a majority of those congregated in any Washington bar-room." Abraham Lincoln was more restrained. "We know the court . . . has often over-ruled its own decisions," he observed, "and we shall do what we can to have it over-rule this." But the decision was sobering. If all territories were now open to slavery, how long would it be before a move was made to reintroduce slavery in the free states? That was precisely what southern Democrats conspired to do, Republican leaders argued.

But the decision also was a blow to Douglas' moderate solution of popular sovereignty. If Congress had no power to prohibit slavery in a territory, how could it authorize a territorial legislature to do so? While the Court did not rule on this point, the clear implication of the *Dred Scott* decision was that popular sovereignty was also unconstitutional. The Court, in effect, had adopted the extreme Calhounite view that slavery was legal in all the territories. In so doing, the Court, which had intended to settle the question of slavery in the territories once and for all, succeeded only in heightening the sense of crisis and strengthening the forces of extremism in American politics.

The Panic of 1857

As the nation grappled with the *Dred Scott* decision, an economic depression aggravated sectional conflict. Once again, boom gave way to bust as falling wheat

Chief Justice Roger Taney.

prices and contracted credit hurt commercial farmers and overextended railroad investors. The Panic of 1857 was nowhere near as severe as the depression of 1837–1843, but the psychological results were far-reaching, for the South remained relatively untouched. With the price of cotton and other southern commodities still high, southern secessionists hailed the panic as proof that an independent southern nation was economically feasible. *DeBow's Review*, the leading commercial journal in the South, argued that southern wealth was real and permanent, whereas northern wealth rested on paper and was fictitious. And James Henry Hammond, a senator from South Carolina, boasted: "What would happen if no cotton was furnished for three years? England would topple headlong and carry the whole civilized world with her save the South. No, you dare not make war on cotton. No power on earth dares to make war on it. Cotton is king."

For their part, northerners sought decisive federal action to bolster the economy—the sort which so many southerners had long opposed. When the North proposed a moderate increase in the tariff duties, which were at their lowest level since 1815, southerners opposed even this moderate measure. Under southern pressure, Buchanan also vetoed bills to improve navigation on the Great Lakes and to give free farms to western settlers. Many businessmen and conservative ex-Whigs concluded that the United States would never be able to develop in the face of southern obstructionism. And the Republicans, hoping to broaden their party's base, began to add economic planks to their platform. Economic issues, in other words, were becoming sectional ones.

The Lecompton Constitution

While the *Dred Scott* decision and economic depression further weakened the bonds of Union, Kansas remained at the center of the political stage. By June 1857, when the territory elected delegates to a convention to draft a state constitution, the worst of the marauding had ended. But free-staters boycotted the election because the voting districts had been unfairly drawn up. As a result, the proslavery majority at the convention meeting in Lecompton promptly drew up a constitution that made slavery legal. Even more boldly, they decided not to allow Kansas voters the chance to reject the constitution. In the referendum that followed, voters could choose only whether to admit additional slaves into the territory; they could not vote against either the constitution or slavery. Once again, free-staters boycotted the election and the Lecompton constitution was approved. In the meantime, however, the free state forces gained control of the territorial legislature and submitted the whole constitution in another referendum, when it was overwhelmingly rejected. In debating the admission of Kansas as a state, Congress had to decide which of the two results to accept.

As an adherent of popular sovereignty, President Buchanan had pledged to support a free and fair vote on the Lecompton constitution. But the outcome offered him the unexpected opportunity to satisfy his southern supporters by pushing the Lecompton constitution through Congress. This was too much for Douglas, who had staked so much on the idea of popular sovereignty. Breaking party ranks, he denounced the Lecompton constitution as a fraud. Nevertheless, the administration prevailed in the Senate. Buchanan now pulled out all the stops

Dred Scott.

to gain the necessary votes in the House, where northern representation was much stronger, to admit Kansas as a slave state. But after one of the fiercest political struggles in American history, the House rejected the Lecompton constitution. In a compromise, Congress, using indirect language, returned the constitution to Kansas for another vote. This time it was decisively defeated, 11,300 to 1788. No doubt remained that as soon as it had sufficient population, Kansas would come into the Union as a free state.

The attempt to force slavery on the people of Kansas drove many conservative northerners to join the Republicans, making that party the most likely victor in 1860. And Douglas, once the Democrats' strongest candidate, now found himself at odds with the Buchanan administration and assailed by the southern wing of his party. On top of that, in the summer of 1858 Douglas faced a desperate fight in his race for reelection to the Senate against Republican Abraham Lincoln.

The Lincoln–Douglas Debates

"He is the strong man of his party . . . and the best stump speaker, with his droll ways and dry jokes, in the West," Douglas commented when he learned of Lincoln's nomination to oppose him. "He is as honest as he is shrewd, and if I beat him my victory will be hardly won." As a Whig, Lincoln had served several terms in the state legislature during the 1830s and 1840s; he had been in Congress two years but had been out of public office for almost a decade. He was a gangly man, with gaunt face, high cheekbones, deep-socketed gray eyes, and a shock of unruly hair. He appeared awkward as he spoke, never knowing quite what to do with his large, muscular hands, and his voice, though strong and clear, sometimes seemed shrill. But his finely honed logic, his simple, eloquent language, and his sincerity carried the audience with him. His sentences, as spare as the man himself, had none of the oratorical flourishes common in that day; they merely laid out propositions to be examined and pondered. "If we could first know *where* we are, and *whither* we are tending, we could then better judge *what* to do, and *how* to do it," Lincoln began, in accepting his party's nomination for senator from Illinois in 1858. And then he went on to dissect Douglas' notion that popular sovereignty could somehow settle the crisis over slavery.

> We are now far into the *fifth* year, since a policy was initiated, with the *avowed* object, and *confident* promise, of putting an end to slavery agitation.
>
> Under the operation of that policy, that agitation has not only, *not ceased,* but has *constantly augmented.*
>
> In my opinion, it *will* not cease, until a *crisis* shall have been reached, and passed.
>
> "A house divided against itself cannot stand."
>
> I believe this government cannot endure, permanently half *slave* and half *free.*
>
> I do not expect the Union to be *dissolved*—I do not expect the house to *fall*—but I *do* expect it will cease to be divided.
>
> It will become *all* one thing, or *all* the other.
>
> Either the *opponents* of slavery, will arrest the further spread of it, and place it where the public mind shall rest in the belief that it is in course of ultimate extinction; or its *advocates* will push it forward, till it shall become alike lawful in all the States, *old* as well as new—*North* as well as *South.*

The message echoed through the hall and across the pages of the national press.

Superb debaters, Douglas (left) and Lincoln nevertheless had very different speaking styles. The deep-voiced Douglas was constantly on the attack, drawing on his remarkable memory and showering points like buckshot in all directions. Employing sarcasm and ridicule rather than humor, he never tried to crack a joke. Lincoln, who had a high-pitched voice and a rather awkward platform manner, developed arguments more methodically, and relied on his sense of humor and unmatched ability as a storyteller to drive his points home to the audience.

Born in the slave state of Kentucky, he had grown up mostly in southern Indiana and central Illinois. He could split rails with the best frontiersman, loved telling stories, and was at home mixing with ordinary folk: lifting weights at a county fair or "standing backs" with a tall man in the crowd to see who had the advantage of height (Lincoln was 6 feet, 4 inches). Yet his intense ambition had lifted him above the rural backwoods from which he came. He compensated for a lack of formal schooling through disciplined self-education, and moving to the capital in Springfield, he became a shrewd courtroom lawyer of respectable social standing. For all that, he stood apart from his society in many ways. He did not drink, and so hated the sight of blood that he did not hunt. He was unswayed by frontier revivalism and, although profoundly sensitive to the power of religion, did not belong to any organized church. Known for his sense of humor, he was nonetheless subject to fits of acute depression, and his eyes often mirrored a deep melancholy.

Lincoln's first love was always politics. At only 25, he entered the state legis-

Daily Lives

PUBLIC SPACE/PRIVATE SPACE

Uncle Tom by Footlights

By 1850 American theaters were a popular, though controversial focal point for public entertainment. The Puritans had roundly condemned plays of any sort, and even in the mid-nineteenth century many ministers and religious critics frowned on theatergoing as an idle diversion. Still, the rise of cities made possible the large audiences needed to support long-run productions. The stage became a medium for mass entertainment, which attracted not only the working classes but, increasingly, the urban middle class.

In 1852 George C. Howard, the head of the Museum Theater in Troy, New York, was casting about for new material. He decided to take up the issue of slavery, which had recently engaged the nation's attention through a controversial new novel, *Uncle Tom's Cabin*. Written by Harriet Beecher Stowe, one of the Reverend Lyman Beecher's energetic daughters, the book's first 5000 copies sold out in two days. Soon four power presses were running night and day (except Sundays) trying to keep up with the demand. Over 300,000 copies were printed in the first year. In the South, although many communities banned the novel, it was read by a remarkable number of the curious.

In trying to turn the novel into a play, Howard faced substantial problems. While full of vivid and dramatic incidents, the plot of *Uncle Tom's Cabin* followed a host of characters to a multitude of locales. When a debt-ridden Kentucky family is forced to sell some of its slaves, George and Eliza Harris, a mulatto slave couple, learn that their young son is to be one of them. Eliza flees north to freedom across the ice-choked Ohio River, her child clinging to her breast. At the same time, Tom, an older slave and a devout Christian, submits to his sale and is taken south. There he meets Evangeline St. Clare, an innocent, golden-haired child, who convinces her father to buy Tom and take him to their home in New Orleans. For a time Tom is treated kindly, but after both Evangeline and her father die, Tom is sold to Simon Legree, a hard-drinking, blasphemous Yankee, who owns a plantation on the Red River in Louisiana. When Tom steadfastly refuses to whip other slaves, Legree beats him to death; Tom is a martyr to his faith in God and his love for his fellow man.

Compressing this complex story was not easy. Then, too, no American play on the subject of slavery had been produced. Many theater managers believed that the public would not accept a black hero. Indeed, black characters were rare on stage except in minstrel shows. But Howard liked the idea of casting his four-year-old daughter Cordelia (already an experienced trouper) as young Eva, and he decided to proceed. A member of the repertory company, George Aiken, wrote an adaptation that focused on Tom's experiences in the St. Clare household.

The play ran successfully for four weeks prompting Aiken to write a sequel, *The Death of Uncle Tom*, based on the Legree section of the novel; finally he combined the two plays into a 6-act, 30-scene epic that took an entire evening to perform. To make the plot coherent would have required almost twice as many scenes, so Aiken actually sacrificed coherence for playability. Aiken's adaptation became the classic stage version of *Uncle Tom's Cabin*. From Troy the production moved to New York City, where it ran for an unprecedented 325 performances and then achieved similar triumphs in other

Daily Lives

CONSOLIDATED WITH

UNCLE TOM'S CABIN

In this playbill advertising a production of *Uncle Tom's Cabin*, vicious bloodhounds pursue Eliza clutching her child as she frantically leaps to safety across the ice-choked Ohio River.

northern cities. No play had ever attracted such large audiences.

Aiken had a good eye for the dramatic: a slave auction, Eva's death after a long illness, and Tom's defiance of Legree when threatened with a whipping. ("My soul a'nt yours, mas'r; you haven't bought it—ye can't buy it.") Eliza's flight across the icy Ohio River—described in two paragraphs in the book—became one of the major scenes, with a pack of bloodhounds added for good measure. Furthermore, since audiences of melodrama were accustomed to comic interludes between dramatic scenes, Aiken expanded the humorous potential of certain characters and added a new one, Gumption Cute, a swindling slavecatcher. As in minstrel shows, blacks were played by whites wearing lampblack.

Despite these additions, the play remained essentially faithful to the book's antislavery message. And Howard worked hard to attract a new middle-class audi-ence. He banned the prostitutes who so often frequented theaters, and in the lobby displayed the endorsements of prominent religious leaders and reformers on posters. A further innovation, matinee performances, attracted women and children. As one reporter for the New York *Atlas* commented, instead of newsboys and apprentices, he saw "many people who have been taught to look on the stage with horror and contempt." Even Harriet Beecher Stowe, who disapproved of having her book turned into a play, at last discreetly attended a performance, her head carefully covered with a shawl. And in a departure from the normal policy of New York theaters, blacks were allowed to attend, seated in a segregated section accessible through a separate entrance.

The play moved audiences of all backgrounds. After wrestling with his religious scruples, John Kirk, a traveling salesman from Chicago, finally went to see a production. He laughed uproariously at the humor, but confessed, "My laughing soon turned to weeping. The appeals of the dying little Eva to her father, for Uncle Tom's freedom, were overwhelmingly affecting. . . . I must confess that I never saw so many white pocket handkerchiefs in use at the same time, and, for the same purpose before. I was not the only one in that large audience to shed tears I assure you." Equally striking, the play affected the workers and apprentices who made up the theater's normal clientele. Traditionally hostile to abolitionism, these groups cheered wildly over Eliza's escape and shouted approval of her antislavery speeches. By providing vivid images of the cruelties and suffering under slavery, theatrical presentations of *Uncle Tom's Cabin*, even more than the book, heightened the sectional tensions that increasingly divided the nation in the 1850s.

lature and went on to become one of the leaders of the Whig party in Illinois. He fervently admired Henry Clay and his economic program. But after 1848, with Illinois staunchly Democratic, his political activities waned until the repeal of the Missouri Compromise rekindled his zeal. He eventually joined the Republican party and became one of its key leaders in the state. In a series of seven joint debates, Lincoln challenged Douglas to discuss the issues of slavery and the sectional controversy. Crowds of 5000, 10,000, and even 15,000 men, women, and children gathered all across Illinois by torchlight, or in drizzling rain, or under a blazing sun, to support their candidate and weigh the issues.

In a state that was antislavery but also strongly racist, Douglas sought to portray Lincoln as a radical whose "House Divided" speech preached sectional warfare. The nation *could* endure half slave and half free, Douglas declared, so long as states and territories were left alone to regulate their own affairs. Accusing Lincoln of believing that the black man was his equal, Douglas suggested sarcastically that his opponent could now accept the black man as "his brother," whereas Douglas was already on record that the American government had been "made by the white man, for the white man, to be administered by the white man."

Lincoln countered by insisting that the spread of slavery was a blight on the Republic. Even though Douglas had voted against the Lecompton constitution, he could not be counted on to oppose slavery's expansion, for he had already admitted that he didn't care whether slavery was voted "down or up." That, after all, was what popular sovereignty was all about. For his part, Lincoln denied any "perfect equality between the negroes and white people" and opposed allowing blacks to vote, hold office, or intermarry with whites. But, he concluded,

> Notwithstanding all this, there is no reason in the world why the negro is not entitled to all the natural rights enumerated in the Declaration of Independence, the right to life, liberty and the pursuit of happiness. . . . I agree with Judge Douglas [that the negro] is not my equal in many respects—certainly not in color, perhaps not in moral or intellectual endowment. But in the right to eat the bread, without leave of anybody else, which his own hand earns, *he is my equal and the equal of Judge Douglas, and the equal of every living man.*

In the debate held at Freeport, Illinois, Lincoln asked Douglas how the people of a territory could lawfully exclude slavery before statehood, since the *Dred Scott* decision seemed to make that impossible. Douglas answered, with what became known as the Freeport Doctrine, that slavery could exist only with the protection of positive law, and that whatever abstract rights slaveowners possessed, they would not bring their slaves into an area that did not have a slave code. Therefore, Douglas explained, if the people of a territory refused to pass a slave code, slavery would never be established there.

In a close race, the legislature elected Douglas to another term in the Senate.* But on the national scene, southern Democrats angrily repudiated him and condemned the Freeport Doctrine. And although Lincoln lost, Republicans thought his impressive performance marked him as a possible presidential contender for 1860.

---

*State legislatures elected senators until 1913, when the Seventeenth Amendment was adopted. While Lincoln and Douglas both campaigned for the office, Illinois voters actually voted for candidates for the legislature who were pledged to one of the senatorial candidates.

The Beleaguered South

While northerners increasingly feared that the Slave Power was conspiring to extend slavery into the free states, southerners worried that the "Black Republicans" would hem them in and undermine their political power.

The very factors that brought prosperity during the 1850s stimulated the South's sense of crisis. As the price of land and slaves rose sharply, fewer small farmers could hope to become slaveowners. The proportion of southerners who owned slaves had dropped almost a third since 1830. Land also was being consolidated into larger holdings. Between 1850 and 1860, the average farm size rose in the South by 20 percent: in Alabama from 289 to 346 acres, and in Mississippi from 309 to 370 acres. Planters were increasing their wealth at the expense of the bottom half of society. In earlier decades, small farm families might have pushed westward, as many continued to do during the 1850s by moving to Texas. But California and Kansas had been closed to southern slaveholders—unfairly, in their eyes—and the *Dred Scott* decision had been negated.

Several possible solutions to the South's internal crisis had failed. Agricultural reform to restore worn-out lands had made significant headway in Virginia and Maryland, but elsewhere the rewards of a single-crop economy were just too great. Like most Americans, southerners preferred to exploit the soil and then move west. In some counties, over half the slaveholders left in a decade. Another alternative—industrialization—had also failed. Indeed, the gap between the North and the South steadily widened in the 1850s. More controversial was the movement to reopen the African slave trade, which became the cry of many fire-eaters after 1850, but which never attracted wide support in the South. A few militant southerners launched their own private military expeditions in the Caribbean during the 1850s, hoping to add Cuba, Mexico, or Nicaragua to the United States as slave territories. But all of these "filibustering" expeditions came to naught. They demonstrated, however, how much the sense of internal crisis made southerners more willing to consider aggressive and extremist solutions.

The South's growing sense of moral and political isolation made this crisis more acute. By the 1850s, slavery had been abolished throughout most of the Americas, and in the United States the South's political power was steadily shrinking. The House had been lost decades ago, the Senate in 1850, and only the expansion of slavery held out any promise of new slave states needed to preserve the South's political power and protect its way of life. For a growing number of southerners, geographic expansion had become a panacea for the section's problems. "The truth is," fumed one Alabama politician, " . . . the South is excluded from the common territories of the Union. The right of expansion claimed to be a necessity of her continued existence, is practically and effectively denied the South."

To defend their embattled way of life, southern whites appealed to the heritage of the Revolution. For them, republicanism consisted of individual liberty, self-government, and equality of opportunity for all whites. Slavery was the linchpin of this system, for it preserved equality among whites and guaranteed all whites, regardless of wealth, a certain pride and status. "Break down slavery," Governor Henry Wise of Virginia maintained, "and you would with the same blow destroy the democratic principle of equality among men." A Georgia newspaper echoed those sentiments: "Slavery," it insisted, "is the best foundation for a *permanent* republican government."

THE ROAD TO WAR

After 1854 a series of blows weakened the forces of compromise and moderation at the nation's political center. But none struck with the force of the news from the quiet town of Harpers Ferry, Virginia. Behind it was none other than John Brown of Pottawatomie.

Harpers Ferry

In 1857 Brown had returned to the East from Kansas, consumed with the idea of attacking slavery in the South itself. Financed by a number of prominent northern reformers (who were unaware of his role in the Pottawatomie killings), Brown gathered a small force of 21 followers, including five free blacks, with the design of fomenting a slave insurrection. On the night of October 16, 1859, they attacked the unguarded federal armory at Harpers Ferry. It fell easily enough, but no slaves rallied to his standard, for the area had few to begin with. Before long the alarm went out and Brown found himself holed up in the armory's engine house with hostile townspeople taking potshots at his army of liberation. Charging with bayonets fixed, federal troops commanded by Colonel Robert E. Lee soon captured Brown and his band.

The "invasion" itself was an ill-planned, dismal failure, as were most of the enterprises Brown undertook in his troubled life. But the old man knew well how to bear himself with a martyr's dignity. At his trial he made an impassioned case against slavery. "Had I so interfered in behalf of the rich, the powerful, the intelligent, the so-called great," he declared, ". . . it would have been all right. Every man in this court would have deemed it an act worthy of reward rather than punishment. . . . I believe that to have interfered as I have done in behalf of [God's] despised poor, is no wrong, but a right." On December 2, 1859, Virginia hanged Brown for treason.

John Brown's enduring legacy sprang not from his ill-conceived raid but from the popular reaction to his cause. With the election of 1860 looming and victory seemingly within their grasp, Republicans sought to distance themselves from abolitionist radicals. Hurriedly they denounced Brown's raid as "the gravest of crimes." But other northerners were less cautious. Ralph Waldo Emerson described Brown as a "saint, whose martyrdom will make the gallows as glorious as the cross," and on the day of his execution, church bells tolled in many northern cities. Only a minority of northerners endorsed Brown, but southerners were shocked by such public displays of sympathy. And they were firmly convinced that the Republican party was secretly connected to the raid. The legislatures of Alabama, Mississippi, and Florida all passed resolutions declaring that the election of a Republican president would justify secession, while countless southerners for the first time seriously considered the prospect. "I have always been a fervid Union man," one North Carolina resident wrote, "but I confess the endorsement of the Harpers Ferry outrage has shaken my fidelity and I am willing to take the chances of every probable evil that may arise from disunion, sooner than submit any longer to Northern insolence and Northern outrage."

John Brown.

A Sectional Election

When Congress convened in December, only three days after John Brown was executed, there were ominous signs everywhere of the growing sectional rift. Intent on destroying Douglas' Freeport Doctrine, southern radicals in Congress issued a platform for the 1860 election which demanded a federal slave code to protect slavery in the territories. Northern Democrats denounced this demand as provocative, since no settlers in any territory had requested such protection. Moreover, for them to support such a platform spelled political death. As one Indiana Democrat put it, "We cannot carry a single congressional district on that doctrine in the state."

The Democratic convention met in April in Charleston, South Carolina, the hotbed of southern extremism. The packed galleries cheered on the fire-eaters, who boldly pressed their demand for a federal slave code as a way to force Douglas out of the race. An angry Senator George Pugh of Ohio spoke for the Douglas forces: "Gentlemen of the South, you mistake us,—you mistake us. We will not do it." After six days of heated debate, the convention adopted the Douglas platform upholding popular sovereignty, whereupon the delegations from the entire Deep South, plus Arkansas, walked out. Unable to agree on a candidate, the convention adjourned to reassemble two months later in Baltimore. There, Douglas was nominated, but most of the remaining southern Democrats left in disgust. Joining with the Charleston seceders, they nominated their own candidate, Vice President John C. Breckinridge of Kentucky, on a platform supporting a federal slave code. With a northern and a southern Democratic candidate in the field, the last major national party had shattered.

In May the Republicans convened in Chicago. In the end, the delegates turned to Abraham Lincoln, who could help carry his doubtful home state of Illinois, was a moderate on slavery, and was acceptable to all factions of the party, including the Germans and the former Know-Nothings. Republicans also sought to

THE ELECTION OF 1860

Although Lincoln did not win a majority of the popular vote, he still would have been elected even if the votes for all three of his opponents had been combined, since he won a clear majority in every state he carried except California, Oregon, and New Jersey (whose electoral votes he split with Douglas).

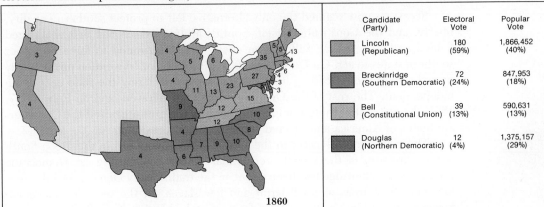

Candidate (Party)	Electoral Vote	Popular Vote
Lincoln (Republican)	180 (59%)	1,866,452 (40%)
Breckinridge (Southern Democratic)	72 (24%)	847,953 (18%)
Bell (Constitutional Union)	39 (13%)	590,631 (13%)
Douglas (Northern Democratic)	12 (4%)	1,375,157 (29%)

1860

broaden their appeal by adding to their platform several economic planks that endorsed a moderately protective tariff, a homestead bill, and a northern transcontinental railroad.

The election that followed was really two contests in one. In the North, which had a majority of the electoral votes, only Lincoln and Douglas had any chance to carry a state. In the South, the race pitted Breckinridge against John Bell of Tennessee, the candidate of the Constitutional Union party, which represented yet another attempt to create a national conservative party. When the votes were counted, Lincoln had less than 40 percent of the popular vote and virtually no support in the South. But he won 180 electoral votes, 27 more than needed for election. Breckinridge ran first in the South and swept the Deep South. The two sectional parties (Lincoln and Breckinridge) had overwhelmed the two Unionist parties (Douglas and Bell). Douglas, the only candidate with support in all areas of the country, finished second in the popular vote but won only 12 electoral votes. For the first time, the nation had elected a president who headed a completely sectional party and who was committed to stopping the expansion of slavery.

Secession

Although the Republicans had not won control of either house of Congress, Lincoln's election struck many southerners as a blow of terrible finality. Lincoln had been lifted into office on the strength of the free states alone. With Republicans opposing slavery in the territories, the South's power base could only diminish. Although the Supreme Court had traditionally checked the abuses of majority rule, Republicans refused to accept the *Dred Scott* decision and had spent the last four years bitterly assailing the Court.

What would Lincoln do, once in office? It was not unrealistic, southern radicals argued, to believe that he would use federal aid to induce the border states to voluntarily emancipate their slaves. Once slavery disappeared there, and new states were added, the necessary three-fourths majority would exist to approve a constitutional amendment abolishing slavery. Or perhaps Lincoln might send other John Browns into the South, to stir up more slave insurrections. The Montgomery (Alabama) *Mail* accused Republicans of intending "to free the negroes and force amalgamation between them and the children of the poor men of the South." Reinforcing these arguments was the comforting opinion held by many white southerners that secession was not only constitutional, but it would also be peaceful.

Secession now seemed the only alternative left to protect southern equality, liberty, and the Constitution itself. South Carolina, which had first challenged federal authority in the nullification crisis, was determined to force the other southern states to act. On December 20, 1860, a popular convention unanimously passed a resolution seceding from the Union and declaring the state once again independent. The rest of the Deep South quickly followed, and on February 7, 1861, the states stretching from South Carolina to Texas organized the Confederate States of America and elected Jefferson Davis president.

The voting for delegates to the secessionist conventions in the Deep South was not a rerun of the recent presidential contest. As the regular Democratic candidate, Breckinridge had been strong in the traditionally Democratic hill counties and other areas of small farms and few slaves. In the secession elections, however, these Democratic yeoman farmers backed Unionist candidates, whereas

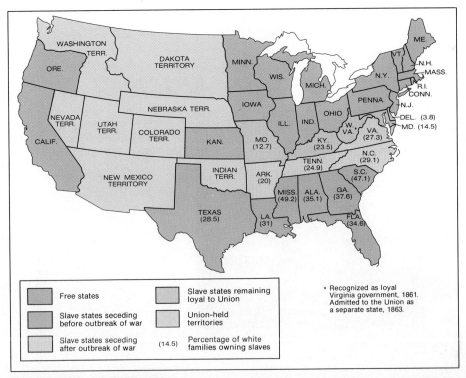

Free states

Slave states seceding before outbreak of war

Slave states seceding after outbreak of war

Slave states remaining loyal to Union

Union-held territories

(14.5)   **Percentage of white families owning slaves**

• Recognized as loyal Virginia government, 1861. Admitted to the Union as a separate state, 1863.

THE PATTERN OF SECESSION
Led by South Carolina, the Deep South seceded between Lincoln's election in November and his inauguration in March. The Upper South did not secede until after the firing on Fort Sumter. The four border slave states never seceded and remained in the Union throughout the war. As the map indicates, secession sentiment was strongest in states where the highest percentage of white families owned slaves.

slaveowners, many of whom had voted for Bell in the presidential election, endorsed secession by decided margins. As a general rule, the higher the concentration of slaves in a county, the greater was its support for secession. When the issue shifted to protecting slavery, slaveholders chose secession. Certainly large numbers of nonslaveholders backed secession also, but in its driving force, secession was a slaveholders' revolution.

But the Upper South and the border states declined to follow, hoping that once again Congress could patch together a settlement. Senator John Crittenden of Kentucky, who now held the seat of the Great Compromiser himself, Henry Clay, proposed extending to the Pacific the old Missouri Compromise line of 36° 30'. Slavery would be prohibited north of this line and given federal protection south of it in all territories, including any acquired in the future. Furthermore, Crittenden proposed an "unamendable amendment" to the Constitution, forever preserving slavery in states where it already existed. To reassure jittery southerners, Crittenden introduced these and several other provisions designed to protect slaveowners as constitutional amendments rather than ordinary statutes.

But the Crittenden Compromise was doomed, for the simple reason that the two groups who were required to make concessions—Republicans and secessionists—had no interest in doing so. "The argument is exhausted," representatives from the Deep South announced, even before Crittenden had introduced his

When Confederate batteries opened fire on Fort Sumter, Charleston civilians climbed to their roofs to witness the bombardment. "The women were wild, there on the housetop," one Charleston woman reported. "Prayers from the women and imprecations from the men, and then a shell would light up the scene." The Civil War had begun.

package. Although President-elect Lincoln maintained a public silence, he privately threw all his influence against any compromise that permitted slavery in new territories. "We have just carried an election on principles fairly stated to the people," he commented. "Now we are told in advance, the government shall be broken up, unless we surrender to those we have beaten, before we take the offices. If we surrender, it is the end of us, and of the government."

The Outbreak of War

As his inauguration approached, Lincoln pondered what to do about secession and the seizure of federal property, including forts, arsenals, and customshouses, by the seceded states. In his inaugural address on March 4, he sought to reassure southerners that he had no intention, "directly or indirectly, to interfere with the institution of slavery in the States where it exists." He pledged to enforce the fugitive slave law. But he maintained that the Union of the states was a solemn compact that no state "upon its own mere motion" could break unilaterally. "The Union of these states is perpetual," he declared, echoing Andrew Jackson's Proclamation on Nullification. He also announced that he intended to "hold, occupy and possess" federal property and collect customs duties under the tariff. Appealing to the "bonds of affection" that united all Americans, he told southerners in closing that the choice between peace and war rested with them.

Lincoln hoped for time to work out a solution, but on his first day in office he learned that Major Robert Anderson, commander of the federal garrison at Fort Sumter, one of the few remaining federal outposts in the South, had just informed the government that he was almost out of food. Located on an artificial island in the middle of Charleston harbor, the fort had been isolated since January by southern forces hoping to starve the occupants into submission. Anderson's dispatch indicated that without additional supplies, he would have to capitulate within six weeks. For a month Lincoln looked for a way out, but he finally sent a relief expedition. As a conciliatory gesture, he notified the governor of South Carolina that supplies were being sent, and that if the fleet were allowed to pass, only food, and not men, arms, or ammunition, would be landed.

The burden of decision now shifted to Jefferson Davis. From his point of view, secession was a constitutional right, and the Confederacy was not a spurious but a real government. To allow the United States to hold property and maintain military forces within the Confederacy would destroy its claim of independence. Lincoln's decision to resupply Fort Sumter, Davis argued, was an act of aggression. After two days of debate with his cabinet, he ordered the commander at Charleston, General Pierre Beauregard, to demand the immediate surrender of Fort Sumter and, if refused, to open fire. When Anderson declined the ultimatum, Confederate batteries began shelling on April 12 at 4:30 a.m. Some 33 hours and 5000 rounds of artillery later, Anderson surrendered. When in response Lincoln called for 75,000 volunteers to put down the rebellion, four states in the Upper South, led by Virginia, also seceded. Matters had passed beyond compromise.

The Roots of a Divided Society

And so the Union was sundered. After 70 years, the forces of sectionalism and separatism had finally outpulled the ties binding "these United States." Why did affairs come to such a pass?

In some ways, we have seen, the revolution in markets, the improving technologies of transportation, the increasingly sophisticated systems of credit and finance, all served to tie the nation together. The cotton planter who rode the steamship *Fashion* along the Alabama River ("Time's money! Time's money!") was wearing ready-made clothes manufactured in New York from southern cotton. Chauncey Jerome's clocks from Connecticut were keeping time not only for commercial planters, to whom time was money, but for Lowell mill workers like Mary Paul, who learned to measure her lunch break in minutes. Wheat farmers in Athens, Tennessee, and Ottumwa, Iowa, were interested in the Crimean War, because the war affected the price of wheat, and the price of wheat affected the profits that could be made shipping their grain by the new railroad lines. American society had become far more specialized, and therefore far more interdependent, since the days of Crèvecoeur's self-sufficient farmer of the 1780s.

But a specialized economy had not brought unity. For the North, specialization meant more factories, a higher percentage of urban workers, and a greater number of cities and towns—themselves signs of specialization. Industry affected midwestern farmers as well, for their steel plows and McCormick reapers allowed them to farm larger holdings and required greater capital investment in the new machines. For its part, the South was transformed by the industrial revolution too, as textile factories made cotton the booming mainstay of its economy. But for all its growth, the region remained largely a rural society. Its prosperity stemmed from expansion westward into new areas of cotton production, and the dominant planter class reinforced the concepts of honor, hierarchy, and deference.

Above all, the intensive labor required to produce cotton, rice, and sugar made slavery an inseparable part of the southern way of life—"so intimately mingled with our social conditions," as one Georgian admitted, "that it would be impossible to eradicate it." An increasing number of northerners viewed slavery as evil, not so much out of high-minded sympathy toward slaves, but as a labor system that threatened the republican ideals of white American society.

If the United States had not grown so dynamically—if its frontier had not swept so quickly toward the Pacific—the nation might have been able to postpone the day of reckoning on slavery. It might have found ways to compromise or to rationalize its creed that "all men are created equal," until some form of gradual emancipation could have been adopted. But the luxury of time was not available. The new territories became the battlegrounds for two contrasting ways of life, with slavery at the center of the debate. Nor did those Americans, North and South, black and white, who saw the issue in moral terms think the question should be postponed.

It fell to the political system to try to adjudicate sectional conflict, through debate within the framework of a democratic republic and through a system of national parties that represented various interest groups. But the political system had critical weaknesses. The American system of electing a president gave the winning candidate a state's entire electoral vote, regardless of the margin of victory. (Lincoln, with a total of 1.9 million ballots cast for him, received 180 electoral votes; Douglas, with 1.3 million, received only 12.) That procedure made a northern sectional party possible, since the Republicans could never have carried an election on the basis of popular vote alone. In addition, the four-year fixed presidential term allowed Pierce and Buchanan to remain in office, pursuing disruptive policies on Kansas, even after the voters had rejected those policies in 1854 and 1858. Finally, since 1844 the Democratic party had required a two-thirds vote to nominate its presidential candidate. Unintentionally, this requirement made it difficult to pick any truly forceful leader and gave the South a veto over the party's candidate. Yet the South, by itself, could not elect a president.

The nation's republican heritage also contributed to the political system's vulnerability. Ever since the Revolution, when Americans accused the king and Parliament of deliberately conspiring to deprive them of their liberties, Americans had been accustomed to suspecting the motives of political opponents. Such an outlook often stimulated exaggerated fears, unreasonable conclusions, and excessive reactions. For their part, Republicans emphasized the existence of the Slave Power bent on eradicating northern rights, while southerners accused the Black Republicans of conspiring to destroy southern equality. Each side viewed itself as defending the country's republican tradition from an internal threat; each side came to feel that defeat would mean the end of republicanism.

In 1850, southerners might have been satisfied if their section had been left alone and the agitation against slavery had ended. But a decade later, many Americans both North and South had come to accept the idea of an irrepressible conflict between two societies, one based on freedom, the other on slavery, in which only one side could ultimately prevail. At stake, it seemed, was control of the nation's future. As a weary Abraham Lincoln looked back to the beginning of the conflict four years later, he noted, "Both parties deprecated war, but one of them would *make* war rather than let the nation survive, and the other would *accept* war rather than let it perish, and the war came."

SIGNIFICANT EVENTS

1834	McCormick patents mechanical reaper
1837	John Deere patents steel plow
1840–1860	Expansion of railroad network
1846–1854	Mass immigration to United States
1849–1860	Cotton boom
1850	Illinois Central is first land grant railroad
1852	Pierce elected president
1853	Gadsden Purchase; Know-Nothings begin expanding
1854	Kansas–Nebraska Act; Republican party organized; Ostend Manifesto; peak of immigration
1854–1855	Height of Know-Nothings' popularity
1855	Fighting begins in Kansas; Republican party organizes in key northern states
1856	Free state "government" established in Kansas; "Sack of Lawrence"; caning of Charles Sumner; Pottawatomie massacre; first railroad bridge built across the Mississippi; Buchanan elected president
1857–1861	Panic and depression
1857	*Dred Scott* decision; Lecompton constitution drafted
1858	Congress rejects Lecompton constitution; Lincoln–Douglas debates
1859	John Brown's raid on Harpers Ferry
1860	Democratic party ruptures at Charleston; Lincoln elected president; South Carolina secedes
1861	Rest of Deep South secedes; Confederate States of America established; Crittenden Compromise defeated; war begins at Fort Sumter; Upper South secedes

16

Total War and the Republic

Off they went, one and all," a congressman reported, "off down the highway, over across fields towards the woods, anywhere, everywhere, to escape." Panic-stricken, their faces streaked and blackened by the powder of their cartridges, they threw away their knapsacks, their canteens, their cartridge boxes, even their rifles—everything—as they fled. In their headlong rush, they shoved aside officers who tried to stop them, ignored congressmen waving revolvers, and raced frantically by the wagons, caissons, and civilians' carriages that clogged the roads. They didn't stop until they reached Washington.

July 21, 1861, had begun as a festive outing. For weeks the drumbeat in Horace Greeley's influential New York *Tribune* had been "Forward to Richmond! The Rebel Congress must not be allowed to meet there on the 20th of July!" As the Union army under the command of General Irvin McDowell moved toward the Confederates concentrated at Manassas Junction, members of Congress, joined by jaunty male and female sightseers, their picnic baskets filled with provisions and fine wines, drove buggies and other conveyances the 25 miles from Washington to see the battle that would crush the rebellion.*

In truth, both armies were composed of raw, undisciplined troops. Few had ever marched together, or fired their rifles in coordinated fashion; indeed, they were more likely to mill about and shoot their own comrades by mistake. Worse yet, neither side had ever deployed such massive bodies of men before: McDowell commanded 30,000 troops against General Pierre Beauregard's 22,000. (During the Mexican War, American armies had usually numbered from 5000 to 10,000.) The fighting surged back and forth near a stream called Bull Run, until Confederate reinforcements under General Thomas "Stonewall" Jackson turned the tide. Railroads had allowed Jackson to transfer his forces in timely fashion; and it was here that he won his nickname, for holding his line so staunchly.

After McDowell ordered a retreat, his green Union soldiers panicked when fired upon while on the road, and the retreat became a rout. Discipline dissolved, the army degenerated into a mob, and a stampede began. All the next day in a drizzling rain, the mud-spattered troops straggled into the capital. The remnants

*The Union and Confederacy often gave different names to a battle. The Confederates called the first battle Manassas; the Union, Bull Run.

Winslow Homer's Rainy Day in Camp, *realistically portrays the tedium and discomfort of camp life. In the world's first total war, victory depended on massing and bringing to bear the North's superior resources.*

of various regiments mingled pell-mell. William Russell, an English reporter, asked one pale officer where they were coming from. "Well, sir, I guess we're all coming out of Virginny as far as we can, and pretty well whipped too," he replied. "I know I'm going home. I've had enough of fighting to last my lifetime."

The rout at Bull Run sobered the North. Gone were dreams of ending the war with one glorious battle. Gone was the illusion that 75,000 volunteers serving three months could crush the rebellion. As one perceptive observer noted, "We have undertaken to make war without in the least knowing how."

Still, it was not surprising that both sides underestimated the magnitude of the conflict. As the conduct of war had evolved in Europe, fighting between armies consisted largely of maneuverings that took relatively few lives, did little damage, respected private property, and left civilians largely unharmed. In that respect, the Mexican War was like the War of 1812 or the American Revolution. The Civil War, on the other hand, was the first war anywhere whose major battles routinely involved over 100,000 troops. So many combatants could be equipped only through the use of factory-produced weaponry; they could be mobilized and moved only with the help of railroad networks; and they could be sustained only through the concerted efforts of civilian society as a whole. The morale of the population, the quality of political leadership, and the utilization of industrial and economic might were all critical to the outcome. By the time the fighting ended, few Americans had not been personally touched by the bloody conflict, and society had been fundamentally transformed. Quite simply, the Civil War was the first total war in history.

THE DEMANDS OF TOTAL WAR

When the war began, the North had an enormous advantage in manpower and industrial capacity. The Union's population was 2.5 times larger, and its advantage in white men of military age even greater. The North had a stronger navy and merchant marine, it produced more iron, firearms, and textiles, and it had in place more railroad track and rolling stock. Creating goods worth $1.5 billion, its 110,000 establishments dwarfed in capacity the 18,000 Confederate manufacturing concerns, whose products were worth $155 million.

From a modern perspective, the South's attempt to defend its independence against such odds would seem a hopeless cause. Yet this view indicates how much the conception of war has changed since then. European observers, who knew the strength and resources of the two sides, believed that the Confederacy, with its large area, poor roads, and rugged terrain, could never be conquered. Indeed, the South enjoyed definite strategic advantages. To be victorious, it did not need to invade the North or capture a single mile of territory—only to defend its own land, prevent the North from destroying its armies, and break the Union's will to fight. Southern soldiers knew the topography of their home country better, and a friendly population regularly supplied them with intelligence about Union troop movements.

The North, in contrast, had to invade and conquer the Confederacy and destroy the southern will to resist. To do so, its armies would be forced to use

Resources of the Union and the Confederacy, 1861

	UNION	CONFEDERACY	UNION ADVANTAGE
Total population	22,300,000	9,100,000*	2.5 to 1
White male population (18–45 years)	4,600,000	1,100,000	4.2 to 1
Bank deposits	$207,000,000	$47,000,000	4.4 to 1
Value of manufactured goods	$1,730,000,000	$156,000,000	11 to 1
Railroad mileage	22,000	9,000	2.4 to 1
Shipping tonnage	4,600,000	290,000	16 to 1
Value of textiles produced	$181,000,000	$10,000,000	18 to 1
Value of firearms produced	$2,290,000	$73,000	31 to 1
Pig iron production (tons)	951,000	37,000	26 to 1
Coal production (tons)	13,680,000	650,000	21 to 1
Corn and wheat production (bushels)	698,000,000	314,000,000	2.2 to 1
Draft animals	5,800,000	2,900,000	2 to 1
Cotton production (bales)	43,000	5,344,000	1 to 124

*Slaves accounted for 3,500,000, or 40 percent.

Sources: U.S. Census 1860; E. B. Long, *The Civil War Day by Day* (New York: Doubleday, 1971), p. 723.

thousands of soldiers to defend long supply lines into enemy territory, a situation that significantly reduced the northern advantage in manpower. Only half the Union troops, compared to three-fourths of the Confederates, were available for combat duty. Yet in the end, the Union's resources and population proved so superior that the Confederacy was not only invaded and conquered but also utterly destroyed. By 1865 the Union forces had penetrated virtually every part of the 500,000 square miles of the Confederacy and were able to move almost at will. The Civil War demonstrated the capacity of a modern society to overcome distance and terrain with technology.

Political Leadership

To sustain a commitment to total war required effective political leadership, especially in a democracy, where coercion of the populace has limits. The task of leadership fell on Abraham Lincoln and Jefferson Davis, who ironically had been born within a hundred miles of each other in Kentucky, before both their families moved west.

The Davises chose Mississippi, where they became part of planter society on the cotton frontier. Assisted in his early life by his wealthy older brother, Jefferson Davis was accustomed to life's advantages. He had been educated at Transylvania University and then West Point. After fighting in the Mexican War, he became one of the South's leading advocates in the Senate, as well as serving as Franklin Pierce's secretary of war. Tall and stately, sensitive about his reputation, the new Confederate president looked and acted like an aristocrat. Although he was extremely hardworking and committed to the cause he led, he quarreled tactlessly with generals and politicians, nursed grudges, and refused to work with those he personally disliked. "He cannot brook opposition or criticism," one member of the Confederate Congress testified, "and those who do not bow down before him have no chance of success with him."

Not surprisingly, a man of such temperament was not well suited to rousing the southern people. His cabinet, with whom he was often at odds, changed constantly; 14 men held its six posts in four years. Yet for all Davis' personal handicaps, he faced an institutional one even more daunting. To meet the demands of total war, he would need to centralize and increase the authority of the government beyond anything the South had ever experienced. And yet the Confederate States of America had seceded in opposition to control by the federal majority. With the doctrine of states' rights so crucial to southern ideology, even a popular leader would have faced serious obstacles in coordinating resistance.

When Lincoln took the oath of office, his national experience consisted of one term in the House of Representatives. He had never held an administrative office, and even his friends worried that his new task was beyond him. But Lincoln was a shrewd judge of character and a superb politician. To achieve a common goal, he willingly overlooked withering criticism and personal slights. (The commander of the Union army, General George McClellan, for one, continually snubbed the president and referred to him as "the original Gorilla.") He was not easily humbugged, overawed, or flattered, and never allowed personal feelings to blind him to his larger objectives. "No man knew better how to summon and dispose of political ability to attain great political ends," one contemporary commented.

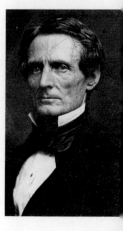

Jefferson Davis.

"This is essentially a People's contest," Lincoln asserted at the start of the war, and few presidents have been better able to communicate with the average citizen. Several times a week, the president opened the White House doors to the general public to hear their praise, complaints, or requests—his "public opinion baths," he called them. He regularly visited Union troops in army hospitals, at field encampments, and on the parade ground, more often than not astride some horse too small to accommodate his lanky frame. "The boys liked him," wrote Joseph Twichell, from a Connecticut regiment, "in fact his popularity with the army is and has been universal." Always Lincoln reminded the public that the war was being fought for the ideals of the Revolution and the Republic. It was a test, he remarked in his famous address at Gettysburg, of whether a nation "conceived in Liberty, and dedicated to the proposition that all men are created equal" could "long endure." The politician in him recognized that without popular support, he could not wage a successful, full-scale war. But his eloquence also sprang from a deep personal anguish, as he witnessed the death and suffering the war produced. Uncorrupted by power, Lincoln remained to the end a man of compassion and humility.

He also proved the more effective military leader. Jefferson Davis took his title of commander-in-chief literally, priding himself on his West Point training and interfering with his generals even on the smallest matters. But he failed to formulate an effective overarching strategy. In contrast, Lincoln read quite clearly the lessons of the disaster at Bull Run. He accepted General Winfield Scott's suggestion that the army and navy surround the Confederacy, cut off its supplies, and slowly strangle it into submission, just as the anaconda snake squeezes its prey. But unlike Scott, he realized that an "anaconda plan" was not enough. As the blockade tightened, the South would have to be invaded and defeated, not only on an eastern front in Virginia, but in the West, where Union control of the Mississippi would divide the Confederacy fatally. Lincoln understood that the Union's superior manpower and matériel would become decisive only when the Confederacy's resources were stretched along a broad front. The Union forces could then break through at the weak points. This novel idea of a simultaneous advance languished several years before the president found generals willing or able to execute it.

Lincoln was not the North's only advantage in leadership. The existence of political parties also contributed to the Union's successful conduct of the war. When southerners seceded, they deliberately suppressed parties, believing that their absence would promote national unity. The result was precisely the opposite. Without parties, Davis lacked the means to mobilize support. Confederate politics deteriorated into a paralyzing system of personal loyalties, while local politicians tended to focus on their own state's narrow interests. In the North, party organizations linked state and local loyalties with a national cause. In addition, elections served as referenda on policy, and every election was a step toward nationalizing the war effort.

The Border States

When the war began, the balance of forces between North and South remained uncertain because four border slave states—Delaware, Maryland, Kentucky, and Missouri—remained in the Union. Only Delaware was certain to stay, and Lincoln's immediate political challenge was to retain the loyalty of the others. Maryland especially was crucial, for if it was lost, Washington itself would have to be abandoned.

The danger became immediately apparent when pro-Confederate forces destroyed the railroad bridges near Baltimore and isolated Washington. Only with difficulty was the administration able to move troops to the city. Once the capital was safe, Lincoln moved vigorously—even ruthlessly—to secure Maryland. He suspended the writ of habeas corpus, the right under the Constitution of an arrested person either to be charged with a specific crime or to be released, and then held without trial prominent Confederate sympathizers (including the mayor and chief of police of Baltimore), suppressed pro-Confederate newspapers, and mounted a massive show of force in Baltimore. As the fall state election approached, Union troops arrested 27 members of the legislature as well as outspoken secessionists who tried to vote on election day. This intimidation ensured that Unionists won a complete victory. The election ended any possibility that Maryland would join the Confederacy.

At the beginning of the conflict, Kentucky officially declared its neutrality. Lincoln was quoted as saying that he hoped to have God on his side, but that he had to have Kentucky. "I think to lose Kentucky is nearly to lose the whole game," he wrote. "Kentucky gone, we can not hold Missouri, nor, as I think, Maryland. These all against us, and the job on our hands is too large for us." Union generals requested permission to occupy the state, but the president refused, preferring to act cautiously and wait for Unionist sentiment to assert itself. After Unionists won control of the legislature in the summer election, a Confederate army entered the state, giving Lincoln the opening he needed. He quickly sent in troops, and Kentucky stayed in the Union.

In Missouri, where controversy over slavery stretched back to the statehood debates of 1820, skirmishing broke out between Union and Confederate sympathizers. Eventually the pro-Confederate governor was deposed by an extralegal Unionist government. Not until March 1862, when the Union scored a victory at Pea Ridge in northern Arkansas, was Missouri secure from any Confederate threat. Even so, guerrilla warfare continued in the state throughout the remainder of the war. In Virginia, internal divisions led to the creation of a new border state, as the hilly western counties where slavery was not strong refused to support the Confederacy. After adopting a congressionally mandated program of gradual emancipation, West Virginia was formally admitted to the Union in June 1863.

The Union scored an important triumph in holding the border states. The population of all five equaled that of the four states of the Upper South that had joined the Confederacy, and their production of military supplies—food, animals, and minerals—was greater. Furthermore, Maryland and West Virginia contained key railroad lines and were critical to the defense of Washington, while Kentucky and Missouri gave the Union army access to the major river systems of the western theater, down which it launched the first successful invasion of the Confederacy.

OPENING MOVES

As with so many Civil War battles, the Confederate victory at Bull Run achieved no decisive military results. But a sobered Congress authorized the enlistment of half a million volunteers, to serve for three years. As public clamor forced Lincoln to replace General Scott, he named a new commander of the Union army, 34-year-old George McClellan, a West Point graduate who had been working as a railroad executive when the war began. Energetic and ambitious, McClellan was a model of businesslike efficiency, and he set to work on the much-needed task of organizing and drilling the Army of the Potomac. Indeed, for the rest of 1861 both sides devoted their energies to assembling and training armies that dwarfed any previously assembled on the continent.

Blockade and Isolate

Assigned the formidable task of blockading some 3550 miles of Confederate coastline, the U.S. Navy had only 42 ships in commission at the beginning of the war. Unlike their army counterparts, however, few naval officers resigned to accept Confederate commissions. By the spring of 1862, the Union fleet had secured several key bases, including Roanoke Island off North Carolina, the sea islands off South Carolina and Georgia, and Fort Pulaski guarding the entrance to Savannah. The navy also began building fleets of powerful gunboats to operate on the rivers. In April 1862, Flag Officer David G. Farragut ran a gauntlet of Confederate fire rafts, armor rams, and shore batteries to capture New Orleans, the Confederacy's largest port. Memphis, another important river city, fell to Union forces in June.

The blockade was hardly leakproof, and Confederates slipped through it using fast, low ships. Still, southern trade suffered badly. Only 800 vessels evaded Union patrols in the first year of war, compared with the 6000 ships that had docked in 1860. Unable to match the Union navy ship for ship, the Confederacy resorted to technological innovation, by converting the wooden U.S.S. *Merrimack* into an ironclad gunboat. Rechristened the *Virginia*, it steamed out in March 1862 to meet the Union fleet at Hampton Roads and damaged a third of the ships before engine trouble forced it to retire. But the next day a new Union ironclad, the *Monitor*, battled it to a standoff; the Confederates were forced to scuttle the *Virginia* when they evacuated Norfolk in May. After that, the Union's naval supremacy was secure.

The South looked to diplomacy as another means to lift the blockade. With cotton so vital to European economies, especially Great Britain's, southerners believed Europe would formally recognize the Confederacy and come to its aid. To increase economic pressure, the Davis administration deliberately withheld cotton that was waiting shipment, rather than rush it overseas before the Union blockade became effective. The North, for its part, claimed that it was merely putting down a domestic insurrection, and Secretary of State William Seward warned European nations against intervening in America's internal affairs. Yet Lincoln's proclamation of a blockade had the effect of giving the Confederacy belligerent status, since a country legally could not blockade itself. European countries extended belligerent status to the government at Richmond, which allowed the Confederacy to purchase supplies abroad and outfit privateers in foreign ports.

A diplomatic crisis erupted in November 1861 when a Union navy ship, acting without orders, stopped a British mail packet, the *Trent*, on the high seas and removed James Mason and John Slidell, two Confederate diplomats who were traveling to Europe. The British government vigorously protested this action, since international law did not authorize the seizure of individuals as contraband.

Amid war talk on both sides of the Atlantic, Lincoln defused the crisis by ordering Mason's and Slidell's release, while refusing to make a formal apology, as the British demanded.

The bumper cotton crop of 1860 initially undermined king cotton diplomacy, for European manufacturers had a large surplus on hand. By 1862, however, supplies were dwindling and the Confederacy mounted a new campaign to win recognition. France was ready to agree, but not unless Britain followed suit. The British prime minister, Lord Palmerston, favored the South, but he hesitated to act until Confederate armies proved themselves strong enough to fend off the North. Meanwhile, new supplies of cotton from Egypt and India enabled the British textile industry to recover. In the end Britain and the rest of Europe refused to recognize the Confederacy. As the blockade continued to tighten, the South was left to stand or fall on its own resources.

Grant in the West

In the western war theater, the first decisive Union victory was won by a short, shabbily dressed, cigar-chomping general named Ulysses S. Grant. An undistinguished student at West Point (he graduated twenty-first in a class of 39), Grant had become lonely and depressed in the army and, drinking heavily, eventually resigned his commission. In civilian life he failed at everything he tried, and when the war broke out he was a store clerk in Galena, Illinois. Almost 39, he enlisted as a colonel in the Illinois militia, and two months later became a brigadier general.

Grant's self-effacing demeanor gave little indication of his military potential. He was a quiet, ordinary-looking man, who disliked ceremony and bore himself in distinctly unmilitary fashion. The gaze of his blue eyes, however, disclosed iron determination. Alert to seize any opening, he remained extraordinarily calm and clear-headed in battle. He absorbed details on a map almost photographically, and in battles that spread out over miles, he was superb at coordinating an attack on horseback. He would "try all sorts of cross-cuts," recalled one staff officer, "ford streams and jump any number of fences to reach another road rather than go back and take a fresh start." Grant also took full advantage of the telegraph to track troop movements, stringing new lines as he advanced and keeping his communications open. (Some of his Union telegraphers were so adept that they could receive messages before a station was set up, by touching the end of the wire to their tongues to pick up Morse code.) Hard-headed and unromantic, Grant grasped that attention to detail and hard fighting, not fancy maneuvering, would bring victory. "The art of war is simple," he once explained. "Find out where your enemy is, get at him as soon as you can and strike him as hard as you can, and keep moving on."

Grant realized that rivers were avenues into the interior of the Confederacy, and in February 1862, supported by Union gunboats, he captured Fort Henry on the Tennessee River and shortly after, Fort Donelson on the Cumberland. These victories forced the Confederates to withdraw from Kentucky and middle Tennessee. Grant continued south with 40,000 men, but he was surprised on April 6 by General Albert Johnston, who had marched his army through dense woodland to Shiloh, just north of the Tennessee–Mississippi border. Johnston was killed in the day's fierce fighting, but by nightfall his army had driven the Union troops back to the Tennessee River, while others huddled disconsolately in the forest as a cold rain fell. William Tecumseh Sherman, one of Grant's subordinates, found the general standing under a dripping tree, his coat collar drawn up against the damp,

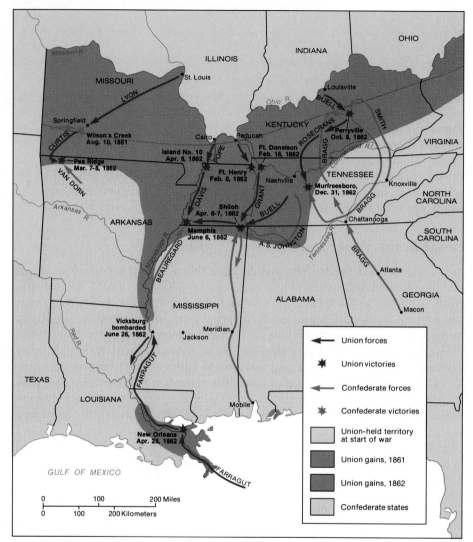

THE WAR IN THE WEST, 1861–1862
Grant's push southward stalled after his costly victory at Shiloh; nevertheless, by the end of 1862 the Union had secured Kentucky and Missouri, as well as most of Confederate Tennessee and the upper and lower stretches of the Mississippi River.

puffing on a cigar. Sherman was about to suggest retreat, but something in Grant's eyes, lighted by the glow of his stogey, made Sherman hesitate. So he said only, "Well, Grant, we've had the devil's own day, haven't we." "Yes," replied Grant. "Lick 'em tomorrow, though." With the aid of reinforcements which he methodically ferried across the river all night, Grant counterattacked the next morning and drove the Confederates from the field.

But victory came at a high price. Shiloh inflicted over 23,000 casualties: virtually as many Americans were killed or wounded in two days as in the Revolution, the War of 1812, and the Mexican War combined. "The scenes on this field would have cured anyone of war," Sherman testified. Grant, who had previously doubted the commitment of Confederate troops, came away deeply impressed by their determined fighting. "At Shiloh," he wrote afterwards, "I gave up all idea of saving the Union except by complete conquest."

Eastern Stalemate

Grant's victories did not impress a number of his envious colleagues, who argued that he drank too much and should be relieved of command. But Lincoln was unmoved. "I can't spare this man. He fights." That was a quality in short supply farther east, where General McClellan directed operations.

The short, handsome McClellan was nicknamed "Little Napoleon" by his admirers, and he did little to discourage the comparison. But beneath his arrogance and bravado lay a self-doubt that rendered him excessively cautious. As the months dragged on and McClellan did nothing but train and plan, Lincoln's frustration grew. "If General McClellan does not want to use the army I would like to *borrow* it," he remarked acidly. In the spring of 1862 the general finally moved against Richmond, the Confederate capital. Transporting 130,000 troops by ship to the mouth of the James River, he began inching his way up the peninsula between the James and York rivers. Habitually overestimating his opponent's strength, he was incapable of seizing the initiative. He threw up siegeworks instead of launching a direct assault, or maneuvered and called for reinforcements instead of striking directly for Richmond. After two and a half months, when he had finally advanced to within five miles of the capital, General Joseph Johnston attacked him near Fair Oaks, from which he barely escaped.* Worse for him, when Johnston was badly wounded, the formidable Robert E. Lee took command of the Army of Northern Virginia.

Lee, an impeccably dressed, gentlemanly commander, had entered the war somewhat reluctantly. ("I must say that I am one of those dull creatures that cannot see the good of secession," he confessed at the beginning of the conflict.) But he could not bring himself to raise his sword against his native Virginia. From his army days, Lee knew McClellan personally and understood how to fight him. Where McClellan was cautious and defensive, Lee was daring and ever alert to assume the offensive. His first name, one of his colleagues commented, should have been Audacity: "He will take more chances, and take them quicker than any other general in this country." Lee was aided by Stonewall Jackson, a deeply religious Calvinist whose rigorous discipline honed his troops to a hard edge. At the Battle of Seven Days McClellan parried the attacks of Lee and Jackson with his own brilliant maneuvering, but he stayed on the defensive. As McClellan retreated to the protection of the Union gunboats, Lincoln ordered the Peninsula campaign abandoned and placed John Pope in command. Lee won another victory, this time over Pope, at the second Battle of Bull Run. As the badly whipped Pope retreated back to Washington, Lincoln restored McClellan to command.

Realizing that the Confederacy needed a decisive victory, Lee convinced Davis to allow him to invade the North, hoping to detach Maryland and isolate Washington. But as his army crossed into Maryland, a copy of Lee's orders, wrapped around three cigars and accidentally left at a campsite by a Confederate officer, fell into Union hands. From this paper McClellan learned that his own forces vastly outnumbered Lee's—yet still he hesitated before launching a series of badly coordinated assaults near Antietam Creek on September 17. Scrambling

---

*Not to be confused with Albert Johnston, the Confederate general in the western theater killed at Shiloh.

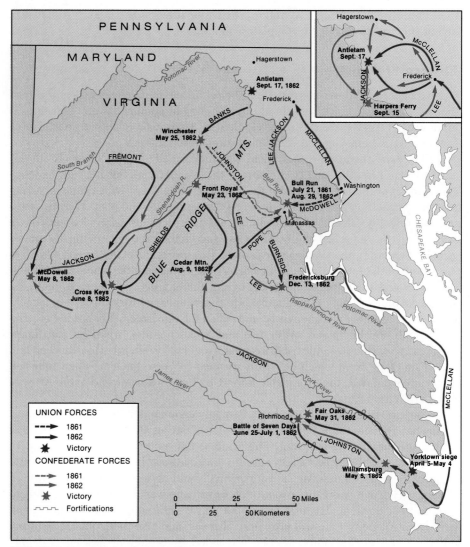

THE WAR IN THE EAST, 1861–1862

McClellan's campaign against Richmond failed when Joseph Johnston surprised him at Fair Oaks. Taking command of the Army of Northern Virginia, Lee drove back McClellan in the Seven Days battles, then won a resounding victory in the second Battle of Bull Run. He followed up by invading Maryland, dividing his forces to take advantage of McClellan's caution, and captured Harpers Ferry. McClellan checked his advance at Antietam. The Army of the Potomac's devastating defeat at Fredericksburg ended a year of frustration and failure for the Union in the eastern theater.

desperately, Lee barely beat back these attacks; the bloody exchanges horrified both sides for their sheer carnage. "Where the line stood the ground was covered in blue," recounted a Georgia soldier. "I could have walked on them without putting my feet on the ground." Within the space of seven hours, nearly 5000 soldiers were killed and another 18,000 wounded, making it the bloodiest single day in American history. When Lee, worried about his overextended supply lines, decided to withdraw, McClellan allowed the Army of Northern Virginia to escape.

With almost 23,000 casualties, Antietam was the bloodiest single day of the war. A group of Confederate soldiers were photographed where they fell along the Hagerstown Pike, the scene of some of the heaviest fighting. Said one Union officer of the fighting there: "Men, I cannot say fell; they were knocked out of the ranks by dozens."

Exasperated beyond measure with McClellan's habitual problem of "the slows," as Lincoln put it, the president relieved him from his command in November.

The winter of 1862 was the North's Valley Forge, as morale sank to an all-time low. It took General Ambrose Burnside, who assumed McClellan's place, little more than a month to demonstrate his utter incompetence. In December at the Battle of Fredericksburg, he ordered a direct assault on an impregnable Confederate position. The disastrous encounter inflicted 12,600 casualties on the North, compared to fewer than 5000 for the Confederates. Lincoln replaced Burnside with "Fighting Joe" Hooker. In the West, Grant had emerged as the dominant figure, but the Army of the Potomac still lacked a capable commander, the deaths on both sides kept mounting, and no end to the war was in sight.

EMANCIPATION

In 1858, Lincoln had proclaimed that an American "house divided" could not stand and that the United States would eventually become either all slave or all free. At the time, he had worried that the movement was toward slavery.

When the house did divide, Lincoln hesitated to move against slavery. He perceived, accurately, that most northern whites were not deeply committed to emancipation. He feared the social upheaval that such a revolutionary step would cause, and he hoped not to alarm the wavering border states. Thus when Congress met in special session in July 1861, Lincoln fully supported a resolution offered by Senator John J. Crittenden of Kentucky, which declared that "this war is not waged for any purpose of overthrowing or interfering with the rights or established institutions of these States, but to defend and maintain the supremacy of the Constitution and to preserve the Union." Even with most of the southern members of Congress gone, the Crittenden Resolution passed the House 117 to 2 and the Senate by 30 to 5.

Still, a minority of Republican radicals like Senator Charles Sumner and Horace Greeley pressed Lincoln to adopt a policy of emancipation. Slavery had caused the war, they argued; its destruction would hasten the war's end. Lincoln, however, placed first priority on saving the Union, not ending slavery. "My paramount object in this struggle *is* to save the Union, and is *not* either to save or to destroy slavery," he affirmed in 1862 in a public letter to Greeley. "If I could save the Union without freeing *any* slave I would do it, and if I could save it by freeing *all* the slaves I would do it, and if I could save it by freeing some and leaving others alone, I would also do that." This statement outlined Lincoln's policy during the first year of the war.

The Logic of Events

As the Union army began to occupy Confederate territory, slaves flocked to the Union camps. Octave Johnson, the runaway who hid in the Louisiana bayous for over a year (page 451), was only one of many slaves who presented themselves to occupying forces. In May 1861, the army adopted the policy of declaring runaway slaves contraband of war, and refused to return them to their rebel owners. In the Confiscation Act of August 1861, Congress provided that slaves used for military purposes by the Confederacy would become free if they fell into Union hands. Lincoln adhered to this position for a year but went no further. When two of his generals, acting on their own authority, abolished slavery in their districts, the president countermanded their orders.

By the time Congress reconvened in December 1861, opinion was beginning to shift. Introduced a second time, the Crittenden Resolution was soundly defeated, with Republicans voting against it almost three to one. Congress also prohibited federal troops from capturing or returning fugitive slaves, banned slavery from all the territories (thus ignoring the *Dred Scott* decision), and freed the 2000 slaves living in the District of Columbia with compensation of their owners. In July 1862 it took even more radical action by passing the Second Confiscation Act, which declared that the slaves of anyone who supported the rebellion would be freed if they came into federal custody. Unlike the first act, it did not matter whether the slaves had been used for military purposes. If vigorously enforced, the law would have led to virtual emancipation throughout the Confederacy.

Lincoln signed this bill, then proceeded to ignore it. Instead, he emphasized state action, since slavery was a domestic institution. In his first annual message to Congress, he proposed that the federal government provide grants to compensate slaveowners in any state-sponsored program of emancipation, to be completed by the year 1900. He also urged delegations of free blacks who visited him to organize colonization programs to Africa. Having lived all their lives in America, the delegates failed to see the virtues of moving to a land they had never seen. Twice the president summoned representatives from the border states and urged them to act before the war destroyed slavery of its own momentum. Both times they rejected his plea.

These failed attempts led Lincoln to suggest a new policy when he met with his cabinet on July 22—to issue a proclamation freeing at least some slaves. He was increasingly confident that the border states would remain in the Union, and he wanted to strike a blow that would weaken the Confederacy militarily. By making the struggle one of freedom versus slavery, such a proclamation would also undermine Confederate efforts to obtain diplomatic recognition. Accepting Seward's advice, Lincoln decided to wait for a Union military victory so that the act would not appear one of desperation.

The Emancipation Proclamation

Two months later, the victory at Antietam provided the opportunity. On September 22, Lincoln announced that all slaves within rebel lines would be freed unless the seceded states returned to their allegiance by January 1, 1863. When that day came, the Emancipation Proclamation went formally into effect. Excluded from its terms were the Union slave states, all of Tennessee, and the areas of Virginia and Louisiana that were under Union control. In all, about 830,000 of the nation's 4 million slaves were not covered by its provisions. Since Lincoln justified his actions on strictly military grounds, he believed that there was no legal right to apply it to areas not in rebellion.

Southerners denounced the proclamation as an attempt to incite their slaves to rebellion. Nor did Europeans immediately praise the move. Its principle, sneered a London paper, was "not that a human being cannot justly own another, but that he cannot own him unless he is loyal to the United States." Yet in the long run, European public opinion swung toward the Union. In the North, Republicans generally favored Lincoln's decision, while the Democrats made it a major issue in the 1862 elections. "Every white man in the North, who does not want to be swapped off for a free Nigger, should vote the Democratic ticket," urged one party orator. While the Democrats improved their showing in the elections that year, the results offered no clear verdict on the proclamation, since the Republicans increased their vote in some areas of the North.

Despite the mixed reaction, the Emancipation Proclamation had immense symbolic importance, for it redefined the nature of the war. The North was fighting, not to save the old Union, but to create a new nation. The war had become remorseless revolution.

Black Americans' Civil War

Contrary to southern whites' fear that a race war would erupt behind the lines, slavery did not explode during the war: it simply disintegrated. Well before federal troops entered an area, slaves took the lead in undermining the institution by openly challenging white authority and claiming greater personal freedom for themselves. For the first time, whites lost control of the slave labor force. One experienced overseer reported in frustration that now the "slaves will do only what pleases them, go out in the morning when it suits them, come in when they please, etc." In addition, the number of instances of slaves refusing to submit to punishment rose. The wife of a Texas planter wrote that she had discontinued whipping, for it only made matters worse. Throughout the Confederacy the vital psychological relationship between master and slave was strained, and sometimes it snapped.

Early in the conflict slaves concluded that emancipation would be one consequence of a Union victory. Perhaps as many as half a million—one-seventh of the total slave population of the Confederacy—fled to Union lines. Even in areas where escape was impractical, a remarkable number of slaves learned the news of the proclamation and rejoiced. One, who found out just before she was to serve her master's dinner, asked to be excused to get water from a nearby spring. Once safely out of earshot of the house, she gave free rein to her feelings. "I jump up and scream, 'Glory, glory hallelujah to Jesus! I'se free! I'se free! Glory to God, you come down an' free us; no big man could do it.' An' I got sort of scared, afeared somebody hear me, an' I takes another good look, an' fall on de groun' an' roll over, an' kiss de groun' fo' de Lord's sake, I's so full o' praise to Masser Jesus."

Slaves who entered the Union lines faced an uncertain reception. Manifesting a deep-seated racism, northern troops were often hostile. The ex-slaves, called freedmen, ended up living in refugee or contraband camps that were overcrowded, disease-ridden, and provided only rudimentary shelter and food. "The poor Negroes die as fast as ever," one northern missionary reported. "The children are all emaciated to the last degree and have such violent coughs and dysenteries that few survive."

Convinced that blacks would not work on their own initiative, the U.S. government put some contrabands to work as cooks, teamsters, woodchoppers, and other unskilled laborers. But their wages fell well below those paid whites for the same work. In the Mississippi valley, where two-thirds of the freedmen under Union control were located, most were forced to work on plantations leased or owned by loyal planters. This policy was officially adopted in the summer of 1863 as a way to free the army from the cost of supporting former slaves and strengthen Unionism in the South. Freedmen had no say in the contracts negotiated between military authorities and planters, found themselves strictly disciplined, and had so many deductions taken from their wages that in the end most received only room and board. In short, the conditions often approximated slavery. The abolitionist Lydia Maria Child was prophetic when she predicted that if the slaves were freed "merely as a war necessity, everything must go wrong, if there is no heart or conscience on the subject."

The Emancipation Proclamation also announced that blacks would be accepted in the navy and, more controversially, the army. Throughout its history, the navy had been hard-pressed to get enough recruits, and as a result that service had always included some black sailors. African-American troops had also fought during the Revolution and the War of 1812, but they had been quickly discharged at the end of the war and had never served in the regular army. Resistance to accepting blacks in the army remained especially strong in the Midwest. Northern blacks themselves were divided over whether to serve, given the hostility of so many whites. But Frederick Douglass spoke for the vast majority of African-American people when he argued that once a black man had served in the army, there was "no power on earth which can deny that he has earned the right of citizenship in the United States."

Black men, including runaway slaves, joined the Union army and navy beginning in 1863. This photograph shows Hubbard Pryor after enlistment. As soldiers, former slaves developed a new sense of pride and confidence.

In the end, over 200,000 black men served in the Union forces, about 10 percent of the Union's total military manpower. Some, including two of Douglass' sons, were free, but most were former slaves who enlisted after escaping to the Union lines. As a concession to the racism of white troops, blacks served in segregated units under white officers. Initially they were relegated to undesirable duties such as heavy labor and burial details. They were paid only $10 a month, with $3 deducted for clothing. Whites, by contrast, received $13 a month plus a $3.50 clothing allowance. After an 18-month struggle, Congress in June 1864 granted equal pay retroactively to African-American soldiers.

After successfully agitating for the chance to fight, black soldiers impressed whites with their courage under fire. It "completely revolutionized the sentiment of the army with regard to the employment of Negro troops," a War Department official reported, after viewing the fierce battle at Millikin's Bend, Louisiana, in June 1863. Ultimately 37,000 African-American servicemen gave their lives, a rate of loss about 40 percent higher than among whites. Blacks had good reason to fight fiercely: they knew that the freedom of their race hung in the balance, they hoped to win civil rights at home by their performance on the battlefield, they resented racist sneers about their loyalty and ability, and they knew that capture might mean death. The effect on African-American pride was also apparent. Slaves admired the confidence of the new black recruits, while for their part, African-American soldiers relished being liberators. One soldier, who discovered his former master among the prisoners he was guarding, summed up the situation succinctly. "Hello, massa!" he called cheerfully, "bottom rail on top dis time!"

THE CONFEDERATE HOME FRONT

Nowhere was the effect of war more complete than within the Confederacy. These changes were especially ironic, since the southern states had seceded in order to preserve their traditional ways. Not only did the war send hundreds of thousands of "Johnny Rebs" off to the front, but it also put extreme burdens on the women and families at home. It fundamentally transformed the southern economy and forced the Confederate government to become more centralized. And of course it ended by destroying the institution of slavery, which the South had gone to war to preserve.

The New Economy

With the Union blockade tightening, the production of foodstuffs became crucial to the South's economy. Many men who normally worked in the fields had gone to fight, and with the lessening of discipline slaves became increasingly assertive, stole livestock, refused to work, or ran off. More and more plantations switched from cotton to raising grain and livestock, and some state and local organizations tried to limit the amount of cotton grown, to encourage the transition. As a result, cotton production dropped from 4.5 million bales in 1861 to 300,000 in 1864, but even so, food production declined. By the last two years of the war, the shortage had become serious.

Southern planters had resisted industrialization before the war, but the Union blockade made it impossible to rely on European manufactured goods. So the Confederate War Department began building and running factories, as well as taking over the region's mines. It also regulated private manufacturers by offering contracts and draft exemptions for their workers if they switched to the production of war goods. Though the Confederacy never became self-sufficient, its accomplishments were impressive. As Josiah Gorgas, head of the Confederate Ordnance Department, noted,

> We began in April, 1861, without an arsenal, laboratory or powder mill of any capacity, and with no foundry or rolling mill except at Richmond, and before the close of 1863, . . . we had built up foundries and rolling mills, smelting works, chemical works, a powder mill far superior to any in the United States, and a chain of arsenals, armories and laboratories equal in their capacity and their improved appointments to the best of those in the United States.

In fact, the Confederacy sustained itself far better in industrial goods than it did in agricultural produce. It was symbolic that when Lee surrendered, his troops had sufficient guns and ammunition to continue, but they had not eaten in two days.

While the Confederacy remained a rural society, its urban areas expanded and became more influential. Richmond more than tripled in population, while Atlanta, a minor upcountry Georgia town, grew into a major urban center because it was located at a critical rail junction. For the first time, urban residents in the South developed a separate identity and a consciousness of their importance.

Southern Women

Southern white women took an active, even an intense role in the war. Some gained notoriety as spies; others smuggled medicine, guns, clothing, and shoes into the South, often taking advantage of the large hoop skirts then in fashion. Women also spent a good deal of time knitting and sewing clothes for soldiers. "We never went out to pay a visit without taking our knitting along," recalled a South Carolina woman. Perhaps most important, with so many men fighting, women took charge of agricultural production. As one Georgia soldier told his wife, "You must be man and woman both while the war lasts." On plantations, the mistress often supervised the slaves, as well as the wrenching shift from cotton to foodstuffs. "All this attention to farming is uphill work with me," one South Carolina woman confessed to her army husband.

The war also opened up new jobs off the farm. Given the manpower shortage, "government girls" became essential to fill the burgeoning Confederate bureaucracy, and with economic conditions so desperate, the secretary of the treasury found he had 100 applications for every vacancy. Initially women were paid half the wages of male co-workers, but by the end of the war they had won equal pay. Women also staffed the new factories springing up on the southern landscape, undertaking even dangerous work that normally would have been considered off limits. A majority of the workers in the South's munitions factories were women, some of whom lost their lives in accidental explosions.

Thus the war brought the harsh realities of hardship and risk to southern women. But when the fighting was over, they had become more assertive, more realistic, and more confident. "Of all the principles developed by the late war," wrote one Alabama planter, "I think the capability of our Southern women to take care of themselves was by no means the least important."

Confederate Finance and Government

The most serious domestic problem the Confederate government faced was finance, for which officials at Richmond never developed a satisfactory program. The South had few banks and only $27 million in specie when the war began. European governments refused to float major loans, which left taxation as the unappealing alternative. Only in 1863 did the government begin levying a graduated income tax (from 1 to 15 percent), a series of excise taxes, and, most controversial, a tax-in-kind on farmers which, after exempting a certain portion, took one-tenth of their agricultural crops. Even more unpopular was the policy of impressment, which allowed the army to seize private property for its own use, often with little or no compensation.

Above all, the Confederacy financed the war effort simply by printing paper money not backed by specie, some $1.5 billion, which amounted to three times more than the federal government issued. The result was runaway inflation, so that by 1865 a Confederate dollar was worth only 1.7 cents in gold and prices soared to 92 times their prewar base. Prices were highest in Richmond, where flour sold for $275 a barrel by early 1864, coats for $350, shoes $125, potatoes $25 per bushel, and butter $15 a pound. By the end of the war, flour had reached an astronomical $1000 a barrel. Inflation that ate away at their standard of living was one of the great wartime hardships borne by the southern people.

In politics even more than finance, the Confederacy exercised far greater powers than those of the federal government before 1861. Indeed, Jefferson Davis strove to meet the demands of total war by transforming the South into a centralized, national state. Backed by the Confederate Congress, he sought to limit state authority over military units and create a truly national army. To do this required a draft, for enlistments had fallen off dramatically after the early rush of enthusiasm. In April 1862 the Confederacy passed the first national conscription law in American history, drafting all white males between 18 and 35 unless exempted. As conditions worsened, those age limits widened to 17 and 50, mobilizing virtually the entire military-age white population. Civilians, too, felt the effects of government control, for in 1862 the Congress authorized Davis to invoke martial law and suspend the writ of habeas corpus. For the duration of the conflict Richmond fell under martial law.

Critics protested that Davis was destroying states' rights, the cardinal principle of the Confederacy. Concerned foremost about their states' safety, governors wanted to be able to recall troops if their own territory was threatened. Governor Joseph Brown of Georgia refused to provide state troops for the defense of Atlanta, since he was afraid they would be placed under Confederate control, while Zebulon Vance of North Carolina insisted that all blankets and uniforms produced by the state's textile mills be reserved for North Carolina troops. When President Davis suspended the writ of habeas corpus, his own vice president, Alexander H. Stephens, accused him of aiming at a dictatorship. Davis, however, used those powers for a limited time, only with the permission of Congress, and only where northern invasion threatened.

But the Confederate draft, more than any other measure, produced an outcry. The original law exempted a number of unimportant occupations, including postmen and editors, and it allowed the rich to provide substitutes, at a cost that eventually rose, on the open market, to as much as $6000. The Confederacy abolished this privilege in the last year of the war, but as one Georgia leader complained, "It's a notorious fact if a man has influential friends—or a little money to spare he will never be enrolled." Most controversially, the draft exempted from service one white man on every plantation with 20 or more slaves (later reduced to 15). This law was designed to preserve control of the slave population, but more and more nonslaveholders complained that it was a rich man's war and a poor man's fight. Denouncing the war as a slaveholders' plot, one Alabama yeoman claimed that "all they want is to git you pumped up and go to fight for their infernal negroes and after you do their fighting you may kiss their hind parts for all they care." In some counties where the draft was unenforceable, conscription officers ventured only at risk to their own safety.

Hardship and Suffering

By the last year of the conflict, food shortages had become so severe that ingenious southerners were brewing parched rye, corn, or acorns instead of coffee, cooking with blackberries and molasses oil instead of vinegar, and using sorghum in place of sugar. One scarce item for which there was no substitute was salt, essential for curing meat. Scarcity bred speculation and hoarding: merchants bought up large quantities of food and supplies to resell at high prices and thus profit from the inflationary spiral. Some states tried to regulate prices and punish extortion, but the laws were unenforceable. The high prices and food shortages led to riots in several southern cities, most seriously in Richmond early in April 1863. About 300 women and children chanting "Bread!" and armed with knives, hatchets, and pistols, marched into the business section, wrecked a number of stores, and helped themselves to bread, food, and other items. Nor were rural areas immune

Precipitated by the high price of food and growing shortages, a series of food riots shook the Confederacy in 1863. In the capital of Richmond, a group of desperate women, some of them armed, ransacked bakeries and other stores until troops rushed to the scene.

from these outbreaks. Country women attacked wagon trains carrying supplies and on several occasions even invaded towns and looted stores.

As always, war corroded the discipline and order of society. With prices rising, the value of paper money dropping, and the future uncertain, many Southerners frantically pursued money and spent it in frenzied haste. The governor of Florida criticized "a wide spread desire for speculation and wealth, which have overcome obligations of patriotism and endangered the very existence of the Confederate States." Gambling halls were crowded with revelers seeking relief, while soldiers on furlough drank heavily, aware of their increasingly poor chances of survival at the front. Even in the army, theft became more common, and during the last two years of the war soldiers could not leave their property unattended. In Richmond, the House of Representatives was robbed and Jefferson Davis' favorite horse stolen.

The search for escape from the grim reality of the war led to a forced gaiety for those who could afford it. "The cities are gayer than before the war," one refugee reported, "—parties every night in Richmond, suppers costing ten and twenty thousand dollars." Walking home at night after spending several hours at the bedside of a dying soldier, Judith McGuire passed a house gay with laughter, music, and dancing. "The revulsion was sickening," she wrote in her diary. "I thought of the gayety of Paris during the French Revolution, and the hall at Brussels the night before the battle of Waterloo, and felt shocked that our own Virginians, at such a time, should remind me of scenes which we were wont to think belong only to a foreign society." The war was a cancer that ate away, not only at southern society, but at the southern soul itself.

THE UNION HOME FRONT

Since the war was fought mostly on southern soil, northern civilians rarely felt its effects directly. Yet to be effective, the North's economic resources had to be organized and mobilized. Stimulated by government purchases, the northern economy boomed and the war accelerated the process of industrialization.

Government Finances and the Economy

To begin with, the North required a comprehensive system to finance its massive campaign. Taxing the populace was an obvious means, and taxes paid for 21 percent of Union war expenses, compared to only 1 percent of the Confederacy's. In August 1861 Congress passed the first federal income tax, 3 percent on all incomes over $800 a year. When that, along with increased tariff duties, proved insufficient, Congress enacted a comprehensive tax law in 1862 that for the first time brought the tax collector into every northern household. Excise fees taxed virtually every occupation, commodity, or service; income and inheritances were taxed, as were corporations and consumers. A new bureaucracy, the Internal Revenue Bureau, oversaw the collection process.

The government also borrowed heavily, through the sale of some $2.2 billion in bonds, and financed the rest of the war by issuing paper money. In 1862 Congress authorized notes known as greenbacks because of their distinctive color on one side. In all, $431 million was printed. Although legal for the payment of debts, they could not be redeemed in specie and therefore their value fluctuated. Congress also established a national banking system, allowing nationally chartered banks to issue notes backed by U.S. bonds. By taxing state bank notes at a steep 10 percent, Congress drove competing paper money out of circulation and for the first time gave the United States a uniform national currency. This arrangement remained the country's banking system until the Federal Reserve System was established in 1913.

During the 1850s, the Republicans appealed to Whigs and commercially minded citizens with measures to develop the national economy. During the war, Lincoln and the Republican-controlled Congress similarly encouraged industry and trade. Tariffs to protect industry from foreign competition rose so sharply that by the end of the war, some duties were 100 percent, and the average rate was 47 percent, compared to 19 percent under the 1857 tariff. To encourage development of the West, the Homestead Act of 1862 granted 160 acres of public land—the size of the traditional American family farm—to those who settled and improved the land for five years. Over a million acres were distributed during the war years alone. And the Land Grant College Act of 1862 donated the proceeds from certain land sales to finance public colleges and universities. Eventually 69 institutions of higher learning were created under its provisions, many in the West.

A Rich Man's War

Over the course of the war, the government purchased more than $1 billion worth of goods and services. The army in particular was a voracious consumer. Shoes wore out every three months and uniforms every six. Goods lost or destroyed on the march and in battle had to be replaced. In response to this heavy demand, many sectors of the economy boomed, fortunes were made, and business prospered. Wages rose 42 percent between 1860 and 1864, but workers did not fully share in the prosperity because inflation and higher tariffs sent the price of consumer goods up 76 percent. Adjusted for inflation, workers' average real income dropped from $363 in 1860 to $261 in 1865, which meant that the working class paid a disproportionate share of the burden of financing the war.

The Republican belief that government should play a major role in the economy also fostered a cozy relationship between business and politics. In the rush to profit from government contracts, some suppliers succumbed to the temptation to sell inferior goods at inflated prices. Uniforms made of "shoddy"—bits of unused thread and recycled cloth—were fobbed off in such numbers that the word became an adjective describing inferior quality. Unscrupulous dealers sold clothing that dissolved in the rain, shoes that fell apart, spoiled meat, broken-down horses, and guns that would not fire. A War Department investigation later revealed that at least 20 percent of government expenditures involved fraud.

Stocks and dividends rose with the economy, as investors scrambled after profitable new opportunities. Cotton especially excited the avarice of speculators, since the Union blockade had driven its price up to $1.90 a pound in Boston. With cotton going begging for 20 cents a pound on southern wharves, smuggled shipments multiplied. Treasury agents and military authorities were either bribed to provide passes to go through the lines or were active participants in the trade. The Confederate government quietly traded cotton for contraband such as food, medicine, and enough arms and equipment to maintain an army of 50,000 men, according to Union investigators. One of them, Charles Dana, reported in 1863 that in the Mississippi valley, "The mania for sudden fortunes made in cotton has to an alarming extent corrupted and demoralized the army. Every colonel, captain or quartermaster is in secret partnership with some operator in cotton."

Speculation during the last two years of the war became particularly feverish and the fortunes made went toward the purchase of ostentatious luxuries. New York City had never seen so much imported foreign finery, while the Chicago *Tribune* admitted: "We are clothed in purple and fine linen, wear the richest laces and jewels and fare sumptuously every day." Like Richmond in the Confederacy, Washington became the symbol of this moral decay. Prostitution, drinking, and corruption reached epidemic proportions in the capital, and for the wealthy, festivities and social gatherings became the means to shut out the numbing horror of the casualty lists.

Women and the Work Force

Even more than in the South, the war opened new opportunities for northern women. Countless wives ran farms while their husbands were away at war. One traveler in Iowa reported, "I met more women driving teams on the road and saw more at work in the fields than men." But the trend toward mechanization and commercial farming made the northern labor shortage less severe. By 1865 three times as many reapers and harvesters were in use as in 1861, while production per agricultural worker increased by a greater percentage from 1860 to 1870 than in any decade before 1890. With the price of grain driven up by government purchases and increased demand in Europe, northern agriculture prospered.

Beyond the farm, women increasingly found work in industry, filling approximately 100,000 new jobs during the war. As in the South, they worked as clerks in the expanding government bureaucracy. The work was tedious, the pace frenzied, the workload heavy: copying reports and correspondence in large volumes, keeping accounts in ledgers often too heavy to lift, counting stacks of currency. Some supervisors would not even allow women to work in the office, instead assigning them papers to take home as "piecework." But the new jobs offered satisfactions as well, including good wages, a sense of economic independence, and a pride in having aided the war effort.

The war also allowed women to enter and eventually dominate the profession of nursing. After the Revolution they had been excluded from medical careers, and army doctors opposed their presence in military hospitals during the Civil War. "Our women appear to have become almost wild on the subject of hospital nursing," protested one physician. He conceded that female volunteers might provide "delicate, soothing attentions . . . which . . . none know so well how to give as do noble, sensible, tenderhearted women"; but he shuddered to "imagine a delicate refined woman assisting a rough soldier to the close-stool, or supplying him with a bedpan." Women lobbied vigorously to overcome such objections, and their service in the wards of the maimed and dying reduced the hostility to women in medicine.

Led by Drs. Emily and Elizabeth Blackwell, Dorothea Dix, who became head of army nurses, and Clara Barton, the founder of the American Red Cross, women fought the bureaucratic inefficiency of the army medical corps. One of the most famous army nurses was Mary Ann "Mother" Bickerdyke, who attacked the

A nurse tends a wounded Union soldier in a military hospital in Nashville, Tennessee. Despite the opposition of army doctors, hundreds of female volunteers worked in army hospitals for each side. Nursing became a female profession after the war.

problem of health care in the western armies head on. Ignoring the established lines of military authority, she ordered hospitals cleaned, kitchens established, bathing facilities constructed, and incompetent employees removed. She became famous for ordering army officers around, prompting Grant to joke that she "outranks everybody, even Lincoln." With her heavyset figure and simple attire, she became a familiar sight at battlefields, aiding those in need.

Clara Barton, like so many other nurses, often found herself in battlefield hospitals, where death and suffering were massive. During the battle of Fredericksburg, she wiped the brows of the wounded and dying, bandaged wounds, and applied tourniquets to stop the flow of blood. She later recalled that as she rose from the side of one soldier, "I wrung the blood from the bottom of my clothing, before I could step, for the weight about my feet." She steeled herself at the sight of amputated arms and legs casually tossed in piles outside the front door as the surgeons cut away, yet she found the extent of suffering overwhelming. She was jolted by the occasional familiar faces among the tangled mass of bodies: the sexton of the church in her hometown, his face drenched in blood; a wayward boy she had befriended years ago; an officer who had kindly assisted her on the way to the front, already dead when she discovered him. Sleeping in a tent nearby, she drove herself to the brink of exhaustion until the last patients were transferred to permanent hospitals. She then returned to her home in Washington where she broke down and wept.

Before 1861 teaching too had been dominated by males, but the war accelerated the profession's transition into a largely female preserve. In both North and South, the shortage of men forced school boards to turn to women, who could be paid half to two-thirds of what men received. As wages were driven down, men increasingly left the educational profession for other occupations, whereas teaching often became not a temporary occupation but a career for women. Women also contributed to the war effort through volunteer work. The United States Sanitary Commission was established in 1861 to coordinate relief efforts and raise money to provide medical supplies and care. Women performed much of the fund-raising at the local level, organizing fairs, collecting supplies, wrapping bandages, and working in hospitals alongside paid nurses. Such activity extended female involvement in humanitarian reform movements.

Civil Liberties and Dissent

With the government attempting to mobilize northern society, Lincoln did not hesitate to curb dissenters. Shortly after the firing on Fort Sumter, he suspended the writ of habeas corpus in specified areas, clearing the way for the detention of anyone suspected of disloyalty or activity against the war. Although the Constitution permitted such suspension in time of rebellion or invasion, Lincoln did so without consulting Congress (unlike President Davis), and he used his power far more broadly, expanding it in 1862 to cover the entire North for cases involving antiwar activities. The president also decreed that those arrested under its provisions could be tried under the stricter rules of martial law by a military court. Eventually at least 14,000 individuals were arrested, most of whom were never charged with a specific crime or brought to trial, and were released as arbitrarily as they had been apprehended.

Democrats attacked Lincoln as a tyrant bent on destroying the Constitution. When Clement Vallandigham, a prominent Ohio Democratic congressman, called for an armistice in May 1863, he was arrested by the local military commander and tried and convicted by a military commission. In the ensuing uproar, Lincoln adroitly sidestepped controversy by commuting the prison sentence to banishment to the Confederacy. Vallandigham eventually made his way to Canada, returning to the United States in 1864 to actively campaign for the Democratic party. Lincoln ignored him, convinced he was doing the Democrats more harm than good. The Supreme Court refused to review the case, which in effect upheld his conviction. Once the war was over, however, the Court changed its position. In *Ex parte Milligan* (1866) it struck down the military conviction of a civilian accused of plotting to free Confederate prisoners of war. The Court ruled that as long as the regular courts were open, civilians could not be tried by military tribunals. The decision became one of the landmarks of constitutional law in defense of civil liberties.

Republicans labeled those who opposed the war Copperheads, conjuring up the image of a venomous snake waiting to strike the Union. Constituting the extreme peace wing of the Democratic party, Copperheads were most often either

In this 1862 painting, Lincoln battles the Copperhead dragon to preserve the Union. He is held back by an Irish Tammany Hall Democrat, who invokes the Constitution and democracy to oppose the war effort. The heavy-handed caricature of the Irish was common in Republican propaganda during the war.

transplanted southerners, who had settled the lower portion of the Ohio valley, or urban Irish Catholics. Both groups hated the Republicans and both had been hurt by the economic changes produced by the war. In protesting the administration's probusiness policies, including the tariff, the national banking acts, and aid to railroads, Copperheads were the forerunners of the Grangers and other agrarian reform movements that developed after 1865.

More than anything else, Copperheads reviled the draft as an attack on individual freedom and an instrument of special privilege. According to the provisions enacted in 1863, a person would be exempt from the present (but not the future) draft by paying a commutation fee of $300, about a year's wages for a worker or ordinary farmer. Or those drafted could hire a substitute, the cost of which was beyond the reach of all but the wealthy. Approximately 118,000 men did so, and another 87,000 paid the commutation fee. In areas of notable Copperhead sentiment, draft officials were shot at and the drawing of names precipitated riots, but the most common form of resistance was draft evasion. Perhaps 160,000 northerners illegally evaded the draft.

In July 1863, when the first draftees' names were drawn in New York, workers in the Irish quarter rose in anger. They hated the rich, who could avoid service, and they resented even more being asked to risk their lives to free black people, who competed with them for the lowest paying jobs. Rampaging through the streets, the mob attacked draft officials and the police, then turned their wrath on a number of prominent Republicans and wealthy individuals. Soon after, they proceeded to African-American neighborhoods, burning the Colored Orphan Asylum and lynching blacks who fell into their hands. The rioting continued for four days until troops rushed from the battle of Gettysburg finally restored order. At least 74 people were killed, the worst loss of life from any riot in American history.

GONE FOR A SOLDIER

By war's end, approximately 2 million men had served the Union cause and another million the Confederate. The common wisdom of the day was that a disproportionate number were poor, but modern research indicates otherwise. In both the North and South, farmers and farm laborers accounted for the largest group of soldiers, whereas unskilled workers, who were poorer than other groups, were actually underrepresented. A study of enlistments for Concord, Massachusetts, reveals that for those under 30, men without property were twice as likely to serve as those with property. But fighting was a job for the young (almost 40 percent of entering soldiers were 21 or younger), and the large majority of males that age, no matter what social class they came from, did not own property.

Camp Life

Soldiers spent most of their time in camp, perhaps as many as 50 days, on average, for every day spent in battle. The near-holiday atmosphere of the early months, when army life seemed like a gigantic campout, soon gave way to dull routine. Men from rural areas, accustomed to the freedom of the farm, complained about the endless recurrence of reveille, roll call, and drill. "When this war is over," one

Soldiers leaving for war often had their picture taken with their loved ones. The Confederate soldier on the left posed with his two sisters. On the right a member of the Union forces sits with his family for a farewell portrait. Such photographs are reminders of how much the war and its mounting death toll touched civilians on both sides as well as soldiers.

Rebel promised, "I will whip the man that says 'fall in' to me." Troops in neither army cared for the spit and polish of regular army men. "They keep us very strict here," noted one Illinois soldier; "it is the most like a prison of any place I ever saw."

Camp life was often unhealthy as well as unpleasant. Poor sanitation, miserable food, exposure, and primitive medical care contributed to widespread sickness and disease. Officers and men alike regarded army doctors as nothing more than quacks and tried to avoid them. It was a common belief that if a fellow went to the hospital, "you might as well say good bye." Twice as many soldiers died from dysentery, typhoid, and other diseases as from wounds.

Treatment at field hospitals was a chilling experience. A Union colonel, wounded at Port Hudson, recounted that as he was taken into a poorly lit cotton press building filled with wounded men. "I could not help comparing the surgeons to fiends. . . . In the middle of the room was some 10 or 12 tables just large enough to lay a man on; these were used as dissecting tables and they were covered with blood; near and around the tables stood the surgeons with blood all over them and by the side of the tables was a heap of feet, legs and arms."

More than anything else, ignorance was responsible for these conditions and practices. Many army doctors were capable by the standards of the time, but nothing was known about germs or how wounds became infected. Having lived through the revolution in medical science, a federal surgeon was appalled as he looked back on his Civil War experience:

> We operated in old blood-stained and often pus-stained coats. . . . We used un-
> disinfected instruments from undisinfected plush-lined cases, and still worse,
> used marine sponges which had been used in prior pus cases and had been only
> washed in tap water. If a sponge or an instrument fell on the floor it was washed
> and squeezed in a basin of tap water and used as if it were clean. Our silk to tie
> blood vessels was undisinfected. . . . We dressed the wounds with clean but
> undisinfected sheets, shirts, tablecloths, or other old soft linen rescued from the
> family ragbag. . . . We knew nothing about antiseptics and therefore used none.

Daily Lives

FOOD/DRINK/DRUGS:

Hardtack, Salt Horse, and Coffee

"If a person wants to know how to appreciate the value of good vi[c]tuals he had better enlist," a Vermont soldier declared. "I have seen the time when I would have been glad to [have] picked the crusts of bread that mother gives to the hogs." Whether in the field or in quarters, food was generally Johnny Reb's and Billy Yank's first concern.

At the beginning of the war, the prescribed daily allowance for each soldier included 12 ounces of pork or 20 ounces of beef, a pound or more of bread or flour, and ample quantities of rice, beans, sugar, and coffee. That allotment was more generous than any received by a European soldier, and for nearly three years, the Union army raised its allowance beyond even that. While both armies experienced serious shortages from time to time, in general northern soldiers had more food and in greater variety than their opponents. By April 1862 the Confederacy was forced to reduce the daily ration, because of shortages, bureaucratic inefficiency, and the lack of adequate transportation. Eventually the allowance for Confederate soldiers dropped to a third of a pound of bacon and a pound of flour or meal—and even this was seldom provided, leaving the average Rebel to complain more about the quartermaster corps than about Yankees.

Meat, bread, and coffee: these were the soldier's mainstays. The meat was either pork or beef and was usually salted to preserve it. Soldiers, who called salt pork "sowbelly" and pickled beef "salt horse," preferred the former, since the beef was so briny it was inedible unless thoroughly soaked in water. Many soldiers left salted beef in a creek overnight before they tried to eat it.

Union soldiers normally were given wheat bread or flour, but for Confederates cornbread was the standby. This monotonous fare prompted a Louisiana soldier near the end of the war to grumble, "If any person offers me cornbread after this war comes to a close I shall *probably* tell him to—go to hell." Both armies often replaced bread with hardtack, crackers half an inch thick that were so hard soldiers dubbed them "teethdullers." Cynics claimed that they were more suitable for building breastworks, and some Yanks insisted that the "B.C." (for Brigade Commissary) stamped on the boxes they came in referred to their date of manufacture. They became moldy and worm-infested

An infantry private from New York eats a meal in camp.

Daily Lives

with age, and hence veterans preferred to eat them in the dark.

Coffee was the other main staple, eagerly and amply consumed. Because of the Union blockade, the Confederacy could not get enough, and Rebel troops resorted to various substitutes, none of which produced a very appealing brew. Despite official opposition, troops often fraternized during lulls in the fighting, swapping tobacco, which was in short supply on the Union side, for coffee and sugar, which Confederates desired most. When the two armies spent the winter of 1862 camped on opposite sides of the Rappahannock River, enlisted men ferried cargoes of sugar and coffee to one bank and tobacco to the other, using makeshift toy boats.

In an effort to create portable rations, the Union War Department produced an experimental "essence of coffee," a forerunner of the instant variety. But the beverage was so vile the men would not drink it, and it was eventually abandoned. More long-lasting was the use of dehydrated potatoes, which few men ever developed a taste for, and desiccated mixed vegetables, which were issued in hard, dry cakes that troops dubbed "baled hay." The only practical way of serving this concentrate was in soup, but the resulting product reminded one officer of "a dirty brook with all the dead leaves floating around promiscuously." The shortage of fruits and vegetables was one of the main deficiencies of the Civil War soldiers' diet.

Troops in both armies supplemented their diet by foraging (the army's polite term for stealing), although Union soldiers, being most often in enemy territory, relied more heavily on this tactic. Hungry troops regularly raided pigpens, poultry houses, orchards, gardens, cornfields, and smokehouses. Attempts to limit this activity to regularly appointed groups were largely ineffective. A Massachusetts soldier serving in North Carolina told his parents in 1862, "When we first started the colonel tried to prevent our foraging but he quickly found out that all that was nonsense and before we got back we were as expert at it as any of the old hands."

During training and in winter quarters, cooks normally prepared food for an entire company. Neither army, however, established a cooks' or bakers' school, and soldiers contended that officers regularly selected the poorest soldiers to be cooks. "A company cook is a most peculiar being," one soldier recalled after the war. "He generally knows less about cooking than any other man in the company. Not being able to learn the drill, and too dirty to appear on inspection, he is sent to the cook house to get him out of the ranks." Once the army went on the march, men usually cooked for themselves or formed a mess of four to eight soldiers, taking turns cooking. Either way, food was rarely prepared with any skill and was laden with grease. In addition, troops often lacked adequate utensils and learned to bake bread on a board, fry food in half a canteen, and roast meat and dough at the end of a stick.

By war's end, soldiers on both sides had developed a new appreciation for food. One hungry Texan promised that when he got home he was going "to take a hundred biscuit and two large hams, call it three days rations, then . . . eat it all at *one* meal." A poetic Yankee summed up the situation succinctly:

The soldiers' fare is very rough,
The bread is hard, the beef is
   tough;
If they can stand it, it will be,
Through love of God, a mystery.

Conditions were even worse in the Confederate hospitals, for the Union blockade produced a shortage of medical supplies, and Confederate doctors often had to resort to native-grown substitutes.

The boredom of camp life, the horrors of battle, and the influence of an all-male society all corrupted morals. Profanity and heavy drinking were widespread, while one Mississippian reported that after payday games of chance were "running night and day, with eager and excited crowds standing around with their hands full of money." As in the gold fields of California, the absence of women stimulated behavior that would have been checked back home by the frowns of family and society. Prostitutes flooded the camps of both armies. An Illinois private stationed in Pulaski, Tennessee, wrote home that there were four brothels in town and added that the price schedule in each was reasonable. "You may think I am a hard case," he conceded, "but I am as pious as you can find in the army."

With death so near, some soldiers sought solace in religion. Devotional activities intensified when troops settled into winter quarters and the fighting let up. Among Confederate troops, a wave of revivals swept the ranks during the last two years of the war, producing between 100,000 and 200,000 conversions. "In all my life, I never witnessed more displays of God's power in the awakening and conversion of sinners," testified a southern Methodist chaplain. These revivals deepened the sense of duty and visibly improved morale. No doubt southern leaders' heavier emphasis on religion contributed to the greater religious fervor in the Confederate camps, but significantly the first major revivals occurred after the South's twin defeats at Vicksburg and Gettysburg. Then too, as battle after battle thinned Confederate ranks, the prospect of death became increasingly real.

Southern Individualism

Despite obvious similarities, Confederate soldiers differed from their northern counterparts in ways that reflected fundamental qualities of southern society. Observers commented on the lack of discipline among Confederate troops—they had "a sort of devil-may-care, reckless, self-confident look." While Union soldiers came grudgingly to accept discipline as a necessity of war, many southerners were "not used to control of any sort and were not disposed to obey anyone except for good and sufficient reason given," one Rebel noted. "There never has been discipline in the armies of the Confederacy," commented one Richmond paper, "but instead thereof a kind of universal suffrage, which fights when it chooses and straggles when it feels like it." Many Confederates discarded equipment on the march and lagged behind, while others left without permission to take care of affairs back home, then returned to the ranks.

This disrespect for authority affected the ordinary soldier's relations with his officers. Like Union soldiers, Confederates complained about officers' special privileges, but they were far more likely to threaten or even physically assault their superiors when dissatisfied. Contributing to the lack of discipline, Confederates insisted on electing all officers through the rank of colonel. The Union army had discarded this democratic tradition soon after the war began, but electioneering constantly disrupted Confederate units. Officers were obliged to court the favor of their troops, and most of those known as strict disciplinarians were eventually defeated. Professional military men unanimously opposed the practice, but the Confederate Congress maintained it out of political considerations. A Confederate general fumed that the law should have been entitled "An act to disorganize and dissolve the army."

Moreover, upper-class southerners often felt that social class should override military rank. "It is galling for a gentleman to be absolutely and entirely subject to the orders of men who in private life were so far his inferiors," declared one socially prominent soldier. Another who was ordered to the guardhouse shouted to his captain, "I will not do it. I was a gentleman before I joined your company and by God you want to make a damned slave of me."

At the beginning of the war, when both armies were little more than disorganized mobs, the rural individualism of southerners was not a severe handicap. But as the Union army became increasingly organized, Confederate indifference to discipline took its toll. Northern soldiers who came from a more economically complex society were more familiar with impersonal organizations and accustomed to greater order and social control, and urban factory workers especially were used to a strict regimen. In a total war, which would be won by superior organization and the mobilization of resources, this difference between the two armies became more significant with each year of the fighting.

The Changing Face of Battle

As in all modern wars, technology revolutionized the conditions under which Civil War soldiers fought. Smoothbore muskets gave way to the rifle, so named because of the grooves etched into the barrel to give a bullet spin, as the basic infantry weapon. A new bullet, the minié ball, allowed the rifle to be easily loaded, and the invention of the percussion cap rendered it serviceable in wet weather. Under these improved circumstances, the number of misfires in 1000 rounds dropped from 411 to fewer than 5. Most significant, however, was the rifle's improved range of 1000 yards—four times greater than that of the old musket.* As a result, soldiers fought each other from greater distances and battles took much longer to fight and produced many more casualties—yet paradoxically they were much less decisive in outcome since modern armies, unless enveloped, are often battered but rarely annihilated in battle.

Under such conditions, the defense became a good deal stronger than the offense. The larger artillery pieces also adopted rifled barrels, but they still lacked good fuses and accurate sighting devices and could not effectively support attacking troops. Loaded with canister or grapeshot, however, they were a deadly defensive weapon, functioning like huge sawed-off shotguns that decimated advancing infantry at close range. Confederate General D. H. Hill described the devastating barrage as his men charged the Union line at Malvern Hill: "As each brigade emerged from the woods, from 50 to 100 guns opened upon it, tearing great gaps in its ranks. Most of them had an open field half a mile wide to cross, under the fire of field artillery and heavy ordnance. It was not war—it was murder."

The rising casualty lists bore down most heavily on the ordinary soldier. During the Crimean War, the charge of the English Light Brigade became notorious as an example of excessive sacrifice. Its casualty rate was a dismaying 37 percent, but that paled beside the experience of the 1st Minnesota or the 26th North Carolina at Gettysburg, which each lost 85 percent of its members, the highest loss sustained by any regiment in a Civil War battle. Over 100 regiments on both sides suffered more than 50 percent casualties in a single battle.

Every battle produced its skulkers and heroes, its miraculous escapes and

*The spin of a bullet leaving a rifle increased not only accuracy, but also velocity, which provided the extra range.

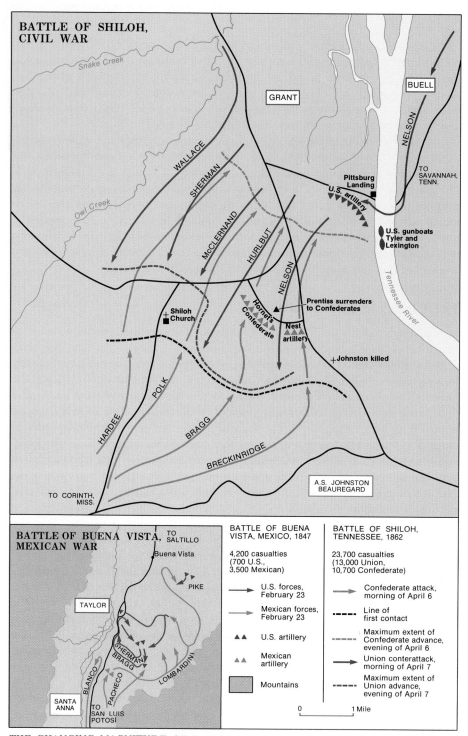

BATTLE OF SHILOH, CIVIL WAR

Snake Creek

GRANT

BUELL

NELSON

Owl Creek

WALLACE

SHERMAN

McCLERNAND

HURLBUT

Pittsburg Landing

U.S. artillery

TO SAVANNAH, TENN.

U.S. gunboats Tyler and Lexington

NELSON

Prentiss surrenders to Confederates

Shiloh Church

Hornet's Confederate

Nest artillery

+Johnston killed

Tennessee River

POLK

HARDEE

BRAGG

BRECKINRIDGE

A.S. JOHNSTON BEAUREGARD

TO CORINTH, MISS.

BATTLE OF BUENA VISTA, MEXICAN WAR

TO SALTILLO

Buena Vista

PIKE

TAYLOR

SHERMAN

BRAGG

BLANCO

PACHECO

LOMBARDINI

SANTA ANNA

TO SAN LUIS POTOSÍ

BATTLE OF BUENA VISTA, MEXICO, 1847

4,200 casualties (700 U.S., 3,500 Mexican)

→ U.S. forces, February 23

→ Mexican forces, February 23

▲▲ U.S. artillery

▲▲ Mexican artillery

Mountains

BATTLE OF SHILOH, TENNESSEE, 1862

23,700 casualties (13,000 Union, 10,700 Confederate)

→ Confederate attack, morning of April 6

- - - - Line of first contact

- - - - Maximum extent of Confederate advance, evening of April 6

→ Union conterattack, morning of April 7

- - - - Maximum extent of Union advance, evening of April 7

0   1 Mile

THE CHANGING MAGNITUDE OF BATTLE

During the Mexican War at Buena Vista, the American army of 4800 men was overextended trying to defend a two-mile line against 15,000 Mexicans. At Shiloh, by contrast, battle lines stretched almost six miles. (The maps are drawn to the same scale.) Against 40,000 Confederates, Grant galloped back and forth, rallying some 35,000 troops organized under five subordinates and coordinating the overnight reinforcement of 25,000 troops. The size of the armies, the complexity of their organization, the length of battle lines, and the number of casualties all demonstrate the extent to which the magnitude of battle had changed.

daring deeds, its gallows humor and wrenching tragedy. But as the haze of gunfire covered the land (smokeless powder had not yet been invented) and the constant spray of bullets mimicked rain pattering through the treetops, soldiers discovered that their romantic notions about war had no place on the battlefield. Men witnessed horrors they had never envisioned as civilians and choked from the acrid stench of decaying flesh and mortal slaughter. They realized that their efforts to convey to those back home the gruesome truth of combat were inadequate. "No tongue can tell, no mind can conceive, no pen portray the horrible sights I witnessed this morning," a Union soldier wrote after Antietam. And yet they tried.

An Indiana soldier at Perryville (7600 casualties): "It was an awful sight to see there men torn all to pieces with cannon balls and bom shells[.] the dead and wounded lay thick in all directions." A Confederate soldier at Shiloh (23,000 casualties): "O it was too shocking too horrible. God Grant that I may never be the partaker of such scenes again. . . . when released from this I shall ever be an advocate of peace." An Ohio soldier at Antietam (23,000 casualties), two days after the fighting: "The smell was offul . . . there was about 5 or 6,000 dead bodes decaying over the field . . . their lines of battle Could be run for miles by the dead[.] they lay long the lines like sheavs of Wheat[.] I could have walked on the boddees all most from one end too the other." A Georgian, the day after Chancellorsville (30,000 casualties): "It looked more like a slaughter pen than anything else. . . . The shrieks and groans of the wounded . . . was heart rending beyond all description." A Maine soldier who fought at Gettysburg (50,000 casualties): "I have Seen . . . men rolling in their own blood, Some Shot in one place, Some another. . . . our dead lay in the road and the Rebels in their hast to leave dragged both their baggage wagons and artillery over them and they lay mangled and torn to pieces so that Even friends could not tell them. You can form no idea of a battle field. . . . I hope none of my brothers will Ever have to go into a fight."

In the face of what Charles Francis Adams, Jr., termed "the carnival of death," soldiers braced themselves with a grim determination to see the war through to the end. Not glorious exploits, but endurance and tenacity became the true measure of heroism.

THE UNION'S TRIUMPH

In the spring of 1863, matters still looked promising for Lee. At the battle of Chancellorsville, he and Stonewall Jackson had brilliantly defeated Lincoln's latest commander, Joseph Hooker. But when Jackson returned from scouting the battle zone, he was accidentally shot by one of his own sentries. He died a few days later—a severe setback for Lee, who mourned that he had lost his "right arm." Determined to take the offensive and perhaps even capture a major northern city, Lee invaded Pennsylvania in June with an army of 75,000. Lincoln's newest general, George Gordon Meade, warily shadowed the Confederates, carefully keeping his forces between them and Washington. On the first of July, advance parties from the two armies accidentally collided at the town of Gettysburg. Both sides rushed up reinforcements, and the war's greatest battle ensued.

For once, it was Lee who had the extended supply lines and was forced to fight on ground chosen by his opponent. After two days of assaults failed to break the Union left or right, Lee made the greatest mistake of his career, sending 15,000 men under General George Pickett in a charge up the center of the Union

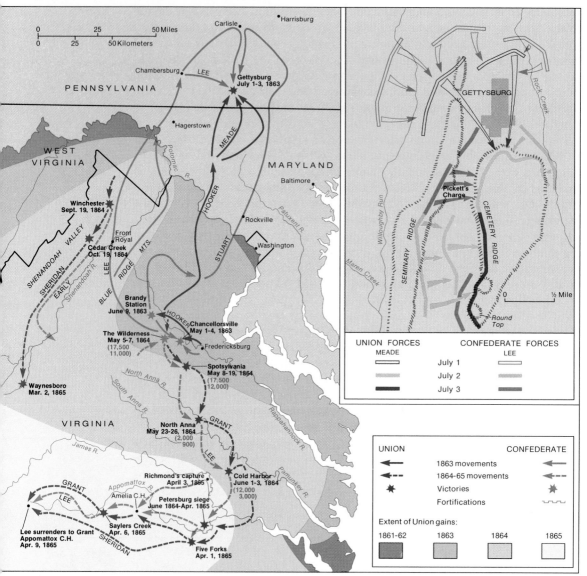

THE WAR IN THE EAST, 1863–1865

Lee won his most brilliant victory at Chancellorsville, then launched a second invasion of
the North, hoping to score a decisive victory. When the two armies accidentally collided at
Gettysburg on July 1, 1863, the Union's Army of the Potomac was driven back through the
town until it took up a strong defensive position, shaped like a fish hook and anchored by a
hill at each end. On July 2 the Confederate attack drove back the Union's left flank, but
failed to dislodge the right. Lee's assault on the center of the Union line July 3 (including
Pickett's charge) ended in a decisive defeat, and the Army of Northern Virginia retreated to
the Confederacy. In 1864 Grant delivered a series of heavy blows against Lee's outnumbered forces in Virginia. Despite staggering losses, Grant relentlessly pressed on in a ruthless demonstration of total war. (Note the casualties listed for the spring and summer of
1864; from mid-May to mid-June Grant lost nearly 60,000 men, equal to Lee's total
strength.) Sheridan's devastating raids against the civilian farms of the Shenandoah Valley
helped deprive Lee of desperately needed supplies. In April 1865, too weak to defend
Richmond any longer, Lee surrendered at Appomattox Courthouse in April 1865.

line on Cemetery Ridge. "Pickett's division just seemed to melt away in the blue musketry smoke which now covered the hill," one Confederate officer wrote. "Nothing but stragglers came back." The Union casualties of more than 23,000 represented a quarter of Meade's effective strength, but Lee lost between 25,000 and 28,000—more than a third of his troops. Never again was he able to assume the offensive.

Lincoln Finds His General

To the west, Grant had been trying for months to capture Vicksburg, one of the two remaining Rebel strongholds on the Mississippi. In a daring maneuver, he left behind his supply lines and marched inland, calculating that he could feed his army largely from the produce of Confederate farms, weakening southern resistance in the process. These were the tactics of total war, and seldom had they been tried before Grant used them. His troops defeated two Confederate armies, then drove the defenders of Vicksburg back into the city and starved them into submission. On July 4, as news of Gettysburg was telegraphed to Lincoln, Vicksburg surrendered to Grant. With the fall of Port Hudson, Louisiana, four days later, the Mississippi was completely in Union hands. Grant had divided the Confederacy and isolated Arkansas, Texas, and part of Louisiana from the rest of the South.

He followed this victory by opening up a supply line over the Tennessee mountains around Chattanooga, relieving Union forces that had been surrounded there. With Chattanooga safe by November, the Union army was poised for a thrust into Georgia. Grant's performance confirmed Lincoln's earlier judgment that "Grant is my man, and I am his the rest of the war," while an enthusiastic Congress now bestowed on him the rank of lieutenant general, held before only by George Washington. In March 1864 Lincoln brought Grant east and put him in command of all the Union armies.

Grant recognized that the Union had always possessed the resources to wear down the Confederacy, but that its larger armies had "acted independently and without concert, like a balky team, no two ever pulling together." He intended to change that. While he launched a major offensive against Lee in Virginia, William Tecumseh Sherman, who replaced Grant as commander of the western army, would drive a diagonal wedge through the Confederacy from Tennessee across Georgia. Grant's orders to Sherman were as blunt as his response had been that rainy night when the two had conferred at Shiloh: "Get into the interior of the enemy's country so far as you can, inflicting all the damage you can against their war resources."

In May and June 1864, Grant fought a series of fierce battles with Lee. Recognizing the importance a breakthrough in Virginia would have on northern morale, Grant tried to maneuver Lee out of the trenches and into an open battle. But Lee was too weak to win head-on, so he opted for a strategy of attrition: entrenching, holding lines dearly, hoping to inflict such heavy losses that the northern will to continue would waver and Lincoln would be defeated at the polls. It was a strategy that nearly worked, for Union casualties were staggering: in a month of heavy fighting, the Army of the Potomac lost 60,000 men—the size of Lee's entire army at the beginning of the campaign. Grant lost two soldiers for every Confederate who fell, yet at the end of the campaign his reinforced army was larger than when it started, whereas Lee's was significantly weaker.

After especially bloody losses at the battle of Cold Harbor, Grant changed tactics. Unable to flank the Confederates any farther to the east, he marched his army south toward Petersburg, which guarded the last remaining rail link between Richmond and the rest of the Confederacy. When the city managed to hold out until Lee arrived, Grant settled into a protracted siege, counting on his numerical superiority to stretch Lee's line to the breaking point. A siege would be agonizingly slow, but he saw no other option. In the west, meanwhile, the gaunt and grizzled Sherman, who was famous for his blunt, unceasing talk and passionate nature, fought his way to the outskirts of Atlanta by July. He had great confidence in his rough-hewn army, which by now had been seasoned by several years of hard campaigning. But Atlanta was heavily defended and gave no sign of capitulating. "Our all depends on that army at Atlanta," wrote Mary Chesnut, based on her conversations with Confederate leaders. "If that fails us, the game is up."

War in the Balance

The game was nearly up for Lincoln as the 1864 election approached. In 1863, the victories at Gettysburg and Vicksburg sparked Republican victories, including the defeat in Ohio of Clement Vallandigham, whom the Democrats had nominated for governor despite his Copperhead record. Public opinion seemed to be swinging toward emancipation. But as the Union draft swept more and more northerners south to death, and Grant and Sherman bogged down on the Virginia and Georgia fronts, even leaders in Lincoln's own party began to mutter out loud that he was not equal to the task.

Perhaps the most remarkable thing about the 1864 election is that it was held at all. Indeed, before World War I, the United States was the only democratic government in history to carry out a general election in wartime. But Lincoln firmly believed that to postpone it would be to lose the priceless heritage of republicanism itself: "We cannot have free government without elections, and if the rebellion could force us to forego or postpone a national election, it might fairly claim to have already conquered and ruined us." Exploiting his control of the party machinery, Lincoln easily won the Republican nomination. Endorsing Lincoln's wartime leadership, the Republican platform stipulated that the Confederacy's unconditional surrender was the only acceptable peace term and, at the president's insistence, called for adoption of a constitutional amendment abolishing slavery. To balance the ticket, Lincoln selected Andrew Johnson, the military governor of Tennessee and a prowar Democrat, as his running mate. The two men ran under the label of the "Union" party.

The Democrats nominated George McClellan, the former Union commander. Their platform, written largely by Vallandigham, pronounced the war a failure and called for an armistice and a peace conference. Warned that a cessation of fighting would lead to disunion, McClellan partially repudiated this position, insisting that "the Union is the one condition of peace—we ask no more." In private he made it clear that if elected he intended to restore slavery. Lincoln was gloomy about his prospects, as well as those of the Union itself. On August 23 he had his cabinet members sign a sealed envelope without revealing its contents. Inside was a statement which declared: "This morning, as for some days past, it seems exceedingly probable that this Administration will not be reelected. Then it will be my duty to so cooperate with the President-elect as to save the Union between the election and the inauguration; as he will have secured his election on such ground that he cannot possibly save it afterwards." But then Admiral Farragut won a dramatic victory at Mobile Bay, and a few weeks later, in early Septem-

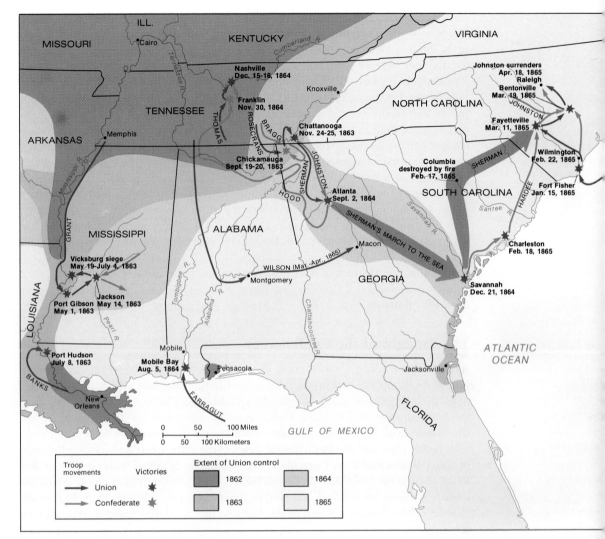

THE WAR IN THE WEST, 1863–1865
The Union continued its war of mobility in the western theater, bringing more Confederate territory under its control. After Grant captured Vicksburg the entire Mississippi lay in Union hands. His victories at Lookout Mountain and Missionary Ridge, near Chattanooga, ended the Confederate threat to Tennessee. In 1865 Sherman divided the Confederacy by seizing Atlanta and marching across Georgia; then he turned north. When Joseph Johnston surrendered, several weeks after Lee's capitulation at Appomattox, the war was effectively over.

ber, Sherman finally captured Atlanta. As Secretary of State Seward gleefully noted, "Sherman and Farragut have knocked the bottom out of the Chicago [Democratic] nominations."

Polling an impressive 55 percent of the popular vote, Lincoln won 212 electoral votes to McClellan's 21. Eighteen states allowed soldiers to vote in the fields, and Lincoln received nearly 80 percent of their ballots. One lifelong Democrat described the sentiment in the army: "We all want peace, but none any but an honorable one. I had rather stay out here a lifetime (much as I dislike it) than consent to a division of our country." As Grant recognized, the victory at the ballot box was "worth more than a victory in the field both in its effect on the Rebels and in its influence abroad." Jefferson Davis remained defiant, but the last hope of a Confederate victory was gone.

Equally important, the election of 1864 ended any doubt that slavery would be abolished in the reconstructed Union. The Emancipation Proclamation had not put an end to the question, for its legal status remained unclear. Lincoln argued that as a war measure, it would have no standing once peace returned; and in any case, it had not freed slaves in the border states or those parts of the Confederacy already under Union control. Thus Lincoln and the Republicans believed that a constitutional amendment was necessary to secure emancipation.

Congress had passed an amendment in the spring of 1864 that freed all slaves without compensating their owners, but the measure did not pass by the necessary two-thirds vote in the House. Following Lincoln's triumph, it came before Congress again. Lincoln threw all his influence behind the drive to round up the necessary votes, and it passed on January 31, 1865. By December, enough states had ratified the Thirteenth Amendment to make it part of the Constitution. Later generations would call Lincoln "the Great Emancipator," a title he merited most from his efforts on behalf of the Thirteenth Amendment.

The Twilight of the Confederacy

In the wake of Lincoln's reelection, the Confederate will to resist rapidly disintegrated. Southerners had never fully united behind the war effort, but the large majority had endured great suffering to uphold it. As Sherman pushed deeper into the Confederacy, and General Philip Sheridan mounted his devastating raid on the Shenandoah Valley, the war came home to southern civilians as never before. "We haven't got nothing in the house to eat but a little bit o meal," wrote the wife of one Alabama soldier in December 1864. ". . . Try to get off and come home and fix us all up some and then you can go back. . . . If you put off a-coming, 'twont be no use to come, for we'll all . . . [be] in the grave yard." He deserted. In the last months of the fighting, over half the Confederacy's soldiers were absent without leave.

After the fall of Atlanta, Sherman gave a frightening demonstration of the meaning of total war. General John Hood moved his Confederate army into Tennessee, in the rash hope of luring Sherman out of Georgia. Instead, Sherman sent only a portion of his forces to keep Hood occupied, and then imitated Grant's strategy by abandoning his supply lines for an audacious 300-mile march to the sea. His 57,000 men proceeded virtually unopposed, not in search of battle, but on an intimidating campaign of total war. Sherman intended to deprive Lee's army of the supplies it desperately needed to continue and to break the southern will to resist. Or as he bluntly put it, "to whip the Rebels, to humble their pride, to follow them to their recesses, and make them fear and dread us."

In four columns the army covered about 10 miles a day, cutting a path of destruction 50 miles wide. "We had a gay old campaign," one of his soldiers wrote. "Destroyed all we could not eat, stole their niggers, burned their cotton and gins, spilled their sorghum, burned and twisted their railroads and raised Hell generally." Sherman paid particular attention to the railroads, so that by the time he had finished tearing up scarce track and burning key bridges, Confederate armies were effectively separated from the resources of their population. Sherman esti-

The war's greatest generals, Ulysses S. Grant (left) and Robert E. Lee (right), confronted each other in the eastern theater during the last year of the war. A member of a distinguished Virginia family, the impeccably dressed Lee was every inch the aristocratic gentleman. Grant, a short, slouched figure with a stubby beard, dressed indifferently, often wearing a private's uniform with only the stars on his shoulders to indicate his rank. But his determination is readily apparent in this picture, taken at his field headquarters in 1864.

mated that his army did $100 million in damage, of which $20 million was necessary to supply his army and the rest was wanton destruction. On December 22 he captured Savannah and turned north. His troops wreaked havoc in South Carolina, which they considered the seedbed of the rebellion.

Meanwhile, General George H. Thomas defeated Hood's forces in December at Nashville, leaving the interior of the Confederacy essentially conquered. Only Lee's army remained, entrenched around Petersburg, Virginia, as Grant relentlessly extended his lines, stretching the Confederates thinner and thinner. In desperation, Lee attacked, hoping to break through the Union defenses, but in vain. The only remaining option was to abandon Richmond, which fell soon after, on April 3.

Westward Grant doggedly pursued the Army of Northern Virginia for another hundred miles. After Union forces captured supplies waiting for Lee at Appomattox Courthouse and also blocked his retreat south, the weary gentleman from Virginia asked to see Grant. As the victorious northern commander rode to where Lee was waiting, a Union band along the road struck up "Auld Lang Syne." His baggage somewhere back in the rear, Grant arrived in a mud-splattered private's shirt with only three stars pinned to the shoulder to signify his rank. Accepting Grant's terms, Lee surrendered on April 9, 1865. As he waited for his horse, Lee looked sadly across the fields and woods in the direction where his army waited— now prisoners. As one of Grant's aides recalled, "He thrice smote the palm of his left hand slowly with his right fist in an absent sort of way," then mounted. Grant saluted by raising his hat; Lee raised his respectfully and rode off at a slow trot. "On our part," one federal officer wrote, there was "not a sound of trumpet . . . nor roll of drum; not a cheer . . . but an awed stillness rather."

With Lee's army gone, remaining resistance throughout the Confederacy collapsed within a matter of weeks. Visiting the captured city of Richmond on April 4, Lincoln was enthusiastically greeted by the black population. He looked "pale, haggard, utterly worn out," noted one observer. The lines in his face showed how much the war had aged him in only four years. Often his friends had counseled rest, but Lincoln had observed that "the tired part of me is *inside* and out of reach." Day after day, the grim telegrams had arrived—so many wounded, so many dead—or the mothers had come to see him in his "public opinion baths," begging him to spare their youngest son because the other two had died in battle. Congressman Isaac Arnold was once shocked to find Lincoln telling one of his innumerable jokes after particularly severe Union losses, and rebuked him for such levity in a time of war. The president broke down, his whole body shaking. If he did not joke or tell stories, he explained as tears flowed down his cheeks, the burden became too much to bear.

Back in Washington, the president received news of Lee's surrender with relief. But massive problems remained. How exactly would the seceded states be brought back into the Union? Could the wounds of a house divided fully heal? The night of April 14, Lincoln, seeking a welcome escape, went to see a comedy at Ford's Theater. In the midst of the performance John Wilkes Booth, an unstable actor and Confederate sympathizer, slipped into Lincoln's balcony box and shot him with a derringer; then he jumped to the stage shouting the state motto of Virginia, "*Sic semper tyrannis*"—Thus be it ever to tyrants—and fled. Lincoln died the next morning without regaining consciousness. As he had called upon others to do in his Gettysburg Address, the sixteenth president had given his "last full measure of devotion" to the Republic.

THE IMPACT OF WAR

The assassination, which capped four years of bloody war, left a tiredness in the nation's bones—a tiredness "*inside*" and not easily within reach. In every way the conflict had produced fundamental, often devastating changes. There was, of course, the carnage. Approximately 620,000 men on both sides lost their lives, almost as many as in all the other wars the nation has fought from the Revolution through Vietnam combined. In material terms, the war cost an estimated $20 billion, or about 10 times the value of all slaves in the country in 1860, and more than 11 times the total amount spent by the federal government from 1789 to 1861. Although northern expenditures slightly exceeded those of the South, white southerners bore a much higher cost per capita. The war's ravages destroyed perhaps $1.5 billion in property, most of it within the Confederacy. Even without adding the market value of freed slaves, southern wealth declined 43 percent, transforming what had been the richest section in the nation (on a white per capita basis) into the poorest.

The staggering demands of total war also stimulated industrialization, especially in the heavy industries of iron and coal, machinery, and agricultural implements, while the probusiness finance and tax policies of the Republican party encouraged the formation of larger corporations and industries in the years ahead. The war also forced manufacturers to supply and equip the army on an unprecedented scale over distances of up to a thousand miles. One consequence was that businesses of necessity became larger, and truly national industries, producing for a national rather than local market, emerged in flour milling, meat packing, clothing and shoe manufacture, and machinery making.

Politically, the war dramatically changed the balance of power. The South lost its substantial influence, as did the Democratic party, while the Republicans emerged in a commanding position. And above the divisions of party, the Union's military victory signaled the triumph of nationalism. No longer could theorists like John C. Calhoun argue that the Union was a voluntary confederacy of sovereign states. It was perpetual, as Andrew Jackson had first suggested—truly an indivisible nation. In an important symbolic change, Americans now spoke of the United States in the singular rather than the plural. Julia Ward Howe's "Battle Hymn of the Republic" had referred to the divine vengeance that would be wreaked by the war's "terrible swift sword"; yet out of this fiery trial, the Republic was reborn stronger and more durable than before.

In the short run, the price was disillusion, ashes, and bitterness. The South faced a painful period of reconstruction in the shadow of its military defeat, while blacks anxiously waited to see whether they would be incorporated into the political and economic life of the nation. The war's corrosive effect on morals left American life and politics more corrupt and made the idealism of antebellum humanitarian reform seem almost innocent by comparison. Millennialism and perfectionism were victims of the war's appalling slaughter, forsaken for a new emphasis on practicality and power, order and discipline, materialism and science. As the war unfolded, the New York *Herald* recognized the deep changes: "All sorts of old fogy ideas, manners, and customs have gone under, and all sorts of new ideas, modes, and practices have risen to the surface and become popular."

George Ticknor, a prominent author and critic who was sensitive to shifting intellectual and social currents, reflected on the changes that had shaken the nation in only a few short years. The war, it seemed to him, had left "a great gulf between what happened before it in our century and what has happened since, or what is likely to happen hereafter. It does not seem to me as if I were living in the country in which I was born."

SIGNIFICANT EVENTS

1861 — Border states remain in the Union; Union blockade proclaimed; Lincoln suspends writ of habeas corpus in selected areas; Battle of Bull Run; Crittenden Resolution; First Confiscation Act; *Trent* affair

1862 — Forts Henry and Donelson captured; *Monitor vs. Virginia (Merrimack);* Battle of Shiloh; slavery abolished in the District of Columbia; Confederacy institutes draft; New Orleans captured; Homestead Act; Union Pacific Railroad chartered; Land Grant College Act; Second Confiscation Act; Union income tax enacted; McClellan's Peninsula campaign fails; second Battle of Bull Run; Battle of Antietam; preliminary Emancipation Proclamation; Lincoln suspends writ of habeas corpus throughout the Union; Battle of Fredericksburg

1863 — Emancipation Proclamation; National Banking Act; Union institutes draft; Confederacy enacts general tax laws, initiates impressment; bread riots in the Confederacy; Battle of Chancellorsville; West Virginia admitted to the Union; Battle of Gettysburg; Vicksburg captured; New York City draft riots

1864 — Grant becomes Union general in chief; Wilderness campaign; Battle of Mobile Bay; fall of Atlanta; Lincoln reelected; Sherman's march to the sea

1865 — Congress passes Thirteenth Amendment; Sherman's march through the Carolinas; Lee surrenders; Lincoln assassinated; Thirteenth Amendment ratified

1866 — *Ex parte Milligan*

17

Reconstructing the Union

O n November 19, 1866, Joseph Davis sold his plantations Hurricane and Brierfield, located on a large bend of the Mississippi River south of Vicksburg. In one sense, there was nothing unusual in this transaction. Like other southern planters financially ruined by the war, Davis had decided to quit agricultural operations. Yet the sale was bound to attract attention, since Joseph Davis was the elder brother of Jefferson Davis. In fact, before the war the Confederate president had operated Brierfield as his own plantation, even though his brother retained legal title to it. In truth, however, this sale was so unusual that the two parties agreed to keep it secret, and with good reason. The purchasers, Benjamin Montgomery and his sons, were black, and Mississippi law prohibited blacks from owning land.

Though a slave, Montgomery had been the business manager of the two Davis plantations before the war. Displaying unusual talent and ambition, he had also obtained Joseph Davis' permission to open a store on Hurricane Plantation and had developed considerable business expertise, operating on his own line of credit in New Orleans and dealing with white as well as black customers. In 1863, when the fighting reached the area around Vicksburg, Montgomery fled to Cincinnati, where his mechanical ingenuity landed him a job in a boatyard. With the coming of peace, however, he returned to Davis Bend, where the federal government had established a settlement of independent black farmers to whom it leased plots of land on confiscated plantations—Joseph Davis' among them. Reopening his plantation store, as well as beginning planting operations, Montgomery emerged as the leader of the African-American community at the Bend.

Then, in 1866, President Andrew Johnson pardoned Joseph Davis and restored his lands. Black hopes of creating a permanent settlement of independent farmers at Davis Bend were thrown into doubt. But when Joseph Davis took possession of Brierfield and Hurricane, he was over 80 years old. He lacked the will and stamina to rebuild and start over again. Unlike many one-time slaveholders, however, Davis still felt bound by obligations to his former slaves, and he remained deeply interested in their welfare. Convinced that with proper encouragement African-Americans could succeed economically in freedom, he sold his land secretly to Benjamin Montgomery in order to promote black self-help. Only when the law prohibiting blacks from owning land was overturned in 1867 did Davis publicly confirm the sale to his ex-slave.

A Visit from the Old Mistress, *by Winslow Homer, captures the conflicting, often awkward emotions felt by both races after the war.*

For his part, Montgomery undertook to fulfill the dream of his former master to create a model society at Davis Bend where African-Americans could prosper through mutual cooperation. Moving with his family into what had once been the home of Jefferson Davis, Montgomery guided the settlement with a paternalistic hand, much like Joseph Davis had earlier. He rented land to black farmers, hired others to work his own fields, sold supplies on credit, and ginned and marketed the crops. To the growing African-American community, he constantly preached the gospel of hard work, self-reliance, and education.

Severe difficulties, including the destruction caused by the war, several disastrous floods, insects, droughts, and declining cotton prices, dogged these farmers. Yet before long, cotton production exceeded that of the antebellum years. In 1870 the black families at Davis Bend produced 2500 bales, more than twice the amount produced by whites on a neighboring plantation with the same acreage. In fact, in that year the Montgomerys accounted for over half of all the cotton bales produced by African-Americans in the state's 20 richest cotton counties. The following year they bought Ursino Plantation, which adjoined their holdings. The addition of 1500 acres to the 4000 they had purchased from Joseph Davis made them reputedly the third largest planters in the state, and they won national and international awards for the high quality of their cotton. Their success was an inspiration and example of what African-Americans, given a fair chance, might accomplish.

The experiences of Benjamin Montgomery during the years after 1865 were not those of most southern blacks, who did not own land or have a powerful white benefactor. Yet Montgomery's dream of economic independence was shared by all African-Americans. As one black veteran noted, "Every colored man will be a slave, and feel himself a slave until he can raise him own *bale of cotton* and put him own mark upon it and say dis is mine!" Blacks could not gain effective freedom simply through a proclamation of emancipation, no matter how well intentioned. They also needed to live in a society where they had economic power of their own—to become the largest cotton planter in the district, like Montgomery, or simply a farmer with a plot of land no one could unfairly take away.

For nearly two centuries, the laws had prevented slaves from possessing such economic power. Inevitably, if such conditions were to be overturned, blacks needed political power too. The whole theory that underlies a democratic republic is that social conflict—between different classes, economic groups, or regions—may be peacefully resolved if all groups share power in the political arena. For 200 years, African-Americans lacked that power, and the conflict and inequality that had built up in American society had led to civil war. In political terms, the Republic would have to be reconstructed in order to share power with a major group of Americans who had been previously denied it.

To achieve that goal in a land where racism had distorted society for so long in both the North and the South would be a major task. War, in its blunt way, had roughed out the contours of a solution, but only in broad terms. Clearly, African-Americans would no longer be slaves. The North, with its industrial might, would be the driving force in the nation's economy and retain the dominant political voice. It had the power to set the terms for admitting the defeated Confederate states back into the Union. But beyond that, the outlines of a reconstructed Republic remained vague. How much effective power would blacks receive? How would the North and South readjust their economic and social relations? These questions lay at the heart of the problem of Reconstruction.

PRESIDENTIAL RECONSTRUCTION

Even in the early months of the war, Abraham Lincoln had considered Reconstruction his responsibility. In devising a program, Lincoln never lost sight of its political consequences. Elected with less than 40 percent of the popular vote in 1860, he was acutely aware that the Republican party had no real strength in the South. Once the states of the Confederacy were restored to the Union, they would again have 22 senators and 63 representatives, as well as 85 votes in the Electoral College. The Republicans inevitably would be weakened unless they evolved into more than a sectional party. Lincoln looked to the old Whigs, who supported many of the Republicans' economic programs, to build up a southern wing of the party. By a generous peace, he hoped to attract white southerners and assure his party's continuing national supremacy.

Lincoln's Plan

As the Union army conquered parts of the Confederacy, Lincoln set up a flexible program of Reconstruction in a Proclamation of Amnesty and Reconstruction, issued in December 1863. A minimum of 10 percent of the qualified voters from 1860, having taken a loyalty oath to the Union, could organize a state government. The new state constitution had to be republican in form, abolish slavery, and provide for black education. High-ranking Confederate leaders were not eligible to take the loyalty oath, although Lincoln did not require that the new state government bar them from public life. Once these requirements had been met, the president would recognize the new civilian state government.

Lincoln also assured southerners that there would be no mass arrests, trials, and executions, for he had no desire to create any Confederate martyrs. He indicated that he would be generous in granting pardons and did not rule out compensation for slave property. Moreover, while he suggested to the Unionist governor of Louisiana that it would be wise to permit a few black men to vote, "as for instance, the very intelligent and especially those who have fought gallantly in our ranks," Lincoln did not demand social or political equality for blacks. Nor did he envision any long-term federal assistance to former slaves. Although he seemed to be moving toward requiring limited black suffrage in the disloyal southern states, he recognized pro-Union governments in Louisiana, Arkansas, and Tennessee that allowed only white men to vote.

The Radical Republicans, who constituted the most militant antislavery wing of the party, found Lincoln's approach much too lenient. Radical members of Congress like Charles Sumner and George W. Julian had been openly condemning slavery and the Slave Power for over a decade. They had led the struggle to make emancipation a war aim and now were in the forefront in advocating rights and privileges for the freedmen. They were also disturbed that Lincoln had not enlisted Congress in devising Reconstruction policy. Lincoln argued that the rebellious states had never left the Union because secession was illegal. Therefore, the executive branch should bear the responsibility for restoring proper relations with the former Confederate states. The Radicals, on the other hand, believed that in seceding, these states had ceased to exist; consequently, it was Congress' duty to set the terms under which they would regain their rights in the Union. Though the Radicals often disagreed with each other on matters of detail, they were united in a determination to readmit southern states only after slavery had been ended, black rights protected, and the power of the planter class destroyed.

Led by Senator Benjamin Wade of Ohio and Representative Henry Winter Davis of Maryland, Congress proposed that Confederate states would be ruled temporarily by a military governor. Under the Wade–Davis bill, state conventions could meet to draft a new state constitution only when fully half the white adult males took an oath of allegiance. The constitution had to renounce secession as illegal, abolish slavery, and repudiate all debts incurred by the Confederate government, ensuring that those who bought Confederate bonds and loaned money to finance the rebellion would not be repaid. To qualify as a voter or to serve as a delegate to the constitutional convention required a second oath, the so-called ironclad oath, attesting that a person had never voluntarily aided or supported the Confederacy. Since only a small minority of white southerners could take this oath in good conscience, this bill would have given political power to the hard-core Unionists in each state.

When the Wade–Davis bill passed on the final day of the 1864 congressional session, Lincoln exercised his right of a pocket veto and the bill died.* The Radicals bitterly assailed the president, but if anything, their strident objections won him wider popular support. Still, his own program could not succeed without the assistance of Congress, which refused to count the electoral votes of the reconstructed states in the 1864 election or seat Unionist representatives who had been elected to Congress from Louisiana or Arkansas. By April 1865, with the war in its last days, Lincoln appeared willing to make concessions to the Radicals. He suggested that he might favor different—and conceivably more rigorous—Reconstruction plans for different states. At his final cabinet meeting, he acknowledged that perhaps he had gone too fast on Reconstruction and approved in principle a proposal by Secretary of War Edwin Stanton to place the defeated South temporarily under military rule.

But only a few days later Booth's bullet found its mark, and Lincoln's final approach to Reconstruction would never be known. Would he have continued to push for moderation? Or being a practical politician, would he have made peace with the Radicals and pushed ahead with a firmer hand? How would the South respond to any plan of "Reconstruction"?

The Mood of the South

Northerners worried about the attitude of ex-Confederates at war's end. During Lincoln's visit to Richmond, he had ridden along deserted, rubble-strewn streets past charred buildings, to be greeted by a dusty silence. Hundreds of white southerners peered out windows, "but it was a silent crowd," recalled one of his guards. "There was something oppressive in those thousands of watchers without a sound, either of welcome or hatred." In the wake of defeat, the immediate reaction among whites was one of shock, despair, and hopelessness. Some southerners, of course, were openly antagonistic. A North Carolina innkeeper remarked bitterly that Yankees had stolen his slaves, burned his house, and killed his son, leaving him only one privilege: "to hate 'em. I git up at half-past four in the morning, and sit up till twelve at night, to hate 'em." Most Confederate soldiers were less defiant, having had their fill of war; and even among hostile civilians there was a pervasive feeling that the South must accept northern terms. A South Carolina paper admitted that "the conqueror has the right to make the terms, and we must submit."

This psychological moment was critical. To prevent a resurgence of resistance, the president needed to lay out in unmistakable terms what white southerners had to do to regain their old status in the Union. A confusion in policy, or a wavering on the terms of how political power was to be shared in the reconstructed Union, could only increase the likelihood that southerners would resist the logic of the war's victory. Perhaps even a clear and firm policy would not have been enough. But Lincoln was no longer president, and as events would prove, the executive power now rested in less capable hands.

Johnson's Program of Reconstruction

Andrew Johnson, the new president, had been born in North Carolina and eventually moved to Tennessee, where he supported himself as a tailor. His wife taught

---

*If a president does not sign a bill after Congress has adjourned, it has the same effect as a veto.

him to read and write. Something of a demagogue, he rose to political power in eastern Tennessee, where there were few slaves, by portraying himself as the champion of the people against the wealthy planter class. "Some day I will show the stuck-up aristocrats who is running the country," he vowed as he began his political career. "A cheap purse-proud set they are, not half as good as the man who earns his bread by the sweat of his brow." In Tennessee, he campaigned for a free, tax-supported public school system, and when he went to Congress, he led the fight for a homestead act to grant free land from the public domain to small farmers. He had not opposed slavery before the war—in fact, he hoped to disperse slave ownership more widely in southern society. Although he accepted emancipation as one of the consequences of the war, Johnson remained an inveterate racist with no concern for the welfare of blacks. "Damn the negroes," he said during the war, "I am fighting these traitorous aristocrats, their masters."

Johnson had been the only southerner to remain in the Senate when his state seceded in 1861. In Congress, he had joined with the Radicals in calling for stern treatment of southern rebels. "Treason must be made odious and traitors must be punished and impoverished," he proclaimed in 1864. After serving as military governor of Tennessee following its occupation by Union forces, Johnson, a Democrat, was tapped by Lincoln in 1864 as his running mate on the rechristened "Union" ticket.

The Radicals expected Johnson to uphold their views on Reconstruction, and upon assuming the presidency he spoke of trying Confederate leaders and breaking up planters' estates. In reality, the grounds of agreement between Johnson and the Radicals were quite narrow. Unlike most Republicans, Johnson strongly supported states' rights and decentralization. He opposed government aid to business and romanticized the self-sufficient yeoman farmer he had championed in Tennessee politics. Given such differences, conflict between the president and the majority in Congress was inevitable. But Johnson's abrasive personality and politi-

Andrew Johnson was a staunch Unionist, but his contentious personality and inflexibility masked a deep-seated insecurity, which was rooted in his humble background. As a young man, he worked and lived in this rude tailor shop in Greenville, Tennessee.

cal shortcomings made the situation worse. Scarred by his humble origins, he remained throughout his life an outsider. When challenged or criticized, he became tactless and inflexible, alienating even those who sought to work with him.

At first, Johnson seemed to be following Lincoln's policy of quickly restoring the southern states to their rightful place in the Union. Like Lincoln, he prescribed a loyalty oath southern whites would have to take to receive pardon and amnesty. Those who took the oath would have their property, except for slaves, restored and would regain their civil and political rights. Like Lincoln, Johnson excluded high Confederate officials from this group, but he added those with property worth over $20,000, which included his old foes in the planter class. These groups had to apply to the president for individual pardons.

Loyal state governments could be formed after a provisional governor, appointed by the president, called a state convention and supervised the election of delegates. Voters and delegates had to qualify under the 1860 state election laws and take the new loyalty oath. Once elections were held to choose a governor, legislature, and members of Congress, Johnson announced he would recognize the new state government, revoke martial law, and withdraw Union troops. Again, the plan was similar to Lincoln's, though more lenient. Johnson did not require southern states to repeal their ordinances of secession, repudiate the Confederate debt, or ratify the proposed Thirteenth Amendment abolishing slavery. He only recommended that they do so.

The Failure of Johnson's Program

The southern delegates who met to construct new governments soon demonstrated that they were in no frame of mind to follow mere recommendations. Several states, instead of repudiating their ordinances of secession, merely repealed them, refusing to yield in principle the right to secede. Mississippi and Texas rejected the Thirteenth Amendment, while Georgia ratified it with the provision that slaveholders be compensated. South Carolina and Mississippi refused to repudiate the Confederate debt.

Most damaging, however, was that none of the new governments allowed blacks any political rights, and none made any effective provision for black education. Mississippi was the first to act in August 1865, but Johnson, instead of pressing harder for change, telegraphed the provisional governor with suggestions on how to appear to comply with his terms without provoking northern public opinion. Give the vote only to the tiny minority of literate black males and those who owned property worth more than $250, he advised. "This you can do with perfect safety and, . . . as a consequence, the radicals, who are wild upon negro franchise, will be completely foiled." But the new southern governments refused to make even that gesture. In addition to denying black political rights, each state passed a series of laws, often modeled on the earlier slave code, that applied only to African-Americans.

The black codes did grant African-Americans some rights they had been denied as slaves. They legalized marriages from slavery and allowed blacks to hold and sell property and to sue and be sued in state courts. Yet their primary intent was to keep African-Americans as propertyless agricultural laborers without political rights and with inferior legal rights. The new freedmen could not serve on juries, could not testify against whites, and could not marry whites. And their freedom to work as they pleased was severely limited. South Carolina forbade blacks from engaging without a special license in anything other than agricultural labor; Mississippi prohibited them from buying or renting farmland; Louisiana required that agricultural laborers make contracts within the first 10 days of January that bound them for the entire year. Most states ominously provided that blacks who were vagrants could be arrested and hired out to landowners.

Although several northern states had narrowly defeated their own proposals to give black men the vote, most northerners were incensed by the restrictive black codes. "We tell the white men of Mississippi that the men of the North will convert the State of Mississippi into a frog pond before they will allow such laws to disgrace one foot of the soil . . . over which the flag of freedom waves," proclaimed the Chicago *Tribune*. Carl Schurz, a Radical Republican orator and politician who toured the South at Johnson's request, wrote that the black codes were "a striking embodiment of the idea that although the former owner has lost his individual right of property in the former slaves, the blacks at large belong to the whites at large."

Southern voters under Johnson's plan defiantly elected governors and members of Congress who were by and large prominent Confederate military and political leaders, headed by Alexander Stephens, the vice president of the Confederacy, who was elected senator from Georgia. At this point, Johnson faced a critical decision. He could have called for new elections or admitted that a different program of Reconstruction was needed. Yet for all his rabble rousing, he recoiled from the prospect of social and economic upheaval in the South. Although he had smarted for years at "the taunts, the jeers, the scowls" of upper-class planters, at the same time, he craved their respect. When they began flocking to the White House, begging for pardons and praising his conduct, he found it enormously gratifying. He began to issue special pardons almost as fast as they could be printed; in the next two years he pardoned some 13,500 Confederates. Confronted with southern defiance, Johnson capitulated and failed to follow through on his original goals.

In private, Johnson warned southerners against a reckless course. Publicly he put on a bold face, announcing that Reconstruction had been successfully completed. But many in the new Congress thought it a failure, and the stage was set for a serious confrontation.

Johnson's Break with Congress

The new Congress was by no means of one mind. The most conservative element, a small number of Democrats and conservative Republicans, backed the president's program of immediate and unconditional restoration. At the other end of the spectrum, a larger group of Radical Republicans, led by Thaddeus Stevens, Charles Sumner, Benjamin Wade, and others, was bent on fundamentally restructuring southern society and making it over on a northern model. Reconstruction must "revolutionize Southern institutions, habits, and manners," thundered Representative Stevens. "The foundations of their institutions must be broken and relaid, or all our blood and treasure have been spent in vain."

As a minority, the Radicals could accomplish nothing without the aid of the Moderate Republicans, the largest bloc in Congress. Led by William Pitt Fessenden, Lyman Trumbull, and John Sherman, the Moderates hoped to avoid conflict

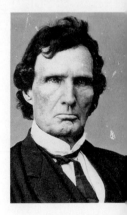

Thaddeus Stevens, Radical leader in the House.

This drawing by Thomas Nast expresses northern condemnation of the black codes enacted in the South after the war. On the left, a black man accused of crime is sold as punishment, while on the right another freedman is whipped in front of a blindfolded justice.

with the president, and they had no desire to foster social revolution in the South. But they wanted to keep Confederate leaders from reassuming power and readmit southern states only after they had fulfilled certain conditions. Finally, while they had no sympathy for the idea of racial equality promoted by many Radicals, the Moderates saw the need to extend federal protection to the freedman, who, Trumbull declared, would "be tyrannized over, abused, and virtually reenslaved without some legislation by the nation for his protection."

The central issue dividing Johnson and the Radicals was the place of African-Americans in American society. Johnson, along with other racists, accused his opponents of seeking "to Africanize the southern half of our country." The Radicals, on the other hand, championed civil and political rights for blacks, particularly the right to vote. Convinced that southern white Unionists were too small a nucleus to build a party around, Radicals believed that the only way to maintain loyal governments and develop a Republican party in the South was to give black men the ballot. Moderates, however, feared too much of an emphasis on black rights would alienate northern voters. But they agreed with Radicals that the new southern governments were too harsh toward blacks and too defiant toward the victorious North. In December 1865, when southern representatives to Congress appeared in Washington, a majority in Congress voted to exclude them. They also appointed a joint committee, chaired by Moderate William Fessenden, to look into Reconstruction.

The growing split with the president became clearer when Congress passed a bill extending the life of the Freedmen's Bureau. Created in March 1865 during the last days of the war, the Bureau provided emergency food, clothing, and medical care to war refugees (including whites) and took charge of settling freedmen on abandoned lands. The new bill not only continued these duties, but also called for the Bureau to supervise special courts to resolve disputes involving freedmen and to set up and support schools for southern blacks. This bill passed with virtually unanimous Republican support, but to the surprise of Moderates, Johnson vetoed the measure, charging that the Bureau's military courts lacked the fundamental guarantees of juries and rules of evidence. (African-Americans, of course, could neither sit on the juries nor testify against whites under the state laws approved by Johnson.) Even more alarming, the president claimed the bill was unconstitutional because southern representatives had been excluded from Congress, which if accepted would mean that any legislation passed by Congress was unconstitutional. Still, Congress failed to override the veto.

Johnson also vetoed a civil rights bill designed to overturn the more flagrant provisions of the black codes. The law made African-Americans citizens of the United States and granted them the right to own property, make contracts, and have access to courts as parties and witnesses. It also provided that federal courts could take jurisdiction if state courts discriminated against blacks. Johnson vetoed the bill on the grounds that it granted greater safeguards to blacks than whites. For most Republicans, Johnson's action was the last straw. In April 1866 Congress overrode his veto, the first major legislation to be enacted into law over a presidential veto in American history. Congress then approved a slightly revised Freedmen's Bureau bill in July and promptly overrode the president's veto. Only three Republicans in the Senate supported the president. "He has broken the faith, betrayed his trust, and must sink from detestation to contempt," observed Senator Fessenden. Johnson's refusal to compromise drove the Moderates into the arms of the Radicals.

The Fourteenth Amendment

To prevent unrepentant Confederates from taking over the reconstructed state governments and denying blacks basic freedoms, the Joint Committee on Reconstruction proposed an amendment to the Constitution, which passed both houses of Congress with the necessary two-thirds vote in June 1866. In effect, the amendment, coupled with the Freedmen's Bureau and civil rights bills, represented the Moderates' terms for Reconstruction.

The amendment put a number of matters beyond the control or discretion of the president. It guaranteed repayment of the national war debt and prohibited repayment of the Confederate debt, which Johnson had not insisted on. To counteract the president's wholesale pardons, the amendment disqualified prominent Confederates from holding office and provided that only Congress by a two-thirds vote could remove this penalty. Radicals had pushed for a provision giving the franchise to blacks, but Moderates balked, convinced that many white northerners would oppose such a provision. Instead, the amendment merely gave Congress the right to reduce the representation of any state that did not have impartial (male) suffrage. The practical effect of this provision, which Radicals labeled a "swindle," was to allow northern states to continue a policy of white suffrage if they wished, for they had few blacks and would not be penalized. Southern states, on the other hand, had significant African-American populations and risked losing part of their representation in Congress by adhering to white suffrage.

The most important provision of the amendment, Section 1, defined an American citizen as anyone who had been born in the United States or naturalized. Blacks thereby automatically became citizens, effectively repealing the Supreme Court's ruling in the *Dred Scott* case. Section 1 also prohibited states from abridging "the privileges or immunities" of citizens, depriving "any person of life, liberty, or property, without due process of law," or denying "any person . . . equal protection of the laws." The framers of the amendment probably intended to prohibit laws that applied to one race only, such as the black codes; or that made certain acts felonies when committed by blacks but not whites; or that decreed different penalties for the same crime when committed by whites and blacks. The framers probably did not intend to prevent African-Americans from being excluded from juries or segregated in schools and public places.

Still, Section 1 used general phrases for the rights it enumerated: "privileges and immunities," "due process of law," and "equal protection of the laws." The authors deliberately made those guarantees broad, to cover unanticipated abuses. And indeed, the first section of the Fourteenth Amendment has been the basis for more litigation than the rest of the Constitution combined, and one of the greatest safeguards of individual liberty and equal rights.

Ratification of a constitutional amendment does not require the president's approval; still, Johnson denounced the proposed amendment and urged southern states not to ratify it. Ironically, the president's own state ignored his advice, and one gleeful foe sent Congress a telegram announcing Tennessee's approval, which concluded, "Give my respects to the dead dog in the White House." Congress readmitted the state with no further restrictions. All the other seceded states rejected the amendment.

The Election of 1866

With Congress and the president at loggerheads, Johnson took his case to the people. In the election of 1866, he hoped to build a new National Union party, rallying Democrats, southern whites, and conservative Republicans on the platform of immediate readmission of the southern states. When a national convention in Philadelphia in August attracted few Republicans, Johnson became a man virtually without a party.

News that summer of major race riots in Memphis and New Orleans heightened northern concern. Forty-six blacks died when white mobs invaded the black section of Memphis, burning homes, churches, and schoolhouses; about the same number were killed in New Orleans when whites attacked both black and white delegates to a convention supporting black suffrage. "The negroes now know, to their sorrow, that it is best not to arouse the fury of the white man," boasted one Memphis newspaper. In the face of such attitudes, Johnson, who launched a tour of the East and Midwest to drum up support for his cause, found it difficult to convince audiences that white southerners were fully repentant. To make things worse, he conducted his campaign "swing around the circle" as if he were stumping the backwoods of Tennessee, trading insults with hostile crowds, responding in kind when they heckled him, and ranting that the Radicals were traitors. Even his supporters found the performance humiliating.

Not to be outdone, the Radicals vilified Johnson as a traitor aiming to turn the country over to rebels and Copperheads. Resorting to the tactic of "waving the bloody shirt," they appealed to voters by reviving bitter memories of the war and sectional distrust. In a classic example of such rhetoric, Governor Oliver Morton of Indiana proclaimed that "every bounty jumper, every deserter, every sneak who ran away from the draft" was a Democrat; everyone "who murdered Union prisoners," every

> New York rioter in 1863 who burned up little children in colored asylums, who robbed, ravished and murdered indiscriminately . . . called himself a Democrat. In short, the Democratic party may be described as a common sewer and loathsome receptacle, into which is emptied every element of treason North and South.

Such rhetoric became a Republican campaign staple for many years.

The voters soundly repudiated Johnson, as the Republicans won over a two-thirds majority in both houses of Congress, every northern gubernatorial contest, and control of every northern legislature. The Radicals had reached the height of their power, propelled by genuine alarm among northerners that Johnson's policies would lose the fruits of the Union's victory and leave the ruling class of the South undisturbed.

CONGRESSIONAL RECONSTRUCTION

With a clear mandate in hand, Republicans devised their own program of Reconstruction. The first Reconstruction Act was passed in March 1867 and, like all other subsequent pieces of Reconstruction legislation, was promptly repassed over Johnson's veto. The 10 unreconstructed states were divided into five military districts, each under a military commander with authority over the provisional state governments. In enrolling voters, officials were to include black adult males but not those former Confederates who were barred from holding office under the Fourteenth Amendment. Delegates to the state conventions would frame constitutions that provided for black suffrage and disqualified prominent ex-Confederates from office; the first state legislatures to meet under the new system were required to ratify the Fourteenth Amendment. Once these steps were completed and Congress approved the new state constitution, a state could send representatives to Congress.

Southern whites found these requirements so obnoxious, they preferred to remain under military rule; thus officials took no steps to register voters. Congress then enacted a second Reconstruction Act, also in March, ordering the local military commanders to enroll voters and put the machinery of Reconstruction into motion. Johnson's efforts to limit the power of military commanders produced a third act, passed in July, which upheld their superiority in all matters and confirmed their power to remove officials and reject voters' loyalty oaths. Southerners then adopted a strategy of delay, hoping that a Democratic victory in the 1868 presidential election would lead to repeal of all the Reconstruction acts. When elections were held to ratify the new state constitutions, southern whites boycotted them in large numbers. In Alabama, the first state to vote on a new constitution, only 43 percent of registered voters participated, less than the required majority. Congress was not to be daunted. It passed the fourth Reconstruction Act

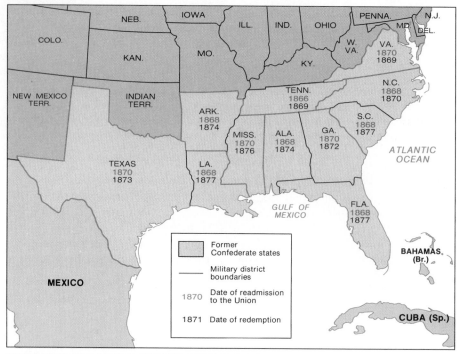

THE SOUTHERN STATES DURING RECONSTRUCTION

(March 1868), which required ratification of the constitution by only a majority of those voting rather than those who were registered. (Congress applied this act retroactively to Alabama and readmitted the state under its new constitution.)

By June 1868, Congress had readmitted the representatives of seven states. Georgia's state legislature expelled its black members once it had been readmitted, granting seats to those barred by Congress from holding office. Congress ordered the military commander to reverse these actions and Georgia was then admitted a second time in July 1870. Texas, Virginia, and Mississippi did not complete the process until 1869.

The Land Issue

While the political process of Reconstruction proceeded, Congress confronted the question of whether it was sufficient to give former slaves political and civil rights alone. Radical Republicans argued that without economic independence, blacks would enjoy only nominal freedom. Certainly many blacks felt that way. At a meeting with Secretary of War Edwin Stanton near the end of the war, African-American leaders declared, "The way we can best take care of ourselves is to have land, and till it by our own labor." Since slaves had been deprived of the right to own property before the war, Congress debated whether they should now be compensated.

During the war, the Second Confiscation Act had authorized the government to seize and sell the property including land of supporters of the rebellion. General Sherman had also issued his Special Order No. 15 in January 1865, granting blacks 40-acre homesteads on abandoned lands along the South Carolina and

Georgia coasts inland for 30 miles. In June 1866 President Johnson ruled that the Second Confiscation Act of 1862 applied only to wartime, and he also overturned Sherman's order. But Congress continued to debate the matter of confiscation from December 1865 until early 1867.

Thaddeus Stevens, the leader of the Radical Republicans in the House, advocated confiscating 394 million acres of land from about 70,000 of what he termed the "chief rebels" in the South, who comprised less than 5 percent of the South's white families. He proposed to give 40 acres to every adult male freedman and then sell the remaining land, which would amount to nine-tenths of the total, to pay off the public debt, compensate loyal southerners for losses they suffered during the war, and fund veterans' pensions. "How can republican institutions, free schools, free churches, free social intercourse exist in a mingled community of nabobs and serfs?" Stevens asked. "If the South is ever to be made a safe Republic, let her lands be cultivated by the toil of the owners or the free labor of intelligent citizens." Land, he insisted, would be far more valuable to blacks than the right to vote.

But even some Radicals believed it sufficient to give black men the ballot and pass laws protecting black rights. With Americans' strong belief in self-reliance, little sympathy existed for the idea that government should support any group or that blacks deserved special consideration. In addition, land redistribution represented an attack on property rights, another cherished American value. "A division of rich men's lands amongst the landless," argued the *Nation*, a Radical journal, "would give a shock to our whole social and political system from which it would hardly recover without the loss of liberty."

By 1867 land reform was dead. Except for property that had already been sold during the war under the Confiscation acts, seized land was returned to its former owners. Few freedmen acquired land after the war, a development that severely limited African-Americans' economic independence and left them vulnerable to white coercion. Certainly the failure to provide an economic foundation for black freedom helped undermine Reconstruction. That this decision was the basic cause of the failure of Reconstruction, however, is doubtful. In the face of white hostility and institutionalized racism, African-Americans probably would have been no more successful in protecting their property than they were in maintaining the right to vote, especially once the federal government refused to use its power to protect them. Southern whites no doubt would have devised ways to dispossess most black landowners.

Impeachment

Throughout 1867 the battle between the executive and legislative branches settled into a predictable rhythm: Congress would pass a bill, the president would veto it, Congress would override. But Johnson had other ways of undercutting congressional Reconstruction. He interpreted the new laws as narrowly as possible. He removed military commanders who vigorously enforced the laws, and his belligerence alarmed even Moderates. "Is the President crazy . . . ?" asked one. "I am afraid his doings will make us all favor impeachment." Congress fought back, directing the president to issue orders to the five military commanders in the southern states only through the general of the army, Ulysses S. Grant. Congress even limited Johnson's control of his cabinet through the Tenure of Office Act, which forbade him from removing any member without the Senate's consent. The

Facsimile of a ticket of admission to the impeachment trial of President Andrew Johnson.

intention of this law was to prevent him from firing Secretary of War Edwin Stanton, the only remaining Radical in the cabinet.

When Johnson tried to dismiss Stanton in February 1868, the determined secretary of war barricaded himself in his office (where he remained night and day for about two months). On February 24, the House of Representatives angrily approved articles of impeachment. The articles focused on the violation of the Tenure of Office Act, but the charge with the most substance was that Johnson had conspired to systematically obstruct Reconstruction legislation. In the trial before the Senate, his lawyers argued that a president could be impeached only for an indictable crime, which Johnson clearly had not committed. They also claimed that the president had fired Stanton merely to test the constitutionality of the Tenure of Office Act, while simultaneously they argued inconsistently that the Tenure of Office Act did not apply to Stanton, since he had been appointed by Lincoln and not Johnson. The Radicals countered that impeachment applied to political offenses and not merely criminal acts, a position James Madison had supported during the drafting of the Constitution.

In May 1868, after a three-month trial at which Johnson did not appear, the Senate voted 36–19 to convict, one vote short of the two-thirds majority needed. The seven Republicans who had joined the Democrats in voting for acquittal were uneasy about using impeachment as a political weapon. In addition, the president pro tempore of the Senate, Benjamin Wade of Ohio, was in line to succeed Johnson, and his Radical views on Reconstruction as well as women's rights and the currency frightened Moderates. Their vote against conviction established the precedent that a president could be removed from office only for indictable offenses, which greatly lessened the effectiveness of the threat of impeachment.

Reconstruction and the Constitution

Impeachment represented an attempt by Congress to establish its supremacy in the federal government. The Supreme Court also became a target of congressional pressure and control. Democrats, who were a hopeless minority in Congress, increasingly looked to the Court to overthrow the Reconstruction acts. For their part, Republicans worried that the *Milligan* decision (page 583), which struck down military trials for civilians during wartime, was a sign that the Court might declare the Reconstruction acts unconstitutional, since they provided for military rule and trials in the southern states. Republicans' fears crystallized when the

Court agreed to hear the appeal of an editor from Mississippi named William McCardle, who had been arrested under the Reconstruction acts and tried by a military commission. The first Reconstruction Act had given federal courts jurisdiction over certain cases, to protect freedmen from state courts. Congress responded by retroactively denying federal courts jurisdiction in such appeals and the Court, unwilling to challenge Congress, ruled in *Ex parte McCardle* (1868) that it had no jurisdiction.

Indeed, throughout this era the Court decided several relevant cases on very narrow grounds and declined to rule on the constitutionality of the Reconstruction acts. In *Texas v. White* (1869) it ruled that secession was illegal and the Union perpetual, and asserted that it was up to Congress to guarantee a republican government in each state. But it perceived, properly, that Reconstruction was an extraordinary situation, one the Constitution had never anticipated. Had the Court challenged Congress on such a highly political matter, it would have precipitated a constitutional crisis that would have led to a concerted effort to restrict the Court, if not destroy its power. Restraint on the Court's part proved wise.

RECONSTRUCTION IN THE SOUTH

The waning power of the Radicals in Congress, evident in the failure to remove Johnson, meant that the success or failure of Reconstruction increasingly hinged on developments in the southern states themselves. Power in these states rested with the new Republican parties, representing a coalition of southern blacks, southern whites, and transplanted northerners.

Black Officeholding

Black men formed the bulk of the Republican voters in the South—perhaps as much as 80 percent. Almost from the beginning, they insisted that they were the only sizable loyal population in the South and lobbied for the right to vote. When they finally received the franchise, they were not about to support the Democratic party and its appeal to white supremacy. As one Tennessee Republican explained, "The blacks know that many conservatives [Democrats] hope to reduce them again to some form of peonage. Under the impulse of this fear they will roll up their whole strength and will go entirely for the Republican candidate whoever he may be."

Yet, even though African-American males eagerly accepted the ballot, they never held office during Reconstruction in proportion to their voting strength. They lacked a majority in any southern legislature; only in South Carolina, where they constituted over 60 percent of the population, did they control even one house of the legislature. No African-American was ever nominated or elected governor. Only in South Carolina did a black judge serve on a state supreme court. Between 15 and 20 percent of the state officers and 6 percent of the congressmen in Reconstruction were black. Two blacks from Mississippi served in the U.S. Senate, and 15 blacks served in the House. In reality, only in South Carolina, where they held 52 percent of all state and federal elective offices, did black officeholding approach their proportion of the population.

This engraving shows a black politician addressing former slaves at a political meeting in the South during the 1868 presidential campaign. Although only men could vote, black women are also in the audience. Commented *Harper's Weekly* when this picture appeared, "Does any man seriously doubt whether it is better for this vast population to be sinking deeper and deeper in ignorance and servility, or rising into general intelligence and self-respect?"

Those who held office came from the top levels of African-American society. Among state and federal officeholders, perhaps four-fifths were literate, and over a quarter had been free before the war, both marks of distinction in the black community. Their occupations also set them apart: two-fifths were professionals (mostly clergy), and of the third who were farmers, nearly all owned their own land. Others were skilled workers or ran small businesses. Among blacks in Congress, all but three had a secondary school education, and four had gone to college. Jonathan Gibbs, the Florida secretary of state, was a graduate of Dartmouth and the Princeton Theological Seminary, and Francis Cardozo, who served as secretary of state and treasurer in South Carolina, had attended several colleges in England. Senator Blanche Bruce of Mississippi was the son of a white planter and had been educated on his father's plantation. In their political and social values, African-American leaders were more conservative than the rural black population, and they showed little interest in land reform. Like whites, they ranged from the talented to the incompetent.

Southern White Republicans

The failure of Congress to disfranchise Confederates meant that the Republican party had to secure white votes to stay in power. Blacks were a majority of the voters only in South Carolina, Mississippi, and Louisiana. Opponents labeled southern whites who allied with the Republican party scalawags, a pejorative term referring to scrubby cattle. An estimated quarter of southern whites at one time voted Republican, including prominent southerners like General James Longstreet, one of Robert E. Lee's key commanders, and James Lusk Alcorn, a wealthy Mississippi planter. Although the party appealed to some wealthy southern Whigs, they were outnumbered by Unionists from the upland counties and hill areas who were largely yeoman farmers. Such voters were attracted to Republican promises to rebuild the South, restore prosperity, create public schools, and open isolated areas to the market with railroads.

The other group of white Republicans in the South hailed originally from the North: carpetbaggers, they were derisively called, allegedly poor and ignorant men who arrived with all their worldly possessions stuffed in a carpetbag, ready to loot and plunder the defeated South. Some did, certainly, but northerners who moved south came for a variety of reasons. Those in political office were especially well educated and, although they constituted only a small percentage of Republican voters, they controlled almost a third of the offices, especially the higher ones. More than half of all southern Republican governors and nearly half of Republican congressmen and senators were originally northerners.

The Republican party in the South had difficulty agreeing on a program or maintaining unity. Scalawags were especially susceptible to the race issue and social pressure. "Even my own kinspeople have turned the cold shoulder to me because I hold office under a Republican administration," testified a Mississippi Republican. As blacks pressed for more recognition and a greater share of the offices, southern whites increasingly defected to the Democrats. Carpetbaggers, by contrast, were less sensitive to race and more strongly committed to the party. A number had previously worked for black rights and education, although most felt that blacks needed guidance and should be content with minor offices. The friction between carpetbaggers and blacks was minor compared to scalawags' resentment of carpetbaggers, intruders who in their eyes had seized offices that rightfully belonged to native southerners. As a result, southern Republicanism was riven by growing factionalism.

The New State Governments

The new state constitutions in the South included a number of significant reforms. In older states the earlier inequitable legislative apportionment, which discriminated against the interior counties, was replaced by a fairer system. Many previously appointive offices were made elective, and property requirements for office-holding were abolished. In South Carolina, for the first time, voters were allowed to vote for the president, governor, and other state officers.* The Radical state governments also assumed some responsibility for social welfare and established the first statewide systems of public schools in the South. The new governments also substantially increased state aid to the insane, the handicapped, and the poor. Women's rights were also enlarged, and divorce was finally legalized in South Carolina.

Although the Fourteenth Amendment prevented high Confederate officials from holding office, virtually all the new state constitutions refused to place any additional penalties on them. Only Alabama and Arkansas temporarily forbade some ex-Confederates from voting. Understandably, the strongest advocates of harsh penalties were southern Unionists, who often had suffered at the hands of

*Previously, presidential electors as well as the governor had been chosen by the South Carolina legislature.

their Confederate neighbors and who believed that political power in the reconstructed South rightfully belonged to them. African-American delegates, on the
other hand, generally opposed any penalties. They argued that blacks and whites
had to live together in the South, and such penalties could lead only to growing
bitterness between the races.

All of the new constitutions proclaimed the principle of equality and granted
black adult males the right to vote, but on social relations they were much more
circumspect. No state outlawed social segregation, and South Carolina and Louisiana were the only states requiring integration in public schools. Even so, that
requirement was ignored except in New Orleans and at the University of South
Carolina. Sensitive to status, mulattoes were more insistent on eliminating social
discrimination, but white Republicans refused to adopt such a radical policy.

Economic Issues and Corruption

The problems of economic reconstruction were as difficult as those of politics.
Major sections of the South lay in ruins; its people, white and black, faced dire
poverty. Charred and gutted buildings scarred cities like Columbia, Atlanta, and
Richmond; rail networks were broken up; central South Carolina, where Sherman's army had struck, was described as "a broad black streak of ruin and desolation."

The Republican governments in the South sought to encourage industry by
providing subsidies, loans, and even exemption from taxes for a certain number of
years. These governments also largely rebuilt the southern railroad system, often
offering lavish aid and privileges to railroad corporations. In the two decades after
1860, the region doubled its manufacturing establishments, and centers like the
Birmingham iron and steel industry became symbols of a new industrial South.
Yet the harsh reality was that the South steadily slipped further behind the economy of the North, which had boomed throughout the war. Between 1854 and
1879, 7000 miles of railroad track were laid in the South, but in the same period
45,000 miles were constructed in the rest of the nation. Social disorder also discouraged outside investment, and southern energy and capital initially were devoted simply to rebuilding what the war had destroyed. The Radical governments
could not create the prosperity that they unrealistically promised in hopes of
gaining the support of upper-class southerners.

The expansion of government services and the cozy relationship with business leaders offered sometimes irresistible temptations for corruption. In many
southern states, officials regularly resorted to fraud and received bribes and kick-
backs for their award of railroad charters, franchises, and other contracts. The tax
rate grew as expenditures went up, so that by the 1870s it was four times the rate
of 1860. By 1872, the debts of the 11 states of the Confederacy had increased $132
million. In Florida between 1868 and 1874 the state debt grew tenfold; in South
Carolina in only three years it increased to almost six times its previous size.

Corruption, however, was not only a southern problem. The decline in morality was nationwide, as scandals in the federal administration and in northern
state governments revealed. During these years, the Democratic Tweed Ring in
New York City stole more money than all the Radical Republican governments in
the South combined. Moreover, corruption in the South was hardly limited to
Republicans. Many Democrats and white businessmen participated in and profited from the corrupt practices, both before and after the Radical governments
were in power. In Louisiana, where corruption had flourished long before Recon-

struction, Governor Henry Warmoth, a carpetbagger, told a congressional committee the legislature was as good as the people it represented. "Why, damn it," he testified, "everybody is demoralizing down here. Corruption is the fashion."

While fraud contributed to the public debt in the South, most of the increase came from the cost of rebuilding. In fact, most of the debt represented grants to railroads. In addition, freeing millions of slaves greatly increased the number of citizens eligible for government services. The new public school systems, even if inadequately funded, meant that state taxes were bound to increase.

Corruption in Radical governments undeniably existed, but southern whites exaggerated its extent for partisan purposes. Conservatives as bitterly opposed the Radical regime in Mississippi, which was untainted by any significant financial scandal, as they did the notoriously corrupt Republican governments in Louisiana and South Carolina. In the eyes of most southern whites, the real crime of the Radical governments was that they recognized blacks in the distribution of offices and tried to protect the civil rights of black Americans. Race was the conservatives' greatest weapon and would prove the most effective means to undermine Republican power in the South.

BLACK ASPIRATIONS

Emancipation came to slaves in different ways. For some it arrived during the war when Union soldiers entered an area; for others it came some time after the Confederacy's collapse when Union troops or officials announced that they were free. On some plantations the news set off a wild celebration—a "Day of Jubilee" and thanksgiving—while other slaves received the news with no outward reaction. But after the initial celebration, what did freedom mean to people who had been in bondage all their lives?

Experiencing Freedom

The first impulse was to think of freedom as a contrast to slavery, to understand the new state of affairs in terms of limitations on white behavior and a release from the most oppressive aspects of bondage—the whippings, the work routine, the breakup of families. Above all, freedom meant that African-Americans were now their own masters and that their labor would be for their own benefit. One Arkansas freedman, who earned his first dollar working on a railroad, recalled that when he was paid, "I felt like the richest man in the world."

Freedom also meant movement, the right to travel without a pass or white permission. In the first months after the war, former slaves clogged the roads of the South. For some, this was a way to experience the thrill of moving about freely. For others, it was an attempt to find lost family members, to visit relatives, or to return to the place where they had grown up either to resettle or just to visit. Some never found the kin they sought, while others wept when reunited at last with husbands, wives, and children.

Freedom also included finding a new place to work. Changing jobs was a concrete way to break the psychological ties of slavery. Blacks especially deserted masters who had been harsh and cruel, but even planters with reputations for kindness and fairness sometimes found most of their former hands had departed. The cook who left a South Carolina family, even though they offered her higher

Daily Lives

PUBLIC SPACE/PRIVATE SPACE

The Black Sharecropper's Cabin

On the plantations of the Old South, slaves had lived in cabins along a central path in the shadow of the white master's "big house" or the overseer's dwelling. These quarters were the center of their community, where marriages and other festivals were celebrated, family life went on, and slaves shared a sense of kinship. With the coming of emancipation, however, freedmen looked to rid themselves of the old quarters, which stood as a symbol of bondage and of close white supervision. Hence when white landowners switched to a system of sharecropping or tenant farming, African-Americans either dismantled their old cabins and hauled them to the plots of land they rented or simply built new housing. This enabled them to live on the land they farmed, just as white farmers and tenants did. It also provided a greater measure of privacy.

In selecting a cabin site, freedmen tried to locate within a convenient distance of their fields, but close to the woods as well, since cutting wood was a year-round task for boys. To improve drainage, cabins were often built on a knoll or had a floor raised above the ground; in low-lying areas, stone or log piers were used. A nearby stream, spring, or well provided not only water but a place to cool butter and other perishable dairy products.

Like slave cabins, sharecroppers' dwellings were one story high with a gable roof, about 16 feet square, and built usually of logs chinked with mud. The few windows had shutters to protect against the weather; glass was rare. Though the inside walls normally lacked plaster or sheeting, they were given a coat of whitewash annually to brighten the dark interior and make the room seem larger. To provide a bit of cheer, the womenfolk often covered the walls with pictures from seed catalogues and magazines. The floor, packed dirt that was as smooth and hard as concrete, was covered with braided rugs made from scraps of cloth and worn-out clothing.

The main room served as kitchen and dining room, parlor, bathing area, and the parents' bedroom. To one side might be a homemade drop-leaf table (essential because of cramped space), which served as a kitchen work counter and a dining table. The other side of the room had a few plain beds, their slats or rope bottoms supporting corn shuck or straw mattresses. (Featherbeds were considered a remarkable luxury.) The social center of the room was the fireplace, the only source of heat and the main source of light after dark. Pots and pans were hung on the wall near the fireplace, and the mother and daughters did the cooking stooped over an open fire. Since the family usually could not afford to buy matches, the fire was rarely extinguished. Some earthen or tin dishes, steel eating utensils, assorted containers, a rifle or shotgun, and a few prized possessions (usually displayed on the mantlepiece over the fireplace) rounded out the family's furnishings. Clothing was hung on pegs in the wall. If the family owned a trunk, the parents' Sunday clothes and valuables would be stored in it.

The fireplace was constructed of smooth stone; the chimney was made of small logs notched together and covered with several layers of clay to protect it from the heat. It often narrowed toward the top, and sometimes its height was extended by empty flour barrels, for a taller chimney drew better. That made for a hot-

Daily Lives

Chimneys on share-croppers' cabins were often tilted deliberately, so they could be pushed away from the house quickly if they caught fire.

ter fire and kept smoke from blowing back down into the house and sparks away from the roof. After the evening meal, the family gathered around the fireplace, the children to play with homemade dolls and toys, the mother to sew, and the father perhaps to play the fiddle. At bedtime, a trapdoor in the ceiling offered access up a ladder to the loft beneath the gabled roof. Being cold and dark, it was used only for sleeping. Normally the parents and infants slept downstairs, older children upstairs until the girls reached puberty, after which they slept downstairs too. The children often slept on pallets on the floor, as had been the case in slavery.

In the summer, cooking was done outdoors over an open fire. Women preferred to cook under a tree, which offered some protection from rain as well as relief from the sun and the high humidity. Sharecropper families rarely had separate cooking rooms attached to or next to the cabin. Separate kitchens, which were a sign of prosperity, were more common among black landowners and white tenant farmers.

Gradually, as black sharecroppers were able to scrape together some savings, the quality of their homes improved. By the end of the century, frame dwellings were more common, and many older log cabins had been covered with wood siding. The newer homes were generally larger, with wood floors, and often had attached rooms such as a porch or kitchen. In addition, glass panes covered the windows, roofs were covered with shingles instead of planking, and stone and brick chimneys were less unusual. A narrow stairwell, often with a door to shut out cold drafts, provided access to the loft; underneath it was a closet for additional storage. Ceramic dishes were more frequently seen, and wood-burning stoves made cooking easier for women and provided a more efficient source of heat.

Without question, the cabins of black sharecroppers provided more space than the slave quarters had, and certainly more freedom and privacy. Still, they lacked many of the comforts that most white Americans took for granted. Such housing reflected the continuing status of black sharecroppers as poverty-stricken laborers in a caste system based on race.

wages than her new job, explained, "I must go. If I stays here I'll never know I'm free." And a black preacher told a group of freedmen in Florida: "So long as the shadow of the great house fall across you, you ain't going to feel like no free man and no free woman. You must all move to new places that you don't know, where you can raise up your head without no fear of Master This and Master The Other."

Symbolically, freedom meant, too, having a full name. As slaves, African-Americans often had no surname, but with the coming of freedom, more than a few took the name of some prominent individual, such as Washington or Jefferson, or else some leading figure in the community. More common, however, was to take the name of the first master in the family's oral history as far back as it could be recalled. Most freedmen, on the other hand, retained their first name in slavery, especially if they had been named by their parents (as most slaves were). It had been their form of identity in bondage, and for those separated from their family it was the only link with their parents. But whatever name they took, it was important to blacks that they made the decision themselves without white interference.

The Black Family

African-Americans also sought to strengthen the family in freedom. Since slave marriages had not been recognized as legal, thousands of former slaves insisted on being married again by proper authorities. Although not required by law, these wedding ceremonies represented a reaffirmation of commitments made earlier. This new right created a dilemma for those who had been forcibly separated from a spouse in slavery and subsequently remarried. Should they return to their first spouse or remain with the current one? The Freedmen's Bureau urged blacks in this predicament to take the spouse with whom they had the greatest number of dependent children, but the final decision rested with the individuals. Laura Spicer, who had been separated from her slave husband, received a series of wrenching letters from him after the war. He had thought her dead, had remarried, and had a new family. "I would come and see you but I know you could not bear it," he wrote.

> You know it never was our wishes to be separated from each other, and it never was our fault . . . I had rather anything to had happened to me most than ever have been parted from you and the children. As I am, I do not know which I love best, you or Anna . . . I do not think I would die satisfied till you tell me you will try and marry some good, smart man that will take good care of you and the children; and do it because you love me; and not because I think more of the wife I have got than I do of you. The woman is not born that feels as near to me as you do.

A family decision that had major economic repercussions for agricultural labor was the insistence of black men that their wives would not work in the fields as they had in slavery. As in white families, black fathers deemed themselves the head of the family and the breadwinner and acted legally for their wives. "The [black] women say they never mean to do any more outdoor work," one planter reported, "that white men support their wives and they mean that their husbands shall support them." African-American families also often withdrew their children from labor. In negotiating contracts, a father demanded the right to discipline his children. All these changes were designed to insulate the black family from white control.

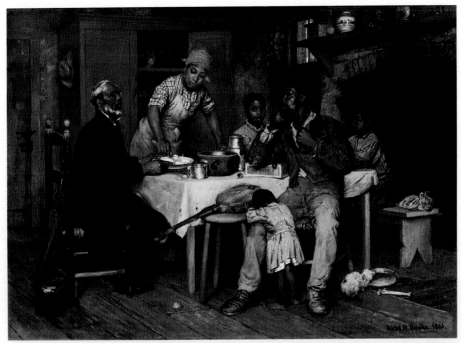

Making the rounds of the parish, a black minister shares a meal with some of his parishioners. Such meals were a welcome supplement to a clergyman's scanty salary. Black ministers were important leaders of the African-American community in freedom.

The Gospel and the Primer

In freedom, the schoolhouse and the black church became essential institutions in the black community. Next to ownership of land, African-Americans saw education as the best hope for advancement. "My Lord, Ma'am, what a great thing learning is!" a South Carolina freedman told a northern teacher. "White folks can do what they likes, for they know so much more than we." Initially, northern churches and missionaries, working with the Freedmen's Bureau, set up black schools in the South. The Bureau also spent over $400,000 to support black colleges, including Howard University in Washington, which were founded to train future African-American leaders and teachers to staff black schools.

The freedmen's schools were not free and required a substantial commitment on the part of the family of those who enrolled. Tuition represented 10 percent or more of a laborer's monthly wages, yet these schools were full. Blacks eagerly came; one school official reported they were simply "crazy to learn." Many parents sent their children to school by day and attended classes themselves at night. Eventually, the freedmen's schools were replaced by the new public school systems, which by 1876 had enrolled 40 percent of African-American children.

Black adults had good reasons for seeking literacy. They wanted to be able to read the Bible, to defend their newly gained civil and political rights, and to protect themselves from being cheated. Slavery had bred a deeply ingrained suspicion of whites, and as one elderly Louisiana freedman explained, giving children an education was better than giving them a fortune, "because if you left them even

$500, some man having more education than they had would come along and cheat them out of it all." White resistance stimulated this desire for education. Black schools were often destroyed, and white teachers threatened and even murdered. Both races saw in the postwar South that education would undermine the old servility that slavery had fostered. More than other Americans, blacks knew that education would overthrow the legacy of slavery.

For the first time in the South, blacks were allowed to establish their own churches. Most slaves had attended white churches or services supervised by whites, and northern organizations like the African Methodist Episcopal Church had been banned. Once free, African-Americans quickly established their own congregations led by black preachers. In the first year of freedom, the Methodist Church South lost fully half of its black members. By 1870, the Negro Baptist Church had increased its membership threefold compared to 1850, and the African Methodist Episcopal Church expanded at an even greater rate.

Indeed, black churches were so important because they were the only social organization in the African-American community actually controlled by blacks. Black ministers were respected leaders. An officer of the American Missionary Association reported that "the Ebony preacher who promises perfect independence from White control and direction carried the colored heart at once." Many of the black men elected to office during Reconstruction were preachers. Just as in slavery, religion offered African-Americans a place of refuge in a hostile white world and provided them with hope, comfort, and a means of self-identification.

New Working Conditions

For blacks, freedom involved more than just receiving pay for labor performed; they sought to remove all the emblems and habits of servitude. Owning land would have best provided them with economic independence, but the few feeble attempts at land reform failed. Blacks remained a largely propertyless class, forced to work for former masters and landowners. Whites insisted, as they had before the war, that blacks would not work without compulsion. Except for paying wages, they tried to retain the old system of labor, including close supervision, gang labor, and discipline by the whip or other physical punishment. African-Americans, however, not only refused to work under this system; they demanded time off to devote to their own work and leisure interests. Convinced that working at one's own pace was part of freedom, they simply would not work as long or as hard as they had in slavery. Because of shorter hours and the withdrawal of children and women from the fields, work output declined by an estimated 35 percent. Blacks also refused to live in the old slave quarters located near the master's house. Instead, they erected cabins on distant parts of the plantation. Wages initially were $5 or $6 a month plus provisions and a cabin; by 1867, they had risen to an average of $10 a month.

Such changes in the labor system eventually led to the rise of the sharecropping system. Under this arrangement, African-American families farmed separate plots of land and then at the end of the year divided the crop with the owner. The farmer's share depended on whether he supplied the seeds, animals, and implements, but the normal arrangement was an equal division of the crop between the sharecropper and the landowner. Although sharecropping was not the same as owning a farm, blacks believed it offered higher status and greater personal freedom than being a wage laborer. One black defended his right to leave the planta-

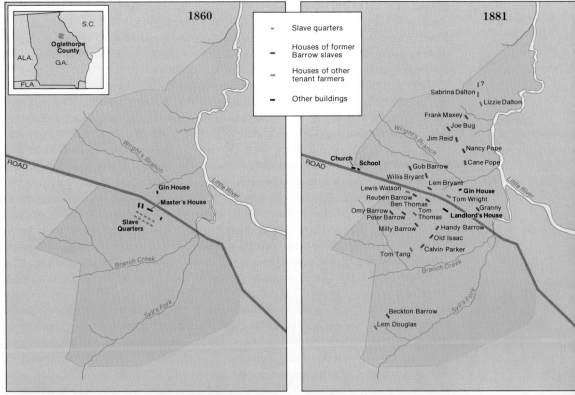

A GEORGIA PLANTATION AFTER THE WAR
After emancipation, sharecropping became the dominant form of agricultural labor in the South. Black families no longer lived in the old slave quarters, but dispersed themselves to separate plots of land that they farmed themselves. At the end of the year each sharecropper turned over part of the crop to the white landowner.

tion at will without permission of the owner. "I am not working for wages," he declared, "but am part owner of the crop and as I have all the rights that you or any other man has I shall not suffer them abridged." Actually, black per capita agricultural income increased 40 percent between 1857 and 1879, since white landlords were unable to expropriate as large a share of black earnings as they had in slavery.

The Freedmen's Bureau

The task of supervising the transition from slavery to freedom on southern plantations fell to the Freedmen's Bureau, a unique experiment in social policy supported briefly by the federal government. Created as an agency of the War Department, the Bureau provided relief for refugees, helped settle freedmen on abandoned lands, and put them back to work. During the summer of 1865 the Bureau provided 150,000 daily rations, a third of which went to whites; from 1865 to 1870 it issued 2 million rations, built 40 hospitals, and treated 450,000 patients. But the Bureau's major task was to protect the freedmen's economic rights. Approximately 550 local agents supervised and regulated working conditions in an attempt to bring order to southern agriculture after the war. The racial attitudes of Bureau agents varied widely, as did their commitment and competence. Since their guidelines were vague, they used their own judgment to settle cases, and they depended on the army to enforce their decisions.

Most agents encouraged or required written contracts between white planters and black laborers, specifying not only wages, but the conditions of employment. Agents adjudicated disputes, sometimes intervening to protect freedmen from unfair treatment. But agents also used their power to get African-Americans who had migrated to the cities back on the plantations. They preached to the freedmen the gospel of work and the need to be orderly and respectful. Given such attitudes, blacks increasingly complained that Bureau agents were mere tools of the planter class. "They are, in fact, the planters' guards, and nothing else," claimed the New Orleans *Tribune*, a black newspaper. Agents did provide important help to planters. They insisted that blacks not desert at harvest time; they arrested as vagrants those who violated their contracts or refused to sign new ones at the beginning of the year. One observer reported, "Doing justice seems to mean seeing that the blacks don't break contracts and compelling them to submit cheerfully."

The primary means of enforcing working conditions were the Freedmen's Courts, which Congress created in 1866 because of persistent discrimination against African-Americans in the state courts. These new courts functioned as military tribunals and often the agent was the entire court, hearing testimony and then rendering a verdict. These courts were more sympathetic to freedmen in some states than others. In 1867 one agent summarized the Bureau's experience with the labor contract system: "It has succeeded in making the freedman work and in rendering labor secure and stable—but it has failed to secure to the Freedman his just dues or compensation."

In 1869, with the Bureau's work scarcely under way, Congress ordered it to prepare to shut down. Even the Radical Republicans did not want to create a permanent welfare agency. By 1872 the Bureau had gone out of business, leaving behind a mixed record. Its major accomplishment was freedmen's schools, but the absence of any program for significant land redistribution ensured that its contributions would be limited. The disbanding of the Bureau, the most effective and efficient agency that protected blacks' civil and political rights, signaled the beginning of the northern retreat from Reconstruction.

Planters and a New Way of Life

Planters and other southern whites faced emancipation with dread. Unwilling to live with free blacks, some planters fled to the North, the West, or even to foreign countries like Mexico and Brazil. Most, however, stayed, searching for a system to replace slavery. "All the traditions and habits of both races had been suddenly overthrown," a Tennessee planter recalled, "and neither knew just what to do, or how to accommodate themselves to the new situation."

The old ideal of a paternalistic planter, which required a facade of black subservience and affection, gave way to an emphasis on strictly economic relationships. Mary Jones, a Georgia slaveholder before the war who did more for her workers than the law required, complained of their disrespectful language, imper-

Black education was one of the significant changes freedom brought during the era of Reconstruction. Here a group of black students pose with their books outside their crude schoolhouse.

tinent gestures, and poor work. But her patience snapped when two workers accused her of trickery and hauled her before a Freedmen's Bureau agent, with whom she won her case. Upon returning home, she announced to the assembled freedmen that "in doubting my word they offered me the greatest insult I ever received in my life; that I have considered them friends and treated them as such but now they were only laborers under contract, and only the law would rule between us." The subservience that planters had demanded and taken for granted—touching one's hat, the obsequious, smiling demeanor, the fawning guise of gratitude—now melted away in freedom. Only with time did planters develop new norms and standards to judge black behavior. What in 1865 had seemed insolence was viewed by the 1870s as the normal attitude of freedom.

Slavery had been a complex institution that welded blacks and whites together in intimate relationships, but under the new system planters increasingly embraced the ideology of segregation. Planters kept dealings with African-Americans to a minimum. Since emancipation significantly reduced the social distance between the races, whites sought psychological separation. Segregation—the legal separation of the races—became an institution to buttress white status. By the time Reconstruction ended, white planters had developed a new set of values to replace those of slavery. Their new way of life was reflected in the institutions of sharecropping and segregation and undergirded by a militant white supremacy. Planters endured, but with emancipation, they lost their pride, confidence, and some of their identity.

Nor did planters regain the economic prosperity of the antebellum years.

Rice plantations, which were not suitable to tenant farming, largely disappeared after the war. The cotton crops in 1865 and 1866 failed, and it was not until 1877 that cotton production consistently exceeded the prewar level. Furthermore, cotton from new areas such as India, Egypt, and Brazil now competed with American cotton, while the world demand grew at a much slower rate after 1865 than it had earlier. Cotton prices began a long decline, and southern per capita income suffered as a result. Cotton plantations continued to dominate southern agriculture, but many planters' income declined sharply. Most escaped total collapse, but by 1880 the value of southern farms had slid 33 percent below the level of 1860.

THE ABANDONMENT OF RECONSTRUCTION

The Radical Republicans had failed to impeach Johnson by one vote—a narrow margin, but effective nevertheless. The Radicals' influence was waning and the Republican party was being drained of the crusading idealism that had stamped its early years. Ulysses S. Grant was hardly the cause of this change, but he certainly came to symbolize it.

The Election of Grant

Grant had not identified with the Radical wing of the party until Johnson used the general as a pawn in his struggle with Congress. In relieving Stanton, Johnson had tried to maneuver Grant to take his place, and in the process drove the general into an alliance with the Radicals. Afraid of sinking into obscurity, Grant yearned to be president, the only office that would be a promotion for him. Immensely popular, he was the natural choice of Republicans in 1868. Since the Republican platform called for repayment of the national war debt in gold, which pleased businessmen but hurt workers and farmers, the Democrats proposed a more inflationary monetary policy. That appealed to many debtor farmers (who were helped by inflation), and the Democrats also hoped to pick up votes of whites who disapproved of Republican policies on behalf of the freedmen.

Grant easily defeated his opponent, former governor Horatio Seymour of New York, in the Electoral College, but his popular margin was only 300,000 votes. With a ticket headed by a great military hero, the close vote shocked Republican leaders. Although Grant would have won in the Electoral College even without the estimated 450,000 votes he received from southern blacks, a majority of whites had voted for Seymour. The 1868 election helped convince Republicans that an amendment securing black suffrage throughout the nation was necessary.

In February 1869 Congress sent the Fifteenth Amendment to the states for ratification. It forbade any state from denying the right to vote on grounds of race, color, or previous condition of servitude. Some Radicals had hoped to forbid literacy or property requirements, to protect blacks further; others wanted a simple declaration that all adult male citizens had the right to vote. But the Moderates feared that only a conservative version could be ratified, since many northerners were increasingly worried about the number of immigrants who were again enter-

Declining to adopt her husband's name, Lucy Stone (right) was a major figure in the women's rights movement after the Civil War. Northern women who had worked for emancipation during the war protested the failure to grant them the right to vote along with male freedmen during Reconstruction.

ing the country. As a result, the final amendment left loopholes that eventually allowed southern states to disfranchise African-Americans.

Radicals saw the Fifteenth Amendment as an antidote to the hypocrisy of the Fourteenth Amendment, which fastened black suffrage only upon the South (and even there, only by indirection). "We have no moral right to impose an obligation on one part of the land which the rest will not accept," one Radical leader declared. Party leaders also felt that the small black vote might be critical to the Republicans in closely contested northern states. The amendment was ratified in March 1870, in part with the votes of the four southern states that had not completed the process of Reconstruction and thus were also required to endorse this amendment before being readmitted to Congress.

Proponents of women's suffrage were gravely disappointed at the refusal of Congress to prohibit voting discrimination on the basis of sex as well as race. Many of the women's suffrage supporters had been associated with the abolitionist movement earlier and had worked hard to get the Thirteenth Amendment ratified. The Women's Loyal League, led by Elizabeth Cady Stanton and Susan B. Anthony, had pressed for first the Fourteenth and then the Fifteenth Amendment to recognize women's public role, but even most Radicals, contending that black rights had to be assured first, were unwilling to back women's suffrage. The Fifteenth Amendment ruptured the feminist movement. While disappointed that women were not included in its provisions, Lucy Stone and the American Woman

Suffrage Association urged ratification of the amendment. Anthony and Stanton, on the other hand, broke with their former allies among the Radicals, denounced the amendment, and organized the National Woman Suffrage Association to work for passage of a new amendment giving women the ballot. This division continued to hamper the women's rights movement in the future.

The Grant Administration

Grant lacked the moral commitment to make Reconstruction succeed. Unsure of himself socially, he gravitated toward the wealthy elements in American society, the businessmen and financiers that the party increasingly aided. He was ill at ease with the political process, lacked trustworthy advisers, and, haunted by his undistinguished career before 1861, had an abiding fear of failure. Grant's simple and taciturn style, while superb for commanding armies, did not serve him as well in politics, and his well-known resolution withered when he was uncertain of his purpose or goal. His bewilderment over the complex political problems he confronted made him appear pathetic, a handicap that even his good intentions could not overcome.

A series of scandals wracked Grant's presidency, so much so that "Grantism" soon became a code word in American politics for corruption, cronyism, and venality. Although Grant did not profit personally, those close to him dipped freely into the public till. Loyal to his friends, he displayed little zeal to root out corruption or bring the guilty to justice. His relatives were implicated in a scheme to corner the gold market, his private secretary escaped conviction for stealing federal whiskey revenues only because Grant interceded on his behalf, and his secretary of war, who was selling Indian trading post contracts, resigned to avoid impeachment. James W. Grimes, one of the party's founders, denounced the Republican party under Grant as "the most corrupt and debauched political party that has ever existed."

Nor was Congress immune from the lowered tone of public life. The Crédit Mobilier, a corporation established to build the Union Pacific Railroad, siphoned huge profits from the coffers into its directors' hands, but a number of bribed congressmen successfully headed off an investigation. In such a climate ruthless state machines, led by men who favored maintaining the status quo, came to dominate the Republican party. Office and power became ends in themselves, and party leaders worked in close cooperation with northern industrial interests.

At the same time, the Radicals who had spearheaded the movement for a rigorous program of Reconstruction were passing from the scene. Thaddeus Stevens died in August 1868, shortly after Johnson's impeachment trial. Benjamin F. Wade and George Julian were defeated, and Charles Sumner, who got into a tug of war with the Grant administration over an attempt to annex the island of Santo Domingo, was stripped of his chairmanship of the foreign relations committee by the Senate. The few Radicals still active in public life increasingly repudiated Grant and the Republican governments in the South. Congress in 1872 passed an amnesty act, removing the restrictions of the Fourteenth Amendment on office holding, except for about 200 to 300 ex-Confederate leaders.

As corruption in both the North and South worsened, reformers in the party became more interested in cleaning up government than in protecting black rights. These liberal Republicans, who considered themselves "the best men," opposed the continued presence of the army in the South, denounced the corrup-

Grant swings from a trapeze while supporting a number of associates accused of corruption. Among those holding on are Secretary of the Navy George M. Robeson (top center), who was accused of accepting bribes in the awarding of navy contracts; Secretary of War William W. Belknap (top right), who was forced to resign for selling Indian post traderships; and the president's private secretary Orville Babcock (bottom right), who was implicated in the Whiskey Ring scandal. Though not personally involved in the scandals during his administration, Grant was reluctant to dismiss supporters accused of wrongdoing from office.

tion of southern governments as well as the national government, and advocated free trade and civil service reform. In 1872 they broke with the Republican party and nominated for president Horace Greeley. The editor of the New York *Tribune* and a one-time Radical, Greeley was disillusioned with Reconstruction and urged a restoration of home rule in the South. Democrats decided to back the Liberal Republican ticket. The Republicans renominated Grant, who, despite the defection of Radicals such as Sumner, Carl Schurz, and E. L. Godkin of the *Nation*, won an easy victory with 56 percent of the popular vote.

Growing Northern Disillusionment

During Grant's second term, Congress passed the Civil Rights Act of 1875, the last major piece of Reconstruction legislation. Up until this time, Congress had refused to challenge segregation and racial discrimination practiced by individuals and corporations. The 1875 law prohibited racial discrimination in all public accommodations, transportation, places of amusement, and juries. Congress, however, rejected a ban on segregation in public schools, which was almost universally practiced in the North as well as the South. While some railroads, streetcars, and public accommodations in both sections were desegregated after the law passed, the federal government made little attempt to enforce the law, and it was ignored throughout most of the South. In 1883 the Supreme Court struck down its provisions except that relating to juries.

Despite passage of this law, northern public opinion was, in fact, growing increasingly disillusioned with Reconstruction. Northerners were bothered by the corruption and dishonesty of the southern governments and tired of the violence and disorder in the South. Even at the height of Reconstruction, the support for black rights owed more to antisouthern than problack motives. "People are becoming tired of abstract questions," one Republican paper commented. "The negro question, with all its complications, and the reconstruction of the Southern states, with all its interminable embroilments, have lost much of the power they once wielded."

At the same time, a number of Republicans were attracted to Lincoln's old strategy of forging an alliance with southern whites. Influential northern business leaders were particularly eager to establish conditions favorable to investment in the South. They began to look to southern conservatives, many of whom were proponents of the idea of a New South based on urbanizaton and industry, to restore order and political stability. William Dodge, a wealthy New York capitalist, wrote in 1875: "What the South now needs is capital to develop her resources, but this she cannot obtain till confidence in her state governments can be restored, and this will never be done by federal bayonets." It had been a mistake, he went on, to make southern blacks feel "that the United States government was their special friend, rather than those with whom their lot is cast, among whom they must live and for whom they must work. We have tried this long enough," he concluded. "Now let the South alone."

As the agony of the war became more distant and Republicans got less mileage out of waving the bloody shirt, economic matters drew public attention away from Reconstruction. The Panic of 1873 marked the beginning of a severe depression that lasted for four years. Some 3 million people were thrown out of work, and much of the wrangling in Congress about how to revive the economy centered on the question of the currency. In 1874 Grant vetoed a bill to increase the supply of greenbacks, and the next year Congress adopted the policy of requiring greenbacks to be convertible to gold by 1878. The question of inflation and the gold standard would remain a central political issue for the remainder of the century (page 782).

But in its immediate political consequences, the depression led to a surge in Democratic strength. Battered by the panic and the corruption issue, the Republicans lost a shocking 77 seats in Congress in the 1874 elections, and along with them control of the House of Representatives for the first time since 1861. The Democrats scored striking gains in every region of the country, even winning the Massachusetts governorship for the first time in 40 years. "The truth is our people are tired out with the worn out cry of 'Southern outrages'!!" one Republican concluded. "Hard times and heavy taxes make them wish the 'ever lasting nigger' were in hell or Africa." Republicans spoke more and more about cutting loose the southern governments to enhance the party's strength in the North.

The Triumph of White Supremacy

As northern commitment to Reconstruction declined, southern Democrats set out to overthrow the remaining Radical governments. Already white southerners were deserting the Republican party by the thousands. A white Republican in Mississippi justified his decision to leave the party on the grounds that otherwise, his children had no future. "No white man can live in the South in the future and act with any other than the Democratic party unless he is willing and prepared to live a life of social isolation and remain in political oblivion."

To poor whites who lacked social standing, the Democratic appeal to racial solidarity offered great comfort. As one explained, "I may be poor and my manners may be crude, but I am a white man. And because I am a white man, I have a right to be treated with respect by Negroes. That I am poor is not as important as that I am a white man; and no Negro is ever going to forget that he is not a white man." The large landowners and other wealthy groups that led southern Democrats objected less to blacks voting, in part because they did not face social and economic competition from them, but also because they were confident that if outside influences were removed, they could control the black vote. When Wade Hampton, a wealthy planter, ran for governor in South Carolina in 1876, he pledged that if elected he would "observe, protect, and defend the rights of the colored man as quickly as any man in South Carolina."

Democrats also resorted to economic pressure to undermine Republican power. The lack of a secret ballot strengthened the hand of white conservatives. White landlords refused to hire or take on as sharecroppers African-Americans who voted Republican. In heavily black counties, white observers at the polls took down the names of blacks who cast Republican ballots and published them in local newspapers. A Mississippi paper urged planters to "discharge . . . every laborer who persists in the diabolical war that has been waged against the white man and his interest ever since the negro has been a voter."

But terror and violence proved the most important means used to overthrow the radical regimes in the South. A number of paramilitary organizations, of which the Ku Klux Klan was the most famous, broke up Republican meetings, terrorized white and black Republicans, assassinated Republican leaders and candidates, and prevented blacks from voting. Founded in 1866 in Tennessee, the Klan represented all social classes, although the leaders were often locally prominent planters. Most of the members were young men in their twenties and thirties, and many were Confederate veterans. The Klan and similar organizations functioned as an unofficial arm of the Democratic party.

Congress finally moved to break the power of the Klan with the Force Act of 1870 and the Ku Klux Klan Act of 1871. These laws made it a felony to interfere with the right to vote; they also authorized use of the army, suspension of the writ of habeas corpus, and removal of Klan supporters from juries. The Grant administration eventually suspended the writ of habeas corpus in nine South Carolina counties and arrested hundreds of suspected Klan members throughout the South. Although these actions weakened the Klan, terrorist organizations continued to operate underground.

What became known as the Mississippi Plan was inaugurated in 1875, when Democrats decided to use as much violence as necessary to carry the state election. Several local papers trumpeted, "Carry the election peaceably if we can, forcibly if we must." Democratic clubs, organized into irregular military companies, paraded in black areas to intimidate voters, dispersed Republican meetings, and assassinated Republican leaders. When Republican Governor Adelbert Ames requested federal troops to stop the violence, Grant's advisers warned that sending troops to Mississippi would cost the party the Ohio election. In the end, the administration told Ames to depend on his own forces. As the attorney general

Two Ku Klux Klan members pose in full regalia. Violence played a major role in overthrowing the Radical governments in the South. One South Carolina paper openly praised Klan attacks on blacks and the Republican Union Leagues:

> Born of the night, and vanish by day;
> Leaguers and niggers, get out of the way!

explained, "The whole public are tired out with these annual autumnal outbreaks in the South, and the great majority are now ready to condemn any interference on the part of the government."

Bolstered by this terrorism, the Democrats swept the election. Violence and intimidation prevented as many as 60,000 black and white Republicans from voting, converting the normal Republican majority into a Democratic majority of 30,000. The victors boasted that Mississippi had been "redeemed."

The Disputed Election of 1876

With the Republican party on the defensive across the nation, the 1876 presidential election was crucial to the final overthrow of Reconstruction. Only three states—Louisiana, South Carolina, and Florida—still remained in Republican hands, and Democrats were prepared to use the Mississippi Plan to carry them in 1876.

The Republicans nominated Ohio governor Rutherford B. Hayes to oppose Samuel Tilden, a Democrat who had won fame by prosecuting the corrupt Tweed Ring in New York City. Once again, violence prevented an estimated quarter of a million Republican votes from being cast in the South, and the outcome was in doubt. Tilden had reported majorities in South Carolina, Florida, and Louisiana, but Hayes' supporters also claimed them. Hayes needed all three states to be elected, for even without them, Tilden had amassed 184 electoral votes, one short of a majority. Tilden also had a clear majority of 250,000 in the popular vote. Although the Democrats also claimed to have carried the governorships and legislatures in South Carolina, Louisiana, and Florida, the Republican canvassing boards in power disqualified enough Democratic votes to give each state to Hayes.

To arbitrate the disputed returns, Congress established a 15-member electoral commission: 5 members each from the Senate, the House, and the Supreme Court. As originally constituted, the commission divided evenly between 7 Republicans and 7 Democrats, with Supreme Court Justice David Davis, who had been a Republican and was now a political independent, as the swing vote. But when Davis was elected to the Senate from Illinois, he declined to serve on the commission and was replaced by a Republican member of the Court. By a straight party vote of 8–7, the commission awarded the disputed electoral votes—and the presidency—to Hayes.

When angry Democrats threatened a filibuster to prevent the electoral votes from being counted, Republicans scrambled to head off a stalemate. On February 26, key Republicans met with southern Democrats at the Wormley Hotel in Washington and reached an informal understanding, later known as the Compromise of 1877. Hayes' supporters agreed to withdraw the troops and not oppose the new white state governments if Democrats would drop their opposition to Hayes' election. Southerners, for their part, pledged to treat blacks fairly and respect their rights. Hayes was quite happy with this deal, for he hoped to rebuild his party in the South by appealing primarily to whites who were former Whigs. Assurances that Republicans would help pass federal aid for a number of southern internal improvement projects also helped in a minor way to ease Democratic objections.

Once in office, Hayes withdrew military support for the Republican governors in South Carolina and Louisiana, who had claimed victory. Those administrations promptly collapsed, and Democrats took control of the remaining two states of the Confederacy. By 1877, the entire South was in the hands of the Redeemers, as they called themselves, and Reconstruction and Republican rule had come to an end.

THE ELECTION OF 1876

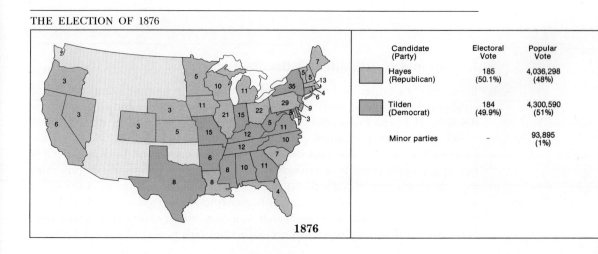

Candidate (Party)	Electoral Vote	Popular Vote
Hayes (Republican)	185 (50.1%)	4,036,298 (48%)
Tilden (Democrat)	184 (49.9%)	4,300,590 (51%)
Minor parties	–	93,895 (1%)

1876

In a crowded Supreme Court chamber, lawyers for both Hayes and Tilden present evidence to the electoral commission (seated on the rostrum at left) created to decide the outcome of the 1876 election. Members of all branches of government listen to the testimony, along with a number of socially prominent women, including Cornelia Adele Fassett, the artist who painted the scene from which this detail is taken.

Racism and the Failure of Reconstruction

Reconstruction failed for a multitude of reasons. The reforming impulse that had created the Republican party in the 1850s had been battered and worn down by the war. The new materialism of industrial America inspired in many a jaded cynicism about the corruption of the age and a desire to forget the uncomfortable issues of the past. In the South, African-American voters and leaders inevitably lacked a certain amount of education and experience; elsewhere, Republicans were divided over policies and options. Yet beyond all these obstacles, the sad fact remains that the ideals of the war and Reconstruction were most clearly defeated by a deep-seated racism that permeated American life. Racism was why the white South so unrelentingly resisted Reconstruction; racism was why most northern whites had little interest in black rights except as a means to an end, to preserve the Union or to safeguard the Republic; racism was why northerners were willing to write off Reconstruction, and with it the welfare of black Americans. Ever since the mid-seventeenth century, the system of slavery had been based on race. While Congress might pass a constitutional amendment abolishing the peculiar institution, it could not overturn at a stroke the social habits of two centuries.

Certainly the political equations of power, in the long term, had been changed. The North had fought tenaciously during the war to preserve the Union, and in doing so, had retained the power to dominate the economic and political destiny of the nation. With the overthrow of Reconstruction, the white South had won back in time of peace some of the power it had lost through war. But even with white supremacy triumphant across the land, African-Americans did not remain on the same social footing as before the war. They were no longer slaves, and blacks who walked dusty roads in search of family members, sent their children to school, or worshiped in churches they controlled, knew what a momentous change this was. Even under the exploitive sharecropping system, black income rose 40 percent in freedom. Then too, the principles of "equal protection" and "due process of law" had been written into the Constitution and would be available for later generations to use in resurrecting the Radicals' goal of racial equality.

But this was a struggle left to future generations. For the time being, the clear trend was away from change, reform, or hope—especially for blacks like Benjamin Montgomery and his sons, the owners of the old Davis plantation in Mississippi. In the 1870s bad crops, falling cotton prices and land values, and other misfortunes undermined the Montgomerys' financial position. At the same time, white violence against blacks made them more dependent than before on white goodwill, and in 1875 Jefferson Davis, who was now in dire economic circumstances himself, sued to have the sale of Brierfield invalidated. Davis acknowledged that he had never received legal title to the land, but he contended that his brother Joseph, who had died in 1870, had given him the plantation years ago to operate as his own.

In 1876, a lower court ruled against Davis, since he had executed his brother's will for four years without challenging its validity. But with the overthrow of Mississippi's Radical government, the political winds in the state shifted, and Davis appealed to the state supreme court, which now had a white conservative majority. The court, in a politically motivated decision, awarded Brierfield to Davis in 1878, and the Montgomerys lost Hurricane as well. The final outcome was not without bitter irony. In applying for restoration of his property after the war, Joseph Davis had convinced skeptical federal officials that he, and not his younger brother, held legal title to Brierfield. Had they decided instead that the plantation belonged to Jefferson Davis, it would have been confiscated.

But the waning days of Reconstruction were times filled with such ironies: of governments "redeemed" by violence, of Fourteenth Amendment rights designed to protect black people being used by conservative courts to protect giant corporations, of reformers searching elsewhere for other causes. Repudiated by its northern supporters and unmourned by public opinion, Reconstruction was over.

Benjamin Montgomery, together with his sons, purchased Jefferson Davis' plantation along the Mississippi River after the war. A former slave, Montgomery pursued the dream of black economic independence by renting land to black farmers at Davis Bend.

SIGNIFICANT EVENTS

1863	Lincoln outlines Reconstruction program
1864	Lincoln vetoes Wade–Davis bill; Louisiana, Arkansas, and Tennessee establish governments under Lincoln's plan
1865	Freedmen's Bureau established; Johnson becomes president; Presidential Reconstruction; Congress excludes representatives of Johnson's governments; Thirteenth Amendment ratified; Joint Committee on Reconstruction established
1865–1866	Black codes enacted
1866	Civil Rights bill passed over Johnson's veto; Memphis and New Orleans riots; Fourteenth Amendment passes Congress; Freedmen's Bureau extended; Ku Klux Klan organized; Tennessee readmitted to Congress; Republicans win decisive victory in congressional elections
1867	Congressional Reconstruction; Tenure of Office Act; Control of the Army Act
1867–1868	Constitutional conventions in the South; blacks vote in southern elections
1868	Johnson impeached but acquitted; Fourteenth Amendment ratified; Grant elected president
1869	Fifteenth Amendment passes Congress; *Ex parte McCardle*
1870	Last southern states readmitted to Congress; Fifteenth Amendment ratified; Enforcement acts
1871	Ku Klux Klan Act
1872	General Amnesty Act; Freedmen's Bureau dismantled; Liberal Republican revolt
1873–1877	Panic and depression
1874	Democrats win control of the House
1875	Civil Rights Act; Mississippi Plan
1876	Disputed Hayes–Tilden election
1877	Compromise of 1877; Hayes declared winner of electoral vote; last Republican governments in South fall

APPENDIX

THE DECLARATION OF INDEPENDENCE

In Congress, July 4, 1776,

THE UNANIMOUS DECLARATION OF THE
THIRTEEN UNITED STATES OF AMERICA

When, in the course of human events, it becomes necessary for one people to dissolve the
political bands which have connected them
with another, and to assume, among the powers
of the earth, the separate and equal station to
which the laws of nature and of nature's God
entitle them, a decent respect to the opinions of
mankind requires that they should declare the
causes which impel them to the separation.

We hold these truths to be self-evident,
that all men are created equal; that they are
endowed by their Creator with certain unalienable rights; that among these, are life, liberty,
and the pursuit of happiness. That, to secure
these rights, governments are instituted among
men, deriving their just powers from the consent of the governed; that, whenever any form
of government becomes destructive of these
ends, it is the right of the people to alter or to
abolish it, and to institute a new government,
laying its foundation on such principles, and
organizing its powers in such form, as to them
shall seem most likely to effect their safety and
happiness. Prudence, indeed, will dictate that
governments long established, should not be
changed for light and transient causes; and, accordingly, all experience hath shown, that mankind are more disposed to suffer, while evils are
sufferable, than to right themselves by abolishing the forms to which they are accustomed.
But, when a long train of abuses and usurpations, pursuing invariably the same object,
evinces a design to reduce them under absolute
despotism, it is their right, it is their duty, to
throw off such government and to provide new
guards for their future security. Such has been
the patient sufferance of these colonies, and
such is now the necessity which constrains

them to alter their former systems of government. The history of the present King of Great
Britain is a history of repeated injuries and
usurpations, all having, in direct object, the
establishment of an absolute tyranny over these
States. To prove this, let facts be submitted to a
candid world:

He has refused his assent to laws the most
wholesome and necessary for the public good.

He has forbidden his governors to pass
laws of immediate and pressing importance,
unless suspended in their operation till his assent should be obtained; and, when so suspended, he has utterly neglected to attend to
them.

He has refused to pass other laws for the
accommodation of large districts of people, unless those people would relinquish the right of
representation in the legislature; a right inesti-
mable to them, and formidable to tyrants only.

He has called together legislative bodies at
places unusual, uncomfortable, and distant
from the depository of their public records, for
the sole purpose of fatiguing them into compliance with his measures.

He has dissolved representative houses
repeatedly for opposing, with manly firmness,
his invasions on the rights of the people.

He has refused, for a long time after such dis-
solutions, to cause others to be elected; whereby the legislative powers, incapable of annihila-
tion, have returned to the people at large for
their exercise; the state remaining, in the
meantime, exposed to all the danger of invasion
from without, and convulsions within.

He has endeavored to prevent the population of these States; for that purpose, obstruct-
ing the laws for naturalization of foreigners,
refusing to pass others to encourage their
migration hither, and raising the conditions of
new appropriations of lands.

He had obstructed the administration of
justice, by refusing his assent to laws for establishing judiciary powers.

He has made judges dependent on his will alone, for the tenure of their offices, and the amount and payment of their salaries.

He has erected a multitude of new offices, and sent hither swarms of officers to harass our people, and eat out their substance.

He has kept among us, in time of peace, standing armies, without the consent of our legislatures.

He has affected to render the military independent of, and superior to, the civil power.

He has combined, with others, to subject us to a jurisdiction foreign to our Constitution, and unacknowledged by our laws; giving his assent to their acts of pretended legislation:

For quartering large bodies of armed troops among us:

For protecting them by a mock trial, from punishment, for any murders which they should commit on the inhabitants of these States:

For cutting off our trade with all parts of the world:

For imposing taxes on us without our consent:

For depriving us, in many cases, of the benefit of trial by jury:

For transporting us beyond seas to be tried for pretended offences:

For abolishing the free system of English laws in a neighboring province, establishing therein an arbitrary government, and enlarging its boundaries, so as to render it at once an example and fit instrument for introducing the same absolute rule into these colonies:

For taking away our charters, abolishing our most valuable laws, and altering, fundamentally, the powers of our governments:

For suspending our own legislatures, and declaring themselves invested with power to legislate for us in all cases whatsoever.

He had abdicated government here, by declaring us out of his protection, and waging war against us.

He has plundered our seas, ravaged our coasts, burnt our towns, and destroyed the lives of our people.

He is, at this time, transporting large armies of foreign mercenaries to complete the works of death, desolation, and tyranny, already begun, with circumstances of cruelty and perfidy scarcely paralleled in the most barbarous ages, and totally unworthy the head of a civilized nation.

He has constrained our fellow citizens, taken captive on the high seas, to bear arms against their country, to become the executioners of their friends, and brethren, or to fall themselves by their hands.

He has excited domestic insurrections amongst us, and has endeavored to bring on the inhabitants of our frontiers, the merciless Indian savages, whose known rule of warfare is an undistinguished destruction of all ages, sexes, and conditions.

In every stage of these oppressions, we have petitioned for redress, in the most humble terms; our repeated petitions have been answered only by repeated injury. A prince, whose character is thus marked by every act which may define a tyrant, is unfit to be the ruler of a free people.

Nor have we been wanting in attention to our British brethren. We have warned them, from time to time, of attempts made by their legislature to extend an unwarrantable jurisdiction over us. We have reminded them of the circumstances of our emigration and settlement here. We have appealed to their native justice and magnanimity, and we have conjured them, by the ties of our common kindred, to disavow these usurpations, which would inevitably interrupt our connections and correspondence. They, too, have been deaf to the voice of justice and consanguinity. We must, therefore, acquiesce in the necessity which denounces our separation, and hold them as we hold the rest of mankind, enemies in war, in peace, friends.

We, therefore, the representatives of the United States of America, in general Congress assembled, appealing to the Supreme Judge of the world for the rectitude of our intentions, do, in the name, and by the authority of the good people of these colonies, solemnly publish and declare, that these united colonies are, and of right ought to be, free and independent states: that they are absolved from all allegiance to the British Crown, and that all political connection between them and the state of Great Britain is, and ought to be, totally dissolved; and that, as free and independent states, they have full power to levy war, conclude peace, contract alliances, establish commerce, and to do all other acts and things which independent states may of right do. And, for the support of this declaration, with a firm reliance on the protection of Divine Providence, we mutually pledge to each other our lives, our fortunes, and our sacred honor.

The foregoing Declaration was, by order of Congress, engrossed, and signed by the following members:

JOHN HANCOCK

New Hampshire
Josiah Bartlett
William Whipple
Matthew Thornton

Massachusetts Bay
Samuel Adams
John Adams
Robert Treat Paine
Elbridge Gerry

Rhode Island
Stephen Hopkins
William Ellery

Connecticut
Roger Sherman
Samuel Huntington
William Williams
Oliver Wolcott

New York
William Floyd
Philip Livingston
Francis Lewis
Lewis Morris

New Jersey
Richard Stockton
John Witherspoon
Francis Hopkinson
John Hart
Abraham Clark

Pennsylvania
Robert Morris
Benjamin Rush
Benjamin Franklin
John Morton
George Clymer
James Smith
George Taylor
James Wilson
George Ross

Delaware
Caesar Rodney
George Reed
Thomas M'Kean

Maryland
Samuel Chase
William Paca
Thomas Stone
Charles Carroll,
   of Carrollton

Virginia
George Wythe
Richard Henry Lee
Thomas Jefferson
Benjamin Harrison
Thomas Nelson, Jr.
Francis Lightfoot Lee
Carter Braxton

North Carolina
William Hooper
Joseph Hewes
John Penn

South Carolina
Edward Rutledge
Thomas Heyward, Jr.
Thomas Lynch, Jr.
Arthur Middleton

Georgia
Button Gwinnett
Lyman Hall
George Walton

Resolved, That copies of the Declaration be sent to the several assemblies, conventions, and committees, or councils of safety, and to the several commanding officers of the continental troops; that it be proclaimed in each of the United States, at the head of the army.

THE CONSTITUTION OF THE UNITED STATES OF AMERICA[1]

We the People of the United States, in Order to form a more perfect Union, establish Justice, insure domestic Tranquility, provide for the common defence, promote the general Welfare, and secure the Blessings of Liberty to ourselves and our Posterity, do ordain and establish this CONSTITUTION for the United States of America.

ARTICLE 1

Section 1. All legislative Powers herein granted shall be vested in a Congress of the United States, which shall consist of a Senate and House of Representatives.

Section 2. The House of Representatives shall be composed of Members chosen every second Year by the People of the several States, and the Electors in each State shall have the Qualifications requisite for Electors of the most numerous Branch of the State Legislature.

No Person shall be a Representative who shall not have attained to the Age of twenty-five Years, and been seven Years a Citizen of the United States, and who shall not, when elected, be an Inhabitant of that State in which he shall be chosen.

[Representatives and direct Taxes[2] shall be apportioned among the several States which may be included within this Union, according to their respective Numbers, which shall be determined by adding to the whole Number of free Persons, including those bound to Service for a Term of Years, and excluding Indians not taxed, three fifths of all other Persons.][3] The actual Enumeration shall be made within three Years after the first Meeting of the Congress of the United States, and within every subsequent Term of ten Years, in such Manner as they shall by Law direct. The Number of Representatives shall not exceed one for every thirty Thousand, but each State shall have at Least one Representative; and until such enumeration shall be made, the State of New Hampshire shall be entitled to chuse three, Massachusetts eight, Rhode-Island and Providence Plantations one, Connecticut five, New York six, New Jersey four, Pennsylvania eight, Delaware one, Maryland six, Virginia ten, North Carolina five, South Carolina five, and Georgia three.

When vacancies happen in the Representation from any State, the Executive Authority thereof shall issue Writs of Election to fill such Vacancies.

The House of Representatives shall chuse their Speaker and other Officers; and shall have the sole Power of Impeachment.

Section 3. The Senate of the United States shall be composed of two Senators from each State, chosen by the Legislature thereof, for six Years; and each Senator shall have one Vote.

Immediately after they shall be assembled in Consequence of the first Election, they shall be divided as equally as may be into three Classes. The Seats of the Senators of the first Class shall be vacated at the Expiration of the second Year, of the second Class at the Expiration of the fourth Year, and of the third Class at the Expiration of the sixth Year, so that one-third may be chosen every second Year; and if Vacancies happen by Resignation, or otherwise, during the Recess of the Legislature of any State, the Executive thereof may make temporary Appointments until the next Meeting of the Legislature, which shall then fill such Vacancies.

No Person shall be a Senator who shall not have attained to the Age of thirty Years, and been nine Years a Citizen of the United States, and who shall not, when elected, be an Inhabitant of that State for which he shall be chosen.

The Vice President of the United States shall be President of the Senate, but shall have no vote, unless they be equally divided.

The Senate shall chuse their other Officers, and also a President pro tempore, in the absence of the Vice President, or when he shall exercise the Office of President of the United States.

The Senate shall have the sole Power to try all Impeachments. When sitting for that pur-

---

[1]This version follows the original Constitution in capitalization and spelling. It is adapted from the text published by the United States Department of the Interior, Office of Education.

[2]Altered by the Sixteenth Amendment.

[3]Negated by the Fourteenth Amendment.

pose they shall be on Oath or Affirmation. When the President of the United States is tried, the Chief Justice shall preside: And no person shall be convicted without the Concurrence of two thirds of the Members present.

Judgment in Cases of Impeachment shall not extend further than to removal from Office, and disqualification to hold and enjoy any Office of honor, Trust, or Profit under the United States: but the Party convicted shall nevertheless be liable and subject to Indictment, Trial, Judgment, and Punishment, according to Law.

Section 4. The Times, Places and Manner of holding Elections for Senators and Representatives, shall be prescribed in each State by the Legislature thereof; but the Congress may at any time by Law make or alter such Regulations, except as to the Places of Chusing Senators.

The Congress shall assemble at least once in every Year, and such Meeting shall be on the first Monday in December, unless they shall by Law appoint a different Day.

Section 5. Each House shall be the Judge of the Elections, Returns and Qualifications of its own Members, and a Majority of each shall constitute a Quorum to do Business; but a smaller number may adjourn from day to day, and may be authorized to compel the Attendance of absent Members, in such Manner, and under such Penalties, as each House may provide.

Each House may determine the Rules of its Proceedings, punish its Members for disorderly Behaviour, and, with the Concurrence of two thirds, expel a Member.

Each House shall keep a Journal of its Proceedings, and from time to time publish the same, excepting such Parts as may in their Judgment require Secrecy; and the Yeas and Nays of the Members of either House on any question shall, at the Desire of one fifth of those Present, be entered on the Journal.

Neither House, during the Session of Congress, shall, without the Consent of the other, adjourn for more than three days, nor to any other Place than that in which the two Houses shall be sitting.

Section 6. The Senators and Representatives shall receive a Compensation for their Services, to be ascertained by Law, and paid out of the Treasury of the United States. They shall in all Cases, except Treason, Felony, and Breach of the Peace, be privileged from Arrest during their Attendance at the Session of their respective Houses, and in going to and returning from the same; and for any Speech or Debate in either House, they shall not be questioned in any other Place.

No Senator or Representative shall, during the Time for which he was elected, be appointed to any civil Office under the Authority of the United States, which shall have been created, or the Emoluments whereof shall have been increased, during such time; and no Person holding any Office under the United States shall be a Member of either House during his continuance in Office.

Section 7. All Bills for raising Revenue shall originate in the House of Representatives; but the Senate may propose or concur with Amendments as on other bills.

Every Bill which shall have passed the House of Representatives and the Senate, shall, before it become a Law, be presented to the President of the United States; If he approve he shall sign it, but if not he shall return it, with his Objections, to that House in which it shall have originated, who shall enter the Objections at large on their Journal, and proceed to reconsider it. If after such Reconsideration two thirds of that House shall agree to pass the bill, it shall be sent, together with the objections, to the other House, by which it shall likewise be reconsidered, and if approved by two thirds of that House, it shall become a Law. But in all such Cases the Votes of both Houses shall be determined by Yeas and Nays, and the Names of the Persons voting for and against the Bill shall be entered on the Journal of each House respectively. If any Bill shall not be returned by the President within ten Days (Sundays excepted) after it shall have been presented to him, the Same shall be a Law, in like Manner as if he had signed it, unless the Congress by their Adjournment prevent its Return, in which Case it shall not be a Law.

Every Order, Resolution, or Vote to which the Concurrence of the Senate and House of Representatives may be necessary (except on a question of Adjournment) shall be presented to the President of the United States; and before the Same shall take Effect, shall be approved by him, or being disapproved by him, shall be repassed by two thirds of the Senate and House of Representatives, according to the Rules and Limitations prescribed in the Case of a Bill.

Section 8. The Congress shall have Power To lay and collect Taxes, Duties, Imposts and Excises, to pay the Debts and provide for the common Defence and general Welfare of the United States; but all Duties, Imposts and Excises shall be uniform throughout the United States;

To borrow money on the credit of the United States;

To regulate Commerce with foreign Nations, and among the several States, and with the Indian Tribes;

To establish an uniform rule of Naturalization, and uniform Laws on the subject of Bankruptcies throughout the United States;

To coin Money, regulate the Value thereof, and of foreign Coin, and fix the Standard of Weights and Measures;

To provide for the Punishment of counterfeiting the Securities and current Coin of the United States;

To establish Post Offices and post Roads;

To promote the Progress of Science and useful Arts, by securing for limited Times to Authors and Inventors the exclusive Right to their respective Writings and Discoveries;

To constitute Tribunals inferior to the Supreme Court;

To define and punish Piracies and Felonies committed on the high Seas, and Offenses against the Law of Nations;

To declare War, grant Letters of Marque and Reprisal, and make Rules concerning Captures on Land and Water;

To raise and support Armies, but no Appropriation of Money to that Use shall be for a longer Term than two Years;

To provide and maintain a Navy;

To make Rules for the Government and Regulation of the land and naval forces;

To provide for calling forth the Militia to execute the Laws of the Union, suppress Insurrections and repel Invasions;

To provide for organizing, arming, and disciplining the Militia, and for governing such Part of them as may be employed in the Service of the United States, reserving to the States respectively, the Appointment of the Officers, and the Authority of training the Militia according to the discipline prescribed by Congress;

To exercise exclusive Legislation in all Cases whatsoever, over such District (not exceeding ten Miles square) as may, by Cession of particular States, and the acceptance of Congress, become the Seat of the Government of the United States, and to exercise like Authority over all Places purchased by the Consent of the Legislature of the State in which the Same shall be, for the Erection of Forts, Magazines, Arsenals, Dock-yards, and other needful Buildings;—And

To make all Laws which shall be necessary and proper for carrying into Execution the foregoing Powers, and all other Powers vested by this Constitution in the Government of the United States, or in any Department or Officer thereof.

Section 9. The Migration or Importation of such Persons as any of the States now existing shall think proper to admit, shall not be prohibited by the Congress prior to the Year one thousand eight hundred and eight, but a tax or duty may be imposed on such Importation, not exceeding ten dollars for each Person.

The privilege of the Writ of Habeas Corpus shall not be suspended, unless when in Cases of Rebellion or Invasion the public Safety may require it.

No bill of Attainder or ex post facto Law shall be passed.

No capitation, or other direct, Tax shall be laid unless in Proportion to the Census or Enumeration herein before directed to be taken.

No Tax or Duty shall be laid on Articles exported from any State.

No Preference shall be given by any Regulation of Commerce or Revenue to the Ports of one State over those of another: nor shall Vessels bound to, or from, one State, be obliged to enter, clear, or pay Duties in another.

No Money shall be drawn from the Treasury, but in Consequence of Appropriations made by Law; and a regular Statement and Account of the Receipts and Expenditures of all public Money shall be published from time to time.

No Title of Nobility shall be granted by the United States: And no Person holding any Office of Profit or Trust under them, shall, without the Consent of the Congress, accept of any present, Emolument, Office, or Title, of any kind whatever, from any King, Prince, or foreign State.

Section 10. No State shall enter into any Treaty, Alliance, or Confederation; grant Letters of Marque and Reprisal; coin Money; emit Bills of Credit; make any Thing but gold and silver Coin a Tender in Payment of Debts; pass any Bill of Attainder, ex post facto Law, or Law impairing the Obligation of Contracts, or grant any Title of Nobility.

No State shall, without the Consent of the Congress, lay any Imposts or Duties on Imports or Exports, except what may be absolutely necessary for executing its inspection Laws; and the net Produce of all Duties and Imposts, laid by any State on Imports or Exports, shall be for the use of the Treasury of the United States; and all such Laws shall be subject to the Revision and Control of the Congress.

No state shall, without the Consent of Congress, lay any duty of Tonnage, keep Troops, or Ships of War in time of Peace, enter into any Agreement or Compact with another State, or with a foreign Power, or engage in War, unless actually invaded, or in such imminent Danger as will not admit of delay.

ARTICLE II

Section 1. The executive Power shall be vested in a President of the United States of America. He shall hold his Office during the Term of four years, and, together with the Vice President, chosen for the same Term, be elected, as follows:

Each State shall appoint, in such Manner as the Legislature thereof may direct, a Number of Electors, equal to the whole Number of Senators and Representatives to which the State may be entitled in the Congress: but no Senator or Representative, or Person holding an Office of Trust or Profit under the United States, shall be appointed an Elector.

[The Electors shall meet in their respective States, and vote by Ballot for two persons, of whom one at least shall not be an Inhabitant of the same State with themselves. And they shall make a List of all the Persons voted for, and of the Number of Votes for each; which List they shall sign and certify, and transmit sealed to the Seat of the Government of the United States, directed to the President of the Senate. The President of the Senate shall, in the Presence of the Senate and House of Representatives, open all the Certificates, and the Votes shall then be counted. The Person having the greatest Number of Votes shall be the President, if such Number be a Majority of the whole Number of Electors appointed; and if there be more than one who have such Majority, and have an equal Number of Votes, then the House of Representatives shall immediately chuse by Ballot one of them for President; and if no Person have a Majority, then from the five highest on the List the said House shall in like Manner chuse the President. But in chusing the President, the Votes shall be taken by States, the Representation from each State having one Vote; a quorum for this Purpose shall consist of a Member or Members from two-thirds of the States, and a Majority of all the States shall be necessary to a Choice. In every Case, after the Choice of the President, the Person having the greatest Number of Votes of the Electors shall be the Vice President. But if there should remain two or more who have equal votes, the Senate shall chuse from them by Ballot the Vice President.][4]

The Congress may determine the Time of chusing the Electors, and the Day on which they shall give their Votes; which Day shall be the same throughout the United States.

No person except a natural-born Citizen, or a Citizen of the United States, at the time of the Adoption of this Constitution, shall be eligible to the Office of President; neither shall any Person be eligible to that Office who shall not have attained to the Age of thirty-five years, and been fourteen Years a Resident within the United States.

In Case of the Removal of the President from Office, or of his Death, Resignation, or Inability to discharge the Powers and Duties of the said Office, the same shall devolve on the Vice President, and the Congress may by Law provide for the Case of Removal, Death, Resignation, or Inability, both of the President and Vice President, declaring what Officer shall then act as President, and such Officer shall act accordingly, until the disability be removed, or a President shall be elected.

The President shall, at stated Times, receive for his Services a Compensation, which shall neither be increased nor diminished during the Period for which he shall have been elected, and he shall not receive within that Period any other Emolument from the United States, or any of them.

Before he enter on the execution of his Office, he shall take the following Oath or Affirma-

---

[4]Revised by the Twelfth Amendment.

tion:—"I do solemnly swear (or affirm) that I will faithfully execute the Office of President of the United States, and will, to the best of my Ability, preserve, protect, and defend the Constitution of the United States."

Section 2. The President shall be Commander in Chief of the Army and Navy of the United States, and of the Militia of the several States, when called into the actual Service of the United States; he may require the Opinion, in writing, of the principal Officer in each of the executive Departments, upon any subject relating to the Duties of their respective Offices, and he shall have Power to Grant Reprieves and Pardons for Offenses against the United States, except in Cases of Impeachment.

He shall have Power, by and with the Advice and Consent of the Senate, to make Treaties, provided two-thirds of the Senators present concur; and he shall nominate, and by and with the Advice and Consent of the Senate, shall appoint Ambassadors, other public Ministers and Consuls, Judges of the supreme Court, and all other Officers of the United States, whose Appointments are not herein otherwise provided for, and which shall be established by Law: but the Congress may by Law vest the Appointment of such inferior Officers, as they think proper, in the President alone, in the Courts of Law, or in the Heads of Departments.

The President shall have Power to fill up all Vacancies that may happen during the Recess of the Senate, by granting Commissions which shall expire at the End of their next Session.

Section 3. He shall from time to time give to the Congress Information of the State of the Union, and recommend to their Consideration such Measures as he shall judge necessary and expedient; he may, on extraordinary occasions, convene both Houses, or either of them, and in Case of Disagreement between them, with respect to the Time of Adjournment, he may adjourn them to such Time as he shall think proper; he shall receive Ambassadors and other public Ministers; he shall take care that the Laws be faithfully executed, and shall Commission all the Officers of the United States.

Section 4. The President, Vice President and all civil Officers of the United States, shall be removed from Office on Impeachment for, and Conviction of, Treason, Bribery, or other high Crimes and Misdemeanors.

ARTICLE III

Section 1. The judicial Power of the United States, shall be vested in one supreme Court, and in such inferior Courts as the Congress may from time to time ordain and establish. The Judges, both of the supreme and inferior Courts, shall hold their Offices during good Behaviour, and shall, at stated Times, receive for their Services, a Compensation, which shall not be diminished during their Continuance in Office.

Section 2. The judicial Power shall extend to all Cases, in Law and Equity, arising under this Constitution, the Laws of the United States, and Treaties made, or which shall be made, under their Authority;—to all Cases affecting ambassadors, other public ministers and consuls;—to all cases of admiralty and maritime Jurisdiction;—to Controversies to which the United States shall be a Party;—to Controversies between two or more States;—between a State and Citizens of another State;[5]—between Citizens of different States—between Citizens of the same State claiming Lands under Grants of different States, and between a State, or the Citizens thereof, and foreign States, Citizens, or Subjects.

In all Cases affecting Ambassadors, other public Ministers and Consuls, and those in which a State shall be Party, the supreme Court shall have original Jurisdiction. In all the other Cases before mentioned, the supreme Court shall have appellate Jurisdiction, both as to Law and Fact, with such Exceptions, and under such Regulations as the Congress shall make.

The trial of all Crimes, except in Cases of Impeachment, shall be by Jury; and such Trial shall be held in the State where the said Crimes shall have been committed; but when not committed within any State, the Trial shall be at such Place or Places as the Congress may by Law have directed.

Section 3. Treason against the United States, shall consist only in levying War against them,

[5]Qualified by the Eleventh Amendment.

or in adhering to their Enemies, giving them Aid and Comfort. No Person shall be convicted of Treason unless on the Testimony of two Witnesses to the same overt Act, or on Confession in open Court.

The Congress shall have power to declare the Punishment of Treason, but no Attainder of Treason shall work Corruption of Blood, or Forfeiture except during the Life of the Person attainted.

ARTICLE IV

Section 1. Full Faith and Credit shall be given in each State to the public Acts, Records, and judicial Proceedings of every other State. And the Congress may by general Laws prescribe the Manner in which such Acts, Records and Proceedings shall be proved, and the Effect thereof.

Section 2. The Citizens of each State shall be entitled to all Privileges and Immunities of Citizens in the several States.

A Person charged in any State with Treason, Felony, or other Crime, who shall flee from Justice, and be found in another State, shall on demand of the executive Authority of the State from which he fled, be delivered up, to be removed to the State having Jurisdiction of the crime.

No Person held to Service or Labour in one State, under the Laws thereof, escaping into another, shall, in Consequence of any Law or Regulation therein, be discharged from such Service or Labour, but shall be delivered up on Claim of the Party to whom such Service or Labour may be due.

Section 3. New States may be admitted by the Congress into this Union; but no new State shall be formed or erected within the Jurisdiction of any other State; nor any State be formed by the Junction of two or more States, or parts of States, without the Consent of the Legislatures of the States concerned as well as of the Congress.

The Congress shall have Power to dispose of and make all needful Rules and Regulations respecting the Territory or other Property belonging to the United States; and nothing in this Constitution shall be so construed as to Prejudice any Claims of the United States, or of any particular State.

Section 4. The United States shall guarantee to every State in this Union a Republican Form of Government, and shall protect each of them against Invasion; and on Application of the Legislature, or of the Executive (when the Legislature cannot be convened) against domestic Violence.

ARTICLE V

The Congress, whenever two-thirds of both Houses shall deem it necessary, shall propose Amendments to this Constitution, or, on the Application of the Legislatures of two-thirds of the several States, shall call a Convention for proposing Amendments, which, in either Case, shall be valid to all Intents and Purposes, as part of this Constitution, when ratified by the Legislatures of three-fourths of the several States, or by Conventions in three-fourths thereof, as the one or the other Mode of Ratification may be proposed by the Congress; Provided that no Amendment which may be made prior to the Year One thousand eight hundred and eight shall in any Manner affect the first and fourth Clauses in the Ninth Section of the first Article; and that no State, without its Consent, shall be deprived of its equal Suffrage in the Senate.

ARTICLE VI

All Debts contracted and Engagements entered into, before the Adoption of this Constitution, shall be as valid against the United States under this Constitution, as under the Confederation.

This Constitution, and the Laws of the United States which shall be made in Pursuance thereof; and all Treaties made, or which shall be made, under the Authority of the United States, shall be the supreme Law of the Land; and the Judges in every State shall be bound thereby, any Thing in the Constitution or Laws of any State to the Contrary notwithstanding.

The Senators and Representatives before mentioned, and the Members of the several State Legislatures, and all executive and judicial Officers, both of the United States and of the several States, shall be bound by Oath or Affirmation to support this Constitution; but no religious Tests shall ever be required as a qualification to any Office or public Trust under the United States.

ARTICLE VII

The Ratification of the Conventions of nine States shall be sufficient for the Establishment of this Constitution between the States so ratifying the same.

Done in Convention by the Unanimous Consent of the States present the Seventeenth Day of September in the Year of our Lord one thousand seven hundred and Eighty seven, and of the Independence of the United States of America the Twelfth. In Witness whereof We have hereunto subscribed our Names.[6]

GEORGE WASHINGTON

PRESIDENT AND DEPUTY FROM VIRGINIA

New Hampshire
John Langdon
Nicholas Gilman

Massachusetts
Nathaniel Gorham
Rufus King

Connecticut
William Samuel
 Johnson
Roger Sherman

New York
Alexander Hamilton

New Jersey
William Livingston
David Brearley
William Paterson
Jonathan Dayton

Pennsylvania
Benjamin Franklin
Thomas Mifflin
Robert Morris
George Clymer
Thomas FitzSimons
Jared Ingersoll
James Wilson
Gouverneur Morris

Delaware
George Read
Gunning Bedford, Jr.
John Dickinson
Richard Bassett
Jacob Broom

Maryland
James McHenry
Daniel of
 St. Thomas Jenifer
Daniel Carroll

Virginia
John Blair
James Madison, Jr.

North Carolina
William Blount
Richard Dobbs
 Spaight
Hugh Williamson

South Carolina
John Rutledge
Charles Cotesworth
 Pinckney
Charles Pinckney
Pierce Butler

Georgia
William Few
Abraham Baldwin

Articles in Addition to, and Amendment of, the Constitution of the United States of America, Proposed by Congress, and Ratified by the Legislatures of the Several States, Pursuant to the Fifth Article of the Original Constitution[7]

[AMENDMENT I]

Congress shall make no law respecting an establishment of religion, or prohibiting the free exercise thereof; or abridging the freedom of speech, or of the press; or the right of the people peaceably to assemble, and to petition the Government for a redress of grievances.

[AMENDMENT II]

A well regulated Militia, being necessary to the security of a free State, the right of the people to keep and bear Arms shall not be infringed.

[AMENDMENT III]

No Soldier shall, in time of peace, be quartered in any house, without the consent of the Owner, nor in time of war, but in a manner to be prescribed by law.

[AMENDMENT IV]

The right of the people to be secure in their persons, houses, papers, and effects, against unreasonable searches and seizures, shall not be violated, and no Warrants shall issue, but

[6]These are the full names of the signers, which in some cases are not the signatures on the document.

[7]This heading appears only in the joint resolution submitting the first ten amendments, known as the Bill of Rights.

upon probable cause, supported by Oath or affirmation, and particularly describing the place to be searched, and the persons or things to be seized.

[AMENDMENT V]

No person shall be held to answer for a capital or otherwise infamous crime, unless on a presentment or indictment of a Grand Jury, except in cases arising in the land or naval forces, or in the Militia, when in actual service in time of War or public danger; nor shall any person be subject for the same offence to be twice put in jeopardy of life or limb; nor shall be compelled in any criminal case to be a witness against himself, nor be deprived of life, liberty, or property, without due process of law; nor shall private property be taken for public use, without just compensation.

[AMENDMENT VI]

In all criminal prosecutions, the accused shall enjoy the right to a speedy and public trial, by an impartial jury of the State and district wherein the crime shall have been committed, which district shall have been previously ascertained by law, and to be informed of the nature and cause of the accusation; to be confronted with the witnesses against him; to have compulsory process for obtaining witnesses in his favour, and to have the Assistance of Counsel for his defence.

[AMENDMENT VII]

In suits at common law, where the value in controversy shall exceed twenty dollars, the right of trial by jury shall be preserved, and no fact tried by a jury, shall be otherwise reexamined in any Court of the United States, than according to the rules of the common law.

[AMENDMENT VIII]

Excessive bail shall not be required, nor excessive fines imposed, nor cruel and unusual punishments inflicted.

[AMENDMENT IX]

The enumeration of the Constitution, of certain rights, shall not be construed to deny or disparage others retained by the people.

[AMENDMENT X]

The powers not delegated to the United States by the Constitution, nor prohibited by it to the States, are reserved to the States respectively, or to the people.

[Amendments I–X, in force 1791.]

[AMENDMENT XI][8]

The Judicial power of the United States shall not be construed to extend to any suit in law or equity, commenced or prosecuted against one of the United States by Citizens of another State, or by Citizens or Subjects of any Foreign State.

[AMENDMENT XII][9]

The Electors shall meet in their respective States and vote by ballot for President and Vice-President, one of whom, at least, shall not be an inhabitant of the same State with themselves; they shall name in their ballots the person voted for as President, and in distinct ballots the person voted for as Vice-President, and they shall make distinct lists of all persons voted for as President, and of all persons voted for as Vice-President, and of the number of votes for each, which lists they shall sign and certify, and transmit sealed to the seal of the government of the United States, directed to the President of the Senate;—The President of the Senate shall, in the presence of the Senate and House of Representatives, open all the certificates and the votes shall then be counted;—The person having the greatest number of votes for President, shall be the President, if such number be a majority of the whole number of Electors appointed; and if no person have such majority, then from the persons having the highest numbers not exceeding three on the list of those

[8]Adopted in 1798.

[9]Adopted in 1804.

voted for as President, the House of Representatives shall choose immediately, by ballot, the President. But in choosing the President, the votes shall be taken by states, the representation from each state having one vote; a quorum for this purpose shall consist of a member or members from two-thirds of the states, and a majority of all the states shall be necessary to a choice. And if the House of Representatives shall not choose a President whenever the right of choice shall devolve upon them, before the fourth day of March next following, then the Vice-President shall act as President, as in the case of the death or other constitutional disability of the President.—The person having the greatest number of votes as Vice-President, shall be the Vice-President, if such number be a majority of the whole number of Electors appointed, and if no person have a majority, then from the two highest numbers on the list, the Senate shall choose the Vice-President; a quorum for the purpose shall consist of two-thirds of the whole number of Senators, and a majority of the whole number shall be necessary to a choice. But no person constitutionally ineligible to the office of President shall be eligible to that of Vice-President of the United States.

[AMENDMENT XIII][10]

Section 1. Neither slavery nor involuntary servitude, except as a punishment for crime whereof the party shall have been duly convicted, shall exist within the United States, or any place subject to their jurisdiction.

Section 2. Congress shall have power to enforce this article by appropriate legislation.

[AMENDMENT XIV][11]

Section 1. All persons born or naturalized in the United States, and subject to the jurisdiction thereof, are citizens of the United States and of the State wherein they reside. No State shall abridge the privileges or immunities of citizens of the United States; nor shall any State deprive any person of life, liberty, or property, without due process of law; nor deny to any person within its jurisdiction the equal protection of the laws.

Section 2. Representatives shall be apportioned among the several States according to their respective numbers, counting the whole number of persons in each State, excluding Indians not taxed. But when the right to vote at any election for the choice of electors for President and Vice-President of the United States, Representatives in Congress, the Executive and Judicial officers of a State, or the members of the Legislature thereof, is denied to any of the male inhabitants of such State, being twenty-one years of age, and citizens of the United States, or in any way abridged, except for participation in rebellion, or other crime, the basis of representation therein shall be reduced in the proportion which the number of such male citizens shall bear to the whole number of male citizens twenty-one years of age in such State.

Section 3. No person shall be a Senator or Representative in Congress, or elector of President and Vice-President, or hold any office, civil or military, under the United States, or under and State, who, having previously taken an oath, as a member of Congress, or as an officer of the United States, or as a member of any State legislature, or as an executive or judicial officer of any State, to support the Constitution of the United States, shall have engaged in insurrection or rebellion against the same, or given aid or comfort to the enemies thereof. But Congress may by a vote of two-thirds of each House, remove such disability.

Section 4. The validity of the public debt of the United States, authorized by law, including debts incurred for payment of pensions and bounties for services in suppressing insurrection or rebellion, shall not be questioned. But neither the United States nor any State shall assume or pay any debts or obligation incurred in aid of insurrection or rebellion against the United States, or any claim for the loss or emancipation of any slave; but all such debts, obligations, and claims shall be held illegal and void.

Section 5. The Congress shall have the power to enforce, by appropriate legislation, the provisions of this article.

[10]Adopted in 1865.
[11]Adopted in 1868.

[AMENDMENT XV][12]

Section 1. The right of citizens of the United States to vote shall not be denied or abridged by the United States or by any State on account of race, color, or previous condition of servitude—

Section 2. The Congress shall have power to enforce this article by appropriate legislation.

[AMENDMENT XVI][13]

The Congress shall have power to lay and collect taxes on incomes, from whatever source derived, without apportionment among the several States, and without regard to any census or enumeration.

[AMENDMENT XVII][14]

The Senate of the United States shall be composed of two Senators from each State, elected by the people thereof, for six years; and each Senator shall have one vote. The electors in each State shall have the qualifications requisite for electors of the most numerous branch of the State legislatures.

When vacancies happen in the representation of any State in the Senate, the executive authority of such State shall issue writs of election to fill such vacancies: *Provided,* That the legislature of any State may empower the executive thereof to make temporary appointments until the people fill the vacancies by election as the legislature may direct.

This amendment shall not be so construed as to affect the election or term of any Senator chosen before it becomes valid as part of the Constitution.

[AMENDMENT XVIII][15]

Section 1. After one year from the ratification of this article the manufacture, sale, or transportation of intoxicating liquors within, the importation thereof into, or the exportation

[12]Adopted in 1870.
[13]Adopted in 1913.
[14]Adopted in 1913.
[15]Adopted in 1918.

thereof from the United States and all territory subject to the jurisdiction thereof for beverage purposes is hereby prohibited.

Section 2. The Congress and the several States shall have concurrent power to enforce this article by appropriate legislation.

Section 3. This article shall be inoperative unless it shall have been ratified as an amendment to the Constitution by the legislatures of the several States, as provided in the Constitution, within seven years from the date of the submission hereof to the States by the Congress.

[AMENDMENT XIX][16]

The right of citizens of the United States to vote shall not be denied or abridged by the United States or by any State on account of sex.

Congress shall have power to enforce this article by appropriate legislation.

[AMENDMENT XX][17]

Section 1. The terms of the President and Vice-President shall end at noon on the 20th day of January, and the terms of Senators and Representatives at noon on the 3d day of January, of the years in which such terms would have ended if this article had not been ratified; and the terms of their successors shall then begin.

Section 2. The Congress shall assemble at least once in every year, and such meeting shall begin at noon on the 3d day of January, unless they shall by law appoint a different day.

Section 3. If, at the time fixed for the beginning of the term of the President, the President elect shall have died, the Vice-President elect shall become President. If a President shall not have been chosen before the time fixed for the beginning of his term or if the President elect shall have failed to qualify, then the Vice-President elect shall act as President until a President shall have qualified; and the Congress may by law provide for the case wherein neither a President elect nor a Vice-President elect shall

[16]Adopted in 1920.
[17]Adopted in 1933.

have qualified, declaring who shall then act as President, or the manner in which one who is to act shall be selected, and such person shall act accordingly until a President or Vice-President shall have qualified.

Section 4. The Congress may by law provide for the case of the death of any of the persons from whom the House of Representatives may choose a President whenever the right of choice shall have devolved upon them, and for the case of the death of any of the persons from whom the Senate may choose a Vice-President whenever the right of choice shall have devolved upon them.

Section 5. Sections 1 and 2 shall take effect on the 15th day of October following the ratification of this article.

Section 6. This article shall be inoperative unless it shall have been ratified as an amendment to the Constitution by the legislatures of three-fourths of the several States within seven years from the date of its submission.

[AMENDMENT XXI][18]

Section 1. The eighteenth article of amendment to the Constitution of the United States is hereby repealed.

Section 2. The transportation or importation into any State, Territory, or possession of the United States for delivery or use therein of intoxicating liquors, in violation of the laws thereof, is hereby prohibited.

Section 3. This article shall be inoperative unless it shall have been ratified as an amendment to the Constitution by conventions in the several States, as provided in the Constitution, within seven years from the date of the submission hereof to the States by the Congress.

[AMENDMENT XXII][19]

No person shall be elected to the office of the President more than twice, and no person who has held the office of President, or acted as President, for more than two years of a term to

which some other person was elected President shall be elected to the office of the President more than once.

But this Article shall not apply to any person holding the office of President when this Article was proposed by the Congress, and shall not prevent any person who may be holding the office of President, or acting as President, during the term within which this Article becomes operative from holding the office of President or acting as President during the remainder of such term.

This article shall be inoperative unless it shall have been ratified as an amendment to the Constitution by the legislatures of three-fourths of the several states within seven years from the date of its submission to the states by the Congress.

[AMENDMENT XXIII][20]

Section 1. The District constituting the seat of Government of the United States shall appoint in such manner as the Congress may direct:

A number of electors of President and Vice-President equal to the whole number of Senators and Representatives in Congress to which the District would be entitled if it were a State, but in no event more than the least populous State; they shall be in addition to those appointed by the States, but they shall be considered, for the purpose of the election of President and Vice-President, to be electors appointed by a State; and they shall meet in the District and perform such duties as provided by the twelfth article of amendment.

Section 2. The Congress shall have power to enforce this article by appropriate legislation.

[AMENDMENT XXIV][21]

Section 1. The right of citizens of the United States to vote in any primary or other election for President or Vice-President, for electors for President or Vice-President, or for Senator or Representative in Congress, shall not be denied or abridged by the United States or any state by reason of failure to pay any poll tax or other tax.

[18]Adopted in 1933.
[19]Adopted in 1961.

[20]Adopted in 1961.
[21]Adopted in 1964.

Section 2. The Congress shall have the power to enforce this article by appropriate legislation.

[AMENDMENT XXV][22]

Section 1. In case of the removal of the President from office or of his death or resignation, the Vice-President shall become President.

Section 2. Whenever there is a vacancy in the office of the Vice President, the President shall nominate a Vice President who shall take office upon confirmation by a majority vote of both Houses of Congress.

Section 3. Whenever the President transmits to the President Pro Tempore of the Senate and the Speaker of the House of Representatives his written declaration that he is unable to discharge the powers and duties of his office, and until he transmits to them a written declaration to the contrary, such powers and duties shall be discharged by the Vice-President as Acting President.

Section 4. Whenever the Vice-President and a majority of either the principal officers of the executive departments or of such other body as Congress may by law provide, transmit to the President Pro Tempore of the Senate and the Speaker of the House of Representatives their written declaration that the President is unable to discharge the powers and duties of his office, the Vice President shall immediately assume the powers and duties of the office as Acting President.

Thereafter, when the President transmits to the President Pro Tempore of the Senate and the Speaker of the House of Representatives his written declaration that no inability exists, he shall resume the powers and duties of his office unless the Vice President and a majority of either the principal officers of the executive departments or of such other body as Congress may by law provide, transmit within four days to the President Pro Tempore of the Senate and the Speaker of the House of Representatives their written declaration that the President is unable to discharge the powers and duties of his office. Thereupon Congress shall decide the issue, assembling within forty-eight hours for that purpose if not in session. If the Congress, within twenty-one days after receipt of the latter written declaration, or, if Congress is not in session, within twenty-one days after Congress is required to assemble, determines by two-thirds vote of both Houses that the President is unable to discharge the powers and duties of his office, the Vice President shall continue to discharge the same as Acting President; otherwise, the President shall resume the powers and duties of his office.

[AMENDMENT XXVI][23]

Section 1. The right of citizens of the United States, who are eighteen years of age or older, to vote shall not be denied or abridged by the United States or by any State on account of age.

Section 2. The Congress shall have power to enforce this article by appropriate legislation.

---

[22]Adopted in 1967.

[23]Adopted in 1971.

PRESIDENTIAL ELECTIONS

Year	Candidates	Parties	Popular Vote	% of Popular Vote	Electoral Vote	% Voter Partici- pation
1789	**George Washington**				69	
	John Adams				34	
	Other candidates				35	
1792	**George Washington**				132	
	John Adams				77	
	George Clinton				50	
	Other candidates				5	
1796	**John Adams**	Federalist			71	
	Thomas Jefferson	Dem.-Rep.			68	
	Thomas Pinckney	Federalist			59	
	Aaron Burr	Dem.-Rep.			30	
	Other candidates				48	
1800	**Thomas Jefferson**	Dem.-Rep.			73	
	Aaron Burr	Dem.-Rep.			73	
	John Adams	Federalist			65	
	Charles C. Pinckney	Federalist			64	
	John Jay	Federalist			1	
1804	**Thomas Jefferson**	Dem.-Rep.			162	
	Charles C. Pinckney	Federalist			14	
1808	**James Madison**	Dem.-Rep.			122	
	Charles C. Pinckney	Federalist			47	
	George Clinton	Dem.-Rep.			6	
1812	**James Madison**	Dem.-Rep.			128	
	DeWitt Clinton	Federalist			89	
1816	**James Monroe**	Dem.-Rep.			183	
	Rufus King	Federalist			34	
1820	**James Monroe**	Dem.-Rep.			231	
	John Quincy Adams	Indep.-Rep.			1	
1824	**John Quincy Adams**	Dem.-Rep.	108,740	31	84	26.9
	Andrew Jackson	Dem.-Rep.	153,544	43	99	
	Henry Clay	Dem.-Rep.	47,136	13	37	
	William H. Crawford	Dem.-Rep.	46,618	13	41	
1828	**Andrew Jackson**	Democratic	647,286	56.0	178	57.6
	John Quincy Adams	National Republican	508,064	44.0	83	
1832	**Andrew Jackson**	Democratic	688,242	54.5	219	55.4
	Henry Clay	National Republican	473,462	37.5	49	
	William Wirt	Anti-Masonic	101,051	8.0	7	
	John Floyd	Democratic			11	
1836	**Martin Van Buren**	Democratic	765,483	50.9	170	57.8
	William H. Harrison	Whig			73	
	Hugh L. White	Whig	739,795	49.1	26	
	Daniel Webster	Whig			14	
	W. P. Mangum	Whig			11	

Year	Candidates	Parties	Popular Vote	% of Popular Vote	Electoral Vote	% Voter Partici- pation
1840	**William H. Harrison**	Whig	1,275,016	53	234	80.2
	Martin Van Buren	Democratic	1,129,102	47	60	
1844	**James K. Polk**	Democratic	1,338,464	49.6	170	78.9
	Henry Clay	Whig	1,300,097	48.1	105	
	James G. Birney	Liberty	62,300	2.3		
1848	**Zachary Taylor**	Whig	1,360,967	47.4	163	72.7
	Lewis Cass	Democratic	1,222,342	42.5	127	
	Martin Van Buren	Free Soil	291,263	10.1		
1852	**Franklin Pierce**	Democratic	1,601,117	50.9	254	69.6
	Winfield Scott	Whig	1,385,453	44.1	42	
	John P. Hale	Free Soil	155,825	5.0		
1856	**James Buchanan**	Democratic	1,832,955	45.3	174	78.9
	John C. Fremont	Republican	1,339,932	33.1	114	
	Millard Fillmore	American	871,731	21.6	8	
1860	**Abraham Lincoln**	Republican	1,866,452	39.8	180	81.2
	Stephen A. Douglas	Democratic	1,375,157	29.5	12	
	John C. Breckinridge	Democratic	847,953	18.1	72	
	John Bell	Constitutional Union	590,631	12.6	39	
1864	**Abraham Lincoln**	Republican	2,206,938	55.0	212	73.8
	George B. McClellan	Democratic	1,803,787	45.0	21	
1868	**Ulysses S. Grant**	Republican	3,013,421	52.7	214	78.1
	Horatio Seymour	Democratic	2,706,829	47.3	80	
1872	**Ulysses S. Grant**	Republican	3,596,745	55.6	286	71.3
	Horace Greeley	Democratic	2,843,446	43.9	66	
1876	**Rutherford B. Hayes**	Republican	4,036,298	48.0	185	81.8
	Samuel J. Tilden	Democratic	4,300,590	51.0	184	
1880	**James A. Garfield**	Republican	4,453,295	48.5	214	79.4
	Winfield S. Hancock	Democratic	4,414,082	48.1	155	
	James B. Weaver	Greenback-Labor	308,578	3.4		
1884	**Grover Cleveland**	Democratic	4,879,507	48.5	219	77.5
	James G. Blaine	Republican	4,850,293	48.2	182	
	Benjamin F. Butler	Greenback-Labor	175,370	1.8		
	John P. St. John	Prohibition	150,369	1.5		
1888	**Benjamin Harrison**	Republican	5,477,129	47.9	233	79.3
	Grover Cleveland	Democratic	5,537,857	48.6	168	
	Clinton B. Fisk	Prohibition	249,506	2.2		
	Anson J. Streeter	Union Labor	146,935	1.3		
1892	**Grover Cleveland**	Democratic	5,555,426	46.1	277	74.7
	Benjamin Harrison	Republican	5,182,690	43.0	145	
	James B. Weaver	People's	1,029,846	8.5	22	
	John Bidwell	Prohibition	264,133	2.2		
1896	**William McKinley**	Republican	7,104,779	52.0	271	79.3
	William J. Bryan	Democratic	6,502,925	48.0	176	
1900	**William McKinley**	Republican	7,218,491	51.7	292	73.2
	William J. Bryan	Democratic; Populist	6,356,734	45.5	155	
	John C. Wooley	Prohibition	208,914	1.5		
1904	**Theodore Roosevelt**	Republican	7,628,461	57.4	336	65.2
	Alton B. Parker	Democratic	5,084,223	37.6	140	
	Eugene V. Debs	Socialist	402,283	3.0		
	Silas C. Swallow	Prohibition	258,536	1.9		

Year	Candidates	Parties	Popular Vote	% of Popular Vote	Electoral Vote	% Voter Partici- pation
1908	**William H. Taft**	Republican	7,675,320	51.6	321	65.4
	William J. Bryan	Democratic	6,412,294	43.1	162	
	Eugene V. Debs	Socialist	420,793	2.8		
	Eugene W. Chafin	Prohibition	253,840	1.7		
1912	**Woodrow Wilson**	Democratic	6,293,454	42.0	435	58.8
	Theodore Roosevelt	Progressive	4,119,538	28.0	88	
	William H. Taft	Republican	3,484,980	24.0	8	
	Eugene V. Debs	Socialist	900,672	6.0		
	Eugene W. Chafin	Prohibition	206,275	1.4		
1916	**Woodrow Wilson**	Democratic	9,129,606	49.4	277	61.6
	Charles E. Hughes	Republican	8,538,221	46.2	254	
	A. L. Benson	Socialist	585,113	3.2		
	J. Frank Hanly	Prohibition	220,506	1.2		
1920	**Warren G. Harding**	Republican	16,143,407	60.4	404	49.2
	James M. Cox	Democratic	9,130,328	34.2	127	
	Eugene V. Debs	Socialist	919,799	3.4		
	P. P. Christensen	Farmer-Labor	265,411	1.0		
1924	**Calvin Coolidge**	Republican	15,718,211	54.0	382	48.9
	John W. Davis	Democratic	8,385,283	28.8	136	
	Robert M. La Follette	Progressive	4,831,289	16.6	13	
1928	**Herbert C. Hoover**	Republican	21,391,381	58.2	444	56.9
	Alfred E. Smith	Democratic	15,016,443	40.9	87	
1932	**Franklin D. Roosevelt**	Democratic	22,821,857	57.4	472	56.9
	Herbert C. Hoover	Republican	15,761,841	39.7	59	
	Norman Thomas	Socialist	881,951	2.2		
1936	**Franklin D. Roosevelt**	Democratic	27,751,597	60.8	523	61.0
	Alfred M. Landon	Republican	16,679,583	36.5	8	
	William Lemke	Union	882,479	1.9		
1940	**Franklin D. Roosevelt**	Democratic	27,307,819	54.8	449	62.5
	Wendell L. Wilkie	Republican	22,321,018	44.8	82	
1944	**Franklin D. Roosevelt**	Democratic	25,606,585	53.5	432	55.9
	Thomas E. Dewey	Republican	22,014,745	46.0	99	
1948	**Harry S Truman**	Democratic	24,105,812	50.0	303	53.0
	Thomas E. Dewey	Republican	21,970,065	46.0	189	
	J. Strom Thurmond	States' Rights	1,169,021	2	39	
	Henry A. Wallace	Progressive	1,157,172	2		
1952	**Dwight D. Eisenhower**	Republican	33,936,234	55.1	442	63.3
	Adlai E. Stevenson	Democratic	27,314,992	44.4	89	
1956	**Dwight D. Eisenhower**	Republican	35,590,472	57.6	457	60.6
	Adlai E. Stevenson	Democratic	26,022,752	42.1	73	
1960	**John F. Kennedy**	Democratic	34,227,096	49.7	303	62.8
	Richard M. Nixon	Republican	34,107,646	49.6	219	
	Harry F. Byrd	Independent	501,643		15	
1964	**Lyndon B. Johnson**	Democratic	43,129,566	61.1	486	61.7
	Barry M. Goldwater	Republican	27,178,188	38.5	52	
1968	**Richard M. Nixon**	Republican	31,785,480	44.0	301	60.6
	Hubert H. Humphrey	Democratic	31,275,166	42.7	191	
	George C. Wallace	American Independent	9,906,473	13.5	46	
1972	**Richard M. Nixon**	Republican	47,169,911	60.7	520	55.2
	George S. McGovern	Democratic	29,170,383	37.5	17	
	John G. Schmitz	American	1,099,482	1.4		

Year	Candidates	Parties	Popular Vote	% of Popular Vote	Electoral Vote	% Voter Partici- pation
1976	**Jimmy Carter**	Democratic	40,830,763	50.1	297	53.5
	Gerald R. Ford	Republican	39,147,793	48.0	240	
1980	**Ronald Reagan**	Republican	43,899,248	51.0	489	52.6
	Jimmy Carter	Democratic	35,481,432	41.0	49	
	John B. Anderson	Independent	5,719,437	7.0	0	
	Ed Clark	Libertarian	920,859	1.0	0	
1984	**Ronald Reagan**	Republican	54,451,521	58.8	525	53.3
	Walter Mondale	Democratic	37,565,334	40.5	13	
1988	**George H. Bush**	Republican	47,917,341	54.0	426	48.6*
	Michael Dukakis	Democratic	41,013,030	46.0	112	

*Estimate

PRESIDENTIAL ADMINISTRATIONS

The Washington Administration (1789–1797)

Vice President	John Adams	1789–1797
Secretary of State	Thomas Jefferson	1789–1793
	Edmund Randolph	1794–1795
	Timothy Pickering	1795–1797
Secretary of Treasury	Alexander Hamilton	1789–1795
	Oliver Wolcott	1795–1797
Secretary of War	Henry Knox	1789–1794
	Timothy Pickering	1795–1796
	James McHenry	1796–1797
Attorney General	Edmund Randolph	1789–1793
	William Bradford	1794–1795
	Charles Lee	1795–1797
Postmaster General	Samuel Osgood	1789–1791
	Timothy Pickering	1791–1794
	Joseph Habersham	1795–1797

The John Adams Administration (1797–1801)

Vice President	Thomas Jefferson	1797–1801
Secretary of State	Timothy Pickering	1797–1800
	John Marshall	1800–1801
Secretary of Treasury	Oliver Wolcott	1797–1800
	Samuel Dexter	1800–1801
Secretary of War	James McHenry	1797–1800
	Samuel Dexter	1800–1801
Attorney General	Charles Lee	1797–1801
Postmaster General	Joseph Habersham	1797–1801
Secretary of Navy	Benjamin Stoddert	1798–1801

The Jefferson Administration (1801–1809)

Vice President	Aaron Burr	1801–1805
	George Clinton	1805–1809
Secretary of State	James Madison	1801–1809
Secretary of Treasury	Samuel Dexter	1801
	Albert Gallatin	1801–1809
Secretary of War	Henry Dearborn	1801–1809
Attorney General	Levi Lincoln	1801–1805
	Robert Smith	1805
	John Breckinridge	1805–1806
	Caesar Rodney	1807–1809
Postmaster General	Joseph Habersham	1801
	Gideon Granger	1801–1809
Secretary of Navy	Robert Smith	1801–1809

The Madison Administration (1809–1817)

Vice President	George Clinton	1809–1813
	Elbridge Gerry	1813–1817
Secretary of State	Robert Smith	1809–1811
	James Monroe	1811–1817
Secretary of Treasury	Albert Gallatin	1809–1813
	George Campbell	1814
	Alexander Dallas	1814–1816
	William Crawford	1816–1817
Secretary of War	William Eustis	1809–1812
	John Armstrong	1813–1814
	James Monroe	1814–1815
	William Crawford	1815–1817
Attorney General	Caesar Rodney	1809–1811
	William Pinkney	1811–1814
	Richard Rush	1814–1817
Postmaster General	Gideon Granger	1809–1814
	Return Meigs	1814–1817
Secretary of Navy	Paul Hamilton	1809–1813
	William Jones	1813–1814
	Benjamin Crowninshield	1814–1817

The Monroe Administration (1817–1825)

Vice President	Daniel Tompkins	1817–1825
Secretary of State	John Quincy Adams	1817–1825
Secretary of Treasury	William Crawford	1817–1825
Secretary of War	George Graham	1817
	John C. Calhoun	1817–1825
Attorney General	Richard Rush	1817
	William Wirt	1817–1825
Postmaster General	Return Meigs	1817–1823
	John McLean	1823–1825
Secretary of Navy	Benjamin Crowninshield	1817–1818
	Smith Thompson	1818–1823
	Samuel Southard	1823–1825

The John Quincy Adams Administration (1825–1829)

Vice President	John C. Calhoun	1825–1829
Secretary of State	Henry Clay	1825–1829
Secretary of Treasury	Richard Rush	1825–1829
Secretary of War	James Barbour	1825–1828
	Peter Porter	1828–1829

Attorney General	William Wirt	1825–1829
Postmaster General	John McLean	1825–1829
Secretary of Navy	Samuel Southard	1825–1829

The Jackson Administration (1829–1837)

Vice President	John C. Calhoun	1829–1833
	Martin Van Buren	1833–1837
Secretary of State	Martin Van Buren	1829–1831
	Edward Livingston	1831–1833
	Louis McLane	1833–1834
	John Forsyth	1834–1837
Secretary of Treasury	Samuel Ingham	1829–1831
	Louis McLane	1831–1833
	William Duane	1833
	Roger B. Taney	1833–1834
	Levi Woodbury	1834–1837
Secretary of War	John H. Eaton	1829–1831
	Lewis Cass	1831–1837
	Benjamin Butler	1837
Attorney General	John M. Berrien	1829–1831
	Roger B. Taney	1831–1833
	Benjamin Butler	1833–1837
Postmaster General	William Barry	1829–1835
	Amos Kendall	1835–1837
Secretary of Navy	John Branch	1829–1831
	Levi Woodbury	1831–1834
	Mahlon Dickerson	1834–1837

The Van Buren Administration (1837–1841)

Vice President	Richard M. Johnson	1837–1841
Secretary of State	John Forsyth	1837–1841
Secretary of Treasury	Levi Woodbury	1837–1841
Secretary of War	Joel Poinsett	1837–1841
Attorney General	Benjamin Butler	1837–1838
	Felix Grundy	1838–1840
	Henry D. Gilpin	1840–1841
Postmaster General	Amos Kendall	1837–1840
	John M. Niles	1840–1841
Secretary of Navy	Mahlon Dickerson	1837–1838
	James Paulding	1838–1841

The William Harrison Administration (1841)

Vice President	John Tyler	1841
Secretary of State	Daniel Webster	1841
Secretary of Treasury	Thomas Ewing	1841

Secretary of War	John Bell	1841
Attorney General	John J. Crittenden	1841
Postmaster General	Francis Granger	1841
Secretary of Navy	George Badger	1841

The Tyler Administration (1841–1845)

Vice President	None	
Secretary of State	Daniel Webster	1841–1843
	Hugh S. Legaré	1843
Secretary of State	Abel P. Upshur	1843–1844
	John C. Calhoun	1844–1845
Secretary of Treasury	Thomas Ewing	1841
	Walter Forward	1841–1843
	John C. Spencer	1843–1844
	George Bibb	1844–1845
Secretary of War	John Bell	1841
	John C. Spencer	1841–1843
	James M. Porter	1843–1844
	William Wilkins	1844–1845
Attorney General	John J. Crittenden	1841
	Hugh S. Legaré	1841–1843
	John Nelson	1843–1845
Postmaster General	Francis Granger	1841
	Charles Wickliffe	1841
Secretary of Navy	George Badger	1841
	Abel P. Upshur	1841
	David Henshaw	1843–1844
	Thomas Gilmer	1844
	John Y. Mason	1844–1845

The Polk Administration (1845–1849)

Vice President	George M. Dallas	1845–1849
Secretary of State	James Buchanan	1845–1849
Secretary of Treasury	Robert J. Walker	1845–1849
Secretary of War	William L. Marcy	1845–1849
Attorney General	John Y. Mason	1845–1846
	Nathan Clifford	1846–1848
	Isaac Toucey	1848–1849
Postmaster General	Cave Johnson	1845–1849
Secretary of Navy	George Bancroft	1845–1846
	John Y. Mason	1846–1849

The Taylor Administration (1849–1850)

Vice President	Millard Fillmore	1849–1850
Secretary of State	John M. Clayton	1849–1850

The Taylor Administration (1849–1850) (continued)

Secretary of Treasury	William Meredith	1849–1850
Secretary of War	George Crawford	1849–1850
Attorney General	Reverdy Johnson	1849–1850
Postmaster General	Jacob Collamer	1849–1850
Secretary of Navy	William Preston	1849–1850
Secretary of Interior	Thomas Ewing	1849–1850

The Fillmore Administration (1850–1853)

Vice President	None	
Secretary of State	Daniel Webster	1850–1852
	Edward Everett	1852–1853
Secretary of Treasury	Thomas Corwin	1850–1853
Secretary of War	Charles Conrad	1850–1853
Attorney General	John J. Crittenden	1850–1853
Postmaster General	Nathan Hall	1850–1852
	Sam D. Hubbard	1852–1853
Secretary of Navy	William A. Graham	1850–1852
	John P. Kennedy	1852–1853
Secretary of Interior	Thomas McKennan	1850
	Alexander Stuart	1850–1853

The Pierce Administration (1853–1857)

Vice President	William R. King	1853–1857
Secretary of State	William L. Marcy	1853–1857
Secretary of Treasury	James Guthrie	1853–1857
Secretary of War	Jefferson Davis	1853–1857
Attorney General	Caleb Cushing	1853–1857
Postmaster General	James Campbell	1853–1857
Secretary of Navy	James C. Dobbin	1853–1857
Secretary of Interior	Robert McClelland	1853–1857

The Buchanan Administration (1857–1861)

Vice President	John C. Breckinridge	1857–1861
Secretary of State	Lewis Cass	1857–1860
	Jeremiah S. Black	1860–1861
Secretary of Treasury	Howell Cobb	1857–1860
	Philip Thomas	1860–1861
	John A. Dix	1861
Secretary of War	John B. Floyd	1857–1861
	Joseph Holt	1861
Attorney General	Jeremiah S. Black	1857–1860
	Edwin M. Stanton	1860–1861
Postmaster General	Aaron V. Brown	1857–1859
	Joseph Holt	1859–1861
	Horatio King	1861
Secretary of Navy	Isaac Toucey	1857–1861
Secretary of Interior	Jacob Thompson	1857–1861

The Lincoln Administration (1861–1865)

Vice President	Hannibal Hamlin	1861–1865
	Andrew Johnson	1865
Secretary of State	William H. Seward	1861–1865
Secretary of Treasury	Samuel P. Chase	1861–1864
	William P. Fessenden	1864–1865
	Hugh McCulloch	1865
Secretary of War	Simon Cameron	1861–1862
	Edwin M. Stanton	1862–1865
Attorney General	Edward Bates	1861–1864
	James Speed	1864–1865
Postmaster General	Horatio King	1861
	Montgomery Blair	1861–1864
	William Dennison	1864–1865
Secretary of Navy	Gideon Welles	1861–1865
Secretary of Interior	Caleb B. Smith	1861–1863
	John P. Usher	1863–1865

The Andrew Johnson Administration (1865–1869)

Vice President	None	
Secretary of State	William H. Seward	1865–1869
Secretary of Treasury	Hugh McCulloch	1865–1869
Secretary of War	Edwin M. Stanton	1865–1867
	Ulysses S. Grant	1867–1868
	Lorenzo Thomas	1868
	John M. Schofield	1868–1869

Attorney General	James Speed	1865–1866
	Henry Stanbery	1866–1868
	William M. Evarts	1868–1869
Postmaster General	William Dennison	1865–1866
	Alexander Randall	1866–1869
Secretary of Navy	Gideon Welles	1865–1869
Secretary of Interior	John P. Usher	1865
	James Harlan	1865–1866
	Orville H. Browning	1866–1869

The Grant Administration (1869–1877)

Vice President	Schuyler Colfax	1869–1873
	Henry Wilson	1873–1877
Secretary of State	Elihu B. Washburne	1869
	Hamilton Fish	1869–1877
Secretary of Treasury	George S. Boutwell	1869–1873
	William Richardson	1873–1874
	Benjamin Bristow	1874–1876
	Lot M. Morrill	1876–1877
Secretary of War	John A. Rawlins	1869
	William T. Sherman	1869
	William W. Belknap	1869–1876
	Alphonso Taft	1876
	James D. Cameron	1876–1877
Attorney General	Ebenezer Hoar	1869–1870
	Amos T. Ackerman	1870–1871
	G. H. Williams	1871–1875
	Edwards Pierrepont	1875–1876
	Alphonso Taft	1876–1877
Postmaster General	John A. J. Creswell	1869–1874
	James W. Marshall	1874
	Marshall Jewell	1874–1876
	James N. Tyner	1876–1877
Secretary of Navy	Adolph E. Borie	1869
	George M. Robeson	1869–1877
Secretary of Interior	Jacob D. Cox	1869–1870
	Columbus Delano	1870–1875
	Zachariah Chandler	1875–1877

The Hayes Administration (1877–1881)

| Vice President | William A. Wheeler | 1877–1881 |
| Secretary of State | William M. Evarts | 1877–1881 |

Secretary of Treasury	John Sherman	1877–1881
Secretary of War	George W. McCrary	1877–1879
	Alex Ramsey	1879–1881
Attorney General	Charles Devens	1877–1881
Postmaster General	David M. Key	1877–1880
	Horace Maynard	1880–1881
Secretary of Navy	Richard W. Thompson	1877–1880
	Nathan Goff, Jr.	1881
Secretary of Interior	Carl Schurz	1877–1881

The Garfield Administration (1881)

Vice President	Chester A. Arthur	1881
Secretary of State	James G. Blaine	1881
Secretary of Treasury	William Windom	1881
Secretary of War	Robert T. Lincoln	1881
Attorney General	Wayne MacVeagh	1881
Postmaster General	Thomas L. James	1881
Secretary of Navy	William H. Hunt	1881
Secretary of Interior	Samuel J. Kirkwood	1881

The Arthur Administration (1881–1885)

Vice President	None	
Secretary of State	F. T. Frelinghuysen	1881–1885
Secretary of Treasury	Charles J. Folger	1881–1884
	Walter Q. Gresham	1884
	Hugh McCulloch	1884–1885
Secretary of War	Robert T. Lincoln	1881–1885
Attorney General	Benjamin H. Brewster	1881–1885
Postmaster General	Timothy O. Howe	1881–1883
	Walter Q. Gresham	1883–1884
	Frank Hatton	1884–1885
Secretary of Navy	William H. Hunt	1881–1882
	William E. Chandler	1882–1885
Secretary of Interior	Samuel J. Kirkwood	1881–1882
	Henry M. Teller	1882–1885

The Cleveland Administration (1885–1889)

Vice President	Thomas A. Hendricks	1885–1889
Secretary of State	Thomas F. Bayard	1885–1889
Secretary of Treasury	Daniel Manning	1885–1887
	Charles S. Fairchild	1887–1889
Secretary of War	William C. Endicott	1885–1889
Attorney General	Augustus H. Garland	1885–1889
Postmaster General	William F. Vilas	1885–1888
	Don M. Dickinson	1888–1889
Secretary of Navy	William C. Whitney	1885–1889
Secretary of Interior	Lucius Q. C. Lamar	1885–1888
	William F. Vilas	1888–1889
Secretary of Agriculture	Norman J. Colman	1889

The Benjamin Harrison Administration (1889–1893)

Vice President	Levi P. Morton	1889–1893
Secretary of State	James G. Blaine	1889–1892
	John W. Foster	1892–1893
Secretary of Treasury	William Windom	1889–1891
	Charles Foster	1891–1893
Secretary of War	Redfield Proctor	1889–1891
	Stephen B. Elkins	1891–1893
Attorney General	William H. H. Miller	1889–1891
Postmaster General	John Wanamaker	1889–1893
Secretary of Navy	Benjamin F. Tracy	1889–1893
Secretary of Interior	John W. Noble	1889–1893
Secretary of Agriculture	Jeremiah M. Rusk	1889–1893

The Cleveland Administration (1893–1897)

Vice President	Adlai E. Stevenson	1893–1897
Secretary of State	Walter Q. Gresham	1893–1895
	Richard Olney	1895–1897
Secretary of Treasury	John G. Carlisle	1893–1897
Secretary of War	Daniel S. Lamont	1893–1897
Attorney General	Richard Olney	1893–1895
	James Harmon	1895–1897
Postmaster General	Wilson S. Bissell	1893–1895
	William L. Wilson	1895–1897
Secretary of Navy	Hilary A. Herbert	1893–1897
Secretary of Interior	Hoke Smith	1893–1896
	David R. Francis	1896–1897
Secretary of Agriculture	Julius S. Morton	1893–1897

The McKinley Administration (1897–1901)

Vice President	Garret A. Hobart	1897–1901
Secretary of State	Theodore Roosevelt	1901
	John Sherman	1897–1898
	William R. Day	1898
	John Hay	1898–1901
Secretary of Treasury	Lyman J. Gage	1897–1901
Secretary of War	Russell A. Alger	1897–1899
	Elihu Root	1899–1901
Attorney General	Joseph McKenna	1897–1898
	John W. Griggs	1898–1901
	Philander C. Knox	1901
Postmaster General	James A. Gary	1897–1898
	Charles E. Smith	1898–1901
Secretary of Navy	John D. Long	1897–1901
Secretary of Interior	Cornelius N. Bliss	1897–1899
	Ethan A. Hitchcock	1899–1901
Secretary of Agriculture	James Wilson	1897–1901

The Theodore Roosevelt Administration (1901–1909)

Vice President	Charles Fairbanks	1905–1909
Secretary of State	John Hay	1901–1905
	Elihu Root	1905–1909
	Robert Bacon	1909
Secretary of Treasury	Lyman J. Gage	1901–1902
	Leslie M. Shaw	1902–1907
	George B. Cortelyou	1907–1909
Secretary of War	Elihu Root	1901–1904
	William H. Taft	1904–1908
	Luke E. Wright	1908–1909
Attorney General	Philander C. Knox	1901–1904
	William H. Moody	1904–1906
	Charles J. Bonaparte	1906–1909
Postmaster General	Charles E. Smith	1901–1902
	Henry C. Payne	1902–1904
	Robert J. Wynne	1904–1905

	George B. Cortelyou	1905–1907
	George von L. Meyer	1907–1909
Secretary of Navy	John D. Long	1901–1902
	William H. Moody	1902–1904
	Paul Morton	1904–1905
	Charles J. Bonaparte	1905–1906
	Victor H. Metcalf	1906–1908
	Truman H. Newberry	1908–1909
Secretary of Interior	Ethan A. Hitchcock	1901–1907
	James R. Garfield	1907–1909
Secretary of Agriculture	James Wilson	1901–1909
Secretary of Labor and Commerce	George B. Cortelyou	1903–1904
	Victor H. Metcalf	1904–1906
	Oscar S. Straus	1906–1909
	Charles Nagel	1909

The Taft Administration (1909–1913)

Vice President	James S. Sherman	1909–1913
Secretary of State	Philander C. Knox	1909–1913
Secretary of Treasury	Franklin MacVeagh	1909–1913
Secretary of War	Jacob M. Dickinson	1909–1911
	Henry L. Stimson	1911–1913
Attorney General	George W. Wickersham	1909–1913
Postmaster General	Frank H. Hitchcock	1909–1913
Secretary of Navy	George von L. Meyer	1909–1913
Secretary of Interior	Richard A. Ballinger	1909–1911
	Walter L. Fisher	1911–1913
Secretary of Agriculture	James Wilson	1909–1913
Secretary of Labor and Commerce	Charles Nagel	1909–1913

The Wilson Administration (1913–1921)

Vice President	Thomas R. Marshall	1913–1921
Secretary of State	William J. Bryan	1913–1915
	Robert Lansing	1915–1920
	Bainbridge Colby	1920–1921
Secretary of Treasury	William G. McAdoo	1913–1918
	Carter Glass	1918–1920
	David F. Houston	1920–1921
Secretary of War	Lindley M. Garrison	1913–1916
	Newton D. Baker	1916–1921
Attorney General	James C. McReyolds	1913–1914
	Thomas W. Gregory	1914–1919
	A. Mitchell Palmer	1919–1921
Postmaster General	Albert S. Burleson	1913–1921
Secretary of Navy	Josephus Daniels	1913–1921
Secretary of Interior	Franklin K. Lane	1913–1920
	John B. Payne	1920–1921
Secretary of Agriculture	David F. Houston	1913–1920
	Edwin T. Meredith	1920–1921
Secretary of Commerce	William C. Redfield	1913–1919
	Joshua W. Alexander	1919–1921
Secretary of Labor	William B. Wilson	1913–1921

The Harding Administration (1921–1923)

Vice President	Calvin Coolidge	1921–1923
Secretary of State	Charles E. Hughes	1921–1923
Secretary of Treasury	Andrew Mellon	1921–1923
Secretary of War	John W. Weeks	1921–1923
Attorney General	Harry M. Daugherty	1921–1923
Postmaster General	Will H. Hays	1921–1922
	Hubert Work	1922–1923
	Harry S. New	1923
Secretary of Navy	Edwin Denby	1921–1923
Secretary of Interior	Albert B. Fall	1921–1923
	Hubert Work	1923
Secretary of Agriculture	Henry C. Wallace	1921–1923
Secretary of Commerce	Herbert C. Hoover	1921–1923
Secretary of Labor	James J. Davis	1921–1923

The Coolidge Administration (1923–1929)

Vice President	Charles G. Dawes	1925–1929
Secretary of State	Charles E. Hughes	1923–1925
	Frank B. Kellogg	1925–1929
Secretary of Treasury	Andrew Mellon	1923–1929
Secretary of War	John W. Weeks	1923–1925
	Dwight F. Davis	1925–1929
Attorney General	Henry M. Daugherty	1923–1924
	Harlan F. Stone	1924–1925
	John G. Sargent	1925–1929
Postmaster General	Harry S. New	1923–1929
Secretary of Navy	Edwin Derby	1923–1924
	Curtis D. Wilbur	1924–1929
Secretary of Interior	Hubert Work	1923–1928
	Roy O. West	1928–1929
Secretary of Agriculture	Henry C. Wallace	1923–1924
	Howard M. Gore	1924–1925
	William M. Jardine	1925–1929
Secretary of Commerce	Herbert C. Hoover	1923–1928
	William F. Whiting	1928–1929
Secretary of Labor	James J. Davis	1923–1929

The Hoover Administration (1929–1933)

Vice President	Charles Curtis	1929–1933
Secretary of State	Henry L. Stimson	1929–1933
Secretary of Treasury	Andrew Mellon	1929–1932
	Ogden L. Mills	1932–1933
Secretary of War	James W. Good	1929
	Patrick J. Hurley	1929–1933
Attorney General	William D. Mitchell	1929–1933
Postmaster General	Walter F. Brown	1929–1933
Secretary of Navy	Charles F. Adams	1929–1933
Secretary of Interior	Ray L. Wilbur	1929–1933
Secretary of Agriculture	Arthur M. Hyde	1929–1933
Secretary of Commerce	Robert P. Lamont	1929–1932
	Roy D. Chapin	1932–1933
Secretary of Labor	James J. Davis	1929–1930
	William N. Doak	1930–1933

The Franklin D. Roosevelt Administration (1933–1945)

Vice President	John Nance Garner	1933–1941
	Henry A. Wallace	1941–1945
	Harry S. Truman	1945
Secretary of State	Cordell Hull	1933–1944
	Edward R. Stettinius, Jr.	1944–1945
Secretary of Treasury	William H. Woodin	1933–1934
	Henry Morgenthau, Jr.	1934–1945
Secretary of War	George H. Dern	1933–1936
	Henry A. Woodring	1936–1940
	Henry L. Stimson	1940–1945
Attorney General	Homer S. Cummings	1933–1939
	Frank Murphy	1939–1940
	Robert H. Jackson	1940–1941
Attorney General	Francis Biddle	1941–1945
Postmaster General	James A. Farley	1933–1940
	Frank C. Walker	1940–1945
Secretary of Navy	Claude A. Swanson	1933–1940
	Charles Edison	1940
	Frank Knox	1940–1944
	James V. Forrestal	1944–1945
Secretary of Interior	Harold L. Ickes	1933–1945
Secretary of Agriculture	Henry A. Wallace	1933–1940
	Claude R. Wickard	1940–1945
Secretary of Commerce	Daniel C. Roper	1933–1939
	Harry L. Hopkins	1939–1940
	Jesse Jones	1940–1945
	Henry A. Wallace	1945
Secretary of Labor	Frances Perkins	1933–1945

The Truman Administration (1945–1953)

Vice President	Alben W. Barkley	1949–1953
Secretary of State	Edward R. Stettinius, Jr.	1945
	James F. Byrnes	1945–1947
	George C. Marshall	1947–1949
	Dean G. Acheson	1949–1953
Secretary of Treasury	Fred M. Vinson	1945–1946
	John W. Snyder	1946–1953
Secretary of War	Robert P. Patterson	1945–1947
	Kenneth C. Royall	1947

Attorney General	Tom C. Clark	1945–1949
	J. Howard McGrath	1949–1952
	James P. McGranery	1952–1953
Postmaster General	Frank C. Walker	1945
	Robert E. Hannegan	1945–1947
	Jesse M. Donaldson	1947–1953
Secretary of Navy	James V. Forrestal	1945–1947
Secretary of Interior	Harold L. Ickes	1945–1946
	Julius A. Krug	1946–1949
	Oscar L. Chapman	1949–1953
Secretary of Agriculture	Clinton P. Anderson	1945–1948
	Charles F. Brannan	1948–1953
Secretary of Commerce	Henry A. Wallace	1945–1946
	W. Averell Harriman	1946–1948
	Charles W. Sawyer	1948–1953
Secretary of Labor	Lewis B. Schwellenbach	1945–1948
	Maurice J. Tobin	1948–1953
Secretary of Defense	James V. Forrestal	1947–1949
	Louis A. Johnson	1949–1950
	George C. Marshall	1950–1951
	Robert A. Lovett	1951–1953

The Eisenhower Administration (1953–1961)

Vice President	Richard M. Nixon	1953–1961
Secretary of State	John Foster Dulles	1953–1959
	Christian A. Herter	1959–1961
Secretary of Treasury	George M. Humphrey	1953–1957
	Robert B. Anderson	1957–1961
Attorney General	Herbert Brownell, Jr.	1953–1958
	William P. Rogers	1958–1961
Postmaster General	Arthur E. Summerfield	1953–1961
Secretary of Interior	Douglas McKay	1953–1956
	Fred A. Seaton	1956–1961
Secretary of Agriculture	Ezra T. Benson	1953–1961
Secretary of Commerce	Sinclair Weeks	1953–1958
	Lewis L. Strauss	1958–1959
	Frederick H. Mueller	1959–1961

Secretary of Labor	Martin P. Durkin	1953
	James P. Mitchell	1953–1961
Secretary of Defense	Charles E. Wilson	1953–1957
	Neil H. McElroy	1957–1959
	Thomas S. Gates Jr.	1959–1961
Secretary of Health, Education, and Welfare	Oveta Culp Hobby	1953–1955
	Marion B. Folsom	1955–1958
	Arthur S. Flemming	1958–1961

The Kennedy Administration (1961–1963)

Vice President	Lyndon B. Johnson	1961–1963
Secretary of State	Dean Rusk	1961–1963
Secretary of Treasury	C. Douglas Dillon	1961–1963
Attorney General	Robert F. Kennedy	1961–1963
Postmaster General	J. Edward Day	1961–1963
	John A. Gronouski	1963
Secretary of Interior	Stewart L. Udall	1961–1963
Secretary of Agriculture	Orville L. Freeman	1961–1963
Secretary of Commerce	Luther H. Hodges	1961–1963
Secretary of Labor	Arthur J. Goldberg	1961–1962
	W. Willard Wirtz	1962–1963
Secretary of Defense	Robert S. McNamara	1961–1963
Secretary of Health, Education, and Welfare	Abraham A. Ribicoff	1961–1962
	Anthony J. Celebrezze	1962–1963

The Lyndon Johnson Administration (1963–1969)

Vice President	Hubert H. Humphrey	1965–1969
Secretary of State	Dean Rusk	1963–1969
Secretary of Treasury	C. Douglas Dillon	1963–1965
	Henry H. Fowler	1965–1969
Attorney General	Robert F. Kennedy	1963–1964
	Nicholas Katzenbach	1965–1966
	Ramsey Clark	1967–1969
Postmaster General	John A. Gronouski	1963–1965
	Lawrence F. O'Brien	1965–1968
	Marvin Watson	1968–1969

The Lyndon Johnson Administration (1963–1969)

Secretary of Interior	Stewart L. Udall	1963–1969
Secretary of Agriculture	Orville L. Freeman	1963–1969
Secretary of Commerce	Luther H. Hodges	1963–1064
	John T. Connor	1964–1967
	Alexander B. Trowbridge	1967–1968
	Cyrus R. Smith	1968–1969
Secretary of Labor	W. Willard Wirtz	1963–1969
Secretary of Defense	Robert F. McNamara	1963–1968
	Clark Clifford	1968–1969
Secretary of Health, Education, and Welfare	Anthony J. Celebrezze	1963–1965
	John W. Gardner	1965–1968
	Wilbur J. Cohen	1968–1969
Secretary of Housing and Urban Development	Robert C. Weaver	1966–1969
	Robert C. Wood	1969
Secretary of Transportation	Alan S. Boyd	1967–1969

The Nixon Administration (1969–1974)

Vice President	Spiro T. Agnew	1969–1973
	Gerald R. Ford	1973–1974
Secretary of State	William P. Rogers	1969–1973
	Henry A. Kissinger	1973–1974
Secretary of Treasury	David M. Kennedy	1969–1970
	John B. Connally	1971–1972
	George P. Shultz	1972–1974
	William E. Simon	1974
Attorney General	John N. Mitchell	1969–1972
	Richard G. Kleindienst	1972–1973
	Elliot L. Richardson	1973
	William B. Saxbe	1973–1974
Postmaster General	Winton M. Blount	1969–1971
Secretary of Interior	Walter J. Hickel	1969–1970
	Rogers Morton	1971–1974
Secretary of Agriculture	Clifford M. Hardin	1969–1971
	Earl L. Butz	1971–1974
Secretary of Commerce	Maurice H. Stans	1969–1972
	Peter G. Peterson	1972–1973
	Frederick B. Dent	1973–1974

Secretary of Labor	George P. Shultz	1969–1970
	James D. Hodgson	1970–1973
	Peter J. Brennan	1973–1974
Secretary of Defense	Melvin R. Laird	1969–1973
	Elliot L. Richardson	1973
	James R. Schlesinger	1973–1974
Secretary of Health, Education, and Welfare	Robert H. Finch	1969–1970
	Elliot L. Richardson	1970–1973
	Caspar W. Weinberger	1973–1974
Secretary of Housing and Urban Development	George Romney	1969–1973
	James T. Lynn	1973–1974
Secretary of Transportation	John A. Volpe	1969–1973
	Claude S. Brinegar	1973–1974

The Ford Administration (1974–1977)

Vice President	Nelson A. Rockefeller	1974–1977
Secretary of State	Henry A. Kissinger	1974–1977
Secretary of Treasury	William E. Simon	1974–1977
Attorney General	William Saxbe	1974–1975
	Edward Levi	1975–1977
Secretary of Interior	Rogers Morton	1974–1975
	Stanley K. Hathaway	1975
	Thomas Kleppe	1975–1977
Secretary of Agriculture	Earl L. Butz	194–1976
	John A. Knebel	1976–1977
Secretary of Commerce	Frederick B. Dent	1974–1975
	Rogers Morton	1975–1976
	Elliot L. Richardson	1976–1977
Secretary of Labor	Peter J. Brennan	1974–1975
	John T. Dunlop	1975–1976
	W. J. Usery	1976–1977
Secretary of Defense	James R. Schlesinger	1974–1975
	Donald Rumsfeld	1975–1977
Secretary of Health, Education, and Welfare	Caspar Weinberger	1974–1975
	Forrest D. Mathews	1975–1977
Secretary of Housing and Urban Development	James T. Lynn	1974–1975
	Carla A. Hills	1975–1977
Secretary of Transportation	Claude Brinegar	1974–1975
	William T. Coleman	1975–1977

The Carter Administration (1977–1981)

Vice President	Walter F. Mondale	1977–1981
Secretary of State	Cyrus R. Vance	1977–1980
	Edmund Muskie	1980–1981
Secretary of Treasury	W. Michael Blumenthal	1977–1979
	G. William Miller	1979–1981
Attorney General	Griffin Bell	1977–1979
	Benjamin R. Civiletti	1979–1981
Secretary of Interior	Cecil D. Andrus	1977–1981
Secretary of Agriculture	Robert Bergland	1977–1981
Secretary of Commerce	Juanita M. Kreps	1977–1979
	Philip M. Klutznick	1979–1981
Secretary of Labor	F. Ray Marshall	1977–1981
Secretary of Defense	Harold Brown	1977–1981
Secretary of Health, Education, and Welfare	Joseph A. Califano	1977–1979
	Patricia R. Harris	1979
Secretary of Health and Human Services	Patricia R. Harris	1979–1981
Secretary of Education	Shirley M. Hufstedler	1979–1981
Secretary of Housing and Urban Development	Patricia R. Harris	1977–1979
	Moon Landrieu	1979–1981
Secretary of Transportation	Brock Adams	1977–1979
	Neil E. Goldschmidt	1979–1981
Secretary of Energy	James R. Schlesinger	1977–1979
	Charles W. Duncan	1979–1981

The Reagan Administration (1981–1989)

Vice President	George Bush	1981–1989
Secretary of State	Alexander M. Haig	1981–1982
	George P. Shultz	1982–1989
Secretary of Treasury	Donald Regan	1981–1985
	James A. Baker, III	1985–1988
	Nicholas Brady	1988–1989
Attorney General	William F. Smith	1981–1985
	Edwin A. Meese, III	1985–1988

Attorney General	Richard Thornburgh	1988–1989
Secretary of Interior	James Watt	1981–1983
	William P. Clark, Jr.	1983–1985
	Donald P. Hodel	1985–1989
Secretary of Agriculture	John Block	1981–1986
	Richard E. Lyng	1986–1989
Secretary of Commerce	Malcolm Baldridge	1981–1987
	C. William Verity, Jr.	1987–1989
Secretary of Labor	Raymond Donovan	1981–1985
	William E. Brock	1985–1987
	Ann D. McLaughlin	1987–1989
Secretary of Defense	Caspar Weinberger	1981–1987
	Frank Carlucci	1987–1989
Secretary of Health and Human Services	Richard Schweiker	1981–1983
	Margaret Heckler	1983–1985
	Otis R. Bowen	1985–1989
Secretary of Education	Terrel H. Bell	1981–1985
	William J. Bennett	1985–1988
	Laura F. Cavazos	1988–1989
Secretary of Housing and Urban Development	Samuel Pierce	1981–1989
Secretary of Transportation	Drew Lewis	1981–1983
	Elizabeth Dole	1983–1987
	James H. Burnley	1987–1989
Secretary of Energy	James Edwards	1981–1982
	Donald P. Hodel	1982–1985
	John S. Herrington	1985–

The Bush Administration (1989–   )

Vice President	J. Danforth Quayle	1989–
Secretary of State	James A. Baker III	1989–
Secretary of Treasury	Nicholas Brady	1989–
Attorney General	Richard Thornburgh	1989–
Secretary of Interior	Manuel Lujan	1989–
Secretary of Agriculture	Clayton Yeutter	1989–
Secretary of Commerce	Robert Mosbacher	1989–
Secretary of Labor	Elizabeth Dole	1989–
Secretary of Defense	Richard Cheney	1989–

The Bush Administration (1989–) (continued)		
Secretary of Health and Human Services	Louis W. Sullivan	1989–
Secretary of Housing and Urban Development	Jack Kemp	1989–

Secretary of Transportation	Samuel K. Skinner	1989–
Secretary of Energy	James Watkins	1989–
Secretary of Veterans Affairs	Edwin Derwinski	1989–

JUSTICES OF THE SUPREME COURT

	Term of Service	Years of Service	Life Span		Term of Service	Years of Service	Life Span
John Jay	1789–1795	5	1745–1829	John M. Harlan	1877–1911	34	1833–1911
John Rutledge	1789–1791	1	1739–1800	William B. Woods	1880–1887	7	1824–1887
William Cushing	1789–1810	20	1732–1810	Stanley Matthews	1881–1889	7	1824–1889
James Wilson	1789–1798	8	1742–1798	Horace Gray	1882–1902	20	1828–1902
John Blair	1789–1796	6	1732–1800	Samuel Blatchford	1882–1893	11	1820–1893
Robert H. Harrison	1789–1790	—	1745–1790	Lucius Q. C. Lamar	1888–1893	5	1825–1893
James Iredell	1790–1799	9	1751–1799	*Melville W. Fuller*	1888–1910	21	1833–1910
Thomas Johnson	1791–1793	1	1732–1819	David J. Brewer	1890–1910	20	1837–1910
William Paterson	1793–1806	13	1745–1806	Henry B. Brown	1890–1906	16	1836–1913
*John Rutledge**	1795	—	1739–1800	George Shiras, Jr.	1892–1903	10	1832–1924
Samuel Chase	1796–1811	15	1741–1811	Howell E. Jackson	1893–1895	2	1832–1895
Oliver Ellsworth	1796–1800	4	1745–1807	Edward D. White	1894–1910	16	1845–1921
Bushrod Washington	1798–1829	31	1762–1829	Rufus W. Peckham	1895–1909	14	1838–1909
Alfred Moore	1799–1804	4	1755–1810	Joseph McKenna	1898–1925	26	1843–1926
John Marshall	1801–1835	34	1755–1835	Oliver W. Holmes	1902–1932	30	1841–1935
William Johnson	1804–1834	30	1771–1834	William R. Day	1903–1922	19	1849–1923
H. Brockholst Livingston	1806–1823	16	1757–1823	William H. Moody	1906–1910	3	1853–1917
Thomas Todd	1807–1826	18	1765–1826	Horace H. Lurton	1910–1914	4	1844–1914
Joseph Story	1811–1845	33	1779–1845	Charles E. Hughes	1910–1916	5	1862–1948
Gabriel Duval	1811–1835	24	1752–1844	Willis Van Devanter	1911–1937	26	1859–1941
Smith Thompson	1823–1843	20	1768–1843	Joseph R. Lamar	1911–1916	5	1857–1916
Robert Trimble	1826–1828	2	1777–1828	*Edward D. White*	1910–1921	11	1845–1921
John McLean	1829–1861	32	1785–1861	Mahlon Pitney	1912–1922	10	1858–1924
Henry Baldwin	1830–1844	14	1780–1844	James C. McReynolds	1914–1941	26	1862–1946
James M. Wayne	1835–1867	32	1790–1867	Louis D. Brandeis	1916–1939	22	1856–1941
Roger B. Taney	1836–1864	28	1777–1864	John H. Clarke	1916–1922	6	1857–1945
Philip P. Barbour	1836–1841	4	1783–1841	William H. Taft	1921–1930	8	1857–1930
John Catron	1837–1865	28	1786–1865	George Sutherland	1922–1938	15	1862–1942
John McKinley	1837–1852	15	1780–1852	Pierce Butler	1922–1939	16	1866–1939
Peter V. Daniel	1841–1860	19	1784–1860	Edward T. Sanford	1923–1930	7	1865–1930
Samuel Nelson	1845–1872	27	1792–1873	Harlan F. Stone	1925–1941	16	1872–1946
Levi Woodbury	1845–1851	5	1789–1851	*Charles E. Hughes*	1930–1941	11	1862–1948
Robert C. Grier	1846–1870	23	1794–1870	Owen J. Roberts	1930–1945	15	1875–1955
Benjamin R. Curtis	1851–1857	6	1809–1874	Benjamin N. Cardozo	1932–1938	6	1870–1938
John A. Campbell	1853–1861	8	1811–1889	Hugo L. Black	1937–1971	34	1886–1971
Nathan Clifford	1858–1881	23	1803–1881	Stanley F. Reed	1938–1957	19	1884–1980
Noah H. Swayne	1862–1881	18	1804–1884	Felix Frankfurter	1939–1962	23	1882–1965
Samuel F. Miller	1862–1890	28	1816–1890	William O. Douglas	1939–1975	36	1898–1980
David Davis	1862–1877	14	1815–1886	Frank Murphy	1940–1949	9	1890–1949
Stephen J. Field	1863–1897	34	1816–1899	*Harlan F. Stone*	1941–1946	5	1872–1946
Salmon P. Chase	1864–1873	8	1808–1873	James F. Byrnes	1941–1942	1	1879–1972
William Strong	1870–1880	10	1808–1895	Robert H. Jackson	1941–1954	13	1892–1954
Joseph P. Bradley	1870–1892	22	1813–1892	Wiley B. Rutledge	1943–1949	6	1894–1949
Ward Hunt	1873–1882	9	1810–1886	Harold H. Burton	1945–1958	13	1888–1964
Morrison R. Waite	1874–1888	14	1816–1888	*Fred M. Vinson*	1946–1953	7	1890–1953
				Tom C. Clark	1949–1967	18	1899–1977

	Term of Service	Years of Service	Life Span
Sherman Minton	1949–1956	7	1890–1965
Earl Warren	1953–1969	16	1891–1974
John Marshall Harlan	1955–1971	16	1899–1971
William J. Brennan, Jr.	1956–	—	1906–
Charles E. Whittaker	1957–1962	5	1901–1973
Potter Stewart	1958–1981	23	1915–
Byron R. White	1962–	—	1917–
Arthur J. Goldberg	1962–1965	3	1908–

	Term of Service	Years of Service	Life Span
Abe Fortas	1965–1969	4	1910–
Thurgood Marshall	1967–	—	1908–
Warren C. Burger	1969–	—	1907–
Harry A. Blackmun	1970–	—	1908–
Lewis F. Powell, Jr.	1971–	—	1907–
William H. Rehnquist	1971–	—	1924–
John P. Stevens, III	1975–	—	1920–
Sandra Day O'Connor	1981–	—	1930–
William H. Rehnquist	1986–	—	1924–
Antonin Scalia	1986–	—	1936–
Anthony M. Kennedy	1987–	—	1936–

*Appointed and served one term, but not confirmed by the Senate.

Note: Chief justices are in italics.

A SOCIAL PROFILE OF THE AMERICAN REPUBLIC

POPULATION

Year	Population	Percent Increase	Population Per Square Mile	Percent Urban/ Rural	Percent Male/ Female	Percent White/ Nonwhite	Persons Per Household	Median Age
1790	3,929,214		4.5	5.1/94.9	NA/NA	80.7/19.3	5.79	NA
1800	5,308,483	35.1	6.1	6.1/93.9	NA/NA	81.1/18.9	NA	NA
1810	7,239,881	36.4	4.3	7.3/92.7	NA/NA	81.0/19.0	NA	NA
1820	9,638,453	33.1	5.5	7.2/92.8	50.8/49.2	81.6/18.4	NA	16.7
1830	12,866,020	33.5	7.4	8.8/91.2	50.8/18.1	81.9/18.1	NA	17.2
1840	17,069,453	32.7	9.8	10.8/89.2	50.9/49.1	83.2/16.8	NA	17.8
1850	23,191,876	35.9	7.9	15.3/84.7	51.0/49.0	84.3/15.7	5.55	18.9
1860	31,443,321	35.6	10.6	19.8/80.2	51.2/48.8	85.6/14.4	5.28	19.4
1870	39,818,449	26.6	13.4	25.7/74.3	50.6/49.4	86.2/13.8	5.09	20.2
1880	50,155,783	26.0	16.9	28.2/71.8	50.9/49.1	86.5/13.5	5.04	20.9
1890	62,947,714	25.5	21.2	35.1/64.9	51.2/48.8	87.5/12.5	4.93	22.0
1900	75,994,575	20.7	25.6	39.6/60.4	51.1/48.9	87.9/12.1	4.76	22.9
1910	91,972,266	21.0	31.0	45.6/54.4	51.5/48.5	88.9/11.1	4.54	24.1
1920	105,710,620	14.9	35.6	51.2/48.8	51.0/49.0	89.7/10.3	4.34	25.3
1930	122,775,046	16.1	41.2	56.1/43.9	50.6/49.4	89.8/10.2	4.11	26.4
1940	131,669,275	7.2	44.2	56.5/43.5	50.2/49.8	89.8/10.2	3.67	29.0
1950	150,697,361	14.5	50.7	64.0/36.0	49.7/50.3	89.5/10.5	3.37	30.2
1960	179,323,175	18.5	50.6	69.9/30.1	49.3/50.7	88.6/11.4	3.33	29.5
1970	203,302,031	13.4	57.4	73.5/26.5	48.7/51.3	87.6/12.4	3.14	28.0
1980	226,545,805	11.4	64.0	73.7/26.3	48.6/51.4	86.0/14.0	2.76	30.0
1990*	250,410,000	9.9	70.8	NA	48.8/51.2	84.1/15.9	NA	32.1**
2000*	268,266,000	7.1	75.8	NA	48.9/51.1	82.6/17.4	NA	NA

NA = Not available.
* Projections.
**1987 figure.

VITAL STATISTICS (rates per thousand)

Year	Births	Year	Births	Deaths*	Marriage*	Divorces*
1800	55.0	1900	32.3	17.2	NA	NA
1810	54.3	1910	30.1	14.7	NA	NA
1820	55.2	1920	27.7	13.0	12.0	1.6
1830	51.4	1930	21.3	11.3	9.2	1.6
1840	51.8	1940	19.4	10.8	12.1	2.0
1850	43.3	1950	24.1	9.6	11.1	2.6
1860	44.3	1960	23.7	9.5	8.5	2.2
1870	38.3	1970	18.4	9.5	10.6	3.5
1880	39.8	1980	15.9	8.8	10.6	5.2
1890	31.5	1987	15.7	8.7	9.9	4.8

NA = Not available.
*Data not available before 1900.

LIFE EXPECTANCY (in years)

Year	Total Population	White Females	Nonwhite Females	White Males	Nonwhite Males
1900	47.3	48.7	33.5	46.6	32.5
1910	50.1	52.0	37.5	48.6	33.8
1920	54.1	55.6	45.2	54.4	45.5
1930	59.7	63.5	49.2	59.7	47.3
1940	62.9	66.6	54.9	62.1	51.5
1950	68.2	72.2	62.9	66.5	59.1
1960	69.7	74.1	66.3	67.4	61.1
1970	70.9	75.6	69.4	68.0	61.3
1980	73.7	78.1	73.6	70.7	65.3
1987	74.9	78.3	75.4	71.5	67.6

THE CHANGING AGE STRUCTURE

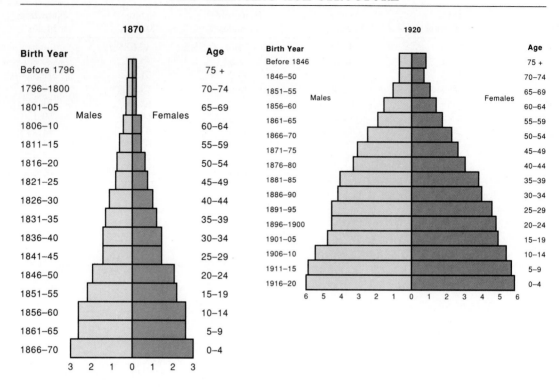

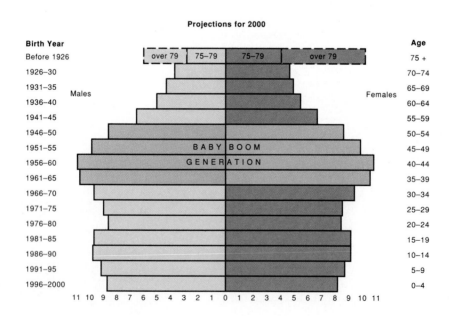

For more explanation of these population pyramids, see pages 714–15 and 1190–91.

REGIONAL ORIGIN OF IMMIGRANTS (percent)

Years	Total Number of Immigrants	Europe				Western Hemisphere	Asia
		Total Europe	North and West	East and Central	South and Other		
1821–1830	143,389	69.2	67.1	—	2.1	8.4	—
1831–1840	599,125	82.8	81.8	—	1.0	5.5	—
1841–1850	1,713,251	93.8	92.9	0.1	0.3	3.6	—
1851–1860	2,598,214	94.4	93.6	0.1	0.8	2.9	1.6
1861–1870	2,314,824	89.2	87.8	0.5	0.9	7.2	2.8
1871–1880	2,812,191	80.8	73.6	4.5	2.7	14.4	4.4
1881–1890	5,246,613	90.3	72.0	11.9	6.3	8.1	1.3
1891–1900	3,687,546	96.5	44.5	32.8	19.1	1.1	1.9
1901–1910	8,795,386	92.5	21.7	44.5	6.3	4.1	2.8
1911–1920	5,735,811	76.3	17.4	33.4	25.5	19.9	3.4
1921–1930	4,107,209	60.3	31.7	14.4	14.3	36.9	2.4
1931–1940	528,431	65.9	38.8	11.0	16.1	30.3	2.8
1941–1950	1,035,039	60.1	47.5	4.6	7.9	34.3	3.1
1951–1960	2,515,479	52.8	17.7	24.3	10,8	39.6	6.0
1961–1970	3,321,677	33.8	11.7	9.4	12.9	51.7	12.9
1971–1980	4,384,000	18.3	4.3	5.6	8.4	44.0	37.3

Dash indicates less than 0.1 percent.

RECENT TRENDS IN IMMIGRATION (in thousands)

	1961–1970	1971–1980	Percent 1961–1970	Percent 1971–1980	1985	1987
All countries	3,321.7	4,493.3	100.0	100.0	570.0	601.5
Europe	1,123.5	800.4	33.8	17.8	69.5	68.0
Austria	20.6	9.5	0.6	0.2	1.9	2.4
Hungary	5.4	6.6	0.2	0.1	0.6	—
Belgium	9.2	5.3	0.3	0.1	0.8	0.9
Czechoslovakia	3.3	6.0	0.1	0.1	0.7	0.7
Denmark	9.2	4.4	0.3	0.1	0.5	0.5
Finland	4.2	2.9	0.1	0.1	0.2	0.3
France	45.2	25.1	1.4	0.6	3.5	3.8
Germany	190.8	74.4	5.7	1.7	10.2	9.9
Great Britain	214.5	137.4	6.5	3.1	15.6	15.9
Greece	86.0	92.4	2.6	2.1	3.5	4.1
Ireland	33.0	11.5	1.0	0.3	1.3	3.0
Italy	214.1	129.4	6.4	7.9	6.4	4.7
Netherlands	30.6	10.5	.9	0.2	1.2	1.3
Norway	15.5	3.9	.5	0.1	0.4	0.4
Poland	53.5	37.2	1.6	0.8	7.4	5.8
Portugal	76.1	101.7	2.3	2.3	3.8	4.0
Spain	44.7	39.1	1.3	0.9	2.3	2.1
Sweden	17.1	6.5	.5	0.1	1.2	1.2
Switzerland	18.5	8.2	.6	0.2	1.0	0.1
U.S.S.R.	2.5	39.0	.1	0.9	1.5	1.1
Yugoslavia	20.4	30.5	.6	0.7	1.5	1.8
Other Europe	9.1	18.9	.2	0.2	4.0	4.0
Asia	427.6	1,588.2	12.9	35.2	255.2	248.3
China	34.8	124.3	1.0	2.8	33.1	18.6
Hong Kong	75.0	113.5	2.3	2.5	10.8	8.8
India	27.2	164.1	0.8	3.7	24.5	26.4

RECENT TRENDS IN IMMIGRATION (continued)

	1961–1970	1971–1980	Percent 1961–1970	Percent 1971–1980	1985	1987
Iran	10.3	45.1	0.3	1.0	12.3	10.3
Israel	29.6	37.7	0.9	0.8	4.3	4.8
Japan	40.0	49.8	1.2	1.1	4.6	4.7
Jordan	11.7	27.5	0.4	0.6	2.7	2.8
Korea	34.5	267.6	1.0	6.0	34.8	35.4
Lebanon	15.2	41.3	0.5	0.9	2.5	3.0
Philippines	98.4	355.0	3.0	7.9	53.1	58.3
Turkey	10.1	13.4	0.3	0.3	1.7	2.1
Vietnam	4.3	172.8	1.1	3.8	20.4	13.1
Other Asia	36.5	176.1	1.1	3.8	50.4	60.0
America	1,716.4	1,982.5	51.7	44.3	225.5	265.0
Argentina	49.7	29.9	1.5	0.7	1.9	2.2
Brazil	29.3	17.8	0.9	0.4	2.6	2.7
Canada	413.3	169.9	12.4	3.8	16.4	16.7
Colombia	72.0	77.3	2.2	1.7	11.8	11.5
Cuba	208.5	264.9	6.3	5.9	17.1	27.4
Dominican Rep.	93.3	148.1	2.8	3.3	23.9	24.9
Ecuador	36.8	50.1	1.1	1.1	4.6	4.7
El Salvador	15.0	34.4	0.5	0.8	10.1	10.6
Guatemala	15.9	25.9	0.5	0.6	4.4	5.8
Haiti	34.5	56.3	1.0	1.3	9.9	14.8
Honduras	15.7	17.4	0.5	0.4	3.7	72.5
Mexico	453.9	640.3	13.7	14.3	61.3	2.8
Panamá	19.4	23.5	0.6	0.5	3.2	5.8
Peru	19.1	29.2	0.6	0.6	4.1	5.8
West Indies	133.9	271.8	4.0	6.1	28.5	48.3
Other America	106.1	125.7	3.1	2.8	22.0	9.7

Figures may not add to total due to rounding.

AMERICAN WORKERS AND FARMERS

Year	Total Number of Workers (thousands)	Percent of Workers Male/Female	Percent of Female Workers Married	Percent of Workers in Female Population	Percent of Workers in Labor Unions	Farm Population (thousands)	Farm Population as Percent of Total Population
1870	12,506	85/15	NA	NA	NA	NA	NA
1880	17,392	85/15	NA	NA	NA	21,973	43.8
1890	23,318	83/17	13.9	18.9	NA	24,771	42.3
1900	29,073	82/18	15.4	20.6	3	29,875	41.9
1910	38,167	79/21	24.7	25.4	6	32,077	34.9
1920	41,614	79/21	23.0	23.7	12	31,974	30.1
1930	48,830	78/22	28.9	24.8	7	30,529	24.9
1940	53,011	76/24	36.4	27.4	27	30,547	23.2
1950	59,643	72/28	52.1	31.4	25	23,048	15.3
1960	69,877	68/32	59.9	37.7	26	15,635	8.7
1970	82,049	63/37	63.4	43.4	25	9,712	4.8
1980	108,544	58/42	59.7	51.5	23	6,051	2.7
1987	119,865	55/45	59.1	55.4	19	4,986	2.0

THE ECONOMY AND FEDERAL SPENDING

Year	Gross National Product (GNP) (in billions)	Foreign Trade (in millions)			Federal Budget (in billions)	Federal Surplus/Deficit (in billions)	Federal Debt (in billions)
		Exports	Imports	Balance of Trade			
1790	NA	$ 20	$ 23	$ −3	$ 0.004	$ +0.00015	$ 0.076
1800	NA	71	91	−20	0.011	+0.0006	0.083
1810	NA	67	85	−18	0.008	+0.0012	0.053
1820	NA	70	74	−4	0.018	−0.0004	0.091
1830	NA	74	71	+3	0.015	+0.100	0.049
1840	NA	132	107	+25	0.024	−0.005	0.004
1850	NA	152	178	−26	0.040	+0.004	0.064
1860	NA	400	362	−38	0.063	−0.01	0.065
1870	$ 7.4	451	462	−11	0.310	+0.10	2.4
1880	11.2	853	761	+92	0.268	+0.07	2.1
1890	13.1	910	823	+87	0.318	+0.09	1.2
1900	18.7	1,499	930	+569	0.521	+0.05	1.2
1910	35.3	1,919	1,646	+273	0.694	−0.02	1.1
1920	91.5	8,664	5,784	+2,880	6.357	+0.3	24.3
1930	90.7	4,013	3,500	+513	3.320	+0.7	16.3
1940	100.0	4,030	7,433	−3,403	9.6	−2.7	43.0
1950	286.5	10,816	9,125	+1,691	43.1	−2.2	257.4
1960	506.5	19,600	15,046	+4,556	92.2	+0.3	286.3
1970	992.7	42,700	40,189	+2,511	195.6	−2.8	371.0
1980	2,631.7	220,783	244,871	+24,088	590.9	−73.8	907.7
1987	4,526.7	252,866	424,082	−171,216	1,015.6	−173.2	2,350.3

80°N

GREENLAND
(KALALLIT-NUNAAT)
(Den.)

ALASKA
(U.S.)

60°N

CANADA

**NORTH
AMERICA**

ATLANTIC
OCEAN

40°N

UNITED STATES

BERMUDA
(Br.)

HAWAII
(U.S.)

MEXICO

BAHAMAS

CUBA

DOMINICAN
REP. 18

CAPE
VERDE

20°N

HAITI

PUERTO 27 26
RICO (U.S.) 25
20 24 23
19
22
28

GUATEMALA
EL SALVADOR
NICARAGUA
COSTA RICA
PANAMA

BELIZE
HONDURAS

29

PACIFIC
OCEAN

VENEZUELA
COLOMBIA

GUYANA
SURINAME
FR. GUIANA

ECUADOR

0° Equator

WESTERN
SAMOA

SOUTH
AMERICA

AMERICAN
SAMOA

FRENCH
POLYNESIA

PERU

BRAZIL

BOLIVIA

20°S
TONGA

PARAGUAY

CHILE

ARGENTINA

URUGUAY

40°S

FALKLAND
IS. (Br.)

60°S

80°S
160°W   140°W   120°W   100°W   80°W   60°W

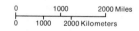

0   1000   2000 Miles

0   1000   2000 Kilometers

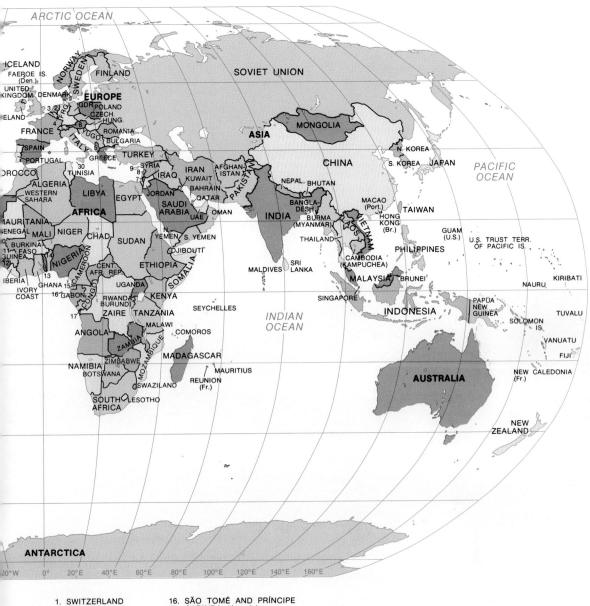

ARCTIC OCEAN

ICELAND
FAEROE IS.
(Den.)
UNITED
KINGDOM DENMARK
ELAND **EUROPE**
GDR POLAND
3 2 1 CZECH.
FRG. HUNG.
FRANCE 6
ITALY ROMANIA
5 BULGARIA
SPAIN
PORTUGAL GREECE TURKEY
ROCCO 30 9 SYRIA
TUNISIA 8 7 IRAN AFGHAN-
ALGERIA 7 IRAQ ISTAN
WESTERN KUWAIT
SAHARA LIBYA EGYPT BAHRAIN
MAURITANIA **AFRICA** JORDAN QATAR
SAUDI UAE OMAN
ENEGAL MALI NIGER ARABIA
BURKINA CHAD N.
11 FASO SUDAN YEMEN S. YEMEN
GUINEA 14
12 NIGERIA DJIBOUTI
IBERIA 13 CAMEROON ETHIOPIA
IVORY GHANA 15 CENT. UGANDA
COAST 16 GABON AFR. REP.
17 CONGO RWANDA KENYA
BURUNDI
ZAIRE TANZANIA
ANGOLA MALAWI
ZAMBIA
NAMIBIA ZIMBABWE MADAGASCAR
BOTSWANA MOZAMBIQUE
SWAZILAND
SOUTH LESOTHO
AFRICA

SOVIET UNION

ASIA MONGOLIA

CHINA N. KOREA
S. KOREA JAPAN

**PACIFIC
OCEAN**

NEPAL BHUTAN

BANGLA-
DESH MACAO
(Port.) TAIWAN
INDIA BURMA HONG
(MYANMAR) KONG
(Br.) GUAM
(U.S.) U.S. TRUST TERR.
THAILAND OF PACIFIC IS.

LAOS VIETNAM
CAMBODIA PHILIPPINES
(KAMPUCHEA)

MALDIVES SRI
LANKA KIRIBATI
NAURU

SEYCHELLES SINGAPORE MALAYSIA BRUNEI

INDONESIA PAPUA
NEW TUVALU
GUINEA
SOLOMON
IS.

**INDIAN
OCEAN** VANUATU
FIJI

COMOROS

MAURITIUS **AUSTRALIA** NEW CALEDONIA
REUNION (Fr.)
(Fr.)

NEW
ZEALAND

ANTARCTICA

20°W 0° 20°E 40°E 60°E 80°E 100°E 120°E 140°E 160°E

1. SWITZERLAND
2. NETHERLANDS
3. BELGIUM
4. LUXEMBOURG
5. ALBANIA
6. AUSTRIA
7. ISRAEL
8. LEBANON
9. CYPRUS
10. GAMBIA
11. GUINEA-BISSAU
12. SIERRA LEONE
13. TOGO
14. BENIN
15. EQUATORIAL GUINEA

16. SÃO TOMÉ AND PRÍNCIPE
17. CABINDA (Angola)
18. VIRGIN IS. (U.S./Br.)
19. BARBADOS
20. NETHERLANDS ANTILLES
21. GRENADA
22. ST. VINCENT
23. ST. LUCIA
24. DOMINICA
25. FRENCH ANTILLES
26. ANTIGUA AND BARBUDA
27. ST. KITTS AND NEVIS
28. TRINIDAD AND TOBAGO
29. JAMAICA
30. MALTA

BIBLIOGRAPHY

CHAPTER 1

Discovery and Exploration in the Sixteenth Century
Kenneth R. Andrews, *Trade, Plunder, and Settlement: Maritime Enterprise and the Genesis of the British Empire, 1480–1630* (1985); K. R. Andrews, N. P. Canny, and P. E. H. Hair, eds., *The Westward Enterprise: English Activities in Ireland, the Atlantic, and America, 1480–1650* (1979); Ralph Davis, *The Rise of Atlantic Economies* (1973); J. H. Elliott, *The Old World and the New, 1492–1650* (1970); James Lang, *Conquest and Commerce: Spain and England in the Americas* (1975); W. H. McNeil, *The Rise of the West* (1963); Samuel Eliot Morison, *The European Discovery of America: The Northern Voyage, 500–1600* (1971), and *The European Discovery of America: The Southern Voyages, 1492–1616* (1974); J. H. Parry, *The Age of Reconnaissance* (1963); David Beers Quinn, *England and the Discovery of America, 1481–1620* (1974), *North America from Earliest Discovery to First Settlements* (1977), and *Set Fair for Roanoke* (1985).

Native American Civilizations
Alfred W. Crosby, Jr., *The Columbian Exchange: Biological and Cultural Consequences of 1492* (1972); Nigel Davies, *The Aztecs* (1973); Harold Driver, *Indians of North America* (2d ed., 1970); Peter Farb, *Man's Rise to Civilization* (1968); R. C. Padden, *The Hummingbird and the Hawk* (1962); M. Leon Portilla, *The Broken Spears: The Aztec Account of the Conquest of Mexico* (1962); Wilcomb E. Washburn, *The Indian in America* (1975).

The Spanish Empire in the Sixteenth Century
Fernand Braudel, *The Mediterranean and the Mediterranean World in the Age of Philip the Second*, Vols. 1 and 2 (1976); J. H. Elliott, *Imperial Spain, 1469–1716* (1963); Charles Gibson, *The Aztecs Under Spanish Rule* (1964); James Lockhart, *Spanish Peru, 1532–1560* (1968); James Lockhart and Stuart B. Schwartz, *Early Latin America: A History of Colonial Spanish America and Brazil* (1983).

The Protestant Reformation
Owen Chadwick, *The Reformation* (1964); Patrick Collinson, *The Elizabethan Puritan Movement* (1967); A. G. Dickens, *The English Reformation* (1974); Richard Dunn, *The Age of Religious Wars, 1159–1689* (1979); Erik Erikson, *Young Man Luther* (1962); Charles George and Katherine George, *The Protestant Mind of the English Reformation* (1961); De Lamar Jensen, *Reformation Europe, Age of Reform and Revolution* (1981); Steven Ozment, *The Reformation in the Cities* (1975); Keith Thomas, *Religion and the Decline of Magic* (1971); Michael Walzer, *The Revolution of the Saints* (1965).

Elizabethan and Stuart England
Trevor Ashton, ed., *Crisis in Europe, 1560–1660* (1965); Carl Bridenbaugh, *Vexed and Troubled Englishmen, 1590–1642* (1968); Mildred Campbell, *The English Yeoman Under Elizabeth and the Early Stuarts* (1942); Peter Laslett, *The World We Have Lost* (1965); Wallace Notestein, *The English People on the Eve of Colonization, 1603–1630* (1954); Laurence Stone, *The Crisis of the Aristocracy, 1558–1641* (1965); Keith Wrightson, *English Society, 1580–1680* (1982).

Ireland in the Sixteenth Century
Nicholas Canny, *The Elizabethan Conquest of Ireland* (1976), and *Kingdom and Colony: Ireland in the Atlantic World, 1560–1800* (1988); David Beers Quinn, *The Elizabethans and the Irish* (1976).

CHAPTER 2

General Histories
Charles M. Andrews, *The Colonial Period in American History, (1934–1938)*; Wesley Frank Craven, *The Southern Colonies in the Seventeenth Century, 1607–1689* (1949); David Galenson, *White Servitude in Colonial America* (1981); Sidney Mintz, *Sweetness and Power: The Place of Sugar in Modern History* (1985); Gary Nash, *Red, White and Black: The Peoples of Early America* (1974); John E. Pomfret, *Founding the American Colonies, 1583–1660* (1970); R. C. Simmons, *The American Colonies* (1976).

Native Americans in the Early South
Karen Kupperman, *Settling with the Indians: The Meeting of English and Indian Cultures in America, 1580–1640* (1980); J. Leitch Wright, Jr., *The Only Land They Knew: The Tragic Story of American Indians in the Old South* (1981); Nancy Lurie, "Indian Cultural Adjustment

to European Civilization," in *Seventeenth-Century America*, ed. James M. Smith (1959); James H. Merrell, *The Indians' New World: Catawbas and Their Neighbors* (1989).

Race and Slavery
Wesley Frank Craven, *White, Red, and Black: The Seventeenth-Century Virginian* (1971); Philip Curtin, *The Atlantic Slave Trade* (1969); Basil Davidson, *The African Genius* (1970); David B. Davis, *The Problem of Slavery in Western Culture* (1966); Carl N. Degler, *Neither White Nor Black: Slavery and Race Relations in Brazil and the United States* (1971); Winthrop Jordan, *White over Black* (1968); Herbert Klein, *The Middle Passage* (1978), and *Slavery in the Americas: A Comparative Study of Virginia and Cuba* (1967); Peter Kolchin, *Unfree Labor: American Slavery and Russian Serfdom* (1987); Richard Olaniyan, *African History and Culture* (1982); Roland Oliver, ed., *The Cambridge History of Africa*, Vol. 3: *c. 1050–c. 1600* (1977); Orlando Patterson, *Slavery and Social Death: A Comparative Study* (1982); James A. Rawley, *The Transatlantic Slave Trade* (1981); Walter Rodney, *West Africa and the Atlantic Slave Trade* (1969); Peter Wood, *Black Majority: Negroes in Colonial South Carolina from 1670 Through the Stono Rebellion* (1974), and "'I Did the Best I Could for My Day': The Study of Early Black History During the Second Reconstruction, 1960 to 1976," *William and Mary Quarterly*, (1978).

The Early Chesapeake Colonies
Philip L. Barbour, *The Three Worlds of Captain John Smith* (1964); Warren M. Billings, John E. Selby, and Thad W. Tate, *Colonial Virginia* (1986); Lois Green Carr, Philip D. Morgan, and Jean B. Russo, *Colonial Chesapeake Society* (1989); Lois Green Carr and Lorena Walsh, "The Planter's Wife: The Experience of White Women in Seventeenth-Century Maryland," *William and Mary Quarterly* (1977); Carville Earle, *The Evolution of a Tidewater Settlement Pattern: All Hallows Parish, Maryland 1650–1783* (1975); Ivor Noel Hume, *Martin's Hundred: The Discovery of a Lost Virginia Settlement* (1979); Allan Kulikoff, *Tobacco and Slaves* (1987); Aubrey C. Land, *Colonial Maryland* (1981); Gloria Main, *Tobacco Colony: Life in Early Maryland, 1650–1720* (1982); Edmund S. Morgan, *American Slavery, American Freedom* (1975); Darrett Rutman and Anita Rutman, *A Place in Time: Middlesex County, Virginia, 1650–1750* (1984); Thad Tate and David Ammerman, eds., *The Chesapeake in the Seventeenth Century* (1979); Alden Vaughan, *American Genesis: Captain John Smith and the Founding of Virginia* (1975).

The English Revolution
Christopher Hill, *The Century of Revolution, 1603–1714* (1961), and *The World Turned Upside Down* (1972); Lawrence Stone, *The Causes of the English Revolution, 1529–1642* (1972).

The Carolinas
Verner Crane, *The Southern Frontier, 1670–1732* (1929); Daniel C. Littlefield, *Rice and Slaves: Ethnicity and the Slave Trade in Colonial South Carolina* (1981); H. T. Merrens, *Colonial North Carolina* (1964); M. Eugene Sirmans, *Colonial South Carolina* (1966); Clarence

L. Ver Steeg, *Origins of a Southern Mosaic* (1975); Robert Weir, *Colonial South Carolina* (1982).

Georgia
Harold E. Davis, *The Fledgling Province: Social and Cultural Life in Colonial Georgia, 1733–1776* (1976); Hardy Jackson and Phinizy Spalding, eds., *Forty Years of Diversity: Essays on Colonial Georgia* (1984); Phinizy Spalding, *Oglethorpe in America* (1977).

The British Caribbean
Richard Dunn, *Sugar and Slaves: The Rise of the Planter Class in the English West Indies, 1624–1713* (1972); Gary Puckrein, *Little England: Plantation Society and Anglo-Barbadian Politics, 1627–1700* (1984).

The Spanish Empire in the Southwest
Sherbune F. Cook, *The Conflict Between the California Indian and White Civilization* (1943); Charles Gibson, *Spain in America* (1966); Edward H. Spicer, *Cycles of Conquest: The Impact of Spain, Mexico, and the United States on the Indians of the Southwest, 1533–1960* (1962).

CHAPTER 3

Native Americans and Northern Colonials
James Axtell, *The European and the Indian* (1981), and *The Invasion Within: The Contest of Cultures in Colonial North America* (1985); Charles E. Clark, *The Eastern Frontier: The Settlement of Northern New England, 1610–1763* (1970); William Cronon, *Changes in the Land: Indians, Colonists and the Ecology of New England* (1983); Francis Jennings, *The Ambiguous Iroquois Empire* (1984), and *The Invasion of America* (1975); Douglas Leach, *Flintlock and Tomahawk: New England in King Philip's War* (1958); Calvin Martin, *Keepers of the Game: Indian–Animal Relationships and the Fur Trade* (1978); Daniel K. Richter and James H. Merrell, *Beyond the Covenant Chain: The Iroquois and Their Neighbors in Indian North America, 1600–1800* (1987); Neal Salisbury, *Manitou and Providence: Indians, Europeans and the Making of New England* (1982); Allen W. Trelease, *Indian Affairs in Colonial New York* (1960); Bruce G. Trigger, *The Children of Aataentsic: A History of the Huron People to 1660* (1976); Alden Vaughan, *The New England Frontier* (1965); Anthony F. C. Wallace, *The Death and Rebirth of the Seneca* (1972).

The French in North America
W. J. Eccles, *The Canadian Frontier, 1534–1760* (1969), and *France in America* (1972); Allan Greer, *Peasant, Lord and Merchant: Rural Society in Three Quebec Parishes, 1740–1840* (1985); Richard Colebrook Harris, *The Seigneurial System in Early Canada* (1966); C. E. O'Neill, *Church and State in French Colonial Louisiana* (1966).

New England Puritanism
Francis Bremer, *The Puritan Experiment* (1976); Stephen Foster, *Their Solitary Way: The Puritan Social Ethic in the First Century of Settlement in New England* (1971); Charles Hambrick-Stowe, *The Practice of Piety: Puritan Devotional Literature in Seventeenth-Century New England* (1982); Robert Middlekauff, *The Mathers* (1971); Perry Miller, *The New England Mind: From Colony to Province* (1953); Edmund S. Morgan, *Visible*

Saints (1963); Harry Stout, *The New England Soul* (1986).

The New England Colonies
Paul Boyer and Stephen Nissenbaum, *Salem Possessed: The Social Origins of Witchcraft* (1974); Richard Bushman, *From Puritan to Yankee: Character and the Social Order in Connecticut, 1690–1765* (1967); David Cressy, *Coming Over: Migration and Communication Between England and New England in the Seventeenth Century* (1987); John P. Demos, *Entertaining Satan: Witchcraft and the Culture of Early New England* (1982), and *A Little Commonwealth: Family Life in Plymouth Colony* (1970); Philip Greven, *Four Generations: Land, Population, and Family in Colonial Andover, Massachusetts* (1970); Stephen Innes, *To Labor in a New Land: Economy and Society in Seventeenth-Century Springfield* (1983); Sydney V. James, *Colonial Rhode Island* (1975); Carol Karlsen, *The Devil in the Shape of a Woman: Witchcraft in Colonial New England* (1987); George Langdon, *Pilgrim Colony* (1960); Kenneth Lockridge, *A New England Town: Dedham, Massachusetts, 1636–1737* (1970); Edmund S. Morgan, *The Puritan Dilemma: The Story of John Winthrop* (1958), and *The Puritan Family*, rev. ed. (1966); Darrett Rutman, *Winthrop's Boston* (1965); David E. Stannard, *The Puritan Way of Death* (1977); Laurel Ulrich, *Good Wives: Image and Reality in the Lives of Women in Northern New England, 1650–1750* (1982).

The Middle Colonies
Patricia Bonomi, *A Factious People: Politics and Society in Colonial New York* (1971); Edwin Bronner, *William Penn's "Holy Experiment"* (1962); Thomas J. Condon, *New York Beginnings* (1968); Wesley Frank Craven, *New Jersey and the English Colonization of North America* (1964); Mary Maples Dunn, *William Penn* (1967); Melvin B. Endy, *William Penn and Early Quakerism* (1973); Joseph Illick, *Colonial Pennsylvania* (1976); Michael Kammen, *Colonial New York* (1975); Gary B. Nash, *Quakers and Politics: Pennsylvania, 1681–1726* (1968); J. E. Pomfret, *Colonial New Jersey* (1973); Oliver A. Rink, *Holland on the Hudson: An Economic and Social History of Dutch New York* (1986); Robert C. Ritchie, *The Duke's Province: A Study of Politics and Society in Colonial New York, 1660–1691*; Alan Tully, *William Penn's Legacy* (1977).

The Imperial Connection
Michael Hall, *Edward Randolph and the American Colonies, 1676–1703* (1960); Richard R. Johnson, *Adjustment to Empire* (1981); Michael Kammen, *Empire and Interest: The American Colonies and the Politics of Mercantilism* (1970); David Lovejoy, *The Glorious Revolution in America* (1972); J. M. Sosin, *English America and the Revolution of 1688* (1982); Ian K. Steele, *Politics of Colonial Policy: The Board of Trade in Colonial Administration* (1968); Stephen Saunders Webb, *The Governors–General: The English Army and the Definition of Empire, 1569–1681* (1979).

CHAPTER 4

General Histories
Patricia Bonomi, *Under the Cope of Heaven: Religion, Society, and Politics in Colonial America* (1986); Philip

Greven, *The Protestant Temperament: Patterns of Childrearing, Religious Experience, and Self in Early America* (1977); James Henretta, *The Evolution of American Society, 1700–1815* (1973); Stephen Innes, ed., *Work and Labor in Early America* (1988); Alice Hanson Jones, *Wealth of a Nation to Be: The American Colonies on the Eve of the Revolution* (1980); John McCusker and Russell Menard, *The Economy of British America, 1607–1787* (1985); Jackson Turner Main, *The Social Structure of Revolutionary America* (1965); D. W. Meinig, *The Shaping of America: A Geographical Perspective on 500 Years of History*, Vol. 1: *Atlantic America, 1492–1800* (1986); Mary Beth Norton, *Liberty's Daughters: The Revolutionary Experience of American Women, 1750–1800* (1980); Gary M. Walton and James F. Shepherd, *The Economic Rise of Early America* (1979); Robert V. Wells, *The Population of the British Colonies in America Before 1776* (1975).

Immigration
Bernard Bailyn, *Voyagers to the West: A Passage in the Peopling of America on the Eve of the American Revolution* (1986); J. M. Bumsted, *The People's Clearance: Highland Emigration to British North America, 1770–1815* (1982); Jon Butler, *The Huguenots in America* (1983); R. J. Dickson, *Ulster Immigration to Colonial America, 1718–1775* (1966); Ned Landsman, *Scotland and Its First American Colony, 1683–1765* (1985).

Rural Society in Eighteenth-Century America
Charles Grant, *Democracy in the Frontier Town of Kent* (1961); James Henretta, "Farms and Families: Mentalite in Pre-Industrial America," *William and Mary Quarterly* (1978); Christopher M. Jedrey, *The World of John Cleaveland* (1979); Sung Bok Kim, *Landlord and Tenant in Colonial New York* (1978); James T. Lemon, *The Best Poor Man's Country: A Geographical Study of Early Southeastern Pennsylvania* (1972); Gregory Stiverson, *Poverty in the Land of Plenty: Tenancy in Eighteenth-Century Maryland* (1978); Michael Zuckerman, *Peaceable Kingdoms: New England Towns in the Eighteenth Century* (1970).

The Frontier
Richard Aquila, *The Iroquois Restoration: Iroquois Diplomacy on the Colonial Frontier, 1701–1754* (1983); Richard Beeman, *The Evolution of the Southern Backcountry* (1984); Richard M. Brown, *The South Carolina Regulators* (1963); David H. Corkran, *The Cherokee Frontier: Conflict and Survival, 1740–1762* (1962), and *The Creek Frontier, 1540–1783* (1967); Robert D. Mitchell, *Commercialism and Frontier: Perspectives on the Early Shenandoah Valley* (1977); Malcolm J. Rohrbough, *The Trans-Appalachian Frontier* (1978).

Provincial Seaports
Carl Bridenbaugh, *Cities in the Wilderness* (1938), and *Cities in Revolt* (1955); Elaine Forman Crane, *A Dependent People: Newport, Rhode Island in the Revolutionary Era* (1985); Thomas Doerflinger, *A Vigorous Spirit of Enterprise: Merchants and Economic Development in Revolutionary Philadelphia* (1986); Christine Leigh Heyrman, *Commerce and Culture: The Maritime Communities of Colonial Massachusetts, 1690–1750* (1984); Gary B. Nash, *The Urban Crucible: Social Change, Political Consciousness, and the Origins of the American*

Revolution (1979); Jacob M. Price, "Economic Function and the Growth of American Port Towns in the Eighteenth Century," *Perspectives in American History* (1974); Marcus Rediker, *Between the Devil and the Deep Blue Sea: Merchant Seamen, Pirates, and the Anglo-American Maritime Works, 1700–1750* (1987); Frederick B. Tolles, *Meetinghouse and Countinghouse: The Quaker Merchants of Colonial Philadelphia* (1948); Gerald B. Warden, *Boston, 1687–1776* (1970); Stephanie Grauman Wolf, *Urban Village: Population, Community, and Family Structure in Germantown, Pennsylvania, 1683–1800* (1976).

Blacks in Eighteenth-Century America
Ira Berlin, "Time, Space, and the Evolution of Afro-American Society in British Mainland America," *American Historical Review* (1980); Thomas J. Davis, *A Rumor of Revolt: The "Great Negro Plot" in Colonial New York* (1985); Herbert Gutman, *The Black Family in Slavery and Freedom, 1750–1925* (1976); Alan Kulikoff, "The Origins of Afro-American Society in Tidewater Maryland and Virginia, 1700–1790," *William and Mary Quarterly* (1978); Jean Butenhoff Lee, "The Problem of the Slave Community in the Eighteenth-Century Chesapeake," *William and Mary Quarterly* (1986); Gerald W. Mullin, *Flight and Rebellion: Slave Resistance in Eighteenth-Century Virginia* (1972); Jean R. Soderlund, *Quakers and Slavery* (1985); Betty Wood, *Slavery in Colonial Georgia, 1730–1775* (1984).

The Eighteenth-Century South
Carl Bridenbaugh, *Myths and Realities: Societies of the Colonial South* (1952); Paul G. E. Clemens, *The Atlantic Economy and Colonial Maryland's Eastern Shore: From Tobacco to Grain* (1980); A. Roger Ekirch, *"Poor Carolina": Politics and Society in Colonial North Carolina, 1729–1776* (1981); Rhys Isaac, *The Transformation of Virginia, 1740–1790* (1982); Jan Lewis, *The Pursuit of Happiness: Family and Values in Jefferson's Virginia* (1983); Daniel Blake Smith, *Inside the Great House: Planter Family Life in Eighteenth-Century Chesapeake Society* (1980); Julia Cherry Spruill, *Women's Life and Work in the Southern Colonies* (1938); Charles Sydnor, *Gentlemen Freeholders: Political Practices in Washington's Virginia* (1956).

The Enlightenment
Henry May, *The Enlightenment in America* (1976); Esmond Wright, *Franklin of Philadelphia* (1986); Louis B. Wright, *The Cultural Life of the American Colonies* (1957).

The Great Awakening
Edwin Scott Gaustad, *The Great Awakening in New England* (1957); Alan Heimert, *Religion and the American Mind: From the Great Awakening to the American Revolution* (1966); Patricia Tracy, *Jonathan Edwards, Pastor* (1979).

Colonial Political Development in the Eighteenth Century
Bernard Bailyn, *The Origins of American Politics* (1968); Edward M. Cook, *The Fathers of the Towns: Leadership and Community Structure in Eighteenth-Century New England* (1976); Jack P. Greene, *The Quest for Power: The Lower Houses of Assembly in the Southern Royal*

Colonies, 1689–1776 (1963); Robert C. Newbold, *The Albany Congress and the Plan of Union of 1754* (1955); Robert Zemsky, *Merchants, Farmers, and River Gods: An Essay on Eighteenth Century American Politics* (1971).

CHAPTER 5

General Histories
Charles M. Andrews, *The Colonial Background of the American Revolution*, rev. ed. (1931); Ian Christie and Benjamin Labaree, *Empire or Independence, 1760–1776* (1976); Edward Countryman, *The American Revolution* (1985); Lawrence Henry Gipson, *The Coming of the Revolution, 1763–1775* (1954); Edmond S. Morgan, *The Birth of the Republic, 1763–1789* (1956); Alfred Young, ed., *The American Revolution: Explorations in the History of American Radicalism* (1976).

The Seven Years' War
Fred Anderson, *A People's Army: Massachusetts Soldiers and Society in the Seven Years War* (1984); France Jennings, *Empire of Fortune: Crown, Colonies, and Tribes in the Seven Years War in America* (1989); Howard H. Peckham, *The Colonial Wars, 1689–1762* (1963); Alan Rogers, *Empire and Liberty* (1974).

British Society and Politics
John Brewer, *Party Ideology and Popular Politics at the Accession of George III* (1976); John Brooke, *King George III* (1972); J. C. D. Clark, *English Society, 1688–1832* (1985); Bernard Donoughue, *British Politics and the American Revolution* (1965); M. Dorothy George, *London Life in the Eighteenth Century* (1965); Lawrence Henry Gipson, *The British Empire Before the American Revolution* (1936–1970); Michael Kammen, *A Rope of Sand: The Colonial Agents, British Politics, and the American Revolution* (1968); Lewis B. Namier, *England in the Age of the American Revolution*, 2d ed. (1961); Richard Pares, *King George III and the Politicians* (1953); J. H. Plumb, *The First Four Georges* (1956); W. A. Speck, *Stability and Strife: England, 1714–1760* (1979).

The Intellectual Sources of Resistance and Revolution
Bernard Bailyn, *The Ideological Origins of the American Revolution* (1967); Trevor Colburn, *The Lamp of Experience: Whig History and the Intellectual Origins of the American Revolution* (1965); Nathan O. Hatch, *The Sacred Cause of Liberty: Republican Thought and the Millennium in Revolutionary New England* (1977); Isaac Kramnick, *Bolingbroke and His Circle: The Politics of Nostalgia in the Age of Walpole* (1968); Edmund S. Morgan, *The Challenge of the American Revolution* (1976), and *Inventing the People: The Rise of Popular Sovereignty in England and America* (1988); J. G. A. Pocock, *The Machiavellian Moment: Florentine Political Thought and the Atlantic Republican Tradition* (1975); Caroline Robbins, *The Eighteenth-Century Commonwealthman: Studies in the Transmission, Development, and Circumstances of English Liberal Thought from the Restoration of Charles II Until the War with the Thirteen Colonies* (1959).

A Decade of Resistance
David Ammerman, *In the Common Cause: The American Response to the Coercive Acts of 1774* (1974); Timothy Breen, *Tobacco Culture: The Mentality of the Great Tidewater Planters on the Eve of the Revolution* (1985); Richard D. Brown, *Revolutionary Politics in Massachusetts: The Boston Committee of Correspondence and the Towns, 1772–1774* (1970); Joseph Ernst, *Money and Politics in America, 1755–1775* (1973); Paul A. Gilje, *The Road to Mobocracy: Popular Disorder in New York City, 1763–1834* (1987); Dirk Hoerder, *Crowd Action in Revolutionary Massachusetts, 1765–1780* (1977); Benjamin Labaree, *The Boston Tea Party* (1964); Pauline Maier, *From Resistance to Revolution* (1972); Edmund S. Morgan and Helen M. Morgan, *The Stamp Act Crisis* (1953); Gregory H. Nobles, *Divisions Throughout the Whole: Politics and Society in Hampshire County, Massachusetts, 1740–1775* (1983); William Penack, *War, Politics, and Revolution in Provincial Massachusetts* (1981); Peter Shaw, *American Patriots and the Rituals of Revolution* (1981); John Shy, *Toward Lexington: The Role of the British Army in the Coming of the American Revolution* (1965); Richard Walsh, *Charleston's Sons of Liberty: A Study of the Artisans, 1763–1789* (1959); Hiller B. Zobel, *The Boston Massacre* (1970).

Leaders of the American Resistance
Richard Beeman, *Patrick Henry* (1982); Eric Foner, *Tom Paine and Revolutionary America* (1976); David Hawke *Paine* (1974); Pauline Maier, *The Old Revolutionaries: Political Lives in the Age of Samuel Adams* (1980); Peter Shaw, *The Character of John Adams* (1976); John J. Waters, *The Otis Family in Provincial and Revolutionary Massachusetts* (1968).

CHAPTER 6

General
John R. Alden, *The American Revolution* (1964); Ira Gruber, *The Howe Brothers and the American Revolution* (1972); Don Higginbotham, *The American War for Independence* (1971); Piers Makesy, *The War for America* (1964); Robert Middlekauff, *The Glorious Cause: The American Revolution, 1763–1789* (1982); John Shy, *A People Numerous and Armed* (1976).

Thomas Jefferson and the Declaration of Independence
Carl Becker, *The Declaration of Independence* (1922); Dumas Malone, *Jefferson the Virginian* (1948); Garry Willis, *Inventing America* (1978).

The Loyalists
Bernard Bailyn, *The Ordeal of Thomas Hutchinson* (1974); Wallace Brown, *The King's Friends* (1966); Robert M. Calhoon, *The Loyalists in Revolutionary America* (1973); Neil MacKinnon, *This Unfriendly Soil: The Loyalist Experience in Nova Scotia, 1783–1791* (1986); Mary Beth Norton, *The British-Americans* (1972).

George Washington and the Continental Army
E. Wayne Carp, *To Starve the Army at Pleasure: Continental Army Administration and American Political Culture, 1775–1783* (1984); James T. Flexner, *George Washington in the American Revolution* (1968); Douglas Southall Freeman, *George Washington* (1948–1957); James Kirby Martin and Mark Lender, *A Respectable Army: The Military Origins of the Republic, 1763–1789* (1982); Charles Royster, *A Revolutionary People at War* (1979).

Diplomacy
Samuel F. Bemis, *The Diplomacy of the American Revolution* (1935); Jonathan R. Dull, *A Diplomatic History of the American Revolution* (1985); Ronald Hoffman and Peter J. Albert, eds., *Peace and the Peacemakers: The Treaty of 1783* (1986); Richard B. Morris, *The Peacemakers: The Great Powers and American Independence* (1965); Gerald Stourzh, *Benjamin Franklin and American Foreign Policy* (rev. ed., 1969).

The North and the American Revolution
Edward Countryman, *A People in Revolution: The American Revolution and Political Society in New York, 1760–1790* (1981); Robert A. Gross, *The Minutemen and Their World* (1976); Robert J. Taylor, *Western Massachusetts in the Revolution* (1954); Donald Wallace White, *A Village at War: Chatham, New Jersey and the American Revolution* (1979); Alfred F. Young, "George Robert Twelves Hewes (1742–1840): A Boston Shoemaker and the Memory of the American Revolution," *William and Mary Quarterly* (1981).

Native Americans and the Revolutionary Frontier
Barbara Graymont, *The Iroquois in the American Revolution* (1972); Isabel Thomson Kelsey, *Joseph Brant, 1743–1807: Man of Two Worlds* (1984); James H. O'Donnell III, *Southern Indians in the American Revolution* (1973); J. M. Sosin, *The Revolutionary Frontier, 1763–1783* (1967).

The South and the American Revolution
John R. Alden, *The South in the Revolution, 1763–1789* (1957); Jeffrey J. Crow and Larry E. Tise, eds., *The Southern Experience in the American Revolution* (1978); Ronald Hoffman, Thad W. Tate, and Peter J. Albert, eds., *An Uncivil War: The Southern Backcountry During the American Revolution* (1985); Jerome J. Nadelhaft, *The Disorders of War: The Revolution in South Carolina* (1981).

The Black Experience and the American Revolution
Ira Berlin and Ronald Hoffman, eds., *Slavery and Freedom in the Age of the American Revolution* (1983); Jeffrey Crow, "Slave Rebelliousness and Social Conflict in North Carolina, 1775–1802," *William and Mary Quarterly* (1980); David Brion Davis, *The Problem of Slavery in the Age of Revolution* (1975); Duncan MacLeod, *Slavery, Race, and the American Revolution* (1974); Benjamin Quarles, *The Negro in the American Revolution* (1961).

Women and the American Revolution
Joy Day Buel and Richard Buel, Jr., *The Way of Duty: A Woman and Her Family in Revolutionary America* (1984); Linda Grant DePauw, *Founding Mothers* (1975); Linda Kerber, *Women of the Republic: Intellect and Ideology in Revolutionary America* (1980).

CHAPTER 7

General

Forrest McDonald, *E Pluribus Unum: The Formation of the American Republic, 1776–1790* (1965); Curtis P. Nettels, *The Emergence of a National Economy, 1775–1815* (1962); Robert R. Palmer, *The Age of Democratic Revolution: A Political History of Europe and America, 1760–1800* (1959, 1964); Gordon Wood, *The Creation of the American Republic* (1969).

State Politics and State Constitutions

Willi Paul Adams, *The First American Constitutions* (1980); Ronald Hoffman and Peter Albert, eds., *Sovereign States in an Age of Uncertainty* (1981); Jackson Turner Main, *The Sovereign States, 1775–1783* (1973), and *Political Parties Before the Constitution* (1973); Stephen E. Patterson, *Political Parties in Revolutionary Massachusetts* (1973); David Szatmary, *Shays' Rebellion: The Making of an Agrarian Insurrection* (1980).

The Articles of Confederation

Joseph L. Davis, *Sectionalism in American Politics, 1774–1787* (1977); E. James Ferguson, *The Power of the Purse: A History of American Public Finance, 1776–1790* (1961); H. James Henderson, *Party Politics in the Continental Congress* (1974); Merrill D. Jensen, *The Articles of Confederation*, rev. ed. (1959), and *The New Nation* (1950); Peter S. Onuf, *The Origins of the Federal Republic: Jurisdictional Controversies in the United States, 1775–1787* (1983); Jack N. Rakove, *The Beginnings of National Politics* (1979).

Society in the New Republic

Nancy Cott, "Divorce and the Changing Status of Women in Massachusetts," *William and Mary Quarterly* (1976); Joseph J. Ellis, *After the Revolution: Profiles of Early American Culture* (1979); Jay Fliegelman, *Prodigals and Pilgrims: The American Revolution Against Patriarchal Authority, 1750–1800* (1982); J. Franklin Jameson, *The American Revolution Considered as a Social Movement* (1962); Benjamin W. Labaree, *The Merchants of Newburyport, 1764–1815* (1962); Jan Lewis, "The Republican Wife: Virtue and Seduction in the Early Republic," *William and Mary Quarterly* (1987); Forrest McDonald and Ellen Shapiro McDonald, "The Ethnic Origins of the American People, 1790," *William and Mary Quarterly* (1980); Donald L. Robinson, *Slavery in the Structure of American Politics, 1765–1820* (1971); Howard Rock, *Artisans of the New Republic: Tradesmen of New York City in the Age of Jefferson* (1979); Charles G. Steffan, *The Mechanics of Baltimore: Workers and Politics in the Age of Revolution, 1763–1812* (1984); Lynne Withey, *Dearest Friend: A Life of Abigail Adams* (1981); Arthur Zilversmit, *The First Emancipation: The Abolition of Slavery in the North* (1967).

The Federal Constitution

Douglass Adair, *Fame and the Founding Fathers* (1974); Lance Banning, "James Madison and the Nationalists, 1780–1783," *William and Mary Quarterly* (1983); Charles Beard, *An Economic Interpretation of the Constitution of the United States* (1913); Richard Beeman, Stephen Botein, and Edward C. Carter II, eds., *Beyond Confederation: Origins of the Constitution and American National Identity* (1987); Irving Brant, *James Madi-son: The Nationalist, 1780–1787* (1948); Robert E. Brown, *Charles Beard and the Constitution* (1956); Linda Grant DePauw, *The Eleventh Pillar: New York State and the Federal Constitution* (1966); John P. Diggins, *The Lost Soul of American Politics: Virtue, Self-Interest, and the Foundations of Liberalism* (1984); Max Farrand, *The Framing of the Constitution* (1913); Ralph Ketcham, *James Madison* (1971); Leonard Levy, ed., *Essays on the Making of the Constitution* (1969); Staughton Lynd, *Class Conflict, Slavery, and the United States Constitution* (1967); Forrest McDonald *We the People: The Economic Origins of the Constitution* (1958), and *Novus Ordo Seclorum: The Intellectual Origins of the Constitution* (1985); Clinton Rossiter, *1787: The Grand Convention* (1973); Gerald Stourzh, *Alexander Hamilton and the Idea of Republican Government* (1970); Garry Wills, *Explaining America: The Federalist* (1981).

The Anti-Federalists

Cecilia Kenyon, "Men of Little Faith: The Anti-Federalists and the Nature of Representative Government," *William and Mary Quarterly* (1955); Jackson Turner Main, *The Anti-Federalists* (1981); Robert A. Rutland, *The Ordeal of the Constitution: The Anti-Federalists and the Ratification Struggle of 1787–88* (1966).

CHAPTER 8

Society

Nancy F. Cott, *The Bonds of Womanhood: "Woman's Sphere" in New England, 1780–1835* (1977); J. Hector St. John de Crèvecoeur, *Letters from an American Farmer* (1782, paper 1981); Joseph J. Ellis, *After the Revolution: Profiles of Early American Culture* (1979); Benjamin Franklin, *The Autobiography and Other Writings* (1986); Reginald Horsman, *The Frontier in the Formative Years, 1783–1815* (1970); Malcolm J. Rohrbough, *The Trans-Appalachian Frontier: Peoples, Societies, and Institutions, 1775–1850* (1978); Charles G. Steffen, *The Mechanics of Baltimore: Workers and Politics in the Age of Revolution, 1763–1812* (1984).

National Government

Ralph Adams Brown, *The Presidency of John Adams* (1975); Manning J. Dauer, *The Adams Federalists* (1953); Richard Hofstadter, *The Idea of a Party System: The Rise of Legitimate Opposition in the United States, 1780–1840* (1969); Richard H. Kohn, *Eagle and Sword: The Federalists and the Creation of a Military Establishment in America, 1783–1802* (1975); Stephan G. Kurtz, *The Presidency of John Adams: The Collapse of Federalism 1795–1800* (1957); Forrest McDonald, *The Presidency of George Washington* (1974); John C. Miller, *The Foundation Era, 1789–1801* (1960).

Party Politics

Richard Beeman, *The Old Dominion and the New Nation, 1788–1801* (1972); William Nisbet Chambers, *Political Parties in the New Nation: The American Experience* (1963); Joseph Charles, *The Origins of the American Party System* (1956); Noble Cunningham, *The Jeffersonian Republicans: The Formation of Party Organization, 1789–1801* (1957); Paul Goodman, *The Democratic Republicans of Massachusetts* (1964); John F. Hoadley, *Origins of American Political Parties, 1789–1803* (1986); Norman Risjord, *Chesapeake Politics, 1781–*

1800 (1978); Thomas P. Slaughter, *The Whiskey Rebellion: Frontier Epilogue to the American Revolution* (1986); Alfred Young, *The Democratic Republicans of New York: The Origins, 1763–1797* (1967).

Party Ideology
Joyce Appleby, *Capitalism and a New Social Order: The Republican Vision of the 1790s* (1984); Lance Banning, *The Jeffersonian Persuasion: The Evolution of a Party Ideology* (1978); Richard W. Buel, Jr., *Securing the Republic: Ideology in American Politics, 1789–1815* (1972); Drew R. McCoy, *The Elusive Republic: Political Economy in Jeffersonian America* (1980); John R. Nelson, Jr., *Liberty and Property: Political Economy and Policymaking in the New Nation, 1789–1812* (1987); Gerald Stourzh, *Alexander Hamilton and the Idea of Republican Government* (1970); John Zvesper, *Political Philosophy and Rhetoric: A Study of the Origins of Party Politics* (1977).

Constitutional Developments
Leonard Levy, *Legacy of Suppression: Freedom of Speech and Press in Early American History* (1960); Robert A. Rutland, *The Birth of the Bill of Rights, 1776–1791* (1955); Bernard Schwartz, *The Great Rights of Mankind: A History of the American Bill of Rights* (1977); James M. Smith, *Freedom's Fetters: The Alien and Sedition Laws and American Civil Liberties* (1956).

Foreign Policy
Harry Ammon, *The Genet Mission* (1973); Jerald Combs, *The Jay Treaty: Political Battleground of the Founding Fathers* (1970); Alexander DeConde, *Entangling Alliance: Politics and Diplomacy Under George Washington* (1958), and *The Quasi-War: The Politics and Diplomacy of the Undeclared War with France, 1797–1801* (1966); Felix Gilbert, *To the Farewell Address: Ideas of Early American Foreign Policy* (1961); Bradford Perkins, *The First Rapprochement: England and the United States, 1795–1805* (1955); William Stinchcombe, *The XYZ Affair* (1980); Paul A. Varg, *Foreign Policies of the Founding Fathers* (1963).

Biographies
Gay Wilson Allen and Roger Asselineau, *St. John de Crèvecoeur: The Life of an American Farmer* (1987); Irving Brant, *James Madison: Father of the Constitution, 1787–1800* (1950); Jacob E. Cooke, *Alexander Hamilton* (1982); Marcus Cunliffe, *George Washington: Man and Monument* (1958); John C. Miller, *Alexander Hamilton: Portrait in Paradox* (1959); Merrill Peterson, *Thomas Jefferson and the New Nation* (1970); Page Smith, *John Adams* (1962); Garry Wills, *Cincinnatus: George Washington and the Enlightenment* (1984).

CHAPTER 9

General Histories
Richard Hofstadter, *The Idea of a Party System: The Rise of Legitimate Opposition in the United States, 1780–1840* (1969); George Dangerfield, *The Era of Good Feelings* (1952), and *The Awakening of American Nationalism, 1815–1828* (1965); Marshall Smelser, *The Democratic Republic, 1801–1815* (1968); James Sterling Young, *The Washington Community, 1800–1828* (1966).

Biographies
Harry Ammon, *James Monroe: The Quest for National Identity* (1979); Leonard Baker, *John Marshall: A Life in Law* (1974); Samuel F. Bemis, *John Quincy Adams and the Foundations of American Foreign Policy* (1949); Noble E. Cunningham, Jr., *In Pursuit of Reason: The Life of Thomas Jefferson* (1987); Ralph Ketcham, *James Madison: A Biography* (1971); Dumas Malone, *Jefferson the President: First Term, 1801–1805* (1970), and *Jefferson the President: Second Term, 1805–1809* (1974); Drew R. McCoy, *The Last of the Fathers: James Madison and the Republican Legacy* (1989); Merrill Peterson, *Thomas Jefferson and the New Nation: A Biography* (1970); Robert Remini, *Andrew Jackson and the Course of American Empire, 1767–1821* (1977).

Jeffersonians in Power
Alexander Balinky, *Albert Gallatin: Fiscal Theories and Policy* (1958); James Banner, *To the Hartford Convention: The Federalists and the Origins of Party Politics in the Early Republic, 1789–1815* (1970); Noble E. Cunningham, Jr., *The Jeffersonian Republicans in Power: Party Operations, 1801–1809* (1963), and *The Process of Government Under Jefferson* (1978); David Hackett Fischer, *The Revolution of American Conservatism: The Federalist Party in the Era of Jeffersonian Democracy* (1965); Paul Goodman, *The Democratic Republicans of Massachusetts* (1964); Linda K. Kerber, *Federalists in Dissent: Imagery and Ideology in Jeffersonian America* (1970); Drew R. McCoy, *The Elusive Republic: Political Economy in Jeffersonian America* (1980); Norman K. Risjord, *The Old Republicans: Southern Conservatism in the Age of Jefferson* (1965); Howard Rock, *Artisans of the New Republic: The Tradesman of New York City in the Age of Thomas Jefferson* (1979).

Indian Affairs and Western Expansion
John Boles, *The Great Revival in the South, 1787–1805* (1972); R. David Edmunds, *The Shawnee Prophet* (1983), and *Tecumseh and the Quest for Indian Leadership* (1984); Reginald Horsman, *Expansion and American Indian Policy, 1783–1812* (1967), and *The Frontier in the Formative Years, 1783–1815* (1970); Donald Jackson, *Thomas Jefferson and the Stony Mountains: Exploring the West from Monticello* (1979); Malcolm J. Rohrbough, *The Trans-Appalachian Frontier: Peoples, Societies, and Institutions, 1775–1850* (1978); Henry Savage, Jr., *Discovering America, 1700–1875* (1979); Bernard W. Sheehan, *Seeds of Extinction: Jeffersonian Philanthropy and the American Indians* (1973).

The Judiciary
Richard E. Ellis, *The Jeffersonian Crisis: Courts and Politics in the Early Republic* (1971); Robert K. Faulkner, *The Jurisprudence of John Marshall* (1968); Morton J. Horowitz, *The Transformation of American Law, 1780–1860* (1977); R. K. Newmyer, *The Supreme Court Under Marshall and Taney* (1968).

Foreign Affairs and the War of 1812
Roger H. Brown, *The Republic in Peril: 1812* (1964); Harry L. Coles, *The War of 1812* (1965); Alexander DeConde, *This Affair of Louisiana* (1976); Reginald Horsman, *The War of 1812* (1969); Ernest R. May, *The Making of the Monroe Doctrine* (1976); Bradford Perkins, *First Rapprochement: England and the United*

States, 1795–1805 (1955), and *Prologue to War: England and the United States, 1805–1812* (1961); Robert A. Rutland, *Madison's Alternatives: The Jeffersonian Republicans and the Coming of War, 1805–1812* (1975); J. C. A. Stagg, *Mr. Madison's War: Politics, Diplomacy, and Warfare in the Early Republic, 1783–1830* (1983).

CHAPTER 10

General Histories
W. Elliot Brownlee, *Dynamics of Ascent: A History of the American Economy* (1974); Stuart Bruchey, *The Roots of American Economic Growth, 1607–1861* (1965); Douglass C. North, *The Economic Growth of the United States, 1790–1860* (1961).

Transportation
Carter Goodrich, *Government Promotion of American Canals and Railroads* (1960); Erik F. Haites et al., *Western River Transportation: The Era of Early Internal Development, 1810–1860* (1975); Louis C. Hunter, *Steamboats on the Western Rivers: An Economic and Technological History* (1949); Philip D. Jordan, *The National Road* (1948); Harry N. Scheiber, *Ohio Canal Era: A Case Study of Government and the Economy, 1820–1861* (1969); Ronald E. Shaw, *Erie Water West: A History of the Erie Canal* (1966); George R. Taylor, *The Transportation Revolution, 1815–1860* (1951).

Industrialization
Alfred D. Chandler, Jr., *The Visible Hand: Managerial Revolution in American Business* (1977); Thomas C. Cochran, *Frontiers of Change: Early Industrialism in America* (1981); Robert F. Dalzell, Jr., *Enterprising Elite: The Boston Associates and the World They Made* (1987); Constance M. Green, *Eli Whitney and the Birth of American Technology* (1956); David J. Jeremy, *Transatlantic Industrial Revolution: The Diffusion of Textile Technology Between Britain and America, 1790–1830* (1981); Nathan Rosenberg, *Technology and American Economic Growth* (1972); Peter Temin, *Iron and Steel in Nineteenth Century America* (1964); Caroline F. Ware, *The Early New England Cotton Manufacture* (1931).

Agriculture
Percy W. Bidwell and John Falconer, *History of Agriculture in the Northern United States* (1925); Clarence Danhof, *Changes in Agriculture: The Northern United States, 1820–1870* (1969); Paul W. Gates, *The Farmer's Age: Agriculture, 1815–1860* (1960); Lewis C. Gray, *History of Agriculture in the Southern United States* (1933).

Workers and Community Studies
Stuart M. Blumin, *The Urban Threshold: Growth and Change in a Nineteenth-Century American Community* (1976); Thomas Dublin, *Women at Work: The Transformation of Work and Community in Lowell, Massachusetts, 1826–1860* (1979); Paul G. Faler, *Mechanics and Manufacturers in the Early Industrial Revolution: Lynn, Massachusetts, 1780–1860* (1981); Bruce Laurie, *Working People of Philadelphia, 1800–1850* (1980), and *Artisans into Workers: Labor in Nineteenth-Century America* (1989); Brian C. Mitchell, *The Paddy Camps: The Irish of Lowell, 1821–61* (1988); Jonathan Prude, *The Coming of Industrial Order: Town and Factory Life in Rural Massachusetts, 1810–1860* (1983); W. J. Rorabaugh, *The Craft Apprentice: From Franklin to the Machine Age in America* (1986); Steven J. Ross, *Workers on the Edge: Work, Leisure, and Politics in Industrializing Cincinnati, 1788–1890* (1985); Christine Stansell, *City of Women: Sex and Class in New York, 1789–1860* (1986); Sean Wilentz, *Chants Democratic: New York City and the Rise of the American Working Class, 1788–1850* (1984).

Society and Values
Daniel J. Boorstin, *The Americans: The National Experience* (1965); Michel Chevalier, *Society, Manners and Politics in the United States* (1839, reprinted 1961); Russel B. Nye, *Society and Culture in America, 1830–1860* (1974); Edward Pessen, *Jacksonian America: Society, Personality, and Politics*, rev. ed. (1978), and *Riches, Class, and Power Before the Civil War* (1973); Alexis de Tocqueville, *Democracy in America* (1945 ed.).

Land and the West
John Mack Faragher, *Sugar Creek: Life on the Illinois Prairie* (1986); Roy M. Robbins, *Our Landed Heritage: The Public Domain* (1942); Malcolm J. Rohrbough, *The Land Office Business: The Settlement and Administration of American Public Lands, 1789–1837* (1968); Dale Van Every, *The Final Challenge: The American Frontier, 1804–1845* (1964); Richard C. Wade, *The Urban Frontier: The Rise of Western Cities, 1790–1840* (1973); David J. Wishart, *The Fur Trade of the American West, 1817–1840* (1979).

Politics and Law
George Dangerfield, *The Awakening of American Nationalism, 1815–1828* (1965); Robert K. Faulkner, *The Jurisprudence of John Marshall* (1968); Morton J. Horwitz, *The Transformation of American Law, 1780–1860* (1977); Glover Moore, *The Missouri Controversy, 1819–1821* (1953); R. Kent Newmyer, *The Supreme Court Under Marshall and Taney* (1968); M. N. Rothbard, *The Panic of 1819: Reactions and Policies* (1962); Charles Sydnor, *The Development of Southern Sectionalism, 1819–1848* (1948).

CHAPTER 11

General Histories
George Dangerfield, *The Awakening of American Nationalism, 1815–1828* (1965); Edward Pessen, *Jacksonian America: Society, Personality, and Politics*, rev. ed. (1978); Arthur Schlesinger, Jr., *The Age of Jackson* (1945); Glyndon G. Van Deusen, *The Jacksonian Era, 1828–1845* (1959).

Biographies
Samuel F. Bemis, *John Quincy Adams and the Union* (1956); Gerald M. Capers, *John C. Calhoun, Opportunist* (1960); Donald Cole, *Martin Van Buren and the American Political System* (1984); Richard N. Current, *Daniel Webster and the Rise of National Conservativism* (1955); Thomas P. Govan, *Nicholas Biddle: Nationalist and Public Banker* (1959); John Niven, *John C. Calhoun and the Price of Union: A Biography* (1988), and *Martin Van Buren: The Romantic Age of American Politics* (1983); Merrill D. Peterson, *The Great Triumvirate: Webster, Clay, and Calhoun* (1987); Robert V. Remini,

Andrew Jackson and the Course of American Freedom, 1822–1832 (1981), and *Andrew Jackson and the Course of American Democracy, 1833–1845* (1984); Glyndon G. Van Deusen, *The Life of Henry Clay* (1937); Charles W. Wiltse, *John C. Calhoun, Nullifier, 1829–1839* (1949).

Society and Values
Michel Chevalier, *Society, Manners, and Politics in the United States* (1961); Charles Dickens, *American Notes for General Circulation* (1842, reprinted 1972); Francis J. Grund, *Aristocracy in America* (1839, reprinted 1959); Harriet Martineau, *Society in America* (1837); Douglas T. Miller, *Jacksonian Aristocracy: Class and Democracy in New York, 1830–1860* (1967); Russel B. Nye, *Society and Culture in America, 1830–1860* (1960); Edward Pessen, *Riches, Class, and Power Before the Civil War* (1973); Alexis de Tocqueville, *Democracy in America* (1945); Frances Trollope, *Domestic Manners of the Americans* (1832, reprinted 1984); John William Ward, *Andrew Jackson: Symbol for an Age* (1955).

The Emergence of Democracy
James S. Chase, *Emergence of the Presidential Nominating Convention, 1789–1832* (1973); Richard Hofstadter, *The Idea of a Party System: The Rise of Legitimate Opposition in the United States, 1780–1840* (1969); Richard P. McCormick, *The Presidential Game: The Origins of American Presidential Politics* (1982); Chilton Williamson, *American Suffrage from Property to Democracy, 1760–1860* (1960).

The Jacksonian Party System
Lee Benson, *The Concept of Jacksonian Democracy: New York as a Test Case* (1961); James C. Curtis, *The Fox at Bay: Martin Van Buren and the Presidency, 1837–1841* (1970); Paul Goodman, *Towards a Christian Republic: Antimasonry and the Great Transition in New England, 1826–1836* (1988); Robert G. Gunderson, *The Log Cabin Campaign* (1957); Mary W. M. Hargreaves, *The Presidency of John Quincy Adams* (1985); Daniel Walker Howe, *The Political Culture of the American Whigs* (1979); Lawrence Frederick Kohl, *The Politics of Individualism: Parties and the American Character in the Jacksonian Era* (1988); Richard B. Latner, *the Presidency of Andrew Jackson: White House Politics, 1829–1837* (1979); Richard P. McCormick, *The Second American Party System: Party Formation in the Jacksonian Era* (1966); Marvin Meyers, *The Jacksonian Persuasion: Politics and Belief* (1957); Robert Remini, *The Election of Andrew Jackson* (1963).

Banking and the Economy
Bray Hammond, *Banks and Politics in America from the Revolution to the Civil War* (1957); John M. McFaul, *The Politics of Jacksonian Finance* (1972); Robert Remini, *Andrew Jackson and the Bank War* (1967); William G. Shade, *Banks or No Banks: The Money Issue in Western Politics, 1832–1865* (1972); James Roger Sharp, *The Jacksonians Versus the Banks: Politics in the States After the Panic of 1837* (1970); Peter Temin, *The Jacksonian Economy* (1969).

Nullification
Richard Ellis, *The Union at Risk: Jacksonian Democracy, States' Rights and the Nullification Crisis* (1987); William W. Freehling, *Prelude to Civil War: The Nullification Controversy in South Carolina* (1966); Merrill D. Peterson, *Olive Branch and Sword: The Compromise of 1833* (1982); Charles S. Sydnor, *The Development of Southern Sectionalism, 1819–1848* (1948).

Indian Removal
Arthur H. DeRosier, Jr., *The Removal of the Choctaw Indians* (1970); Michael D. Green, *The Politics of Indian Removal: Creek Government and Society in Crisis* (1982); John K. Mahon, *History of the Second Seminole War, 1835–1842* (1967); William G. McLoughlin, *Cherokee Renascence in the New Republic* (1986); Francis P. Prucha, *American Indian Policy in the Formative Years* (1962); Ronald N. Satz, *American Indian Policy in the Jacksonian Era* (1975).

CHAPTER 12

General Histories
Perry Miller, *The Life of the Mind in America: From the Revolution to the Civil War* (1966); Russel B. Nye, *Society and Culture in America, 1830–1860* (1974); Alice Tyler, *Freedom's Ferment: Phases of American Social History from the Colonial Period to the Outbreak of the Civil War* (1944); Ronald G. Walters, *American Reformers, 1815–1860* (1978).

Revivalism
Whitney R. Cross, *The Burned-Over District: The Social and Intellectual History of Enthusiastic Religion in Western New York, 1800–1850* (1950); Paul Johnson, *A Shopkeeper's Millennium: Society and Revivals in Rochester, New York, 1815–1837* (1978); William G. McLoughlin, *Modern Revivalism: Charles Grandison Finney to Billy Graham* (1959).

Women's Sphere and Feminism
Nancy F. Cott, *The Bonds of Womanhood: "Woman's Sphere" in New England, 1780–1835* (1977); Carl Degler, *At Odds: Women and the Family in America from the Revolution to the Present* (1980); Ann Douglas, *The Feminization of American Culture* (1977); Ellen C. DuBois, *Feminism and Suffrage: The Emergence of an Independent Women's Movement in America, 1848–1869* (1978); Keith E. Melder, *Beginnings of Sisterhood: The American Women's Rights Movement, 1800–1850* (1977); James Reed, *From Private Vice to Public Virtue: The Birth Control Movement in America* (1978); Mary P. Ryan, *Cradle of the Middle Class: The Family in Oneida County, New York, 1790–1865* (1981); Nancy Woloch, *Women and the American Experience* (1984).

American Romanticism
Paul F. Boller, Jr., *American Transcendentalism, 1830–1860: An Intellectual Inquiry* (1974); F. O. Matthiessen, *American Renaissance: Art and Expression in the Age of Emerson and Whitman* (1941); Anne C. Rose, *Transcendentalism as a Social Movement, 1830–1850* (1981).

Utopian Communities
Arthur Bestor, *Backwoods Utopias: The Sectarian and Owenite Phases of Communitarian Socialism in America, 1663–1829* (1950); Maren L. Carden, *Oneida: Utopian Community to Modern Corporation* (1971); Henri Destroche, *The American Shakers from Neo-Christianity to Pre-Socialism* (1971); Lawrence Foster, *Religion*

and Sexuality: Three American Communal Experiments of the Nineteenth Century (1981); J. F. C. Harrison, Quest for the New Moral World: Robert Owen and the Owenites in Britain and America (1969); Louis Kern, An Ordered Love: Sex Roles and Sexuality in Victorian Utopias (1981).

Reform Movements
Lawrence A. Cremin, American Education: The National Experience (1980); Ellen Dwyer, Homes for the Mad: Life Inside Two Nineteenth-Century Asylums (1987); Barbara Leslie Epstein, The Politics of Domesticity: Women, Evangelism, and Temperance in Nineteenth-Century America (1981); Carl F. Kaestle, Pillars of the Republic: Common Schools and American Society, 1780–1860 (1983); Stephen Nissenbaum, Sex, Diet, and Debility in Jacksonian America: Sylvester Graham and Health Reform (1980); W. J. Rorabaugh, The Alcoholic Republic: An American Tradition (1979); David Rothman, The Discovery of the Asylum: Social Order and Disorder in the New Republic (1971); Ian R. Tyrrell, Sobering Up: From Temperance to Prohibition in Antebellum America, 1800–1860 (1979); Rush Welter, Popular Education and Democratic Thought in America (1962).

Abolitionism
R. J. M. Blackett, Building an Antislavery Wall: Black Americans in the Abolitionist Movement, 1830–1860 (1983); Aileen Kraditor, Means and Ends in American Abolitionism: Garrison and His Critics on Strategy and Tactics, 1834–1850 (1967); Donald G. Mathews, Slavery and Methodism (1965); John R. McKivigan, The War Against Proslavery Religion: Abolitionism and the Northern Churches (1984); Russel B. Nye, Fettered Freedom: Civil Liberties and the Slavery Controversy, 1830–1860, rev. ed. (1963); Benjamin Quarles, Black Abolitionists (1969); Leonard Richards, "Gentlemen of Property and Standing": Anti-Abolition Mobs in Jacksonian America (1970); James B. Stewart, Holy Warriors: The Abolitionists and American Slavery (1976).

Biographies
Robert Abzug, Passionate Liberator: Theodore Dwight Weld and the Dilemma of Reform (1980); Lois Banner, Elizabeth Cady Stanton: A Radical for Woman's Rights (1980); Betty Fladeland, James Gillespie Birney: Slaveholder to Abolitionist (1955); Keith J. Hardman, Charles Grandison Finney, 1792–1875: Revivalist and Reformer (1987); Nathan Huggins, Slave and Citizen: The Life of Frederick Douglass (1980); Gerda Lerner, The Grimké Sisters of South Carolina: Rebels Against Slavery (1967); Katherine Kish Sklar, Catharine Beecher: A Study in American Domesticity (1973); James Brewer Stewart, Wendell Phillips: Liberty's Hero (1986); John L. Thomas, The Liberator: William Lloyd Garrison (1963); Robert D. Thomas, The Man Who Would Be Perfect: John Humphrey Noyes and the Utopian Impulse (1977); Bertram Wyatt-Brown, Lewis Tappan and the Evangelical War Against Slavery (1969).

CHAPTER 13

General Histories
Monroe Billington, The American South (1971); Clement Eaton, A History of the Old South, 3d ed. (1975); Charles S. Sydnor, The Development of Southern Sectionalism, 1819–1848 (1948).

Southern Society
Ira Berlin, Slaves Without Masters: The Free Negro in the Antebellum South (1976); Dickson D. Bruce, Jr., Violence and Culture in the Antebellum South (1979); Everett Dick, The Dixie Frontier: A Social History of the Southern Frontier from the First Transmontane Beginnings to the Civil War (1948); Clement Eaton, The Growth of the Southern Civilization, 1790–1860 (1961); Drew Gilpin Faust, James Henry Hammond and the South: A Design for Mastery (1967); John Hope Franklin, The Militant South, 1800–1861 (1956); Lewis C. Gray, History of Agriculture in the Southern United States to 1860 (1933); J. William Harris, Plain Folk and Gentry in a Slave Society: White Liberty and Black Slavery in Augusta's Hinterlands (1985); Michael P. Johnson and James L. Roark, Black Masters: A Free Family of Color in the Old South (1984); Donald G. Mathews, Religion in the Old South (1977); John Hebron Moore, The Emergence of the Cotton Kingdom in the Old Southwest: Mississippi, 1770–1860 (1988); James Oakes, The Ruling Race: A History of American Slaveholders (1982); Frederick Law Olmsted, The Cotton Kingdom (1861, reprinted 1984); Frank L. Owsley, Plain Folk of the Old South (1949); Theodore Rosengarten, Tombee: Portrait of a Cotton Planter (1986); Steven M. Stowe, Intimacy and Power in the Old South: Ritual in the Lives of the Planters (1987); Gavin Wright, The Political Economy of the Cotton South: Households, Markets, and Wealth in the Nineteenth Century (1978); Bertram Wyatt-Brown, Honor and Violence in the Old South (1986).

Southern Women
Jane Turner Censer, North Carolina Planters and Their Children, 1800–1860 (1984); Catherine Clinton, The Plantation Mistress: Woman's World in the Old South (1983); Elizabeth Fox-Genovese, Within the Plantation Household: Black and White Women of the Old South (1988); Frances Anne Kemble, Journal of the Residence on a Georgian Plantation in 1838–1839 (1863, reprinted 1961); Suzanne Lebsock, Free Women of Petersburg: Status and Culture in a Southern Town, 1784–1860 (1984); Anne Firor Scott, The Southern Lady: From Pedestal to Politics, 1830–1930 (1970); Deborah G. White, Ar'n't I a Woman? Female Slaves in the Plantation South (1985); C. Vann Woodward, ed., Mary Chesnut's Civil War (1981).

Slavery
Carl N. Degler, Neither Black Nor White: Slavery and Race Relations in Brazil and the United States (1971); Ulrich B. Phillips, American Negro Slavery (1918), and Life and Labor in the Old South (1929); Kenneth M. Stampp, The Peculiar Institution: Slavery in the Antebellum South (1956); Robert S. Starobin, Industrial Slavery in the Old South (1970); William L. Van Deburg, The Slave Drivers: Black Agricultural Labor Supervisors in the Antebellum South (New York, 1988); Richard C. Wade, Slavery in the Cities (1964).

Slave Culture
John W. Blassingame, The Slave Community: Plantation Life in the Ante-Bellum South, rev. ed. (1979); Frederick Douglass, My Bondage and My Freedom (1855, reprint 1969); Eugene D. Genovese, Roll, Jordan, Roll: The World the Slaves Made (1974); Herbert G. Gutman, The Black Family in Slavery and Freedom, 1750–1925 (1976); Charles Joyner, Down by the Riverside: A South

Carolina Slave Community (1984); Lawrence Levine, Black Culture and Black Consciousness: Afro-American Folk Thought from Slavery to Freedom (1977); Albert J. Raboteau, Slave Religion: The "Invisible Institution" in the Antebellum South (1978); Sterling Stuckey, Slave Culture: Nationalist Theory and the Foundations of Black America (1987).

The Defense of Slavery
William J. Cooper, Jr., The South and the Politics of Slavery, 1828–1856 (1978); Clement Eaton, Freedom of Thought in the Old South (1940); Drew Gilpin Faust, A Sacred Circle: The Dilemma of the Intellectual in the Old South (1977); George M. Fredrickson, The Black Image in the White Mind: The Debate on Afro-American Character and Destiny, 1817–1914 (1971); Alison Good-year Freehling, Drift Toward Dissolution: The Virginia Slavery Debate of 1831–1832 (1982); Kenneth S. Green-berg, Masters and Statesmen: The Political Culture of American Slavery (1985).

CHAPTER 14

General Histories
Ray A. Billington, The Far Western Frontier, 1830–1860 (1956); Ray A Billington and Martin Ridge, Westward Expansion, 5th ed. (1982); Frederick Merk, History of the Westward Movement (1978).

American Expansionism
Bernard De Voto, The Year of Decision: 1846 (1943); John Mack Faragher, Women and Men on the Overland Trail (1979); Norman A. Graebner, Empire on the Pacific: A Study of American Continental Expansionism (1955); Thomas R. Hietala, Manifest Design: Anxious Aggrandizement in Late Jacksonian America (1985); Reginald Horsman, Race and Manifest Destiny: The Origins of American Racial Anglo-Saxonism (1981); Frederick Merk, Manifest Destiny and Mission in American History (1963), The Monroe Doctrine and American Expansionism, 1843–1849 (1966), and The Oregon Question: Essays in Anglo-American Diplomacy and Politics (1967); John D. Unruh, Jr., The Plains Across: The Overland Emigrants and the Trans-Mississippi West, 1840–60 (1979).

Societies in the West
Leonard J. Arrington, Great Basin Kingdom: An Economic History of the Latter-Day Saints (1958); Leonard J. Arrington and Davis Bitton, The Mormon Experience: A History of the Latter-Day Saints (1979); Gunther Barth, Instant Cities: Urbanization and the Rise of San Francisco and Denver (1975); William C. Binkley, The Texas Revolution (1952); John W. Caughey, Gold is the Cornerstone (1948); Malcolm Clark, Jr., Eden Seekers: The Settlement of Oregon, 1812–1862 (1981); Robert F. Heizer and Alan J. Almquist, The Other Californians: Prejudice and Discrimination under Spain, Mexico, and the United States to 1920 (1971); Donald D. Jackson, Gold Dust (1980); Julie Roy Jeffrey, Frontier Women: The Trans-Mississippi West, 1840–1860 (1979); Dorothy O. Johansen and Charles M. Gates, Empire on the Columbia: A History of the Pacific Northwest, 2d ed. (1967); Sandra L. Myres, Westering Women and the Frontier Experience, 1800–1915 (1982); Rodman Paul, California Gold: The Beginning of Mining in the Far

West (1947); Leonard Pitt, The Decline of the Californios: A Social History of the Spanish-Speaking Californians, 1846–1890 (1966); David J. Weber, The Mexican Frontier, 1821–1846: The American Southwest Under Mexico (1982).

Expansion and the Party System
Paul B. Bergeron, The Presidency of James K. Polk (1987); William R. Brock, Parties and Political Conscience: American Dilemmas, 1840–1850 (1979); Frederick Merk, Slavery and the Annexation of Texas (1972); Robert J. Morgan, A Whig Embattled: The Presidency Under John Tyler (1954); James C. N. Paul, Rift in the Democracy (1961); George R. Poage, Henry Clay and the Whig Party (1936).

The War with Mexico
K. Jack Bauer, The Mexican War, 1846–1848 (1974); Seymour V. Connor and Odie B. Faulk, North America Divided: The Mexican War, 1846–1848 (1971); Neal Harlow, California Conquered: The Annexation of a Mexican Province, 1846–1850 (1982); Robert W. Johannsen, To the Halls of the Montezumas: The Mexican War in the American Imagination (1985); David M. Pletcher, The Diplomacy of Annexation: Texas, Oregon, and the Mexican War (1973); John H. Schroeder, Mr. Polk's War: American Opposition and Dissent, 1846–1848 (1973).

The Sectional Crisis and the Expansion of Slavery
John Barnwell, Love of Order: South Carolina's First Secession Crisis (1982); Eugene H. Berwanger, The Frontier Against Slavery: Western Anti-Negro Prejudice and the Slavery Extension Controversy (1967); Frederick J. Blue, The Free Soilers: Third Party Politics, 1848–1854 (1973); William J. Cooper, Jr., The South and the Politics of Slavery, 1828–1856 (1978); Holman Hamilton, Prologue to Conflict: The Crisis and Compromise of 1850 (1964); Michael F. Holt, The Political Crisis of the 1850s (1978); Chaplain W. Morrison, Democratic Politics and Sectionalism: The Wilmot Proviso Controversy (1967); Allan Nevins, Ordeal of the Union (1947); David M. Potter, The Impending Crisis, 1848–1861 (1976); Joseph G. Rayback, Free Soil: The Election of 1848 (1970); Richard H. Sewell, Ballots for Freedom: Antislavery Politics in the United States, 1837–1860 (1976).

Biographies
Leonard J. Arrington, Brigham Young: American Moses (1985); K. Jack Bauer, Zachary Taylor: Soldier, Planter, Statesman of the Old Southwest (1985); Robert F. Dalzell, Daniel Webster and the Trial of American Nationalism, 1843–1852 (1972); Holman Hamilton, Zachary Taylor: Soldier in the White House (1951); Robert W. Johannsen, Stephen A. Douglas (1973); Charles G. Sellers, Jr., James K. Polk: Continentalist, 1843–1846 (1966); Glyndon G. Van Deusen, The Life of Henry Clay (1937).

CHAPTER 15

General Histories
Avery Craven, The Coming of the Civil War, 2d ed. rev. (1957), and The Growth of Southern Nationalism, 1848–1861 (1953); Allan Nevins, Ordeal of the Union (1947), and The Emergence of Lincoln (1950); David M. Potter, The Impending Crisis, 1848–1861 (1976).

Biographies
David Donald, *Charles Sumner and the Coming of the Civil War* (1960); Don E. Fehrenbacher, *Prelude to Greatness: Lincoln in the 1850s* (1962); Robert W. Johannsen, *Stephen A. Douglas* (1973); Philip Shriver Klein, *President James Buchanan* (1962); Roy F. Nichols, *Franklin Pierce: Young Hickory of the Granite Hills*, 2d ed. rev. (1958); Stephen B. Oates, *To Purge This Land With Blood: A Biography of John Brown* (1970), and *With Malice Toward None: A Life of Abraham Lincoln* (1977); Benjamin P. Thomas, *Abraham Lincoln* (1952).

Economic Development
Alfred D. Chandler, ed., *The Railroads: The Nation's First Big Business* (1965); Albert Fishlow, *American Railroads and the Transformation of the Antebellum Economy* (1965); Paul W. Gates, *The Farmer's Age: Agriculture, 1815–1860* (1960); James Huston, *The Panic of 1857 and the Coming of the Civil War* (1987); Douglass C. North, *The Economic Growth of the United States, 1790–1860* (1961); John F. Stover, *Iron Road to the West: American Railroads in the 1850s* (1978).

Immigration and Nativism
Ray A. Billington, *The Protestant Crusade, 1800–1860* (1938); John P. Dolan, *The Immigrant Church: New York's Irish and German Catholics, 1815–1865* (1975); Robert Ernst, *Immigrant Life in New York City, 1825–1863* (1949); Oscar Handlin, *Boston's Immigrants: A Study of Acculturation*, rev. ed. (1959); Michael F. Holt, "The Antimasonic and Know Nothing Parties," in Arthur M. Schlesinger, Jr., ed., *History of U.S. Political Parties* (1973), vol. 1, 575-737; W. Darrell Overdyke, *The Know-Nothing Party in the South* (1950); Philip D. Taylor, *The Distant Magnet: European Emigration to the U.S.A.* (1971).

Southern Sectionalism and Nationalism
Fred Bateman and Thomas Weiss, *A Deplorable Scarcity: The Failure of Industrialization in the Slave Economy* (1981); Charles H. Brown, *Agents for Manifest Destiny: The Lives and Times of the Filibusterers* (1979); William J. Cooper, Jr., *The South and the Politics of Slavery, 1828–1856* (1978); Robert E. May, *The Southern Dream of a Caribbean Empire, 1854–1861* (1973); John McCardell, *The Idea of a Southern Nation: Southern Nationalists and Southern Nationalism, 1830–1860* (1979); William R. Taylor, *Cavalier and Yankee: The Old South and American National Character* (1961).

Sectionalism and National Politics
Eugene H. Berwanger, *The Frontier Against Slavery: Western Anti-Negro Prejudice and the Slavery Extension Controversy* (1967); Don E. Fehrenbacher, *Slavery, Law, and Politics: The Dred Scott Case in Historical Perspective* (1981); Eric Foner, *Free Soil, Free Labor, Free Men: The Ideology of the Republican Party before the Civil War* (1970); Paul W. Gates, *Fifty Million Acres: Conflict Over Kansas Land Policy, 1854–1890* (1954); William E. Gienapp, *The Origins of the Republican Party, 1852–1856* (1987); Michael F. Holt, *The Political Crisis of the 1850s* (1978); Robert W. Johannsen, ed., *The Lincoln-Douglas Debates* (1965); Roy F. Nichols, *The Disruption of American Democracy* (1948); James A. Rawley, *Race and Politics: "Bleeding Kansas" and the*

Coming of the Civil War (1969); Richard H. Sewell, *Ballots for Freedom: Antislavery Politics in the United States, 1837–1860* (1976); Mark W. Summers, *The Plundering Generation: Corruption and the Crisis of the Union, 1849–1861* (1987).

Secession and the Outbreak of War
William L. Barney, *The Secessionist Impulse: Alabama and Mississippi in 1860* (1974); Steven A. Channing, *Crisis of Fear: Secession in South Carolina* (1974); Daniel W. Crofts, *Reluctant Confederates: Upper South Unionists in the Secession Crisis* (1989); Richard N. Current, *Lincoln and the First Shot* (1963); George N. Knoles, ed., *The Crisis of the Union, 1860–1861* (1965); David M. Potter, *Lincoln and His Party in the Secession Crisis* (1942); Kenneth M. Stampp, *And the War Came: The North and the Secession Crisis, 1860–1861* (1950); Ralph Wooster, *The Secession Conventions of the South* (1862).

The Causes of the Civil War
David M. Potter, *The South and the Sectional Conflict* (1969); Thomas J. Pressly, *Americans Interpret Their Civil War* (1954); Kenneth M. Stampp, ed., *The Causes of the Civil War*, rev. ed. (1974).

CHAPTER 16

General Histories
Richard E. Beringer et al., *The Elements of Confederate Defeat: Nationalism, War Aims, and Religion* (1989); David Donald, *Why the North Won the Civil War* (1960); Allan Nevins, *The War for the Union*, 4 vols. (1959–1971); James M. McPherson, *Battle Cry of Freedom* (1988); James G. Randall and David Donald, *The Civil War and Reconstruction*, 2d ed. (1961); Edmund Wilson, *Patriotic Gore: Studies in the Literature of the American Civil War* (1962).

Biographies
Bruce Catton, *Grant Moves South* (1960), and *Grant Takes Command* (1969); Douglas Southall Freeman, *R. E. Lee* (1934–1935); Lloyd Lewis, *Sherman: Fighting Prophet* (1932); William S. McFeely, *Grant: A Biography* (1981); Stephen B. Oates, *With Malice Toward None: The Life of Abraham Lincoln* (1977); James G. Randall and Richard N. Current, *Lincoln the President* (1945–1955); Hudson Strode, *Jefferson Davis*, 3 vols. (1955–1964); Benjamin P. Thomas, *Abraham Lincoln* (1952); Benjamin P. Thomas and Harold Hyman, *Stanton: The Life and Times of Lincoln's Secretary of War* (1962); Glyndon G. Van Deusen, *Willian Henry Seward* (1967).

Military History
Bern Anderson, *By Sea and by River: The Naval History of the Civil War* (1962); Bruce Catton, *The Centennial History of the Civil War* (1961–1965); Thomas L. Connelly, *Army of the Heartland: The Army of Tennessee, 1861–1862* (1967), and *Autumn of Glory: The Army of Tennessee, 1862–1865* (1971); Thomas L. Connelly and Archer Jones, *The Politics of Command: Factions and Ideas in Confederate Strategy* (1973); Burke Davis, *Sherman's March* (1980); Herman Hattaway and Archer Jones, *How the North Won: A Military History of the Civil War* (1983); Gerald F. Linderman, *Embattled Courage: The Experience of Combat in the American*

Civil War (1987); Reid Mitchell, *Civil War Soldiers: Their Expectations and Their Experiences* (1988); Bell I. Wiley, *The Life of Johnny Reb* (1943), and *The Life of Billy Yank* (1952); T. Harry Williams, *Lincoln and His Generals* (1952).

The Confederacy
Thomas B. Alexander and Richard E. Beringer, *The Anatomy of the Confederate Congress* (1972); Curtis A. Amlund, *Federalism in the Southern Confederacy* (1966); Paul D. Escott, *After Secession: Jefferson Davis and the Failure of Confederate Nationalism* (1978); Drew Gilpin Faust, *The Creation of Confederate Nationalism: Ideology and Identity in the Civil War South* (1988); Mary Elizabeth Massey, *Refugee Life in the Confederacy* (1964); Robert M. Myers, ed., *Children of Pride: A True Story of Georgia and the Civil War* (1972); Frank L. Owsley, *State Rights in the Confederacy* (1925); Charles W. Ramsdell, *Behind the Lines in the Southern Confederacy* (1944); James L. Roark, *Masters Without Slaves: Southern Planters in the Civil War and Reconstruction* (1977); Emory M. Thomas, *The Confederate Nation, 1861–1865* (1979); Richard C. Todd, *Confederate Finance* (1954); Bell I. Wiley, *The Plain People of the Confederacy* (1943), and *The Road to Appomattox* (1956); Wilfred B. Yearns, *The Confederate Congress* (1960).

The Union
Ralph Andreano, ed., *The Economic Impact of the American Civil War* (1962); Adrian Cook, *The Armies of the Streets: The New York City Draft Riots of 1863* (1974); Leonard P. Curry, *Blueprint for Modern America: Non-Military Legislation of the First Civil War Congress* (1968); George Fredrickson, *The Inner Civil War: Northern Intellectuals and the Crisis of the Union* (1965); Paul W. Gates, *Agriculture and the Civil War* (1965); William B. Hesseltine, *Lincoln and the War Governors* (1948); Harold M. Hyman, *A More Perfect Union: The Impact of the Civil War and Reconstruction on the Constitution* (1973); Frank L. Klement, *The Copperheads in the Middle West* (1960); James H. Moorhead, *American Apocalypse: Yankee Protestants and the Civil War, 1860–1869* (1978); Philip S. Paludan, *A Covenant with Death: The Constitution, the Law, and Equality in the Civil War Era* (1975), and *"A People's Contest": The Union and Civil War, 1861–1865* (1988); James A. Rawley, *The Politics of Union: Northern Politics During the Civil War* (1974); Joel H. Silbey, *A Respectable Minority: The Democratic Party in the Civil War Era* (1977); George Winston Smith and Charles Burnet Judah, *Life in the North During the Civil War* (1966); Hans L. Trefousse, *The Radical Republicans: Lincoln's Vanguard for Racial Justice* (1969).

Women and the Civil War
Mary Elizabeth Massey, *Bonnet Brigades: American Women and the Civil War* (1966); George C. Rable, *Civil Wars: Women and the Crisis of Southern Nationalism* (1989); C. Vann Woodward, ed., *Mary Chesnut's Civil War* (1981); Agatha Young, *Women and the Crisis: Women of the North in the Civil War* (1959).

Emancipation and the Black Experience
Dudley Cornish, *The Sable Arm: Negro Troops in the Union Army, 1861–1865* (1956); LaWanda Cox, *Lincoln and Black Freedom: A Study in Presidential Leadership* (1981); Barbara Jeanne Fields, *Slavery and Freedom on the Middle Ground: Maryland During the Nineteenth Century* (1985); John Hope Franklin, *The Emancipation Proclamation* (1963); Louis Gerteis, *From Contraband to Freedman: Federal Policy Toward Southern Blacks, 1861–1865* (1973); Leon Litwack, *Been in the Storm So Long: The Aftermath of Slavery* (1979); James M. McPherson, *The Struggle for Equality: Abolitionists and the Negro in the Civil War and Reconstruction* (1964); Clarence L. Mohr, *On the Threshold of Freedom: Masters and Slaves in Civil War Georgia* (1986); Willie Lee Rose, *Rehearsal for Reconstruction: The Port Royal Experiment* (1964); V. Jacque Voegli, *Free but Not Equal: The Midwest and the Negro During the Civil War* (1967).

Diplomacy
David P. Crook, *Diplomacy During the American Civil War* (1975); Norman Ferris, *The Trent Affair: A Diplomatic Crisis* (1977); Brian Jenkins, *Britain and the War for the Union* (1974); Frank L. Owsley, *King Cotton Diplomacy*, rev. ed. (1959).

CHAPTER 17

General Histories
Eric Foner, *Reconstruction: America's Unfinished Revolution, 1863–1877* (1988); James McPherson, *Ordeal by Fire: The Civil War and Reconstruction* (1982); James G. Randall and David Donald, *The Civil War and Reconstruction*, 2d ed. (1961); Kenneth M. Stampp, *The Era of Reconstruction, 1865–1877* (1965).

Biographies
Fawn M. Brodie, *Thaddeus Stevens: Scourge of the South* (1959); David Donald, *Charles Sumner and the Rights of Man* (1970); William S. McFeely, *Yankee Stepfather: General O. O. Howard and the Freedmen* (1968), and *Grant: A Biography* (1981).

National Politics
Richard H. Abbott, *The Republican Party and the South, 1855–1877: The First Southern Strategy* (1986); Herman Belz, *Emancipation and Equal Rights: Politics and Constitutionalism in the Civil War Era* (1978); Michael Les Benedict, *A Compromise of Principle: Congressional Republicans and Reconstruction* (1974), and *The Impeachment and Trial of Andrew Johnson* (1973); W. R. Brock, *An American Crisis: Congress and Reconstruction, 1865–1867* (1963); John Cox and LaWanda Cox, *Politics, Principles, and Prejudice, 1865–1866* (1963); Eric L. McKitrick, *Andrew Johnson and Reconstruction* (1966); James M. McPherson, *The Struggle for Equality: Abolitionists and the Negro in the Civil War and Reconstruction* (1964); John G. Sproat, *"The Best Men": Liberal Reformers in the Gilded Age* (1968); Hans L. Trefousse, *The Radical Republicans: Lincoln's Vanguard for Racial Justice* (1969).

Reconstruction and the Constitution
William Gillette, *The Right to Vote: Politics and the Passage of the Fifteenth Amendment* (1965); Harold M. Hyman, *A More Perfect Union: The Impact of the Civil War and Reconstruction on the Constitution* (1973); Joseph James, *The Framing of the Fourteenth Amendment*

(1956); Stanley I. Kutler, *Judicial Power and Reconstruction Politics* (1968).

The Black Experience in Reconstruction
Herbert G. Gutman, *The Black Family in Slavery and Freedom, 1750–1925* (1976); Janet Sharp Hermann, *The Pursuit of a Dream* (1981); Thomas Holt, *Black Over White: Negro Political Leadership in South Carolina* (1977); Leon Litwack, *Been in the Storm So Long: The Aftermath of Slavery* (1979); Howard Rabinowitz, ed., *Southern Black Leaders in Reconstruction* (1982); Willie Lee Rose, *Rehearsal for Reconstruction: The Port Royal Experiment* (1964); Vernon L. Wharton, *The Negro in Mississippi, 1865–1890* (1947); Joel Williamson, *After Slavery: The Negro in South Carolina During Reconstruction* (1966).

Reconstruction in the South
Dan T. Carter, *When the War Was Over: The Failure of Self-Reconstruction in the South, 1865–1867* (1985); Richard N. Current, *Those Terrible Carpetbaggers: A Reinterpretation* (1988); William C. Harris, *Day of the Carpetbagger: Republican Reconstruction in Mississippi* (1979); Elizabeth Studley Nathans, *Losing the Peace: Georgia Republicans and Reconstruction, 1865–1871* (1968); Michael Perman, *Reunion Without Compromise: The South and Reconstruction, 1865–1868* (1973), and *The Road to Redemption: Southern Politics, 1869–1880* (1984); George C. Rable, *But There Was No Peace: The Role of Violence in the Politics of Reconstruction* (1984); James Sefton, *The United States Army and Reconstruction, 1865–1877* (1967); Allen Trelease, *White Terror: The Ku Klux Klan Conspiracy and Southern Reconstruc-*

tion (1967); Ted Tunnell, *Crucible of Reconstruction: War, Radicalism, and Race in Louisiana, 1862–1877* (1974); Sarah Woolfolk Wiggins, *The Scalawag in Alabama Politics, 1865–1881* (1977).

Social and Economic Reconstruction
George R. Bentley, *A History of the Freedmen's Bureau* (1955); Eric Foner, *Nothing But Freedom: Emancipation and Its Legacy* (1983); Steven Hahn, *The Roots of Southern Populism: Yeoman Farmers and the Transformation of the Georgia Upcountry, 1850–1890* (1983); Jacqueline Jones, *Soldiers of Light and Love: Northern Teachers and Georgia Blacks, 1865–1873* (1980); Donald Nieman, *To Set the Law in Motion: The Freedmen's Bureau and the Legal Rights of Blacks, 1865–1868* (1979); Lawrence N. Powell, *New Masters: Northern Planters During the Civil War and Reconstruction* (1984); Roger L. Ransom and Richard Sutch, *One Kind of Freedom: The Economic Consequences of Emancipation* (1977); James Roark, *Masters Without Slaves: Southern Planters in the Civil War and Reconstruction* (1977); Mark W. Summers, *Railroads, Reconstruction, and the Gospel of Prosperity* (1984).

The End of Reconstruction
Paul Buck, *The Road to Reunion, 1865–1900* (1937); William Gillette, *Retreat from Reconstruction, 1869–1879* (1980); Keith Ian Polakoff, *The Politics of Inertia: The Election of 1876 and the End of Reconstruction* (1973); C. Vann Woodward, *Reunion and Reaction: The Compromise of 1877 and the End of Reconstruction* (1951).

PHOTO CREDITS

Art (Rogers Fund, 1942); **244** Courtesy of the New York Historical Society, New York City; **247** Culver Pictures; **252** Independence National Historical Park; **254** Independence National Historical Park; **256** Colonial Williamsburg Foundation.

GENERATIONS OF THE REPUBLIC

258-L The Library Company of Philadelphia; **258-R** Thomas Coram, "View of Mulberry Plantation." Oil on paper, 10 × 17.6 cm. The Gibbes Museum of Art/Carolina Art Association; **259-L** The Detroit Institute of Arts, Founders Society Purchase, Gibbs-Williams Fund; **259-C** Maryland Historical Society, Baltimore, Md. Bequest of Miss Ellen C. Gaingerfield; **259-R** Maryland Historical Society, Baltimore, Md.; **260-L** Colonial Williamsburg Foundation; **260-C** Collection of Dr. Alexander A. McBurney; **260-R** The Valentine Museum, Richmond, Va.; **261-L** Abby Aldrich Rockefeller Folk Art Center; **261-R** "Renty, Congo. Plantation of B. F. Taylor, Esq." Original daguerrotype by J. T. Zealy, Columbia, S.C., 1850. Courtesy of the Peabody Museum, Harvard University.

CHAPTER 8

263 Courtesy of the New York Historical Society, New York City; **264** American Antiquarian Society; **269** Addison Gallery of American Art, Phillips Academy, Andover, Mass.; **277-L** Independence National Historical Park; **277-R** National Gallery of Art, Washington, D.C.; **281** Culver Pictures; **284** Courtesy of the New York Historical Society, New York City; **289** U.S. Department of the Interior, National Park Service. Adams National Historic Site, Quincy, Mass.; **294** Courtesy of The Henry Francis Du Pont Winterthur Museum (detail).

CHAPTER 9

299 New York State Historical Association (detail); **300** Courtesy of the New York Public Library; **301** Library of Congress; **306** Boston Athenaeum (detail); **313** Library of Congress; **319** George Catlin, "The Open Door, known as The Prophet, brother of Tecumseh," 1830. Oil on canvas, 29 × 24 in. National Museum of American Art, Smithsonian Institution. Gift of Mrs. Joseph Harrison, Jr.; **324** The Historical Society of Pennsylvania; **328-L** New Orleans Museum of Art. Gift of Edgar William and Bernice Chrysler Garbish; **328-R** Yale University Art Gallery, Mabel Brady Garvan Collection; **331** New York State Office of Parks, Recreation and Historic Preservation. Philips Manor Hall State Historic Site; **334** Bibliothèque Nationale (detail); **335** Bildarchiv Preussischer Kulturbesitz.

CHAPTER 10

339 The Bettmann Archive; **342** Smithsonian Institution, Textile Division; **343** Courtesy of the New York Historical Society, New York City; **349** Anglo-American Art Museum, Louisiana State University, Baton Rouge. Gift of Mrs. Mamie Persac Lusk; **353** Beinecke Rare Book and Manuscript Library, Yale University; **357** Missouri Historical Society; **361** Baker Library Manuscripts & Archives, Harvard Business School. Harvard University; **369** Alfred Jacob Miller, "Caravan en Route." Courtesy Boatmens BancShares, Inc. St. Louis, Mo.

CHAPTER 11

375 Roosevelt Library; **377** Courtesy of the Historical Society of York County, Penna.; **377** Courtesy of the New York Historical Society, New York City; **384** The St. Louis Art Museum; **390** New Orleans Museum of Art. Gift of William E. Groves; **391** Historical Picture Service, Inc.; **395-L** Fogg Art Museum, Harvard University (detail); **395-R** Collection of Jay P. Altmayer; **398** Boston Art Commission, Office of the Arts and Humanities; **404** Museum of the City of New York, The Clarence Davies Collection; **407** Courtesy of The Cincinnati Historical Society.

CHAPTER 12

413 Print Collection, Miriam and Ira D. Wallach Division of Arts, Prints and Photographs. New York Public Library, Astor, Lenox, and Tilden Foundations; **414** The Stowe-Day Foundation, Hartford, Conn.; **416** Allen Memorial Art Museum. Gift of Lewis Tappan; **421** Historical Picture Service, Inc.; **423** Bettmann ArchiveBBC Hulton; **425** Library of Congress; **427** Rare Book Division, New York Public Library, Astor, Lenox, and Tilden Foundations; **428** Culver Pictures; **436-L** Rare Books and Manuscripts, Boston Public Library. Photo courtesy Geoffrey Stein Studios; **436-R** The Bettmann Archive; **438** The Bettmann Archive; **441** Courtesy of Rhoda Barney Jenkins.

GENERATIONS OF THE REPUBLIC

446-L Colonial Williamsburg Foundation; **446-C** Fraktur. Andrew Mayberry-Margaret Trott Family Record, Heart & Hand artist, Windam, Me. Watercolor and ink on woven paper, 13⅜" × 9⅜". Collection of the Museum of American Folk Art, New York City. Gift of Mr. and Mrs. Philip M. Isaacson; **446-R** The Nelson-Atkins Museum of Art, Kansas City Missouri. Gift of Mrs. Edith Gregor Halpert; **447-L** Colonial Williamsburg Foundation; **447-C** Gift of Belle Greene and Henry Copley Greene, in memory of their mother, Mary Abbey Greene. Courtesy of the Museum of Fine Arts, Boston; **447-R** "The Emerson School" by Southworth and Hawes, American Daguerreotype (1840–1862). The Metropolitan Museum of Art. Gift of I. N. Phelps Stokes, Edward S. Hawes, Alice Mary Hawes, Marion Augusta Hawes, 1937; **448-L** The Bettmann Archive; **448-R** Library of Congress; **449-L** Library of Congress; **449-C** National Archives; **449-R** Division of Photographic History, National Museum of American History. Smithsonian Institution, Washington, D.C.

CHAPTER 13

451 Historic New Orleans Collection; **454–455** Museum of the City of New York, Harry T. Peters Collection; **465** Historic New Orleans Collection; **467** San Antonio Museum Association, San Antonio, Tex.; **475** Kennedy Galleries, New York City; **477** Courtesy of The Charleston Museum, Charleston, S.C.; **483** Courtesy of the New York Historical Society, New York City.

CHAPTER 14

487 Library of Congress; **491** Alfred Sully, "Monterey, California Rancho Scene," n.d. Watercolor, 8" × 10". Kahn Collection. The Oakland Museum, Oakland, Calif.; **494** Courtesy, Archives Division, Texas State Library; **497** J. Goldsborough Bruff. Courtesy of the Yale University Library; **503** George Peter Alexander Healy, "James K. Polk." In the collection of The Corcoran Gallery of Art, Museum Purchase, Gallery Fund;

506 Courtesy of the New York Historical Society, New York City; 519 Library of Congress.

CHAPTER 15

523 Culver Pictures; 525 Kansas State Historical Society, Topeka, Kans.; 531 Museum of the City of New York; 541 Print Collection, Miriam and Ira D. Wallach Division of Arts, Prints and Photographs. New York Public Library, Astor, Lenox, and Tilden Foundations; 545 Missouri Historical Society; 545 Library of Congress; 547-L The Bettmann Archive; 547-R Illinois State Historical Library; 552 Boston Athenaeum; 556 *Harper's Weekly;* 549 Library of Congress.

CHAPTER 16

561 Winslow Homer, "A Rainy Day in Camp." The Metropolitan Museum of Art. Gift of Mrs. William F. Milton, 1932; 562 *Harper's Weekly;* 563 Chicago Historical Society; 571 Library of Congress; 574 Library of Congress; 578 Frank W. and Marie T. Wood Print Collection, Alexandria, Va.; 582 U.S. Army Military History Institute, Carlisle Barracks, Penna.; 583 M. and M. Karolik Collection. Courtesy, Museum of Fine Arts, Boston; 586 Dale S. Snair Collection, Richmond, Va.; 585 Larry B. Wilford Collection, Civil War Photohis-torian; 597-L Library of Congress; 597-R The Valentine Museum of the Life and History of Richmond, Cook Collection.

CHAPTER 17

603 Winslow Homer, "A Visit from the Old Mistress," 1876. Oil on canvas, 18″ × 24⅛″. National Museum of American Art, Smithsonian Institution. Gift of William T. Evans; 607-L Library of Congress; 607-R U.S. Army Military History Institute, Carlisle Barracks, Penna.; 609 Library of Congress; 610 The Library Company of Philadelphia; 616 Library of Congress; 618 Library of Congress; 623 Courtesy of the New York Historical Society, New York City; 625 Richard Norris Brooke, "A Pastoral Visit, Virginia." In the collection of The Corcoran Gallery of Art, Museum Purchase, Gallery Fund; 629 The Valentine Museum of the Life and History of Richmond, Cook Collection; 631-L Courtesy of the American Antiquarian Society; 631-R Sophie Smith Collection, Smith College; 633 The Granger Collection; 636 Rutherford B. Hayes Presidential Center; 638 United States Senate, Committee on Rules and Administration; 639 Library of Congress, Division of Rare Books and Manuscripts; 642 The Bettmann Archive; 643 Courtesy of The British Library, London.

INDEX

Note: Page numbers in *italic* indicate illustrations.

ABOUT THE AUTHORS

JAMES WEST DAVIDSON received his Ph.D. from Yale University. A historian who has pursued a full-time writing career, he is the author of numerous books, among them *After the Fact: The Art of Historical Detection* (with Mark H. Lytle), *The Logic of Millennial Thought: Eighteenth-Century New England*, and *Great Heart: The History of a Labrador Adventure* (with John Rugge).

WILLIAM E. GIENAPP has a Ph.D. from the University of California, Berkeley. He is Professor of History at the University of Wyoming, where he was the 1988–1989 Seibold Professor. In 1988 he was given the Avery O. Craven Award for his work, *The Origins of the Republican Party, 1852–1856*. Currently he is at work on *Abraham Lincoln and Civil War America*.

CHRISTINE LEIGH HEYRMAN is Associate Professor of History at Brandeis University. She received a Ph.D. in American Studies from Yale University and is the author of *Commerce and Culture: The Maritime Communities of Colonial Massachusetts, 1690–1750*. Her professional activities include serving on the Editorial Board of the *Journal of American History* and as Council Secretary for the Institute of Early American History and Culture.

MARK H. LYTLE, who was awarded a Ph.D. from Yale University, is Professor of History and Environmental Studies and Chair of the American Studies Program at Bard College. He is also Director of the Master of Arts in Teaching Program at Bard. His publications include *The Origins of the Iranian–American Alliance, 1941–1953* and *After the Fact: The Art of Historical Detection* (with James West Davidson). In 1989 he received the Horace Kidger Award of the New England History Teachers Association. He is now at work on *The Uncivil War: America in the Vietnam Era*.

MICHAEL B. STOFF is Associate Professor of History at the University of Texas at Austin, where he directs the honors program in history. The recipient of a Ph.D. from Yale University, he wrote *Oil, War, and American Security: The Search for a National Policy on Foreign Oil, 1941–1947* and the forthcoming *Manhattan Project: A Documentary Introduction to the Development and Use of the Atomic Bomb*.